South-West China

Bradley Mayhew
Korina Miller
Alex English

LONELY PLANET PUBLICATIONS
Melbourne • Oakland • London • Paris

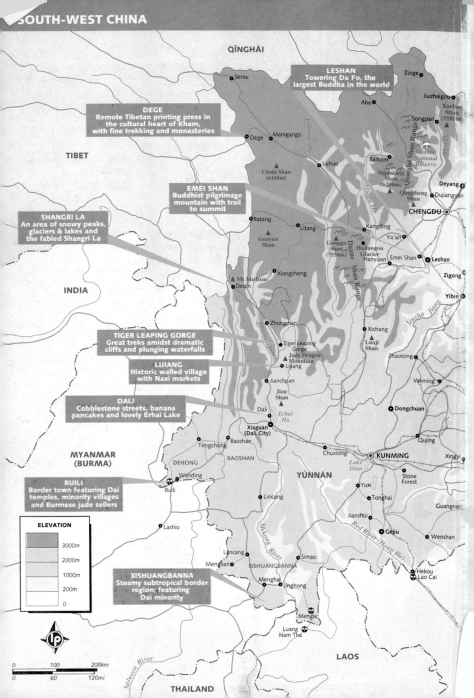

SOUTH-WEST CHINA

QĪNGHǍI

• Serxu

LESHAN
Towering Da Fo, the
largest Buddha in the world

Zoige

Jiuzhaigou

Aba

Xuebao
Shan
(5588m)

DEGE
Remote Tibetan printing press in
the cultural heart of Kham,
with fine trekking and monasteries

Songpan

• Dege • Manigango

TIBET

Luhuo

Chola Shan
(6168m)

Barkam

Siguniang
Shan
(6250m)

Wolong
National
Reserve

Deyang

Qingcheng
Shan

Dujiangyan

CHENGDU

EMEI SHAN
Buddhist pilgrimage
mountain with trail
to summit

Batang

Litang

Kangding

Ya'an

SHANGRI LA
An area of snowy peaks,
glaciers & lakes and
the fabled Shangri La

Genyen
Shan

Gongga
Shan
(7556m)

Hailuogou
Glacier

Hanyuan

Emei Shan

Leshan

INDIA

Xiangcheng

Zigong

▲ Mt Meilixue
• Deqin

Yibin

Zhongdian

Xichang

Luoji
Shan

TIGER LEAPING GORGE
Great treks amidst dramatic
cliffs and plunging waterfalls

Tiger Leaping
Gorge

Jade Dragon
Mountain

Lijiang

Zhaotong

LIJIANG
Historic walled village
with Naxi markets

Jianchuan

Jizu
Shan

Weining

DALI
Cobblestone streets, banana
pancakes and lovely Erhai Lake

Dali

Erhai
Hu

Dongchuan

Xiaguan
(Dali City)

**MYANMAR
(BURMA)**

Tengchong

Baoshan

DEHONG

BAOSHAN

Chuxiong

Qujing

KUNMING

Xingyi

RUILI
Border town featuring Dai
temples, minority villages
and Burmese jade sellers

Wanding

Ruili

Lincang

Yuxi

Lake
Dian

Stone
Forest

Tonghai

Guangnan

Lashio

Jianshui

Red River (Hong He)

Gejiu

Wenshan

ELEVATION

3000m

2000m

1000m

200m

0

Lancang

Menglian

Simao

XISHUANGBANNA

Menghai

Jinghong

Hekou
Lao Cai

XISHUANGBANNA
Steamy subtropical border
region; featuring
Dai minority

Menghan

Mengla

Luang
Nam Tha

0   100   200km

0   60   120mi

LAOS

THAILAND

Salween River

Mekong River

Yalong He

Dadu He

Min He

Yinsha Jiang

Daxue Shan Range

Shan Range

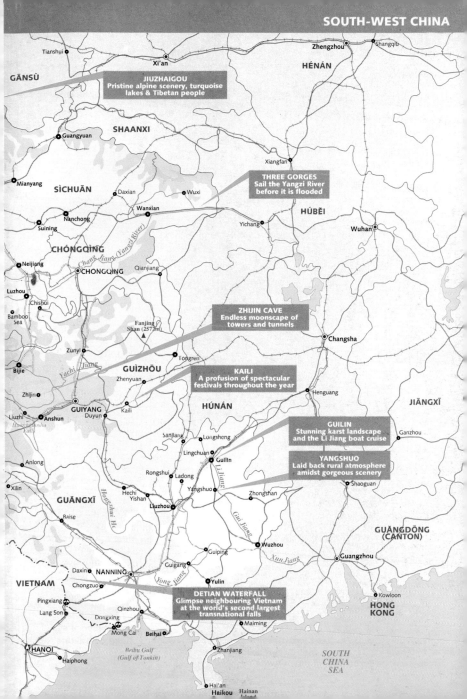

JIUZHAIGOU
Pristine alpine scenery, turquoise lakes & Tibetan people

THREE GORGES
Sail the Yangzi River before it is flooded

ZHIJIN CAVE
Endless moonscape of towers and tunnels

KAILI
A profusion of spectacular festivals throughout the year

GUILIN
Stunning karst landscape and the Li Jiang boat cruise

YANGSHUO
Laid back rural atmosphere amidst gorgeous scenery

DETIAN WATERFALL
Glimpse neighbouring Vietnam at the world's second largest transnational falls

GĀNSÙ
SHAANXI
SÌCHUĀN
CHÓNGQÌNG
GUÌZHŌU
GUĂNGXĪ
VIETNAM
HÉNÁN
HÚBĚI
HÚNÁN
JIĀNGXĪ
GUĂNGDŌNG
(CANTON)
HONG KONG
SOUTH CHINA SEA

Tianshui
Xi'an
Zhengzhou
Shangqiu
Guangyuan
Xiangfan
Mianyang
Daxian
Wuxi
Nanchong
Wanxian
Yichang
Wuhan
Suining
Neijiang
CHONGQING
Qianjiang
Luzhou
Chishui
Bamboo Sea
Fanjing Shan (2571m) ▲
Changsha
Zunyi
Tongren
Bijie
Zhenyuan
Zhijin
GUIYANG
Duyun
Kaili
Henguang
Liuzhi
Anshun
Ganzhou
Anlong
Sānjiāng
Longsheng
Xilin
Lingchuan
Guìlín
Rongshui
Ladong
Hechi
Yishan
Yangshuo
Zhongshan
Shaoguan
Liuzhou
Baise
Guiping
Wuzhou
Guangzhou
Daxin
NANNING
Guigang
Chongzuo
Yulin
Pingxiang
Qinzhou
Lang Son
Dongxing
Maiming
Mong Cai
Beihai
Kowloon
HANOI
Haiphong
Beibu Gulf (Gulf of Tonkin)
Zhanjiang
Hai'an
Haikou
Hainan Island

Chang Jiang (Yangzi River)
Yachi Jiang
Hongshui He
Li Jiang
Gui Jiang
Xun Jiang
Yong Jiang

South-West China
2nd edition – January 2002
First published – November 1998

Published by
Lonely Planet Publications Pty Ltd ABN 36 005 607 983
90 Maribyrnong St, Footscray, Victoria 3011, Australia

Lonely Planet offices
Australia Locked Bag 1, Footscray, Victoria 3011
USA 150 Linden St, Oakland, CA 94607
UK 10a Spring Place, London NW5 3BH
France 1 rue du Dahomey, 75011 Paris

Photographs
Many of the images in this guide are available for licensing from
Lonely Planet Images.
email: lpi@lonelyplanet.com.au
Web site: www.lonelyplanetimages.com

Front cover photograph
Lijiang, Yunnan, China (Juliet Coombe)

ISBN 1 86450 370 X

Printed by The Bookmaker International Ltd
Printed in Malaysia

Contents – Text

Contents – Maps

MAP INDEX

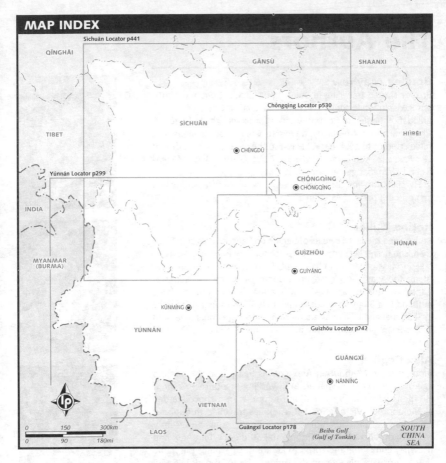

QÍNGHĂI

GĀNSÙ

SHAANXI

Sìchuān Locator p441

TIBET

SÌCHUĀN

● CHÉNGDŪ

HÚBĚI

Chóngqìng Locator p530

CHÓNGQÌNG
● CHÓNGQÌNG

Yúnnán Locator p299

INDIA

HÚNÁN

GUÌZHŌU

● GUÌYÁNG

MYANMAR
(BURMA)

KŪNMÍNG ●

YÚNNÁN

Guìzhōu Locator p242

GUĂNGXĪ

● NÁNNÍNG

VIETNAM

0   150   300km
0   90   180mi

LAOS

Guăngxī Locator p178

Beibu Gulf
(Gulf of Tonkin)

SOUTH
CHINA
SEA

5

The Authors

Bradley Mayhew

Bradley started travelling in South-West China, Tibet and northern Pakistan while studying Chinese at Oxford University. Upon graduation he fled to Central America for six months to forget his Chinese and now regularly travels to China's borderlands in a futile attempt to get it back. He is also the co-author or author of LP's *Pakistan*, *Karakoram Highway*, *Tibet*, *Central Asia*, *Mongolia* and *Shanghai* guides, amongst others.

He splits his time between Sevenoaks in south-east England and obscure parts of Montana.

Korina Miller

Korina lived the first 18 years of her life on Vancouver Island. Since then, she hasn't lived in any one place for very long, managing to take in parts of Japan, India, Egypt, Europe, and South America. Along the way she picked up a degree in Communications & Canadian Studies, an MA in Migration Studies and a Limey husband in a Brighton discotheque. In 1997 she spent six months in Shànghǎi and Lìjiāng as an intern researching cooperatives and eco-tourism. She has recently fled to Central America to thaw.

Alex English

Brought up in Melbourne, Alex got his first job at the ripe old age of 10, selling newspapers and working in a butcher's shop. He then spent four years eating the profits in a chocolate deli at Melbourne's Victoria market. Alex has travelled throughout Asia, Europe and the Indian subcontinent, and is presently working on his PhD in Environmental Studies. When Alex and his wife, Eunkyong and son, Oscar, are not roaming the globe they are usually playing on the swings at a local park in Seoul or in Melbourne.

FROM THE AUTHORS

Bradley

Thanks again to Calum 'our man in Běijīng' MacLeod for sending steaming loads of China information and for expertise on booze and minorities, travel with children and loads of other great stuff. Special thanks to Lijia for the continued use of her Miáo aside and to Andre for his good cheer in difficult circumstances in Western Sìchuān. Thanks also to my trusty co-authors Alex and Korina. Thanks and love as ever to Kelli.

Korina

Thanks and love to Paul, a fantastic travelling companion, for braving the frozen bus rides, the chunky butter tea, my moodiness and the manic schedule and still managing to survive with (most of) his sanity intact. Thank you to Jocelyn Harewood, Anastasia Safioleas, Sophie Reed, my co-authors and all the others at Lonely Planet who have been supportive and patient – especially with my computer afflictions and Chinese-challenged ways. Thanks to Xiao Ning for his help with translations, to Samuel Yue for doling out his knowledge of the region to a writer undercover and to all of the readers and travellers who shared their insight and experiences. Finally, to the local people I met on the road: thank you for your kindness, and keenness to help, not to mention the mighty stare-downs.

Alex

Thanks to all the infinite number of patient and polite Chinese who endured my many inquisitions around Guǎngxī. I look forward to catching up again soon with some of the great people I met along the way. The biggest thanks have to go to my favourite travelling companions, Eunkyong and Oscar, who had to let me go off all by myself this time – thanks for your love and care!

This Book

The first edition of this book was written by Bradley Mayhew, who coordinated the book, wrote the introductory chapters and concentrated on Sìchuān and Guìzhōu, and Thomas Huhti, who wrote the Yúnnán and Guǎngxī chapters. For this edition Bradley again coordinated the book, updated Yúnnán and expanded parts of Western Sìchuān. Korina Miller updated Sìchuān and Guìzhōu and Alex English concentrated on Guǎngxī.

From The Publisher

This 2nd edition of South West China was produced in Lonely Planet's Melbourne office. Anastasia Safioleas coordinated the editing. She was assisted by a small army of editors, which included Kyla Gillzan, Michael Day, Yvonne Byron, Janine Eberle and the inimitable Jocelyn Harewood. Newcomers Simone Egger and Gina Tsarouhas helped with the proofing. When Sophie Reed was not tackling the snowfields of New Zealand with a snowboard she was coordinating cartography, design and layout. She was assisted by Chris Tsismetzis and Chris Thomas, as well as Meredith Mail, Chris Love, Corinne Waddell and Jack Gavran. Thanks to George Dunford for his contribution to the Sìchuān chapter, Charles Qin for all things pinyin and script related, Emma Koch and Quentin Frayne for the language section, and LPI for providing the photos. Matt King coordinated the illustrations, which were drawn by Sophie Reed, Mic Looby, Clint Curé, Enjarn Lin, Don Hatcher, Tamsin Wilson and Mick Weldon. Thank you Daniel New and Jane Hart for creating the cover.

Acknowledgment

Extract from The Songlines by Bruce Chatwin published by Jonathan Cape. Used by permission of The Random House Group Limited. Copyright (c) Bruce Chatwin 1987

Thanks

Many thanks to the travellers who used the last edition and wrote to us with helpful hints, useful advice and interesting anecdotes:

Luke Arnold, Natasha & Daniel Barker, Dr Ajit Bhalla, Cindy & Maggie Blick, Becky Boltz, D Bowland, Maureen Breslin, Kimberley Bryden, Linda Burgin, Clifford Chan, Danny Chang, Fritz Chavez, Lawrence Chin, Louisa Chui, Simon Coffey, Bill Coleman, Chris Cummins, Keith Davies, Wayne Dealy, Jaap Fahrenfort, Richard Fish, Barbara Forbes, Matthew Grant, Peter Jacklyn, Eldon Kendrew, Peter Klein, Andrew Kwee, Jerome Le Tourner, Matt Lee, Patrick Leonard, David Leung, Aimee Linnett, Marcel Maessen, Jock & Janice Moilliet, Matthew Murphy, Joanne Nicel, Gezina Oorthuys, Norma Pearce, Antoni Peris, Andrew Perlstein, Barry Peters, Hong Xiu Ping, Juan Recio, John Ronan, Bojan Rotovnik, Lex Schrama, Saskia van der Zande, Karen Wang, Joe Wood, Oliver Zoellner.

Foreword

ABOUT LONELY PLANET GUIDEBOOKS

The story begins with a classic travel adventure: Tony and Maureen Wheeler's 1972 journey across Europe and Asia to Australia. Useful information about the overland trail did not exist at that time, so Tony and Maureen published the first Lonely Planet guidebook to meet a growing need.

From a kitchen table, then from a tiny office in Melbourne (Australia), Lonely Planet has become the largest independent travel publisher in the world, an international company with offices in Melbourne, Oakland (USA), London (UK) and Paris (France).

Today Lonely Planet guidebooks cover the globe. There is an ever-growing list of books and there's information in a variety of forms and media. Some things haven't changed. The main aim is still to help make it possible for adventurous travellers to get out there – to explore and better understand the world.

At Lonely Planet we believe travellers can make a positive contribution to the countries they visit – if they respect their host communities and spend their money wisely. Since 1986 a percentage of the income from each book has been donated to aid projects and human rights campaigns.

Updates Lonely Planet thoroughly updates each guidebook as often as possible. This usually means there are around two years between editions, although for more unusual or more stable destinations the gap can be longer. Check the imprint page (following the colour map at the beginning of the book) for publication dates.

Between editions up-to-date information is available in two free newsletters – the paper *Planet Talk* and email *Comet* (to subscribe, contact any Lonely Planet office) – and on our Web site at www.lonelyplanet.com. The *Upgrades* section of the Web site covers a number of important and volatile destinations and is regularly updated by Lonely Planet authors. *Scoop* covers news and current affairs relevant to travellers. And, lastly, the *Thorn Tree* bulletin board and *Postcards* section of the site carry unverified, but fascinating, reports from travellers.

Correspondence The process of creating new editions begins with the letters, postcards and emails received from travellers. This correspondence often includes suggestions, criticisms and comments about the current editions. Interesting excerpts are immediately passed on via newsletters and the Web site, and everything goes to our authors to be verified when they're researching on the road. We're keen to get more feedback from organisations or individuals who represent communities visited by travellers.

Lonely Planet gathers information for everyone who's curious about the planet – and especially for those who explore it first-hand. Through guidebooks, phrasebooks, activity guides, maps, literature, newsletters, image library, TV series and Web site we act as an information exchange for a worldwide community of travellers.

Research Authors aim to gather sufficient practical information to enable travellers to make informed choices and to make the mechanics of a journey run smoothly. They also research historical and cultural background to help enrich the travel experience and allow travellers to understand and respond appropriately to cultural and environmental issues.

Authors don't stay in every hotel because that would mean spending a couple of months in each medium-sized city and, no, they don't eat at every restaurant because that would mean stretching belts beyond capacity. They do visit hotels and restaurants to check standards and prices, but feedback based on readers' direct experiences can be very helpful.

Many of our authors work undercover, others aren't so secretive. None of them accept freebies in exchange for positive write-ups. And none of our guidebooks contain any advertising.

Production Authors submit their manuscripts and maps to offices in Australia, USA, UK or France. Editors and cartographers – all experienced travellers themselves – then begin the process of assembling the pieces. When the book finally hits the shops, some things are already out of date, we start getting feedback from readers and the process begins again ...

WARNING & REQUEST

Things change – prices go up, schedules change, good places go bad and bad places go bankrupt – nothing stays the same. So, if you find things better or worse, recently opened or long since closed, please tell us and help make the next edition even more accurate and useful. We genuinely value all the feedback we receive. A well-travelled team reads and acknowledges every letter, postcard and email and ensures that every morsel of information finds its way to the appropriate authors, editors and cartographers for verification.

Everyone who writes to us will find their name listed in the next edition of the appropriate guidebook. They will also receive the latest issue of *Planet Talk*, our quarterly printed newsletter, or *Comet*, our monthly email newsletter. Subscriptions to both newsletters are free. The very best contributions will be rewarded with a free guidebook.

We may edit, reproduce and incorporate your comments in all Lonely Planet products, such as guidebooks, Web sites and digital products, so let us know if you don't want your comments reproduced or your name acknowledged.

Send all correspondence to the Lonely Planet office closest to you:

Australia: Locked Bag 1, Footscray, Victoria 3011
USA: 150 Linden St, Oakland, CA 94607
UK: 10a Spring Place, London NW5 3BH

Or email us at: talk2us@lonelyplanet.com.au

For news, views and updates see our Web site: www.lonelyplanet.com

HOW TO USE A LONELY PLANET GUIDEBOOK

The best way to use a Lonely Planet guidebook is any way you choose. At Lonely Planet we believe the most memorable travel experiences are often those that are unexpected, and the finest discoveries are those you make yourself. Guidebooks are not intended to be used as if they provide a detailed set of infallible instructions!

Contents All Lonely Planet guidebooks follow roughly the same format. The Facts about the Destination chapters or sections give background information ranging from history to weather. Facts for the Visitor gives practical information on issues like visas and health. Getting There & Away gives a brief starting point for researching travel to and from the destination. Getting Around gives an overview of the transport options when you arrive.

The peculiar demands of each destination determine how subsequent chapters are broken up, but some things remain constant. We always start with background, then proceed to sights, places to stay, places to eat, entertainment, getting there and away, and getting around information – in that order.

Heading Hierarchy Lonely Planet headings are used in a strict hierarchical structure that can be visualised as a set of Russian dolls. Each heading (and its following text) is encompassed by any preceding heading that is higher on the hierarchical ladder.

Entry Points We do not assume guidebooks will be read from beginning to end, but that people will dip into them. The traditional entry points are the list of contents and the index. In addition, however, some books have a complete list of maps and an index map illustrating map coverage.

There may also be a colour map that shows highlights. These highlights are dealt with in greater detail in the Facts for the Visitor chapter, along with planning questions and suggested itineraries. Each chapter covering a geographical region usually begins with a locator map and another list of highlights. Once you find something of interest in a list of highlights, turn to the index.

Maps Maps play a crucial role in Lonely Planet guidebooks and include a huge amount of information. A legend is printed on the back page. We seek to have complete consistency between maps and text, and to have every important place in the text captured on a map. Map key numbers usually start in the top left corner.

Although inclusion in a guidebook usually implies a recommendation we cannot list every good place. Exclusion does not necessarily imply criticism. In fact there are a number of reasons why we might exclude a place – sometimes it is simply inappropriate to encourage an influx of travellers.

Introduction

Without going outside, you may know the whole world.
Without looking through the window, you may see the ways of heaven.
The farther you go, the less you know.

Laotzu, Tao Te Ching

China's south-west has long been a favourite among backpackers, anthropologists and other explorers. Its highlights are China's greatest highlights, whether you're making a pilgrimage to the Buddhist mountain of Éméi Shān, taking a boat ride to the biggest Buddha in the world, cycling around the sublime karst landscapes of Guìlín, or taking in the spectacular minority festivals of Guìzhōu. The turquoise lakes of Jiǔzhàigōu national park rank as the most beautiful scenery in the country, and the traveller-friendly Meccas of Dàlǐ and Yángshuò still offer the only places in China where you can get a blueberry muffin for breakfast and learn taichi in the afternoon. This is the China of most foreign visitors' dreams.

Beyond this, China at its most traveller-friendly becomes China at its most remote. The south-west has always formed the fringe of China, and here at the southern gates live a diverse range of ethnic groups, who give the region much of its colour and charm. Up in the snowy peaks of western Sìchuān you'll meet Tibetans with gold teeth and cowboy hats, while down in the tropical forests of Xīshuāngbǎnnà you can eat sticky Thai rice out of a pineapple. The region holds an astonishing array of landscapes and cultures, blowing the lid off the myth of a monochrome China.

The recent boom in trade connections to South-East Asia has brought good news for travellers. You can now fly direct to Kūnmíng from most regional capitals without the need to hit Hong Kong or Běijīng. If you're heading overland, join the jade traders on the interesting bus and train routes from Laos and Vietnam. You can even enter the south-west from Laos, check out China and then head back south into Vietnam.

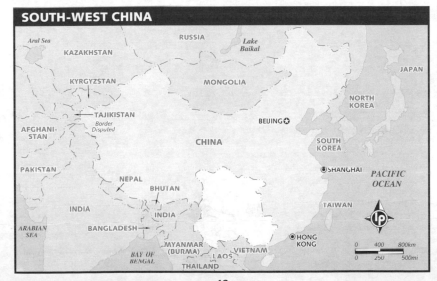

SOUTH-WEST CHINA

China is changing fast. Yet, while Chéngdū and Chóngqìng share Shànghǎi's mania for neon and cellular phones, traditional life in the countryside continues, unimpressed by the modern economic miracle. Minority women still wear traditional embroidery and make the trek down from the hills to shop in the bustling weekly markets.

Alas, some things don't change. China is still not the easiest place to travel, though it's undoubtedly easier than it was 10 years ago. The linguistic and cultural barriers can be daunting, at times infuriating. And yet somehow this just adds to China's appeal. The more you learn about China, the more fascinating it becomes. Love it or hate it, the one thing you can't do is ignore it.

Facts about South-West China

HISTORY

For much of its early history the empires of central China held only nominal sway over the South-West. When dynasties were strong, they expanded and conquered; whenever they grew weak and withdrew, independent kingdoms sprang up in their wake. To the Chinese emperors the region south of the Yangzi was a barbarian and pestilent borderland populated by wild and uncivilised tribes known collectively as the *mán*. They were the first to rebel and the last to be brought back into the fray.

The South-West provided a kind of sub-tropical Siberia, a place of dissidents, rebels and exiled officials, where the last fragments of outgoing empires fought on and rising empires consolidated their rule. As time went by, waves of Han migrants fleeing war, famine and the barbarian invasions of the north slowly shifted the demography of the region and brought it into the Chinese fold. It was a process that began in Sìchuān and eastern Guăngxī 2000 years ago and only ended in the remotest regions of Yúnnán and western Sìchuān with the formation of the People's Republic of China in 1949.

Early History

Recent scientific discoveries continue to push back the time frame of the region. Some of the earliest multi-celled organisms ever discovered were found in Weng'an county, Guìzhōu, in 1998. One

Chinese Dynasties & Republics

Xia	**2200 – 1700 BC**		**Northern**	**386 – 581**
Shang	**1700 – 1100**		Northern Wei	386 – 534
Zhou	**1100 – 221**		Eastern Wei	534 – 577
Western Zhou	1100 – 771		Western Wei	535 – 556
Eastern Zhou	770 – 221		Northern Qi	550 – 577
Spring & Autumn Period	722 – 481		Northern Zhou	557 – 581
Warring States Period	453 – 221		**Sui**	**589 – 618**
Qin	**221 – 207**		**Tang**	**618 – 907**
Han	**206 BC – AD 220**		**Five Dynasties**	**907 – 960**
Former Han	206 BC – AD 24		Later Liang	907 – 923
Later Han	25 – 220		Later Tang	923 – 936
Three Kingdoms Period	**220 – 280**		Later Jin	936 – 946
Wei	220 – 265		Later Han	947 – 950
Shu Han	221 – 263		Later Zhou	951 – 960
Wu	222 – 280		**Liao**	**916 – 1125**
Jin	**265 – 420**		**Song**	**960 – 1279**
Western Jin	265 – 316		Northern Song	960 – 1126
Eastern Jin	317 – 420		Southern Song	1127 – 1279
Southern & Northern			**Western Xia**	**1038 – 1227**
Dynasties	**420 – 589**		**Jin**	**1115 – 1234**
Southern	420 – 589		**Yuan (Mongol)**	**1271 – 1368**
Song	420 – 479		**Ming**	**1368 – 1644**
Qi	479 – 502		**Qing (Manchu)**	**1644 – 1911**
Liang	502 – 557		**Republic of China**	**1911 – 1949**
Chen	557 – 589		**People's Republic of China**	**1949 –**

fossil encased a 580-million-year-old embryo. The Chengjiang region of Yúnnán has been the site of particularly rich finds of soft-bodied fossils, which have revealed so much about the evolutionary process that they have been listed as world cultural relics by Unesco. In the 1960s two-million-year-old human fragments were found in Yúnnán, as ancient as anything found in China. Then in 1980 an eight-million-year-old anthropoid skull was discovered, showing that Yúnnán was one of Asia's earliest centres of human activity.

Sìchuān was one of the earliest settlements in China, and was populated by settlers from the Yellow River basin, the oldest cradle of Chinese civilisation. At this time the whole of southern China was inhabited by Thai-related tribes, who were joined by Miáo and other migrating tribes around 2000 to 3000 years ago. Much of the west of the region was inhabited by Qiang tribes, ancestors of the Tibetans. Han Chinese settlers started to trickle into the region in the 5th century BC.

By around 3000 BC a distinct culture, separate from the Zhou dynasty farther north, had evolved in modern day Sìchuān around the kingdoms of Shu (taking in Chéngdū, parts of north-west Yúnnán and north-west Guìzhōu) and Ba (centred on the region between Yíbīn and Three Gorges). By 1200 BC these kingdoms had been joined by the agriculturally sophisticated Dian culture around Kūnmíng.

The first incursion from the north came in 339 BC when a Chinese general from the state of Chu, in the central Yangzi plain, conquered territory all the way down to Yúnnán. When it came time for the general and his army to return home, they found their path cut by the encroaching rival Qin armies and so set up the early kingdom of Dian, an island of Chinese culture cut off and isolated from its source.

Qin Dynasty

The state of Qin to the north grew in power during the 5th and 4th centuries BC. In 246 BC the state conquered the kingdom of Shu in present day Sìchuān as well as parts of

the Baiyue kingdom in eastern Guǎngxī. Though the Qin empire failed to spread to Yúnnán or Guìzhōu, suzerainty was acknowledged and by 221 BC the state of Qin had united the Chinese for the first time into a single empire. The ruler Qin Shihuang honoured himself with the newly coined title *huángdì*, or emperor.

The First Emperor Qin Shihuang ruled only from 221 to 207 BC but the Qin dynasty bequeathed administrative institutions that were to remain features of the Chinese state for the following 2000 years. Weights, measurements and the writing system were standardised and the empire was divided into provincial units, which were administered by centrally appointed scholars.

The Qin's most important engineering legacy in the south was the construction of the Dūjiāngyàn irrigation system in 256 BC, which cast Sìchuān as the granary of China for the next 2000 years. Their other great engineering construction (apart from the Great Wall) was the Ling Canal in Guǎngxī, which linked the Yangzi and Pearl River systems for the first time, creating a north-south waterway that initiated the absorption of the South-West into the rest of the empire.

Qin Shihuang's heir to the imperial throne proved ineffectual and, shaken by rebellion, the Qin capital near Chāng'ān (Xī'ān) fell to an army led by the commoner Liu Bang in 207 BC. Liu lost no time in taking the title of emperor and establishing the Han dynasty.

Han Dynasty

The Han dynasty ruled China from 206 BC to AD 220. While it held the reins of power less tightly than the preceding Qin dynasty, it nevertheless maintained many of the institutions of the dynasty that it followed.

The Western Han was a period of consolidation, notable for the true establishment of the Chinese state and the military extension of the empire's borders.

The South-West at this time still held the independent kingdoms of Shu and Ba in Sìchuān, Dian in Yúnnán, Nanyue around Guǎngxī (and northern Vietnam) and numerous smaller kingdoms like the Yelang kingdom of Guìzhōu. As the Han dynasty consolidated control in 112 BC the lands of Guǎngxī and Guìzhōu were subsumed into the Han province of Lingnan, while the region in general became known as Nanyue, all the way down to Vietnam.

Exploratory Han missions to open up trade routes beyond the empire's southern gate were at first blocked by the local king of Dian, which was then a tributary state to the Han empire. Over the years, though, the southern Silk Routes from Téngchōng and Mángshì to India were established; channels of commerce which would eventually provide a path for the introduction of Hinayana Buddhism from Burma.

Another far-reaching innovation was the introduction of the *tusi* system, which was to dominate imperial China's relations with the South-West for the next two millennia. The system involved bestowing a hereditary imperial rank and title onto local chieftains or headmen, or, as the Chinese saw it, 'ruling barbarians with barbarians'. As long as local rulers maintained peace and paid their taxes or tribute they were largely left to their own devices.

The Three Kingdoms

The Eastern Han, after a brief period of stability, fell prey to a process of a weakening and decentralisation of power. From the collapse of the Han dynasty in AD 220 to the establishment of the Sui in 581, China was riven by more than four centuries of internal conflict that saw some of the most terrible wars in the nation's history.

Between AD 220 and 280 China was divided into three kingdoms, of which the most important in the South-West was the kingdom of Han Shu, centred upon modern day Chéngdū. The kingdom was ruled first by Liu Bei, a member of the Han royal family, and then by his chief minister Zhuge Liang. (You can visit their tombs in Chéngdū.) The era was later romanticised in the 17th century novel *Romance of Three Kingdoms*, which featured fictionalised characterisation of all the main kings.

The Han Shu enjoyed control over much of Guìzhōu and Yúnnán through garrisons at Zhènyuán and Kūnmíng, but the region's clan-based settlements were largely left undisturbed. It is in historical texts of this period that the first reference is made to 'Yúnnán' or 'south of the clouds' of foggy Sìchuān.

The kingdom of Shu was eventually eclipsed by the Wei, which was itself replaced by the Western Jin. For the next 300 years the territory of the South-West fragmented into petty kingdoms and clan bases.

Sui Dynasty

By 589 the Sui had control of southern China, and the country was once again reunified under a single government. The Sui dynasty (589–618) was short-lived but its accomplishments were many: administrative reform and land reform were undertaken, and the civil service was strengthened at the expense of aristocratic privilege. All this, along with revisions of the law code, was to serve as the basis for the institutions of the Tang dynasty that followed fast on the heels of the Sui's collapse.

Tang Dynasty

Faced with disastrous military setbacks and revolt on the streets, the Sui Emperor Yangdi was assassinated by one of his high officials. A former Sui official Li Yuan (known posthumously as Gaozu), established the Tang dynasty (618–907). The Tang is commonly regarded by Chinese as the most glorious period in their history.

As Central China grew strong again, it once again surged towards the South-West from its capital at Chāng'ān. In a move to discourage the development of regional power bases, the empire was divided into 300 prefectures (*zhōu*) and 1500 counties (*xiàn*), a regional breakdown that persists to this day.

Strengthened by mass migrations and the building of garrison towns like Guìyáng and Anlong, the Guìzhōu-Guǎngxī region became known once again as Lingnan. Chinese control resumed all the way down to Annan ('the pacified south') in northern Vietnam.

The Tang dynasty saw a grand flourishing of Buddhism as Silk Road contacts with the people of Central Asia reached a cross-cultural crescendo. At a later stage in the dynasty foreign contact was extended to Persia, India, Malaysia, Indonesia and Japan during what was a cosmopolitan golden age.

For Chinese, the apex of Tang dynastic glory was the reign of Xuanzong (685–761). His capital of Chāng'ān became one of the greatest cities in the world, with a population of over one million. His court was a magnet to scholars and artists throughout the country, and home for a time to Sìchuān's two most famous poets, Du Fu and Li Bai. Xuanzong's reign also saw a flourishing of the arts, dance and music, as well as a remarkable religious diversity.

Nánzhaō Kingdom

During the time of the early Tang, Yúnnán was divided into six kingdoms, of which the most powerful was the Nánzhaō (Southern kingdom) of the Bai people, based at Dàlǐ. In 731 the Nánzhaō king took control of Yúnnán when he coldly buried alive his five rivals. He confirmed his power by marrying an imperial princess from Chāng'ān, a time-honoured means of establishing political alliances.

By 751 the Nánzhaō kingdom was getting too big for its boots and a Tang punishment squad of 80,000 troops swept south to Dàlǐ. The Tang army was soundly whipped (60,000 were massacred outside Xiàguān) and the Nánzhaō kingdom expanded south into Burma. Before long the kingdom reached as far as Hanoi in the south-east, Sìchuān in the north, Zūnyì in the north-east and Nánníng (Guǎngxī) in the east.

The Nánzhaō, which had formerly allied itself with the Tang Chinese against the Tibetans, now switched allegiances, joining forces with the Tibetans to sack Chéngdū in 829. Tens of thousands of scholars and artisans were transported back to the capital at Dàlǐ, and the kingdom ruled as the most important in the South-West for the next six centuries.

The rulers of Nánzhaō were much influenced by the glories of the Tang to the north and Chinese culture spread quickly to the region. In the 10th century the local Bai dynasty was deposed by ethnic-Chinese rulers, but the independent kingdom of Dàlǐ continued right up until the Mongol invasion in 1252, when it was finally incorporated into the Yuan dynasty.

Song Dynasty

Meanwhile, the Tang dynasty, weakened by the An Lushan Rebellion and repeated Tibetan incursions, had fallen and a period of smaller kingdoms had filled the political vacuum. In 934 the lands of northern Vietnam (Annan) were lost, never again to form part of the Chinese empire.

In 959 Zhao Kuangyin, the leader of the palace corps of one of the so-called Five Dynasties (the Later Zhou), usurped power from a seven-year-old head of state. By 976 Zhao Kuangyin had conquered the dozen or so other kingdoms, one of them Sìchuān, that stood in the way to reunifying China and established yet another dynasty: the Song (960–1279).

The Song is remembered for its strong centralised government, a renewal of Confucian learning, a restoration of the examination system that fostered a civilian-dominated bureaucracy, and what has been referred to as a commercial revolution. The rise of a merchant class and the introduction of paper money facilitated the growth of more urban centres nourished by the influx of goods from around the country. Historians point to the Song dynasty as the turning point in China's development of an urban culture.

The Song profoundly influenced the development of Chinese culture, which in turn profoundly influenced the South-West, but the Song had little direct influence on the region. While the Song emperor incorporated Sìchuān into the empire proper, he was also supposed to have drawn a line across the Dadu River on a map of Sìchuān and told his generals to forget about the lands to the south. The Song had few dealings with Yúnnán and for a while Zhuang rebels set up a short-lived kingdom in Guǎngxī.

Mongol Reign (Yuan Dynasty)

In 1206, after 20 years of internal war, Genghis Khan united the roaming Mongol tribes into a new national entity. He turned his gaze eastwards and the epitome of all barbarians came crashing through the Great Wall of China.

South-West China felt shock waves of refugees but it was not until 1252 that Kublai Khan, Genghis Khan's grandson, swept into Yúnnán (via Lugu Lake) as part of a pincer movement to outflank the southern Song troops. In 1258 Kublai's brother Möngke invaded Sìchuān but died in mid-campaign, giving the region pause for breath.

In the wake of the Mongols as many as one million Muslim mercenaries settled in Yúnnán to control and repopulate the devastated countryside. The Mongols set up two ruling centres, at Kūnmíng (Yúnnánfu) and Dàlǐ. Kublai's son and grandson ruled the region until power was finally handed to a Muslim governor from Bukhara. In the employ of the Khans came Marco Polo, who travelled on a fact-finding mission from Sindafu (Chéngdū) to Yachi (Kūnmíng), recording a marvellous land of crocodiles, rice wine and tattooed tribespeople.

Eventually the great Khan bought southern China under his sway and established the Yuan dynasty (1271–1368). Both Yúnnán and Guǎngxī were formally brought into the imperial fold and the latter received its modern name for the first time. The China ruled by Kublai was the vastest empire the world has ever seen.

The Mongols were harsh in administering their rule, but on the economic front at least they were less interfering than the Chinese dynasties that had preceded them. More work was carried out on China's canal system and roads, offering a further stimulus to trade. The commercial revolution that had gathered pace in the Song continued unabated in the Yuan, with inter-regional and even international trade flourishing. Taxes were heavy, however, except for people of Mongol descent, who were exempt.

The grip of the Yuan dynasty over its vast empire remained strong almost until the very end, but by the middle of the 14th century the country had become convulsed by rebellion. By 1367 Zhu Yuanzhang, originally an orphan and Buddhist novice, had climbed to the top of the rebel leadership, and in 1368 he established the Ming dynasty and restored Chinese rule.

Ming Dynasty

Upon establishing the Ming (1368–1644), Zhu Yuanzhang took the name of Hongwu. Hongwu is remembered for his despotism (he had some 10,000 scholars and their families put to death in two particularly paranoid purges of his administration), but he was also a strong leader who did much to set China back on its feet in the aftermath of the Yuan collapse.

The Ming dynasty based at Nánjīng (the 'Southern Capital') and later Běijīng (the 'Northern Capital') saw the formal incorporation of the rest of the South-West into the Chinese empire. Political and military control of the region tightened and mass migration started in earnest. In 1381 a pacification campaign launched from Ānshūn gained control of Yúnnán. Guìzhōu was formally made a province in 1413.

In reality, semi-independent local fiefdoms still commanded their own armies and raised their own taxes. Imperial rule was propped up by a web of agricultural garrison-communities run by governors-general whose thankless job it was to extend the control of the empire. They did this through various 'pacification campaigns' among the local minorities. One of the bloodiest battles in Guǎngxī's history was fought between imperial troops and Yao tribesmen near Guìpíng in 1465. Yúnnán was no better behaved and Guìzhōu grew as a heavily garrisoned base for incursions into both provinces.

The subsequent reign of Yongle saw, for the first time, China developing into a strong maritime nation. Zheng He (Cheng Ho), an eunuch general of Muslim descent from Yúnnán, undertook seven great expeditions to South-East Asia, Persia, Arabia and even eastern Africa as head of the largest naval fleet in the world.

In the final years of Ming rule, official corruption, excessive eunuch power, intellectual conservatism and costly wars brought the nation to virtual bankruptcy. A famine in Shaanxi province, coupled with governmental neglect, was the spark for a massive peasant rebellion that brought the Ming to a close. The remnants of the declining dynasty clung desperately to power in the South-West, as the remnants of the Song had done before them. The last Ming prince made a desperate last stand in the Gāolígòng Shān near the current border with Burma before finally fleeing to Mandalay.

Qing Dynasty

The Manchus, a separate ethnic group to the north of China proper, had long been growing in power and lost no time in inflicting a decisive defeat on the weakened empire. In June 1644 they marched into the Ming capital and proclaimed their new dynasty the Qing (1644–1911), although it was to be four decades before they finally cleared the south of Ming loyalist forces and pacified the whole country.

A brief rebellion in 1674 by the warlord Wu Sangui, the man responsible for pacifying most of Guìzhōu and Yúnnán for the Manchus, was a short-lived attempt at local rule. As the empire grew in confidence, the Manchu nobleman Oertai was promoted to the governor-generalship of Guìzhōu, Yúnnán and Guǎngxī and given a mission to bring the local tribes under imperial control, to pacify the Miáo and to abolish the powerful local tusi headmen who had been effectively ruling the region for centuries. Over the next six years he ruthlessly expanded the power of government and quashed the local headmen, sparking a series of local rebellions. During one rebellion at Leigong in 1726 over 10,000 Miáo tribespeople are said to have been beheaded, and another 400,000 starved to death in an ensuing famine. A similar rebellion took place in 1797, this time among the Bouyi.

Today's Chinese 'triads' (the modern secret societies generally thought to be involved in criminal activity, especially drug trafficking) are the descendants of secret societies originally set up in southern China to resist Manchu control.

Although the Manchus concentrated power in their own hands and alienated the Han Chinese, the reign of the early Qing emperors from 1663 to 1796 was a period of great prosperity. The throne was occupied by three of the most able rulers China has known: Kangxi, Yongcheng and Qianlong. The Qing expanded the empire to its greatest limits since the Han dynasty. Reduced taxation and massive flood control and irrigation projects benefited the peasants.

However, China continued to be an inward-looking nation, oblivious to the technological and scientific revolutions taking place in Europe. By 1760 the barbarians were banging at the gate.

Foreign Incursions & Domestic Rebellions

As the British, Dutch and Spanish pried open the Chinese markets from their bases in Guǎngzhōu, trade began to flourish – in China's favour. British purchases of tea, silk and porcelain far outweighed Chinese purchases of wool and spices. In 1773 the British decided to balance the books with sales of opium. Despite imperial declarations of wars against drugs, opium addiction in China skyrocketed and with it so did sales. Opium gradually became the main crop amongst the warlords and minorities of the South-West and the land and its people became saturated in it. Opium was even used as local currency in some places.

Triad pirates, forced inland by the British, shipped opium up and down the waterways of Guǎngxī and Guìzhōu. Increasing Han migration continued to force many of the local minorities off the best lands. Taxes were crippling.

In the face of so much hardship and humiliation it was inevitable that a series of rebellions spread through the region like wildfire. The first major rebellion was the Taiping, which burst out of Jintian village (near Guiping in Guǎngxī) in 1851, swept through Guìzhōu and ended up taking Nánjīng three years later. The rebellion was led by Hong Xiuquan, a failed scholar whose encounters with Western missionaries had given rise to a series of religious visions, in one of which he ascended to heaven, was given a new set of internal organs by a golden-bearded Jehovah and then proceeded to battle the evil spirits of the world with his elder brother Jesus Christ.

The Taipings owed much of their ideology to Christianity. They forbade gambling, opium, tobacco and alcohol; advocated agricultural reform; and outlawed foot-binding, prostitution and slavery. Before long the Taipings commanded forces of around 600,000 men and 500,000 women. Ironically, they were defeated by a coalition of Qing forces and Western mercenaries – the Europeans preferring to deal with a corrupt and weak Qing government than a powerful, united China governed by the Taipings.

In 1855 a Muslim rebellion lead by Sultan Suleiman rocked Yúnnán. Initial sparks came from rivalries between the Muslim and Chinese tin miners of Yúnnán, but this quickly took an anti-government nature when the Qing authorities sided with the Chinese. A Muslim army (armed by the British) rose up but was eventually crushed by the Chinese (armed by the French), who slaughtered tens of thousands of Muslims in retaliation.

In 1854 a large Miáo rebellion in Guìzhōu, led by Zhang Xumei, gained many military victories and even linked up with the Taiping Rebellion. By 1871 this too had been defeated but at the cost of several million deaths.

More Foreign Incursions

As imperial control loosened, the encroaching Western powers moved in to pick off China's colonial 'possessions'. A war with France in 1858 (to avenge the murder of a French missionary in Guǎngxī) and another from 1883 to 1885 ended Chinese suzerainty in Indochina and allowed the French to both maintain control of Indochina and carve out Yúnnán and Guǎngxī as their designated sphere of influence. Wúzhōu to the east was prised open to foreign trade in 1897 and Nánníng followed 10

years later. In 1903 France started to build the railway line from Haiphong and Hanoi to Kūnmíng, a line which would soon become the province's main link to the outside world. By 1911 one million Chinese were riding the train every year; by 1992 a handful of backpackers were doing the same.

The British crept closer to Yúnnán when they occupied the Kachin state of northern Burma and even managed to persuade one of Yúnnán's local tusi headman to defect to the British cause, thus snatching a strategic section of land in north-west Yúnnán. In 1891 500 British troops briefly occupied Jǐnghóng, when it was known as Cheli. They further toyed with the idea of building a railway line from Burma to Yúnnán. When a British commercial agent in Bhamo, north Burma, was killed during an exploratory mission to the Yúnnán-Burma border, the British used his murder as a means to extract more trade concessions from the Qing. In 1900 a British gunboat docked in Chóngqìng for the first time.

By 1898 the European powers were on the verge of carving up China for dinner, a feast that was thwarted only by a US proposal for an 'open-door' policy that would leave China open to trade with any foreign power.

Fall of the Qing

Farther north, the Boxer Rebellion was defeated in 1900 by a combined British, US, French, Japanese and Russian force of 20,000 troops, and the foreign forces levied yet another massive indemnity on the Qing government.

With the defeat of the Boxer Rebellion, the empress fled from Běijīng to Xī'ān and began to realise that China was too weak to survive without reform. But, while the civil service examinations based on irrelevant 1000-year-old Confucian doctrines were abolished, other court-sponsored reforms proved to be a sham.

Furthermore, by now secret societies aimed at bringing down the Qing dynasty were legion, even existing overseas, where they were set up by disaffected Chinese who had left their homeland. To make matters worse for the Qing, in 1908 the empress dowager died and the two-year-old Emperor Puyi ascended to the throne. The Qing was now rudderless and quickly collapsed. Two months later representatives from 17 provinces throughout China gathered in Nánjīng to establish the Provisional Republican Government of China. China's long dynastic cycle had come to an end.

Early Days of the Republic

The Provisional Republican Government was set up on 10 October 1911 by Sun Yatsen and Li Yuanhong, a military commander in Wuchang. Lacking the power to force a Manchu abdication, they had no choice but to call on the assistance of Yuan Shikai, head of the imperial army, who promptly placed himself at the head of the Republican movement and forced Sun Yatsen's resignation.

Yuan lost no time in dissolving the Republican government and amending the constitution to make himself president for life. When this met with regional opposition, he took the natural next step in 1915 of declaring an imperial restoration and pronouncing himself China's latest emperor.

With this Yúnnán seceded, taking Guǎngxī, Guìzhōu and much of the rest of the south with it. What followed was an era of domination by warlords, with no single power strong enough to hold the country together until the Communists established the People's Republic of China (PRC) in 1949.

Kuomintang & Communists

By 1920 the Kuomintang (also called the Guomindang, KMT or Nationalist Party), headed by Chiang Kaishek, had emerged as the dominant political force in eastern China. Between 1926 and 1928 the KMT wrested control of the country from the north Chinese warlords during the Northern Expedition and established a national government in Běijīng.

Nevertheless, only about half the country was under direct Kuomintang control; the rest, including the entire South-West, was still ruled by local warlords. China's social problems were legion: children were used as

---

Warlords

In the first half of the 20th century, as central government control waned, large areas of South-West China slipped into the hands of warlords, private armies and bandit gangs.

In 1920 Guǎngxī alone was controlled by over a dozen separate warlord armies and Sìchuān was controlled by no fewer than 17. The three most powerful warlords in Guǎngxī came to be known as the Guǎngxī clique. They controlled over 230,000 troops and played a crucial part in the rise of Chiang Kaishek until they finally withdrew their support in 1929.

Warlords became particularly powerful during WWII. Leaders like Tang Qiyao and Long Yun in Yúnnán ruled like kings and exacted crippling taxes, often years ahead of production. Central to warlord control was the huge opium trade, which had mushroomed to become the South-West's single largest industry. One field of poppies could produce over six times as much profit as a field of wheat, and few farmers could afford not to switch crops, especially as some warlords even imposed an opium tax on 'lazy' farmers who wouldn't produce their quota.

When the warlords squeezed their subjects too hard rebellions erupted, like the Jian Tang Rebellion that ripped through Guìzhōu from 1941 to 1944. Most warlords, however, continued to rule until 1949.

The warlords faced an uncertain future with the declaration of the PRC. Many fled to Taiwan with the Kuomintang or established drug baronies in the Golden Triangle of Burma and Laos. Some, like the infamous Wei brothers, continued to pass intelligence to the Kuomintang from bases among the head-hunting Wa tribes of northern Burma. Later, during the Vietnam War, they would also keep the CIA informed as Chinese supply convoys headed to the Pathet Lao and Viet Minh.

The warlords who stayed behind in China were subsequently vilified by the Communists and, more often than not, executed, while their families were branded as class enemies for decades to come.

slave labour in factories; domestic slavery, prostitution and opium addiction were rife; the destitute and starving died on the streets; and strikes were ruthlessly suppressed by foreign and Chinese factory owners.

In 1921 the Chinese Communist Party (which became the CCP) was formed in Shanghai and, under the advice of the Soviet Comintern, joined a temporary alliance with the Kuomintang, largely to prevent Japanese expansion. After the death of Sun Yatsen in 1925, Chiang became obsessed with countering the influence of the Communists, and in 1927 he showed his true colours by ordering the massacre of over 5000 Shanghai Communists and trade union representatives. The Reds were on the run.

Civil War

After the 1927 massacre, the Communists were divided between an insurrectionary policy of targeting large urban centres and one of basing their rebellion in the countryside. Communist-led uprisings in parts of the South-West met with some success, notably at Bose in Guǎngxī under the leadership of Deng Xiaoping.

The Communist armies were still small and hampered by limited resources. They adopted a strategy of guerrilla warfare, emphasising mobility and deployment of forces for short attacks on the enemy, followed by swift separation once the attack was over. Pitched battles were avoided except where their force was overwhelmingly superior. The strategy was summed up in a four-line slogan:

The enemy advances, we retreat;
The enemy camps, we harass;
The enemy tires, we attack;
The enemy retreats, we pursue.

By 1930 the ragged Communist forces had been turned into an army of perhaps 40,000, and presented such a serious challenge to the Kuomintang that Chiang had to wage a number of extermination campaigns against them. He was defeated each time, and the Communist army expanded its territory.

The Long March

When Chiang's fifth extermination campaign began in October 1933, the Communists suddenly changed their strategy. The authority of the Communist leaders Mao Zedong and Zhu De, who championed rural revolt from their base in the Jinggǎng Shān, was being undermined by other members of the Party who advocated meeting Chiang's troops in pitched battles; this strategy proved disastrous. By October 1934 the Communists had suffered heavy losses and were hemmed into a small area in Jiāngxī.

On the brink of defeat, the Communists decided to retreat from Jiāngxī and march north to Shaanxi to join up with other Communist armies in Sìchuān, Shaanxi and Gānsù. In the course of the next year the Long March took the ragbag Communist army over 9500km to safety in Shaanxi, where they consolidated their position at the famous base at Yán'ān.

Japanese Invasion

In September 1931 the Japanese took advantage of the confusion in China to invade and occupy Manchuria in the north-east. Chiang, still obsessed with the threat of the Communists, went ahead with his fifth extermination drive, but in 1936 Chiang's own generals took him hostage, and an anti-Japanese alliance was formed after negotiations led by Zhou Enlai.

But it did little to halt the advance of the Japanese, who in 1937 launched an all-out invasion; by 1939 they had overrun most of eastern China and reached Nánníng in central Guǎngxī.

Ironically, this was in many ways a huge boost to the economy and industrialisation of the South-West, which became the main base for resistance to the Japanese. The Kuomintang moved their entire base of operations up the Yangzi to Chóngqìng, which became the new seat of the Nationalist government from 1938 to 1945. Entire factories were shifted upstream and China's best universities relocated to Kūnmíng and Chéngdū, along with an estimated 60 to 80 million Chinese. Guìlín became a major airforce base.

The Long March

On 16 October 1934, a 100km-long trail of 90,000 men and 30 women burst out of Kuomintang encirclement and embarked on what would become known as the Long March. Over the next 12 months they covered 9500km, passed through 11 provinces, traversed 18 mountain ranges and crossed 24 major rivers. En route the group took 64 major cities and battled the armies of 10 warlords. Marching under cover of night, they averaged more than 30km a day for a year.

Two months later the Red Army reached Lìpíng in south-east Guìzhōu and convened its first meeting – it had already lost two-thirds of its troops. From Lìpíng the Reds crossed the Wuyang River near Shībīng and arrived at Zūnyì by January 1935.

The meeting at Zūnyì, from 7 to 18 January, marked a turning point for the march and a critical juncture in the history of the Communist Party. It ended with the dominance of Mao's views over the Soviet adviser Otto Braun (Li De) and the forging of a uniquely Chinese brand of Communism. It was also the point where Mao took charge of the Chinese revolution.

From Zūnyì the marchers zigzagged around Guìzhōu in a series of feints and double-backs in an attempt to confuse Chiang Kaishek, who was directing operations against them from a base in Guìyáng. They were beaten back from Chìshuǐ but finally took the Loushan Pass north of Zūnyì after a desperate race to the top between the troops of Peng Dehuai on one side of the pass and the local Guìzhōu warlord on the other. The Reds got there first, by five minutes, and smashed the warlord army below.

From Loushan the Reds made many about turns between Xishui and Tongzi before heading south to Guìyáng and Xīngyì. As they moved they were continually harassed by Nationalist planes – a 'cloud of steel mosquitos' – which supposedly dropped boulders whenever they ran out of bombs.

The goal of the march was to meet up with the Fourth Route Army that was somewhere in north-west Sìchuān. Mao chose to head south-west, via Xīngyì and Panxian, coming close enough to Kūnmíng to persuade the small foreign community there (including Joseph Rock – see the boxed text in the Yunnan chapter) to evacuate to Hanoi. Mao's plan was to draw the Kuomintang troops away from their real goal, the Yangzi River, and the ruse worked like a dream. The Reds sprinted north to the Jinsha River at Jiaopingdu and for the next nine days and nights ferried their troops across the Yangzi.

To the north lay the 'Cool Mountains' of the Liang Shān and the tribal areas of the Yi people, one of the most dangerous tribes in the South-West. Here the army had a stroke of luck. The Red Commander Liu Bocheng spoke a little Yi and managed to win over the Yi chieftain with promises of autonomy (and free guns). The agreement was sealed with a toast of chicken blood and wine, and a safe passage was secured.

The heroics were just beginning. At the Lúdìng Bridge 22 soldiers hauled themselves across bare iron chains, avoiding both crossfire from the Kuomintang troops and real fire from the burning bridgehead, in order to secure the crossing of the Dadu River.

From this point on, nature became the marchers' worst enemy. As the Great Snowy Mountains rose up ahead of the army there was a choice of two paths – one east of the mountains, the other west. Mao decided to go over the top. Wearing little more than hemp sandals or cloth wrapped around their feet, the marchers dragged themselves over 4000m passes, with strips of cloth bound across their eyes to prevent snow blindness. Many suffered from the low temperatures and high altitude; the March's chief historian had his legs amputated after frostbite set in.

At Xiaojin, on the other side of the mountains, to their great relief the marchers met up with the Fourth Route Army of Zhang Guotao. However, relief soon turned to anger as conflict between Zhang and Mao tore the two groups apart. Zhang headed west to set up a revolutionary base at Gānzī, while Mao's troops continued north.

As the Communists passed the mountains near Barkam, they headed into the marshlands of Hóngyuán and Zöigê in northern Sìchuān in an attempt to avoid the Kuomintang troops at Sōngpān. This was to prove the worst stretch of the march. According to local historians, 'every step gained

The Long March

cost a man's life'. For seven days the soldiers floundered through the bogs, an effort likened to 'walking through beancurd'. Food was especially scarce and many soldiers ruptured their bowels by eating raw millet, while the soldiers at the back of the march washed the faeces of those at the front in order to get a little extra grain. Zhou Enlai came close to death from acute hepatitis.

The struggles of the Long March would soon turn to legend. Years afterwards, stories circulated of how cloth Chinese characters were tacked onto soldiers' backs in order to help the comrades behind learn to read and write; of how Mao was constipated for weeks at a time during most of the March; and of how, when the Reds passed through Maotai, the dastardly Comintern adviser drank so much that he fell unconscious for a week. A series of revolutionary paintings depict Mao and Zhou leading the March from the front. In reality, they covered most of the ground asleep in two-man litters.

When the ragtag group eventually arrived at the safety of Gānsù and then Yán'ān, the Long Marchers were a decimated force. Over 60,000 had perished, including Mao's wife and his infant child, who was abandoned in Guìzhōu. Some marchers deserted, some died in battle, others simply dropped dead from fatigue.

Even so, the march proved that will could prevail over circumstance, and that the Chinese peasants could fight if they were given a method, organisation, leadership, hope and weapons. The journey was invaluable in providing the leadership with insights into the vast countryside and the minority tribes who lived there. Moreover, it offered a golden opportunity to spread the Communist good word. Along the way the Communists confiscated the property of officials, landlords and tax-collectors; redistributed land; armed thousands of peasants with weapons captured from the Kuomintang; and left soldiers behind to organise guerrilla groups to harass the enemy.

The hardened and experienced core who completed the march (including Lin Biao, Liu Shaoqi, Peng Dehuai, Zhou Enlai, Zhu De and Deng Xiaoping) was to form the backbone of the revolutionary aristocracy for the next 40 years. The march also established Mao as the paramount leader of the Chinese Communist movement and created a moral prestige and untarnished revolutionary myth that would endure until the great disasters of the 1960s.

In 1941 the Japanese assault on Pearl Harbor brought the Americans into the conflict. Hoping to use Chiang's troops to tie down as many Japanese as possible, the Americans, headed by General Stillwell, poured medicine, weaponry and supplies into the crucial South-West supply corridor. Between 1937 and 1939 hundreds of thousands of local workers toiled over the construction of the epic 1154km-long Burma Road. The supply line connected Lashio in northern Burma with Xiaguan and finally Kūnmíng, which rapidly became a major US air base. For more on the Burma Road see the boxed text in the Yúnnán chapter.

In 1942 the Japanese overran Burma and cut off the Burma Road and the allies were forced to build another road, this time from Ledo in north-east India. They also started running a plane service from British India over the Himalayan 'hump' into the airfields of Kūnmíng and Lìjiāng. American Flying Tigers were stationed across Yúnnán under the command of officer Claire Lee Chennault. A military airfield was even built just north of Lìjiāng. The run was extremely hazardous (an average of 13 planes were lost a month) but a supply line was kept open until the new road was opened in 1944 and supply trucks once again made the long haul to Kūnmíng. The Japanese eventually reached Téngchōng in Yúnnán and even got as far as taking Guìlín, Liǔzhōu and Wúzhōu in 1944 before their surrender in 1945.

Defeat of the Kuomintang

The Kuomintang-Communist alliance had collapsed by 1941 and by the end of WWII China was in the grip of an all-out civil war. By 1948 the Communists had captured so much US-supplied Kuomintang equipment and had recruited so many Kuomintang soldiers that they equalled the Kuomintang in both numbers and supplies. Three great battles were fought in 1948 and 1949, which saw the Kuomintang defeated and hundreds of thousands of Kuomintang troops join the Communists. The Communists moved south and crossed the Yangzi – by October all the major cities in southern China had fallen to them.

In Běijīng on 1 October 1949, Mao Zedong stood atop Tiananmen Gate, announced that the Chinese people had stood up, and proclaimed the foundation of the People's Republic of China (PRC). Chiang Kaishek fled to the island of Formosa (Taiwan), taking with him the entire gold reserves of the country and what was left of his air force and navy, to set up the Republic of China (ROC), naming his new capital Taipei.

As Mao celebrated the new republic in Běijīng, the Kuomintang leader Ding Zuoshou was still very much at large in southern Yúnnán, and it was not until two months later that the Communists finally pushed through to Kūnmíng. Ding finally fled to Burma and then northern Thailand with 1000 of his best troops. Taiwanese supply planes, aided by the CIA, started to fly arms and ammunition into this small base to prepare for a counter-attack on Yúnnán (returning with cargo-loads of opium to help finance the cause), and soon Kuomintang troops numbered 12,000. The Kuomintang made a total of seven attempts to retake Yúnnán between 1951 and 1953 but was never successful. Thousands of Kuomintang troops remained in the region until 1961, when 20,000 Communist troops crossed into Burma, swept through the Golden Triangle and broke the back of the remaining Kuomintang.

Early Years of the PRC

The PRC began its days as a bankrupt nation. Its economy was in chaos and inflation rampant – one cup of coffee in 1949 Shanghai cost a cool three million yuan. The country had just 19,200km of railways and 76,800km of usable roads, all in bad condition. Irrigation works had broken down and livestock and animal populations were greatly reduced. Industrial production fell to half that of the prewar period and agricultural output plummeted.

With the Communist takeover, China seemed to become a different country. Unified by the elation of victory and the immensity of the task before them, and further bonded by the Korean War and the necessity to defend the new regime from possible US invasion, the Communists made the 1950s a dynamic period. The drive to become a great nation very quickly was awesome.

By 1953 inflation had been halted, industrial production had been restored to prewar levels and the land had been confiscated from the landlords and redistributed to the peasants. Party workers penetrated into the most remote corners of the South West, persuading tribal groups like the head-hunting Wa and the slave-raiding Yi that their antisocial activities were incompatible with the brotherhood of nationalities. On the basis of earlier Soviet models, the Chinese embarked on a massive five-year plan that was successful in lifting production on most fronts.

At the same time, the Party increased its social control by organising the people according to their work units *(dānwèi)* and dividing the country into 21 provinces, five autonomous regions, two municipalities (Běijīng and Shanghai) and around 2200 county governments with jurisdiction over approximately one million Party sub-branches. In the South-West the province of Xikang was incorporated into Sìchuān (1955) and Guǎngxī became an autonomous region (1958). The south-western borderlands saw an intriguing and often tense mixture of traditional tribal culture and Soviet-inspired reform.

Hundred Flowers

While the early years of the PRC saw rapid economic development, immense problems remained in the social sphere, particularly with regard to the question of intellectuals. Many Kuomintang intellectuals had stayed on rather than flee to Taiwan, and still more overseas Chinese, many of them highly qualified, returned to China soon after liberation to help in the enormous task of reconstruction. Returning Chinese and those of suspect backgrounds were given extensive re-education courses in special universities put aside for the purpose, and were required to write a self-critical 'autobiography' before graduating. For many it was a traumatic experience.

In the upper echelons of the Party itself opinions were divided as to how to deal with the problem of the intellectuals. But Mao, along with Zhou Enlai and other influential figures, felt that the Party's work had been so successful that it could roll with a little criticism, and in a closed session Mao put forward the idea of 'letting a hundred flowers bloom' in the arts and 'a hundred schools of thought contend' in the sciences.

It was to be a full year before Mao's ideas were officially sanctioned in April 1957, but once they were, intellectuals around the country responded with glee. Complaints poured in on everything from Party corruption to control of artistic expression, from the unavailability of foreign literature to low standards of living; but most of all, criticisms focused on the CCP monopoly on power and the abuses that went with it. The Party quickly had second thoughts about the flowers, and an anti-rightist campaign was launched. Within six months 300,000 intellectuals had been branded rightists, removed from their jobs and, in many cases, incarcerated or sent to labour camps.

The Great Leap Forward

The first five-year plan had produced satisfactory results on the industrial front, but growth of agricultural yields had been a disappointingly low 3.8%. The state faced the difficult problem of how to increase agricultural production to meet the needs of urban populations. As with the question of dealing with intellectuals, the Party leadership was divided on how to respond. Some, such as Zhou Enlai, favoured an agricultural incentive system. Mao favoured mass mobilisation of the country and inspirational exhortations that he believed would jump-start the economy to overtake Great Britain within 15 years.

In the end it was Mao who won the day, and the Chinese embarked on a radical program of creating massive agricultural communes and drawing large numbers of people from both rural and urban areas into enormous water control and irrigation projects. Mao perceived the Chinese masses as a 'blank piece of paper' and believed that revolutionary zeal and mass cooperative effort could overcome any obstacle. At the same time he criticised the earlier emphasis on heavy industry, and pushed for small local industry to be developed in the communes, with profits going back into agricultural development.

China embarked on one of the greatest failed economic experiments in human history. The Communists tried to abolish money and all private property, and told everyone to build backyard blast furnaces to increase steel production. Lacking iron ore, peasants had to melt down farm tools, pots, pans and even their bronze festival drums in order to meet the quota of steel 'production'. Villages that proudly met their quota soon discovered that the steel ingots were basically worthless.

Despite the enthusiastic forecasts for agricultural production, at the end of the day the lack of incentive to work in the common field and the large numbers of rural workers engaged in the worthless blast furnaces project resulted in a massive slump in grain output. Bad weather in 1959 and the withdrawal of Soviet aid in 1960 made matters worse. Every effort was made to cover up the ensuing disaster and no foreign assistance was sought. China plunged into a famine of staggering proportions: an estimated 30 million Chinese starved to death, and some put the figure at 60 million.

Sino-Soviet Split

As the Soviet Union inched towards peaceful coexistence with the USA and vilified the personality cult of Stalin, Mao increasingly began to regard the Soviet leadership as 'revisionist'. Sino-Soviet relations became ever frostier, with the unpredictable Khrushchev reneging on a promise to provide China with a prototype atomic bomb and siding with the Indians in a Sino-Indian border dispute.

In 1960 the Soviet Union removed all 1390 of its foreign experts working in China. With the experts went the blueprints for some 600 projects that the two powers had been working on together, including China's nuclear bomb program.

The Cultural Revolution

Although the official scapegoats were the Gang of Four, most non-partisan scholars now agree that the prime mover in the Cultural Revolution was Mao. The Cultural Revolution (1966–70) was another Great Leap Forward, an attempt to create new socialist structures overnight by destroying everything that had gone before, while allowing Mao to claw his way back into power.

Mao's extreme views, his recent disastrous policy decisions and his opposition to bureaucratisation led to his increasing isolation within the Party. In response, he began to cultivate a personality cult with the assistance largely of Lin Biao, the minister of defence and head of the People's Liberation Army (PLA).

In the early 1960s, Lin had a collection of Mao's sayings compiled into a book that was to become known simply as the 'little red book', though its real title was *Quotations from Chairman Mao*. The book became the subject of study sessions for all PLA troops and eventually this practice was extended into the general education system.

The result was that Mao's opponents were purged and simultaneously wall posters went up at Beijing University attacking the university administration. Mao officially sanctioned the wall posters and criticisms of Party members by university staff and students, and before long students were being issued red armbands and taking to the streets. By August 1966 Mao was reviewing mass parades of these Red Guards (*Hóngwèibīng*), chanting and waving copies of his little red book.

Nothing was sacred as the Red Guards rampaged through the country. Universities and secondary schools were shut down; intellectuals, writers and artists were dismissed, killed, persecuted or sent to labour in the countryside; publication of scientific, artistic, literary and cultural periodicals ceased; and the movement to destroy the 'Four Olds' smashed everything from Dǎi pagodas and Huí mosques to Tibetan monasteries. Minority areas were among the worst affected because they were the most traditional. In 1955 there were more than 2000 temples in Yúnnán; by the end of the Cultural Revolution there were fewer than half that.

Rival gangs of Red Guards fought pitched battles to prove their revolutionary purity. In Guǎngxī rival groups even robbed an ammunition train headed for Vietnam and fought each other with machine guns, bazookas and anti-aircraft guns. Dead bodies began to flow down the Xi River, to be picked up by the British authorities in Hong Kong.

A Revolution is not a Dinner Party – Mao Zedong

According to research by the dissident Chinese writer Zheng Yi (corroborated by John Gittings in his book *Real China: From Cannibalism to Karaoke*), it appears that over a six-week period in 1968 some 75 people in a remote corner of Guǎngxī province were killed and then, incredibly, devoured in the name of revolution.

Like the rest of the country, by 1968 Guǎngxī was in a state of near civil war. As the Cultural Revolutionary madness intensified, political cliques fought pitched battles for control of the province. Orders then came from Běijīng for the warring factions to turn up the heat to a 'force twelve typhoon' and foment 'merciless class struggle'.

The town of Wuxuan in central Guǎngxī was no different to other Chinese towns in that it was the site of countless 'struggle sessions'. During mass meetings class enemies were paraded in dunce caps to the sounds of drums and cymbals, placed in the aeroplane position (bent double with their arms behind their back) and forced to confess their political crimes, while the revolutionary mob whipped itself into a fury. Some of the interrogations ended in death: between May and June 1968 factional infighting in Wuxuan county alone led to the deaths of over 575 people. But the compelling horrors of what happened next makes Wuxuan almost unique.

During struggle sessions in Wuxuan, class enemies from one political faction were dragged down to the river side by their rivals. Here their chests were cut open and their hearts and livers cut out, cooked and eaten in barbecues, stews and even communal hotpots, in scornful revenge for previous factional murders. Feasting took place in secret at first but gradually came to be held publicly, with ceremonies and rituals celebrating the 'victory of the mass dictatorship'. One victim's head and feet were even put on display in the market. Two geography teachers were killed and their livers were eaten by their students.

The spiralling descent into mass madness was only halted when one local resident bravely sneaked a letter out to the authorities in Běijīng. In July a convoy of army troops won control of the town, only to find decomposing body parts adorning the town centre.

These atrocities, some of which were so barbaric as to defy credulity, were officially investigated in 1981. Twenty-seven cadres from Wuxuan and neighbouring Shanglin were subsequently expelled from the Party for eating human flesh and 15 were jailed.

Just what made the people of Wuxuan violate society's strongest taboo? Well, the reasons are still far from clear. Academics point out the perceived medicinal benefits amongst Chinese of eating certain animal organs, highlight the historical and mythological examples of justified cannibalism, and even search for ancient cannibalistic practices among the local Zhuang people. Perhaps more relevant was the political climate of the time – mass hysteria, anarchy, the polarisation of good and evil, and a state-sponsored climate of chaos which preached that no fate was too severe for the enemies of the people. The murderers were mostly people with 'bad class backgrounds' desperate to prove their revolutionary zeal, while others joined in simply to prevent the same thing from happening to them.

Not surprisingly, the Chinese government is reluctant to admit to the events in Wuxuan, and the work of dissident author Zheng Yi has been instrumental in bringing the story to light. The horror cannot be confined solely to the past. The events are *living* history and some of those who took part in the eating of human flesh still live and exercise power in the quiet town of Wuxuan to this day.

By January 1967 the PLA had been ordered to break up all 'counter-revolutionary organisations'. The struggles continued through to September 1967, and even Mao and Jiang Qing began to feel that enough was enough, especially in the sensitive border regions of Guǎngxī and Yúnnán – the main logistical link between Communist China and the Communist Viet Minh. 'Ultra-left tendencies' were condemned and the PLA was championed as the sole agent of 'proletarian dictatorship'.

The Cultural Revolution took a new turn as the Red Guards slipped from power and the PLA began its own reign of terror. Anyone with a remotely suspect background – this could mean anything from having a college education to having a distant cousin who lived overseas – was sent to the countryside, often in remote areas of Yúnnán or Guìzhōu, for re-education: intensive study, self-criticism and hard labour.

Significance & Repercussions Like most of Mao's well-intentioned experiments, the Cultural Revolution was a disaster of vast proportions. One of the few elements to benefit was the PLA, which ended up with a deeper penetration of most government organisations. Vast numbers of Chinese were victims of the revolution and later became known as the 'Lost Generation'. According to official figures 14,000 people were killed in Yúnnán alone.

A major victim of the Cultural Revolution was the man who had done so much to get it started: Lin Biao. In the aftermath of the Cultural Revolution, Mao was troubled by the powers of the PLA, and demanded self-criticisms from senior PLA officers. It is thought that a desperate Lin Biao sought support for an assassination attempt on Mao and, failing to find it, fled with his family to the USSR in a Trident jet. The 'renegade and traitor', as the Chinese press labelled him, died when his plane mysteriously crashed in Mongolia on 13 September 1971.

After the Cultural Revolution
The years immediately following the Cultural Revolution saw a return to some measure of political stability. Zhou Enlai had the most influence in the day-to-day governing of China and, among other things, worked towards restoring China's trade and diplomatic contacts with the outside world. In 1972 US President Nixon visited Běijīng and normalised relations between the USA and the PRC. And in 1973, Deng Xiaoping, vilified as China's 'No 2 Capitalist Roader' during the Cultural Revolution, returned to power.

Nevertheless, Běijīng politics remained factional and divided. On the one side were Zhou, Deng and a faction of 'moderates' or 'pragmatists'; on the other were the 'radicals', 'leftists' or 'Maoists' led by Jiang Qing. As Zhou's health declined, the radicals gained the upper hand. By the time of Zhou's death in January 1976, Hua Guofeng, Mao's chosen protege, was made acting premier and Deng disappeared from public view.

Tiananmen Incident
The death of Zhou Enlai and public anger towards Jiang Qing and her clique culminated in the Tiananmen Incident of March 1976. During the Qingming Festival, when Chinese traditionally honour the dead, crowds began to gather in Běijīng's Tiananmen Square to lay wreaths for Zhou, recite poems, make speeches and brandish posters. The content of the speeches, poems and banners was as critical of Jiang as it was eulogistic of Zhou.

The Politburo (the policy making authority of the Communist Party) met in an emergency session and, with the approval of Mao, branded them counter-revolutionary. Through the day of 5 April the crowd fought with police and police vehicles were burnt. Tiananmen Square was occupied by some 30,000 militia during the night and the remaining several hundred protesters were beaten and arrested. The incident was blamed on Deng, who was relieved of all his posts and fled to Guǎngzhōu before disappearing altogether.

Mao's Death & the Gang of Four
Mao had been a sick man for many years. In 1974 he was diagnosed as having Lou

Gehrig's disease, an extremely rare motor-neuron disorder. For the last few years of his life he was immobilised and fed through a tube into his nasal passage and his speech was indecipherable. On 8 September 1976 he died.

Mao Zedong's chosen successor was Hua Guofeng, an obscure party member whose first action was to arrest the ultra-leftist 'Gang of Four'. There were celebrations all throughout China when the news of the arrests was formally announced three weeks later.

The Gang did not to come to trial until 1980, and when it took place it provided a bizarre spectacle, with the blame for the entire Cultural Revolution falling on their shoulders. Jiang Qing remained unrepentant, hurling abuse at her judges and holding famously to the line that she 'was Chairman Mao's dog – whoever he told me to bite, I bit'. Its meaning was not lost on most Chinese, and privately whispers circulated that the problem had been not a Gang of Four but a 'Gang of Five'. Jiang Qing's death sentence was commuted and she lived under house arrest until 1991, when she committed suicide by hanging.

Third Coming of Deng

In the middle of 1977 Deng Xiaoping returned to power for the third time and was appointed to the positions of vice-premier, vice-chairman of the Party and chief of staff of the PLA. His next step was to remove Hua Guofeng. In September 1980 Hua relinquished the post of premier to Zhao Ziyang, a long-standing member of the CCP whose economic reforms in Sìchuān (including dissolving the first communes) in the mid-1970s overcame the province's bankrupt economy and food shortages and won him Deng's favour. In June 1981 Hu Yaobang, a protege of Deng's for several decades, was named Party chairman in place of Hua.

Final power now passed to the collective leadership of the six member Standing Committee of the CCP, which included Deng, Hu and Zhao. The China they took over was racked with problems, a backward

country in desperate need of modernisation. A short, sharp 16-day war with Vietnam in 1979 didn't help.

The need for order had to be reconciled with the popular desire for more freedom; the crisis of faith in the Communist ideology had to be overcome; and a regime now dependent on the power of the police and military for its authority had to be legitimised.

1980s – Economics in Command

With Deng at the helm, China set a course of pragmatic reforms towards economic reconstruction. In rural Sìchuān the so-called 'Responsibility System' allowed agricultural households and factories to sell their quota surpluses on the open market. And in coastal China, Special Economic Zones (SEZs) were established at Zhūhǎi (next to Macau), Shēnzhèn (next to Hong Kong) and Shàntóu and Xiàmén. The results have been nothing short of spectacular: over the last 15 years China has managed average annual growth rates of 9%.

In Communist China, however, the rush of economic reform has generated very little in the way of political reform. In fact, the reforms of the last 15 years might be thought of as a trade-off: increased economic opportunities in return for a continued Communist monopoly on power. The Party, one way or another, controls virtually every facet of public life: it is accountable to nobody but itself; it controls the army; and it controls the government, the courts and industry. In short, very little gets done in China without the approval of the Party. It is hardly surprising that official corruption and nepotism has become a major problem.

Tiananmen Massacre

The immediate catalyst of the protests of 1989 was the death of Hu Yaobang, a reforming element and protege of Deng's who had been attacked and forced to resign by hard-liners in early 1987. Behind the scenes, double-digit inflation, rampant official corruption and a purge of reformist Party members like Hu had given rise to massive social discontent. On 22 April 1989, a week after Hu's death, China's leaders gathered in the

Hall of the People for an official mourning service. Outside, approximately 150,000 students and other activists held an unofficial service that soon became a massive pro-democracy protest.

All through April, crowds continued to fill Tiananmen Square so that by the middle of May the number of protesters in and around the square had swelled to nearly one million. Workers and even members of the police force joined in. Protests erupted in at least 20 other cities. Approximately 3000 students staged a hunger strike for democracy in the square. Railway workers assisted students travelling to Běijīng by allowing them free rides on the trains. Students enrolled at Běijīng's Art Institute constructed the 'Goddess of Democracy' in Tiananmen Square – a statue which bore a striking resemblance to America's Statue of Liberty. The students made speeches demanding a free press and an end to corruption and nepotism. The arrival of the foreign press corps turned the 'Běijīng Spring' into the media event of 1989.

Through much of May, the CCP was unable to quell the protests, and the imminent arrival of Mikhail Gorbachev for the first Sino-Soviet summit since 1959 precluded the use of arms to dispel the crowds. On 20 May, however, immediately after Gorbachev's departure, martial law was declared, and by 2 June, 350,000 troops had been deployed around Běijīng. In the early hours of the morning on 4 June the 27th Army division attacked. Other units loyal to Deng were also employed. Heavy tanks and armoured vehicles made short work of the barricades, crushing anyone who got in their way, while troops with automatic weapons strafed the crowds on the streets.

The number of deaths that resulted from the action is widely disputed. Eyewitness accounts have indicated that hundreds died in the square alone, and it's likely that fighting in the streets around the square and in the suburbs of Běijīng may have led to several thousand casualties. What is certain is that the Party lost whatever remaining moral authority it had.

Holding It Together

He who stands on tiptoe is not steady, he who strides cannot maintain the pace.
Laotzu, 7th century BC

The empire, long united, must divide; long divided, must unite. Thus it has always been.
Romance of the Three Kingdoms

The Deng years brought political stability and rising living standards, but Deng died in early 1997. Jiang Zemin heads both the government and the Party as state president and Communist Party general secretary. But Jiang's power is held in place by a fragile web of alliances and compromises. China has never had a system for orderly succession.

Faced with a looming inner-Party power struggle and increasingly uneven economic development, both Chinese and foreign experts have begun to voice concerns that China might break up. Certainly the problems facing the current regime make it ripe for radical change, if not total collapse.

Despite spectacular economic growth rates on paper, the South-West has not been a winner in the glorious race to get rich. Spiralling prices in the region have not been met with a rise in income and most people, while they are better off in real terms, have fallen relatively in the social hierarchy.

Rural incomes have stagnated in recent years, while the end of the 'iron rice bowl' and dissolving state subsidies have pushed up prices of basic foodstuffs, leading to widespread social unrest. Official corruption permeates the entire system despite occasional widely publicised drives to stamp it out. Unemployment is rising at a rapid rate and up to 30% of the people of rural Sìchuān are classified as unemployed. The government has nightmares of widespread peasant unrest – the very force that brought it to power 50 years ago – and it has good reason to be fearful. Isolated rioting involving up to 20,000 people rocked the Sìchuānese cities of Minyang, Renshou, Nanchong, Yíbīn and Zígòng throughout 1997 and 1998.

[continued on page 37]

ETHNIC MINORITIES OF SOUTH-WEST CHINA

1	Tibetan
2	Qiang
3	Yi
4	Mosu
5	Naxi
6	Drung
7	Nu
8	Lisu
9	Pumi
10	Bai
11	Jingpo
12	Wa
13	Lahu
14	Dai (Thai)
15	Hani (Akha)
16	Bulang
17	Mongolian
18	Miao (Hmong)
19	Bouyi
20	Tujia
21	Shui
22	Dong
23	Yao (Mien)
24	Maonan
25	Mulam
26	Zhuang

ETHNIC MINORITIES

KRAIG LIEB

The ethnic minorities of the South-West present a fascinating kaleidoscopic compression of Chinese, Tibetan, Thai and Burmese peoples. They add a vibrant, colourful dimension to a region often perceived as monotonously peopled by Mao-suited Han Chinese. A visit to some of these minority areas, especially during market days or festivals, is often the highlight of a trip to the South-West. The ethnic diversity ranges from the Tibetans and Qiang of western Sìchuān to the one-time slave-raiding Yi and head-hunting Wa of Yúnnán. Visual highlights range from the colourful embroidery of the Miáo to the subtropical colours of the Thai-related Dǎi, Bulang and Jingpo of Xīshuāngbǎnnà.

Some 36.8% of South-West China is made up of minorities (compared to 8.2% nationwide) and the region contains almost 50% of China's entire 'minority nationality' population – about 45 million people. China's 100 million strong minority people are divided into 56 ethnic groups, of which 26 are found in the South-West, though even these only touch the tip of the iceberg. In remote areas of Yúnnán random geographical features such as a fast-flowing river or mountain range can result in sharp cultural and ethnic divides. When minority classifications were first drawn up in the early 1950s, Yúnnán alone nominated 260 groups, of which 25 were formally recognised. Some minorities, including the Baima of northern Sìchuān and the Kemu of Yúnnán, remain officially unrecognised to this day. Group populations range from the 15-million-strong Zhuang of Guǎngxī to the fragile pocket of 5000 Drung people in south-western Yúnnán.

The minorities are far more strategically important to China than mere numbers suggest. Not only do they inhabit sensitive border areas but many also have ethnic kin on the other side of these borders. The Guìzhōu Miáo are ethnically the same as the Hmong of Laos and Vietnam; the Yao of Guǎngxī are the Mien of Laos and Thailand; and the Jingpo are known in northern Burma as the Kachin. Also, minority lands contain large reserves of untapped minerals and other natural resources.

Relations between the minorities and the Han Chinese have always been dicey at best and today the different communities remain quite separate. The Chinese have traditionally regarded non-Han groups as *yěmán*, or 'barbarians', even though China was itself ruled by two of these 'minorities' – the Mongols during the Yuan Dynasty and the Manchu during the Ming. All nationalities in China are referred to as 'equal brothers', with the Han as the 'eldest brother' (big brother?). History has seen several minority rebellions against Han control, particularly the Muslim and Miáo rebellions of the 19th century. Great Han chauvinism remains rife.

Most minorities speak their own languages among themselves but also speak Mandarin Chinese, as this is taught in all the schools. Most

Front page: Nàxī women dancing in front of a poem by Mao. (Photograph by Hilary Smith)

also employ Chinese script, though others, such as the Yí, Tibetans and Náxī, have their own ancient scripts. Some, like the Miáo, have a written code that was established by missionaries during the 18th century. Most cling to ancient animist beliefs and have an elaborate set of festivals closely linked to fertility and courtship.

Music is central to many of the nationalities, with lúshēng pipes a particular favourite, never more so than at the lúshēng festivals of the Miáo in Guìzhōu during the first lunar month (usually February). The other main festivals of the region include the Torch Festival of the Yí and the Water-Splashing Festival of the Dǎi in Xīshuāngbǎnnà.

The Chinese authorities continue to paint the minorities as happy, smiling colourful people. In reality they are often at the lowest rung of the social and economic ladder. Most groups originate from the richer agricultural lands of central China and were pushed first south into the valleys and then up into the mountains of the South-West by Han expansion. Minority areas remain the remotest and least developed parts of China and have generally been passed by in the race to get rich quick. Opium used to be a major cash crop for many minorities (as it is still for their cousins over the border) but the Communists clamped down hard on this and most are now subsistence farmers. Integration of the minorities into modern Chinese society is happening fast but is still far from complete.

The minorities of the South-West enjoy a wide ethnic spread. Some, such as the Zhuang of Guǎngxī or the Tujia of Guìzhōu, have been largely sinofied while others, like the Dong of Guìzhōu, retain their traditional culture. Many, such as the Miáo, have several internal subgroups, which are defined by their dress (eg, the Black Miáo, Flowery Miáo etc). The Huí nationality are ethnic Chinese and only considered a minority because of their Islamic faith.

Western Sìchuān is made up of Tibetans, mostly Khambas from eastern Tibet or Goloks from the northern Amdo region of Qīnghǎi. Also resident here are small numbers of Tibetan-related Qiang. The south of the province is home to the fascinating Yí people of the Liáng Shān (Cool Mountains), who remained a slave-raiding society strictly divided along caste lines until the end of the 1950s.

Left: Bai women with baskets out shopping in Měnghùn, Yúnnán. (Photograph by Kraig Lieb).

Guìzhōu is dominated by the seven million strong Miáo (Hmong) but also populated by the Dong, known for their dramatic wooden drum towers and bridges, and the Bouyi, the batik masters of central Guìzhōu. The border with Guǎngxī is home to small groups of Yao and Shui.

North-west Yúnnán has large numbers of the matrilineal Náxī and Mosu. The Bai of Dàlǐ have been largely sinofied over the centuries but they were the most powerful ethnic group in the region during the height of the Nanzhao kingdom, 1200 years ago. The Bai and the Yi are the two largest minority groups in Yúnnán. The remote border valleys of the Salween River near to Assam in India are Drung, Lisu, and Nu areas.

Xīshuāngbǎnnà has the densest collection of ethnic groups, of which the largest are the Hani (or Akha) and Dǎi. Many smaller groups such as the Lahu, Wa, Jingpo and Khmer-speaking Bulang live in remote settlements. Many still practice slash-and-burn agriculture. Tiny communities of Pumi, Achang, Jinuo and Deang still exist. The Lisu, Lahu, Akha and Jinuo all have communities south of the border in Myanmar and Laos.

Guǎngxī is the most sinofied province of the South-West but it has communities of Dong, Yao and Mulao in the north.

Minority Nationalities under Communism

In the early years of the PRC local headmen usually became local party cadres, mostly under the watchful assistance of a more influential Han official. Nationalities Institutes were set up to train minority party cadres and the Nationalities Press began to publish books in minority languages, often for the first time in their history. Minority areas were organised into various autonomous units, according to the dominant ethnic group. Today approximately 64% of China's land is an autonomous unit.

The Cultural Revolution and the Great Leap Forward were dark times for the minorities and assimilation sped up. Local languages were

Right: A Yi woman tending to her market stall. (Photograph by Hilary Smith)

outlawed and the 'four olds' (old ideas, old culture, old customs and old habits) were criticised. Religious freedoms were suppressed and shamans, priests and holy men were arrested. Minorities were forced to cremate their dead, a practice that broke traditional taboos. Local headmen or chiefs were subject to self-criticism and re-education.

Since the 1980s there has been something of an ethnic revival in the South-West. Minorities remain exempt from the one-child policy (they are allowed two) and receive preferential weighting for educational placement – two good reasons why more and more people are registering as belonging to a minority nationality. Local festivals and cultural life in general is growing in strength.

Yet the Han nationalism seems to grow. Demographic dilution is having a large effect on many minority areas, and economic freedoms are speeding up the assimilation process. Economic advancement in the South-West generally only comes from immersion in the Han language and social system. Rapid economic development of the region appears to be the greatest threat to the survival of its rich ethnic and cultural diversity.

[continued from page 32]

In July 2000 a disgruntled silk-worm worker blew up a town hall in south-west Sìchuān killing six, including the mayor. The central government meanwhile complains of increasing regional power – one of the main reasons that Chóngqìng was taken from the control of powerful Sìchuān in 1997 – and has difficulties collecting its taxes. Yúnnán looks south to the neighbouring countries of South-East Asia for its economic future. However, hand in hand with the rise in trade has come a disturbing increase in prostitution, drug addiction and AIDS.

Ironically, if the Western press is not announcing the coming collapse of China (with attendant consequences for the world economy), it's warning of the dangers of an ascending, newly empowered China. Defence spending has been on the rise in recent years and foreign sources currently place figures at anywhere between US$10 billion and US$75 billion annually. Both the USA and China's Asian neighbours are watching the situation with intense interest.

The next few years will be critical for China. The handover of Hong Kong and Macau to Chinese rule passed relatively smoothly but the problem of increasingly independent-minded Taiwan has yet to be resolved (the Communist mainland and the Kuomintang government of Taiwan have technically been at war ever since 1949). Běijīng refuses to rule out the prospect of an armed invasion.

Ongoing disputes with the USA over trade issues and human rights threaten China's export industries, and tensions were further inflamed by NATO's bombing of the Chinese embassy in Yugoslavia in 1999 and the US spy plane collision with a Chinese fighter jet off China's southern coast in 2001. Slowly dismantling the bankrupt state sector is a delicate process that must continue if the government wants to deliver the affluent lifestyle that more and more Chinese are demanding as their right. And the central government will probably find itself under increasing pressure to provide greater freedom and to undertake some democratic reform. Without continued economic freedom, the Party's days are numbered; with continued economic freedom, Party influence will continue to diminish.

GEOGRAPHY

China's South-West consists of the provinces of Sìchuān, Yúnnán and Guìzhōu, the Zhuang Autonomous Region of Guăngxī and the municipality of Chóngqìng. The entire region comprises 1.36 million sq km, roughly the size of France, Germany and Spain combined. The region is bordered by the Beibu Gulf and the South China Sea, the countries of Vietnam, Laos and Myanmar (Burma) and the Chinese provinces of Tibet, Qīnghăi, Gānsù, Shaanxi, Húběi, Húnán and Guăngdōng (Canton). North-western Yúnnán lies within 100km of the Indian state of Arunachal Pradesh.

The region holds an incredible geographic variety. Yúnnán alone has 6000m peaks, mile-deep river gorges, volcanoes, karst formations and tropical jungle, while Guăngxī has over 1500km of coastline.

Sìchuān Basin

Known as the Red Basin due to its purple sandstone and shale deposits, this fertile plain averages only 500m in altitude and supports over 100 million people. It is as hot and humid as a greenhouse; there are so many foggy days that one local saying goes that the dogs bark in shock whenever they see the sun. The Sìchuān Basin is bordered by the Qinling Mountains to the north and the Chéngdū plain to the west. At the far east are the Three Gorges of the Yangzi River.

Yúnnán-Guìzhōu Plateau

The limestone Yúnnán-Guìzhōu Plateau takes in eastern Yúnnán, Guìzhōu and west Guăngxī.

It is a 1000m- to 2000m-high dissected limestone plateau of soluble carbonate rock, which decreases in height from north-west to south-east. The eroded carbonate rock produces the weird karst formations of the Stone Forest, the caves and waterfalls of Guìzhōu and the famous landscapes of Guìlín and Yángshuò.

Cháng Jiāng – The Long River

The Yangzi is China's longest river and the third longest in the world at 6300km (3900 miles). From its source in the mountains of Tibet's Tanggula Shān it falls 5000m (16,400 ft) to the sea. In its upper reaches in the Hengduan Shān the water is too rough even for fish to survive.

Just where the real source of the Yangzi is remains a controversial question. Is it the highest source, the Gelandandong Glacier; or, as is now widely believed, the point where the river is furthest from the sea, at Damqu? The official source at Tuotuo Heyan is of more practical importance as it for years enabled countless backpackers to sneak into neighbouring Tibet on a hooky travel permit.

You won't find the name 'Yangzi' on many Chinese maps. At the river's source it is the Dri Chu (Yak River) in Tibetan or the Tōngtiān Hé (Crossing to Heaven River) in Chinese. For the next 2308km it becomes the Jīnshā or 'Golden Sands' before reaching Yíbīn in Sìchuān, where it joins the Min River. From here it is known as Cháng Jiāng or 'Long River', its most common Chinese name.

During its course it flows through 10 provinces, drains an area inhabited by 300 million people and cuts China in two. It is central China's lifeline and its spinal cord. It has been exploited as a highway for centuries and was even used as a political symbol by Mao, who swam across it at the height of the Cultural Revolution to prove his revolutionary energy and political control. Like other Chinese rivers it has its darker side: a flood in 1931 killed 145,000 and displaced over 28 million people.

Its lower reaches are also home to Chinese river dolphins, one of the world's rarest species of river dolphins. Only 300 remain in the world.

Only about 5% of Yúnnán and Guìzhōu can be considered flat. To the north are the steep Dalou Mountains bordering the Sìchuān Basin, and to the west are the Wumeng Mountains. The otherwise obscure Miaoling Mountains of Guìzhōu form the historically important watershed between the Yangzi and Pearl drainage systems. The major river in Guǎngxī is the Xi, which flows east to Guǎngzhōu.

Subtropical South

Southern Yúnnán and Guǎngxī sit astride the tropic of Cancer. Southern Yúnnán is protected from cold northern winds by the Himalaya mountains, and receives moisture-laden air from the Indian Ocean, resulting in high levels of precipitation and a monsoon climate. The region still contains isolated pockets of rainforest and tropical monsoon forest.

Western Mountains

The western parts of Sìchuān and Yúnnán are dominated by the Hengduan Shān, a north-south extension of the Himalaya incorporating the Qionglai, Daxue (Great Snowy) and Gāolígòng ranges. The highest mountain in the South-West is Gònggā Shān, at 7556m; other notable peaks include Kawa Karpo (Méilǐ Xuěshān; 6740m), near Déqīn, and Jade Dragon Mountain (Yùlóng Xuěshān; 5596m), near Lìjiāng.

These mountains are really an extension of the Qīnghǎi-Tibet Plateau, which drops down to the Sìchuān Basin and Yúnnán-Guìzhōu Plateau. Melting snow from the plateau tumbles down into a concertina landscape to form some of the most dramatic gorges in the world, including the famous Tiger Leaping Gorge. In this part of north-west Yúnnán the Nùjiāng (Thanlwin or Salween), Láncāng (Mekong) and Jīnshā (upper Yangzi) rivers all pass parallel within 150km, separated by huge mountains.

From north-west Yúnnán the Mekong flows through Laos, Cambodia and southern Vietnam to the South China Sea; the Salween flows through Myanmar to the Andaman Sea and the Red River (Hong He) flows south-east to Hanoi and the Gulf of Tonkin. The Dadu, Min and Yalong all drain into the Yangzi, which empties into the East China Sea near Shànghǎi.

GEOLOGY

The geology of the South-West has been greatly affected by the collision of the Indian and Asian continents. The impact of the collision created a great crumpling in the earth's crust and subsequent erosion resulted in the great gorges of north-western Yúnnán.

The region is still seismically active, as was highlighted by the major earthquake that hit Lìjiāng in 1996, killing 228 people. A quake in January 2000 destroyed over 10,000 homes in Yao'an county, 100km east of Dàlǐ. Western Sìchuān was hit by a powerful quake in 2001. The region's worst quake was in 1970, at the height of the Cultural Revolution, when 15,500 were killed around Tōnghǎi.

Tectonic uplift has also caused the volcanic activity and hot springs around Téngchōng, whose 600m Daying Shān was last active 360 years ago.

Yúnnán's lakes were formed when grabens (areas that dropped between fault lines) filled with water. A few rivers, such as the Red River, follow geological faults.

The Sìchuān Basin was under water in the Paleozoic Era, 570 to 200 million years ago, as indicated by the layers of rich sandstone and huge reserves of salty brine and natural gas.

The Yúnnán-Guìzhōu Plateau was also originally a vast, shallow sea, as testified by the marine fossils at the Stone Forest in Yúnnán. The subsequent dramatic karst formations have been formed over the millennia by chemical erosion. When water mixes with carbon dioxide it forms carbonic acid. As this acidic ground water percolates through the rock, it dissolves the calcium carbonate of the limestone, thus creating the many caves, subterranean rivers, gorges, caves and sinkholes of the region. Add a little wind erosion and you get the whimsical karst landscape of Guìlín.

CLIMATE

The South-West generally enjoys a pleasant climate (Kūnmíng is known as the 'city of eternal spring') but there are some large regional differences, and as a general rule temperature is ruled by altitude.

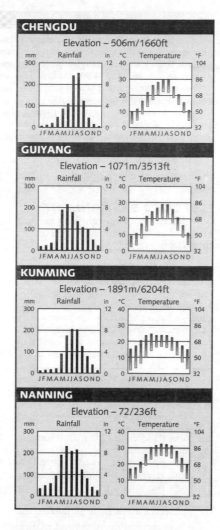

Summer lasts from around May to August. Xīshuāngbǎnnà in southern Yúnnán experiences a mild monsoon during this time. Summer is also when the most rain falls in Guìzhōu. Sìchuān is foggy and cloudy all the time. Summers are very long and hot in Chóngqìng, which has been dubbed one of the 'three furnaces' of China. High spots like Éméi Shān are a great relief from the heat.

Winter is short and cold north of Kūnmíng and Nánníng, from November to February, with temperatures dropping to freezing. Temperature statistics don't really indicate how cold it can get, so bring warm clothes. The mountainous areas in the west of Sìchuān freeze at this time, as does much of Guìzhōu and northern Guǎngxī. The warmest regions in winter are found in Xīshuāngbǎnnà and the south coast of Guǎngxī, which remains a balmy 24° to 27°C (75° to 80°F).

Spring (March, April) and autumn (September, October) are the best times to visit the region.

ECOLOGY & ENVIRONMENT

Given the fact that the South-West has such a range of vertical distribution and climatic zones, there is great diversity in its plant and animal life. Moreover, many of the region's ethnic groups have traditionally maintained a close and sustainable relationship with their natural environment.

Unfortunately, in a land that has sustained a large population for such a long time, humans have had a considerable impact on the environment and much of China's rich natural heritage is now either rare, endangered or extinct. With one-quarter of the world's population living on only 7% of the earth's cultivable land there is incredible pressure on the land's resources. The high mountain wilderness of western Sìchuān and north-western Yúnnán conceals some of China's last remaining natural sanctuaries.

To the government's credit, more than 150 nature reserves have been established in the South-West alone, protecting about 7% of China's land area. Many animals are officially protected, although illegal hunting and trapping continues. The trade in endangered species is particularly a problem along the borders with Myanmar, Laos and Vietnam.

A bigger problem is habitat destruction, caused by agriculture, urbanisation and industrial pollution. The tensions between environmental conservation and economic development remain particularly acute, especially as wildlife and natural resources have long been considered as mere economic commodities to be exploited. Plants have fared somewhat better than animals under the crunch of more than a billion people, but deforestation, grazing and intensive cultivation have taken a toll.

Logging and its incumbent erosion have long been pressing problems in western Sìchuān, where many of China's largest river systems rise. China's devastating floods of 1998, which killed over 4000 people and caused US$20 billion worth of damage, was blamed squarely on deforestation and led to the Sìchuān government's ban on commercial logging in 1998. Yúnnán soon followed and in 2001 introduced a ten-year campaign to stop illegal logging. The two provinces jointly agreed to invest the equivalent of US$14 billion over ten years in forest conservation. It is hoped that a rise in tourism can earn back some of the US$1 billion that Yúnnán reaped annually from the lumber trade.

Under Mao much of the land was ravaged in the name of revolution. Tropical rainforests in Yúnnán were clear-cut to make way for rubber plantations that quickly exhausted the soil. Today only small pockets of Xīshuāngbǎnnà's rainforest remain. During the Great Leap Forward the movement to destroy the 'Four Pests' caused a rapid decrease in the sparrow population and an environmental imbalance which resulted in a huge increase in the bug population.

As a result of the open door policy, China is now a member of Unesco's Man and Biosphere Programme (1979), a signatory to the Convention on the International Trade in Endangered Species and a member of the World Conservation Union. World Wildlife Fund cooperates in the park management of Wòlóng and Xīshuāngbǎnnà, and the International Crane Foundation operates a conservation program at Cǎohǎi Lake. (For more information see the Cǎohǎi Lake section in the Guìzhōu chapter.)

Taoist thought contains elements of ecology in its belief in the harmony of nature, but this seems *very* subconscious in today's society. China has a fledgling environmental movement though, much of it a response to the country's most environmentally

Wealth Hazards

China's current economic boom has come at the expense of controls on pollution and most of the major cities lie smothered under great canopies of smog. Nine of the world's ten most polluted cities are in China.

The first problem is coal. It provides for some 70% of China's energy needs and around 900 million tonnes of it go up in smoke every year. Some of it comes back to earth in the form of acid rain. Then there is the ever-expanding fleet of motor vehicles. Meanwhile, China's state-run factories dump three billion tonnes of untreated water into its rivers annually. Some reports indicate that half the population is supplied with polluted water. Few cities in the South-West have any form of sewage treatment.

None of this is good for anyone's health, and the government has made noises about doing something. The problem is not that China lacks legislation designed to curb the worst excesses of industry (the central government recently established 230 new environmental standards), but that these laws designed to safeguard the environment are rarely implemented. Even when they are, it's often more cost-effective for the polluting companies to pay a fine than clean up their operations.

Most Chinese have no concept of litter. Trash is simply thrown in the street and magically swept away at dawn by a small army of little masked ladies. What happens to the polystyrene boxes and disposable chopsticks that are thrown out the train window is another matter entirely.

The Chinese people seem to be taking the attitude that China can get rich and dirty, and then spend some of the proceeds on cleaning up. It's a time-honoured tradition, but then China is perhaps unique in the grand scale on which it is abusing its environment in a race against time to get rich. And anything the world's most populous and third largest country does has global repercussions.

controversial project, the Three Gorges Dam. For more information on this see the 'Damned Yangzi' boxed text in the Sìchuān chapter. In 1996 environmental activists managed to halt logging in Déqīn county that was threatening the environment of the endangered golden monkey. How long the government will tolerate this kind of environmental dissent remains to be seen.

FLORA & FAUNA
Flora

The South-West has a particularly rich flora that has been well utilised over the years. Tea-oil trees, camphor, lacquer, betel nuts, tangerine, pomelo, orange, longan, lychee, kiwis (also known as the Chinese gooseberry), tea, chillies and garlic all grow wild in the region. Xīshuāngbǎnnà has plantations of rubber trees, oil palms, coconuts, cashews, coffee, cocoa, avocados and sapodillas as well as wild tea trees up to 1700 years old. Three thousand species of medicinal plants are harvested in Sìchuān alone, the most important of which are ginseng, golden hairpin, angelica, fritillary and gastrodia.

The area around Xīshuāngbǎnnà in the tropical south has a diverse and rich flora, with over half of China's protected plants found there. Over 5000 species are known to grow here – up to 100 species in a 250 sq metre area. The tropical forest is, however, under intense pressure from slash-and-burn agriculture and is today mostly secondary growth. Only 20% to 30% of the original forest remains.

Most of the world's rhododendrons, azaleas, roses, magnolias, orchids, chrysanthemums, and camellias are indigenous to the mountains of western Sìchuān and northwest Yúnnán and were tracked down by intrepid botanist-explorers such as Kingdon Ward and Ernest Henry Wilson who carted off samples in the 19th and 20th centuries. Azaleas are native to China – of the 800 varieties in the world, 650 are found in Yúnnán. Gentian and primroses are also common. The deep mountain valleys of the north-west provide countless biotic niches and a wide range of vertical distribution, both of which encourage a wide variety of plants in a small area. Six hundred species of rhododendron are found in north-western Yúnnán alone.

Perhaps the most beautiful cultivated plant is the bamboo. Bamboo – which is a grass – comes in many varieties and has for centuries supplied the Chinese with almost everything they have needed. For some examples see the 'Bamboo' boxed text in the Around Yíbīn section of the Sìchuān chapter.

Of the flora endemic to the South-West, one of the rarest trees is the magnificent Cathay silver fir, found in isolated groups at Huaping in Guǎngxī (between Lóngshèng and Lingui) and at Jinfo Shān (Nanchuan). Only about 400 trees remain.

The dove tree *(Davidia involucata)* gets its popular name from spring blossoms that resemble white doves roosting in the branches. Another name is the handkerchief tree. Other endemic trees include the eucommia, ginkgo and the dawn redwood *(Metasequoia glyptostroboides)*; the latter has existed in eastern Sìchuān for over 70 million years. Yúnnán's 'Dragons Blood Tree' has a lifespan of up to 8000 years, making it the longest-lived tree on earth. It is also used in Chinese medicine.

Another prehistoric plant is *Cyathea spinulosa*, a large woody fern which existed as far back as the Jurassic period.

The Chinese parashorea, discovered in the 1970s, is found in Xīshuāngbǎnnà and parts of Guǎngxī. It is much sought after for its timber and is so fast-growing that the Chinese call it the Wàngtiānshú, or 'Looking at the Sky' tree.

Fauna

Animals are animals – in the wild they wisely avoid humans. Other than some pathetic specimens in zoos, you probably won't get to see many exotic animals in China.

Bird-watching is a possibility, especially at Cǎohǎi Lake in north-west Guìzhōu and at the lakes Bìtǎ Hǎi and Nàpà Hǎi in north-west Yúnnán. All three are important wintering sites for rare species of migratory birds. See the Cǎohǎi Lake section for more information. Two useful books for bird lovers in South-West China are the 850 page paperback *A Field Guide to the Birds*

of China by John Mackinnon, and the hardback *A Guide to the Birds of Southeast Asia* by Craig Robson.

The lakes of the Yúnnán Plateau are particularly rich in carp: of China's 13 species, 12 are found only here.

If you're interested in delving further into China's flora and fauna, two good books on the subject are *Living Treasures* by Tang Xiyang and *The Natural History of China* by Zhao Ji et al.

Endangered Species

Three hundred and seventy nine species of vertebrates are protected in China, of which just over 100 are 'class one', meaning endemic, rare or endangered. Likewise, there are 389 species of protected plants, of which eight are class one protected. Many of these are hovering on the brink of extinction. Several people are executed every year for trading in pandas or other endangered species. A common sight in the South-West is groups of Tibetans selling dried tiger's or bear's paws for their medicinal properties. China has been a traditional market for rhino's horn and ivory, as well as a major exporter of cat skins.

Perhaps no animal better represents both the beauty and the struggle of wildlife in China than the giant panda. These splendid animals are endangered by a combination of hunting, habitat encroachment and natural disasters. China has 28 panda reserves, of which 22 are in Sìchuān. For more information see the boxed text 'Pandas: Elusive & Endangered' in the Chéngdū section of the Sìchuān chapter. Red pandas are also found in north-west Yúnnán.

Another of China's rarest animals is the golden monkey (Guìzhōu and Yúnnán both have varieties), often described as the most beautiful monkey in the world for its orange fur, upturned nostrils and blue-blush eyes. Other endangered primates include the Rhesus macaque, Biet's snub-nosed monkey and the black gibbon of Xīshuāngbǎnnà. The endangered slow loris is a comically slow and impossibly cute relative of the sloth, whose huge eyes are ringed in black fur.

The Chinese infatuation with tiger-related medicine has decimated the big cat population of the South-West. Only 40 South China tigers remain in the world (down from 4000 in the 1950s and 250 in 1982), which makes the tiger one of the world's ten most endangered species. A tiger sperm bank was set up recently in Chóngqìng in a last ditch attempt to prevent extinction. Equally at risk are the snow leopard and clouded leopard, both found in the remotest parts of western Sìchuān. The region is also home to Indian civets.

Other weird and wonderful animals include the takin, found in western Sìchuān and north-western Yúnnán (especially the Laba River Nature Reserve); the ox-like gaur, an almost extinct form of wild bull found in Xīshuāngbǎnnà; the Asiatic Indian elephant, of which only around 300 remain, also in Xīshuāngbǎnnà; and the scaly anteater-like pangolin, a culinary delicacy.

The Sika deer and Thorold's (or white-lipped) deer are both endangered. The lesser mouse deer is one of the smallest deer in the world, around the size of a small rabbit. The giant Chinese salamander, on the other hand, is one of the largest amphibians in the world. The brown bear is found in the Himalaya up to 5000m and the smaller Asiatic black bear, with its penchant for honey, is found at slightly lower altitudes.

Endangered birds include the red-crowned crane, black-necked crane, crested ibis, Reeve's pheasant, various other forms of pheasant and the stunningly beautiful tragopan.

Nature Reserves

Wildlife management started in China in 63 BC with a Han dynasty decree ordering the protection of certain birds. Modern wildlife protection started in 1959 with protection laws for the giant panda and golden monkey, the establishment of nature reserves in Xīshuāngbǎnnà and, in 1961, the Huaping Reserve for the Cathay Silver Fir. Environmental protection was enshrined in the 1982 constitution.

Today there are 926 nature reserves in China. There has been a recent explosion of nature reserves in the South-West. Yúnnán alone has over 100 nature reserves, more than any other province. The region's showcase reserves are at Wòlóng, Fànjìng Shān and Xīshuāngbǎnnà. There is no formal national park system but many parks, such as Jiǔzhàigōu in northern Sìchuān province, function as one. A few privately funded reserves are beginning to get off the ground in far-western Sìchuān.

Some reserves protect whole ecosystems. Examples of these include the Baima Mountain Reserve in north-west Yúnnán, the Gāolígòng Shān Reserve near Téngchōng, and the Xīshuāngbǎnnà Reserve. Some are set up to protect specific rare animals (eg, the Tiebu Reserve for the endangered Sika deer and Garqu Reserve for the golden monkey, both near Jiǔzhàigōu), while others protect rare flora (eg, the Huaping Cathay Silver Fir Reserve in Guǎngxī). Still others protect geological wonders such as the limestone terracing at Huánglóng and Báishuǐtái (north-west Yúnnán). Reserves of the last kind tend to be as much tourist attraction as protected area, eg, the Stone Forest in Shílín.

There is also a breeding centre for pandas at Wòlóng and one for golden monkeys at Fànjìng Shān. The largest and most famous panda reserve is at Wòlóng but there are others at Wanglang, Baishui River and Xiaozhaizigōu (all in northern Sìchuān, near Jiǔzhàigōu).

The Nature Conservancy is working to promote environmental protection and sustainable development in north-west Yúnnán. You can find out more about the agency's work by contacting Nature Conservancy directly (☎ 703-841 5300) 4245 N Fairfax Dr, Arlington, Virginia, USA, or through its Web site (W www.tnc.org). The Nùjiāng River Project is another foreign-inspired organisation that strives to protect the Nùjiāng Valley through ecotourism developments. See the Organised Tours section in the Getting There & Away chapter for contact details.

Environmentalists shouldn't cheer too loudly though. Most of China's park lands are under heavy commercial development pressure from hotels, restaurants, logging companies, souvenir vendors and even the odd airport or superhighway. Most reserves lack staff, funds, infrastructure and even a basic management plan. One problem is that there is no central government agency responsible for protected areas; many of the government bureaus that control the parks, such as the forestry department, have their own agendas for protected area management.

The South-West's main reserves include:

Xīshuāngbǎnnà Nature Reserve (2420 sq km, established 1986) Half of all China's protected plant species can be found in this lush reserve, which was formed by merging five existing nature reserves. Around one-eighth of Xīshuāngbǎnnà is protected in the reserve. The main habitat is tropical monsoon rainforest, replete with lianas, epiphytes, strangling vines and parasitic plants. The lofty fig, with its many buttresses and aerial roots is common and its fruit is favoured by the local Dǎi people. There are also three hundred types of medicinal plants, several of which are used to cure hypertension and cancer.

Sixty-two species of mammals and 400 species of birds have been recorded, including the great pied hornbill, green peafowl, parakeets, Hoolock gibbon, Asiatic elephant, gaur (Indian bison), slow loris and python.

Wòlóng Nature Reserve (2000 sq km, established 1976) This reserve is most famous for its population of giant pandas but the wide range of ecosystems also provides a home to 46 species of animals, including endangered species such as the golden monkey, red panda, snow leopard, Thorold's deer, Chinese monal pheasant, Temminck's tragopan, takin and clouded leopard. The park has 380 employees and 59 specialists. Some 4000 people, mostly Tibetan, live within the park boundaries. Recent attempts to relocate them have proved largely unsuccessful.

Jiǔzhàigōu Nature Reserve (600 sq km, established 1978) Partly set up to preserve stunning alpine scenery, this park is the most popular with foreign tourists and rightly so. With a vertical range of 2000m, the park has a mix of temperate and tropical environments. Many rare animals live at the higher elevations, such as red pandas, takins, river deer, golden monkeys and blue-eared pheasants.

Excessive tourism is the greatest threat the park faces.

Fànjìng Shān Nature Reserve (419 sq km, established 1978) This nature park preserves a range of mountain ecosystems, with important communities of Guìzhōu golden monkey (plus a breeding centre) and dove trees.

Cǎohǎi Lake Nature Reserve (5334 hectares, established 1985) This is an important wetland and wintering site for the black-necked crane and other rare migratory birds.

Gāolígòng Shān A total of 485 bird species, 60% of Yúnnán's total, have been recorded in this mountain reserve in south-west Yúnnán, along with takins, gibbons, pangolins and 600 species of rhododendron, some up to 25m tall.

Great Rivers National Park This proposed park would protect most of north-west Yúnnán. The region contains 15,000 species of plants, including 40% of the plants used in Chinese medicine and 75% of those used in Tibetan medicine. Animals include the snub-nosed monkey, of which there are less than 1000 in the wild, the red panda and clouded leopard. There are several environmental dangers to the park: the province plans to build a string of 14 hydropower stations on the Mekong, including the 1000-foot tall Xiaowan dam south of Déqīn county. There are also several large zinc, copper, lead, silver and cobalt mines in the Déqīn region.

GOVERNMENT & POLITICS

Precious little is known about the inner workings of the Chinese government, but what is known is that the entire monolithic structure, from grass-roots work units to the upper echelons of political power, is controlled by the Communist Party. The current top man in China is President and Communist Party Chief Jiang Zemin, while No 2 is Chairman Li Peng. Rising political star Hu Jintao, widely tipped to succeed Jiang Zemin as general secretary in 2002, is the former party chief of Guìzhōu.

The day-to-day running of the country lies with the State Council, which is directly under the control of the CCP. The State Council is headed by the premier (formerly Li Peng, currently Zhu Rongji). At grass-roots level the Party forms a parallel system to the administrations in the army, universities, government and industries. Real authority is exercised by the Party representatives at each level in these organisations.

Rubber-stamping the decisions of the CCP leadership is the National People's Congress (NPC). It theoretically comprises a 'democratic alliance' of both Party and non-Party members who include intellectuals, technicians and industrial managers.

The South-West is divided into three provinces (Yúnnán, Guìzhōu, Sìchuān), one autonomous region (Guǎngxī) and one municipality (Chóngqìng). These are subdivided into prefectures *(zhōu)*, regions *(dìqū)* and townships *(shì)*, which are then further divided into counties *(xiàn)*. Thus the town of Jiǔzhàigōu is in Nánpíng County, in the Aba Tibetan Autonomous Prefecture, in Sìchuān province. Some autonomous areas, eg, Ganzi and Aba in western Sìchuān, are huge areas of land but the word 'autonomous' has little real meaning.

Cadres

The Chinese government is equipped with a massive bureaucracy. The term 'cadre' *(gànbù)* is usually applied to bureaucrats, and their monopoly on power means that wide-ranging perks are a privilege of rank for all and sundry – from the lowliest clerks to the shadowy puppet masters of Běijīng's Zhongnanhai. China's bureaucratic tradition is a long one. In a country without a proper legal framework the patronage of officials becomes extremely important, and many cadres have used their power to get rich on the back of economic liberalisation.

Dānwèi

At grass-roots level, the basic unit of social organisation outside the family is the work unit *(dānwèi)*. Every worker in a state-run company or government bureaucracy (until recently, this meant everyone) is theoretically a member of one, whether he or she works in a hospital, school, office, factory or village. Nowadays, though, many Chinese slip through the net by being self-employed *(xiàhǎi*, or 'jumping into the sea' in Chinese), working in a private operation or migrating to find work in the booming coastal cities.

The work unit is a perfect organ of social control, with leaders exercising tight controls over members. The dānwèi approves marriages, divorces and even childbirth. It assigns housing, sets salaries, handles mail, recruits Party members, keeps files on each unit member, arranges transfers to other jobs or other parts of the country, and gives permission to travel abroad. As soon as you forsake your dānwèi you also lose your housing allocation, your health benefits and even your bus pass. The work unit's control still extends into every part of the individual's life but its days are undoubtedly numbered.

People's Liberation Army (PLA)

'Political power grows out of the barrel of a gun.'

Mao Zedong

South-West China is one of the nation's seven military regions. Comprising land forces, the navy and the air force, the People's Liberation Army *(Jiěfàng Jūn)* has a total of around 2.9 million members and is the largest army in the world. Numbers have been streamlined by over a million in the last few years but military spending has risen, prompting neighbouring Japan to reconsider its pacifist constitution.

The PLA tarnished its reputation during the Tiananmen massacre in 1989 but control of the army is still vital to China's senior leaders. Until recently the PLA was also a huge business venture consisting of over 20,000 enterprises. Jiang Zemin ordered the PLA to dismantle its business ventures in 1999.

Political Dissidence & Repression

The brutal massacre in Tiananmen Square in 1989 focused world attention on China's political repression, but it was not the end of the story. The mid-1990s did see a few cases of high-profile, relatively organised dissent. In mid-1995, a total of 12 petitions had been signed by prominent intellectuals, largely calling for greater freedom of speech and, specifically, a re-evaluation of the Tiananmen Square protests.

The petitions resulted, predictably, in a round of arrests, and at the time of writing the hardliners seemed to be reasserting themselves and China was cracking down once again. Wang Dan, a leader in the Tiananmen Square protests, was released in 1993, just before the decision on where to hold the 2000 Olympics; Běijīng lost out to Sydney and Wang was re-arrested. In 1996 he was sentenced to another 11 years in prison but was released into exile in 1998 in the wake of Jiang Zemin's trip to the USA. Wei Jingsheng received another 14-year sentence but was also released into exile in the USA in January 1998. Many other dissidents are being held under house arrest.

According to Amnesty International, '1999 saw the most serious and wideranging crack-down on peaceful dissent in China for a decade'. Běijīng's current target is the Falun Gong religious group, or cult. The group, whose adherents number 100 million worldwide, was formally banned in China in 1999. Over 100 Falun Gong members are thought to have died so far in police custody.

Another bone of contention with the West is the 260,000 Chinese undergoing *láogǎi* (re-education through labour) in the gulags of Qīnghǎi and Tibet. The government has the power to sentence suspects to up to three years forced labour without a trial.

It is thought that China executes around 1800 people a year, more than the rest of the world combined. The method is normally shooting or lethal injections, a method that first took place in Kūnmíng in 1997 and is gaining prevalence. A disturbing twist on the theme came in March 1998, when two Chinese officials were arrested in New York by the FBI for trying to sell the livers, corneas, pancreas, kidneys and lungs of executed Chinese prisoners. Around 90% of organ transplants in China come from executed prisoners, since Confucian ethics deter most Chinese from donating organs.

Check out Amnesty International's annual China report at W www.amnesty.org/ailib /index.html or at W www.amnesty-usa.org /asa/china/contents.html or get it in print. Another Web site is Human Rights in China (W www.hrichina.org).

Democracy – the Fifth Modernisation?

While the foregoing description of China's government makes it look anything but democratic, there is one curious anomaly. In the 1990s, a little-noticed reform permitted small villages to elect their own leaders.

Optimists have suggested that it's the beginning of a major movement towards democracy throughout China.

Pessimists note that the central government has squashed all attempts to extend democratic elections to larger towns and cities. Certainly, the case of Hong Kong is not encouraging; its democratically elected Legislative Council was dismissed on the day the British handed over the colony to China. Many argue that the Chinese simply have no tradition of democracy, that a strong central government is actually preferred by many Chinese and that a country like China needs a central authoritarian government to stop it sliding into warlord anarchy or cracking up altogether.

ECONOMY

Under Mao, China's economy was a prisoner to ideology and incompetence, and politics ruled over pragmatism. The reign of Deng Xiaoping (essentially 1977 to 1997) was a period of pragmatic reforms aimed at achieving the so-called 'Four Modernisations': of China's industry, agriculture, defence, and science and technology.

Since then economic growth has hovered between 10% and 14%, although 1998 levels are projected to be around 8%. The Chinese economy is already the third largest in the world, behind the USA and Japan.

Rural Sìchuān was the birthplace of Deng's pioneering economic reforms. Having been forcibly collectivised during the Mao era, the 'household responsibility system' of the late 1970s allowed farmers to sell whatever they wanted on the free market after government quotas had been filled. Productivity rose and a new era of plenty was heralded for rural China.

One of the most spectacular Sìchuānese success stories has been the Hope group, a family business set up with a Y1000 investment in 1982 to supply animal feed. The business empire is now worth US$800 million, making the owners the second richest family in China.

The transition from the centrally controlled, ideologically motivated economy of the Mao years to Deng's vast free-enterprise experiment has not, however, been an entirely smooth one. Rural earnings in the South-West lag far behind the urban incomes of the booming eastern coastal cities. According to government statistics 2.5 million people in Yúnnán alone live without adequate food and clothing. Increased mechanisation and fertiliser use have led to increased productivity but also to a scarcity of work. There are perhaps as many as 40 million farm labourers in the region without regular employment, a figure that could rise nationwide to an incredible 400 million by the middle of the next decade. Eight million migrants from Sìchuān alone currently work in China's coastal cities – often working long hours in poorly paid factory jobs – and their remittances provide up to a quarter of Sìchuān's rural income.

The state is also saddled with some 100,000 state-owned firms, which between them lose around US$10 billion a year. Restructuring in 1997 and 1998 resulted in the laying-off of some 14 million state workers throughout China, and this is only the tip of the unemployment iceberg.

China also faces a banking crisis. The state-run banks continue to pour money into near-bankrupt state companies that will never be able to repay the loans. Technically, China's banks are already insolvent – disaster has been staved off by the high savings rate. The system can stay afloat as long as the masses do not try to withdraw their savings from the banks. It's this thought that keeps China's financiers awake at night. That and the estimated US$4.4 billion that China loses each year through tax fraud.

In an attempt to redress the serious economic imbalance between the east and the South-West, Běijīng has undertaken a program of infrastructure developments in its western regions, including the construction of several major airports, highways and railways.

Yúnnán in particular is looking increasingly out of its 'southern gate' towards South-East Asia. Thousands of square kilometres have been cleared of mines set during the Sino-Vietnamese War and 25 border trade sites and nine local ports of entry have been opened with Vietnam. Plans abound to dredge the Mekong and permit large-scale navigation into the so-called economic 'Golden Quadrangle' of Indochina. A series of highways will eventually cut the drive to the ports around Bangkok down to 48 hours. Yúnnán is a major player in Myanmar's economy.

Tourism is becoming increasingly important to Yúnnán in particular; in 1999 the province earned US$20 billion from tourists (mostly from Thailand and Taiwan). Officials estimate that almost one million people in Yúnnán and Guìzhōu have been lifted above the poverty line as a result of tourism revenues. By 2020 China is expected to be the world's most popular tourist destination.

China's imminent entry into the World Trade Organisation (WTO) could have far-reaching and destabilising effects on China's economy as state-run companies are faced with stiff competition from foreign companies.

POPULATION & PEOPLE

The four provinces of the South-West have a combined population of 236 million out of a national total of 1260 million (1.26 billion) people. China's population is greater than those of the USA, Russia and Europe combined.

Officially, only 30% of the total population is classified as urban, which is low by any standards (Australia's population is 86% urban). The figures are changing, though, as the countryside urbanises and farmers abandon the land and migrate into the cities in search of work.

The huge population has to be fed with the produce of around 15% to 20% of the land they live on, the sum total of China's arable land. This arable land is shrinking at an alarming rate: industrialisation, urbanisation and erosion are robbing the country of valuable farmland while the population continues to grow.

The Malthusian prospect of a growing population with a shrinking capacity to feed itself led the government to promote a limited birth control program in the 1950s, but this was abandoned during the Cultural Revolution. The responsibility lies with Mao Zedong, and this decision was probably his greatest mistake. He believed that birth control was a capitalist plot to make China weak and that the country would find strength in a large population. His ideas very much reflected his background – that of the peasant farmer for whom many hands make light work in the fields. It was not until 1973 that a strict nationwide birth-control program was instituted, with each couple permitted to have just one child.

The current plan is to limit growth to 1.25 billion people, hold that figure steady somehow, and allow birth control and natural mortality to reduce the population to 700 million, which China's leaders estimate would be ideal. Current projections, however, indicate that China's population will be close to 1.5 billion by the year 2030, and that the present population could double within 50 years. The latest census was held in November 2000.

In recent years the main thrust of the campaign in the cities has been to encourage married couples to sign a one child pledge by offering them an extra month's salary per year until the child is 14 years old, plus housing normally reserved for a family of four (a promise sometimes not kept because of the housing shortage). If the couple have a second child, then the privileges are rescinded, and penalties such as demotion at work, a fine of up to a year's salary or even loss of job are imposed. If a woman has an abortion it entitles her to a vacation with pay. Minority nationalities and many rural families are allowed two children before penalties are imposed and there are noticeably more babies in the countryside, especially in minority areas.

The South-West has one of the highest birth rates in the country – Guìzhōu province has the third highest birth rate after Tibet and Qīnghǎi. Unfortunately it also has the highest infant mortality rates: in some parts of Yúnnán infant mortality is seven times the national average. Rural health costs in China increased on average 500% between 1990 and 1997 and it is thought that only about 6% of women in remote counties can now afford hospital deliveries. In China as a whole four babies are born every second.

Birth-control measures appear to be working in the cities. An estimated 300 million extra people (more than the entire population of the USA) would have been born in China during the last 20 years had there been no form of family planning.

On the other hand, families who do abide by the one-child policy will often go to great lengths to make sure their child is male. This is particularly true in rural China, where the ancient custom of female infanticide continues to this day. In parts of China, this is creating a serious imbalance of the sexes. The national average is 120 males for every 100 females, meaning that there are now at least 60 million more men than women in China.

If China's one child policy does succeed, one soon-to-be-felt consequence will be a rapidly ageing population. The baby boom generated by Mao's policies has created a population that is today overwhelmingly young. The baby bust of the one child policy will create the opposite. The consequence of having to support a large number of retired geriatrics is yet another challenge that China will soon be facing.

EDUCATION

China records an official literacy rate of 80%, but Guìzhōu and Yúnnán have the lowest rates in the country, well below this figure. Many minority people cannot read Chinese characters, but may be literate in their own native scripts. By 2010, nine-year compulsory schooling will be universal in China.

Until very recently, all education right through university level was 100% state-funded. In return, university graduates had to accept whatever job the state wished to assign them to. However, the past couple of years have seen a radical new experiment – students can pay their own way through school and are then free to take a job of their own choosing. Of course, most Chinese cannot afford this, though some manage by borrowing money from their relatives.

China has belatedly recognised the economic value of having an educated population at least semi-fluent in foreign languages. English is by far the most popular foreign language, and many young Chinese will be anxious to practise with you. If you want to meet English-speaking Chinese, go to the 'English corners' which have developed in many large cities.

ARTS

Artistic creativity in post-1949 China has been (and to some extent still is) greatly hampered by ideological controls. Mao's 'Yán'ān Talks on Art & Literature' edict basically reduced art, literature and film to the status of a revolutionary tool. Works that did not show peasants triumphing over huge odds were condemned as bourgeois.

Worse was to come during the Cultural Revolution, when many of China's ancient art treasures were razed to the ground and precious pottery, calligraphy and embroidery were defaced or destroyed.

Fortunately, since the early 1970s a great deal of work has been done to restore what was destroyed. Initially, restoration was carried out only on major attractions with foreign tourism in mind, but with local tourism emerging as a major money-spinner, tourist attractions all over the South-West are now being restored.

Dance

Many of South-West China's minorities have a rich tradition of dance, which has evolved from religious rituals and even exorcism rites. Lúshēng (see Music, following) dances are common amongst the Miáo and Lahu, and the Wa have a wooden drum dance. China's most famous dancer is the Bai nationality Yang Liping.

Music

Possibly the most famous ensemble in the South-West is the Lìjiāng Traditional Music Ensemble, which plays a mixture of traditional Tang dynasty Dongjing Taoist religious music and traditional Náxī songs.

Taoists used existing music from other traditions and religions to enliven their services and to provide a ritual structure. Confucianism also used music in its rituals. Many of the original melodies derive from classical poems, all of which would originally have been performed to music by itinerant or court-based bards. Few of the tunes were written down.

Traditional Chinese musical instruments include the two stringed fiddle *(èrhú)*, three stringed lute *(sānxuán)*, four stringed banjo *(yuèqín)*, two stringed fiddle *(húqín)*, vertical flute *(dòngxiāo)*, horizontal flute *(dízi)*, piccolo *(bāngdí)*, four stringed lute *(pípá)*, zither *(gǔzhēng)*, the ceremonial trumpet *(suōnà)* and ceremonial gongs *(dàluó)*. Some of these, such as the *pípá* from Central Asia and the Persian lute, were introduced into the region, the latter along the southern Silk Route from Myanmar. Instruments are accompanied by a range of percussion, including gongs, drums, clappers and bells. In Daoist music, the striking of a gong marks a new chapter of the Dongjin text.

Music is central to the lives of many minority peoples of the South-West and features heavily in festivals, weddings and courtship rituals. Epic oral ballads which recount the exploits of historical rebel heroes are especially popular. The main instruments used are the *lúshēng*, a reed pipe, and the *yuèqín*, a round lute. The Náxī have a small, seven-holed bamboo pipe known as a *bebe*. Even leaves are used among Yúnnán's minorities.

You can purchase tapes of Chinese music in most Xinhua or foreign language bookstores. The following collections of minority music have been published in the West:

Dongjing Music in Yúnnán (Nimbus Records) Traditional Confucian and Taoist ceremonial music by the Dayan Ancient Music Ensemble of Lìjiāng

The Music of Small Ethnic Groups in Yúnnán Features Náxī, Bai and Jingpo music

A Happy Miáo Family (Pan) Miáo festival music

China – It's Time to Listen (Ellipsis) A good three-CD overview of many different music styles, including Dong, Jingpo and Miáo folk songs. There's also a condensed one-CD version.

Yunnan Instrumental Music (Hugo) Includes folk pieces from Hani, Jingpo, Munao and Yi people Ð www.hugocd.com

Baishibai: Songs of the Minority Nationalities of Yúnnán (Pan) A collection of music from various ethnic groups

Popular Music

China is beginning to develop a thriving music industry. Much of it is heavily influenced by the already well-established music industries in Taiwan and Hong Kong, but these are in turn influenced by Western musical trends.

Cui Jian (the 'Bruce Springsteen of China') was a pioneer in bringing rock 'n' roll to China in the late 1980s, and he is still very popular, though his concerts are still watched over by hundreds, if not thousands, of PLA soldiers. Popular singers like Li Jie, Da Wei, Wei Hua and Tian Zhen are played everywhere and you'll soon be humming their songs. Both Chéngdū and Kūnmíng have music scenes that are worth checking out.

Literature

'Confucius said, 'Be dutiful at home, brotherly in public; be discreet and trustworthy, love all people, and draw near to humanity. If you have extra energy as you do that, then study literature.''
I Ching (Book of Changes)

China has a rich literary tradition. Unfortunately, without many years of intensive study, much of it is inaccessible to Western readers. Many important Chinese classics are available in translation, but much of the Chinese literary heritage (in particular, its poetry) is untranslatable (though scholars continue to try).

Prior to the 20th century there were two literary traditions: the classical and the vernacular. The classical tradition, largely Confucian in nature, consisted of a core of texts written in classical Chinese that had to be mastered thoroughly by all aspirants to the Chinese civil service, and was the backbone of the Chinese education system. It was all but indecipherable to the masses. The vernacular tradition arose in the Ming dynasty and consisted largely of prose epics written for entertainment.

Classical Literature Tang China's two greatest poets have strong connections to the South-West. Li Bai (or Li Bo) is a particular favourite among Westerners for his eccentric individuality. By all accounts he was a drunkard, womaniser, spontaneous genius, immortal and rebel with a deep disregard for authority – a Jim Morrison among Chinese poets. He was banished to Guìzhōu early in his career for backing the wrong side in the An Lushan Rebellion. Many of his poems deal with friendship, loneliness and being drunk. Legend attributes his death to drowning in a lake after trying to embrace a reflection of the moon. Li Bai was born in Central Asia but moved to Sìchuān when he was five. His family home was at Jiangyou, north of Chéngdū and die-hard fans can visit a temple complex there dedicated to his memory.

Du Fu, Sìchuān's other great poet, is widely regarded as China's greatest. Though Du Fu was a friend of Li Bai's, his style couldn't be more different, with dense poems full of literary and historical allusion that make them hard to appreciate in translation.

Awakening on a Spring Day After Getting Drunk

Life is only a dream. Why all the unrest?
To me wisdom
Lies in being drunk perpetually
And sleeping the rest of the time.
And that I did one day:
When I awoke and looked around me,
I saw a bird chirping among the flowers.
I asked what day it was. They told me:
'It's spring. An oriole is singing.'
I sighed deeply, for the voice had touched me.
I helped myself to a copious draught.
And sang a cheerful song, while waiting for the moon;
When I had ended, it was all forgotten.
Li Bai (701–762)

Vernacular Literature Most of China's vernacular texts are available in translation and provide a fascinating insight into life in China centuries past. Perhaps the three most famous early 'novels' are: *The Water Margin (Shuǐhú Zhuàn)*, also translated as *Rebels of the Marsh*; *The Dream of the Red Chamber (Hónglóu mèng)*, also translated as *The Dream of Red Mansions* and *The Story of the Stone*; and *Journey to the West (Xīyóu Jì)*.

Another classic is the *Jin Ping Mei*, an erotic tale of a wealthy Chinese man and his six wives. It's banned in China but available elsewhere in English. *The Art of War (Bīngfǎ)* by Sun Tzu was studied by Mao and is still required reading for modern military strategists in the West.

Modern Literature By the early 19th century, Western novels had begun to appear in Chinese translations in increasing numbers. Chinese intellectuals began to look at their own literary traditions more critically. Calls for a national literature based on vernacular Chinese rather than the stultifying classical language grew in intensity.

The first of the major Chinese writers to write in colloquial Chinese as understood by the masses was Lu Xun (1881–1936), and for this reason he is regarded by many as the father of modern Chinese literature. Most of his works were short stories that looked critically at the Chinese nation's inability to drag itself into the 20th century. His first set of short stories was entitled *Call to Arms*, and included his most famous tale, *The True Story of Ah Q*. His second collection was entitled *Wandering*, and his last collection was called *Old Tales Retold*.

Other Chinese writers and their works worth looking into include Lao She, Wang Meng, Ba Jin, Shen Congwen and Zhang Xianliang. Most of these works are available inside China in English translation from foreign language bookstores or larger tourist hotels.

Calligraphy

Calligraphy has traditionally been regarded in China as the highest form of visual art. Children were trained at an early age to write beautifully, and good calligraphy was a social asset and an essential art of the scholar and official. A person's character was judged by their handwriting; if it was elegant it revealed great refinement.

All over China, decorative calligraphy can be found in temples, adorning the walls of caves and on the sides of mountains and monuments.

Painting

Chinese painting is the art of brush and ink. The basic tools are those of calligraphy, which influenced painting in both technique and theory. Shading is regarded as a foreign technique (introduced to China via Buddhist art from Central Asia between the 3rd and 6th centuries), and colour plays only a minor symbolic and decorative role. Until the end of the Tang dynasty, the human figure occupied the dominant position in Chinese painting but since the 11th century landscape has dominated Chinese painting.

When the Communists came to power, much of the country's artistic talent was turned to glorifying the revolution and bombarding the masses with political slogans. Colourful billboards of Mao waving to cheering crowds holding up the 'little red book' were once popular, as were giant Mao statues standing above smaller statues of enthusiastic workers and soldiers. 'Pop art' inspired by the revolution and Mao iconography have made something of an ironic comeback in the 1990s.

Since the late 1970s, the Chinese art scene has gradually recovered. The work of traditionally influenced painters can be seen for sale in shops and galleries all over China, while in the major cities a flourishing avant-garde scene has emerged. Art collecting has become a fashionable hobby among China's new rich, and many of China's young artists have been exhibited overseas.

Yúnnán has pioneered its own style of art and several Náxī painters have been exhibited overseas. Several well-known Běijīng artists, among them Fang Lijun and Yue Minjun, have set up studios in relaxed Dàlǐ, far from the political shackles of Běijīng. A good place to get in touch with the local art scene in Dàlǐ is the MCA (Mekong Culture and Art) Guesthouse, which also doubles as an artists studio. Kūnmíng also has a flourishing art scene.

The work of Chinese painters has been arguably more innovative and dissident than that of writers, possibly because the political implications are harder for the authorities to interpret.

Architecture

Modern China is not exactly an architectural treasure trove, and since 1949 this situation has been exacerbated by the widespread construction of concrete socialist-style buildings. The current drive for modernisation often translates into bulldozing traditional buildings to make space for blocks of blue reflective glass and white bathroom tiles. Nevertheless, temples are being restored throughout the country and the occasional rural village such as Jiànshuǐ, Héshùn (near Téngchōng) and even Lìjiāng, all in Yúnnán, have emerged unscathed from the ravages of soviet socialism.

Traditional Chinese architecture, from the lowliest village homestead to imperial palace, follows certain principles. A north-south-oriented, walled compound (with the main entrance to the south) that houses one or more structures was the basic form. As Chinese lived together in extended family groups, a walled home would generally house the living quarters for the head of the family in the north, with housing for children and their families on the side.

Minorities have some distinct and varied architecture. The Dong are famous for their wooden drum towers and wind and rain bridges, and the Miáo have beautiful traditional wooden houses. The traditional Náxī houses of Lìjiāng have been placed under the protection of Unesco's World Heritage Programme. The Qiang have characteristic fortress-like stone residences, while the Dǎi have houses on stilts. The Bouyi are famed for their excellent stonemasonry.

Bronze Vessels

Yúnnán's Dian kingdom was a major independent centre for bronze and copper work over 2500 years ago. A collection of some 48 tombs discovered in 1955, 40km south of Kūnmíng, revealed a cache of bronze figurines, mirrors and statuettes depicting mythological beasts, head-hunting and slave-raiding practices and human sacrifice, among daily scenes of domestic and agricultural life. Other bronze implements such as cowrie holders and particularly bronze drums have been found elsewhere in Yúnnán, around Chǔxióng and Jiāngchuān and also in Guǎngxī.

Bronze drums are still used during festivals by many of the region's minorities such as the Shui, Miáo and Yi.

Jade

Nephrite and less valuable jadeite stone have been revered since Neolithic times. While the pure white jade is the most highly valued, the stone varies in translucency and colour, including many shades of green, brown and black. Most of China's modern jade comes across the border from Myanmar, where it is described as the area's most profitable commodity, after heroin.

Jade is also thought to be empowered with magical and life-giving properties, and was considered a guardian against disease and evil spirits. Taoist alchemists, hoping to become immortal, ate an elixir of powdered jade – a 'high-fibre' diet if there ever was one. Plugs of jade were placed over the orifices of corpses to prevent the life force from escaping. Opulent jade suits, meant to prevent decomposition, have been found in Han tombs.

Cinema

In the last decade, films from mainland China have enjoyed great success in the West. They are regularly shown in art house cinemas and even, at times, in more mainstream venues.

Sadly, the best Chinese films cannot be produced in China. Because of its status as a 'mass' medium, film has faced stricter censorship than literature or drama. Any film dealing with the more seedy side of life is almost certain to be clipped by the censors or banned outright. As if the political

Chinese Temples

Temple architecture in China also tends to follow a certain uniformity. There is little external difference between Buddhist, Confucian and Taoist temples, all of which are comprised of groups of buildings, arranged in courtyards and aligned north-south.

The main entrance complex usually consists of two stone guardian lions, an impressive main gate adorned with calligraphy and two painted celestial guardians. A spirit wall blocks the passage of evil spirits who it is believed can only travel in straight lines.

Inside is a small courtyard with a large bronze basin where incense and paper offerings are burnt. Beyond is the main hall with an altar table, often with an intricately carved front. Depending on the size and wealth of the temple there are gongs, chimes, drums, side altars and adjoining rooms with shrines to different gods, chapels for prayers to the dead and displays of funerary plaques. There are also living quarters for the temple keepers. There is no set time for prayer and no communal service except for funerals. Worshippers enter the temple whenever they want to make offerings, pray for help or give thanks.

Architecturally, the roof is the dominant feature of a Chinese temple. It is usually green or yellow and is decorated with figures of divinities and lucky symbols such as dragons and fish (sons of the dragon king). Cantilevered and bracketed upturned eaves are common.

Statues include the Four Heavenly Kings (holding between them the flag of Buddhist truth, a lute, a sword and the pearl of perfection), the guardian general Wei Tuo, Sakyamuni (historical Buddha), Dipamkara (Buddha of the past) and Maitreya (future Buddha). Maitreya is often portrayed as fat and smiling, with long ear lobes, which symbolise wisdom, and bushy eyebrows, which indicate happiness and wisdom. Sakyamuni has set hand-positions to symbolise meditation, teaching etc. Buddhas are often seated on a lotus, a symbol of purity.

Other religious beings include Bodhisattvas who, though they have reached Buddhahood, forego the path to nirvana in order to help people remaining on earth. The Bodhisattva Puxian (Samantabhadra) is said to have journeyed from India on a white elephant and today resides on Éméi Shān. Another popular deity is Avalokiteshvara, known to the Chinese as Guanyin, the Goddess of Mercy, and to Tibetans as Chenresig, the Bodhisattva of Compassion. You will also see statues of the 500 Luohan (or Arhats), men who have achieved their own salvation through meditation but who are selfishly only concerned with their own salvation.

Taoist temples have statues of the Three Immortals, the Eight Immortals, the Yellow Emperor and other historical characters.

The most striking feature of the Buddhist temple is the pagoda. It was probably introduced from India along with Buddhism in the 1st century AD. Pagodas were originally built to house relics of the Buddha and later to hold religious artefacts and documents, to commemorate important events, or to store the ashes of the deceased.

Drum towers (gǔlóu) and bell towers (zhōnglóu) are usually two-storey pavilions whose function is to mark prayer time. They are also found forming a secular function in larger cities.

LPP

Spirit money is often burnt during funerals to ensure safe passage through the gates of hell.

'Electric Shadows' – The Fifth Generation

Chinese cinema has been revitalised in the last 10 years by the so-called 'Fifth Generation' of Chinese directors. Two of them in particular, Zhang Yimou and Chen Kaige, have planted Chinese cinema firmly on the map.

The first film by Fifth Generation directors to come to the attention of film buffs in the West was *Yellow Earth* (*Huáng Tǔdì*; 1984) directed by **Chen Kaige**, with Zhang Yimou as cinematographer. It wasn't a big hit in the theatres but *Yellow Earth* was noticed at festivals abroad for its stark style, political ambiguity and gorgeous use of colour.

Chen's most notable work since has been *Farewell My Concubine* (1993), which was nominated in the category of best foreign film in the 1994 Academy Awards and received the Palme D'Or in Cannes. The film featured homosexual love, opium smoking, love triangles and Cultural Revolution fanaticism, and was banned on release (though later re-released within China with several cuts). This was followed by *Temptress Moon* (1997), featuring Gong Li and Leslie Cheung, and *The Emperor and the Assassin* (1999), again featuring Gong Li in a historical drama set in the Qin dynasty. Chen's most recent project was his first English-language film, *Killing Me Softly*, an erotic thriller starring Joseph Feinnes and Heather Graham. Earlier movies by Chen include *Life on a String*, *The Big Parade* (1986) and *King of the Children* (1987).

Zhang Yimou, the cinematographer of *Yellow Earth*, later brought his visual talents to full force in his own first film *Red Sorghum* (*Hóng Gāoliang*; 1987), which was adventurous by Chinese standards in portraying an illicit love affair against the backdrop of the Sino-Japanese War. Zhang has since emerged as China's foremost director (and sometimes cameraman) with award-winning and visually sumptuous releases, such as *Ju Dou* (1990), *Raise the Red Lantern* (1991), *The Story of Qiu Ju* (1992), *To Live* (1994), *Shanghai Triad* (1995), *Not One Less* (1999) and *The Road Home* (1999). Zhang's most recent films have moved away from sumptuous visuals to a starker mood, as seen in *Keep Cool*, an urban comedy. China's most popular movie pin-up, Gong Li, appeared in most of Zhang's films until the erstwhile couple split up in 1996, and remains China's premier actress.

Zhang received a lot of publicity in China and abroad for the (temporary) banning of *Ju Dou* and

---

restrictions weren't enough, home-grown cinema has also been considerably weakened on the commercial front by Hollywood films and entertainment alternatives. In 1998 Jiang Zemin officially endorsed the film *Titanic*, which was subsequently shown in almost every cinema in China.

Mao's straight-jacketing of art for politics' sake became especially acute when Mao's wife Jiang Qing, a former screen actor in 1930s Shanghai, took an active role in designing China's policies for cultural production during the Cultural Revolution.

The major turning point took place with the graduation of students following the end of the Cultural Revolution from the Běijīng Film Academy in 1982. This group of adventurous directors became known as the 'Fifth Generation' (see the boxed text 'Electric Shadows – The Fifth Generation').

In the early '90s, a younger generation of directors emerged, quickly dubbed the 'Sixth Generation', with a very different cinematic touch and without the foreign financial backing that Chen Kaige and Zhang Yimou enjoy. The most notorious of these rebel directors is Zhang Yuan, whose film *Beijing Bastards* (1993) concerns itself with aimless youth and cynicism, centred around performances by China's biggest rock star, Cui Jian. Zhang's gritty 1996 film *Sons* charts the effect on a family of their father's descent into alcoholism and mental illness. The realism is heightened by the fact that the family played themselves on screen and the film was shot entirely on location in their flat. Zhang's most recent films are *East Palace, West Palace* (1997), the story of a gay man under police interrogation in Běijīng, and *Seventeen Years* (1999), a family drama.

'Electric Shadows' – The Fifth Generation

Raise the Red Lantern, both of which received Oscar nominations. Both films were eventually screened in China, but Zhang and other directors continually face restrictions and Zhang is regularly refused permission to show his films in or even attend film festivals. He is also regularly accused by both Party officials and Chinese intellectuals of pandering to foreign tastes and portraying China as a backward and insidious society. These simplistic conclusions must be very frustrating for an artist who above all wants his films to be appreciated in his native land. Zhang was also the cinematographer of *The One & the Eight* (1984) made at Guāngxī film studio.

The openness in expression and fresh talent of the Fifth Generation invigorated older directors, some of whom began to re-examine the Chinese experience under socialism. In 1986 veteran director Xie Jin utilised his trademark flair for melodrama and a style well grounded in the Hollywood tradition with the film *Hibiscus Town*, which presented a critical view of how political opportunism and extremism affect the lives of ordinary people.

Many of Chen and Zhang's contemporaries also came out with provocative films that explored new territory. **Tian Zhuangzhuang**'s film *The Blue Kite* (*Lán Fēngzhēng*; 1993) won many awards in foreign film festivals but was banned in China because of its indictment of the Great Leap Forward and Cultural Revolution. Tian also directed *The Horse Thief* (1985), a haunting story set in Tibet.

Huang Jianxin directed *Stand Up, Don't Bend Over* (1992) and *The Black Cannon Incident* (1985). The latter is without a doubt the sharpest satire released by any of the Fifth Generation directors.

Wu Tianming, who was the head of the Xian film studio that gave these young directors their start, returned from six years in the USA to make a new masterpiece, *King of Masks*. His other films include *Life* (1984) and *The Old Well* (1987), which also saw Zhang Yimou as cinematographer.

Other notable Fifth Generation films include: *Swan Song* (1986), the tragic story of a Cantonese opera composer who dies neglected after his best work is stolen and made famous by a music student; *The Women from the Lake of Scented Souls* (1992), which portrays the unhappiness of a woman who runs a sesame-oil mill; and *Sacrificed Youth* (1985), which tells the story of a woman who is sent during the Cultural Revolution to live with the Dǎi people of Xīshuāngbǎnnà.

Other 'Sixth Generation' directors include He Jianjun, Jiang Wen, Ning Ying, Wu Wenguang. Jiang Wen directed the acclaimed *In the Heat of the Sun* (1994), whose screenplay was written by one of China's hippest modern writers Wang Shuo, and the recent historical drama *Devils on the Doorsteps* (1999). Jiang is also one of China's best regarded actors, most recently starring in Zhang Yimou's *Keep Cool*.

Tragedy (often linked to political movements) is a central element of Chinese art films, and plots tend to move slowly. Ge You is arguably China's most popular actor, and Gong Li the most popular actress.

Theatre

Chinese theatre draws on very different traditions to Western theatre. The crucial difference is the importance of music to Chinese theatre, and thus it is usually referred to as opera. Contemporary Chinese theatre, of which the most famous is Běijīng opera, has a continuous history of some 900 years, having evolved from a convergence of comic and balladic traditions in the Northern Song period. From this beginning, Chinese opera has been the meeting ground for a disparate range of forms: acrobatics, martial arts, poetic arias and stylised dance. Local varieties of opera such as Sìchuān, Ānshùn and Nuo opera arose in the South-West from the contact between Han Chinese garrison communities and local minority rituals and oral ballads.

Operas were usually performed by travelling troupes whose social status was very low in traditional Chinese society. Chinese law forbade mixed-sex performances, forcing actors to act out roles of the opposite sex. Opera troupes were frequently associated with homosexuality in the public imagination, as depicted in the film *Farewell My Concubine*.

Despite this, opera remained a popular form of entertainment, though it was considered unworthy of the attention of the scholar class. Performances were considered an obligatory adjunct to New Year celebrations, local festivals and marriages, and sometimes to funerals and ancestral ceremonies.

Opera performances usually take place on a bare stage, with the actors taking on stylised roles that are instantly recognisable to the audience. For more information on local forms of opera see the boxed text 'Ground Opera' in the Ānshùn section of the Guìzhōu chapter.

Red Theatre was used by the early Communists in the 1930s to help disseminate their ideology and was the only form of art to be sanctioned during the Cultural Revolution. The Cultural Revolution opera *The Detachment of Red Women* is great fun if you can find a performance of it.

Tàijíquán & Kung Fu

Known in the West as 'taichi', *tàijíquán* is sometimes referred to as shadow boxing. Strictly speaking it is one of China's martial arts, and the ideas behind its movements share much with those behind kung fu (*gōngfū*). Tàijíquán, however, is only a true martial art in the hands of an exponent who has studied it for decades.

For most Chinese, particularly old people, whom you might see executing fluid movements in parks at the crack of dawn, tàijíquán is a form of exercise. The set patterns of movements are beneficial to muscle tone and the circulatory system, and its exponents claim a host of other pay-offs such as flexibility, good circulation, leg strength, good balance and an antidote to stress.

After learning the empty hand form (a smooth, continuous set of movements), the practitioner goes on to learn weapons forms, generally including the taiji sword and maybe the taiji pole. The student will also be introduced to pushing hands, a two person exercise that opens the door to the martial, or fighting, side of tàijíquán.

SOCIETY & CONDUCT
Traditional Culture

Chinese culture literally took a beating during the Cultural Revolution and the country has yet to recover completely. Yet these traditions run deep and have even flourished in recent years, along with a renewed interest in popular religion and ethnicity, much to the dismay of Communist Party bosses.

Family The family is the cornerstone of Chinese society. Extended families often share the same house, especially in the cities where housing space is tight (a major factor influencing the sex life of China's youth). Every member has a clearly defined position or rank in the family and there is a clear set of Confucian responsibilities and deferences. While English only has a single word for brother, grandmother etc, Chinese has totally separate words to define more clearly 'second elder brother', 'grandmother-on-the-maternal-side' etc. Children have a strong Confucian responsibility to obey their parents and look after them in old age.

Marriage is still as much a union of families as individuals, especially in the countryside. In traditional areas astrologers are often brought in to determine whether two individuals are astrologically suitable for each other and, if so, to fix an auspicious wedding date. Many marriages are still arranged by parents, though some modern touches such as white wedding dresses and

The ancient art of kung fu

Wives for Sale

As China continues to shed the austerities of the hardline Communist years, many of the old ways are returning. Chinese are going back to their temples, burning paper money for their ancestors and playing mahjong. In rural China, the sale of wives and children is coming back into fashion.

Accurate figures are difficult to obtain, but according to officials 110,000 women and 13,000 children were freed during one crackdown in 2000. One gang alone in Zūnyì (Guìzhōu) was found guilty of kidnapping 84 women and children. Chinese sources further admit that this number probably represents only a small percentage of actual cases. Unicef is so concerned that it has set up awareness projects in south-western Yúnnán, one of the worst affected areas.

The central problem seems to be the gangs of Chinese men who abduct young women and children from rural areas of Yúnnán and Guìzhōu and take them thousands of kilometres to the eastern provinces. The women and children are then sold for between US$450 and US$550 to rural communities, where there is often a chronic lack of single women and/or a strong desire for male heirs. Others are sold to factories for cheap labour or forced into prostitution. The women are often drugged and raped by the gangs. It is suspected that the shame prevents many of the women from reporting what has happened to them, though in some cases local authorities are in cahoots with the smugglers.

Strong efforts are being made in China to stamp out the practice (in January 2001 eight men were executed for trafficking a total of 140 women) but the roots of the problem lie deep in social policies, economic disparities and traditional attitudes, and that requires profound change.

even divorce are creeping in. The groom's parents normally pay for the wedding.

In minority areas the oldest son often moves out to start a new household while the second son remains at home. A woman often doesn't live with her husband until she becomes pregnant, though when she does move house, she shifts her responsibilities and allegiances to her new family and, in particular, her mother-in-law. This is partly why daughters are traditionally seen as a financial liability. The traditional custom of keeping concubines has largely died out.

Names Most Chinese have three names (some have two), of which the first is the surname. (Thus Jiang Zemin would be called Mr Jiang in the West.) One of China's most unexpected problems is a chronic shortage of names. A quarter of China's population, some 300 million people, share just five surnames – Li, Wang, Zhang, Liu and Chen. In big cities thousands of people may share the same surname and given name, written in exactly the same characters. Chinese newspaper reports frequently bemoan wrongful arrests, bank account errors and even unwanted surgery performed – all due to mistaken identity.

Chinese Symbols Chinese culture is suffused with a great number of symbols, partly because of the large number of homonyms, or multiple meanings for a single word or sound. For example, one commonly stylised character is *fu*, meaning happiness; as the sound 'fu' can also mean a bat, this animal has in turn become a symbol of happiness. Other common stylised symbols include the character *shou*, or longevity, and the double happiness symbol found pasted on many doorways.

Colours carry great symbolic meaning. Red signifies happiness and is worn during weddings or used on New Year cards. White symbolises death and mourning, green signifies harmony, while yellow is the colour of the emperor (and also pornography – blue movies are 'yellow movies' in Chinese!).

Animals also have great symbolic power and are often found as statues in temples; a crane symbolises wisdom, tortoises show longevity, dragons symbolise rain and the emperor, and a phoenix denotes peace and prosperity and is a symbol of the empress.

Mandarin ducks are a symbol of fidelity. Lions are benevolent protectors: a male lion is often seen playing with a ball; a female, with its young. The peacock is an important symbol to the Dǎi people of Xīshuāngbǎnnà and is painted on many roof eaves.

Numbers are often symbolic rather than literal. Department stores or *bǎihuòlou* are 'buildings of 100 goods'; the masses are referred to as the *laǒbǎixìng* or 'old 100 names'. As Mao once said, 'let a hundred flowers bloom and a hundred schools of thought contend'. The character *wàn* or 'ten thousand' is also used as a set phrase to signify a large number, as seen in the numerous '10,000 Buddha' caves.

Fēngshuǐ The Chinese word *fēngshuǐ* literally means 'wind-water'. Westerners call it geomancy, the art (or science if you prefer) of manipulating or judging the environment to produce good fortune. If you want to build a house or find a suitable site for a grave then you have to call in a geomancer. The Chinese warn that violating the principles of good fēngshuǐ can have serious consequences. Fēngshuǐ originated in burial rites and the location of an ancestor's grave remains an especially serious matter. Before Hong Kong's mass transit could be built, geomancers had to be called in to placate the spirits that might be displaced by the construction.

Cultural Concepts

Diūliǎn – Losing Face

Face can be loosely described as 'status', 'ego' or 'self-respect', and is a concept by no means alien to foreigners. Essentially it's about avoiding being made to look stupid or being forced to back down in front of others. In the West it's somewhat important; in China, it's critically important. A negotiated settlement of differences that provides benefits to both parties is always preferable to confrontation. Outright confrontation should be reserved as a last resort (Chinese are not shy of using it), and problems should first be tackled with smiling persistence. If one tack fails, try another. Circumvent a problem rather than tackle it straight on, and always give your adversary a way out. Displays of anger and emotion are great losses of face. The reaction to such displays is often a smile, which doesn't mean happiness.

Linked to this is the tendency of people not necessarily to say what they think, but rather what they think you want to hear or what will save face for them. Thus, the staff at the CAAC office may tell you that your flight will be here 'very soon' even if they know it will be delayed for two days; or reception may deny the existence of the cheapest rooms in the hotel if those rooms haven't been cleaned yet.

Kèqi – Politeness

Linked to face are displays of politeness and respect. Always offer gifts, cigarettes and food to be shared several times, and expect them to be refused several times before finally being accepted. It's good to refer to elders with the appellation lǎo, eg, 'lǎo Wang' ('old Mr Wang'). One good way of conveying respect is to hand things over with both hands.

Guānxì – Connections

In their daily life, Chinese often have to compete for goods or services in short supply, and many have been assigned jobs in which they have zero interest and, often, have had no training. Those who have guānxì (connections) usually get what they want because the connections network is, of course, reciprocal. Obtaining goods or services through connections is informally referred to as 'going through the back door' (zǒu hòu mén).

Cadres are well placed for this activity; foreigners will have to resort to some sort of gift giving (bribery?) to achieve the same result. Imported goods have much prestige value and will help you

Fēngshuǐ took a beating when the Communists came to power – the Soviet engineers that China imported in the 1950s hardly cared about offending the spirits. However, fēngshuǐ still has a strong following in Hong Kong and Macau.

Cruelty to Animals

Giant salamanders (grade one endangered species) are of great interest and importance and are used in laboratory experiments and medicine as well as entertainment in the zoo.
Guìzhōu Tourism Manual

China's treatment of animals is not the best, though not the worst either. In general, Chinese society shows very little awareness of even the concept of animal suffering. Travellers most frequently come up against the hard reality when they visit markets, many of which resemble take-away zoos. Some of the less exotic varieties – snake, turtle, monkey, pangolin, bear, giant salamander and raccoon, as well as dog, cat and rat – are traditionally eaten in China and can be found on restaurant menus.

In Western countries, shoppers are usually shielded from the messy business of slaughtering animals, while in China it's often done in front of the customer. Ducks are killed en masse in most markets in Guìzhōu, and you will often come across dogs being skinned for lunch.

Cultural Concepts

win points in the face game. Cigarettes make an excellent subtle bribe, though be warned that prestigious foreign brands such as Marlboro and 555 are almost mandatory if you partake in this kind of tobacco diplomacy. Half a packet of Panda cigarettes will get you nowhere.

Businessmen donate endless hours to cultivating and massaging their guānxì, normally through business dinners and banquets. Proposals which were 'impossible' a few hours earlier can suddenly become very possible when discussed over a plate of Běijīng duck and a bottle of Johnny Walker.

Zhōngguó – the Middle Kingdom

The Chinese have historically viewed their country as the centre (zhōng) of the world, even the limits of the civilised world. This (often well deserved) sense of cultural superiority is reflected in the ancient view that the peoples outside the gates of the empire are barbarians (including what are now called 'minority peoples'). Many travellers in modern China still find it hard to break down the emotional distance between themselves and the people whose land they are travelling through.

The notion of territorial integrity is important to China. Taiwan is an integral part of the country, even if the Taiwanese don't happen to agree. Ditto for Tibet, the Spratly Islands and perhaps Chinatown in San Francisco. Han nationalism is in fact perhaps the fastest growing ideology in modern China. In short, if you have any pro-independence sentiments about Tibet and Taiwan, you'd best keep them to yourself.

Rènào – Hot & Noisy

Rènào means 'hot and noisy', and this is how the Chinese like it, whether it be an evening meal out or a walk up Éméi Shān. Often the first thing Chinese tourists do when arriving in a new hotel room is turn the TV on full volume and open the door to get rid of the oppressively quiet atmosphere. Banquets that feature eardrum-blowing drinking games and karaoke sessions are about as hot and noisy as you can get.

Linked to this is a cultural preference for the group over the individual (especially in the form of group travel), a preference that may be part Communism, part Confucianism. People who travel alone are generally to be pitied.

The Chinese Dragon

Dragons are an important symbol in Chinese mythology and are the fifth creature in the zodiac. Good natured and benign, as opposed to the fiercesome version of European mythology, they are considered a male symbol, closely linked to the emperor. Only the emperor was allowed to have images of dragons with five claws on his robes; everyone else had dragons with only three claws.

The dragon has come to symbolise the Chinese nation and the Chinese refer to themselves as descendants of the dragon, one reason why the millennium celebrations (which heralded the year of the dragon) carried such significance in China. The earliest image of the dragon in China dates back over 6000 years. It was the yellow dragon that gave the Chinese the gift of writing.

Dragons are also intimately connected with water and especially rain – thunderstorms are said to be caused whenever dragons ascend to heaven. The image of a dragon playing with a pearl symbolises thunder storms. The dragon and the phoenix embody male and female characteristics respectively.

You will see dragons everywhere on a trip to China, from Hong Kong's Kowloon ('Nine Dragons' in Cantonese) district to the Dragon Boat races held in both Miáo and Han regions, and from the carvings on temple roofs in Kūnmíng to designs on Miáo embroidery.

LPP

Things can get especially nasty down on the farm: the way in which deer are confined in dark hovels doesn't look very humane. The notorious bear-bile extraction industry has come in for some particularly virulent condemnation by animal rights activists. Economic pressures are also taking their toll: in 1999 some 230 fish and mammals were killed in debt-ridden Chéngdū Aquarium when the electricity was cut off.

RELIGION

Chinese religion has been influenced by three great streams of human thought: Taoism, Confucianism and Buddhism. Although each has separate origins, all three have been inextricably entwined in popular Chinese religion along with ancient animist beliefs, much to the consternation of foreigners who are often confused to see the Taoist and Buddhist deities together in the same temple. Religion in China is nothing if not eclectic and pragmatic.

Popular Religion

Beyond the formal tenets of their religions, the founders of Taoism, Confucianism and Buddhism have been deified and placed next to mythical and historical figures, such as the Yellow Emperor, the Eight Immortals and even Mao Zedong. To these the Chinese further tack on a pantheon of other gods and ghosts, such as the spirits of the hearth, of sickness (even of latrines) and spirits connected to certain professions. This is rounded off by the extremely common practice of ancestor worship.

It's often said that many Chinese are Confucianists during their education, Taoists in retirement and Buddhists as they approach death. Tradition has it that the body contains two souls, the *hun* and the *po*. The hun soul enters the body sometime in the month following birth and relinquishes the body 49 days after death, to be judged in various stages of hell. The po soul remains with the body after death and can cause a lot of problems for the deceased's relatives if funeral arrangements and sacrifices are not satisfactorily carried out. 'Hungry ghosts' have no-one to care for them and roam the earth creating havoc. Spirit money is often burnt during the funeral to help the souls bribe their way through the various gates of hell (Daoism has ten of these, Buddhism has 18). Shrines to deceased family members are common and usually consist of a picture of the deceased, an ancestral tablet and various offerings of food. In many temples fortune tellers divine visitors' futures from sticks drawn out of a jar.

In general, modern Chinese religious practices are concerned with the pursuit of worldly success, the appeasement of spirits and the securement of good fortune.

Religion in all its forms seems to be on the rise in China, perhaps in reaction to the spiritual vacuum and political cynicism created by the Mao years and to the materialism of the 1990s.

Taoism

It is said that Taoism *(Dào Jiào)* is the only true 'home-grown' Chinese religion – Buddhism was imported from India and Confucianism is mainly a philosophy. According to tradition, the founder of Taoism was a man known as Laotzu *(Lǎozi)*, whose name has been variously misspelled in Western literature as 'Laotse' and 'Laotze'. He is said to have been born around the year 604 BC, making him a contemporary of Confucius, but there is some doubt that he ever lived at all. His main record was a slim volume of only 5000 characters, the *Tao Te Ching (Dao De Jing)*, or *The Way & Its Power*.

It's doubtful that Laotzu ever intended his philosophy to become a religion. Chuang Tzu *(Zhuāngzi)*, who lived between 399 and 295 BC, picked up where Laotzu left off. Chuang Tzu is regarded as the greatest of all Taoist writers, and *The Book of Chuang Tzu* is still required reading for those studying Taoism.

At the centre of Taoism is the concept of Dao. Dao cannot be perceived because it exceeds senses, thoughts and imagination; it can be known only through mystical insight, which cannot be expressed with words. Dao is the way of the universe, the driving power in nature, the order behind all life, the spirit which cannot be exhausted.

Dao is the way people should order their lives to keep in harmony with the universe.

The most famous Taoist notion is that of the duality of a universe divided into Yin (feminine, dark, passive) and Yang (masculine, bright, busy), symbolised by a circle divided into swirls of black and white.

One important aspect of Taoism was its search for immortality through meditation, exercise, alchemy and various other techniques. To this were added many gods, ceremonies, saints, special diets to prolong life and offerings to the ghosts. As time passed, Taoism increasingly became wrapped up in the supernatural, self-mutilation, witchcraft, exorcism, fortune telling, magic and ritualism. Taoists eventually produced a collection of over 1400 baffling scriptures known as the *Daozang*.

Confucianism

More a philosophy than a religion, Confucianism *(Rújiā Sīxiǎng)* has nevertheless become intertwined with Chinese religious beliefs.

With the exception of Mao, the one name that has become synonymous with China is Confucius *(Kǒngzi)*. He was born to a poor family around the year 551 BC, in what is now Shāndōng province. His ambition was to hold a high government office and to re-order society through the administrative apparatus. At most he seems to have had several insignificant government posts, a few followers and a permanently blocked career. At the age of 50 he perceived his divine mission, and for the next 13 years tramped from state to state offering unsolicited advice to rulers on how to improve their governing, while looking for an opportunity to put his own ideas into practice. That opportunity never came, and he returned to his own state to spend the last five years of his life teaching and editing classical literature. He died in 479 BC, aged 72.

The glorification of Confucius began after his death. Mencius (372–289 BC), or Mengzi, helped raise Confucian ideals into the national consciousness with the publication of *The Book of Mencius*. Eventually, Confucian philosophy permeated every

You Are What You Eat

The Chinese notion of 'health food' *(yàoshàn)* differs somewhat from that of the West. While Western health food emphasises low fat content, high fibre and fewer chemical additives, the Chinese version puts its main emphasis on the use of traditional ingredients and herbs. It is a widely held belief in China that overwork and sex wear down the body and that such 'exercise' will result in a short life. To counter the wear and tear, some Chinese practice *jinbu* (the consumption of tonic food and herbs). This can include, for example, drinking raw snake blood (the more venomous the better) or bear bile, or eating deer antlers, all of which are claimed to improve vision, strength and sexual potency. In a literal interpretation of 'you are what you eat', it's widely believed that consuming tiger meat will produce a miraculous increase in one's vigour and virility. Rhinoceros horn has long been touted as a tonic for whatever ails you. Eating monkey's brain is said to increase intelligence.

Environmentalists are not too happy about the consumption of such things as tiger meat and rhinoceros horn, given that both tigers and rhinos are endangered species. To be fair, the Chinese government has cracked down on the practice, and much of what gets passed off nowadays as ultra-expensive tiger meat and rhino horn is in fact fake.

Animal rights activists have sharply criticised the way that bear's bile is obtained – by strapping a living bear into a metal vest and running a tube into the creature's liver. It is estimated that some 7000 bears are held like this in farms across China. (See Useful Organisations in the Facts for the Visitor chapter for information on the Animals Asia Foundation).

However, China has reacted to such criticism the same way the country reacts to reports of human rights violations – by telling everyone that this is one of China's 'internal affairs'. If the animal rights activists happen to be British, the Chinese remind them of Britain's rude behaviour in the Opium War of 1841; if the critics are Americans, they are reminded of 19th-century slavery in the southern states of the USA; the Aussies are reminded about mistreatment of the Aborigines. No word yet on just what the bears are told.

level of Chinese society. To hold government office presupposed a knowledge of the Confucian classics, and spoken proverbs trickled down to the illiterate masses. The Confucian bible, *The Analects*, became the basis of all education, along with the other Confucian classics the *Book of Songs* and *Spring and Autumn Annals*.

It is not hard to see why Confucianism took hold in China. Confucianism defines codes of conduct and patterns of obedience. Women obey and defer to men, younger brothers to elder brothers and sons to fathers. Respect flows upwards, from young to old, from subject to ruler. Certainly, any reigning Chinese emperor would quickly see the merits of encouraging such a system.

All people rendered homage to the emperor, who was regarded as the embodiment of Confucian wisdom and virtue – the head of the great family-nation. There is no rigid code of law, because Confucianism rejected

the idea that conduct could be enforced by some organisation; taking legal action implied an incapacity to work things out by negotiation. Government by moral example was central to Confucianism as was that of the gentleman ruler well versed in the arts, literature and Confucian rites *(lǐ)*. The result, however, was often arbitrary justice and oppression by those who held power.

The family retains its central place as the basic unit of Confucian society. The key to family order is filial piety – children's respect for and duty towards their parents. Teaming up with traditional superstition, Confucianism reinforced the practice of ancestor worship and the keeping of genealogical tables. Confucius himself is worshipped and temples are built for him; one of the best examples of this in the South-West is at Jiànshuǐ in Yúnnán.

Confucius has often been used as a political symbol, his role 'redefined' to suit the needs of the time. In its early years, Confucianism was regarded as a radical philosophy, but over the centuries it has come to be seen as conservative and reactionary. At the end of the 19th century he was upheld as a symbol of reform because he had worked for reform in his own day. After the fall of the Qing dynasty, Chinese intellectuals vehemently opposed him as a symbol of a conservative and backward China. In the 1930s he was used by Chiang Kaishek and the Kuomintang as a guide to proper, traditional values.

During the Cultural Revolution Confucius was denounced by the Communists (along with Lin Biao) as yet another incorrigible link to the bourgeois past. Confucian temples, statues and Confucianists themselves took quite a beating at the hands of rampaging Red Guards. Today Confucius is back in favour, with the Chinese government seeing much to be admired in the neo-Confucianist authoritarianism espoused by Lee Kuan Yew of Singapore.

Buddhism

Buddhism *(Fó Jiào)* was founded in India by Siddhartha Gautama (563–483 BC). Siddhartha was his given name, Gautama his surname and Sakya the name of the clan to which his family belonged. His title 'Buddha' means 'the awakened' or 'the enlightened one'.

The story goes that though he was a prince brought up in luxury, Siddhartha became discontented with the world when he was confronted with the sights of old age, sickness and death. Around the age of 30 Siddhartha broke from the material world and sought 'enlightenment' by following various yogic disciplines.

The cornerstone of Buddhist philosophy is the view that all life is suffering. Everyone is subject to the traumas of birth, sickness, decrepitude and death; to what they most dread (an incurable disease or an ineradicable personal weakness); and to separation from what they love.

The cause of suffering is desire – specifically the desires of the body and the desire for personal fulfilment. Happiness can only be achieved if these desires are overcome, and this requires following the 'eightfold path'. By following this path the Buddhist aims to attain nirvana. Volumes have been written in attempts to define nirvana; the *suttas* (discourses of the Buddha) simply say that it's a state of complete freedom from greed, anger, ignorance and the various other 'fetters' of existence.

The first branch of the eightfold path is 'right understanding'. the recognition that life is suffering, that suffering is caused by desire for personal gratification and that suffering can be overcome. The second branch is 'right-mindedness': cultivating a mind free from sensuous desire, ill will and cruelty. The remaining branches of the path require that one refrain from abuse and deceit; show kindness and avoid self-seeking in all actions; develop virtues and curb passions; and practise meditation.

The Buddha wrote nothing; the Buddhist writings that have come down to us date from about 150 years after his death. By the time these texts came out, divisions had already appeared within Buddhism. Some writers tried to emphasise the Buddha's break with Hinduism, while others tried to minimise it. At some stage Buddhism split into two major schools: Theravada and Mahayana.

The Theravada, or 'doctrine of the elders', school (also called Hinayana or 'little vehicle' by non-Theravadins) is the more conservative of the two and holds that the path to nirvana is an individual pursuit. It centres on monks and nuns who make the search for nirvana a full-time profession (the practice of the first-born son becoming a monk has always sat particularly uneasily with the Confucian notion of filial duty). This school maintains that people are alone in the world and must tread the path to nirvana on their own; Buddhas can only show the way. Many of the minorities of Xīshuāngbǎnnà, such as the Dǎi, are Theravada Buddhists, as are the peoples of the neighbouring countries of Myanmar, Thailand, Laos and Cambodia.

The Mahayana, or 'big vehicle', school holds that since all existence is one, the fate of the individual is linked to the fate of others. The Buddha did not just point the way and float off into his own nirvana, but continues to offer spiritual help to others seeking nirvana. The Mahayana school is the Buddhism of Vietnam, Japan, Tibet, Korea, Mongolia and China.

Mahayana Buddhism is replete with innumerable heavens, hells and descriptions of nirvana. Prayers are addressed to the Buddha and combined with elaborate ritual. There are deities and Bodhisattvas – a rank of supernatural beings in their last incarnation before nirvana. Temples are filled with images such as the future Buddha, Maitreya (often portrayed as fat and happy over his coming promotion) and Amitabha (a saviour who rewards the faithful with admission to the Western Paradise). The ritual, tradition and superstition that Buddha rejected came tumbling back in with a vengeance. Chan, or Zen Buddhism, China's main home-grown contribution to the religion, has since become the most popular form of Buddhism in the West.

In Tibetan areas of western Sìchuān and north-western Yúnnán, a unique form of the Mahayana school is practised: Tibetan or Tantric Buddhism (*Lǎmā Jiào*), sometimes called Lamaism. Tibetan Buddhism, often called Vajrayana or 'thunderbolt vehicle' by its followers, has been practised since the early 7th century AD and is heavily influenced by Tibet's pre-Buddhist Bön religion, which relied on priests or shamans to placate spirits, gods and demons. It is much more mystical than other forms of Buddhism, relying heavily on *mudras* (ritual postures), *mantras* (sacred speech), *yantras* (sacred art) and secret initiation rites to jolt the follower towards enlightenment. Priests called lamas are often believed to be reincarnations of highly evolved beings.

Tibetan Buddhism has itself split into two separate orders – known in the West as the Red Hat (Kagyupa) or Yellow Hat (Gelugpa) sects. The Dalai Lama is the supreme patriarch of Tibetan Buddhism.

Yúnnán is unique in that it has strong centres of Tibetan, Mahayana and Theravada Buddhism.

Islam

The South-West has a prominent community of Huí, ethnic Chinese Muslims who trace their descent from Arab traders or mercenaries who settled in the region in the wake of the 13th-century Mongol invasion of Kublai Khan. They are set apart from the Han Chinese by their white skullcaps and abhorrence of pork (China's main source of meat). Many towns in the South-West have at least one mosque and several Muslim restaurants, recognisable by the strips of beef drying out the front. China's Muslims suffered greatly during the Cultural Revolution when many were forced to eat pork and mosques were turned into pigsties.

The proper name of the religion is Islam (*Yīsīlán Jiào* in Mandarin), derived from the word *salaam*, which primarily means 'peace', and in a secondary sense 'surrender'. The full connotation is something like 'the peace which comes by surrendering to God'. The corresponding adjective is 'Muslim'. Mohammed said that there is only one God, Allah. The name derives from joining *al*, which means 'the', with *Illah*, which means 'God'.

Christianity

(*Jīdū Jiào*)
Christianity came to China when large numbers of Catholic and Protestant missionaries established themselves in the South-West following the invasion of China by the Western powers in the 19th century. French Catholics were prevalent in north-west Yúnnán and western Sìchuān and Methodist missions were especially popular amongst the Miáo of Guìzhōu. You can still find prominent Protestant and Catholic churches in Guìyáng, Zūnyì, Móxī, Yíbīn, Kāngdìng, the Nùjiāng Valley and elsewhere.

Minority Religions

Most of the minority groups of South-West China have their own animist and shamanistic belief system, which has subsequently been overlaid with Buddhist, Taoist and Confucian elements.

A belief in spirits, which must be propitiated with charms and sacrifices in order to ensure a good harvest, is almost universal. Many groups offer thanks to water spirits after the rice seedlings are transplanted. The

Dàlǐ is known for its weekly markets

Acupuncture clinic in Kūnmíng

Going for a ride at Tiger Leaping Gorge

Selling vegetables at a Chéngdū market

Bread on the road to Lijiāng

Playing the traditional two-stringed Èrhú in Dàlǐ

Lighting candles by the Grand Buddha, Lèshān

Ducks going for a ride Sìchuān-style, near Chéngdū

local village shaman is the main mediator between the human and spirit worlds. Burial rituals are especially important to ensure the deceased's soul makes it to the correct home. Many nationalities, including the Bouyi and Shui, have elaborate burial taboos and a system of sacrifices to appease angry spirits.

Religion & Communism

Today the Chinese Communist government professes atheism. It considers religion to be base superstition, a remnant of old China used by the ruling classes to keep power. This is in line with the Marxist belief that religion is the 'opiate of the people'.

Nevertheless, in an effort to improve relations with the Muslim, Buddhist and Tibetan minorities, the Chinese government is once again permitting open religious activity. However, only atheists are permitted to be members of the CCP. Since almost all of China's 55 minority groups adhere to one religion or another, this rule precludes most of them from becoming Party members. It is illegal for under-18s to participate in religious activities in China.

Traditional Chinese religious beliefs took a battering during the Cultural Revolution when monasteries were disbanded, temples were destroyed and the monks were sometimes killed or sent to the fields to labour.

Since the death of Mao, the Chinese government has allowed many temples (sometimes with a limited contingent of monks and novices) to reopen as active places of worship. All religious activity is firmly under state control and many of the monks are caretakers within renovated shells of monasteries, which serve principally as tourist attractions.

Christians are estimated to comprise about 1% of China's total population. It is still officially frowned upon by the government as a form of spiritual pollution, but nevertheless you can see new churches being built. What the Chinese government does, however, is make it difficult for Chinese Christians to affiliate with Christians in the West. Churches are placed under the control of the government: the Three-Self Patriotic Movement was set up as an umbrella organisation for the Protestant churches, and the Catholic Patriotic Association was set up to replace Rome as the leader of the Catholic churches. Churches which are not registered with the government are illegal.

Proselytising is forbidden and Western missionaries are routinely denied visas to enter China, though many simply enter on tourist visas or as English teachers. Yúnnán is a favourite haunting ground for Christian development organisations.

There is much friction between the government and the Chinese Catholic church because the church refuses to disown the Pope as its leader. The one child policy doesn't sit well with the Catholic stand on abortion. For this reason, the Vatican maintains diplomatic relations with Taiwan, much to China's consternation.

Facts for the Visitor

HIGHLIGHTS
Backpacker Getaways

Unlike the South-East Asian trail, which seems to harbour some little getaways with travellers' breakfasts, walks, waterfalls and fabulous beaches at every turn, in China such rest-up retreats are few and far between. In fact, there are only three places that have achieved a legendary status on the travel circuit: Yángshuò (Guǎngxī), Dàlǐ (Yúnnán) and Lìjiāng (Yúnnán).

Yángshuò is a village set amid the famous karst scenery of Guìlín. The surrounding countryside alone, which can be explored by bicycle, makes Yángshuò worth a stay of a few days, but there are also river trips, nearby rural markets, caves to explore, cheap accommodation and banana pancakes for breakfast.

Dàlǐ is arguably more exotic but is essentially a similar deal. The old walled town, home to the Bai minority, nestles beside Ěrhǎi Jiang (lake) and the Cāng Shān (mountains). It is a superb place to rest up for a few days.

Lìjiāng, home to the matriarchal Nàxī minority, is arguably more exotic but still offers creature comforts like cappuccino and pizza. Nearby Tiger Leaping Gorge is fast becoming a major attraction.

Xīshuāngbǎnnà, on the border of Laos and Myanmar, is also favoured for its minority colours and subtropical weather.

Minority Regions

South-West China is home to some of the most colourful and vibrant parts of China. Yúnnán alone is home to around 20 different minority groups. In large urban areas these minorities are difficult to distinguish from the Chinese, but in the country many still dress in traditional costumes and regularly hold colourful festivals and markets.

Notable minority areas in South-West China include Yúnnán's Xīshuāngbǎnnà and Měnglián (mainly Dǎi), Dàlǐ (Bai), Lìjiāng (Nàxī) and Déhóng (Burmese, Dǎi

and Jingpo). The other main centre for minority nationalities is Guìzhōu, particularly around Kǎilǐ (Miáo), Róngjiāng and Zhàoxing (Dong), Huángguǒshù (Bouyi) and Xīngyì (Black Miáo).

Many minorities live in remote regions where bus services and hotels are generally poor and there are few creature comforts. If this is your thing, head to the Liáng Shān region around Xīchāng in southern Sìchuān (Yi), to Wēiníng (Yi and Miáo) in north-western Guìzhōu or the Hónghé and Wénshān regions of Yúnnán (Hani, Dǎi and Miáo).

Greater Tibet

Much of western Sìchuān and north-western Yúnnán were once part of the Tibetan Empire and are still very much culturally Tibetan, perhaps even more so these days than many places in Tibet proper. They offer breathtaking mountain scenery, remote monasteries and interesting and friendly people.

Kāngdìng and the roads west to Gānzī and Lǐtáng (the roads to Lhasa) are very much Tibetan, as are the Aba grasslands and the valleys around Barkam in northern Sìchuān and destinations in the far north-west of Yúnnán such as Zhōngdiàn and Déqīn.

These areas are now open to foreigners but you'll need a flexible itinerary as travel is hard here. The roads to Tibet from Chéngdū are wild and spectacular but largely off-limits past the Sìchuān border. Likewise it is currently not allowed to travel independently into Tibet from Yúnnán.

It's possible to travel up the wild north-eastern routes into Qīnghǎi or Gānsù, thus combining the region with a visit to Labrang Monastery at Xiàhé (Gānsù) or Ta'er Monastery near Xīníng (Qīnghǎi). For details on these last two monasteries see Lonely Planet's *China* guide.

Markets

South-West China has some great markets. The best ones are a colourful blur of local minorities who have made the trek into town from the surrounding countryside to trade, catch up on gossip and maybe visit the local palm reader. They are normally the best places to see genuine minority cultural life, spot traditional dress and taste a wide variety of local foods.

Many markets in minority areas are held on a five- or six-day cycle, making it a bit hit-and-miss for foreigners to know when they are on. Others like Kǎilǐ, Róngjiāng and Dàlǐ have fixed dates, often on a Sunday.

The best markets are in Róngjiāng, Táijiāng, Kǎilǐ, Chóng'ān and Weīníng in Guìzhōu and Shāpíng (Dàlǐ), Zhōngdiàn, Fúgòng (Nùjiāng Valley), Měnghùn and Xīdìng in Yúnnán.

Natural Beauty

The mountains of western Sìchuān rank among the highest in China (and thus the world) and feature spectacularly beautiful areas. Hǎiluógōu Glacier, Wòlóng Nature Reserve, Jiǔzhàigōu National Park and Huánglóng Sì are the most accessible places in north-west Sìchuān. Yúnnán has equally stunning alpine scenery in the north-west, particularly at the Míngyǒng Glacier near Déqīn and Tiger Leaping Gorge around Lìjiāng. All offer a mix of high mountains and a spread of ecosystems ranging from sub-tropical to glacial.

The limestone plateau further south-east has a very different type of beauty. There's the stunning karst landscape of Yángshuò, the weird eroded splinters of the Stone Forest in Yúnnán and the huge caves and waterfall complexes of Huángguǒshù, Zhījīn and Chìshuǐ in Guìzhōu.

Cǎohǎi Lake in north-western Guìzhōu has a subtle beauty and is one of the best bird-watching sites in China.

River Trips

Cruises on the Yangzi River (Cháng Jiāng) have long been touted as one of China's premier attractions. In reality they get mixed reports. Some travellers have even found the Three Gorges (the whole reason for cruising the river) overrated. In any event the area will soon be submerged by the Three Gorges Dam project so if you want to see it you'd better get a move on.

The Li River cruise from Guìlín to Yángshuò is probably the country's premier scenic river trip, passing through a superb karst landscape. Other less touristy river trips worth checking out can be found on the Wuyang Jiang around Zhènyuán (Guìzhōu), the Mǎlǐng Gorge near Xīngyì (Guìzhōu) and the Zuo Jiang in Guǎngxī.

Hiring a Bike

Cycling is one of the best ways to get around villages. You can pass some sublime days peddling around the sleepy villages of Yángshuò, Lìjiāng, Dàlǐ and Xīshuāngbǎnnà, stopping at a minority village or local pagoda for lunch.

Temples & Buddhas

The Grand Buddha at Lèshān in Sìchuān is the largest Buddha in the world. Seventy-one metres high, it is carved into a cliff face overlooking the confluence of the Dadu and Min rivers. You can go to the top, opposite the head, and then descend a short stairway to the feet for a Lilliputian perspective. Tour boats pass by for a frontal view.

Dàzú, not far from Chóngqìng, has some Buddhist caves (not as good as Dūnhuáng). One of the most beautiful traditional buildings in China can be found at the Shānxī Merchants Guild in Zígòng (southern Sìchuān). Other tourist favourites include the vibrant Yuántōng and Bamboo Temples in Kūnmíng. For something completely different check out the Burmese-style pagodas of Xīshuāngbǎnnà.

Yúnnán and Sìchuān have some of the largest and most active Tibetan monasteries, including Ganden Songtseling Gompa in Zhōngdiàn and the monasteries around Dégé.

SUGGESTED ITINERARIES

There are an infinite variety of itineraries to choose from in the South-West. One important thing to remember is not to try to pack too much in if your time is limited. Travel times in rural Guìzhōu and western Sìchuān are much longer than any map could suggest. There's nothing worse than spending all your time in China on a Chinese bus. Except maybe on a hard-seat train.

Generally, it's better to concentrate your time in one area or province. Travel in China is difficult enough without stretching things to the limit. For the same reasons it's a good idea to build in a rest day every now and then.

The Loop Route

The South-West loop has long been China's most favoured backpacker trail. The standard routine is a brief stay in Guǎngzhōu (one or two nights), followed by a ferry to Wúzhōu, and from there a direct bus to Yángshuò (very few travellers bother with Guìlín).

Onward travel to Kūnmíng in Yúnnán can be undertaken by train or by plane. From Kūnmíng, there is a wide range of choices – south to the subtropical areas of Xīshuāngbǎnnà and Déhóng or north-west to Dàlǐ and Lìjiāng (or both). From Kūnmíng, many travellers opt to travel on to Chéngdū via Dàlǐ, Lìjiāng, a couple of days climbing Éméi Shān and a brief stop at the giant Buddha of Lèshān. An increasingly popular option is the tough five-day trip from Zhōngdiàn in Yúnnán to Kāngdìng in Sìchuān

From Chéngdū there are many options: back to Běijīng or Guǎngzhōu by rail, eastwards to Chóngqìng and from there down the Yangzi River or south-eastwards, looping back to Guìzhōu, Guìlín and Hong Kong.

Two months is a good amount of time to spend on this, though you can speed things up with a flight or two.

Other Options

Other onward options from Kūnmíng include a flight to Chiang Mai or Bangkok in Thailand, a train to Hanoi in Vietnam or overland routes into Laos. Come up from Hanoi by train to Nánníng, take in Yángshuò and some minority areas in Guìzhōu, take a train to Kūnmíng, see something of Yúnnán and then head back to Indochina through Laos to Thailand.

From Chéngdū there are many options. A 10-day loop can take you around the Tibetan areas of Jiǔzhàigōu, Sōngpān and Huánglóng

Park. Alternatively, head west from Chéngdū to visit Wolong Panda Sanctuary and then loop north to Barkam or south to Kāngdìng. An increasingly popular Tibetan taster is to travel from Kāngdìng west to Lǐtáng and then south via Xiāngchéng to Zhōngdiàn and Lìjiāng in Yúnnán.

From Kūnmíng take in Xīshuāngbǎnnà. You can also head up to the border with Tibet via the scenic Tibetan areas of Zhōngdiàn and Déqīn.

An overland option from Guìyáng to Kūnmíng takes you through some interesting minority areas around Huángguǒshù Falls and the town of Xīngyì. Alternatively, journeying north takes you to the offbeat natural scenery of Chìshuǐ and the Bamboo Sea before reaching the interesting cities of Yíbīn and Zígòng in Sìchuān and the Great Buddha at Lèshān.

For more detailed provincial options see Suggested Itineraries in each provincial chapter.

Great Journeys

There are some great journeys to be made within South-West China. The greatest of course was the Long March (see the boxed text 'The Long March' in the Facts about South-West China chapter).

An interesting week or 10-day trip can take you from Yángshuò in Guǎngxī to Kǎilǐ in Guìzhōu, passing through some fascinating Dong and Miáo minority villages.

Another rugged 10-day trip takes you north of Chéngdū up into the Tibetan areas of Sōngpān and Jiǔzhàigōu. From here you can loop back to Chéngdū or continue north-west into the Tibetan grasslands of Aba and on to Lánzhōu in Gānsù province.

There are many interesting comparisons to be made between South-West China and Indochina. Many of the minority peoples of the South-West are also found in Vietnam, Thailand and Laos. From Kūnmíng you can travel by road or rail to Hanoi via Jiànshuǐ and Yuányáng in south-east Yúnnán and the interesting market town of Sapa in north Vietnam. Road routes also lead via Xīshuāngbǎnnà to Laos. Kūnmíng to Myanmar is also an interesting trip as it follows the old Burma Road. This route is not quite yet possible.

Chéngdū-Lhasa is the ultimate high-altitude roller coaster trip into Tibet. Unfortunately it is currently out of bounds unless you have several thousand dollars to blow on an organised trip. Still, you can make it as far as the Tibetan border with a bit of perseverance. An increasingly popular Tibetan taster is to travel from Chéngdū to Lǐtáng via Kāngdìng and then swing south via Xiāngchéng to Yúnnán. For details see the Western Sìchuān & the Road to Tibet section in the Sìchuān chapter.

Two Weeks

In 14 days you could fly to Guìlín, take in the scenery and Yángshuò, then fly to Kūnmíng and visit Dàlǐ and Lìjiāng.

Alternatively, fly to Kūnmíng and travel overland to Chéngdū via Dàlǐ, Lìjiāng and Lèshān.

One Month

In a month you could do a loop from Guìlín to Kūnmíng, Dàlǐ, Lìjiāng, Éméi Shān and Lèshān before arriving in Chéngdū.

PLANNING
When to Go

There is never a bad time to visit South-West China. Whenever you go, somewhere is always at its best.

That said, summers can be uncomfortably hot in the Sìchuān basin, Chóngqìng and Xīshuāngbǎnnà, and the latter also has a mild monsoon season from June through August. Local tourism has taken off in a big way in China and in the summer months, when it hits its peak, getting around and finding accommodation can become quite a headache.

Winter (November to February) is the quietest time of year to visit the region, with airfares to China often much cheaper during this time. Southern Yúnnán and southern Guǎngxī are balmy in winter, though most of Guìzhōu and north Guǎngxī is shrouded in freezing fog, and temperatures in western Sìchuān and north-eastern Yúnnán plummet way below freezing. Many travellers succumb to diabolical flus in winter.

Spring (March, April, May) and autumn (September, October, November) are probably the best months to be on the road. Flowers bloom throughout the region in spring and the autumn colours in north-west Sìchuān are particularly stunning.

See the Climate section in the Facts about South-West China chapter for more information on regional weather variations.

Another thing to consider is the timing of festivals, especially if you are planning to visit Guìzhōu and, to a lesser extent, other minority areas. Festival dates are listed at the beginning of each province chapter. In general, winter is a quiet time, though February is chock-a-block with festivals in south-east Guìzhōu.

Major public holidays are also to be avoided if possible. Chinese New Year is a terrible time of year to be travelling (nearly two million tourists visited Yúnnán during the week of Chinese New Year 2001!) and many hotels are booked solid.

Maps

Inside China Top quality maps of almost every Chinese city, even many small towns, are readily available. Some of these show incredible detail – bus routes (including names of bus stops), the locations of hotels, shops and so on. Unfortunately most are in Chinese characters only. Provincial atlases are available in all provincial capitals.

Maps are most easily purchased from bookstalls or street vendors around train and bus stations, from branches of the Xīnhuá Bookstore or from hotel front desks (even cheap Chinese hotels where foreigners can't stay). Most cost from around Y2 to Y4.

It is only in tourist centres that you will find English maps. The places to look are hotel giftshops, entrances to tourist sites and sometimes foreign-language bookshops. English-language editions invariably cost more than their Chinese equivalents.

Abroad Some of the most detailed maps of China available in the West are the aerial survey 'Operational Navigation Charts' (Series ONC). These are prepared and published by the Defence Mapping Agency Aerospace

Center, St Louis Air Force Station, Missouri 63118, USA. Cyclists and mountaineers have recommended these maps highly because of their extraordinary detail.

Good general maps of South-West China are hard to come by. Nelles' *Southern China* or Hilderbrand's *China* are both pretty good. Tourist offices abroad sometimes carry stock of the National Tourist Administration's excellent *Tourist Map – Southwest of China*.

Ordering Maps Several map suppliers have Web sites where you can view catalogues or even the actual maps. Mail order suppliers include:

Australia
Mapland (☎ 03-9670 4383) 372 Little Bourke St, Melbourne, Vic 3000
The Travel Bookshop (☎ 02-9241 3554) 20 Bridge St, Sydney, NSW 2000

Germany
GeoCenter ILH (☎ 0711-788 93 40, fax 788 93 54, ℮ geocenterilh@t-online.de) Schockenriedstrasse 44, D-70565 Stuttgart

UK
Edward Stanford Ltd (☎ 020-7836 1321, fax 836 0189) 12-14 Long Acre, Covent Garden, London WC2E 9LP
ⓦ www.stanfords.co.uk
Maps Worldwide (☎ 01225-707 004) Datum House, Lancaster Road, Melksham, SN12 6TL
ⓦ www.mapsworldwide.co.uk
Upton Map Shop (☎ 01684-593146, fax 594 559) 15 High St, Upton-upon-Severn, Worcestershire WR8 0HJ

USA
Chessler Books (☎ 800-654 8502, 303-670 0093, fax 303-670 9727, ℮ chesslerbk@aol.com) PO Box 4359, Evergreen, CO 80437
ⓦ www.chesslerbooks.com
Map Link (☎ 805-692 6777, fax 692 6787, ℮ custserv@maplink.com) 30 S La Patera Lane, Unit 5, Santa Barbara, CA 93117
ⓦ www.maplink.com

What to Bring

As little as possible. It's much better to buy things as you need them than to throw things away because you've got too much to carry. Lightweight and compact are two words that should be etched in your mind when you're deciding what to bring. Drill holes in the handle of your toothbrush if you have to – anything to keep the weight down!

Backpacks Invest in a good backpack. Increasingly popular are packs that convert into a carry bag by way of a hood that zips over the shoulder and waist straps – these are less likely to be damaged on airport carousels and more presentable if you ever need to discard the backpacker image.

Check whether at least some compartments can be locked, usually by locking the two zips together. Otherwise you can make it a bit more thief-proof by sewing on tabs so that you can padlock pockets shut. True, any backpack can be slashed open with a razor blade but a couple of padlocks will deter most opportunist crime on buses and in dormitories.

A day-pack is essential for carrying things around after you've dumped your backpack at the hotel or train station. Some large rucksacks even have a detachable day-pack. Some travellers travel with two large day-packs and travel with one for a week or two while the other (full of refills and luxuries) sits in hotel storage. You need to have a pretty clear idea of your itinerary to do this though.

A beltpack is OK for maps, extra film and other miscellanea, but don't use it for valuables such as your travellers cheques and passport – it's an easy target for pickpockets.

If you don't want to use a backpack, a shoulder bag is much easier to carry than a suitcase. Bring suitcases only if you know you won't be carrying your luggage on buses and trains.

Chinese-made backpacks are generally terrible. If you are passing through Běijīng, check out the Xishui Silk Market, just off Jianguomen Wai Dajie, where you can normally find pukka Western backpacks at bargain prices.

Clothes In theory, you need only two sets of clothes – one to wear while the other is washed. Dark coloured clothing is preferable because it doesn't show the dirt. Clothing is one of the best cheap buys in China, so don't feel compelled to bring everything from home. The only problem might be finding large Western sizes, especially shoes.

China is pretty informal, although fashionable clothing is in vogue in big cities like Chéngdū and Kūnmíng. Shorts and T-shirts are respectable summer wear, but try to look clean. Most hotel rooms provide flip-flops for the shower. Trekking sandals are becoming increasingly popular and are a good idea for subtropical areas like Xīshuāngbǎnnà.

If you're travelling at the height of winter, prepare yourself for severe cold in certain areas. Few hotels south of the Yangzi have any heating during winter. Good down jackets are available in China, but it's hard to find good quality hats, mittens and boots (at least in Western sizes). PLA shops are often a good place to find cheap, warm clothes, though only if you look good in army green. Western long johns are more comfortable and warmer than the Chinese variety.

A light raincoat or windbreaker is useful outside of winter or during the relatively mild winters in Yúnnán and Guǎngxī.

Sleeping Bag A sleeping bag isn't strictly necessary unless you plan to go camping. However, if you're staying in remote, basic hotels or planning to climb Éméi Shān in winter, a snug sleeping bag can be a real luxury. Hotels provide copious bedding during the winter months, as do the sleeper carriages on trains.

Toiletries Outside the major cities, some pharmaceutical items are hard to find, such as shaving cream, sunscreen (UV lotion), decent razor blades, mosquito repellent (especially useful in Xīshuāngbǎnnà), deodorant, dental floss, Western tampons and contact lens solution. Bring condoms, as the quality of locally made condoms may be suspect. Cold medicines and throat pastilles such as Strepsils throat pastilles are essential if you are travelling in winter. Shampoo is available everywhere in convenient one-use sachets, so you can buy these as you go along. Laundry soap and travel packs of tissues are also available everywhere.

Necessities A portable, lightweight alarm clock is essential for getting up on time to catch your flight, bus or train. A padlock is useful for securing bags to buses and trains and for securing hotel rooms or lockers in budget hotels. A torch (flashlight) is essential in rural areas. Earplugs are essential if you want to sleep at any time during your trip.

Packets of instant soup, coffee and cold remedies can be lifesavers in winter as every hotel room has a flask of boiling water. A water bottle is essential if you plan to do any walking or trekking. A metal one will enable you to cool hotel *kāishǔi* (boiling water) giving you a reliable drinking water source. Leak proof plastic containers and Ziploc bags are useful for transporting things like half-opened packs of soap powder. Stuff bags are useful for dividing clean and dirty clothes or keeping things dry in the rain. A sarong can be used as a bed sheet, skirt, emergency towel and pillow.

The following is a comprehensive checklist of things to consider packing, but do not feel compelled to bring *all* these things:

Passport, visa, documents (vaccination certificate, diplomas, marriage licence photocopy, student ID card), money, money belt or vest, air ticket, copy of your address book, reading matter, pen, notepad, name cards, visa photos, Swiss army knife (with bottle opener for beers), camera and accessories, extra camera battery, colour slide film, video camera and blank tapes, radio, Walkman and rechargeable batteries, small battery recharger (220V), padlock, cable lock (to secure luggage on trains), sunglasses, glasses prescription, contact lens solution, alarm clock, clothes line, leak-proof water bottle, torch (flashlight) with batteries and bulbs, comb, compass, daypack, long pants, short pants, long shirt, T-shirt, nylon jacket, sweater, raincover for backpack, umbrella or rain poncho, razor, razor blades, shaving cream, sewing kit, spoon, sun hat, sunscreen (UV lotion), toilet paper, tampons, toothbrush, toothpaste, dental floss, deodorant, underwear, socks, thongs, nail clipper, tweezers, mosquito repellent, vitamins, laxative, Lomotil, condoms, contraceptives, special medications you use and medical kit (see the Health section later in this chapter).

Gifts Many Chinese people study English and appreciate old English books and magazines. Stamps make good gifts; the Chinese are avid collectors, congregating outside the philatelic sections of the post offices. Foreign postcards make popular gifts. Pictures of you and your family are great for breaking the ice when no-one speaks English, especially in minority areas.

RESPONSIBLE TOURISM

Think about the impact you may be having on the environment and the people who inhabit it. One very simple way of minimising your impact is to reduce the amount of plastic you use; recycle plastic bags and try to recycle plastic drinking bottles or purify your bottle.

Try to support local services and guides whenever possible rather than paying a large agency (like China International Travel Service) in the capital. Support eco-friendly tourist initiatives.

Don't give out pens and sweets to children – you'll turn them into beggars. Similarly, handing out medicines can encourage people not to visit doctors. If you wish to contribute something constructive it's better to give the pens directly to schools and the medicines to rural clinics. Avoid buying products or medicines that are made from endangered species.

Don't pay to take a photo of someone and don't photograph someone if they don't want you to. If you agree to send someone a photograph make sure you follow through it.

Act with respect when visiting temples or monasteries. In Tibetan monasteries always circle a statue or *chörten* (stupa) in a clockwise direction. In Dǎi temples in Xīshuāngbǎnnà always take your shoes off before entering. Don't take photos inside temples unless you have permission.

TOURIST OFFICES
Local Tourist Offices

State travel agencies such as CITS can often help with information on off-the-beaten track sites but in general they exist primarily to book you onto one of their tours. In more popular destinations, CITS operates

an FIT (Family and Independent Travellers) office that is of more use to independent travellers. Most useful of all are the backpacker cafes in centres like Lìjiāng, Dàlǐ and Yángshuò, which offer advice, information and books full of advice from previous travellers.

Tourist Offices Abroad

China National Tourist Office (CNTO) and China National Tourist Administration (CNTA) offer brochure maps and information. Their offices abroad include:

Australia
(☎ 02-9299 4057, fax 9290 1958) CNTO, 19th floor, 44 Market St, Sydney, NSW 2000

France
(☎ 01 56 59 10 10, fax 01 53 75 32 88) Office du Tourisme de Chine, 15 rue Berri, 75008 Paris

Germany
(☎ 069-520 135, fax 528 490) CNTO, Ilkenhans Strasse 6, D 60433 Frankfurt-am-Main

Israel
(☎ 03-522 6272, fax 522 6281) CNTO, 19 Frishman St, PO Box 3281, Tel Aviv 61030

Japan
Tokyo: (☎ 03-3591 8686, fax 3591 6886) CNTA, 6th floor, Hamamatsu cho Bldg, 1-27-13 Hamamatsu cho, Minato-ku
Osaka: (☎ 06-6635 3280, fax 6635 3281) CNTA, 4th floor, OCAT Bldg, 1-4-1 Minatomachi, Naniwa-ku, Osaka

Singapore
(☎ 221 8681, fax 221 9267) CNTO, No 17-05 Robina House, 1 Shenton Way, Singapore 0106

Spain
(☎ 01-548 0011, fax 548 0597) CNTO, Gran Via 88, Grupo 2, Planta 16, 28013 Madrid

UK
(☎ 020-7935 9787, fax 7487 5842) CNTO, 4 Glenworth St, London NW1

USA
Los Angeles: (☎ 818-545 7505, fax 545 7506) CNTO, Suite 201, 333 West Broadway, Glendale, CA 91204
New York: (☎ 212-760 9700, fax 760 8809) CNTO, Suite 6413, Empire State Building, 350 Fifth Ave, New York 10118

The China National Tourist Association has a somewhat dated Web site at **W** www .cnta.com.

VISAS & DOCUMENTS
Passport
The Chinese government requires that your passport *(hùzhào)* must be valid for at least six months after the expiry date of your visa. You will need at least one entire blank page in your passport for the visa. Your country's embassy or consulate can usually add additional pages to your passport if need be.

Losing your passport is very bad news indeed. Getting a new one takes time and money. However, if you will be staying in China or any foreign country for a long time, it helps tremendously to register your passport with your embassy. This will eliminate the need to send telexes back to your home country to confirm to authorities that you really exist.

If you lose your passport, you should certainly have some ID card with your photo – many embassies require this before issuing a new passport. Some embassies will accept a driver's licence, but others will not – an expired passport will often save the day.

Visas
A visa *(qiānzhèng)* is required for the People's Republic of China (PRC) but these are normally easy to get. The Chinese will even issue visas to individuals from countries that do not have diplomatic relations with the PRC. Chinese embassies abroad have been known to stop issuing visas to independent travellers during summer or in the run up to sensitive political events or con-

The Hong Kong and Macau SARs
At the time of writing, visas were not required for most Western nationals to visit Hong Kong or Macau. However, now that Hong Kong has been reunified with China, be aware that new visa regulations could be issued at any time. If you cross from China into Hong Kong or Macau you will be stamped out of China and you will need another visa or a double entry visa to re-enter China.

ferences in an attempt to control the numbers of tourists entering China during the high season.

There are six types of visas, as follows:

L	Travel *(lǚxíng)*
F	Business or Student (less than six months) *(fǎngwèn)*
D	Resident *(dìngjū)*
G	Transit *(guòjìng)*
X	Long-term Student *(liúxué)*
Z	Working *(rènzhí)*

For most travellers, the type of visa is 'L', from the Chinese word for travel *(lǚxíng)*. This letter is on the visa.

Visas are readily available from Chinese embassies and consulates in most Western and many other countries. It's best to get an application form in person at the embassy or consulate, though it is possible to obtain one online at embassy Web sites. This will ask you to list exit/entry points, your itinerary in China and means of transport but don't worry, you won't be forced to stick to this. Don't give your occupation as writer or journalist, don't list Tibet as a destination and don't mention bicycles. Regulations state that you should have a ticket out of the country but this is rarely enforced.

A standard 30-day, single-entry visa from most Chinese embassies can be issued in three to five working days. A visa mailed to you will take up to three weeks. Express services cost twice the normal fee. Fees must be paid in cash and you'll need two passport photos.

Rather than going through an embassy or consulate, you can also make arrangements at some travel agencies, especially Chinese government-owned agencies (such as CITS and CTS) that have overseas representatives. Fees vary according to how much your country charges Chinese citizens for a visa.

You can easily get a visa in Hong Kong. The standard 30-day visa can be obtained from almost any travel agency. The cheapest visas are available from the Visa Office (☎ 2827 1881) at the Ministry of Foreign Affairs of the PRC, 5th floor, Low Block, China Resources Building, 26 Harbour Rd,

Wanchai. It charges HK$100 (HK$150 for double entry) for next-day service and an extra HK$150 for same-day service. US citizens (unless of Chinese descent) face an additional surcharge of HK$160. The office is open Monday to Friday from 9am to 12.30pm and from 2pm to 5pm, and on Saturday from 9am to 12.30pm.

Visas valid for more than 30 days are often difficult to obtain anywhere other than in Hong Kong, though some embassies abroad (for example the UK) may give you 60 days out of high tourist season if you ask nicely. If you do have troubles getting more than 30 days or a multiple-entry visa, head to one of the branches of CTS in Hong Kong or Macau (see the boxed text 'Stopover Survival Information' in the Getting There & Away chapter).

Prices range from HK$160 for a single-entry, 90-day visa issued in 2½ days to HK$1300 for a six-month, multiple-entry visa. CITS will get you a 90-day tourist visa in two days for HK$180, by the next day for HK$250 or the same day for HK$380 (hand in your passport before noon and you'll get it back at 6.30pm). You can get passport photos made at the office. Some Hong Kong travel agencies can also get you 60- and 90-day and multiple-entry visas. Two reliable ones are Phoenix services (☎ 2722 7378), 6th floor, Milton Mansion, 96 Nathan Rd, Tsimshatsui, Kowloon, and Shoestring Travel (☎ 2723 2306), 4th floor, Block A, Alpha House, 27 Peking Rd, Tsimshatsui, Kowloon.

A 30-day visa is activated on the date you enter China, and must be used within three months of the date of issue. Officials in China are often confused over the validity of the visa and look at the 'Valid Until' date. On most 30-day visas, however, this is actually the last date by which you must have *entered* the country, not left. Your visa expires the number of days that your visa is valid for after the date of entry into China (but note that you must enter China within three months of the date the visa was issued). Longer-stay visas normally start from the day they are issued, not the day you enter the country, so you should check this.

Multiple-entry visas allow you to enter and leave the country an unlimited number of times and are available through CTS and some travel agencies in Hong Kong and Macau. The cheapest multiple-entry visas cost HK$350 and are valid for 90 days; six month multiple-entry visas cost HK$500 for next day pick-up or HK$600 for same day pick-up. CITS will arrange a six-month business visa for HK$850 in three days, HK$1050 for the next day and HK$1300 for the same day. You will need the business card of your (or any) contact in China. The latter are business or short-term student (F) visas and normally will be issued only if you've been to China at least once before and have a stamp in your passport to prove it. Extensions are close to impossible.

It is possible to obtain single-entry visas at the border at Shēnzhèn (next to Hong Kong) and Zhūhǎi (next to Macau). Unfortunately, they are valid for travel only within the Shēnzhèn Special Economic Zone or the Zhūhǎi Special Economic Zone respectively and so are of no use to a trip to South-West China. It won't be long before visas are not even required for trips to Shēnzhèn, but you will of course still need one for the rest of China.

There are tentative plans to introduce a visa upon arrival system at Chéngdū, though this will probably only be good for a stay of 48 hours or less. Check at a Chinese embassy beforehand.

Visa Extensions All visa extensions are handled by the Foreign Affairs Branch *(Wàishìkē)* of the local Public Security Bureau (PSB; *Zhōu Gōngānjú*). Government travel organisations, like CITS, have nothing to do with extensions, so don't ask them. Visa extensions can cost nothing for some, but Y200 to Y320 for most nationalities.

The situation with visa extensions seems to change frequently and varies from town to town. Recently, travellers who entered China with a 30-day visa have routinely been able to extend their visa twice, each time by 30 days, giving a total stay of 90 days.

The penalty for overstaying your visa in China is Y500 *per day*.

Travel Permits

Alien Travel Permits (*Tōngxíng Zhèng* or *Lǚxíng Zhèng*) are pretty much defunct as almost every county in Yúnnán, Sìchuān, Guìzhōu and Guǎngxī is now open to foreigners.

Travel Insurance

Although you may have medical insurance in your own country, it is probably not valid in China. But ask your insurance company anyway – you might already be covered. You also might be automatically covered if you hold a valid International Student Identity Card (ISIC), GO 25 International Youth Travel Card or International Teachers' Identity Card (ITIC) – ask at the place where you purchased the card.

A travel insurance policy is a very good idea. The best ones protect you against cancellation penalties on advance-purchase flights, medical costs through illness or injury, theft or loss of possessions and the cost of additional air tickets if you get really sick and have to fly home. Cover depends on the insurance and your type of ticket, so ask both your insurer and the ticket-issuing agency to explain where you stand.

Ticket loss is also covered by travel insurance. Paying for your airline ticket with a credit card often provides limited travel accident insurance and you may be able to reclaim the payment if the operator doesn't deliver. Ask your credit-card company what it's prepared to cover.

Some policies offer both high and low medical-expense options; the high category is chiefly for countries such as the USA that have extremely high medical costs – China should be in the low one. There is a wide variety of policies available so check the small print.

Some policies specifically exclude 'dangerous activities', which can include scuba diving, motorcycling, and even trekking. Check that the policy covers ambulances or an emergency flight home.

You may prefer a policy that pays doctors or hospitals directly rather than you having to pay on the spot and claim later. If you have to claim later make sure you keep all documentation. Some policies ask you to call back (reverse charges) to a centre in your home country where an immediate assessment of your problem is made.

Some policies offer a cheaper option, which includes only medical cover and not baggage loss. This can be worthwhile if you're not carrying any pricey valuables. Many policies require you to pay the first US$100 or so anyway and only cover valuables up to a set limit (thus if you lose a US$1000 camera you might find yourself only covered for US$300 and having to pay the first US$100!). In case of loss of baggage or valuables you will almost certainly need an official police report to show the insurance company.

Buy travel insurance as early as possible. If you buy it the week before you fly, you may find that you're not covered for delays to your flight caused by strikes or other industrial action that may have started or been threatened before you took out the insurance.

Insurance policies can usually be extended while you are on the road by calling the insurance company or agency you bought it from. Make sure you extend the policy *before* it expires or you may have to buy a new policy, often at a relatively higher premium.

Student travel offices are one place to inquire about relatively inexpensive insurance policies. Better travel agencies also sell travel insurance policies – do a little checking around before you buy. Again, read the fine print – the coverage may be cheap, but very limited.

Driving Licence

As a tourist you are not allowed to drive in China. An International Driving Permit is not recognised by the Chinese authorities. Nor will you get any use out of your home country's licence unless you have a Chinese residence permit.

Hostel Cards

We only found one place in South-West China where you can use an International Youth Hostel Federation (IYHF) card, and this only gives you a Y5 discount on accommodation! If you already have a valid card, you can bring it along on the odd chance you might actually get to use it, but it certainly would not be advisable to buy one just for China.

Student & Youth Cards

If you are studying in China, you'll be issued a student card by your school. These are often useful to get a discount on admission fees or to bargain down overpriced hotel rooms, though only if you speak some Chinese to back this up.

Even a Taiwanese student card can sometimes be useful. If you do encounter any obstruction you can at least smugly point out that 'Taiwan is an inalienable part of the People's Republic of China...isn't it?'.

International student cards and youth cards can sometimes get you a discount on international flights to China and occasionally admission discounts in China itself. The cost to buy one of these cards varies according to country, but is typically between US$10 and US$20.

As mentioned above, you may be automatically covered by a travellers' health insurance policy if you hold one of these cards (be sure to ask). Another supposed benefit is access to a 24-hour toll-free help line that can provide emergency medical, legal and financial services (such as finding a doctor or lawyer, replacing lost or stolen documents and arranging an emergency flight home).

To qualify for an International Student Identity Card (ISIC), you need to be a full-time student, but there are no age limits. Full-time teachers and faculty staff can apply for an International Teacher Identity Card (ITIC). To get these cards you need an official letter from your school confirming that you are indeed a student (or teacher, as the case may be).

If you are not a student or teacher, but aged 25 or under, then you can qualify for a GO 25 International Youth Travel Card (just call it a 'GO 25 Card'). These are issued by representative offices of the Federation of International Youth Travel Organisations (FIYTO).

These cards offer essentially the same benefits as the ISIC and ISTC. Student travel offices in various cities and university campuses in most countries can provide you with application forms for them.

Vaccination Certificates

Useful, although not essential, is a yellow International Health Certificate to record your vaccinations. It's unlikely you'll ever be asked to show it, unless you've been in an epidemic area.

Resident Permits

The 'green card' is a residence permit issued to English teachers, foreign experts and students who live in China. The green card is not really a card, but resembles a small passport. Green cards must be renewed annually. If you lose your card you'll have to pay a hefty fee to have it replaced.

Besides having to have all the right paperwork, you must also pass a health exam to obtain a residence permit. Bring your passport and two photos. Besides a general health exam, ECG and an x-ray, you will be tested for HIV. The staff should use disposable syringes which are unwrapped in front of you.

A few hotels (even five star hotels!) offer major discounts to green-card holders.

Copies

If you're thinking about working or studying in China or anywhere else along the way, photocopies of university diplomas, transcripts and letters of recommendation could prove helpful.

Married couples should have a copy of their marriage certificate with them, especially if either husband or wife is ethnic Chinese (or looks Chinese). It's worthwhile carrying photocopies of the front and back pages of your passport, as well as your Chinese visa. There are photocopiers on most street corners in Chinese cities.

EMBASSIES & CONSULATES

Addresses of China's embassies and consulates overseas include:

Australia (☎ 02-6273 4780, 6273 4781)
15 Coronation Dr, Yarralumla, ACT 2600

Consulates: Melbourne, Perth and Sydney
W www.chinaembassy.org.au
Cambodia (☎ 426271) 150 Mao Tse Toung
Blvd, Phnom Penh
Canada (☎ 613-789 3509/3434) 515 St Patrick
St, Ottawa, Ontario K1N 5H3
Consulate-Generals: Calgary, Toronto and
Vancouver
W www.chinaembassycanada.org
France (☎ 01 47 36 02 58, fax 01 47 36 34 46)
9 Avenue Victor Cresson, 92130 Issy Les
Mounlineaux, Paris
W www.amb-chine.fr
Germany (☎ 0228-361 095) Kurfislrstenallee
125-300 Bonn 2
Consulate: Hamburg
W www.china-botschaft.de
Japan (☎ 03-3403 3380, 3403 3065)
3-4-33 Moto-Azabu, Minato-ku, Tokyo 106
Consulates: Fukuoka, Osaka and Sapporo
Laos (☎ 021-315103) Thanon Wat Nak Nyai,
Vientiane
Malaysia (☎ 03-242 8495) 229 Jalan Ampang,
Kuala Lumpur
Consulate: Kuching
Myanmar (Burma) (☎ 01-221280)
1 Pyidaungsu Yeiktha Lan, Yangon
Netherlands (☎ 070-355 1515) Adriaan
Goekooplaan 7, 2517 JX, The Hague
New Zealand (☎ 04-587 0407) 104A Korokoro
Rd, Petone, Wellington
Consulate: Auckland
W www.chinaembassy.org.nz
Singapore (☎ 734 3361) 70 Dalvey Road
South Korea (☎ 319 5101, fax 319 5103)
83 Myŏng-dong 2-GA, Chunggu, Seoul 100022
Consulate: Pusan
Thailand (☎ 02-245 7032/49)
57 Th Ratchadaphisek, Bangkok
UK (☎ 020-7636 8845, 7631 1430, 24-hour
premium rate visa information ☎ 0891-
880808, fax 020-7436 9178,) 31 Portland
Place, W1N 5AG, London; visas cost £30,
plus £20 for same-day or £15 for 24-hours
service; double-entry visas cost £45
Consulate-Generals: Edinburgh, Manchester
W www.chinese-embassy.org.uk
USA (☎ 202-338 6688, fax 588 9760, faxback
265 9809, e visa@china embassy.org) Room
110, 2201 Wisconsin Avenue, NW Washing-
ton DC, 20007
Consulates: Chicago, Houston, Los Angeles,
New York and San Francisco
W www.china-embassy.org has downloadable
visa forms
Vietnam (☎ 04-845 3736) 46 Hoang Dieu St,
Hanoi
Consulate: Ho Chi Minh City

For embassies not listed here, consult the
Foreign Ministry's Web site at W www
.fmprc.gov.cn.

Embassies & Consulates in China For
information on the Lao, Myanmar and Thai
consulates in Kūnmíng and the US consulate in Chéngdū see those cities in the
main text.

In Běijīng (☎ area code 010) there are
two main embassy compounds – Jianguomenwai and Sānlǐtún.

The following embassies are in Jianguomenwai, east of the Forbidden City:

Austria (☎ 6532 2061, fax 6532 1505)
5 Xiushui Nanjie
India (☎ 6532 1908, fax 6532 4684)
1 Ritan Donglu
Ireland (☎ 6532 2691, fax 6532 2168)
3 Ritan Donglu
Israel (☎ 6505 2970, fax 6505 0328) Room
405, West Wing, China World Trade Centre,
1 Jianguomenwai Dajie
Japan (☎ 6532 2361, fax 6532 4625) 7 Ritan Lu
New Zealand (☎ 6532 2731, fax 6532 4317)
1 Ritan Dong Erjie
Singapore (☎ 6532 3926, fax 6532 2215)
1 Xiushui Beijie
South Korea (☎ 6505 2608, fax 6505 3458) 3rd
and 4th floors, China World Trade Centre,
1 Jianguomenwai Dajie
Thailand (☎ 6532 1903, fax 6532 1748) 40
Guanghua Lu
UK (☎ 6532 1961, fax 6532 1937)
11 Guanghua Lu
USA (☎ 6532 3831, fax 6532 6057)
3 Xiushui Beijie
Vietnam (☎ 6532 5414, fax 6532 5720)
32 Guanghua Lu

The Sānlǐtún Compound, north-east of the
Forbidden City, is home to the following
embassies:

Australia (☎ 6532 2331, fax 6532 6957)
21 Dongzhimenwai Dajie
Belgium (☎ 6532 1736, fax 6532 5097)
6 Sānlǐtún Lu
Cambodia (☎ 6532 1889, fax 6532 3507)
9 Dongzhimenwai Dajie
Canada (☎ 6532 3536, fax 6532 4072)
19 Dongzhimenwai Dajie
Denmark (☎ 6532 2431, fax 6532 2439)
1 Sānlǐtún Dong Wujie

Finland (☎ 6532 1817, fax 6532 1884)
1-10-1 Tayuan Diplomatic Bldg,
14 Liangmahe Nanlu
France (☎ 6539 1300, fax 6539 1301) Unit
1015, Tower A, 21 Gongti Beilu, Chaoyangqu
Germany (☎ 6532 2161, fax 6532 5336)
17 Dongzhimenwai Dajie
Italy (☎ 6532 2131, fax 6532 4676)
2 Sānlǐtún Dong Erjie
Laos (☎ 6532 1224, fax 6532 6748)
11 Sānlǐtún Dong Sijie
Malaysia (☎ 6532 2531, fax 6532 5032)
13 Dongzhimenwai Dajie
Myanmar (☎ 6532 1584, fax 6532 1344)
6 Dongzhimenwai Dajie
Netherlands (☎ 6532 1131, fax 6532 4689)
4 Liangmahe Nanlu
Spain (☎ 6532 1986, fax 6532 3401)
9 Sānlǐtún Lu
Sweden (☎ 6532 3331, fax 6532 5008)
3 Dongzhimenwai Dajie
Switzerland (☎ 6532 2736, fax 6532 4353)
3 Sānlǐtún Dong Wujie

The following countries also have consulates in Guǎngzhōu (☎ area code 020):

Australia (☎ 9331 2738) Room 1503-4, Main
Bldg, GITIC Plaza, 339 Huanshi Donglu
France (☎ 8667 7522) Unit 1160, China Hotel,
Liuhua Lu
Germany (☎ 8192 2566) 103 Shamian Beijie,
Shamian Island
Japan (☎ 8333 8999) Garden Hotel Tower,
368 Huanshi Donglu
Thailand (☎ 8188 6968) Room 316, White
Swan Hotel, Shamian Island
UK (☎ 8335 1354) CITIC Plaza, 339 Huanshi
Donglu
USA (☎ 8188 8911) 1 Shamian Nanjie,
Shamian Island
Vietnam (☎ 8652 7908, 8368 1000) 13 Taojin
Beilu (behind Guǎngzhōu Friendship Store)

CUSTOMS

Chinese border crossings have gone from being severely traumatic to exceedingly easy. Although there may seem to be lots of uniformed police around, the third degree at customs seems to be reserved for pornography-smuggling Hong Kongers rather than Western travellers.

Note that there are clearly marked 'green channels' and 'red channels'; you should take the red channel only if you have something to declare.

You're allowed to import 400 cigarettes (or the equivalent in tobacco products), 2L of alcoholic drink and 50g of gold or silver. Importation of fresh fruit is prohibited. You can legally only bring in or take out Y6000 in Chinese currency. There are no restrictions on foreign currency except that you should declare any cash that exceeds US$5000 (or its equivalent in another currency).

A very peculiar restriction is the Y300 limit (Y200 if going to Hong Kong or Macau) on taking herbal medicines out of the country. Our favourite Chinese regulation is the one that strictly forbids anyone bringing more than 20 pieces of underwear into the People's Republic.

Cultural relics, handicrafts, gold and silver ornaments and jewellery purchased in China theoretically have to be shown to customs on leaving. If these items are deemed to be 'cultural treasures' they will be confiscated (see Antiques in the Shopping section later in this chapter). All bags are x-rayed. A few foreigners have had nearly worthless pottery and paintings seized by overzealous customs agents but in general you won't even be checked. Still, make sure that you have a receipt for any valuable items.

It's illegal to import any printed material, film, tapes, etc, 'detrimental to China's politics, economy, culture and ethics'. But don't be too concerned about what you take to read. As you leave China, things such as tapes, manuscripts and books 'which contain state secrets or are otherwise prohibited for export' can be seized.

MONEY
Currency

The Chinese currency is known as Rénmínbì (RMB), or 'People's Money'. Formally the basic unit of RMB is the *yuán*, which is divided into 10 *jiǎo*, which again is divided into 10 *fēn*. In spoken Chinese the yuán is referred to as *kuài* and jiǎo as *máo*. The fēn has so little value these days that it is rarely used.

The Bank of China issues RMB bills in denominations of two, five, 10, 20, 50 and

100 yuán. The new Y20 note was introduced in 2000 and features the scenery of Guilín on one side and Chairman Mao on the other. A new red Y100 bill was introduced in 1999. Older bills feature the communist pantheon of Mao Zedong, Zhou Enlai, Zhu De and Liu Shaoqi. Both are legal tender.

Coins are in denominations of one yuán, five jiǎo and one, two and five fēn. There are still a lot of paper versions of the coins floating around, but it is likely that these will gradually disappear in favour of the coins.

Currency Exchange

Exchange rates for Chinese RMB are as follows:

country	unit		yuán
Australia	A$1	=	Y4.31
Canada	C$1	=	Y5.31
Euro	€1	=	Y7.33
France	1FF	=	Y1.11
Germany	DM1	=	Y3.75
Hong Kong	HK$1	=	Y1.06
Japan	¥1	=	Y0.06
New Zealand	NZ$1	=	Y3.58
Singapore	S$1	=	Y4.72
Switzerland	SFr1	=	Y4.85
Thailand	1B	=	Y0.18
UK	UK£1	=	Y12.06
USA	US$1	=	Y8.27

Exchanging Money

Foreign currency and travellers cheques can be changed at border crossings, international airports, main branches of the Bank of China and sometimes the Industrial and Commercial Bank of China (ICBC), the larger tourist hotels and a few of the big department stores. Top-end hotels will generally change money for hotel guests only. You need to fill most forms out in triplicate but the process is relatively speedy. The official rate is given almost everywhere, so there is little need to shop around looking for the best deal. A standard commission of 0.75% is charged.

Australian, Canadian, US, UK, Hong Kong, Japanese and most Western European currencies are acceptable in China. In some

of the backwaters, it may be hard to change lesser known currencies – US dollars are the easiest to change.

Keep at least a few of your exchange receipts. At the end of your trip you can change any remaining RMB into foreign currency but only up to the amount covered by your receipts. Those travelling to Hong Kong can change RMB for Hong Kong dollars there.

Cash A lot of Chinese vendors and taxi drivers can't make change for even a Y50 note, so stock up on Y10 notes.

If you are travelling off the beaten track it's always worth carrying enough cash to last you a minimum of several days. Some small town banks get very nervous at the sight of a sweaty wad of crunched travellers cheques. Don't be caught out by a weekend or public holiday – even top-end hotels are reluctant to change money at these times as they can't verify the official rates. It's a good idea to carry a small stash of small denomination US dollars, say US$100 in tens and twenties, especially if you'll be crossing borders. Note that in the last few years the USA has introduced new cartoon-like US$100 and US$50 bills; the old bills are still legal tender.

If you don't like the idea of turning up in China without Chinese currency you can buy it in Hong Kong and at some branches of the Bank of China abroad (for example in New York, Singapore and London's Chinatown).

Counterfeit bills are a problem in China. In February 2001 seven Chinese were executed for forging banknotes worth 640 million yuán, or US$77 million. (At one time the forgers even set up shop in a Communist Party office cafeteria!) Very few Chinese will accept a Y50 or Y100 bill without checking first to see if it's a fake. Locals use a variety of methods for checking bills. First of all, they look for the watermark – obviously, if it doesn't have one it's a fake. Many people maintain that colours tend to be more pronounced in counterfeit notes and the drawn lines less distinct. The texture of a note is another tell-tale sign counterfeits tend to be smoother than authentic bills.

Travellers Cheques Besides the advantage of safety, travellers cheques are useful to carry in China because the foreign exchange rate is generally higher than what you will get for cash. There is a 0.75% commission for changing travellers cheques.

Cheques from most of the world's leading banks and issuing agencies are now acceptable in China – stick to the major companies such as Thomas Cook, VISA, American Express and Citibank and you'll be OK. You can even buy Renminbi travellers cheques from the Bank of China, though there's little to gain by this.

ATMs Most Automatic Teller Machines (ATMs) in Chinese cities only work with the Chinese banking system and foreign cards will be rejected. However you may get lucky with ATMs in major cities like Chéngdū and Kūnmíng and tourist towns like Lìjiāng – ask the bank first. Chinese ATMs dispense yuán only. Keep all your receipts and compare them to statements back home. In general, don't come to South-West China relying on ATMs for your cash.

An exception, of course, is Hong Kong, where you'll find ATMs advertising international bank settlement systems such as GlobalAccess, Cirrus, Interlink, Plus, Star, Accel, The Exchange and Explore. The rear side of your ATM card should tell you which systems will work with your card. Visa, MasterCard and American Express will work in many Hong Kong machines as well.

Credit Cards Plastic is gaining more acceptance in China for use by foreign visitors in major tourist cities. Useful cards include Visa, MasterCard, American Express, JCB and Diners Club. They can be used in most mid-range to top-end hotels (three-star and up) and some department stores. You still can't use your credit card to pay for train tickets but more and more airlines and travel agencies will accept credit cards as payment for flights (though often with a surcharge of up to 3%).

Credit card cash advances have become fairly routine at head branches of the Bank of China. Bear in mind, however, that a 3% commission is generally deducted and usually the minimum advance is Y1200.

If you are embarking on a long trip check the expiry date of your credit card. Keep a record of the card number separate from the card itself.

International Transfers Except in Hong Kong, Běijīng and Shànghǎi, having money sent to you via a bank in China can be a time-consuming and frustrating task that is best avoided. If dealing with the Bank of China, the funds may have to be routed via a clearing bank and the process can take weeks.

Western Union can wire money via EMS (see Post & Communications) in Kūnmíng, Chéngdū, Guìlín, Nánníng. See their Web site at W www.westernunion.com.

Bank Accounts Foreigners can open bank accounts in China – both Chinese currency and US dollar accounts (the latter only at special foreign-exchange banks). You do not need to have resident status, a tourist visa is sufficient documentation. Note that you can often only access funds in the city where you opened the account.

Black Market The abolition of Foreign Exchange Certificates (FEC) in 1994 basically knocked China's flourishing black market on its head. Black market moneychangers still attempt to eke out a meagre living in some major cities but the rates they offer are not much more than bank rates. Given the very likely risk of short-changing and rip-offs, and the abundance of counterfeit currency floating about, it would be wise to avoid changing money on the streets. Be careful if moneychangers hand you back a US$100 note and tell you it's a fake – it may have been discreetly swapped for a US$1 note.

Most borders have a branch of Bank of China. If these are shut, duty-free shops will often change money at the same rate.

Security

A money belt or pockets sewn inside your clothes is the safest way to carry money.

Velcro tabs sewn to seal your pockets shut will also help thwart roving hands.

Keeping all your eggs in one basket is not advised – you could leave a small stash of money (say US$100) in the hotel safe or buried in your backpack, with a record of the travellers cheque serial numbers and a photocopy of your passport. Never leave cash lying about your hotel room.

Costs

How much will a trip to South-West China cost? Well, that's largely up to the degree of comfort you need, how much travelling you do and how much time you spend in cities as opposed to the countryside. One thing's for sure though – it will cost a lot less than in the economic boomtowns of eastern China. While it's now hard to travel from Běijīng to Shànghǎi for less than US$35 a day, it's generally not too difficult to keep costs down to US$15 per day in the South-West, especially in rural areas.

Food costs remain reasonable throughout China, and if you are careful they can be as little as US$4 per day. Transport costs can be kept to a minimum by travelling by bus wherever possible or by travelling hard-seat on the train. You can normally get a bed in a two- or three-bed room, with communal bathroom, for around US$4. Budget double rooms start from around US$7. On average, mid-range hotels cost around US$20 to US$35 for a double with air-con, bathroom, TV etc. It is usually possible to eat well in hotel restaurants for around US$5 to US$10.

The main drain on savings will be the long train journeys, on which generally only the hardiest of travellers can face hard-seat. Transport costs have actually fallen for foreigners with the demise of the dual-pricing system. Train travel is reasonable and costs about half the price of flying. Newly introduced luxury express coaches are significantly more expensive than normal buses.

Top-end travel in China? It's possible to hit the major attractions of the South-West staying in four- or five-star hotels (US$60 upwards for a double), flying long distances, taking taxis to and from airports, dining on Chinese haute cuisine and enjoying a few drinks in the lobby bar in the evenings for between US$150 and US$200 per day.

China used to have a separate currency for foreigners and a dual-pricing system for bus, train and air travel and entry tickets but these have been dismantled in the last few years. A few government hotels in rural areas charge foreigners double the local rate for rooms but that's about it. After so many years of official support for overcharging, it's not surprising that many ordinary Chinese consider overcharging foreigners as their patriotic duty and certainly justified. It's worth checking what locals are paying, especially on private transport.

One thing not to lose sight of is the relative value of money. China can be a draining place to travel in, especially if you are trying to keep costs at a bare minimum. If you're going to be on the road for more than a couple of weeks it's worthwhile throwing in the occasional bout of luxury like a soft-seat train ride or an express bus ride. Remember – you're on holiday.

Tipping & Bargaining

China is one of those wonderful countries where tipping is not done and almost no-one asks for it. When tips are offered in China, they are offered before you get the service, not after – that will ensure (hopefully) that you get better service. All things considered, tipping isn't a good idea because it will make it rough for foreigners who follow you.

Since foreigners are so frequently overcharged in China, bargaining becomes essential. You can bargain in shops, hotels, with taxi drivers, with most people – but not everywhere. In large shops where prices are clearly marked, there is usually no latitude for bargaining. In small shops and street stalls, bargaining is expected, but there is one important rule to follow – be polite.

There is nothing wrong with asking for a discount, if you do so with a smile. Some foreigners seem to think that bargaining should be an exercise in intimidation. This is not only unpleasant for all concerned, it seldom results in getting a lower price – indeed, in 'face-conscious' China, intimidation is likely to make the vendor more recalcitrant and you'll be overcharged.

You should keep in mind that entrepreneurs are in business to make money and aren't going to sell anything to you at a loss. Your goal should be to pay the Chinese price, as opposed to the foreigners' price.

Taxes

Although big hotels and top-end restaurants may add a tax or 'service charge' of 10% to 15%, all other consumer taxes are included in the price tag.

For information on departure and airport taxes see the Getting There & Away and Getting Around chapters.

POST & COMMUNICATIONS
Postal Rates

Postage for domestic letters up to 20g is Y0.50; domestic postcards are Y0.30. International letters cost Y5.40 up to 10g and Y6.40 for 11g to 20g.

International postal rates are as follows: for the final airmail letter rate add Y1 *for every 10g* for international destinations, and Y0.50 to Hong Kong, Macau and Taiwan.

letters (weight)	inter-national	HK, Macau & Taiwan	Asia-Pacific
11-20g	Y4.40	Y1.50	Y3.70
21-50g	Y8.20	Y2.80	Y6.20
51-100g	Y10.40	Y4.00	Y8.80
101-250g	Y20.80	Y8.50	Y17.60
251-500g	Y39.80	Y16.70	Y33.80
501g-1kg	Y75.70	Y31.70	Y64.30
1-2kg	Y123.00	Y55.80	Y104.00
Postcards	Y4.20	Y2.00	Y3.70
Aerograms	Y5.20	Y1.80	Y4.50

There are discounts for printed matter *(yìnshuāpǐn)* and a small packet *(xiǎobāo)* rate. As a rough guide, a 1kg airmail package costs around Y175 letter rate, Y135.50 printed matter rate and Y147 small packet rate. A 5kg packet to the UK costs Y523 airmail, Y368 surface mail and Y201 sea mail. Sea and land mail takes around two months. The maximum weight you can send or receive is 30kg.

Post offices are very picky about how you pack things; don't finalise your packing until the parcel has its last customs clearance. Most post offices offer materials for packaging, including padded envelopes, boxes and heavy brown paper

If you have a receipt for the goods, put it in the box when you're mailing it, since it may be opened again by customs further down the line.

Express Mail Domestic Express Mail Service (EMS) parcels up to 200g cost Y15; each additional 200g costs Y5. For international EMS, the charges vary according to country and take between four and seven days. Some sample minimal rates (up to 500g parcels) are as follows:

destination	rate
Asia (South)	Y255
Asia (South-East)	Y136
Australia	Y166
Europe (Eastern)	Y382
Europe (Western)	Y226
Hong Kong & Macau	Y96
Japan & Korea	Y121
North America	Y186

Registration Fees The registration fee for letters, printed matter and packets is Y6.50. Recorded delivery is Y2.30. Acknowledgment of receipt is Y5 per article.

Sending Mail

The international postal service is efficient, and air mail letters and postcards will probably take around five to 10 days to reach their destinations. If possible, write the country of destination in Chinese characters, as this should speed up the delivery.

As well as the local post offices, there are branch post offices in many of the major tourist hotels where you can send letters, packets and parcels. Even at cheap hotels you can usually post letters from the front desk – reliability varies, but in general it's OK. In some places you may only be able to post printed matter from these branch offices. Other parcels may require a customs form attached at the town's main post office, where their contents will be checked.

The post office requires that you use an envelope of an approved size. If you bring envelopes from abroad, these might not meet the standard. They will still be delivered, but given low priority and will take a long time to arrive at the intended destination.

Receiving Mail

Poste restante services only really work in the main cities and towns where a lot of foreigners stay. Services at Kūnmíng, Dàlǐ, Lìjiāng and Yángshuò seem to work well.

Elsewhere you may find yourself being pushed from post office to post office like a pinball. The collection system differs from place to place, but one thing all post offices seem to agree on is the Y1 to Y2.30 charge for each item of poste restante mail you collect. It's important to check every possible combination of names your letter could be filed under, including 'M' for Mr, Miss or Mrs. You will need your passport to retrieve your letters or parcels, so be sure to bring it along when you head for the post office.

Some major tourist hotels will hold mail for their guests, but this is generally a less reliable option. Smaller backpacker hotels will usually pin your letter up on a notice board and this seems to work. In general poste restante is fast losing adherents to Web-based email accounts like Hotmail.

Receiving a parcel from abroad is a bit complicated. The mail carrier will not deliver the parcel to your address – what you get is a slip of paper (in Chinese only). Bring this to the post office (indicated on the paper) along with your passport. One good thing about this system is that it mostly eliminates the possibility of your goods being pinched by corrupt customs officials.

Officially, the PRC forbids certain items from being mailed to China – the regulations specifically prohibit 'reactionary books, magazines and propaganda materials, obscene or immoral articles'. You also cannot mail Chinese currency abroad or receive it by post. As elsewhere, mail order hashish and other recreational chemicals will not amuse the authorities.

Telephone

China's phone system is undergoing a major overhaul and, given the size of the task, it has so far been reasonably successful. Both international and domestic calls can be made with a minimum of fuss. Card phones are becoming increasingly widespread.

Most hotel rooms are equipped with phones from which local calls are free. Alternatively, local calls can be made from public pay phones or from privately run phone booths (there's one of these on every corner nowadays). Long-distance domestic calls can also be made from the phone booths, but usually not international calls. In the lobbies of many hotels, the reception desks have a similar system – free calls for guests, Y1 for non-guests, and long-distance calls are charged by the minute. Bear in mind that hotels generally levy a 30% surcharge on long-distance calls.

You can also place both domestic and international long-distance phone calls from China Telecom offices. Generally you pay a deposit of Y50 for domestic calls and Y200 for international calls and are given a card with the number of the phone booth you call from. The call is timed by computer, charged by the minute and a receipt will be provided. Booths are rarely sound-proof.

Domestic long-distance rates in China vary according to distance, but are fairly cheap. International calls are relatively expensive at around Y12 per minute (Y5 to Hong Kong), although with the introduction of IP cards in larger cities, this is quickly changing (see Phone Cards following). There is sometimes a minimum charge of three minutes, though you can normally pay by the minute – check before you dial. Reverse-charge (collect) calls are often cheaper than calls paid for in China. You don't pay if no-one answers but you will be charged if you get through to an answering machine. There is no call cancellation fee. Calls are generally cheaper at the weekend and after 9pm.

If you are expecting a call to your hotel, either international or domestic, try to advise the caller beforehand of your room number. The operators frequently have difficulty understanding Western names and the hotel receptionist may not be able to locate you. If this can't be done, then try to inform the hotel receptionist that you are expecting the call and write down your name and room number – this should increase your chances of success.

The National Tourist Authority has set up a series of information and complaint telephone hotlines for tourists that you will see posted up in hotels across the region. Don't expect too much (if anything) from them.

Card Phones There's a wide range of local and international phonecards.

Lonely Planet's eKno Communication Card is aimed specifically at independent travellers and provides budget international calls, a range of messaging services, free email and travel information – for local calls you are usually better off with a local card. You can either join online at ⓦ www.ekno .lonelyplanet.com, or by phone from China by dialling ☎ 10800 180 0073. Once you have joined, to use eKno from China dial ☎ 10800 180 0072. Check the eKno Web site for joining and access numbers from other countries and updates on super budget local access numbers and new features.

The introduction of the IP (Internet Phone) system slashed the cost of international calls by about two-thirds to Y4.8 per minute. In March 2001 rates were further reduced to Y2.40 per minute to the USA and Canada and Y3.60 to Western Europe, Australia, Japan, Singapore, Malaysia and Thailand. 'Domestic' calls cost Y1.50 per minute to Hong Kong, Macau and Taiwan and Y0.30 elsewhere in China. The service is only available in cities and large towns.

To take advantage of these rates you have to buy an IP card (known by a variety of names, such as a 201 card), which are available in increments of Y100 and less. The cards aren't all that common but you can buy them at most China Telecom offices. You dial a local number, then punch in the card number, then a password number that is sealed under foil on the card, followed by the number you wish to call. Most cards require you to dial the # symbol after each

number. You can use some public phones (you normally have to pay the public phone a service fee of Y1 or around Y0.2 per minute) and most private phones for this but not regular card phones (see information following). You may have to search around for a phone that will accept the number you are trying to ring. English-language service is usually available.

Regular card phones (IC cards) are also found in most China Telecom buildings and major hotels. They cost the standard rate of about Y15 per minute. Note that most phonecards can generally only be used in the province you buy them.

Calls made on card phones are charged by the minute but you may be left with up to US$2 of unusable credits on a card if it's less than the minimum one minute charge.

Direct Dialling To dial into China, first dial your country's international access code (normally 00) + 86 + the Chinese local code (minus the 0) + the local number.

To dial out of China, dial the international access code (00) + your country code + the local area code (minus the first 0) + the number.

Another option is to dial the home country direct dial number (☎ 108) and then your country code, which puts you straight through to a local operator there. You can then make a reverse-charge (collect) call or a credit card call with a telephone credit card valid in the destination country.

Sound too good to be true? Well it is. Firstly, most telecom offices don't seem to be aware that the system exists. If they are the tiniest bit unsure they will normally deny it exists. Another problem is that the phone you are normally given to use is right by the main enquiry desk – the noisiest part of one of the noisiest offices in one of the noisiest countries in the world. Thirdly, the direct dial number seems to change according to where you dial out from. During the course of research the access number for US Sprint varied from 108-13 to 108-130 to 108-013. Telecom staff rarely know which number is the correct one.

Dialling codes include:

country	direct dial	country direct
Australia	☎ 00-61	☎ 108-610
Canada	☎ 00-1	☎ 108-186
France	☎ 00-33	☎ 108-33
Hong Kong	☎ 00-852	☎ 108-852
Japan	☎ 00-81	☎ 108-81
Netherlands	☎ 00-31	☎ 108-31
New Zealand	☎ 00-64	☎ 108-64
UK	☎ 00-44	☎ 108-440
USA	☎ 00-1	☎ 108-1*

* For the USA you can dial ☎ 108-11 (AT&T), ☎ 108-12 (MCI) or ☎ 108-13 (Sprint).

Fax

Faxes can be sent from most telecom centres and main post offices but they are expensive. Not only is there a three minute minimum, even for a one page fax, but there is also an additional per page fee, bringing the cost of a one page fax to the USA to around Y54. At the end of transmission you should be given a print out confirming the fax went through and a receipt for monies paid. If you subsequently find the fax didn't go through you can, in theory at least, get a refund or try again at no charge. Problems arise if you are sending a fax to a combined fax/phone and someone at the other end picks up the phone.

Major hotels usually operate a business centre complete with telephone and fax service, not to mention photocopying and perhaps the use of typewriters and computers. Beware that some hotels charge up to US$10 *just to receive a fax*.

Essential Numbers

There are several telephone numbers that are the same for all major cities. Only international directory assistance is likely to have English speakers:

Ambulance	☎ 120
Fire	☎ 119
International assistance	☎ 115
Local directory assistance	☎ 114
Long-distance assistance	☎ 113/173
Police	☎ 110

Email & Internet Access

Email has taken off in China. Not only will you find Internet cafes in most tourist towns such as Lìjiāng, Dàlǐ and Yángshuò, but Internet access is offered in even the smallest town by the 'business centres' of China Telecom. Internet access costs around Y15 per hour at a private cafe to as low as Y5 at China Telecom in some towns, though this figure varies a lot around the region.

Probably the cheapest way to keep in touch while on the road is to sign up for a free email account with Hotmail (W www.hotmail.com), Rocketmail (W www.rocketmail.com) or with Yahoo! (W www.yahoo.com) and access your account from an Internet cafe. These services are free because you have to put up with advertising. If you're willing to spend US$15 per year, you can get all your email forwarded to any address of your choice by signing up with Pobox (W www.pobox.com) – this service can also be used to block advertising and mail bombs.

If you want to use a foreign-based Internet Service Provider (ISP), you'll have much difficulty getting online in South-West China. If you're travelling with a portable computer and want to access your email, your only alternative may be to make an expensive call to Hong Kong or abroad.

If you're travelling with a portable computer and modem, you'll need an IDD line with an RJ-11 phone jack to call to your favourite email service abroad. However, it's risky to attach your modem to the phone in your hotel room and dial out through the switchboard – if the switchboard is digital (as opposed to analog) you risk frying your modem. Ironically, this is a bigger problem at newer hotels – old hotels usually have analog equipment. One of the few companies to market a solution to this problem is Konexx (W www.konexx.com) – it sells a device called a 'mobile konnector', which not only protects the modem, but also allows you to hook up to the phone's handset cord.

You do have to put up with some censorship as the Chinese government has blocked access to certain sites that peddle pornography or contain political content deemed unsuitable for the masses (such as the BBC's Web site).

INTERNET RESOURCES

The Internet changes so fast that almost anything we can recommend about it is liable to be out of date tomorrow. You could try going online and compiling a search using the words 'China' or 'Chinese', but this will turn up many thousands of hits, most of them worthless.

Lonely Planet has information on China on its Internet site at **W** www.lonelplanet .com.au, as well as the Thorn Tree, where you post and reply to queries about travel in China and elsewhere.

Many Chinese Web sites require that you have a Chinese-enabled Web browser to see the Chinese characters, but find an icon that changes the display to English.

A few China-related Web sites include:

Aweto Has an awesome collection of links to China-related sites.
  W www.chinasite.com
China Business World A travel guide with a hotel booking facility, flight timetables and general travel information.
  W www.cbw.com/tourism
China News Current affairs and news reports on China with lots of links.
  W www.chinanews.bfn.org
China Now A site featuring travel information, nightlife and restaurant listings, with sections on Kūnmíng and Sìchuān and articles on travel in the region.
  W www.chinanow.com
China Online Good for general and business news.
  W www.chinaonline.com
China Tour Good general travel information.
  W www.chinatour.com
China Vista Everything from business to virtual tours of China, culture and travel information.
  W www.chinavista.com
Inside China Another useful news site, with links to other areas of China-related information.
  W www.insidechina.com
Kham Aid Web site of a charity that promotes literacy and health levels in Western Sìchuān. Features excellent travel articles on remote destinations in western Sìchuān.
  W www.khamaid.org
Mr China's Son Cultural and travel guide to Dàlǐ and around, run by the author and cafe of the same name in Dàlǐ (see the Dàlǐ section in Places to Eat and Recommended Reading in this chapter).
  W www.homestead.com/yndali/homepage2.html

BOOKS

Fathoming the enigma of China is such a monumental task that the need for 'China-watchers' and their publications will probably never dry up. Indeed, just keeping up with the never-ending flood of conjecture on the Middle Kingdom would be a full-time job in itself. Few books concentrate exclusively on China's South-West but most general books on China are relevant. The following is an abbreviated tour of the highlights.

Bookstores

Some Web sites such as Amazon (**W** www .amazon.com), or Waterstone's (**W** www .waterstones.co.uk) and Barnes & Noble (**W** www.bn.com) can be a useful resource for tracking down books.

The following bookshops specialise in travel.

UK
Edward Stanford (☎ 020-7836 1321, fax 836 0189) 12–14 Long Acre, Covent Garden, London WC2E 9LP
The Travel Bookshop 13 Blenheim Crescent, London W11 2EE

USA
Adventurous Traveller Bookstore (☎ 1-800-282 3963, **e** info@AdventurousTraveler.com) 245 S Champlain Street, Burlington, VT 05401. American online travel bookstore, which claims to have the world's largest collection of travel books and guides.
  W www.adventuroustraveller.com
Chessler Books (☎ 800-654 8502, 303-670 0093, fax 303-670 9727, **e** chesslerbk@aol.com) PO Box 4359, Evergreen, CO 80437. New and used books and maps.
  W www.chesslerbooks.com
The Complete Traveller (☎ 212-685 9007) 199 Madison Avenue, New York 10016
Distant Lands (☎ 626-449 3220, fax 310 3220) 56 So. Raymond Ave, Pasadena, CA 91105
  W www.distantlands.com

Lonely Planet
Other Lonely Planet guides to the region include *China, Běijīng, Shànghǎi, Hong Kong*

& *Macau*, and *Tibet*. Also published by Lonely Planet is *Read This First: Asia & India* and *Healthy Travel Asia & India*.

Guidebooks

The Hong Kong publisher Odyssey is gradually producing a series of illustrated provincial guides to China. South-West China is currently covered by guides to *Yunnan, Guizhou, Sichuan* and *The Yangtze River*.

Odyssey's *Guizhou* guide by Gina Corrigan (2nd edition, 2001) has particularly good background information on minorities, festivals and religion but is firmly aimed at tourists travelling on group tours, with frustratingly little information on how to get to the places mentioned.

Trekking in Tibet by Gary McCue (2nd edition, 1999) has useful maps and trail notes for intrepid treks around Minya Konka (Gonga Shan) and the Dégé region of Sìchuān.

Travel

When the wall came tumbling down in the early 1980s, two eminent travel writers got in there quick: Colin Thubron with *Behind the Wall* and Paul Theroux with *Riding the Iron Rooster*. Although only partly set in the South-West, these remain the best recent travel books written on China. Thubron's is the more thoughtful of the two; Theroux the more provocative.

For a more recent and localised travelogue try *Yak Butter and Black Tea* by Wade Brackenbury – an account of the author's two-year adventure with a French photographer trying to hike into the Drung Valley in north-western Yúnnán.

River Town: Two Years on the Yangtze by Peter Hessler is the highly praised record of the two-year stay of a Peace Corps worker in the town of Fuling in Sìchuān.

Simon Winchester's *The River at the Centre of the World* is a thoughtful and companionable wander up the Yangzi, past the Three Gorges Dam, Lìjiāng, Tiger Leaping Gorge and up to the river's source in Tibet. It is subtitled 'A Journey up the Yangtze and Back in Chinese Time' and comes recommended.

Soul Mountain by Gao Xingjian is a rich, challenging and often difficult story of a voyage through the wilds of Sìchuān and Yúnnán in search of Ling Shan, or Soul Mountain. Gao, who now lives in France, recently became the first ever Chinese winner of the Nobel Prize for Literature. Predictably, the novel was banned in China. A second novel entitled *One Man's Bible*, telling his experiences in the Cultural Revolution, is due to be published in 2002.

Several classic travel books from the old school are hard to find outside libraries but worth tracking down. *The Yangtse and Beyond* by Isabella Bird is a classic. Originally published in 1899 it has been reissued by Virago.

Forbidden Kingdom (John Murray, 1957) by Peter Goullart is an expert account of his nine-year stay in Lìjiāng and the customs of the people he met while there. *The Ancient Na-khi Kingdom of Southwest China* (1947) by the inimitable Dr Joseph Rock is also worth digging out if you have a strong interest in north-west Yúnnán.

Slaves of the Cool Mountains by Alan Winnington is a fascinating account of an expedition in 1959 into the slave-owning Yi region of the Liáng Shān bordering Sìchuān and Yúnnán.

Tibetan Marches by Andre Migot is a 1954 account of a trip from Kūnmíng to Kāngdìng, Gānzī and Dege, when travel was on foot, the only guesthouses were in the homes of resident missionaries and bandits lurked around every corner (Migot had everything stolen near Kāngdìng).

Village Life in China. A Community Study of Kao Yao, Yúnnán (Ronald Press, 1963) by Cornelius Osgood is better than the ponderous name would suggest. It's part village survey, part travel story.

History & Politics

A Traveller's History of China by Stephen G Haw is a portable overview of Chinese history, as is *The Walled Kingdom: A History of China from 2000 BC to the Present* by Witold Rodzinsky. Both are paperbacks.

The best recent history of modern China is Jonathan Spence's *The Search for Modern*

China. It covers China's history from the late Ming through to the Tiananmen Massacre in lively prose that is a pleasure to read. Another of Spence's books, *God's Chinese Son*, charts the course of the Taiping Rebellion, which left some 20 million Chinese dead in its wake, and is a biography of its leader Hong Xiuquan, who believed himself to be the younger brother of Jesus Christ.

The Great Chinese Revolution 1800–1985 by John King Fairbank is another highly rated modern history. An updated version by the same author is *China: A New History*, though ironically it is harder to find.

Both Harrison Salisbury and Dick Wilson have produced books entitled *The Long March*, which provide plenty of human details and personal accounts on the epic trek around the South-West and make for gripping reading.

A polemical overview of what Chinese history has been about and where it is all heading is provided in *The Tyranny of History: The Roots of China's Crisis* by WJF Jenner. The essential argument that China's history has been one of tyranny, and that China's attachment in history continues to tyrannise it, is a fascinating one, if perhaps a little too clever for its own good.

A story of the political history of the Deng years has already appeared in *Burying Mao* by Richard Baum. For anyone seriously interested in China's stop-go reforms of the last 20 years, this is the book to read. Merle Goldman also looks at the tortuous course of democratic reform over recent years in *Sowing the Seeds of Democracy in China: Political Reform in the Deng Xiaoping Era*.

Hungry Ghosts: Mao's Secret Famine by Jasper Becker is perhaps the best book on the disastrous Great Leap Forward. The book focuses on the 1958–62 famine that killed 30 million people. China's leaders still try to hide this disaster because it was largely caused by them.

For two alarmist looks at the future try *The Coming Conflict with China* by Richard Bernstein & Ross H Munro or *Pacific Nightmare* by Simon Winchester. The latter is a fictional (but only just) account of the break up of China, ensuing civil war and World War III.

General

Insights *Wild Swans* by Jung Chang is one of the more ambitious of what is a long line of I-survived-China (but only just) books. *Life and Death in Shanghai* by Nien Cheng focuses largely on the Cultural Revolution and is also recommended.

Red Azalea by Anchee Min is a strange and racy account of what it was like to grow up in the Cultural Revolution.

Daughter of the River by Hong Ying, an emigre writer who was born in Sìchuān, is a personal narrative that recalls a childhood and coming of age in the depressing slums of Chóngqìng. Her previous work *Summer of Betrayal* tells the sexual awakening of a young poet during the 1989 Tiananmen protests.

Less riveting, perhaps, is a fine account of life in rural China (mostly Yúnnán) in *Mr China's Son: A Villager's Life* by He Liuyi. The author continues to live in Dàlǐ and now owns a cafe there (where the book is for sale), offering a rare opportunity to ask the author all the questions you wanted to ask during the reading of the book. The author is currently writing a sequel.

State of the nation accounts of contemporary Chinese politics and society by Western scholars and journalists are thick on the ground and tend to become repetitive if you read too many of them. One of the best recent works is *China Wakes* by Nicholas D Kristof & Sheryl Wudunn. Orville Schell has also been diligently tracking China's awakening in several books, the latest being *Mandate of Heaven*.

Read *Real China: From Cannibalism to Karaoke* by John Gittings. It's informative and entertaining, with a tendency towards the scholarly, with chapters on the outbreak of cannibalism in Guǎngxī during the Cultural Revolution, the Yangzi dam and other topics from outside the South-West.

The Chinese by Jaspar Becker, a long-term foreign correspondent in China, paints an engaging picture of modern China and is bang up to date.

China Remembers by Calum Maceod & Lijia Zhang is an excellent and recommended compilation of biographical essays that expertly tells the history of the last tumultuous 50 years through the words of the people who lived it.

Looking for Chengdu: A Woman's Adventure in China by Hill Gates is an anthropologist's look at women's life in Sìchuān as she travels around the province.

The Age of Wild Ghosts: Memory, Violence and Place in Southwest China by Erik Mueggler is an ethnographic study of a Yi community. It portrays the political upheavals of the last 50 years ('The Age of Wild Ghosts') through the eyes of a traditional culture on the fringes of Chinese society.

Human Rights *Eighteen Layers of Hell: Stories from the Chinese Gulag* by Kate Saunders blows the lid off China's human rights violations.

Harry Wu, imprisoned by Chinese authorities for 19 years, exposes China's *laogai* (forced labour camps) in his eloquently written *Bitter Winds: A Memoir of My Years in China's Gulag*. Wu returned to China again in 1995 and was immediately arrested and tried for espionage, but was expelled after intervention by the US congress and President Clinton. He wrote about that experience in his sequel, *Troublemaker: One Man's Crusade Against China's Cruelty*.

The smuggled prison letters of dissident Wei Jingsheng have been collected and published in *The Courage to Stand Alone: Letters from Prison and Other Writings*, edited by Kristina Torgeson.

Some earlier works can be tracked down in libraries. Two excellent examples are *Prisoner of Mao* by Bao Ruo-Wang (Jean Pasqualini) and *Seeds of Fire – Chinese Voices of Conscience*, edited by Geremie Barmé & John Minford.

Biography Immensely popular are biographical appraisals of China's shadowy leaders. Mao, of course, has been the subject of countless biographies. The classic is *Red Star over China* by Edgar Snow, but it was his personal physician, Zhisui Li, who finally blew the lid on the world's most famous dictator cum pop icon. Li's *The Private Life of Chairman Mao* is absolutely compelling in its account of Mao as a domineering manipulator who hypocritically flouted the authoritarian and puritanical rules he foisted on his people – fascinating stuff.

Mao gets similar treatment in *The New Emperors* by Harrison E Salisbury. The book covers the lives of Mao and Deng, but it is Mao who gets the bulk of the book. Deng Xiaoping himself remains elusive. Richard Evans has written an excellent book in *Deng Xiaoping and the Making of Modern China*, which has a particularly good synopsis of the events leading up to the killings in Tiananmen Square in 1989.

Religion Being able to make sense out of Chinese religion will require considerable patience and perseverance. One book that gives a readable overview with an emphasis on places and icons that travellers will encounter is *Travels in Sacred China* by Martin Palmer.

Aside from the Taoist classics, such as the *Tao Te Ching* and *I Ching,* there are hundreds of books on Taoism and fengshui, though many of them tend towards the New Age end of the spectrum.

One of our personal favourites is the *Tao of Pooh* by Benjamin Hoff, which explains Taoism remarkably well in terms of Winnie the Pooh, Piglet and Christopher Robin. Honest!

Art *Chinese Art* by Mary Tregear is an excellent introduction to Chinese art.

FILMS

Movies produced by Westerners and filmed in China are thin on the ground, largely because the Chinese government demands huge fees for the privilege. For Chinese films see the Facts about South-West China chapter.

The definitive classic has to be *The Last Emperor,* released in 1988 by Columbia Pictures and directed by Bernardo Bertolucci.

A more recent production is the film *Red Corner*, starring Richard Gere, not known for his pro-Chinese stance.

Xiu Xiu: the Sent-Down Girl is a Chinese-language film directed by Joan Chen (of *Twin Peaks* fame), which tells the story of a Chéngdū girl sent down to the Tibetan countryside of north-western Sìchuān during the Cultural Revolution. Chen filmed without permission in China and later had to pay a fine of around US$20,000 to the Chinese authorities.

On the other hand, documentaries about China are numerous, although tracking down a video tape to rent or buy might take some effort. The *Gate of Heavenly Peace* by Carma Hinton & Richard Gordon is a well-balanced video about the democracy protests and bloodshed at Tiananmen Square in 1989. Another serious video is *The Dying Rooms* by Kate Blewett and Britain's Channel 4, which explores the practice of infanticide in China.

If nature documentaries are your style, you could try *The Amazing Panda Adventure*. The National Geographic Society has produced a number of excellent videos on China, including *The Mountain Sculptors*, a beautifully shot look at the Hani farmers of Yúnnán's Ailao Mountains.

Phil Agland's absorbing nine hour epic *Beyond The Clouds* is a recommended peek at daily life in Lìjiāng – perfect for all those who ever wanted to know what the old women of Lìjiāng talk about all day.

Lonely Planet also has a video available on travel in *South-West China*.

CD-ROMS

There are plenty of CD-ROMs about China, but finding those published in English will take some effort. Some digging around will find titles on learning Chinese, Chinese art, travel and even a multimedia version of the Taoist text the *I Ching*!

If you are into games, Abacus produce *Wings Over China*, a flight simulation game that enables you to fly missions with the Flying Tigers into wartime South-West China.

In the USA, check out the China Guide Company (☎ 718-389 4876, 888-242 8805, W www.china-guide.com), 642 Leonard St, 2R, Brooklyn, NY 11222.

In Canada, there's BIS Information Systems (☎ 604-688 8916, W www.voyagerco .com), No 203-124 E Pender St, Vancouver, BC V6A 1T3.

Hong Kong and Taiwan are good places to shop for CD-ROMs, but you'll have to look hard to find titles in English.

NEWSPAPERS & MAGAZINES
Chinese-Language Publications

Newspapers in China contain little hard news. Mostly, they are devoted to sloganeering and editorialising. It's hard to say how many Chinese believe what they read, but certainly most Chinese are familiar with the official line: 'the Dalai Lama is a counter-revolutionary splittist', 'Taiwan is a revisionist dictatorship', and so on. When Hong Kongers held a candlelight vigil for the students who were massacred by Communist troops in Tiananmen Square, the Chinese press showed the photo with the caption 'Hong Kong people are expressing their joy and happy feelings at being reunited with the motherland'.

There are more than 2000 national and provincial newspapers in China. The main one is *Renmin Ribao (People's Daily)*, with nationwide circulation. Every city worth its salt has its own local version of the *People's Daily*, and like the banner publication they serve chiefly as a propaganda vehicle. The Letters to the Editor section in the *People's Daily* provides something of a measure of public opinion, and complaints are sometimes followed up by reporters. However, the sports page usually attracts the most interest.

At the other end of the scale is China's version of the gutter press – several hundred 'unhealthy papers' and magazines hawked on street corners and bus stations in major cities with nude or violent photos and stories about sex, crime, witchcraft, miracle cures and UFOs. These have been criticised by the government for their obscene and racy content. They are also extremely popular. Movie and fashion magazines are also becoming increasingly

Notice Boards

Apart from the mass media, the public notice board retains its place in China as an important means of educating the people and influencing public opinion. Wall posters (dàzìbào, or 'big character posters') in public places has long been a traditional form of communicating ideas in China. Deng Xiaoping personally stripped from China's constitution the right to put up wall posters after the Democracy Wall movement of 1979.

Today the notice boards in China are operated by the government and two of the most common subjects are crime and accidents. In China it's no holds barred – before-and-after photos of executed criminals are plugged up on these boards along with a description of their heinous offences. Other popular themes include industrial safety and family planning. You'll often see people reading the *People's Daily*, which is posted up free on notice boards.

popular, as are Chinese-language versions of Elle, Marie-Claire and the like.

There are also about 40 newspapers for the minority nationalities.

Foreign-Language Publications

China publishes various newspapers, books and magazines in a number of European and Asian languages. The *China Daily* (W www.chinadaily.net) is China's official English-language newspaper but it's hard to find in the South-West – even top-end hotels rarely have more than a neglected business section, three months out of date.

China also publishes a large number of very dull magazines in English and other languages. They are seldom seen in China itself, but often clutter up periodical racks in university libraries around the world. They have titles like *China Philately* (for stamp collectors), *China's Patents & Trademarks*, *China's Tibet* (the name says it all) and *Women in China*.

In top-end tourist hotels you might score copies of the popular imported English-language magazines, such as *Time*,

Newsweek, Far Eastern Economic Review or the *Economist*, though don't count on it. If you're *really* lucky you might find European magazines like *Le Point* and *Der Spiegel* or foreign newspapers such as the *Asian Wall Street Journal, International Herald-Tribune* and Hong Kong's *South China Morning Post*.

To China's credit, foreign-language magazines and newspapers are seldom, if ever, censored, even when they contain stories critical of the PRC. Of course, a different set of rules applies to Chinese-language publications from Taiwan and overseas Chinese communities – essentially, these cannot be brought into China without special permission.

RADIO & TV

Domestic radio broadcasting is controlled by the Central People's Broadcasting Station (CPBS). Broadcasts are made in *pǔtōnghuà*, the standard Chinese speech, plus local Chinese dialects and minority languages.

If you want to keep up with the world news, a short-wave radio receiver would be worth bringing with you. You can buy these in China, but the ones from Hong Kong are usually more compact and better quality. You can check frequencies at the following organisations:

Radio Australia (☎ 03-9626 1825),
  e raust@ozemail.com.au) PO Box 428G, Melbourne, Vic 3001
  W www.abc.net.au/ra/
Voice of America (fax 202-619 0211)
  Washington, DC 20547
  W www.voa.gov/
BBC (☎ 020-7240 3456) PO Box 76, Bush House, London WC2B 4PH
  W www.bbc.co.uk/worldservice/tuning/

Chinese Central Television (CCTV) began broadcasting in 1958, and colour transmission began in 1973. Many provinces have their own channel, such as Yúnnán or Guìzhōu TV. Major cities and even small towns in South-West China have their own channel! (Many show pirated videos of Western films!). There is little of interest here for foreigners but as almost every hotel room in China now has a television as standard, most foreigners eventually start flicking optimistically through the channels. If you do succumb, then CCTV's Channel 5 (sports channel) and Channel 8 (music and culture) are the most rewarding. CCTV broadcasts a daily English news program at around 10.30pm and CCTV4 normally has some kind of English news around 7pm. CCTV9 is an international channel available only by satellite.

Hong Kong's STAR TV does satellite broadcasts to China. There are both Chinese- and English-language shows, and a few are actually worth watching. In order to get the right to broadcast in China, STAR TV had to agree to remove the BBC World News (though CNN is normally available).

VIDEO SYSTEMS

China subscribes to the PAL broadcasting standard, the same as Australia, New Zealand, the UK and most of Europe. Competing systems not used in China include SECAM (France, Germany, Luxembourg) and NTSC (Canada, Japan, Taiwan, Korea, Latin America and the USA). However, VCDs and DVDs are much more widely used in China than videotapes.

PHOTOGRAPHY & VIDEO

South-West China is a mixed bag when it comes to photography. Minority areas with their bustling local markets, technicolour costumes and spectacular festivals rank among the most photogenic places in China, but good timing is everything here. Most villages are dead on non-market days and even the minorities swap their Sunday best for a cheap Chinese suit outside festival days.

The weather is also unpredictable, especially during winter, when the sun only shines a few times a month in most parts of Guìzhōu and Sìchuān. It's worth bringing a range of film speeds for the varying levels of light.

Cities and towns are pretty grey and bleak at this time, though you can get some gritty black and white socialist realist shots at this time. In general, black and white film gives good results in China.

Film & Equipment

Imported film and cameras are expensive, but major Japanese companies such as Fuji, Konica and Kodak now have factories in China, bringing film prices down to less than you'd pay in the West. China's most reliable film is the (gulp) Lucky brand.

Colour print film is available widely at around Y20 for 100 ASA (21 DIN) or Y30 for 200 ASA; 400 ASA is harder to find. Slide film such as Ektachrome is available in Kūnmíng, Lìjiāng and Chéngdū and costs between Y68 and Y88 but supplies are patchy and almost impossible to find elsewhere, so try to bring all you need and more. Black and white film is quite easy to find and is cheap to buy (Y10 for 36 exposures) but expensive to develop. Check the expiry date on all film and try to avoid anything that looks like it's been sitting out in the sun for too long.

There are now Kodak and Fuji one-hour developing centres in every large town, though if your film is valuable to you it's probably best to wait until you return home.

Cameras are still mostly pricey, although there are some made-in-China models, like the famous Seagull brand.

Finding the special lithium batteries used by many cameras is generally not a problem, but it would be wise to bring a spare. Some cameras have a manual mode, which allows you to continue shooting with a dead battery, although the light meter won't work. Fully automatic cameras totally drop dead when the battery goes, which can happen in cold weather even if the battery is new.

You're allowed to bring in 8mm movie cameras; 16mm or professional equipment may raise eyebrows with customs.

Video

Video cameras were once subject to shaky regulations, but there seems to be no problem now, at least with the cheap camcorders that tourists carry. A large professional video camera might raise eyebrows – the Chinese government is especially paranoid about foreign TV crews filming unauthorised documentaries.

For the average video hobbyist, the biggest problem is recharging your batteries off the strange mutations of plugs in China – bring all the adaptors you can, and remember that it's 220V.

Restrictions

Photography from planes and photographs of airports, military installations, harbour facilities and railroad terminals are prohibited; bridges may also be a touchy subject. With the possible exception of military installations, these rules are rarely enforced.

Photography most definitely is prohibited, however, in many museums, at archaeological sites and in some temples, mainly to protect the postcard and colour slide industry. It also prevents valuable works of art from being damaged by countless flash photos, but in most cases you're not allowed to take even harmless natural light photos or time exposures. Many places will let you take photos if you pay an often hefty photography fee. There should be a sign in English advising of such restrictions, but ask at the ticket desk if you're not sure.

If you're caught taking photos where you shouldn't, generally the film is ripped out of your camera. Start with a new roll if you don't want to lose any previous shots.

Photographing People

If you have befriended a Chinese, he or she is generally more than happy to be a model. Candid shots of people, however, are viewed with suspicion by many Chinese. Many people in rural areas don't want their picture taken if they are not wearing their Sunday best or if they are doing something menial like working the fields. Payment is rarely demanded and you shouldn't offer and set a precedent.

Make contact with people you want to photograph – often a smile and a wave will do the trick. If you want to take a picture of someone in a market then maybe buy some of their produce first. On the other hand, don't be surprised if a total stranger asks to have his or her picture taken with you; there seems to be a certain kudos in this.

The idea of using photography as a creative outlet is alien to most Chinese. For them, cameras are used to snap friends and family at get-togethers or posed stone-faced in front of (and often blocking out) major tourist sights. It's not uncommon to haul yourself up to the top of a Taoist peak, only to find yourself slap-bang in the middle of a noisy group of excitable Chinese tourists in matching fluorescent hats, busily conscripting a sweaty *laowai* (foreigner) into their group photo. Freelance photographers regularly stalk popular tourist sites to snap up any punters who passed up the opportunity of having their picture taken at a revolutionary monument, in full minority costume, next to a cardboard cut out of Zhou Enlai.

Airport Security

Most X-ray machines in China are marked 'film safe', and this seems to be the case. However, films with a very high ASA rating could be fogged by repeated exposures to airport X-rays – you may wish to put the film in a lead-lined bag or carry it by hand.

As elsewhere in the world, airport security personnel don't want travellers taking photographs and they're especially protective about the area around the baggage X-ray machines.

TIME

Time throughout China is set to Běijīng local time, which is eight hours ahead of GMT/UTC. There is no daylight-saving time. When it's noon in Běijīng the time in other cities around the world is:

Auckland	4pm
Bangkok	11am
Frankfurt	5am
Hanoi	11am
Hong Kong	noon
London	4am
Los Angeles	8pm*
Montreal	11pm*
New York	11pm*
Paris	5am
Sydney	2pm
Vientiane	11am
Yangon	10.30am

* the day before

ELECTRICITY

Electricity is 220V, 50 cycles AC. Plugs come in at least five designs: three-pronged angled pins (like in Australia), three-pronged round pins (Singapore style), two flat pins (American style, but without the ground wire), two narrow round pins (European style) and three rectangular pins (British style). For the most part, however, you can safely travel with two plugs: American style and Australian style.

Conversion plugs are easily purchased in Hong Kong, but are more difficult to find in China. Battery chargers are widely available, but these are generally the bulky style which are not suitable for travelling – buy a small one in Hong Kong.

Electricity can be dicey in the countryside and the low wattage of bulbs in many cheap hotels makes the light difficult to read by. It's wise to have a torch (flashlight) and a couple of spare candles if you're travelling in rural areas.

WEIGHTS & MEASURES

The metric system is widely used in China. However, the traditional Chinese measures are often used in local markets. Fruit and vegetables are weighed by the *jīn* (500g). Smaller measurements (eg, for *shuǐjiǎo* ravioli) are measured in *liǎng* (50g). The following equations may help.

metric	Chinese	imperial
1m (*mǐ*)	3 *chi*	3.28 feet
1km (*gōnglǐ*)	2 *lǐ*	0.62 miles
1L (*gōngshēng*)	1 *gōngshēng*	0.22 gallons
1kg (*gōngjīn*)	2 *jīn*	2.2 pounds

Land is often measure in *mǔ*, which is about 1/30 of a hectare.

LAUNDRY

Backpacker guesthouses in popular tourist destinations like Yángshuò, Dàlǐ and Lìjiāng offer a laundry service which costs around Y3 for a T-shirt and Y5 for trousers.

Each floor of just about every hotel in China has a service desk, usually near the elevators. The attendant's job is to clean the rooms, make the beds and collect and deliver laundry. Almost all tourist hotels have a laundry service, and if you hand in clothes one day you should get them back a day or two later.

Most towns also have a dry cleaners (*gānxǐ diàn*), which will normally do regular laundry for a fraction of what the big hotels charge. Prices range from Y2 to Y8 for a pair of trousers or Y1 to Y4 for a T-shirt.

Most travellers hand-wash their own clothes and you can buy small packets of soap powder (eg, Tide) everywhere. Most hotel rooms supply a washing basin and boiling water, which makes hand washing much easier.

TOILETS

Some travellers have given up eating (for a while at least) just to avoid having to use Chinese toilets. Unfortunately, unless your stay in China is extremely brief, you'll have to learn to cope.

Public toilets in China are not the healthiest looking places – basically they're holes in the ground or ditches over which you squat, and some look like they haven't been cleaned since the Han dynasty. Many cannot be flushed at all while others are flushed with only a bucket of water.

Public toilets can often be found in train stations and the side streets of the cities and towns – many now charge a fee of one or two máo. Some have very low partitions (without doors) between the individual holes and some have none. And no, the staring doesn't stop just because you're going for a crap! Toilet paper is sometimes offered at public toilets but you're better off keeping a stash with you. Dormitory-style hotel rooms are also not equipped with toilet paper.

While it takes some practice to get proficient at balancing yourself over a squat toilet, at least you don't need to worry about whether the toilet seat is clean. Furthermore, experts who study such things (scatologists?) claim that the squatting position is better for your digestive system. Tourist hotels have foreign-style 'sit-down' toilets, a luxury you will come to appreciate. Some Chinese seem to have problems with these though – it's not uncommon to see muddy footprints on the toilet seat.

The issue of what to do with used toilet paper has caused some concern. In general, if you see a wastebasket next to the toilet, that is where you should throw the toilet paper. The problem is that in many hotels, the sewage system cannot handle toilet paper. This is especially true in old hotels where the antiquated plumbing system was designed in the pre-toilet paper era. Also, in rural areas where there is no sewage treatment plant the waste empties into an underground septic tank and toilet paper will really create a mess in there. For the sake of international relations, be considerate and throw the paper in the wastebasket.

The symbols for men and women are:

men   women

男   女

HEALTH

Your health while away depends on your predeparture preparations, your daily health care while travelling and how you handle any medical problem that does develop. While the potential dangers can certainly seem quite frightening, in reality few travellers experience anything more than upset stomachs.

Although South-West China presents a few particular health hazards that require your attention, overall it's a healthier place to travel than many other parts of the world. Large cities such as Chéngdū have decent medical facilities, but in the backwaters of Guìzhōu or western Sìchuān facilities are more basic.

Medical services are generally very cheap in China, although random foreigner surcharges may be exacted. At least foreigners get better service – Chinese patients usually have to wait for hours in long queues.

The main things you have to worry about are intestinal problems, never-ending colds, bronchitis and being run over by China's mad traffic.

In case of accident or illness, it's best just to get a taxi and go to the hospital directly – try to avoid dealing with the authorities (police and military) if possible.

Medical Kit Check List

Following is a list of items you should consider including in your medical kit – consult your pharmacist for brands available in your country.

☐ **Aspirin or paracetamol (acetaminophen in the USA)** – for pain or fever

☐ **Antihistamine** – for allergies, eg, hay fever; to ease the itch from insect bites or stings; and to prevent motion sickness

☐ **Cold and flu tablets, throat lozenges and nasal decongestant**

☐ **Multivitamins** – consider for long trips, when dietary vitamin intake may be inadequate

☐ **Antibiotics** – consider including these if you're travelling well off the beaten track; see your doctor, as they must be prescribed, and carry the prescription with you

☐ **Loperamide or diphenoxylate** –'blockers' for diarrhoea

☐ **Prochlorperazine or metaclopramide** – for nausea and vomiting

☐ **Rehydration mixture** – to prevent dehydration, which may occur, for example, during bouts of diarrhoea; particularly important when travelling with children

☐ **Insect repellent, sunscreen, lip balm and eye drops**

☐ **Calamine lotion, sting relief spray or aloe vera** – to ease irritation from sunburn and insect bites or stings

☐ **Antifungal cream or powder** – for fungal skin infections and thrush

☐ **Antiseptic (such as povidone-iodine)** – for cuts and grazes

☐ **Bandages, Band-Aids (plasters) and other wound dressings**

☐ **Water purification tablets or iodine**

☐ **Scissors, tweezers and a thermometer** – note that mercury thermometers are prohibited by airlines

☐ **Sterile kit** – in case you need injections in a country with medical hygiene problems; discuss with your doctor

Acupuncture

Chinese acupuncture (*zhēnjiū*) has received enthusiastic reviews from many satisfied patients who have tried it. Of course, one should be wary of overblown claims. Acupuncture is not likely to cure terminal cancer or heart disease, but it is of genuine therapeutic value in the treatment of chronic back pain, migraine headaches, arthritis and other ailments.

Acupuncture is a technique employing needles which are inserted into various points of the body. In former times, needles were probably made from bamboo, gold, silver, copper or tin. These days, only stainless steel needles of hair-like thinness are used, causing very little pain when inserted. Dirty acupuncture needles can spread disease rather than cure, so good acupuncturists sterilise their needles or use disposable ones. As many as 2000 points for needle insertion have been identified, but only about 150 are commonly used.

One of the most amazing demonstrations of acupuncture's power is that major surgery can be performed using acupuncture alone as the anaesthetic. The acupuncture needle is inserted into the patient and a small electric current is passed through the needle. The current is supplied by an ordinary torch battery.

The exact mechanism by which acupuncture works is not fully understood by modern medical science. The Chinese have their own theories, but it is by no means certain they really know either. Needles are inserted into various points of the body, each point believed by the acupuncturist to correspond to a particular organ, joint, gland or other part of the body. These points are believed to be connected to the particular area being treated by an 'energy channel', also translated as a 'meridian', but more likely it has something to do with the nerves. By means not fully understood, it seems the needle can block pain transmission along the meridian. No matter how it works, many report satisfactory results.

Acupuncture is practised in hospitals of traditional Chinese medicine, which can be found all over China. Some hospitals in major cities such as Guǎngzhōu, Běijīng and Shànghǎi also train Westerners in the technique. And if you need some emergency acupuncture, even hotels (up-market ones, at least) provide such services at their in-house clinics.

If you're (justifiably) concerned about catching disease from contaminated acupuncture needles, you might consider buying your own before undergoing treatment. Good quality needles are available in major cities in China. Needles come in a bewildering variety of gauges – try to determine from your acupuncturist which type to buy.

One traveller who broke his leg near Dàlǐ made the mistake of calling on the police for help. They took him to the military hospital, where a cast was put on his leg – he was then charged Y20,000 for this service! A civilian hospital would have charged much less – about Y100. This particular foreigner didn't have that much cash, so the police took his passport away and basically held him for ransom until his family could come up with the cash.

Most hospitals offer both Western and traditional Chinese medicines. In fact, the best thing about getting sick in China is getting the chance to try out herbal medicines and acupuncture.

The Chinese do not have Rh-negative blood and their blood banks don't store it.

Predeparture Planning

Immunisations Plan ahead for getting your vaccinations: some of them require more than one injection, while some vaccinations should not be given together. Note that some vaccinations should not be given during pregnancy or in people with allergies – discuss with your doctor. It is recommended you seek medical advice at least six weeks before travel. Be aware that there is often a greater risk of disease with children and during pregnancy.

Discuss your requirements with your doctor, but vaccinations you should consider for this trip include the following (for more details about the diseases themselves, see the individual disease entries later in this section). Whatever vaccinations you get should be recorded in an International Health Certificate. The only vaccination requirement for travellers to China is yellow fever if coming from an infected area (parts of Africa and South America).

Diphtheria & Tetanus Vaccinations for these two diseases are usually combined and are recommended for everyone. After an initial course of three injections (usually given in childhood), boosters are necessary every 10 years.

Polio Everyone should keep up to date with this vaccination, which is normally given in childhood. A booster every 10 years maintains immunity.

Hepatitis A The vaccine (eg, Avaxim, Havrix 1440 or VAQTA) provides long-term immunity (possibly more than 10 years) after an initial injection and a booster at six to 12 months. Alternatively, an injection of gamma globulin can provide short-term protection against hepatitis A – two to six months, depending on the dose given. It is not a vaccine, but is ready-made antibody collected from blood donations. It is reasonably effective and, unlike the vaccine, it is protective immediately, but because it is a blood product, there are current concerns about its long-term safety. Hepatitis A vaccine is also available in a combined form, Twinrix, with hepatitis B vaccine. Three injections over a six-month period are required, the first two providing substantial protection against hepatitis A.

Typhoid Travellers to China are at risk from this disease, especially if travelling to rural areas. It is now available either as an injection or as capsules to be taken orally.

Cholera The current injectable vaccine against cholera is poorly protective and has many side effects, so it is not generally recommended.

Meningococcal Meningitis A single injection gives good protection against the major epidemic forms of the disease for three years. Protection may be less effective in children under two years.

Hepatitis B China is one of the world's great reservoirs of hepatitis B infection, which is spread by blood or by sexual activity. Vaccination involves three injections, with a booster at 12 months. More rapid courses are available if necessary.

Rabies Vaccination should be considered by those who will spend a month or longer in Tibetan areas of western Sìchuān, especially if they are cycling, handling animals, caving or travelling to remote areas. Pretravel rabies vaccination involves having three injections over 21 to 28 days. If someone who has been vaccinated is bitten or scratched by an animal, they will require two booster injections of vaccine; those not vaccinated require more and within a shorter period of time.

Tuberculosis The risk of TB to travellers is usually very low. Vaccination against TB (BCG) is recommended for children and young adults living in these areas for three months or more.

Japanese B Encephalitis Consider vaccination against this mosquito-borne disease if spending over a month in rural China, making repeated trips to a risk area or visiting during an epidemic. It involves three injections over 30 days.

Malaria Medication Antimalarial drugs do not prevent you from being infected but kill the malaria parasites during a stage in their development and significantly reduce the risk of becoming very ill or dying. Expert advice on medication should be sought, as there are many factors to consider, including the risk of exposure to malaria-carrying mosquitoes, the side effects of medication, your medical history and whether you are a child or an adult or pregnant. Travellers to isolated areas in high risk countries may like to carry a treatment dose of medication for use if symptoms occur.

Health Insurance Make sure that you have adequate health insurance. See Travel Insurance under Visas & Documents in the Facts for the Visitor chapter for details.

Chinese Medicine

Many foreigners visiting China never try Chinese herbal medicine *(zhōng yào)* because they either know nothing about it or simply don't believe in it. Prominent medical authorities in the West often dismiss herbalists as no better than witch doctors. The ingredients, which may include, apart from herbs, such marvellous things as snake gall bladder or powdered deer antlers, will further discourage potential non-Chinese customers.

Chinese medicine is holistic in that it seeks to treat the whole body rather than focusing on a particular organ or disease. It seems to work best for the relief of unpleasant symptoms (pain, sore throat etc) and for some long-term conditions that resist Western medicines, such as migraine headaches, asthma and chronic backache. But for acute life-threatening conditions, such as a heart attack, it would be foolish to trust your life to herbs.

Another benefit of Chinese medicine is that there are relatively few side effects. Compared with a drug like penicillin, which can produce allergic reactions and other serious side effects, herbal medicines are fairly safe. Nevertheless, herbs are still medicines, not candy, and there is no need to take them if you're feeling fine. In fact, some herbs are mildly toxic and if taken over a long period of time can actually damage the liver and other organs.

Before shopping for a cure, keep in mind that although a broad-spectrum remedy such as snake gall bladder may be good for treating colds, there are many different types of colds. The best way to treat a cold with herbal medicine is to see a Chinese doctor and get a specific prescription. Otherwise, the medicine you take may not be the most appropriate for your condition. However, if you can't get to a doctor, you can just try your luck at the pharmacy.

If you visit a Chinese doctor, you might be surprised by what he or she discovers about your body. For example, the doctor will almost certainly take your pulse and then may tell you that you have a slippery pulse or perhaps a thready pulse. Chinese doctors have identified more than 30 different kinds of pulses. The doctor may then examine your tongue to see if it is slippery, dry, pale or greasy, or has a thick coating or maybe no coating at all. The doctor, having discovered that you have wet heat, as evidenced by a slippery pulse and a red greasy tongue, will prescribe the herbs for your condition.

Beware of quackery – there is one Chinese herbal medicine, for instance, which pregnant women take to ensure that their foetus will develop into a boy. Other herbal tonics promise to boost your

---

Even with insurance, hospitals may require payment *before* they treat you. Make sure that your health insurance covers repatriation, as least as far as Běijīng.

Travel Health Guides Lonely Planet's *Healthy Travel Asia* is a handy pocket size and packed with useful information, including pretrip planning, emergency first aid, immunisation and disease information and what to do if you get sick on the road. *Travel with Children* by Maureen Wheeler, also from Lonely Planet, includes advice on travel health for younger children.

Other detailed health guides include:

CDC's Complete Guide to Healthy Travel Open Road Publishing, 1997. The US Centers for

Disease Control & Prevention recommendations for international travel.
Staying Healthy in Asia, Africa & Latin America by Dirk Schroeder, Moon Publications, 1994. Detailed and well organised.
Travellers' Health by Dr Richard Dawood, Oxford University Press, 1995. Comprehensive, easy to read, authoritative and highly recommended, although it's rather large to lug around.
Where There Is No Doctor by David Werner, Macmillan, 1994. A very detailed guide intended for someone, such as a Peace Corps worker, going to work in an underdeveloped country.

There are also a number of excellent travel health sites on the Internet. From the Lonely Planet home page you will find links at Ⓦ www.lonelyplanet.com/weblinks/wlheal.htm to the World Health Organization

Chinese Medicine

IQ or sexual prowess and cure baldness. All sorts of overblown claims have been made for herbal medicines, especially by those who make and sell them. Most of these miracle herbs are expensive, and the promised results have never been confirmed by any scientific studies. Yet some gullible Westerners have persuaded themselves that Chinese herbs can cure any disease. A visit to any of China's hospitals will quickly shatter this myth.

Another point to be wary of when taking Chinese medicine is the tendency of some manufacturers to falsely claim that their product contains numerous potent and expensive ingredients. For example, some formulas may list rhinoceros horn as one of the ingredients. Rhinoceros horn, widely acclaimed as a cure for fever, is practically impossible to buy. Any formula listing rhinoceros horn may, at best, contain water buffalo horn. In any case, the rhino is a rare and endangered species, and you will not wish to hasten its extinction by demanding rhino horn products.

Counterfeiting is another problem. Everything gets copied in China, and the problem extends even to medications. If the herbs you take seem to be totally ineffective, it may be because you've bought sugar pills rather than medicine.

If you spend a good deal of time on buses and boats, you'll see how the Chinese deal with motion sickness, nausea and headaches – usually by smearing liniments on their stomach or head. Look for White Flower Oil (Báihuā Yóu), probably the most popular brand. A variation on the theme are salves, the most famous being Tiger Balm, which originated in Hong Kong. And should you strain yourself carrying that heavy backpack around, try applying 'sticky dog skin plaster' (gǒupí gāoyào) to your sore muscles. You might be relieved to know that these days it's no longer made from real dog skin.

and the US Centers for Disease Control & Prevention.

Other Preparations Make sure you're healthy before you start travelling. If you are going on a long trip make sure your teeth are OK. If you wear glasses take a spare pair, your prescription and an ample supply of lens-cleaning solution If you require a particular medication take an adequate supply, as it may not be available locally. Take part of the packaging showing the generic name rather than the brand, which will make getting replacements easier. It's a good idea to have a legible prescription or letter from your doctor to show that you legally use the medication to avoid any problems.

Basic Rules
Food There is an old colonial adage which says: 'If you can cook it, boil it or peel it you can eat it...otherwise forget it'. Vegetables and fruit should be washed with purified water or peeled where possible. Beware of ice cream that is sold anywhere as it might have been melted and refrozen; if there's any doubt steer well clear. Shellfish such as mussels, oysters and clams should be avoided as well as undercooked meat, particularly in the form of mince. Steaming does not make shellfish safe for eating.

If a place looks clean and well run and the vendor also looks clean and healthy, then the food is most probably safe. Chinese food is generally stir-fried quickly over a high heat, which kills most germs. In general, places that are packed with travellers or locals will be fine, while empty restaurants are questionable. The food in busy restaurants is cooked and eaten quite quickly with little standing around and is probably not reheated.

Water The No 1 rule is *be careful of the water* and especially ice. Tap water is not considered safe to drink anywhere in China, though in most cities it's chlorinated and won't kill you. If you don't know for certain that the water is safe, assume the worst. Reputable brands of bottled water or soft drinks are generally fine, although in some places bottles may be refilled with tap water. Only use water from containers with a serrated seal – not tops or corks. Take care with fruit juice, particularly if water may have been added. Milk should be treated with suspicion as it is often unpasteurised, though boiled milk is fine if it is kept hygienically. Tea or coffee should also be OK, since the water should have been boiled.

Water Purification The simplest way of purifying water is to boil it thoroughly. Vigorous boiling is satisfactory in most circumstances; however, at high altitude water boils at a lower temperature, so boil it for longer in these environments.

Consider purchasing a water filter for a long trip. There are two main kinds of filter. Total filters take out all parasites, bacteria and viruses, and make water safe to drink. They are often expensive, but they can be more cost effective than buying bottled water. Simple filters take out dirt and larger foreign bodies from the water so that chemical solutions work much more effectively; if water is dirty, chemical solutions may not work at all. It's very important when buying a filter to read the specifications, so that you know exactly what it removes from the water and what it doesn't. Simple filtering will not remove all dangerous organisms, so if you cannot boil water it should be treated chemically.

Chlorine tablets (Puritabs, Steritabs or other brand names) will kill many pathogens, but not some parasites like giardia and amoebic cysts. Iodine is more effective in purifying water and is available in tablet form (such as Potable Aqua). Follow the directions carefully and remember that too much iodine can be harmful. Boiled water *(kāishǔi)* is available everywhere in China and is safe to drink hot or cold.

Medical Problems & Treatment
Self-diagnosis and treatment can be risky, so you should always seek medical help. Although we do give drug dosages in this section, they are for emergency use only. Correct diagnosis is vital.

An embassy, consulate or five-star hotel can usually recommend a good place to go for advice. In some places standards of medical attention are so low that for some ailments the best advice is to get on a plane and go to Běijīng or Hong Kong.

Antibiotics should ideally be administered only under medical supervision. Take only the recommended dose at the prescribed intervals and use the whole course, even if the illness seems to be cured earlier. Stop immediately if there are any serious reactions and don't use the antibiotic at all if you are unsure that you have the correct one. Some people are allergic to commonly prescribed antibiotics such as penicillin or sulphur drugs; carry this information (eg, on a bracelet) when travelling.

Environmental Hazards
Altitude Sickness Lack of oxygen at high altitudes (over 2500m) affects most people to some extent. The effect may be mild or severe and occurs because less oxygen reaches the muscles and the brain at high altitude, requiring the heart and lungs to compensate by working harder. Symptoms of Acute Mountain Sickness (AMS) usually develop during the first 24 hours at altitude but may be delayed up to three weeks. Mild symptoms include headache, lethargy, dizziness, difficulty sleeping and loss of appetite. AMS may become more severe without warning and can be fatal. Severe symptoms include breathlessness, a dry, irritative cough (which may progress to the production of pink, frothy sputum), severe

headache, lack of coordination and balance, confusion, irrational behaviour, vomiting, drowsiness and unconsciousness. There is no hard and fast rule as to what is too high: AMS has been fatal at 3000m, although 3500 to 4500m is the usual range.

Many of the towns in western Sìchuān are over 3500m and some of the passes take you over 4500m so this is definitely a place to take things slowly.

Treat mild symptoms by resting at the same altitude until recovery, usually a day or two. Paracetamol or aspirin can be taken for headaches. If symptoms persist or become worse, however, *immediate descent is necessary*; even 500m can help. Drug treatments should never be used to avoid descent or to enable further ascent.

The drugs acetazolamide (Diamox) and dexamethasone are recommended by some doctors for the prevention of AMS, however their use is controversial. They can reduce the symptoms, but they may also mask warning signs; severe and fatal AMS has occurred in people taking these drugs. In general we do not recommend them for travellers.

To prevent acute mountain sickness:

• Ascend slowly – have frequent rest days, spending two to three nights at each rise of 1000m. If you reach a high altitude by trekking, acclimatisation takes place gradually and you are less likely to be affected than if you fly directly to high altitude.
• Sleep at a lower altitude than the greatest height reached during the day if possible. Also, once above 3000m, care should be taken not to increase the sleeping altitude by more than 300m per day.
• Drink extra fluids. The mountain air is dry and cold and moisture is lost as you breathe. Evaporation of sweat may occur unnoticed and result in dehydration.
• Eat light, high-carbohydrate meals for more energy.
• Avoid alcohol as it may increase the risk of dehydration.
• Avoid sedatives.

Fungal Infections Such infections occur more commonly in hot weather and are usually found on the scalp, between the toes or fingers, in the groin and on the body (ringworm). You get ringworm (which is a fungal infection, not a worm) from infected animals or other people. Moisture encourages these infections.

To prevent fungal infections wear loose, comfortable clothes, avoid artificial fibres, wash frequently and dry carefully. If you do get an infection, wash the infected area at least daily with a disinfectant or medicated soap and water, and rinse and dry well. Apply an antifungal cream or powder like tolnaftate (Tinaderm). Try to expose the infected area to air or sunlight as much as possible and wash all towels and underwear in hot water, change them often and let them dry in the sun.

Heat Exhaustion Dehydration and salt deficiency can cause heat exhaustion. Take time to acclimatise to high temperatures, drink sufficient liquids and do not do anything too physically demanding.

Salt deficiency is characterised by fatigue, lethargy, headaches, giddiness and muscle cramps; salt tablets may help, but adding extra salt to your food is better.

Anhydrotic heat exhaustion, caused by an inability to sweat, is quite rare. It is likely to strike people who have been in a hot climate for some time, rather than newcomers.

Heatstroke This serious, occasionally fatal, condition can occur if the body's heat-regulating mechanism breaks down and the body temperature rises to dangerous levels. Long, continuous periods of exposure to high temperatures and insufficient fluids can leave you vulnerable to heatstroke.

The symptoms are feeling unwell, not sweating very much (or at all) and a high body temperature (39°C to 41°C or 102°F to 106°F). Where sweating has ceased, the skin becomes flushed and red. Severe, throbbing headaches and lack of coordination will also occur, and the sufferer may be confused or aggressive. Eventually the victim will become delirious or convulse. Hospitalisation is essential, but in the interim get victims out of the sun, remove their clothing, cover them with a wet sheet or towel and then fan continually. Give fluids if they are conscious.

Hypothermia Too much cold can be just as dangerous as too much heat. If you are trekking at high altitudes or simply taking a long bus trip over mountains, particularly at night, be prepared. In western Sìchuān you should always be prepared for cold, wet or windy conditions, even if you're just out walking or hiking. There is often a dramatic drop in temperature when the sun dips behind the valley sides.

Hypothermia occurs when the body loses heat faster than it can produce it and the core temperature of the body falls. It is surprisingly easy to progress from very cold to dangerously cold due to a combination of wind, wet clothing, fatigue and hunger, even if the air temperature is above freezing. It is best to dress in layers; silk, wool and some of the new artificial fibres are all good insulating materials. A hat is important, as a lot of heat is lost through the head. A strong, waterproof outer layer (and a 'space' blanket for emergencies) are essential. Carry basic supplies, including food containing simple sugars to generate heat quickly and fluid to drink.

Symptoms of hypothermia are exhaustion, numb skin (particularly toes and fingers), shivering, slurred speech, irrational or violent behaviour, lethargy, stumbling, dizzy spells, muscle cramps and violent bursts of energy. Irrationality may take the form of sufferers claiming they are warm and trying to take off their clothes.

To treat mild hypothermia, first get the person out of the wind and/or rain, remove their clothing if it's wet and replace it with dry, warm clothing. Give them hot liquids – not alcohol – and some high-kilojoule, easily digestible food. Do not rub victims, instead allow them to slowly warm themselves. This should be enough to treat the early stages of hypothermia. The early recognition and treatment of mild hypothermia is the only way to prevent severe hypothermia, which is a critical condition.

Jet Lag This condition is experienced when a person travels by air across more than three time zones (each time zone usually represents a one hour time difference). It occurs because many of the functions of the human body (such as temperature, pulse rate and emptying of the bladder and bowels) are regulated by internal 24-hour cycles. When we travel long distances rapidly, our bodies take time to adjust to the 'new time' of our destination, and we may experience fatigue, disorientation, insomnia, anxiety, impaired concentration and loss of appetite. These effects will usually be gone within three days of arrival, but to minimise the impact of jet lag:

• Rest for a couple of days prior to departure.
• Try to select flight schedules that minimise sleep deprivation; arriving late in the day allows you to sleep soon after you arrive. For very long flights, try to organise a stopover.
• Avoid excessive eating (which bloats the stomach) and alcohol (which causes dehydration) during the flight. Instead, drink plenty of non-carbonated, non-alcoholic drinks such as fruit juice or water.
• Avoid smoking.
• Make yourself comfortable by wearing loose-fitting clothes and perhaps bringing an eye mask and ear plugs to help you sleep.
• Try to sleep at the appropriate time for the time zone you are travelling to.

Motion Sickness Eating lightly before and during a trip will reduce the chances of motion sickness. If you are prone to motion sickness try to find a place that minimises movement – near the wing on aircrafts, close to midships on boats, near the centre on buses. Fresh air usually helps; reading and cigarette smoke don't. Commercial motion-sickness preparations, which can cause drowsiness, have to be taken before the trip commences. Ginger (available in capsule form) and peppermint (including mint-flavoured sweets) are natural preventatives.

Prickly Heat An itchy rash caused by excessive perspiration trapped under the skin, prickly heat usually strikes people who have just arrived in a hot climate. Keeping cool, bathing often, drying the skin and using a mild talcum or prickly heat powder or resorting to air-conditioning may help.

Sunburn In the tropics of Xīshuāngbǎnnà and the high altitudes of western Sìchuān you can get sunburnt surprisingly quickly, even through cloud. Use a sunscreen, hat, and barrier cream for your nose and lips. Calamine lotion or Stingose are good for mild sunburn. Protect your eyes with good quality sunglasses, particularly if you will be near water, sand or snow.

Infectious Diseases

China Syndrome Upper respiratory tract infections (URTIs), or the common cold, are the most common ailment to afflict visitors to China. The Chinese call it *gǎnmào* and it is a particular problem here.

China also has a special relationship with the influenza virus. You may not remember the notorious 'Hong Kong flu' of 1968, but you may have heard of the more recent 'Shànghǎi flu' epidemic of 1989 or the 'Chicken Flu' that hit Hong Kong in winter 1997. There have been various other influenza strains named after Chinese cities because China is the production house for new strains of influenza virus. The reason for this is thought to be the proximity in which people live to ducks and pigs, which are the reservoirs for the two other main populations of the virus. This provides the opportunity for the viruses to chop and change, reappearing in different forms or strains.

During winter, practically the entire population of 1.2 billion is stricken with gǎnmào. URTIs are aggravated by cold weather, poor nutrition and China's notorious air pollution. A particular culprit in the South-West are the noxious coke briquettes that are burned during winter. Smoking makes it worse, and half the population of China smokes. Overcrowded conditions increase the opportunity for infection. Another reason is that Chinese people spit a lot, which helps spread the disease. It's a vicious circle: they're sick because they spit and they spit because they're sick.

Winter visitors to China should bring a few favourite cold remedies. These can easily be purchased from any good pharmacy in Hong Kong or Macau. Such items can be found in South-West China, but with considerably more difficulty.

Symptoms of influenza include fever, weakness, sore throat and a feeling of malaise. Any URTI, including influenza, can lead to complications such as bronchitis and pneumonia, which may need to be treated with antibiotics. Seek medical help in this situation. Finally, if you can't get well in China, leave the country and take a nice holiday on a warm beach in Thailand.

Diarrhoea Simple things like a change of water, food or climate can all cause a mild bout of diarrhoea (*lādùzi* or 'spicy stomach' as the Chinese call it), but a few rushed toilet trips with no other symptoms is not indicative of a major problem. Even Marco Polo suffered from the runs.

Dehydration is the main danger with any diarrhoea, particularly in children or the elderly where dehydration can be rapid. Under all circumstances *fluid replacement* (at least equal to the volume being lost) is the most important thing to remember. Weak black tea with a little sugar, soda water, or soft drinks allowed to go flat and diluted 50% with clean water are all good.

With severe diarrhoea a rehydrating solution is preferable; it replaces minerals and salts lost. Commercially available oral rehydration salts (ORS) are very useful; add them to boiled or bottled water. In an emergency you can make up a solution of six teaspoons of sugar and a half teaspoon of salt to a litre of boiled or bottled water. You need to drink at least the same volume of fluid that you are losing in bowel movements and vomiting. Urine is the best guide to the adequacy of replacement – if you have small amounts of concentrated urine, you need to drink more. Keep drinking small amounts often. Stick to a bland diet as you recover.

Gut-paralysing drugs such as Lomotil or Imodium can be used to bring relief from the symptoms, although they do not actually cure the problem. Only use these drugs if you do not have access to toilets, ie, if you must travel. For children under 12 years Lomotil and Imodium are not recommended.

In certain situations antibiotics may be required: diarrhoea with blood or mucus (dysentery), any fever, watery diarrhoea with fever and lethargy, persistent diarrhoea not improving after 48 hours and severe diarrhoea. In these situations gut-paralysing drugs like Imodium or Lomotil should be avoided.

A stool test is necessary to diagnose which kind of dysentery you have, so you should seek medical help urgently. Where this is not possible the recommended drugs for dysentery are norfloxacin 400mg twice daily for three days or ciprofloxacin 500mg twice daily for five days. These are not recommended for children or pregnant women. The drug of choice for children would be co-trimoxazole (Bactrim, Septrin, Resprim) with dosage dependent on weight. A five-day course is given. Ampicillin or amoxycillin may be given in pregnancy, but medical care is necessary. **Giardiasis** is caused by a common parasite, *Giardia lamblia*. Symptoms include stomach cramps, nausea, a bloated stomach, watery, foul-smelling diarrhoea and frequent gas. Giardiasis can appear several weeks after you have been exposed to the parasite. The symptoms may disappear for a few days and then return; this can go on for several weeks. **Amoebic dysentery**, caused by the protozoan *Entamoeba histolytica*, is characterised by a gradual onset of low-grade diarrhoea, often with blood and mucus. Cramping abdominal pain and vomiting are less likely than in other types of diarrhoea, and fever may not be present. It will persist until treated and can recur and cause other health problems. You should seek medical advice if you think you have giardiasis or amoebic dysentery, but where this is not possible, tinidazole (known as Fasigyn) or metronidazole (Flagyl) are the recommended drugs. Treatment is a 2g single dose of Fasigyn or 250mg of Flagyl three times daily for five to 10 days.

Hepatitis A general term for the inflammation of the liver, Hepatitis is a common disease worldwide. The symptoms are fever, chills, headache, fatigue, feelings of weakness and aches and pains, followed by loss of appetite, nausea, vomiting, abdominal pain, dark urine, light-coloured faeces, jaundiced (yellow) skin and yellowing of the whites of the eyes. People who have had hepatitis should avoid alcohol for some time after the illness, as the liver needs time to recover. **Hepatitis A** is transmitted by contaminated food and drinking water. You should seek medical advice, but there is not much you can do apart from resting, drinking lots of fluids, eating lightly and avoiding fatty foods. **Hepatitis E** is transmitted in the same way; it can be very serious in pregnant women.

There are almost 300 million chronic carriers of **Hepatitis B** in the world, and China has more cases than any other country – almost 20% of the population are believed to be carriers. It is spread through contact with infected blood, blood products or body fluids, for example through sexual contact, unsterilised needles and blood transfusions, or contact with blood via small breaks in the skin. Other risk situations include having a shave, tattoo, or body piercing with contaminated equipment. The symptoms of type B may be more severe than type A and may lead to long term problems such as chronic liver damage, liver cancer or a long term carrier state. Hepatitis C and D are spread in the same way as hepatitis B and can also lead to long term complications. There are vaccines against hepatitis A and B, but there are currently no vaccines against the other types of hepatitis. Following the basic rules about food and water (hepatitis A and E) and avoiding risk situations (hepatitis B, C and D) are important preventative measures.

HIV & AIDS Infection with the human immunodeficiency virus (HIV) may lead to acquired immune deficiency syndrome (AIDS), which is fatal. Any exposure to blood, blood products or body fluids may put the individual at risk. The disease is often transmitted through sexual contact or dirty needles – vaccinations, acupuncture, tattooing and body piercing can be potentially as dangerous as intravenous drug use. HIV/AIDS can also be spread through infected blood transfusions; China is notorious

Taking A Stance On AIDS

Until recently, the outbreak of AIDS in China has been rigorously avoided by Chinese media and masked with inaccurate statistics by the Chinese government. Although China's AIDS-related death toll has risen dramatically since the first victim succumbed to the illness in 1986, AIDS has consistently been viewed as a 'foreign problem' that could be contained by denying entry to foreigners infected with HIV. Within China, negligible funds have been spent on awareness, education or prevention – with deadly consequences.

One of the most prevalent routes for transmission of the disease in China is through contaminated blood supplies. China's chronic shortage of blood and plasma has led hospitals to offer money for donations, mainly attracting donors such as prostitutes and drug-users who are at high risk of being HIV positive. It's also led to the development of a black-market blood trade, supplying the hospitals with unscreened blood. Added to this is the frightening fact that most hospitals outside urban centres reuse syringes; in 1996, it was reported that up to 90% of syringes were reused in Chinese hospitals nationwide.

Recent efforts by the Chinese government to fight back against AIDS through education and awareness have been thwarted by the more prudish elements of Chinese society. Condom ads were banned almost immediately by the entertainment industry who claimed they violated existing rules that prohibit contraception from being advertised on television. Actors refused to play AIDS victims even with a pay incentive of five times the normal wage. Attempts to hand out condoms on university campuses were greeted with disapproval by students.

Yet, following the media's recently revealed statistics, the pressure on the government to do something has grown alongside public fear. And so China has fallen back on its old standby – tough legislation – and Chéngdū has been the first city to bring it into force. As of May 2001, it has become illegal for HIV positive residents to marry or hold such occupations as kindergarten teachers or surgeons. The legislation also suggests that pregnant women who are HIV positive may be 'persuaded' to abort their child if medicine to prevent transmission of the disease is not available.

More unusual for China than this harsh and seemingly absurd legislation, is the public outcry it has provoked from within the country. The *Chengdu Worker's Daily* newspaper and Chinese AIDS experts have opposed the legislation on public health and moral grounds, arguing that controlling AIDS patients doesn't constitute control over the disease and that the law amounts to punishment of AIDS patients rather than prevention. So far, this opposition has managed to remove only one stipulation of the law which was to prohibit HIV positive residents from entering public pools and baths. While this may be only a small step, it hints that there may be a growing potential for public dissent in China.

The fight against AIDS in China has turned into something more akin to a fight against AIDS victims. Unless it is redirected, the results could be catastrophic with the UN predicting that, left unchecked, HIV will spread to 10 million people in China before 2010.

Korina Miller

for not screening blood donors (see the boxed text 'Taking a Stance on AIDS').

While the government maintains that only 20,711 Chinese people are HIV positive (up 30% from last year), the number is likely closer to one million, with the largest percentage of these people living in the South-West. Almost all of the early cases originated from Ruìli, on the Yúnnán-Myanmar border, and most are directly attributable to intra-venous drug use, though prostitution is helping to spread the disease. All foreigners applying to stay in China for more than nine months must have a certificate verifying that they are AIDS-free.

If you do need an injection, ask to see the syringe unwrapped in front of you, or take a needle and syringe pack with you. Fear of HIV infection should never preclude treatment for serious medical conditions.

Intestinal Worms These parasites are most common in rural, tropical areas. The different worms have different ways of infecting people. Some may be ingested on food, including undercooked meat, and some enter through your skin. Infestations may not show up for some time, and although they are generally not serious, if left untreated some can cause severe health problems later. Consider having a stool test when you return home to check for these and determine the appropriate treatment.

Sexually Transmitted Diseases Gonorrhoea, herpes and syphilis are among these diseases; sores, blisters or rashes around the genitals, discharges or pain when urinating are common symptoms. In some STDs, such as wart virus or chlamydia, symptoms may be less marked or not observed at all, especially in women. Chlamydia infection can cause infertility in men and women before any symptoms have been noticed. Syphilis symptoms eventually disappear completely but the disease continues and can cause severe problems in later years. While abstinence from sexual contact is the only 100% effective prevention, using condoms is also effective. The treatment of gonorrhoea and syphilis is with antibiotics. The different sexually transmitted diseases each require specific antibiotics. There is no cure for herpes or AIDS.

Typhoid A dangerous gut infection, typhoid fever is caused by contaminated water and food. Medical help must be sought.

In its early stages sufferers may feel they have a bad cold or flu on the way, as early symptoms are a headache, body aches and a fever that rises a little each day until it is around 40°C (104°F) or more. The victim's pulse is often slow relative to the degree of fever present – unlike a normal fever where the pulse increases. There may also be vomiting, abdominal pain, diarrhoea or constipation.

In the second week the high fever and slow pulse continue and a few pink spots may appear on the body; trembling, delirium, weakness, weight loss and dehydration may occur. Complications such as pneumonia, perforated bowel or meningitis may occur.

The fever should be treated by keeping the victim cool and giving them fluids as dehydration should be watched for. Ciprofloxacin 750mg twice a day for 10 days is good for adults.

Chloramphenicol is recommended in many countries. The adult dosage is two 250mg capsules, four times a day. Children aged between eight and 12 years should have half the adult dose; and younger children one-third the adult dose.

Insect-Borne Diseases

Filariasis, leishmaniasis, lyme disease and typhus are all insect-borne diseases, but they do not pose a great risk to travellers. For more information on them see Less Common Diseases at the end of the Health section.

Malaria This serious and potentially fatal disease is spread by mosquito bites. It has nearly been eradicated in China but if you are travelling in parts of Yúnnán's Xīshuāngbǎnnà and the Guǎngxī coast, especially during the summer monsoon season, it is important to avoid mosquito bites and to take the precautions listed in this section. Check with your doctor to decide which antimalarial tablets to take and remember that most tablets need to be taken for a week prior to visiting a malarial area and for a month after leaving it. Symptoms range from fever, chills and sweating, headache, diarrhoea and abdominal pains to a vague feeling of ill-health. Seek medical help immediately if malaria is suspected. Without treatment malaria can rapidly become more serious and can be fatal.

If medical care is not available, malaria tablets can be used for treatment. You need to use a malaria tablet which is different to the one you were taking when you contracted malaria. The treatment dosages are Mefloquine (two 250mg tablets and a further two six hours later), Fansidar (single dose of three tablets). If you were previously taking Mefloquine and cannot obtain Fansidar, then other alternatives are Malarone (atovaquone-proguanil; four tablets once daily for three days), Halofantrine (three doses of two 250mg tablets every six hours) or quinine sulphate (600mg every six hours). There is a greater risk of side effects with these dosages than in normal use if used with Mefloquine, so medical advice is preferable. Be aware also that Halofantrine is no longer recommended by the WHO as emergency standby treatment, because of side effects, and should only be used if no other drugs are available.

Travellers are advised to prevent mosquito bites. The main messages are:

- Wear light coloured clothing.
- Wear long pants and long-sleeved shirts.
- Use mosquito repellents containing the compound DEET on exposed areas (prolonged overuse of DEET may be harmful, especially to children, but its use is considered preferable to being bitten by disease-transmitting mosquitoes).
- Avoid using perfumes or aftershave.
- Use a mosquito net impregnated with mosquito repellent (permethrin) – it may be worth taking your own.
- Impregnating clothes with permethrin effectively deters mosquitoes and other insects.

Japanese B Encephalitis This viral infection of the brain is transmitted by mosquitoes. Most cases occur in rural areas as the virus exists in pigs and wading birds. Symptoms include fever, headache and alteration in consciousness. Hospitalisation is needed for correct diagnosis and treatment. There is a high mortality rate among those who have symptoms; of those that survive many are intellectually disabled.

Cuts, Bites & Stings
See Less Common Diseases for details of rabies, which is passed through animal bites.

Cuts & Scratches Wash well and treat any cut with an antiseptic. Where possible avoid bandages and sticking plasters, which can keep wounds wet.

Bedbugs & Lice Bedbugs live in various places, but particularly in dirty mattresses and bedding, evidenced by spots of blood on bedclothes or on the wall. Bedbugs leave itchy bites in neat rows. Calamine lotion or sting relief spray may help.

All lice cause itching and discomfort. They make themselves at home in your hair (head lice), your clothing (body lice) or in your pubic hair (crabs). You catch lice through direct contact with infected people or by sharing combs, clothing and the like. Powder or shampoo treatment will kill the lice and infected clothing should then be washed in very hot, soapy water and left in the sun to dry.

Bites and Stings Bee and wasp stings are usually painful rather than dangerous. However, in people who are allergic to them severe breathing difficulties may occur and require urgent medical care. Calamine lotion or sting relief spray will give relief and ice packs will reduce the pain and swelling. There are some spiders with dangerous bites but antivenins are usually available.

Leeches & Ticks Leeches may be present in the damp rainforest conditions of Xīshuāngbǎnnà; they attach themselves to your skin to suck your blood. Trekkers often get them on their legs or in their boots. Salt or a lighted cigarette end will make them fall off. Do not pull them off, as the bite is then more likely to become infected. Clean and apply pressure if the point of attachment is bleeding. An insect repellent may keep them away.

You should always check all over your body if you have been walking through a potentially tick-infested area as ticks can cause skin infections and other more serious diseases. If a tick is found attached, press down around the tick's head with tweezers, grab the head and gently pull upwards. Avoid pulling the rear of the body as this may squeeze the tick's gut contents through the attached mouth parts into the skin, increasing the risk of infection and disease. Smearing chemicals on the tick will not make it let go and is not recommended.

Snakes If you're going to be hiking around the subtropical areas of Yúnnán and

Guǎngxī, keep an eye out for snakes as there are several potentially dangerous varieties that may be encountered. To minimise your chances of being bitten always wear boots, socks and long trousers when walking through undergrowth where snakes may be present. Be careful when collecting firewood.

Snake bites do not cause instantaneous death and antivenins are usually available. Immediately wrap the bitten limb tightly, as you would for a sprained ankle, and then attach a splint to immobilise it. Keep the victim still and seek medical help, if possible with the dead snake for identification. Don't attempt to catch the snake if there is a possibility of being bitten again. Tourniquets and sucking out the poison are now comprehensively discredited.

Less Common Diseases

The following diseases pose a very small risk to travellers in South-West China. Seek medical advice if you think you may have any of these diseases.

Cholera This is the worst of the watery diarrhoeas and medical help should be sought. Outbreaks of cholera are generally widely reported so you can avoid such problem areas. **Fluid replacement is the most vital treatment** – the risk of dehydration is severe as you may lose up to 20L a day. If there is a delay in getting to hospital then begin taking tetracycline. The adult dose is 250mg four times daily. It is not recommended for children under nine years or pregnant women. Tetracycline may help shorten the illness, but adequate fluids are required to save lives.

Rabies This is a fatal viral infection found in many countries. Many animals can be infected (such as dogs, cats, bats and monkeys) and it is their saliva that is infectious. Any bite, scratch or even lick from a warm-blooded, furry animal should be cleaned immediately and thoroughly. Scrub with soap and running water, and then apply alcohol or iodine solution. Medical help should be sought promptly to receive a course of injections to prevent the onset of symptoms and death.

Tetanus This disease occurs when a wound becomes infected by a germ which lives in soil and in the faeces of horses and other animals. The germ enters the body via breaks in the skin. All wounds should be cleaned promptly and adequately and an antiseptic cream or solution applied. Use antibiotics if the wound becomes hot, throbs or pus is seen. The first symptom may be discomfort in swallowing, or stiffening of the jaw and neck; this is followed by painful convulsions of the jaw and whole body. The disease can be fatal.

Tuberculosis (TB) A bacterial infection, TB is usually transmitted from person to person by coughing but may be transmitted through consumption of unpasteurised milk. Milk that has been boiled is safe to drink, and the souring of milk to make yoghurt or cheese also kills the bacilli. Travellers are usually not at great risk as close household contact with the infected person is usually required before the disease is passed on.

Typhus Spread by ticks, mites or lice, typhus begins with fever, chills, headache and muscle pains followed a few days later by a body rash. There is often a large painful sore at the site of the bite and nearby lymph nodes are swollen and painful.

Typhus can be treated under medical supervision. Seek local advice on areas where ticks pose a danger and always check your skin (including hair) carefully for ticks after walking in a danger area such as a tropical forest. A strong insect repellent can help, and serious walkers in tick areas should consider having their boots and trousers impregnated with benzyl benzoate and dibutylphthalate.

Women's Health

Gynaecological Problems Antibiotic use, synthetic underwear, sweating and contraceptive pills can often lead to fungal vaginal infections, especially when travelling in hot climates. Fungal infections are characterised by a rash, itch and discharge and can be treated with a vinegar or lemon-juice douche, or with yoghurt. Nystatin, miconazole or clotrimazole pessaries or vaginal cream are the usual treatment. Maintaining good personal hygiene and wearing loose-fitting clothes and cotton underwear help prevent these infections. Sexually transmitted diseases are a major cause of vaginal problems. Symptoms include a smelly discharge, painful intercourse and at times a burning sensation when urinating. Medical attention should be sought and male sexual partners must also be treated. For more details see the section on Sexually Transmitted Diseases earlier. Besides abstinence, always practise safer sex using condoms.

Pregnancy It is not advisable to travel to some places while pregnant as some vaccinations normally used to prevent serious diseases are not advisable in pregnancy. In addition, some diseases are much more serious for the mother (and may increase the risk of a stillborn child) in pregnancy (eg, malaria).

Most miscarriages occur during the first three months of pregnancy. Miscarriage is not uncommon, and can occasionally lead to severe bleeding. The last three months should also be spent within reasonable distance of good medical care. A baby born as early as 24 weeks stands a chance of survival, but only in a good modern hospital. Pregnant women should avoid all unnecessary medication, though vaccinations and malarial prophylactics should still be taken where needed. Additional care should be taken to prevent illness and particular attention should be paid to diet and nutrition. Alcohol and nicotine, for example, should be avoided.

WOMEN TRAVELLERS

As something of a novelty, women may receive some unwanted attention while travelling in China. However, they are unlikely to suffer serious sexual harassment. When Chinese men do pester, something that is much more likely to happen in the cities, it seems to be based on their ideas of foreign women gathered from imported films. If you don't respond like they do in the movies, they're likely to give up quickly and leave you alone.

Wherever you are, it's worth noticing what the local women are wearing and how they are behaving and making a bit of an effort to fit in, as you would in any other foreign country. Wearing skimpy clothes or going topless on the beach is asking for trouble. While women in China's cities are hip to the latest fashions, as a foreigner, you will be more closely examined and may want to play down the hyper-short miniskirt look. Tank tops are a no-go all over China. The countryside in general and minority regions in particular are much more conservative.

The police investigate crimes against foreigners much more closely and more severe penalties (like execution) are imposed if the perpetrator is caught. While this gives foreign women a small but important aura of protection, it certainly hasn't removed all possibility of hostility and it's important to stay alert. It's also not wise to wander out alone at night or into the wilderness. While rape is uncommon, it does happen and robbers and pick-pockets tend to see women as easier targets. In the spring of 2000 a British woman was stabbed to death while hiking alone on Pǎomǎ Shān in Kāngdìng; the alleged motive was theft.

On another note, you can buy sanitary pads galore in China, however, tampons are a rare find – come prepared.

GAY & LESBIAN TRAVELLERS

The official attitude to gays and lesbians in China is ambiguous, with responses ranging from draconian penalties to tacit acceptance.

Certainly there is greater tolerance in the big cities than in the more conservative countryside. However, even the big cities are not good places for gays and lesbians to flaunt their sexual preferences in public, as police or local officials might respond to this 'provocation' with a crack down on local meeting places. Note that Chinese men routinely hold hands and drape their arms around each other without any sexual overtones.

In 1996 British organisation War on Want reported that China was jailing gays for up to five years for 'disturbances against the social order' (a violation of Penal Code section 158). Other gays are reportedly treated with electric shocks to 'cure' their homosexuality.

Similarly, Chinese writers and film producers who try to deal with the topic of homosexuality routinely see their works banned.

On the other hand, there are many recognised gay discos, bars and pubs in cities like Běijīng and Guǎngzhōu, which appear to function without official harassment, although they tend to keep a fairly low profile.

As far as most Chinese people are concerned, homosexuality is a 'foreign problem' – for them, it just doesn't exist in China. A more realistic recent estimate puts the number of gays in China at about 2% of the population, or 26 million people.

Check out W www.utopia-asia.com/tipschin.htm for tips on travelling to China.

DISABLED TRAVELLERS

China has few facilities geared for the disabled. But that doesn't necessarily make it out of bounds for those who do have a physical disability (and a sense of adventure). On the plus side, most hotels have lifts, so booking ground-floor hotel rooms is not essential. In bigger cities, some hotels at the four- and five-star level have specially designed rooms for people with physical disabilities.

On the other hand, just getting up the steps to enter the hotel lobby could present a challenge. Persons whose sight, hearing or walking ability are impaired must be extremely cautious of China's crazy drivers who almost never yield to pedestrians. Travelling by car or taxi is probably the safest transport option.

Organisations

Get in touch with your national support organisation (preferably the 'travel officer' if there is one) before leaving home. They often have travel literature to help with holiday planning and can put you in touch with travel agents who specialise in tours for the disabled.

If any specialised travel agency might be interested in arranging trips to South-West China, the best bet is Accessible Journeys (☎ 800-846 4537, 610-521 0339, fax 521 6959, e sales@disabilitytravel.com), 35 West Sellers Avenue, Ridley Park, PA 19078, USA, who have some experience of disabled travel in China. There is a Web site at W www.disabilitytravel.com.

The following organisations offer general travel advice for the disabled but provide no specific information on China:

Australia
NICAN (☎ 02-6285 3713, fax 6285 3714) PO Box 407, Curtin, ACT 2605

France
CNFLRH (☎ 01 53 80 66 66) 236 bis rue de Tolbiac, Paris

UK
Holiday Care Service (☎ 01293-774535, fax 784647) Imperial Bldgs, Victoria Rd, Horley, Surrey RH6 7PZ.
Travelcare (☎ 020-8295 1797, fax 8467 2467) 35A High St, Chislehurst, Kent BR7 QAE. Specialises in travel insurance for the disabled.
RADAR (Royal Association for Disability & Rehabilitation; ☎ 020-7250 3222, fax 7250 0212) 12 City Forum, 250 City Rd, London EC1V 8AF. Produces three holiday fact packs for disabled travellers.

USA
Access (The Foundation for Accessibility for the Disabled; ☎ 516-887 5798) PO Box 356, Malverne, NY 11565.
Mobility International (☎ 541-343 1284 V/TTY, fax 343 6812, e info@miusa.org) PO Box 10767, Eugene, OR 97440. They organise international exchanges, have several publications and have a Web site at W www.miusa.org.
SATH (Society for the Advancement of Travel for the Handicapped; ☎ 212-447 0027, 447 7284, fax 725 8253) 347 Fifth Ave No 610, New York, NY 10016. The good Web site at W www.sath.org contains tips on how to travel with diabetes, arthritis, visual and hearing impairments, and wheelchairs.

For general advice, bulletin boards and searchable databases on the Internet try:

W www.access-able.com
W www.newmobility.com
W www.travelhealth.com
W www.dpi.org

SENIOR TRAVELLERS

In China, older people are revered. To be called elderly is a compliment, a tribute to your maturity and wisdom. China even has legislation to reinforce the duty of children to support their parents.

The main threat to senior travellers is the dreaded 'China Syndrome', or 'chronic bronchitis' as it's commonly known in the West. See the Health section earlier in this chapter for more details. If you are less flexible in your joints than you used to be, you may have difficulties with squat toilets. Some travellers have suggested bringing a light but strong and collapsible stool.

Lonely Planet's *Read This First: Asia & India* has chapters on Niche Travellers (including Senior Travellers) and on Health.

CITS organises group tours for seniors, as do some private travel agencies. ElderTreks (☎ 1 800 741 7956, 416-588 5000, fax 588 9839, ℮ eldertreks@eldertreks.com) 597 Markham St, Toronto, Ontario, Canada M6G 2L7 run groups tours to Yúnnán for the over 50s only, taking in Dàlǐ, Lìjiāng, Zhōngdiàn, Déqīn and Chéngdū. Their Web site is at W www.eldertreks.com.

USEFUL ORGANISATIONS

'With one monkey in the way, not even 10,000 men can pass'

Chinese saying

For foreigners and Chinese alike, the major monkey governing everyday life in China is the Public Security Bureau (PSB).

The PSB is the name given to China's police, both uniformed and plain-clothed. Its responsibilities are varied and include the suppression of political dissidence, crime detection, mediating family quarrels and directing traffic. Related forces include the Economic Police, Traffic Police and the Chinese People's Armed Police Force (CPAPF), which was formed several years ago to absorb cuts in the People's Liberation Army (PLA; *Jiěfàng Jūn*).

The Foreign Affairs Branch (*Wàishìkē*) of the PSB deals with foreigners. This branch (also known as the 'entry-exit' branch) is responsible for issuing visa extensions and Alien Travel Permits.

The PSB is responsible for introducing and enforcing regulations concerning foreigners. So, for example, they bear responsibility for exclusion of foreigners from certain hotels. If this means you get stuck for a place to stay, they can offer advice. Don't pester them with trivia or try to 'use' them to bully a point with a local street vendor. Do turn to them for mediation in serious disputes with hotels, restaurants, taxi drivers etc. This often works since the PSB wields God-like power – especially in remote areas. Most PSB stations have at least one English-speaking officer who is genuinely willing to help a traveller in need.

There are a few ways you can inadvertently have an unpleasant run-in with the PSB. The most common way is to overstay your visa. Foreign males who are suspected of being 'too friendly' with Chinese women could have trouble with the PSB.

Charities

Many travellers feel that they would like to contribute something to the countries they have visited. The following charities operate organised development programs in South-West China:

Animals Asia Foundation (☎ 852-2791 2225, fax 2791 2320, ℮ info@animalsasia.org) PO Box 82 Sai Kung Post Office, Kowloon, Hong Kong. Works against mistreatment of animals. Recently purchased 500 imprisoned bears to form the new Panyu Bear Sanctuary in Sìchuān.
W www.animalsasia.org
DORS (☎ 1452-522 328, fax 331 843, ℮ dors @ya-public.sc.cninfo.net) 17 Denmark Rd, Gloucestershire G11 3HZ, UK. A development organisation that works toward poverty alleviation in Sìchuān.
W www.newmind.co.uk/dors

Kham Aid (☎ 213-489 7688, fax 489 7686, e khamaid@khamaid.org) 619 South Olive St, Suite 204, Los Angeles, CA 90014, USA. Runs international assistance to western Sìchuān in the form of educational grants, medical supplies and cultural preservation. Contact Pamela Logan.
W www.khamaid.org

TRAFFIC International (☎ 01223-277427, fax 01223-277237, e info@trafficint.org) 219c Huntingdon Rd, Cambridge CB3 0DL, UK. *China office* (☎ 852-2530 0587, fax 2530 0864, e tea@asiaonline.net) Room 2001, Double Bldg, 22 Stanley Street, Central, Hong Kong. Works to prevent the illegal trade in endangered species and offers information on the trade in China, how you can help prevent trade in endangered species and how to contribute to TRAFFIC's work.
W www.traffic.org

Other Organisations

A very useful contact in the UK is the Great Britain China Centre (☎ 020-7235 6696, e contact@gbcc.org.uk) 15 Belgrave Square, London SW1X 8PS. The centre offers business and cultural links with China, advertises job vacancies and runs lectures, an excellent China-related library and Chinese language courses. Annual membership is £25. For details see their Web site (W www.gbcc.org.uk).

DANGERS
Crime & Punishment

Outwardly, China is booming, with gleaming new skyscrapers, superhighways and department stores bulging with the latest consumer goods. Yet beneath the con-

Travelling with Children

South-West China is not the easiest place to travel with kids. First off, there's the dreaded 'China Syndrome' and nothing is worse than having sick children to take care of while travelling.

Health problems aside, travel in China tends to be uncomfortable and uncompromising – picture long distances by train, often in hard-seat carriages where everyone smokes and spits. China's crowds can be overpowering and blonde-haired, blue-eyed or black children will often receive far more attention than they want.

Xiǎo lǎowài and *yáng wáwá* ('little foreigner' and 'foreign baby') are prime targets for cheek-pinching and head-patting. Extended families doting on the little emperors and empresses of China's one-child policy mean Chinese children are rarely out of someone's arms. If you speak Chinese you can also expect continuous advice ('he's cold, put more clothes on!').

The big cities and their 'adult' cultural attractions can be hard work with children, so take time to seek out bustling markets, parks with boating lakes and playgrounds and, in more and more cities, Western-style funfairs with lots of cotton candy, Ferris wheels, merry-go-rounds and other nauseating rides.

Of more obvious appeal than the cities are South-West China's colourful villages, peoples, weekend markets and exciting festivals with folk games, song and dance. After long bus and rail trips, the traveller-friendly centres of the south-western trail – Yángshuò, Dàlǐ and Lìjiāng – may well be what the whole family needs: beautiful locations, thinner crowds, child-friendly food (banana porridge!), swimming, boat trips, videos, country walks and bike rides. Yúnnán is probably the most child-friendly region of the South-West.

Children's prices are rarely available for foreign children, who simply get lumped in with foreign adults and charged at the same inflated level. Even student prices are not available for children unless they have a student card! So, ridiculous though it may seem, it's worth getting your child, even at kindergarten age, an ISIC card to wave at temple, garden and museum entrance counters.

Much of the South-West is hilly and even mountainous, and it's worth bringing some kind of child backpack. The minorities of the South-West often use colourful embroidered cloth to tie babies to their backs – a good souvenir at the very least. A stroller (pushchair) is essential for town movement, despite poor pavements. A combined backpack/stroller that metamorphoses with ease is an

sumerism and glittering office towers is poverty on a massive scale. The cities are filled with poor people, often newly arrived from the countryside and desperate to find work. Not everyone gets a job, and some turn to crime.

Although crime is certainly on the rise in China, the scary reports in the press exaggerate the danger. Providing you are sensible, keep your wits about you and make it difficult for thieves to get at your belongings, you shouldn't have any problems.

Pickpocketing is the most common form of theft and the one you need to carefully guard against. The wholesale theft of luggage is unusual (unless you leave it lying around unattended), but razoring of bags and pockets in crowded places like buses is fairly common. Certain cities are worse than others – Guìyáng is notorious.

The high risk areas in China are train and bus stations, city and long-distance buses and hard-seat sections of trains. The hard-seat sections of trains in particular can become very anarchic with the onset of darkness – they are sometimes worked by gangs who use knives to persuade travellers to hand over their valuables. Some foreign travellers who have tried to resist have been stabbed in incidents such as these.

Recently there have been reports of druggings and thefts on sleeper buses between Kūnmíng and Jǐnghóng (Xīshuāngbǎnnà). On this and other popular tourist routes (ie, Kūnmíng-Lìjiāng etc) don't accept any food

Travelling with Children

excellent solution: Chinese-made models sell for around US$20 in some large department stores, but it is safer to bring one with you.

Bring a cotton sheet, a blanket and some soft toys to offer your child something familiar in a strange environment. A portable cot is impractical, and hotels can rarely provide one, but a comfortable bed can be made on the floor between two beds from the copious quantities of blankets and quilts that even budget hotels readily supply. Check every room for common hazards such as unprotected radiators and electric sockets hanging off the wall.

Thankfully (from an environmental point of view), only about 1% of China's babies currently use disposable nappies. Split pants are employed on most – eager guardians rush to spread the child's legs whenever a look of concentration takes over! But you will find disposables in larger cities such as provincial capitals. Chinese-made ones are cheaper and more widely available; joint-venture products are more expensive but better quality, while imported nappies cost far more than back home. Older children are liable to raise hell when faced with all those fun squat toilets – even adults have trouble dealing with these.

Bring all basic medicines for fever, cold and upset stomachs, sterilising pills for bottles and disposable syringes too, as medical care in remote areas is poor. Even small towns have clinics, but check the expiry date of all medicine. An advantage of Chinese hotels is the constant supply of flasks of hot water to help keep babies' cups and spoons clean. It is best to bring your own small plastic spoons as restaurants only offer chopsticks and large spoons.

Baby food in jars can be found in supermarkets in China's larger cities, at higher prices than in the West. Formula, infant cereal and Chinese-made milk powders are available all over the country. Fresh milk is nowhere to be seen in towns and rural areas. Chinese food seems to go down all right with foreign children, provided you can teach the toddlers how to use chopsticks (bring a set of plastic cutlery). Older children will marvel at more exotic fare such as the sticky rice-stuffed pineapples of Xīshuāngbǎnnà.

Lonely Planet's *Travel with Children* by Maureen Wheeler has many useful tips for travelling with children and precautions to take during pregnancy.

With information from Lijia & Calum MacLeod

and drink from strangers and never leave your bags unattended.

Be careful in public toilets. A few foreigners have laid aside their valuables, squatted down to business, and then straightened up again to discover that someone had absconded with the lot.

Hotels are generally safe. There are theoretically attendants on every floor keeping an eye on the rooms and safeguarding the keys (though in reality they are often huddled together, knitting on the 5th floor). Dormitories obviously require more care. Don't leave anything you can't do without (passport, travellers cheques, money, air tickets etc) lying around in communal rooms and don't be overly trusting of your fellow travellers – many of them are considerably less honest than the Chinese. All hotels have safes and storage areas for valuables – use them. Some attendants will ask you to sign a form saying that you have no valuables in the room.

The biggest problem is what to do with your moneybelt when you use communal showers. One solution is to take it in with you in a waterproof bag. Another inconvenience for solo travellers arises when you need to use the bathroom and don't have the key to your room. You just have to lock the door and keep bugging the room attendant to let you back in.

Small padlocks are useful for backpacks and some dodgy hotel rooms. Bicycle chain locks (preferably not Chinese-made) come in handy not only for hired bikes, but for attaching backpacks to railings or luggage racks. The trendy waist-pouches often used by Hong Kongers are definitely not advisable for valuables. Street tailors are skilled at sewing inside pockets to trousers, jackets and shirts usually for a few yuán, and these can even be sealed with zippers.

Loss Reports If something of yours is stolen, you should report it immediately to the nearest Foreign Affairs Branch of the PSB. They will ask you to fill in a loss report before investigating the case and sometimes even recovering the stolen goods.

If you have travel insurance (highly recommended), it is essential to obtain a loss report so you can claim compensation. Be warned, however, many travellers have found Foreign Affairs officials very unwilling to provide one. Be prepared to spend many hours, perhaps a couple of days, to organise it.

Violence
Street arguments are common in China, though they seldom lead to serious injury; mostly there's just lots of arm-waving, screaming and threats. Fights between women are invariably the most vicious. The reasons are generally simple enough: people are pushing and shoving their way to the front of a queue, the traffic is forever noisily colliding and finally someone just flips out.

Sometimes it's the foreigners who flip out, pouring out their frustrations on to a hapless ticket seller or eight-year-old kid who said one 'Hello!' too many.

Most Chinese carry knives (at least the men do), but these are seldom used for anything other than peeling fruit. Guns are impossible to buy legally but some hunters in remote areas have home-made versions.

Scams
There's no need to be paranoid about this but be aware that scams exist.

Guìlín is probably the scam centre of China. One common ruse is for a student to invite you for dinner, order for you both and then suddenly run out of money when the Y200 bill arrives. Keep your guard especially high in karaoke bars, and remember that most women who offer to sit with you will charge for the pleasure.

ANNOYANCES
China can be a frustrating place to travel at the best of times and the South-West is less sophisticated than many of the coastal cities. There are times when most people want to leave or lash out at an unsuspecting bystander. You'll gain nothing by venting your frustration, though, and will in fact only alienate yourself further. Try not to swear, in particular, as locals and kids will soon pick this up and practice their new-found English on other foreign friends.

Kill the Rooster to Frighten the Monkey

'To get rich is glorious', Deng once famously said. But in the scramble for glory, more and more Chinese are turning to crime. Locals all over the country fret at the increasing incidence of theft and kidnappings. Crime, they mutter, extends from train station platforms to the corridors of power. No one is immune to temptation in get-rich-quick China.

In 2000 the former governor of Guǎngxī province, Cheng Kejie, was found guilty of taking US$5 million in bribes and was executed, the most senior official to be executed for bribery since the 1949 revolution. The execution of two vice-chairmen of the Guǎngxī government quickly followed. Later that year the former police chief of Liǔzhōu city, again in Guǎngxī, was executed for taking US$275,000 in bribes, possession of arms and running gambling operations.

As Jiang Zemin himself has admitted, cracking down on crime is a priority for the government if it is to stay in power. Official corruption was a major factor in the Tiananmen Square crisis, and most Chinese claim that the problem is worse now than it was then. Widely publicised arrests and drives against corruption, such as the one held in 2000, are met with public cynicism: the problem is the government itself. Its monopolistic hold on power and broking of all business deals puts it in a perfect cream-skimming position. Besides, privilege for high officials and their relatives is an age-old tradition in China.

Meanwhile, widespread unemployment and social disaffection is leading to a growing problem in juvenile crime. Murder, rape and theft head the list of juvenile crimes. The official view is that Chinese youngsters are victims of 'spiritual pollution' – influenced by the Western disease of greed and general depravity.

Justice in China is for the most part the domain of the police, who also decide the penalty. The ultimate penalty is execution, which serves the purpose of 'killing the rooster to frighten the monkey' or, to phrase this in official terms, 'it is good to have some people executed so as to educate others'. Before execution, the prisoner is typically paraded through the streets on the back of a truck. The standard manner of execution is a bullet in the back of the head, often at a mass gathering in a sports stadium. Afterwards a mugshot and maybe even a photo of the extinguished body gets pinned up on a public notice board. The prisoner's family often has to pay the cost of imprisonment, as well as the cost of the bullet.

Try to remember that as a foreigner you are treated better and with more respect than local Chinese. Most irritations stem from nothing more than cultural miscomprehension and linguistic frustration.

Personal Space

Years of Communist communalism, Confucian deference and living in the same house as your grandma has resulted in the fact that personal space is generally not as highly valued in China as it is in the West. No-one is ever going to get a lot of personal space in a country of 1.3 billion but the reasons for this are often as much cultural as physical.

After 15 years of tourism, the Chinese will still often stop what they are doing, grab the kids, call out to their friends and gawp at the passing foreigner. It's less likely to occur in major urban centres and tourist sites, but in most rural centres things are the same as they ever were.

Crowds soon gather around you as you sit, especially if you are reading or writing. Don't be surprised if someone nonchalantly takes the book out of your hands to get a better look, even while you are reading it. Men in shorts will have kids queuing up to feel their Yeti-style hairy legs. Attention on the street is one thing; staring in the communal showers or toilets is even more off-putting! As people stare, laugh, point, bring their children out to look at you and even walk up and poke you, you'll soon feel a deep bond of sympathy growing between you and the crazed pandas of Chéngdū zoo.

There is no easy recipe for dealing with crowds of staring strangers. Some travellers take it in their stride, others turn into nervous wrecks and flee to Thailand. There's nothing you can do about it; smiling, laughing, waving, scowling or screaming hysterically is all part of the show. It becomes more bearable if you have a travelling companion – solitary travellers can sometimes end up feeling like the elephant man cast adrift in Victorian London.

The best advice is to keep moving. Some travellers swear by a Walkman – it helps insulate you from the caterwauls of locals trying to get your attention as they summon their friends. In close quarters, on trains and buses, try befriending the people closest to you. In almost all cases the staring is pure uninhibited curiosity, and the starers would like nothing more than to strike up a conversation and find out where you are from and how much you earn a month, if only they could break through the language barrier.

Laowai!

Get outside the cities or traveller centres such as Dàlǐ and Yángshuò and you will hear the exclamation *lǎowài*, or alternatively 'Hellawooo, *lǎowài*, hello'. You'll probably hear this a couple of dozen times a day, often in an irritating falsetto voice and accompanied by a lot of sniggering. *Lǎo* means 'old' in Chinese and is a mark of respect, *wài* means 'outside', and together they constitute the politest word the Chinese have for 'foreigner'.

Chinese speakers will hear it used in many ways, sometimes with a thick overlay of irony that undermines the respect implied in the word, but generally it is used in startled surprise at suddenly encountering a foreigner in a world that is overwhelmingly Chinese. You may very occasionally hear the word *wàiguǐ*, or Foreign Devil, a pejorative phrase dating from the end of the Qing dynasty.

There is no point getting annoyed by it. If you answer by saying hello, they (the audience) will often as not break into hysterical laughter.

Noise

In recent years the Chinese government has launched an anti-noise pollution campaign. Look out for billboards emblazoned with a huge crossed-through ear presiding over busy intersections swarming with honking traffic. The government is really onto a loser with this one. China is quite possibly the noisiest country in the world.

The Chinese are generally far more tolerant of noise than most Westerners. People watch TV at ear-shattering volumes (to drown out the karaoke from a nearby restaurant), drivers habitually lean on the horn, telephone conversations are conducted in high-decibel rapid-fire screams and most of China seems to wake uncomplainingly to the sound of jackhammers. If it's peace and quiet you want, head for a remote part of western Sìchuān. At the very least bring a good set of earplugs.

Spitting

When China first opened to foreign tourism, many Western travellers were shocked by the spitting, which was conducted noisily by everyone everywhere. Government campaigns to stamp out the practice have been reasonably successful in the major urban centres of the east – there is a lot less public spitting in Guǎngzhōu, Shànghǎi and Běijīng these days – but here in the South-West the early morning 'HOIK!' is still a national sport.

Apart from the fact that it is very unpleasant to be stuck in, say, a bus with 50 people who feel impelled to pave the floor with gob, the spitting spreads flu and bronchitis. Early mornings are the worst times for stomach-turning throat clearing; hotel carpets are the worst affected. You can actually see the panic in some people's eyes when they board a plane and realise that there is nowhere to smoke or spit (most people eventually use the air sickness bag).

Most Chinese spit for health reasons. They believe that the mucus is better out than in and that spitting is a way to clear the respiratory system, particularly important in cities where the air quality is bad. Some Taiwanese like to joke that the mainlanders spit because they've had a bad taste in their mouths ever since the Communists took power.

Racism
There is no racism in China because we don't have any black people.
Student, Chéngdū University

Racism in China is a knotty problem. Most Chinese will swear blind that neither they nor their government is racist. But then very few Chinese you meet will have thought very deeply about the issue, and the Chinese government itself would never allow lively public debate on China's racist policies and attitudes. But, of course, as in most other countries around the world, racism is alive and kicking in China.

The Chinese are a proud people. Being Chinese links the individual to a long historical lineage, for the most part of which, Chinese believe, their country was the centre of the world (*zhōngguó*, or China, literally means 'The Middle Kingdom'). There's nothing new here, except that being Chinese is defined by blood, not nationality (and where does that leave China's ethnic minorities?). Chinese public discourse is littered with metaphors of racial purity and fulsome praise for the achievements of the great race of Chinese people.

Take the dual-pricing system, remnants of which exist here and there. Whether it is motivated by greed or not, it is fundamentally racist, especially since exceptions can be made for 'overseas Chinese' (that is, anyone who looks Chinese and claims to have Chinese ancestry). But most Chinese don't see this as racism – to them, it's simply the rules. Yet surely the Chinese would

The Chinese People Light Up

Both Mao Zedong and Deng Xiaoping were both chain smokers. Deng died aged 93; Mao aged 83. Nevertheless, awareness of tobacco's harmful effects are slowly sinking in (one million Chinese men die prematurely each year of smoking-related diseases). The Chinese government is beginning to make good on a long-held promise to do something about public smoking, banning cigarettes in airports and many train stations, and both President Jiang Zemin and Premier Li Peng have publicly condemned the habit. In private though, few treasury officials in Yúnnán or Guìzhōu want to see a cut in an industry that provides up to 60% of provincial revenues and US$12 billion nationwide in taxes and employs some 10 million tobacco farmers nationwide.

Even if they want to do something, the authorities have a real battle on their hands. One out of every three cigarettes in the world is smoked in China, and in some parts of the countryside over 90% of males above the age of 15 are addicts. Offering a cigarette is still the major social and commercial ice-breaker in China.

In rural China you can expect buses and trains to be thick with wafting cigarette smoke. The continual 'flick flick' of countless cigarette lighters will soon grate on any non-smoking nerves you have left. To compound the problem, most Chinese abhor opening bus windows as the cold air is thought to be bad for one's health. Hotel rooms and sleeper buses often smell like the inside of an ashtray.

As with drinking hard liquor, smoking in public has traditionally been a male activity, though more women are starting to smoke. If you cannot tolerate smoking in crowded public places like buses and restaurants, you will either have to leave the country or buy a gas mask. The Chinese will be surprised if you tell them not to smoke but subtle signs like wafting a newspaper in front of their faces seem to work.

For smokers, on the other hand, the good news is that cigarettes are cheap (around US$1 per pack for foreign brands) and you can smoke almost anywhere. Chinese cigarettes are a mixed bag. The cheapest brands can cost less than Y2, while the best brands (such as Red Pagoda Mountain – Hóngtǎshān) cost double the most expensive foreign cigarettes. Regardless of the price, they all taste very much the same.

call it racist if Western countries adopted rules saying blond-haired blue-eyed people could receive discounts on admission fees and hotel rooms.

Then there's the interesting case of non-Chinese Hong Kong residents. There are many 'foreigners' who were born in Hong Kong and hold Hong Kong passports, and in fact have never lived anywhere else. Some are one-half Chinese or one-quarter Chinese, but Běijīng flatly refused to grant citizenship to anyone who was not of 'pure Chinese descent'. In other words, racial purity was the deciding factor, not place of birth. This rendered all these people stateless in July 1997. Like others born in Hong Kong, they hold 'British National Overseas' (BNO) passports, which allows them to travel, but gives them no right of abode in Britain. Since a BNO passport does not confer nationality, the non-Chinese Hong Kongers are now stateless. The 30,000 Hong Kong-born Indians are the largest affected group, but there are many others born in Hong Kong who have 'mixed blood' and are thus racially unqualified to become Chinese citizens.

Gripes aside, foreigners in China are generally treated well. It is very unusual to encounter direct racism in the form of insults (although it does happen) or be refused service in China (except to be excluded from 'Chinese-only hotels'). It does help, however, if you are from a predominantly white and prosperous nation. Other Asians and blacks often encounter discrimination in China. The most famous outright racist incident occurred in 1988 when Chinese students in Nanjing took to the streets to protest black overseas students dating local Chinese women.

When a Chinese person tells you that racism is a 'foreign problem', bear in mind that homosexuality too is a 'foreign problem' – in fact almost everything the Chinese government considers 'unhealthy' is a foreign problem. And if that sounds a little racist, it isn't, because there's no racism in China.

Queues

Forget queues. In China a large number of people with a common goal (a bus seat, a train ticket etc) generally form a surging mass. It is one of the more exhausting parts of China travel, and sometimes it is worth paying a little extra in order to be able to avoid train and bus stations. That said, queuing is less of a problem today than a few years ago. This is China and you have to accept the fact that there's nothing you can do about a population of a billion people!

Beggars

Yes, beggars do exist in China and their numbers are increasing. Some squat on the pavement beside large posters, which detail their sad story. Professional beggars are common – sometimes women clutching babies who regurgitate stories about having lost their train tickets and all their money.

The adults tend not to pounce on foreigners, but it's a different situation with the kids, who have to be removed with a crowbar once they've seized your leg. Child beggars are usually organised, working under instructions from nearby older women who supervise them and collect most of the cash. There have even been stories of children being kidnapped, taken hundreds of kilometres from their homes and forced into these begging gangs.

Prostitution

The world's oldest profession is on the rise in China. If you are male and staying alone in a hotel, chances are high that you'll either receive a phone call from a prostitute asking you if you'd like a massage or prostitutes will actually come knocking on your hotel room door in the middle of the night. It's also not uncommon for men to be approached by prostitutes on the street and in certain bars and karaoke lounges. A polite bú yào (no) should be enough to deter them, though in hotel rooms you may have to disconnect your phone.

EMERGENCIES

See the Post and Communications section earlier in this chapter for a list of emergency telephone numbers.

If you are arrested or run into legal problems you should contact your embassy or consulate for assistance.

LEGAL MATTERS
Judicial System

China is relying increasingly on laws to govern their civil and commercial activities, where once neigbourhood committies would handle disputes between ordinary citizens.

That said, only the most serious cases are tried in front of a judge (never a jury). Most lesser crimes are handled administratively by the PSB. The PSB acts as police, judge and executioner – they will decide what constitutes a crime regardless of what the law says, and they decide what the penalty will be.

If you do have a run-in with the PSB, you may have to write a confession of your guilt and pay a fine. Fines vary from Y50 for being in a closed area to whatever they think you can afford. There is some latitude for bargaining in these situations, and you should request a receipt (shōujù). In more serious cases such as overstaying your visa, you can be expelled from China (at your own expense). In general, if you aren't doing anything particularly nasty, like smuggling suitcases of dope through customs, the PSB will probably not throw you in prison.

In theory, if foreigners breach Chinese law they are prosecuted like locals and will be punished according with China's criminal law. The foreigner's home country may request the extradition of the foreigner from China but the final decision is up to the Chinese government. Note that China does not recognise dual nationality.

In China, prisons generally operate at a profit, either by using prison labour to manufacture goods or by forcing the prisoners' families to cough up some cash. If you do get tossed into prison for anything, don't be surprised if the terms of your release require you to pay the cost of your imprisonment – if you don't pay, you don't get released.

Drugs

China takes a particularly dim view of opium and all of its derivatives. The Chinese suffered severely from an opium epidemic, which was started by British traders in 1773 and lasted until the Communists came to power, and they haven't forgotten.

Indeed, China is always fond of bringing up the issue of opium every time the British criticise China's frequent human rights violations. Not much is said about the fact that China's current booming heroin trade is run exclusively by Chinese gangs, often with help from corrupt local police. If current trends continue China will once again become one of the world's biggest consumers of heroin.

South-West China has become a major smuggling route and even a market in its own right for the heroin warlords of the Golden Triangle just over the border in Myanmar and Laos. The Chinese government takes the drugs problem extremely seriously. Never carry packages or bags for other people, especially when going through customs.

Marijuana is often seen growing by the roadside in South-West China (it's very poor quality). Hashish is smoked by some of China's minority groups, who have historically had a long relationship with opium.

If a traveller is arrested with drugs, he or she can be sentenced to three to 15 years imprisonment for trafficking, selling, transporting or manufacturing drugs. It's difficult to say what attitude the Chinese police will take towards foreigners caught using small amounts of marijuana – they often don't care what foreigners do if Chinese aren't involved. Then again, you have to remember the old story about 'kill the rooster to frighten the monkey'. If you plan to use drugs and don't want to become the rooster, discretion is strongly advised!

BUSINESS HOURS

China officially converted to a five-day work week in 1995, although some businesses still force their workers to put in six days. Banks, offices and government departments are normally open Monday to Friday. As a rough guide, most open around 8.30am, close for one to two hours in the middle of the day, then reopen until 5pm or 6pm. Saturday and Sunday are both public holidays, but most museums stay open on weekends and make up for this by closing for one or two days during the week, usually Monday.

In Xīshuāngbǎnnà most government buildings operate on the siesta system and working hours are normally around 8am to 11.30am and then 3pm to 6pm or even 8pm.

Travel agencies and the foreign-exchange counters in the tourist hotels and some of the local branches of the Bank of China have similar opening hours, but are generally open on Saturday and Sunday as well, at least in the morning. Post offices and telecommunication offices usually stay open to at least 7pm and many are open 24 hours.

Many parks, zoos and monuments are also open on weekends and often at night. Shows at cinemas and theatres end around 9.30pm to 10pm.

Restaurants keep long hours and it is always possible to find something to eat at any hour of the day, especially around train and bus stations.

Long-distance bus stations and train stations open their ticket offices around 5am or 5.30am, before the first trains and buses pull out. Apart from a one- or two-hour break in the middle of the day, they often stay open until midnight.

PUBLIC HOLIDAYS & SPECIAL EVENTS

The PRC has nine national holidays:

New Year's Day 1 January
Spring Festival February – lasts up to a week
International Women's Day 8 March
International Labour Day 1 May – a worldwide Communist holiday
Youth Day 4 May – commemorates the student demonstrations in Běijīng on 4 May 1919, when the Versailles Conference decided to give Germany's 'rights' in the city of Tianjin to Japan
International Children's Day 1 June
Birthday of the Chinese Communist Party (CCP) 1 July
Anniversary of the founding of the PLA 1 August
National Day 1 October – celebrates the founding of the PRC on 1 October 1949. You may find many shops and offices are also closed the following day

Much of the Chinese culture took a beating during the Cultural Revolution and still has not fully revived. Nevertheless, hanging around the appropriate temples at certain times will reward you with special ceremonies and colourful events.

Special prayers are held at Buddhist and Taoist temples on days when the moon is either full or just the thinnest sliver. According to the Chinese lunar calendar, these days fall on the 15th and 16th days of the lunar month and on the last (30th) day of the month just ending and the first day of the new moon.

Except for Spring Festival, festivals that don't qualify as national holidays include the following:

February

Spring Festival *(Chūn Jié)* Usually in February – this is otherwise known as Chinese New Year and starts on the first day of the first month in the lunar calendar. Although officially lasting only three days, many people take a week off from work and enjoy big family get-togethers. This is the time when the gods of the kitchen and hearth ascend to heaven to make their annual report on the family – so debts are settled and houses are cleaned in preparation. Families also paste red couplets up on doorways to welcome benevolent spirits and add posters of ferocious house guardians to ward off evil ones. During the Cultural Revolution spring couplets were temporarily replaced by political slogans. Firecrackers are normally set off at midnight, both to welcome the new year and to ward off any bad spirits who weren't put off by the door posters. Be warned: this is China's biggest holiday and all transport and hotels are booked solid. Although the demand for accommodation skyrockets, many hotels close down at this time and prices rise steeply. If you can't avoid being in China at this time, then book your room in advance and sit tight until the chaos is over! The Chinese New Year will fall on the following dates: 12 February 2002, 1 February 2003, 22 February 2004 and 9 February 2005.

Lantern Festival *(Yuánxiāo Jié)* It's not a public holiday, but it is very colourful. People take the time to make (or buy) paper lanterns and walk around the streets in the evening holding them. You may also see dragon dances, lion dances and stilt walking, though this is more common in southern China. People make *yuánxiao* or *tángyuán*, sweet dumplings made of glutinous rice with sweet fillings, which are particularly auspicious as the character 'yuán' can also mean a family reunion. The festival falls on the 15th day of the first lunar month, and will be celebrated on the following dates: 26 February 2002, 15 February 2003, 5 February 2004 and 23 February 2005.

March/April
Guanyin's Birthday (*Guānshìyīn Shēngrì*) The birthday of Guanyin, the goddess of mercy, is a good time to visit Taoist and Buddhist temples. Guanyin's birthday is the 19th day of the second moon and will fall on the following dates: 1 April 2002, 2 March 2003, 9 March 2004 and 28 March 2005.

April
Tomb Sweeping Day (*Qīngmíng Jié*) A day for worshipping ancestors; people visit the graves of their departed relatives and clean the site. They often place flowers on the tomb and burn ghost money for the departed. Party faithful also visit statues of revolutionary martyrs, one famous example being after the death of Zhou Enlai in 1976. The festival also has traditional links with Cold Food Day, a separate festival commemorating the death of a Zhou dynasty official, but this has been forgotten in recent years. The festival falls on 5 April in the Gregorian calendar in most years, or 4 April in leap years.

April/May
Mazu's Birthday (*Māzǔ Shēngrì*) Mazu, goddess of the sea, is the friend of all fishing crews. She's called Mazu in Fujian Province and Taiwan, Tianhou in Guangdong and Tin Hau in Hong Kong. Her birthday is widely celebrated at Taoist temples in coastal regions as far south as Vietnam. Mazu's birthday is on the 23rd day of the third moon, and will fall on the following dates: 5 May 2002, 24 April 2003, 11 May 2004 and 1 May 2005.

June
Dragon Boat Festival (*Duānwǔ Jié*) This is the time to see dragon boat races. It's a fun holiday despite the fact that it commemorates the sad tale of Qu Yuan, a 3rd century BC poet and statesman who hurled himself into the Miluo River in Hunan province to protest against the corrupt government. Pyramid shaped packets of glutinous rice wrapped in bamboo or banana leaves, called *zōngzi*, are handed out, as symbols of the rice packets that were originally thrown into the river to stop the fish from eating Qu Yuan's body. Lèshān and Nánníng are good places to see the festival in the South-West. This holiday falls on the fifth day of the fifth lunar month, which corresponds to the following dates: 15 June 2002, 4 June 2003, 22 June 2004 and 11 June 2005.

August
Ghost Month (*Guǐ Yuè*) The devout believe that during this time the ghosts from hell walk the earth and it is a dangerous time to travel, go swimming, get married or move to a new house. If someone dies during this month, the body will be preserved and the funeral and burial will be performed the following month. The Chinese government officially denounces Ghost Month as a lot of superstitious nonsense. The Ghost Month is the seventh lunar month, or really just the first 15 days and culminating on the 15th day. The first day of the Ghost Month will fall on: 9 August 2002, 29 July 2003, 16 August 2004 and 5 August 2005.

September
Mid-Autumn Festival (*Zhōngqiū Jié*) This is also known as the Moon Festival, and is the time to eat moon cakes, sold in most shops in flavours ranging from bean paste to duck's egg. Yúnnán's cakes are particularly good. The cakes are a reminder of an uprising against the Mongols in the 14th century when plans for the revolution were passed around in cakes. Gazing at the moon and lighting fireworks are popular activities, and it's also a traditional holiday for lovers. The festival takes place on the 15th day of the eighth lunar month during the full moon, and will be celebrated on the following dates: 21 September 2002, 11 September 2003, 28 September 2004 and 18 September 2005.

South-West China's various minorities each have their own colourful festivals and these are an excellent time to see traditional dress and foods. With the exception of the Water Splashing Festival in Jinghong, they are rarely visited by foreigners. Many take place during the winter period when there is little work to be done in the fields and people have more time for festivals. Almost all are dated by the lunar calendar and fall on auspicious dates such as the third day of the third lunar month.

Chinese Lunar Calendar

While the solar Gregorian calendar (gōngli) is used for most dates in China, the traditional lunar calendar (nōngli) is used by both Han Chinese and minorities to date festivals and to mark auspicious dates for a wedding, funeral, house-moving etc. Conversions between the two calendars are listed in special red almanacs, which are almost always consulted before an important decision is made.

The lunar calendar is based upon the movements of the moon; every month begins with a new moon and the 15th day is a full moon. One lunar year has 12 months, each of 29 or 30 days, thus totalling 354 days, 11 days less than the solar calendar. To bridge the gap the Chinese added an extra, or intercalary, month, inserted seven times in a 19 year cycle. The year 2001 thus has 13 months in the lunar calendar. This was all sorted out some 3000 years ago.

As festivals are held according to the lunar calendar, every year they fall on a different date in the Gregorian calendar, making it difficult for tourists to know when exactly festivals start. To make matters worse, many festivals aren't fixed at all. Some minorities, like the Shui, have their own separate calendars and calculate their festivals according to this. Other festivals fall upon days named after the 12 signs in the Chinese zodiac, such as a hai or 'pig' day.

There are several Web sites that you can use to convert between Gregorian and lunar dates. Try W www.mandarintools.com/calconv.html.

The best thing you can do to track down accurate festival dates is to ask as many people as possible and then just turn up and be prepared to hang around for a few days for the festivities to begin.

Guìzhōu (especially around Kǎilǐ) and Yúnnán (Dàlǐ and Xīshuāngbǎnnà) have the best of these festivals. For details of local and minority festivals see the beginning sections of each province chapter.

Chinese and Tibetan Buddhist monasteries mark several auspicious dates, including Saga Dawa, the date of Buddha's enlightenment, on the 15th day of the 4th lunar month. This will occur on 26 May 2002, 15 May 2003 and 2 June 2004 in the Chinese lunar calendar. The Tibetans use their own separate calendar.

The 15th of the 5th month is another auspicious date that creates a lot of activity at Buddhist monasteries. This will occur on 25 June 2002, 14 June 2003 and 2 July 2004.

ACTIVITIES
Cycling
The South-West is ripe for two-wheeled exploration, either on short trips with a hired bike or long-distance trips with your own set of wheels. See the Highlights section in this chapter and the Bicycle section in the Getting Around chapter for more information.

Hiking & Trekking
As opposed to mountaineering (which requires equipment such as ropes and ice axes), normal hiking activities can usually be pursued without permits. There are three distinct types of trekking available in South-West China.

First and most common are the holy mountains such as Éméi Shān, Jīzú Shān and Fànjìng Shān. These are major tourist attractions, complete with an admission gate (charging a fee), handrails, concrete steps, trailside souvenir vendors, cable cars, photo props, restaurants and perhaps a hotel or two. This doesn't mean that they are not worth the effort, in fact they're an essential part of the 'China experience'; simply that the climber gets few solitary, contemplative moments.

The second type includes hikes along defined routes. Excellent treks of this type can be found along the dramatic Tiger Leaping Gorge (with the option to continue up to Bìtǎ Hǎi), up to the glaciers and snowy peaks of Hǎiluógōu Glacier Park, Yàdīng Nature Reserve, Wòlóng Nature Reserve around Dégé and through the minority villages and jungle of Xīshuāngbǎnnà from

Dàměnglóng to Bùlǎngshān. These all take around two or three days and have at least basic places to stay and eat en route so you don't need a tent or stove.

The third type is wilderness experience or as close as this gets in China. Treks in these areas are unsupported, there is no food or accommodation en route and no trails, just beautiful scenery and the odd village or nomad. You will need to bring all your maps with you as well as a tent, stove, sleeping bag, waterproofs, everything in fact. Western Sìchuān offers unrivalled trekking of this sort if you are fully self-sufficient or supported by a local or foreign travel agency. The area around Gōnggā Shān offers some stunning treks in remote Tibetan areas, as does Sìgūniáng Shān (Four Girl Mountain), though you have to know what you are doing in these remote and unforgiving mountains.

Some local travel agencies can arrange guides and porters (though this isn't Nepal). Several Western adventure travel agencies also offer supported treks in these regions, although they aren't cheap. See the Organised Tours section in the Getting There & Away chapter for some contact addresses.

There are endless opportunities in the South-West for village walks set in stunning scenery, the best of which are around the sublime karst landscapes of Xīngyì (Guìzhōu) and Yángshuò (Guǎngxī), and the alpine scenery of Jiǔzhàigōu or Sōngpān (Sìchuān).

Horseback Riding

The venues are not numerous, but South-West China does offer some opportunities. Sōngpān, Hǎiluógōu and monasteries around Dégé in Sìchuān and Dàlǐ, Lìjiāng, Déqīn, Bìtǎ Hǎi and Tiger Leaping Gorge in Yúnnán all offer horseback trails around snow-capped peaks. Most of the time you'll have to be led around by a guide, which takes much of the fun out of it. The hire of a horse and guide for a day can cost anything from Y70 to Y100 per day.

More common are photo-prop camels and horses, where Chinese tourists dress up like Genghis Khan, mount their steed and have their photo taken.

Golf

Golf ranks right up there with Remy Martin XXX Cognac, cellular phones and Chicken McNuggets as one of China's hippest status symbols.

Manicured green lawns are sprouting up all over Yúnnán, in particular, in an attempt to attract Thai and other South-East Asian tourists. In 1998 Kūnmíng opened two 18-hole championship courses (one designed by Jack Nicklaus) 50km out of town, and even Lìjiāng has plans to get in on the act. Green fees are extremely steep.

Skiing

Skiing in the tropical South-West? Well, one of Lìjiāng's more harebrained schemes is to build a ski resort on Jade Dragon Mountain north of town, despite Swiss advice that it's unfeasible.

Exercise & Gymnastics

Swimming pools, gymnasiums and some weightlifting rooms are catching on in China but still don't rival the old stalwarts of table tennis and badminton.

For a fee, a few top-end hotels in big cities like Chéngdū, Kūnmíng, Jǐnghóng and Ruìlì permit non-guests to join their 'health club', which entitles you to use the workout rooms, pools, saunas or tennis courts. Monthly membership fees at four- or five-star hotels typically start at around Y500 but smaller hotels sometimes offer one-off use of the pool for as low as Y15.

Public swimming pools and gymnasiums are generally overcrowded and in poor condition. Many public swimming pools in China require foreigners to have a recent certificate proving they are AIDS-free before they are allowed to swim.

Massage

Legitimate massage (as opposed to prostitution) has traditionally been performed by blind people in China. The Chinese can take credit for developing many of the best massage techniques that are still employed today.

Most five-star hotels have a massage service at five-star prices (typically Y300 per hour). You can get a massage for around

Y50 per hour at small specialist massage clinics, but you'll need a Chinese person to direct you to one. See the entries in Chéngdū, Jǐnghóng and Kūnmíng.

Watersports

Places such as Hongfeng Lake outside Guìyáng, Qionghai Lake near Xichang, Manfeilong Lake in Xīshuāngbǎnnà and Beihai's Silver Beach in Guǎngxī have windsurfers and sailing boats for hire during the summer, though you shouldn't get your hopes up too high.

You can take rafting trips at Mǎlǐng Gorge (near Xīngyì) and at Ziyuan near Guìlín. More intrepid white water can be found in western Sìchuān and north-west Sìchuān, where some of Asia's greatest rivers tumble off the Tibetan plateau into two-mile deep gorges of raging white water. For the moment however logistics are hard to arrange and most people arrange white water rafting trips through professional but pricey Western adventure tour companies such as Mountain Travel

Sobek (see Getting There & Away Organised Tours).

Adventure Sports

Western Sìchuān in particular offers the type of topography to entice mountaineers, white water rafters, hang-gliding enthusiasts and others who want to pursue their adventurous hobbies in some of the world's highest mountains.

The problem, as always, are those faceless, sombre figures known collectively as 'the authorities'. High-ranking cadres, the PSB, the military, CITS and others in China with the power to extort money know a good business opportunity when they see it. Foreigners have been asked for as much as US$1 million for mountaineering and rafting permits. The amount demanded varies considerably depending on who you're dealing with but the price is always negotiable.

COURSES

As China continues to experiment with capitalism, universities have found it increas-

---

Massage

Massage (ànmó) has a long history in China. It's an effective technique for treating a variety of painful ailments, such as chronic back pain and sore muscles. To be most effective, a massage should be administered by someone who has really studied the techniques. An acupuncturist who also practises massage would be ideal.

Traditional Chinese massage is somewhat different from the increasingly popular do-it-yourself techniques practised by people in the West. One traditional Chinese technique employs suction cups made of bamboo placed on the patient's skin. A burning piece of alcohol-soaked cotton is briefly put inside the cup to drive out the air before it is applied. As the cup cools, a partial vacuum is produced, leaving a nasty-looking but harmless red circular mark on the skin. The mark goes away in a few days. Other methods include blood-letting and scraping the skin with coins or porcelain soup spoons.

A related technique is called moxibustion. Various types of herbs, rolled into what looks like a ball of fluffy cotton, are held close to the skin and ignited. A slight variation of this method is to place the herbs on a slice of ginger and then ignite them. The idea is to apply the maximum amount of heat possible without burning the patient. This heat treatment is supposed to be good for such diseases as arthritis.

However, there is no real need to subject yourself to such extensive treatment if you would just like a straight massage to relieve normal aches and pains. Many big tourist hotels in China offer massage facilities, but the rates charged are excessive – around Y180 per hour and up. You can do much better than that by inquiring locally. Alternatively, look out for the blind masseuses that work on the streets in many Chinese cities, especially in Chéngdū, Kūnmíng and Jǐnghóng.

ingly necessary to raise their own funds and not depend so much on state largesse. For this reason, most universities welcome fee-paying foreign students.

Most of the courses offered are Chinese language study, but other possibilities include Chinese medicine, acupuncture, brush painting and music. If you've got the cash, almost anything is possible.

Prices for four hours of instruction per day, five days a week, range from around US$700 to US$1300 for a four-month semester, and perhaps half that for a six-week summer session. The spring semester starts just after Chinese New Year and the autumn semester starts in mid-September. Dormitory housing starts at around US$8 a day for private room, or half that amount to share the room. There have been complaints from students that universities try to hit foreigners with all sorts of various hidden surcharges – 'study licences', health certificates and so on. Other schools try to coerce you into teaching English for little or nothing.

If possible, don't pay anything in advance. Show up at the school to assess the situation yourself and talk to other foreign students to see if they're satisfied. Once you've handed over the cash, don't expect a refund. It is often possible to find a freelance teacher at major universities for around Y30 to Y50 per hour.

Probably the most popular place in the South-West to study Chinese is Yúnnán University, more specifically the Yúnnán University Center for Chinese Studies (☎ 503 3624, ⓔ ccfs.ynu.edu.cn), which has a vibrant foreign student community. Tuition costs around US$700 per semester. Chéngdū's Sichuan University (Chuanda), Southwest Jiaotong University and Southwest University of Finance and Economics are also worth a try.

The China Scholarship Council (☎ 10-6641 1324, fax 6641 3198), 160 Fuxingmennei Dajie, Běijīng 100031, offers information on arranging study at Chinese universities. Try their Web site at ⓦ www.csc.edu.cn.

The cheapest way to learn *taijiquan* (tai chi), how to cook dumplings etc is to get a local to teach you, although this can be difficult to arrange. Some cafes at backpacker centres like Lèshān, Yángshuò, Dàlǐ and Lìjiāng can arrange cheap courses in calligraphy, mahjong etc as well as short Chinese-language courses.

WORK

There are opportunities to teach English and other foreign languages, or other technical skills if you're qualified. Teaching in China is not a way to get rich – the pay is roughly Y1200 to Y2500 a month. While this is several times what the average urban Chinese worker earns, it won't get you far after you've left China. There are usually some fringe benefits like free or low-cost housing and special ID cards that get you discounts at some hotels.

In order to qualify for the high end of the salary range, you need to be declared a 'foreign expert'. It's not totally clear what makes you an expert, but points in your favour could include a graduate degree, TESL (Teacher of English as a Second Language) certificate, other credentials and/or experience. The final decision is made by the State Bureau for Foreign Experts. Many Americans who teach in the South-West (particularly Sìchuān) do so through the Peace Corps.

It's become fairly typical for universities to pressure foreigners into working excessive hours. A maximum teaching load should be 20 hours per week, and even this is a lot. You can insist on no more than 15 hours and some teachers get away with 10. Chinese professors teach far fewer hours than this, some hardly show up for class at all since they often have outside business interests.

The main reason to work in China is to experience the country at a level not ordinarily available to travellers. Unfortunately, just how close you will be able to get to the Chinese people depends on what the local PSB allows. In some towns where the PSB is almost hysterical about evil foreign 'spiritual pollution', your students may be prohibited from having any contact with you beyond the classroom, although you may secretly meet them far away from the campus.

Foreign teachers are typically forced to live in separate apartments or dormitories. Chinese students wishing to visit you at your room may be turned away at the reception desk; otherwise they may be required to register their name, ID number and purpose of visit. Since many people are reluctant to draw attention to themselves like this, they may be unwilling to visit you at all.

In other words, teaching in China can be a lonely experience unless you spend all your free time in the company of other expats, but this deprives you of the 'foreign experience' you may be seeking. A lot depends on where you'll be teaching – things are fairly open in Chéngdū, but it's a different story in the hinterlands of Sìchuān.

Two topics that cannot be discussed in the classroom are politics and religion. Foreigners teaching in China have reported spies being placed in their classrooms. Other teachers have found microphones hidden in their dormitory rooms.

China is opening up slowly, and some provinces are liberalising faster than others. In the city where you live, you may find that conditions are better than what is described here.

If you are interested in working in China, contact a Chinese embassy or the universities directly. One useful Web site on teaching English in China is W www.teflchina.com.

ACCOMMODATION

In the more developed east of China, hotel prices have leapt up to near Western levels in recent years. The good news is that in the backwaters of South-West China accommodation is still pretty cheap and there are few towns or cities where the cheapest bed is more than US$7. The trend is clear, however, and prices are rising everywhere.

On the other hand, quality has improved. Rooms are more luxurious, service has improved and hotel staff are friendlier and more used to dealing with foreigners than a few years ago. In the past, it was common for the staff to simply deny that rooms were available, even when the hotel was empty.

Foreigners are still controlled by strict rules (enforced by the PSB) concerning which accommodation they may or may not stay in. Dirt cheap accommodation exists everywhere but many of these hotels do not have permission from the PSB to accept foreigners and will turn them away. It's not worth getting angry with the reception staff as this is a PSB decision and both staff and hotel will be fined by the PSB if they accept foreigners. You will probably only run up against these problems if you are searching for the cheapest hotel in town.

If you arrive late at a hotel and promise to leave early the next day some hotels may let you stay. Some cheap hotels off the beaten track are unaware of the regulations and you may encounter no problems. Some towns are stricter enforcing these rules than others, while small villages often only have one hotel and so can't turn you away. Only very small villages have no accommodation at all.

If you get to a town not covered in this guide there will normally only be one hotel that will accept foreigners and you will be directed here automatically if you ask for a hotel (try adding the word 'Binguan' to the name of the town). Generally speaking the cheapest hotels cluster around bus and train stations, though these areas are rarely the quietest or safest parts of town.

If you are really stuck for a place to stay, it may help to phone or visit the local PSB and explain your problem. Just as the PSB makes the rules, the PSB can break them. A hotel not approved for foreigners can be granted a temporary reprieve by the PSB and all it takes is a phone call from the right official. Unfortunately, getting such an exemption is not the usual practice.

When you check into a hotel you must fill in a registration form. A copy of this is sent to the local PSB. There is usually a question on the registration form asking what type of visa you have. Most travellers aren't sure how to answer. For most, the type of visa is 'L', from the Chinese word for travel (lǚxíng). For a full list of visa categories, see the Visas & Documents section earlier in this chapter.

Hotels

After you've handed over your foreigner's mark-up rate, filled in the registration form in triplicate and idly noticed that the clocks in the hotel foyer for New York, London, Paris and Běijīng all display the same time, it's time to find the xiǎojiě (female attendant) to open the door to your room. As you search for your room down spittoon-lined corridors, you will notice that all the doors along the corridor are open and the occupants are channel hopping with the TV on full volume. Welcome to a typical Chinese budget hotel.

As you inspect the bathroom, you notice that the lavatory is draped with a ribbon that says 'sterilised'. This actually means nothing of the sort, so don't pay much attention to it. Occasionally you will find that, with space-saving ingenuity, the extractor fan from your bathroom runs directly into the bathroom of the adjacent room and vice-verse. The scorch marks of ground-out cigarettes on the carpet of the main room makes the room smell and look like the headquarters of the local Triad; you will find little solace in the overhead smoke alarm that probably houses a rusty battery and a cockroach nest.

As you dive into bed, the door crashes open and xiǎojiě marches in with a thermos flask and a technician to mend the TV. As she crashes out again, the telephone rings and a sultry voice asks if Mr Wang is still there; you say you hope not, and put the phone down. Finding a sock a moment later in your bed, you are not so sure.

They tell you that hot water is from 6pm to 8pm. When you turn on the tap at 7pm, nothing emerges except the hiss of escaping air, or a trickle of water the colour of coffee. You hunt for xiǎojiě, who assures you that hot water is imminent; hot water alternates with cold till 7.30pm, when it stops altogether.

After chasing an engorged mosquito around your room with a flip-flop in one hand, you turn off the TV at 11pm and get ready to hit the sack. This is the signal they've been waiting for directly below in the karaoke lounge; someone snaps their fingers with a '... and a one, two, three ...', the amplifier goes on with a Whummpf and there's a collective clearing of throats. Half an hour later, you run out of your room with a pillow pressed to each ear, looking for xiǎojiě. Xiǎojiě is nowhere to be found – she's singing downstairs.

Damian Harper

The 'Visa Valid Until' section can cause confusion. Just write the date on the visa, even though this is strictly the date by which you need to have entered the country, not left it.

Camping

You have to get a long way from civilisation before camping becomes feasible in China. Camping within sight of a town or village in most parts of China would probably result in a swift visit by the PSB or at least hordes of staring children (and adults). Wilderness camping is more appealing, but most such areas in China require special permits and are difficult to reach. Many travellers have camped successfully in remote north-western Sìchuān and in national parks such as Hǎiluógōu. In general, the Chinese are not great campers.

The trick is to select a couple of likely places about half an hour before sunset, but keep moving (by bicycle, foot or whatever) and then backtrack so you can get away from the road at the chosen spot just after darkness falls. Be sure to get up around sunrise and leave before sightseeing locals take an interest. Camping carries an inherent security risk in China.

University Accommodation

In theory, university dormitories are for students, teachers and their guests, or others with business at the university. In practice, universities are trying to make money, and they are simply entering into the hotel business just like many other state-run organisations.

While staying at a university sounds like a great idea, in practice many university dorms appear to be perpetually full, while others have upgraded their facilities and charge foreigners prices similar to a three-star hotel. A final problem is that many university dormitories have restrictions such as lights out by 10pm and no visitors in your room.

In short, you should probably only consider staying at a university if you have some interest in the campus itself – maybe to hang out with the students or foreign teachers, or participate in some on-campus activities.

Hotels

Chinese hotels have improved dramatically in the last few years and there are lot more options, many private. It is wise, however, not to expect too much, no matter how much you are spending. Many of the finer details of the hotel business still elude Chinese management and staff.

The vast majority of rooms in China are 'twins', which means two single beds placed in one room. 'Single rooms' (one bed per room) are less common and often much smaller than twins without a noticeable difference in price. 'Double rooms' (a room with one large double bed shared by two people) are less common still and often much more expensive. In most cases two people are allowed to occupy a twin room for the same price as one person, so sharing is one good way to cut expenses.

Something to be prepared for is lack of privacy. What happens is that you're sitting starkers in your hotel room, the key suddenly turns in the door and the room attendant casually wanders in. Don't expect anyone to knock before entering. Some of the better hotels have a bolt that will lock the door from the inside, but most budget hotels are not so well equipped. Your best protection against becoming an unwilling star in a live nude show is to prop a chair against the door.

Most hotels have an attendant (fúwùyuan) on every floor, whom you address as xiǎojiě or 'Miss'. The attendant keeps a sharp eye

on the hotel guests and a firm hand on all the room keys. This is partly to prevent theft and partly to stop you from bringing locals back for the night (this is not a joke).

Budget and even mid-range hotels rarely entrust you with a key and this can be a real pain when you need to keep popping in and out of your room. It's worth trying to get hold of one by giving a Y50 or Y100 deposit (yājīn). Some hotels may also require a room deposit to ensure you don't steal the ratty flip-flops.

Second only to the bed, the most important piece of furniture in any Chinese hotel is without doubt the television, and you will rarely be without one, or out of earshot of one. Other room standards include a thermos of boiling water, some cups and tea leaves, a bowl for washing, a pair of flip flops and four or five dim lights, of which one may work. Always check the hardness of the bed, and the ability of the toilet to flush and the windows to be locked before committing to a room.

Almost every hotel has a left-luggage room (jìcún chù or xínglǐ bǎoguǎn), and in many hotels there is such a room on every floor. If you are a guest in the hotel, use of the left-luggage room might be free (but not always).

The Chinese method of designating floors is the same as that used in the USA, but different from, say, Australia. What would be the 'ground floor' in Australia is the '1st floor' in China, the 1st is the 2nd, and so on. The upper floors generally hold the best rooms in Chinese hotels.

The policy at every hotel in China is to require that you check out by noon to avoid being charged extra. If you check out between noon and 6pm there is a charge of 50% of the room price, after 6pm you have to pay for another full night.

Budget Hotels Lǚguǎn or lǚshè are the cheapest dosshouses in China, although few are open to Western guests. Zhāodàisuǒ are mostly reception guesthouses for visiting government officials, although the title has spread to include most cheap hotels. Many are off-limits to foreigners but in rural areas government zhāodàisuǒ are sometimes the only place to stay. Government guesthouses are generally cheap but tend to charge foreigners double the local price.

Fàndiàn or jiǔdiàn are the next step up. Their Chinese names respectively mean 'restaurant' and 'inn'. These vary from cheap threadbare hotels to mid-range joints. In the early days of China travel, many of these government-run hotels had dormitories (duō rén fáng) but most of these have long since gone. The cheapest option you are left with is a bed in a three- four- or five-bed room, with a communal bathroom down the hall. The cheapest rooms will have a concrete floor, more upscale cheap rooms will have a horrible stained carpet.

Some hotels charge per room, others per bed and this can make a big difference if you are travelling alone. Rooms charged by the bed can be a bargain as most hotels will not put other Chinese guests in the room (the PSB don't allow Chinese and foreigners to share a room), thus giving you a spacious three-bed room for the price of the cheapest bed in the hotel. There is often no difference between paying for a bed in a two-bed room or a four-bed room, except the latter is cheaper and gives you more space. The downside is that hotels will sometimes demand that you pay for the whole room (baōfáng), regardless of how many beds there are.

Even if a hotel looks expensive it's still worth asking if it has any cheaper rooms. Newly converted mid-range hotels often have older buildings (lǎolóu) with basic rooms (pǔtōng jiān) at a fraction of the price.

Where these cheaper rooms or old blocks exist, the reception staff are often reluctant to tell you. Most will assume that as a foreigner you will want the best room in the house. A little persistence will often reveal a cheaper room; anger rarely achieves anything.

To conserve energy, in many cheaper hotels hot water for bathing is available only in the evening, sometimes only for a few hours, or every other day. It's worth asking when or if the hot water will be turned on. Some cheap hotels have separate shower blocks, though most are located at the end of the corridor, often with separate floors for men and women.

Mid-Range Hotels China's mid-range hotels have improved immensely in the last few years. Service standards are better, the toilets may actually flush and sometimes there are even minibars and 24-hour hot water. Prices are reasonable at around US$15 to US$40 for most mid-range 'standard' rooms (biāozhǔn jiān).

Fàndiàn and jiǔdiàn are often mid-range joints. Bīnguǎn (guesthouse) are usually enormous government-run hotels, often with many wings in spacious grounds. Most of them were set up in the 1950s for travelling government officials and overseas dignitaries. Most of these have been renovated over the last decade or so and are being rented out as mid-range accommodation – you no longer have to be a government official or dignitary. Bīnguǎn are most definitely not the kind of inexpensive, family-run guesthouses you find all over Thailand, Indonesia and other parts of Asia.

Top-End Hotels Four- and five-star hotels start at about US$50 and are often equipped with business centres, saunas, limousine service, bars etc. Most budget travellers will use them to pick up a free *China Daily* and use the marble-clad Western-style toilets. Top-end hotels are called either bīnguǎn, dàjiǔdiàn or dàjiǔlòu.

Top-end hotels are supposed to add a 15% tax to all room and board costs but you often get away without paying this, or negotiate a discounted rate that includes tax.

Reservations & Discounts In a big city like Chéngdū or Guìyáng, it's wise to call ahead first to see if there are any vacant rooms. Of course, at budget hotels there's only a 50% chance that the person answering the phone will speak anything other than Chinese.

It's possible to book rooms in advance at up-market hotels through overseas branches of CITS, CTS and some other travel agencies.

Often you actually get a discount by booking through an agency.

Several Web sites will book hotels throughout the South-West. The discounts they offer are normally available to walk-in guests but at least you know that you have a room.

There are so many hotels in the south-west (particularly Yúnnán) that almost every hotel offers discounts of between 20% and 50% on the published room rates. This is particularly true in the quieter season from November to March. The most common Chinese phrase for 'discount' is *yōuhuì jiàgé* or 'preferential' price.

If you're studying in the PRC, you can sometimes get an additional discount on room prices by showing your government-issued 'green card'.

FOOD

For Chinese script and pronunciation of epicurean words and phrases, see the Food Vocabulary in the Language chapter.

Chinese cooking is justifiably famous, a fine art perfected through the centuries, and one of the things that makes travelling in China a real joy.

Eating out is about more than just food though. It is a social lubricant, a time when families get together, and the major leisure activity of around a billion people. While friends in the West go out for a beer, the Chinese will opt for a meal punctuated with numerous shots of *bāijiǔ* (rice wine). One method of saying 'how are you?' *(nǐ chīfàn le méiyǒu?)* translates literally as 'Have you eaten yet?'.

Chinese tend to order far more than they could possibly eat. The bill is hardly ever split and diners compete for the privilege of paying the bill. Going Dutch is almost un-heard of amongst Chinese, except amongst very close friends. If you are invited for a meal, don't insist on paying your part of the bill (though you should offer at least once) and certainly don't pass money to your host in front of other guests or restaurant staff as this would cause a massive loss of face.

Quality, availability of ingredients and cooking styles vary, but you'll almost always find something to suit your tastes. That said, vegetarians may find their choices limited in rural Guìzhōu in winter. Your biggest problems are likely to be figuring out the menus and being overcharged.

Restaurants

There are 2.58 million restaurants in China so you should be able to find at least one that you like. The cheapest ones are little more than a hole in the wall, a fire (barely under control) and a wok, and seating consists of a couple of midget-sized seats and tables less than a foot tall. Up a grade come canteens, where you pay for your food in advance, get a little chit and hand this to the waitress. Most restaurants these days, however, are small family-run business, beneficiaries of Deng Xiaoping's free market reforms.

Outside hotel restaurants, prices are generally low. Beware, however, of overcharging and always check the bill – many places think nothing of charging foreigners double or more.

Most restaurants provide a packet of napkins with your chopsticks, for which you will be charged five máo or one yuán. Better restaurants sometimes do the same with sunflower seeds, flashy disposable chopsticks and the like. If you don't want these things, send them back or they will appear on your bill, even if you didn't use them! Tea is normally free, even in the cheapest places, though don't count on it. Most waiters will ask you what kind of alcohol you want. Most Chinese accompany their meal with a shot or two of bāijiǔ or a bottle of beer.

The language barrier can be formidable since English menus are a rarity. A phrasebook is a big help, but the alternative is to point at something one of the other diners is eating. Remember to determine the price before you order. In this guide we list the most common dishes that can be found almost anywhere, as well as some unusual dishes that you may see in better restaurants.

In rural China many restaurants have pick-and-choose kitchens where you wander out back, select your vegetables and meat and have the chef fry it all up. Chinese are often very surprised by the ingredients

Chopstick Etiquette

If you haven't mastered using chopsticks before going to China, you probably will by the time you leave. In up-market restaurants, sometimes the staff will bring out the cutlery for foreign guests but generally you will have to click your chopsticks along with the locals. Cheap places offer disposable bamboo chopsticks (an environmental nightmare), which most users rub together to get rid of splinters. Other types of chopsticks are used over and again so it might be an idea to sterilise them with boiling water or tea. Some travellers prefer to carry their own.

Chopsticks are relatively easy to use and are employed for picking items from communal dishes and for shovelling rice (with the bowl held to the lips) in rapid flicking motions into the mouth – that's a tricky one to master. The key is to hold the chopsticks high; you know you've got a problem when the sticks keep crossing. If you're feeling cocky try the peanut test; to pick up one peanut in your chopsticks is pretty good; two peanuts is impressive for a big nose; three peanuts entitles you to be addressed reverently as 'maahstaah'.

In rural China, table manners leave a lot to be desired, and large groups often wreak carnage and desolation wherever they dine. However, this does not mean you can bring to the big cities the bad habits you have acquired in the backwoods. Spitting bones across the table on to the floor and shouting through mouthfuls of rice may be OK in the backstreet stalls of Guìzhōu, but is frowned upon in an up-market Chéngdū restaurant. One thing you should never do is stick your chopsticks vertically into a bowlful of rice. This is considered a very bad omen as it resembles the incense sticks that are burnt at a Chinese funeral.

If eating in a group, remember to fill your neighbour's tea cups when they are empty, as yours will be by them. You can thank the pourer by tapping your middle finger on the table gently. On no account serve yourself tea without serving others first.

Chinese toothpick etiquette is similar to other nearby Asian countries. One hand wields the toothpick and does the picking, the other hand shields the mouth from prying eyes.

One other thing to bear in mind is that restaurant staff get severely aggravated if you stand around the entrance to a restaurant while checking out the menu. It's best to take a seat, even if you don't intend to eat.

foreigners choose to throw together, but they will usually oblige all the same. You will have to make it very clear that you want them cooked together *(yīkuàir)* or you'll get three separate dishes. Unless you're vegetarian, you may get a chance to meet your dinner face to face – choose your chicken, duck or fish and it will be slaughtered on the spot.

The main snag with point-and-choose technique is that you'll miss out on many of the most interesting dishes and sauces and will be stuck with the same dishes over and over again. Moreover, Chinese meals are essentially a group affair with everyone dipping their chopsticks into many different communal dishes and flavours. Solo travellers in particular tend to suffer from chronic culinary monotony.

Snacks

South-West China has some great snacks *(xiǎo chī* or literally 'little eats')* and it's worth trying as many of them as possible. They are cheap, quick and there's no need to labour through any difficult Chinese menus. What's more, the best places to track them down – weekly produce markets, night markets and old town backstreets – are often great fun in themselves.

The following is a rundown of the main street snacks you will find:

shuǐjiǎo Chinese ravioli, stuffed with meat, spring onion and greens. It's sometimes served by the bowl in a soup, sometimes dry by the weight (250g or half a *jīn* is normally enough). It's often served with rice gruel *(xīfàn)*. Locals mix chilli *(làjiāo)*, vinegar *(cù)* and soy sauce *(jiàngyóu)* in a little bowl according to taste and dip the ravioli in. Watch out, vinegar and soy sauce look almost identical! The slippery buggers can be tricky to eat with chopsticks. Don't wear white as you'll get sprayed in soy whenever you drop them in the bowl. Shuǐjiǎo are often created by family mini-factories – one stretches the pastry, another makes the filling and a third spoons the filling into the pastry and makes a little twist to finish it off.
zhēngjiǎo a steamed version of a shuǐjiǎo
guōtiē a fried version of a shuǐjiǎo
bāozi steamed dumplings filled with pork and spring onions, again normally served with rice

The art of eating noodles

gruel, soy sauce etc. These are normally bought by the *lóng*, or steamer basket, though large versions are sold individually.
mántou steamed dumplings without the filling or the taste (and also Chinese slang for a woman's breasts!)
húntún known in the West as wonton soup, these are small savoury ravioli served by the bowl.
niúròu miàn beef noodles in a soup
jīdàn miàn noodles with egg
dàpái miàn beef noodles with a rib or bone in it
rán miàn literally 'burning noodles'; dry with onions, peanuts and chillies.
fěn miàn gelatinous rice noodles
jiānbǐng an egg and spring onion omelette made to order on a black hotplate and served folded up with chilli sauce
chǎomiàn fried noodles or 'chaomein', not as popular as in the West. There is no such thing as 'Chop Suey' in China.
chǎofàn fried rice
qìguō an earthenware pot with a hole in the centre, whose soupy contents are heated by steam coming through the hole
shāguō a stewed casserole cooked in an earthenware pot
shǎokǎo an upturned skillet on which you can fry your own meat or vegetables
huǒguō hotpot (literally 'firepot'), a huge bowl of bubbling, spicy broth into which you dip various vegetable and meats on skewers. For the spicy version ask for *làwèi*; *báiwèi* is a milder version.
málàtàng a variant of hotpot but more spicy, with ginger, garlic, chilli, pepper and herbs

Look out also for sticky rice in a bamboo tube in Xīshuāngbǎnnà, for delicious baba flatbread in Lìjiāng and Uyghur shashlyk (kebabs) in most major towns. Market snacks that most foreigners turn down inclue fried birds, chicken's feet, pig's ears, pig's trotters and even pig's faces. Noodles are either rice noodles (mǐxiàn or mǐfěn), found mostly in the southern provinces of Yúnnán and Guǎngxī, or flour noodles (miàntiáo).

Baked sweet and normal potatoes are available in many markets. Fried potatoes can be found outside many schools – Chinese kids love them almost as much as Western backpackers do. Vendors usually douse them in chilli, soy sauce and more chilli so step in quickly if you don't want your mouth to burn.

Western-style cakes and sweetbreads are on sale everywhere but they rarely taste very good. The Chinese are considerably better at making their traditional breads – steamed buns (mántóu), clay-oven bread (shāobǐng) and fried bread rolls (yínsī juǎn) are notable examples.

Favourite travelling snacks are peanuts, melon seeds and sesame seeds.

Main Dishes

China harbours a diverse range of culinary styles and between them all almost everything edible ends up in the wok. For the most part, however, the pangolins, raw monkey brains and bear paws of legend rarely find their way on to the tables of Chinese restaurants (very few people can afford such delicacies), and the Chinese trick is to do ingenious things with a limited number of ingredients.

Several of China's various cooking styles can be found in the South-West. Most restaurants serve a standard range of jiācháng, or 'home-style' cuisine.

Most Cantonese cooking in the region is done in Guǎngxī, though most good hotels will have a Cantonese restaurant. Cantonese food has its origins in Canton (Guǎngzhōu) and Hong Kong and tends to be lighter and less spicy than other cuisines in the South-West. Its most popular creations are sweet and sour dishes and dimsum (diǎnxīn in mandarin). Most restaurants abroad tend to be Cantonese, though, as you'll soon discover, the Chinese food served abroad is very different from that enjoyed in China.

Sìchuānese cuisine is the most fiery of all the cuisines of the South-West, using huājiāo, or flower pepper, to add subtlety to the blast of the red chillies. Popular dishes include pork with peanuts, fish-resembling chicken and 'strange tasting' chicken. See the Chéngdū section for more information on Sìchuānese cuisine.

Guìzhōu is heavily influenced by neighbouring Sìchuānese cuisine and has a lot of hotpot, especially in winter. It's also traditionally one of the poorest parts of China and so has developed 'famine cuisine'. Many parts of Guìzhōu (and Guǎngxī) specialise in preparing dog and rural areas may even offer rat. Duck is also another popular meat in minority areas.

Yúnnánese cuisine is harder to pin down, though you tend to find sweeter dishes that make use of local tropical fruits and vegetables. Yúnnán also has good dairy goods (rare in most parts of China) such as roasted goat's cheese, as well as roasted tofu and excellent cured hams.

You will also find a few Běijīng-style restaurants, mostly specialising in delicious Běijīng Duck (tender duck meat that has been basted in honey and vinegar, winddried and grilled). The meat is eaten in pancakes with shallots and plum sauce and the bones are boiled up into soup.

Epicureans will tell you that the key to ordering Chinese dishes is to get a variety and balance of textures, tastes, smells, colours and even temperatures. Most Chinese will order at least one cold dish, a main dish and a watery soup to finish off with. Meals are almost always accompanied by rice. The character for 'eating' translate literally as 'eat rice'.

Pork and chicken are the main meats throughout China, but you will also find beef and mutton, especially in Huí Muslim restaurants. Most dishes are stir-fried quickly under extreme heat ('explode-frying'), sealing in most of the nutrients. Other cooking styles include hóngshāo ('red soaked' in soy sauce), yúxiāng (cooked in a spicy, piquant sauce that is supposed to 'resemble fish') and tiěbǎn (served sizzling on a hot plate).

You may also get the chance to sample minority dishes. Dǎi dishes are among the tastiest and include black glutinous rice, sticky rice steamed in a bamboo tube, pineapple and coconut rice, beef with lemon grass and steamed pork. Huí Muslim restaurants offer a good alternative, often serving the best noodles and cured beef, though never pork. You can recognise a Muslim restaurant from the Arabic calligraphy, and strips of beef drying outside. They often have a green pendant hanging outside. Miáo regions offer glutinous rice cakes and dishes stir-fried with zesty tangerine peel. Other regional specialities include edible bamboo fungi from southern Sìchuān, fried river moss in Xīshuāngbǎnnà and Nàxī flat bread in Lìjiāng.

Vegetarian

There are plenty of vegetables in China, the most common being eggplant, báicài (a kind of cabbage, known as bok choy in Cantonese), various types of green beans, tomatoes and mushrooms. The latter are a joy, with at least five different types regularly on offer including mùěr, or wooden ears, a delicious rubbery fungus. Vegetables vary with the season and can be scarce in remoter Guìzhōu or Sìchuān during winter. Dòufu (tofu in the West) or bean curd is a trusty vegetarian option. People seem to either love it or hate it.

The major problem for strict vegetarians is that chefs often sneak little bits of meat into your meal when you are not looking. Furthermore, most dishes are stir-fried in animal fat or oil, while soups and soupy noodles are often derived from animal stock.

The best vegetarian restaurants are normally attached to Buddhist monasteries or nunneries. Strict Buddhists are strict vegetarians and even though many of the dishes are especially designed to physically resemble meat (with names like 'fish-resembling chicken') there is never any meat present.

Western

Big Macs and pizzas have arrived in the PRC, but they have been slow to make it down to the South-West – most are still Chinese versions. The Chinese attach no stigma to eating fast food, and in fact it actually has some snob appeal.

Opportunities to indulge in a Western meal are decidedly limited in rural areas. Backpacker centres like Yángshuò, Dàlǐ and Lìjiāng offer passable imitations of Western dishes, but generally speaking you're better off sticking to Chinese food, unless the desire to chew becomes overpowering. Top-end hotels offer international food at international prices.

Breakfast

While the Chinese make outstanding lunches, dinners and snacks, many foreigners are disappointed with breakfast. The Chinese do not seem to understand the Western notion of eating lightly in the morning – a typical breakfast could include fried peanuts, pickled vegetables, pork with hot sauce, fried breadsticks (yóutiáo) and rice porridge, all washed down with a glass of beer. Just what you had in mind at 7am.

One breakfasty dish you can get any time of the day is scrambled eggs and tomatoes (fānqié chǎo jīdàn). A popular breakfast drink is soybean milk (dòujiàng or dòunǎi). Many street vendors also offer bottles of delicious sweet yoghurt (suānnǎi), which you drink through a straw, though these seem to be disappearing fast under the free market onslaught. Backpacker centres can rustle up the ubiquitous banana pancake and even muesli, yoghurt and fruit.

Desserts & Sweets

The Chinese do not generally eat dessert, but fruit is considered an appropriate end to a good meal. Western influence has added ice cream to the menu in some up-market establishments, but in general sweet food is consumed as snacks and is seldom available in restaurants.

One exception to the rule is caramelised fruits, such as apple (bāsī píngguǒ), banana (bāsī xiāngjiāo) and even potato (bāsī tǔdòu), which you can find in a few restaurants. Other sweeties include tángyuán, small sweet glutinous balls filled with sugar or bean paste; Eight Treasure Rice *(bābaófàn)*, a sweet sticky rice pudding; and various types of steamed buns filled with sweet bean paste.

The Chinese have yet to discover the deep spiritual joy that can come from eating chocolate. Most Chinese versions have the consistency of chalk and won't melt under a blowtorch. If you get desperate then try the small chocolate footballs sold in most department stalls or anything expensive from Shànghǎi.

Toffee crab apples *(bīngtáng fulu)* on a stick are a popular winter treat.

Fruit

South-West China in general and Yúnnán in particular has some great fruit. Supply and price vary regionally; apples are cheapest in northern and western Sìchuān, tangerines and mandarins are best in south-eastern Guìzhōu, bananas are best in Yúnnán and pineapples are best in Xīshuāngbǎnnà. Some exotic Chinese fruits to try include lychees (small red-skinned fruit with white pulpy flesh and a large seed), pomelos (large sweet grapefruit), longan (similar to lychees but with a brown skin), rambutan (like a hairy lychee) and the occasional durian *(bōluómì)* and sapodilla *(xīfānlián)*. The area around Lìjiāng has fine persimmons (somewhere between a kiwi fruit and a tomato) and walnuts.

Sugarcane is the traditional poor person's candy in China. It is sold at train and bus stations and is a common on-the-road snack. The idea is not to eat the purple skin (this is usually shaved off anyway) and not to swallow the pulp – chew on it until it tastes like string, then spit it out.

The Chinese peel all fruit, which is probably a good idea considering the pesticides that are used in China. Canned and bottled fruit is readily available everywhere, in department and food shops as well as in train stations.

DRINKS

For Chinese script and pronunciation of names of common drinks, see the Drinks Vocabulary in the Language chapter at the back of the book.

Nonalcoholic Drinks

Tea is the most commonly served brew in the PRC; it didn't originate in China but in South-East Asia. Although black (fermented) tea is produced in China, green (unfermented) is by far the most widely drunk. Indian and Sri Lankan black tea (often Liptons) is available only in international supermarkets.

Tea bags can be hard to find. Tea leaves are much more common, though it can be hard to get them to sink, and therefore difficult to avoid straining the tea through your teeth and spitting the leaves out afterwards.

Boiled water is supplied in every hotel and so hot drinks are easy to prepare yourself. Familiar brands of Western instant coffee are for sale everywhere, though fresh-brewed coffee is only available in Kūnmíng. Many department stores now sell 'three in one' sachets of instant coffee, creamer and sugar, which avoids having to lug around a huge jar of coffee in your rucksack. The Chinese are still experimenting with these drinks and you'll often see beer and coffee being drunk together.

Coca-Cola, first introduced into China by American soldiers in 1927, is now produced in China under the Chinese name *kěkǒu kělè* ('tastes good, tastes happy'). Chinese attempts at making similar brews include Tianfu Cola, which has a recipe based on the root of herbaceous peony, but this is hard to find in the South-West. Pepsi and Sprite are widely available – both genuine and copycat versions. Sugary Chinese soft drinks are cheap and sold everywhere, some are so sweet they'll turn your teeth inside out. Jianlibao is a Chinese soft drink made with honey rather than sugar and is one of the better brands. Lychee-flavoured carbonated drinks are unique to China and get rave reviews from foreigners.

Mineral water *(kuàngquánshuǐ)* is available everywhere, although some of the 'minerals' involved might raise a few eyebrows.

Fresh milk and dairy products used to be rare in China (the Chinese lack the enzyme that aids the digestion of milk products) but the Robust brand is now becoming increasingly popular under Taiwan's influence. A surprising treat is sweet yoghurt, sold on street corners in what looks like small milk bottles and drunk with a straw rather than eaten with a spoon. Street vendors also sell delicious coconut milk (from Hainan Island), soybean milk and even peanut milk (ever tried squeezing the milk out of a peanut?).

Alcoholic Drinks

If tea is the most popular drink in the PRC, then beer must be number two. By any standards the top brands are great stuff. Indeed the word for beer *(píjiǔ)* is the only Chinese phrase that many travellers truly master, the word for 'cold' coming a close second.

China is a beer superpower and, at over 16 million tonnes per year, is tipped to overtake the USA as the world's largest brewer. The best known is Tsingtao (Qingdao), made with a mineral water which gives it its sparkling quality. It's really a German beer since the town of Qīngdǎo (formerly spelled 'Tsingtao'), where it's made, was once a German concession and the Chinese inherited the brewery. Experts in these matters claim that draft Tsingtao tastes much better than the bottled stuff but it's about four times the price.

All the world's top brewers – Budweiser, Becks, Bass, Carlsberg, Foster's, Heineken, Kirin, SAB, San Miguel, and so on – have established mainland operations. In addition, there is licensed production of the Scottish & Newcastle brand McEwans Ale 1856, which is sold in Newcastle Arms pubs in Chéngdū and Lèshān. Other foreign brewers in the South-West include Belgium's Interbrew joint venture with Blue Sword in Deyang and Pabst's Blue Ribbon at the Emei Brewery. San Miguel *(Shènglì Píjiǔ)* has a brewery in Guǎngzhōu, so you can enjoy this 'imported' beer at Chinese prices.

A long train ride will yield countless (warm) domestic brands to sample en route: Liquan (Li Spring) in Guìlín, Yufeng (Fish Hill) in Guìyáng, Bailongtan (White Dragon Pool) and KK Beer in Kūnmíng, Guangming in Hónghé, Lancanjiang (Mekong River) in Bǎoshān and Wanli in Nánníng. Elsewhere try the products of the Dàlǐ Brewery, honey beer and even prickly pear beer from Yúnnán's Mengzi region. In the Tibetan regions of the Sìchuān and Yúnnán, look out for chang, an alcoholic drink made from barley.

Most Chinese beer is sold in green 640ml bottles *(píng)*, though there is also an increasing use of more expensive can *(tíng)* and draught *(zhā)* varieties.

Save grain, drink wine! This patriotic call has spurred grape wine *(pútaojiǔ)* consumption in China, combined with the new-found belief that red wine (always a lucky colour) is good for you. China has probably cultivated vines and produced wine for more than 4000 years but it's still not very good at it. Or at least as far as Western expectations are concerned. Dynasty and Great Wall wines are results of a joint venture with French companies and are generally available in top-end hotels. Yúnnán has a tradition of making red wine that dates from the Catholic missionaries of the 19th century. Yúnnán Rouhong red wine is bottled in Mílè and Shangri-La red wine is made in Déqīn, where vineyards have grown for 90 years since French missionaries introduced them.

The word 'wine' gets rather loosely translated. Many Chinese 'wines' are in fact spirits. Rice wine, a favourite with Chinese alcoholics due to its low price, is intended mainly for cooking rather than drinking. Hejie Jiu (lizard wine) is produced in the southern province of Guǎngxī; each bottle contains one dead lizard suspended perpendicularly in the clear liquid. Wine with dead bees or pickled snakes is also desirable for its alleged tonic properties. In general, the more poisonous the creature, the more potent the tonic effects.

Maotai, a favourite of the Chinese, is a spirit made in north-west Guìzhōu from sorghum (a type of millet) and is used for toasts at banquets. It tastes rather like rubbing alcohol and makes a good substitute for petrol or paint thinner. Anshun in western Guìzhōu produces a similar brew. For more information on these white spirits, *báijiǔ*, see the boxed text 'Evil Spirits' in the Yíbīn section of the Sìchuān chapter.

As a rule, Chinese men are not big drinkers, however toasts are obligatory at banquets. Minorities like the Dong and Miáo are fearsome drinkers and, more to the point, hospitable and generous with it. Foreign guests will be expected to keep up with copious toasts of face-numbing bāijiǔ rice wine, accompanied to loud cries of *gānbēi* or 'dry the cup'. Chinese generally don't clink classes and drain their glass in one hit. If you really can't drink, fill your wine glass with tea and say you have a bad stomach. In spite of all the toasting and beer drinking, public drunkenness is strongly frowned upon.

Imported booze, such as XO, Johnny Walker, Kahlua and Napoleon Augier Cognac, is highly prized by the Chinese for its prestige value rather than exquisite taste. The snob appeal plus steep import taxes translates into absurdly high prices; don't walk into a hotel bar and order this stuff unless you've brought a wheelbarrow full of cash.

ENTERTAINMENT

As on all other fronts, China's entertainment options are expanding rapidly. Bars, discos and karaoke parlours are springing up in all the major cities, and more cultural entertainment is also being resurrected.

Cultural Shows

If you watch enough Chinese TV you'll soon notice the Chinese obsession with cultural song-and-dance shows, particularly those by minority nationalities (though many on TV are performed by Han Chinese dressed up to appear like minorities. Live cultural shows are common throughout the south-west region, from colourful song and dance routines at the Stone Forest to dinner performances at the Dǎi restaurants in Xīshuāngbǎnnà. In general you are better off trying to see a real troupe like the Song and Dance Ensemble of Yúnnán in Kūnmíng or the Nàxī Music Academy in Lìjiāng. Better still try to catch a minority festival when you'll see the real McCoy.

Teahouses

Teahouses have traditionally served the same role as pubs in the West. These are the places where people (normally men) went to relax, catch up on news, and in the not so distant past, discuss the latest political line. It was also a place for entertainment and storytellers, opera singers, musicians and even communist Red Theatre propaganda would regularly perform at teahouses, which often had a stage especially for this purpose. Chéngdū's teahouses were particularly famous.

These days many teahouses have closed under pressure from town redevelopment and the popularity of karaoke bars and pool halls. However you can still find a few left (in Chéngdū, Zígòng and Yíbīn in particular), often in former temples or parks, where you can sit with a cup of tea, read a book and watch the old men playing cards, Chinese chess and mahjong.

Discos

Despite being somewhat unfashionable in the West, discos are very much alive and well in China and should not be confused with nightclubs. Discos (*dìsìkè*) are places for dancing, while nightclubs (*jiǔlèbù*) are places for drinking, usually with a floor show thrown in.

Discos have taken China by storm, or at least in eastern cities such as Běijīng and Guǎngzhōu. South-West China is a few years behind the east and few Chinese are really sure of the appropriate moves to make to a pounding bass. It's not unusual to see huge crowds dancing in formation, everyone looking over their shoulders to see what everyone else is doing. Ruili is one of the hottest night spots outside of Chéngdū and Kūnmíng. Dàlǐ has even seen the occasional rave.

Karaoke

Nowadays karaoke (*kǎlā OK*) requires little in the way of introduction, even in the West. The word 'karaoke' is a combination of the Japanese words kara, meaning 'empty', and oke, a Japanese contraction of the English word 'orchestra'. Today karaoke is *the* entertainment option for moneyed Chinese. 'Let's get together and sing some songs' is what they say to each other when it's time to unwind. The results will probably leave you with the impression that 99% of Chinese are completely tone deaf.

It's easy to recognise a karaoke parlour: they are usually lit up in neon and have a Chinese sign with the characters for kǎlā (a phonetic rendering of the Japanese) followed by the English letters 'OK'. Sometimes clubs can be identified by the acronym KTV – 'karaoke television'. The latter normally have private booths.

A recent development is the poor-person's karaoke bar, a TV (a video with a bouncing ball following the lyrics) set up by the roadside, where you pay a few máo to sing into a small PA system.

Much maligned by Westerners, karaoke can be fun with enough drinks under your belt. It's not unusual for inebriated Westerners who claim to hate karaoke to have to be pried loose from the microphone once they get going.

There are two menus: one for the drinks and one for the songs. Don't expect much in the way of English songs. It usually costs around Y10 to get up on stage and sing a song. It doesn't matter how badly you sing. You'll get a polite round of applause from the audience when you finish, probably a rapturous round of applause if you are a foreigner.

Warning One thing to watch out for in karaoke parlours is rip-offs. In some heavily touristed areas, young women work as touts. You may not even realise that they are touts – they will 'invite' any likely looking male to join them at a nearby karaoke bar, but no sooner than the bottle of XO is ordered then the woman 'disappears' and the hapless male is presented with a bill for US$200.

It is not sensible to accept invitations to clubs from young women on the streets. In clubs themselves, if you invite a hostess to sit with you, it is going to cost money. The same rules apply in China as anywhere else in the world of paid entertainment and sex.

Bars

There are a few Western type bars in the South-West, notably in Chéngdū, Kūnmíng and Lìjiāng. Bottled beer is generally much cheaper than draught but in up-market bars you don't get a choice. In most places you can get a draught beer for around Y20, though pitchers (zhā píjiǔ) are better value.

Cinemas

Up-market hotels have in-house English-language movies, but elsewhere the situation is fairly dire. Foreign movies are dubbed into Chinese, and Chinese movies – well, they're in Chinese. Hong Kong movies at least usually have inventive English subtitles: 'she my sister you call watermelon fool!', and can be entertaining when you are in the mood for historical kung fu epics and fast-paced cop dramas. You may find a few Western movies playing on video in backpacker centres such as Yángshuò and Dàlǐ.

Comedy

Back in the days before karaoke and MTV, the Chinese had to entertain themselves with pun-laden stand-up comedy acts and storytelling. This is known as xiàngshēng (crosstalk). Unfortunately, you'd have to be extremely fluent at Mandarin to make any sense out of this. It's extremely difficult to translate because it relies to a great extent on Chinese sound-alike words. Much of the unintelligible noise emanating from the loudspeaker on the trains and buses is just this sort of crosstalk.

Another form of comic dialogue known as duǎnzi is enjoying a resurgence in the form of political jokes, often laced with sexual overtones. Premier Li Peng is a particular butt of jokes mocking his intelligence.

SPECTATOR SPORTS

If there is any spectator sport the Chinese have a true passion for, it's football (soccer). Games are devoutly covered in the mass media, even those from the British, Brazilian and Italian leagues. China has dreams of taking the World Cup eventually, and the government has been throwing money into the project by importing players and coaches.

Chéngdū's home side, known as Quanxing, is probably the most successful in the South-West. Whole sections of the crowd are often made up of PLA crowd-control troops who do their best to suppress any attempts at a Mexican wave. The troops came in useful in July 2000, when thousands of fans in Xī'ān fought with police after a game between Chéngdū Wuniu and Shaanxi Guoli ended in a draw after a dubious referee decision.

Although it hasn't quite fired the Chinese imagination the way soccer has, basketball does provide the masses with entertainment during the long winter when playing outdoors means risking frostbite. There are now two professional leagues, and players have been recruited from the USA.

The Chinese are aces at table tennis and badminton (often played in the middle of a busy thoroughfare) and have recently begun to dominate women's long-distance running as well as swimming and gymnastics. Pool tables were the latest craze in the 1980s but these have been superseded in the hipster stakes by ten pin bowling.

China made bids for the 2000 and 2008 Olympics, each time releasing several prominent political prisoners just before the bid in an attempt to bolster its chances. Apparently it worked and Běijīng is due to host the games in 2008.

SHOPPING

The Chinese produce some interesting export items – tea, clothing, Silkworm missiles (the latter not generally for sale to the public).

Gone are the days of ration cards and empty department stores. China is in the grip of a consumer revolution and the big cities of the South-West are furiously trying to catch up with the east.

The so-called 'Friendship Stores' (not notable for friendly staff) were set up to cater for foreign needs back in the days when ordinary Chinese basically had no access to imported luxury items. It is a measure of just how far China has come when you think how, just 10 years ago, many Chinese dreamed of simply getting through the doors of a Friendship Store.

Nowadays, Friendship Stores are an anachronism and have become one of the many chains of department stores stacked to the rafters with cheap goods. Big department stores are economic barometers to the pace of change in China and are well worth a visit.

Foreign-language bookstores can be good places to stock up on cards, posters, Chinese dictionaries and learning aids, Chinese music and even Western pop music.

Hotel gift shops are still useful to pick up hard to find things such as slide film and imported magazines. On the whole, they tend to be expensive though.

On blankets spread on the pavement and in pushcarts in the alleys is where you'll find the lowest priced products. In street markets, all sales are final; forget about warranties and, no, they don't accept American Express. Nevertheless, the markets are interesting, but be prepared to bargain hard.

Service standards have been steadily improving in China over the last few years. In the recent past it was usual to be ignored by shop assistants as they read comics and chatted over jam jars of tea. Now with some real competition, shops are pushing their staff to be polite and attend to customers. The authorities have got in on the act, with public campaigns urging workers in service industries not to spit and to try smiling at customers. Even train staff now manage the occasional tight-lipped smile as they toss passengers a rice-box lunch for the afternoon meal.

Buying goods in state-run stores can still be a lesson in socialist bureaucracy. Firstly you must tell the sales assistant that you want to buy something. You will then receive two copies of a bill, which you must take to a separate cashier's desk. Here you hand over the cash and receive two copies of a stamped receipt, which you take back to the first sales assistant. She then keeps one of these before finally handing over the goodies.

Antiques

Many of the Friendship Stores have antique sections and some cities have antique shops, but in the case of genuine antiques you can forget about bargains. Chinese are very savvy when it comes to their own cultural heritage. Only antiques which have been cleared for sale to foreigners may be taken out of the country.

When you buy an item over 100 years old it will come with an official red wax seal attached. This seal does not necessarily indicate that the item is an antique though. You'll also get a receipt of sale, which you must show to customs when you leave the country; otherwise the antique will be confiscated. Imitation antiques are sold everywhere. Some museum shops sell replicas, usually at extravagant prices.

Most touristy stuff in the South-West is actually mass produced in Guìlín and sold outside popular tourist sites.

Stamps & Coins

China issues quite an array of beautiful stamps, which are generally sold at post offices in the hotels. Outside many of the post offices you'll find amateur philatelists with books full of stamps for sale; it can be extraordinarily hard bargaining with these guys! Stamps issued during the Cultural Revolution make interesting souvenirs, but these rare items are no longer cheap. Old coins are often sold at major tourist sites, but many are forgeries.

Paintings & Scrolls

Watercolours, oils, woodblock prints, calligraphy – there is a lot of art for sale in China. Tourist centres such as Guìlín, Chéngdū and Dàlǐ are good places to look out for paintings.

Prices are usually very reasonable, even some of the high quality work available in galleries. In the eyes of connoisseurs, the scrolls selling for Y200 are usually rubbish, but remain popular purchases all the same.

Minority Products

Minorities produce some of the most skilful handicrafts in the South-West. The Miáo (Hmong) of south-east Guìzhōu are expert embroiderers and many sell examples of their work. Jackets, baby hats, baby carriers, bags and silverware are all for sale. Kǎilǐ, Shidong, Taijiang and Zhaoxing in Guìzhōu are probably the best places to find handicrafts. Enterprising hawkers in Lìjiāng even sell embroidered Miáo mobile phone covers.

Guìzhōu is also famous for its batik, made mostly by the Bouyi around Anshun and sold as far away as Yángshuò and Dàlǐ. Dàlǐ produces its own indigo and white batik. Xīshuāngbǎnnà has a range of embroidered and woven bags.

Tibetan areas produce jackets, hats and yak-lined overcoats. Yi areas have woollen capes and laquerware.

More Than Meets the Eye...

Once upon a time in China you got what you paid for. If the sales clerk said it was top-quality jade then it was top-quality jade. Times have changed. Now there are all sorts of cheap forgeries and imitations about, from Tibetan jewellery to Qing coins, phoney Marlboro cigarettes, fake Sony Walkmans (complete with fake Duracell batteries with the battery tester painted onto the side!), imitation Rolex watches, even fake sticks of Wrigley's gum and tubes of Pringles.

China has implemented a major crackdown on counterfeiting, though efforts have been directed mainly towards items that flout international intellectual copyright laws: CDs, pirated software and, most recently, video CDs. Microsoft is particularly peeved. It's a big country, however, and there are still a lot of illegal consumer goods out there, most emanating from underground factories in Shēnzhèn and Guǎngzhōu. The government confiscated over 600 million packets of illegal cigarettes in 1999 alone!

At the same time, the government has to contend with more localised problems: the manufacture of fake train tickets, fake lottery tickets and fake Y100 notes. Cadres frequently paid their expense accounts with fake receipts, one of the many reasons why state-run companies are losing money.

Take care buying anything in China, particularly if you are forking out a large sum for it. Watch out for counterfeit Y100 notes. And if you are after genuine antiques, try to get an official certificate of verification – just make sure the ink is dry.

High quality goods can be hard to find. Some towns have minority department stores, which stock some interesting goods. Weekly markets are another good place to look. Hotels and museums have a good selection but are normally pricey.

Oddities

China abounds in wacky souvenirs and specialises in communist revolutionary kitsch. Popular souvenirs from the golden past include little red books of Chairman Mao's quotations, Mao badges, Mao watches (hard to get outside Běijīng) and even Cultural Revolution alarm clocks. Now that Deng Xiaoping too has shuffled off to the great socialist paradise in the sky, Deng memorabilia is popping up all over the place, though the Deng personality cult is nowhere near reaching the proportions of the Great Helmsman's.

Other cheesy highlights of the South-West include scale models of both Long March and The East is Red space rockets (available from Xichang in southern Sìchuān). People's Liberation Army outfitters can be a great source of offbeat presents like Mao caps and jackets (China actually calls Mao jackets 'Sun Yatsen jackets'). Need a gift for a special friend? How about a pair of skin-tight olive-green PLA underpants, fully equipped with a handy zipped pocket at the front (for ammunition?)!

Other Items

Lots of shops sell medicinal herbs and spices. Export tea is sold in extravagantly decorated tins (you can often get a very good deal buying the same thing at train stations). Tuocha Tea from Xiguan near Dàlǐ, Pu'er Tea from Menghai and Xishan Tea from Guiping are reputed to be the best.

Getting There & Away

AIR

There are an increasing number of direct international flights to South-West China, though at present all are from destinations within North-East and South-East Asia. (If you're interested in the North/South-East Asia option see Flying Direct to South-West China later in this section.)

Most long-haul international flights to China go via Běijīng or Hong Kong, and there's little difference between the two when it comes to air fares. Though once again part of China, flights from Hong Kong to China's South-West are still classed as international. (For long-haul international flights see Flying via Běijīng & Hong Kong later this section.)

Airports

Kūnmíng airport currently has the most international connections (to/from Thailand, Laos, Vietnam, Myanmar and Singapore), followed by Chéngdū airport (Thailand and Singapore). Guìyáng has a new airport capable of receiving international jets, though there were no international flights. Nánníng airport in Guǎngxī currently has a single international flight to Hanoi, though there are plans to introduce a Bangkok connection.

Airlines

The Civil Aviation Administration of China (Zhōngguó Mínháng), also known as CAAC, is the official flag carrier of the People's Republic of China (PRC), though it has now been broken up into various subsidiary and competing companies. On most long-haul international routes CAAC is known as Air China but in the South-West many international routes are handled by Yunnan Airlines (Yúnnán Hángkōng) based in Kūnmíng, China Southern Airlines (Zhōngguó Nánfāng Hángkōng) based in Guǎngzhōu or China Southwest Airlines (Zhōngguó Xīnán Hángkōng) based in Chéngdū. All are International Air Transport Association members with international fleets made up of new Boeing and Airbus jets, and their service is of a relatively high standard.

Other airlines that fly direct into South-West China include Thai Airways, Myanmar Airways, Lao Aviation and Silk Air, a subsidiary of Singapore Airlines.

Cathay Pacific Airways (Guótài Hángkōng) is a Hong Kong-based company partly owned by British Airways and CAAC. Except for Hong Kong, Cathay doesn't fly into China under its own name, but runs a joint venture with CAAC to operate Hong Kong's other airline, Dragonair (Gǎnglóng Hángkōng).

Dragonair started operations in 1985 with a single aircraft. Owned 100% by the PRC, it probably would have gone bankrupt had Cathay Pacific not bought into it in 1990. Cathay's influence is certainly visible – these days Dragonair's service is top-notch.

You can book Dragonair flights from Cathay Pacific offices around the world. You can also book combined tickets. For example, a flight from Vancouver to Kūnmíng, flying Cathay Pacific from Vancouver to Hong Kong and then switching to a Dragonair flight on to Kūnmíng. Both can be included on a single ticket.

Chinese Airline Offices Abroad

Air China
Australia
Melbourne: (☎ 03-9642 1555) Suite 2, 5th Floor, 422 Collins St, Melbourne, Vic 3000
Sydney: (☎ 02-9232 7277, 9232 7465) Level 4, 70 Pitt St, Sydney, NSW 2000
Austria
(☎ 1-586 8008) Operngasse 5, A-1010, Vienna
Canada
Toronto: (☎ 416-5818833, fax 5810056) Suite 1005, 655 Bay St, Toronto, MSG 2K4
Vancouver: (☎ 604-6850921, 6855892) 660-1040 West Georgia St, Vancouver, BC V6E 4H1
France
(☎ 01 42 66 16 58, fax 01 47 42 67 63) 10 Blvd Malesherbes, Paris 75008
Germany
Frankfurt: (☎ 69-233038, fax 236976) Düsseldorfer Str 4, D-60329, Frankfurt-am-Main
Berlin: (☎ 30-283 4181, fax 283 4225) Ziegel Str, 2-3, Berlin 10117
Italy
(☎ 06-855 2249, fax 854 1074) Corso D'Italia 29, Rome 00198
Japan
(☎ 3-52510711, fax 52510856) Air China Bldg, 2-5-2, Toranomon, Minato-ku, Tokyo 105
Myanmar
(☎ 1-65187) 112B, Pyay Rd Mayangon, Yangon
Singapore
(☎ 65-225 2177, fax 225 7546) 01-53 Anson Centre, 51 Anson Rd, Singapore 0207
South Korea
(☎ 2-774 6886, fax 773 9233) 47-2 (Han-sung B/D 1.2F), Seosnmun dong Jung-gu, Seoul
Switzerland
(☎ 1-2111617, 2120736) Nuscheler Str 35, CH8001, Zurich
Thailand
(☎ 2-631 0728, fax 238 2205) CP Tower 2/F, 313 Silom Rd, Bangrak, Bangkok 10500
UK
(☎ 171-7630 0919, fax 7630 7792) 41 Grosvenor Gardens, London SWIW 0BP

USA
New York: (☎ 212-371 9898, fax 656 4785) 45E 49th St, New York, NY 10017
San Francisco: (☎ 415/650-392 2162, fax 392 6214) 2nd Floor, 185 Post St, San Francisco, CA 94108

China Southern Airlines
Indonesia
(☎ 21-520 2980, fax 520 2979) Suite 102, Tamara Centre, JL, Jend Sudirman Kav 24, Jakarta 12920
Laos
(☎ 21-312642) KM, 3 Thadeua Road, Vientiane
Malaysia
(☎ 3-241 6978, fax 244 4580) Ground floor, Mui Plaza, Jaian P Ramlee, Kuala Lumpur 50250
Singapore
(☎ 65-223 3233, fax 223 3112) 01-02 Keck Seng Tower, 133 Cecil St, Singapore 0106
Thailand
(☎ 2-266 5688) 1st floor, Silom Plaza Bldg, Silom Rd, Bangkok 10500
USA
(☎ 323-653 8088, 888-338 8988, fax 818-795 6669) Suite 101, 6300 Wilshire Blvd, Los Angeles 90048
Vietnam
Hanoi: (☎ 4-269233/4, fax 269232) Binh Ming Hotel, 27 Ly Thai To Street, Hanoi
Ho Chi Minh City: (☎ 8-298417, fax 296800) 52B Pham Hong Thai Qi, Ho Chi Minh City

China Southwest Airlines
Nepal
(☎ 1-419 770, 411 302, 416 541) Kamaladi, Kathmandu
Singapore
(☎ 65-333 9566, fax 333 9466) 01-06 Stamford Court, 61 Stamford Rd, Singapore 178892
Thailand
(☎ 2-662 1940/5, fax 662 1937) 179/337–338 Supalai Place Bldg, Sukhumvit Soi 39, Bangkok 10110
175–177 Ground floor, Bangkok Union Bldg, Surawongse Rd, Bangrak, Bangkok 10500

Yunnan Airlines
Singapore
(☎ 65-324 0188, 346 7356) ICS Bldg, 137 Cecil St, 1-2, Singapore 0106
Thailand
(☎ 2-216 3067/8) 200/9 2A Phaynthai Rd (near Asia Hotel), Bangkok

REGIONAL FLIGHTS

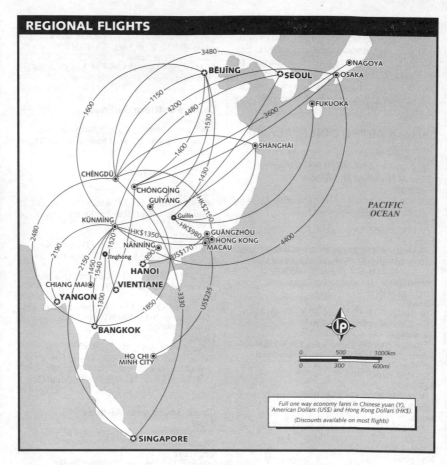

Full one way economy fares in Chinese yuan (Y),
American Dollars (US$) and Hong Kong Dollars (HK$).

(Discounts available on most flights)

Buying Tickets

There are several route options to consider, depending on where you are flying from. If you are flying long haul or round-the-world and can find a cheap ticket to Bangkok (not all that difficult), you can buy an onward ticket from Bangkok or Chiang Mai to either Kūnmíng or Chéngdū. This gives you the flexibility to fly into one city (eg, Chéngdū) and out of another (Kūnmíng) or to combine your trip with one or more regional countries (eg, fly into Kūnmíng then overland to Vietnam).

A more common option is to fly long haul to either Běijīng or Hong Kong and then buy a domestic ticket onwards to almost anywhere in South-West China. Běijīng has traditionally been more expensive to fly to but this is not always the case these days. Prices from the UK to Běijīng or Hong Kong, for example, are now roughly the same. If fares to the two cities are similar then your choice depends upon which city you would rather stopover in, the ease of finding accommodation and whether you want to get your China visa in Hong Kong. For further details see the boxed text

'Stopover Survival Information' later in this chapter. Domestic tickets to the South-West are marginally more expensive from Hong Kong than from Běijīng.

A further option to consider with long-haul flights is whether to buy the domestic leg of your ticket in your home country or wait until you are inside China. Generally speaking, it is easier and cheaper to buy the domestic ticket in China, but this does mean that you will have to spend a minimum of a day, possibly two, organising and waiting for the flight. Most travel agencies abroad that specialise in China can book a domestic ticket, but it will cost you more as they buy it through local agents and then add on a service charge. However, sometimes you can get a reduction if you book the domestic section in conjunction with the international section. For example, China Travel Service & Information Centre (CTSIC) in London offers a 30% reduction on any domestic Air China ticket booked at the same time as an international Air China ticket.

If you are travelling via Běijīng, you should buy a return ticket as international flights purchased within China are invariably more expensive (usually much more) than those purchased elsewhere. Hong Kong and Macau are exceptions – air fares from those two cities are as cheap as anything you can find in the West.

When you're looking for bargain air fares you have to go to a travel agent rather than directly to the airline. Airlines can only sell fares at the full list price. But watch out – many discount tickets have restrictions (eg, the journey must be completed in 60 days, no flights during holidays, no change of date). It's important to ask the agent what restrictions, if any, apply to your ticket, and whether or not there is a charge to change the return date.

A small minority of ticket discounters are unsound. Sometimes backstairs-over-the-shop travel agents fold up and disappear after you've handed over the money and before you've got the tickets. When purchasing a ticket from a small-time operator, it's wise to take a few precautions.

You're safer if you pay with a credit card – if they don't accept credit cards, that's a danger sign (though not absolute proof of dishonesty). Agents who only accept cash should hand over the tickets straight away, not tell you to 'come back tomorrow'. After you've made a booking or picked up the tickets, call the airline and confirm that the booking was made. All this might sound like excessive paranoia, and perhaps it is – but remember that it's your money on the line.

If you purchase a ticket and later want to make changes to your route or get a refund, you need to see the original travel agent not the airline. Many travellers do in fact change their dates and route halfway through their trip, so think carefully about buying a ticket that is not easily refunded.

Stopovers There are plenty of discount tickets that are valid for 12 months, allowing multiple stopovers with open dates. These tickets allow maximum flexibility. All sorts of special packages are available that allow you a prolonged stopover in Hong Kong on the way to somewhere else. The Hong Kong stopover may cost nothing, or perhaps US$50 extra. Return-trip tickets are usually significantly cheaper than one way. Few such tickets are available in China, but look for these bargains in Hong Kong and Macau.

Back-to-Front Tickets These should be avoided. Back-to-front tickets are best explained by an example. If you are living as an expat in Běijīng (where tickets are very expensive) and you want to fly to London for a holiday (where you'll find tickets are much cheaper), you can (theoretically) pay a London-based travel agent by cheque or credit card and have a London friend or the travel agent mail the ticket to you.

The problem is that the airlines have computers and will know that the ticket was issued in London rather than Běijīng and they will refuse to honour it. Consumer groups have filed lawsuits over this practice with mixed results, but in most countries the law protects the airlines, not consumers.

Air Travel Glossary

Alliances Many of the world's leading airlines are now intimately involved with each other, sharing everything from reservations systems and check-in to aircraft and frequent-flyer schemes. Opponents say that alliances restrict competition. Whatever the arguments, there is no doubt that big alliances are the way of the future.

Courier Fares Businesses often need to send urgent documents or freight securely and quickly. Courier companies hire people to accompany the package through customs and, in return, offer a discount ticket which is sometimes a bargain. However, you may have to surrender all your baggage allowance and take only carry-on luggage.

Fares Airlines traditionally offer 1st class (coded F), business class (coded J) and economy class (coded Y) tickets. These days there are so many promotional and discounted fares available that few passengers pay full fare.

Frequent Flier Most airlines offer frequent flier deals that can earn you a free air ticket or other goodies. To qualify, you have to accumulate sufficient mileage with the same airline or airline alliance. Many airlines have 'blackout periods', or times when you cannot fly for free on your frequent-flier points (Christmas and Chinese New Year, for example). The drawback with frequent-flier programs is that they tend to lock you into one airline, and that airline may not always have the cheapest fares or most convenient flight schedule.

Lost Tickets If you lose your airline ticket, an airline will usually treat it like a travellers cheque and, after inquiries, issue you with another one. Legally, however, an airline is entitled to treat it like cash and if you lose it then it's gone forever. Take very good care of your tickets.

Onward Tickets An entry requirement for many countries is that you have a ticket out of the country. If you're unsure of your next move, the easiest solution is to buy the cheapest onward ticket to a neighbouring country or a ticket from a reliable airline which can later be refunded if you do not use it.

Open-Jaw Tickets These are return tickets where you fly out to one place but return from another. If available, this can save you backtracking to your arrival point.

Overbooking Since every flight has some passengers who fail to show up, airlines often book more passengers than they have seats. Usually excess passengers make up for the no-shows, but occasionally somebody gets 'bumped' onto the next available flight. Guess who it is most likely to be? The passengers who check in late. If you do get 'bumped', you are normally offered some form of compensation.

Reconfirmation Some airlines require you to reconfirm your flight at least 72 hours prior to departure. Check your travel documents to see if this is the case.

Restrictions Discounted tickets often have various restrictions on them – such as needing to be paid for in advance and incurring a penalty to be altered or cancelled. Others are restrictions on the minimum and maximum period you must be away.

Round-the-World Tickets RTW tickets give you a limited period (usually a year) in which to circumnavigate the globe. You can go anywhere the carrying airlines go, as long as you don't backtrack. The number of stopovers or total number of separate flights is decided before you set off and they usually cost a bit more than a basic return flight.

Ticketless Travel Airlines are gradually waking up to the realisation that paper tickets are unnecessary encumbrances. On simple one-way or return trips, reservations details can be held on computer and the passenger merely shows ID to claim their seat.

Transferred Tickets Airline tickets cannot be transferred from one person to another. Travellers sometimes try to sell the return half of their ticket, but officials can ask you to prove that you are the person named on the ticket. On an international flight, tickets are compared with passports.

In short, a ticket is often only valid starting from the country where it was issued. The only exception is if you pay the full fare, thus foregoing any possible discounts that London travel agents can offer. Having said this, China Travel Service & Information Centre (see the UK entry later in this chapter) can arrange through a local agent for a Běijīng-London ticket to be paid for in London and picked up in Běijīng (known as a PTA ticket).

Be careful that you don't fall afoul of these back-to-front rules when purchasing air tickets by post or through the Internet.

Student, Teacher & Youth Fares Student travel agencies and some airlines offer student discounts on their tickets of up to 25% for holders of student cards, youth cards and teacher cards. In addition to the card, some airlines may even ask for a letter from your school.

Buying Tickets Online Numerous airlines and travel agents have Web sites, which can make the Internet a quick and easy way to compare prices. Online ticket sales can work well if you are doing a simple one-way or return trip on specific dates. Beyond this you can spend an awfully long time tracking down the ticket you want, only to find you could have got it cheaper by visiting your nearest travel agent. Travel agency Web sites are given in the individual country listings later in this chapter.

Airline Web sites rarely offer discounted tickets but they do have office contact details and schedules. Sites include:

Aeroflot
W www.aeroflot.org
Air China
W www.airchina.com
Air France
W www.airfrance.fr
Asiana Airlines
W www.asiana.co.kr
British Airways
W www.british-airways.com
CAAC
W www.caft.com

Canadian Airlines International
W www.cdnair.ca
Cathay Pacific
W www.cathaypacific-air.com
China Southern
W www.cs-air.com/en/
China Southwest Airlines (Web site is Chinese only)
W www.cswa.com
Dragonair
W www.dragonair.com
Japan Airlines (JAL)
W www.jal.co.jp
Shanghai Airlines
W www.shanghai-air.com
Singapore Airlines
W www.singaporeair.com
Thai Airways
W www.thaiairways.com
Yunnan Airways (Web site is Chinese only)
W www.yunnanair.com

Travellers with Special Needs

Most international airlines can cater for special needs – travellers with disabilities, people with young children and even children travelling alone. Special dietary preferences (eg, vegetarian, kosher) can also be catered for with advance notice.

Airlines usually allow babies up to two years of age to fly for 10% of the adult fare, although a few may allow them to fly free of charge. For children between the ages of two and 12, the fare on international flights is usually 50% of the regular fare or 67% of a discounted fare.

Reputable international airlines usually provide nappies (diapers), tissues, talcum powder and all the other paraphernalia needed to keep babies clean, dry and happy.

If you are travelling in a wheelchair, most international airports can provide an escort from check-in desk to plane where needed, and ramps, lifts, toilets and phones are generally available.

Departure Tax

If leaving China by air, the departure tax is Y90. This has to be paid in local currency before you go through airport security, so be sure you have enough yuán to avoid a last-minute scramble at the airport money-changing booth.

Flying Direct to South-West China

Japan Air China and China Eastern fly frequently from Běijīng to Tokyo, Osaka, Fukuoka and Sendai. Some of these flights are direct and others are via Shànghǎi. Japan Airlines flies from Běijīng and Shànghǎi to Tokyo, Osaka and Nagasaki. In Tokyo, you can try Council Travel (☎ 03-3581 5517).

Otherwise, Japan Airlines (JAL) has flights between Kūnmíng and Osaka (Y4400) with connections to Tokyo (Y5100) twice a week. There are twice-weekly flights between Guìlín and Fukuoka (Fùgāng in Chinese), flights between Chéngdū and Tokyo (Y5200) and Osaka (Y4200), and between Chóngqìng and Nagoya (Y3600).

Laos Yunnan Airlines and Lao Aviation fly once or twice a week between Vientiane and Kūnmíng for Y1520.

Myanmar (Burma) Both Air China and Myanmar Airways International offer weekly flights between Yangon (Rangoon) and Kūnmíng (Y2190), which then carry on to Běijīng. To board a flight you must have a visa for Myanmar, which is obtainable in Kūnmíng.

Singapore Yunnan Airlines and Silk Air (part of Singapore Airlines) both have two flights a week between Singapore and Kūnmíng for around Y2150. China Southwest has two flights a week between Singapore and Chéngdū (Y3330).

STA Travel (☎ 737 7188), Orchard Parade Hotel, 1 Tanglin Rd, offers competitive discount fares. Chinatown Point shopping centre on New Bridge Rd has a good selection of travel agents to choose from.

South Korea Yunnan Airlines has two flights weekly between Kūnmíng and Seoul (Hànchéng in Chinese; Y4480). There are flights four times weekly between Seoul and Guìlín. China Southwest flies twice weekly between Chéngdū and Seoul (Y3480).

Otherwise, Asiana Airlines, Korean Air and Air China operate routes from Seoul to Běijīng, Shànghǎi and other Chinese cities.

Recommended discount travel agencies in Seoul include: Joy Travel Service (☎ 776 9871, fax 756 5342), 10th floor, 24-2 Mukyo-dong, Chung-gu, Seoul (directly behind City Hall). There is also discounters on the 5th floor of the YMCA building on Chongno 2-ga (next to the Chonggak subway station), including Korean International Student Exchange Society (KISES; ☎ 733 9494) in room 505 and Top Travel (☎ 739 5231) in room 506. In Itaewon, you can try O&J Travel (☎ 792 2303, fax 796 2403), on the 2nd floor just above the Honey Bee Club.

Thailand Yunnan Airways (Y1540) and Thai Airways (Y1750) each have a daily flight between Kūnmíng and Bangkok. Tickets seem to cost slightly more in Kūnmíng than in Bangkok.

The Thai Airways flight stops three times a week in Chiang Mai and it's possible to buy tickets for the Kūnmíng-Chiang Mai leg. The flight is a popular one and costs around US$100 in Chiang Mai and Y1450 in Kūnmíng. Yunnan Airlines also has two flights a week between Jǐnghóng (Xīshuāngbǎnnà) and Bangkok for Y1300.

China Southwest has four flights a week between Bangkok and Chéngdū; it costs Y2480 in Chéngdū or US$255 in Bangkok. The small Thai airline Angel Airways has flights from Bangkok to Chéngdū and, perhaps, Kūnmíng. China Southwest has three flights weekly between Guìyáng and Bangkok (Y1850). There are occasional flights between Bangkok and Guìlín.

Khao San Rd in Bangkok is budget traveller headquarters and the place to look for bargain ticket deals. Bangkok has a number of excellent travel agents, but there are also some suspect ones; ask the advice of other travellers before handing over your cash. STA Travel (☎ 02-236 0262), 33 Surawong Rd, is a good and reliable place to start. In Chiang Mai try the Thai Airways office near Wat Chiang Man on Phra Pokklao Rd.

Vietnam China Southern flies twice weekly between Hanoi and Běijīng via Nánníng in Guǎngxī province. A Nánníng-Hanoi ticket costs Y890. It also flies twice a week between Ho Chi Minh City and Guǎngzhōu. Vietnam Airlines flies from both Hanoi and Ho Chi Minh City to Guǎngzhōu three times a week. The Guǎngzhōu-Hanoi flight (US$170 one way) takes 1½ hours; Guǎngzhōu-Ho Chi Minh City (US$235 one way) takes five hours. Return air fares cost exactly double.

Vietnam, like China, is not a good country for buying cheap air tickets.

Flying via Běijīng & Hong Kong

This is still the most popular way of getting to the South-West. For information on flights to these two gateway cities see the various country entries in this section and the boxed text 'Stopover Survival Information' in this section.

From Běijīng there are daily flights to Beihai (Y1800), Chéngdū (Y1150-1300), Chóngqìng (Y1400), Guìlín (Y1430), Guìyáng (Y1530), Kūnmíng (Y1600) and Nánníng (Y1790), as well as two flights a week to Yíbīn (Y1400) in Sichuan.

From Hong Kong there are daily scheduled flights to Chéngdū, Chóngqìng and Kūnmíng with China Southwest, China Southern and Dragonair. There are also charter flights to Chéngdū (daily), Nánníng (three weekly), Chóngqìng (five weekly), Guìlín (daily) and Guìyáng (two weekly), which can be booked by travel agents in Hong Kong and specialist travel agents abroad. Charter flights offer no refund for cancellation and cannot be changed.

Sample one-way fares from Hong Kong include Chéngdū (HK$2150), Chóngqìng (HK$1950), Guìlín (HK$980), Guìyáng (HK$1280), Kūnmíng (HK$1350) and Nánníng (HK$1200). Dragonair fares are about HK$100 cheaper. For fares from South-West China see the relevant section of the destination chapters.

You might save a little money by booking a flight in Hong Kong from Guǎngzhōu to Kūnmíng, Chéngdū etc and then making your own way across the border. A Guǎngzhōu-Kūnmíng flight at time of research was Y1160, while a Hong Kong-Kūnmíng flight was Y1870. Getting from Hong Kong to Guǎngzhōu by train can cost as little as Y100.

You can also save money by flying from Shēnzhèn, just across the border. At time of research a flight ticket from Shēnzhèn to Chéngdū, for example, was HK$1250 from Shēnzhèn (sometimes discounted to as low as HK$900) and HK$2330 from Hong Kong. A turbojet catamaran from Hong Kong's Tsimshatsui direct to Shēnzhèn airport costs HK$189 but when bought with an air ticket out of Shēnzhèn from CITS costs HK$100, making this a very good deal.

There are also a few direct international flights to Shànghǎi, Guǎngzhōu and Macau, from where there are connections to most places in South-West China. Shànghǎi has flights to Lìjiāng (Y1940) and Jǐnghóng (Y1670), which involve a quick stop (but no change of plane) in Kūnmíng. You can normally buy same-day tickets at the airport for these flights.

The USA Discounters in the USA are known as 'consolidators'. San Francisco is the ticket consolidator capital of the USA, though some good deals can be found in Los Angeles, New York and other cities. Consolidators can be found through the *Yellow Pages* or the major daily newspapers. The *New York Times*, the *Los Angeles Times*, the *Chicago Tribune* and the *San Francisco Examiner* all produce weekly travel sections in which you will find a number of travel agency ads. Ticket Planet is a leading consolidator and is recommended. Visit its Web site at W www.ticketplanet.com.

Another way is to wander around San Francisco's Chinatown, where most of the shops are located, especially in the Clay St and Waverly Place area. Many of these are staffed by recent migrants from Hong Kong and Taiwan. Inquiries are best made in person, and be sure to compare prices, as cheating is not unknown.

There are good-value tickets between the West Coast and Hong Kong, with stopovers in Japan, Korea or Taiwan; for a little extra money the departure dates can be changed and you have one year to complete the journey.

Be careful during the high season (summer and Chinese New Year) because seats will be hard to come by unless reserved months in advance.

Council Travel (☎ 800-226 8624) is the USA's largest student travel organisation, but you don't have to be a student to use it. Council Travel has an extensive network in all major US cities – look in the phone book or check out its Web site (W www.council travel.com).

STA Travel (☎ 800-777 0112) has offices in Boston, Chicago, Miami, New York, Philadelphia, San Francisco and other major cities. Its Web site is at W www.sta.com.

One of the cheapest and most reliable travel agents on the US West Coast is Overseas Tours (☎ 800-323 8777, 650-692 4892) in Millbrae, California. Its Web site is at W www.overseastours.com. Another good agent is Gateway Travel (☎ 214-960 2000, 800-441 1183), headquartered in Dallas, Texas, but with branches in many major US cities.

A good Web site with information on international and domestic air fares is W www.flychina.com.

From the West Coast, budget one-way fares to Hong Kong start at around US$385 and return tickets begin at US$750 – these fares increase dramatically during the summer and Chinese New Year. To Běijīng, re-

---

Stopover Survival Information

Běijīng From the airport, the cheapest way into the centre of town is on one of the many airport buses (Y16). A taxi should cost from Y70. Běijīng is very spread out and the easiest way to get around this city is by subway or bike.

Hotels are not cheap and private double rooms cost a minimum of Y300. Favourite backpacker hotels are the *Jinghua Hotel* (☎ 6722 2211, Nansanhuan Zhonglu) and the *Lihua Hotel* (☎ 6721 1144, 71 Yangqiao, Yongdingmenwai). Both are in the south of the city, near the third ring road, and have dorm beds for around Y30 and doubles for around Y190.

Tickets for all domestic airlines can be bought at the Aviation Building (Mínháng Dàshà; ☎ 6601 6667 international, ☎ 6601 3336 domestic), 15 Xichang'an Jie, Xicheng District, south-west of the Forbidden City. Most trains to the South-West depart from Běijīng West train station and this is where you should buy tickets, as far in advance as possible.

Some of Běijīng's sightseeing 'musts' include the Forbidden City, Tiananmen Square, Mao's Mausoleum, Lama Temple and Temple of Heaven. A second full-day trip could take in the Great Wall (preferably the Huánghuā section) and Summer Palace. One good place to try Běijīng duck is the *Qiánmén Quànjùdé Kǎoyādiàn*, (32 Qianmen Dajie) 500m south of Tiananmen Square.

For more details see Lonely Planet's *Běijīng* guide.

Hong Kong Hong Kong was handed back to China on 1 July 1997, though for most practical purposes the ex-colony (now Special Administrative Region; SAR) still acts as an independent territory. Hong Kong has a new flag but the currency, the HK$, remains the same.

Flights to Hong Kong are considered international – the departure tax will cost you Y90. You will also have to go through Chinese immigration and customs when you travel between the SARs and China proper, though at the time of writing most nationalities did not require a visa to visit Hong Kong.

Hong Kong's Chek Lap Kok Airport has efficient bus and rail connections to the city centre. Airport bus number A21 runs direct to Tsimshatsui, the home of most budget accommodation, for HK$33. The useful airport tourist information centre (as you exit customs) has hotel price lists, free phones and bus maps. You can change money and use ATMs at the airport. The airport Thomas Cook branch changes money at rates about 10% lower than most banks in town but doesn't charge commission. Free maps of Hong Kong are also available from the Hong Kong Tourist Association alongside the Star Ferry Terminal.

turn fares from San Francisco begin at US$858. From New York–Hong Kong, fares start at US$408 one way and US$900 return. New York–Běijīng fares start at US$1100 return.

Canada As in the USA, Canadian discount air ticket sellers are known as consolidators. Air fares from Canada tend to be about 10% higher than from the USA. The *Globe and Mail*, the *Toronto Star*, the *Montreal Gazette* and the *Vancouver Sun* carry travel agent ads and are a good place to look for cheap fares.

Travel Cuts (toll-free ☎ 800-667 2887) is Canada's national student travel agency and has offices in all major cities. You don't have to be a student to use its services. You can find it in the phone directory, or visit the Web site (W www.travelcuts.com). Major cities also have Flight Centre branches.

Canadian Airlines is worth trying for cheap deals to Hong Kong, although Korean Air may still be able to undercut it. Canadian Airlines has long had the cheapest flights from Vancouver to Běijīng.

Besides the numerous flights to Hong Kong, Air China provides two flights weekly that originate in Toronto, then fly onward to Vancouver, Shànghǎi and Běijīng (in that order).

Stopover Survival Information

Hong Kong is a more expensive place to stop over than Běijīng. Budget accommodation is largely restricted to the infamous Chungking Mansions - a huge, claustrophobic rabbit warren holding around 80 guesthouses. Dormitories cost around HK$80; the cheapest private rooms range from HK$150 to HK$250. One of the most popular places for dormitories is the **Traveller's Hostel** (☎ 2368 7710, 16th floor, A Block), which has dormitories for HK$40. A similar but cleaner collection of guesthouses is at the **Mirador Arcade** (58 Nathan Rd). Dormitory beds can be found for HK$60 at the **New Garden Hotel** (☎ 2311 2523, 13th floor, Flat F4). Even crummy hotels are expensive for what you get.

A decent mid-range choice, however, is the **Evergreen Hotel** (☎ 2780 4222, 42-52 Woosung St), which has small but comfortable doubles for HK$406, including tax, breakfast, and free use of Internet and laundry facilities. You can save yourself money on mid-range or top-end hotels by booking them through a travel agency.

China Southwest and China Southern air tickets can be bought at the CAAC office (☎ 2739 3666) at 10 Queen's Rd, Central. Dragonair and charter flight tickets can be bought at most travel agencies. Many travellers use the Hong Kong Student Travel Bureau (☎ 2730 3269), 8th floor, Star House, Tsimshatsui. You could also try Phoenix Services (☎ 2722 7378), 7th floor, Milton Mansion, 96 Nathan Rd, Tsimshatsui.

Hong Kong is a convenient place to get a Chinese visa. The cheapest visas are available from the Visa Office (☎ 2827 1881), Ministry of Foreign Affairs of the PRC, 5th floor, Low Block, China Resources Bldg, 26 Harbour Rd, Wanchai. CTS (☎ 2315 7188), 1st floor, Alpha House, 27-33 Nathan Rd, Tsimshatsui (enter from Peking Rd), is a convenient and popular place to get a visa. See the Visa & Documents section in the Facts for the Visitor chapter for more information.

For things to do while waiting for your visa, take the Star Ferry across from the Kowloon side to Hong Kong Island's Central District. You can then take a tram up to Victoria Peak. Both trips offer fantastic views, especially at night. It's worth trying lunchtime dim sum at one of the Cantonese restaurants. Just order snacks off the passing trolleys.

The easiest way to get around is by Mass Transit Railway (MTR), Hong Kong's underground metro. For information on getting from Hong Kong to South-West China by bus or train via Guǎngzhōu see the Land section later in this chapter. For information on boats to Guǎngzhōu and Guǎngxī province see the Sea & River section in this chapter.

For more information on Hong Kong see Lonely Planet's *Hong Kong & Macau* guide.

For a low season return fare in winter from Vancouver to Běijīng you're looking at around US$800. The high season is from June to September.

Australia Quite a few travel offices specialise in discount air tickets. Some travel agents, smaller ones in particular, advertise cheap air fares in the travel sections of weekend newspapers, such as the *Age* and the *Sydney Morning Herald*.

The high season for most flights from Australia to Asia is from 22 November to 31 January; if you fly during this period expect to pay more for your ticket.

Cheap flights from Australia to China generally go via one of the South-East Asian capitals, such as Kuala Lumpur, Bangkok or Manila. If a long stopover between connections is necessary, transit accommodation is sometimes included in the price of the ticket, but if it's at your own expense it may work out cheaper buying a slightly dearer ticket.

STA Travel has offices in all major cities and on many university campuses, but you don't have to be a student to use its services. Call ☎ 131 776 Australia-wide for the location of your nearest branch, or visit its Web site (W www.statravel.com.au).

Flight Centre has a central office at 82 Elizabeth St, Sydney and dozens of offices throughout Australia and New Zealand. Call ☎ 131 600 Australia-wide, or visit the Web site (W www.flightcentre.com.au) for your nearest office.

The minimum low-season return fare from Australia's east coast to Hong Kong or Běijīng starts at about A$980.

New Zealand The *New Zealand Herald* has a travel section in which travel agents advertise fares. Flight Centre (☎ 09-309 6171) has a large central office at 3A National Bank Towers, 205-225 Queen St, Auckland, and many branches throughout the country.

STA Travel (☎ 09-309 0458) has its main office at 10 High St, Auckland, and has other offices in Auckland as well as Hamilton, Palmerston North, Wellington, Christchurch and Dunedin.

At the time of research, low-season one-way/return fares to Hong Kong were NZ$990/1345. Return low-season fares to Běijīng start at NZ$1645 with Malaysia Airlines.

The UK Air ticket discounters are affectionately known as 'bucket shops' in the UK. There are a number of magazines in the UK that have good information about flights and agents. These include *Trailfinder*, free from the Trailfinders Travel Centre in Earl's Court, and *Time Out*, a London weekly entertainment guide widely available in the UK. The best deals are available in London.

When purchasing a ticket from a bucket shop that looks a little unsound, make sure they are bonded and belong to the Association of British Travel Agents as well as the Air Travel Organiser's Licensing (ATOL). The latter is a government agency.

London's best-known bargain-ticket agencies include:

Bridge the World (☎ 020-7911 0900) 47 Chalk Farm Road, Camden Town, London NW1 8AH
Council Travel (☎ 020-7478 2000, fax 734 7322, e infouk@councilexchanges.org.uk) 52 Poland Street, London W1V 4JQ
  W www.ciee.org
Flight Bookers (☎ 020-7757 2444)
  W www.flightbookers.co.uk
STA Travel (☎ 020-7432 7474) 85 Shaftesbury Ave, London W1V 7AD
  W www.statravel.co.uk
Trailfinders (☎ 020-7938 3366, fax 937 9294) 42-50 Earl's Court Rd, Kensington, London W8 6EJ; (☎ 020-7938 3939) 194 Kensington High St, W8 7RG
  W www.trailfinders.com
Usit Campus Travel (☎ 020-7730 8111) 52 Grosvenor Gardens, London SW1W 0AG. Campus is also found in many YHA shops.
  W www.campustravel.co.uk

These agents can't book Chinese domestic air tickets, for that you'll need a specialist travel agency. China Travel Service & Information Centre (☎ 020-7388 8838, fax 7388 8828), 124 Euston Rd, London NW1 2AL, has some of the lowest air fares to

China and offers a 30% discount on any domestic Air China ticket booked in conjunction with an international Air China ticket. They have a Web site at W www.china travel.co.uk.

The similarly named China Travel Service (CTS; ☎ 020-7836 9911), 7 Upper St Martins Lane, can also book most domestic flights, but at prices approximately 20% higher than those bought in China. Travel agencies specialising in flights to Hong Kong and China are as thick as flies in Soho, London's Chinatown.

British Airways (☎ 0845-77 333 77) is worth checking for excellent excursion fares direct to Běijīng, although these tickets normally have tight restrictions on the duration of stay in China. Air China (☎ 020-7630 7678) is also worth contacting direct to see if it has any specials.

The cheapest low season (winter) return fares to Běijīng at the time of research included a UK£329 special to Běijīng with British Airways and a UK£340 three-month return ticket with Air China. High season or longer excursion fares were around UK£300 one way or UK£500 return. Virgin Airlines offers excellent fares to Shànghǎi for about UK£400 return.

Low season indirect return fares to Hong Kong were around UK£400. The best deals were usually with the Middle Eastern airlines, such as Gulf or Emirates. At other times you can expect a one-way direct London-Hong Kong ticket to cost around UK£330 and a return ticket around UK£500. It's also possible to fly to Melbourne or Sydney via Hong Kong for UK£385 one way or UK£690 return.

Continental Europe A reliable European source of bargain tickets is NBBS Travels (☎ 20-620 7051), Leidsestraat 53, 1017 NV Amsterdam; it has another office at Rokin 38 in Amsterdam (☎ 20-624 0989).

STA Travel has offices in Paris; the main one is at 49 Rue Pierre Charron (☎ 01 43 59 23 69). STA Travel has dozens of offices in Germany, including Bergerstrasse 118 Frankfurt/Main, 60316 (☎ 49-69 430 1910). In Switzerland try SSR Travel (☎ 41-31 302

0312), Falkenplatz 9 BERN, 3012, affiliated with STA Travel.

Council Travel's headquarters in Europe is at 1, Place de l'Odéon, F-75006 Paris (☎ 01 44 41 74 74, fax 01 43 26 97 45, e infofrance@ciee.org). It also has a Web site at W www.ciee.org. Council also has offices in Germany (☎ 030-2884 8590, fax 2809 6180, e info@councilexchanges.de), Oranienburgerstr 13-14, 10178 Berlin, and Italy (☎ 39-06 4620 431, fax 8535 5407, e info@councilexchanges.it), Corso Trieste 133, 00198 Rome.

Air China has flights between Běijīng and Berlin, Frankfurt, London, Milan, Moscow, Paris, Rome, Stockholm and Zurich. Other international airlines operate flights out of Běijīng, but there are very few, if any, cut-rate fares from the Chinese end.

Eastern European countries with functioning airlines that fly to China include Poland (LOT Polish Airlines) and Serbia (JAT-Yugoslav). Both airlines are reputed to be cheap, but travellers have reported problems with lost luggage.

Asia Běijīng and Hong Kong are well connected with air services to the rest of Asia.

Indonesia Air China and China Southern have flights originating in Jakarta that continue to Surabaya and then to Guǎngzhōu, Xiàmén or Běijīng. Garuda Indonesia has a twice-weekly flight from Jakarta to Guǎngzhōu. Jakarta, Jalan Jaksa is the place for travel agencies specialising in discounts.

Malaysia China Southern has direct flights from Kuala Lumpur to Běijīng, Guǎngzhōu, and Hong Kong, and from Penang to Guǎngzhōu. Malaysia Airlines flies from Kuala Lumpur to Běijīng and Guǎngzhōu.

The Philippines China Southern has a twice-weekly flight from Běijīng to Manila and a weekly flight from Guǎngzhōu to Manila.

LAND
If you're heading overland from Europe or Asia, it's entirely possible to travel all the way to China and back without having to

leave the ground. There are numerous interesting routes, including the Vietnam-China border crossing, the Trans-Siberian Railway from Europe, or the exotic Tibet to Nepal, Xīnjiāng to Pakistan and Xīnjiāng to Kazakhstan routes. For more on these routes see Lonely Planet's *China* guide.

It's not possible to bring your own vehicle into China unless you are part of an organised rally or special tour. Bicycles are allowed on some routes but not others – the regulations governing the use of bicycles is in a constant state of confusion, though you shouldn't have a problem bringing a bike into Guǎngzhōu or Běijīng.

There are innumerable connections between the South-West and other provinces in China. See the individual cities and towns in the destination chapters for details on some of these.

Hong Kong & Guǎngzhōu

Hong Kong is now part of China, but there is nevertheless a real border crossing at Lo Wu with customs, immigration and the whole routine. This has long been the most popular entry point to the PRC.

Train The cheapest way to get from Hong Kong into China is to take the Kowloon-Canton Railway (KCR) from Hunghom to the border at Lo Wu (HK$33), walk across the border and then catch the popular local train from Shēnzhèn to Guǎngzhōu (Y58 hard seat, three hours). The last train from Hunghom is at 9.45pm. Note that some trains go to Guǎngzhōu main railway station, others go to Guǎngzhōu East railway station.

There are also four or five direct express trains a day to Guǎngzhōu's East station (HK$180 to HK$190, three hours) from the KCR station in Kowloon. Note that customs and immigration formalities for the direct service are done at Hunghom KCR station, so make sure you arrive about 45 minutes before departure.

Guǎngzhōu has rail connections to everywhere in the South-West, but it's a major rail bottleneck and it can sometimes be difficult to get an onward ticket leaving the same day or even the next day. This is one

city where it's worth trying the CITS (located on the eastern side of the main railway station). Ticket scalpers and pickpockets abound so be careful. Note that Guǎngzhōu has two railway stations, the main one and Guǎngzhōu East station, which is a long way from the centre of town.

Bus You can also get from Hong Kong to Guǎngzhōu by road on the recently completed six-lane superhighway. Citybus in Hong Kong (☎ 2736 3888) runs buses (HK$150, three hours) from the China Hong Kong City bus station in Kowloon. Buses return from Guǎngzhōu's Garden Hotel on Shamian Island. Guangdong Tours Transportation (☎ 2576 9995) also has frequent departures to Guǎngzhōu's Liúhuā Bīnguǎn (opposite Guǎngzhōu's main train station). Buses depart from Hong Kong's New Cathay Hotel, 17 Tung Lo Wan Rd, Causeway Bay; the fare is HK$150.

There are also frequent minibuses between Shēnzhèn and Guǎngzhōu railway stations (Y30, 2½ hours). Luxury buses shuttle all day between Shēnzhèn's Luohu bus station (next to the railway station) and Guǎngzhōu's long-distance bus station on Huanshi Xilu, near the railway station for Y55. There are also direct buses to take you to Guangzhou Airport for Y60.

Overnight sleeper buses run from Guǎngzhōu's Liúhuā bus station to Yángshuò and Guìlín (Y100, 13 hours).

Macau

On the other side of the border from Macau is the Special Economic Zone (SEZ) of Zhūhǎi. The Macau-Zhūhǎi border is open from 7.30am to 11.30pm, and cyclists can ride across. Most people just take a bus to the border and walk across. From here you will have to take a bus to Guǎngzhōu to get decent land connections to South-West China.

Laos

From the Mengla district in Yúnnán it is legal to enter Laos via Boten in Luang Nam Tha province if you possess a valid Lao visa. There are morning and afternoon buses between Boten and the Lao provincial capitals of Luang Nam Tha and Udomxai, three and four hours away, respectively.

At the time of writing, the Lao consulate in Kūnmíng was issuing 15-day transit tourist visas for Laos, available in three days. See the Kūnmíng section in the Yúnnán chapter for more details.

Most travellers from Kūnmíng go via Jǐnghóng to Mengla and then to the border at Mohan. As the bus journey from Jǐnghóng will take the better part of the day, you will probably have to overnight at Mengla. If you are travelling from China into Laos, note that you will get better rates changing US dollars or yuán into Lao kip on the Laos side.

Myanmar

At time of writing it was still not yet possible to travel overland from Myanmar to China. The border is supposedly open in the opposite direction between China and Myanmar, via the Ruili-Muse checkpoint, but very few, if any, travellers have been successful in crossing here (though there are plenty of Chinese tours crossing the border). See the Ruili section in the Yúnnán chapter for details.

Vietnam

Travellers to Vietnam no longer require a special visa for entering or exiting overland from China.

The only place in the South-West to get a Vietnam visa is at Nánníng CITS in Guǎngxī province. See the Nánníng section in the Guǎngxī chapter for more details. Vietnam has a consulate in Guǎngzhōu, but most people apply for their visa in Běijīng.

The Vietnam-China border crossing is open from 7am to 4pm (Vietnam time) or 8am to 5pm China time. Set your watch when you cross the border – the time in China is one hour later than in Vietnam. Neither country observes daylight-saving time.

There are currently three border checkpoints where foreigners are permitted to cross between Vietnam and China. There is a possibility that others will open in the future.

Friendship Pass The busiest border crossing is at the Vietnamese town of Dong Dang,

---

Mekong Dreaming

The governments of Thailand, Laos, China and Myanmar have agreed to the construction of a ring road through all four countries. The western half of the loop will proceed from Mae Sai, Thailand, to Jǐnghóng in Xīshuāngbǎnnà, via Myanmar's Tachilek (opposite Mae Sai) and Kengtung (near Daluo on the China-Myanmar border), while the eastern half will extend from Chiang Khong, Thailand, to Jǐnghóng via Huay Xai and Boten in Laos. It's difficult to predict when it will happen but 2005 seems to be the target date.

The Mekong Tourism Forum has further plans to introduce a single visa that would enable a visit to Yúnnán, Laos, Myanmar, Thailand and Vietnam, though this is expected to be a long way off. Other dreams include a future Pan-Asian Railway, which will link Yúnnán, Laos, Thailand, Malaysia and Singapore.

164km from Hanoi. The closest Chinese town to the border is Píngxiáng, in Guǎngxī province, but it's about 10km north of the actual border gate. The crossing point (Friendship Pass) is known as Huu Nghi Quan in Vietnamese or Yǒuyì Guān in Chinese.

Dong Dang (Tóngdēng in Chinese) is an obscure town. The nearest city is Lang Son, 18km to the south. Buses and minibuses on the Hanoi–Lang Sön route are frequent. The cheapest way to cover the 18km between Dong Dang and Lang Sön is to hire a motorbike for US$1.50. There are also minibuses cruising the streets looking for passengers. Just make sure they take you to Huu Nghi Quan – there is another checkpoint but this is the only one where foreigners can cross.

There is a customs checkpoint between Lang Sön and Dong Dang, and sometimes there are long delays while officials gleefully rip apart the luggage of Vietnamese and Chinese travellers. For this reason, a motorbike might prove faster than a van since you won't have to wait for your fellow passengers to be searched. Note that this is only a problem when you're heading south towards Lang Sön, not the other way.

There is a walk of 600m between the Vietnam and China border posts.

On the Chinese side, it's a 20-minute bus ride or shared taxi from the border to Píngxiáng. A Train connects Píngxiáng to Nánníng in Guǎngxī. Trains to Nánníng depart from Píngxiáng (Y20 to Y30 hard seat, five to six hours) at 4.40am and 1.37pm. Buses are more frequent and run every 30 minutes or so and take about four hours (Y35) to Nánníng. The bus station is a five-minute walk north of Píngxiáng's north train station.

If you are headed to Vietnam, an early morning bus or train from Nánníng will get you into Píngxiáng around noon, time enough to find transport to the Friendship Pass.

Trains on the Hanoi–Dong Dang route run according to the following schedule:

no	dept. Dong Dang	arr. Hanoi
HD4	8.30am	8.00pm
HD2	5.40pm	1.50am

no	dept. Hanoi	arr. Dong Dang
HD3	5.00am	1.30pm
HD1	10.00pm	5.10am

A twice-weekly international train runs between Běijīng and Hanoi (Hénèi in Chinese), though passengers actually have to change trains on the Vietnamese side at Dong Dang. You can board or exit the train at several stations in South-West China, including Nánníng, Liǔzhōu and Guìlín. The train numbers change along the route. From Běijīng to Nánníng the train is T5/6, then from Nánníng to Dong Dang it becomes T905/6 and finally from Dong Dang to Hanoi it is the M1/2.

The Běijīng-Hanoi run is 2951km and takes approximately 55 hours, including a three-hour delay (if you're lucky) at the border checkpoint. Schedules are subject to change, but at present, trains depart from Běijīng West on Monday and Friday, arriving in Hanoi on Wednesday and Sunday.

Going the other way, trains depart from Hanoi on Tuesday and Friday, arriving in Běijīng west on Thursday and Sunday. At the time of writing the train schedule was as follows:

station	to Hanoi
Běijīng	dept. 10.51am
one day/night elapses	
Guìlín Nth	10.43am
Guìlín	11am
Liǔzhōu	1.29pm
Nánníng	8.20pm
Píngxiáng	arr. 12.15am
	dept. 3.34am
Dong Dang	arr. 3.30am*
	dept. 6am*
Hanoi	11.30am*

station	to Běijīng
Hanoi	dept. 2pm*
one night/day elapses	
Dong Dang	arr. 8.30pm*
	dept. 11pm*
Píngxiáng	arr. 12.56am
	dept. 4.40am*
Nánníng	11.02am
Liǔzhōu	3.10pm
Guìlín	5.27pm
Guìlín Nth	5.48pm
one night/day elapses	
Běijīng	5.18pm

*Vietnam Time

Lao Cai-Hékǒu The 762km metre-gauge Dian-Viet railway, inaugurated in 1910, links Hanoi with Kūnmíng in Yúnnán. The border town on the Vietnamese side is Lao Cai, 294km from Hanoi. On the Chinese side, the border town is called Hékǒu, 468km from Kūnmíng. Hékǒu has a couple of hotels that accept foreigners.

An international train runs between Kūnmíng and Hanoi every Friday and Sunday, departing at 4pm. Only four-person soft sleeper berths are currently available and these cost Y298 for the 30-hour ride. Trains arrive in Hanoi at 8.10pm local time.

Domestic trains also run daily on both sides of the border. On the Chinese side,

Kūnmíng-Hékǒu takes about 16 hours. A hard-sleeper ticket costs Y72 to Y77; soft sleepers are sometimes available for Y207. Trains depart and arrive at Kūnmíng's north railway station according to the following schedule:

no	dept. Kūnmíng	arr. Hékǒu
5933	4pm	8.15am

no	dept. Hékǒu	arr. Kūnmíng
5934	2.20pm	7.25am

On the Vietnamese side, trains run according to the following schedule:

no	dept. Lao Cai	arr. Hanoi
LC4	9.40am	8.10pm
LC2	6.00pm	4.10am

no	dept. Hanoi	arr. Lao Cai
LC3	5.10am	3.35pm
LC1	9.45pm	7.55am

Mong Cai-Dōngxīng Vietnam's third but little-known border crossing is at Mong Cai, just opposite the Chinese city of Dōngxīng. The crossing was officially opened to foreign travellers in mid-2000 but very few foreign travellers cross here. There are buses between Dōngxīng and Qinzhou, Nánníng (via Qinzhou) or Běihǎi, on the Chinese side, and between Mong Cai and Hon Gai (Halong Bay) on the Vietnamese side.

SEA & RIVER

International options into China include boat services between Osaka and Shànghǎi (starting at Y1300, two days), and between Kobe in Japan and Tánggū, near Tiānjīn (starting at US$250). International ferries also connect the South Korean port of Incheon with Shànghǎi, Wēihǎi (Shandong), Qīngdǎo (Shandong), Tiānjīn, and Dàlián, from where there are rail and air links into South-West China. For more details see Lonely Planet's *China* guide.

Hong Kong

Hovercrafts run between Guǎngzhōu and Hong Kong from the China Hong Kong City ferry terminal in Kowloon. There are two daily departures, at 8.15am and 1.30pm. Tickets cost HK$189 for economy class and HK$198 for 1st class. The trip takes just over two hours, and passengers can take a shuttle bus to the Garden Hotel in Guǎngzhōu from the Huángpǔ ferry terminal.

Catamarans for Guǎngzhōu also leave from the China Hong Kong City ferry terminal at 7.30am and 2pm. Tickets are HK$198/293 and the trip takes 2½ hours. In Guǎngzhōu, shuttle buses transport passengers from the Dōngjiāng ferry terminal to the White Swan Hotel and Hotel Landmark Canton.

Turbojet catamarans also run to Shēnzhèn airport (also marked as Fuyong) for HK$189, or HK$289 in 1st class. Departures are at 7.30, 9 and 10.30am and 12.45, 3.45, 6 and 7pm; travel time is one hour. From the ferry there is a free five-minute shuttle bus to Shēnzhèn airport. Tickets can be booked at the Hong Kong China City ferry terminal or at CITS. Catamarans from Shēnzhèn airport back to Guǎngzhōu depart at 9am and 10.30am and 2.15, 4 and 5.15pm. There are also night sailings to the Hong Kong Macau Ferry Terminal at 7.30pm and 8.45pm. You can get more information by ringing ☎ 2921 6688 in Hong Kong or ☎ 20-8222 2555 in Guǎngzhōu. There is a Web site (Chinese only) at Ⓦ www.turbojet.com.hk.

From Guǎngzhōu you can catch other ferries on to Wúzhōu (see the Guǎngzhōu entry following), though you'll have to transfer first to the Dashatou wharf.

The ferry services between Hong Kong and Wúzhōu, and – for the time being – Guǎngzhōu and Liǔzhōu, have been discontinued.

Guǎngzhōu

There are a couple of different services from Guǎngzhōu to Wúzhōu in Guǎngxī, the jumping-off point for Yángshuò and Guìlín. You can even buy a combined boat/bus ticket, though there are plenty of buses in

Wúzhōu on to Yángshuò and Guìlín. This is one of the most popular ways of getting to South-West China from Hong Kong, though you'll have to get yourself from Hong Kong to Guǎngzhōu by train or boat.

The quickest service from Guǎngzhōu to Wúzhōu is the high-speed ferry service, which costs Y80 and takes five hours. Departures are at 7.30am and 9am, and 12.30pm and 2pm. Take a morning service and you should be in Yángshuò in time for a late dinner and a cold beer. Tickets are sold at the Dashatou wharf and departures are from the Rapid Ferry terminal, 100m east of Dashatou. Bus No 7 travels from the railway station to the wharf.

The slower, old service is still running but most of the ferries have been upgraded, so you can do the 24-hour trip in comparative comfort. A two-bed cabin will cost Y77; Y57 in a four-bed cabin; penny pinchers can sleep with the masses for Y45. Boats depart from Dashatou wharf at 12.30, 2.30 and 9pm.

There used to be a daily boat service from Dashatou wharf to Liuzhou (Guǎngxī) via Guìpíng, though this had stopped at the time of research. Boats used to depart at 8am and cost around Y100 for the 12-hour trip. Check at the docks to see if it is running again.

Yangzi River (Cháng Jiāng)

Passenger ships cruise up and down the Yangzi between Shànghǎi and Wǔhàn (Húběi province) and between Wǔhàn and Chóngqìng. Tickets in Wǔhàn can be bought from the Yangzi ferry terminal on the Hankou side of Wǔhàn. You can also pick up a boat farther west at Yíchāng. For more details see the Down the Cháng Jiāng (Yangzi River) section in the Chóngqìng chapter.

Vietnam

For some time now there have been rumours of a planned boat service connecting the three Vietnamese ports of Haiphong, Halong and Mong Cai with the Chinese city of Běihǎi, though nothing has so far materialised.

Also in the pipeline is a boat service from Haiphong to the port of Fangcheng in Guǎngxī province.

ORGANISED TOURS

Are tours worth it? Unless you simply cannot make your own way around, then probably not. Apart from the expense, they tend to screen you from some of the basic realities of China travel. Most people who come back with glowing reports of the PRC never had to travel proletariat class on the trains or battle their way on board a local bus in the whole five days of their stay. On the other hand, if you want to get off the beaten track in a limited amount of time or don't want to travel alone, an adventure tour might be for you.

If you wish to travel around by yourself but have limited time, you can give yourself a skeleton itinerary by pre-booking a few hotels and train tickets through a China-specialist travel agency in your own country and then make the rest up when you get to China. This needs to be arranged several months before you travel, as most arrangements are done through faxes with the mother ship in China. Even if you do arrange everything well in advance, snags can still arise: like when you arrive in Kūnmíng with a flimsy voucher for a soft-sleeper train ticket to Chéngdū and no-one has ever even heard of you. The following foreign travel agents offer tours and can book Family & Independent Traveller (FIT) itineraries in China:

China Overseas Travel Service (☎ 212-925 7729, fax 925 7784) Suite 501, 109 Lafayette St, New York, NY 10013-4143, USA

Regent Holidays Ltd (☎ 0117-921 1711, fax 925 4866, e regent@regent-holidays.co.uk) 15 John St, Bristol BS1 2HR. It can cobble together an individual itinerary, including flights and hotels.
  w www.regent-holidays.co.uk

Silk Steps (☎ 0117-940 2800, fax 940 6900, e info@silksteps.co.uk) 83 Quakers Rd, Downend, Bristol BS16 6NH. It also arranges tours to Yúnnán.
  w www.silksteps.co.uk

If you are interested in a top-end Three Gorges cruise the following companies operate Yangzi cruises:

Regal China Cruises (☎ 212-768 3388, 800-808 3388, fax 212-768 4939, e info@regal chinacruises.com) 57 West 38th St, New

York, NY 10018, USA
w www.regalchinacruises.com
Victoria Cruises (☎ 800-348 8084, 212-818
1680, fax 818 9889, **e** contact@victoria
cruises.com) 57-08 39th Avenue, Woodside,
New York, NY 11377. Cruises from US$680,
with an office in Chongqing
w www.victoriacruises.com

Chinese State Travel Agents Abroad

CITS and CTS, the main Chinese state
travel bureaus, will also book hotels, domestic flights, train tickets and tours, usually with a service charge. This won't save
you any money, except perhaps if you are
booking top-end hotels, but it can save you
time and hassle in China if you have a tight
itinerary. Overseas representatives include
the following:

CITS There are offices (**w** www.cits.net)
worldwide:

Australia
(☎ 03-9621 2198, fax 9621 2919) 99 King St,
Melbourne, Vic 3000
w www.travman.com.au
Canada
(☎ 604-267 0033, fax 267 0032) 5635 Cambie
St, Vancouver BC V5Z
w www.citscanada.com
Denmark
(☎ 039-3391 0400, 3312 3688) Ved Vester-
port 4, DK-1612, Copenhagen V
w www.cits.dk
France
(☎ 01 42 86 88 66, fax 01 42 86 88 61) 30 rue
de Gramont, 75002 Paris
Hong Kong
(☎ 852-2732 5888, fax 2721 7154, **e** marketing
@cits.com.hk) New Mandarin Plaza, Tower A,
12th floor, 14 Science Museum Rd, Tsim Sha
Tsui East
w www.cits.com.hk
Japan
Tokyo: (☎ 03-3499 1245, fax 3499 1243) 6th
floor, 24-2 Shu Bldg, Shibuya 1-Chome,
Shibuya-Ku, Tokyo 150
Osaka: (☎ 06-6910 6635, fax 6910 6640,
e cits-osk@magical.egg.or.jp) 9th Floor, 2-16
YK Bldg, Hinomachibashi, Chuo-Ku, Osaka
Fukuoko: (☎ 92-441 8180, fax 441 8160,
e cits-fuk@magical3.egg.or.jp) 7th floor, SS
Building 3-21-15, Hakada, Fukuoko
w www.citsjapan.co.jp

Sweden
(☎ 08-702 2280, fax 702 2330,
e tinaxz@swipnet.sc) Gotgatan, 41, 1tr,
11621 Stockholm
USA
New York: (☎ 718-261 7329, fax 261 7569,
e citsusa@aol.com) Suite 204, 71-01 Austin
St, Forest Hills, NY 11375
Pasedena: (☎ 626-568 8993, fax 568 9207,
e citslaz@aol.com) Suite 101,
975 East Green St, Pasadena, CA 91106
w www.citsusa.com

CTS Overseas representatives include the
following:

Australia
(☎ 02-9211 2633, fax 9281 3595) 757–759
George St, Sydney, NSW 2000
Canada
Vancouver: (☎ 1-800-663 1126, 604-872
8787, fax 873 2823) 556 West Broadway,
Vancouver, BC V5Z 1E9
Toronto: (☎ 1-800-387 6622, 416-979 8993,
fax 979 8220) Suite 306, 438 University Ave,
Box 28, Toronto, Ontario M5G 2K8
France
(☎ 01 44 51 55 66, fax 01 44 51 55 60)
32 rue Vignon, 75009 Paris
Germany
Frankfurt: (☎ 69-223 8522) Düsseldorfer
Strasse 14, D-60329, Frankfurt-am-Main
Berlin: (☎ 30-393 4068, fax 391 8085)
Beussel Strasse 5, D-10553, Berlin
Hong Kong
(☎ 2853 3888, fax 2541 9777,
e ctsdmd@ctshk.com) 4th floor, CTS House,
78-83 Connaught Rd, Central;
(☎ 2315 7188, fax 2721 7757) 1st floor, Alpha
House, 27-33 Nathan Rd, Tsimshatsui
w www.ctshk.com
UK
(☎ 020-7836 9911, 7836 3121,
e cts@ctsuk.com) 7 Upper St Martin's Lane,
London
USA
San Francisco: (☎ 1-800-899 8618, 415-398
6627, **e** info@chinatravelservice.com) 575
Sutter St, San Francisco, CA 94102
Monterey Park: (☎ 1-800-890 8818, fax 626-
457 8955, **e** usctsla@aol.com) Suite 303, 119
S Atlantic Blvd, Monterey Park, CA 91754
w www.chinatravelservice.com

Adventure Tours

Mountaineering, trekking, camping, cycling, whitewater rafting and kayaking

tours to China are organised by various agents in the West, but the prices are too high for low-budget travellers.

Various travel agents will book you through to these operators. Scan their literature carefully as sometimes the tours can be done just as easily on your own. What you want is a company that can take you to places that individuals have trouble getting to.

The best adventure travel companies operating in South-West China include:

Australia
Adventure World (☎ 02-8913 0755, fax 9956 7707, Ⓔ info@adventureworld.com.au) 3rd floor, 73 Walker St, North Sydney, NSW 2060. Agent for Explore Worldwide (see UK listing) and others
Ⓦ www.adventureworld.com.au

Intrepid Travel (☎ 1300 360 667) 13 Spring St, Fitzroy, Melbourne, Vic 3065. Trips include ROAM trips for 18-35 year olds, billed as the cheapest adventure holidays in the world. Lots of trips to Yúnnán, Sìchuān and Guǎngxī, with a 14-day Yúnnán Explorer tour to Lìjiāng, Tiger Leaping Gorge and Zhōngdiàn; trips north from Sōngpān, from Zhōngdiàn to Kāngdìng and from Guǎngxī to Vietnam.
Ⓦ www.intrepidtravel.com.au

Peregrine Adventures (☎ 613-9663 8611, fax 9663 8618, Ⓔ websales@peregrine.net.au) 258 Lonsdale Street, Melbourne, VIC 3000. Allied with Exodus (see UK listing).
Ⓦ www.peregrine.net.au

World Expeditions (☎ 02-9264 3366) 3rd floor, 441 Kent St, Sydney, NSW 2000. Has an eight-day bicycle trip from Zhaoqing to Guìlín.
Ⓦ www.worldexpeditions.com.au

Canada
Access China Tours (☎ 800-788 1399, 604-522 2550, fax 522 2551, Ⓔ info@accesschina tours.com) 6-774 Columbia St, New Westminster, BC V3M 1B5
Ⓦwww.accesschina.net

China Hiking Adventures (☎ 1-800-363 0745, 416-605 7479, fax 605-7479), PO Box 5967, Toronto, Ontario M5W 1P4

Concepts East (☎ 1-888-302 1222, 416-322 3387, fax 322 3129, Ⓔ info@concepts east.com) Suite 904, 120 Eglinton Ave East, Toronto, Ontario M4P 1E2. Shangrila trip to Yángshuò, Kǎilǐ, Dàlǐ, Lìjiāng and Zhōngdiàn; plus a Three Gorges trip and a week-long cookery class in Chéngdū.

Maple Leaf Adventures (☎ 1-888-599 5323, 250-715 0906, fax 250-715 0912, Ⓔ maple leaf@mapleleafadventures.com) 2087 Indian Crescent, Duncan, BC V9L 5L9. Small company that runs two tours a year to Xīshuāngbǎnnà and north-west Lìjiāng, staying with local communities.
Ⓦ www.bcadventure.com/mapleleaf/

World Expeditions (☎ 613-241 2700, fax 241 4189, Ⓔ info@worldexpeditions.com) 78 George St, Ottawa, Ontario KIN SW1, with an office in Montreal. General China tour.
Ⓦ www.worldexpeditions.com

China
Bike China Yúnnán-based company that specialises in bicycle tours of South-West China
Ⓦ www.bikechina.com

Edward Adventures (☎/fax 872-267 0222, Ⓔ edad@public.km.yn.cn) 21 Guangwu Lu, Dàlǐ, Yúnnán. Off the beaten track tours throughout the region and to eastern Tibet.

Haiwei Trails (UK number ☎ 020-797 0358, in Lìjiāng ☎ 0888-512 2114/1350-888 6126, Ⓔ haiweitrails@chinamail.com) New British company that operates out of Lìjiāng and runs jeep trips and charters to north-western Yúnnán and Kham.
Ⓦ www.haiweitrails.com

Wild China (10-6528 7781, fax 6528 7791, Ⓔ info@wildchina.com) Room 702, 3 Dong-dan Beidajie, Dongcheng District, Běijīng 100005. Well-run tours to remote scenic and culturally interesting corners of the South-West.
Ⓦ www.wildchina.com

UK
Exodus (☎ 020-8675 5550, fax 8673 0779, Ⓔ websales@exodus.co.uk) 9 Weir Rd, London SW12 OLT. Many trips, including one to south-east Guìzhōu
Ⓦ www.exodustravels.co.uk

Explore Worldwide (☎/fax 01252-760001) 1 Frederick St, Aldershot, Hants GU11 1LQ. Offers well-run group tours to Yúnnán, which include a five-day trek in Tiger Leaping Gorge.
Ⓦ www.exploreworldwide.com

Imaginative Traveller (020-8742 3049, fax 8742 3045, Ⓔ info@imaginative-traveller .com) 14 Barley Mow Passage, Chiswick, London W4 4PH. Small group tours to Yúnnán and Sìchuān.
Ⓦ www.imaginative-traveller.com

Occidor Adventure Tours (☎ 01243-582178, fax 01243-587239) 10 Broomcroft Rd, Bognor

Regis, Sussex PO22 7NJ. Offers small group tours specialising in minorities, embroidery tours and festivals in Guìzhōu.

Silk Steps (☎ 0117-940 2800, fax 940 6900, e info@silksteps.co.uk) 83 Quakers Rd, Downend, Bristol BS16 6NH. Tours to Yúnnán
W www.silk-steps.co.uk

Travelbag Adventures (☎ 01420-541007, fax 541002, e info@travelbag-adventures.co.uk) 15 Turk St, Alton, Hampshire GU34 1AG. Small group adventure tours to Yúnnán and Guìzhōu.
W www.travelbag-adventures.co.uk.

Voyages Jules Verne (☎ 020-7723 4084, 7616 1000) 21 Dorset Square, London NW1 6QG. Good for upmarket tours (though these only touch on the South-West) and Yangzi cruises.
W www.vjv.co.uk

USA

Abercrombie & Kent (☎ 800-323 7308, 800-757 5884) 1520 Kensington Rd, Oak Brook, ILL 60523-2141. Top-end independent tours to Yúnnán and other destinations, plus Yangzi cruises.
W www.abercrombiekent.com

Adventure Center (☎ 800-228 8747, 510-654 1879, fax 654 4200) Suite 200, 1311 63rd St, Emeryville, CA 94608. Can book passengers for several travel companies including Explore Worldwide and Intrepid(see UK listing).
W www.adventurecenter.com

Asian Pacific Adventures (☎ 800-825 1680, 818-886 5190, fax 818-935 2691, e aoausa@earthlink.net) 9010 Reseda Blvd, Suite 227, Northridge, CA 91324. Tours incorporate festivals in Guìzhōu, and tours around Lìjiāng.
W www.asianpacificadventures.com

Earth River Expeditions (☎ 800-643 2784, fax 914-626 4423, e earthriv@ulster.net) 180 Towpath Rd, Accord, NY 12404. Offers rafting and trekking around Tiger Leaping Gorge.
W www.earthriver.com

Geographic Expeditions (☎ 800-777 8183, 415-922 0448, e info@geoex.com) 2627 Lombard Street, San Francisco CA 94123. Tours in north-west Yúnnán and onto Laos.
W www.geoex.com

High Asia (☎/fax 800-809 0034, e travel@highasia.com) PO Box 2438, Basalt, CO 81621. Offers a wide range of exciting trekking, climbing and cultural trips in the wilds of western Sìchuān, including treks in the Min Shan around Songpan, around Minya Konka and Siguniang Shan,

trips around Dege and Mùlǐ, and botany tours of western Sichuan.
W www.highasia.com

Journeys International (☎ 800-255 8735, 734-665 4407, fax 734-665 2945, e info@journeys-intl.com) Suite 3, 107 Aprill Dr, Ann Arbor, MI 48103. Tours that take in the highlights of the South-West.
W www.journeys-intl.com

Minzu Explorations (☎ 503-684 9531, e pctncls@aol.com) 18444 Tualata Ave, Lake Oswego, OR 97035. Small company offering tours to Miáo and Dong festivals in Guìzhōu and to the Zhōngdiàn region.
W www.minzuexplorations.com

Mountain Travel-Sobek (☎ 888-MTSOBEK, 510-527 8100, fax 525-7710, e info@mtsobek.com) 6420 Fairmount Ave, El Cerrito, CA 94530. Specialises in rafting and trekking, and has an adventurous tour from Bagan (Myanmar) to Lashio, Ruìlì and Lìjiāng. Runs occasional photo trips to Guìzhōu.
W www.mtsobek.com

REI Adventures (☎ 800-622 2236, 206-395 8111) PO Box 1938, Sumner, WA 98390. Offers cycling tours from Nánníng to Hanoi and around Guìlín.
W www.rei.com/travel

White Pearl Associates (fax 303-449 7605, e whitepearl@gci-net.com) Suite 315, 1705 14th St, Boulder, CO 80302. Runs tours in the Nùjiāng region of Yúnnán that directly benefit local community organisations and protected areas.
W www.chinarivers.com

MOVING TO CHINA

If you're going to be moving something heavy like furniture, you'll need the services of an international mover or freight forwarder. Crown Worldwide is reliable and has a Chéngdū office (☎ 28-612 0046, fax 612 0046, e general.cncdu@crownworldwide.com) at Room 608, Yi Yuan Bldg, 8 Shao Cheng Section, Shu Du Jie, Chéngdū 610015, as well as offices in Běijīng and Shànghǎi. For more details see the Web site (W www.crownworldwide.com).

In Běijīng you can try Sino Santa Fe (☎ 010-6514 1180, fax 6514 8080, e santafe@ssf-bjg.eac.btmail.com). In Hong Kong there's Asian Express (☎ 2893 1000, e hongkong@aemovers.com.hk); the Web site is at W www.aemovers.com.hk, or call Jardine Logistics (☎ 2563 6653).

Getting Around

AIR

The Civil Aviation Administration of China (CAAC; Zhōngguó Mínháng) is the civil aviation authority for China's numerous private airlines, including Air China (CA), China Eastern (MU), China Southern (CZ), China Southwest (SZ), China Northwest (WH), Sichuan Airlines (3U) and Yunnan Airlines (3Q). China Southwest is based in Chéngdū and China Southern is based in Guǎngzhōu.

The last few years have also seen a rapid increase in the number of airports in the South-West, with new ones appearing at Xiàguān (Dàlǐ), Lìjiāng, Líncāng, Zhōngdiàn and Guìyáng.

CAAC publishes a combined international and domestic timetable in English and Chinese in April and November each year. This can be bought at some CAAC offices in China, but are free in Hong Kong and overseas (though it may take a month to arrive). The private airlines also publish their own timetables.

Booking offices have become increasingly computerised over recent years. In larger cities different airlines have their own booking offices, although most smaller towns have only one main CAAC booking office, where you can buy tickets for any domestic airline. These offices allow you to purchase a ticket to or from any other destination on the computer reservation system. If the city you want to fly from is not on the system, however, you'll have to wait until you get there to buy your ticket from the local booking office.

Buying Tickets

You need to show your passport when reserving or purchasing a ticket, and you definitely need it to board the aircraft. Some airports will even check your Chinese visa, and if it has expired you will be prohibited from boarding.

Tickets are usually available for next-day travel. To book a ticket you must first fill in a booking form. At CAAC offices outside the main cities it is still impossible to use credit cards to finance your transport costs, though this will probably change soon. All flights currently have to be paid for in cash.

The government can't seem to make its mind up about price controls, which come and go. At present most domestic fares are fixed, so there's little difference between flying on, say, Yunnan Airlines or China Southwest. Yet every now and then airlines will discount fares, especially for inter-provincial flights. In Kūnmíng, for example, Yunnan Airlines flights out of the province are 25% cheaper than all other airlines. It can pay to shop around, though it is the airlines that will directly offer discounts, not travel agencies. Full fares are listed in this book, unless otherwise stated. Travel agencies and the service desks in better hotels (three star and up) can reserve and even issue air tickets with a little advance notice, but the latter will probably tack on an additional fee.

Business-class tickets cost 25% more than economy class and 1st-class tickets cost an extra 60%. Babies under two are charged 10% of the adult fare; children aged two to 12 are charged 50% of the adult fare; those over 12 are charged adult fare.

Cancellation fees depend on how long before departure you cancel. On domestic flights, if you cancel 24 to 48 hours before departure you lose 5% of the fare; if you cancel between two and 24 hours before the flight you lose 10%; and if you cancel less than two hours before the flight you lose 20%. If you don't show up for a domestic flight, you are entitled to a refund of 50%.

When purchasing a ticket, you may be asked to buy luggage insurance (about Y20). It's certainly not compulsory though some staff give the impression it is – the amount you can actually claim if your bags are lost is pathetically low.

The Flight

Airlines often ask you to check in two hours before departure but for most domestic

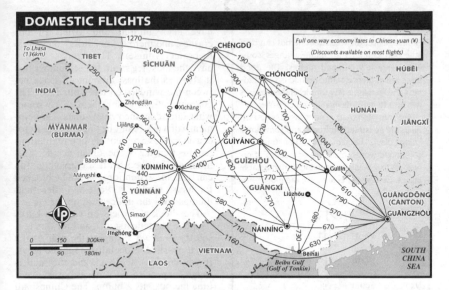

DOMESTIC FLIGHTS

Full one way economy fares in Chinese yuan (¥)

(Discounts available on most flights)

flights one hour is more realistic. Airport buses usually leave the CAAC office two hours or so before flight time. There is an airport tax of Y50 on domestic flights that must be paid before you go through airport security.

On domestic and international flights the free baggage allowance for an adult passenger is 20kg in economy class and 30kg in 1st class. You are also allowed 5kg of hand luggage, though this is rarely weighed. The charge for excess baggage is 1% of the full fare for each kilogram.

On domestic flights longer than an hour, you might get a 'real meal' if you're flying on an Airbus or Boeing aircraft, but if the plane is Soviet built there will be no facilities for hot food. In that case, you'll probably be given a little bag or two of sweets and a key ring as a souvenir.

Exiting from a Chinese aircraft can be hazardous – everyone grabs their oversized hand luggage and storms for the door before the aircraft even rolls to a stop. It's best to just sit back and let them fight it out. Window seats are better because your fellow passengers won't be climbing over you in the scramble for the door. Few people bother to check in

luggage on a domestic flight. It's quicker to just lug your bag on and off the plane.

BUS

Long-distance buses are one of the best means of getting around the country. Services are extensive and main roads are improving rapidly. Also, since the local buses stop every so often in small towns and villages, you get to see parts of the countryside you wouldn't see if you travelled by train.

Of course, the buses provide stops in places you had never counted on visiting; breakdowns are frequent and can occur anywhere. This is a special treat for the locals, who are temporarily entertained by the rare spectacle of a small herd of 'big noses' while the bus is being repaired (or stripped and sold for scrap metal). It also creates some economic opportunities – enterprising locals are quick to produce baskets of fruit, biscuits and soft drinks to sell to the waiting passengers.

Safety is another consideration. Accidents are frequent, especially on winding mountain roads. An astonishing 67,000 people died in traffic accidents in China in 2000, including 21 in a single crash in

Navigating Chinese Cities

At first glance, Chinese street names can be a little bewildering, with name changes common every few hundred metres. The good news is that there is some method in the madness and learning a few simple Chinese words will help to make navigating much easier.

The most common generic words used on maps are *jiē* (street), *lù* (road) and sometimes *xiàng* (alley). The names of longer streets are compound words, made up of a series of directions that break the street into manageable pieces. Compass directions are the most common locator:

Dōng	East	东
Xī	West	西
Běi	North	北
Nán	South	南

Another way of dividing roads is between *shàng* (upper), *xià* (lower) and, most commonly, *zhōng* (middle). Thus Beijing Xilu is Beijing West Road; as it heads east it will become Beijing Zhonglu and then Beijing Donglu. The word *huánchéng* (encircling city) denotes a ring road.

Marxist-inspired street names are common in the People's Republic. The following are translations of the most common street names in China:

Jiěfàng	Liberation
Guānghuá	Splendour
Mínzú	National/Nationality
Rénmín	People's
Dōngfēng	East Wind
Xīnhuá	New China
Shènglì	Victory
Mínzhǔ	Democracy
Yǒuyì	Friendship
Wénhuà	Culture
Hépíng	Peace
Tuánjié	Unity

Guǎngxī in February 2000. Foreigners have been injured and killed in bus crashes, and there is very little you can do to protect yourself. The front seat may have the most leg room but remember that it also has the least amount of space between the windscreen and your face. The government-run buses seem to be somewhat safer than the private ones – government drivers can be imprisoned for causing a bus accident. Police regulations require that the scene of an accident remain undisturbed until an investigation can be held, so minor roads can be blocked for hours while everyone twiddles their thumbs until the police turn up.

The shock absorbers on Chinese buses are poor (or nonexistent), and for this reason try to avoid sitting at the rear of the bus if possible, especially in remote areas. If you do sit in the back and the road is rough, expect to become airborne every time the bus hits a bump. The Chinese all know this, and there is much competition for seats at the front of the bus. Legroom is tight everywhere, even for the Chinese. Anyone over a metre tall might want to grab an aisle seat.

Many long-distance buses are equipped with cassette tape players and stereo speakers that allow the drivers to blast out your eardrums with sickly sweet Chinese pop music; select a seat as far away from these sinister speakers as possible and bring earplugs. Alternatively, try buying some Chinese or Western rock tapes that you like (as middle-of-the-road as possible) and giving them to the driver in the hope that they will be played.

Rural bus rides can be a riot with the bus crammed with cargo and livestock. As soon as the bus departs everyone simultaneously seals the windows, lights up a cigarette and turns up the stereo. At the end of a long trip the interior of the bus is almost destroyed.

Long-distance rides usually have food and toilet stops, though it's wise to carry a few snacks and water in summer. Drivers often develop cast-iron bladders from a life of slurping cold tea out of jam jars, so toilet stops can be few and far between.

Living on the Edge

Foreign regulars on Chinese buses develop a kind of 1000-yard stare that betrays the tattered fragments of what we call innocence. They display the 'been there, done that' mentality of the veteran – they cross the road without looking (even in Guǎngzhōu), fly on Friday the 13th (even Guangxi Air) and smoke 60 a day (even Temple of Heaven brand). They have eluded death and feel chosen, somehow. Life is not the same after a long-distance bus trip in China; it is a rite of passage, a journey into the heart of darkness, a life on the edge and to some, I am sure, a drug that must be regularly imbibed.

Our driver drove like Mr Death himself. If the road ahead was obstructed by an ever-so-slightly-slower moving vehicle, he'd be up with his full weight on the gas pedal like a deranged jockey. Our bus would creep by the other like two sprinting snails, around countless bends in the road and blind corners. You'd find yourself standing up, white-knuckle grip on your travellers bible, screaming the increasingly shrill mantra 'come on, come on'. Eventually the driver would slump back in his seat and light a victory cigarette and our bus would ease by, slotting into the hard-won gap in front. Five minutes later the other bus would pass on the inside, and the process would repeat itself.

I remember getting to Lijiāng and leafing through the travellers book in Pete's Café (when it was there), and coming across an entry from one poor bloke who had been in a minibus accident in the locality. The distillation of his experience yielded the tragic advice to 'sit at the back of the bus, so that when there is a collision you will have time to slow down before you hit the windscreen'.

Damian Harper

Chinese law requires drivers to announce their presence to cyclists (and any other living creature within a square kilometre), and for this they use a tweeter for preliminaries, a bugle or bullhorn if they get annoyed and an ear-wrenching airhorn when they're really stirred up.

While the roads and condition of the buses have improved in recent years, traffic is getting worse, making bus travel a rather slow means of transport. In a luxury coach on an expressway in Yúnnán or Sìchuān you can break 100km/h but in rural Guìzhōu you'll be lucky to average 25km/h. Much of the South-West is undergoing massive road construction and until it's finished traffic moves at a snail's pace. Things are slowed down further by Chinese driving techniques – drivers are loath to change gears and appear to prefer coming to an almost absolute standstill on a slope rather than changing from third into second. Petrol-saving ploys include getting up to the highest speed possible and then coasting to a near standstill, before starting the process again. Engines are switched off for stops of any kind, even if it's only a matter of seconds.

Costs & Classes

Bus travel generally works out to be comparable to hard-seat train travel in terms of expense. Compulsory insurance in northern Sìchuān province can push foreigner's prices up to almost triple the local price.

Most buses are government run and should have been sold for scrap decades ago. They are the cheapest and slowest way of travelling but sometimes there's no other choice.

On most popular routes, sleeper buses (wòpùchē) have been introduced – they are usually around double the price of a normal bus service. Many travellers swear by them, while others liken the experience to being locked in an ashtray for 12 hours. Some have reclining seats, while others even have two-tier bunks and a comfy duvet thrown in. You are expected to remove your shoes (sometimes there's a plastic bag provided for this) before taking your berth.

The main problem with these berths is the lack of luggage storage. Be careful with your valuables as you sleep, especially if you have a window berth. Sleeper routes popular with travellers include Kūnmíng-Lìjiāng (Y100),

Chéngdū-Kāngdìng (Y110) and Kūnmíng-Xīshuāngbǎnnà (Jǐnghóng, Y120).

On runs of over 12 hours where sleeper buses have not been introduced there should be an overnight stop, but this is not always the case.

Privately-owned minibuses (zhōngbā) are increasingly competing with public buses on medium-length routes. Although they're often a bit cramped, you always get a seat (or at least a knee to sit on) and they are faster than most government buses. If there's only one long-distance bus for your destination and it leaves at 5am you can often cobble together several minibus rides and even get there before the big bus. This also enables you to break your trip in interesting villages.

On the downside there are few fixed departures and you may have to wait some time for the minibus to fill up (to bursting point). If not enough people turn up, then the bus won't go. You may also have to bargain to get the Chinese price. Drivers will sometimes try to make you pay extra for bulky luggage.

On some rural routes you will also find microbuses, no bigger than a car and seating around seven. Examples of these can be found on the Ānshùn-Huángguǒshù and Táijiāng-Shīdòng (Guìzhōu) routes.

Some luxury coaches (háohuá dàbā) also ply popular routes, particularly in Yúnnán. Notable examples are the Chéngdū-Lèshān, Ānshùn-Guìyáng, Kūnmíng-Jǐnghóng, Kūnmíng-Dàlǐ and Kūnmíng-Lìjiāng routes. These are normally at least twice the price of the local bus but are worth it every now and then for the sake of your sanity (most are nonsmoking!). The only downside is that many of the coaches show low-grade action movies at high volume (it was only a question of time before China discovered video buses!). Coaches are generally listed on timetables by their make, either Volvo (wòěrwò) or Daewoo (dàyú). Iweco (yīwéikē) buses are high-speed, but cramped, white minibuses. Other services you might see advertised at bus stations include air-con buses (háoba) or 'wide-seat' class (kuānwèi).

Astronaut-type backpacks are a nightmare to stow on buses as there's little space under the seats, the overhead racks are hardly big enough to accommodate a loaf of bread, and there is sparse space in the aisles. If you intend to do a lot of bus travel, then travel light! In China, unlike other Asian countries, people do not ride on the roof, although luggage and even livestock is sometimes stowed there.

Buying Tickets

It's a good idea to book a seat the day before you want to travel. All seats are numbered and most bus stations are now computerised. You don't actually have a reservation until you've got a fully paid ticket in hand. While some hotels and travel agents book bus tickets, it's often easier and less error-prone to head for the bus station and do it yourself.

Bus stations are often large affairs with numerous ticket windows and waiting halls. Each destination has its specific ticket window. If you don't recognise the characters you'll just have to guess (and be redirected).

In northern Sìchuān you may be required to purchase local travel insurance. Ticket sellers won't sell you a ticket and drivers won't let you board the bus without it.

Some large towns have more than one bus station. One might serve destinations north, the other south. In smaller towns, where there are different stations or many through-buses, it can often be easiest to head out of town to the nearest junction and pick up the first bus that comes, though you stand less chance of getting a seat this way.

If you are exploring some wild and woolly minority areas it's worth bearing in mind that bus services to small towns normally only run to and from the county capital and often once a day, so you may have to overnight. Cross-county buses are much less frequent.

Local Chinese maps have a special symbol for a bus station, meant to resemble the steering wheel of the bus. The symbol is:

LPP

TRAIN

China's trains are small towns in themselves, with populations typically well over 1000. Although crowded, trains are the best way to get around in reasonable speed and comfort.

There are an estimated 68,000km of railway lines in China, with most built after 1949 from scratch, and new lines are still being laid. The industry is mind-bogglingly huge; between 1998 and the year 2000 over 1.1 million railway workers were laid off, and that was only from the railway's subsidiary businesses! New services expected to come into operation soon include the Kūnmíng-Xiàguān (Dàlǐ) and Kūnmíng-Nánníng lines.

The safety record of the railway system is good. Other than getting your luggage pinched or dying from shock when you see the toilets, there isn't much danger on trains. However, the Chinese have a habit of throwing rubbish out the windows even as the train moves through a station. Avoid standing too close to a passing train or sitting too close to an open window, lest you get hit by flying beer bottles or chicken bones.

Classes

In socialist China there are no classes; instead you have hard seat, hard sleeper, soft seat and soft sleeper.

Hard Seat Except on the trains that serve some of the branch or more obscure lines, hard seat *(yìngzuò)* is not in fact hard, but padded. However, it is hard on your sanity and you'll get little sleep on the upright seats. Since hard seat is the only thing the locals can afford, it's packed to the gills, the lights stay on all night, passengers spit on the floor and the carriage speakers endlessly drone news, weather, good tidings and music.

Hard seat is OK for a day trip, but most foreigners can't take more than five hours of it, although some have a threshold of 12 hours or even longer. A few brave, penniless souls have even been known to travel long distances this way – some roll out a mat on the floor under the seats and go to sleep on top of the gob and cigarette butts. Experienced hard-seat travellers always

position themselves upstream of Chinese babies, just in case.

As bad as it is, you should try to experience hard seat at least once, and the more crowded the better. This is China as it exists for the masses, a very different world from the glittering tourist hotels.

Hard Sleeper These are comfortable and only a fixed number of people are allowed in the sleeper carriage. The carriage is made up of doorless compartments with half a dozen bunks, or hard sleepers *(yìngwò)*, in three tiers and little foldaway seats by the windows. Sheets, pillows and blankets are provided and it does very nicely as a budget hotel. The best bunk to get is the middle berth *(zhōngpù)* since the lower berth *(xiàpù)* is invaded by all and sundry who use it as a seat during the day, while the top one has little headroom. The top berths *(shàngpù)* are also where the cigarette smoke floats about and it's close to the endless drone from the infernal loudspeakers.

Lights and speakers in hard sleeper go out at around 9.30pm to 10pm. Competition for hard sleepers has become keen in recent years, and you'll be lucky to get one on short notice.

Soft Seat On shorter journeys and in tourist *(lǚyóu)* class some trains have softseat *(ruǎnzuò)* carriages. The seats are comfortable and overcrowding is not permitted. Smoking is prohibited but if you want to smoke you can go out into the corridor between cars. You get free tea and sometimes even a packet of dried plums.

Soft seat costs about the same as hard sleeper and is well worth it. Unfortunately, soft-seat cars are a rarity. Some useful routes include Guìyáng-Zūnyì, Guìyáng-Liùpánshuǐ and Píngxiáng-Nánníng.

Soft Sleeper Luxury. Softies get the works, with four comfortable bunks in a closed compartment – complete with straps to keep the top-bunk fatso from falling off in the middle of the night, wood panelling, potted plants, lace curtains, teacup set, clean washrooms, carpets (so no spitting) and often air-con. As for those speakers, not only do you have a volume control, you can turn the bloody things off!

Soft sleeper *(ruǎnwò)* costs around twice as much as hard sleeper. It's comparatively easy to get soft sleeper because few ordinary Chinese can afford it. However, the growing class of nouveaux riches plus high-ranking cadres has upped the demand for soft sleepers, so you might wind up in hard seat no matter how much cash you have.

Travelling in soft sleeper should be experienced once – it gives you a good chance to meet the ruling class.

Reservations & Tickets

Buying hard-seat tickets at short notice (up to half an hour before departure) is usually no hassle, although you will not always be successful in getting a reserved seat. Buying a ticket for a sleeper can be more problematic.

Trains are graded according to the speed and this determines the price of tickets. Generally the fastest trains have a K in front of the number. Apart from this, the numbers don't really tell you much else about the train. As a general rule, the outbound and inbound trains have matching numbers; thus train Nos 207/208 divide into No 207 leaving Chéngdū and going to Kūnmíng, and No 208 leaving Kūnmíng and going to Chéngdū.

If you try to buy a sleeper ticket at the train station and the clerk just says *'meiyou'* ('not have') you'll have to seek the assistance of a travel agent. This can mean a government travel agency like China International Travel Service (CITS; Zhōngguó Guójì Lǚxíngshè), the travel booking desk in your hotel, or even the private travel agencies in towns such as Chéngdū or Yángshuò. You'll pay a service charge of perhaps Y20 to Y40, but it's probably worth it to avoid 30 hours in hard-seat hell.

Tickets for sleepers can easily be obtained in major cities, but not in quiet backwaters as they have no ticket allocation. There is a six- to 21-day, advance-purchase limit, depending on the station, presumably to prevent tickets being hoarded by scalpers. Still you will often find touts at stations offering tickets for popular routes. If you find there is no

choice but to buy your ticket this way make sure you at least check the train number, class, departure time, destination and seat or berth number. If you can't read the Chinese then get someone to check it for you before you hand over the cash. Ticket counterfeiting is not uncommon and you could be buying a worthless piece of cardboard.

You can buy tickets the night before departure or on the day of departure from the train station. Most stations are well run, with computers that spit out tickets fast and efficiently, resulting in queues that move quickly. Others are bedlam with formidable numbers of people scrumming around a postcard-sized, waist-height ticket window. In this case it helps to have the details written in Chinese.

Reserved tickets normally have a thin slip of paper stuck over them detailing the carriage and berth number. Computer tickets have their own format; still others come as a separate sheet of paper.

Hard-seat tickets bought on the same day will usually be unreserved – you get on board and try to find a seat. If there are no seats, you'll either have to stand, find a place for your bum among the peanut shells, cigarette butts and spittle or try to upgrade (see the separate entry below).

If you have a sleeper ticket the carriage attendant will take it from you and give you a metal or plastic chit – when your destination is close he or she will swap it back for the original ticket. Keep your ticket until you get through the barriers at the other end, as you'll need to show it there.

Getting Aboard Some large train stations require that luggage be x-rayed before entering the waiting area. The reason has less to do with terrorism than with the fact that China has to deal with people transporting huge quantities of explosive chemicals – there have been several disastrous explosions. Just about all train stations have left-luggage rooms *(jìcún chù)* where you can safely dump your bags for a few yuán.

As soon as the train pulls into the station, all hell breaks loose. Hoping to get a seat, hard-seat passengers with no reservation charge at the train, often pushing exiting passengers back inside. Some would-be travellers climb through the windows. Railway attendants – often female – try to keep order, sometimes using sticks or bamboo poles. To limit the chaos hard-seat passengers are not usually allowed onto the platform until the train has already pulled in.

If you have a reserved seat or sleeper, you can let the crowd fight it out for a while, then peacefully find your carriage and claim your rightful place. If you've got a soft-seat or soft-sleeper ticket you can even wait in a separate soft-class waiting room. If you don't have a reserved seat, you're going to have to join the fray. The sensible option is to head for either the very front or the very rear of the train. Most passengers attack the middle of the train – the part closest to the platform entrance gate.

On Board Food is available both on board and at stations. It's not gourmet but the prices are certainly reasonable. If the journey time is more than 12 hours then the train qualifies for a dining car, which is often located between the hard-seat and hard-sleeper/soft-sleeper carriages. Aside from the dining cars, railway staff regularly walk through the trains with pushcarts offering *miàn* (instant noodles), *miànbāo* (bread), *héfàn* (boxed rice lunches), *huǒtuǐ* (bologna sausage), *píjiǔ* (beer), *kuàng quán shuǐ* (mineral water) and *qìshuǐ* (soft drinks). After about 8pm when meals are over you can probably wander back into the dining car. The staff may want to get rid of you, but if you just sit down and have a beer it may be OK.

All classes except hard sleeper supply Thermoses of boiling water, which are refilled from urns at the ends of the hard-class sections. Hardened travellers will quickly unpack an enamel cup the size of a small basin and hang up a little face towel above their seat to wash their hands with. Toilets are generally locked in stations. On long trips the water often runs out.

If your train is an overnighter it's a good idea to pack your alarm clock, flip-flops and a bottle of water, easily accessible in your luggage. By the way, the little towels on top of your pillow are to protect the pillow, not to wash your face with. Wet wipes are a good idea as trains can be pretty dirty.

Upgrading If you get on the train with an unreserved seating ticket, you can seek out the conductor and upgrade *(bǔpiào)* yourself to a hard sleeper, soft seat or soft sleeper if there are any available. There are obvious risks involved (no sleepers left), but it is sometimes the only way to get a sleeper or even a seat. On some trains it's easy to do, but others are notoriously crowded, like the Kūnmíng-Chéngdū service. A lot of intermediary stations along the railway lines can't issue sleepers, making upgrading the only alternative to hard seat.

If the sleeper carriages are full then you may have to wait until someone gets off. That sleeper may only be available to you until the next major station that is allowed to issue sleepers, but you may be able to get several hours' sleep. The sleeper price will be calculated for the distance that you use it.

Another option is to head for the dining car where you can sometimes wangle a seat, depending on how busy things are. Sometimes the staff will let you sit for a few hours for a 'fee' of Y10 to Y20, other times you will have to buy dinner (up to Y40) or at the very least nurse a beer.

As far as foreigners are concerned, many railway staff in China are exceedingly polite and can be very helpful. The staff may bend over backwards to assist you, particularly if you smile, are friendly and look lost. Sometimes they'll invite you to sit with them or even give you their own train seats. Even when all the sleepers are supposedly full, they sometimes manage to find one for foreigners, so it pays to be nice. Unfortunately, many foreigners take out their frustration on the railway staff – this just makes it tough for all who follow.

Ticket Validity Tickets are valid for one to seven days, depending on the distance travelled. On a cardboard ticket the number of days is printed at the bottom left-hand corner. If you go 250km it's valid for two days; 500km, three days; 1000km, three days; 2000km, six days; and about 2500km, seven days.

If you miss your train, your ticket is not refundable. However, if you return your ticket at least two hours before departure, you are entitled to an 80% refund. If you are travelling two weeks before or after the Spring Festival, you must return your ticket at least six hours before departure for a 50% refund.

Timetables

There are paperback train timetables in Chinese, but nothing in English. No matter how fluent your Chinese, the timetables are so excruciatingly detailed that it's a drag working your way through them. Even the Chinese complain about this. Thinner versions listing the major trains can sometimes be bought at major train stations. Hotel reception desks and CITS offices have copies of the timetable for trains out of their city or town.

Costs

Calculation of train prices is a complex affair based on the length of the journey, speed of the train and possibly the relative position of the sun and moon. There are a few variables, such as air-con charges or whether a child occupies a berth or not, but nothing worth worrying about. The express surcharge is the same regardless of what class you use on the train.

Some sample fares for the fastest trains at time of research were Guìyáng-Kūnmíng (Y150 hard sleeper, Y309 soft sleeper), Kūnmíng-Chéngdū (Y256 hard sleeper, Y389 soft sleeper) and Guìlín-Kūnmíng (Y198 hard sleeper, Y309 soft sleeper).

CAR & MOTORCYCLE

For those who would like to tour China by car or motorbike, the news is bleak. Basically it's impossible unless you go with a large group – accompanied by the Public Security Bureau (PSB; Zhōu Gōngānjú) the whole way – apply for permits months in advance and pay through the nose for the privilege. It's not like India, where you can simply buy a motorbike and head off on your own.

Only resident foreigners may drive in China (either car or motorcycle), once they obtain a Chinese driver's licence. However, there are often restrictions on how far you can drive from your place of residence – the local PSB can inform you of the latest regulations.

On the other hand, it's easy enough to book a car with a driver. Travel agencies like CITS or even hotel booking desks can make the arrangements, though they generally ask excessive fees – the name of the game is to negotiate. One new company that claims to arrange self-drive tours of Yúnnán and Sìchuān is DriveinChina.com; check out its Web site at W www.drivein china.com or email at e ddiao@drivein china.com. If you can communicate in Chinese or find someone to translate, it's not particularly difficult to find a private taxi driver to take you wherever you like for less than half CITS rates.

Some taxis run along fixed routes for a fixed fare, for example Kāngdìng-Lúdíng in Sìchuān. The price is per seat and you'll have to wait for the other three seats to fill up unless you pay for them yourself. Shared taxis are twice the bus fare but are also twice as quick and twice as comfortable.

If you travel much around China, you'll periodically encounter road blocks where the police stop every vehicle and impose arbitrary fines for driving with sunglasses, driving without sunglasses, scratching your nose while driving etc. The fine must be paid on the spot or the vehicle will be impounded. Basically, these are fundraising events.

Rental

Tourists are not yet permitted to rent either cars or motorbikes in China. Rental companies do exist (Hertz has a branch in Shanghai), but none have offices in the South-West. In any case they are only for the domestic market or for foreigners armed with a Chinese driver's licence.

PASSENGER TRACTOR

Yes, that's right, tractors. In several places in rural Guìzhōu (for example, around Róngjiāng and Shīdòng) tractors run set routes between villages, pulling a cart equipped with seats – or not. They are not quick, not very comfortable and certainly not very safe, but sometimes they are your only option to an isolated village. Most seem to be driven by teenagers with a death wish, and few have fully mastered changing gear. Locals will often advise against using tractors.

BICYCLE

Probably the first time the Chinese saw a pneumatic-tyre bicycle was when a pair of globe-trotting Americans called Allen and Sachtleben bumbled into Beijing around 1891 after a three-year journey from Istanbul. They wrote a book about it called *Across Asia on a Bicycle*. The novelty was well received by the Qing court, and the boy-emperor Puyi was given to tearing around the Forbidden City on a bike.

Today there are over 300 million bikes in China, more than in any other country. The traditional Chinese bicycle and tricycle are workhorses, used to carry anything up to a 100kg slaughtered pig or a whole couch. Until very recently, Chinese bikes all looked the same – heavy, gearless monsters like the Flying Pigeon brand made out of black waterpipe. Although these are still the most popular design (because they last a long time and are relatively cheap), sleek new multi-geared models in a variety of colours are available. The Chinese are even having success in exporting these.

Most of South-West China is ideal for biking. Minority and rural areas are particularly rewarding, though normally pretty hilly.

In Western countries, travel agencies organising bicycle trips advertise in cycling magazines. Some are mentioned under Adventure Tours in the Organised Tours section of the Getting There & Away chapter. Bicycle clubs can contact CITS (or its competitors) for information about organising a trip.

Rental

There are established bicycle-hire shops in most traveller centres in South-West China, the best being at Yángshuò, Dàlǐ, Lìjiāng and Jǐnghóng. In touristy places like Yángshuò it's even possible to rent sharp-looking mountain bikes, but elsewhere it's the old black clunkers.

Most hire shops operate out of hotels popular with foreigners, but there are also many independent hire shops. Even in towns that don't see much tourist traffic there are often hire shops catering to Chinese who are passing through. Unfortunately these are rapidly disappearing as the increasingly affluent Chinese switch to 'modern' transport such as taxis.

Day hire, 24-hour hire and hire by the hour are usual options. You can hire for a stretch of several days, so touring is possible if the bike is in good condition. Rates for Westerners are typically Y2 per hour or Y10 to Y20 per day – the price depends more on competition than anything else. Some big hotels charge ridiculous rates, although this may get you a mountain bike.

If you hire over a long period you should be able to reduce the rate. Most hire places will ask you to leave a deposit of at least a couple of hundred yuán or some sort of ID. Sometimes they ask for your passport, which is asking a lot. It's wiser to leave some other form of ID, like a student card, driver's licence or expired passport.

If you're planning on staying in one place for more than about five weeks, it's probably cheaper to buy your own bike and either sell it or give it to a friend when you leave.

Before taking a bike, check the brakes (are there any?), get the tyres pumped up hard and make sure that none of the moving parts are about to fall off. Get the saddle raised for maximum leg power. It's also worth tying something on – a handkerchief, for example – to identify your bicycle amid the zillions at the bicycle parks. If something falls off or is stolen then you will be expected to pay for a new part. If this happens it's almost always cheaper to buy the new part yourself than to hand over cash.

A bike licence is obligatory for Chinese, but is not necessary for a foreigner. Bike repair shops are everywhere and repairs are cheap – from three máo to pump up your tyres to Y10 to fix a bent wheel rim. Overcharging of foreigners is common, so ask the price first.

Purchase

Some travellers have saved themselves the bother of bringing bikes across the border by buying mountain bikes or racers in China. Most department stores sell Flying Pigeons for around Y300 and cheap mountain bikes from about Y750.

In Hong Kong, Flying Ball Bicycle Shop (☎ 0852-2381 5919, e cflying@netvigator .com) at 201 Tung Choi St (near Prince Edward MTR station) in Mongkok is the place to go for both hardware and information about cycling in China.

Touring

The legalities of cycling from town to town are open to conjecture. There is absolutely no national law in China that prohibits foreigners from riding bicycles. That said, Chinese officials don't really understand why foreigners would want to bicycle around China and are suspicious of your motives. You shouldn't have any run-ins unless you are in a 'closed' area or are suspected of having come from a closed area.

One potential problem is finding accommodation en route. In most areas this isn't a problem as most towns or villages have at least one guesthouse, though it may be unsavoury. Out in the wilds of Sìchuān you may have to cycle for a couple of days between towns. Camping is possible but only in really remote areas. The trick is to select a couple of likely places about half an hour before sunset, keep pedalling and then backtrack so you can pull off the road at the chosen spot just after darkness falls.

One problem with Western bikes is that they attract a lot of attention. Another problem is the unavailability of spare parts. One Westerner brought a fold-up bicycle with him – but in most places it attracted so much attention that he had to give it to the locals to play with until the novelty wore off, and fold-up bikes just aren't practical for long-distance riding.

It's essential to have a kickstand for parking. A bell, headlight and reflector are good ideas. Make sure everything is bolted down, otherwise you'll invite theft. A cageless water bottle, even on a Chinese bike, attracts too much attention. Adhesive reflector strips get ripped off.

Hazards

It's difficult to miss the ubiquitous picture displays around Chinese cities exhibiting the gory remains of cyclists who didn't look where they were going and wound up looking like Y10 worth of fried dumplings.

Night riding is particularly hazardous. Many drivers in China only use their headlights to flash them on and off as a warning for cyclists up ahead to get out of the way. On country roads look out for tractors, which often have no headlights at all. Chinese bicycles are rarely equipped with lights.

Your fellow cyclists are another factor in the hazard equation. Most Chinese cyclists have little more than an abstract grasp of basic road courtesy and traffic rules. Be prepared for cyclists to suddenly swerve in front of you, to come hurtling out of a side road or even to head straight towards you against the flow of the traffic. This is not to mention situations where you yourself are the traffic hazard: Beware of the cyclist who spots you, glides by staring wide-mouthed, crashes into something in front and causes the traffic following to topple like tenpins.

Dogs, the enemy of cyclists the world over, are less of a problem in China than elsewhere but can be a real menace in Tibetan areas of Western Sìchuān and northeastern Yúnnán.

In most large towns and cities bicycles should be parked at designated places on the sidewalk. This will generally be a roped off enclosure, and bicycle-park attendants will give you a token when you park there; the charge is usually a few máo. If you don't use this service, you may return to find that your bike has been 'towed' away. Confiscated, illegally parked bicycles make their way to the police station. There will be a fine to retrieve it, though it shouldn't bankrupt you.

Bicycle theft does indeed exist. The bicycle parks with their attendants help prevent this, but keep your bike off the streets at night, or at least within the hotel gates. If the hotel has no grounds then take the bike up to your room. Most hired bicycles have a lock around the rear wheel, which can be prised open with a screwdriver in seconds. You can increase security by using a cable lock, widely available from shops in China, but your best bet is to bring along a secure lock from your home country.

Off the Road

Most travellers who bring bikes take at least a couple of breaks from the rigours of the road, during which they use some other means of transport. The best option is bus. It is generally no problem stowing bikes on the roof of buses and there is seldom a charge involved. Air and train transport is more problematic.

Bikes are not cheap to transport on trains; they can cost as much as a hard-seat fare. Boats are cheaper, if you can find one. Trains have quotas for the number of bikes they can transport. As a foreigner you will get preferential treatment in the luggage compartment and the bike will go on the first available train. But your bike won't arrive at the same time as you unless you send it on a couple of days in advance. At the other end it is held in storage for three days free, and then incurs a small charge.

The procedure for putting a bike on a train and retrieving it at the other end is as follows:

• Railway personnel would first like to see a train ticket for yourself (not entirely essential).
• Go to the baggage transport section of the station. Get a white slip and fill it out to get the two or three tags for registration. Then fill out a form (it's only in Chinese, but just fill it out in English) which reads: 'Number/to station x/send goods person/receive goods person/total number of goods/from station y'.
• Take the white slip to another counter, where you pay and are given a blue slip.
• At the other end (after delays of up to three days for transporting a bike) you present the blue slip, and get a white slip in return. This means your bike has arrived. The procedure could take from 20 minutes to an hour depending on who's around. If you lose that blue slip you'll have real trouble reclaiming your bike.

Chinese cyclists spend ages at stations mummifying their bicycles in cloth for transport. For the one scratch the bike will get, it's hardly worth going through this elaborate procedure.

The best bet for getting your bike on a bus is to get to the station early and put it on the roof. Strictly speaking, there shouldn't be a charge for this, but in practice the driver will generally try to get a few yuán out of you. You can generally bypass this by putting it on the roof and unloading it yourself. The driver won't like it, but you'll normally be allowed to proceed all the same.

Transporting your bike by plane can be expensive, but it's often less complicated than by train. Some cyclists have not been charged by CAAC; others have had to pay 1% of their fare per kilogram of excess weight.

HITCHING

Hitching is never entirely safe in any country in the world, and we don't recommend it. Travellers who decide to hitch should understand that they are taking a small but potentially serious risk. People who do choose to hitch will be safer if they travel in pairs and let someone know where they are planning to go.

Many people have hitchhiked in China, and some have been amazingly successful. It's not officially sanctioned and the same dangers that apply elsewhere in the world also apply in China. Exercise caution, and if you're in any doubt as to the intentions of your prospective driver, say no. A woman travelling alone would be wise to hitch with a male companion.

Hitching in China is rarely free, and passengers are expected to offer at least the equivalent bus fare. Some drivers might even ask for an unreasonable amount of money, so try to establish a figure early on in the ride to avoid problems later. Even when a price is agreed upon, don't be surprised if the driver raises it when you arrive at your destination and creates a big scene (with a big crowd) if you don't cough up the extra cash. Indeed, your driver may even pull this scam halfway through the trip, and if you don't pay up then you get kicked out in the middle of nowhere.

In other words, don't think of hitching as a means to save money – rarely will it be any cheaper than the bus. The main reason to do it is to get to isolated outposts where public transport is poor. There is, of course, some joy in meeting the locals this way, but communicating is certain to be a problem if you don't speak Chinese. The best rides in rural areas are on market days when truckloads of highlanders from the surrounding regions head into town for the monthly shop. In rural Guìzhōu hitching on passenger tractors is often the best way to get to small minority villages.

The surest way to get a lift is, like anywhere else, to head out to main roads on the outskirts of town. There are usually lots of trucks on the roads, and even postal trucks and army convoys are worth trying, though not on the roads to Tibet. There is no Chinese signal for hitching, so just try waving down the trucks. Unless you speak the local language, you'll need to have where you want to go written down in Chinese characters.

BOAT
For better or worse, China's boats are fast disappearing. Many services have been cancelled – victims of improved bus and air transport. Safety is a particular concern on Chinese ferries, which are often poorly maintained and overcrowded. In June 2000, 170 people were killed when two ferries capsized in separate incidents in Sìchuān. In November of the same year 280 people were killed in a ferry accident in Shāndōng.

The best-known river trip is the fantastic three-day boat ride along the Yangzi River from Chóngqìng to Wǔhàn (Y684/320/229 2nd/3rd/4th class). The six-hour Lí Jiāng boat trip from Guìlín to Yángshuò (Y460 or Y420) is also popular. Less trafficked are river trips on the Wǔyáng Hé, around Zhènyuán and Shībǐng in Guìzhōu.

The Guǎngzhōu to Wúzhōu route along the Xī Hé (West River) is popular with low-budget travellers as it is the cheapest way to get from Guǎngzhōu to Guìlín and Yángshuò, disembarking at Wúzhōu and then continuing on by bus to Guìlín or Yángshuò.

There are also ferries in summer between Lèshān and Yíbīn, Yíbīn and Luzhou, Luzhou and Chóngqìng and Chóngqìng and Chìshuǐ (Guìzhōu). One day there may even be passenger ferries from Yúnnán down the Mekong to Laos and Thailand.

For more details on these services see the relevant destination sections of this book.

LOCAL TRANSPORT
Long-distance transport in China is not really a problem – the dilemma occurs when you finally make it to your destination. The bicycle is the key to getting around Chinese cities and if you don't have one, life is more difficult. Walking is not usually recommended, since Chinese cities tend to be very spread out.

Bus
Apart from bikes, buses (gōnggòng qìchē) are the most common means of getting around in the cities. Services are fairly extensive and the buses go to most places you want to go. The problem is that they are almost always packed. If an empty bus pulls in at a popular stop then a fierce battle for seats ensues. Even more aggravating is the slow traffic. You just have to be patient, never expect anything to move rapidly, and allow lots of time to get to the station to catch your train.

Another problem is that, in the big cities at least, bus routes are fiendishly complicated. Furthermore, minibuses also use the same numbers as the buses but follow different routes. One consolation is that buses are cheap – rarely more than five máo for old-style buses or Y1 for newer versions. Minibuses are more expensive (Y1 to Y2) and faster, but you'll spend more time hanging around waiting for passengers.

Good maps of Chinese cities and bus routes are readily available and are often sold by hawkers outside the train stations. When you get on a bus, point to where you want to go on the map and the conductor (who is seated near the door) will sell you the right ticket. They usually tell you where to get off, provided they remember. Most city buses have separate entrances for getting on (the front) and off (the back).

Taxi

Taxis (chūzūqìchē) cruise the streets in most large cities, but elsewhere they may simply congregate at likely spots (such as bus stations) and hassle every foreigner who walks past. Rather than speak to you in Chinese, the drivers typically grab foreigners by the arm, get all agitated and start grunting 'Laowai, OK, hey, ooh, aaahh, arrghh' and so on. This seems to be a special dialect peculiar to taxi drivers.

You can always summon a taxi from the tourist hotels, which sometimes have separate booking desks. You can hire them for a single trip or on a daily basis – the latter is worth considering if there's a group of people who can split the cost.

Most taxis have meters and increasing numbers of drivers stick to them, especially in large cities. In some towns meters only get switched on by accident. In this case you should negotiate the fare before you get into the taxi, and don't be afraid to bargain (though keep it friendly as nastiness on your part will result in a higher price). Don't be surprised if the driver attempts to change the price when you arrive, claiming that you 'misunderstood' what he said. If you want to get nasty, this is the time to do it. If your spoken Chinese is less than perfect, write the price down clearly and make sure the driver agrees at the start to avoid 'misunderstandings' later.

Some cities have a set rate for a ride anywhere in the city, normally between Y5 and Y10. These rates can be good value if there are a couple of you. Some taxi routes also have set fares.

Most Chinese cities impose limitations on the number of passengers that a taxi can carry. The limit is usually four and drivers are normally unwilling to break the rules and risk trouble with the police.

Motorcycle Taxi

The deal for a motorcycle taxi (chūzū mótuōchē) is that you get a ride on the back of someone's motorcycle for about half the price of what a regular four-wheeled taxi would charge. If you turn a blind eye to the hazards, this is a quick and, sometimes, cheap way of getting around. It's required that you wear a helmet – the driver will provide one. Obviously, there is no meter, so fares must be agreed in advance.

Motor-tricycle

The motor-tricycle (sānlún mótuōchē), or motorised rickshaw, is an enclosed three-wheeled vehicle with a driver at the front, a small motorbike engine below and seats for two passengers behind. They congregate outside the train and bus stations in larger towns and cities. Some of these vehicles have trays at the rear with bench seats along the sides so that four or more people (plus a few chickens) can all be accommodated. They are usually priced somewhere between a taxi and a pedicab.

Pedicab

A pedicab (sānlúnchē) is a pedal-powered tricycle with a seat to carry passengers. Chinese pedicabs have the driver in front and passenger seats in the back, the opposite of some countries (Vietnam, for example).

Pedicabs are gradually disappearing in China, victims of the infernal combustion engine. However, pedicabs congregate outside train and bus stations or hotels in many parts of China. In a few places, pedicabs cruise the streets in large numbers and are surprisingly cheap (for example in Yíbīn and Lèshān).

Unfortunately, many drivers are aggressive. A reasonable fare will often be quoted, but when you arrive at your destination it'll be multiplied by 10. So if you're quoted a fare of Y5 it becomes Y50, and if you're quoted Y50 it becomes Y500. Another tactic is to quote you a price like Y10 and then demand US$10 – the driver claims that you 'misunderstood'.

The best bet is to write down a price (be sure to specify Renminbi, not US dollars), get the driver to agree three or four times and sign it, and then when he tries to multiply it by 10, hand over the exact change and walk away. It's worse if there are two of them, so never get into a pedicab if the driver wants his 'brother' to come along for the ride (a common strategy).

The situation is less likely to turn ugly when the driver is female, but women pedicab drivers are very rare indeed. And if she happens to have a 'brother' who wants to come along for the ride, find another driver. In many cases, a taxi works out to be cheaper than a pedicab because the chances of being ripped off are much lower.

ORGANISED LOCAL TOURS

Some of the one-day tours are reasonably priced and might be worth the cost as they can save you a lot of trouble. Some remote spots are difficult to reach and a tour might well be your only option.

Some tours are very informal and even popular with budget travellers. Examples of these include tours from Guìyáng to Huángguǒshù Falls, from Chéngdū to the Panda Research Centre and from Dàlǐ to sites around Ěrhǎi Lake.

Another low-cost option is to go on a tour with a local Chinese group. The tour bus could be an old rattletrap and you'll get to visit a few souvenir shops (which invariably pay under-the-table commissions to the bus drivers), but these tours can be interesting if you keep a sense of humour about it. Don't expect the guides to speak anything but Chinese.

Sometimes the buses will whiz through what Westerners would consider interesting spots and make long stops at dull places for the requisite photo sessions. You might have difficulty getting a ticket if your Chinese isn't good and they think you're too much trouble. The Chinese tours are often booked through hotel service desks or from private travel agencies. In some cases, there is an established tour bus meeting spot – you just roll up in the morning and hop on board.

CITS

The China International Travel Service (CITS; Zhōngguó Guójì Lǚxíngshè) deals with China's foreign tourist hordes, and mainly organises travel arrangements for group tours. CITS existed as far back as 1954, when there were few customers; now it's inundated with a couple of hundred thousand foreign tourists a year. Sadly, after 40 years of being in business, CITS has still not got its act totally together.

Nowadays, many solo travellers make their way around China without ever having to deal with CITS. In many remote regions CITS does not offer much in the way of services. In other places, it may sell hard-to-get-hold-of train tickets or perhaps provide tours of rural villages or factories. It really depends on where you are.

There will usually be a small service charge of Y20 to Y40 added to the price of train, boat or plane tickets purchased through CITS.

CITS is a frequent target of ire for all kinds of reasons: rudeness, inefficiency, laziness and even fraud. Bear in mind, however, that service varies enormously from office to office. The staff at the Guìyáng, Xīchàng and Nánníng offices, for example, are pleasant, knowledgeable and helpful. Expect the worst, but be prepared to be pleasantly surprised.

One useful recent development has been the introduction of Family and Individual Traveller (FIT) departments in a few CITS branches, specifically aimed at independent travellers' needs.

CTS

China Travel Service (CTS; Zhōngguó Lǚxíngshè) was originally set up to handle tourists from Hong Kong, Macau and Taiwan as well as foreign nationals of Chinese descent (Overseas Chinese). These days your gene pool and nationality make little difference – CTS has now become a keen competitor with CITS.

Many foreigners use the CTS offices in Hong Kong and Macau to obtain visas and book trains, planes, hovercraft and other transport to China. CTS can sometimes get you a better deal on hotels booked through its office than you could obtain on your own (of course, this doesn't apply to backpackers dormitories).

CYTS

The name China Youth Travel Service (CYTS; Zhōngguó Qīngnián Lǚxíngshè) implies that this is a student organisation, but these days CYTS performs essentially the same services as CITS and CTS. Being a small organisation, CYTS seems to try harder to compete against the big league. This can mean better service, but not necessarily lower prices.

Private Travel Agencies

There are a few private agencies in the South-West, mostly in travellers' centres such as Chéngdū, Dàlǐ or Yángshuò. They are usually small, friendly operations, happy to help backpackers with information. They can often book train and long-distance bus tickets and can sometimes arrange Yangzi cruise tickets, guides, transport, horses etc at more competitive prices than CITS. The best ones offer trips to the opera, tai chi lessons and the like. As they are in backpacker centres it's relatively easy to get a small group together to share costs. See individual destination sections for details.

Guăngxī 广西

Guăngxī at a Glance

Guăngxī p179

Lóngjĭ Tītián p234
Lóngshèng p233
Guìlín p214
Yángshuò p226
Liŭzhōu p240
Around Yángshuò p229
Bǎisè p202
Wúzhōu p210
Guìpíng p207
Nánníng p184
Běihǎi p192

Area: 236,300 sq km

Population: 47.2 million

Capital: Nánníng

Highlights

- Yángshuò, a backpackers' Mecca, famous for its gorgeous scenery and laid-back rural atmosphere

- Lóngshèng, Sānjiāng and Róngshuĭ, mountain towns and gateways to minority villages, spectacularly terraced rice fields and beautiful scenery

- Běihǎi, a sleepy seaside town boasting white sand beaches that attract sun-seeking Chinese tourists

- Guìlín, one of China's favourite tourist cities, famous for its karst scenery and the Lí Jiāng boat cruise

- Guìpíng's Xīshān Park, one of Guăngxī's favourite mountain retreats; there's also Dragon Pool National Forest Park in the area, and nearby is Jīntián, birthplace of the leader of the Taiping Rebellion

- Détiān Waterfall, straddling the Sino-Vietnamese border, the world's second-largest transnational cascade

Guăngxī's most famous attraction is Gùilín, perhaps the most eulogised of all Chinese sightseeing areas. While most travellers spend some time in the nearby town of Yángshuò, few make it to other parts of Guăngxī, and the province remains mostly unexplored. For the adventurous, there are minority regions in the northern areas bordering Guìzhōu, and less-touristed karst rock formations throughout the province, but most notably around the Zuǒ Jiāng, and Língyún and Jìngxī regions. Guăngxī also has an easily accessible border crossing with Vietnam near the town of Píngxiáng.

Guăngxī first came under Chinese sovereignty when a Qin-dynasty army conquered what is now Guăngdōng province and eastern Guăngxī. Like the rest of the South-West, the region had never been firmly under Chinese control; the eastern and southern parts of Guăngxī were occupied by the Chinese, while a system of indirect rule through chieftains of the aboriginal Zhuang prevailed in the west.

The situation was complicated in the northern regions by the Yao (Mien) and Miáo (Hmong) tribespeople, who had been driven there from their homelands in Húnán and Jiāngxī by the advance of Han Chinese settlers. Unlike the Zhuang, who easily assimilated Chinese customs, the Yao and Miáo remained in the hill regions, and were often cruelly oppressed by the Han. The tribes and the Han were involved in continuous conflicts. In the 1830s there was a major uprising, and another coincided with the Taiping Rebellion, which began in Guăngxī.

Today the Zhuang are China's largest minority, with well over 15 million people concentrated in Guăngxī. In 1955 Guăngxī province was reconstituted as the Guăngxī Zhuang Autonomous Region. The Zhuang are, however, virtually indistinguishable from the Han Chinese, the last outward vestige of their original identity being their linguistic links with the Thai people. Besides the Zhuang, Miáo and Yao minorities,

GUĂNGXĪ 广西

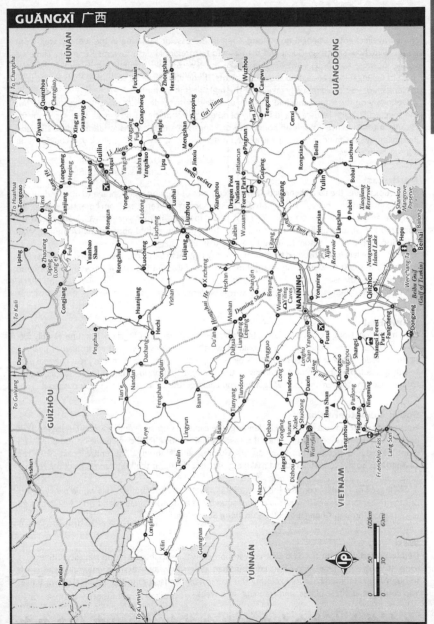

GUĂNGXĪ

Suggested Itineraries

Most travellers enter Guǎngxī from Hong Kong in the east or Kūnmíng in the west. A well-worn path is Wúzhōu-Yángshuò-Gùilín and then a mad transregional dash towards Kūnmíng. There's a whole lot more out there, however, if you take the time to poke around. Not many travellers remain in Guǎngxī long enough to see all the sights; if you choose to do so, without too long a spell in Yángshuò, you could leisurely take in all the highlights in a month.

Definitely on the list is **Yángshuò**. Yes, it's unbelievably crowded with foreigners in summer, but the spectacular karst landscape and friendly people in surrounding villages make this place tops for cycling in China. Since it's only an hour north of Yángshuò and is a transportation hub, **Gùilín** and its similarly world-famous landscape is also considered a must-see. With a week you could take in a lot in both places.

North-East

Most books cover the **Lóngshèng** and **Sānjiāng** counties of the north-east, home to outstanding minority cultures. Lóngshèng is also famous for its spectacular rice terraces. From here, travellers often take the seriously low-budget route into Guìzhōu. However, if your goal isn't Guìyáng, head for Lóngshèng, Sānjiāng, and ultimately bend south to **Róngshuǐ**, a third node on the Dong and Miáo minority-culture route, before heading back to Liǔzhōu or Gùilín.

Other travellers have absorbed their fill of minority culture in Sānjiāng, and returned to Lóngshèng to catch a bus east to **Zīyuán** for river rafting and waterfalls. On the return trip you might stop in **Xīng'ān** to see the Ling Canal.

Either itinerary requires a minimum of a week, preferably 10 days.

South-East

Coming in from Hong Kong via **Wúzhōu**, travellers generally head for Yángshuò. Don't necessarily forsake Wúzhōu, a time-locked town that could be worth a day or even two. Then, instead of heading north, consider hopping on a bus west to explore **Guìpíng**'s nearby mountain and great national park – with a side trip to the site of the genesis of the Taiping Rebellion in **Jīntián** – before looping north through Liǔzhōu, Gùilín and then Yángshuò. You could do this all in one week if you pushed it.

South & Southern Coast

Here's the neglected part of Guǎngxī. **Nánníng**, the capital, is up and coming and often leaves travellers with a positive impression. From the east, **Běihǎi**, at roughly the midpoint on the province's coast, is easy to get to from Wúzhōu via Guìpíng and Nánníng. The entire coast from the Guǎngdōng border to Vietnam could make a great sunbelt trip, if the Vietnamese relax the regulations a little.

Coming from Yúnnán, consider the Nánkūn Railway directly to Nánníng. This would give you lots of time to explore the coast. You could even squeeze in a trip to **Hǎinán Island** from Běihǎi and go for a traipse through **Chóngzuǒ** to the **Zuǒ Jiāng Scenic Area**.

West

Détiān Waterfall, along the Sino-Vietnamese border, will undoubtedly be on travellers' itineraries soon. If you've got time, stop off at **Lónghú Shān** along the way. After the waterfall, head north through **Jìngxī** (a good base for exploring the scenic karst landscape) to the historical city of **Bǎisè**. You could see all these places, and Nánníng, in a week.

Guǎngxī is home to smaller numbers of Dong, Maonan, Mulao, Jing (Vietnamese Gin) and Yi peoples. Until very recently, 75% of Guǎngxī's population was non-Han.

China's first canal was built in Guǎngxī during the Qin dynasty, but the scattered Han were unable use it for economic advantage and the province remained comparatively poor until the 20th century. The first attempts at modernising Guǎngxī were made in 1926–27 when the 'Guǎngxī Clique' (the main opposition to Chiang Kaishek within the Kuomintang) controlled much of Guǎngdōng, Húnán, Guǎngxī and Húběi. After the outbreak of war with Japan, the province was the scene of major battles and substantial destruction.

Despite improvements in the quality of life in Guǎngxī during the past few years, the province remains one of China's less affluent, though you might be forgiven for not realising this if you only visit Nánníng, Liǔzhōu, Wúzhōu and Gùilín. In these cities industry, trade, tourism and foreign investment have brought great changes. This is especially so since the Chinese government embarked on a 'develop the west program', which has resulted in large public works expenditure on roads, communications, water conservancy and housing.

FESTIVALS

Numerous festivals are celebrated by the minorities of Guǎngxī, particularly the Dong, Yao and Miáo. These take place according to the lunar calendar and some of the best areas to see them include the villages around Sānjiāng and Róngshuǐ (see these sections for more details).

Festivals popular with foreign and local tourists alike include the many Firecracker Festivals, which are spread throughout the year; festivals based around the *lusheng* (traditional bamboo instrument); Dragon-Boat and Rocket festivals; and various singing festivals. Travellers may wish to avoid the bullfighting, horse-fighting and bird-fighting festivals.

In recent years many of these festivals have been adopted by the tourism authorities and moved to Nánníng to coincide with the annual Festival of Folk Songs and Folk Arts held in November. Even some within China are starting to question the authenticity and legitimacy of many of these tourism-culture events. One academic criticised these urban re-enactment festivals as a 'disjointed mosaic' of once 'time-honoured traditional customs'. Furthermore, fake cliff inscriptions and misrepresentations of local folk tales and performances have also been witnessed throughout the province. One cannot be too critical, however, when considering the incredible events China has experienced over the past 50 years. It can only be hoped that the pursuit of cultural tourism will become more sensitive in the future and assist in the preservation of the rich and diverse cultures inhabiting the province.

NÁNNÍNG 南宁

☎ 0771 • pop 1.3 million

Nánníng is one of those provincial centres that provide an insight into just how fast China is developing. The country's new affluence leaps out at the visitor at every turn: New department stores are brimming with electronic goods and fashionable clothes, and many of the old backpackers' stand-bys have transformed themselves into upmarket retreats for well-heeled tour groups or overseas Chinese investors. In recent years, most of the city's main streets and river banks have been beautifully landscaped and restored. The local promotional slogan is, appropriately, 'A city half of buildings and half of trees'. Nánníng is an interesting place to walk around and an important transit point for travellers moving on to Vietnam. You can even arrange a Vietnamese visa here.

The area around Nánníng was populated early on by the Baiyue, progenitors of the Zhuang. Nánníng's settlement and first serious development occurred between the Qin and Han dynasties, with the Jinxing prefecture established simultaneously with the Eastern Jin (AD 318). Nánníng was effectively a mere backwater market town at the start of the 20th century. From the 1920s it gained increasing importance, along with Bǎisè, as an operations base for the growing communist movement, and has become the

Festivals in Guǎngxī

festival	location	lunar date	2002	2003
(The following events occur in the vicinity of Sānjiāng.)				
Bamboo Instrument Competition	Sānjiāng/Dùtóng	1st of 1st	12 Feb	1 Feb
Firecracker & Opera Festivals	Chéngyáng	7th of 1st	18 Feb	7 Feb
	Méilín	2nd of 2nd	15 Mar	4 Mar
	Dōujiāng	15th of 2nd	28 Mar	17 Mar
	Fùlù/Gǔyí	3rd of 3rd	15 Apr	4 Apr
	Shāyi'	4th of 3rd	16 Apr	5 Apr
Dragon Boat Festival	Lǎobǎo	13th of 5th	23 June	12 June
Bullfighting	Pínglíu/Bāxié	15-16th of 6th	24-25 Jul	14-15 Jul
Firecracker Festival	Línxī	26th of 10th	30 Nov	19 Nov
(The following festivals occur in the vicinity of Róngshuǐ.)				
Bamboo Instrument Festival	Róngshuǐ	13th of 1st	24 Feb	13 Feb
Ancient Dragon Hill Festival	Xiāngfén	16th of 1st	27 Feb	16 Feb
Mangge Festival	Ānchuí	17th of 1st	28 Feb	17 Feb
Firecracker Festival	Róngshuǐ/Dòngtóu	2nd of 2nd	15 Mar	4 Mar
	Hémù	24th of 4th	4 Jun	24 May
Dragon Pavilion Songfest	Lóngtíng	3rd of 3rd	15 Apr	4 Apr
New Tree Festival	Yuànbǎo Shān	6th of 6th	15 Jul	5 Jul
Horse-fighting Festival	Róngshuǐ	6th of 6th	15 Jul	5 Jul

NB *Festival dates are subject to change – check before you head off for one.*

capital of Guǎngxī. Apart from the urban expansion the post-1949 railway-construction boom induced in the South-West, Nánníng became an important staging post for shipping arms to Vietnam in the 1960s and 1970s. It's now a centre for the thriving border trade that has sprung from Běijīng's increasingly friendly ties with Hanoi.

The train line to the border town of Píngxiáng was built in 1952, and was extended to Hanoi, giving Vietnam a lifeline to China. The link was cut in 1979 with the Chinese invasion of Vietnam. Today the line is open again, and it is already possible, with the appropriate paperwork, to travel to Píngxiáng by train, cross the Vietnam border and continue by train or bus to Hanoi from Lang Son just over the border.

The population of Nánníng is more than 64% Zhuang, though for the most part it is impossible to distinguish them from their Han compatriots. Over 30 minority groups are represented in the city and its surroundings. The only colourful minorities you're likely to encounter in town are the occasional Miáo or Dong selling silver bracelets and earrings on the overhead pedestrian passes near the train station.

Orientation

Nánníng's grids require only a few blocks to work out. In the north are the bus and train stations. The main artery from there – Chaoyang Lu – runs roughly north-south towards the Yōng Jiāng, which bisects the city. Halfway down Chaoyang Lu is Cháoyáng Garden (*Cháoyáng Huāyuán*), essentially the geographic centre of town. This is a good place for people-watching and for bus connections to scenic sights, like Lónghú Shān, Dàmíng Shān, Qīngxiù Shān and Liángfèng Jiāng. Just before the river Chaoyang Lu splits into Jiangnan Lu, which heads over the Yōng Jiāng Bridge, and

2004	2005	2006
22 Jan	9 Feb	30 Jan
28 Jan	15 Feb	5 Feb
21 Feb	11 Mar	1 Mar
5 Mar	24 Mar	14 Mar
21 Apr	11 Apr	31 Mar
22 Apr	12 Apr	1 Apr
30 Jun	19 Jun	8 Jun
31 Jul-1 Aug	20-21 Jul	10-11 Jul
8 Dec	27 Nov	16 Dec
3 Feb	21 Feb	11 Feb
6 Feb	24 Feb	14 Feb
7 Feb	25 Feb	15 feb
21 Feb	11 Mar	1 Mar
11 Jun	31 May	21 May
21 Apr	11 Apr	31 Mar
22 Jul	11 Jul	1 Jul
22 Jul	11 Jul	1 Jul

Minzu Dadao, which heads east towards the Bank of China and the provincial museum.

Maps Nánníng city maps are available at shops and stalls in the train and bus stations.

Information
Tourist Office The China International Travel Service office (CITS; ☎ 280 4960) is at 40 Xinmin Lu. The new Family and Individual Traveller (FIT) department on the 2nd level is good news. The English-speaking staff is friendly, helpful and, perhaps best of all, can help you get your hands on a Vietnam visa. FIT also offers five-day individual or group tours to Hanoi and Haiphong, and a nine-day tour that takes in Saigon as well. The office is open 8.30am to noon and 2.30pm to 5pm weekdays.

Vietnam Visas The staff at the FIT department can set you up with a one-month visa

for Y650. Whereas in Hong Kong more money means a quicker visa, in Nánníng you will have to wait 10 – yes, that's 10 – working days. It is important to note that if you only have a single-entry visa and would like to return to China, then you will need to apply for a re-entry Chinese visa from the PSB.

PSB The Foreign Affairs office of the Public Security Bureau (PSB; ☎ 280 4530) is to the left of the entrance of the main building on the northern corner of the intersection of Chaoyang Lu and Minzu Dadao. It's open 8am to noon and 2.30pm to 5pm Monday to Thursday, 8am to noon only on Friday.

Money The main Bank of China is on Minzu Dadao, just east of the PSB. This is the place to change travellers cheques. The bank is open 8am to 6pm daily.

Post & Telecommunications Opposite the main Bank of China, the main post office is open 8.30am to 11pm daily. You can make international telephone calls and send faxes from the main post office. There are plans to set up an Internet cafe on the 2nd floor.

The most convenient place to surf the Web and check your email is on the 5th level of the Nánníng Department Store (Bǎihuò Dàlòu). China Telecom has an Internet bar here and charges Y10 per hour.

Bookshops Xīnhuá Bookshop on Xinhua Lu is one of the largest in China, with four levels jam-packed with books. The entrance resembles an airport hangar.

Guǎngxī Provincial Museum
广西省博物馆 Guǎngxī Shěng Bówùguǎn
On Minzu Dadao, the museum sits within the larger National Minorities Cultural Relics Park. Although dark and decaying, the museum offers an interesting insight into the highlights of Guǎngxī's rich history and culture. It features a wealth of minority costumes and artefacts, and one of the most exhaustive collections of Dong bronze drums in the world, including the largest one in existence. A third hall on the 2nd level usually exhibits a more contemporary

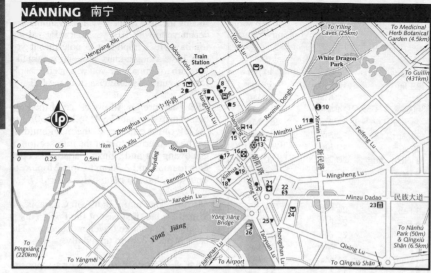

NÁNNÍNG 南宁

PLACES TO STAY

2 Tiědào Fàndiàn
  铁道饭店
3 Yíngbīn Fàndiàn
  迎宾饭店
5 Nánfāng Dàjiǔdiàn
  南方大酒店
8 Yínhé Dàjiǔdiàn
  银河大酒店
11 Xiángyún Dàjiǔdiàn
  翔云大酒店

PLACES TO EAT

4 Hángzhōu Lù
  Fruit Market;
  Row of Restaurants
  杭州路水果市场和餐厅
15 Canine Cuisine District
  狗肉区
18 Muslim Restaurant
  清真饭店
25 Food Street
  夜市

OTHER

1 Post Office
  邮局
6 Main Bus Station
  南宁客运总站
7 CAAC
  中国民航
9 Nánníng Passenger
  Centre
  南宁客运中心
10 CITS (FIT)
  中国国际旅行社
12 Cháoyáng Gardens
  Bus Stop
  朝阳花园
13 Cháoyáng Gardens
  朝阳花园
14 Bus to Yangmei
16 Nánníng Department
  Store;
  Internet Bar
  南宁百货大楼
  网吧

17 Night Market
  Area
  夜市
19 Xinhua
  Bookshop
  新华书店
20 Bicycle
  Rental
  出租单车
21 PSB
  公安局
22 Bank of
  China
  中国银行
23 Guǎngxī
  Provincial
  Museum
  广西省博物馆
24 Main Post
  Office
  电信大楼
26 Ferry Dock
  南宁客运码头

display. In the recent past, this has included an extraordinarily graphic exhibition on opium and its dangers to society and, less disturbing, a scenic photo collection.

In the tree-filled rear garden sit several full-size examples of Dong and Miáo houses and a nail-less bridge, complete with pond and an enormous version of a Dong drum.

The museum is a quiet, relaxing break from the hectic city streets. There are some English descriptions or you may chance upon one of the modest English-speaking guides. To get there, walk or take a No 6 bus. Opening hours are 8.30am to 12pm and 3pm to 6.30pm daily. Admission is Y8.

White Dragon Park
白龙公园 **Báilóng Gōngyuán**

Also known as Renmin Park, the park has now reverted to its old name, White Dragon. It's a pleasant enough place for a stroll, with a lake, a couple of pagodas, a restaurant and boat hire. Close to the main entrance on Xinmin Lu, is a flight of stairs leading up Wangxian Slope and to the remains of a fort. A viewing platform, complete with funny mirrors and an old cannon, gives a fairly decent view of the city. More interesting is the botanical garden, which features some rare herbs, exotic flowers, a hothouse with local flower varieties, and the requisite 1000-year-old banyan tree. By the lake is a restaurant specialising in chafing dish (a variant of hotpot). Entry is Y3.

Guǎngxī Medicinal Herb Botanical Garden 广西药用植物园
Guǎngxī Yàoyòng Zhíwùyuán

On the far-eastern outskirts of town, this fascinating garden is one of the largest of its kind in China, with over 2400 species of medicinal plants (Guǎngxī has more than 5000 species). If you're lucky enough to tag along with one of the centre's few English guides, or you can read Chinese, then you'll be impressed. Entry is Y5. It takes about 30 minutes to get there on bus No 101 or 102 from Cháoyáng Garden.

Qīngxiù Shān Park 清秀山风景区

This largish 'scenic area' to the south-west of Nánníng on the Yōng Jiāng is full of lakes, ponds, pavilions, cable cars, viewing platforms and tour groups. A favourite summer retreat since the Sui and Tang dynasties, the park offers verdant woods, springs and landscaped gardens with modest but scenic peaks of up to 180m that can be easily scaled.

Local bus No 10 goes to the park, but you still have a fair walk to the entrance. Buses depart when full from the northern side of Cháoyáng Garden. It cost Y3 to the front gate or Y11 into the park including admission.

Dragon Boat Races

As in other parts of the South-West (and Guǎngdōng and Macau), Nánníng has dragon boat races on the fifth day of the fifth lunar month (sometime in June), when large numbers of sightseers cheer the decorated rowing vessels along the Yōng Jiāng. The rowers pull to a steady cadence of drum beats maintained by a crew member at one end of the boat.

Organised Tours

Boats depart at 9.30am, and occasionally at 9.30pm, from a pier off Linjiang Lu, south of the Yōng Jiāng Bridge for two-hour river tours (Y30). The pier is at the head of a lovely new riverside walk with river-view teahouses and an excellent 500m-long mural depicting Guǎngxī's history and attractions.

Special Events

If you arrive in Nánníng during November, be sure to check out the **Nánníng International Festival of Folk Songs and Folk Arts.** For one whole week, the city explodes with colour, song and dance. The main attraction is the profusion of singers in colourful traditional attire and the incredible variety of sounds. Usually there are representatives from at least 24 different Guǎngxī minorities, as well as groups from other provinces and even overseas. The festival has been held annually since 1993 in Nánhú Park.

If you are worried that this is just another exploited-minority performance, then just allow the organisers to explain, 'They sang their melodies with singers from other nationalities and countries to woo tourists and investors'. If you miss the festival, then don't despair as you may be fortunate enough to encounter one of the many weddings, birth ceremonies, funerals and harvest festivals that take place throughout the province. For more festival details check with CITS.

Places to Stay – Budget

Nánníng is getting expensive, and most hotels are pricing themselves out of the backpacker market, but there are still a few cheap picks around the train station. However, many travellers may find the noise factor too much.

Top choice is the well-run, friendly *Tiĕdào Fàndiàn (Railway Hotel; ☎ 243 8600, fax 242 2572, 84 Zhonghua Lu)*, just west of the train station. It has beds from Y25 or Y45 in a spiffy double with bath.

Opposite the station is *Yíngbīn Fàndiàn (☎ 241 2299, ext 3688, e yingbin@public .info.gx.cn)*, probably the cheapest place open to foreigners, with basic beds in dorms from Y18 and doubles starting at Y28; for a splurge, the Y80 singles/doubles are quite reasonable. There's no English sign for this place and it looks a bit shabby, but it is clean and friendly all the same. The hotel also produces a useful tourist map with some English.

Places to Stay – Mid-Range & Top End

For Y150 and up, there are more options. In the train-station area, *Nánfāng Dàjiŭdiàn (☎ 243 1662, fax 242 1599, e nanfang@nn .col.com.cn)* is a good choice with rooms often discounted by 50%. Discounted twins are Y138 and Y154 and doubles are Y254, although you would be better off going for the luxury twins at Y252.

Nearby, *Yínhé Dàjiŭdian (Milky Way Hotel; ☎ 243 8223, ext 4001, fax 242 0303)* has fairly comfortable doubles with air-con and bathroom for Y140 to Y150. It often offers discounts of up to 50% on rooms. A bad omen is the use of mops to clean the carpet, so it won't be long before things start looking a bit tacky.

Less conveniently located, three-star *Xiángyún Dàjiŭdiàn (☎ 210 1999)* has twins starting at Y380 and singles starting at Y320. Outside of summer all rooms are discounted by 50%.

Places to Eat

Nánníng, like Gùilín and Liŭzhōu, is famous for its dog hotpot *(gŏuròu huŏguō)*. The *canine cuisine district* is just over the Chaóyáng Stream and south along Chaoyang Lu. In the evenings this area teems with roadside stalls specialising in dog hotpot.

The most raucous *food street*, rife with open-air stalls serving cuisine other than dog,

Heading West?

Westerners trying to travel between Kūnmíng and Guìlín soon discover what locals have long since known: everyone else is trying to get there too. In early 1998 the Chinese government drove the final spike into its pet project – the Nánkūn Railway, linking Kūnmíng with Nánníng, offering a crucial alternative route between Guāngxī☐, Guìzhōu, and Yúnnán.

This extraordinary project may seem tame when compared with the Three Gorges Dam, but it's also another perfect representation of the new can-do spirit of China. The government poured over 20 billion yuán into the project, and a small army of workers spent more than seven years toiling non-stop on the project. Engineers had a field day with the geography, a rough jumble of mountain ranges and steep valleys, 899km long. Nearly one-third of the route is bridge or tunnel, but you can still catch the occasional glimpse of scenic waterfalls and other natural sights. The all-electric railroad sports all the features they could cram in, including modern sensors built into the track to sense conditions and make adjustments.

The government had a secondary motive for the railroad. Some of the areas the train roars through are among the most 'backward' in China; already officials have touted that fresh fruit and vegies are now available year-round in previously isolated villages. The government is counting on tourism and, more particularly, mining to boom in the region.

Travellers, though, are most concerned with one other highlight: At the time of writing, hard-sleeper tickets were relatively easy to procure, even for next-day travel!

Thomas Huhti

is probably Zhongshan Lu. Here you will find a variety of tasty local snacks including, *juàntŏngfĕn* (steamed noodle pancake wrap with pork and coriander filling served in steaming broth), *lăoyŏumiàn* and *lăoyŏufen* (literally 'old friend' wheat or rice noodles).

For some excellent food and cheap beer try **Muslim Restaurant** *(Qīngzhēn Fàndiàn)*. It has a limited English menu, but the friendly staff will probably also let you into the kitchen to point out what you want. The restaurant is just on the left beyond Xīnhuá Bookstore.

Nánníng also specialises in fast food like nowhere else in China; seemingly every 50m is a restaurant with signs touting 'fast' food, either in Chinese or English, though menus are inevitably monolingual. There's also a lively row of **restaurants** offering a variety of dishes at the northern end of Hangzhou Lu. Not many of them have English menus, but that doesn't stop the owners from trying to lure you off the street. This is where you will also find the **Hàngzhōu Lù Fruit Market,** offering a delicious variety of China's best fruit year-round.

For self-caterers there is a good **supermarket** in the basement of the Nánníng Department Store.

Getting There & Away

Air Domestic airlines fly daily to Guǎngzhōu (Y670), Shànghǎi (Y1480), Shēnzhèn (Y710), Kūnmíng (Y580) and Běijīng (Y1790). Other flights include Chéngdū (Y820), Chóngqìng (Y700), Guìyáng (Y570), Hǎikǒu (Y560), Wǔhàn (Y1000) and Zhūhǎi (Y740).

There are also connections to Hong Kong (Y1880, Tuesday, Friday and Sunday) and to Hanoi (Hénèi; Y890, Monday and Thursday).

The Civil Aviation Administration of China office (CAAC; ☎ 243 1459) is at 82 Chaoyang Lu and is usually efficient. It may be worth checking with some travel agencies as they often sell discount tickets.

Bus Nánníng has two central bus stations *(qìchēzhàn):* Nánníng Bus Station (Nánníng Kèyùn Zŏngzhàn) and the Nánníng Passenger Centre (Nánníng Kèyùn Zhōngxīn). The bus station should satisfy most travellers with the passenger centre serving mostly regional destinations. Like the rest of the province's bus stations there is a left-luggage facility.

Highway construction in Guǎngxī, means bumpy bus rides around the province have been replaced by a growing number of express services. These new, luxury express buses are equipped with reclining seats, TVs showing bad Hong Kong movies, aircon and attendants.

Frequent express *(kuàibànchē)* buses depart from the bus station to: Bǎisè (Y45, three hours), Běihǎi (Y50, three hours), Guǎngzhōu (Y180, 10 hours), Gùilín every 20 to 30 minutes (Y80, 4½ hours), Guìpíng (Y40, four hours), Liǔzhōu (Y50, three hours) and Wúzhōu (Y80, six hours). There are still one or two regular snail buses prowling these routes for less, but these are now few and far between.

If you want to head south-west to Chóngzuŏ, Níngmíng or Píngxiáng (Y60, 4½ hours), then you should really consider the infinitely more convenient morning train. Heading towards Détiān Waterfall (on the Vietnam border), buses leave for Jìngxī (Y50, seven hours) at 7.50am and there is also a bus direct to Détiān Waterfall at 8.30am (Y50, four hours).

It's likely that the main bus station will offer all the routes you need, but if not, wander a giant block east of the train station to the round-the-clock Nánníng Passenger Centre on the corner of You'ai Lu. It has zillions of departures to mostly regional destinations, and also provides a few long-distance services to places such as Guìzhōu.

Train Since the advent of express buses, the train is more useful for longer hauls. Major destinations with direct rail links with Nánníng are shown over the page.

The T6 bound for Běijīng also passes through Liǔzhōu (four hours), Gùilín (six hours), Wǔhàn (18 hours), Zhèngzho (24 hours) and Shíjiāzhuāng (27½ hours). The K142 to Chéngdū passes through Guìyáng (19 hours) and Chóngqìng (29 hours).

destination	train no	departure	duration
Běijīng	T6	11.02am	32 hours
Chéngdū	K142	6.57pm	39 hours
Guăngzhōu	L240	2.12pm	18 hours
Kūnmíng	2005	3.40pm	16 hours
Shànghăi	1380	5.52pm	36 hours
Xī'ān	1316	7.05am	38 hours

The T905/M2 from Nánníng to Dong Dang (Tóngdēng) departs at 8.20pm, but is very slow with delays in the middle of the night in Píngxiáng and at customs.

Getting tickets for the next day doesn't seem to be too problematic. Foreigners can use window 15 and window 16 to change tickets.

Getting Around

To/From the Airport The CAAC buses to the airport cost Y15 (40 minutes) and are the most efficient way to get there. They depart regularly from the Chaoyang Lu CAAC office.

Local Transport A bicycle-hire place can be found along Chaoyang Lu, north of the Yōng Jiāng Bridge; rentals are available from 7am to 11pm and cost Y0.60 per hour. There is an abundance of taxis and motorcycle taxis (that offer a ride on the back or in the sidecar of a motorcycle or motor-tricycle). Taxi rides usually start at Y10; the motorcycle taxis, around Y5.

Buses generally run from 6am to around 11pm and fares start at Y0.70.

AROUND NÁNNÍNG
Liángfèng River Park 良丰河公园
Liángfèngjiāng Sēnlín Gōngyuán

Eight kilometres south of Nánníng, this is basically your average park – albeit a national park – with a standard, if a bit wider than usual, waterfall and a nice wooded area with over 125 subtropical tree species, many nearing extinction. The authorities are currently preparing to break ground on a new Chinese Primitive Culture Village and promise it will be more academic than kitsch.

Your best bet is to catch bus No 301 from in front of the train station. Otherwise, buses depart sporadically, more frequently on weekends, from Chaóyáng Garden. There is usually one bus at 8.30am, but at other times they won't leave until all the seats are taken.

Yángměi 杨梅

This 17th-century traditional town has been beautifully preserved and has become a popular day trip from Nánníng for Chinese tourists. The town is just 26km west of Nánníng on the Yōng Jiāng. You could spend a couple of hours just wandering the cobblestone streets admiring the beautiful, historic buildings. There are some descriptions of the history of the town's buildings, but not too much English. Guides will offer their services and you may be lucky to find someone who speaks some English. The best way to get around the town is to hire an ox cart for the half-day (Y10). Lunch is available at a couple of restaurants in town or take a packed lunch.

The village used to be a pleasant boat trip away but now a bus makes the run. Buses depart from a small bus station north of Chaóyáng Garden just south of the small bridge, on the eastern side of Chaoyang Lu.

Yílíng Cave 伊岭岩
Yílíng Yán

Twenty-five kilometres to the north of Nánníng is Yílíng Cave. A bit of a tourist trap, but fun all the same with its stalagmites and galactic lights; don't forget to take your imagination. Once you have mastered the art of closing one eye and blurring the other, the cave will reveal its previously hidden secrets of animals, sages and monsters. The use of coloured fluorescent lights adds to the experience.

When you first arrive at the front gate, wait around for a group to form for a guided tour of the **Zhuang-minority Culture Park**. This is an atypical introduction to Chinese-style minority tourism, not so much reflecting cultural tourism, but rather a tourism culture. You will first receive an introduction to popular Zhuang culture, including festivals, songs, ornaments, crafts, cuisine and dating habits. Remember that it is all meant to be fun. Some of the guides speak English, but going with a Chinese group adds to the entertainment. Entry is Y14 and an extra Y25 to enter the cave.

If you have any time left, then the surrounding countryside is worth exploring.

If you are feeling peckish, the first restaurant to the north of the entrance is famous for its *níngmáyā*, a spicy Zhuang speciality duck dish. It costs Y15 per half-kilo *(yi jin)* serving.

To get to either Wǔmíng or Yílíng Cave head over to the Nánníng Passenger Centre. Express buses depart from inside the main gates, which are to the right of the old waiting area. Tickets (Y6) should be bought from the nearby tin shed. These buses drop you off at the entrance to Yílíng Cave, but check first with the driver. It is also possible to reach the cave on these buses as they return from Wǔmíng.

Minibuses run from Chaóyáng Garden on the left-hand side of Chaoyang Lu just over Chaóyáng Stream on most weekends, especially during summer. And finally, the daily Nánníng to Dàmìng Shān bus also passes by the cave at around 4pm (Y8, 1½ hours).

Língshuǐ Springs

Língshuǐ, meaning soul water, is essentially a big swimming pool a few kilometres from Wǔmíng, which is 45km from Nánníng, on the same road that leads to Yílíng Cave. In summer this mineral outdoor pool is a popular spot with locals and tourists alike.

To get to Língshuǐ, first catch a bus to Wǔmíng (see the above directions for Yílíng Cave). From Wǔmíng bus station hop on a motorcycle taxi (Y3) to the springs.

Dàmìng Shān 大明山

Another 1½ hours north-east of Wǔmíng, 90km from Nánníng, is what most Nánníng residents consider their rest-and-relaxation spot come summer – Dàmìng Shān. Averaging 1200m above sea level and reaching a maximum height of 1760m, it's a great vacation spot in summer. The temperate climate allows the region to support more than 1700 species of plants.

On the plateau is a small tourist village with a couple of hotels and a restaurant. There are several relatively easy walks to nearby scenic lookouts. Most people head up to Dàmìng Shān to take in some of the scenery: the deep valley of **Shēnshān Shāngǔ;** the ancient Song pine trees, **Bùlǎosōng** and **Yíngkèsōng;** one of the three waterfalls **(Lóngwěi Pùbù); Sacred Girl Peak** (Shénnǚ Fēng); and of course the highest peak, Dàmìng Shān. The majority of these spots are accessible within a day's hike, however most visitors organise a guide as paths are poorly marked. If you want to explore more of the mountain, then you should inform the forestry workers at the ticket office. Entry to Dàmìng Shān costs Y8.

Dàmìng Shān Resort *(Dàmìngshān Dùjiācūn;* ☎ 986 0902, mobile ☎ 137 0781 8397) offers a restaurant and log cabins and a couple of inns for accommodation. Prices are reasonable, but vary depending on the season. Twin cabins with water and toilets go for Y100 and beds in larger dorms are Y25. Ring before you go so that arrangements can be made for a guide, food and lodging. The Forestry Bureau also has **Línyè Zhāodàisuǒ** with very basic dorm beds (Y15).

There is one daily public bus that terminates at the small forestry town at the base of the mountain (Y14). This is where you will find the ticket office. Accommodation and a small shop can also be found here. It is, however, another 27km up to the top from here. This bus departs from Nánníng's Chaóyáng Garden at 3.10pm and returns to Nánníng the next morning at 7.30am. It will only continue the final 27km up to the resort if there are enough paying passengers. If you don't want to walk, then it would be better to hop off 5km earlier in **Léijiāng**, where you can arrange a motorbike lift (Y50) to take you up to the top early the next day. In Léijiāng, accommodation can be found at **Dàmìng Shān Lüshè**. There are also a couple of restaurants and shops here. It is much easier to get to Léijiāng on any of the regular buses heading for Dàhuà, Mǎshān or Liǎngjiāng from either Wǔmíng or Nánníng.

On weekends another service makes the run to Dàmìng Shān, but again will terminate at the ticket office if there aren't enough passengers to continue to the top. This bus heads back to Nánníng at 2.30pm from the ticket office. During summer, sporadic minibuses leave from Chaóyáng Garden on Chaoyang Lu. However, these are hit or miss and even on the weekends you may have a long wait.

A good plan for visiting Dàmìng Shān could include a visit to Yílíng Cave. If you make it to the cave by lunchtime, try the local speciality, *níngmáyā,* have a tour of the Zhuang-minority Culture Park and the cave, before hopping on the regular Dàmìng Shān bus, which passes the main entrance to Yílíng Cave at around 4pm.

Lónghú Shān 龙虎山

If you don't have enough time to go to Dàmìng Shān *and* to Détiān Waterfall (west of Nánníng, on the Sino-Vietnamese border), you might want to visit Lónghú Shān. It's closer to Nánníng (about 65km west), and you get both waterfall and mountain.

In 2000 the nature reserve that encompasses Lónghú Shān held China's first **Wild Monkey Festival**. The occasion was organised to celebrate the continued existence of about 3000 wild monkeys living in the reserve and to publicise the plight of the many endangered monkey species and their threatened habitats in southern China.

The reserve covers an area of 1000 hectares and is home to over 200 animal species and more than 1200 plant species.

It is possible to stop off here on your way to Détiān Waterfall. Despite there being no direct public transport, you could hop on a bus to the small village of Pīngshān and then arrange local transport from there. Otherwise, from late spring to late summer, tours (Y45) depart from Chaóyáng Garden at 8.30am and return around 4.30pm on Saturday and Sunday.

BĚIHĂI 北海
☎ 0779 • pop 560,000

This friendly, tree-lined port community 229km south of Nánníng is best-known for its ferry to Hăinán Island and its famous Silver Beach. More than 2000 years old, Běihăi was settled and developed during the Qin dynasty and became famous – as it still is today – as one of the world's greatest fisheries (though pearls really put it on the

international map). The town, its shady, expansive boulevards draped with widebranched *róngshù* trees, is easy-going, and the locals seem pretty friendly.

The main tourist attraction, Silver Beach (Yíntān), is a good place to see how the Chinese pursue their fun in the sun. If you are looking for China's best beaches, then purchasing a boat ticket to Hăinán Island is your answer. It seems this is what happened to all the investment in town. You will notice a large number of hotels, buildings and resort-style accommodation lying vacant or half built.

The waterfront, a few kilometres west of the bus station, has some fascinating old architecture. The old town, with its exceedingly long concrete wave breakers around the harbour and old-style fishing boats make for great photos.

Orientation

Běihăi sits on a small peninsula on the western end of a larger, east-to-west peninsula jutting off Guăngxī. The northern coast of the town is home to the bus terminal, most of the population, shops and budget lodging options. The southern strip has the new International Ferry Terminal, a couple of up-market hotels and that famous stretch of white sand.

Information

The most convenient Bank of China is opposite the entrance to Zhongshan Park. It can change travellers cheques and cash from 8am to 6pm daily. The main Bank of China branch is on the corner of Beihai Dadao and Sichuan Lu.

There are Internet bars on the 3rd floor of the two largest department stores in Běihăi. At Y2 per hour don't expect much; actually it may be quicker writing a postcard home.

Silver Beach
Yíntān

Southern Thailand it is not, but 1.6km-long Silver Beach, about 10km south-east of Běihăi city centre in Silver Beach Park, does have white sand and fairly clean water, not to mention eclectic architecture.

From Běihǎi, walk west from the bus station, bear right at Woping Lu, which branches off behind Běihǎi Yíngbīnguǎn, and catch bus No 3 on the corner of Jiefang Lu (Y2, 20 minutes). On the way you pass the International Ferry Terminal and a large number of half-built apartments and holiday guesthouses. Just behind Silver Beach are numerous restaurants and hotels. All are reasonably cheap and simple. The most lively time to visit is between May and September and during national holidays. Entry to the beach costs Y25.

Hǎibīn Park
Hǎibīn Gōngyuán

If the popular Zhongshan Park is rocking too much with senior citizens disco dancing, then head north-east to the more derelict part of town and the northern waterfront where you will find little Haibin Park. Inside the park is one of China's largest **aquariums** (Shuǐchǎn Zhǎnlǎn Guǎn). Two buildings house seven spacious exhibition halls filled with tanks of strange and colourful fish. Most of the exhibits feature local marine life from the Gulf of Tonkin (Běibùwán) with the main highlight being the rare *dogzong*, more commonly known as mermaid. Entry is a little steep at Y60.

Places to Stay

Běihǎi has a few touts hanging about the bus terminal who will likely lead you to the run-down, but exceedingly cheap, small hotels in the vicinity of the terminal. Expect to pay as little as Y40 for a double at the more pungent options, and you can probably still bargain this down. Give the cheap-looking Chinese hotels a shot, as they mostly all seem amenable to foreign friends.

A very good mid-range hotel is *Táoyuán Dàjiǔdiàn* (☎ 202 0919), across from the bus station and down a small alley – good for noise reduction. It has reasonably clean doubles with air-con and 24-hour hot water from Y70, including breakfast. It also has some cheaper beds in twins and triples. It's definitely worth it for the cleanliness and especially for the service. The restaurant is also good.

For a more sentimental stay, try *Běihǎi Yíngbīnguǎn* (☎ 202 3511). In pleasant surroundings, it has clean and quiet rooms from Y100 and friendly staff. It is even possible to stay in the former French consulate situated within the hotel grounds, which is where the cadres used to stay when they came for a dose of Běihǎi's sea breezes.

Today, most well-heeled and self-respecting cadres choose to stay at the *Shangri-La Hotel* (☎ 206 2288, fax 205 0085, e sbhi@shangri-la.com), Běihǎi's most luxurious abode, but oddly located in the northern, more dilapidated part of town. Room rates range from Y960 for a sea-view double to Y12,800 for the Guǎngxī suite. These prices are often heavily discounted.

Silver Beach If you have come to Běihǎi to see how the Chinese frolic in the sun, then you should stay at Silver Beach; most hotels will gladly put you up. There are quite a few grubby, budget options like the *Yíntān Zhāodàisuǒ*, down an alley near the beach entrance. It's pretty clean and cheap with beds from Y25 in a room with shared shower. A good mid-range option is *Beach Hotel* (Hǎitān Bīnguǎn; ☎ 388 8888, fax 389 8168, e bhht@bh.gx.cninfo.net). Comfy twins and doubles start from Y630, or Y360 outside of summer. The hotel is just opposite the huge, cylindrical musical sculpture and fountain at the entrance to Sea Beach.

Places to Eat

Being a port and fishing town, it's odd that Běihǎi doesn't have more sit-down, outdoor seafood places. But you won't go hungry. Around the bus station are clusters of nondescript eateries and noodle shops.

A five-minute walk west of the bus station is *Jìnxìng Fàndiàn* with some outdoor seating (look for the white sign with red letters). There's no English menu, but you can get *dānghuā rìběn dòufǔ* (sweet-and-sour bean curd) and great *hóngshāo dòufǔ* (braised bean curd).

Around the corner from the bus station is *Èrgēlǎojī Fàndiàn*, a popular and often rowdy place specialising in *huǒguō* (hotpot), *tiánsuān páigǔ* (sweet-and-sour pork

GUĂNGXĪ

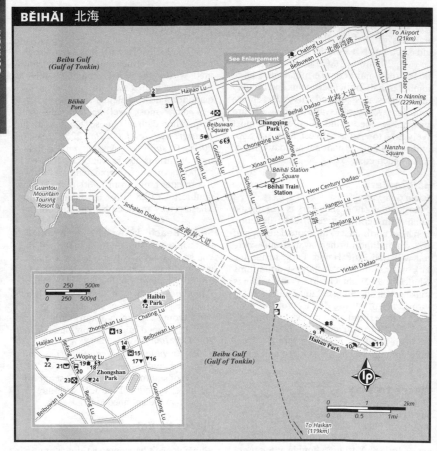

ribs) and *báisījī*, a free-range chicken dish also called *tǔjībǎn*.

Opposite is a good ***market*** with a row of stalls and tents selling local snacks and lots of fresh produce.

Just west of the Woping Lu post office is a good little ***teahouse*** serving beverages and small snacks.

In the northern section of Yunnan Lu, close to the wharf is Běihǎi's large ***Seafood Market***. This is the place to come if you need to stock up on dried squid or any other seafood. Bus Nos 2 and 8 from in front of the bus station pass by the market.

Getting There & Away

There is a helpful ticket office (☎ 202 8618) on the ground floor of the Shangri-La Hotel. Its hours are 8am to 10pm and it sells boat, bus, train and plane tickets. There are plenty of more conveniently located travel agencies around town offering the same services.

Air The major connections with Běihǎi include daily flights to: Běijīng (Y1800), Guǎngzhōu (Y630), Guìyáng (Y730), Hǎikǒu (Y350) and Guìlín (Y480). CAAC buses (Y10, 30 minutes) meet arriving planes and leave two hours before departure

BĚIHǍI

PLACES TO STAY
1 Shangri-La Hotel
香格里拉大饭店
8 Beach Hotel
海滩宾馆
11 Yíntān Zhāodàisuǒ
银滩招待所
14 Táoyuán Dàjiǔdiàn
桃园大酒店
19 Běihǎi Yíngbīnguǎn
北海迎宾馆

PLACES TO EAT
3 Seafood Market
海产市场
16 Market
市场
17 Èrgēlǎojī Fàndiàn
二哥佬鸡饭店

22 Tea House
茶园
24 Jīnxíng Fàndiàn
饭店

OTHER
2 Ferry Passenger Office
海运客运站
4 Huálián Department
Store (Internet)
华联商厦（网吧）
5 CAAC
民航大厦
6 Main Bank of China
中国银行
7 International Ferry
Terminal
北海国际客运码头

9 Sea Beach
海滩
10 Silver Beach
银滩
12 Aquarium
水产展览馆
13 PSB
公安局
15 Main Bus Station
汽车总站
18 Bank of China
中国银行
20 Buses to Silver Beach
往银滩的汽车
21 Post Office
邮局
23 Department Store
(Internet)
国通购物中心（网吧）

from the CAAC building (Mínháng Dàshà; ☎ 305 1899) on Beibuwan Xilu. This is also the best place to purchase plane tickets.

Bus Express buses connect Běihǎi with Dōngxīng (Y35, three hours), Guǎngzhōu (Y180, 9½ hours), Guìlín (Y150, seven hours), Liǔzhōu (Y110) and Nánníng (Y50, three hours).

To visit either the nature reserve or the tourist resort of Nánguóxīng Island Lake (see the Around Běihǎi section for details), you will need to first catch one of the many buses to Hépù and then change (Y4, 30 minutes).

Train Travelling by train means more hassles than the bus since the completion of the expressway to Nánníng. Train No K140 departs from Běihǎi for Chéngdū, via Nánníng, Guìyáng and Chóngqìng. Hard-sleeper fares are Y277 for the 43-hour trip to Chéngdū.

Boat Despite its name, the International Ferry Terminal (Guójì Kèyùn Mǎtou) is yet to offer any international departures. Services include Hǎikǒu on Hǎinán Island and the nearby island of Wèizhōu. Boats for the 11-hour journey to Hǎikǒu leave twice daily (7.30am and 6pm) on even days and once only on odd days. Tickets cost from Y100 for a seat to Y250 for a cabin.

There is one daily boat to Wèizhōu departing at 8.30am (Y46 for 3rd class to Y60 for sleeper, 2¼ hours).

At the time of research, you were able to purchase tickets at the old terminal (Běihǎi Kèyùnzhàn), but this may soon be discontinued. It's also possible that your hotel will book your tickets.

Getting Around
To/From the Airport Comfortable, large buses meet planes at the airport, which is 21km north of town. The fare is Y10 for the half-hour ride. A taxi should cost about Y50.

Bus Běihǎi's buses mostly congregate north of Zhongshan Park along Jiefang Lu. Besides being the place to catch the No 3 bus to Silver Beach, this is also where you can pick up the No 2 that goes west to the ferry docks and seafood market. Local buses cost Y2.

Motorcycle Taxi For the best way of getting around in a hurry, try a cheap motorcycle taxi. It will cost Y6 to get to Silver Beach from the town centre or Y3 for around town.

AROUND BĚIHǍI
Běihǎi's surroundings are wide open for exploration – there's a whole coastline out there. With so much of Guǎngxī opening

up to foreign travellers, if Vietnam relaxes border regulations, a great trip may be to skirt the coast all the way from Guǎngdōng to Vietnam, with Běihǎi as your midpoint.

North-east of Běihǎi, a good road crosses the peninsula via Hépù, where you could try to arrange transport to **Shānkǒu Mangrove Reserve**, a Unesco-designated Biosphere Reserve. The reserve is quite large at 8000 hectares, but there is only a small mangrove stand of 72 hectares left after decades of neglect. Tourist facilities are being improved and there are plans to develop the area as a marine ecotourism site.

Halfway along the road between Běihǎi and the reserve, head south towards the coastal town of **Báilóng**, or 'Pearl City'. It has some interesting traditional buildings.

You can take the Nánníng Highway to the north of Běihǎi, and detour 10km east to **Nánguóxīng Island Lake** (Nánguóxīng Dǎohú). This iridescent-blue body of water is dotted with verdant, sand-edged islands.

At Hépù, you can visit **Dōngpō Pavilion** (Dōngpō Tíng), 2km to the north, and then head 2km south to **Wénchāng Pagoda** (Wénchāng Tǎ). The pavilion was constructed in memory of the famous Song dynasty scholar and poet, Su Dongpo. Wénchāng Pagoda stands 36m high and was built over 300 years ago during the Ming dynasty. Both sites are easily accessible by motorbike taxi (Y4).

CHÓNGZUǑ 崇左
☎ 0771 • pop 330,000

At the 122km point along the Nánníng-Píngxiáng train line is this friendly city, known for its diminutive Stone Forest and its Guīlóng Pagoda, also called the Leaning Pagoda. As you disembark the train, Chóngzuǒ appears to be a fly-speck town, at least by Chinese standards, but as you walk along the main street, you realise it's actually one very thin – but very long – city. And it's worth an overnight stay before hitting the Zuǒ Jiāng Scenic Area to the south.

Guīlóng Tǎ

Easily one of the most often painted sights in south-west Guǎngxī, this pagoda (also

known as Shuǐ Tǎ, or 'Water Pagoda') is approximately 5km north-east of town on Phoenix Lake. Built in 1621 and one of only eight of its kind in the world – leaning, that is – the silvery 18m tower sits atop a rocky outcrop in the lake. It's connected to the shore by a makeshift path. The tower's 1m lean is discernible from the shore.

Lolling nearby will be a couple of fishermen in skiffs. They'll barely raise their heads as they offer you rides around the lake for a couple of yuán. Don't bother making this trip during winter as the water level in the lake is so low that the area looks more like a neglected quarry site.

Catch a motorcycle taxi for around Y5. It's a long, bumpy ride with lots of turnoffs. After 5km or so, a gravel road appears; you probably won't be able to see it, but your driver will. Take this road, then, just when you start to worry your driver's going to rob you, nope, another 100m on is the entrance. Admission is Y3.

Stone Forest
Shílín

No one would ever confuse Chóngzuǒ's diminutive Stone Forest with Kūnmíng's grand menagerie of stone, but there are a few nooks and crannies within this geological spectacle that for a moment might make you think you've seen it before. Even better – it doesn't have the crowds or high admission fees that take some of the shine off of the better-known version.

It's over an hour's walk from town. A motorcycle taxi is about Y5. Admission is Y10.

Places to Stay

Across the street and east of the train station is *Nánzhèn Lǚguǎn,* which has friendly staff and good budget rooms. Beds in quads start at Y10 or Y18 with a shower; the cheapest single is Y28. For these prices, this place is magnificent. Beds are clean and, best of all, the showers have real pressure and reliable hot water. (Check out the odd footbridge crossing the river behind the hotel.)

Turning left out of the train station and walking for five minutes or so brings you to *Xīnhuá Zhāodàisuǒ* on the right. A bit cleaner than the Nànzhèn but with similar tariffs: Y15 per bed in a five-person room, or Y30 in a dorm with bathroom, and Y48 for a double. The small entrance is next door to Xīnhuá Bookstore and is lined with plants.

Farther west along Jianguan Lu past Xinmin Lu but on the other side of the road is *Zuǒjiāng Dàshà* (☎ 782 1601), where beds in triples start at Y20. Basic twin rooms cost Y50 with more comfortable ones for Y128.

Places to Eat

Chóngzuǒ is not known for its culinary appeal, but you shouldn't starve. The first grubby-looking *restaurant* to the right as you exit the bus station has tasty dumplings, while the next one puts together a tasty and cheap vegetable stir-fry. More evening, *outdoor hot-pot restaurants* are just west of the train station. There's a fairly good, small *bakery* on Xinmin Lu, on the right just past the market.

Getting There & Away

Chóngzuǒ is accessible by train from Nánníng and Píngxiáng. From Nánníng, the 8.00am No 5517 arrives at 10.07am and continues on to Níngmíng (11.12am) and Píngxiáng (12.10pm). The 11.08am No 8511 takes an extra hour to all destinations. In the other direction, the No 5518 passes through at 3.36pm and the No 8512 at 11.39am.

Buses are more frequent than the train to Nánníng (Y40, 4½ hours), Níngmíng (Y6.5, 1½ hours) and Píngxiáng (Y14, 2½ hours).

Regular buses connect Chóngzuǒ and Dàxīn (Y15, 2½ hours), from where you can change for a bus to Shuòlóng (Détiān Waterfall) and Jìngxī. To Shàngsī (Y12, three hours), five buses depart between 8am and 2.30pm. If you're heading to the untouristed coastal region between Fángchéng and Dōngxìng on the Vietnamese border, Shàngsī would be a logical stopover. You could get to Shàngsī on the 10am bus to Fángchéng (six hours).

AROUND CHÓNGZUǑ
Shàngsī

The three-hour bus trip to Shàngsī is worthwhile as a stopover if you're heading south-east to explore the coast. The main highlight is **Shàngsī Forest Park** (Shàngsí Sēnlín Gōngyuán, also known as Shíwàn Dàshān Guójiā Sēnlín Gōngyuán), where you can swim in medicinal pools and hike in the mountains. From here you could go on to Fángchéng and then along the coast to Dōngxìng on the Vietnamese border or continue all the way to Běihǎi.

ZUǑ JIĀNG SCENIC AREA
左江风景区 Zuǒjiāng Fēngjǐngqū

About 190km south-west of Nánníng, Zuǒ Jiāng Scenic Area provides the opportunity to see karst rock formations like those in Gùilín, with the added attraction that the region is home to around 80 groups of Zhuang-minority rock paintings. The area is also the last habitat of the rare white-headed leaf monkey. Midway along the river is Pānlóng, a funky village to stay, which adjoins an outstanding nature reserve for backcountry hiking.

Níngmíng 宁明

There's only one reason people come to Níngmíng – to get out. This town is the launching point for a Zuǒ Jiāng adventure but, to be brutally honest, you do not want to spend any time here.

Just next to the train station is *Tiělù Zhāodàisuǒ*, with OK rooms from Y25 per bed in a dorm to Y60 for a single with bath. A Y2 motorcycle-taxi ride from the train station will take you to *Huāshān Bīnguǎn* (☎ 0771-862 132), with much nicer twins from around Y80. This is the place to stay if you have arrived by bus. The hotel is to the right as you exit the bus terminal.

The River Route

At first, the river scenery is nothing to write home about, unless you happen to catch the early-morning or late-afternoon sun. It's the river life that really makes the experience – lots of little bullet-shaped dugouts criss-crossing the river, locals tending vegetable and flower plots in riverside pools edged with bamboo, and little kids splashing about in the mud. The banks start out flat and wide and it isn't until about 30 minutes into the journey from Níngmíng that the interesting geology appears. The oversized karst formations are followed by almost-imposing ruddy cliffs, some of which have Zhuang-minority rock paintings.

Just over an hour into the puttering boat journey, is the cheerful village of **Pānlóng**, with wandering chickens, pigs and oxen. Behind the village is *Huāshān Ethnic Culture Village (Huāshān Mínzú Shānzhài Dújiàcūn;* ☎ *862 8195)*, more of a low-key tourist resort that offers decent rooms in Dong-style wooden cabins. Rooms start at Y120 for a single/double/triple/quad. Hot water for showering is available in the evening. The grounds and architecture are lovely, but the noisy crowds can be a bit of a downer, so try to avoid national holidays. When there is enough of a crowd it is possible to see some traditional Zhuang dancing (Y18). A restaurant on-site serves traditional local fare for about Y25 per person. To save you lugging your bags around, leave them at Níngmíng's bus station if you plan to overnight at Pānlóng.

A Circular Tale

Only 750 of the white-headed leaf monkeys are left in the world, most in the Lóngrì Nature Reserve. Legend has it that the ancestors of these monkeys were local children who were taken here to eat the fruits of the forest during a food shortage in surrounding villages. When the parents returned after several days to collect them, their children had adapted to the forest way of life and had grown tails. The children refused to return to the village.

Today, the problem has reversed itself with the nearby villages continuing to expand their cultivated land so much that they have reduced the habitat of the monkeys and thus reduced their numbers. According to one researcher, more than 70% of the monkeys' habitat has been lost to agriculture. As a result, the reserve was established to help alleviate the pressure. It is also hoped that ecotourism will offer a joint solution of increasing the livelihood opportunities for the locals while preserving the monkeys' habitat.

Even better than the cultural village is the **Lóngruì Nature Reserve** (Lóngruì Zìrán Bǎohùqū). It's directly behind the village – follow the concrete path until it ends and then plunge into the undergrowth. Continue up, up, up along a hard scrabble path and you get a splendid view of the river valley and surrounding area. A hike up and back takes just over an hour. After passing a gazebo at the summit the trail then descends and degrades simultaneously into the thickness. There are some tough sections, but you could definitely spend a whole day poking around in this reserve. Most tourists come with the hope of spying the rare **white-headed leaf monkey** *(bǎitóu yèhóu)*, also known as the white-headed langur. The resort can easily arrange a guide, if you prefer (Y30). Entry to reserve is Y6.

The largest of the Zhuang paintings is in the **Huā Shān Bìhuà** area, another hour's boat ride along the river. A fresco, 170m high and 90m across, groups nearly 2000 figures of hunters, farmers and animals. It is now believed that the Luoyue, the ancestors of the Zhuang, painted these cliffs 2000 years ago during the early Han period (AD 25–220), although it's unclear why. Stand at the bottom of the cliffs and figure out how in the world whoever painted them *did* it on those vertiginous rock faces! It takes five minutes to walk along a path to the end of the cliff.

On the 2nd floor of the administration building is a small, dilapidated **museum** with displays explaining the history of the site, but they're all in Chinese and run down. Admission is Y5.

Boat Tours

This area is still relatively unexplored by Western travellers, however it is quite easy to independently organise a trip. If you don't want to go down to the river and arrange a boat yourself, then one of the tour operators or touts will soon find you.

Tour operators in Níngmíng are found along the main road straight out of the train station. They offer tours for Y80 for one or two people, and Y100 for three or four. Add Y50 if you want to stop overnight in

Pānlóng. One or two workers at these agencies speak a little English, but the guides generally don't.

Getting There & Around

First, make your way to Níngmíng and then head down to the small 'wharf' – nothing more than a muddy river bank – on the Zuǒ Jiāng. This is where most of the tourist boats congregate. From the train station, continue straight along the main road and wander down the path to the right of the bridge. From the bus terminal catch a motorcycle taxi (Y2) and ask the driver to take you to Tuólóng or Huā Shān chuán mǎtóu. The boats wait below the bridge you cross when coming from town.

It will cost about Y70 for the return trip to hire the boat and driver. Add another Y50 for a night in Pānlóng. The more passengers the cheaper the trip. From Níngmíng's wharf it is a 1¼-hour boat journey to Pānlóng and another hour downstream to Huāshān.

It would be better to get from Nánníng to Níngmíng and then head down to the wharf or hook up with a tour for the trip to Pānlóng and Huāshān. Stay overnight in Pānlóng and the next morning explore Lóngruì Nature Reserve before taking the boat on to Huāshān and then back to Níngmíng later that afternoon.

If you are pressed for time or dislike puttering boats, a new road runs along the river from Níngmíng to Pānlóng. A taxi takes about 20 minutes (Y30). There are frequent buses connecting Níngmíng with Píngxiáng, Chóngzuǒ and Nánníng. Otherwise you could get back to Níngmíng in time for the last train out. You could do the whole trip in one extremely long day, but it would preclude any exploration of the Lóngruì Nature Reserve.

Trains depart from Níngmíng for Píngxiáng at 11.12am and 3.31pm. Going north to Chóngzuǒ or Nánníng, trains depart at 10.06am and 2.30pm. Since trains are generally empty, they're preferable to buses.

Buses leave from the bus station, a Y2 motor-taxi ride from the train station. The last reliable bus to Chóngzuǒ departs at 3.10pm (Y8, 1½ hours).

PÍNGXIÁNG 凭祥

☎ 0771 • pop 100,000

Píngxiáng is the staging post for onward travel to Vietnam. It's basically a border trading town and, after you've taken a wander through the bustling markets, there's not a lot to see.

There are heaps of banks in Píngxiáng, so changing money is no problem.

The cheapest accommodation is *Yínxīng Bīnguǎn,* inside the bus station. Basic beds in twins cost Y20, Y25 or Y45. A slightly more comfortable option is *Xīnníng Bīnguǎn,* behind the bus station.

There's no real need to stay in Píngxiáng. An early-morning bus or train from Nánníng will get you into Píngxiáng around midday, and at this point you should be able to find transport to the Friendship Pass (Yǒuyì Guān) on the Vietnamese border. Minibuses and private vehicles wait near the bus and train stations – charging between Y5 and Y20 depending on the number of passengers. From the Friendship Pass it's another 600m to the border post. Onward transport to Hanoi by train or bus is via the Vietnamese town of Lang Son (Liàngshān), which is 18km from the Friendship Pass.

If you're heading into China, after crossing the Vietnamese border catch one of the minibuses into Píngxiáng to the bus station, from where you can catch one of the regular buses onto Níngmíng (Y6.5) or Nánníng (Y35). The bus station (qìchēzhàn) is a five-minute walk north of Píngxiáng's northern train station.

DÉTIĀN WATERFALL 德天瀑布
Détiān Pùbù

Guǎngxī's tourist authorities like to boast that Détiān Waterfall is the world's second-largest transnational cataract. While it's not Niagara Falls, Détiān is still captivating, with its many levels and an impressive cacophony of water. Plus, you can surreptitiously cross the Vietnamese border (at least for a few metres) and nobody will shoot you.

At the 53rd boundary marker between China and Vietnam, the waterfall drops only 40m, but makes up for it by a more than modest breadth. The Vietnamese got the

Troubled Waters: Sino-Vietnamese Relations

Quintessential uneasy neighbours, China and Vietnam have been at odds, if not actually skirmishing, for over 2100 years. Han-dynasty armies conquered the first Vietnamese patriot, Tire Da, in the 2nd century BC, making Vietnam one of many countries devoured by China as it tried to expand its commercial influence. This had a significant cultural and social impact on Vietnam. The introduction of a patriarchal Confucian social and governmental system was a double-edged sword. It made the elite more inclined to tolerate Chinese rule, but later also gave the Vietnamese the framework to encourage revolt. Vietnam eventually threw off the yoke of imperialism in the 10th century AD, after dozens of revolts.

After WWII, Western forces sent a 200,000-strong force of Chinese Nationalists to northern Vietnam to demobilise Japanese troops. The two nations have regularly been at war ever since, apart from when China supported Vietnam during the (American) Vietnam war.

In 1979 open war broke out after years of sporadic skirmishes. The Chinese crossed the border for several reasons. In 1978 the Vietnamese had rebuffed China and signed a treaty with (and accepted military and monetary support from) the Soviet Union – another border country with a Chinese love-hate relationship. Vietnam had also invaded Cambodia to topple the Khmer Rouge and, most importantly, had seized the assets of and deported (or forced out) up to 250,000 overseas Chinese, most of them to the Chinese provinces of Yúnnán and Guǎngxī.

The Chinese say Vietnamese forces crossed the border first, necessitating their own incursion. The Vietnamese deny this (most Western sources back this version). Over 16 days scores of people were killed and five provincial border towns in Vietnam were heavily damaged. Both sides claim to have won this battle.

It didn't end there, though. The border was sealed and major battles erupted again in 1984 in Láoshān, Zhèyóushān and Bālǐdōnghé in Yúnnán and along much of Guǎngxī's border. This time the Vietnamese used up to 10 expanded divisions to attack Chinese border forces. They shelled the Chinese with up to 10,000 rounds a day and, while they didn't seize any land in this conflict, they did inflict a humiliating lesson on China. It's quite common when travelling in Guǎngxī to run into China's own Vietnam veterans, many of whom openly talk about the war.

Things have long since cooled down; border points at Hékǒu in Yúnnán and the Friendship Pass in Píngxiáng hardly show any lingering effects, and the only disagreements for a decade have been between haggling Vietnamese and Chinese traders. All is not exactly cosy, however. In 1997 Vietnam took its protests over China's sale of oil-exploration rights in its waters to Asean (which sided with Vietnam), and in January 1998 the Vietnamese daily newspapers ran front-page banner headlines accusing China of major border transgressions. The focal point was a 1km-long river embankment in Guǎngxī, which the Vietnamese claim the Chinese had deliberately built 10m into Vietnamese territory and which now floods the Vietnamese side of the river.

The Chinese initially laughed off the accusations. Then, to everyone's surprise, made a concession, agreeing to clear land mines along the border and in Vietnam (at a cost of US$10 million) as a goodwill gesture. Cynics argue that China did this as much to facilitate further trade – which had quadrupled from 1992 to 1997 along the border – as to encourage friendly relations. The job was completed by August 1999 and, in all, more than 600,000 mines were removed. This is from an estimated 2.2 million land mines that were laid along the 673km-long border. The first high-level contingent of Vietnamese since 1990 then travelled to Běijīng to try to stabilise relations. Later that year historic sites in Dōngxìng (Guǎngxī), dating Sino-Vietnamese ties to the 19th century, were restored and opened to the public. Perhaps most symbolic of all, in mid-1999 direct postal links – they were previously through Singapore – were finally restored through Guǎngxī.

short end of the cascade stick, with a paltry few ribbons of water falling on their side of the border, while the Chinese have the earth-shaking majority of water flow. The best time to visit is July, though water levels will be fairly high from May to late September. Show up in November or December and be thoroughly underwhelmed by the lack of water and constant cloud and fog.

From the entrance, a road runs alongside the river and several trails descend to the banks, where you'll be gently harassed by raft operators offering to take you right into the spray.

The trail also follows the river a short distance away from the falls before hooking up with the road again. You can continue along the road several hundred metres more to another cluster of hawkers. Here you'll find the boundary marker between the two countries. Chinese can wander across at will and, though technically you cannot, nobody will arrest you for walking a few metres into Vietnam for an obligatory photo shoot. In November or December you could probably use the stepping-stones to cross the river into Vietnam. Admission to the falls is Y30.

Places to Stay

Just behind the ticket office is a new *guesthouse* on a rise above the falls with a great view of the falls and river. If you want to stay here ensure you first book with its Nánníng (☎ 0771-362 7088) or Dàxīn (☎ 0771-262 4540) office. Not only can you ask for a room with a view, but you will receive a discounted rate. If you just turn up at the door, twins cost Y450 and a quad suite is Y680. There's solar hot water and a restaurant.

Back towards Shuòlóng is the very average *Détiān Bīnguǎn*. Incredibly, prices are the same, despite a lack of character or views.

If you get stuck in Shuòlóng, then there are a few grubby *guesthouses* at the main intersection.

Getting There & Away

Coming from Nánníng, or even from Píngxiáng, you'll probably have to first get to Dàxīn and arrange transport from there. From Dàxīn, hop on a bus heading to Xiàléi

and get off in Shuòlóng. The 47km ride costs Y8 and takes 1½ hours (sometimes more depending on bus quality). For travellers coming from Jìngxī, any bus to Dàxīn should pass through Shuòlóng, but verify this before getting on. In Shuòlóng, the bus will probably deposit you in front of the 'minibus tree', where rattletrap minibuses or motorbike taxis run the final lovely 14km – full of eye-catching coloured pools – for Y2. If you're the only passenger going all the way to the falls the driver may ask for Y4.

When you leave the falls, walk down to the main road from the guesthouse and towards Shuòlóng for about 10 minutes. Buses usually wait at the little cluster of stands there – you can get a bus in the morning, even in the low season. If you do want to leave in the evening, you can never really be sure when buses to/from Shuòlóng stop running. There isn't much movement after 5pm.

From Shuòlóng, you stand by the road and wait for a bus to pass – there's no way to tell when the next one's coming. Semi-regular service is found towards Dàxīn, and therefore Nánníng, but if you want to go towards Jìngxī, the best thing to do is leapfrog villages. First take a Y2 minibus north-west to Xiàléi and then another Y2 minibus to Húrùn (pronounced Fuyuan here). From there you can get a proper bus for the hour-long ride to Jìngxī. All up, the trip should take around two hours, though three isn't unheard of.

AROUND DÉTIĀN
Dàxīn
☎ 0771 • pop 350,000

Dàxīn is the usual staging point for Détiān Waterfall. A sleepy town, there's not much to see here besides the fall, but there are worse places to have to stay overnight. On the western edge of town, left at the big intersection, is the **South Gate** (Nánmén), which locals claim dates from the Zhou dynasty.

Places to Stay & Eat Everything is found *left* out of the bus station. *Xīndu Dàjiǔdiàn* (☎ 362 2011) is a clean and friendly place 100m past the first intersection. It has dorm beds from Y10 and doubles with air-con for Y68.

The best choice in town is ***Táoyuán Dàjiǔdiàn*** (☎ *362 1018),* where beds in quad dorms are Y20 and singles/doubles start at Y39. More comfy twins/doubles are Y108/116. All rooms are spacious and as clean as you'll find anywhere for the price. It's just a bit farther down on the same side of the street.

There are heaps of places to eat – mostly point-and-choose stir-fries and hotpot – out on the street.

Getting There & Away Express buses to Nánníng (Y40, 3½ hours) flow pretty much constantly from 5am to 5.30pm. Buses to Xiàléi, which get you to Shuòlóng and Détiān Waterfall, depart half hourly (Y8, 1½ hours). Otherwise, show up at the station and wait for buses to depart when full.

Hēishuǐ Hé 黑水河
Halfway between Shuòlóng and Dàxīn, the road hugs one of the bends of the Hēishuǐ Hé (Black Water River). There's a minor path that leads down to the river where a couple of small tour boats can take you for a cruise along this picturesque section of the river where limestone peaks soar above. It is also possible to arrange for the boats to take you downstream to Nà'ān, from where you can hook up with one of the regular buses back to Dàxīn.

JÌNGXĪ 靖西
☎ 0776 • pop 570,000
Jìngxī sits somewhat isolated midway between Détiān Waterfall and Bǎisè. It looks ugly coming in from the south, but a stroll along the main drag reveals it to be modestly well off, if a bit unkempt. Jìngxī has nothing much in the centre of town itself, but nearby are some fine sights.

Things to See
If you need to kill time while waiting for a bus, exit the rear of the bus station into the car park. Look up to the right (north-east). The **dragon statue** atop the hill can be reached via steps and a moderately strenuous climb, though don't expect a breathtaking vista.

Also nearby is **Dragon Pool** (Lóngtán), a few ponds joined by streams with a small temple at the head of the pools. Just keep asking for directions or it's a Y3 motorcycle-taxi ride from the bus terminal.

Better is **Wòlóng Cave** (Wòlóng Dòng), 5km from the city centre, by the TV tower. However, it was closed to the public when we last visited to allow it to recuperate from overuse.

Places to Stay
The frenetic bus station has a flophouse *guesthouse* with rooms from Y10, but there's no need to resort to that, since any number of cheap places accept foreigners. Exit the northern bus station, turn left and wander along for a bit. There are quite a few reasonably priced new inns along here.

Bīngān Sùshè is 250m down from the bus terminal on the left and is a pleasant, quiet and clean place with twins for Y30. Its ground-floor restaurant is not bad.

The best digs in town are found at the decent *Xīngyuán Dàjiǔdiàn* (☎ *621 6300).* Turn left out of the northern bus station and walk down the main drag to the first intersection. The hotel is on the corner. Doubles are Y60 and beds in twins/triples cost Y25/20. Some triples and quads have more reasonable per-bed prices, but you can't split up rooms. The staff is quite friendly.

Most places in Jìngxī have hot water in the evening.

Places to Eat
You'll notice lots of woks frying the local favourite snack, *yóu zhā* (triangular rice-flour wrappers stuffed with fresh greens, bean sprouts, and mostly beef). For five máo they're pretty cheap and filling. They also fry duck legs in these wrappers.

Opposite the northern bus terminal is a good, cheap fast-food restaurant. Just point and choose your dishes.

Just north of Bīng'ān Sùshè are a couple of restaurants serving a tasty local favourite, *juàntǒngfěn* (steamed noodle pancake wrap with a pork and coriander filling served in a steaming broth, Y0.40 per roll). Add extra chilli, spring onion and coriander to taste.

Another good little restaurant is farther south down the road on the left before E'quan Jie. There is no sign, but it's next door to Ruìfēng Bǐngshì, a birthday-cake bakery.

For self caterers, there is a large fresh-produce *market* behind the Xīngyuán Dàjiǔdiàn. A *supermarket* is also here.

Getting There & Away
There are two bus stations in Jìngxī: northern and southern. The southern is for local or regional buses and you may be dropped off there. The northern station is more long-distance oriented and has departures to Bǎisè every 20 minutes (Y20, four hours) or hourly express buses (Y30, 3½ hours). There are also frequent buses to Nánníng (Y70, five hours). The entrance is to the right past the reception for the station's hostel.

Most buses, not express, that depart from the northern station pass by the southern station on their way out of town. It may be just as easy to wait around out the front for your bus. Useful departures from the southern station include: Xiàléi, Dàxīn (for Détiān Waterfall) and Húrùn (for Tōnglíng).

AROUND JÌNGXĪ
Jìngxī is regarded as a 'little Gùilín' with its fine karst scenery and rustic country atmosphere. The countryside around Jìngxī is gradually becoming more popular and an increasing number of areas are being developed or receiving a face-lift.

Tōnglíng, 32km east of Jìngxī, is one of these areas – a scenic valley with impressive scenery boasting cascades, rock formations, waterfalls, natural pools, canyons and boating. To get there catch any bus going to Húrùn, Xiàléi or Dàxīn. Ask the driver to drop you off at the entrance to Tōnglíng (Y5) and make suer it is not at the nearby town of Xīnqún. You will need to head back around 4pm as buses are less frequent after that.

One trip you might want to consider is to the semi-preserved town of Jiùzhōu, 16km south of Jìngxī along the road to Dìzhōu. The main attraction is Jiùzhōu Pavilion (Jiùzhōu Wénchāng Gé). This is the pagoda

you'll see on lots of murals in Jìngxī and across the entire county. This is also the place to shop for **xiùqiú**, little needlepoint globes that are the handicraft speciality of the Zhuang in western Guǎngxī. Wander through the town passing all the small workshops where the women meticulously carry out their embroidery and needlework. Xiùqiú cost between Y5 and Y20 depending on their size.

To get to Jiùzhōu from Jìngxī, hop on one of the frequent (every 15 minutes) No 1 local buses from the intersection next to the Xīngyuán Dàjiǔdiàn (Y1.50, 15 minutes). The bus drops you off just a short walk from the village. You may need to wander through the village for a while to see the pagoda, depending on where you are dropppcd off.

Calling Rock (Jiàohǎnyán) is another popular local site. It's an impressive limestone cave full of caverns, stalactites, stalagmites and fluorescent lights.

If you need some fresh air after the cave, continue along the main road over the hill to **Goose Spring** (É'quán), a natural spring where you can sit and drink tea while absorbing the surroundings and watching the fish in the spring. The restaurant specialises in *é'dàn tāng*, (goose-egg soup) and also makes a tasty dish of the local fish.

Calling Rock and Goose Spring are both reached on the No 2 local bus that leaves every 30 minutes (Y1.50, 15 minutes). Just ask the driver to drop you off at the cave and then it's a 600m walk to the entrance. Entry to both attractions is Y6.

BǍISÈ 白色
☎ 0776 • pop 120,000
Bǎisè (Bose) is the largest city in western Guǎngxī. Despite its size and historical significance, most travellers don't seem to know it's there. Definitely worth a stop, this trim, up-and-coming city has a minor buzz to it and has some worthy sights. Bǎisè was as much of a backwater as the rest of the province until Deng Xiaoping and the Seventh Red Army combined two divisions of men in Nánníng and steamed north west up the Yōng Jiāng into the hills and established

GUǍNGXĪ

its base of operations in the city. On 11 December 1929 – a date chosen to commemorate an uprising in Guǎngdōng – the communist flag was raised above Bǎisè, signalling a great expansion of the revolution into the hinterlands. This would eventually result in a long march through Guǎngxī, Húnán, Guǎngdōng and Jiāngxī that in many ways paralleled Mao's famous Long March.

Bǎisè's historical significance has given it a solid tourism base. It is also a useful transit point for further explorations of the minority towns north of Bǎisè towards Língyún.

Orientation

Cradled in a nook at the confluence of Dèngbì Hé and Yòu Jiāng, the city centre is quite compact. It is laid out in a quadrant that basically runs north-west to south-east, with Xiangyang Lu running through the centre. The bus station sits at the top of the quadrant. The train station is inconveniently 6km east of downtown.

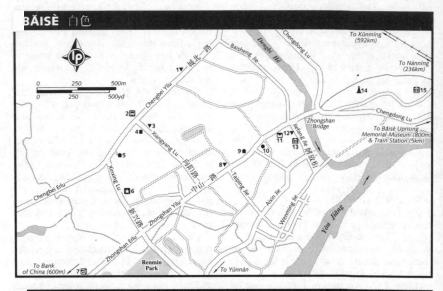

BĂISÈ 白色

PLACES TO STAY
4 Xiánlì Fàndiàn
贤丽饭店
5 Co-op Hotel
供销大厦
9 Bǎisè Fàndiàn
白色饭店

PLACES TO EAT
1 Guìzhōu Héwèi Cānguǎn
贵州合味餐馆
3 Jīnfēnghuá Restaurant
金丰华餐馆

8 Xīnměi Restaurant & Bakery
新美饭店、饼屋
12 Tea House
灵洲会馆

OTHER
2 Bǎisè Bus Station
百色汽车站
6 PSB
公安局
7 China Post & Telecom (Internet Bar)
邮电局（网吧）

10 Xinhua Bookstore
新华书店
11 China Post & Telecom
中国电信
13 Bǎisè Uprising Museum
粤东会馆
14 Bǎisè Uprising Memorial
白色起义烈士纪念碑园
15 Yòu River Minorities Museum
右江民族博物馆

The older section of town between Zhongshan Yilu and Aixin Jie is worth a wander. Sadly most of the older buildings in this area are earmarked for demolition. One area that has been preserved from the ravages of the white-tiled and reflective blue-glass buildings is the historical Jiefang Jie. Before the 1949 revolution this street was the business-activity centre for visiting traders from Guǎngdōng.

Information

Public Security Bureau The PSB office is south-west of the bus station on Xinxing Lu. The foreign affairs office (Wàishìkē) is on the left inside the entrance. It's open 8.30am to noon and 2.30pm to 6pm weekdays.

Money The only place to change travellers cheques is the distant Zhongshan Erlu branch of the Bank of China. Continue past the China Post & Telecom building for another 600m; it's on the right.

Post & Communications The main China Post & Telecom building is on Zhongshan Yilu. Long-distance calls can be made from the 2nd floor. The Zhongshan Erlu branch also has an Internet bar (Y6 per hour) next door.

Bǎisè Uprising Museum
粤东会馆 Yuèdōng Huìguǎn

This interesting museum occupies one of the best surviving examples of old architecture in Bǎisè. On Jiefang Jie, south of Zhongshan Bridge, the museum traces every movement of Deng Xiaoping and the Seventh Red Army during the 1920s and 1930s. Heavy on historical photos, and also featuring display cases of uniforms, documents and other detritus of military offices, the museum unfortunately has no forcign-language translations. You may, however, enjoy the paintings and cool diorama of old Bǎisè, along with a display of the army's progress in 1930–31.

The museum is open 8am to noon and 3pm to 6pm Monday to Saturday, and 9am to 5pm Sunday from 1 April to 30 October. The afternoon hours are 2pm to 5pm from 1 November to 31 March. Admission is Y5.

Deng Xiaoping used the Qingfeng Building, down an alley off Xiangyang Lu, as an office when holed up in Bǎisè.

Bǎisè Uprising Memorial & Yòu River Minorities Museum
Bǎisè Qǐyì Lièshì Jìniànbēi & Yòu Jiāng Mínzú

As you cross the Zhōngshān Bridge from the city centre, you cannot help but notice the newish Bǎisè Uprising Memorial. It's a tall white – Bǎisè is called 'White City' after all – spire, overlooking the town from a hill and reached by lots and lots of steps.

Continue east a few minutes along the paved path and you'll come to the Yòu River Minorities Museum, another place with a staff so eager to see foreigners you may find yourself with an entourage leading you around. The building's exterior is a bit weary-looking, but the museum's holdings and displays are well worth a visit. The first room includes a mock-up of a Pinguo excavation of a 15th-century temple site. Other rooms examine each of western Guǎngxī's minorities in minute detail. Fabrics, weaving, clothing, pottery, bronze drums, ornamental wares and lots more line the walls. There's even a full-sized dwelling and a dugout canoe. Of particular interest are the cases displaying puppets, large masks and early script. Admission is Y8.

Bǎisè Uprising Memorial Museum 百色起义纪念博物馆
Bǎisè Qǐyì Jìniànguǎn

This impressive new museum inside Yínglóngshān Park is another reminder of the central place of Bǎisè as a revolutionary base for the Communists. The collection includes a variety of revolutionary memorabilia and is a popular place for school politics classes.

The museum is open 9am to 5pm daily. Entry costs Y10. Bus Nos 1, 4 and 9 run from the bus station past the museum.

Renmin Park 人民公园
Rénmín Gōngyuán

This micro-sized park is on the west side of the city centre along Zhongshan Lu. Its tree-lined paths pass by croquet-playing seniors.

Deng Xiaoping & the Seventh Red Army in Guǎngxī

By the late 1920s, the Chinese Communist Party had still failed to make any serious inroads into South-West China. All that changed after Deng Xiaoping was sent to Guǎngxī in April 1929 to execute the general plans agreed at the 6th Chinese Communist Party Congress in Moscow. In essence he was sent to organise the peasantry into 'soviets' and incite rural insurrections in support of growing numbers of urban uprisings.

With the help of Ho Chi Minh, Deng arrived in Guǎngxī, which historically was among the most isolated of China's south-west provinces. Han Chinese – Nationalist or otherwise – controlled virtually none of the province. When Deng arrived in Nánníng in 1929, along with Zhang Yunyi, he began a cordial relationship with the governor. Eventually Zhang was appointed commander of a provincial garrison, which in time gave the pair access to an astonishing cache of weapons. They also began funnelling assistance to Zhuang rebels in the Yòu Jiāng region, and Deng dispatched a battalion into the mountainous area. By September 1929 a Communist Congress in Nánníng had decided to establish a Red Army. Two forces remained in southern Guǎngxī and were routed by Nationalist forces, but they bought enough time for Deng and Zhang to lead their 1000-soldier-strong force north-west into Bǎisè (known then as Bose).

Organising a headquarters at Bǎisè made a great deal of sense. In the 1920s it was still among China's most backward and ignored towns and the citizens needed little encouragement to sympathise with the Communists. Soon Deng's new Seventh Red Army had grown to over 7000 men.

On 11 December 1929, a date chosen to mark the anniversary of another uprising in Guǎngdōng, a red flag was raised over Bǎisè and the Yòu River Soviet Government was declared, with Deng as political commissar. The movement spread rapidly and eventually over a million people declared themselves part of the soviet. Bǎisè's 'uprising' was a bloodless event, but another in Lóngzhōu was definitely not.

The charm of the new movement didn't last forever and the Communists eventually met resistance to their plans. Initial land reforms were rebuffed when they caused greater problems for the peasants than before. Further, the Chinese Communist Party leadership went too far, too quickly. They expected newly formed Red Armies to almost immediately march throughout Guǎngxī and establish a strong channel into Guǎngdōng – something Deng thought was suicidal, but which he dutifully undertook nonetheless in early 1930. The armies disintegrated quickly and were defeated, necessitating Deng's own version of the 'Long March' to Jiāngxī to hook up with Mao's army. For nearly two years, the little army wandered through Guǎngdōng, Guǎngxī, Húnán and Jiāngxī, losing huge numbers of men to desertion and attrition by Nationalist forces. They didn't arrive until the middle of 1931, when they were absorbed by Mao's army.

Though the Guǎngxī uprisings did not create the Soviet utopias hoped for, 11 December 1929 was significant, as it signalled an expansion of the communist strongholds into South-West China.

A pond with paddleboats lies at the rear of the park. Admission is five máo.

Places to Stay

Bǎisè has a good range of budget options, but is a little thin on mid-range and top-end possibilities at present.

A good option is the clean and quiet *Xiànlì Fàndiàn* (☎ 284 2718) along Xiangyang Lu, the street opposite the bus station. Beds start at Y30 in a triple with bathroom. All rooms have 24-hour hot water and all advertised rates are readily discounted.

Another good choice is *Co-op Hotel* (*Gōng-xiāo Dàshà;* ☎ 282 4292), a well-run outfit with clean rooms from Y40. The hotel is just off the street down a small lane near the corner of Cheng Beilu and Xinxing Lu.

Bǎisè Fàndiàn (☎ 284 7781) is probably the best mid-range place in town with reasonably priced and newly refurbished rooms. Doubles cost Y158 or Y180 while twins range from Y108 to Y238; triples go for Y120. Discounts of 30% to 40% are usually available on walk-in prices. The reception desk is hidden in the middle of one of the wings, around to the right of the entrance – just follow the signs.

Places to Eat

Bǎisè is within spitting distance of Guìzhōu, so 'hot' is the default setting for food. The local delicacy is huā jiāng gǒuròu, dog meat dipped in hot oil and slathered with chillies.

Budget eaters should head a block southeast of the bus station on Xiangyang Lu. *Jīnfēnghuá Restaurant,* on the left side of the street, is a set-meal place with just about every phrasebook entree represented, starting at around Y7. Sadly, vegetarians aren't catered for. The restaurant claims its across-the-bridge noodles are the speciality, along with Yangzhou fried rice and *mápó dòufǔ* (spicy tofu).

Bǎisè's young and hip seem to all eat at *Xīnměi,* probably the trendiest place in town with a bakery downstairs and a restaurant upstairs serving a mixture of Taiwanese and Western dishes. The Taiwanese mini-hotpot (Y18) is pretty popular for couples, but you will need to order extra ingredients, like mushrooms, tofu etc. Otherwise try the Sichuanese noodles (*dānzimiàn,* Y5), sandwiches (Y5) or a steak (Y18). Most Taiwanese-style drinks are available, as well as filtered coffee (Y9).

North-east of the bus station are two Guìzhōu restaurants serving lots of dishes other than doggie. The best is *Guìzhōu Héwèi Cānguǎn,* with a copious menu devoid of English, but a cheery, helpful staff. There is at least one full page of tofu and vegetable dishes for nonmeat eaters.

A great little *teahouse* has recently opened in Língzhōu Huìguǎn, a restored 19th-century meeting hall on historic Jiefang Jie. Traditional musical performances are often staged here between May and October or when a Chinese tour group drops in. The building used to be a meeting place for visiting wealthy southern businessmen and dates

from 1876. Try the famous white-hair green tea (*língyún bǎihǎo chá,* Y28) from nearby Língyún county and the local Máojiān tea (Y58). There are also plans for traditional tea-ceremony classes to be held here.

Getting There & Away

Bus Express buses leave Bǎisè for Nánníng at 7.30am and 2.50pm (Y45, four hours). Regular buses (Y23) or sleepers (Y32) depart five times daily until 11am. Some of these buses pass through Dàxīn, from where you can visit Détiān Waterfall. To Jìngxī, buses leave up to three times hourly between 6am and 5.30pm (Y30, 3½ hours). A daily sleeper departs for Liǔzhōu (Y95, seven hours). Express-bus tickets should be purchased from the ticket window inside the waiting area, near the bus parking area.

Buses for the 96km trip to Língyún depart from the local bus stand next door. Exit the bus station and go to the left gate. Useful express buses to Língyún depart at 7.40pm and 1.40pm (Y20, two hours). Regular buses to Língyún leave every 30 minutes, but take three hours.

Train Bǎisè has daily connections to Nánníng (Nos 1166, 2006, 5514 and 8566, four hours), Kūnmíng (Nos 1165 and 2005, 11 hours) and Guǎngzhōu (No 1166, 21 hours). The train station is way out of town, so try to buy your tickets from your hotel. Bus No 1 connects the bus and train stations, via Zhongshan Lu.

Getting Around

Bǎisè is small enough to get around on foot. Bus No 1 to the train station passes the Bǎisè Uprising Memorial Museum.

AROUND BǍISÈ
Dèngbì Reservoir 澄碧水库
Dèngbì Shuǐkù

Technically outside the city limits, massive Dèngbì Reservoir – the name means 'clear blue' – is still close enough to reach by local bus. The third-largest impoundment of its kind, obviously water recreation is the attraction here. A boat trip is required to see anything of interest on the lake's shoreline.

Things slow to a halt in late October, so plan for a summer visit.

Bus No 7 (Y1) runs out past the reservoir. You can hop on just outside the Co-op Hotel or anywhere along Zhongshan Lu. Hop off at either the Zhangba Lu stop or farther on at Paihong stop (30 minutes).

Língyún 凌云

A scenic two-hour drive through the mountains following the Dèngbì Hé 80km north of Bǎisè brings you to the town of Língyún. The windy road passes some absolutely stunning scenery full of beautiful minority villages with humble abodes, many of which are made of mud brick and wood. Língyún is a useful staging post for adventures to visit nearby caves, tea plantations and colourful minority villages.

If you have more time you could continue on north to Lèyè county where there are some impressive karst landscapes. One recent discovery is a funnel-shaped limestone formation that is more than 500m deep and around 550m across. This karst funnel, believed to be the third largest in the world, includes an underground river and some primitive forests. Most of these landscapes require professional caving equipment to explore and permission from the authorities, but you can appreciate the beauty of the area through off-the-track exploring.

Língyún Caves
Língyún Dòng

North of Língyún are **River Source Caves** (Shuǐyuán Dòng) and **Nàlíng Cave** (Nàlíng Dòng). They're as impressive as the caves in Seven Star Park in Gùilín, though not nearly as developed (and thus covered in graffiti).

River Source Caves feature a 2.5km trek underground and you might get a chance to see the rare *wawa* fish. Half the cave has been closed for renovations, no doubt for installing more dazzling special effects. Entry costs Y60 including a guide.

Not far away, Nàlíng Cave is equally impressive and entertaining. Entry is a more modest Y20.

A motorcycle taxi is the best way to get to either cave (Y2) from the bus station.

Língyún Tea Plantations 凌云茶园
Língyún Chàyuàn

If you have a day to spare, then a trip to the nearby terraced tea plantations is well worth it. Sadly the local bus only goes halfway, but it is possible to walk the final leg. Otherwise there are plenty of hitching opportunities. Just ask at the bus station for the next local bus. If you don't have the time, try a cup of the local white-hair green tea in town at one of the teahouses or restaurants. This tea leaf is regarded as one of China's finest.

Getting There & Away To get to Língyún from Bǎisè, catch one of the buses departing from the left gate of the bus station every half-hour or so (Y12, two hours). Express buses depart at 7.40am and 1.40pm (Y20). Heading back to Bǎisè is the same, with express buses departing at 4.30pm and 7pm.

GUÌPÍNG 桂平
☎ 0775

For a break in the journey between Nánníng and Wúzhōu, Guìpíng definitely warrants a stop. The wonderful mountain scenery of Xīshān Park, on the western fringes of town, lures most visitors. An hour to the north is the birthplace of the bloody Taiping Rebellion. Beautiful **Dragon Pool National Forest Park** and **Tàipíngshān Nature Reserve** are both an hour to the north-west.

Guìpíng comes alive at night and the locals are definitely friendly.

Information

The main China Post & Telecom office is on the corner of Renmin Zhonglu and Guigui Beilu. There is an Internet bar (Y3 per hour) on the 2nd floor of China Telecom.

The main Bank of China branch is the only place to change travellers cheques. The numerous other branches will generally only change US cash.

Xīshān Park 西山公园
Xīshān Gōngyuán

On the western fringes of town, Xīshān (880m) is considered one of the prettiest mountains in Guǎngxī. If the haze has lifted, you can get some decent views from

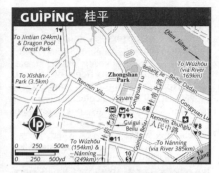

GUÌPÍNG 桂平

GUÌPÍNG

1 Tiānkèténg
   天客逢
2 Bus Station
   汽车站
3 Small Claypot
   Restaurant
   保火粉
4 China Post & Telecom
   (Internet)
   邮电局（网吧）
5 Night Market
   夜市
6 Guìpíng Fàndiàn
   桂平饭店
7 PSB
   公安局
8 Bǎoyǎng Fàndiàn
   保养饭店
9 Restaurant
   餐厅
10 Bank of China
   中国银行
11 Forestry Department;
   Travel Agency
   林业局、旅游联络处

the summit. Xīshān is popular year-round and there are a few temples along the trails (most cost Y2 to enter). If you walk quickly, you can get to the top – your goal, sadly, is a TV tower – in an hour, but the last part of the climb is difficult, with rough, slippery steps. If you are not interested in working up a sweat, then you can ride the chair lift (*zuòsù*). It costs Y31 for a return trip, including the entry fee of Y10. In times past you were treated to the bizarre

spectacle of acrobats performing on a high-wire next to you as you ascended. Sadly, the show has been brought to an end.

While at the park, you will no doubt notice the local speciality – Xīshān tea. Purportedly, certain rare, perfect examples of the tea can sell for as much as Y2000 per kilogram. Pricewise, you're probably best haggling with one of the innumerable tea hawkers back in town.

To get to the park, take one of the buses (Y1) departing from the square every 15 minutes between 7am and 4pm, sometimes later in summer. A motorcycle-taxi ride costs Y2 to the car park or Y5 to the entrance. The park is open 8am to 5pm and entry costs Y11.

Places to Stay

The local authorities have simplified accommodation options in Guìpíng. The only place open to foreigners is the enormous ***Guìpíng Fàndiàn*** (☎ 338 2775, fax 338 3919). This isn't as bad as it seems, as there is a mind-boggling array of rooms ranging from Y20 per bed in a quad, to Y45 in a single and Y250 for superior offerings. Rooms are a little spartan, but the environment is pleasant enough. Some of the singles in the older No 2 building even have balconies. The hotel is just south of the square on Renmin Zhonglu.

Staying the night at Xīshān is a better option than in town, as the air is clearer and the environment more peaceful. There are a couple of basic inns around the base of the hill. However, foreigners are only officially allowed to stay at the posh ***Gōngdé Shānzhuāng*** (☎ 339 3399, fax 339 3618). Rooms are not cheap, at Y298 for a double. Discounts of 20% are usually available and the service here is impeccable. Furthermore the grounds of the hotel are nicely landscaped. From the car park continue along the main road beyond the stairs up to the cable car to get to the hotel.

Places to Eat

Directly across the street from the bus station is a ***small restaurant***, firing up clay pots of rice casserole.

Bǎoyǎng Fàndiàn is 100m beyond the PSB and is a fine place to try some local flavours. The restaurant on the opposite side of the road is just as popular and offers a similar menu. A little farther down is *Róngzǐ Huāyuán Fànzhuāng*, a teahouse overlooking the river and wharf.

The restaurant inside the Guìpíng Fàndiàn is reputedly one of the best in town. Some of its speciality dishes include *shengjiān huáishān* (fried dried yam root), *xiǎojuān sǔnsī* (spring bamboo shoots) and *xiāngzāo muchang* (pickled pig stomach).

For once vegetarians aren't left out. At Xīshān Park, next to Xīshīan Hermitage – right of the entrance to the park manager's office and the cable car – is *Cāntīng Cházuò*, a vegetarian restaurant on the 2nd floor. Its entrees are creatively prepared to resemble meat-based dishes. There is also an outstanding restaurant at the *Gōngdé Villa*.

Entertainment

In the evenings the *night market* is a popular social spot for a late snack. Try some of the local noodles, one of which resembles a bowl of spaghetti bolognaise. A more popular evening activity is to head north along Renmin Xilu to the edge of town where you'll find *Tiānkèféng,* which is literally dozens of outdoor drinking huts. Beer, karaoke, tea and spicy snacks are the order. These places are a hive of activity during the warmer months.

Getting There & Away

To Nánníng, express buses leave every three hours (Y50). If you want to get to Gùilín or Liǔzhōu, you need to first travel to Guìyáng (Y12) and change. There are four express buses daily to Wúzhōu (Y30, three hours) and one to Guǎngzhōu at 1pm (Y90, six hours)

AROUND GUÌPÍNG
Jīntián

Just 25km north of Guìpíng is the town of Jīntián, the birthplace of Hong Xiuquan. Hong was a schoolteacher who declared himself a brother of Jesus Christ and led an army of over a million followers against the Qing dynasty in what came to be known as the Taiping Rebellion, one of the bloodiest civil wars in history. A **museum** (Qǐyì Jìniànguǎn) now stands at the site of Hong's home.

The museum has two floors of artefacts and displays tracing the history of the movement, all a little neglected. There are no English explanations, but a few diagrams and maps will keep you guessing which army went where and when. The assorted weaponry may keep you interested. Next to the museum is a glorified replica of the rebel's fortress, built by China Central Television in 1998.

East of the museum is a statue of Hong, and even farther east is a small pond in which the group hid its weapons to keep them from being confiscated. Entry is Y3.

Back towards the village 100m or so, then along a rough dirt road and into the brush is the decaying **old home** of Wei Cheng Hui, another leader of the movement. Here the plotters met and forged their weapons, using the cacophony of flocks of honking geese to mask the sounds of their hammering. The Qing army burned the house, and it wasn't until 1974 that artefacts and fragments of the group's efforts were unearthed. Most relics and memorabilia are kept in Nánjīng, the Taiping kingdom (1853–64) capital. Today the house lies enshrouded in weeds, behind a locked iron gate.

To get to Jīntián, take one of the green buses from inside the Guìpíng bus terminal gates (Y2, 40 minutes). From where the bus terminates in Jīntián you'll have to backtrack 500m or so over the bridge to where you see motorcycle taxis grouped. Go through the red gate there and continue another 4km – a pleasant walk if you've got the time – or a Y6 or so round trip in a sidecar. If you want a side trip to Wei's house, the driver will tack on another Y3. The last bus back to Guìpíng departs around 6pm.

Dragon Pool National Forest Park 龙潭国家森林公园
Lóngtán Guójiā Sēnlín Gōngyuán

Though Xīshān and Jīntián have always been the attraction for most travellers, the opening of this new national forest reserve and park could bring in the throngs. Opened only recently and still lacking much trailside infrastructure – including maps – this park is approximately 20km north-west of Guìpíng. It features rough trails, odd-ball stone formations, valleys everywhere and a host of waterfalls. The park is so diverse in ecology – over 1000 species of plants and 100 of animals – that it's been dubbed a 'Little Xīshuāngbǎnnà'. (It's also known as the 'Shining Pearl' and the 'Plant Treasure Box'.) For once the hype isn't hyperbole – this is one of the most extensive pockets of original forest left in Guǎngxī. You might even be so lucky as to spot the rare wawa fish.

Accommodation is available for about Y20 to Y30 per night.

The only problem with getting to this park is that there's no direct transport. From Guìpíng hop on the bus to Jīntián (Y2) and ask the driver to drop you off where the Lóngtán Park (Lóngtán Lùkǒu) access road turns off. There are usually motorbike taxis waiting at the intersection. They should be able to take you to Lóngtán for about Y20, or Y50 for the round trip.

It is possible to organise a tour to Lóngtán with the Forestry Department's travel agency, Lǚyóu Liánluòchù (☎ 0775-338 0413), inside the Forestry building in Guìpíng. The staff's a friendly bunch and it offers a two-day trip to Lóngtán for Y180 including guide, food, transport and accommodation. Nobody speaks English, but an English-speaking guide can be organised if you give some warning. The agency also organises boat cruises through a scenic gorge along the Zhū Jiāng (Pearl River) Valley.

WÚZHŌU 梧州
☎ 0774 • pop 330,000

For most travellers, Wúzhōu is a pit stop on the road between Yángshuò and Guǎngzhōu or Hong Kong. Although it's not one of Guǎngxī's major attractions, Wúzhōu has some pleasant parks and interesting street life. Give it an overnight stay, as it's an interesting contrast if coming from Hong Kong via the chaos of Guǎngzhōu.

At the confluence of Guì Jiāng and Xún Jiāng, it is effectively two cities: the more modern and developed Héxī (west of the river) and the more interesting Dōnghé (east of the river).

Wúzhōu's strategic position led the British to set up steamer services in 1897 from Wúzhōu to Guǎngzhōu, Hong Kong and later to Nánníng. A British consulate was established, which gives some idea of the town's importance as a trading centre at the time, and the town was also used by British and US missionaries as a launching pad for the conversion of the 'heathen' Chinese.

The period after 1949 saw some industrial development, including the establishment of a paper mill, food-processing factories and machinery and plastics manufacturing works. During the Cultural Revolution, as most places in China, Wúzhōu found itself a battleground of Red Guard factions claiming loyalty to Mao; only here half the city was reportedly destroyed or seriously damaged.

Today, Wúzhōu has some fine street markets (absolutely everywhere you walk, in fact), tailors, tobacco, herbs, roast duck and river life to discover. Wúzhōu also has one of Guǎngxī's more unusual sights in the Snake Repository.

Information

The post office is on Nanhuan Lu, east of the bridge. Next door is China Telecom and hidden behind is an Internet bar. The main Bank of China is nearby on the corner of Zhongshan Lu. Good maps of the city, with bus routes, are available at the shops inside both bus stations.

Snake Repository
Shéchǎng

Wúzhōu has what it claims is the world's largest snake repository, a major drawcard for overseas Chinese tourists and a sight that pulls in the occasional Western traveller. More than one million snakes are transported annually to Wúzhōu (from places like Nánníng, Liǔzhōu and Yúlín) for export to the kitchens of Hong Kong, Macau and other snake-devouring parts of

GUÁNGXĪ

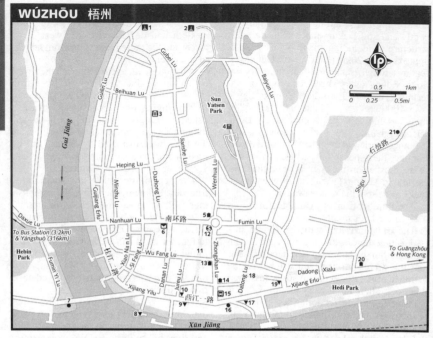

WÚZHŌU 梧州

the world. To get there, walk along Shigu Lu from Wúzhōu Dàjiǔdiàn for about 2km. A motorbike taxi will charge Y2 from the Dōnghé bus station. Snake and cat fights are staged – something you may wish to avoid if you have any respect for animals. The repository is open 8am to 6pm daily. Admission is Y5 or Y10 including an English-speaking guide.

Sun Yatsen Park 中山公园
Zhōngshān Gōngyuán

Sun Yatsen Park is the site of China's earliest memorial hall for the founder of the Republic of China. The hall was constructed in 1928 and commemorates an important speech given by Sun Yatsen in Wúzhōu. The park costs Y1 to enter.

Western Bamboo Temple 西竹寺
Xīzhú Yuán

Just north of town, bordering Sun Yatsen Park, is Western Bamboo Temple, where around 40 Buddhist nuns live. The temple sits above the town and has a lot of character.

The vegetarian restaurant is usually open for lunch on weekends and is highly rated by travellers who have taken the time to wander up here. The restaurant doesn't exactly keep regular hours but, whenever it is open, the earlier you get there, the more likely you'll get food.

To get to the temple continue straight up Wenhua Lu to the top end of Sun Yatsen Park. On the left is a small path that follows a brick wall all the way around to the temple. After visiting the temple you can wander down the back lanes to the Dragon Mother Temple on the river. From the Bamboo Temple turn right out the gate and wander down the zigzag staircase. Halfway down at the large bike rack go right and continue down some more stairs to the first road (Gubei Lu) and turn right. At the intersection with Guilin Lu, turn right and the temple is 300m on your right.

WÚZHŌU

PLACES TO STAY
5 Dōngxìn Bīnguăn
   东信宾馆
13 New World Hotel
   新世界大酒店
14 Gōnghuì Bīnguăn
   工会宾馆
20 Wúzhōu Dàjiŭdiàn
   梧州大酒店

PLACES TO EAT
8 Huālì Jiŭjiā
   花利酒家
9 Fēngyuán
   Huŏguōchéng
   丰源火锅城

10 Street Restaurant
   餐厅
17 Huánán Qīngpŭ
   Mĕiròuchéng
19 Salon of Moto Player

OTHER
1 Dragon Mother
   Temple
   龙母太庙
2 Western Bamboo
   Temple
   西竹园
3 Museum
   博物馆
4 Sun Yatsen Memorial
   中山纪念堂

6 China Post & Telecom
   (Internet)
   邮电局 (网吧)
7 Yuanjiang Pavilion
   鸳江亭
11 Fruit Market
   水果市场
12 Bank of China
   中国银行
15 Dōnghé Bus Station
   东河汽车站
16 Supermarket
   东盛货仓超市
18 Market
   市场
21 Snake Repository
   蛇园

Dragon Mother Temple 龙母太庙

Lóngmŭtàimiáo

Dating from the Northern Song dynasty, but recently renovated, the temple was built in memory of the dragon mother of a mythical female chieftain of the Southern Yae, who is believed to be the mother of the descendants of the dragon. The temple has thus become a popular pilgrimage spot because of the belief that it will help all those in need, especially those born in the year of the dragon.

A good time to visit is during the temple's main festival, which is held on the seventh and eighth day of the fifth lunar month and 15th of the eighth lunar month. Entry costs Y3.

Places to Stay

Budget options are a little scarce in Wúzhōu. Official tourist hotels have a steady flow of overseas Chinese and Hong Kong travellers, so prices are not really low. You may get lucky at one of the cheaper hostels (lŭguăn), but don't count on it.

Out the front of the Dōnghé bus station is *Gōnghuì Bīnguăn,* where the cheapest twins and doubles are Y60 to Y78. An interesting option is the Y65 double without a window – perhaps a little damp, but you would be hard pressed to find a quieter room in town.

The newest place in town is *Dōngxìn Bīnguăn* (☎ 283 888, fax 282 5461, 28 Wenhua Lu), at the top of Zhongshan Lu.

Doubles go for Y186, twins are Y203 and suites are Y350. These prices are already discounted by 50% off the walk-in rate, which seems standard.

New World Hotel (Xīnshìjiè Dàjiŭdiàn; ☎ 282 8222, fax 282 4895) is a good mid-range option. Rooms are a little old, but they are clean. Standard twins and doubles cost Y388, but are usually discounted to Y195.

Similar is the *Wúzhōu Dàjiŭdiàn* (☎ 202 2193, fax 202 4905), with recently renovated good-value rooms with a fridge for Y260. Cheaper rooms (Y118) are a little worn, but still OK.

If you arrive at the Héxī bus station and have an early-morning departure, then you could always try the budget *Mínháng Bīnguăn*. Officially it doesn't take foreigners, but is willing to bend the rules if you speak a bit of Chinese. The hotel is 100m to the right as you exit from the bus station.

Places to Eat

Wúzhōu's riverside restaurants seemed to be going through a tough period when we last visited. Half were rusting hulks stuck in the mud and the other half were on their way to it. There is still a great variety of eateries around town, none too hard to find.

One of the seafood palaces is *Huā Lì Jiŭjiā*, which specialises in game meats and raw fish. Another similar-style eatery is *Huánán Qīngpŭ Mĕiròuchéng,* where you will find a variety of cuisine, including goat, dog, hotpot and seafood. For local flavours at more affordable prices try the popular small *street restaurant* on the corner of Juren Lu and Xijiang Yilu. Opposite on the waterfront is the very popular hotpot restaurant, *Fēngyuán Huǒguōchéng*. The eating area is on the roof so as to allay the heat that is created within. An interesting option is the strangely named *Salon of Moto Player,* offering Western-style food in a try-hard trendy cafe-restaurant.

There is a large *supermarket* on the waterfront opposite the Dōnghé bus station for self-caterers. Otherwise there are plenty of fresh-produce *markets* along the backstreets.

Getting There & Away

Wúzhōu has two bus stations, Dōnghé (east of the river) and the main bus station in Héxī (west of the river). Each serves different destinations, so make sure you check which station your bus is departing from. In general buses heading east leave from Dōnghé and those heading west or north depart from Héxī bus station. Attendants will stamp the ticket if the bus is departing from the other station. You will then need to hop on the free connecting shuttle bus that goes every 30 to 40 minutes. It may be quicker to walk two small blocks north along Zhongshan Lu to the bus stop for bus No 2, which terminates opposite the Héxī bus station (Y1.20, 20 minutes). A taxi will cost around Y20.

It's a bumpy seven hours to Yángshuò (Y70) and another 1½ hours to Guìlín (Y75) from Wúzhōu. Buses depart Héxī bus station at 8.40am, 12.30pm, 4.30pm and 11pm.

There are also express buses to Guǎngzhōu at 10am (Y80, 5½ hours), Liǔzhōu (Y80, seven hours), Nánníng every two hours (Y80, six hours) and Shēnzhèn at 8.30am and 4pm (Y150, six hours). There is also a night bus to Guǎngzhōu (Y45, 6½ hours).

Getting Around

Bus No 3 (Y1.20, 25 minutes) runs between Wúzhōu's Héxī and Dōnghé bus stations. There's also a free shuttle bus departing every 30 to 40 minutes from inside the Dōnghé bus station.

GUÌLÍN 桂林

☎ 0773 • pop 620,000

Guìlín has always been famous in China for its scenery. The city has been eulogised in innumerable literary works, paintings and inscriptions as the most beautiful spot in the world – the world, of course, meaning China. The city can be used as a base for exploring the region, with its dozen or so minority cultures, including large populations of Zhuang, Yao, Miáo, Huí and Dong. Rapid economic growth and a booming tourist trade have diminished some of Guìlín's charm – photographers quickly discover the maddening, seemingly permanent haze that hovers on summer days – but it is still one of China's greener, more scenic cities.

If you can handle the hectic traffic, most of Guìlín's limestone karst peaks and parks are a short bicycle ride away. There is also a wealth of restaurants – particularly of the outdoor point-and-choose variety – and a few now have English menus to boot. Unfortunately, locals don't shy from cashing in on Guìlín's popularity. Most tourist sights levy exploitative entry fees for foreigners, and many travellers tell of being grossly overcharged at restaurants throughout town. Near the train and bus stations, touts appear at every turn. All this means you'll hear plenty of 'best of/worst of' tales of Guìlín.

The prefecture was established in 214 BC during the Qin dynasty but the city was not founded until 111 BC. It developed as a transport centre with the building of the Ling Canal linking the important Pearl and Yangzi river systems. Under the Ming it was the provincial capital, a status it retained until 1914 when Nánníng became the capital. During the 1930s and throughout WWII, Guìlín was a communist stronghold, and its population grew from about 100,000 to over a million as people sought refuge here. Today it's home to around 600,000.

The average temperature seems balmy at 20°C, but don't let that fool you. Come winter (December to February), Guìlín can be chilly and exceedingly damp, thanks to 1900mm of annual precipitation.

If you're itching to get to the heart of karst country, you may do best to skirt the crowds, high prices and heat of the city and go straight to Yángshuò, approximately one hour south of Guìlín by bus. But for those in the mood for a bit of city life, a day or two of cycling around Gùilín can be enjoyable.

Orientation

Most of Guìlín lies on the western bank of the Lí Jiāng. The main artery is Zhongshan Lu, which runs roughly parallel to the river on its western side. At the southern end of this street – that is, Zhongshan Nanlu – is Guìlín's main train station, where most trains pull in. Zhongshan Zhonglu is a rapidly developing stretch of tourist-class hotels, opulent department stores and expensive restaurants – be sure to check prices before you order a bite to eat.

Closer to the centre of town is Róng Hú, to the west of Zhongshan Zhonglu, and Shān Hú on the eastern side. On the other side of the lakes, heading north-east, you'll find Gùilín's new Central Square (Zhōngxīn Guǎngchǎng) and the main shopping and eating district. Farther along Zhongshan Beilu is the main commercial area of the city, the PSB and a few restaurants. Along the Lí Jiāng near Elephant Trunk Hill is the spanking-new CITS office.

Jiefang Lu runs east-west across Zhong-shan Zhonglu. Heading east, it runs over Liberation (Jiefang) Bridge to the large Seven Star Park, one of the town's chief attractions. Most of the limestone pinnacles form a circle around the town, though a few pop up within the city limits. For the best views of the surrounding karst formations you should climb the hills.

Maps There are a couple of reliable maps for Guìlín, but the best one with some English is *The Tourist Maps of Guìlín* (Y4).

Information

Tourist Offices A welcome addition to Guìlín is the appearance of several tourism booths. They vary in their usefulness, but it is a positive sign of things to come. As well as helping you with directions and transport, they may be able to assist with booking accommodation and tour information

(☎ 282 7491). Staff even speak a little English. The main booths are in front of the train station and inside the bus station. Most of the others are at park entrances and are usually only open during summer.

CITS's FIT department (☎ 286 1623, fax 282 2936, 41 Binjiang Lu) has friendly and reasonably helpful staff offering a range of tours. See the Organised Tours section later for details.

PSB The PSB office (☎ 582 9930) for visa extensions (Shì Gōngānjú Chūrùjìng Guǎnlǐsuǒ) is in the Shíjiāyuán area, south off Longyin Lu. It's open 8.30am to noon and from 3pm to 6pm weekdays.

Money The main branch of the Bank of China is on Shanlu Beilu. For changing money and travellers cheques, you can use the branches at the corner of Shanghai Lu and Zhongshan Nanlu – next to the train station – and at Zhongshan Nanlu near Yinding Lu. Most tourist hotels also have foreign-exchange services, which you can usually use even if you're not staying at the hotel.

Post & Communications The main China Post & Telecom building is on Zhongshan Beilu. There is a second post office on the northern corner of the large square in front of the train station.

There's a 24-hour Internet bar inside the southern entrance of Xīnhuá Bookstore on Zhongshan Beilu (Y4 per hour). Another is opposite the main China Post office and is open 9am to 10pm (Y3 per hour).

Bookshops Guìlín's Xīnhuá Bookstore, north along Zhongshan Beilu, has a foreign-language section. Besides an array of English classics and photo-travel books on Gùilín, you could pick up the latest release of *The Evil Cult of Falun Gong* on VCD.

Solitary Beauty Peak 独秀峰

Dúxiù Fēng

This 152m pinnacle is at the centre of the town. The climb to the top is steep, but there are good views of the town, Lí Jiāng and surrounding hills. At the foot of the peak is

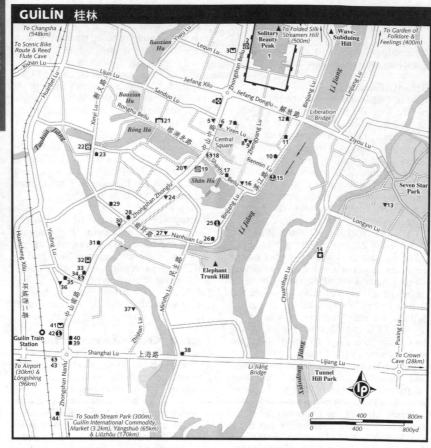

GUÌLÍN 桂林

Wáng Chéng, a 14th-century Ming prince's mansion that was built by the nephew of the emperor, Jing Jiang. Wáng Chéng is now a theatre where there are nightly traditional and minority performances at 7.30pm (Y35). Surrounding the peak are the restored walls and gates of Jing Jiang's palace, now occupied by Guǎngxī Normal University.

Entry to the park costs Y15. Bus Nos 1 and 11 go up Zhongshan Beilu past the western side of the peak. Alternatively, take bus No 2, which goes past the eastern side along the river. Both buses leave from Guìlín train station.

Wave-Subduing Hill 伏波山
Fúbō Shān

Close to Solitary Beauty and beside the western bank of Lí Jiāng, this peak offers a lovely view of the town. One explanation for its name is that the peak descends into the river, blocking the waves. The other is that a temple was established here for a Tang-dynasty general called Fúbō Jiangjun, also known as the wave-subduing general. Upon entering the gate, look out for the large rice pot left behind from the Dìngyuè Sì – it's big enough to cook rice for 1000 people.

GUÌLÍN

PLACES TO STAY

7 Jǐnfēng Bīnguǎn
   锦丰宾馆
10 Guìlín International
   Youth Hostel
   桂林国际青年旅馆
11 Sheraton Guilin
   Hotel
   文华大酒店
12 Universal Hotel
17 Líjiāng Fàndiàn
   漓江饭店
23 Brave Hotel
   桂林宾馆
26 Golden Elephant
   金象大酒店
28 Guìlín Fàndiàn
   桂林饭店
29 Bǎilèmén Jiǔdiàn
   百乐门酒店
31 Osmanthus
   Hotel
   丹桂大酒店
33 Huáli Hotel
   华丽酒店
35 Xīnguì Fàndiàn
   新桂饭店
39 Nánxī Fàndiàn
   南溪饭店
40 New City Hotel
   新城市饭店
44 Overseas Chinese
   Hotel
   华侨大厦

PLACES TO EAT

4 Nikodo Plaza
   微笑堂
5 Good Aunt;
   Bāguì Mansion
   好大妈、八桂大厦
6 MFW
   桂林人/旺角
8 MFW
   桂林人/旺角
9 Chéngdū Xiǎochī
   成都小吃
13 Crescent Mansion
   月乐楼
16 Coffee-Language 110
   名典
20 Forest of Flowers
   花之林茶坊
24 Táilián Hotel
   台联酒店
27 Yìyuán Restaurant
   怡园饭店
30 Jiǔlóng Jiǔjiā
   九龙酒家
36 Dōngběi Fàndiàn
   东北饭店
37 Shèngfā Fàndiàn
   胜发饭店

OTHER

1 Wáng Chéng
   土城
2 Internet Bar
   网吧
3 China Post
   & Telecom
   中国电信
14 PSB
   (visa extensions)
   市公安局出入境管理所
15 Tourist Wharf
   漓江游览船码头
18 Bank of China
   (Main Branch)
   中国银行
19 Xinhua Bookstore;
   Internet Bar
   新华书店
   网吧
21 South City Gate
   南门
22 Guìlín Children's Palace
   桂林少年宫
25 CITS (FIT)
   中国国际旅行社
32 Main Bus Station
   汽车总站
34 Bank of China
   中国银行
38 CAAC
   中国民航
41 Post Office
   邮局
42 Tourist
   Information
   旅游咨询服务中心
43 Bank of China
   中国银行

On the southern slope of the hill is **Returned Pearl Cave** (Huánzhū Dòng). The story goes that the cave was illuminated by a single pearl and inhabited by a dragon; one day a fisherman stole the pearl but he was overcome by shame and returned it. A 1000-year-old Buddha image is etched into the wall somewhere in the cave, along with more than 200 other images of the Buddha, most dating from the Song and Tang dynasties. Somewhere, too, is a portrait and autograph by Mi Fu, a famous calligrapher of the Song dynasty. A sad sight are the Sword Testing Stones, which are remnants of stalactites hacked off by soldiers of the warlord showing off their metal and mettle.

Nearby is **Thousand Buddha Cave** (Qiānfó Yán), though the name's an exaggeration – there seem to be a couple of dozen statues at most, dating from the Tang and Song dynasties. There is a pleasant cafe inside the park overlooking the flowing Lí Jiāng.

Admission is Y10. Bus No 2 runs past the hill.

Folded Silk Streamers Hill
Diécǎi Shān
Also called Folded Brocade Hill, this hill is still farther to the north, and has vistas equal to that of Fúbō Shān, as well as rebuilt pavilions dating as far back as the Ming dynasty. It's also known informally as 'Cassia Hill' for the once-numerous trees that lined

its paths. Overlooking the Lí Jiāng are Mǔlóng Cave and nearby stone pagoda.

Climb the stone pathway that takes you through the cooling relief of Wind Cave, its walls decked with inscriptions and Buddhist sculptures. Some of the damage to faces on the sculptures is a legacy of the Cultural Revolution. Entry costs Y13. Bus Nos 1 and 2 run past the hill.

Seven Star Park 七星公园
Qīxīng Gōngyuán

One of China's nicer city parks, 137-hectare Seven Star Park is on the eastern side of the Lí Jiāng. Cross Liberation Bridge (Jiěfàng Qiáo) and continue to the end of Jiefang Donglu.

The park was one of the original tourist spots in South-West China, and was first opened to sightseers as far back as the Sui dynasty. It takes its name from its seven peaks, which are supposed to resemble the Ursa Major (Big Dipper) constellation. There are several caves in the peaks, where visitors have inscribed graffiti for centuries, including a recent one that says, 'The Chinese Communist Party is the core of the leadership of all the Chinese people'.

Groups of stalagmites and stalactites have been named, though it takes a lot of imagination to see the 'Monkey Picking Peaches', 'Two Dragons Playing Ball', and especially 'Melon and Fruits Woven into Satin'. Seven Star Park and its caves have undergone a recent overhaul. State-of-the-art laser effects have replaced some of the fluorescent lights in the caves and the park's gardens have received a much-needed landscaping. Lots of trails wind in and around the hills and you can picnic on the sprawling lawns. To ensure you don't get lost there is also good English signage. Otherwise, head up to **Round Viewing Pavilion** (Kuàngguān Tíng) to get your bearings and a view of the park.

For lunch visit the **Crescent Mansion** (Yuèlèlōu) where there is a good range of vegetarian food on offer. Try the local speciality *gūzi miàn* or nun noodles.

General admission to the park costs Y20 and an extra Y25 for entry to the caves (Y30 in summer). The park is open 7am to 9.30pm daily and the caves 8am to 5pm.

To get to the park, take bus No 9, 10 or 11 from the train station. From the park, No 3 runs across the Lí Jiāng, past Wave-Subduing Hill and to Reed Flute Cave.

Tunnel Hill Park 穿山公园
Chuān Shān Gōngyuán

South of Seven Star Park and still on the eastern side of the Lí Jiāng, Tunnel Hill

---

Dangers & Annoyances

In Guìlín it's always hunting season, and your wallet is the quarry. Whether it's a fourfold price hike in the cost of a meal, a wildly circuitous taxi ride or exorbitant entry fees, almost every traveller can count on having to deal with overcharging. Stay alert to potential rip-offs and calmly negotiate prices first. And keep the word 'calm' in mind no matter what, because it's easy to lose your cool and that makes things worse.

Be wary of students wanting to practise English with you. Signs of possible scam artists include a willingness to discuss ways of spending your money. Also, watch out for pickpockets, especially around the train station. We receive a steady stream of letters from fellow travellers warning of scam tour guides and bad experiences. All of the letters have one thing in common – Guìlín.

A recent and more disturbing phenomenon is the explosion of touts in Guìlín. In the past it was always someone offering accommodation, a taxi ride, a tour of Guìlín or perhaps even changing money, but now touting has become more bold with offers of massage, freak shows, escort services and even sex. Most of these more spicy offers pop up in the evening around the bus and train stations or at the entrance to top-end hotels. If you want to stay out of trouble, then keep your hands in your pockets, preferably on your valuables, and your nose to the ground.

Park rates a mention since most locals claim its cave is superior to those of Seven Star Park in every way. The cave is interesting, but the park is quite run down. If you tire of the cave, you can cross the Xiǎodōng Jiāng (a small branch of the Lí) and can hike up to a fairly interesting pagoda. Near the summit of the hill is a wind-eroded chasm that supposedly resembles a moonscape from afar.

Reed Flute Cave 芦笛岩
Lúdí Yán
Some of the most extraordinary scenery Guìlín has to offer is 240m underground at the Reed Flute Cave, where multicoloured lighting and fantastic stalactites and stalagmites resemble a set from *Journey to the Centre of the Earth*. At one time the entrance to the cave was distinguished by clumps of reeds used by the locals to make musical instruments, hence the name.

The **Crystal Palace of the Dragon King** grotto can comfortably hold about 1000 people, though many more crammed in here during the war when the cave was used as an air-raid shelter for protection by the locals.

Despite the high entrance price (Y40), the cave is worth visiting. Consider some of the surrounding walks, including those up to Half-Hill Pavilion and across to Lotus Pond.

The cave is on the north-western outskirts of town. Take bus No 3 (Y1.50) from the train station to the last stop. Otherwise, it's a pleasant bicycle ride. Follow the bus route along Lijun Lu, which runs into Xishan Lu and then Taohua Jiāng Lu. The latter parallels the small river, Táohuā Jiāng, and winds through fields and karst peaks – a welcome break from the traffic of Zhongshan Lu. At Ludi Lu turn left and continue for another 1.2km.

Other Sights
At the southern end of town, one of Guìlín's best-known sights is **Elephant Trunk Hill** (Xiàngbí Shān), which actually does resemble an elephant dipping its snout into the Lí Jiāng. Visit Water Moon Cave and head up the peak walk to Púxiǎn Pagoda for

---

Legends of the Caves

Many legends surround the limestone formations for which Reed Flute Cave is famous. In the grotto known as the Crystal Palace of the Dragon King, the dominant feature is a great slab of white rock hanging from a ledge like a cataract.

The slab is said to be the Dragon King's needle, used as a weapon by his opponent the Monkey King. The Monkey King used the needle to destroy the dragon's army of snails and jellyfish, leaving their petrified remains scattered around the floor of the cave.

Opposite this stands a huge stalactite resembling an old scholar. It's said that a visiting scholar wished to write a poem worthy of the cave's beauty. After a long time he had composed only two sentences and, lamenting his inability to find the right words, turned to stone.

You can no doubt invent your own stories! In all, over 30 other 'scenes' have been isolated and given fanciful names – my favourite has to be 'Giant Lion Seeing off Guests'.

---

a view of the park and the picturesque Lí Jiāng. Entry costs Y15.

At the southern end of Guìlín, **South Stream Park** (Nánxī Gōngyuán) is a pretty place. You can contemplate the mythological immortal who is said to have lived in one of the caves here; look for his statue.

There are two lakes near the city centre, **Róng Hú** on the western side of Zhongshan Zhonglu and **Shān Hú** on the eastern side. Róng Hú is named after an 800-year-old banyan tree on its shore. The tree stands by the restored **South City Gate** (Nán Mén) originally built during the Tang dynasty. These lakes and their surrounds have recently received a face-lift making it one of the nicer neighbourhoods in town for a stroll.

Organised Tours
CITS's FIT department can organise a number of tours, including a half-day city tour (Y200) and a full-day Lí Jiāng tour (Y460 or Y420) to Yángshuò. This includes

the drive to Zhújiāng Pier and the four-hour river trip. You will have about 1½ hours in Yángshuò before returning by bus to Guìlín. CITS also organises longer trips, but prefers larger groups.

Places to Stay – Budget

For those on a backpacker's budget, Guìlín is lacking – the lower end of the market is served primarily by Yángshuò.

A very welcome addition to Guìlín is *Guìlín International Youth Hostel* (Guìlín Guójì Qīngnián Lǚguǎn; ☎ 282 7115, fax 282 7116, e magùilíniyh@263.net, 90 Binjiang Lu). This clean and friendly place has beds in quads for Y50 (Y35 for YHA members). Twin rooms are Y150 and suites cost Y258, however these are readily discounted to Y120 and Y200 respectively. The hostel also organises a number of tours (through CITS) in and around Guìlín. Bike rental is available for Y20 per day and there's an Internet bar next to the cafe (Y10 per hour). Washing facilities are available and the staff will also help book train and plane tickets.

The central *Guìlín Fàndiàn* (☎ 282 2754) is a tad weary, but there are cheap beds from Y30 in a twin or triple with shared bathroom or from Y140 in a double with bathroom. Hot water is available from 6pm. Rooms are discounted by 20% outside of summer.

Just around the corner *Bǎilèmén Jiǔdiàn* (☎ 282 5492, 42 Nanhuan Lu) has basic but OK doubles and twins for Y70 and Y80. Hot water is available after 7pm.

Overseas Chinese Hotel (Huáqiáo Dàshà; ☎ 383 5753, ext 2001) is an old backpackers' stand-by. Despite being a little inconveniently located south of the train station, it does offer reasonable beds in twins for Y44 with shared bathroom. Beds in twins with bath start at Y70.

Across from the train station, *Nánxī Fàndiàn* has doubles from Y100, twins from Y120 and beds in triples for Y40 (although you may be asked to take the whole room). Hot water is available in the evening from 7pm to 11.30pm.

A five-minute walk north of the train station, on Yinding Lu, *Xīnguì Fàndiàn* has singles/doubles starting at Y60/100. You can try to wrangle a room in a reported 'secret' old wing, which has four-bed rooms for Y16 each and triples for Y20 each, but don't count on it.

Places to Stay – Mid-Range

Most of the budget places mentioned above have nicer rooms for Y100 to Y200, but there are also a couple of mid-range spots for those setting their sights a bit higher.

The convenient *Huálì Hotel* (Huálì Jiǔdiàn; ☎ 383 6409, fax 382 7103) is a well-kept, quiet and clean place just 180m south of the bus station. Twins, triples and doubles are available from Y130/150/120, but they are often discounted to Y100 or less.

Jǐnfēng Bīnguǎn (☎ 283 8919), down a lane off Central Square, offers good mid-range rooms that fill up quickly. Twins are Y180 or Y214 for a larger room and doubles are also Y214.

Golden Elephant (Jīnxiàng Dàjiǔdiàn; ☎ 280 8888, fax 280 9999, 36 Binjiang Lu) is one of Guìlín's better run three-star hotels. Very comfortable twins and doubles cost Y320. It also offers very stylish, traditional Korean *ondol* suites for Y960. Some of the rooms also have nice views of the Lí Jiāng and Elephant Trunk Hill. Attached to the hotel is a fine Korean restaurant, an Asiana Airlines office and even a Korean bathhouse.

Places to Stay – Top End

No shortage of choice here, at least in terms of price, but only some of the top-enders are worth it. One brand-new place that several readers have rated highly is *New City Hotel* (Xīnchéngshì Jiǔdiàn; ☎ 343 2511, fax 383 3340), just across from the train station. Its immaculate singles/doubles start at US$60 and the service is reportedly great.

Universal Hotel (Huánqiú Dàjiǔdiàn, ☎ 282 8228, 1 Jiefang Donglu), is a little worn, yet the pleasant rooms have some nice river views. Twins and doubles are Y380 and suites cost Y650.

Líjiāng Fàndiàn (1 Shanhu Beilu) overlooks the picturesque waterways of Shān Hú and the Lí Jiāng. However, when we last visited the whole area was covered in construction scaffolding and dust, and the hotel had been gutted for a complete overhaul. No doubt, every effort will be made to make this one of Guìlín's best hotels.

Just north of the bus station on Zhongshan Zhonglu, *Osmanthus Hotel (Dānguì Dàjiǔdiàn; ☎ 383 4300)* is one of the main hotels for tour groups, with nicely furnished doubles from US$70. It usually offers 40% off the walk-in rate, which makes rooms reasonable value.

The four-star *Brave Hotel (Guìlín Bīnguǎn; ☎ 282 3950, fax 282 2101, 14 Ronghu Nanlu)* has taken over the Holiday Inn Guìlín and is arguably one of the city's best. The only swimming pool in town is here as well. Comfy doubles with balcony are US$120 and smaller twins and doubles go for US$110. Discounts of 20% only negate the service tax. You will find good meals at the Chinese, Japanese and Western restaurants.

Five-star *Sheraton Guìlín Hotel (Guìlín Dàzì Dàfàndiàn; ☎ 282 5588)* has consistently received poor reports from readers who have suggested that at least a star should be pared from its ranking. After our last visit we have to agree. For the record a twin or double costs Y916 plus 20% tax.

Places to Eat

Guìlín is traditionally noted for its snake soup, wild cat or bamboo rat, washed down with snake-bile wine. You could be devouring some of these animals into extinction, and we don't recommend that you do. The pangolin (a sort of armadillo) is a protected species but still crops up on restaurant menus. Other protected species include the muntjac (Asian deer), horned pheasant, mini-turtle, short-tailed monkey and gem-faced civet. Less rare are such delicacies as wild boar, lynx, bamboo partridge, giant salamander, crocodile and bamboo rat. Generally the most exotic food you should come across is eel, catfish, pigeon and dog.

Guìlín has been legendary since the Qing dynasty for its white fermented bean curd, used most often to make a sauce for dipping roast pork or chicken in. Sanhua Wine, actually more like mellow rice fire water, is distilled in northern Guăngxī and is a favourite local drink.

The main eating area seems to be around Central Square, with a good variety ranging from buffet-style cafeterias, standard restaurants and trendy cafes to small hole-in-the-wall eateries. All are very popular.

On the corner of Yiren Lu and Zhengyang Lu is *Chéngdū Xiăochī*, serving heaps of tasty noodle dishes, including *dāndān miàn-lèi* (Sichuanese noodles, Y3) and *Chéngdū lěngmiàn* (cold noodles, Y3).

MFW, otherwise known as *Wāngjiǎo* and *Gùilínrén,* has two outlets nearby offering tasty fast-food Chinese meals. Photo menus help you order and the food is good value. Of similar style is *Aunt (Hǎodàmā),* an enormous food gallery on the 4th level of Bāguì Mansion on Zhongshan Zhonglu. Here you will find an amazing smorgasbord of every Chinese provincial speciality cuisine as well as some Western dishes and a Japanese sushi bar. Ordering is easy, just point and choose.

Coffee-Language 110 (Míngdiǎn) is a trendy cafe with a variety of Chinese and Western food and beverages, including set breakfast meals, tea, coffee and draught beer. Prices are reasonable, but not cheap.

Forest of Flowers offers a nice eating environment with a cafe and restaurant in one. There is an English menu offering a fusion of Western and Chinese cuisine and drinks. The restaurant is opposite Xīnhuá Bookstore on Zhongshan Zhonglu on the 2nd level.

Shèngfā Fàndiàn is just a 15-minute walk from the bus station down Zhishan Lu. It is very popular with the locals who come to eat *píjiǔyú* (Y18), literally beer fish, which is wok fried on your table and usually knocked down with the local Liqun Beer. Noodles are added at the end to mop up the sauce.

There is an outstanding, inexpensive Sichuanese restaurant on Nanhuan Lu called *Yíyuán Restaurant (Yíyuán Fàndiàn).* Although there is no English sign, you'll easily spot the place by its tasteful all-wood exterior. The owner speaks excellent English and will be happy to explain and help you choose. She imports all her spices from Sìchuān and you can taste the difference. The restaurant serves meals from 11.30am to 2.30pm and again from 5.30pm to 9.30pm.

One of the most well-known of Guìlín's large tourist restaurants is *Jiŭlóng Jiŭjiā*. It actually has three branches, all just north of the train station. One of these is on Zhongshan Zhonglu, but budget travellers may be shocked at the prices. However, if you're on a splurge, it's a fairly good introduction to Chinese tourists out on the town.

For a dim sum or yum cha buffet, *Táilián Hotel (Táilián Jiŭdiàn)* is considered by locals and overseas Chinese as the best place in town. Lunch costs Y20 and is served between 12pm and 2pm. Dinners cost Y28 and run from 6pm to 8pm, but you may be hard pressed to find an empty seat on weekends.

Closer to the train and bus stations is *Měishí Wénhuàchéng,* a small eateries district with a dozen restaurants serving up a wide variety of cuisine. A good choice is *Dōngběi Fàndiàn* for a taste of northeastern cuisine. Try some of the tasty dumplings, like *jiŭcài jiăozi* (with pork and chives) or *guōtiē jiăozi* (dry fried). There's also *sùshè jiăozi* (vegetarian dumplings) using chives and egg.

For the self-caterers there are a number of *supermarkets* around town, but by far the most convenient is in the basement of Nikodo Plaza.

Entertainment

In addition to the traditional and minority performances at *Wáng Chéng Theatre* (Y35), there are also daily shows at the *Garden of Folklore and Feelings (Mínsú Fēngqíngyuán)* at 8.30am, 2pm, 7.30pm and 8.30pm (Y50). Another good choice for some daily minority singing and dancing performances is the *Guìlín Children's Palace (Shì Shàoniángōng).* The show begins at 7.30pm daily (Y80).

For those looking for a Disneyland with Chinese characteristics, then head for *Guìlín Merryland (Guìlín Lèmăndi Xiūxián Shìjiè),* a brand-new theme park 60km from Guìlín. This is definitely for those with children or the young at heart. In addition to all the adrenaline-pumping rides, you will discover Hawaii World, the Wild West, traditional China, Caribbean pirates and Fantasy

World. Entry is a steep Y150. It is even possible to stay the night at Merryland Resort (☎ 622 9988) for those that need more than a day of thrills. Express buses depart for Merryland from Guìlín's bus station every 40 minutes from 7am to 12.20pm.

For something more local, then try *Crown Cave (Guān Yán)* and the adjacent island folk and minority theme park of *Xiāngba Dăo.* Crown Cave is 29km south of Guìlín near Căopíng Village. You can either walk to the entrance of the cave from the car park or ride the high-speed train cart (Y16) the 3.2km into the cave. Once inside the cave you can take a tourist train, an elevator, or navigate along the 3km of waterways by canoe. The cave itself is 12km long and no doubt more attractions are in store. If you are lucky enough you may even have time to admire some limestone formations.

Xiāngba Dăo is another monolithic theme park of more traditional character focusing on the province's ethnic minority folklore and customs. The island is studded with traditional minority architecture, a central performance area, craft shops, minority-cuisine restaurants, workshops and an entertainment stadium. The unfortunate motto, 'A Place nearest from Nature', aptly describes what awaits travellers. Xiāngba Dăo is 500m south of Crown Cave in the middle of the Lí Jiāng and accessed by boat from Crown Cave. Some of the Lí Jiāng tour boats stop off at both the cave and island on their way to Yángshuò.

Shopping

Guìlín is Guăngxī's number-one tourist spot, so there is always a plethora of cheap tourist junk available and an even greater number of fake antiques. However, more and more visitors to Guìlín are now frequenting the new department stores and designer and famous-label clothes stores. The best place to find these is around Central Square.

Guìlín and its back-alley workshops are the source of many of South-West China's crafts for tourist consumption. The Guìlín International Tourist Commodity Market, in the far southern part of town, is a huge place – as big as several city blocks. While a good share of the 'craft' is made up of kitsch souvenirs or simple household wares, many locals come here to buy their socks, underwear and fluffy slippers. You could easily spend a day wandering the labyrinthine network of stalls and drowning in the whir and whine of small carving tools.

Of note are the massive sculptures and furniture wrought from huge trees (it makes you weep to imagine the tree felled for an incredibly expensive, bizarre-shaped coffee table). Entire sections of the market are devoted to stonework, including exotic haematite and jade, jade, jade and more jade.

This is the spot buy a tea set. Avoid the scroll artwork, judging by the work of the few vendors offering it. You can even get a Christmas tree, greeting cards, hair curlers or panda slippers.

To get there, take the No 11 bus that runs between Seven Star Park and the southern part of town. Get off at the last stop (just after the bus turns left off the main road) and walk south. You can't miss the street-long sign welcoming you and your bulging wallet.

Getting There & Away

Air CAAC has an office (☎ 384 7252) on the corner of Shanghai Lu and Minzhu Luopen 7.30am to 8.30pm. Dragonair (☎ 282 5588, ext 8895) has an agency in the Brave Hotel.

Guìlín is well connected and adequately serves the rest of China by air. Destinations include: Běijīng (Y1580), Chéngdū (Y900), Chóngqìng (Y670), Hǎikǒu (Y710), Guǎngzhōu (Y610), Guìyáng (Y500), Hong Kong (Y1710), Kūnmíng (Y770), Shànghǎi (Y1190) and Xī'ān (Y1000). You should purchase tickets in advance; Guìlín is one of China's most popular tourist spots and, with a billion people competing for seats, airlines can't handle the load. That said, spot checks revealed seats were available for next-day purchase on most flights.

Two international connections are to Seoul (Hànchéng) on Monday, Tuesday, Friday and Saturday and to Fukuoka (Fùgāng) on Tuesday and Saturday. Tickets cost at least Y2800 one way for either destination. Flights to Bangkok seem to be off and on – presently off.

Bus For short local runs (such as Yángshuò and Xīng'ān), buses depart from in front of the train station, as well as from the bus station. The trip to Yángshuò takes just over an hour (Y6). You just have to exit the train-station doors and people start offering you buses to Yángshuò.

Guìlín's bus station is north of the train station on Zhongshan Nanlu. There are hourly buses to Lóngshèng (Y10 or Y15 for expresses, three to four hours). There are several really slow buses to Sānjiāng (Y17) between 6am and 7.30pm. There is one bus daily for Xīng'ān at 11.40am (Y6, two hours). You can also catch the hourly express buses to Quánzhōu (Y10, one hour). Express buses to Zīyuán depart every two hours (Y18, 2½ hours). Buses to Lìpǔ (for Dàyáo Shān) leave every 20 minutes (Y6, 1½ hours).

Departures for Liǔzhōu are every 20 minutes (Y40, two hours) and for Nánníng every 20 to 30 minutes (Y80, 4½ hours).

Express and sleeper buses to Guǎngzhōu and Shēnzhèn are available. Even with the rapid improvement in roads, the expresses are usually more reliable and smoother. Express buses head for Guǎngzhōu hourly (Y150, eight hours) and to Shēnzhèn at 8.30am and 8pm (Y180, 10 hours). Buses for Wúzhōu leave at 8.20am, 12.30pm, 4.30pm and 11pm (Y75, 6½ hours).

Train Guìlín is not as convenient as Nánníng or Liǔzhōu for train connections and tickets are therefore harder to come by. Outside of national holidays, the demand for tickets is lower, but be prepared to wait an extra day or two for hard-sleeper tickets. Guìlín has direct trains to Běijīng, Guǎngzhōu, Guìyáng, Kūnmíng and Shànghǎi.

Train No T6 to Běijīng departs at 5.27pm (24 hours), No 35/38 to Guǎngzhōu at 6pm (14 hours), No 150 to Shànghǎi at 12.52pm (26½ hours) and train No 1316 to Xī'ān departs at 2.24pm (30 hours). For Chóngqìng and Chéngdū change trains at Guìyáng.

Train No K154/155 to Kūnmíng departs at 1.55pm (via Guìyáng, 30 hours). You can also catch train Nos K181 and 1337, which depart from Guìlín's northern station (Guìlín Běizhàn), but these are pretty slow, so it might be worth your while to first go to Nánníng and buy a ticket there for the direct Nánkūn line to Kūnmíng (15 hours).

Window 5 is for foreigners to buy tickets.

Getting Around

To/From the Airport Guìlín's international airport is 30km west of the city. CAAC runs buses from its Shànghǎi Lu office (Mínháng Dàshà) to the airport, leaving half-hourly from 6.30am (Y20). A taxi to the airport costs about Y80.

Bus & Taxi Most of the city buses that stop in front of Guìlín's bus and train stations will get you to the major sights, but a bicycle is definitely better, especially in the summer heat. Bus No 2 is one of these, running from South Stream Park through town passing Elephant Hill Park, Seven Stars Park, Wave-Subduing Hill, Folded Silk Streamers Hill and Guānyīn Pavilion. Bus No 15 runs from the train station around the city's main tourist highlights. Local buses cost Y1 to Y1.5.

Taxis cost about Y10 to Y20 per trip, depending on the distance. Pedicabs, if you can find them, charge Y5 to Y10 per trip.

Motorcycle taxis charge Y4 to Y5 and are a good way of getting to the nearby parks.

Bicycle Cycling is the best way to get around Guìlín. There are plenty of bicycle-hire shops – just look along Zhongshan Zhonglu. There are some near the bus and train stations and one next to the Overseas Chinese Hotel. Most charge between Y10 and Y20 per day, and require Y200 or your passport as security. Try to avoid handing over your passport.

Tours If you want to leave the transport details to someone else then there is no shortage of tour operators offering half- or full-day tours of Guìlín's major sights. They charge around Y35, not including entry tickets.

AROUND GUÌLÍN
Ling Canal

Líng Qú

The Ling Canal is in Xīng'ān county, about 70km north of Guìlín. Locals say, 'The north has the Great Wall, the South has the

Ling Canal'. It was built between 219 and 214 BC in the reign of the first Qin emperor, Qin Shihuang, to transport supplies to his army. It is considered to be one of the three great feats of Chinese engineering (the others are the Great Wall and the Du Jiāng irrigation system in Sìchuān). The 34km canal links the Xiāng Hé – which flows into the Yangzi River and the Lí Jiāng, which flows into the Zhū Jiāng – thus connecting two of China's major waterways and aiding China's expansion to the south-west.

You can see the Ling Canal at **Xīng'ān**, a market town of about 30,000 people. Two branches of the canal flow through the town, at the northern and southern ends. Come springtime, you'll be elbow to elbow with photographers jockeying for position to snap shots of the peach blossoms lining the canals and spillway. There is one bus daily for Xīng'ān at 11.40am (Y6, two hours). It is also possible to catch any of the hourly express buses to Quánzhōu (Y10, one hour). Minibuses to Xīng'ān may also leave from in front of the train station.

LÍ JIĀNG 漓江

This beautiful river is the connecting waterway between Guìlín and Yángshuò and is one of the main tourist attractions of the area. A thousand years ago a poet wrote of the scenery around Yángshuò, 'The river forms a green gauze belt, the mountains are like blue jade hairpins'. The 83km stretch between the towns is hardly that, but you do see some extraordinary peaks, sprays of bamboo lining the river banks, fishers in small boats and picturesque villages.

As is the Chinese habit, every feature along the route has been named. **Paint Brush Hill** juts straight up from the ground with a pointed tip like a Chinese writing brush. **Cock-Fighting Hills** stand face to face like two cocks about to engage in battle. **Mural Hill**, just past the small town of Yángdī, is a sheer cliff rising abruptly out of the water; there are supposed to be the images of nine horses in the weathered patterns on the cliff face.

A popular tourist trip is the boat ride from Guìlín down the Lí Jiāng to Yánshuò.

Budget travellers have been put off by the exorbitant ticket prices, presently around Y500, including lunch and the bus trip back to Guìlín from Yángshuò. This is one of Guìlín's worst cases of price gouging. It you don't mind joining a Chinese tour group, then you will only have to pay around Y180 for the same service, just without the English-speaking guide.

Tour boats (Y460) depart from Guìlín from a jetty across the road from the Golden Elephant Hotel each morning at around 8am, although when the water is low you have to take a shuttle bus to Zhújiāng or Mópánshān wharf downriver. For trips booked through hotels, buses usually pick you up at around 7.30am to 8am, and take you to the boat. The ticket office for the trip is across the road from the park entrance, on the same side of the street as the Golden Elephant. The trip lasts all day, and some people find that the time drags towards the end. It's probably not worth it if you're going to be spending any length of time in Yángshuò, where you can organise personalised trips through villagers and more picturesque boat trips to nearby villages.

YÁNGSHUÒ 阳朔
☎ 0773 • pop 300,000

Just 65km south of Guìlín, Yángshuò has, along with Dàlǐ in Yúnnán, become one of those legendary backpacker destinations that most travellers have heard about long before they even set foot in China. Set amid limestone pinnacles, it's a small town growing bigger on the back of its popularity. In an attempt to preserve the appearance of the place, extensive renovations have been recently carried out along and around Xi Jie. Some travellers have criticised the move as an attempt to destroy the soul of the area, others commend it for keeping the white tiles and blue glass of modern Chinese architecture at bay. Although not as quaint as it once was, Yángshuò is still a great laid-back base from which to explore small villages in the nearby countryside.

With its Western-style cafes, Hollywood movies and banana pancakes, Yángshuò may not seem like the 'real China', but who cares?

It's a great spot to relax, see the scenery and grab a good cup of coffee – the perfect antidote to weeks on the road. Don't make this your first stop coming from Hong Kong. Save it for after knocking around Guǎngzhōu, Guìzhōu or Guǎngxī. You'll appreciate it much more. Despite the strong Western influence, Yángshuò still contains some strong local flavours.

Either way, for sheer scenic beauty, it's hard to top a leisurely bike ride around Yángshuò and its surrounding villages; some travellers wind up extending their stay by up to two weeks or more! A lot of people have even stayed overnight in the villages, and if you want to go camping in the mountains you shouldn't have any problem. It's probably not permitted to camp out, but who's going to climb a 200m peak to bring you down?

Orientation

You'll only need to know two streets. The first, Pantao Lu, forms the south-western boundary of Yángshuò centre and is the main artery to/from Guìlín. The second, Xi Jie, is known as 'Foreigner Street'. It runs northeast to Lí Jiāng, and is lined with Western-style cafes, hotels and tourist shops. The farther you go from Xi Jie or from Pantao Lu at its intersection with Xi Jie, the closer you get to Chinese group-tour reality.

Although a loop road's been built around Yángshuò's fringes to ease traffic on Pantao Lu, trucks and buses still roar through town. However, Xi Jie is a pedestrian mall, free from bicycles, traffic and those infamous tractors.

Maps A reasonably good street map of Yángshuò and surrounds is available everywhere (Y2.50). The regional map is limited for anything in the surrounding area. Then again, half the fun of Yángshuò is following some obscure rice-paddy path and getting lost.

Information
Tourist Offices Most travel agents seem to work for CITS nowadays or just use the acronym. Either way, travellers seldom avail

themselves of their services, as enterprising locals working from the cafes are generally more in touch with the needs of independent travellers, and levy lower service charges.

PSB The Yángshuò PSB is well versed in dealing with travellers. That said, don't go in expecting whatever visa extension you want to be stamped in your passport. Reports have been mixed – some people have received an extension pronto, others have been given a serious run-around. Consider getting a friendly cafe representative to act on your behalf if your business is important.

Money The Bank of China on Binjiang Lu will change cash and travellers cheques, as well as do credit card advances (3% commission) and receive wire transfers (can take up to 15 days). On weekends, there's a small counter open next to the bank. Opening hours are 8am to 5pm.

Post & Communications The post office, on Pantao Lu across from Xi Jie, has English-speaking staff and long-distance phone services. You can also purchase IP cards here that only cost Y2.40 to Y3.60 per minute for international calls, rather than the standard Y12 on China Telecom IC cards. It's open 8am to 5pm.

Internet bars are springing up all over town. The standard charge is Y10 per hour. Connection speeds and service vary considerably.

Bookshops No bookshops per se exist in Yángshuò. A few cafes deal in used books, but the selection is usually quite limited. On the whole, though, Yángshuò concentrates on movies.

Medical Services An array of medical services are available in Yángshuò and you should be able to find somebody who can speak basic English. The People's Hospital is north of the main tourist centre, not far from the PSB. Any accommodation in Yángshuò will find a doctor for you, including those practising traditional Chinese

medicine. There are a number of clinics on the northern side of Pantao Lu offering therapeutic massage, acupuncture and traditional medicine. It is even possible to enrol in brief courses at some of these centres.

Work & Study For short courses in Chinese language, taichi or medicine try Merry Planet Language Club on Xi Jie. You can also enrol in some of the courses offered by Buckland School. It welcomes volunteer teachers in exchange for a bed and food.

Things to See & Do

You can't help but notice the peaks surrounding Yángshuò, and you'll likely work up a big desire to try to hoof it up one or more of them. They're not all accessible, but quite a few can be climbed. Get specific instructions from locals before you set off – there's no search-and-rescue service for foreigners stranded on a karst cliff face. **Green Lotus Peak** (Bìlián Fēng) rises up beside the Lí Jiāng in the south-eastern corner of town, in the **Mountain Water Garden** (Shānshuǐyuán). It's also called Bronze Mirror Peak (Tóngjìng Fēng) because it has a flat northern face, which is supposed to look like an ancient bronze mirror. A path leads along the river; entry costs Y18.

Yángshuò Park (Yángshuò Gōngyuán) is in the west of the town, and here you'll find **Man Hill** (Xīláng Shān), which is meant to resemble a young man bowing and scraping to a shy young girl represented by **Lady Hill** (Xiǎogū Shān). Entry costs Y6. Other hills nearby are named after animals: **Lion Riding Carp Hill** (Shìzì Qí Lǐyu' Shān), **Dragon Head Hill** (Lóngtóu Shān) and the like.

It's amazing how many travellers come to Yángshuò and don't really see the town – they're too preoccupied with the karst peaks and Pantao Lu's beer and movies. But to the north and west of Pantao Lu are great small-town trekking opportunities: back alleys, small markets and throngs of Chinese tourists poking about dozens of shops.

A popular evening activity is to take in the **cormorant fishing** on the Lí Jiāng that usually begins around 7pm to 7.30pm. It is a show for the tourists, but is still entertaining.

The pinnacles at sunset near Yángshuò in Guăngxī

Guăngxī's stunning rice terraces

The colourful people of Ruìlì

Xīshuāngbănnà's young Buddhist monks

Lèshān's dignified Grand Buddha carved into a cliff face overlooking the Dàdù and Mín rivers

Guǎngxī's majestic Détiān Waterfall straddles the Sino-Vietnamese border

Eroded by wind and split by rain, the grey pinnacles and peaks of Yúnnán's Stone Forest

Hotels and restaurants usually charge around Y25 per person.

Places to Stay – Budget & Mid-Range

Travellers always seem to arrive in Yángshuò expecting bargain room prices, but it's the market that dictates. Competition keeps things somewhat sane, but show up in high season (summer) and you'll have to pay the asking price for a bed. In winter, negotiation seems to re-enter the picture in most places. On arrival you will no doubt be met by touts wielding name cards and photo albums of their abodes. Feel free to check them out because new places keep springing up and old stand-bys keep on renovating.

Outside of budgetary constraints, there are generally three choices of accommodation. The first, along Pantao Lu, is probably the noisiest because of trucks hurtling down the main road to Guìlín. The second and probably most popular is along Xi Jie, although this can also be quite noisy because of late-night drinking binges by travellers in the cafes below. The final choice is in the Chinese section of town where there are more white-tiled, mid-range options available and more internal noise with all-night tour-group karaoke shows.

Among the most popular places to stay in Yángshuò are the travellers hang-outs nestled together on Xi Jie. Most of the budget backpacker options also offer very reasonably priced mid-range options, although during summer all rooms become pretty pricey. A number of travellers complain that many of the older hostels suffer from winter damp. To avoid this check out your room thoroughly before dumping your bags.

Yángshuò International Youth Hostel (Xījiē Guójì Qīngnián Lǚguǎn; ☎ 882 0933, fax 882 0988) is a new addition to Xi Jie offering spotless YHA-standard rooms. Despite appearing a tad sanitary for some travellers and lacking in ambience, it offers very good-value dorm beds for Y18 and twins for Y80.

Bamboo House Inn & Café (Zhúlín Fàndiàn; ☎ 882 3222) is another newie in Yángshuò. Down a small lane off Xi Jie, this place is quiet and pleasant and the staff is reasonably friendly. Beds in dorms are Y15 and in doubles and triples Y20 to Y25. Beds in rooms with air-con cost from Y30 to Y60. All rooms have good bathrooms.

Sìhǎi Hotel (Sìhǎi Fàndiàn; ☎ 882 2013, **e** SiHai@hotmail.com) is popular mainly for its convenience to the cafes on Xi Jie and, apart from the noise in the evenings, it's a good spot. This labyrinthine hotel is still reasonably new after a major renovation. Dorm beds start at Y15 and the cheapest doubles with bathroom start at Y50 or with air-con from Y80. There's also a good family room for Y200 to Y500 depending on the time of year. This is also where you will find Uncle Bob, a travel agent with a wealth of local knowledge and helpful advice.

Not far away, the popular cafe, *Lisa's,* has completely renovated rooms. Plastering was in progress when we last dropped by, but prices are expected to be from budget to mid-range.

Another cafe, *Blue Lotus,* has just recently extended its accommodation. Rooms looked promising, but prices were not available at the time of writing. *White Lion* is also in the construction phase and will be offering both budget dorm and more comfortable options.

Hotel Explorer (Wénhuà Fàndiàn; ☎ 882 8116, fax 882 7816) is a fusion of backpacker and Chinese white-tile-style accommodation. Rooms are clean and good value and the staff is friendly. Beds in dorms range from Y25 to Y45 with bathroom and twins from Y100 to Y150 a room.

Places to Stay – Top End

New Century Hotel (Xīnshìjì Jiǔdiàn; ☎ 882 9822, fax 882 9823) is a new three-star, Chinese-style hotel with good-quality rooms and service. Singles and doubles cost US$60, while triples are US$75. It usually provides 20% discount on these rates.

For more ambience try *Yángshuò Resort Hotel* (Yángshuò Bǎilèlái Dùjiā Fàndiàn; ☎ 882 2109, fax 882 2106), complete with swimming pool, bar and three-star rating. The best thing about this place is its gardens. Standard rooms start at US$48 and

GUĂNGXĪ

YÁNGSHUÒ 阳朔

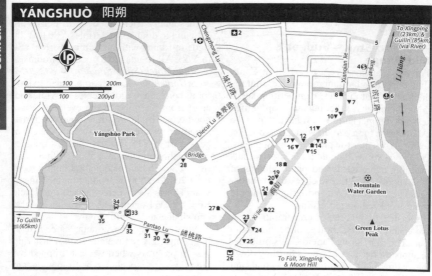

very comfortable luxury rooms go for US$110. Some travellers have complained of deteriorating standards, but the hotel has recently caught onto the renovation craze and rooms are receiving a much needed face-lift. It has nice rooms and a serious slate of amenities, including a fitness centre, satellite TV, pool tables, a business centre, restaurants and lounges.

Places to Eat

Xi Jie teems with tiny cafes offering interesting Chinese, Western and fusion cuisine as well as perennial travellers' favourites, such as banana pancakes, muesli and pizza. For anyone who has been wandering around China for a while it's a good chance to have a break from oily, stir-fried vegetables and grab a cup of coffee. At night, movie junkies are in heaven, since all the cafes try to woo travellers with Hollywood flicks over dinner.

Because most cafes serve reasonable to very good fare, travellers will be attracted by the atmosphere. Like accommodation, most travellers opt for the more laid-back and quieter part of town down Xie Jie. Sheer numbers make for fierce competition – by the time you read this it's a safe bet

some names will have changed, but at least you won't be lacking for choice.

Red Star Express produces a pretty mean pizza with a good range of toppings, especially vegetarian choices. The nearby *Drifter's* is another favourite haunt, especially in the evenings. Across the road, *Lisa's* used to be quite a popular place, but was undergoing renovations when we last visited. *Meiyou Café* promises 'mei you bad service, mei you warm beer' ('méiyǒu' means 'don't have'), and it delivers.

Café Under the Moon opts for ambience to accompany its friendly service and tasty food. There are also tables on a lovely 2nd-level balcony. Just next door, *Minnie Mao's* has won travellers' praise for tasty dishes, especially the satay chicken with rice.

Off a side street just north-west of the Sihai Hotel, *Susannah's* also draws a steady stream of customers. Its claim to fame is that it was the first Western restaurant in town and Jimmy Carter ate there in 1987! Do try the *zuì yā*, or 'drunk duck', an appealing dish of duck cooked in a sauce of local red wine.

The nearby *Karst Café* is the place for enthusiastic rock climbers. It provides

YÁNGSHUÒ

PLACES TO STAY
- 8 Hotel Explorer
  文化饭店
- 14 Sìhǎi Hotel
  四海饭店
- 18 Bamboo House Inn
  & Cafe
  竹林饭店
- 21 Yángshuò
  International
  Youth Hostel
  阳朔国际青年旅馆
- 27 Yángshuò Resort Hotel
  阳朔白乐来度假饭店
- 32 Fawlty Towers
  Guesthouse
  宝泉饭店
- 36 New Century Hotel
  新世纪酒店

PLACES TO EAT
- 7 Karst Cafe
- 9 Drifter's
- 10 Blue Lotus

- 11 Red Star Express
- 12 Susannah's
- 13 Lisa's Cafe
- 15 Le Vôtre Cafe
- 16 Cafe Under the Moon
- 17 Minnie Mao's
- 19 Meiyou Cafe
  没有饭店
- 23 Tent City Market
- 24 Momozi Cafe
- 25 MC Blues Bar & Cafe
- 28 Night Market
- 29 Planet Yángshuó
- 30 Ebo's Cafe
- 31 Hard Seat Cafe
- 35 Farmer's Trading
  Market
  农贸市场

OTHER
- 1 People's Hospital
  人民医院
- 2 PSR
  公安局

- 3 Fresh Produce
  Market
  农贸市场
- 4 Bank of China
  中国银行
- 5 Tourist Market
  旅客市场
- 6 Wharf
  码头
- 20 Merry Planet
  Language Club
  快乐星球
- 22 Buckland School
- 26 Post Office
  邮电局
- 33 Main Bus
  Station
  汽车总站
- 34 Private Buses to
  Guìlín, Fùlì,
  Yángdī
  & Xīngpíng
  往桂林、福利、
  杨堤和兴坪的班车

good food and beverages, and is also the place to find out about climbing possibilities around Yángshuò and organise climbing guides.

Le Vôtre Café appears a little grand, but has won the praise of many travellers for its fine French cuisine and delectable bakery.

Other popular places include the cluster of cafes on the corner of Xi Jie and the main road, including the fusion Japanese-Chinese *Momozi*, *Paris Café* and *MC Blues Bar*. They all have outdoor seating and are good places to sit and watch the world go by. MC Blues has the added attraction of over 150 tapes, and serves up a tasty hamburger – the house speciality.

Pantao Lu is the site of some of Yángshuò's original cafes and, while they don't enjoy the popularity of the Xi Jie strip, *Planet Yángshuò*, *Ebo's Café* and *Hard Seat* are all friendly spots for a meal or a cup of coffee.

Don't forget that you *are* in China: Wander the labyrinth of back alleys and you'll discover many small markets and restaurants catering to locals and Chinese travellers. If you get tired of the 'international'

spots, Yángshuò's two day markets and two night markets offer an array of tasty delights.

On Pantao Lu through the archway, *Farmer's Trading Market* (*Nóngmào Shìchǎng*) is open all day and late into the evenings. *Píjiǔyú* (beer fish, Y30 per kilogram) is Yángshuò's most famous dish and in fact this may be the best budget place to buy it. Local Lí Jiāng fish are cooked up with chillies, spring onion, tomato, ginger and beer. A good winter alternative is *qīngshuǐyú huǒguǒ*, a hotpot of Lí Jiāng catfish in a tasty broth of garlic, spring onions and chives. The price starts at Y15 for the hotpot and extras (tofu, spinach, mushrooms, fensi noodles etc) are charged separately. For the more adventurous, there is also *lǎoshǔgān* (fried dried rat with chillies and garlic, Y20). If you like the game-meat taste then why not also try *sōngshǔgān* (fried squirrel, Y20). Other interesting cuisine available in Yángshuò includes *yútóutāng huǒguǒ* (fish-head broth hotpot), *qīngwādàn* (frogs eggs), *zhūcháng* (pig intestines), *tùzi* (wild rabbit) and *yějī* (wild hen).

At the fresh-produce *market (Sāngmào Shìchǎng)* small snacks are the daily speciality. In the morning its hard to beat a stick of *yóutiáo* (deep-fried batter, Y0.50 each) dipped in a bowl of *dòujiāng* (soy milk, Y1). Pyramid *zōngzi* are a local winter favourite and usually contain green beans, pork and peanuts wrapped in a lotus leaf served under a tofu and chilli sauce (Y0.50). There are a couple of fast-food stalls frying up rice, meat and vegies for between Y2 and Y5. This is also the place to stock up on some fresh or dried fruit, like *shìbīng* (dried persimmons, Y5 per 500g).

Another great *night market* for larger meals starts about 5.30pm on Diecui Lu. Tasty dishes on offer here include *tiánluóniàng* (stuffed field snails, Y10 to Y15), *yāohuā chànlóng* (fried pig kidneys with garlic stems and chilli, Y15), *niàng xiānggǔ* or *niàng làjiāo* (stuffed mushrooms or capsicum) and *hóngshāo páigǔ* (braised pork spare ribs, Y10).

On Xi Jie, about a quarter of the way to the river from Pantao Lu, is an evening *tent city* of outdoor grills and woks – this is the real China. These stalls serve mainly snacks, such as *húntun* (dumpling soup, Y3), *yóutiáo* (fried bread sticks), *tāngyuán* (sweet balls, Y2), *tiánjiǔdan* (boiled egg soup with red jujubes, lotus seeds and fermented rice, Y2 to Y3) and the local speciality *mǐfěn* (rice-flour noodles), which are usually served with crispy fried soy beans and spicy sour pickles.

Shopping

Yángshuò is a good place for souvenir shopping. Best buys include silk jackets (at much cheaper prices than in Hong Kong), hand-painted T-shirts, scroll paintings and batiks (from Guìzhōu). Name chops cost Y10 to Y60 on average. If you are in the market for a chop, bear in mind that it is not the size of the stone that is important in determining a price but the quality of the stone itself. Often the smaller pieces are more expensive than the hefty chunks of rock available. Bargain for everything! The paintings available in Yángshuò, for example, are generally poor quality (even if you think they look good) and a starting price of Y150 can easily go below Y100. Most travellers suggest shopping in the early evening after all the tour groups have left.

Don't forget too that Yángshuò is not simply Xi Jie. Wander around the backstreets, especially north along Binjiang Lu around the Bank of China. There are many places that may not be especially better, but do offer the shopper lots more to compare.

Getting There & Away

Air The closest airport is in Guìlín, and any of the numerous CITS outlets and cafes dispense air tickets relatively cheaply. Check the Guìlín Getting There & Away section earlier in this chapter for details on available flights. Cafes and hotels can organise taxi rides from Yángshuò directly to the airport (Y75, one hour).

Bus Most travellers arrive in Yángshuò via Guìlín, from where there are good connections to domestic and even international destinations. Regular buses and minibuses run between Yángshuò and Guìlín through the day. A popular option is the minibus service that operates from in front of the bus station. Buses leave as soon as they fill up, which could take anywhere from five to 15 minutes, and the trip is a little over an hour. The cost is Y5 per person, and Y1 per piece of luggage. The occasional weasel will try to charge you Y10. Buses also regularly depart from inside the bus station (Y6).

There are express buses to Guǎngzhōu (Y150, 7½ hours), Wúzhōu (Y70, six hours) and Shēnzhèn (Y180, nine hours), from where you can hop on a bus, boat or train to Hong Kong. These express buses – equipped with reclining seats, violent or comic Hong Kong movies, air-con and hostesses – now rule the road. In times past it was possible to take a bus/boat combination to Guǎngzhōu and Hong Kong via Wúzhōu. However, with the arrival of express buses and the construction and upgrading of more roads, this option has pretty much been ruled out. If you arrive in Yángshuò on one of the express buses heading for Guìlín, then you might be deposited at the petrol station on the edge of town. Don't despair as there will most likely be a welcoming party of hostel touts wielding photo albums to lead or follow you into town.

To visit Dàyáo Shān, you should aim for the small town of Jīnxiù. But to get there you will probably need to first catch a bus to Lìpǔ (Y3.50, one hour) and then transfer to another bus to Tóngmù (Y5.50). You can then hop in a share minivan taxi to Jīnxiù (Y4). Altogether this should take about four hours.

For Liǔzhōu it is quicker to first go to Gùilín and then transfer. See the Gùilín section for more details.

If you prefer the smoky atmosphere, haphazard driving, excruciatingly slow and rustic feel of the junket sleepers, then don't despair as they still ply most of these routes. Check at the bus station for details.

Train The nearest train station is in Gùilín. Almost any cafe or travel outfit around Yángshuò will organise train tickets, and some offer hard sleepers for high-demand routes like Gùilín to Kūnmíng for around Y270. When eyeing these prices, bear in mind that locals usually have to go through 'the back door' in Gùilín to get the tickets. Doing it yourself requires an hour trip to Gùilín, buying your own ticket, and an hour trip back. To get any of these tickets you'll have to book at least two to three days in advance. Outside of national holidays, train tickets to most destinations are reasonably easy to obtain.

Getting Around
Yángshuò itself is small enough to walk around without burning up too many calories, but if you want to get farther afield you should hire a bicycle. Most hotels and cafes will point you in the right direction. Otherwise look for rows of bikes and signs near the intersection of Xi Jie and the main road. The charge is about Y10 per day plus a deposit. Before taking a bike out check its gears, brakes, tyres, handlebars, cranks and anything else that could possibly fall off. The farmers' paths around Yángshuò put all bikes to the test and you don't want to have to walk home.

AROUND YÁNGSHUÒ
There are weeks and weeks of possible exploration out there for travellers, including bike, boat, foot or any combination thereof.

Moon Hill Area 月山地区
Yuèliàng Shān
The highway from Gùilín turns south out of Yángshuò and after a couple of kilometres crosses Yùlóng Hé. Continue on for another few kilometres, until you see Water's Café & Restaurant. The entrance to Moon Hill is opposite, just south of Jīnbǎo Hé and to the west of the highway. It is a limestone pinnacle with a moon-shaped hole. To get to Moon Hill by bicycle, take the highway out of town towards the river and turn right onto the road about 200m before the bridge. Moon Hill is 8.5km from town on your right and the views from the 320m peak (after 1251 steps, so reports one focused Frenchman) are incredible! You can see **Moon Hill Village** and the 1500-year-old **Big Banyan**

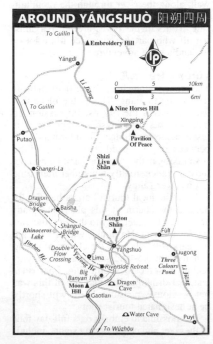

Tree (ask the hawkers to point it out). Entry costs Y18.

A series of caves have been opened up not far from Moon Hill: the **Black Buddha Caves** (Hēifó Dòng) and **Water Caves** (Shuǐ Yán). On the way to Moon Hill, you will undoubtedly be intercepted and invited to enjoy the caves. Both caves are worth a visit and Water Caves have become especially popular. Entry costs Y50 and includes guide and lights. It is quite easy to get to the caves on a bike, but you can also join one of the many tours from Yángshuò. Chufa Tours, at Moon Hill, offers both independent and group tours of the caves. Its two- and four-hour tours cost Y78 to Y108 per person including transport, entry and equipment. Other tours cost from Y25 per head depending on the size of your group and the length of time spent in the caves. You go through the caves and then climb down a steep chimney via a rope and ladder to an underground pool fed by a river. You can walk along the river through the mountain for a few hours and come out on the other side. Tours of the caves are not bargains, but all who partake guarantee it's a lot of fun and a good adventure.

Yùlóng Hé 玉龙河

The scenery along here equals or even beats that of the Lí Jiāng. This is the place that usually leaves the biggest impression on most visitors to Yángshuò. Whether it is just meandering along a small farmers' path between the rice paddies or sitting by the river taking in the rural and karst landscape, most travellers fondly remember their time in this river valley.

Even the local tourist bureau has finally noticed the charm of this place and plans are currently under way to develop the valley for tourism. No doubt, within a couple of years you will have the choice of eating banana pancakes and staying out here, partaking in some rock climbing, boat rides and beer drinking. Not that any of this was not previously possible, but it will shortly be at designated tourist spots.

It is possible to embark on a full-day tour of the river and neighbouring sights, including **Double Flow Crossing** (Shuāngliúdù), **Shànguì Bridge** (Shànguì Qiáo), nearby **Rhinoceros Lake** (Xīniú Hú) and **Dragon Bridge** (Yùlóng Qiáo). This impressive last bridge was built in 1412 during the Ming dynasty and is among Guǎngxī's largest at 59m long, 5m wide and 9m high. It would be a full day to head up to Dragon Bridge and back on the trails, but definitely worth it. Pack your lunch and some water and enjoy a picnic along the banks of Yùlóng Hé.

From Yángshuò, head out towards Moon Hill and, before crossing the bridge over Yùlóng Hé, turn right down the dirt trail. It is possible to continue along this path (in a variety of its forms) all the way to the Dragon Bridge and Bāishá. Don't worry too much if you take a wrong turn as there are innumerable paths running between Yùlóng Hé and the Yángshuò-Bāishá road. Don't be tempted by the Bāishá road as it's busy, noisy and dusty. The best part of this trip is not worrying about whether you wander down the wrong path but, rather, just enjoying the scenery.

If you seem to be going around in circles, then just ask one of the locals the way back to Yángshuò or follow one of the other independent guides who frequent this area. If you don't fancy heading off independently, then this is a popular trek with Yángshuò's guides who will take you out for the day and even sometimes stop at their home for lunch. This is a good way to see the scenery with an informed local (see the Tours section below for more details).

Finally a note of warning: Take care riding along some of those bumpy narrow paths between paddy fields, as it only takes one mistake to end up covered in mud!

Tours

In Yángshuò several locals offer guided tours of Moon Hill, the caves and other famous spots, as well as their home villages. Some will even bring you home and cook you lunch! These minitours have received rave reviews from some travellers and may be worth a try. For Y50 to Y70 you can get almost a whole day's tour, which provides a glimpse of the real Yángshuò via its back roads and rice paddies. Prices rise in summer, when tour guides become more popular.

Lately, some travellers with limited time have been hiring a motorbike side-car to see all the sights in a day.

Do-it-yourself tours are also possible along the many village paths and trails. For a great day trip, head out of Yángshuò towards Gùilín; before you get to the toll booths on the main highway, cut over to your left onto the ring road. Take the first road (that isn't a path) to the right, leading into the rice paddies and towards all those grand peaks. Now get lost; when you've exhausted all the branches and serpentine trails in this area, you can just continue straight ahead until you hook up with the road to Moon Hill.

River Excursions

If you're keen on a river trip, the best thing to do is ask around. There are dozens of touts and guides who will chat you up on the streets of Yángshuò, so ask them for advice on the good, bad and boring stretches of the river.

There are many villages close to Yángshuò that are worth checking out. A popular river-boat trip is to the picturesque village of Fùlǐ, a short distance down the Lí Jiāng, with its stone houses and cobbled lanes. There are a couple of boats a day to Fùlǐ from Yángshuò for around Y40, although most people tend to cycle there – it's a pleasant ride and takes around an hour.

Another way to get to Fùlǐ is by inner tube, available for about Y10 per day. It takes around three or four hours to get to Fùlǐ this way. Several places also offer rafting trips and kayak hire, which are both popular options in the warm summer months. Ask at your hotel or at one of the restaurants.

On market days in Fùlǐ, be very careful of pickpockets; young males work in groups of three or four, brushing up against travellers in the press of the crowd and relieving their pockets of valuables.

Many cafes and travel agents also organise boat trips to Yángdī and Xīngpíng, about three hours upstream from Yángshuò. The mountain scenery around Xīngpíng is even more breathtaking than around Yángshuò, and there are many caves.

Official prices for all boat trips are now Y100 a ride. Local boats charge Y2 for the same trip, but are deemed too dangerous for foreigners and the owners are not allowed to take foreigners. If the danger is real, it is a sad blight upon the official value placed on the local populace. No doubt of more concern is how to ensure tourism remains the main cash cow of the region.

A good alternative is to cycle to Xīngpíng and then put your bike on the boat coming back – it's a picturesque ride of about three hours. Any number of places in Yángshuò or Xīngpíng can organise boat tickets (Y20 to Y45 per person). It's also possible to catch a local bus to Xīngpíng (Y3, one hour) from the minibus car park opposite the bus station in Yángshuò.

For a panoramic view of the surroundings wander up the 1159 steps to the **Pavilion of Peace** (Hépíng Tíng). The steep path begins south of the wharf and takes about 30 to 40 minutes.

You could spend the night in Xīngpíng. There are a couple of hotels around the wharf. *Róngtán Fàndiàn* (☎ 870 2248) is the first one up from the wharf on the left. Beds with bathroom go for Y20 or Y30 with air-con. Next door, *River View Hotel* (Wàngjiāng Fàndiàn; ☎ 870 2276) is also reasonably priced with beds in quads for Y25 and twins for Y80.

More and more places to stay and eat are popping up every year in Xīngpíng offering a wider range of accommodation and cuisine. *Bamboo Café* (Zhúlín Fàndiàn) is right on the river and is a good spot for a meal and refreshing drink. Just up from the river is *One World Café*, a friendly and helpful place serving tasty meals. Also nearby is *Cottage Café*, another good place offering fine food.

Markets

The villages in the vicinity of Yángshuò are best visited on market days, and these operate on a three-day, monthly cycle. Thus, markets take place every three days starting on the first of the month for Bāishá (Day 1,

4, 7 etc), starting on the second of the month for Fùlǐ (Day 2, 5, 8 etc) and on the third of the month for Yángshuò and Xīngpíng (Day 3, 6, 9 etc). Yángshuò is on the same cycle as Xīngpíng. There are no markets on the 10th, 20th, 30th and 31st of the month.

JĪNXIÙ 金秀

If you're coming from Wúzhōu or any-where south of Yángshuò, you might want to consider stopping in Lìpǔ and wrangling a bus towards the small town of Jīnxiù. The town is a good base for exploring the nearby scenic mountain, **Dàyáo Shān**.

The main attractions are a fair distance from town, but most transport options depart from Jīnxiù. The town also has the cheapest official accommodation in the area.

Shèngtáng Shān (1979m) is the main peak of Dàyáo Shān, which is 42km south from Jīnxiù. Transport to the peak involves hiring a minivan taxi for an overnight trip (Y150 to Y200). This will allow you to climb to the peak and view the sunset, sleep on the mountain and watch the sunrise, as well as enjoy the nearby scenery before heading back. Entry costs Y50.

Another local attraction is the **Primitive Forest Resort** (Yuánshǐ Sēnlín Dùjiā), 16km to the east of Jīnxiù. This is the location of Guǎngxī's largest old-growth forest and is a hot spot of biodiversity. In fact, the area has been protected to preserve the grand Cathay Silver Fir tree and the Yaoshan crocodile, both of which are rare species in China. There are a couple of winding trails through the forest. Traditional Yao singing and dance performances are also held at the resort for tour groups. Entry costs Y20 and performance tickets are Y50. A minivan taxi would cost between Y30 to Y40 for the return trip from Jīnxiù.

Accommodation on Dàyáo Shān includes **Yúnhǎi Zhuāng,** which is 300m from the peak and has Y200 twins with bath. There are also rooms available right on the peak for Y150 but without a bathroom. **Shèngtáng Shānzhuāng** has twins with bathrooms for Y180 or you can stay at **Shùnjǐng Shānzhuāng** at the base of the mountain for Y90 with bath.

Accommodation is available in Jīnxiù at **Wǔzhuāngbù Zhāodàisuǒ** where decent but simple beds in singles are Y38 and in twins Y30. Hot water is available in the evening. There is a reasonable restaurant opposite with cheap and wholesome set-price meals (Y2 to Y7).

Jīnxiù's CTS (☎ 0772-621 2606) offers tours of these and other sights, but is mainly geared towards groups. However, during summer you may be able to tag along with a Chinese tour group.

Buses make the 155km run to Liǔzhōu throughout the day (Y15, four hours). There are also a couple of departures for Lìpǔ (Y9.5, 2½ hours). See the Yángshuò Getting There & Away section for more details.

LÓNGSHÈNG 龙胜
☎ 0773 • pop 170,000

About four hours by bus to the north-west of Gùilín, Lóngshèng is close to the border of Guìzhōu and is a good introduction to the rich minority cultures of this region. The Lóngshèng area is home to a colour-ful mixture of Dong, Zhuang, Yao and Miáo. Lóngshèng's main attraction is definitely not the town – a cluster of concrete hulks that clash with the mountain back-drop. Not far out of town, however, are the Dragon's Backbone Rice Terraces and a nearby hot spring (wēnquán). The hot spring is a tacky tourist highlight and can be safely missed, although buses (Y5) run-ning out there pass through rolling hills sculptured with rice terraces and studded with Yao and Zhuang minority villages. The area is reminiscent of Banaue in North Luzon, in the Philippines. It's possible to desert the bus around 6km to 7km from the hot spring and take off into the hills for some exploring.

Information
The China Post & Telecom office is on Gu-long Lu. Just 50m beyond is an Internet cafe open 9am to midnight (Y4 per hour).

Lóngshèng Travel Service (☎ 751 7566) is next to the bus station and should be able to help you arrange transport, guides and tours to the surrounding sights.

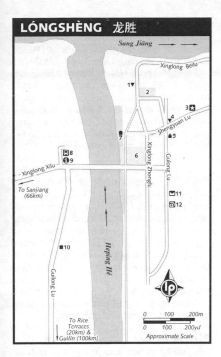

LÓNGSHÈNG 龙胜

LÓNGSHÈNG

1 Lóngshèng Green Food
  Restaurant
  绿色茶馆
2 Square
  广场
3 PSB
  公安局
4 Tea House
  茶馆
5 Lǚyóu Bīnguǎn
  旅游宾馆
6 Market
  市场
7 Foreign Trade Hotel
  外贸宾馆
8 Bus Station
  汽车站
9 Lóngshèng Tourist
  Corp
  龙胜县旅游公司
10 Riverside Hotel
   凯凯旅舍
11 China Post & Telecom
   邮电局
12 Internet Bar
   网吧

Dragon's Backbone Rice Terraces
Lóngjǐ Tītián 龙脊梯田

Though the region around Lóngshèng is covered with terraced rice fields, in the Dragon's Backbone Rice Terraces these feats of farm engineering reach all the way up a string of 500m peaks. A half-hour climb to the top delivers an amazing vista – if the Yao women who invariably tag along to peddle their trinkets give you a moment's peace to enjoy it.

The Zhuang village of **Píng'ān**, on the central main ridge of the backbone, is rapidly becoming a small travellers centre and in a couple of years has accumulated a host of guesthouses, bars, restaurants and no doubt will soon have Internet cafes.

The cause of this boom was the construction of a 6km zigzag road from the riverside at the bottom of the valley up to Píng'ān. In order to build this road a large number of rice terraces had to be blasted away and serious environmental damage has resulted. In any case, it is still possible to avoid using the

road as Píng'ān is only a half-hour's walk up a beautiful stone path from **Huángluò**.

Despite the proliferation of buildings in Píng'ān, the town remains a very attractive place to base yourself for a couple of days of exploring the area. Walking possibilities include the one-hour circuit from the village to the clearly marked Viewpoint 1 and Viewpoint 2. More extensive day-walks are also possible along the dragon's backbone and down to Hépíng or over the ridge and down into the valley beyond. The best time to visit the area is during summer when water is plentiful, although some travellers have remarked at the beauty of the terraces covered in snow. Winter and early spring are not the best due to the heavy fogs and mist that often shroud the terraces.

There's a Y20 entry charge to the terraces collected on the main road along the valley bottom and checked just before the beautiful covered bridge at the entrance to Píng'ān.

Buses to the terraces leave infrequently between 7am and 5.30pm from Lóngshèng's

GUÁNGXĪ

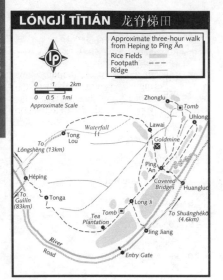

LÓNGJĪ TĪTIÁN 龙脊梯田

Approximate three-hour walk
from Heping to Píng'ān
Rice Fields
Footpath ---
Ridge

0   1   2km
0   0.5 1mi
Approximate Scale

Zhonglu
Tomb
Uhlong
Lawai
Waterfall
Goldmine
Tong
Lou
To
Lóngshèng (13km)
Píng
'An
Héping
Covered
Bridges
Huangluc
To
Guilin
(83km)
Tonga
Long Ji
Tea
Plantation
Tomb
To Shuānghékǒu
(4.6km)
Jing Jiang
River
Road
Entry Gate

bus station. The 9.20am, 10.40am and 4pm buses are most regular and usually make the trip to the top, whereas the other buses will drop you off at the base of the terraces and continue on to Shuānghékǒu. Buy your tickets on the bus (Y4.50 to the base or Y6.50 to the top). Though the trip is only about 20km, some of the buses stop midway at the town of Héping to try to pull in more passengers, which can make the ride last up to 1½ hours! Returning to Lóngshèng, buses usually depart from the car park near the covered bridge at 7.30am, 10.30am and 2pm.

Places to Stay

By far the best choice for accommodation is found in the small village of Píng'ān at the Dragon's Backbone Rice Terraces. Most of the other villages in the area also offer accommodation in traditional wooden homes. A basic dorm bed costs Y15 in Píng'ān or Y10 elsewhere. Most of the hostels in Píng'ān have 24-hour hot water and will serve meals (Y5 to Y10 per meal). Many travellers have raved about their time staying and eating with the locals here. The owners are generally friendly and very helpful about suggested itineraries. There is

little difference between most of the hostels, except for their views. Two worthy hostels include *Liǎoměilū Lǚguǎn* (☎ 758 2542) and *Lóngyíng Lǚguǎn* (☎ 758 2410).

Foreign Trade Hotel (*Wàimào Bīnguǎn;* ☎ 751 2078), which you can't miss, thanks to the many signs around town, is good value and the staff is friendly. Beds in a twin or triple with toilet, but no hot water, cost Y10. A bed in a good twin with shower and 24-hour hot water costs Y25.

Another very good mid-range option is the newly renovated *Lǚyóu Bīnguǎn* (☎ 751 7206) where clean doubles are Y80 or Y100 and twins cost Y100 and Y120. It also has a quad room for Y160. All of these prices are usually discounted by 20% and include bathrooms, air-con and 24-hour hot water.

Down the road to Gùilín is *Riverside Hotel* (*Kǎikǎi Lǚshè*). It's run by an English teacher who seems happy to give travellers information on how to get to the local sights. Rooms are very basic and cost Y10 per bed.

There are plenty of places to stay around the bus station, but it is quite noisy.

Places to Eat

Lóngshèng is not a culinary wonderland. Although plenty of restaurants have opened up in recent years, most don't have any English menus or speakers. Past the Moon Hotel, *Lóngshèng Green Food Restaurant* (*Lüsè Cháguǎn*) serves up decent local speciality dishes. There is a photo board to help you order, but check the prices first as some dishes aren't cheap. This is a good place to have a group hotpot (Y30 for the basic plus extras). The *xiānggū ròupiàn* (beef strips with shitake mushrooms and red capsicum) is quite tasty.

Up Shengyuan Lu towards the PSB is a pleasant little traditional building with a *teahouse* serving local teas and snacks.

Just past the bridge on Xinglong Xilu, *street stalls* appear around 8pm, offering point-and-choose meals by lantern light. There are also some *noodle shops* on Xinglong Beilu.

The new *Zhuang-Minority Flavours Restaurant* has opened in Píng'ān offering a wide range of traditional Zhuang snacks, meals and drinks. Traditional performances were also planned for the restaurant on special occasions.

Getting There & Away

Buses leave the bus station every 10 to 15 minutes for Gùilín (Y10, four hours) and express buses depart every two hours (Y15, three hours). Buses depart from Lóngshèng for Sānjiang hourly (Y7, two hours). There is one daily bus to Zīyuán at 7.20am (Y17, 4½ hours)

ZĪYUÁN 资源

While most tourists come to Gùilín to placidly float down the Lí Jiāng, at Zīyuán you can get a more adrenaline-inducing ride. Located 107km north-east of Gùilín in Māor Shān (Cat Mountains), Zīyuán is the jump-off point for the wild rafting trip along the Wŭpái Hé. This takes you floating or roaring – depending on water levels – on a trip of around 30km with a drop of about 300m. Another trip of up to 90km along the Zī Jiāng passes by lots of villages, cliffs and caves, but requires an overnight.

Those who don't want to go rafting can visit nearby **Bàodǐng Falls** (Bàodǐng Pùbù). Zīyuán's been on a few European tour agencies' itineraries for a number of years, but for the most part it's gone unnoticed by Western travellers. Part of the problem is cost – it's prohibitive by most travellers' standards. You won't even get in the water without paying a minimum of Y100, and the same goes for lodging: Beds under Y100 or Y150 are often impossible to find until you get far down the river.

Gùilín's youth hostel offers one- and two-day tours to Zīyuán during the warmer months. It charges Y180 for one day and Y300 for an overnight, however weekends are often more expensive. Prices are often higher during summer, but it is easier to hook up with a larger tour group. Otherwise head for Zīyuán during summer and make inquires with some of the tour operators in town.

Buses depart from Gùilín every two hours (Y18, 2½ hours). You might also consider heading to Lóngshèng from Zīyuán if you've already visited Gùilín.

SĀNJIĀNG DONG MINORITY AUTONOMOUS COUNTY

三江侗族自治县　Sānjiāng Dongzu Zìzhìxiàn

☎ 0772 ● pop 330,000

If arriving in the town of Sānjiāng leaves you wondering why you made the trip, don't worry. Like Lóngshèng, the idea is to get out and about. Approximately 20km to the north of town, Chéngyáng Wind and Rain Bridge and the surrounding Dong villages are peaceful and attractive. About seven hours by bus from Gùilín, Sānjiāng is inhabited mostly by Dong, who comprise over 50% of the county's population. See also the boxed text 'The Dong' in the Eastern Guìzhōu section of the Guìzhōu chapter.

Chéngyáng Wind & Rain Bridge

程阳　Chéngyáng Qiáo

Built in 1912, this 78m-long, elegant covered bridge is considered by the Dong to be the finest of the 108 such structures in Sānjiāng county, and took villagers 12 years to build. The five towers feature multiple storeys with exquisite eaves and were theoretically made without nails. The bridges are characterised by design flexibility, allowing them to be built on any topography. This bridge looks over a lush valley dotted with Dong villages and water wheels. The inevitable minority women hawking wares are there as well. An admission fee of Y10 is charged.

Chéngyáng is a great place to base yourself for a couple of days to explore the surrounding countryside and minority villages. Chéngyáng Bridge National Hostel is a good option (see the following Places To Stay section).

From the Sānjiāng bus station, you can catch hourly buses to Línxī, which go right past the bridge, or otherwise take one of the frequent minivan taxis (both Y3) that gather outside the bus station. Bus services stop around 6pm in each direction, so if you need to get back to Sānjiāng later than that you'll have to hitch. The first bus of the day to Sānjiāng passes by the bridge around 7.40am.

Minority Villages

The bridge and the fantastic water wheels dotting the countryside aren't the only attractions of the Sānjiāng area. Due north of Sānjiāng is **Mǎpàng**, with one of the largest drum towers in Guǎngxī province. The road north to Dùtóng takes you through minority villages abounding with traditional architecture and offering plenty of photo opportunities. A few villages north is **Bātuán Bridge**, not quite as large as Chéngyáng Bridge, but equally impressive. A good day trip would be to set out early to Sānjiāng and change to a bus to Dùtóng (Y7.50, two hours), hop off at Bātuán and walk down to the village of **Mèngsāi**. There are regular buses and minivan taxis from Mèngsāi back to Sānjiāng (Y5.20, 70 minutes).

If you decide to stay at Chéngyáng Bridge, then a popular full-day circuit walk is to wander up to Píngyán and then continue on to Jíchāng, via Píngpù. Many of Píngpù's people continue to wear their traditional attire. From Jíchāng you can wander down to Línxī and then catch a bus back to the bridge. The hostel will give you directions or can arrange for a guide and translator to accompany you.

Buses depart to all these villages from the Sānjiāng bus station.

Festivals The villages around Sānjiāng have no fewer than six versions of the Firecracker Festival spread throughout the year. In addition, in the first lunar month is a festival and *lúshēng* (traditional bamboo instrument) competition. In the fifth lunar month is the Dragon-Boat Festival. Some travellers may wish to avoid the eighth lunar month's bullfighting festival and the ninth lunar month's bird-fighting festival.

Places to Stay

The best place for accommodation in the area is easily **Chéngyáng Bridge National Hostel** (*Chéngyáng Qiáo Zhāodàisuǒ*; ☎ 861 2444, fax 861 1716), which is just to the left of the Chéngyáng Bridge, over the river. The entrance is on the far side of the building. Opened in mid-1994, this hotel is an all-wood, Dong-style building with beds for Y20 and nice doubles with shared bathroom for Y60. The owners are friendly,

informative and welcoming. Even if you don't spend the night, a cup of tea or a simple meal on the hostel's riverside balcony is a great way to enjoy the scenery.

Some other hotels have sprung up around the bridge, including **Dong Village Hotel**, but they don't really offer any competition.

There's no need to stay in Sānjiāng unless you are catching a very early bus out of town. If so, your quietest option by far is the **Guesthouse of the People's Government of the Sānjiāng Dong Autonomous County** (*Sānjiāng Dòngzú Zìzhìxiàn Rénmín Zhéngfǔ Zhāodàisuǒ*). Doubles are Y40, or Y60 with bath. To get there, follow the road that runs between the Department Store Hotel and the bus station uphill, and bear left. Walk about 10 minutes and the guesthouse is on your right, across from a Dong drum tower.

Right in town on the opposite corner to the bus station, **Bǎihuò Zhāodàisuǒ** has beds in quads/twins from Y6/12, and doubles with bath for Y18. There is every chance that staff will tell you that there are no cheap rooms available.

Farther down the street, the **Chéngyáng Bridge Hotel** (*Chéngyáng Qiáo Bīnguǎn*) has slightly more upmarket rooms starting at about Y100.

Getting There & Away

The Sānjiāng bus station has several buses to Gùilín (Y18.5, five hours) between 7.10am and 2.30pm and Liǔzhōu (Y23, six hours) between 7.50am and 4pm. These usually pass through Róngshuǐ (Y4.50), a scenic trip of 3½ hours. Buses to Lóngshèng (Y7) leave every 40 to 50 minutes between 6.30am and 5.10pm.

Sānjiāng to Kǎilǐ If you have time on your hands, it's worth considering entering Guìzhōu province through the back door, using local buses. From Sānjiāng take the 6.50am or 2pm bus to Dìpíng (Lóng'é) (Y10), which is just across the Guìzhōu border. Though the journey is only about three hours, if you catch the later bus and there are delays you'll almost certainly have to stay overnight in Dìpíng. There are frequent buses from Dìpíng to Lìpíng (Y15, five hours).

The journey to Lìpíng passes through some beautiful mountains, as well as the town of Zhàoxīng, which is worth a visit. For more information on these areas, see the Dong Region section of the Guìzhōu chapter.

Another possibility is to take a train to Tōngdào in Húnán province and from there travel on by bus to Lìpíng. Minibuses run every half-hour throughout the day to the train station a few kilometres west of Sānjiāng.

RÓNGSHUǏ
☎ 0772 • pop 450,000

Lóngshèng and Sānjiāng get most of the press, but Róngshuǐ is another town central to Guǎngxī's minority culture. Travellers who don't want to cross into Guìzhōu could make this town a possible third node on a Lóngshèng-Sānjiāng-Róngshuǐ loop trip out of Gùilín. Within the county 13 minority groups are represented, with Miáo making up 37% of the total. Large numbers of Yao, Zhuang and Dong also live in the county.

Apart from the minority cultural experience, Róngshuǐ's most famous attraction is Yuànbǎo Shān, a couple of hours to the north-west, a rustic mountain. The loveliest Guǎngxī sunrises are viewed from this mountain. The town itself has a quickly climbed Buddhist mountain to occupy your time while you plan your getaway to the surrounding areas.

Orientation

Róngshuǐ is a small town with only two main streets, Shouxing Zhonglu and Chaoyang Lu. The train line hugs the northern part of town with the station in the north-west about a 20-minute walk from the centre. The bus station is in the south-west about 10 minutes' walk from downtown. All of the sights are out of town and require a visit to either one of the travel agencies or the bus station.

Lǎozi Shān

The only sight within the town proper is this tiny hillock, which locals refer to as a 'mountain'. A temple, some pavilions, and the odd cave are found around this hump, whose summit you can reach in about 20

sweatless minutes. The park is on the southern edge of the central part of town. Admission is Y3.

To get there, head south-east from the town's only traffic roundabout until the road ends, then local paths will take you by pretty riverside scenes and through village gardens. After 10 minutes you'll cross a stream and see the first of the pedlars at the entrance. Local bus No 2 also passes by Lǎozi Shān.

Minority Villages

Many of the minority villages are accessed only via waterways. This is not so easy to do, however, at least not for solo travellers. There is a pier near Róngshuǐ and you could theoretically arrive, take a motorcycle taxi to the pier and try to hook up with a Chinese group tour. However, in practice, this rarely works and you generally wind up haggling over outrageous prices with a boat owner yourself. Even if you arrive in the high summer season and find a group that will take you, the trip will still be expensive. You might have luck negotiating directly with a boat guide if there are a few of you. Otherwise, take an organised tour – for details see that section following.

There's also no shortage of Miáo culture in the countryside; pick a local bus to anywhere north and you'll be likely to pass at least relatively close to a Miáo village. Just jump off the bus and look around.

Festivals Taking place throughout the year, festivals don't lack for Chinese tourist attendance. These often include local varieties of a 'firecracker festival', held around here in the second and fourth lunar months. Otherwise, the first lunar month starts with the Lunar Festival, followed by the Ancient Dragon Hill Meeting, and ends with the Lost Brother Festival. The festival that few foreigners wish to take in is the horse-fighting festival in the sixth lunar month.

Organised Tours

A couple of tour operators are on Shouxing Lu. The Guǎngxī Autonomous County Travel Service (Máozú Zìzhìxiàn Mínzú Lǚxíng; ☎ 512 7733), at 36 Shouxing

Zhonglu, offers boat tours to minority villages. Count on a minimum charge of Y120 per person for a 9am to 5pm tour that includes all transportation and lunch. Tours only operate on weekends from the middle of March to early November. This office also runs three-day tours to Yuànbǎo Shān (Y350 minimum) and other places, and some multiday offerings. The folk here are friendly enough, but are not really prepared to offer any advice or assistance to independent travellers. Furthermore there's an additional 100% charge for foreigners. All tours require a four-person minimum.

Places to Stay

The nicest rooms in town are definitely at *Dìshuì Zhāodàisuǒ* (☎ 512 7744). This new guesthouse has very good, clean rooms with 24-hour hot water. Beds in quads/triples cost Y38/48 and doubles are Y68 with larger twins for Y168. Turn left as you exit the bus station and then turn right over the bridge at the first road. Continue down here for about 400m and the hotel is on your left.

Gōngxiāoshè Zhāodàisuǒ (☎ 512 2589) is a bit farther along at the roundabout intersection. Beds in quads here are Y12, with more comfy options at Y58 for a twin and Y78 for a double with air-con and individual heating – a godsend on those cold December nights.

Both of these places are preferable to the official *Shòuxīng Dàshà* (☎ 512 2463), where twins cost Y60, Y90 or Y110. Hot water is available from 6.30pm to 11pm. The Shòuxīng is at the northern end of Shouxing Zhonglu.

Places to Eat

Ròngshuǐ is famous for its *sūanyǔ* (sour-vinegar meat) and *sūanrò* (fish) dishes. They are most easily available in summer. Many dishes will also feature *dōngxiānggū*, a flavourful winter mushroom. You can find very good *zhútóng fàn* (rice steamed in bamboo); you peel the bamboo and eat the cooked rice like bread. No one restaurant really stands out as the best, but off Shouxing Zhonglu a few metres down an alley is a little *open-air restaurant* that is consistently packed with locals.

For a lighter meal, turn left out of the bus station and then right at the first intersection and cross the bridge. The first little restaurant on the right cooks up some tasty *xiǎolóngbǎo* (steamed pork dumplings, Y1.50) and the second and third places do a pretty spicy bowl of *luósīfěn* (the regional rice-noodle soup speciality, Y2).

Getting There & Away

Bus Lots of buses ply the route between Ròngshuǐ and Liǔzhōu (Y12, three hours). If you are heading for Ròngshuǐ, then first go to Liǔzhōu and catch one of the expresses to Gùilín. Buses for Sānjiāng are a little sporadic and it is better to share a ride in a minivan taxi to Ròng'ān (Y3, 50 minutes) and then jump on one of the regular buses that connect Ròng'ān and Sānjiāng (Y8, 2½ hours).

Train Ròngshuǐ is served by trains between Ròng'ān to the north, and Liǔzhōu to the south.

Three trains a day connect Liǔzhōu and Ròngshuǐ, departing at 7.30am, 1.20pm and 4.40pm, arriving in Ròngshuǐ at 10.22am, 4.11pm and 8.21pm respectively. The first two then continue on to Sānjiāng arriving at 12.28pm and 6.47pm. If you catch the later train to Sānjiāng, then you will have to stay in town as the last bus to the Chéngyáng Bridge is around 6pm.

Heading south, trains to Liǔzhōu from Ròngshuǐ depart at 7.42am, 9.54am and 5.47pm, arriving at 11.26am, 12.51pm and 8.38pm respectively.

Getting Around

Except for the train station, any motorcycle-taxi ride in Ròngshuǐ should be Y1; the train station will be Y1.50 to Y2 as it's 2km from the town centre. Otherwise the town is small enough to walk around.

AROUND RÒNGSHUǏ
Yuànbǎo Shān

This is the king of the Ròngshuǐ side trips. The summit of Yuànbǎo Shān rises 2100m over the surrounding plain, about 75km from Róngshuǐ.

While it isn't a killer mountain – you can climb it in four to six hours – it has a lot to offer on the way up. The 3900 hectares of national park surrounding Yuànbǎo Shān feature several ambitious trails (lots of steps) and plenty of waterfalls. One famous mountain highlight is the 'Sea of Clouds', which often shrouds the summit overnight. At dawn, when the clouds clear, Yuànbǎo reddens in what is arguably Guǎngxī's best sunrise scene.

Due to the current transport situation you'll have to stay overnight at one of the wooden huts (Y15 to Y20 a bed) on the mountain, since there's no way you could explore the mountain and get back in a day.

You should visit Róngshuǐ's forestry office (Sénliú) to obtain a permit before heading up to Yuànbǎo Shān. The office is 500m from the bus station and is open 8am to noon and 2.30pm to 5.30pm weekdays. Turn right out of the bus station and continue until the second intersection. Turn right and the entrance to the department is on your right. You might even get help organising a guide (Y60 per day) if you were planning on staying longer. This office will try to tell you to organise the trip through a travel agency, but most agencies are only interested in groups. You will also need to take enough food with you unless other arrangements have been made.

To get there, catch the daily bus departing at noon from Róngshuǐ to the park entrance town of Xiǎosāng (Y8.10, two hours).

LIǓZHŌU 柳州
☎ 0772 • pop 880,000

Liǔzhōu, is the largest city on the Liǔ Jiāng and is one of South-West China's important train junctions. The place dates back to the Tang dynasty, when it was a dumping ground for disgraced court officials. Largely left to its mountain wilds until 1949, Liǔzhōu has since been transformed into a major industrial city.

Liǔzhōu is Gùilín's poor cousin, with similar, but less impressive, karst scenery on the outskirts of town. Most mornings eagle-eyed travellers can witness taichi sessions atop the peaks ringing Liǔzhōu. The town sees few foreigners, and the locals are thus far from jaded in their dealings with travellers. Liǔzhōu has received a recent boost in spending on public infrastructure, resulting in a much needed face-lift for many of the rivers and roads and transforming the place into a modern Chinese city.

Information
China Post & Telecom is south of Liǔzhōu Square and is open 8am to 8pm. Next door is an Internet bar, which is open until 10pm daily and charges Y3 per hour. There are a couple of Bank of China branches that can exchange travellers cheques. There is a useful ticket office on Longcheng Lu that sells plane and train tickets.

City Parks
Liǔzhōu may be lacking in big tourist drawcards, but the city retains a certain charm with its picturesque river banks and urban parks. Entry to each of these parks costs Y3.

Pleasant Liǔhòu Park (Liǔhòu Gōngyuán) is in the north of the city and has a lake and small temple erected to the memory of Liu Zongyuan (772–819), a famous scholar and poet. Bus No 2, 5 or 6 will get you to the park.

Along Feie Lu near the main bus station is Yúféng Shān, or Fish Peak Mountain, in Yúféng Park. It's very small as mountains go (33m!), and derives its name from the fact that it looks like a 'standing fish'. Climb to the top for a smoggy vista of Guǎngxī's foremost industrial city or ride the cable car from Yúféng Park up to the peak of neighbouring Mǎ'ān Shān. Otherwise known as Horse Saddle Mountain, Mǎ'ān Shān has several temples and pavilions and the peak provides better views. A return ticket on the cable car costs Y20, including the Y3 entry, and runs until 8pm.

Bǎotáshān Park is to the south-east of town with two beautiful seven-storey pagodas perched upon the peaks of this pleasant park.

Liǔzhòu's riverside parks have only recently been landscaped and beautified with a number of pleasant trails. Plans are in place for tourist boats to start making tours along the Liǔ Jiāng during summer, departing from the wharf on the river.

Places to Stay

Opposite the main train station is *Tiān'é Fàndiàn* where beds in a triple/double/twin cost Y30/55/35. More expensive rooms with damp carpet are also available and are usually discounted by 30%.

A more preferable option is friendly *Jīn'é Dàjiǔdiàn* (☎ 361 1888, ext 2100) where

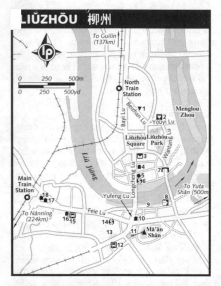

LIǓZHŌU 柳州

To Guìlín (137km)

North Train Station

Bàyì Lù
Bèihǎn Lù

Menglou Zhou

Liǔzhōu Square

Liǔzhōu Park

Youyi Lu

Wàntàng Lù

Liǔ Jiāng

Longcheng Lu

Main Train Station

To Yuta Shān (500m)

Yufeng Lu

To Nánníng (224km)

Feie Lu

Ma'ān Shān

0   250   500m
0   250   500yd

twins/triples start at Y50/60. The hotel is just to the left as you exit the south bus station. Staff will also purchase bus, train and air tickets for you (20% commission).

No hotels around the main bus station accept foreigners, forcing travellers to make the hike to *Yúfēng Dàshà* (☎ 787 8177, ext 3108), which is the cheapest official option. Twins/triples/singles go for Y118/125/130. Its rooms are a little tired but should be OK for a night.

Farther down Feie Lu towards the train station is the mid-range *Nánjiāng Fàndiàn* (☎ 361 2988, fax 361 7575), a three-star outfit with good comfy rooms. Tariffs start at Y153 for a double and Y180 for a twin. It also has a good family room with a separate bedroom for Y266. These prices are already discounted and, with the exception of public holidays, are readily available. There is also a nice cafe in the foyer.

Liǔzhōu's top-end hotel is definitely the central *Lìjīng Dàjiǔdiàn* (☎ 280 8888, fax 280 8828). It's brand new, with luxurious twins for Y338 and Y418, depending on their size. A 20% discount is usually available.

Places to Eat

Your best bet may be the lively *night market* across from the Foreign Language Bookstore. From around 8pm numerous stalls serve tasty dumplings and noodles fried with your choice of fresh ingredients – just point to what you want.

LIǓZHŌU

PLACES TO STAY & EAT
1 Time Bar
   时间酒吧
4 Lìjīng Dàjiǔdiàn
   丽晶大酒店
10 Yúfēng Dàshà
   鱼峰大厦
16 Jīn'é Dàjiǔdiàn
   金鹅大酒店
17 Nánjiāng
   Fàndiàn
   南疆饭店
18 Tiān'é
   Fàndiàn
   天鹅饭店

OTHER
2 Popular Cafes
   热闹的酒吧和餐厅
3 China Post
   & Telecom,
   Internet Bar
   中国电信
   网吧
5 Train & Plane
   Ticket Office
   售票处
6 Bank of China
   中国银行
7 East Gate
   东门城楼

8 Ferry Dock
   航运码头
9 Riverside Park
   江滨公园
11 Yufeng Park
   鱼峰公园
12 Main Bus Station
   汽车总站
13 Night Market
   夜市
14 Bank of China
   中国银行
15 Liǔzhōu South
   Bus Station
   柳州南站

The train-station area also has dumpling and noodle places. There is a string of trendy and popular cafes and bars on Youyi Lu near the Liǔzhōu Hotel serving Western food and cocktails.

Off to the west from here up Beizhan Lu is *Time Bar (Shíjiān Jiǔbā)*, a Western-style bar. It serves up a few decent Western dishes and has draught beer!

Getting There & Away
Air There is one daily flight to Guǎngzhōu (Y570) at 8.50pm. Tickets for this flight and other flights departing from Gùilín and Nánníng can be purchased at window No 13 in the main bus station.

Bus The Liǔzhōu south bus station is actually north of the main bus station, but let's not quibble. It's along Feie Lu and is much closer to budget lodgings and the train station, so it's likely to become the main terminus for travellers. The other station is a fair hike from the train station, and is south of Yúféng Park. The stations have different schedules entirely, so if you arrive and one doesn't have a convenient departure time, check the other.

If you want to get to Yángshuò, then it is quicker to first travel to Gùilín and change buses there. Frequent express buses run to Gùilín (Y40, 1½ hours) and Róngshuǐ (Y16, four hours). Other services include hourly buses to Sānjiāng (Y22, five hours) and Jīnxiù (Y15 to Y20, 4½ hours).

Train Liǔzhōu is a main railway junction connecting Nánníng to Gùilín. There are a number of good connections including Běijīng, Chángshā, Chéngdū, Guǎngzhōu, Guìyáng, Shànghǎi and Xī'ān.

Boat There are no longer boats connecting Liǔzhōu with Wúzhōu and Guǎngzhōu. The only services are tour-boat cruises on the Liǔ Jiāng.

Getting Around
Bus Nos 2 and 24 connect Liǔzhou Square and the train station; bus Nos 10 and 25 run past the main bus station to Liǔzhōu Square and No 11 goes to the train station.

Guìzhōu 贵州

Guìzhōu at a Glance

Guìzhōu p243

Zūnyi p295   Tóngrén p286

Weining p264   Zhènyuǎn p284

Guìyáng p248 ⊙   Kǎilǐ p274

Ānshùn p254

Huángguǒshù Falls p260

Eastern Guìzhōu p271

Xīngyì p267

Around Xīngyì p268

Area: 170,000 sq km

Population: 35.6 million

Capital: Guìyáng

Highlights

- Huángguǒshù Falls, China's premier cataract surrounded by scenic countryside

- Traditional minority villages, especially Xījiāng, China's largest Miáo (Hmong) village, and the remote Dong village of Zhàoxìng in the south-east

- Festivals, countless celebrated throughout the region, notably in and around Kǎilǐ in February

- Zhījīn Cave, China's largest cavern; an endless moonscape of towers, tunnels and huge, open rooms

Terraced crops climb the sides of rolling mountains that eventually stretch out into wide plateaus. These give way to jagged karst hills dotted with giant limestone caves and countless waterfalls plunging to the ground. Guìzhōu's landscape is that of traditional Chinese paintings; a delicate beauty of moss-greens and grey-blues.

Within this setting lives a vibrant and colourful mix of people. Around 35% of Guìzhōu's population is made up of over 80 different ethnic minorities. While the majority Han cluster mainly in the province's cities, communities of Miáo, Bouyi, Dong, Yi, Shui, Huí, Zhuang, Bai, Tujia, Gelao and Gejia populate the more remote villages where, between them, they celebrate nearly 1000 festivals each year. These festivals preserve fascinating customs and elaborate skills in architecture, dress and handicrafts.

Surprisingly, for a province so rich in minority culture, Guìzhōu is still neglected by most travellers. The well-worn path from Guìlín to Kūnmíng cuts through the province, and yet if you hop off the train in Guìyáng, other Westerners look at you as if you're daft. The only attraction to draw relatively large numbers is the Huángguǒshù Falls, China's largest.

One reason for this lack of interest is probably the perceived difficulty of travel in the province, perhaps due to its reputation as one of China's more hard done by provinces. A Chinese proverb has it enshrined as a land 'without three li of flat country, three days of fine weather or three cents to rub together'. While Guìzhōu is one of the poorest areas of China, in reality travel here is no more difficult than in other, more popular regions of the country. If you head out into the sticks, you will have to rough it, the food ain't so great and not a word of English is uttered, but if you're an adventurer with an interest in minority cultures, Guìzhōu's outback can be an extremely rewarding destination and may be the surprise highlight of your trip.

The south-east of Guìzhōu is particularly worth exploring. Around 72% of the population in this region is Miáo or Dong or a mixture of other minorities. Travelling in this area takes you through countless tiny villages with drum towers and 'wind and rain' bridges. With the exception of the buses and trucks that ply the roads, life in

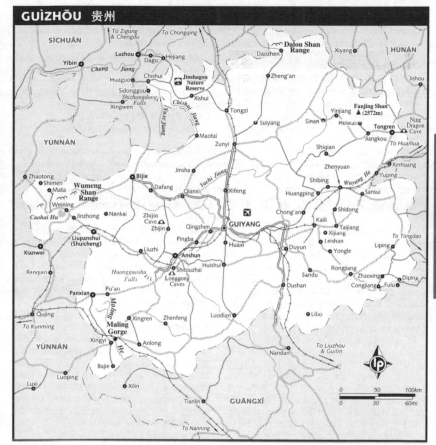

GUÌZHŌU 贵州

this part of China seems to go on much as it has for centuries past.

History

Although Chinese rulers set up an administration in the area as far back as the Han dynasty (206 BC to AD 220), they merely attempted to maintain some measure of control over the non-Chinese tribes who lived here. Chinese settlement was confined to the north and east of the province and the western areas were not settled until the 16th century, when the native minorities were forced out of the most fertile areas. Another wave of Chinese immigration in the late 19th century brought many settlers from overpopulated provinces of Húnán and Sìchuān. However, with poor communication systems and transport, development in Guìzhōu was sluggish and the province remained impoverished.

It wasn't until the Japanese invasion in 1931 forced the Kuomintang to retreat to the south-west of China that the development of Guìzhōu began in earnest: Roads to the neighbouring provinces were constructed, a rail link was built to Guǎngxī, and industries were set up in Guìyáng and Zūnyì. Most of

Suggested Itineraries

Guìzhōu is not a great place to be on a tight itinerary, and it's worth building in a couple of days to allow for bus breakdowns or the unexpected but booming village market.

One Week

From Guìyáng, head east by bus to **Kǎilǐ** and spend a couple of days visiting **minority villages**, such as Xījiāng, Chóng'ān and Lángdé, especially if there are festivals scheduled. Return to Guìyáng and make an overnight visit to **Huángguǒshù Falls**, staying one night in Ānshùn. You can try to catch the **Sunday market** here and tack on another day to head north to **Zhījīn Cave**.

Two Weeks

To the week above, add a further week exploring the Dong villages, in particular **Zhàoxīng**, to the south of Kǎilǐ. From there you can continue south into Guǎngxī province. Alternatively, you can head west from Ānshùn to **Wēiníng** and see the wintering birds at **Cǎohǎi Hú**, then south to **Mǎlǐng Gorge**, outside Xīngyì. You can then continue west to Kūnmíng in Yúnnán.

this activity ceased with the end of WWII and it wasn't revived until the Communists began construction of the railways. Today the province's most famous export is Maotai liquor, named for the village of its origin in Renhuai county. This fiery white spirit is sold in distinctive white bottles with a diagonal red label. Guìzhōu is also, like Yúnnán, a major tobacco-producing area.

Despite advances, Chinese statistics continue to paint a grim picture of underdevelopment and poverty for Guìzhōu. Eight million of the province's population still live below the national poverty line, between 60% and 70% of the population are illiterate, and many of the province's more remote villages are not accessible by road. Blame is often laid unfairly at the door of the minorities, who may well be self-sufficient but are nonetheless viewed as backward and as choosing to embrace poverty rather than consumer life and assimilation. The government, for its part, is attempting to change all this, mostly by laying down roads in every place possible to facilitate travel to Huángguǒshù Falls and by promoting minority cultures as a local attraction.

The vast majority of Guìzhōu is open to foreign travellers. Nevertheless, restrictions change frequently and if you're planning to visit anywhere extremely remote, in particular along the provincial borders, you might be wise to check with the Public Security

Bureau (PSB; Zhōu Gōngānjú) in Guìyáng before heading out as permits can only be issued in the province's capital. Unfortunately, you need to know your exact destinations as the PSB has only a long list of where you can go – not a list of where you are not allowed.

Festivals

Festivities among the minority communities in Guìzhōu offer plenty of scope for exploration. Taking place throughout the lunar calendar at various sites, these vibrant celebrations can feature bullfighting, horse racing, pipe playing, comic opera, singing contests and gigantic courting parties. Oh yes, and basketball matches.

The majority of festivals are held on auspicious lunar dates such as the third day of the third lunar month, the sixth of the sixth, the fifth of the fifth and the ninth of the ninth. Most are annual events, though some are held every few years, and others just once a decade.

Courtship is the drive behind most festivals. There are many elaborate ploys to get boys and girls together, ranging from handing out rice packets with secret messages inside to less subtle games of catch, where crowds of adolescents line up and 'inadvertently' throw the ball at their favourite potential partner until the object of this affection gets the point. Festivals

Festivals in Guìzhōu

festival	location	lunar calendar	2002	2003	2004
Caigetang	Dong Areas	beg of 1st	mid-Feb	early Feb	late Jan
Taiguanren	Dong areas (near Zhàoxìng, Longtu)	3rd–4th of 1st	14–15 Feb	3–4 Feb	24–25 Jan
Flower Dance	Tongmuling (Huāxī)	9th of 1st	20 Feb	9 Feb	30 Jan
Ground Opera	Dazhai (near Huāxī)	15th of 1st	26 Feb	15 Feb	5 Feb
Dragon Lantern	Táijiāng	15th of 1st	26 Feb	15 Feb	5 Feb
Huapao	Cóngjiāng	28th of 1st	11 Mar	28 Feb	18 Feb
Eryueer	Fǎnpái	2nd of 2nd	15 Mar	4 Mar	21 Feb
Drum Beating (near Qīngmàn)	Qinglang of 2nd lunar	1st 'hai' day	20 Mar	3 Mar	26 Apr
Flower Dance	Nankai (near Lìùpánshuǐ)	13–15th of 2nd	26–28 Mar	15–17 Mar	3–5 Mar
Sanyuesan	Baojing (near Zhènyuǎn)	2nd–4th of 3rd	14–16 Apr	3–5 Apr	20–21 Mar
Maoshanshu	Dewo (near Anlong)	3rd of 3rd	15 Apr	4 Apr	21 Apr
Sisters' Meal Festival	Shīdòng	15–17th of 3rd	27–29 Apr	16–18 Apr	3–5 May
Siyueba	Feiyun Dong, Huángpíng, Guìyáng	8th of 4th	19 May	8 May	26 May
Dragon Boat	Zhènyuán	5th of 5th	15 Jun	4 Jun	22 Jun
Flower Dance	Nankai (near Lìùpánshuǐ)	5th of 5th	15 Jun	4 Jun	22 Jun
Flower Dance	Mata (near Wēiníng)	5th of 5th	15 Jun	4 Jun	22 Jun
Dragon Boat	Shīdòng, Chóng'ān	24–27th of 5th	4–7 Jul	23–26 Jun	11–14 Jul
Liuyueliu	Huāxī	6th of 6th	15 Jul	5 Jul	22 Jul
Eating New Rice	Xījiāng, Zhouxi, Qīngmàn	16th of 6th	25 Jul	15 Jul	1 Aug
Hill Climbing	Incense Burning Hill, Kǎilǐ		28 Jul	18 Jul	4 Aug
Chabai Singing	Dingxiao (near Xīngyì)		30 Jul	20 Jul	6 Aug
Torch	Pugu (near Panxian)	24th of 6th	2 Aug	23 Jul	9 Aug
Qiyueban	Kǎilǐ	13th of 7th	21 Aug	10 Aug	28 Aug
Drum Beating	Liuhe (near Shīdòng)	14–15th of 7th	22–23 Aug	11–12 Aug	29–20 Aug
Eating New Rice	Zhouxi, Qīngmàn	2nd week of 7th	mid- to late Aug	1st week of Aug	end of Aug
Chongyang	Qīngmàn (near Zhouxi)	9th of 9th	14 Oct	4 Oct	22 Oct
Double Ninth	Yongxi (near Zhènyuǎn)	9th of 9th	14 Oct	4 Oct	22 Oct
Duan	Around Sāndū	end of 9th	early Nov	late Oct	2nd week of Nov
Miáo New Year	Xījiāng, Zhouxi, Lángdé	end of 10th	beg of Dec	3rd week of Nov	2nd week of Dec

NB *Dates are based on information compiled from tourism and local sources. However, some festivals are notoriously hard to pin down to a fixed date. Moreover, many festivals (like Miáo New Year) are held on different dates at different villages. It's best to check with CITS before setting off and to leave an extra few days in your itinerary.*

Lusheng Festivals

location	lunar calendar	2002	2003	2004
Ongyi (near Zhouxi)	3rd to 5th of 1st	14–16 Feb	3–5 Feb	24–26 Jan
Yatang (near Zhouxi)	6–7th of 1st	17–18 Feb	6–7 Feb	27–28 Jan
Xinguang (near Zhouxi)	7–9th of 1st	18–20 Feb	7–9 Feb	28–30 Jan
Dazhong (near Zhouxi)	10–12th of 1st	21–23 Feb	10–12 Feb	31 Jan–1 Feb
Tonggu, Shiqing (near Zhouxi)	13–15th of 1st	24–26 Feb	13–15 Feb	3–5 Feb
Longchang	15–16th of 1st	26–27 Feb	15–16 Feb	5–6 Feb
Sānjiāng	17–18th of 1st	28 Feb–1 Mar	17–18 Feb	7–8 Feb
Zhouxi	19th–21st of 1st	2–4 Mar	19–21 Feb	9–11 Feb
Xījiāng	24th of 3rd	6 May	25 Apr	12 May
Panghai (near Kǎilǐ)	21st of 7th	29 Aug	18 Aug	5 Sep
Luoxiang (near Cóngjiāng)	13–15th of 8th	19–21 Sep	9–11 Sep	26–28 Sep
Chóng'ān	26–27th of 9th	31 Oct–1 Nov	21–22 Oct	8–9 Nov
Gulong (near Huángpíng)	27–29th of 9th	1–3 Nov	22–24 Oct	9–11 Nov
Xījiāng	20th of 11th	23 Dec	13 Dec	31 Dec

are therefore a time to look your best and flaunt your wealth, which in Guìzhōu means silver jewellery and exquisite embroidery. Girls spend hours preparing for a festival and will often attend accompanied by their mothers, who continually fuss over their daughters' and offer advice.

Festivals also serve as a time to meet other clans, pick up news from other villages and generally to relax and enjoy life while there is little work to be done in the fields. Glutinous rice cakes, pounded in wooden troughs and dyed with bright colours, are an important festival food. Guests are toasted continually with rice wine, either out of buffalo horns or through straws from a large jug. Important groups are denied entry to some villages until they have downed several shots of rice wine and sung a song.

One of the most common events is the Lusheng Festival, usually held during the first lunar month. The *lusheng* is a reed instrument that ranges in length from 1m to 7m. Lusheng competitions are common and various acrobatic styles are performed to the music, such as 'Earthworm Crossing the Mountain'. Activities include playing the lusheng (of course), traditional dancing, beating bronze drums, bullfighting and horse racing. Most dances are little more than slow monotonous shuffles, which peo-

ple join one by one over the course of an hour or more. Antiphonal singing (echoing duets) is also popular.

Some festivals are held at traditional sites or hills, often called dancing or flower grounds, though many are now held in the less glamorous surroundings of the municipal basketball courts.

Two other common events are the Flower Dance (Tiàohuā), centred around a special flower tree decorated in red silks, and Eating New Rice (Chīxīn Jié) festivals, held to celebrate the harvest by hanging ears of rice and corn in doorways and brewing buckets of rice wine.

A good starting point for festival forays is Kǎilǐ, east of Guìyáng. A profusion of festivals are held in other minority areas such as Ānshùn, Nankai, Shīdòng and Xīngyì. See those sections for information on specific festivals and the following table for approximate dates in the Gregorian calendar.

Central Guìzhōu

Central Guìzhōu is the most developed part of the province and holds its only established tourist attraction, Huángguǒshù Falls, along with Lónggōng and Zhījīn Caves. The land is a pleasant mix of limestone hills and intensively farmed terraces, which explode in spring with a burst of yellow rape (canola) flowers. On the way to Huángguŏshù there are some traditional villages worth exploring – though, in general, the minorities here have been more influenced by Han culture than in other parts of the province.

GUÌYÁNG 贵阳
☎ 0851 • pop 3.5 million • elevation 1070m

Although the capital of Guìzhōu province has a mild climate year-round, its name means Precious Sun and may be a reference to the fact that the sun rarely seems to shine through the clouds and drizzle. Most travellers give the place a miss, however, as you're likely to pass through at least once in your travels around Guìzhōu, it's worth lingering for a day or so. There's good food available, lively market and shopping areas, some pleasant parks and a few interesting sights around town.

The city appears to be getting a face-lift, meaning the usual uncountable number of construction sites, scaffolding and mushrooming high-rises. Nevertheless, a few of the older neighbourhoods and temples have held on and some of the new areas, including the riverside and Rénmín Square, provide enjoyable areas to wander, mingle and relax.

Guìyáng is also Guìzhōu's transport hub with a brand new, state-of-the-art train station and good bus connections in every direction. The city is therefore a good jumping-off point for the Huángguŏshù Falls, 100km west, or the minority villages to the east around Kăilĭ.

Orientation
While Guìyáng is a somewhat sprawling kind of place, it remains a manageable size and is easy enough to get around. The main commercial district is found along Zhonghua Lu and Zhonghua Nanlu, spreading out along the main roads they intersect. In the south of this area, you'll find the main Bank of China, China Telecom and China Post. If you continue south, you'll reach Zunyi Lu and Rénmín Square. To the east of here is Jiăxiù Pavilion, a symbol of the city that hovers over Nanming Hé.

Information
Tourist Offices The CITS office (☎ 581 4829), at 20 Yan'an Zhonglu, is one of the South-West's most helpful and friendly branches. The staff have maps, timetables and information on minority areas.

Staff at the Guìzhōu Overseas Travel Company (GOTC; ☎ 582 5328), next door, have less time to chat but are more reliable if you want to make travel arrangements.

Near the train station, the Guìzhōu Railway International Tour Service (☎ 575 3505) is also helpful in handing out info on nearby sights and for booking train travel. It also arranges regular tours to Huángguŏshù Falls and nearby minority villages. The staff here don't speak English.

Money The Bank of China has several branches around town with ATMs accepting all major credit and bank cards. A number of the branches also exchange money. The main branch on Dusi Lu is the best place to go for credit card advances and wire transfers.

Post & Communications The main China Post and Telecom building is at the intersection of Zunyi Lu and Zhonghua Nanlu. You can make international phone calls from the international and long-distance hall, to the left of the main doors. Collect calls are made from the inquiry desk by the front door.

China Telecom offers Internet access in the office farthest round to the left (north) from the main doors of China Post. Access is available until 5.30pm for Y5 an hour. Across the street, on the 4th floor of the

GUIZHOU

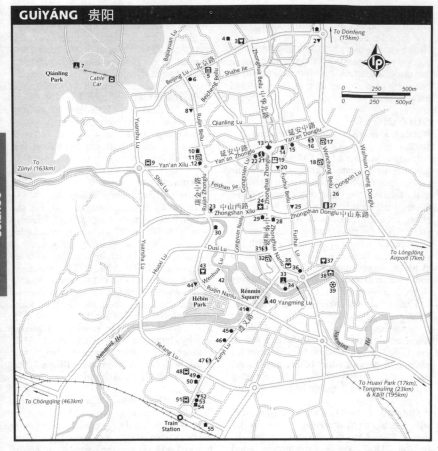

GUÌYÁNG 贵阳

Telecommunications Business Centre, there are more computers where you can go online for the same price until 6.30pm.

A number of private Internet cafes are opening throughout Guìyáng, offering access for Y3 per hour. You'll find two on Wenchang Beilu and another at the southern end of Ruijin Beilu. They're often insanely busy with students cranking the speakers of each computer to a different Chinese dance tune.

Bookshops The Foreign Languages Bookstore on Yan'an Donglu isn't particularly

well stocked, but if you're desperate for reading material, there may be something worth picking up. Several employees of the store hold an English-speaking lecture session here every Sunday morning and warmly welcome any foreign visitors.

Farther west, on the roundabout with Yan'an Xilu, the Xīnhuá Bookstore has a wider selection of Chinese-language maps and posters.

Emergencies The PSB office (☎ 682 1231) is in a white-tiled building on Zhongshan Xilu, close to the intersection with Zhonghua

GUÌYÁNG

PLACES TO STAY

1 Crown Plaza
   Holiday Inn
   神奇假日酒店
4 Guizhou Park
   Hotel
   贵州公园饭店
10 Gōnglù Dàshà
   公路大厦
14 Trade-Point Hotel
   柏顿酒店
28 Guiyang Baicheng
   Fandian
29 Jǐnjiāng Fresh
   Flower Hotel
   锦江鲜花大酒店
30 Jīnqiáo Fàndiàn
   金桥饭店
50 Tǐyù Bīnguǎn
   体育宾馆
54 Tōngdá Fàndiàn
   通达饭店
55 Míngzhū Fàndiàn
   明珠饭店

PLACES TO EAT

2 Miáo Nationality
   Restaurant
   苗苗寨
8 New Zealand
   Western Restaurant
   纽西兰西餐厅
20 Juéyuán Cāntīng
   觉园餐厅
23 Shakey's
25 Outdoor Restaurants
   夜市
44 Night Market
   夜市场
52 Guìzhōu Běijīng
   Kǎoyādiàn
   贵州北京烤鸭店
53 Guizhou Railway
   International
   Tour Service
   贵州铁路
   国际旅行社

OTHER

3 Legends of the Fall Bar;
   The Little Beer House
5 Provincial Museum
   省博物馆
6 China
   Southwest Airlines
   贵阳启明航空服务公司
7 Hóngfú Sì
   弘福寺
9 Long-Distance
   Bus Station
   贵阳长途汽车站
11 Internet Café
   网吧
12 Xinhua Bookstore
   新华书店
13 Penshuichi Fountain
   喷水池
15 Foreign
   Languages
   Bookstore
   外文书店
16 Bank of China
   中国银行
17 Internet Café
   网吧
18 Internet Café
   网吧
19 Cinema
   电影院
21 CITS
   中国国际旅行社
22 Guizhou Overseas
   Travel Company
   (GOTC)
   贵州海外旅游总公司
24 PSB
   公安局
26 Dongxin Lu
   Produce Market
   市场
27 Wénchāng
   Pavilion
   文昌阁
31 Bank of China
   中国银行

32 Telecommunications
   Business Centre
   电信商场
33 Qiánmíng Sì
   黔明寺
34 Yángmíng Lù Market
   阳明路市场
35 China Post
   & Telecom
   邮电大楼
36 Bakery
   面包房
37 Norway Forest
   萝威森林
38 Jiǎxiù Pavilion
   甲秀楼
39 Cuìwēi Garden;
   Tiandi Culture and
   Arts Company
   翠微园
40 Mao Statue
   人民广场
41 China Southern
   Air Booking Office
   南方航空（集团）
   贵州航空有限公司
42 Wénhuà Lù
   Produce Market
   文化路市场
43 No-Name Coffee Bar
   无名咖啡厅
45 CAAC
   中国民航
46 Guizhōu
   Exhibition Centre
   省展览馆
47 Bank of China
   中国银行
48 Bus Stand (Ānshùn,
   Kǎilǐ & South-East)
   汽车站（至安顺、
   凯里和东南地区）
49 Guizhōu
   Gymnasium
   省休育馆
51 Bus Stand
   汽车站

Zhonglu. This is the place to report thefts or seek travel permits and visa extensions.

Walking Tour

Guìyáng is a pleasant enough place to stroll around and, apart from the markets and shopping districts, there are a few pavilions and temples worth visiting. Try to take the more interesting backstreets – not only will you escape the hair-raising intersections and roundabouts, you'll also avoid the retired old guards who maniacally wave red flags at you every time you attempt to inch off the pavement.

Beginning at **Rénmín Square**, north of the train station, you'll find one of China's largest, glistening-white statues of Mao Zedong, as well as two new Louvre-like glass pyramids. The square itself, extending onto both sides of Zunyi Lu, is a favourite hang-out for Guìyángese to fly kites, practise taichi or visit in the small gazebos.

Just north of here, a wander along **Yangming Lu** takes you through an interesting market of birds, plants, goldfish, antiques and incense. Take a staircase down, closer to the river, to see herbal medicine sellers peddling their wares and prescribing concoctions of snakes and herbs.

Follow a small alley branching left off Yangming Lu to find the Buddhist **Qiánmíng Sì**. Friendly monks and worshippers will welcome you into this peaceful oasis with its eclectic collection of Buddha statues.

Continue up Yangming Lu, cross a large roundabout, and follow a set of stairs down to the riverside. This walkway is filled with older people playing cards and mahjong. At the end, another set of stairs leads you up to the bridge on which rests **Jiǎxiù Pavilion** (Jiǎxiù Lóu).

On the other side of the river is **Cuìwēi Garden**, a collection of several small pavilions set in a charming garden of bonsai trees, Chinese stones and miniature plum blossoms. The garden was originally a Buddhist abbey built during the Ming dynasty (1425–35), however nowadays it's essentially home to a group of shops selling traditional Miáo embroidery; interesting to browse through but extremely pricey. Admission to the garden is Y3.

Backtracking across the bridge and heading north up Wenchang Beilu brings you to the Ming dynasty **Wénchāng Pavilion** (Wénchāng Gé), now a small coin museum.

Parks
Gōngyuán

In the north of the city, **Qiánlíng Park** is worth a visit for its forested walks and for the 17th-century, Qing-dynasty **Hóngfú Sì**, perched near the top of 1300m Qiánlíng Shān. A path winds uphill from inside the entrance gate, or if that seems like hard work, there's a cable car that takes you straight to the top (Y12 one way). The monastery has a vegetarian restaurant in the rear courtyard that's open 11am to around 4pm, making the park a good place for lunch. From the train station area take a No 2 bus. The park is open 8am to 10.30pm and admission is Y2.

Not far from Rénmín Square is **Hébīn Park**, which has benches under shady trees along the river and a Ferris wheel that offers good views of Guìyáng for Y6.

Kebabs & Raisins

On many street corners in Guìyáng, and many other towns in the South-West, you'll see (and smell, long before you see) the occasional hard-nosed entrepreneur grilling delicious mutton kebabs over a crackling rack of coals. On the other side of the street there'll often be another swarthy-looking guy lovingly piling Turpani raisins into a conical mound.

These guys are Uighurs, Turkic-speaking Muslims from Xīnjiāng in Chinese Central Asia, recognisable by their Mediterranean or Middle Eastern appearance, their black or green skullcaps and the knife that hangs perennially by their side.

On Saturday in Guìyáng, keep an eye out for *matang*, a wonderful chewy walnut and fruit nougat loaf that some Uighurs sell near the Penshuichi Fountain. It's a bit pricey at Y15 for 500g, but it's worth its weight in gold.

Most Uighurs know as much Chinese as you do. If you really want to impress, try out the Muslim greeting a *salaam aleikum* (May peace be upon you.) or the Turkic *yakshimisis?*, meaning 'How are you?'. If that doesn't get you cheap kebabs, nothing will.

Bradley Mayhew

Provincial Museum
Shěng Bówùguǎn
In the northern part of town, on Beijing Lu, this museum has good displays on various aspects of the province's minorities. Exhibitions encompass architecture, textiles, silverware, clothing, festivals and marriage customs, local fossil finds and grave finds dating from the ancient Yelang kingdom. Few exhibits were previously labelled in English however, at the time of writing, the museum was closed for renovations so perhaps this will change. It should have reopened by the time you read this.

Festivals
On the eighth day of the fourth lunar month (Siyueba), Miáo from surrounding villages congregate at the Penshuichi Fountain in the centre of town to commemorate Miáo heroes who died in uprisings against the Chinese government. The mythological Miáo hero Yanu is also said to be buried near the fountain. Lusheng playing and singing continues late into the night.

Several festivals are held around Huāxī Park, 17km south of town. There's a Bouyi gathering here on the sixth of the sixth lunar month and on the 15th of the first lunar month (around Feb) there are performances of Bouyi opera at Dazhai, near Huāxī.

There are also minor festivals at Tongmuling, 23km south of Guìyáng, on the ninth of the first lunar month and at Dongfeng, 15km north-east of Guìyáng, on the 15th of the second lunar month. For details on these and other minor festivals in the region visit the CITS office in Guìyáng.

Places to Stay – Budget
There isn't much to choose from when it comes to budget accommodation in Guìyáng. *Míngzhū Fàndiàn* (☎ 579 3389), a couple of minutes' walk east of the train station, is a good choice, especially if you're catching an early-morning train. Beds in three- to five-bed dorms with shared bathroom range from Y35 to Y40. Comfortable doubles with bath start at Y120.

Gōnglù Dàshà (☎ 599 2524, 12 Ruijin Beilu) is an easy walk from the long-distance bus station. The guesthouse is divided into two; reception desks for both are on the ground floor, next to each other. One has beds for Y25 with common bathroom on the 13th floor but you may be directed to the other, on the 5th floor, which has doubles/triples with bath for Y148/165. You might not mind being on the 5th floor after 11pm when the elevator stops running.

Places to Stay – Mid-Range
Across from the train station, *Tōngdá Fàndiàn* (☎ 579 0484, fax 579 0235) has good service and clean, comfortable doubles with heating and new showers from Y148, including breakfast. These rooms are great value when you consider how closely they resemble those in many of Guìyáng's top-end hotels. Room prices rise with each floor, however the rooms stay the same. Try to get a room at the back of the hotel where you can't hear the booming train announcements.

North on Zunyi Lu, *Tǐyù Bīnguǎn* (☎ 579 8777, fax 579 0799) has clean, enormous doubles with bath from Y138. You'll find the hotel in the grounds of the Guìzhōu Gymnasium, next door to the restaurant, on the train station side of the complex.

Jīnqiáo Fàndiàn (☎ 582 9958, fax 581 3867, Ruijin Zhonglu) has OK standards with balconies from Y248. Finally, *Bǎichéng Fàndiàn* (☎ 586 6888, fax 582 4985, 246 Zhonghua Beilu) is a four-star hotel in the centre of town. Although its prices are definitely top-end, at the time of writing it was permanently offering standards marked down from Y480 to Y260.

Places to Stay – Top-End
While there are loads of top-end hotels in Guìyáng, few are worth the splurge. The most tempting is *Trade-Point Hotel* (Bǎidùn Jiǔdiàn; ☎ 582 7888, fax 582 3118, [e] fotph@public.gx.cn) in the centre of town on Ya'an Donglu. Beautiful standards start at Y800, however you may get them for Y428 in the off season.

In the north of town, Guìzhōu *Park Hotel* (Guìzhōu Fàndiàn; ☎ 682 2888, fax

682 4397, **W** *www.gzhotel.com, 66 Beijing Lu)* has plush standards from Y320 to Y680. Ask about the presidential suite for Y4800 – maybe there are special rates for backpackers!

Jìnjiāng Fresh Flower Hotel *(Jǐngjiāng Xiānhuādā Jiǔdiàn;* ☎ *586 7888, fax 587 3010, 1 Zhonghua Nanlu)* is in the heart of the commercial district, above the Parkson Shopping Centre. Singles/doubles are Y198/428, however you're paying more for location than anything else. Enter the hotel off Zhongshan Xilu and take the lift up to the 12th floor reception.

Finally, the ***Crown Plaza Holiday Inn*** *(*☎ *677 1888, fax 677 1688,* **e** *hlgybc @public1.gy.gz.cn, 1 Guikai Lu)* on the corner of Beijing Lu, offers its usual, comfortable rooms from Y750.

Places to Eat

Traditional Restaurants Next door to the Tǐyù Bīnguǎn, on the grounds of the Guìzhōu Gymnasium, is a good restaurant with fairly reasonable prices. There's no English menu, but do try other forms of communication, as this place is a treat. Attentive staff serve the traditional form of Eight Treasures Tea (Bābǎo Chá), by swirling hot water from a long-stemmed copper kettle.

Many Guìyáng restaurants specialise in duck. One that comes highly recommended is ***Guìzhōu Běijīng Kǎoyādiàn*** *(Guìzhōu Beijing Duck Restaurant),* opposite the Tǐyù Bīnguǎn near the train station. The duck here is excellent and, although you'll be looking at around Y60 for a whole duck, it's money well spent.

Across from the Holiday Inn is the ***Miáo Nationality Restaurant*** *(Miáo Miǎ Zhāi)* where you can try authentic Miáo cuisine. Follow the staircase down to a courtyard.

Vegetarians should try ***Júeyuán Cāntīng*** *(Awakening Palace Restaurant, 51 Fushui Beilu)*. This Buddhist restaurant, originally constructed in 1862, forms part of the adjacent temple and promises meals 'free of worldly dust'. All food is strictly vegetarian, though the restaurant specialises in dishes that resemble meat – at least in appearance. Opening hours are 11.30am to 2.30pm and 4.30pm to 7pm.

Street Snacks Guìyáng, like Kūnmíng, is a great city for snack tracking. Just follow Zunyi Lu up to Zhonghua Nanlu and peer into the side alleys for noodle, dumpling and kebab stalls. One alley definitely worth trying is just north-east of the train station. On the first block off Zunyi Lu are lots of fresh noodles and *jiǎozi* (Chinese ravioli). If you take the first left towards Jiefang Lu, you will find stalls with chefs cooking all sorts of veggies, tofu and meat on huge table-top grills. You eat straight off the grill, dipping your food into chilli and barbecue-type sauces. It is extremely tasty, filling and inexpensive.

North of Zhongshan Donglu, along Fushui Beilu, is a bustling street of ***outdoor restaurants*** – lots of hotpot in all its incarnations but plenty of others as well, including grill your own.

There is also a decent, if small, ***night market*** on Ruijin Lu, just north of Hébīn Park. You can select from the local varieties of *shāguō fěn*, a noodle and seafood, meat or vegetable combination put in a casserole pot and fired over a flame of rocket-launch proportion. All of these market stalls offer filling meals for around Y10.

Western Restaurants The ***New Zealand Western Restaurant*** *(Niǔxīlánxī Cāntīng;* ☎ *651 2086),* north on Ruijin Beilu, has salads, soups, burgers and pasta, not to mention Baked Alaska, for reasonable prices. It also serves a few Japanese dishes and has a full bar.

In addition to an amazing number of fried-chicken, fast-food outlets, Guìyáng now boasts a ***Shakey's***, which has deep-pan pizzas from Y26. You'll find it on Zhongshan Xilu, next to the overpass.

For amazing, freshly baked cinnamon buns, head for the ***bakery*** at the bottom of Fushui Lu. The ***cafe*** at the Holiday Inn serves croissants, cheesecake and sells fantastic loaves of banana bread for Y16.

If you're looking for something a little more classy (or filling), try the ***Western***

Buffet on the 2nd floor of the Trade-Point Hotel for Y78.

Entertainment
Bars & Cafes The cosy *No-Name Coffee Bar* (*Wúmíng Kāfēitīng*), across from Hébīn Park on Ruijin Nanlu, has coffee from Y10, a stocked bar and serves small plates of snacks. This is a comfortable place to lounge for a while.

Norway Forest (*Mèngwēisēnglín*) is a cafe/bar near Jiǎxiù Pavilion with a wide range of beer, including Carlsberg, Heineken and Sol, along with Irish coffees and Baileys. You can relax here until 2am.

Along Beijing Lu, between Ruijin Beilu and Zhonghua Beilu, is a plethora of bars and cafes, including *Legends of the Fall Bar* and *The Little Beer House*. Be fore-warned however, most local Guìzhōu beers have a fairly bad reputation among travellers – unless bottled river sludge is your thing.

Shopping
Guìyáng is not a particularly good place to buy handicrafts. What's available is of good quality but it's also expensive. There are several souvenir shops along Beijing Lu that sell wooden dolls, batiks and opera masks. You'll also find shops at Hóngfú Sì and top-end hotels.

For the highest quality Miáo and Dong embroidery (and prices to match), head for the Cuìwēi Garden.

Getting There & Away
Air The CAAC office (☎ 584 4534 to book, ☎ 581 2138 to reconfirm), at 264 Zunyi Lu, is open 8.30am to 9pm. The English-speaking staff are really helpful. China Southern Air has a booking office on the corner of Ruijin Nanlu and Zunyi Lu (☎ 582 8429).

Destinations from Guìyáng's shiny Lóngdòng Airport, 7km east of town, include Chóngqìng (Y420, Wednesday and Saturday), Guìlín (Y500, Tuesday, Thursday and Sunday) and Xī'ān (Y770, Monday, Wednesday and Friday). There are also daily flights to (as well as from) Chéngdū (Y570), Kūnmíng (Y400), Guǎngzhōu (Y790),

Běijīng (Y1530), Shànghǎi (Y1430) and Shēnzhèn (Y860).

Tickets to Hong Kong (Y1850, Tuesday and Friday) and Bangkok (Y1850, Wednesday, Thursday and Sunday) can be arranged through China Southwest Airlines at its booking office on the corner of Beijing Lu and Ruijin Beilu.

Bus There are three major stations for long-distance buses in Guìyáng. The main bus station is quite a long trek from the train station, and if you're looking at getting out of Guìyáng quickly from the train, you're better off using the two stands that operate from just north of the train station.

From the long-distance bus station on Yan'an Xilu, buses travel between Ānshùn and Guìyáng between 8am and 7pm (Y20, two hours). To and from Zūnyì, buses depart every 30 minutes from 7am to 9pm (Y50, 2½ hours). There is also a morning bus to Zhījīn at 8am (six hours), afternoon sleepers to Chìshuǐ at 2pm and 5pm (Y138, 14 hours) and an evening sleeper heads to Xīngyì at 8pm (Y106).

The bus stand just north of the train station is a convenient place to hop on a bus, as they seem to be leaving almost continuously. Tickets can be bought on the bus or from the stand at the western end of the road, nearest the train station. Buses and minibuses head to and from Zūnyì from 7am until as late as midnight. Officially the price is Y49 but shop around, you may be able to find one for around Y30. To Ānshùn, buses leave from 7am until late (Y23) and there is a sleeper at 5pm for Xīngyì (Y105).

The bus stand on Jiefang Lu, serves buses that connect Guìyáng with Ānshùn via the Guihang Expressway every 20 minutes from about 7am to 7.30pm (Y18/Y20 luxury/super-luxury). Frequent buses to (8am to 7pm) and from (6.40am to 6pm) Kǎilǐ also use this stand (Y35 to Y50). Sleeper buses both to and from Róngjiāng leave at 4pm. Departures for Huángpíng are at noon and 5pm.

Tour buses travel to Huángguǒshù Falls and Lónggōng Caves regularly during summer. See the Getting There & Away information in the Huángguǒshù Falls section for details.

Train Guìyáng's glossy, new train station has a modern computerised ticket office, making it one of the more pleasant places in China to buy a train ticket. Keep an eye open in the ticket hall for the extremely helpful retired official 'in charge of social order', who speaks flawless English and has an interesting history.

A direct train, No 2079, departs for Kūnmíng at 6.50pm (Y60/250 hard/soft sleeper, 12½ hours). To Chéngdū, train No K922 leaves at 3.40pm (Y170/250 hard/soft sleeper, 18 hours) and to Chóngqìng train No 5608 leaves at 7.30pm (Y100/150 hard/soft sleeper, 10 hours).

There are also connections to Zūnyì (7.07am and noon) and Liùpánshuǐ (9.20am and 5pm). The 7.40am train to Kǎilǐ originates in Guìyáng and is therefore easiest to get a seat on (Y25). Most of the trains to Ānshùn leave Guìyáng in the late evening, so it's easier to take the bus.

Daytime trains depart for Guìlín at 10am (four hours) and for Guǎngzhōu at 10.50am (Y240, seven hours).

For a longer haul, train No K112 takes three days to reach Shànghǎi, leaving Guìyáng at 8pm (Y360/400 hard/soft sleeper). To Běijīng, catch No T88, departing at 10pm and arriving three days later (Y500/650 hard/soft sleeper).

Getting Around

To/From the Airport Buses to the airport depart from the CAAC office two hours before flight departures and meet incoming flights. Buses cost Y10 and take 20 minutes.

Bus For city-tour loops take bus Nos 1 and 2 from the train station (they also pass close to the long-distance bus station). Bus No 1 travels up Zhonghua Beilu and heads west along Beijing Lu. Buses cost Y1 and recorded announcements boom out stops in Chinese and English.

Taxi There is a flat Y10 fare charge to anywhere in the city.

ĀNSHÙN 安顺
☎ 0853

Having Ānshùn as your base is not the worst of fates. In addition to giving you fairly easy access to Huángguǒshù Falls and Lónggōng Caves, Ānshùn itself is set in a pleasant limestone karst region. Markets abound and are often host to minority entrepreneurs in traditional dress. Many of these markets are held in the town's narrow streets, which are lined with interesting old, wooden buildings. While it may not be Shangri-La, you can easily while away an afternoon.

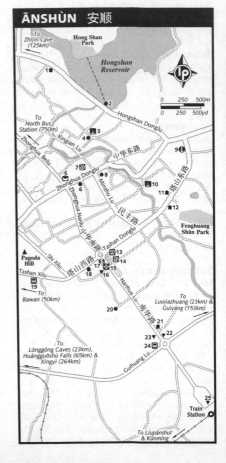

Once an important tea and opium-trading centre, Ānshùn remains the commercial hub of western Guìzhōu. Today it's most famous as a producer of batiks, although the Chinese know the town better for its kitchen knives and the lethal Anjiu brand of alcohol made here. The nearby aviation factory is also well known, and recently diversified production from fighter planes to family hatchbacks.

Orientation

The long-distance bus and train stations are 3km and 4km south of downtown respectively. The main commercial and shopping area is found on Zhonghua Donglu, Minzhu Lu and Zhonghua Nanlu.

Information

Tourist Office Ānshùn lacks a CITS branch, but China Travel Service (CTS; ☎ 322 4379) has an office at the northern end of Tashan Donglu (3rd floor). It organises trips to Huángguǒshù and the surrounding area, and has information on attractions and festivals. Outside the tourist season, the office's opening hours can become somewhat sporadic.

Money You can change money at the Bank of China's main branch, across the street from the China Telecom office.

Post & Communications The main China Post is on the corner of Zhonghua Donglu and Zhonghua Beilu. China Telecom is south of here, at the intersection of Zhonghua Nanlu and Tashan Donglu.

Next door to its main office, China Telecom offers Internet access for Y5 per hour from 8.30am to 10pm. On the corner of Xingian Lu and Zhonghua Donglu, there are three or four Internet cafes on the 2nd floor, offering access for Y3 per hour.

Things to See & Do

The town's main attraction is the **Dōnglín Sì**, a small Buddhist temple dating back to the Ming dynasty (1405) and restored in 1668. A string of vendors sell incense outside to the growing number of local worshippers. Inside, the fragrant sticks are lit before three large, bright gold Buddhas, or *arhats*, which are flanked by equally bright gold Buddhas. Entry is a mere five máo.

North of here, the **Wén Miào** (Confucian Temple) is a more recent concrete temple that is dilapidated and deserted however, the narrow market streets that surround it are worth exploring.

Ānshùn has a huge **Sunday market** where you can buy anything – modern or traditional – from dried beef to human hair (bought by young Miáo women to boost

ĀNSHÙN

PLACES TO STAY
1 Hóngshān Bīnguǎn 虹山宾馆
11 Mínzú Fàndiàn 民族饭店
12 Golden Pheonix Mountain Hotel 凤凰山大酒店
18 Huáyóu Bīnguǎn 华油宾馆
21 Xīxiùshān Bīnguǎn 西秀山宾馆

PLACES TO EAT
16 Food Market 食品市场
22 Restaurants 饭馆
23 Restaurants 饭馆
25 Noodle Stalls

OTHER
2 Dock 码头
3 Wén Miào 文庙
4 Market 市场
5 China Post 邮电局
6 Xinhua Bookstore 新华书店
7 Internet Cafes 网吧
8 Bakery 面包房
9 CTS 中国旅行社
10 Dōnglín Sì 东林寺
13 China Telecom 邮电大楼
14 Internet Cafe 网吧
15 Department Store 百货大楼
17 Bank of China 中国银行
19 Local Bus Station 客车西站
20 Market 市场
24 Long-Distance Bus Station 长途汽车站

their hairdos). The market completely takes over the centre of town, though the most traditional part lies along Shi Xilu. Watch out for an interesting alley of tobacco vendors midway along the western side of the street.

Festivals
A few minor festivals are held in the Ānshùn area, though they're generally not as spectacular as those held around Kǎilǐ. You'd be wise to double-check with local tourism officials before heading off into the wilds to attend any of the following festivities.

Sanyuesan At Pogong (Guanling county), 80km south-west of Ānshùn, and at Huohua (Ziyun county), 100km south of Ānshùn, on the third day of the third lunar month.

Liuyueliu A Bouyi festival at Luohe (Ziyun county), 67km south-east of Ānshùn and Lazhai (near Huangla town), 56km east, on the sixth of the sixth lunar month. Activities include ground opera and singing competitions.

Tiàohuā Flower Dance Festival Held in Miáo villages during the first lunar month. The main location in Ānshùn is Flower Dance Hill, a few kilometres north-west of town from the fourth to the sixth of the first lunar month. Other gatherings are held at Machang and Gaofeng villages (Pingba county), halfway between Ānshùn and Guìyáng, and in Qingzhen town.

Siyueba 'Ox King' Festival Held at Jiuzhou and Shuangbao villages, both about 25km east of Ānshùn on the eighth day of the fourth lunar month.

Eating New Rice Festival Held at Huolong and Dagouchang villages, 55km east of Ānshùn, south of main highway, sometime during the seventh or eighth lunar months.

Guìzhōu Batik Festival A state-sponsored festival set up to display (and flog) batik to the tourists. Ānshùn, 28–29 September.

Places to Stay
The nicest and cheapest rooms in town can be found at *Golden Phoenix Mountain Hotel* (Fēnghuǎngshā Dā Jiǔdiān; ☎ 322 5663, Tashan Donglu), where clean, wooden, next-to-new twin rooms without bath are only Y80. Rooms with bath are a bit steeper at Y180. Bus No 1 will take you there from the long-distance bus or train station.

If you're looking for something closer to the long-distance bus station, try *Xīxiùshān*

Bīnguǎn (☎ 322 3900). Clean standard rooms with bath start at Y98, suites are Y138. You may be able to cut a deal in the off season. Staff are friendly and rooms at the back give a view over a small garden and karst hills beyond.

Huáyóu Bīnguǎn (☎ 322 6020, 15 Tashan Xilu), near the local bus station, is now open to foreigners. However you won't be let near the cheap rooms. Instead you'll be shown to the somewhat overpriced doubles for Y120 to Y260.

Ānshùn's two old stand-bys, to which you may be directed, have both seen better days and cater mainly to tour groups. *Mínzú Fàndiàn* (☎ 322 2500, 67 Tashan Donglu) has clean, nondescript standards with bath for Y180 but appears deserted. In the far north of town, *Hóngshān Bīnguǎn* (☎ 322 3101, 43 Hongshan Donglu) has been given a new paint job on the outside, but inside it's damp, less than clean and overpriced with standards from Y200 to Y500. At least you get a view of the dried-up reservoir across the street.

Places to Eat
Food-wise, there's little to recommend in Ānshùn. If you're hunting down cheap eats, outside the train station are a row of forgetable *noodle stalls* and around the long-distance bus station are some friendly *point-and-choose* places, a few of which do hotpot as well. Along many of Ānshùn's streets, vendors sell fried potatoes with onion and chilli, fried bread or meaty barbecues. There is also a popular *bakery* on the corner of Minzhu Lu and Zhonghu Donglu.

Be forewarned: Dog is eaten in these parts – lots of dog. You'll see the skinned animals propped up outside restaurants as an enticement to come in for lunch. If you haven't got a taste for canine meat or a desire to try it, check the Food Vocabulary in the Language chapter for how to say 'I don't eat dog' and practise it well.

Getting There & Away
Bus The trip to Guìyáng takes about two hours along the Guihuang Expressway, Guìzhōu's premier highway. It was built

Green fields in Jǐnghóng thanks to the rapid flow of the neighbouring Mekong River

Monks wearing colourful dress in the grounds of a Sìchuān monastery

Tending the fields of sleepy Dàměnglóng in Xīshuāngbǎnnà

BRADLEY MAYHEW

A breathtaking view of Déqīn's Miacamu from a stupa

BRADLEY MAYHEW

A traditional teahouse in Yùxī

KRAIG LIEB

Smile! You're in Měnghǎi

KRAIG LIEB

Bai women in Yúnnán

RICH PROHASKA

Loading a horse on Da Xue Shān in Sìchuān

specifically to whisk tourists straight up to Huángguǒshù Falls.

Luxury buses (Y18) and super-luxury Daewoo coaches (Y20) whip between Ānshùn's long distance bus station and the bus station on Guìyáng's Jifang Lu (near the train station). Private operators around Ānshùn's long distance bus station also run this route until late into the night. Local buses take a lot longer and stop everywhere en route.

There is a 1pm direct sleeper bus to Kūnmíng (Y126, 19 hours) via Panxian. You can also reach Kūnmíng via Xīngyì in Guìzhōu's south-west, from where you can catch a direct bus or train. Buses leave Ānshùn for Xīngyì (via Xīngrén) between 8.30am and 11am (Y46). From Xīngrén, minibuses depart for Ānshùn in the morning.

To Huángguǒshù Falls there is a slow 10am bus (Y6) or you can take a Xīngyì-bound bus that will let you off on the highway, about a 15-minute walk down to Huángguǒshù village.

If you're heading to Zhījīn Cave, buses depart from Ānshùn's north bus station between 8am and 6pm, more or less hourly (Y20, three hours).

The local bus station on Tanxhan Xilu has buses between Ānshùn and Lónggōng (Y5 to Y8) running hourly between 8am and 5pm. There are also services to and from Langdai and Bawan.

Train It is virtually impossible to get sleeper reservations to Kūnmíng in Ānshùn. If that's what you're after, you may have to backtrack to Guìyáng and make one there. If you are willing to brave a hard seat for the 11-hour journey, the train pulls out of Ānshùn at 8.20pm (Y68).

Trains for Guìyáng (Y15, two hours) leave at 10.50am and 7.20pm, however most people hop on a bus. Coming from Guìyáng, most trains depart for Ānshùn in the late evening; you're better off on the bus.

A train for Lìupánshuǐ departs daily at 11.20am (Y16). Another leaves at 6.29pm, arriving around 9pm. From Lìupánshuǐ, the 8am and 4.40pm trains for Guìyáng pass through Ānshùn.

Getting Around

The No 1 minibus is the most useful – it zips around town from the train station, up Tashan Donglu and on past the Hóngshān Bīnguǎn. Bus No 2 travels between the train station and the north bus station. A seat on a bus costs Y1.

AROUND ĀNSHÙN
Lónggōng Caves 龙宫洞
Lónggōng Dòng

About 23km south of Ānshùn is a series of underground caverns called Lónggōng, or Dragon Palace, which forms a huge network through 20 hills. At present, only 1km of the cave system is open to tourists. While it's dolled up like many Chinese tourist sites with recorded music and coloured spotlights, on a quiet day a glide through here in a hand-paddled boat can be an impressive and peaceful experience.

The caverns lie around the Bouyi settlement of Lóngtǎn Zhài. From the bus drop-off point at the car park, follow the road down to the right and cross the bridge to the ticket office. From there, the trail follows the river, across another bridge and on to **Dragon's Gate Waterfall**. To the right is a staircase marked 'No 1', which climbs through a number of tunnels.

From the pagoda at the top of this staircase, bear right down the hill for a more direct route to **Paradise Pool** or follow the sign-posted trails over the hills to **Lalong Ground** and on to Paradise Pool from there.

Once at Paradise Pool, you will be given a guided boat tour through the 840m Dragon Palace Caves. During the dry season you will return by boat, however, when the water level is higher, your boat will continue out the other end of the cavern where you can disembark and climb to the small **Tiger's Lair Cave**. There is also a number of short trails from there that can keep you busy for the better part of a day. Eventually, you can return to Paradise Pool by foot.

An exit/entrance gate at Paradise Pool leads you back down to the car park. If you're really short of time, or only want to see the Dragon Palace Caves, you can head directly up to this gate from the bus stop.

GUIZHOU

Follow the stairs up from a side road to the right, just before the car park.

A second site, 4km before Lónggōng, is **Guānyīn Cave**. Here you can see a whirlpool pond, take a boat trip through some whimsical karst scenery and visit a couple of shallow caves with statues of Buddha and the goddess Guānyīn. It's pleasant but not really worth the admission fee. If you do decide to stop here and have bought a joint admission ticket for here and Lónggōng, show your ticket to the site workers on the 2nd floor of the gate you reach *after* the boat ride (not the original ticket gate). They'll whisk you over to Lónggōng in a van free of charge and save you the 4km or 5km hike.

Admission is Y35 to Lónggōng Caves and Y25 to Guānyīn. Both include boat rides. Joint admission to both sites is Y50. There are a couple of very pricey hotels at Lónggōng entrance, primarily for tour groups.

There are other attractions worth seeing en route to Lónggōng Caves, if you have time to make a day of it. Halfway between Ānshùn and Lónggōng lies the village of **Caiguan**, famous for its traditional local opera (see the boxed text 'Ground Opera'). There's a small **Ground Opera Museum** (Dìxì Bówùguǎn) here, which displays many wooden masks used during performances. A farther 6km brings you to **Shítou Zhài**, or Stone Stockade village, 17km from Ānshùn and 6km before Lónggōng. This pretty Bouyi village, crafted entirely from stone, is worth exploring, along with the surrounding countryside. See the boxed text 'The Bouyi' later in this chapter.

Getting There & Away Local buses to Lónggōng (via Shítou Zhài and Caiguan) depart hourly from Ānshùn's local bus station on Tashan Xilu, between 8am and 5pm. The trip takes just under an hour and costs Y5. Buses return hourly until 5pm.

Buses from Ānshùn will more than likely drop you at Guānyīn Caves even if you've asked for Lónggōng. If you aren't planning to visit Guānyīn, be sure you've been taken all the way to Lónggōng (the final stop) or you'll have a 4km hike ahead of you.

Many of the tours from Guìyáng or Ānshùn to Huángguǒshù also stop in Lónggōng for an hour or so. (See the Huángguǒshù Falls section for details.) Unfortunately, there is no public transport between Lónggōng and Huángguǒshù other than via Ānshùn. Private microvans will take you – bargaining begins at Y50.

Zhījīn Cave 织金仙洞
Dǎjī Dòng
At around 10km long and up to 150m high, Zhījīn Cave ranks as the largest in China

---

Ground Opera

In addition to the cultural arts of Běijīng Opera and Sìchuān Opera, Ānshùn has its own version of opera, which dates from the Ming dynasty. It's called *dìxì* – ground or open-air opera.

As part of the performance, actors wrap black see-through cloth over their foreheads and don traditional masks made from bamboo shoots. Up to 50 masks may be used in one opera. The colours of the masks are very symbolic: black denotes righteousness, red symbolises loyalty and bravery, while white indicates evil. Blue and green masks are reserved for monsters or particularly nasty bandits. Banners are also worn on the actors' backs to denote rank, as in the Běijīng Opera.

The operas originally served to drive out evil spirits but have merged with local religious dramas and Han classics such as the *Romance of Three Kingdoms* and *History of the Sui and Tang Dynasties*. The plots are livened up by gongs, drums, stilts, flags and displays of martial arts to keep the audience's mind from wandering during the slow bits.

The best time to catch ground opera is during festivals, especially the Spring Festival in January or February. It's also worth inquiring at Ānshùn CTS or at Caiguan Village, which also has a dìxì museum.

Another form of local opera, *nuo*, is practised by the Tujia people of north-eastern Guìzhōu. There's a Nuó Opera Museum in Tóngrén.

and one of the biggest in the world. At the edge of a small village some 15km outside of Zhījīn, this place is impressive even if you're not a cave fanatic. Small passageways open up into giant room after room where calcium deposits have created a moonscape with spectacular shapes and spirals, often reaching from floor to ceiling. Not surprisingly, coloured lights have found their way into this tourist site, but it's still worth a visit.

Tickets to the site are steep – Y60. This includes a compulsory tour and if you're not travelling with a posse, this can mean a bit of a wait as tours depart with a minimum of 10 people. While the tour itself is in Chinese only, you'll likely be glad to have someone around who knows the way back out of the maze of trails. The tour lasts for around three hours – possibly more.

Places to Stay If you're planning to overnight here, it would be a good idea to check with CTS in Ānshùn about accommodation – basically, whether or not there is any.

There is a tourist hotel on the right as you enter the village however it was closed when we last visited. There are a couple of guesthouses in Zhījīn but the only one open during the low season will not accept foreigners. Your options are likely to be better in the summer months.

Getting There & Away A visit to the cave can be made as a day trip from Ānshùn – just. Buses depart from Ānshùn for Zhījīn between 8am and 6pm (Y20) and take 2½ to 3½ hours, depending on whether you're on a bus that can reach speeds of over 50km per hour. Once in Zhījīn, another bus takes you to the cave from the local bus station, however it's unreliable and slow. Shared taxis can do the trip in 20 minutes and cost around Y5 per person or you can take a taxi for Y20. The last bus leaves Zhījīn for Ānshùn at 6pm from a small lot, 10 minutes' walk north of the main long-distance bus station.

The scenery between Ānshùn and Zhījīn is very picturesque and the bus passes through a number of small villages. Keep a look out for other huge caves en route.

The Bouyi

The Bouyi (Bouyei), the 'aborigines' of Guìzhōu, are of Thai origin and closely related to the Zhuang of Guǎngxī. Most travellers will come upon them in the Huángguǒshù and Ānshùn areas.

The Bouyi are generally very poor, in sharp contrast with the postcard minority image of starched and ironed costumes or the ring-of-confidence sparkling teeth. Bouyi dress is dark and sombre, with colourful trimmings. Both men and women wear white or blue checked head scarves.

Batik cloth dyeing is one of the many skills of the Bouyi. Batik is made by drawing designs with molten beeswax on a strip of cloth. A variety of instruments are used to produce different shapes with the wax. The fabric is dyed, normally in indigo, and then boiled to remove the beeswax. After it has been rinsed, the pattern of the beeswax remains as the original colour of the fabric. The beeswax is collected and re-used.

The Bouyi are also fine stonemasons. The masonry at Huángguǒshù is intriguing – houses are composed of stone blocks but no plaster is used, and roofs are finished in slate. Bouyi villages often have arched stone bridges and elaborate house entrances. One good place to see stonework is Shítou Zhài (Stone Stockade village) on the road to the Lónggōng Caves, near Ānshùn.

Bouyi festivals are held on the Double Third (third day of the third lunar month) and Double Sixth. The Siyueba or Ox King Festival is held on the eighth day of the fourth month, when glutinous rice cakes are offered to ancestors and cattle. The Big Year Festival is held from the third to the fifth of the 12th month. Festivities include lion and dragon dances on top of seven upturned tables, plus courtship games and singing of love songs. Bouyi open-air opera is especially popular during the Big Year and Spring festivals.

Tōngdá Fàndia also in Guìyáng offers a daily tour to Zhījīn Cave for Y98 per person.

Traditional Villages

If you're interested in visiting more traditional villages and have plenty of time to endure local transport, you can head out to **Loujiazhuang**, a Miáo village 23km northeast of Ānshùn, **Langdai**, 45km west of Huángguǒshù, or **Bawan**, about 50km west of Ānshùn (just south of the Ānshùn-Liuzhi road). Both Langdai and Bawan are Bouyi villages.

HUÁNGGUǑSHÙ FALLS 黄果树瀑布
Huángguǒshù Dàpùbù

Reaching a width of 81m and plunging 74m down into Rhinoceros Pool, it is not surprising that this huge cascade of water is Guìzhōu's number-one tourist attraction. The Chinese explored this area in the 1980s, as a preliminary to harnessing the region's hydroelectric potential. They discovered about 18 falls, four subterranean rivers and 100 caves, many of which are now being gradually opened to visitors. The massive waterfall, cave and karst complex covers some 450 sq km, however the area near Huángguǒshù village, home to the massive Huángguǒshù (Yellow Fruit Tree) Falls, is closer to 6km in length and easily explored in an afternoon.

The thunder of the falls can be heard for some distance and, during the rainy season (May to October), the mist from the falls carries up to Huángguǒshù Village. The cascade is most spectacular about four days after heavy rains. The dry season lasts from November to April and during March and April the flow of water can become a less impressive trickle.

There are three entrances to the main falls: at the top of the presently closed cable car, next to Huángguǒshù Bīnguǎn and just before Huángguǒshù village. Admission is Y30. Once inside, you can get up close to the falls, both by trapezing across a stone path over **Rhinoceros Pool** and by visiting **Water Curtain Cave** where, for an extra Y10, you can walk through a tunnel behind the falls and view them streaming past.

During the rainy season, both of these explorations can turn into wades and prove treacherous. Good footwear and waterproofs are necessary at any time of year.

There's a number of other waterfalls in the area that you can visit. One kilometre above the main falls and a couple of kilometres' walk north of town, is **Steep Slope Falls** (Dǒupō Pùbù), which are 105m wide and 23m high and get their name from the crisscross patterning of sloping waters. One kilometre downstream of the main falls is the **Luósītàn Falls** (Luósītàn Pùbù), which can be reached on foot from the car park by following the main road south. The pretty **Dishuitan Falls**, actually a cluster of smaller cascades, are on the road to Langdai.

While most things are within walking or hiking range, if you wish to go farther, motor rickshaws roam the main roads of Huángguǒshù village looking for passengers.

Eight kilometres below Huángguǒshù Falls is the **Star Bridge Scenic Area** (Tiānxīng Qiáo Jǐngqū), which includes 'potted landscape', a cave and **Silver Chain Falls** (Yínliàn Zhuìtān Pùbù), all set in a pretty karst landscape of pools and banyan trees. Entrance to this area is an additional Y30.

HUÁNGGUǑSHÙ FALLS

1 Pharmacy 药房	7 Restaurants 饭馆	12 Footbridge 人行桥
2 Catholic Church 天主教堂	8 Huángguǒshù Gōngshāng Zhāodàisuǒ 黄果树工商招待所	13 Cable Car 缆车
3 Pùbù Bīnguǎn 瀑布宾馆		14 Ticket Office 售票处
4 Restaurants 饭馆	9 New Huángguǒshù Bīnguǎn 新黄果树宾馆	15 Snack Bars 小吃店
5 Huángguǒshù Waterfall; Water Curtain Cave 黄果树瀑布、水帘洞	10 Ticket Office 售票处	16 Information Centre 问讯处
	11 Huángguǒshù Bīnguǎn 黄果树宾馆	17 Bus Stand 汽车站
6 Ticket Office 售票处		18 Snack Bar 小吃店

The occasional minibus and motor rickshaw run to here from the bus stand. You can haggle the price down to around Y10.

In addition to its impressive falls, the area around Huángguǒshù also provides an excellent chance to ramble through nearby rural minority areas on foot.

Places to Stay & Eat
While choices of hotels open to foreigners in Huángguǒshù village have recently risen, so have the prices. Accommodation is fairly grim and very overpriced.

Halfway between the bus stand and Huángguǒshù village is *Huángguǒshù Bīnguǎn*, located in two separate buildings. The newer part (☎ 0853-359 2110) is on the left of the main road and has pricey standards from Y380. The older section (☎ 0853-359 2226), off to the right of the main road (look for the parking sign), has slightly cheaper standards for Y280, which are somewhat musty but have peaceful surroundings and tip-toe views of the falls.

A little farther up the road is the police-run *Huángguǒshù Gōngshāng Zhāodàisuó* (☎ 0853-359 2583), where reasonable standards/triples are available from Y160/220. You may be able to cut a deal.

In town, *Pùbù Bīnguǎn* (☎ 0853-359 2520) is also overpriced. Basic, clean triples without bath are Y120 and bare standards with TV and bath are Y200.

Along the main road in town are several *restaurants* with verandas at the back where you can eat, sip a cold beer and enjoy a great view of the falls. There are also *snack bars* and souvenir stalls scattered along the path from the bus station to the falls viewing area.

Getting There & Away
Unless you're on a tour, Huángguǒshù is easiest to reach from Ānshùn, from where a bus departs daily at 10am (Y6). During the summer months, additional buses as well as tour buses run from the long-distance station and some of Ānshùn's major hotels.

Buses from Ānshùn to Zhenfeng and Xīngyì also pass by Huángguǒshù, leaving you about a 15-minute walk from the highway down to the village. If you're coming from Xīngyì, morning buses to Guìyáng will also drop you at this point. Be sure to let the driver know that you want off at the falls.

Coming from Guìyáng, the only direct transport to Huángguǒshù is by tour bus. Tours to here and the Lónggōng Caves leave from the train station, the long-distance bus station or many of the hotels in Guìyáng. They generally only run in summer, depart in the early morning and cost Y55 to Y68, depending on the type of bus. This does not include admission. These buses will get you to Huángguǒshù in around three hours, as opposed to the five hours required if you take public transport. If you don't want to stay overnight at Ānshùn or the falls, this is definitely the most hassle-free way of getting out there.

GUÌZHŌU

Heading out of Huángguǒshù, minibuses and buses for Ānshùn, and occasionally for Guìyáng, depart between 7am and 7pm. Buses for Xīngyì leave in the morning. Buses leave as soon as they are full and often drive around town looking for prospective passengers. Local buses often take the old road to Ānshùn that stretches out the journey to 1½ hours, passing through small villages. If you're heading directly to Ānshùn or Guìyáng, you may want to find a bus taking the expressway.

You can look for tour buses en route to Lónggōng Caves at the bus stand, however there is no public transport from here to Lónggōng other than via Ānshùn. Private microvans and even rickshaws will offer to take you. Bargaining begins at Y50.

Western Guìzhōu

West of Ānshùn there aren't many 'sights'. The main attraction is the nature reserve at Cǎohǎi Hú, famous among bird-watchers as the wintering site for the black-necked crane. If you're heading overland to Kūnmíng, this route also passes through fascinating minority regions. Many sub-branches of the Miáo (Hmong) live here, including the Long-Horned Miáo around Liuzhi, named after their enormous protruding hairstyles; the Flowery Miáo in the north-west around Wēiníng; and the Black Miáo in the south-west around Xīngrén and Xīngyì. See the boxed text 'The Miáo' in the Around Kǎilǐ section later in this chapter.

LIÙPÁNSHUǏ 六盘水

The large, ugly industrial town of Liùpánshuǐ (also known as Shuicheng) isn't high on anyone's list of places to visit but it's the gateway to Wēiníng and Cǎohǎi Hú. It's hard to get there without spending one night in Liùpánshuǐ.

The Liùpánshuǐ region is named after its three main towns – Liuzhi, Panxian and Shuicheng – but is also the name used to refer to Shuicheng town. The main industries in the region are coal mining and steel production. Add some interesting karst formations, plenty of pollution and freezing fog during winter, and that's pretty much it.

Orientation

The train station is a couple of kilometres north-east of the town centre. China Post and the post office are halfway between the train station and centre. The main Liùpánshuǐ bus station is 1km east of the post office.

Festivals

The village of Nankai, 37km north-east of Liùpánshuǐ, has a large Tiàohuā or **Flower Dance Festival** in the middle of the second lunar month. The local Miáo dress mainly in red and white, while the lusheng players wear special embroidered capes and feathered caps.

Places to Stay

The cheapest beds can be found at *Yíng Bīnguǎn* (☎ 822 2333), where a bed in a double/triple costs Y30/20. Rooms are OK but fairly smoky. The hotel also has standards with bath from Y98. To find the hotel from the train station, head right (west) at the crossroads after China Post and continue for a couple of kilometres.

A better option is *Xīnlǒng Dàjiǔdiàn* (☎ 822 3378, ext 8888), conveniently across from the train station. Beds in clean, spacious doubles/triples go for Y45/35. Singles with bath aren't as good a deal at Y118 and doubles start at Y138.

Yi'ngshānhóng Bīnguǎn (☎ 868 2109), a few doors west of the main bus station, has clean, comfortable doubles/triples without bath for Y90/60 and standards with bath from Y80.

Getting There & Away

Bus The most comfortable bus to Wēiníng is the postal bus, which departs from outside China Post daily at 8am (Y17, three hours). Try to buy your ticket early as there is a limited number of seats. Buses to Wēiníng from the main bus station are crowded and decrepit and cost a whooping Y40. Buses run every couple of hours between 8am and 4pm. This route crosses some frozen territory; if you're not on the postal bus, dress warmly.

Buses to Nankai depart from China Post at 8am. There is also a sleeper from the main bus station that leaves each night at 9.40pm for Guìyáng.

Train The easiest way to or from Lìùpánshuǐ is by train. The most comfortable option to Guìyáng is the No 620 that leaves at 8am, which originates in Lìùpánshuǐ and therefore has the most empty seats (hard/soft seats Y25/42, four hours). In the afternoon, the 4.40pm train to Guìyáng is the next least crowded. You aren't likely to get a seat on the 7pm train heading to Chóngqìng or the 8.50pm train to Shànghǎi. All trains to Guìyáng stop at Ānshùn.

Trains to Kūnmíng (eight hours) depart at 8.47am, 12.17pm and 11.20pm. It's difficult to secure a seat or bunk so try to book before you head off to Wēiníng.

To reach Lìùpánshuǐ from Guìyáng, a train departs at 9.20am, stopping at Ānshùn at 11.20am. A faster train leaves Guìyáng at 5pm, reaching Ānshùn at 6.29pm and arriving in Lìùpánshuǐ around 8.30pm.

Getting Around
Buses shuttle between the train station and the town centre. Taxis charge a flat rate of Y5 during the day, double at night.

WĒINÍNG 威宁
☎ 0857
The area around Wēiníng is Guìzhōu's wild west. It's a harsh, rugged and sometimes sullen plateau of Hàn, Miáo, Huí and Yi minorities. It's also one of the most conservative and underdeveloped districts in Guìzhōu, and one of the last places in the province to be opened to foreign tourists.

The town of Wēiníng is caked with mud and not likely to be the most beautiful place you will visit, however it has an interesting mix of minority peoples. A large market is held here every three or four days and is attended by the Flowery Miáo. At other times there is a quieter market street in the old eastern part of town. Evidence of the Huí includes a modern mosque in the north of town and several Muslim restaurants nearby.

Apart from exploring some of the South-West's most remote villages, the main reason to visit the plateau is to go to Cǎohǎi Hú, one of China's premier bird-watching sites.

Cǎohǎi Hú 草海湖
About a 15-minute walk from downtown Wēiníng is Cǎohǎi Hú, a 20 sq km freshwater wetland, which became a national nature reserve in 1992. The lake is an important wintering site for many migratory birds, the most famous of which is the black-necked crane. The lake is considered a wetland because its average depth is only 2m. Grasses cover 60% of the lake, giving rise to the name Cǎohǎi or Grass Sea.

The lake has a fragile history. It once drained into the Yangzi River (Cháng Jiāng) and has even disappeared several times in the last 3000 years. The lake was drained during the Great Leap Forward and then again during the Cultural Revolution in order to provide farmland (which turned out to be unusable). Dry for a decade, action was taken to refill the lake in 1980. In 1992, Chinese Premier Li Peng donated a painting of Cǎohǎi Hú to the United Nations Conference on Environment and Development at Rio de Janeiro, to commemorate the lake's return from an environmental grave.

The government has poured Y4 million into lake conservation, but some pressing problems remain. Almost a third of Wēiníng's sewage runs into the lake and more than 20,000 people live in the reserve. One result is that many birds remain relatively unconcerned by humans. To encourage local interest in park conservation, some villagers have been hired as park workers, a conservation education program has been set up and grants have been made available to farmers who wish to set up alternative businesses. One plan for sustainable development involves ecotourism or, more to the point, you.

The park management office (☎ 622 2524), behind the Cǎohǎi Bīnguǎn, provides information on the lake and, during the summer months, can put on slide shows.

The best way to see the lake – and the birds – is by punt. Boatmen (punters?) will more than likely find you. They'll start bargaining at Y30 per person for an hour. To find the boat launch, go west past the Cǎohǎi Bīnguǎn until the road becomes a dirt track. Follow the trail left, down to the water.

For a peaceful walk, wander the paths along the northern shore of the lake to the villages of Huolongshan, Dengjia and Miaojia. Take the dirt track past the path to the boat launch, making your way south, down towards the lake. Farmers' fields border the lake so you can't get right up close, however you're likely to spot a number of birds in these fields. The cacophony of their many calls is fantastic.

If you are feeling fit, you can walk to the far-western corner of the lake, where a bridge crosses a side creek, then turn north to meet the main road and hitch a ride back to town. It's possible to walk to the lakeshore but you'll soon end up in muddy swampland.

The best time to visit the lake is December to March, when the birds are wintering. During this time the north-west enjoys much better weather than the rest of Guìzhōu and there are often clear blue skies in Wēiníng when visibility in nearby Liùpánshuǐ is down to 200m. The lake is particularly beautiful at dusk when the jagged Wumeng Shān Range frames the silvery sunset. The elevation here is higher though, so bring warm clothes for the cold nights.

Places to Stay

Cǎohǎi Bīnguǎn (☎ 622 1511) has beds in basic four-bed dorms without bath for Y38. Doubles/triples with bath and electric blankets are Y58. Although the place is convenient to the lake, it's fairly musty and cold. Your chance of getting a view is minimal.

Better accommodation is available in town. Friendly *Hóngyàn Bīnguǎn* (☎ 622 4755), next to China Post, has dorm beds in clean triples for Y20. Bright, comfortable standards with bath (but no heat) are Y80.

Jiàngōng Bīnguǎn (☎ 622 4438) is where you'll most probably be directed. Doubles/triples without bath are Y50/60 and singles/doubles with bath are Y90/120. The hotel's biggest seller is its central heating, which kicks in each night at 8pm.

The only other place in town that will take you is *Zhēngfù Zhāodàisuǒ,* which is poorly maintained and not very clean. Dorms with bath are Y15/20 and singles/doubles with bath are Y70/80. Don't be fooled by the heaters – they don't work.

Places to Eat

There are a number of restaurants around the Cǎohǎi Bīnguǎn including the *Cǎohǎi Cāntīng,* 200m east of the hotel, which is cheap and friendly.

Near the mosque are a number of *Muslim restaurants* that serve good beef noodles. *Sīxiāngjiǔjiā,* situated next to the Jiàngōng Bīnguǎn, serves great stir-fried dishes (try the smoked tofu) and also has hotpot.

There are several point-and-choose restaurants south of the Xīnhuá Bookstore and lots of people selling roasted potatoes along the streets.

Getting There & Away

Wēiníng appears to have buses departing from all over town. The daily postal bus (Y17, three hours) to Liùpánshuǐ departs daily around 1pm. Tickets are sold from outside China Post from about 11am, after

WĒINÍNG

1 Mosque
清真寺

2 Muslim Restaurants
回族饭店

3 Minibuses to Zhāotōng
到昭通的中巴

4 Sīxiāngjiǔjiā
思乡酒家

5 Jiàngōng Bīnguǎn
建工宾馆

6 Long-Distance
Bus Station
长途汽车站

7 Market
市场

8 Zhèngfǔ
Zhāodàisuǒ
政府招待所

9 Minorities'
Department Store
民族百货商店

10 Xinhua Bookstore
新华书店

11 Minibuses to
Jīnzhōng
到金钟的中巴

12 Hóngyàn
Bīnguǎn
鸿雁宾馆

13 China Post
邮电局

14 Postal Bus
to Liùpánshuǐ
到六盘水的邮车

15 Produce
Market
市场

16 Restaurants
饭馆

GUÌZHŌU

Birding on the Grass Sea

Cǎohǎi Hú is one of the best places to bird-watch in China; in fact, the World Wide Fund for Nature (WWF) has listed it as one of the top 10 bird-watching destinations in the world.

Up to 100,000 birds winter at the lake between December and March, with 179 different species having been recorded. These include a number of protected species, such as the black-necked and hooded cranes, black and white storks, golden and imperial eagles, white-tailed sea eagle, Eurasian crane and white spoonbill. More common birds easily spotted at the lake include the bar-headed goose, Eurasian widgeon, common pochard, Eurasian coot and black-headed gull.

Black-necked cranes are without doubt the lake's most celebrated visitor. The least known of the 15 types of crane, they are listed by the IUCN (World Conservation Union) as vulnerable, with a global population of around 6000. The birds breed at high altitudes in Tibet, Qīnghǎi and western Sichuān, and then spend the winter basking in the relative warmth of southern Tibet and the Yúnnán-Guìzhōu plateau. It is thought one important local migration route takes birds from Cǎohǎi to Zöigê in northern Sichuān. Four hundred black-necked cranes currently winter at the lake – the highest ever recorded and a great improvement on the mid-1970s, when numbers plummeted to only 35.

The cranes have little fear of people and you can often approach to within 10m without disturbing them. Perhaps part of the reason for this is that cranes have long enjoyed an exalted place in Chinese culture as a symbol of happiness and good fortune. You may see statues of cranes in many of China's imperial palaces, such as the Forbidden City in Běijīng.

South-West China has several other important crane wintering sites at Dashanbao, Bitahai, Napahai and Huize in neighbouring Yúnnán, but Cǎohǎi remains by far the easiest and best place to spot them.

The Tuoda Forest, 60km north-west of Cǎohǎi, has been set aside as a nature reserve for the protection of the endangered **Reeves' pheasant**. This bird is unique to China, but owing to widespread deforestation its numbers have declined in recent years and its total population is probably no more than 5000. The male has striking plumage in autumnal golds and browns boldly crisscrossed with black and white; its tail can be up to three times its body length.

Tuoda is a plantation of deciduous and evergreen trees that provides safe feeding and nesting for the pheasants. However, despite its protected status, Tuoda continues to suffer from illegal clearing; recent visitors reported only saplings of oak and pine where once a mature forest supported a good diversity of birds. Reeves' pheasant appears to hang on in Tuoda, but parts of the forest are being converted to agriculture, which almost certainly means local extinctions of the bird.

the bus pulls into town. Buy yours as soon as possible as there are limited seats.

Your other option for getting back to Liùpánshuǐ are crowded public buses from the main bus station that depart irregularly from about 8am until 4pm and cost Y40.

From the main bus station, a 9am bus heads to Xianwei (Y30) in Yúnnán for connections to Kūnmíng. A sleeper departs from here at 8.30pm for the long trip back to Guìyáng (Y100).

Minibuses to Jīnzhōng leave from near the post office whenever full between 8am and 4.30pm (Y4).

Minibuses leave from the north of town to Zhàotōng in Yúnnán (Y30, five hours) between 8am and 4pm. From Zhàotōng you can head onto Xīchāng in southern Sìchuān and connect with the train to Lèshān, Éméi Shān and Chéngdū, or Kūnmíng in Yúnnán.

Wēiníng is most easily accessible via Liùpánshuǐ. See the Getting There & Away section of Liùpánshuǐ for details.

AROUND WĒINÍNG

Wēiníng is useful as a base to visit remote Yi and Miáo villages in the region, though you'll really have to rough it as facilities are very limited in this area.

If you want to do some exploring, locals recommend **Longjie**, 60km north-west of Wēiníng. The town of **Jīnzhōng**, 16km east on the road to Shuicheng, has a great market every three or four days.

On the fifth of the fifth lunar month there is **horse racing** in several Yi villages around Wēiníng and a **Flower Dance Festival** at Mata, featuring crossbow shooting and antiphonal singing. Mata is 80km north-west of Wēiníng and buses to Yungui and Longjie pass nearby.

Also nearby is the ruined mission at **Shi-men** (Stone Gate), which the Methodist missionary Samuel Pollard set up in the 1890s in his attempt to convert the Flowery Miáo and rescue them from opium addiction and slavery at the hands of the Yi. During his 25 years in the South-West, he also devised the first written system for the Miáo language (primarily so he could translate the Bible into Miáo). You will find little of

the mission remaining, due to the ravages of the Cultural Revolution.

XĪNGYÌ 兴义
☎ 0859
Mainly a stopover for those travelling between Guìyáng and Kūnmíng by bus, Xīngyì has some interesting side streets and worthwhile attractions nearby. It also has some of the finest weather in Guìzhōu. Xīngyì is mainly populated by Han Chinese and Huí Muslims, though the surrounding villages are largely made up of Black Miáo and Bouyi.

Xīngyì is one of the most pleasant cities in Guìzhōu, although the region is developing quickly with new railway connections, cheap electricity from the nearby Tianshengqiao hydroelectric plant and a new industrial zone centred at nearby Dingxiao.

Information
Tourist Offices Xīngyì Travel Service is inconveniently located in the east of town. The staff here, however, are friendly and helpful and will dole out information on nearby sights, villages and train schedules. They also offers rafting tours of Mǎlíng Gorge for Y98 per person (2½ hours) and tours of nearby minority villages.

Money Bring your yuán with you as there is no place to exchange or access money here.

Post & Communications You can post your letters from the main China Post office, a five-minute walk north-west of the Pánjiāng Bīnguǎn. Internet access is available from any one of the six Internet cafes along the upper floor of the ring of buildings surrounding the town's central plaza.

Things to See & Do
The most interesting area of town lies in the pedestrian alleys and side streets, north-east of Chuanyundong Park and leading to the central plaza. Here you'll find markets and small shops where you'll see women making chopsticks from freshly cut bamboo. The central plaza and the small riverside square across from the park are popular meeting places for locals, especially in the evenings.

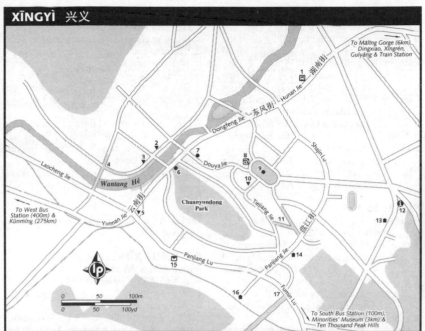

XĪNGYÌ 兴义

XĪNGYÌ

1 East Bus
   Station
   汽车东站
2 Huí Muslim
   Restaurants
   回族饭馆
3 Noodle &
   Jiǎozi
   Restaurants
   面条水饺店
4 Market
   市场
5 Snack Stalls
   小吃摊

6 Entrance to
   Chuanyundong Park
   公园入口
7 Xinhua Bookstore
   新华书店
8 Internet Cafés
   网吧
9 Central Plaza
   噴泉广场
10 The Shu's
   Gàngzi Noodles
   舒记杠子面
11 Market
   市场

12 Xīngyì Travel
   Service
   兴义旅行社
13 Yínhé Jiǔdiàn
   银河酒店
14 Jīnsuì Bīnguǎn
   金穗宾馆
15 China Post
   & Telecom
   邮电局
16 Pánjiāng Bīnguǎn
   盘江宾馆
17 Market
   市场

Chuanyundong Park itself isn't really worth your time – especially when the attendants insist that the price is Y5 despite signs at the entrance stating Y2.

The most worthwhile sights in this area are outside of Xīngyì city (see the Around Xīngyì section).

Places to Stay

Pánjiāng Bīnguǎn (☎ 322 3456) is the official tourist hotel. While it has cheap twins/triples without bath for Y38/48 and standards/triples with bath for Y88/98, these are often full. They're also rather dingy if you're paying the higher price and you might want to consider splurging on comfortable standards for Y138. The staff is friendly and the hotel is well located; the only real downside is the surround-sound karaoke that pelts out until 11pm.

There are two other hotels in Xīngyí that might accept you. Just down the road from Pánjiāng Bīnguǎn, the *Jīnsuì Bīnguǎn* has clean, basic standards with/without bath for Y60/30. No hot water to speak of, however.

South of town, *Yínhé Jiǔdiàn (☎ 323 2001)* has standards with bath for Y90 although the price seems a little steep for what's on offer. There are cheaper rooms but you're unlikely to get near them.

Places to Eat
Across the river from Chuanyundong Park are a number of good restaurants. To the west of the footbridge are a couple of *noodle* and *jiǎozi restaurants* and east you'll find a string of *Huí Muslim restaurants* that specialise in beef dishes.

For excellent noodles for as little as Y2 a bowl, try *The Shu's Gāngzhī Noodles,* just off the central plaza.

On Panjiang Lu, just south of Yunnan Jie, a number of *stalls* open at night, serving noodles and barbecue. You'll also find numerous stands throughout town selling cakes and steamed breads.

Getting There & Around
Bus Sleeper buses leave for Guìyáng from the east bus station at 3pm and 6pm (Y84, eight hours). If you don't want to arrive in the middle of the night, consider taking one of the morning minibuses that depart at 6am, 8am and 9am (Y78). These buses also stop at Xīngrén, Huángguǒshù Falls and Ānshùn. Outside the east bus station are minibuses for Zhenfeng and Ānlóng.

From Guìyáng, there is a sleeper for Xīngyí at 5pm, departing from the bus stand just north of the train station. From Ānshùn there are buses for Xīngyí at 8.30am and 11am.

Heading west, buses to Kūnmíng (Y91, 10 hours) leave from the west bus station every half-hour between 6am and 8am. There is also a sleeper bus that departs at

8pm; the bus arrives before dawn but most passengers sleep on the bus until daylight.

If you're going to the Stone Forest at Shílín in Yúnnán, you can get off the bus a couple of hours before Kūnmíng and save yourself doubling back (plus Y10 on the bus fare).

Buses south to Bajie leave from the south bus station frequently throughout the day.

Train Xīngyí's nearest train station is 10km north-east of town at Dingxiao. Buses will take you there for Y10 from outside Xīngyí's east bus station.

Trains to Kūnmíng depart at 9.07am and 1.32pm. A train also stops here en route to Nánníng at 1.52pm.

Taxi At Y5 a ride to anywhere in town, taxis are good value.

AROUND XĪNGYÍ 兴义四周
Minorities Museum
民族婚俗博物馆 Mínzú Hūnsú Bówùguǎn
This museum is formally devoted to the wedding customs of Guìzhōu's minorities but the displays also encompass costume, festivals and social structure. The wonderful complex housing the museum was once

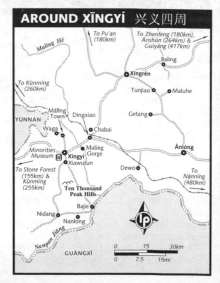

the home of the local Qing official and is worth a visit.

The exhibits are interesting and self-explanatory, which is just as well because the labels in English are a trifle obscure. We dare you to make sense of 'Beautiful parcels and exquisite embroidered handkerchiefs with pleasantly surprising put up and invisible magpie bridge' or the equally intriguing 'Girls control their pleasure sowing seeds of love on the village road'.

To get to the museum, walk or catch a taxi (Y15) past the south bus station along the road to Xiawutun and Bajie. After about 1km, branch right and continue for another kilometre to a small village.

The museum is open 8.30am to 11am and 2.30pm to 5.30pm Monday to Friday and 8.30am to 11.30am Saturday. Entry is Y8.

Ten Thousand Peak Hills 万峰陵
Wànfēnglíng

South of Xīngyì is a beautiful landscape of karst hills that could have been transplanted directly from Guìlín. (For more about karst formations see the Geology section of the Facts about South-West China chapter.) You can make a pleasant half-day trip here or combine it with a trip to the museum for a full day.

Getting yourself among the hills is no easy feat and, while you might find a taxi to take you on a minitour for Y50, the nearer you get to the peaks, the less you see anyway. You're better off admiring them from the nearby villages, 5km to 10km from Xīngyì, where you can find some great walks.

To reach this area from the museum, head back to the main road and turn south towards the village of Xiawutun. During the walk you'll pass a small **outdoor noodle factory** where you can watch the entire noodle-making process; from boiling and squeezing, to separating and hanging the final strands.

From Xiawutun continue south along the main road to Bajie by foot or passenger tractor. Just flag one down, get off where the scenery looks good, and go for a wander.

There's another similar set of peaks 45km south-east of Xīngyì.

Mǎlíng Gorge
Mǎlínghé Xiágǔ

As the major scenic attraction in the area, the 15km Mǎlíng Gorge is being groomed for an onslaught of tourists but, as yet, it remains peaceful and well worth a visit. With stunning scenery, many travellers find it more interesting than Huángguǒshù Falls and you can spend the better part of a day following the winding path into the lush gorge, across bridges and up to and behind high, cascading waterfalls.

From the ticket gate, follow the newly laid stone trail down into the gorge. At the fork, take a right and continue to the southern bridge, crossing to the eastern side of the gorge. At the next break in the trail, you can follow the more direct lower path to the northern bridge or stay on the top path, which takes you up and up, through a number of tunnels and directly under a couple of smaller waterfalls, eventually descending to the bridge.

On the other side of the northern bridge, the trail leading north (right), will take you farther along the gorge a kilometre or so. The trail then splits in three with the left-hand path taking you up to the top of the hill, the right-hand path down to a platform on the river, and the middle, somewhat hidden, trail leads 500m beyond the gorge. Backtracking to the bridge and heading south will take you up behind the largest waterfall and then return you to the entrance.

With the copious amounts of water and mist in the gorge, the trail can become extremely slippery and treacherous, especially during the rainy season. Sturdy shoes and waterproofs are essential. You may also want to bring a torch for the tunnels.

You can raft on the river at several points but don't expect white-water rapids, this is a slow descent. Xīngyì Travel Service arranges 2½-hour trips for Y98 per person.

Getting There & Away To reach Mǎlíng Gorge from Xīngyì, you can attempt to catch a Xīngrén- or Dingxiao-bound bus however, at the time of writing, these buses were being diverted away from the gorge due to construction on the bridge over

Mǎlǐng Gorge. If this is still the case, taxis will take you the 6km for Y15.

Returning to Xīngyì from the gorge can be tricky. Once the bridge reopens, you should be able to flag down a bus. Otherwise, you can take a pleasant stroll through the countryside to the edge of the first village. Here an unnumbered Xīngyì public bus makes its final stop before heading back into town (Y1).

Minority Villages & Festivals
民族村和民族节日

The region around Xīngyì has a couple of interesting festivals and is great to explore.

Chabai Singing Festival takes place on the 21st of the sixth lunar month in a village a few kilometres north of Dingxiao, just off the main road to Xīngrén. The thwarted ardour of the lovers, Cha and Bai, is marked by an antiphonal singing contest and an improvised love song competition.

Maoshanshu Festival is commemorated on the third day of the third month in the village of Dewo with a large gathering of musicians, dancing and courting ceremonies.

The region around Xīngyì is remote and traditional. There are a number of nearby Bouyi villages you can explore such as **Waga**, 7km from Mǎlǐng town, or **Nanlong**, in the south near Bajie. There are also many remote Black Miáo and Yi villages scattered between Xīngyì and Pu'an.

XĪNGRÉN & AROUND

The modern town of Xīngrén is a good base for exploring the surrounding country and Black Miáo, Bouyi and Yi villages. The village of **Baling**, 21km east of Xīngrén on the road to Ānshùn, has a particularly interesting market every six days, frequented mainly by Black Miáo and Bouyi people.

Other villages south-east of town with weekly markets include Tunjiao (18km towards Ānlóng, every Saturday), Maluhe (22km towards Ānlóng then 6km east of the main road, with a market every Wednesday) and Getang (41km towards Ānlóng, then 9km west of the main road, every six days). You might also head out to the town of **Zhenfeng**, 65km east of Xīngrén.

Trekking out to these villages by bus, tractor and foot can be arduous and, while the villages are humming with life on market day, you run the risk of finding them virtually deserted most other days.

From Xīngrén, there are buses to Baling and Zhenfeng. To reach the other villages, take any Ānlóng-bound bus, get off at the relevant junction and hitch.

Places to Stay & Eat

There are two main places to stay in Xīngrén: the army-run **Jūnxìng Zhāodàisuǒ**, five-minutes' walk north and then west of the bus station; and **Xiānewi Zhāodàisuǒ**, five minutes south-west of the station. While rooms at the latter are grimmer, they're also cheaper.

The recommended **Sanjin Restaurant**, opposite the Xiānewi Zhāodàisuǒ serves cheap, tasty food.

Getting There & Away

All buses between Xīngyì, Ānshùn and Guìyáng stop in Xīngrén, so finding transport is rarely a problem (though finding a seat might be). Minibuses from Xīngrén run regularly to Xīngyì, Baling, Zhenfeng and Ānlóng and are generally the fastest mode of transport.

Eastern Guìzhōu

The rich minority areas of south-eastern Guìzhōu, technically the Qiandongnan Miáo and Dong Autonomous Prefecture, are surprisingly unexplored by Western travellers. The forested hillsides and river valleys hide a rich mesh of Dong, Shui, Miáo and Gejia villages, many of which hold epic weekly markets and annual festivals and retain a unique way of life relatively untouched by China's modernising mania.

If you're interested in catching a glimpse of the ethnic diversity that rural China has to offer and don't mind roughing it a bit, this can be one of the most rewarding places to visit in the South-West. Little (if any) English is spoken, there are few concessions to Western tastes and you're not likely to bump into many other travellers, but if

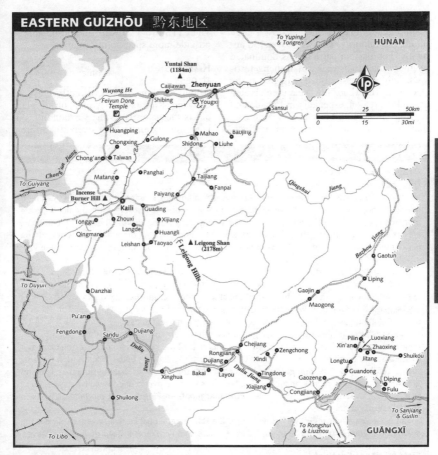

EASTERN GUÌZHŌU 黔东地区

that's your kind of thing, then get the map out and catch a local bus.

Transport in this region is slow but relatively plentiful. Most towns and villages have at least one basic guesthouse, often attached or next to the bus station. If you wander around looking lost, someone will either put you on the next bus or take you to the local hotel. There are no places to change money in Kǎilǐ's outlying areas, so bring plenty of Rénmínbì with you.

If your time is limited, then there are many interesting villages that can be reached as a day trip from Kǎilǐ. If you have

more time, it's possible to explore a number of Miáo villages in a loop north-east of Kǎilǐ, limiting the amount of backtracking you'll have to do. A journey south-east into Dong territory can also take you in a loop from Róngjiāng, eventually bringing you back to Kǎilǐ or across the border into Guǎngxī province. Chóng'ān, Zhènyuǎn, Xījiāng and Zhàoxìng are all villages and towns that are definitely worth a visit and it's worthwhile planning your trip around at least one of the local festivals. In the summer, you might also visit Fánjìng Shān Nature Reserve, near Guìzhōu's eastern border.

Festivals

Kǎilǐ and surrounding villages host a large number of minority festivals – over 130 annually. February in particular is dominated by more than two weeks of lusheng festivals, held successively in villages in the Zhoī area. The Miáo New Year is celebrated around the region, especially in Lángdé and Xījiāng, in the 10th lunar month. Approximate Western dates for the main festivals are given at the beginning of this chapter. The CITS office in Kǎilǐ should be able to provide more specific information.

KǍILǏ 凯里
☎ 0855

About 195km almost directly east of Guìyáng, Kǎilǐ is a fairly uninspiring place but is the gateway to the surrounding villages throughout which over 80 different

---

Festivals

Dragon Boat Festival
Lóngchuán Jié

Up to 40,000 people from the surrounding area attend Shídòng's Dragon Boat Festival, making it one of the biggest in the region. Preparations start days before the festival – food and rice wine are prepared and villagers rush around, trying to finish any outstanding chores. The 20m dragon boats are taken out from their specially constructed shelters and a willow dragon's head is added and decked with horns and red pendants. You can see these dragon boat shelters any time of the year in villages around Shídòng.

On the date of the festival a team of 40 rowers directed by the drumming of the Gutou, a respected community elder in charge of organising the festival, pushes the dragon boat out onto the river. As the rowers head downstream they call at all of the riverside villages to pick up presents of ducks, geese and even pigs, while fending off copious toasts of rice wine. Villagers toast the benevolent dragon and ask for happiness and good fortune for the year ahead.

The festival commemorates the slaying of a bloodthirsty dragon by a local fisherman, in retaliation for the dragon's fatal attack on his son. It is said that all the villagers from the region came out to celebrate the death of the dragon and to take a share of the dragon's body. Villagers from Pingzhai village got the head, Tanglong got the body, Laotun got the tail, while Shídòng turned up late and got stuck with the heart, liver and lungs. The festival is still held over four consecutive days in these four villages, starting on the 24th of the fifth lunar month in Pingzhai and reaching a climax in Shídòng on the 27th.

This Miáo Dragon Boat Festival has no links to the Han Dragon Boat Festival, which celebrates the death of the Chinese poet Qu Yuan, on a different date, and with races instead of visits to relatives.

Sisters' Meal Festival
Zīmèifàn Jié

In a culture devoid of nightclubs and singles bars, Sisters' Meal is a rare opportunity for Miáo men and women to meet, flirt and find a partner. On the eve of the festival, groups of girls get together to dye packets of glutinous rice with berry juice. After putting on their best embroidery and silver jewellery, the girls and boys sing love songs to each other and gradually pair off.

Men who want to know whether they are barking up the right tree unwrap the packet of rice they have been given to see what has been placed inside. A pair of red chopsticks brings good news and marriage is definitely on the cards. Leaves and pine needles are also a positive sign, though the man needs to come up with a few gifts of silks, satins and threads to cement the alliance. A clove of garlic or a chilli pepper is the Miáo cold shoulder and is a polite signal to pursue true love elsewhere.

The following morning, successful pairings are celebrated with much beating of drums and playing of the lusheng, as well as bullfights and horse races.

minority groups are scattered. Coming from Guìyáng the place may seem like a shambolic backwater. Coming from the surrounding minority areas it seems a decadent metropolis.

Information

Tourist Office The Kǎilǐ CITS office (☎/fax 822 2506) is in the Yìngpánpō Mínzú Bīnguǎn complex. Helpful English-speaking staff can fill you in on minority destinations and festivals as well as possible boat trips on the Wǔyáng Hé.

Also inside the hotel complex is Nation Culture Ecology Travel which, unfortunately, was closed at the time of research but might be worth a look.

Money The main branch of the Bank of China on Beijing Donglu changes travellers cheques and money without any fuss. The branch on Zhoashan Nanlu now houses the train ticket office but continues to have an ATM outside that accepts Mastercard.

Post & Communications You can post mail, send faxes and make international phone calls until around 7pm from China Post, diagonally opposite the Lántiān Jiǔdiàn. China Telecom has an office upstairs.

There are Internet cafes around town where you can surf for Y2 to Y3 per hour.

Things to See & Do

Kǎilǐ itself has a few attractions. There's a pagoda in **Dàgé Park**, which is not surprising as the park's name means 'big pagoda park'. The other main park is the **Jīnquánhú Park**, at the very southern end of town, where there's a Dong minority drum tower, built in 1985.

Also in the south is the moderately interesting **Minorities Museum** (Zhōu Mínzú Bówùguǎn), with displays on local handicrafts, costume and festivals. The museum is theoretically open 9am to 4pm daily, but it all really depends on whether anyone turns up to unlock the doors. Entrance to the museum is off Ningbo Lu, at the end of Zhaoshan Nanlu. Don't be deterred by what appears to be a furniture shop on the 1st

floor. Continue upstairs another flight to purchase your Y10 ticket.

Kǎilǐ also has a good **Sunday market** that swamps the streets with traders from nearby minority villages. Even on other days the market in the west of town is worth a visit.

Organised Tours

CITS can arrange tours of the villages around Kǎilǐ, although they are on the pricey side, with a day tour without transport costing Y200 per person. Two- or three-day tours north through Miáo areas or south to the Dong region cost Y100 per person per day for the guide, Y2.5 per kilometre for transport, plus meals and accommodation for you, the guide and the driver.

Places to Stay

Shíyóu Zhāodàisuǒ (☎ 823 4331, Jianpan Donglu) currently has the cheapest beds in town for Y12 in a five-person dorm. Triples/doubles with bath, electric blankets and TVs are Y69/68. Rooms are big and clean but freezing cold in winter.

Near the museum, *Jīnxīn Bīnguǎn* (☎ 825 1910) has basic, clean rooms in a building out back for Y40 per bed. Doubles with heat and bath are a pricey Y180.

Lántiān Jiǔdiàn (☎ 823 4699), in the heart of town, has a great location and 24-hour hot water, however you may have a struggle to get a bed in its three- to four-bed dorms for Y30 to Y35. Instead you'll be offered the heated doubles for Y168 with an extremely clean bath and a nice view. The hotel's entrance is down the side of the building off Beijing Xilu.

Zhènhuá Zhāodàisuǒ (☎ 823 4600), in the east of town, has nice refurbished doubles for Y60 per person, including a heater, hot water and a shower. This is a better deal than *Yìngpánpō Mínzú Bīnguǎn* (☎ 823 4600), which has doubles at the same price but is somewhat more run down.

Finally, *Kǎilǐ Bīnguǎn* (☎ 827 5000), near the Minorities Museum, is a two-star hotel working hard to gain its next star. Rooms are clean and comfortable but somewhat overpriced at Y218/228 for a double/triple.

GUÌZHŌU

Places to Eat

While not boasting a great number of notable restaurants, Kǎilǐ has some fantastic *snack stalls* lining its streets. Savoury crepes, potato patties, barbecues, tofu grills, noodles, hotpot, *shuijiao* (a form of steamed jiǎozi), and wonton soup overflow for extremely reasonable prices. Check out Beijing Donglu, east of the China Post or the northern end of Zhaoshan Beilu, especially its night market.

Lǎodìfang Jiǔjiā (Yingpang Donglu), between the Yìngpànpō Mínzú Bīnguǎn and the Shíyóu Zhāodàisuó, has OK food for around Y12 a dish and is worth a try if you can get the staff to unplug the karaoke.

There are a number of *noodle shops* around Kǎilǐ. Try the one near the museum or on Beijing Donglu or east of the bank for fresh rice noodles.

Bakeries are plentiful throughout town. The one on Beijing Donglu, behind a staircase and across from the bank, sells instant hot drinks and cakes in a heated cafe.

A backpacker-friendly cafe has opened in Kǎilǐ on Wenhua Nanlu. *Lǐxiǎng Miànshí Diàn* has an English menu (with pictures!) and serves Chinese dishes along with some creative takes on Western dishes, including a pizza that'll stick to your ribs for Y2.20.

Shopping

Two shops inside the Yìngpànpō Mínzú Bīnguǎn complex, and a number along Zhoufu Lu, sell embroideries, bags, batik and the like. You may even have the seamstresses themselves invite you into their homes to see their work. Much of it is very good quality, however you can get the same things cheaper in the surrounding villages such as Táijiāng and Shídòng.

Entertainment

Night-time is pretty quiet in Kǎilǐ, however, if you're looking for a local beer or a Carlsberg or Heineken, go over to the *Jane Story Bar (Jīndē Gùshì Jiǔbā)* off Zhaoshan Lu.

Getting There & Away

Bus Frequent buses run between Kǎilǐ's long-distance bus station and Guìyáng's Zunyo Lu bus stand from 6.40am until 6pm (Y35 to Y50, three hours). There are also lots of minibuses and vans leaving for Guìyáng in the mornings from the local bus station in the west of town.

A bus for Chóng'ān (then Huángpíng, Shībǐng and Zhènyuǎn) departs from the long-distance bus station at 6.50am, however more frequent buses also leave for here from the local bus station between 6.50am and 5pm.

Buses run between the long-distance bus station and Léishān (Y9.50, 1½ hours) more or less hourly from 7am to 6pm, with a cou-

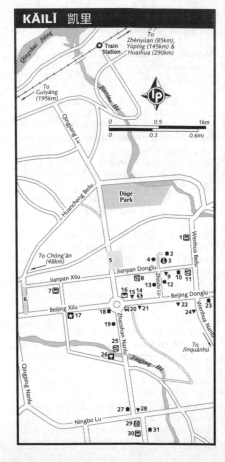

ple of them continuing on to Xījiāng. Sleepers leave for Cóngjiāng and Lìpíng at 7pm (Y71). There may also be a couple of morning buses along this route, however the schedule is 'flexible'. A number of buses leave for Róngjiāng (Y29) from 7.40am until early afternoon. Hourly buses also leave for Táijiāng (Y12) from 7am, with a couple of morning buses continuing on to Shīdòng.

The Wànbó local bus station in the south of town, near the museum, has frequent services to Dānzhài (Y30) via Zhoī and Qīngmàn between 8am and 3pm or 4pm.

Train Kǎilǐ's train station is a couple of kilometres north of town, however you can buy hard-seat tickets from an office on Zhaoshan Nanlu that is effectively disguised as the Bank of China.

The first of five trains to Guìyáng (Y25) departs from Kǎilǐ at 8am. The afternoon trains are faster (four hours), with the final one leaving at 6.30pm. From Guìyáng, the 7.40am train to Kǎilǐ is the easiest to get seats on. A train to the north-east to Yùpíng departs at 10.40am (Y27, three hours). This is also the train you need to board for Zhènyuǎn (Y14).

For longer distances it's worth stopping in Guìyáng to secure a reservation. Trains to Kūnmíng and Chóngqìng pass through Kǎilǐ at 5.30pm and 5.08pm respectively. You can't get a sleeper reservation in Kǎilǐ so you'll have to pray for intervention from a higher power (the conductor guard). The same advice is valid for eastbound services to Běijīng and Shànghǎi.

Getting Around
Buses in Kǎilǐ cost five máo and almost all of those departing from the train station follow the same route up Qingjiang Lu, past the long-distance bus station, along Bejing Donglu and down Zhaoshan Nanlu to the museum.

GUÌZHŌU

KǍILǏ

PLACES TO STAY
2 Yíngpánpō Mínzú Bīnguǎn
   营盘坡民族宾馆
10 Shíyóu Zhāodàisuǒ
   石油招待所
18 Lántiān Jiǔdiàn
   蓝天酒店
23 Zhènhuá Zhāodàisuǒ
   振华招待所
27 Jīnxīn Bīnguǎn
   金鑫宾馆
31 Kǎilǐ Bīnguǎn
   凯里宾馆

PLACES TO EAT
9 Lǎodìfang Jiǔjiā
   老地方酒家
15 Snack Stalls
   小吃摊
21 Bakery
22 Noodle Bar
   面条店

24 Lǐxiǎng Miànshí Diàn
   理想面食店
28 Noodle Bar
   面条店

OTHER
1 Long-Distance Bus Station
   长途汽车站
3 CITS
   中国国际旅行社
4 Minorities Souvenir Shop
   民族纪念品商店
5 Night Market
   夜市
6 Market
   市场
7 Local Bus Station
   汽车站
8 Internet Café
   网吧
11 Internet Café
   网吧
12 Minorities Souvenir Shop
   民族纪念品商店

13 Minorities Souvenir Shop
   民族纪念品商店
14 Bank of China
   中国银行
16 China Post
   邮电局
17 PSB
   公安局
19 Train Ticket Office
   火车售票处
20 Buses to Guading & Train Station
   到火车站的中巴
25 Internet Café
   网吧
26 Jane Story Bar
   金的故事酒吧
29 Minorities Museum
   贵州民族博物馆
30 Wànbó Local Bus Station
   万博汽车站

The Miáo

The Miáo, or Hmong as they prefer to be called, are thought to have migrated 2000 years ago from an area north of the Yellow River. During the course of their migrations the Miáo diversified into subgroups, known as Black, Red, White, Blue, Long-Horned and Flowery Miáo, after their style of dress. This is, however, largely a Han classification and few Miáo use these names among themselves. Many Miáo continued their migration beyond China, into Laos, Thailand and Vietnam where they are known as the Hmong (or Mong).

The Miáo have a reputation as independent-minded and rebellious highlanders. Many Miáo joined the armed uprising against the Qing government, from 1840 to 1870, which became known as the Miáo Rebellion. Numerous Lao Hmong worked covertly for the US Government during the American (Vietnam) War and settled in the USA after the fall of Saigon.

A significant number of Miáo were converted to Christianity by 19th-century missionaries, who created the first Miáo script. Most Miáo remain animist, however with strong elements of ancestor worship. Miáo creation stories tell of an ancient flood and also of a mythical bird that hatched the first humans. Tradition also states that the sky is propped up by 12 silver pillars. Miáo oral history is full of warrior heroes, many of whom died in uprisings against the Chinese.

Miáo women are famous for their embroidery and silver jewellery, with each subgroup employing unique styles. Black Miáo, for example, wear 10m-long black turbans, black and purple clothes, and silver 'sideburns', while the Flowery Miáo dress predominantly in red, white and yellow. All wear long skirts pleated like an accordion. These skirts, up to 6m long, are starched with rice water and then folded, rolled and stored in a bamboo tube to set the desired number of pleats.

At festival time, Miáo women wear stunning silver jewellery, often piling on five or six neck rings, as well as chains, coins, chest locks and multiple headdresses. Girls wear huge horned, silver headdresses and silver crowns resplendent with delicate silver birds, flowers and coins. Silver was originally obtained from melting coins, though the Miáo later received an annual silver stipend from the government. Today most of the silver is alloy and, outside festival time, wooden combs and plastic flowers and hairpins are worn as a substitute.

Long hair is particularly sought after, and old or fake hair is sometimes woven into a large headdress. You can even see Miáo women buying and selling big bunches of hair in some traditional markets.

AROUND KǍILǏ

There are dozens of Miáo villages within an hour's bus ride of Kǎilǐ that can be visited as day trips. The main attraction is the chance to wander around the countryside, explore traditional wooden villages and see the colourful Miáo. Few villages have any 'sights' as such, and can appear almost deserted outside of festival time.

Lángdé, on the road south to Léishān, is a lovely wooden village with traditional bridges and water wheels. It's the darling of the few tour groups that make it here. From the main turn-off, Lángdé is a several-kilometre walk or hitch west. The village has a basic hotel.

Zhōi, on the road south-west to Dānzhài and Duyun, is another picturesque wooden

village that has a large lusheng festival in the first lunar month. Nearby **Qīngmàn** shares the festival and provides many musicians for the gathering. In fact, the entire region is a riot of smaller lusheng festivals throughout the first lunar month (usually February), which shifts every couple of days between the surrounding villages of Shiqing, Dazhong, Xinguang, Sanjiang and Yatang.

The village of **Tónggǔ**, 30km west of Kǎilǐ on the road to Majiang, specialises in a form of colourful painting, partly an extension of traditional embroidery designs.

North of Kǎilǐ, the road to Chóng'ān passes the turn-off to **Mátáng**, a quiet Gejia minority village. The village is about 6km north of the main Kǎilǐ-Huángpíng road. To get there, hitch or take a Yudong, Longchang or Wanshui-bound bus from the road junction at Huzhuang or from Kǎilǐ. The road climbs over a pass, descends and then bears to the left. Get off here and walk east for 10 minutes.

Nearby is **Incense Burner Hill** (Xiānglú Shān), which hosts a Hill Climbing Festival on the 19th of the sixth lunar month. People flock here to commemorate those who used the hill as a base for the mid-19th-century Miáo Rebellion. The one-time temples on the hill have either fallen into disrepair or were razed during the Cultural Revolution.

LÉISHĀN 雷山
☎ 0855

This village on the road south to Róngjiāng is a good base from which to visit Xījiāng (see the following entry) or Taóyaòcun, 8km from Léishān on the road to Xījiāng. Nearby Leigong Shān (2178m) also offers some interesting hiking, however getting there could be a problem. Ask at the CITS office at Kǎilǐ.

Places to Stay & Eat

Next door to the bus parking lot, *Yóuyú Bīnguǎn* (☎ *333 1436*) has standards with bath for Y60. If you're on your own you should be able to get these for Y30. Despite heaters, the rooms are cold.

Fēitiān Dàjiǔdiàn (☎ *333 2568*) has doubles with/without bath for Y44/30 per person. Business is evidently pretty slow as the owners couldn't find the keys to show us a room. If the pictures are anything to go by, however, it's worth checking out. To find the hotel, turn right out of the bus station parking lot and take the first left. The hotel is on your left.

If you carry on up the road and turn right, you'll be confronted by the huge, peach *Léishān Bīnguǎn* (☎ *333 2338*). Nice new rooms with bath go for Y40 a bed. Excellent value for your yuán.

There isn't much to recommend for food in Léishān. On the main road through town are a couple of small restaurants with noodles, hotpot or dog brewing up.

Getting There & Away

Léishān doesn't have a bus station as such but rather a large bus parking lot. The women selling fruit along the road in front seem to have schedules down pat and are the ones to ask for information.

Buses to Kǎilǐ (Y9.50, 1½ hours) depart from 7am to 6pm. Minibuses run between Léishān and Xījiāng every hour or two with the last returning to Léishān at 4pm. You can also pick up southbound buses from Kǎilǐ to Róngjiāng and beyond.

XĪJIĀNG
☎ 0855

Hidden in the folds of the Leigong hills, Xījiāng is thought to be the largest Miáo village. It's a superbly picturesque place, set in a natural basin and bordered by paddy fields drenched in green, with wooden houses rising up the hillside.

The town is the site of a major Miáo **New Year Festival** at the end of the 10th lunar month, when there are lusheng competitions, dances, bullfights and feasting. Local Miáo wear their best silver-horned headdresses. The festival is held over five days, with most activities taking place on the basketball court in the centre of the village.

The village itself is the attraction here and there are also plenty of pleasant walks around the hillsides.

Places to Stay & Eat

If you continue through the village, about 200m from the bus drop-off, on the left is *Yóudiàn Zhāodàisuǒ* (☎ *334 8206*). Beds in clean, basic rooms without bath are Y15.

Zhēngfù Zhāodàisuǒ (☎ *334 8121*) is possibly a second option. It also has cheap beds in basic rooms, however it was closed at the time of writing. The hotel is on the right, about 150m from the bus drop-off. Look for a sign saying 'Otel Yinp Onpl'. Head past the first building; the guesthouse is behind it.

There are a couple of small *restaurants* near the bus drop-off.

Getting There & Away

There are one or two direct buses every day between Kǎilǐ and Xījiāng (Y20, four hours) but it's generally easier to take a minibus to Léishān (Y8, two hours), which runs every hour or two until 4pm, and change there. You could visit Xījiāng as a day trip from Kǎilǐ if you left *really* early, but it's far better to spend at least one night here.

TÁIJIĀNG 台江
☎ 0855

The built-up town of Táijiāng is worth a visit for its large **market**, held every five days. The Kǎilǐ CITS office staff might be able to tell you exactly when the market will be held. The market takes over the main street, but also spills into the interesting backstreets.

Táijiāng is a centre for Miáo handicrafts and many Miáo women will offer to show you their work at their workshop or house. You can also visit the **Wénchāng Gōng**, a small temple in the east of town dating from 1892 that now houses a small **Embroidery Museum**. On display are traditional clothing, hats and shoes, all hand-stitched with intricate, beautiful patterns and pictures. On the road from Kǎilǐ, turn right at the bus station and head into the centre of town, bearing right at the T-junction. Continue on for a couple of hundred metres to find the museum on your right. Admission is Y5.

You can also use Táijiāng as a base to visit the nearby villages of Fǎnpái or Shīdòng (see the following entries). Finally, Táijiāng hosts an interesting lantern festival halfway through the first lunar month.

Places to Stay & Eat
Táijiāng is best visited as a day trip from Kǎilǐ. If you do decide to spend the night, *Gōng'an Zhāodàisuǒ* (☎ 532 2229) has beds in clean, basic triples for Y12. From the bus station, head into the town centre and turn left at the T-junction. Take the first right and the hotel is on the corner of the second block, on the right.

If you continue up the hill another 50m, you'll find *Jiehong Zhāodàisuǒ* on the left. The hotel may be closed during winter. When it is open for business, beds in cement, bare rooms go for Y20 a piece. Enter the building around the back, which doesn't appear quite as derelict as the front.

Nonji Zhaodàisuǒ, across from the bus station on the road to Kǎilǐ, is reported as having clean rooms at reasonable prices, however it was closed at the time of writing.

There are a few hotpot and noodle places along the main street and at the central T-junction. A few restaurants specialise in a kind of communal stir-fry that's worth trying if there's more than one of you.

Getting There & Away
The main bus station is in the south-west of town, from where buses run to and from Kǎilǐ every hour or so from 7am until 6pm (Y10, 1½ hours).

To reach Shīdòng, head up to the main T-junction and bear left. Minibuses run this route from 7am until 2pm or 3pm (Y8, two hours), every other hour. There are also tractor-truck type vehicles that run the same route for the same price. This isn't the safest mode of transport though – doors have been known to fly open and breakdowns aren't uncommon.

If you're heading to Fǎnpái, you'll find transport along the right-hand branch of Táijiāng's T-junction.

FǍNPÁI 反排
This traditional Miáo village, hidden high in the hills around Táijiāng, is often shrouded in a fog that makes it seem even more isolated from the rest of the region. The village consists of several hundred **traditional wooden dwellings**, which cloak the steep valley like green moss. In spring, villagers are busy tending the surrounding terraced fields. In the winter chill the kids head off to school carrying mini-braziers full of glowing coals.

The town is noted for its wooden drum dances and has a **festival** on the second day of the second lunar month.

Explore the village and hike in the surrounding hills, following farmers' trails. It's a peaceful, harmonious place where time seems to have stood still – an increasingly rare find in 21st-century China.

To get to Fǎnpái, take an hourly minibus heading from Táijiāng to Nangong and ask the driver to let you off at Fǎnpái (not Fanzhài

– that's another village on the same road). The journey costs around Y7 and takes 90 minutes. There are no hotels or restaurants in the village so bring some supplies.

SHÍDÒNG

Shídòng is a small **Miáo** village on the banks of the Qingshui River, and is famous for its festivals. The two biggest are the **Dragon Boat Festival** held from the 24th to the 27th of the fifth lunar month and the **Sisters' Meal Festival** on the 15th of the third lunar month. For more information on these two festivals, refer to the boxed texts 'Festivals' in the Kǎilǐ section and 'Festivals in Guìzhōu' at the start of this chapter.

At other times this village is quiet except for the **local market**, held every six days. The backstreets of the old town, east of the main road, and even the banks of the river are filled with stalls and traders.

Women sell inexpensive embroidery and silver all year, and Shídòng is a pretty good place to buy them. There's also a handicraft shop in Laotun, a few kilometres out of town, along the road to Táijiāng.

Places to Stay & Eat

Shídòng is definitely best visited as a day trip. The one *hostel* here is not a pretty sight. Ice-block triples with broken windows are Y30 – you have to pay for all three beds. Water supplies are iffy, as is cleanliness. But don't despair – embroidery sellers may offer to put you up in a spare room for around Y10.

There are a couple of basic *restaurants* near where the bus drops you.

Getting There & Away

Minibuses and tractor-trucks run between Táijiāng and Shídòng every hour or two between 7am and 2pm or 3pm for a pretty, two-hour drive through rural countryside (Y10). There are also one or two morning buses between here and Kǎilǐ.

Travel between Shídòng and Zhènyuǎn is fairly difficult. Unless you have got lots of time, you had be better off travelling via Kǎilǐ. Nevertheless, if you are up for it, a bus or two passes through Zhènyuǎn each morning, en route to Mahao village. Its ap-

pearance is somewhat haphazard. From Mahao, walk downhill 800m to the river and catch the small ferry (two máo) across to Shídòng. Buses for the return trip to Zhènyuǎn supposedly depart from Mahao bus station between 7.30am and 8am.

CHÓNG'ĀN 重安

☎ 0855

About two hours north of Kǎilǐ by bus, this hamlet's main claim to fame is its bustling **market**, held every five days. Set along the river, Chóng'ān retains its village size and atmosphere as well as many of its wooden homes and buildings. Among these are **Longevity Hall**, recently reincarnated as a pool hall, and the nearby **Cultural Pavilion**, which still holds a 1st-floor library.

The area around Chóng'ān offers some enjoyable short walks. Head east from town, towards the bridge to Kǎilǐ, to find wooden ferry boats along the river bank. These will take you across to the south side of the river for five máo. On the other side are a number of **traditional houses**, some of which still have faded red political slogans from the Cultural Revolution blazoned across their fronts. One by the dockside reads: 'In our hearts Chairman Mao is the reddest of the reddest red suns'. No one seems to be in any particular hurry to get rid of it.

Chóng'ān has a **Lusheng Festival** on the 26th of the ninth lunar month and celebrates the **Dragon Boat Festival** on the 26th of the fifth month, although these celebrations aren't as major as at Shídòng.

Walks

Longer walks around Chóng'ān will take you to minority villages. From the traditional houses on the south bank of the river, paths lead up the hillside to several Miáo villages. If you continue right along the river bank for a couple of minutes and then uphill to the left, you eventually come to **Xinzai**, an interesting Gejia village.

A second walk begins at the Jianxinlou Bīnguǎn in the town centre, from where you head east over the bridge and out of town, following the main river downstream. You will pass several water wheels grinding grain in the middle of the river and a workshop of stone carvers by the road.

The road sweeps to the left heading north to the Gejia village of **Chongxing**. If you continue straight, you'll pass a carpenters' village. On a hilltop to the left is the village of **Taiwan**, a blacksmiths' village recognisable by the rhythmic hammering of iron. Chongxing is 9km farther along this road – your best bet is to hitch with the occasional tractor or truck.

Another hike from Chóng'ān takes you west and upstream. If you continue west along the river bank, you will come to a modern road bridge and a chain suspension bridge, built in 1873 with 16 iron chains.

From here you can follow paths along the river bank for about 5km to the **Shēngǔ Pool** (Shēngǔ Yōuchí) scenic spot. For more information on this site, see the manager at Xiǎojiān-gnán Lǚyóu Fàndiàn.

Places to Stay

Xiǎojiāngnán Lǚyóu Fàndiàn (☎ 3266) is pleasantly situated on the river bank between the town and the bridge over Chóng'ān Jiāng. The hotel has two buildings. Coming from town, the first one is on the right; stairs lead up to a courtyard with rooms backing onto a fruit garden. About 100m farther down the road, towards the bridge to Kǎilǐ, is the second building with

---

The Story of Long Yuqiong

For generations, my family has been living in Xījiāng. My mother was only 27 when my father passed away, leaving her to raise three young children and work the fields alone.

Under the Nationalist Kuomintang regime, bandits often attacked good-looking women and took them as wives. Consequently, my mother always kept a knife with her, which she also used to cut fish. In time, I grew up and also turned into a pretty girl. Like my mother, I lived in constant fear, particularly after my older brother left home to study, leaving no man to protect us. My mother thought it a good idea for me to marry early, so I became a wife at age 17, not particularly young for a Miáo bride.

After her own bitter and hard life, my mother was determined I should marry into a rich family. When I danced to the lusheng at New Year and other festivals, everyone said how pretty and good I was. But my mother chose a good family with plenty of livestock and land. Who could have expected that only four years after my wedding day, China would be liberated and my husband's family decried as landlords. We both suffered later, as a result of his 'bad' class background.

Despite her poverty, my mother managed to give me 7.5kg of silver jewellery for my wedding, some from her own in-laws, but mostly from growing opium. Although it was illegal, and anyone caught growing opium would be thrown in jail, she crept out secretly at night to cultivate poppies on a distant mountain so she could give her only daughter a decent dowry and prevent my in-laws from looking down on me. At my lavish wedding I wore all the painfully heavy jewellery – one large necklace alone weighed 2.5kg!

The marriage was arranged by my mother and my husband's parents. I did not know him beforehand and I didn't see him at all for three years after the wedding. According to Miáo practice, new brides continue to stay with their mothers until they become pregnant. Women only go to their husbands' houses to live at busy times, such as planting and harvest. My husband was studying in town at first and only came back during the slack summer and winter holidays. I had no excuse to go to visit him. He also lacked the nerve to come to my house to see me. Only after graduation, when he became a teacher in a neighbouring village, did we have the chance to meet. We now have four children. Miáo people are extremely shy about sex or anything related to sex, such as childbirth. We are taught that sex is dirty and ugly. Couples are laughed at if they are seen together in public. At home, they usually avoid talking or making contact with each other.

My pregnant aunt was working in the fields when she had contractions. She told her husband, 'I have to go home'. She was too embarrassed to say she was about to go into labour.

rooms built over the river. Rooms in both buildings are basic with beds for Y20 to Y25. In winter, prices are more flexible and the riverside rooms may well be closed. Meals are available at the hotel.

The manager of the hotel can help organise boat trips to Shēngǔ Pool (Y30 a boat) and full-day guided treks to remote Mulao minority villages. The hotel reception displays plenty of photos of the surrounding area to whet your appetite.

The other hotel in town, *Jianxinlou Bīnguǎn,* is on the main highway at the T-junction in the centre of town. Basic rooms go for around Y8. The owners, however, are likely to refuse you with reasons such as a lack of running water or locked doors – more than likely a polite way of getting around their restriction against accepting foreigners.

Getting There & Away

Buses between Shībǐng, Huángpíng and Kǎilǐ all pass through Chóng'ān, which means there's a bus almost every half-hour in either direction. Buses to Kǎilǐ run until around 6.30pm.

HUÁNGPÍNG 黄平
☎ 0855

Huángpíng is home to a huge **market** that transforms the town every five days and

GUÌZHŌU

The Story of Long Yuqiong

On her way home, she met my mother. She said, 'Help me to have my baby now'. Horrified, my mother dragged her home, as Miáo people believe newborn babies are half human and half devil. If they are born outdoors, they will be taken away by the devil. When my aunt's husband got home and realised he had become a father, he did not even care to look at his wife and child, let alone to help them, since raising children was women's business.

I too received little help from my husband, as he was not around most of the time. I only lived with him for a few years, before he went to Běijīng for further studies at university. That was the best time in my life. After university, he was assigned to a job in another province. Seven years later, he finally moved back to teach at nearby Kǎilǐ. It was only a short spell of half a year before he was sent away to undergo re-education at a labour camp. My mother burst into tears when I broke the news to her: 'I suffered all my life. Why does my child have to suffer, too?'.

Just like her, I had to do all the men's and women's work. I don't know how we got over the incredible hardships. During the Great Leap Forward my family lost four members – my husband's parents and two brothers. A severe famine forced us to eat wild grass.

One day when I was collecting river weeds, one of my children ran to me crying, 'Grandad is dead'. I found him on a slope and carried him home. He was not dead yet and hung on through the night. My mother-in-law said to him, 'Go. Poor you, I know you miss your youngest son, but he is too far away to see you off'. He died straight away. Before he shut his eyes, he told us he had seven yuán hidden inside his pocket. With the money, we bought some rice so that my children survived.

Looking back, the best time I had was with my girlfriends. In Miáo society women rarely have fun with their husbands – couples of the older generation do not even talk, and sleep in separate rooms. We love getting together as it is the only time we can completely relax and enjoy ourselves. We weave or do embroidery work together, gossiping, venting our bitterness, telling jokes, singing and sometimes drinking. Young girls embroider on their clothes and expectant mothers work on the slings we use to carry babies on our backs. From these gatherings, we learn singing, cooking, embroidery and about life. I was in a group of nine women. We often wore the same clothes, went out together and had lots of fun. We had deep affection for each other. We Miáo women know how to endure hardships but also know how to enjoy life.

The oral history of Long Yuqiong, adapted by Lijia MacLeod

attracts both Miáo and Gejia people from the surrounding villages.

Also worth a visit is the Taoist temple complex of **Feiyun Dong**, built in 1443 and only 12km north-east of town. **Siyueba**, a large festival, is held here on the eighth day of the fourth lunar month. To reach the temple, take any Shībǐng-bound minibus.

Places to Stay & Eat

If you need to stay in Huángpíng for the night, take a right out of the bus station and walk two minutes up the road to *Línyè Zhāodàisǔo* (☎ 243 2044). Beds in clean, two-bed dorms without bath – but with electric blankets – are great value at Y10. Doubles with bath range from Y40 to Y60 per bed, depending on whether you want a heater.

If you want to do your respiratory system a favour, the bus station's *Chēzhàn Yíng Bīnguǎn* is best avoided. Rooms with bath are cheap at Y10 to Y15 per bed, however there is mildew spreading its way across the walls and the place is fairly unpleasant.

Getting There & Away

The central bus station has departures to Kǎilǐ from 7.20am until 4.30pm (Y16, 2½ hours) and to Zhènyuǎn from 7am until 4.30pm (Y22). From Kǎilǐ, buses run to Huángpíng from the western bus station from 6.50am until 5pm. For Shībǐng, catch a Zhènyuǎn-bound bus, which run until about 5.30pm.

SHĪBǏNG 施秉
☎ 0855

What was once the large Miáo village of Shībǐng has quickly transformed itself into a concrete town. Nevertheless, there are still opportunities for walks in the surrounding countryside as well as visits to smaller Miáo settlements.

The major attraction in the area is a cruise through the Guìlín lookalike countryside of the **Wǔyáng Hé**. Boats once continued all the way to Zhènyuǎn but these have been discontinued and no longer go any farther than the **Zhuge Gorge**. For more information ask at the CITS office (☎ 422 1177) at Minfu Bīnguǎn in town, or at the dock, 9km

east of Shībǐng near Caijiawan. See Wǔyáng Hé in the Around Zhènyuǎn section for information on cruises from Zhènyuǎn.

The CITS office can also give information on rafting and inner-tube floating on the **Shanmu Jiāng**, a couple of kilometres east of town.

Yuntai Shān, 15km east of town, is a pretty landscape of limestone peaks making it a great place for some hiking. To get there, take a Zhènyuǎn-bound bus and then hitch.

Places to Stay

Your best bet for accommodation is the friendly *Minfu Bīnguǎn* (☎ 422 2888), where a bed in a basic but clean triple goes for Y30. Doubles with bath and hot water are Y80 to Y100. To find the hotel, turn left as you leave the bus station and then right at the roundabout, onto Huancheng Donglu. The hotel is a further five-minute walk north.

Getting There & Away

A daily bus leaves for here from Kǎilǐ at 6.50am; the return bus leaves Shībǐng at 6.30am. Buses to Huángpíng and Zhènyuǎn run from about 8am until 5.30pm.

ZHÈNYUǍN 镇远
☎ 0855

Zhènyuǎn is a 2000-year-old Han town set on a bend in the Wǔyáng Hé. The pretty turquoise ribbon of river splits the town in half, with the original town site on the northern side (traditionally known as Fucheng) and the more recent additions in the south (known as Weicheng). While modern construction is swallowing up much of Zhènyuǎn, some of the more traditional wooden buildings and mazes of cobbled streets can still be found in the north-east.

Zhènyuǎn grew up as a garrison outpost on the trade route from Yúnnán to Húnán. Today it's a pleasant place and worth a day's exploration. Sunday brings the weekly market when the streets are especially interesting.

Information

CITS (☎ 572 2556; fax 572 2916) has an office opposite the Lèróng Bīnguǎn in the

Clothing

The variety of clothing worn by the minorities of South-West China, and Guìzhōu in particular, provides travellers with a daily visual feast. Clothes are as much a social and ethnic denominator as pure decoration. They also show whether a woman is married or not; if unmarried, clothes are a further pointer to a woman's wealth and skills in weaving and embroidery.

Many women in remote areas weave their own hemp and cotton cloth, though mass-produced cloth is commonly bought in the local markets or department stores. The same is true for dyes. Many women will not attend festivals in the rain for fear that the dyes in their fabrics will run. Some families, especially in Dong areas, still ferment their own indigo paste, and you will also see this for sale in traditional markets. Methods of producing indigo are greatly treasured and kept secret, but these are increasingly threatened by the introduction of artificial chemical dyes.

Embroidery is central to minority costume and is a tradition, passed down from mother to daughter. Until recently, embroidery was never bought and sold but rather handed down through generations. The designs include many important symbols and references to Miáo myths and history. Birds, fish and a variety of dragon motifs are popular symbols. Today the best designs are copied onto paper-cuts and sold.

The highest-quality work is often reserved for baby carriers, and many young girls work on these as they approach marrying age. Older women will often spend hundreds of hours embroidering their own funeral clothes. You may see women embroidering small strips or panels of cloth – these are then added to jackets piecemeal. Particularly elaborate sleeve panels can then be removed after the main festivals or when the jacket gets old. Baby hats are also embroidered and decorated with silver symbols to protect the infant. Embroidered insoles were once popular, but are becoming less so. A great place to get a close look at some traditional work is the small embroidery museum in Táijiāng, as well as in the shops of Guìyáng's Cuìwēi Garden.

Costumes move with the times. In larger towns, Miáo women often substitute their embroidered smocks with a good woolly jumper and their headdresses look suspiciously like mass-produced pink and yellow Chinese towels.

Bradley Mayhew

southern half of town. It arranges boat trips down the Wǔyáng Hé for Y100 per boat with a maximum of 10 people per boat. If there's already a boat going, you may be squeezed in. No one in the office speaks English.

Things to See & Do

The town's most famous attraction is the **Black Dragon Cave** (Qīnglóng Dòng), a pretty Taoist and Buddhist complex of pavilions, temples and grottoes that appears to have fused with the mountainside over time.

Buy your Y10 ticket at a booth near the Zhùshèng Bridge and follow the twisting stairways past the Hall of the Great Buddha and Zhongyuan Cave to the two-storey Ziyang Academy and the Jade Emperor Pavilion (Yùhuáng Gé). The last two offer good views over the old town.

Most of the shrines and statuary were destroyed during the Cultural Revolution, but it's still a peaceful and pleasant place to visit. Just by the exit is the Wanshou (Longevity) Theatre, currently home to an interesting **Minority Nationalities Architecture Museum**.

From the complex, cross over the Zhusheng Bridge, through the **Kuixing Pavilion**, to the old town. Near the bridge is a former temple that now serves as a wood workshop. The best way to explore the old town is to head along either Sifangjing or Fuxiang Xiang and wander around the tall, layered stone buildings. Many of the houses have quotations from Chairman Mao painted over the entrance archways.

Farther west along the northern river bank is the **Tianhougong Sì**. Although the

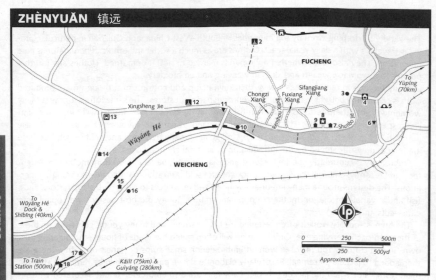

ZHÈNYUǍN 镇远

building itself is closed, old-aged bird fanciers flock here every Sunday to admire each other's birds and cages.

For an energetic hike, head up the hill north of town to the **Sìgōng Sì**, named after four generals of the Warring States Period (453–221 BC). Bear right near the top, and you'll come to the **old city walls** (Gǔchéng), snaking over the countryside like a shrunken Great Wall of China. There are more defences snaking over hillsides south of town.

Festivals

The town's mainly Han residents celebrate the Han **Dragon Boat Festival** on the fifth day of the fifth lunar month. The Dong minority village of Baojing, 41km south-east of Zhènyuǎn, celebrates **Sanyuesan** on the third of the third lunar month with a barbecue fish banquet. The Miáo town of Yongxi, 12km west, celebrates **Double Ninth** on the ninth of the ninth lunar month.

Places to Stay

Lèróng Bīnguǎn, on the southern side of town is probably the best accommodation option at the moment. A bed costs Y30 in a comfortable and carpeted double with bath-

room. Doubles without bathroom aren't nearly as good value at Y15 a bed.

Nearby, *Wǔyáng Bīnguǎn* and *Xīxiù Bīnguǎn* are both somewhat overpriced. The Wǔyáng has doubles with grim bathrooms for Y60 per bed or beds in bathless triples for Y20. The Xīxiù has beds in bathless triples for Y30 or doubles/triples with bath for Y50/60.

Across the river, *Ténglóng Bīnguǎn* (☎ 572 7188) has cosy, heated doubles with bath for Y128 or triples for Y28 per bed.

North-east of here, *Zhènyuǎn Bīnguǎn* (☎ 572 2592) has clean, well-priced triples for Y90 or doubles with bath starting at Y68. Next door, the *Míngchéng Bīnguǎn* (☎ 572 6028) has heated triples/doubles for Y189/188. Rooms are clean and comfortable but the beds are tiny.

Places to Eat

The restaurant at the Lèróng Bīnguǎn is a good place for dinner. For a daytime snack or cup of tea, try the *wooden restaurant* on Xingsheng Jie by the main bridge. There are other snack bars in the eastern part of town.

For the classiest surroundings try the *Qīnglóng Restaurant* by the Black Dragon

ZHÈNYUǍN

1	Old City Walls 老城墙	7	Míngchéng Bīnguǎn 名城宾馆	13	Long-Distance Bus Station 长途汽车站
2	Sìgōngdiàn 四宫殿	8	PSB 公安局	14	Ténglóng Bīnguǎn 腾龙宾馆
3	Fire God Temple 火神庙	9	Zhènyuǎn Bīnguǎn 镇远宾馆	15	Lèróng Bīnguǎn 乐容宾馆
4	Kuixing Pavilion; Zhùshèng Bridge 祝圣桥	10	Market 市场	16	CITS 中国国际旅行社
5	Black Dragon Cave; Ticket Booth 青龙洞、售票处	11	Restaurant 饭馆	17	Wǔyáng Bīnguǎn 舞阳宾馆
6	Qīnglóng Restaurant 青龙餐厅	12	Tianhougong Sì 天后宫	18	Xīxiù Bīnguǎn 西秀宾馆

Cave, though you'd be wise to check prices first. You can get there by ferry from the northern shore or over the Zhùshèng Bridge.

Getting There & Away
Bus There are several buses to and from Kǎilǐ via Shībīng regularly during the day. Departures for Shībīng are between 7am and 4pm from the local bus station in the north-west of town. There are also some through buses to Huángpíng or you can change at Shībīng.

If you're going to Shīdòng, there are morning buses to Mahao from the road outside Zhènyuǎn's train station. From Mahao's bus station, head downhill 800m to Mahao village and catch the small ferry across to Shīdòng. If you're coming from Shīdòng, a bus or two supposedly departs from Mahao's bus station between 7.30am and 8am. This route is time consuming and unreliable – travelling via Kǎilǐ is much easier.

Train The train station is a little tricky to find. It's up a small driveway and out of view from the main road. Ticket booths only open at the station about half an hour before departures, turning the waiting crowd into a bit of a frenzied mob and creating a long and frustrating queue. It's therefore best to get your tickets as soon as you can.

Trains to Yùpíng (1½ hours) depart at 8am, 8.59am, noon, 12.31pm and 1.59pm. Southbound trains to Kǎilǐ (two hours) and Guìyáng (six hours) pass through at around

1.50pm and 3.45pm. From Kǎilǐ, a train departs for Zhènyuǎn at 10.40am (Y14).

Getting Around
Armoured rickshaws will take you anywhere in town for Y1 per person. Derelict taxis will also take you for the same price (and at the same speed).

Ferries cross the Wǔyáng Hé near the marketplace for a couple of máo.

AROUND ZHÈNYUǍN
Wǔyáng Hé 舞阳河
The Wǔyáng Hé runs through a scenic area packed with white limestone gorges and weirdly shaped rocks cut by waterfalls and topped with lush green vegetation. There are three mini-gorges along the river: West Gorge, Dragon King Gorge and Zhuge Gorge, plus plenty of spuriously named peaks, the most famous of which is Peacock-Tailed Peak. Boats tour the main river gorges and the side creeks of the Xiangjian and Baishui Rivers.

The docks are 17km west of Zhènyuǎn and 1km off the main road to Shībīng. In summer it's worth taking a Shībīng-bound bus to see if any boats are leaving that day. Alternatively, ask at the CITS office (☎ 572 2556, fax 572 2916) in Zhènyuǎn about boat trips.

TÓNGRÉN 铜仁
☎ 5231
Tóngrén is the largest town in the north-east of Guìzhōu and is of interest to tourists

mainly as a base to visit nearby Fànjìng Shān (see the following Around Tóngrén section). It's a pleasant place on the Jīn Jiāng and is a manageable size. You can also pass through here when leaving the region for neighbouring Húnán province. Visit the Tóngrén Tourism Bureau (☎ 521 1000) in the courtyard behind the Fànyǔ

Dàjiǔdiàn for more information on the Fàn-jìng Shān Nature Reserve.

Information

The main branch of the Bank of China is on Huangcheng Xilu and changes money and travellers cheques. Internet access is available on the 2nd floor of a shopping arcade just off Minzhu Lu as well as on Jiefang Lu, both for Y3 an hour.

Things to See

The small **Nuó Museum** in the south-east of town at Dongshān Sì (East Hill Monastery) is worth a visit. Nuó is a local form of religious opera, with animist overtones, similar in many ways to the Bouyi Ground Opera. It is performed at festivals around Ānshùn. Admission to the museum is Y2. To reach the museum, take the second right off Jiefang Lu, after Minzhu Lu, and follow the staircase on the left up the hill. Turn left at a group of yellow buildings and continue up the stairs to the top.

Places to Stay & Eat

Jīnlóng Dàjiǔdiàn has a good central position and clean, large basic rooms with bath for Y40 a bed. You may be able to sweet-talk your way into cheaper dorms. The hotel has central heating, but if that doesn't work staff will bring a coal fire right into your room. Farther down Huangcheng Xilu, *Chéngōngguǎn Jiǔlóu* has similar prices.

Across the river and north of the centre, *Jīn Jiāng Bīnguǎn* was once the established

TÓNGRÉN

1 Jīn Jiāng Bīnguǎn 锦江宾馆	7 Jīnlóng Dàjiǔdiàn 金龙大酒店	11 Main Bus Station; Taxis to Yùpíng & Jiāngkǒu 汽车总站、到玉屏、 江口的出租车
2 Night Market 夜市场	8 Bank of China 中国银行	
3 China Post 中国电信	9 Local Bus Station 市客车站	12 Chéngōngguǎn Jiǔlóu 陈公馆酒楼
4 Internet Café 网吧		13 Internet Café 网吧
5 Grocery Store 超市	10 Fànyǔ Dàjiǔdiàn; Tóngrén Tourism Bureau 梵宇大酒店、 铜仁旅游局	14 Nuó Museum 傩文化博物馆
6 Xinhua Book Store 新华书店		15 Tóngyán Pavilion 铜岩阁

tourist headquarters of Tóngrén, however singles/doubles in the redone north building are severely overpriced at Y150/218. Rooms in the west building are slightly cheaper but appear harder for foreigners to obtain.

Across the street from the bus station, the two-star *Fányǔ Dàjiǔdiàn* (☎ 998 3002) is also overpriced with somewhat run-down standards with bath starting at Y238.

A great place to eat is the *night market*, which spreads down a small alley and into a courtyard across from China Post. Here you can sample fresh noodles, hotpot, jiǎozi and barbecue. The friendly Jīnlóng Dàjiǔdiàn also has a decent *restaurant*.

If you're stocking up for Fànjìng Shān, there is a large grocery store on Minzhu Lu.

Getting There & Away

The easiest way to get to Tóngrén is to take a train to the railhead at Yùpíng and then a minibus or taxi from outside the train station. Comfortable Aveco vans (Y30) run from about 8am until 6pm. Taxi drivers will start bargaining at Y50 but will go at least as low as Y30. There is fierce competition for passengers; be prepared for an aggressive sales pitch. The trip takes approximately two hours, however once current roadworks are completed, this should be reduced. En route you'll pass by a number fields with tea bushes snaking their way over the hills.

Leaving Tóngrén, Aveco vans and shared taxis huddle at the bus station. If you're heading to Jiāngkǒu (for Fànjìng Shān), you can get a shared taxi from here (Y20, 2 hours).

Trains from Yùpíng to Kǎilǐ depart at 10.25am, 2.14pm and 7.19pm. An overflowing train from Shànghǎi passes through at 3.46pm en route to Kūnmíng but your chances of finding a seat are slim. One train also leaves daily for Huáihuà in Húnán province at 9.40am. From Kǎilǐ, a train departs for Yùpíng at 10.40am.

AROUND TÓNGRÉN
Fànjìng Shān Nature Reserve
梵净山自然保护区

Fànjìng Shān Zìrán Bǎohùqū
This 2572m mountain in the Wuling Shān range is Guìzhōu's most important conser-

vation area, providing a home to over half the province's protected plants and two-thirds of its protected animals. The area was declared a nature reserve in 1978 and incorporated into Unesco's Man and the Biosphere Programme in 1986. (See the Ecology & Environment and Flora & Fauna sections in the Facts about South-West China chapter for more information.)

One of the rarest of its 300 species of animals is the golden monkey *(jinsihou)*, with a breeding centre at the base of the mountain that has been trying to boost the animal's population since 1995. The mountain is home to about 170 of the 15,000 left in the wild. Famous in Chinese mythology as a symbol of longevity, the golden monkey is immediately distinguishable by its blue face. Other animals found on the mountain include protected giant salamanders, musk deer, pangolins (scaly anteater), rhesus monkeys and several varieties of pheasant.

The mountain's most famous flora is the dove tree *(Davidia involucrata)*, 'discovered' by the French missionary Père David. When the tree blossoms in April/May, the flowers look like huge handkerchiefs or doves ready to fly. The vertical 2km forest that blankets the mountain also features subtropical magnolias, Mao bamboo, oaks, myrtles, China fir trees, azaleas and rhododendrons.

Fànjìng means the 'state of enlightenment and freedom from earthly worries' and has its origins in the 16th century when the mountain was an important Buddhist pilgrimage site. Most of the Ming-dynasty temples on the mountainside have since been ruined, though a few were restored in 1992 when access to the mountain was also improved and Chinese tourists gained a renewed interest in the area.

Spring and autumn are the best times to visit the mountain. Spring in particular enlivens the summit with azalea blossom. Summers are generally wet and humid, and winters freezing.

From the park entrance at Heiwan you will have to take a minivan, hitch or walk the 7km to the Copper Mine, and then a farther 2.7km to the beginning of the steps at Yu'ao. From here it's a four or more hour climb up 6800 steps past Huixiangping to **Wanbao** (Ten Thousand Treasures), where most people stay overnight. From Wanbao there are another 300 or so steps to the summit at **Jǐndǐng** (Golden Summit) and the weird, layered Mushroom Rocks beyond.

The rocky summit has the remains of an old monastery and offers more hiking to nearby sites such as Baiyun and Zhenguo monasteries to the east and Nine Dragon Pool to the west.

Some sections of the staircase are narrow and in bad shape and all sections are a killer on your legs. Give yourself a day to haul yourself up the mountain, another to climb back down, and maybe a third to have a look around the summit.

It is theoretically possible to descend the mountain on the other side to Shizhuyan, but it's hard to find transport on to Zhangjiaba and the town of Yinjiang, 39km from Shizhuyan.

Admission to the mountain is Y15.

Places to Stay & Eat There are several places to stay at the park entrance in Heiwan. *Heiwanhe Bīnguǎn* has rooms for Y70 to Y100.

There is also a number of options on the mountain. Most people stay at the *guesthouse* at Wanbao, though there are *hotels* lower down the mountain at Copper Mine, Huixiangping and Yu'ao. A sleeping bag would be useful from November until at least March.

It's a good idea to check with the Tóngrén Tourism Board, especially if you're visiting out of season, to make sure hotels are open for business. It may even be able to book you a room.

You'll find a few basic *noodle places* and *stalls* along the trail but it's a good idea to bring along some of your own food.

Getting There & Away To get to the park entrance, first take a shared taxi from Tóngrén to Jiāngkǒu (Y20, 1½ hours), and then a minibus or shared taxi 23km north to the park entrance at Heiwan (Y20, one hour).

Nine Dragon Cave 九龙洞
Jiǔlóng Dòng

This 1400m-long karst cave is said to be able to hold 10,000 people. It's really off the beaten track but if you're a cave fanatic, it's got to be worth it. To get there, take a bus from Tóngrén's local bus station to Yangtou and get off a couple of kilometres past the town of Mayan, 15km east of Tóngrén. From here you can cross the Jǐn Jiāng by ferry and walk 15 minutes to the cave entrance. Guānyīn Shān lies behind the cave and is also worth exploring.

DONG REGION 侗族地区

South-east of Kǎilǐ, the road climbs into the hills before finally descending into the subtropical Róngjiāng Basin. This is the land of the Dong minority, instantly recognised by its distinctive drum towers, and one of the most interesting parts of Guìzhōu to explore.

Most travellers who come here are en route to or from Guǎngxī province. If this isn't in your plans, you can do an interesting loop from Róngjiāng, visiting Lìpíng, Zhàoxìng and Cóngjiāng. The most interesting area is between Cóngjiāng and Zhàoxìng.

It's worth travelling as lightly as possible in these areas, so you can jump off the bus when a particularly interesting village catches your eye. Roads around here are still pretty rough but are slowly being improved. Buses, however, are another matter – they remain decrepit monsters chugging along in a vain attempt to keep to the schedule.

Doing any kind of banking in these parts is not possible so bring your Rénmínbì with you.

RÓNGJIĀNG 榕江
☎ 0855

Róngjiāng is a small market town serving the nearby Dong villages. It has its fair share of concrete mess and is mainly of interest as a base to visit nearby villages. You are likely to see a number of traditionally dressed villagers here who have come to town to buy or sell goods. The highlight of Róngjiāng is undoubtedly its **Sunday market** (see the boxed text 'Market

Day') and it's worth trying to arrange your itinerary to catch it. The market takes over a couple of streets just east and parallel to the main road.

The town is clustered around a north-south road with a roundabout and the long-distance bus station at the northern end, and a local minibus stop in the south. About midway along the main road is **Xiànwén Wùguǎnlǐsuǒ**, a restored hall that has become enshrined as a Communist Revolutionary site. You can pop in for a look.

A 20-minute walk north-east of Róngjiāng's main roundabout brings you to the large, wooden Dong village of **Chejiāng**. The paths in the village are fascinating to stroll along, especially as they actually lead somewhere, unlike those in most Dong villages in the region, which simply end at someone's front door.

Places to Stay & Eat

There are two decent hotels near the bus station. *Lántiān Bīnguǎn* (☎ 662 2479) has the best rooms in town, with heated doubles with bath for Y50 per bed. If you opt for no heat, you can save Y10. To find the hotel, turn left out of the bus station, take the first left and the hotel is on the right.

Qìngfēng Bīnguǎn (☎ 662 3088) has basic clean, though somewhat musty, doubles with heat and bath for Y50 a bed. Without bath it's Y30. Turn right out of the bus station, left at the roundabout and the hotel is on your immediate right.

In the centre of town, next door to the Revolutionary site, is *Róngjiāng Bīnguǎn* (☎ 662 4188). OK singles/doubles/triples without bath are Y30/60/90. Rather plush, comfortable doubles with bath and heat are Y160. From the bus station, turn right at the

---

Market Day

Sunday morning is no day of rest in Róngjiāng. The streets are clogged, buses are backed up for miles and tractor loads of people just keep pouring into town. Pigs are stuffed squealing into bamboo cages; there's even a guy with a dead pig on the back of his bike. It's carnage. It's the Sunday market.

The range of goods for sale is amazing: duck eggs transported in bamboo and straw packages; huge baskets of dried chillies; long strings of mushrooms; tobacco; brooms made of sorghum; and more dried roots than you ever thought possible.

Rat-catchers do a brisk trade, proving the efficiency of their poisons with a bubonic pile of dead rats. There are also stalls selling everything you might need to worship your ancestors – from incense sticks to spirit money, burnt when important decisions have to be made to check if the spirits have any major objections. Young guns in sunglasses ogle the posters of Hawaii, the Party faithful prefer the latest Deng Xiaoping calendars.

In one corner a group of Dong women with half-shaved heads sell indigo dye in small vats or plastic bags. Customers who come up to feel its texture walk away unsatisfied, with blue stained hands. Many Dong men come to sell charcoal to buyers from other regions. Other itinerant vendors to look out for are the music sellers, who crouch behind prehistoric stereos playing tapes of tinny Dong music recorded in someone's kitchen, and the hairdressers and dentists who set up portable shops on the pavement.

There's always plenty of food on offer, though once you've found it you might soon lose your appetite. Pickled raw fish is a firm favourite, followed up with fried, sweet, glutinous rice balls covered in sesame seeds. The meat market is the hard-core place to get lunch, though beware that the most popular dishes are normally dog meat, thought to bestow strength and virility. Preparation techniques are not for the squeamish; dogs are often part-cooked with a blowtorch. Ducks have their throats cut and are plunged into boiling tar and cold water to help remove the feathers. The stench can be nauseating – but not as nauseating as the row of pink pigs' faces hung above a curtain of lungs and stomachs. Still hungry?

Bradley Mayhew

roundabout and walk about 10 minutes into town. The hotel is on the right.

There are a number of small *restaurants* around the bus station and roundabout. There is also a two- or three-stall *night market* near the local minibus station that serves great fried noodles for Y3 a plate. It's open until at least midnight.

Getting There & Away
Róngjiāng's main bus station is in the north of town near the main roundabout. Sleeper buses run between here and Guìyáng, departing from Róngjiāng at 4pm and simultaneously from Guìyáng (Y80, 14 hours).

A range of buses, minibuses and sleepers leave for Kǎilǐ between 6.30am and 12.30pm. From Kǎilǐ, buses depart from Róngjiāng from 7.40am until early afternoon. Around mid-afternoon, buses from Kǎilǐ continue south to Cóngjiāng. Other buses depart Róngjiāng for Cóngjiāng from 6.40am until 4.30pm. These buses return to Róngjiāng from 7am until 5pm. Minibuses between Lìpíng, Sāndū and Róngjiāng run from 6.30am to 9.30am.

A small minibus stand in the south-west of town has frequent westbound departures between 7am and 5.30pm for Xinghua (Y15) via Bakai. There are numerous connections from there to Sāndū. To find the minibus stand, head south on Róngjiāng's main road and turn right at the first crossroad past the Revolutionary site. Continue to the end of the road.

AROUND RÓNGJIĀNG
On the road to Sāndū, 25km west of Róngjiāng, **Bakai** is a small Dong village with a traditional Sunday market. The one-hour bus ride also passes the villages of **Dujiang**, set at a strategically important bend in the river, and **Layou**, a picturesque village on the southern side of the river recognisable by its old hump-backed bridge. You could stop off in these towns and go for a wander if you're interested in exploring some Dong villages. Bakai has a small guesthouse if you miss your ride, though you should be able to make it back to Róngjiāng in a day trip.

A more demanding excursion takes you to the villages of **Xindi** and **Zengchong**. Xindi is said to have the largest drum tower in the region, and Zengchong the oldest at 300 years old. There's little, if any, public transport here and you'll have to hitch or hire a taxi to get there and back. Follow the Cóngjiāng road 23km south to Tingdong, from where a side road leads 23km north to the two villages.

CÓNGJIĀNG 从江
☎ 0855
Cóngjiāng is a fairly nondescript town set on the banks of the Duliu Jiāng. You'll likely have to change buses here if you're heading south to more interesting Dong villages and may have to spend the night if you're aiming for Guǎngxī.

The town is divided by the river. The western side is built up while the eastern side, once a small Dong village, is at an interesting point of convergence between traditional wooden structures and tiled, modern giants.

There is a CITS office in the Ténglónggé Bīnguǎn (☎ 641 2468) that gives out maps of the area and can help with some basic information. No one speaks English.

Places to Stay & Eat
Ténglónggé Bīnguǎn (☎ 641 2468), opposite the bridge on the eastern side of the river, has comfortable doubles with bath and with/without heat for Y130/100. Singles/doubles without bath or heat are Y70/90. Unfortunately, your foreignness qualifies you to pay a special, higher rate than prices posted for Chinese nationals.

Just down the road, across from the bus station, *Běmèizhèn Zhāodàisuǒ (☎ 641 4395)* has beds in basic, clean doubles with bath for Y25 each. It also has a beauty parlour on the 2nd floor where you can get your hair slicked back into a Dong figure-eight do.

On the western side of town, a five-minute walk north of the bridge, *Mínfù Zhāodàisuǒ (☎ 641 2900)* has cleanish doubles with bath and heat for Y60 a bed. It also has beds in triples without bath for Y15 – the cheapest deal in town.

If you're looking for a meal in Cóngjiāng, it's best not to leave it too late as the town shuts around 7pm or 8pm. Across the street from the bus station is a row of small *restaurants*. We enjoyed one of our tastiest meals in Guìzhōu at the restaurant fourth from the southern (right-hand) end. A small *night market* sets up with a few barbecue and hotpot stalls, 15-minutes' walk north of the bridge on the western side of town. Ténglónggé Bīnguǎn also has a decent *restaurant*.

Getting There & Away

Cóngjiāng has a new bus station about 150m south of the bridge on the eastern side of the river.

Between here and Kǎilǐ there are a couple of early morning buses each way, with the ones from Cóngjiāng leaving at 6am and 7.20am. A sleeper leaves Cóngjiāng for Kǎilǐ at 6pm (Y71) and a return bus leaves Kǎilǐ for Cóngjiāng at 7pm. This is a popular route and you'd be wise to buy your tickets a day in advance. To and from Róngjiāng, buses depart almost hourly between 6.30am and 5pm.

Heading east, there are buses to and from Lìpíng between 6.30am and 11.30am. There is no direct link with Zhàoxìng – use the Lìpíng route and change at Pilin. Alternatively, you can take buses to Luoxiang, which depart between 7.30am and 4.30pm (Y11, two hours), and walk the final hour or so to Zhàoxìng.

To Guǎngxī, there are five departures for Sānjiāng between 5.40am and 8.20am and then again at 11.30am, 12.30pm and 2.30pm. To Róngshuǐ, a bus leaves at 6.30am. There are two departures daily for Liǔzhōu at 1.30pm and 5pm.

CÓNGJIĀNG TO ZHÀOXÌNG

The beautiful three-hour bus journey east from Cóngjiāng towards Zhàoxìng winds its way over rolling hills and lush terraced fields, passing groves of tangerine trees and riverboats gliding along the turquoise waters. This route also passes through some of the most interesting villages in south-eastern Guìzhōu and it's well worth breaking your trip in at least one.

As the road starts to climb into the hills, about 8km from Cóngjiāng, you'll see the three drum towers of **Gaozeng**, a settlement of three small villages. Another 20km or so brings you to **Guandong**, the largest village en route, equipped with a basic *Zhēngfù Zhāodàisuǒ* offering beds for Y7, a couple of restaurants and a market every five days. Don't be put off by the ugly concrete blocks on the main street – behind this is an interesting village offering good walks in the surrounding countryside.

Longtu is another Dong village with several drum towers. A festival, featuring mock battles, is held here over New Year in memory of the ancestral goddess Sasui. North of Longtu the road splits left to **Xin'an**, a small village with a drum tower on the road to Lìpíng, and right to **Luoxiang**, on the road to Zhàoxìng and Sānjiāng.

The region holds a lusheng festival and competition in successive villages from the middle of the seventh to the middle of the eighth lunar month.

Transport in this area shouldn't be a problem. Morning buses run from Cóngjiāng to Lìpíng and Xin'an, and between Cóngjiāng and Luoxiang from 7.30am and 4.30pm.

ZHÀOXÌNG

Zhàoxìng is a lively, traditional Dong minority village with a remarkable five drum towers. Having somehow eclipsed the rash of modern buildings that has taken over many of China's villages, Zhàoxìng still boasts its traditional wooden structures. Surrounded by lush fields and hills, Zhàoxìng is a small oasis and well worth a day's stopover. If you only visit one Dong village, this should be it.

Things to See & Do

The main attraction is the village itself. The five **drum towers**, each built by a different clan, as well as a number of **wind and rain bridges** and **theatre stages**, make Zhàoxìng a beautiful place to wander around. The village is very active and you'll see people weaving baskets, building homes and embroidering. Many of the town's inhabitants continue to wear traditional clothing and speak only their native Dong language.

The Dong

You will easily spot the Dong by their clothing, headgear and hairdos. Dong men commonly don a black turban, white headband or a black-and-white scarf. In a few traditional villages you may even see men with a shaved head and topknot. On the feet may be straw sandals, and trousers are generally short indigo pants reaching mid-shin. Men working in the fields often tie a wooden tool holder shaped like a boot behind their back.

Dong women wear a pleated skirt over skin-tight indigo trousers and embroidered gaiters (or puttees), topped off with an embroidered jacket, buttoned to the right, and a blue and black headscarf. The indigo often has a reddish tinge, due to the addition of egg white and blood, and a sheen that comes from beating the cloth with a mallet. The indigo is so dark that many women seem almost drenched in it. Most women wear their hair oiled, wound up in a figure eight and held in place with a comb. Many wear silver neck rings.

The Dong are famed for their wooden architecture, in particular their drum towers and wind and rain bridges, traditionally constructed without nails from the timber of at least 300 fir trees.

Most villages have at least one drum tower, traditionally used for meetings and festivals. Larger drum towers have a fireplace underneath the tower, to act as a social centre and meeting point for village elders. The 2m-long drum suspended from the roof rouses the village in case of attack or fire. Drum towers can be up to 15 storeys tall with four, six or eight sides. Multiple towers in a single village indicate that there were originally several settlements, or groupings of clans, which have merged into a larger village unit.

Wind and rain bridges or 'flower bridges' are named after the pavilions that shelter people from the elements, and provide a place to meet, rest and hang out. The best bridges are at Dìpíng in Guìzhōu and Chengyang in Guǎngxī. Both drum towers and bridges are decorated with painted Buddhist carvings, often of guardians or symbolic protective animals such as dragons or phoenixes.

The Dong replenish the timber they fell; with each new baby that is born, the parents traditionally plant a tree to be used to build a house when the child reaches adulthood. Because most buildings are made of wood, villages have many fish ponds that double as a water source in case of fire.

Many Dong villages have festivals during the first lunar month. During the **Tiaguanren Festival,** men from a neighbouring village, dressed as government officials and guards, visit local people who are dressed as bandits, goblins, spiders, beggars and fishermen. Gifts of money are eventually handed out to the actors and to the groups of women who come to sing songs. It's really just an excuse for a huge party.

Another festival, the **Caigetang,** is held on the second day of the first lunar month and features singing and dancing competitions. Folk songs and oral histories are particularly important to the Dong, as they have no written language.

During the New Year many Dong women who were married the previous year return with their husband's family to their parents' home, bearing gifts. The New Year in general is a time to remember ancestors, especially the ancient Dong heroine and ancestral goddess **Sasui** (Grandmother). There are many memorial services to her during this time, especially around Lìpíng and Cóngjiāng.

Another activity organised by the Dong, especially in Guǎngxī, is **huapao**. During a game of huapao an iron ring wrapped in red floss is blasted out of a metal tube, and in the ensuing rugby-like chaos teams of 12 to 13 players try to wrench it from the opposition and hand it to a judge.

The Dong are especially renowned for their hospitality and fearsome drinking ability. Important guests are often toasted as they enter a village. One spectacular farewell ritual quoted by a local tourism brochure obliges the Dong to 'hang pig heads and tails over the guests, put intestines on everybody and chase after one another with severed pig heads'.

There are also a number of pleasant walks around the village and into the countryside. One excellent hour-long walk takes you to the nearby village of **Jitang**, high in the hills. Follow the dirt road at the edge of town, heading west to Luoxiang. The road climbs uphill and then branches right, snaking around the terraced valley. Jitang has an old drum tower and good views over the valley floor.

From Jitang, return by the same route or follow a road that bears right halfway down the hill. Cross into the next valley and then descend slippery paths into the hamlet of **Jilun**, up a side valley from Zhàoxìng. Jilun is a tiny but beautiful Dong village with a single drum tower. Plan half a day for the round trip.

There are also good views of Zhàoxìng from the eastern end of town as the road climbs out of the valley. The hills offer endless opportunities for exploration.

Places to Stay & Eat

Your best bet is the wooden *Wénhuàzhàn Zhāodàisuǒ*, east of the drum tower and 50m south off the main road in the centre of town. The owners are friendly and rooms are basic but cosy and clean and still smell of timber. Beds are Y20 each with communal bath and showers. The hotel also offers tours of Zhàoxìng, the surrounding area and nearby villages for extremely reasonable rates. (We were quoted Y8 per person.) There are lots of photos of possible tour destinations and festivals on the walls of the hotel's little-known souvenir shop. There isn't any English spoken here.

Mínzú Zhāodàisuǒ, nearby on the corner, has beds from Y30 but the rooms aren't half as nice as the wooden exterior suggests. Once you get inside, the place is actually a concrete bunker with far from clean, common toilets.

Next door is a *restaurant*, (which also serves as the hotel's reception) that has pretty good food. Be sure to check on the meat of the day though; the restaurant has been known to purchase it's daily special from the local rat-catcher. Rat meat *(lǎoshǔ ròu)* is quite a common dish in this area.

Other options for eating are limited – especially in winter – to hotpot, noodles and savoury rice cakes. You can eat good, spicy, glutinous rice noodles for Y3 a bowl, seated on a comfy sofa in a little shop in the centre of town. If you plan to do some day walks, it might be a good idea to take some snacks.

Getting There & Away

From Cóngjiāng, take a Lìpíng bus and change at Pilin for a Lìpíng-Dìpíng minibus that passes through Zhàoxìng. These run until around 4pm.

Alternatively, if you're looking to stretch your legs, take a Luoxiang-bound bus from Cóngjiāng. Buses are supposed to run from 7.30am until 4.30pm (Y11, two hours) but may start later and end sooner. From Luoxiang, it's a lovely 1½-hour walk along a dirt road to Zhàoxìng, passing through a number of smaller villages en route. This makes for an excellent overnight trip from Cóngjiāng where you can store your bags at Ténglónggé Bīnguǎn.

From Zhàoxìng, there are a few buses daily to Lìpíng (four hours) and at least one Lìpíng-Sānjiāng bus passing through each way. The trip to Sānjiāng takes about five hours. There are no direct buses to Cóngjiāng.

ZHÀOXÌNG TO GUǍNGXĪ

There are several buses daily south from Lìpíng to Zhàoxìng and on to **Dìpíng** (also known as **Lóngé**). The trip takes around four hours. Dìpíng is a Dong village with the best **wind and rain bridge** in the region. If you do break your trip here, you'll probably have to stay the night, as the bus to Sānjiāng in Guǎngxī doesn't leave until the next morning. The hotel at the square where the buses stop has reasonably priced dorm beds.

From Sānjiāng there are buses to Lóngshèng or Guìlín. See the Sānjiāng section of the Guǎngxī chapter for more information.

LÌPÍNG 黎平
☎ 0855

Lìpíng is famous in communist mythology for a Long March meeting on 18 December 1934, when Zhou Enlai, Mao and other

Communist Party luminaries sat here and discussed their next move – to storm Zūnyì. Other than that, there is little of interest.

Around Lìpíng, there's a wind and rain bridge at **Maogong** and also a Dong village at **Gaojin**, both on the road to Róngjiāng. Near **Gaotun**, you can explore a number of limestone caves in a scenic area along the Bazhou Jiāng, about 10km north-east of Lìpíng.

Lìpíng has basic accommodation at *Lìpíng Zhāodàisuǒ* for around Y10 per person. You'll find it at the traffic circle at the centre of town, near the long-distance bus stop.

There are several morning buses to Róngjiāng and Dìpíng as well as a few daily Kǎilǐ-bound buses. There's also an overnight sleeper bus to Kǎilǐ (Y71, nine hours). From Kǎilǐ, a sleeper departs at 7pm for Lìpíng. You may also find a few morning buses on this route, depending on the demand. Minibuses from Róngjiāng depart for Lìpíng from 6.30am to 9.30am.

The Shui

This small ethnic group, originally from the Pearl River region in Guǎngxī, now lives mainly along the Duliu Jiāng around Sāndū. They are most easily recognised by their white turbans. While the majority speak and write Chinese, there is an ancient Shui script of about 100 pictographs that is used during shaman practices. Elaborate death taboos and funeral rites ensure a Shui's 12 souls return to their correct place at death.

The **Shui Duan New Year Festival** is held at the end of the year according to the Shui calendar, around the 10th lunar month. Festivities are held in Shuipan, Dūjiāng and other villages, and feature fish banquets, drumming and horse racing. The Shui are famous for their bronze drums, many of which were melted down for scrap during the Great Leap Forward.

Jiemao is a singing and courting festival held in the ninth and 10th month of the Shui calendar. It is held in several villages south of Sāndū, including Shuipu and Jiuqian.

SĀNDŪ 三都
☎ 0855

Sāndū is a medium-sized town about 100km west of Róngjiāng, which could be visited on the way back from Róngjiāng to Kǎilǐ. It's the capital of a Shui autonomous prefecture and a major market town. Sāndū itself is fairly uninteresting but can be used as a base to visit surrounding Shui villages such as **Pu'an**, 26km north, or **Shuilong**, 30km south.

If you want to stay the night, try *Gúosúi Zhāodàisuǒ*, just near the bus station or *Xiànzhēngfù Zhaòdàisuǒ* in the town centre.

Sāndū's bus station is little more than a random collection of vehicles loitering at the eastern end of town. Minibuses depart at least every hour for Dānzhài and Duyun. Buses run between Sāndū and Róngjiāng from 6.30am to 9.30am. Failing this, there are also many minibuses east to Xinghua, where you can hop on a connecting bus to Róngjiāng. Early morning and lunchtime buses run between Sāndū and Kǎilǐ, Dushan and Libo.

Northern Guìzhōu

Northern Guìzhōu is seldom visited by foreign travellers other than communist-history buffs heading to the pleasant city of Zūnyì and its abundance of revolutionary sites. Farther north, the remote, scenic area of Chìshuǐ offers natural wonders minus the crowds, and can be visited as you head for the backdoor into southern Sìchuān.

ZŪNYÌ   遵义
☎ 0852 • pop 6.7 million

Around 160km north of Guìyáng, Zūnyì is a pleasant enough city in which to break your journey north. As the site of the famous Zūnyì Conference, the city is also something of a Mecca for those with an interest in Communist Party history.

History

On 16 October 1934, hemmed into the Jiāngxī soviet by Kuomintang forces, the Communists set out on a Herculean, one-year, 9500km Long March from one end of

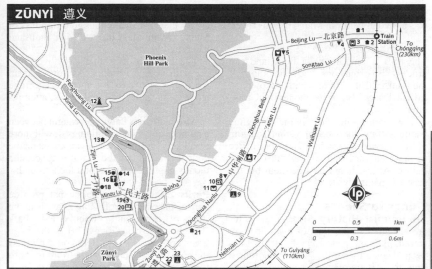

ZŪNYÌ 遵义

PLACES TO STAY
1 Lántiān Bīnguǎn
   蓝天宾馆
2 Jīnhóng Dàjiǔdiàn
   金虹大酒店
13 Zūnyì Bīnguǎn
   遵义宾馆
21 Huáhǎi Dàjiǔdiàn
   华海大酒店

PLACES TO EAT
4 Hotpot &
   Grill Stalls
   火锅烧烤摊
5 Hotpot Restaurants
   火锅餐馆
8 Dōng Dōng Bāo
   东东包
22 Hotpot & Grill
   Restaurants
   火锅烧烤店

OTHER
3 Long-Distance
   Bus Station
   长途汽车站
6 Bar 1950
7 PSB
   公安局
9 Báiyún Sì
   白云寺
10 China Telecom
   Internet Cafe;
   Workers
   Cultural Palace
   网吧、
   工人文化宫
11 China Post
   邮电局
12 Monument to
   the Martyrs of
   the Red Army
   红军烈士纪念碑

14 Red Army
   General Political
   Department
   红军总政治部旧址
15 Residence of
   Bó Gǔ
   博古旧居
16 Catholic Church
   天主教堂
17 State Bank of
   the Red Army
   红军银行
18 Zūnyì
   Conference Site
   遵义会议会址
19 Bank of China
   中国银行
20 Cinema
   电影院
23 Xiāngshān Sì
   湘山寺

China to the other. By mid-December they had reached Guìzhōu and marched on Zūnyì, a prosperous mercantile town. Taking the town by surprise, the Communists were able to stock up on supplies and take a breather. Between 15 and 18 January 1935, the top-level Communist leaders took stock of their situation in the now-famous Zūnyì Conference. Its resolutions largely reflected the views of Mao Zedong, who was elected a full member of the ruling Standing Committee of the Politburo and Chief Assistant to Zhou Enlai in military planning. This was a pivotal factor in Mao's rise to power.

Information

The PSB is on Zhonghua Beilu and can process visa extensions. The main branch of the Bank of China, in the centre of town, on Minzu Lu, will change money and travellers cheques.

The main China Post is on Zhonghua Nanlu. A few doors down, China Telecom offers Internet access in a 2nd-floor office in the courtyard of the Workers Cultural Palace. Access is only Y4 per hour but the server is painfully slow.

Things to See

Communist-History Sites These sites are clustered in the west of town, in a restored, pleasant, pedestrian district that has been cleaned up for the burgeoning tourist industry. All are open 8.30am until 5pm.

The most celebrated site is the **Zūnyì Conference Site** (Zūnyì Huìyì Huìzhǐ) where the famous meeting took place. Open to the public are rooms filled with CCP memorabilia, as well as the meeting rooms and living quarters of the bigwigs. Admission is Y5.

Nearby is the original headquarters of the **Red Army General Political Department** (Hóngjūn Zǒngzhèngzhìbù). In the Catholic Church that has stood here since 1866, Mao Zedong, Zhang Wantian and Zhou Enlai held a meeting of cadres to publicise the resolutions passed at the Zūnyì Conference. It was also here that the Revolutionary Committee of Zūnyì was established – the largest political power set up at county level during the Long March. A couple of rooms are open to the public with displays on the Long March. Admission is Y2.

Across the street are two more sites – the **Residence of Bó Gǔ** and the original home of the **State Bank of the Red Army** (Huìyìqíjiān), today's Bank of China. Entry to these sites is Y2 each.

Temples Up on a hill, south of the revolutionary-history area, **Xiāngshān Sì** is a peaceful place to visit. Built in the 1920s, this temple remains an active place of worship.

In addition to a number of gold buddhas and arhats, there is a marvellous gold **Goddess of Mercy (Avalokitesvara)** with her thousand hands and heads.

The temple is off a small alley overflowing with veggie vendors. As you head up the hill, you'll pass by numerous fortune tellers with their cards and bones, attempting to entice you with a reading.

Also in town is **Báiyún Sì**, caught between a number of concrete buildings. It will more than likely be closed, but if you knock on the door to the left of the main entrance, the monks might let you in for a look around.

Parks Zūnyì has two parks that provide ample space for a stroll. **Zūnyì Park** is in the west of town and **Phoenix Hill Park** (Fènghuáng Shān Gōngyuán) is the huge green area in the north. Here you can't miss the epic soviet-socialist style **Monument to the Martyrs of the Red Army**.

Another interesting spot for a rest is the pedestrian bridge and surrounding square at the southern end of Zhonghua Nanlu. This is where local people come to fly kites, play cards, have their ears cleaned, or float along the river in small duck-shaped boats.

Places to Stay

Next to the bus station is the *Jǐnghóng Dàjiǔdiàn* (☎ 882 2925, ext 30199) – also known as the Zūntiě Dàshà – a friendly place with comfortable and immaculate singles/doubles without bath for Y30/50 or with bath and air-con for Y80/90. Try to get a room at the back where you won't hear the bus and train station noise all night.

Across the street, *Lántiān Bīnguǎn* (☎ 862 2916, ext 9810) might let you stay but you'll only be offered the overpriced doubles with basic bathrooms for Y138.

In the city centre, *Huáhǎi Dàjiǔdiàn* (☎ 883 7660) has singles/doubles with bath for Y100/120 or twins for Y160. The rooms are nice enough but the bathrooms need a good clean. Look for a sign over the hotel's entrance that reads 'Zūnyì Huahai Entertainment Service'.

North of the communist-history area, *Zūnyì Bīnguǎn* (☎ 822 4902, fax 822 1497) is the official three-star, tourist hotel with singles/doubles from Y326/388. Rooms are spacious and comfortable but overpriced.

Places to Eat

There is nothing to rave about in Zūnyì, culinarily speaking. Come dinnertime, Beijing Lu at Waihuan Lu comes alive with *hotpot and grill stalls*. You'll also find similar grills during the day along Zhonghua Nanlu – devoted mainly to meat lovers. The alleys running south-east off Zhonghua Nanlu are crowded with noodle stalls.

If you want to eat indoors, try the *hotpot restaurants* at the western end of Beijing Lu or the *hotpot and grill restaurants* along Neihuan Lu. *Dōng Dōng Bāo* is a popular noodle restaurant on Zhonghua Nanlu (near the pedestrian overpass) that makes delicious rice noodles and dumplings.

Zūnyì Bīnguǎn has more upmarket Chinese and Western restaurants, however these were closed at the time of research.

Entertainment

On Beijing Lu, *Bar 1950* is a pretty close rendition of an American pub with live music, pool tables and muted *Tom & Jerry* cartoons on the TV. With a well stocked bar, it's a great place to enjoy a cocktail – although if you want anything beyond a rum and coke you may have to show the bartender how to make it.

Getting There & Away

Bus Between 7am and about midnight, buses and minibuses zip along the expressway between Guìyáng and Zūnyì. The trip takes 3 hours. You'll find buses at the long-distance bus station in Zūnyì and at the bus stand north of the train station in Guìyáng. Prices vary drastically but you should be able to get a seat in a comfy Aveco van for Y30.

Also from this bus station, sleepers depart for Chìshuǐ (11 hours) at 5pm (Y102) and 7pm (Y89). Despite government plans to link Guìyáng with Chóngqìng and Chéngdū with new expressways, nothing has yet materialised. Consequently, no bus runs to Chéngdū and only one heads to Chóngqìng (Y80) at 4pm – a 10-hour journey that'll

dump you off in the middle of the night. You might be better off on the train.

Train Zūnyì is on the main northern rail line connecting Guìyáng with Chóngqìng, Chéngdū and the rest of China. It can be a pleasant stopover on any of these routes.

Morning trains depart from Guìyáng for Zūnyì (Y10) at 7.07am and noon. From Zūnyì, trains head for Guìyáng at 8.04am and 11.49am, and 8.35pm and 9pm.

A train for Chóngqìng passes through Zūnyì at 3.49pm (Y23) and for Chéngdū at 6.32pm (Y60).

CHÌSHUǏ 赤水

Perched on the border with Sìchuān, the town of Chìshuǐ has more links with the fertile red basin of that province than the rocky limestone plateau of Guìzhōu. It's mainly a stopover on the way to or from southern Sìchuān, but there are some scenic spots nearby. These are rarely visited by foreigners, but are worth the effort to reach them.

The town has some interesting old backstreets near the eastern docks. To get there from the Chìshuǐ Dàjiǔdiàn, walk downhill towards the Chìshuǐ Hé, turn right just before the bridge and continue for about 500m. The river was an important conduit for salt transported from Zigong in Sìchuān to Guìzhōu.

Places to Stay & Eat

Chìshuǐ Dàjiǔdiàn, halfway between the river and the east bus station, is the most convenient place to stay. Carpeted doubles with TV, fan and bathroom are around Y60.

Suǒluó Jiǔdiàn, in the centre of town, isn't as nice or as convenient, but has passable clean doubles with bathroom for a reasonable price and cheap beds in triples. To get there from the east bus station, walk downhill past the Chìshuǐ Dàjiǔdiàn, turn right at the main roundabout, walk up the hill and turn left. There's a decent *restaurant* on the ground floor.

Getting There & Away

The main bus station for destinations in Guìzhōu is in the east of town. Some buses

GUIZHOU

to southern Sìchuān leave from the Sìchuān (west) bank of the Chìshuǐ Hé.

Chìshuǐ is really a long haul from anywhere. Sleeper buses leave for Chìshuǐ from Guìyáng at 2pm and 5pm (Y138, 14 hours) and Zūnyì at 5pm (Y102, 11 hours) and 7pm (Y89). Buses to these cities depart from Chìshuǐ in the late afternoon. If you're heading to Xīngrén or Yíbīn in southern Sìchuān, take a bus to Dagu or Lúzhōu and get off at the road junction at Huaguo (see the Southern Sìchuān section in the Sìchuān chapter for details). Beware that some buses to Lúzhōu do not travel west via Huaguo, but north via Hejiang.

AROUND CHÌSHUI
Sìdònggōu 四洞沟
The lovely, small Four Cave Valley is soaked in a thousand shades of green and studded with four pretty waterfalls. The valley is especially famous for its *Spinulosa* plants *(suōluó)*, huge woody ferns that grow up to 10m with large umbrella-like leaves. The ferns date from the Jurassic period, 200 million years ago, and have been dubbed 'living fossils' or 'the food of dinosaurs'.

Trails lead up both sides of the valley to the waterfalls, so you can walk up one side of the valley and return via the other. You can cover most of the valley in a couple of hours, though intrepid hikers can explore side valleys after the fourth waterfall.

Sìdònggōu is the most accessible of the scenic spots around Chìshuǐ. Buses to Sìdòng (45 minutes) leave Chìshuǐ from a roundabout halfway up the hill, on the way to the bus station. If there aren't any direct

buses, take one to Datong and hitch the remaining 3 or 4km.

Shízhāngdòng Waterfall 十丈洞瀑布
Shízhāngdòng Pùbù
Farther south-east on the Fuxi River, this waterfall is China's second largest after Huángguǒshù. (See that section earlier in this chapter.) At 72m high and 68m wide, Shízhāngdòng is only a metre or so shorter than Huángguǒshù but sees far fewer tourists. This is most likely due to the lack of transport. You may find a bus to Shizhang Village, next to the falls, however you'll more than likely be stuck there overnight and there is no hotel in the vicinity. In summer you might find a tour group to hook up with in Chìshuǐ. Otherwise, your only other option is to travel by taxi; a day's hire is around Y500. Tours from the Railway Travel Service in Guìyáng also go to Shízhāngdòng Waterfall, but with a minimum of 16 people. Admission to the falls is Y30.

Another large cascade, the **Zhongdong Waterfall**, is nearby. Remember that during winter (November to April) water levels at the falls are at their lowest.

Jīnshāgōu Nature Reserve
Jīnshāgōu Zìrán Bǎohùqū
金沙沟自然保护区
This is the third of Chìshuǐ's nature reserves, set up in 1984 to protect a large area of pristine *Spinulosa* forest. There is also a bamboo forest *(zhúhǎi)* nearby. Buses to Jīnshāgōu (Y8) from Chìshuǐ run all day from the east bus station.

Yúnnán

Yúnnán at a Glance

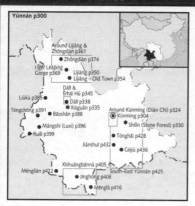

Yúnnán p300

Around Lìjiāng &
Zhōngdiàn p361
● Zhōngdiàn p374
Tiger Leaping
Gorge p369   Lìjiāng p350
● Lìjiāng – Old Town p354
Dàlǐ &
Ěrhǎi Hú p345
Liùkù p385 ●   ● Dàlǐ p338
● Xiàguān p335
Téngchōng p391 ● Bǎoshān p388   Around Kūnmíng (Diān Chí) p324
◉ Kūnmíng p304
● Mángshì (Luxi) p396   Shílín (Stone Forest) p330
Ruìlì p399 ●   ● Tōnghǎi p428
Jiànshuǐ p432 ● ● Gèjiù p436
Xīshuāngbǎnnà p405
South-East Yúnnán p425
Ménglián p422 ●   ● Jǐnghóng p408
● Měnglà p416

Area: 394,000 sq km

Population: 40.4 million

Capital: Kūnmíng

Highlights

- Kūnmíng, a modern city with great food and good sights

- Lìjiāng's old town, the narrow stone streets give a fascinating glimpse into Nàxī culture and history

- Tiger Leaping Gorge, a short trek amid dramatic cliffs and waterfalls

- Dàlǐ, one of China's best places to kick back and relax in the midst of wooden buildings and flagstone streets

- Téngchōng, a quaint town with nearby hot springs, Lisu minority villages and dormant volcanoes

- Ruìlì, a sometime wild border town surrounded by plenty of Dǎi temples, minority villages and Burmese jade sellers

- Jiànshuǐ, home to an abundance of traditional architecture

- Xīshuāngbǎnnà, a taste of tropical South-East Asia and home to the Dǎi people

- Déqīn, self-proclaimed 'Shangri La', the next best thing to Tibet

Yúnnán is without doubt one of the most alluring destinations in China. It's the most varied of all China's provinces, with terrain ranging from tropical rainforest to snow-capped peaks and peoples ranging from Thai to Tibetan. It is also the sixth-largest province and home to a third of China's ethnic minorities (nearly 50% of the province is non-Han) and half of China's plant and animal species. If you could only go to one province, this one might well be it. The province has nearly three quarters of a million foreign tourists annually and lists a collective of hotels, travel agencies, and parks as its first offering on the Hong Kong stock exchange.

Yúnnán is well known for its mild climate year-round – its name means 'South of the Clouds'. The provincial capital, Kūnmíng, is similarly referred to as the 'Spring City'.

Despite the best government efforts, numerous pockets of the province have resisted Chinese influence and exhibit strong local identities. Even Kūnmíng has a flavour all its own, though this individual identity is in danger of being quashed by rapid economic growth.

Nicknames are attached to everything in China, and Yúnnán boasts more than it's fair share. Since the province contains the nation's greatest diversity of flora and fauna – including 2500 varieties of wild flowers and plants – it has been given nicknames like 'Kingdom of Plants', 'Garden of Heavenly Marvellous Flowers', and 'Hometown of Perfume'. Officials are less thrilled with the new tag: 'Treasure House of Crude Drugs'.

HISTORY

In the 1960s scientists rocked the anthropological world when they determined that fragments of human-like teeth discovered by railway engineers in Yuánmóu, north-west of Kūnmíng, belonged to hominids who lived 1.75 million to 2.5 million years ago. This and further discoveries proved what was once considered a wild, isolated region was habited before any other in China.

Yúnnán's other great anthropological discovery was of sophisticated Bronze Age cultures around Lake Dian. First discovered in the 1950s, excavations throughout south-east Yúnnán are filling gaps in a previously unknown period of the province.

It wasn't until the Warring States Period (453–221 BC) that the rest of China became interested in the frontiers. Armies invaded twice before Chu general Zhuang Qiao put himself into power as the emperor of the Dian kingdom near Kūnmíng. Though regular contact with the rest of China was still a long way off, it was Zhuang who facilitated eventual expansion and the first large-scale migration.

Qin dynasty emperor Qin Shihuang extended a road from Sìchuān to Qūjìng in north-east Yúnnán and established the first 'jun' (prefecture). As the Qin dynasty ceded to the Han dynasty, western Yúnnán was organised within prefectures and the famed Southern Silk Route into Burma and India was established. Meanwhile, Yúnnán was occupied by large numbers of non-Chinese aboriginal people. They lacked good political organisation and their chieftains either obeyed or ignored the emperor

Festivals in Yúnnán

festival	location	lunar calendar	2002	2003	2004
Water-Splashing Festival	Jǐnghóng, Xīshuāngbǎnnà	(13–15 April fixed in Western calendar)			
Sanyuesan	Western Hills, Kūnmíng	3rd of 3rd	15 April	4 April	21 April
Fertility Festival	Lìjiāng	13th of 3rd	25 April	14 April	1 May
Third Moon Fair	Dàlǐ	15th 21st of 3rd	27 April–May 3	16–22 April	3–9 May
Guanyin Pavilion Festival	Dàlǐ	19th of 3rd	1 May	20 April	7 May
Raosanling	Dàlǐ	23rd–25th of 4th	3-5 June	23-25 May	10-12 June
Guanyin Pavilion Festival	Dàlǐ	19th of 6th	28 July	18 July	4 August
Torch Festival	Shílín, Dàlǐ, Lìjiāng, Chǔxióng	24th of 6th	2 August	23 July	9 August
Guanyin Pavilion Festival	Dàlǐ	19th of 9th	24 October	14 October	1 November

NB *Festival dates are subject to change – check before you head off for one.*

In the Three Kingdoms period (AD 220–280), a kingdom including parts of Sìchuān was formed when a rebellion by Yúnnán's up and coming elite was put down. From this time and throughout the Western Jin period (AD 265–316), Yúnnán crept ever closer to consolidation, and came under the jurisdiction of some sort of Chinese control.

The power base of Yúnnán also shifted slowly – first eastward to Qūjìng, then westward. By the 7th century AD the Bai people had established a powerful kingdom, the Nánzhāo, south of Dàlǐ. Initially allied with the Chinese against the Tibetans, this kingdom extended its power until, in the middle of the 8th century, it was able to challenge and defeat the Tang armies. It took control of a large slice of the south-west and established itself as a fully independent entity, dominating trade routes from China to India and Burma.

The Nánzhāo kingdom fell in the 10th century and was replaced by the kingdom of Dàlǐ, an independent state overrun by Kublai Khan and the Mongols in the mid-13th century. Kublai's armies also brought in many of South-West China's Muslims, who were warriors from Central Asia.

The Ming dynasty purged the Mongols but Yúnnán resisted capitulation to the emperor's armies. Finally, after 15 centuries of resistance to northern rule, the Qing emperor cowed enough local power-brokers into submission to gain a modicum of control. In 1658 this part of the South-West was finally integrated into the empire as the province of Yúnnán.

Even so it remained an isolated frontier region, with scattered Chinese garrisons and settlements in the valleys and basins, a mixed aboriginal population occupying the highlands, and various Dǎi (Thai) and other minorities along the Láncāng Jiang (Mekong River). Like the rest of the South-West, Yúnnán was always one of the first regions to break with the northern government. During China's countless political purges, fallen officials often found themselves exiled here, which added to the province's rebellious character.

Right up to the 20th century, Yúnnán looked as much to its neighbours Indochina

Suggested Itineraries

These four regions could be done in a week each; if you plan to leapfrog all the way to Déqīn after Dàlǐ, plan on two weeks minimum. To see everything with a sense of justice, plan six weeks, minimum.

North-West

This is the area that lures most travellers – its visitor numbers are second only to Xīshuāngbǎnnà. Don't get mired in Dàlǐ as most travellers do, since **Lìjiāng's Old Town** is just as good and puts you closer to the Tibetan-heavy regions of **Zhōngdiàn** and **Déqīn**. There are lots of side trips from Lìjiāng and Zhōngdiàn so even two weeks is pushing it for this trip.

Bǎoshān-Déhóng Regions

Starting from **Kūnmíng**, the road to Ruìlì in Déhóng is improving but still laborious; consider a day of rest in **Dàlǐ** and a flight back to Kūnmíng from Mángshì. If you've only got a week, after Dàlǐ, bypass Bǎoshān and head for **Téngchōng**, home of old architecture, volcanoes and gorgeous **Lisu villages** peppering the countryside. After that, go directly to **Ruìlì** for a couple of days of heady border life. If you want to add the remote **Nùjiāng Valley** you'll need an extra week.

Xīshuāngbǎnnà

Yúnnán's version of tropical rainforest is always a favourite. Transport has dramatically improved so you can now easily fly to **Jǐnghóng**, and the once awful bus ride is a manageable 16 hours in a luxury coach. A week gives you enough time to cycle to **Gǎnlǎnbà** and nearby villages, visit a local market in **Xīdìng** or **Měnghùn**, see the **Tropical Botanic Plant Gardens** in **Měnglún**, and take one long-ish bus ride north-west to **Měnglián**.

South-East

From Xīshuāngbǎnná take a long bus ride over to **Gèjiù** and from there take a week to head back up to Kūnmíng. Alternatively, make a week-long loop from Kūnmíng, taking in **Tōnghǎi**, **Jiànshuǐ**

and Burma, as it did to the Chinese emperor. Wracked by ethnic disturbances, including the bloody 1855 Muslim uprising and even bloodier Chinese army put-down, Yúnnán was exploited by local warlords, European powers along the border, and the emperor. It was the death of China, at least in the east, with the arrival of Japanese forces in 1937 that was to ironically augur a better future for Yúnnán. Strategically located away from Japan's forces in the east, the province was used to shuttle material for the allied war machine. Later, the Red Army would be welcomed by a peasantry that felt it had been ignored long enough.

Today, Yúnnán province looks firmly back in the Chinese fold. It is a province of 40 million people, including a veritable constellation of minorities (25 registered): the Zhuang, Huí, Yi, Miáo, Tibetans, Mongols, Yao, Bai, Hani, Dǎi, Lisu, Lahu, Wa, Nàxī, Jingpo, Bulang, Pumi, Nu, Achang, Bulang, Jinuo and Drung. These groups make up more than a third of the population, but they occupy two-thirds of the land.

CLIMATE

Though Guǎngdōng's southernmost peninsular juts a bit farther south than Yúnnán's own border with Laos, to most, Yúnnán is the real 'south' China. The Xīshuāngbǎnnà borderline with Laos lies on the 21° latitude – meaning steamy subtropics. Factor in the stunning range of geomorphology – 76.4m above sea level in Hékǒu to 6740m in the Tibetan plateau with an average of 2000m – and Yúnnán is a nearly perfect getaway weatherwise, year-round.

The official classification as 'subtropical highland monsoon' really translates as

and **Gèjiù**, or go there en route to Vietnam. You'll find a large enclave of **Mongols**, one of South-West China's grandest hill climbs, and one of its most intact traditional towns (Jiànshuǐ).

With a couple of extra days you could take in the stunning rice terraces of **Yuányáng**, a four-hour drive south of Jiànshuǐ.

Combinations

You could cover Dàlǐ and Lìjiāng and then meander south-west to Ruìlì in the Déhóng region in two to three weeks. You could also combine the Déhóng and/or Bǎoshān regions with Xīshuāngbǎnnà for a two or more week trip, though the bus ride between either Ruìlì or Bǎoshān and Jǐnghóng can be miserable.

You could do an all-Yúnnán extravaganza in a month but you'd certainly be rushing it and one or two flights would be required. Six weeks would be better. Assuming you fly into Kūnmíng – another place nobody gives enough time – the most obvious route is to take a bus immediately to Dàlǐ, Lìjiāng and Zhōngdiàn in north-west Yúnnán, then on to the Bǎoshān and Déhóng regions, an epic journey to Xīshuāngbǎnnà (stopping in Mènglián along the way), and from there to Kūnmíng. This would probably put you off long-distance buses for a long, long time.

Instead of this painful experience, from Lìjiāng or Dàlǐ you could take the useful direct flight to Xīshuāngbǎnnà.

If possible add a visit to under-appreciated Téngchōng before the provincial authorities knock it all down. Plan to be enchanted by Ruìlì and hang out in the surrounding countryside. Head to Déqīn, north-west of Zhōngdiàn, before Shangri La gets run over by tour groups. The south-east is quicker; every city's great but you could do each pretty much in a full day. And don't forget to give Kūnmíng a couple of days.

If you are headed up to Sìchuān, most people bus from Lìjiāng to Jǐnjiāng and catch a train there. Alternatively, take the high back road from Zhōngdiàn to Kāngdìng via the wild Tibetan lands of western Sìchuān.

dozens of microclimates. In the grip of summer you'll freeze your tail off in the north, and in the midst of winter you can get by with a light coat within a 12-hour ride south of Kūnmíng. Kūnmíng, the capital, seemingly lacks 'weather', its mean temperature never fluctuates more than 10°C throughout the year.

FLORA & FAUNA

Hands down, Yúnnán is China's treasure-trove of plants and animals. Yúnnán's timber reserves account for 10% of China's total, over a billion cubic metres of wood. Eighteen-thousand species of higher plants inhabit the province, well over half of China's total. There are 2500 species of ornamental plants, particularly flowers and herbs. In one Yúnnán mountain range over half of China's azalea species can be found.

The province's eight key flowers – camellia, azalea, primrose, *Gentiana scabra*, lily, magnolia, orchid and *Meconopsis integrifolia* – are prized throughout the world.

Half of China's 1700 fauna species are found in Yúnnán and 80 of the country's endangered species are found only in Yúnnán.

KŪNMÍNG 昆明

☎ 0871 • pop 3,838,200

While Kūnmíng and its surrounding districts boast several interesting sights, they pale in comparison with some of Yúnnán's jewels – Lìjiāng or Xīshuāngbǎnnà for example. But the city is still a fine place to wander around, once you get off the wide boulevards.

Unfortunately Kūnmíng's charm is under threat. The city has been treated to a ruthless face-lift, much of it thrown up for 1999's International Horticultural Expo. This means

KŪNMÍNG 昆明

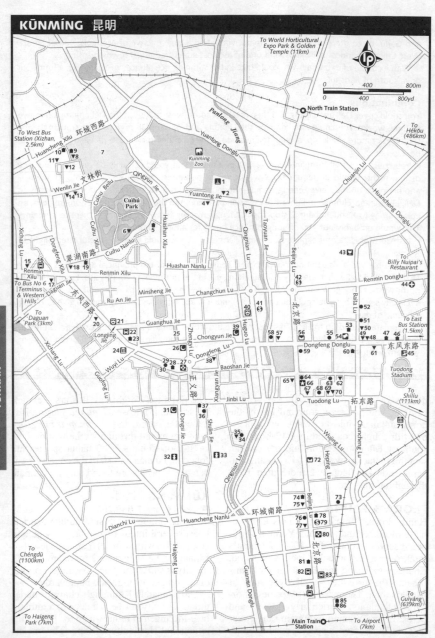

To World Horticultural
Expo Park & Golden
Temple (11km)

Panlong Jiang

North Train Station

Yuantong Donglu

环城西路 Huancheng Xilu

To West Bus
Station (Xizhan,
2.5km)

Huancheng Xilu

10 ▲9
▼8
11▼ ▼12

7

文林街 Wenlin Jie

14▼13

Kunming
Zoo

▣1

Yuantong Jie
4▼ ▼2

Qingyun Jie

Taoyuan Jie

Qingnian Lu

▼3

Cuihu Beilu

Cuihú
Park

6▼ ⬤5

Huashan Xilu

Cuihu Nanlu

43 ▣

To Billy Nuipai's
Restaurant

Cuihu Xilu

Dongfeng Xilu

Xichang Lu

15 16
⬤
Renmin
Xilu
To Bus No 6
Terminus
& Western
Hills

翠湖南路 Cuihu Nanlu

▼18 19

Renmin Xilu

Huashan Nanlu

42 ⊗

Renmin Donglu

44 ✚

To
Daguan
Park (3km)

17⬤

Daguan Jie 大观西路

Ru An Jie

Minsheng Jie

Changchun Lu

Batai Lu

To East
Bus Station
(1.5km)

20▼ ▣21

Guanghua Jie

41 ⊗
40 ▣

52 ⬤

47 46
45 ▣

东风东路 Dongfeng Donglu

Longjing
Jie

⬤22
▼23

25

Chongyun Jie

39 ▣

Huguo Lu

53
50

51 ⬤
54 ⬤

49
48

Zhengyi Lu

58 ▼57
56

55 ⬤

61

Tuodong
Stadium

24 ▣

26 ▣

Dongfeng Lu

59 ⬤

Dongfeng Donglu

60 ▣

To
Shíliú
(111km)

Wuyi Lu

29▲28 27
30▼

38▼

Baoshan Jie

正义路 Zhengyi Lu

Xiangyun Jie

Jinbi Lu

65 ▼64
66
67 ▼68
62
63
70

Tuodong Lu

拓东路 Tuodong Lu

Guolong Lu

31 ▣

37
36

Dongsi Jie

Shulin Jie

71 ▣

35▼
34

32 ▣

▣33

Qingnian Lu

72 ▣

Heping Lu

Chuncheng Lu

74 ▼
75▼

73 ⬤

Dianchi Lu

Huancheng Nanlu

环城南路 Huancheng Nanlu

76 ▣
77▼

78
⬤79

80 ▣

北京路 Beijing Lu

Haigeng Lu

To
Chéngdū
(1100km)

Guannan Donglu

81 ⬤
82 ▣ ▣83

84 ▣

To
Guìyáng
(639km)

To Haigeng
Park (7km)

Main Train
Station

To Airport
(7km)

85
86 ▣

Chuanjin Lu

环城东路 Huancheng Donglu

To
Hékǒu
(486km)

0   400   800m
0   400   800yd

KŪNMÍNG

PLACES TO STAY
5 Green Lake Hotel
翠湖宾馆
9 Yúndà Bīnguǎn
云大宾馆
10 Yúndà Zhāodàisuǒ
云大招待所
19 Kūnmíng Harbour
Plaza
昆明海逸酒店
23 Yúnnán Fàndiàn
云南饭店
28 Chūnchéng Jiǔlóu
春城酒楼
37 The Hump
驼峰客栈
46 Báiyún Dàjiǔdiàn
白云大酒店
47 Camellia Hotel;
Lao Consulate;
Myanmar Consulate
茶花宾馆;
老挝领事馆;
缅甸领事馆
53 Kūnmíng Hotel
樱花酒楼
60 Holiday Inn Kūnmíng;
Charlie's Bar
樱花假日酒店
74 Kūnhú Fàndiàn
昆湖饭店
78 Golden Dragon
Hotel
金龙饭店
81 King World Hotel
锦华大酒店
85 Kūnmíng Railway
Building
昆明铁路旅行社

PLACES TO EAT
2 New World Over the
Bridge Noodle
Restaurant
新世界过桥城
3 The Brothers Jiang
江氏兄弟
4 Yùquánzhāi
Vegetarian
Restaurant
玉泉斋

6 Lǎozhīqīng Shíguǎn
老知青食馆
8 Journey to the
East Cafe
往东方旅行
11 Travellers Home Cafe
12 French Cafe
兰白红
13 Teresa's Pizzeria;
Dove Email
信鸽
14 Paul's;
Face to Face Bar
堡利、面对面
15 Měngzì
Across-the-Bridge
Noodles Restaurant
蒙自过桥米线
17 Yúnnán Fēngwèi
Kuàicān
云南风味快餐
18 Bluebird Cafe
青鸟
20 Bluebird Cafe
青鸟
30 Muslim Restaurants
清真饭店
35 1910 La Gare Du Sud
火车南站
38 Běijīng Fàndiàn
北京饭店
48 City Cafe
厦门陈氏小吃
49 Zhènxīng Fàndiàn
振兴饭店
50 Mǎ Mǎ Fū's 2
马马付
57 The Brothers Jiang;
Orient Cafe
江氏兄弟
61 Cooking School
学厨饭店
62 Báitǎ Dǎi Flavour
Restaurant;
Dōngběi Jiǎozidiàn
白塔傣味餐厅；
东北饺子店
65 Měngzì
Across-the-Bridge
Noodles Restaurant
蒙自过桥米线

67 King Dragon
Food Village
元龙风味城
69 Yuèlái Píjiǔguǎn
悦来啤酒馆
70 Wei's Pizzeria
哈哈餐厅
75 Lìlái Restaurant;
Happy Cafe;
Mr Balls
利来啤酒馆、
快乐餐厅
77 Dicos
得卡斯

ENTERTAINMENT
21 Arts Theatre
艺术剧院
34 Upriver Club
上河会馆
40 Kūnmíng
Theatre
昆明剧院
43 Camel Bar
骆驼酒吧

THINGS TO SEE
1 Yuántōng Sì
圆通寺
24 Yúnnán Provincial
Museum
云南省博物馆
25 Flower & Bird
Market
花鸟市场
26 Nánchéng
Mosque
南城清真古寺
31 Mosque
清真寺
32 West Pagoda
西寺塔
33 East Pagoda
东寺塔
39 Mosque
清真寺
63 Flower Market
尚义花鸟市场
71 Kūnmíng City
Museum
昆明市博物馆

continued over

YÚNNÁN

KŪNMÍNG

TRANSPORT

16 Xiǎoxīmén
     Bus Station
     小西门汽车客运站

22 Buses to
     Western Hills &
     Bamboo Temple
     往西山、筇竹寺的车

29 Kunming United
     Airlines
     昆明联合航空公司

55 Shanghai
     Airlines
     上海航空公司

59 China Southern
     Airlines
     西南航空公司

68 Yunnan
     Airlines/CAAC
     云南航空公司、
     中国民航

76 China Southwest
     Airlines
     西南航空公司

82 Long Distance
     Bus Station
     长途汽车总站

83 Bus Station
     客运站

84 Sleeper Bus Stand
     卧铺汽车站

86 Train Ticket
     Office
     火车站售票处

OTHER

7   Yúnnán University
     云南大学

27 Kūnmíng
     Department Store
     昆明百货大楼

36 Foreign Languages
     Bookstore
     外文书店

41 Bank of China
     中国银行

42 Bank of China
     (Main Branch)
     中国银行

44 Yán'ān Hospital
     延安医院

45 Tuòdōng
     Swimming Pool
     拓东游泳池

51 Postar Outdoor &
     Equipment Collection

52 Manchester United
     Shop
     球迷用品

54 Royal Thai Consulate
     泰王国总领事馆

56 Post Office;
     Telecom Business
     Centre
     邮电电信营业厅

58 Climber Outdoors
     攀登者

64 Tiēn Fú
     Famous Teas
     天福茗茶

66 PSB
     公安局

72 International Post
     Office
     国际邮局

73 CITS
     中国国际旅行社

79 Bank of China
     中国银行

80 Kai Wah Plaza
     International

the quaint back alleyways lined with fascinating wooden buildings are rapidly disappearing. In a country possessed by the spirit of modernisation even the locals have criticised the overzealous knocking down of anything not constructed of steel. There are enough pockets to still make it worth getting lost in the backstreets, but the last remnants of old Kūnmíng will probably soon succumb to the demolition ball.

For now, the city remains an interesting place to linger for a few days. There is great food, and the streets are vibrant with shoppers, peddlers, roadside masseurs and karaoke stalls.

Kūnmíng's total population is around 3.5 million, though only about a million inhabit the urban area. At most, minorities account for 6% of Kūnmíng's population, although the farming areas are home to some Yi, Huí and Miáo groups. There are also Vietnamese refugees-turned-immigrants who fled the Sino-Vietnamese border clashes

that started in 1977. It's an enormous municipality at some 6100 sq km.

The city is surrounded on three sides by the mountain ranges of the Yúnnán-Guìzhōu Plateau; Lake Dian lies to the south. At an elevation of 1891m, Kūnmíng has a mild climate and can be visited at any time of year. Light clothes will usually be adequate, but bring some woollies during the winter months, when temperatures can suddenly drop, particularly in the evenings. There have even been light snowfalls here in recent winters. There's a fairly even spread of temperatures from April to September. Winters are short, sunny and dry. In summer (June to August) Kūnmíng offers cool respite, although rain is more prevalent.

History

The region of Kūnmíng has been inhabited for around 2000 years, though nearby areas have been populated for millions of years. The tomb excavations around Lake Dian, particularly at Shizhai Shān near Jìníng on the southern shore, have unearthed thousands of artefacts from the Bronze Age – weapons, drums, paintings, and silver, jade and turquoise jewellery – that suggest a well-developed culture and provide clues to a very sketchy early history of the city.

During the Warring States period the kingdom of Dian was established close to present-day Kūnmíng. The first Chinese prefecture, the Yizhou Jun, was set up in Kūnmíng in 109 BC during the Western Han dynasty. Until the 8th century the town was a remote Chinese outpost, but the kingdom of Nánzhāo, centred to the north-west of Kūnmíng at Dàlǐ, captured it and made it their second capital.

In 1274 the Mongols came through, sweeping all before them. Marco Polo gives us a fascinating picture of Kūnmíng's commerce in the late 13th century:

At the end of these five days journeys you arrive at the capital city, which is named Yachi, and is very great and noble. In it are found merchants and artisans, with a mixed population, consisting of idolaters, Nestorian Christians and Saracens or Mohametans...The land is fertile in rice and wheat...For money they employ the white porcelain shell, found in the sea, and which they also wear as ornaments about their necks. Eighty of the shells are equal in value to...two Venetian groats. In this country also there are salt springs...the duty levied on this salt produces large revenues to the Emperor. The natives do not consider it an injury done to them when others have connection with their wives, provided the act is voluntary on the woman's part. Here there is a lake almost a hundred miles in circuit, in which great quantities of fish are caught. The people are accustomed to eat the raw flesh of fowls, sheep, oxen and buffalo...the poorer sorts only dip it in a sauce of garlic...they eat it as well as we do the cooked.

In the 14th century the Ming set up shop in Yunnanfu, as Kūnmíng was then known, building a walled town on the present site. From the 17th century onwards, the history of the city becomes rather grisly. The last Ming resistance to the invading Manchu took place in Yúnnán in the 1650s and was crushed by General Wu Sangui. Wu in turn rebelled against the king and held out until his death in 1678. His successor was overthrown by the Manchu emperor Kangxi and killed himself in Kūnmíng in 1681.

In the 19th century, the city suffered several blood baths, as the rebel Muslim leader Du Wenxiu, the Sultan of Dàlǐ, attacked and besieged the city several times between 1858 and 1868. It was not until 1873 that the rebellion was finally and bloodily crushed.

The intrusion of the West into Kūnmíng began in the middle of the 19th century and by 1900 Kūnmíng, Hékǒu, Sīmáo and Měngzì had been opened to foreign trade. The French were keen on exploiting the region's copper, tin and timber resources, and in 1910 their Indochina railway, started in 1898 at Hanoi, reached the city.

Kūnmíng's expansion began with WWII, when factories were established here and refugees fleeing the Japanese poured in from eastern China. In a bid to keep China from falling to Japan, Anglo-American forces sent supplies to Nationalist troops entrenched in Sìchuān and Yúnnán. Supplies came overland on a dirt road carved out of the mountains in 1937–38 by 160,000 Chinese with virtually no equipment. This was the famous Burma Road, a 1000km haul from Lashio to Kūnmíng. Today, the western extension of Kūnmíng's Renmin Lu, leading in the direction of Heilinpu, is the tail end of the road. For more on the Burma Road, see the boxed text later in this chapter.

In early 1942 the Japanese captured Lashio, cutting the supply line. Kūnmíng continued to handle most of the incoming aid during 1942–45 when US planes flew the dangerous mission of crossing the 'Hump', the towering 5000m mountain ranges between India and Yúnnán. A black market sprang up and medicines, canned food, petrol and other goods intended for the military and relief agencies were siphoned off.

The face of Kūnmíng has been radically altered since then, with streets widened and office buildings and housing projects flung up. With the coming of the railways, industry has expanded rapidly, and a surprising range of goods and machinery now bears a 'Made in Yúnnán' stamp. The city's exports include steel, foodstuffs, trucks, machine tools, electrical equipment, textiles, chemicals, building materials and plastics.

Orientation

The jurisdiction of Kūnmíng includes four city districts and eight rural counties, which supply the city with fruit and vegetables. The centre of the city is the traffic circle at the intersection of Zhengyi Lu and Dongfeng Lu. Surprisingly, you can still find a few rows of old wooden houses in nearby neighbourhoods.

To the south-west of the intersection, down to Jinbi Lu, there are some interesting old alleys and great places to eat. Sadly, tree-lined and funky old Jinbi Lu, the last large-scale bastion of old architecture in Kūnmíng, fell to the wrecking ball in October 1997.

To the north of the intersection is Cuìhú Park, a pleasant place for a wander, Yuántōng Sì and the Kunming Zoo. East of the intersection is Kūnmíng's major north-south road, Beijing Lu. At the southern end is the main train station, the long-distance bus station and the Kūnhú Fàndiàn, one of the few cheap places to stay in Kūnmíng. At about the halfway point, Beijing Lu is intersected by Dongfeng Donglu, where the luxurious Kunming Hotel and Holiday Inn Kunming can be found.

Maps Shop around as there are many varieties of maps, some with a smattering of English names. The *Kunming Tourist Map* has street and hotel names in English and shows bus lines, while the *Yunnan Communications and Tourist Map* has the names of nearly every town in the province written out in English.

Information

Tourist Offices There is a Kunming Tourist Information office opposite the main train station. Kūnmíng has a 'Tourist Complaint and Consultative' telephone number at ☎ 316 4961.

Consulates Thailand, Laos and Myanmar (Burma) now all have visa-issuing consulates in Kūnmíng – but (sigh) still not Vietnam. The following visa details were current at the time of writing but visa regulations change frequently.

Laos The Lao consulate (☎ 317 6624, 669 2751) is in room 120 on the ground floor of the main building of the Camellia Hotel. Standard 15-day tourist visas are issued in three working days or you can pay a surcharge for an express 24-hours service. Seven- and 15-day visas cost the same. Fifteen/30 day visas cost Y320/440 for Germans and Americans, and Y270/400 for most Western European countries and Australians. You must bring one photo. Neither visa can be extended and you currently cannot get a Lao visa at the border. Note that Lao visa regulations change frequently. Office hours are Monday to Friday, 8.30am to 11.30am and 2.30pm to 4.30pm.

Myanmar The office (☎ 317 6609, fax 317 6309) is on the 3rd floor of Building No 3 of the Camellia Hotel. The consulate can grant you a four-week visa in three days for Y185, in 12 hours for Y235 or in three hours for Y285. You must enter Myanmar within four weeks of getting the visa. There are two catches: you must change US$300 into Myanmar kyat at the government's scandalously low rate; and the visas are not good for land crossings: you are supposed to fly in via Yangon (Rangoon) only. The consulate is open Monday to Friday 8.30am to noon and 1pm to 4.30pm.

Thailand The Thai consulate (☎ 316 2033, ext 62105), on the ground floor of the building next to the Kunming Hotel, can arrange 60-day visas for Y110 generally by the next day. Travellers from most countries won't need a visa unless they plan to spend more than 30 days in Thailand. Office hours are weekdays 9am to 1.30pm, closed all Chinese and Thai holidays.

Money The main Bank of China is at 448 Renmin Donglu. Other branches with a foreign-exchange counter are on Beijing Lu near the Golden Dragon Hotel and on Qingnian Lu. Most branches are open weekdays 9am to noon and 2pm to 5.30pm. All the main hotels, including the Camellia and Kūnhú hotels, have foreign-exchange counters, but may offer lower rates than the banks.

There are still one or two hopeful moneychangers in front of the Kunming Hotel, but beware of rip-offs, which occur frequently by sleight of hand.

Post & Communications There is an international post office on the east side of Beijing Lu, halfway between Tuodong Lu and Huancheng Nanlu. It has a very efficient poste restante and parcel service. Every poste restante letter or parcel is listed in a ledger that's kept on the counter. To claim a letter, you must show your passport or ID. Usually, at least one of the clerks speaks English. This is also the city's Express Mail Service (EMS) and Western Union agent. You can also make telephone calls here

There is another China Post and China Telecom office to the north of this one, at the intersection of Beijing Lu with Dongfeng Donglu. The postal service hours here are 8am to 8pm, the telecommunication service from 8am to 5pm.

Email & Internet Access The Telecom Business Centre on the corner of Beijing Lu and Dongfeng Donglu has fast hookups and cheap rates – Y10 per hour. You'll need to hand over a Y20 refundable deposit before you get connected. Printing costs five máo an A4 page. The centre is open weekdays 8am to 6.30pm and weekends 9am to 5pm.

Most cafes frequented by travellers also offer email, although at slightly higher rates. A couple of cheaper places include The Hump (see Places to Stay) and Dove Email, near Yúnnán University, at 47 Wenlin Jie. Both charge Y4 per hour.

Travel Agencies China International Travel Service (CITS; ☎ 314 8308) is just east of Beijing Lu in a large white-tiled building at 220 Huancheng Nanlu. Like CITS offices elsewhere in China, it concentrates on group tours and is not able to offer much to individual travellers.

Better for independent travellers would be CITS' new Family & Independent Traveller (FIT) office (☎ 313 8888, 313 3104) adjoining the King World Hotel on Beijing Lu.

Mr Chen, formerly of Chéngdū, recently moved to the Camellia Hotel and now arranges flight tickets from Zhōngdiàn to Lhasa along with the requisite Tibet Tourism Bureau (TTB) permit and three day 'tour' in Lhasa. Prices are currently around Y2000 to Y2500 for the package (the ticket is Y1250) but prices and tour requirements change regularly. Moreover, several budget travel agencies in Kūnmíng and Lījiāng are planning to offer the fascinating ten-day overland trip from Yúnnán into Tibet. Nothing had been established at the time of research but you can expect this to become a popular option over time. See Lonely Planet's *Tibet* guide for details.

PSB The Foreign Affairs Branch of the Public Security Bureau (PSB; ☎ 313 0139) on Beijing Lu is open weekdays 8am to 11.30am and 1pm to 5.30pm (4.30pm Friday). Duty officers speak English, and are quite friendly. While they will happily reply '*dōu kěyǐ*' ('everywhere is OK') when asked about open areas, when pressed further they will roll their eyes, groan, and tell you those rumours of the road to Tibet from Yúnnán opening up have been greatly exaggerated.

First visa extensions are pretty straightforward, but you'll probably need a good reason for a second extension. A one-month extension costs Y320 for Brits and the French, Y250 for Americans, Y200 for Australians and Y310 for Canadians.

Medical Services The Yán'ān Hospital (Yán'ān Yīyuàn) on Renmin Donglu has a foreigners' clinic (☎ 317 7499, ext 311) on the 1st floor of Building No 6, at the back of the compound.

Dangers & Annoyances Kūnmíng is one of the safest cities in China but take extra special precaution near the train and long-distance bus stations. Seemingly, every day someone has a bag razored or pilfered in the train station or on a Dàlǐ-bound bus.

Tang Dynasty Pagodas 大理国古幢

To the south of Jinbi Lu are two Tang pagodas, of which the **West Pagoda** (Xīsì Tǎ) is more interesting. The **East Pagoda** (Dōngsì Tǎ) was, according to Chinese sources, destroyed by an earthquake; Western sources say it was destroyed by the Muslim revolt. It was rebuilt in the 19th century, but there's little to see.

The West Pagoda is on Dongsi Jie, a bustling market street – you'll probably have to walk your bicycle through the crowds. Its compound is a popular spot for old people to drink tea and play cards and mahjong. You can even get a haircut and shave at the base of the pagoda. It's not a bad stop to catch your breath and sip a cup of tea. The temple is open 9am to 9pm and admission is Y2.

Yúnnán Provincial Museum 云南省博物馆 Yúnnán Shěng Bówùguǎn

This museum, on Wuyi Lu, has three exhibition halls covering the province's ancient bronzes, Buddhist art and ethnic minorities.

The first hall is the **Bronze Drums Hall**, which has a collection of artefacts from tomb excavations at Jìnníng (Lake Dian), Wanjiaba (Chǔxióng) and Lijiashan (near Jiāngchuān). The drums themselves date from the Warring States period and Western Han periods and are superb. Of 1600 such drums known to exist in the world, China has 1400 and Yúnnán 400 itself, most unearthed at Shizhai Shān near Lake Dian. The ancient drums are brought into a modern context by their continued use amongst minorities such as the Yi. For more on Yúnnán's bronze drums see the Art section in the Facts about South-West China chapter.

The **Ancient Buddhist Art Hall** has examples of the art at Shíbǎoshān, near Dàlǐ, and the murals of Báishā outside Lìjiāng, which are useful if you are thinking of visiting either site.

The **Minority Nationality Hall** mostly consists of photos and fairly tacky shop mannequins (some with blond hair!) dressed in minority clothes, with examples of embroidery, bags and hats. It gives an idea of Yúnnán's ethnic diversity but you are better off going to Kūnmíng's Nationality Museum (see Around Kūnmíng section further on).

The museum is open Tuesday to Sunday 9am to 5pm and entry is Y5. Bus No 5 goes here from the Camellia Hotel.

Kunming City Museum 昆明市博物馆 Kūnmíngshì Bówùguǎn

Located along Tuodong Lu, opposite the sports stadium, this museum is worth a trip if you've exhausted all other Kūnmíng options. The first room, a chilly examination of Lake Dian region Bronze Age artefacts, is the best since it has glorious English captions.

The English has disappeared by the next room, a fascinating look at modern Kūnmíng. 'Development' is the theme here, and there are even displays of store shelves, a karaoke machine, and an enormous scale model of the city. The next room traces Kūnmíng's history from early hominids through liberation but it's pretty difficult to understand anything. The incomplete 2nd floor palaeontology display is a surprise – it includes very large model skeletons of dinosaurs, including, I kid you not, *Yúnnánosaurus robustus*, complete with rib and tail bones wrapped in tinsel.

The museum is open Wednesday to Sunday, 10am to 4pm and admission is Y5.

Yuántōng Sì 圆通寺

This temple, to the north-east of the Green Lake Hotel and at the base of Luófēng Hill, is the largest Buddhist complex in Kūnmíng, and attracts a fair number of pilgrims. An excellent example of Tang dynasty design, it is 1200 years old and has been renovated many times. Leading up to the main hall is an extensive display of flowers and potted landscapes. The central courtyard holds a large square pond intersected by walkways and bridges, and has an octagonal pavilion at the centre. Built by General Wu Sanqui in the early Qing dynasty, the pavilion houses a 3m golden Maitreya statue.

To the rear of the temple a new hall enshrines a statue of Sakyamuni, a gift from the king of Thailand. Two dragon sculptures here are a big attraction for pilgrims and lots of stories and poems about them have been carved into the temple walls.

Behind the hall is a cliff, Putuo Rock, with steps leading up and then inexplicably stopping. Along the way are carved scholastic inscriptions dating back to the Tang dynasty. A brick platform at the base covers two caves inhabited by dragons. It's said the temple was constructed in part to subdue the beasts. There's a wonderful vegetarian restaurant opposite the main temple entrance (see the Places to Eat section).

The temple is open 8am to 5pm and admission is Y4. Watch out for pickpockets outside the temple and for the elderly women inside who stop foreigners taking pictures of the Buddhist statuary.

Kunming Zoo 昆明市动物园
Kūnmíng Dòngwùyuán

Close to Yuántōng Sì is the zoo, and it's not too shabby. High up on an oddly-shaped hill (the name means 'spiral'), the grounds are pleasantly leafy and provide a vista of the city. Most travellers will still find the 700 animals' living conditions depressing – animal lovers should give the place a miss. If you do go, you can see such Yúnnán rarities as Xīshuāngbǎnnà wild oxen, lesser (red) pandas, leaf monkeys, and black-tail pythons; from greater China you'll get the obligatory pandas, tigers, Yangzi alligators, golden monkeys and others. The grounds also use existing city architecture, including a Ming dynasty city wall. The pavilions were constructed to feature all the architectural styles seen throughout Kūnmíng.

The main entrance is at the corner of Yuantong Jie and Qingnian Lu. Entry is Y6.

Cuìhú Park 翠湖公园
Cuìhú Gōngyuán

A short distance south-west of the zoo at the base of Wuhua Hill, Cuìhú (Green Lake) Park is worth a stroll. The park is at its liveliest on Sunday, when it is host to an English Corner, colourful paddleboats and hordes of families at play. The area was once a morass of swamp and reeds used for cultivation. Show up in winter and you might see the red-beaked seagulls that migrate to this park from the north. Admission is Y2.

Mosques 清真寺
Qīngzhēnsì

Kūnmíng's Buddhist shrines, desecrated during the Cultural Revolution, have been mostly 'rehabilitated'. Now it seems the locals are focusing on the hitherto left-out Muslim community.

The oldest of the lot, the 400-year-old **Nánchéng Ancient Mosque** (Nánchéng Gǔsì) was ripped down in 1997 in order to build a larger version. The new mosque, at 51 Zhengyi Lu, immediately north of the Kūnmíng Department Store, couldn't be further from the aesthetics of the original. Looking vaguely like a bad Las Vegas casino, it is a hybrid of white-tiled Chinese high-rise with a mosque's green onion-domes. (It has office and business convention space on its upper floors!) Not too far away is a lively strip of Muslim restaurants and shops selling skullcaps, Arabic calligraphy and pictures of Mecca. To get there, walk west past the Chūnchéng Jiǔlóu and then bear left a half-block to a small alley.

There's another mosque nearby, wedged between Huguo Lu and Chongyun Jie, and another on the corner of Jinbi Lu at Dongsi Jie, though both are more historical landmarks rather than places of active worship.

Organised Tours

Several tour outfits cover the area faster than public minibuses would, but you must pay and they generally feature sights that most Western travellers find rather boring. Some local tour operators refuse to take foreigners, claiming the language barrier causes too much trouble. In general, the central sights like Yuántōng Sì are just a short bicycle ride away and it hardly makes sense to join a tour.

For tours to the Stone Forest see the Shílín section.

Activities

The **Spring City Golf and Lake Resort**, 48km from Kūnmíng on the north-eastern shore of Lake Yangzong, is generally recognised as China's best golf course. It features one championship 18-hole course designed by Jack Nicklaus and another designed by Robert Trent Jones Jr, as well as a five-star resort (singles/doubles US$138/168) and water sports centre. China's first Club Med is attached. A round of 18 holes costs around US$56/78 weekdays/weekends including cart and caddie if you are staying at the hotel, otherwise it's over double this. Club hire is an additional Y200. A one-way taxi from Kūnmíng costs around Y150. For more information, contact the course (☎ 767 1188, e springct@kepland.com.sg, W www .springcitygolf.com).

If swimming is your thing, try the Tuòdōng ('Open Up the East') **Swimming Pool** (Tuòdōng Yóuyǒngguàn), next to the Tuòdōng Stadium, near the Camellia Hotel. A swim costs Y8 and the pool is open daily 6.30am to 10.30pm.

There are plenty of sporting activities at **Hǎigěng Park** – tennis costs from Y15/30 for an hour daytime/evening during the week to Y20/40 for the weekend. Racket hire costs Y15. The golf range costs Y0.50 per ball, plus Y10 for the hire of two clubs. There are also expensive boats for hire

At the end of a hard day's sightseeing let the blind masseurs in front of Camellia Hotel ease your aching limbs.

Places to Stay – Budget

Long frequented by budget travellers is the *Camellia Hotel (Cháhuā Bīnguǎn;* ☎ *316*

Yúnnán's Muslims

Unlike Muslims in other parts of China, who generally settled at the centres of trade routes used by Arab traders, Yúnnán's sizeable Muslim population dates back to the 13th-century Mongol invasion of China, when the great Khan's armies swooped into the province to outflank the Song dynasty troops. After establishing a base, Muslim traders, builders and craftsmen settled. Yúnnán didn't have the largest population of Muslims, but it was the only region to have been put under a Muslim leader immediately after Kublai Khan's armies arrived – Sayyid Ajall being named governor in 1274.

All over China mosques were simultaneously raised with the new Yuan dynasty banner. A Muslim was entrusted to build the first Mongol palace in Běijīng. An observatory based on Persian models was constructed in Běijīng, and later copied by the Ming emperor. Dozens of Arabic texts were translated and consulted by Chinese scientists, influencing Chinese mathematics more than any other source. The most famous Yúnnán Muslim was Cheng Ho, the famed eunuch admiral who opened up Chinese sea lanes to the Middle East.

Ethnically indistinguishable from the Han Chinese, the *Huí*, as ethnic Chinese Muslims are known, have had an unfortunate history of repression and persecution. Heavy land taxes and disputes between Muslims and Han Chinese over land confiscations and local gold and silver mines triggered a Muslim uprising in 1855, which lasted until 1873. A recent low point was the Cultural Revolution.

The Muslims made Dàlī the centre of their operations and laid siege to Kūnmíng, overrunning the city briefly in 1863. Du Wenxiu, the Muslim leader, proclaimed his newly established kingdom the Nánpíng Guó (Kingdom of the Pacified South) and he took the name Sultan Suleyman. But the Muslim successes were short-lived. In 1873 Dàlī was taken by Qing forces and Du Wenxiu was captured and executed.

Up to a million people died in Yúnnán alone, the death toll rising to 18 million including Gānsú and Qínghǎi provinces. While the Muslim uprisings had been quelled, one of the lasting effects was to elicit sympathy from Burma and foment a passion for culture among many of South-West China's ethnic minorities, most of whom had supported the Huí.

Muslim man reading from the Koran.

3000/2198, fax 314 7033, 154 Dongfeng Donglu). You can get a bed in a three-, four- or seven-person room for Y30, but demand can be heavy sometimes. Most rooms are in Building No 3 across the compound; ask for 3rd-floor rooms, as these are generally in better shape.

The Camellia has bicycle hire, a foreign-exchange counter, poste restante, free luggage and valuables storage and a reasonably priced laundry service. They also have four free bus transfers a day to the airport. The hotel used to fill up quickly, but with more rooms opening up, the situation isn't quite so severe. When you check in you'll have to hand over a refundable Y50 key deposit.

To get there from the train station, take a No 2 or 23 bus to Dongfeng Lu, then change to the No 5 bus heading east and get off at the second stop.

The new kid on the block is *The Hump* (*Tuófēng Kèzhàn;* ☎ 364 4638/4197), which should shake up the budget accommodation scene. Youth-hostel-style dorm beds on the 3rd floor cost from Y15 in an eight- or 17-bed room to Y40 in a double. All beds come with a locker and the clean common showers and toilets have 24-hour hot water. Best of all is the fine sun terrace on the roof. The bars and restaurant downstairs have cheap beer – pick up some travel tips as the owners are keen travellers.

Near the train and bus stations on Beijing Lu, the *Kūnhú Fàndiàn* (☎ 313 3737, 202 Beijing Lu) has dorm beds in triples/quads for Y25/26. Unfortunately, most of the dorm rooms look out onto Beijing Lu, so they're quite noisy. The hotel has singles/doubles for Y60/68. Beyond this dingy doubles with bathroom go for Y128. Some travellers have been unnerved by the common washrooms *and* showers but they are fairly clean. Next door are several cafes where you can sip coffee and trade tales with the large numbers of travellers that pass through. The hotel is two stops from the train station on bus No 2, 23 or 47, though it's easy enough to walk it.

Slightly higher in price but still good value is the *Yúndà Zhaōdaìsuǒ* (*Yúnnán University Center for Chinese Studies;* ☎ 503

3624, fax 514 8513). Singles cost Y40, though there are some bigger and brighter rooms for Y60. Doubles and triples cost Y80 and Y120. All rooms have bathrooms. Some rooms are in the front block, others are in the back garden. Rooms are clean and it's a good place to meet foreign students who live here long-term.

Don't confuse the student guesthouse with the much plusher *Yúndà Bīnguǎn* just up the road, which has comfortable rooms for Y238, discounted to Y120.

Places to Stay – Mid-Range

The Camellia Hotel (see Places to Stay – Budget) has decent doubles from Y220, but first take a look at the Y140 doubles with bathroom and satellite TV in the older wing as they've been spruced up.

The swanky three-star *Báiyún Dàjiǔdiàn* (*White Cloud Hotel;* ☎ 318 8688, 112 Dongfeng Lu), opposite the Tuodong Stadium, has been offering comfortable rooms in its old block for Y100 (the top-floor rooms are even cheaper at Y80 as there's no lift!). Rooms are small but carpeted and the immaculate bathrooms have 24-hour hot water; some rooms are better than others. Beyond this standard rooms start at Y440, discounted to Y320.

A trusty stand-by is the *Chūnchéng Jiǔlóu* (☎ 363 3271, fax 363 3191) at 11–17 Dongfeng Xilu. Also known as the Spring City Hotel, it has clean doubles with bathroom for Y90 or Y128 – take a look at a few rooms as we've seen some clunkers. There are also acceptable doubles with common washroom for Y54, which are a quiet alternative to other budget dorms (corner rooms are generally the most pleasant). The showers are clean and there's 24-hour hot water. Friendly, attentive service is the norm and the restaurant gets good reviews.

Next to the main train station, the *Kunming Railway Building* (*Tiělù Dàshà;* ☎ 351 1996, fax 351 3421) has doubles with bathroom for Y160 and Y198. The cheaper rooms are not for foreign travellers. The hotel is fairly new, so it's not a bad place to stay if you don't mind the train station crowds on your way in and out of the building.

YUNNAN

The *Yúnnán Fàndiàn* (☎ 313 7667) on Dongfeng Xilu, was Kūnmíng's first tourist hotel. Singles/doubles cost around Y180/220, discounted to Y100/150 in winter. There are still a few doubles with common bathroom for Y80 (discounted to Y60). All in all, you'll probably get better value at the city's other budget hotels.

Places to Stay – Top End

Thanks to the city's hosting of the 1999 International Horticultural Expo an astonishing number of shiny new hotels dot the city centre and proletarian stand-bys have received luxury face-lifts.

The *Kunming Hotel* (*Kūnmíng Fàndiàn;* ☎ 316 2063, fax 316 3784, 50–52 Dongfeng Donglu) has doubles starting at US$66 and rising to US$128. Facilities include: airline ticket bookings, poste restante, post office, photocopying, a snooker room, bike hire, several high-end restaurants including Korean and Chaozhou eateries, and a couple of shops. Discounts of 20% are available if you book online (W www.kmhotel.com.cn).

Diagonally opposite Kunming Hotel is the *Holiday Inn Kunming* (*Yīnghuā Jiàrì Jiǔdiàn;* ☎ 316 5888, fax 313 5189, 25 Dongfeng Donglu). It is still one of Kūnmíng's best hotels, sporting an excellent 18th-floor Thai restaurant, a Western-style pub, a small health club and pool, a super-chic disco and one of the better breakfasts in town. You can expect the usual Holiday Inn standards and room rates (singles/doubles Y800/950 plus 15% tax, and then into the stratosphere at US$888 for a suite). Rooms come with a Western buffet breakfast. Non-guests can also use the exercise room for Y25, towel included.

Green Lake Hotel (*Cuìhú Bīnguǎn;* ☎ 515 8888, fax 515 3286, 6 Cuihu Nanlu) used to be quiet and quaint, in an older section of Kūnmíng, but has lost some of its character with the construction of a 20-floor, four-star addition in the back. Doubles in the old building are nothing special at Y280. Rooms in the new section cost US$100, often discounted to US$75. The hotel has a bar, a coffee shop and good Western and Chinese restaurants.

Kunming Harbour Plaza (*Hǎiyì Jiǔdiàn;* ☎ 538 6688, e kunming@harbour-plaza.com, 20 Cuihu Nanlu) is part of the popular Hong Kong chain. Rooms start at US$78.

Golden Dragon Hotel (*Jīnlóng Fàndiàn;* ☎ 313 3015, 575 Beijing Lu), was once Kūnmíng's premier upmarket hotel, is a Hong Kong–China joint venture. Doubles start at Y580, discounted in winter to Y460, including breakfast and taxes. Dragonair has an office here and there is a pool, gym, sauna, tennis courts and business centre on the premises. You can get discounts of 50% by booking online (W www.dragonhotels.com).

King World Hotel (*Jǐnhuá Dàjiǔdiàn;* ☎ 313 8888, fax 313 1910, W www.kingworld.com.cn, 98 Beijing Lu), down the road from the Golden Dragon, is another four-star hotel. Doubles that cost Y460 in wing A and Y625 in wing B can be discounted as low as Y288 and Y388, including breakfast. The hotel features an expensive revolving restaurant (the highest above sea level in China, the hotel proudly points out), currently offering Brazilian food. Rooms also come with fruit baskets. The best rooms even have computer modules, some of the first in China. A free shuttle is offered to the airport.

Kai Wah Plaza International (*Jiāhuá Guǎngchǎng Jiǔdiàn;* ☎ 356 2828, fax 356 1818, 157 Beijing Lu) is Kūnmíng's first five-star hotel. Rooms start at US$140.

Places to Eat

Chinese Cuisine There are several eating places with bilingual menus near the Kūnmíng and Camellia hotels on Dongfeng Donglu. The *Cooking School* (*Xuéchú Fàndiàn*) on Dongfeng Lu specialises in local fish and vegetable dishes, but it must save its novice chefs for the foreigners; it gets mixed reviews.

The *Zhènxīng Fàndiàn* (*Yúnnán Typical Local Food Restaurant*) has a good range of dishes and gets good reviews from locals and foreigners. Service is spotty and they may ignore you. Across-the-bridge noodles costs Y15, Y20 or Y25 depending on the size and ingredients mixed with the noodles. The place is supposedly open 24 hours a day.

Kūnmíng Food

Kūnmíng has some great food, especially in the snack line. Regional specialities are *qìguōjī* (herb-infused chicken cooked in an earthenware steampot), *xuānwèi huǒtuǐ* (Yúnnán ham), *guòqiáo mǐxiàn* (Across-the-bridge noodles), *rǔbǐng* (goat cheese) and various Muslim beef and mutton dishes. *Qìguōjī* is served in dark brown casserole pots from Jiànshuǐ county and is imbued with medicinal properties depending on the spices used – caterpillar fungus *(chóngcǎo)* or pseudo-ginseng is one. Some travellers wax lyrical about toasted goat cheese – the cheese is actually quite bland and sticks to your teeth.

Gourmets may be interested in a whole banquet based on Jizhong fungus (mushrooms) or 30 courses of cold mutton, not to mention fried grasshoppers or elephant trunk braised in soy sauce.

The chief breakfast in Kūnmíng is noodles (choice of rice or wheat), usually served in a meat broth with a chilli sauce.

Yúnnán's best-known dish is Across-the-bridge noodles. You are provided with a bowl of very hot soup (stewed with chicken, duck and spare ribs) on which a thin layer of oil is floating, along with a side dish of raw pork slivers (in classier places this might be chicken or fish), vegetables and egg, and a bowl of rice noodles. Diners place all of the ingredients quickly into the soup bowl, where they are cooked by the steamy broth.

Across-the-bridge noodles is the stuff of which fairy tales are made:

Once upon a time there was a scholar at the South Lake in Měngzì (Southern Yúnnán) who was attracted by the peace and quiet of an island there. He settled into a cottage on the island, in preparation for official examinations. His wife, meanwhile, had to cross a long wooden bridge over the lake to bring the bookworm his meals. The fodder was always cold in winter by the time she got to the study bower. Oversleeping one day, she made a curious discovery. She'd stewed a fat chicken and was puzzled to find the broth still hot, though it gave off no steam – the layer of oil on the surface had preserved the temperature of the broth. Subsequent experiments showed that she could cook the rest of the ingredients for her husband's meal in the hot broth after she crossed the bridge.

Prices generally vary from Y5 to Y15 depending on the side dishes. It's usually worth getting these, because with only one or two condiments it lacks zest.

One of the best places for cheap Chinese food is the **Yuèlái Píjiǔguǎn**. There's an extensive menu of Chinese dishes in English that enables you to try something different. There's not much over Y15 a dish. The mini hotpots are excellent but are not on the English menu. There's also an extensive list of foreign food like muesli and yoghurt and burgers, which the chef learned in Dàlǐ. The restaurant is down an alley off Tuodong Lu.

If you want real Yúnnánese food real fast, an outstanding new option is **Yúnnán** *Fēngwéi Kuàicān (Yúnnán Flavour Fast Food)*, near the intersection of Renmin Xilu and Dongfeng Xilu; look for Yúnnán's first Wal-Mart (as if you could ever miss one). The restaurant is also known as Happy Fish *(Xīngfùyǔ)* and displays an big piscine fibreglass statue outside. You pay first, then wander along a pan-Yúnnán line of food stations, point and drool as chefs prepare food in front of you. You can get dishes for as little as Y5.

A similar venture just west of Yunnan Airlines, is the **King Dragon Food Village**

(*Yuánlóng Fēngweìchéng*) is harder to deal with as the cooks are behind high counters.

For something a little classier, ***1910 La Gare Du Sud*** (*Huǒchē Nánzhàn;* ☎ *316 9486*) serves traditional local Yúnnánese specialties in a pleasant neo-colonial-style atmosphere. There's no English menu but most dishes are moderately priced. It's hidden down an alley next to the Upriver Club, south of Jinbi Lu.

One of the better known places for steampot chicken is the Chūnchéng Jiǔlóu (see Places to Stay). Several small, private restaurants on Beijing Lu opposite the long-distance bus station sell cheaper versions of steampot chicken.

Sadly, lots of places specialising in Kūnmíng's favourite noodles are disappearing. Fortunately a few options have held out. The ***Měngzì Across-The-Bridge-Noodles Restaurant*** (*Měngzì Guòqiáo Mǐxiàn*) has noodles for Y5 to Y20. There's one branch on Beijing Lu, not far from the Public Security Bureau (PSB) office; another is on Renmin Xilu, west of the Xixiaomen bus station.

East of Yuántōng Sì is the popular ***New World Over the Bridge Noodle Restaurant*** (*Xīnshìjìe Guòqiáochéng*). Half the restaurant is an expensive seafood joint but the other serves great Across-the-bridge noodles in an upscale environment.

A more recent phenomenon in Kūnmíng is the discovery of ethnic cuisines. At present there are at least two Dǎi minority restaurants in Kūnmíng. The food is spicy and uses sticky rice as its staple. Popular with overseas students studying in Kūnmíng is the ***Lǎozhīqíng Shíguǎn***, near the entrance to Cuìhú Park.

The ***Báitǎ Dǎi Flavour Restaurant*** (*Báitǎdǎiwèi Cāntīng*), nestled down an alley near the Kunming Hotel, has tasty food, an English menu and cold draught beer (though the beer is flat at times). Prices are a bit high, but it's a good place to try Dǎi cuisine – an opportunity you won't get again unless you head down to Xīshuāngbǎnnà. The 'pork in bamboo steamer' is otherworldly.

Next door is the ***Dōngběi Jiǎozidiàn***, which serves dozens of varieties of tasty dumplings from north-east China.

There is a string of eateries on Xiangyun Jie between Jinbi Lu and Nanping Jie. At the Nanping end at No 77 is the ***Běijīng Fàndiàn***, where northern-style roast seafood, chicken and duck is dished through windows at the front. They've also got pretty decent pictures of all offerings. Farther down are lots of street vendors and small private restaurants.

Vegetarian Apart from the various temples in and around town, most of the restaurants near the Kūnhú and Camellia hotels that cater to foreigners have decent veggie selections.

Right opposite Yuántōng Sì is the outstanding ***Yùquánzhāi Vegetarian Restaurant***. It doesn't have aesthetic charm and prices are high (though there are still dishes for Y10), but it's definitely worth it. This restaurant takes on the practice of 'copying' meat-based dishes to a new level, with an encyclopaedic menu. Staff highlight the duck in fermented bean curd. Also check out the *tiěbǎn* (sizzling iron-pot) meals for around Y20.

Snacks Kūnmíng used to be a good place for bakeries and arrhythmia-inducing Vietnamese-style coffee, but most of these have disappeared. Exploration of Kūnmíng's backstreets might turn up a few lingerers.

There are roadside *noodle stands* near the long-distance bus station and in many of the side streets running off Beijing Lu. Generally you get a bowl of rice noodles for Y2 to Y4 and a bewildering array of sauces with which to flavour the broth – most of them are hot and spicy.

Another place to go snack hunting is Huguo Lu, north of Dongfeng Donglu, with *noodle stands* and a *teahouse*. The intersection of Changchun and Huguo yields lots of small eateries.

Shuncheng Jie, an east-west street running south of Dongfeng Xilu near the Chūnchéng Jiǔlóu, is one of the most interesting streets in Kūnmíng. Here you'll find dozens of ***Muslim restaurants***, *kebab stalls* and *nan bread stalls*, dried beef, Arabic calligraphy and skullcaps, all visible through a haze of kebab smoke. Try *bānmiàn*, a kind of spaghetti, or Uighur *suoman*, fried noodle squares with peppers, tomato and cumin.

The Brothers Jiang (*Jiāngshì Kèdì*) has good noodles (ask for the *shāoguō mǐxiàn*) and a range of Across-the-bridge noodles from Y5 to Y60. There are several branches, all popular at lunchtime. Pay up front at the cash register. One convenient branch is at Dongfeng Donglu, opposite the government square and another is just south of the zoo on Qingnian Jie.

Upstairs from the government square branch, the *Orient Café* (*Hérùn Lùtái*) has a pleasant open-air seating area that is great for people-watching. Teas and coffee are around Y10, beers Y15 and small meals about the same.

Western Food Kūnmíng hasn't yet experienced the friendly invasion of KFC à la Chéngdū, but a passable local approximation *Dicos* (*Dékèshì Huǒjī*) has outlets in front of the Kūnmíng Department Store and just south of the Kūnhú Fàndiàn.

There are several places catering to backpackers around the main backpacker hotels. A few doors down from the Kūnhú Fàndiàn on Beijing Lu are several pleasant cafes, currently the *Lìlái Restaurant*, *Happy Café* and *Mr Balls*, serving food at budget conscious prices.

Near the Camellia Hotel are more places catering to foreigners. *City Café* (*Chéngshì Xiǎochī*) doesn't look like much but it serves good portions of authentic Western food ranging from lasagne to brownies. Prices are reasonable. There are even some Chinese dishes, with a few Fujianese specialties such as fish ball soup (the owners are from Xiàmén).

Mǎ Mǎ Fū's 2 (*Māmāfu Cāntīng*), a legendary Lìjiang cafe, recently opened up around the corner east of the Camellia Hotel and is now run by the original Mama and Papa, it's still got the same to die for fresh breads and apple pie.

A giant block south of the Camellia Hotel is *Wei's Pizzeria* (☎ *316 6189*), off Tuodong Lu down a small alley (look for arrows on the wall). Unbelievable Italian food is around Y12 a dish, and the wood-

fired pizzas (Y20 to Y25) are unspeakably good. You can also get tasty Chinese dishes, such as good *qìguōjī* (medicinal-herb chicken in a pot). Frosted beer mugs (or try a glass of Yúnnán red wine) and eclectic Western music top off the effect.

The environs of Yúnnán University and nearby Cuìhú Park have restaurants catering to foreign students and they are a good place to find out what's going on where in Kūnmíng. Between the university and park at 40 Wenlin Jie is the pleasant *Teresa's Pizzeria* (☎ *538 66725*), with excellent pizzas, calzones, salads and a great atmosphere.

Wenlin Jie and its surrounding alleys has several other restaurants and bars, including *Paul's* (*Bǎolì Shāngdiàn*), a grocery specialising in Western gourmet and hard to find imports like Cornflakes and real cheese.

The alley that leads north of Wenlin Jie, near the Face to Face pub, leads to Yúnnán University and is crammed with restaurants and bars. The *French Café* (*Lánbáihóng*; ☎ *538 2391*) here is a fine place, offering hard to find goodies like salads, sandwiches, crepes (salty and sweet) and lots of different teas and coffees, all served up with typical Gallic charm. It's a great place to read during the day and the place gets lively at night with good music and a nice mix of foreign and Chinese crowd. There's Internet access and books for loan.

The nearby *Travellers Home Café* is a cosy place that will even let you cook your own food. It also claims to offer Chinese language and cookery classes.

Farther along the alley towards Yúnnán University is the town's original Western cafe, *Journey to the East Café* (*Wàngdōngfāng Lüxíng*), with good and cheap food, email and a ton of books.

One of the most popular Western-inspired restaurants in town is the *Bluebird Café* (*Qīngniǎo*), so popular in fact that is now has a couple of branches. The branch at 150 Cuihu Lu (☎ *531 4071*) is the cosiest; the larger branch is down an alley at 127 Dongfeng Xilu (☎ *361 0478*) but is blighted by the occasional karaoke fiesta.

If your stomach is crying out for Western food that tastes like the real thing, there is one option apart from the Holiday Inn's tasty but expensive restaurants. Tucked away in the north-eastern Xinying Xiaoqu district is **Billy Niupai's** *(Bǐlì Niúpá;* ☎ *331 1748, 47 Tianyuan Lu)*, where you can get steaks, burgers, pasta and even tacos that should successfully satisfy a homesick appetite. Figure on around Y50 for a full Western meal. The decor is American cowboy, but pleasant for all that. Take a taxi so the cab driver can help you find the place. It should cost around Y15 from the Kūnhú Fàndiàn, less from the Camellia.

The big hotels all sport coffee shops. For a no-holds-barred breakfast buffet for Y65, head down to the second floor of the Holiday Inn Kūnmíng from 6.30am to 10am. Buffet lunches/dinners cost Y55/86.

The Camellia Hotel does an excellent-value breakfast buffet for Y10, served from 7am to 10am.

Entertainment

Once restricted to dismal karaoke bars, Kūnmíng is exploding with night-time options, most of the boozing rather than dancing variety. Any of the Western cafes mentioned in the previous section double as drinking holes.

The Hump (see Places to Stay) has three bars that offer regular drink specials and low priced domestic beer.

The **Camel Bar** *(Luòtuō Jiǔbā;* ☎ *337 6255, 274 Baita Lu)* is north of the Camellia Hotel along Baita Lu. Run by Li Du, a local rocker of some repute, it's got cheap Tsingtao beer and live music on weekends.

Near Yúnnán University are a couple of bars hidden in the back streets. **Face to Face** *(Miànduì'miàn)* on Wenlin Jie is a pleasant little place for a quiet drink and snack.

At the Holiday Inn, **Charlie's** is frequented by Kūnmíng's expat community, but prices are considerably higher – stick to beer, since a mixed drink costs about Y80. There's normally a happy hour from 4pm to 7pm.

You might see displays of minority dancing (more often held for group tours), travelling troupes or Yúnnán Opera. The CITS office sometimes has information. The Song and Dance Ensemble of Yúnnán performs most weekdays at 8.30pm at the **Kūnmíng Theatre** *(Kūnmíng Jùyuàn)*.

Around the corner from the Běijīng Fàndiàn there's a number of *cinemas*, usually with at least one Hollywood offering and normally in English; admission is Y10 to Y15.

One unique place is the **Upriver Club** *(Shànghé Huìguǎn)*, a cafe/art gallery set up by painter Ye Yongqing. Drinks are pricey at around Y20 a tea but the Western food is reasonably priced and there's plenty of art to look at. The club is hidden down an alley off Houxin Jie, south of Jinbi Lu and close to the Panlong Jiāng.

Shopping

You have to dig to come up with inspiring purchases in Kūnmíng; even locals will tell you the city will never be famed for its shopping. Specialities are jade (related to Burmese jade), marble (from the Dàlǐ area), batik, minority embroidery, musical instruments and spotted brass utensils.

Some functional items make good souvenirs: the *qíguō* or ceramic steampot, the large bamboo waterpipes for smoking angel-haired Yúnnán tobacco, or local herbal medicines such as *Yúnnán Báiyào* (Yúnnán White Medicine), which is a blend of over 100 herbs and highly prized by Chinese throughout the world.

Tea from Yúnnán comes in several varieties, from bowl-shaped bricks of smoked green tea called *tuóchá*, around since at least Marco Polo's time, to leafy black tea that rivals some of India's best. One tea shop worth checking out is Tiēn Fú Famous Teas (Tiānfù Míngchá), next to the PSB on Beijing Lu.

One of the main shopping drags is Zhengyi Lu, especially the traffic circle at the intersection of Zhengyi Lu and Dongfeng Lu, which has several huge department stores such as the Kūnmíng Department Store, Parksons and even Walmart. Other shopping areas are Jinbi Lu near the Zhengyi Lu intersection (where there are lots of small speciality shops), and Dongfeng Donglu, between Zhengyi Lu and Huguo Lu.

The Flower and Bird Market (Huāniǎo Shìchǎng) is definitely worth a visit. It's tucked away on Tongdao Jie, one of the numerous alleys lying between Zhengyi Lu and Wuyi Lu, north of the Kūnmíng Department Store. Pet supplies, fishing gear and flowers dominate the cramped rows of tiny stalls, but there is a bizarre assortment of other items such as old coins, wooden elephants, tacky wall murals and so-called 'antiques' on sale. Just walking around here is rewarding; if you actually find something to buy, it's a bonus.

For antiques look among the privately run shops on Beijing Lu and Dongfeng Donglu. Outside the Kunming Hotel you will be ambushed by minority women flogging handiwork – bargain if you want a sane price. Both the Green Lake and Kūnmíng hotels sell batik that you can also find in Dàlǐ. Delve into the smaller shops around Jinbi Lu if you're into embroidery. For Yúnnán herbal medicines, check the large pharmacy on Zhengyi Lu (on the east side, several blocks up from the Kūnmíng Department Store). The southern end of Beijing Lu also has a few herbal medicine shops.

If you need warm clothes or camping gear try Climber Outdoors (Pāndēngzhe; ☎ 313 2783), just down an alley at 20 Dongfeng Donglu next to the Brothers Jiang restaurant, or Postar Outdoor and Equipment Collection (Jíxīng) on Baita Lu, not far from the Camellia Hotel. Both sell a mixture of Western and local trekking shoes, Gore-Tex jackets, stoves, sandals, water bottles and sleeping bags. Inspect everything carefully.

For a surreal lesson in the power of English football and China's modernity pay a visit to the Manchester United Shop (!) on Baita Lu.

Getting There & Away

Air The Yunnan Airlines/CAAC office (☎ 316 4270 domestic; 312 1220 international) is the large office on Tuodong Lu. You can buy air tickets for any Chinese airline but the office only offers discounts (of around 20%) on Yunnan Airlines flights. It's open 24 hours, though only the small ticket window on the left side of the building is open between 8pm to 8am. You can pay for tickets with a Visa credit card but there's a 3% surcharge.

Other airline offices in Kūnmíng include:

China Southern Airlines (☎ 310 1831)
433 Beijing Lu
China Southwest Airlines (☎ 353 9702)
160 Beijing Lu
Kunming United Airlines (☎ 362 8592)
13 Dongfeng Xilu
Shanghai Airlines (☎ 313 8502)
46 Dongfeng Donglu

Kūnmíng is well connected by air to the rest of China, and most flights (even within Yúnnán) are on Boeing 737 and 757 jets. Popular destinations include Běihǎi (Y710), Běijīng (Y1600), Chéngdū (Y640), Chóngqìng (Y660), Guǎngzhōu (Y1160), Guìlín (Y770), Guìyáng (Y400), Nánjīng (Y1710), Nánníng (Y580), Qīngdǎo (2140), Shànghǎi (Y1670), Shēnzhèn (Y1400), Xiàmén (Y1540), Xī'ān (Y970) and Yíbīn (Y470).

Flights within the province on Yunnan Airlines include Bǎoshān (Y440), Jǐnghóng (Y520), Lìjiāng (Y420), Mángshì/Déhóng (Y530), Xiàguān/Dàlǐ (Y340), Zhāotōng (Y390) and Zhōngdiàn (Y560).

Service on this surprisingly comprehensive network is quite good. Most destinations are served at least three times a week, and within Yúnnán, Jǐnghóng and Mángshì have numerous daily flights. Bigger cities such as Běijīng and Shànghǎi have up to four flights per day.

It's now often possible to book flights to Xīshuāngbǎnnà, the Déhóng region and most other popular destinations at short notice. However, during the high season it pays to book at least a week in advance. During April (Water Splashing Festival), the flights to Xīshuāngbǎnnà can be booked rock solid for a week, and the airline offices jammed with maniacs pushing and shoving. During this time make your plans for Xīshuāngbǎnnà as flexible as possible: consider the bus option, or book your flight ahead and spend the intervening time in Dàlǐ or elsewhere.

Yunnan Airlines and several foreign carriers have international flights to Hong Kong (Y1870, daily), Macau (Y1770), Bangkok (Y1540, daily), Yangon (Rangoon; Y2190,

YÚNNÁN

once a week), Vientiane (Y1520, twice a week), Osaka (Y4400), Singapore (Y3580, discounted to Y2150, twice a week) and Seoul (Y5860, discounted to Y4480). It's also possible to fly from Jǐnghóng to Bangkok for Y1300.

Foreign airline offices and connections include the following:

Dragonair (☎ 313 8592) in the Golden Dragon Hotel; twice-weekly flights to Hong Kong.
JAS (☎ 316 1230) Room 633, 6th floor, Holiday Inn
Lao Aviation. Entrance to the Camellia Hotel; weekly flights to Vientiane
Silk Air/Singapore Airlines (☎ 313 2334) 2nd floor, Holiday Inn
Thai Airways International (☎ 313 3315, fax 316 7351) 28 Beijing Lu, next to the King World Hotel, close to the train station. Flights to Bangkok (Y1750) leave daily; the Tuesday, Thursday and Sunday flights stop off in Chiang Mai (Y1450).

See the Getting There and Away chapter for more information on international connections.

Bus In Kūnmíng bus transportation can be a little confusing, with buses leaving from all over the place. However, the long-distance bus station on Beijing Lu is the best place to organise bus tickets to almost anywhere in Yúnnán or further afield. Departures listed in this section are from the long-distance bus station. Exceptions to this are local destinations like Lake Dian or towns south-east of Kūnmíng.

Other bus stations include the eastern bus station, and a second bus station across Beijing Lu from the long distance bus station. Apart from the services listed here, private sleeper buses for all kinds of destinations congregate in front of the train station. Most sleeper departures are in the early evening. You usually don't even need to purchase in advance. Fares are negotiable here and at their lowest just before departure.

Certain destinations are now served by super luxury express buses, costing lots more but sometimes cutting travelling time by 40%. Services offer an occasional English

movie, a bottle of mineral water and other souvenirs and sometimes even a decent lunch midway. There are express buses to Dàlǐ, Lìjiāng, Bǎoshān, Jǐnghóng, Qūjìng, Gèjiù, Yùxī, Kāiyuán and Hékǒu.

Dàlǐ Express buses to Xiàguān/Dàlǐ (Y104, five hours) depart every hour or so from 7.30am to 7.30pm. Slower minibuses cost from Y55 to Y64 and depart all day from both the long-distance bus station and the bus stand in front of the train station. The latter also has sleeper buses (Y68, 7½ hours) but these are generally a poor option.

Check where the bus is heading as sometimes buses marked 'Dàlǐ' terminate in Xiàguān, a 30-minute bus ride from Dàlǐ. A few buses terminate in Xiàguān at the Cāngshān Bīnguǎn. From Xiàguān it's no problem to either catch the big, lumbering local bus, or hop on one of the many private minibuses to Dàlǐ for Y5.

Lìjiāng & Zhōngdiàn Lìjiāng is just nine hours away on a comfortable Korean bus (Y152). Express buses depart at 7.30am, 9.15am, 10.20am and noon. Normal sleeper buses depart in the early morning or evening around 7pm, and take longer (Y100, 11 hours).

A daily express bus leaves for Zhōngdiàn (Y171, 12 hours) at 8.20am but most travellers break the trip in Lìjiāng or Dàlǐ.

Xīshuāngbǎnnà The marathon trip to Jǐnghóng in Xīshuāngbǎnnà is now 18 to 22 hours, depending on the length of the numerous meal breaks and unscheduled stops.

Ordinary sleeper buses to Jǐnghóng cost around Y120 and leave between 6pm and 9pm from both the long-distance bus station and in front of the train station. Luxury express coaches depart at 4pm and 6.30pm from the long-distance bus station (Y150, 15 hours).

There are a couple of private operators outside the train station who go to Měnglà (Y138), the jump-off point for Laos, bypassing Jǐnghóng, adding another 130km onto an already insane ride. There are also a few sleeper buses to Mènglián.

Déhóng Both options for getting to the Déhóng region involve long hauls, so it's worth considering doing at least one leg of the trip by air (to Mángshì). Sleeper buses for Bǎoshān (Y97, 14 hours) leave from the long-distance bus station four times between 4.30pm and 6.20pm. An express bus to Bǎoshān leaves sometime between 7.30am and 9am (Y116).

Sleeper buses direct to Ruìlì (Y148, 22 to 26 hours) leave six times daily between 10am and 7.30pm. To Mángshì (Y128) there's a direct sleeper at 10am. More options can be found in front of the train station, where there are also sleepers to Téngchōng (Y127).

South-East Yúnnán The easiest place to start a loop of south-eastern Yúnnán is Yùxī, as express buses run every 30 minutes or so (Y33.50, 1½ hours). To Jiànshuǐ, small buses (Y30 to Y41, five hours) depart hourly 7.30am to 8.30pm.

There is one express service to Gèjiù (Y61, five hours) at 8.30am and plenty of speedy white Iwecos (Y51, 6½ hours) and slower minibuses (Y41) all day.

If you can't get a Gèjiù bus, Kāiyuán has multiple departures in small buses (Y35, six hours). Express buses to Kāiyuán (Y52, three hours) run three times a day. There are morning and evening sleeper buses to Hónghé (Y60).

To Qūjìng there are loads of express buses (Y35.50, two hours) and minibuses (Y21).

For other destinations in the south-east, take the No 25 local bus to the east bus station (Dōngmén Qìchēzhàn), at the intersection of Tuodong Lu and Huangcheng Lu, where buses run to most destinations from 7am to 7pm.

Buses run every 20 to 30 minutes to Jiāngchuān (Y17), Tōnghǎi (Y21), Lúxī (Y26), Qūjìng (Y20), Yùxī (Y18) and Shílín/Lùnán (Y14). For Chéngjiāng (Y13) cross the main road to a smaller bus station where there are departures every 15 minutes via Chénggòng (Y7).

For more information on getting to the Stone Forest see the Shílín – Getting There & Away section later in this chapter.

Neighbouring Provinces It is possible to travel by bus from the long-distance bus station to several destinations in neighbouring provinces. Sleeper buses to Guìyáng (Guìzhōu) leave at 7.40am, 1.20pm and 7pm (Y101, 18 hours). Break the trip by travelling first to Xīngyì, an interesting town just over the border (see the Guìzhōu chapter). Five sleeper buses to Xīngyì leave five times between 7.30am and 6pm (Y64, ten hours). There are also less frequent sleepers to Xīngrén and Bìjié, also in Guìzhōu.

Another interesting option is the bus service to Nánníng in Guǎngxī province. There are around four sleeper buses a day bumping to Nánníng (Y161, 25 to 32 hours). If you can't buy a ticket for Nánníng, get a bus to Guǎngnán, a border town with onward connections to Nánníng; one sleeper leaves at 8.20pm. There are even occasional buses to Guǎngzhōu that take forever.

Neighbouring Countries If you are headed to Vietnam, a single express bus runs to the Chinese border town of Hékǒu (Y95, 11 hours) in the morning from the long-distance bus station. There are also daytime and overnight sleepers (Y83 to Y88, 14 hours). Before buying a ticket, check at the train station: a hard-sleeper train ticket to Hékǒu would assure you of an infinitely more pleasant journey.

Travellers going overland to Laos will probably want to go to Jǐnghóng first, from where there are buses to Měnglà, near the border crossing. See the Xīshuāngbǎnnà section earlier.

Train The city can become a real trap for train travellers during the high season. The main station sells both hard-sleeper and hard-seat tickets from 8.30am, up to eight days in advance. Staff at counter No 5 sometimes speak some English. In the high season you should book at least a couple of days ahead. Take your passport or a passport copy when reserving train tickets. A few touts lurk outside but you shouldn't need to use them. The train station ticket office is open 6.30am to 11.10pm.

Inter-Provincial Rail options out of Kūnmíng include Běijīng, Chéngdū, Chóngqìng, Guǎngzhōu, Shànghǎi and all points between. The Kūnmíng-Shànghǎi train (No K80) travels 3069km via Guìyáng, Zhūzhōu, Nánchāng and Hángzhōu. Trains to Běijīng route via Guìyáng, Chángshā and Zhèngzhōu. Trains to Chóngqìng generally travel via Guìyáng and Zūnyì.

For details and prices of the most convenient and popular long-distance trains see the table. For Éméi Shān take a Chéngdū-bound train. The fastest trains take about 17 hours and cost Y215 to Y230 for a hard sleeper and Y336 to Y351 for a soft sleeper. Almost any train headed east (for Běijīng, Chóngqìng, Guǎngzhōu, Shànghǎi etc) passes through Guìyáng.

If you're headed to Guìlín, consider the impressive new Nánkún Railway, which links Nánníng and Kūnmíng. The line bypasses some fine scenery, including at least one great waterfall. For information on the line see the boxed text 'Heading West?' in the Nánníng section of the Guǎngxī chapter.

Within Yúnnán The two most popular services with tourists are the overnight service to Xiàguān (for Dàlǐ) and the day return train to Shílín. For details of these services see the Dàlǐ and Shílín sections.

You can also take a train down the narrow-gauge line to the border crossing with Vietnam at Hékǒu. Train No 5933 leaves from the north train station *(huǒchē běi zhàn)* daily at 4pm and arrives the next morning at 8.15am (Y72/207 hard/soft sleepers). On Friday and Sunday the train continues on to Hanoi (see International Trains, following). The north train station ticket office is open 7am to 7pm.

Also departing from the north train station is a night train, the No 5931/5935 departing at 10.45pm, which follows the Hékǒu route, but then switches west from Kāiyuán to Jiànshuǐ (13 hours, compared with 5½ hours by bus), and Shípíng (14½ hours). You could avoid a hotel room's cost but since a sleeper is roughly twice a dorm bed, you're not actually saving anything. If you're headed to Gèjiù, hop off in Kāiyuán at 6.50am and catch one of the zillions of minibuses. A hard sleeper to Kāiyuán is around Y50.

International Trains Every Friday and Sunday at 4pm trains depart from the north train station for Hanoi (*Hénèi* in Mandarin; 30 hours). Only four-person soft-sleeper berths (Y298) are available and trains arrive in Hanoi at 8.10pm local time the following day. For more information see the Getting There & Away chapter.

Getting Around

Most of the major sights are within a 15km radius of Kūnmíng. Local transport tends to

destination	train no	duration	hard sleeper	soft sleeper
Shànghǎi	K80	46	Y485–518	Y763–798
	K182	56	Y325–350	Y528–553
Běijīng	T62		Y538–577	Y851–889
Guǎngzhōu	1166/1163	31	Y329	Y515
Chéngdū	K166	19	Y239–256	Y373–389
	K114	18½	Y239–256	Y373–389
	2512	20	Y193–207	Y309–323
Chóngqìng	K160/K168	23	Y212–226	Y330–345
Guìyáng	K156	12	Y96–102	Y150–157
	2080	12½	Y141–150	Y222–233
Guìlín	K182	17½	Y184–198	Y296–309
Nánníng	2060/2057	15	Y156–168	Y249–261
	2006	14½	Y113–122	Y184–193
	1166	14	Y180–194	Y287–301

NB *Only the popular trains are shown. Fares vary according to the type of train and route taken.*

be an out-and-back job, with few crossovers for combined touring. If you wish to take in everything, you'd be looking at something like five return trips, which would consume three days or more.

You can simplify this by pushing Black Dragon Pool, Ānníng Hot Springs and the Golden Temple to the background, and concentrating on Bamboo Temple and Western Hills, both of which have decent transport connections. Lake Dian presents engrossing circular-tour possibilities of its own (for details see the Around Kūnmíng section). Better yet, buy a map, hire a good bicycle and tour the area by bike (though there are some steep hills lurking out there...).

To/From the Airport An efficient bus shuttles between the Kūnmíng airport and the CAAC/Yunnan Airlines office. Service is supposed to be from 6am to 8pm. Buses run from the airport when full, and pretty much every 15 minutes. The driver will normally drop off passengers at the Camellia and Kūnhú hotels. This is well worth the Y5.

You can also exit the airport, walk past the taxis, a traffic roundabout and a hotel to the main road. Bus No 52 runs along this road to/from the city centre. From Beijing Lu bus No 67 runs to the airport.

Better still, treat yourself to a taxi – it's only Y15 between the airport and city centre.

Bus Public buses run out to most of the major sights. Options include No 10 to the Golden Temple and the No 9 to Black Dragon Pool, both from the north train station; the No 44 from Kūnmíng train station to Hǎigěng Park; and the No 4 from the Zoo to Dàguān Park. Bus No 63 runs from the east bus station to the Camellia Hotel and on to the train station. Bus No 23 runs from the north train station south down Beijing Lu to the main train station. Fares range from Y0.50 to Y4. The main city buses have no conductors and require exact change.

Taxi Flag falls are Y8 for the first 2km or so, with an additional Y1.8 per km after that.

Bicycle Bikes are a fast way to get around town. The Camellia Hotel has a decent selection for Y2 per hour or Y15 for the day (Y200 deposit). The Kūnhú also has a few bikes for rent for Y8 per day, (Y100 deposit), though they've seen better days.

Fat Tyres Bike Shop (☎ 530 1755) at 61 Qianju Jie, just off Cuihu Nanlu, has superb equipment including mountain bikes to rent, and organises Sunday morning bike rides – you need to make reservations ahead of time.

AROUND KŪNMÍNG
Golden Temple 金殿
Jīn Diàn

This Taoist temple is perched amid a pine forest on Mingfeng (Phoenix Song) Hill, 11km north-east of Kūnmíng. The original Ming dynasty temple was purportedly built by the governor of Yúnnán who in a dream saw Lu Dongbin, one of Chinese mythology's eight Immortals, appear at this spot. This construction was carted off to Jīzú Shān near Dàlǐ; the present one dates from 1671 and was the brainchild of General Wu Sangui, who was dispatched by the Manchus in 1659 to quell the uprisings in the region. Wu Sangui turned against the Manchus and set himself up as a rebel warlord, with the Golden Temple as his summer residence.

Though a Taoist temple, elements of Buddhism and even Confucianism were introduced in extensions. The pillars, ornate door frames, walls, fittings and roof tiles of the 6m-high temple are all made of Yúnnán bronze. The entire temple structure, laid on a white Dàlǐ marble foundation, is estimated to weigh more than 250 tonnes. A sword weighing 20kg sits in the temple; Zhen Wu, a Taoist superhero whose image graces the central statue, is said to have used it. In the courtyard are ancient camellia trees, one reputedly dating back 600 years. Around Míngtěng Hill is a large arboretum divided into 12 sections. At the back is a 14-tonne bronze bell, cast in 1432. In the temple compound are teahouses and a noodle stand.

To get to the Golden Temple, take bus No 10 or 71 from Kūnmíng's north train station. Many travellers ride hired bikes to the temple – it's fairly level to the base of the hill and an easy hill path to the temple compound. A cable car (Y15) runs from the temple to the Horticultural Expo Garden, or you can take a bus. Admission to the temple costs Y15 (no student discounts).

World Horticultural Expo Garden
世博园 Shìjiè Yuányì Bólǎnyuán

This 218-hectare garden complex (☎ 501

AROUND KŪNMÍNG (DIĀN CHÍ) 昆明地区（滇池）

2367), near the Golden Temple, was built in April 1999 for the World Horticultural Exposition. A mix of pleasant Disneyland-style gardens and pointless exhibits left over from the expo, the place is worth a visit if you are interested in gardens and plants, otherwise give it a miss.

The best exhibits are the Grand Greenhouse, which has absorbing displays of Yúnnán's tropical plants and flowers, and the bonsai and vegetable and fruit garden. The butterfly garden is worth a look from April to October.

Entry is a staggering Y100. A better deal is the Y50 ticket available after 2pm. You'll miss some of the folk shows at 10am and 11am but that's no real hardship. The complex is open daily from 8am to 5pm, with the last ticket sold at 4pm. There are restaurants and a hotel on the grounds.

To get there take bus No 47 from the main train station or No 71 from Kūnmíng's north train station; the same bus continues to the Golden Temple. A cable car at the back of the gardens can take you to the Golden Temple for Y15.

Black Dragon Pool 黑龙潭
Hēilóng Tán

This mediocre garden is 11km north of Kūnmíng, with old cypress trees, dull Taoist pavilions and springs without bubbles. It gets mixed reports but the view of the mountains from the garden is inspiring. The name comes from another legend: 10 'flood dragons', a scourge to the countryside, were stopped by the mythological

AROUND KŪNMÍNG

1	Golden Temple 金殿	6	Yúnnán Minorities Village 云南民族村	11	Tàihuá Sì 太华寺
2	World Horticultural Expo Village 世博园	7	Yúnnán Nationalities Museum 云南民族博物馆	12	Huàtíng Sì 华亭寺
3	Bamboo Temple 笻竹寺	8	Hǎigěng Park 海埂公园	13	Ānníng Springs 安宁温泉
4	Dàguān Park 大观公园	9	Lóngmén Village 龙门	14	Cáoxī Sì 曹溪寺
5	Gaoyao Bus Station 高峣汽车	10	Sanqing Temple 三清阁	15	Zheng He Park 郑和公园
				16	Stone Village Hill 石村

Immortal Lu Dongbin, who buried nine dragons beneath an ancient pagoda, with the tenth relegated to this pond.

Within walking distance is the **Kunming Botanical Institute**. It has over 4000 species of tropical and subtropical plants, though the camellia is particularly prized here. Take the No 9 bus here from the north train station; admission is Y1.

Bamboo Temple 筇竹寺
Qióngzhú Sì

About 12km north-west of Kūnmíng, this temple dates back to the Tang dynasty and marks the site of the introduction of Mahayana Buddhism from central China. (Up until then, Tibetan Buddhism had influenced the region.) Burned down and rebuilt in the 15th century, it was restored from 1883 to 1890 when the abbot employed the master Sìchuānese sculptor Li Guangxiu and his apprentices to fashion 500 *luohan* (arhats or noble ones). These life-size clay figures are a stunning sculptural tour de force.

Down one huge wall come the incredible surfing Buddhas, some 70-odd, riding the waves on a variety of mounts – blue dogs, giant crabs, shrimp, turtles, unicorns. One gentleman has metre-long eyebrows; another has an arm that shoots to the ceiling.

In the main section are housed row upon row of standing figures, captured with the precision of a photograph – a monk about to chomp into a large peach (the face contorted almost into a scream), a figure turning to emphasise a discussion point, another about to clap two cymbals together. The old, the sick, the emaciated – nothing is spared; the expressions of joy, anger, grief or boredom are extremely vivid.

The sculptures were considered in bad taste by Li Guangxiu's contemporaries (some of whom no doubt appeared in caricature), and upon the project's completion he disappeared.

As for the bamboo of the temple's name, there was actually none until very recently, when bamboo from Chéngdū was transplanted here. (The name came from the bamboo walking stick of an old sage who appeared to two brothers in this spot.) The main halls were restored in 1958 and again, extensively, in 1981.

The easiest way to get there is to take a bus from in front of the Yúnnán Fàndiàn. According to the schedule, buses run from 7am to 4.30pm, but you'll be lucky to find much going after around 10am. Buses leave as soon as they are full. The ride takes 30 minutes and costs Y8. Admission is Y3.

Ānníng Hot Springs 安宁温泉
Ānníng Wēnquán

Most travellers sensibly give this place, 44km south-west of Kūnmíng, a wide berth. Local tourist authorities proclaim the hot spring as 'No 1 under the heavens' and describe it as a 'Jade Spring', but green water is still green water. Some hotels pipe the hot spring water into their rooms. Reports also have it that couples are not accepted – this rule may have changed.

Across the Tanglang River bridge 1km, then up Cong Hill in a bamboo grove, is the **Cáoxī Sì**. Inside are Song dynasty wooden statues, including one of Sakyamuni Buddha. On the night of Mid-Autumn Festival, the moon's first beams of light fall directly on the statue's mirrored forehead and slowly trace down. North of the temple and down the slope is another spring famed for, believe it or not, toads. Supposedly three times a day golden toads leave their holes and the geyser gushes. You can imagine the heavenly nicknames the Chinese have thought up for that one.

Buses to the springs run approximately hourly from the Xiǎoxīmén bus station between 8am and 6pm; the trip costs Y4. Returning, the last bus is at 5pm. There is another bus station west of Xiǎoxīmén bus station that may also have buses.

Lake Dian 滇池
Diān Chí

The shoreline of Lake Dian, to the south of Kūnmíng, is dotted with settlements, farms and fishing enterprises; the western side is hilly, while the eastern side is flat country. The southern end of the lake is industrial, but there are lots of possibilities for

YÚNNÁN

Lake Dian is dotted with fishing enterprises.

extended touring. The lake is elongated; about 150km in circumference, about 40km from north to south, and covering 300 sq km. Plying the waters are *fanchuan*, pirate-sized junks with bamboo-battened canvas sails. It's mainly an area for scenic touring and hiking, and there are some fabulous aerial views from the ridges up at Dragon Gate in the Western Hills.

Dàguān Park 大观公园
Dàguān Gōngyuán

Also known as Grand View Park, this recreational area is at the northernmost tip of Lake Dian, 3km south-west of the city centre. The park covers 60 hectares and includes a nursery with potted plants, children's playground, rowing boats and pavilions. It's most famed for its access to and views of Lake Dian and the Western Hills, particularly on the evening of Mid-Autumn Festival. Work began on the park in 1690 after a Buddhist temple was constructed here in 1682.

The **Grand View Tower** (Dàguān Lóu) provides good views of Lake Dian. Its façades are inscribed with a 180-character poem – perhaps the most famous 'couplet' in South-West China – by Qing poet Sun Ranweng (1700–75). The poem rapturously extols the beauty of the lake; the official English translation drones on for two pages. You'll also probably be told that Queen Elizabeth II planted three English rose bushes here in 1986.

Bus No 4 runs to Dàguān Park from Yuántōng Sì via the city centre; bus No 52 departs from near the Kunming Hotel. Entry is Y5.

At the south-eastern end of the park you can take a boat to Hǎigěng Park and Lóngmén village. Boats leave when full and the 40-minute ride costs Y5. From Lóngmén village you can hike up the trail to Dragon Gate and the Western Hills, and then catch a minibus back into town near the summit at the Tomb of Niè Ěr. From Hǎigěng, take the No 44 bus to Kūnmíng's main train station.

Western Hills
Xī Shān

This range of mountains spreads across a 40km-long wedge of parkland on the western side of Lake Dian. They're also known as the Green Peacock Mountains or more commonly, the Sleeping Beauty Hills, a reference to their undulating contours resembling a reclining woman with tresses of hair flowing into the sea.

The path to the summit passes a series of famous temples – it's a steep approach from the north side. The hike from Gāoyáo bus station at the foot of the Western Hills to the summit at Dragon Gate takes 2½ hours, though most people take a connecting bus from Gāoyáo to the top section, or take a minibus direct to Niè Ěr's Tomb. The initial hike up to Niè Ěr's Tomb is only worth doing if you take the shortcut paths through the lovely forest. It is also possible to cycle to the Western Hills from the city in about

---

The Legend of the Hills

The Chinese legend describing the creation of the Western Hills is one of the most engaging and sad. Before they married, two young lovers who lived in Dragon Gate village at the foot of Luohan Mountain decided to chip stone from the mountain to form a dragon gate, emulating one in northern China. For years the two toiled but just before completion, the man accidentally broke the tip of a calligraphy brush on a carving. Devastated, he leapt from the cliffs to his death. The young girl was so grief-stricken that her tears filled Lake Dian. She lay down and turned to stone, forming the rest of the Western Hills.

an hour – consider doing the return route across the dykes of upper Lake Dian.

Locals traditionally visit the Western Hills on the third day of the third month of the lunar calendar, a custom dating from the Warring States period.

At the foot of the climb, about 15km from Kūnmíng, is **Huátíng Sì**, one of the largest and oldest groupings of surviving Buddhist structures in northern Yúnnán. A country temple of the Nánzhāo kingdom, it's believed to have been constructed in the 11th century, rebuilt in the 14th century, and extended in the Ming and Qing dynasties. The present temple was finished in 1920. The temple has some fine statues, a dozen or so stupas and excellent gardens. The main hall features 500 arhats (Buddhists who have passed to nirvana after death), representations of disciples of Buddha. The Indian heritage of South-West China is more obvious here than anywhere else in the region.

The Y4 entry fee is worth it.

The road from the Huátíng Sì winds 2km up to the Ming dynasty **Tàihuá Sì**, which boasts a fine collection of magnolias and camellias. The temple is comprised of six temples and halls. The original temple, the first built in the Western Hills, was constructed in 1306 by Xuan Jian, a monk from Qūjìng who travelled 9000km just to study Mahayana Buddhism in Zhèjiāng province. The statues of the Four Heavenly Kings here are a very different style to those at the Huátíng Sì. The views of Lake Dian are a bonus. Entry costs Y3.

Farther along the road, near the minibus and cable car terminus is the **Tomb of Niè Ěr** (Nièěr Zhīmù; admission Y1). Niè Ěr (1912–36) was a talented Yúnnán musician who composed the national anthem of the PRC before drowning in Japan on his way for further training in the Soviet Union. From here you can catch a chairlift (Y15) if you want to skip the fairly steep ascent to the summit. Alternatively a tourist tram takes passengers up to Dragon Gate (see following) for Y2. You can also catch a cable car (Y30) here down to Hǎigěng Park and Yúnnán Nationalities Village.

The **Sanqing Temple** (Sānqīng Gé), actually a group of temples, halls and pavilions, was a country villa for a prince of the Yuan dynasty and was later turned into a temple dedicated to the three main Taoist deities. There is a small spring behind Zhenwu Hall.

Farther up is **Dragon Gate** (Lóngmén), a group of grottoes, sculptures, corridors and pavilions hacked from the cliff between 1781 and 1853 by a Taoist monk and co-workers, who must have been hanging up there by their fingertips. At least that's what the locals do when they visit, seeking out views of Lake Dian. Some of the vistas are truly spectacular. The tunnel along the outer cliff edge is so narrow that only one or two people can squeeze by, so avoid public holidays and weekends! It's possible to walk up to Dragon's Gate along the cliff path and return via the back paths. Entry to the Dragon Gate area (which includes Sanqing Temple) costs Y20. All the temples are open as long as there are visitors.

Getting There & Away From Kūnmíng to the Western Hills the most convenient transport is minibus (Y6 to Y8, 30 minutes). These leave from outside the Yúnnán Fàndiàn between 7.30am and 1pm, though you won't find much after 10am.

A more reliable option is to use local buses: take bus No 5 from the Kunming Hotel to the terminus at Liǎngjiāhé, and then change to bus No 6, which will take you to the Gāoyáo bus station at the foot of the hills. Minibuses (Y5 to Y6) also leave from Liǎngjiāhé and drop passengers off at the Niè Ěr Tomb.

Returning to Kūnmíng, you can either take the bus or scramble down to Lóngmén village (also known as Shānyí Cūn), on the lake side. A thousand steps wind forever down from the main road, 200m before the Dragon's Gate and Sanqing Temple area ticket office. When you reach the road, turn right and walk about 100m to a narrow spit of land that leads across the lake. You'll arrive at a narrow stretch of water and a small bridge. (You can also take the cable car from Niè Ěr's Tomb to Hǎigěng Park for Y30). You can proceed by foot through

Hǎigěng Park (admission Y8) to the far entrance, and catch the No 44 bus to the Kūnmíng train station.

The tour can easily be done in reverse; start with the bus No 44 to Hǎigěng Park, either walk to Lóngmén village and climb straight up to Dragon Gate or take the cable car for Y30, then when you are finished make your way down through the temples to the Gāoyáo bus station, where you can get bus No 6 back to the Liǎngjīahé terminus and then the No 5 bus to the Yúnnán Hotel. Note that if you don't want to pay Y8 to walk through Hǎigěng Park you'll have to walk 3km from the entrance of the Yúnnán Nationalities Village or take a taxi.

Alternatively, bus No 33 runs along the western lake shore through Dragon Gate Village, or take a boat from Dàguān Park.

Yúnnán Nationalities Village
云南民族村　Yúnnán Mínzú Cūn

On the north-eastern side of the lake, is a string of model minority villages that aim to represent all 26 of Yúnnán's minority groups (12 have been built so far). It's a rather expensive cultural experience, with a Y45 general entry fee (students Y25). There are also song-and-dance performances during the day such as a Lisu sword climbing and a Wa wood-drum dance. An evening ticket (Y20), issued after 6pm, gets you into an evening bonfire and song and dance performance.

As for the villages, while they show you what the minorities' architecture and costumes look like, it's impossible to get any feel for how these people really live. Add in the hordes of gawking tourists, and the place feels more like a zoo – spend an extra day in Xīshuāngbǎnnà or Déhóng, where you can see the real thing.

Hǎigěng Park 海埂公园
Hǎigěng Gōngyuán

After the Nationalities Village, what little remains of nearby Hǎigěng Park – on a narrow peninsula of greenery jutting into and separating the lake – has become a good place to escape the crowds and enjoy the scenery. Most of the lakefront restaurants are shuttered, giving the place a ghost town feel, but there are plenty of recreational activities (see the Activities section earlier). There are great views of the lake and the Western Hills, and plenty of spots to kick back or have a picnic. The park even has a sandy beach for swimming. Then you can tackle the hike up to Dragon Gate or walk to the east end of the park and take the cable car up to the Niè Ěr Tomb (Y30 one-way, Y50 return). The last car leaves at 5pm.

Bus No 44 runs to Hǎigěng Park from one street north of the Kūnmíng Train Station.

Yúnnán Nationalities Museum
云南民族博物馆　Yúnnán Mínzú Bówùguǎn

If you are headed into Yúnnán's minority areas this large and modern museum is worth a visit. There are eight main halls that take in festivals, folk art, jewellery, costume, social structure, writing, handicrafts and musical instruments. Displays range from spirit traps of the Jingpo and totems of the Wa to a set of Yi shaman clothes and a monkey skin pouch made by the Lisu of the Nùjiāng Valley.

The museum has a good bookshop and a couple of shops that sell some of the best examples of minority clothing, though prices are high. Opening hours are Tuesday to Sunday, 9am to 4.30pm. Entry is Y10 (students Y4).

Zhèng Hé Park 郑和公园
Zhènghé Gōngyuán

At the southern edge of the lake, this park commemorates the Ming dynasty navigator Zhèng Hé (also known as Admiral Cheng Ho). A mausoleum here holds tablets describing his life and works. Zheng He, a Muslim, made seven voyages to over 30 Asian and African countries in the 15th century in command of a huge imperial naval fleet.

Near the eastern gate a museum to Zheng He's exploits is housed in a Ming dynasty temple. Besides the obligatory bust of Zheng He, the small museum mostly comprises paintings of the admiral's fleets. West of here is a mausoleum containing Zheng He's father.

From the Xiǎoxīmén station take the bus to Kúnyáng: the park is on a hill overlooking the town. For a change of pace, take a train from the north train station to Hǎikǒu, and then a local bus to Kúnyáng. You can complete a full circuit by catching a bus onto Jìnchéng and Chénggòng. There's accommodation in Kúnyáng for around Y20 per bed.

Chénggòng

This is an orchard region on the eastern side of the lake. Climate has a lot to do with Kūnmíng's reputation as China's flower capital; cultivation in the province has grown at 30% per annum, currently producing over 200 million sprays of flowers annually. Flowers bloom all year round, with the 'flower tide' in January, February and March. This is the best time to visit, especially **Dòunán village** near Chénggòng. Once one of Yúnnán's poorest villages, Dòunán now sells more than 400,000 sprays of flowers *each day* at its massive 1000-stall market, raking in Y300,000 daily. In four years, the village's per capita annual income has jumped from US$13 to US$445; even Yunnan Airlines has set up an office in the village to facilitate the daily shipments of 200,000 flowers out of Kūnmíng to northern and eastern cities.

During the Spring Festival (February to March) blooming species can be found at temple sites around Kūnmíng – notably the Tàihuá, Huátíng, Bamboo and Golden temples, as well as Black Dragon Pool.

Take the No 5 bus east to the terminus at Juhuacun, and change there for the No 12 bus to Chénggòng.

SHÍLÍN 石林
☎ 0871

Shílín, or the Stone Forest, about 100km south-east of Kūnmíng, is a massive collection of grey limestone pillars, the tallest 30m high, split by rain water and eroded to their present fanciful forms. Marine fossils found in the area suggest that it was once under the sea. Legend has it that the immortals smashed a mountain into a labyrinth for lovers.

The maze of grey pinnacles and peaks, with the occasional pool, is treated as an oversized rockery – with a walkway here, a

pavilion there, some railings along paths and some mind-bending weeds. You'd certainly need some chemical stimulants to make out such formations as General Zhao Guan Pitching a Camp (a bunch of rocks) or Moon-Gazing Rhino (another bunch of rocks). The maze is cooler and quieter by moonlight, and would enthral a surrealist painter. It's a great wander with a cold beer.

The Stone Forest is essentially a tourist attraction for Chinese. The important thing, if you venture here, is to get away from the main tourist area – there are some idyllic, secluded walks within about 2km of the centre.

The villages are inhabited by the Sani branch of the Yi tribespeople. Since so many ethnically interesting areas of Yúnnán are now open, you might be disappointed if you make the trip just to see the Sani who live in this area. Their craftwork (embroidery, purses, footwear) is sold at stalls at the forest entrance, and Sani women act as tour guides. You are more likely to see genuine Sani culture at Lùnán's Wednesday or Saturday market (see the Lùnán entry later in this chapter). On the 24th of the sixth month of the lunar calendar, the Sani hold their Torch Festival.

Off to the side is Five-Tree Village, which is an easy walk and has the flavour of a Mexican pueblo, but it's been commercialised. For those keen on genuine village and farming life, well, the Stone Forest is a big place – you can easily get lost. Just take your butterfly net and a lunch box along and keep walking – you'll get somewhere eventually.

There is a Y55 entry fee for foreigners into the main Stone Forest, though you should be able to get in for Y30 with any student card. Amazingly, the ticket office is open 24 hours. English-speaking guides cost Y80 for a 2½ hour tour.

Places to Stay

Most people visit the Stone Forest as a day trip from Kūnmíng, though it's not a bad idea to stay the night. It's also possible to stay in Lùnán, a ten-minute minibus ride away.

The *Shílín Bīnguǎn* (☎ 771 1405), near the main entrance to the Stone Forest, is a villa-type place with a souvenir shop and dining hall. A double room costs Y260 or Y300 and triples are Y350. Before you despair, there's a 'Common Room Department' (Pǔtōng Kèfáng) at the back, with basic doubles for Y30 per bed, though you may have to bargain. Singles have to pay for the room but can probably get away with Y40. You don't get a lot for your money. Grubby doubles with bathroom cost Y100. To find the rooms follow the circular road clockwise to the other side of the hill.

The *Shílín Bìshǔyuán Bīnguǎn* (☎ 771 1088) is a new hotel right where the main forest trails start. Rooms are clean and pleasant, with a nice bathroom and views over the Stone Forest. Doubles/triples cost Y300/360 but were as low as Y150/180 when we were there, making it the best-value mid-range choice.

Rates are a bit cheaper at the *Yúnlín Bīnguǎn* (☎ 771 1410), which is about 1km down the road that forks to the right after you cross the bridge. Rooms range from Y100 to Y150 in the old block (the first building you come to) to Y250 to Y350 in the new block, where you'll find the reception.

The only other place inside the forest is the *Holiday Hotel* (Jiàrì Jiǔdiàn; ☎ 771 0888), by the main entrance, which has rooms for Y210, discounted to Y170.

On the main highway, 400m from the main entrance is the *Shílín Tiānyù Jiǔdiàn* (☎ 771 0898), with three-star rooms for Y218, discounted to Y158.

Places to Eat

Several *restaurants* next to the bus terminal specialise in duck roasted in extremely hot clay ovens fuelled with pine needles. A whole duck costs Y40 to Y50 and takes about 20 minutes to cook – have the restaurant staff put a beer in their freezer and it'll be just right when the duck comes out. The ducks are massaged with a local sesame oil mixture before roasting.

Near the main Stone Forest entrance is a cluster of *restaurants* and *snack bars* that are open from dawn to dusk. Check all prices before you order as overcharging is not uncommon. The hotels also have decent restaurants.

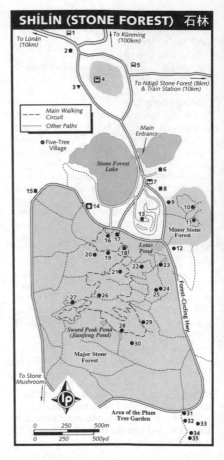

Entertainment

Sani song-and-dance evenings are organised when there are enough tourists. Surprisingly, these events turn into good-natured exchanges between *Homo ektachromo* and *Sani dollari* and neither comes off worse for wear. The short performances display ethnic costumes and musical instruments. Shows start at around 8pm at a stage next to the mini stone forest but there are sometimes extra performances so ask at the hotels. Performances are free.

There are also Sani performances between 2pm and 3pm. Occasional bull-fighting

SHÍLÍN (STONE FOREST)

PLACES TO STAY & EAT

2 Shílín Tiānyù Jiǔdiàn
石林天裕酒店

3 Restaurants
餐厅饭店

6 Holiday Hotel
石林节日酒店

8 Shílín Bīnguǎn
(Old Building)
石林宾馆（老楼）

13 Shílín Bīnguǎn;
CITS
石林宾馆;
中国国际旅行社

15 Yúnlín Bīnguǎn
云林宾馆

17 Shílín Bìshǔyuán
Bīnguǎn
石林避暑园宾馆

OTHER

1 Microbuses to
Lùnán;
Horse Carts
中巴车到路南、
马车

4 Bus Departures
汽车出发处

5 Buses to the
Train Station
到火车站的汽车

7 Post Office
邮局

9 Stage
舞台

10 Inscription of Mao
Zedong's Poem
'Ode to the
Plum Blossom'
咏梅石

11 Rock Arrowhead
Point to the Sky
石柱擎天

12 Monk Tanseng
唐僧石

14 PSB
公安局

16 Lion Pond
狮子池

18 Stone Screen
石屏风

19 Baby Buffalo
小牛

20 Sweet Water Well
甜水井

21 Open Stage
舞场

22 Resting Peak for
Wild Geese
落雁峰

23 Stone Prison
石监狱

24 Phoenix Combing
Its Wings
凤凰梳翅

25 Stone Mushroom
灵芝石

26 Steps to the Sky
耸天阶

27 Lotus Peak
莲花峰

28 Two Birds Feeding
Each Other
双鸟渡食

29 Stone Bell
石钟

30 Moon-Gazing
Rhino
犀牛望月

31 Wife Waiting
for Her
Husband
望夫石

32 Goddess of Mercy
观音石

33 Camel Riding
on an Elephant
骆驼骑象

34 Swan Gazing Afar
天鹅远嘱

35 Old Man
Taking a Stroll
漫步从容

takes place between 1pm and 2pm at a natural outdoor amphitheatre by Hidden Lake at the back of the Stone Forest. Wrestling, bullfighting, singing and dancing is held here during the Torch Festival – see the 'Festivals' boxed text at the beginning of the chapter for dates.

Getting There & Away

There are plenty of day tours from Kūnmíng from the front of the train station, and from near the King World Hotel – choose these with extreme caution. You may spend the whole morning rummaging around in various caves (a national obsession), followed by a marathon lunch. If you're lucky you may even get an hour or so in the Stone Forest before being whisked back to Kūnmíng. That said, the occasional traveller has come back satisfied – an interesting initiation into Chinese tourism rituals

It's easy to visit the forest from Lùnán or to combine it with a visit to other towns in south-east Yúnnán.

Train Currently, the most popular way to get to the Stone Forest is the express tourist train from Kūnmíng. Services currently depart Kūnmíng's main train station at 8.32am, arriving at 10.06am. Return services depart Shílín at 4.30pm, arriving back in Kūnmíng at 6.04pm. Tickets cost Y20/30 one-way/return for a hard seat or Y25/40 for a soft seat. Buses meet the trains to take passengers the extra 10km or so to the Stone Forest. The Camellia Hotel normally runs a morning bus from the hotel to catch the morning departure. You can buy admission tickets to the Stone Forest on the train.

Bus Alternatively, buses leave Kūnmíng's long-distance bus station at 7.30am and 8.40am to Shílín (Y18.50). There are also plenty of buses from Kūnmíng's east bus station (Y15). Getting back from the Stone Forest to Kūnmíng is fairly simple. In the afternoon there are usually minibuses waiting at the car park outside the entrance, leaving when full (Y10 to Y15). In the morning you'll have less choice and you may have to take a horse cart or microbus 2km to the main highway and flag down a Kūnmíng-bound bus there. Better yet, continue into Lùnán county or further afield into south-east Yúnnán.

AROUND SHÍLÍN

If you want to get away from the tourist crowds there are less visited sights around Shílín. Larger (300 hectare) rock formations called the **Nǎigǔ Stone Forest** (Nǎigǔ Shílín Fēngjǐngqū), with karst caves, a large waterfall and impressive causeway of black volcanic blocks (*nǎigǔ* means black in the local Yi dialect) is 8km north-east of the main Stone Forest. The easiest way to get to Nǎigǔ is to take a microbus (Y15 one-way) or more relaxing horse cart (Y10 return, 45 minutes) from the main road. Entry is Y25.

Another day trip is the impressive **Dàdiéshuǐ Waterfall**, 18km from the Stone Forest. Hire a microbus for Y30 from Lùnán, otherwise walk 2km south-west of Lùnán centre, turning left when you see a blue sign, to a small bus stand where microbuses leave for Bǎnqiáo (Y2) and then change for a less frequent microbus to the falls. Entry is Y18.

Other places include **Yuè Hú** (Moon Lake), 15km away and accessible only by hired minibus, and **Cháng Hú** (Long Lake). To get to Cháng Hú take a bus bound for Guìshān or Lúxī, and get off at Wéizé, from where it's 1.5km to the lake. Entry is Y6.

Guìshān itself is an interesting town that has an excellent Sunday market full of Sani traders and completely unfrequented by foreign tourists. There is also a remarkable blue church in town that looks like it's been lifted straight from St Petersburg.

LÙNÁN 路南
☎ 0871

Lùnán is a small market town about 10km from the Stone Forest. It's not worth making a special effort to visit, but if you do go, try to catch a market day (Wednesday or Saturday), when Lùnán becomes a colossal jam of donkeys, horse carts and bicycles. The streets are packed with produce, poultry and wares, and Sani women are dressed in their finest. The main market entrance is opposite the Kēxīng Bīnguǎn.

Places to Stay & Eat

The **Kēxīng Bīnguǎn** (☎ 779 6725) on the south-west side of the roundabout is a good budget bet with rooms with bathroom for Y50 and beds in a triple for Y10, though it's in need of renovation.

The high-profile **Stone Forest Hotel** (Shílín Dàjiǔdiàn; ☎ 779 8888, fax 779 4887) is right on the central roundabout and has three-star rooms for Y228/368, plus 15% but including breakfast and transfer from the train station.

There are plenty of restaurants on the street next to the Stone Forest Hotel. The **Línlǎowū Fàndiàn** serves good food at bargain prices and there's plenty of fresh produce to point at.

Getting There & Away

Minibuses shuttle between Lùnán and Shílín regularly (Y2, ten minutes). In Lùnán, flag down anything heading north of the main traffic circle. At Shílín, minibuses leave from a stand on the main road.

Minibuses to Kūnmíng (Y14, 1½ hours) depart regularly from the west side of Lùnán's main roundabout until around 7pm. For Lúxī (Y12, two hours), catch a through bus at the south-east corner of the roundabout.

JIǓXIĀNG 九乡

The Jiǔxiāng Scenic Area consists of a series of caves, river gorges and waterfalls. It's an up-and-coming destination for local Chinese but few foreigners make it out here. Most visitors take a short boat trip through the Yīncuìxiá gorge and then follow walkways into the Jīnghúnxiá gorge. After that you enter the main cave hall and proceed through the complex, passing the **Cíxióng Waterfall** and some impressive limestone terraces. From the exit of the cave a Y15 cable car takes visitors back to the entrance. Entry to the caves is Y30. There are several other caves in the area.

The area is best visited as a day trip but if you want to spend the night, the *Jiǔxiāng Bīnguǎn* has decent rooms for Y80.

In Yíliáng, 38km away, the *Shuānglú Dàjiǔdiàn (☎ 0871-753 9444)* on the main highway is a good bet if you can't get back to Kūnmíng. Rooms cost Y260 but may be discounted as low as Y80.

To get to Jiǔxiāng take a minibus from Kūnmíng to Yíliáng (Y8, one hour) and then another from Yíliáng bus station or the road junction to Jiǔxiāng (Y5, one hour)

CHǓXIÓNG 楚雄
☎ 0878

Most travellers have probably been to this river-side town and not known it. The county seat and centre of the Yi nationality, Chǔxióng is 185km and two-plus hours west of Kūnmíng on the road to Dàlǐ. Originally called Elu in the Yi language, the city is also known today as Lùchéng, or Deer City. It isn't pretty on the main highway in the northern part of the city along the river, but the town's centre and ambitiously upgraded city can be fairly interesting.

The Yi account for nearly 20% of the city's 400,000 residents – for more information on the Yi see the boxed text in the Around Xīchāng section of the Sìchuān chapter. Other minorities with significant populations include Huí, Bai and Miáo.

Things to See

Chǔxióng's city sights include **Longjiang Park** in the northern section of the city and **Elu Park** in the western part of town. The latter has good views.

Just south of town is the 25m-high **Yan Pagoda**, based on the design of the Dayan Pagoda of Xī'ān and dating from the Ming dynasty. It collapsed in an earthquake during the Qing dynasty and was rebuilt.

Digging in the Dirt

Budding palaeontologists and anthropologists will love the Chǔxióng region. Near Lùfēng to the east, bone fragments of palaeanthropoids two to eight million years old have been unearthed. Over 120 dinosaurs dating back up to 200 million years have also been found here in what is though to be one of the world's largest dinosaur burial grounds, and a dinosaur museum has recently been established.

The famed Yuanmou Man was unearthed near Shangnabang village in Yuánmóu bordering Chǔxióng county, dating Yúnnán's earliest human-like ancestor to 1.7 million years ago. A large scale excavation near the Long River unearthed the Dadunzi Neolithic Village. In March 2001 fossilised tusk fragments from a stegadon, or sabre-toothed elephant, were unearthed in nearby Wēishān county.

Most Chinese museums have bronze drums and other relics from nearby Wanjiaba's 2500-year-old Eastern Zhou excavation sites. Many of these sites can be visited, though transport is tricky.

Getting There & Away

Buses constantly depart from Kūnmíng's main bus station between 7am and 5.50pm; though you may have to take a Xiàguān/Dàlǐ-bound bus and get off at the road junction (Y25/Y32, three hours). You're not supposed to get off the Dàlǐ-bound express bus in Chǔxióng, but they don't seem to mind.

Chǔxióng is served by Xiàguān-bound trains but all trains currently arrive in the middle of the night.

AROUND CHǓXIÓNG
Zǐxī Shān 紫金山

This isolated peak in a 12km-long range is 20km west of town. The prime minister of the kingdom of Dàlǐ used the mountains as a retreat. When he retired, he built nearly 100 temples, pavilions and nunneries, but earthquakes and wars have left only one – Zǐdìng Sì. The mountain is known for its two resident flocks of wild peacocks and a 600-year-old camellia tree.

Dàyáo 大姚

About 100km north-west of Chǔxióng is Dàyáo. The feature of this town is one of the oddest-looking pagodas you'll see – the **Bái Tǎ**, or White Pagoda, to the west in Báitǎ Shān. It's hard to ignore its phallic shape, designed to resemble a mallet used to strike an inverted Buddhist bell. The base is an octagonal *samara* while the upper level, reaching 18m, is organised into three structures. The pagoda has a small chink in it, rumoured to be for once-hidden treasure, dislodged during an earthquake.

A **Confucian Temple** dating from the Ming dynasty is 33km north-west of Dàyáo, in Shíyáng. It's famed for having supposedly the only intact, original bronze temple statue of Confucius on mainland China.

It might be a good idea to go to Xiàguān and/or Dàlǐ via Bīnchuán from Dàyáo if you don't want to slog all the way back to Chǔxióng or Kūnmíng.

Yuánmóu Earth Forest 元谋土林

Yuánmóu Tǔlín

Located about 100km north of Chǔxióng, Yuánmóu is the site of famed anthropological excavations and this unique landform. Bizarrely striated sand and clay spires and pillars rise from the flat plains – some formations are so huge they actually resemble cathedrals – and they're given the usual weird names. It's one of Yúnnán's 'Three Forests' along with Kūnmíng's Stone Forest and Xīshuāngbǎnnà's Rain Forest. This freak geology can be found around the region, but is best at Bānguǒ, north-west of Yuánmóu, near the Dongsha River.

Buses depart from Yuánmóu to the Earth Forest. In summer you might do the last leg in a donkey cart. Though Yuánmóu is technically in Chǔxióng county, it's just as close to Kūnmíng and is probably most easily accessed from the capital on any Chéngdū-bound train (4½ hours).

XIÀGUĀN 下关

☎ 0872

Xiàguān lies at the southern tip of Ěrhǎi (Ear-Shaped) Lake, about 400km west of Kūnmíng. It was once an important staging post on the Burma Road and is still a key transport centre for north-west Yúnnán. Xiàguān is the capital of Dàlǐ prefecture and is also referred to as Dàlǐ Shí (Dàlǐ City). This confuses some travellers, who think they are already in Dàlǐ, book into a hotel and head off in pursuit of a banana pancake only to discover they haven't arrived yet. Nobody stays in Xiàguān unless they have an early bus the next morning.

To go straight to Dàlǐ, upon arriving in Xiàguān, turn left out of the long-distance bus station, and at the first intersection turn left. Just up from the corner, diagonally opposite the Dàlǐ Hotel, is the station for the No 4 local bus, which runs to the real Dàlǐ (Y1.2, 30 minutes) until around 8pm. If you want to be sure, ask for Dàlǐ Gǔchéng (Dàlǐ Old City). Alternatively, minibuses run from a block west of the bus station (turn right out of the entrance) but you'll spend a lot of time waiting for other passengers.

Information

Public Security Bureau The regional PSB office on 21 Tianbao Jie now handles all visa extensions for Xiàguān and Dàlǐ. It's a five- to ten-minute walk north and then west of the bus station. See the Dàlǐ section for more details.

Things to See & Do

There are good views of the lake and mountains from **Ěrhǎi Park** (Ěrhǎi Gōngyuán). You can reach the park on foot or by motortricycle for around Y3. Bus No 6 goes to the park from the centre of town.

Travel agents around the bus station also sell tickets for day trips up and down Ěrhǎi Lake, taking in all the major sights. Prices for the all-day tours range from Y60 to Y80.

At the south end of Black Dragon Bridge over the Xi'er River, along Tianbao Lu, is Tiānbǎo Park, which holds the repaired tombs of the **Pit of 10,000 War Victims**. The pit probably contains the remains of at least as many soldiers who perished under the Tianbao emperor of the Tang dynasty. He repeatedly sent troops here in attacks on the Nánzhāo kingdom but his armies were slaughtered each time. Following these hu-

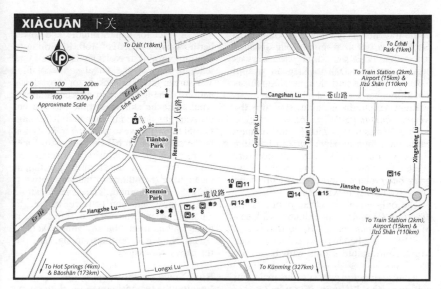

XIÀGUĀN 下关

XIÀGUĀN

1   Erhǎi Bīnguǎn
    洱海宾馆
2   PSB
    公安局
3   Yúnnán
    Airlines
    云南航空公司
4   Dàlǐ Fàndiàn
    大理饭店
5   Bus No 4
    Terminus
    (to Dali)
    四路车到大理古城

6   China Post
    邮电局
7   Xiàguān Fàndiàn
    下关饭店
8   Main Bus Station
    汽车客运站
9   Kèyùn Fàndiàn
    客运饭店
10 Dàyùn Bīnguǎn
    大运宾馆
11 Xiàguān Prefecture
    Bus Station
    州汽车站

12 Minibuses
    to Dàlǐ
    中巴到大理古城
13 Xiàguān
    Bīnguǎn
    下关宾馆
14 Bus Station
    汽车客运站
15 Jiāotōng
    Fàndiàn
    交通饭店
16 East Bus Station
    汽车运东站

miliations, one general purportedly drowned himself and his spirit haunts a cave on Xieyang Peak west of town. Locals built a temple to house his spirit. A park has grown around the peak and it has good views of Xiàguān.

Snake-Bone Pagoda 蛇骨塔
Shégú Tǎ
This pagoda stands 3km north of Xiàguān in Yangping village at the base of Ma'er Peak. You can see it from the bus ride north to Dàlǐ. It was built to commemorate a

heroic Bai man who strapped knives to his body and allowed a boa constrictor dragon terrorising Ěrhǎi Lake to devour him, killing the beast. Just south of here, at the base of Xieyang Peak, is **Bǎolìng Sì**, which houses a statue of the local hero and the God of the White Dragon King he killed.

Xiàguān Hot Spring 下关温泉
South-west of Xiàguān, a few kilometres in the suburbs, is this hot spring in the Si'er River valley. A small 'resort' with marble bathtubs below waterfalls has been built.

Places to Stay

Some travellers stay a night in Xiàguān to catch an early bus from the long-distance bus station, but it's not strictly necessary as buses start from Dàlǐ to Xiàguān around 6.30am. Accommodation in Xiàguān is generally overpriced and mid-range.

Right next to the main bus station is the **Kèyùn Fàndiàn** (☎ 212 5286), with singles/doubles/triples for Y38/50/48 with common bathroom. Slightly better but still box-like singles/doubles/triples with bathroom are available at Y68/80/90. The hotel is a bit grim but probably the cheapest option if you have to stay in Xiàguān.

The only other dirt cheap option is the **Jiāotōng Fàndiàn**, a five-minute walk east of the main bus station. Basic rooms cost Y8/10/15 for a bed in a single/double/quad. More comfortable rooms with bathroom are Y100.

Almost directly opposite the main bus station is the **Xiàguān Bīnguǎn** (☎ 217 4933). Rooms in the glitzy main building cost Y120 to Y168 for singles and Y240 for doubles but these are often discounted by up to 40%. The separate west wing of the hotel has triples for Y45 to Y60 and doubles for Y60 to Y80 without bathroom, which are OK but still overpriced.

The **Dàlǐ Fàndiàn**, near the No 4 bus stop, has been transformed into a three-star monster with rooms for Y168, discounted to Y100.

There are several other similar hotels with rooms for around Y100, including the **Xiàguān Fàndiàn** and **Dàyùn Bīnguǎn**.

Getting There & Away

Air Xiàguān's new airport is 15km from town. Flights leave daily to Kūnmíng (Y340) and Xīshuāngbǎnnà/Jǐnghóng (Y540). The Yunnan Airlines ticket office (☎ 216 6588) is next to the Dàlǐ Fàndiàn. There are no public buses to the airport; taxis cost Y40 to Y50 from Xiàguān or Y80 from Dàlǐ.

Train The railway link between Kūnmíng and Xiàguān was finally opened in 1999. Overnight sleeper trains leave Kūnmíng's main train station at 10.10pm, arriving in Xiàguān at 6.45am. Hard sleepers are Y75, Y85 or Y95 for upper, middle and lower berth. A soft sleeper is Y160. Returning to Kūnmíng trains leave Xiàguān at around 9.30pm.

You can buy train tickets for most destinations (Chéngdū etc) from Kūnmíng at a window at the entrance to the bus station, but stupidly, not from Xiàguān to Kūnmíng. For that you'll have to go to the train station in the eastern suburbs! For tickets to Éméi Shān, Chéngdū etc you will normally be sold a ticket departing from the junction at Guǎngtōng, two-thirds of the way between Xiàguān and Kūnmíng. This saves you time and money but you'll have to get to Guǎngtōng in time for the train; ask if there's a bus when you buy your ticket.

Bus No 1 goes to the train station from the centre of town.

Bus Xiàguān has several bus stations. Luckily, the two main ones are on the same street, on the same side, approximately two blocks apart. Both have departures throughout the province, so if the main one doesn't have a good departure time for you, wander along to the other. Xiàguān also has a north bus station (for Zhōngdiàn) and an east bus station (for Bīnchúan).

The main bus station has luxury Royale Express buses and this is the quickest way to travel. Buses to Lìjiāng (Y50, 3½ hours) depart at 8.30am and 9.30am, and at 2pm and 7pm. There are two buses to Zhōngdiàn (seven hours, via Lìjiāng) at 9am and 3pm (Y85). There are express buses to Kūnmíng every 30 minutes between 7.30am and 8.30pm (Y89 to Y103, six hours). There are also plenty of minibuses to Kūnmíng.

Other bus departures from the main bus station include Bǎoshān (Y26, six hours) at 7.30, 8.30, 9.30 and 10.30am and Mángshì (Lúxī; 12 hours) at 7am (Y50) and 7pm (sleeper bus; Y80). The Mángshì buses continue to Ruìlì (Y90, 15 hours). Consider breaking the journey by staying in Bǎoshān. Sleeper buses to Téngchōng leave at 7.30pm (Y70). To Liùkù, in the Nùjiāng Valley, there are morning buses for Y30 to Y40, sleepers for Y45 or a single daily express bus for Y60 that pulls in from Kūnmíng around 1.30pm.

Buses north for Lìjiāng leave at 6.40am, 10am and 12.30pm and cost Y40 to Y50 (these stop in Dàlǐ to pick up passengers, and tickets can also be booked in Dàlǐ). To Zhōngdiàn you are better off taking the express bus as normal buses depart from the north bus station. It would make sense to break the trip in Lìjiāng.

There are occasional direct sleeper buses to Jǐnghóng in Xīshuāngbǎnnà (Y145, 30 hours). Alternatively you could take local buses, breaking the trip at Líncāng and Láncāng. Roads are very bad along this route, and travel times have been known to stretch to three days.

To get to Jīzú Shān, minibuses run from the east bus station to Bīnchúan (Y10, two hours) frequently all day.

AROUND XIÀGUĀN
Jīzú Shān   鸡足山

Jīzú Shān (Chicken Foot Mountain) is one of China's sacred mountains and a major attraction for both Chinese and Tibetan Buddhist pilgrims. The mountain is about 110km north-east of Xiàguān. At the time of the Qing dynasty there were approximately 100 temples on the mountain and 5000 resident monks. The Cultural Revolution's assault did away with much that was of interest, though the temples have been undergoing renovation since 1979 and the area is now a nature reserve. More than 150,000 tourists and pilgrims clamber up the mountain every year to watch the sunrise. Jīndǐng, the Golden Summit, is at a cool 3240m so you will need some warm clothing.

Sights along the way include the **Zhùshèng Sì**, the most important temple on the mountain, about an hour's walk up from the bus stop at Shāzhǐ. **Zhōngshān Sì** (Mid-Mountain Temple), about halfway up the mountain holds little of interest. Just before the last ascent is the **Huáshǒu Mén** (Magnificent Summit Gate). At the summit is the **Lèngyán Tǎ**, a 13-tier Tang dynasty pagoda that was restored in 1927. There's some basic accommodation at the **Jīndǐng Sì** (Golden Summit Temple) next to the

pagoda – a sleeping bag might be a good idea at this altitude.

A popular option for making the ascent is to hire a pony. Travellers who have done the trip claim it's a lot of fun. Again, as with all Chinese mountains, a cable car (Y22) to the summit is a good way to cheat, though the ride only starts halfway up. Entry to Jīzú Shān is Y40.

Places to Stay Accommodation is available at the base of the mountain, about halfway up and at the summit. Prices average Y10 to Y15 per bed. Food gets fairly expensive once you reach the summit so you may want to bring some of your own.

If you need to stay in Bīnchúan, there's hotels, such as the **Bīnchúan Bīnguǎn**, with dorm beds for as cheap as Y15.

Getting There & Away From Xiàguān take a bus to Bīnchúan, 70km north-east of Xiàguān (Y10, two hours), from there you'll have to take another bus or minibus to Shāzhǐ at the foot of the mountain (Y10, one hour).

Some travellers have hiked from Wāsè on the eastern shore of Ěrhǎi Lake to Jīzú Shān. This should only be undertaken by experienced hikers. Locals claim that it is easy to get lost in the mountainous terrain and in bad weather the hike could turn into a bad experience. Take care, and talk to locals in Dàlǐ about your plans before you go.

Wēishān   巍山
Wēishān is famous for the Taoist temples on nearby Wēibǎo Shān, about 7km south of town. There are reportedly some fine Taoist murals here. It's 61km south of Xiàguān, so it could be done as a day trip.

DÀLǏ   大理
☎ 0872

Dàlǐ is a perfect place to tune out for a while. The stunning mountain backdrop, Ěrhǎi Lake, the old city, cappuccinos, pizzas and the herbal alternative to cheap Chinese beer (you can pick it yourself) make it, alongside Lìjiāng and Yángshuò, one of the few places in China where you can well and truly take a vacation from travelling.

Dàlǐ lies on the western edge of Ěrhǎi Lake at an altitude of 1900m, with the imposing Cāng Shān mountain range (average 4000m) behind it. For much of the five centuries in which Yúnnán governed its own affairs, Dàlǐ was the centre of operations, and the old city still retains a historical atmosphere that is hard to come by in other parts of China.

Dàlǐ has become a Mecca for travellers – escape the crowds on the narrow backstreets lined with old stone houses. Recently Dàlǐ's character has started to change, with the influx of Chinese tour groups. The southern part of town has been radically renovated to create a new 'old Dàlǐ', complete with original gates and renovated city walls. The wrecking balls have inched their way up Fuxing Lu, which is now lined with shops catering to Chinese tourists led around by guides dressed up in Bai costumes. The gentrification has been less successful than Lìjiāng's and has certainly taken some of the city's historical charm and authenticity.

History

In the early 8th century the Bai grouped together and succeeded in defeating the Tang imperial army, establishing the Nánzhāo kingdom. The kingdom held power throughout South-West China and, to a lesser extent, south-west Asia, since the kingdom ruled over upper Burma for much of the 9th century. This established Dàlǐ as an end node on the famed Burma Road. In the mid-13th century, the Nánzhāo kingdom fell before the undefeatable Mongol hordes of Kublai Khan, bringing Yúnnán back into the imperial Chinese ambit.

At the base of Zhōnghé Shān, just outside Dàlǐ, is a 1km-long section of wall from the town of Yangjumie, an ancient capital of the Nánzhāo and Dàlǐ kingdoms. At the base of Fódǐng Shān, 7km from Xiàguān, are the ruins of Taihe town, another Nánzhāo city.

Orientation

Dàlǐ is a midget-sized city that has preserved some cobbled streets and traditional stone architecture within its old walls. You can get your bearings just by taking a walk for about half an hour from the recently renovated South Gate (Nán Mén) across town to the North Gate (Běi Mén). You can also get a good overview of the town and its surroundings by walking around the town walls. The walls were renovated in 1998 after every government employee in Dàlǐ was forced to fork over a Y500 'contribution' to the rebuilding work.

Huguo Lu is the main strip for cafes – locals call it Yángrén Jiē (Foreigner's Street) – and this is where to turn for your cafe latte, burritos, ice-cold beer and other delicious treats. Dàlǐ is so popular that in 1996 this street was widened and made pedestrian-only.

Maps Dàlǐ and Ěrhǎi Lake area maps are available at street stalls near the corner of Huguo Lu and Fuxing Lu, though none of them are all that useful.

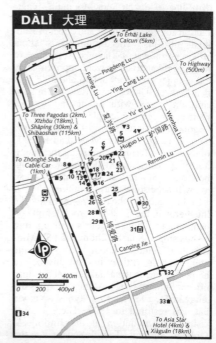

YÚNNÁN

Information

PSB Exhausted by a deluge of demands for visa extensions, the Dàlǐ PSB office has finally retreated to the relative safety of Xiàguān. This probably won't affect visa extensions too much, you'll just have to take bus No 4 to Xiàguān. Just after the bus crosses the river in Xiàguān, by the Ěrhǎi Bīnguǎn, get off, walk south down Renmin Lu and then take a right into Tianbao Jie. The office is on the right.

Money The Bank of China is in the centre of town, near the corner of Huguo Lu and Fuxing Lu. The bank changes cash and travellers cheques and will give cash advances on a credit card. It's open daily from 8am to 7.30pm, so there's no longer any reason to keep track of what day it is in Dàlǐ. Bank staff say that Western cards can be used in the ATM just outside the entrance to the bank.

The Industrial & Commercial Bank (ICBC) right on Huguo Lu also changes cash and travellers cheques daily and is open until 9pm.

Post & Communications The post office is at the corner of Fuxing Lu and Huguo Lu. This is the best place to make international calls, as it has direct dial and doesn't levy a service charge. You still can't use an international calling card, however. It's open until 8.30pm.

Email & Internet Access A number of places offer Internet access for Y10 per hour. One of the most professional places is Tim's Internet Shop, at 82 Boai Lu. Other places offering Internet access include the MCA Guesthouse, as does its shop at 69 Huguo Lu.

Laundry Most hotels offer cheap 24-hour laundry at around Y2 for a T-shirt or Y3 for trousers. The Ting Ting laundry on Boai Lu has roughly the same prices and a three-hour express service at double the normal charge. For Y40 it will wash and dry an entire load in three hours.

There are dozens of shoe repairers at the intersection of Huguo Lu and Fuxing Lu.

DÀLǏ

YÚNNÁN

PLACES TO STAY	PLACES TO EAT	OTHER
9 Yú'ān Garden 第四招待所 (榆安园)	3 Old Bai House Restaurant 白里香	5 China Post 邮电
10 Sunny Garden 第三招待所 (桑尼园)	4 Yúnnán Café 云南咖啡馆	8 Noodles Books
22 Jīnhuā Dàjiǔdiàn 金花大酒店	6 Tibetan Cafe 西藏餐厅	13 Ting Ting Laundry
24 No 2 Guesthouse 第二招待所	7 Old Wooden House 如意饭店	15 CITS 中国国际旅行社
25 Dàlǐ Bīnguǎn 大理宾馆	11 Marley's Cafe 马丽咖啡馆	16 Michael's Travel
26 Jim's Tibetan Peace Guesthouse; Jim's Peace Cafe 和平饭店	12 Sister's Cafe 14 Mr China's Son Cafe	18 Dàlǐ Passenger Service Ticket Office 大理客运售票处
28 Old Dàlǐ Four Seasons Inn 大理四客栈	17 Cafe de Jack; Tim's Internet Shop 樱花阁	23 Bank of China 中国银行
29 Xīngyuè Bīnguǎn 星月宾馆	19 Sunshine Cafe 20 Star Cafe 21 La Pizzeria La Stella	27 Local Buses to Shaping 往沙坪的公共汽车
33 MCA Guesthouse	**OTHER** 1 North Gate 北门	30 Wǔhuá Lóu 五华楼
	2 Vegetable Market 菜市场	31 Dàlǐ Museum 大理博物馆
		32 South Gate 南门
		34 Pagoda 三塔公园

Bookshops Noodles Books on Huguo Lu has the best selection of books and you can get a coffee while you browse. Mr China's Son Café has a large selection of books for rent or sale but sale prices are high. You can normally get copies here of He Liuyi's *Mr China's Son* (see Facts for the Visitor – Books for details).

Dàlǐ Museum 大理博物馆
Dàlǐ Bówùguǎn

This small collection of archaeological pieces relating to Bai history is worth a browse in between coffees or fruit shakes on Huguo Lu. See the boxed text 'The Bai' in the Around Dàlǐ section for more information on this minority group. There's an exhibit on marble handicrafts; a number of marble steles grace one wing.

There's an interesting permanent art exhibition at the back of the museum, featuring artists who have leapt onto the Yúnnán school of art bandwagon. It also has copies of scroll paintings by famous Chinese artists of old. These include Shun Huazhen's 5.75m-long scroll depicting the establishment of the Nánzhāo kingdom and, even better, a 30m-long scroll painting depicting old Dàlǐ Buddhist practices, flora and fauna, boats and houses.

The museum is open 8.30am to 5pm and admission is Y5.

Three Pagodas
Sān Tǎ Sì

Standing on the hillside 2km north-west of Dàlǐ, the three pagodas are an obligatory photo opportunity, particularly when seen reflected in the nearby lake. They are among the oldest standing structures in South-West China. The tallest of the three, **Qianxun Pagoda**, has 16 tiers that reach a height of 70m. It was originally erected in the mid-9th century by Xī'ān engineers. It is flanked by two smaller 10-tiered pagodas, each of which are 42m high.

The temple behind the pagodas, **Chongsheng Sì**, is laid out in a traditionally Yúnnánese style, with three layers of buildings lined up with a sacred peak in the background. The temple was recently restored and converted into a museum that chronicles the history, construction and renovation of the pagodas. Also on exhibit are marble slabs cut and framed so that the patterns of the marble appear to depict landscapes.

Many travellers find the pagodas more impressive from a distance. There's an admission fee of Y10 (some have been charged Y30) at the main entrance on the highway.

Organised Tours/Travel Agencies

Numerous travel agencies, cafes and individuals around town can arrange tours to sights around Ěrhǎi Lake. Most are boat trips across Ěrhǎi Lake to the market at Wāsè for Y20 to Y30 per person, which includes a horse cart trip to the lakeshore. Private entrepreneurs run cruises around the lake daily if there is enough demand.

During festivals, many of the cafes arrange transport to festival sites at nearby villages. Other possibilities include cormorant fishing trips and escorted hikes in the Cāng Shān.

A new activity is horse riding to waterfalls around the base of the Cāng Shān. Horsemen congregate at the main highway and offer escorted horse-riding for Y20 per hour or Y70 per day, though initial offers will start much higher.

Jim's Peace Café and Café De Jack both offer a bus trip to a Yi minority market, about a two-hour drive from Dàlǐ, held every 10 days on the 10th, 20th and 30th of the Western calendar. The interesting trip costs Y40 per person with three hours at the market.

Michael's Travel on Boai Lu can arrange calligraphy or taìjíquán (taichi) lessons for Y40 per hour, and almost everything else, including bus and train tickets.

CITS (☎ 266 1701, ⓔ ptcitsdl@ynmail .com) has a branch at 77 Boai Lu, though it offers nothing that the private companies don't and prices are much higher. They will get air tickets for Y20 commission.

Festivals

Dàlǐ, Xiàguān, and the Ěrhǎi Lake region hold 11 different festivals from February to October. If you don't mind crowds, the best time to be in Dàlǐ is during the **Third Moon Fair** (Sānyuè Jiē), which begins on the 15th day of the third lunar month (usually April) and ends on the 21st day. The origins of the fair commemorate a fabled visit by Guanyin, the Buddhist goddess of mercy, to the Nánzhāo kingdom. Today it's an extra festive market; people from all over Yúnnán arrive to buy, sell and make merry. The main fair ground is north-west of town, near the three pagodas.

The **Ràosānlíng** (Three Temples) **Festival** is held between the 23rd and 25th days of the fourth lunar month (usually May). The name refers to touring three temples. The first day involves a walk from Dàlǐ's South Gate to the Shèngyuán Sì at the foot of Wǔtái Shān in Xǐzhōu. Here the walkers stay up until dawn, dancing and singing, before moving on to Jīnguì Sì temple on the shore of Ěrhǎi Lake. The final day involves walking back to Dàlǐ by way of Majiuyi Temple.

The **Torch Festival** (Huǒbǎ Jié) is held on the 24th day of the sixth lunar month (usually July). Flaming torches are paraded at night through homes and fields. Other events include fireworks displays and dragon boat racing. If you're around, Mr China's Son Café has a get-together usually, part educational tour and part party.

Markets

See the Around Dàlǐ section for information on the Shāpíng market held on Monday. Wāsè also has a popular market every five days with trading from 9am to 4.30pm. To get there, haggling with ferries is possible but it's probably easier to let local cafes organise transport for around Y20 a head.

Dàlǐ has a weekly market outside town at the Third Moon Fair festival ground to the east of town. The market is fixed according to the lunar calendar, on the second, ninth, 16th and 23rd of each month.

Local markets are pegged to the lunar calendar so clueless tourists have an idea when and where to go. Markets around Ěrhǎi Lake take place in Shuānglǎng (Tuesday), Shābā (Wednesday, near Shāpíng), Yòusuǒ (Friday, the largest in Yúnnán) and Jiāngwěi (Saturday).

Places to Stay – Budget

Places tend to fill quickly, and those visiting during the peak summer months may find themselves trekking around town in search of that perfect bed on their first day.

A popular place to see and be seen on the backpacker circuit Dàlǐ stop is the **MCA Guesthouse** (☎ 267 3666/1999), south of the South Gate on Fuxing Lu. This self-contained little community has spacious dorms with hardwood floors. Beds in a five-bed dorm are Y10. The bathrooms are across the compound but at least the showers have 24-hour hot water. Spartan doubles without bath cost Y50 and there are a couple of singles round the back for Y30.

The main building has a common area and a bar that's very easy to hang out in. The guesthouse has book rental, laundry service (and a washing machine), poste restante, Internet access (free for guest except those staying in dorms), and bikes for rent (Y10 to Y15 per day). The restaurant is good and cheap and weekends occasionally feature a Tibetan brunch.

The newest and most unique place to stay is the **Old** Dàlǐ **Four Seasons Inn** (Sìjì Kèzhàn; ☎ 267 0382, 51 Boai Lu), also known as the No 5 Guesthouse. Opened by a Taiwanese investor, it makes use of one of the street's most distinctive traditional-style buildings, a former school. Two wings of the two-storey complex face a flower-laden courtyard and gazebo. Dorm rooms start at Y10 per hard bed in clean quads; for an extra Y5, you can get the 'luxury dorm', which means a soft bed. A bed in a triple costs Y20. Singles/doubles with common bath cost Y30. The communal squat toilets are fairly clean (though not very private) and the showers have reliable hot water 18-hours a day. The cafe shows the occasional video. A comfortable veranda lines the complex and makes for great lazy days. Bicycles can be rented here and the laundry service is cheap.

Still popular is the old favourite **Yú'ān Garden** (Yúān Yuán; ☎ 267 2093), or No 4 Guesthouse. Perched at the top of Huguo Lu, this pleasant little spot has 24-hour hot water, Internet access, mountain bike hire (Y10 per day), a lovely Thai-style cafe, washing machines, a score of laundry lines, friendly staff, and dorm beds for Y10 to Y15 (the latter are worth the extra money). Doubles without bathroom are available for Y25 per bed but look at a few options, since there's a wide variety. Small singles cost Y30. The only problem is that the best rooms are always full.

Just down from the Yu'an Garden, the friendly *Sunny Garden (Sāngní Yuán; ☎ 267 0213)*, or No 3 Guesthouse is being renovated so might be a good new option (though prices might have risen).

Jim's Tibetan Peace Guesthouse (Jímǔ Hépíng Fàndiàn) is tacked onto the back of his fine Peace Café on Boai Lu. A bed in a cramped triple costs Y15 but there's a nice common bathroom with (gasp) a Western toilet. There's also a single room with an awesome bathtub for Y50 and doubles for Y60 to Y80.

Closest to all the action on Huguo Lu, the *No 2 Guesthouse (Dìèr Zhāodàisuǒ; ☎ 267 0423)*, also known as the Red Camellia Hotel, has long been Dàlǐ's old stand-by. Though devoid of the charm of the smaller guesthouses, it's actually not a bad place, especially if you get a room on the 2nd or 3rd floor of the old wing. First-floor rooms tend to be damp and dark. A bed in a double/ triple costs Y15/12 and a single costs Y30. Hot water is available 8pm until around midnight, and there may even be some in the morning.

The *Xīngyuè Bīnguǎn (Star and Moon Hotel; ☎ 267 3798)* is a more unusual accommodation choice in that it's part of, and owned by, the local mosque. The rooms have seen better days but are a bargain at Y50 a double with bathroom. The hotel is the Islamic-looking building next to the Old Dàlǐ Four Seasons Inn.

Places to Stay – Mid-Range

A couple of the budget guesthouses have recently added comfortable doubles with bathroom that enjoy all the charm and sociability of the guesthouses with a bit more comfort and privacy. They are sometimes booked out by 'adventure travel' companies. For more details see the previous entries.

MCA Guesthouse has good doubles with bath for Y120, discounted to Y80 in low season, facing the popular pool area. New doubles at the back cost Y150, discounted to Y100.

Old Dàlǐ Four Seasons Inn has small but pleasant upscale doubles with bath for Y125, which includes breakfast.

Yu'an Garden recently added doubles with bathroom for Y120 or Y150, often discounted to Y100 and Y120.

The new building of the No 2 Guesthouse has standard Chinese hotel style identikit doubles with 24-hour hot water for Y200 to Y220.

Dàlǐ Bīnguǎn (☎ 267 0386, fax 267 0551) is a bit farther away, on Fuxing Lu, but you'll earn your banana pancake walking the five minutes or so to Huguo Lu. It has doubles for Y110, Y200 and Y240, which are often discounted to Y80, Y120 and Y150.

Sticking out at the corner of Huguo Lu and Fuxing Lu, *Jīnhuā Dàjiǔdiàn (☎ 267 3343, fax 267 0573)* probably won't see much backpacker traffic. Standard singles/ doubles with air-con, satellite TV and all the rest, start at Y168/198. Sporting red-capped doormen and a marble staircase, and yet more hostesses with colourful and ill-fitting headgear, the Jīnhuā definitely seems out of sync with the rest of Dàlǐ. But if you're in the mood for luxury, or are toting the kids around, this might be a good choice.

Dàlǐ also has its own five-star hotel, the *Asia Star Hotel (Yà'īng Dàfàndiàn; ☎ 267 0009)*, an enormous luxury monster that is thankfully parked several kilometres south of town. A China-Taiwan joint venture, it stands out clearly against the mountain backdrop when viewed from the lake.

Places to Eat

Most of the travellers' hang-outs are at the top section of Boai Lu and on Huguo Lu. Most are good value for money, with good food and pleasant staff, and are a welcome relief if you've been on the road for a while. There are many more than listed here, but many restaurants in places like Dàlǐ (and Yángshuò in Guǎngxī) are much the same –

not bad, simply unremarkable. It's a good idea to share your patronage around until you hit on a favourite.

If you want to avoid other travellers, eat with the locals in Chinese restaurants around town. You would be surprised how many little, very local places way off the main drags have English menus so go experiment. Several places serve up Bai specialities such as grilled Dàlǐ cheese, claypot fish (*shāguōyú*) and 'three course tea' (*sāndàochá*) – one bitter, one sweet and the other bittersweet, with an aftertaste to mirror life's experiences.

One nice place that sees hardly any foreigners is the *Old Bai House Restaurant* (*Báilǐxiāng*), opposite the park on Yu'er Lu. The restaurant has a traditional interior (a shame about the plastic awning on the roof) and an English menu, with Chinese and Bai dishes for Y10 to Y15.

One place drawing a crowd for over a decade is *Marley's Café*. The place recently located to an ugly building on the corner of Boai Lu and Huguo Lu and houses a popular Chinese and Western restaurant. Hopefully the popular Sunday Bai-food group dinner will continue in the new location (make reservations). Marley herself is a good source of local information.

Nearby, on Boai Lu, the number one choice for hip music and a congenial atmosphere is *Café de Jack*, known for its amazing chocolate banana cake with ice cream; it also has good pizza and comfy couch seating worth a mention.

For an interesting afternoon of conversation, you can try *Mr China's Son Café*, a cafe opened by an old gentleman who has penned an English-language account of his trials and tribulations during the Cultural Revolution. This place bills itself as providing 'Food for the Mind', and it delivers. The inside is a mini-museum of regional culture and the highlights are personal letters from Prince Charles and a photograph of the owner standing near Zhou Enlai. Best of all, the cafe organises lots of cultural get-togethers. There's a wide selection of Western dishes, as well as good-value set Bai meals for Y13 to Y15 per person (the more

people the better the selection). The place also has a thorough collection of maps and tips on Dàlǐ and its environs – and a minor guidebook of its own.

The *Sister's Café* on the corner of Boai Lu and Huguo Lu serves the Japanese travellers' market and is a good place to meet wandering souls from Tokyo, Osaka and so on.

Huguo Lu is lined with restaurants serving up Western food, though many are frequented mainly by Chinese tourists. The friendly folks at the *Sunshine Café* serve everything from burritos to doner kebabs and whip up the best brownies in town. Their couch, under a skylight, is possibly the most comfortable seat in Dàlǐ.

Nearby, the *Old Wooden House* has good outside seating and its bolognaise is definitely worth trying – an itinerant Italian gave them the recipe.

Another long popular place is the *Tibetan Café*, though it plans to move from its current location. Across the street, the *Star Café* is dark but cosy and has good Japanese food. Next door is *La Pizzeria La Stella*, which serves good pizzas and Italian dishes.

The *Yúnnán Café* (☎ 267 9014), recently under new management, is about a five-minute walk down Huguo Lu. Formerly called the Coca Cola Restaurant (until the long arm of Coca-Cola Inc dispatched warnings), it has served consistently good food. Travellers plant themselves on the rooftop sun deck until closing time drives them away. The cafe also has an extensive CD collection, book exchange and rental service.

True party-goers should head to *Jim's Peace Café* for rock 'n' roll and late-night sessions. Jim is part-Tibetan, a very cool guy, and mixes up some potent concoctions – look out for his No 1 Special. Food is served and there's plenty of travel information.

Shopping

One rule of thumb for Dàlǐ is *shop around*; don't just stick to Huguo Lu. Batik is a good example: Huguo Lu's shops will have mark-ups noticeably higher (around 20%) than those on Fuxing Lu. This isn't a hard and fast rule, but check and you'll see the trend.

YÚNNÁN

You'll need to bargain hard for most things. For those roving sales ladies badgering you, don't feel bad to pay *one-fifth* of their asking price – that's what locals advise. For marble from street sellers, 40% to half price is fair. In shops, two-thirds of the price is average. And don't fall for any expert advisers; go back later and strike your own deal.

Dàlǐ is famous for its marble, and while a slab in your backpack might slow you down a bit, local entrepreneurs produce everything from ashtrays to model pagodas in small enough chunks.

Huguo Lu has become a mini Khao San Rd in its profusion of clothes shops – you could outfit yourself for a time-machine jaunt back to Woodstock here but the shopkeepers can also make clothes to your specifications, so you're not stuck with the ready-made hippie stuff. Prices are very reasonable.

Most of the 'silver' jewellery sold in Dàlǐ is really brass. If it *is* silver this will be reflected in the starting price.

Batik wall hangings and Miáo embroidery are popular in Dàlǐ. Several places near the No 2 Guesthouse on Huguo Lu have a good collection, but don't believe the proprietors make the stuff themselves. Most of the batik, as in Yángshuò, comes from Guìzhōu, where it can be bought for a song. Some batik is made locally, particularly in Xǐzhōu. Authentic Dàlǐ batik is the blue and white printed on cotton and silk. Cotton batik usually should be Y11 to Y14 per metre, the silk version Y13 to Y15 per metre. In general you can probably aim for about 25% less than the asking price.

Getting There & Away

Xiàguān's new airport has, for better or worse, brought Dàlǐ to within 45-minutes flying time from Kūnmíng. There are several flights daily to Kūnmíng (Y340) and daily to Jǐnghóng in Xīshuāngbǎnnà (Y540). For any flight after about 8.30am it's easy enough to catch an early morning local bus to Xiàguān and then take a taxi to the airport from there.

Probably the most popular means of getting to Dàlǐ is the overnight sleeper train from Kūnmíng (Y75 to Y95 for a hard sleeper). For details on the train and plane, and for additional bus options see the previous Xiàguān entry.

The golden rule about getting to Dàlǐ by bus is to find out in advance, preferably several times, whether your bus is for Dàlǐ or Xiàguān. Many buses advertised to Dàlǐ actually only go as far as Xiàguān. For information on getting to Dàlǐ from Kūnmíng see the Kūnmíng – Getting There & Away section.

Most travellers take the daytime express buses from Kūnmíng. If you do take the overnight sleeper bus take care, as someone always seems to find a bag pinched or razored; chain them securely and cram them under the lower bunk as far back as possible.

Coming from either Xiàguān or Lìjiāng by express bus, along the express highway to the east of Dàlǐ, you may find yourself dropped off next to the highway at the eastern end of Dàlǐ. From here it's a 20-minute walk to the main guesthouses, or take a horse cart for around Y5.

Leaving Dàlǐ, the best thing is to shop around. Plenty of tour and travel agencies means plenty of options and competitive prices. Most buses for Lìjiāng and Kūnmíng depart from Dàlǐ; for other destinations you can buy tickets in Dàlǐ but must return to Xiàguān to get on the bus.

Buses to Kūnmíng generally leave between 6.30am and 9am and take eight hours. Most agencies also run sleeper buses, generally leaving in the evening (Y40 to Y55).

Buses to Lìjiāng leave between 7am and 2.30pm. Tickets (Y35/Y40 minibus/express, three hours) can be bought from the Passenger Service Ticket Office (see later) or any travel agency on Huguo Lu. You can also catch any one of numerous buses to Lìjiāng that originate in Xiàguān. Buses to Zhōngdiàn pass through Dàlǐ between 7.30am and 10am (Y50, seven hours).

Tickets for public buses are available at the Dàlǐ Passenger Service Ticket Office (Dàlǐ Kèyùnzhàn Shòupiàochù) on Boai Lu; this office also sells tickets for the Xiàguān long-distance bus station.

To catch buses to other points, such as Bǎoshān, Ruìlì or Jǐnghóng, you have to go to Xiàguān. The No 4 local bus to Xiàguān (Y1.20, 30 minutes) starts early enough – around 6.30am – runs every 15 minutes, and there are stops along Boai Lu. If your bus leaves Xiàguān earlier than 7.30am, you'll have to stay overnight there.

Getting Around

Bikes are the best way to get around. Prices average Y2 per hour or Y5 per day for clunky Chinese models, Y2 per hour and Y10 per day for better mountain bikes. The Old Dàlǐ Four Seasons Inn, Yu'an Garden and MCA Guest House all rent bikes and several other places on Boai Lu are getting into the business.

A taxi to Xiàguān airport should take around 45 minutes and costs Y80; to Xiàguān train station costs Y30.

AROUND DÀLǏ

There is plenty of scope for extended touring around Ěrhǎi Lake either by ferry, bicycle or bus. If you need to stretch your legs there are some fine walks in the Cāng Shān behind Dàlǐ. Be aware that solo walkers have been robbed here and in 1997 a German traveller was killed (though no problems have been reported since). To be safe find a hiking partner and be back before dusk.

Ěrhǎi Lake 洱海湖
Ěrhǎi Hú

Ěrhǎi Lake is the seventh largest in China at 250 sq km but it doesn't have a large volume. The lake is a 50-minute walk from town, a 10-minute downhill zip on a bike or a short hop on the No 2 minibus.

From Cáicūn, a lakeside village east of Dàlǐ, there's a ferry at 4pm to Wāsè on the other side of the lake. You can stay overnight at the *Wāsè Zhāodàisuǒ* and catch a ferry back at 6am. Close to Wāsè is **Putuo Island** (Pǔtuó Dǎo) and the **Xiǎopǔtuó Sì** (Lesser Putuo Temple), set on an extremely photogenic rock island that was said to have been created by a Bodhisattva who forgot to finish a bridge between the two islands.

Ferries also crisscross the lake between Lóngkān and Hǎidōng, and between Xiàguān

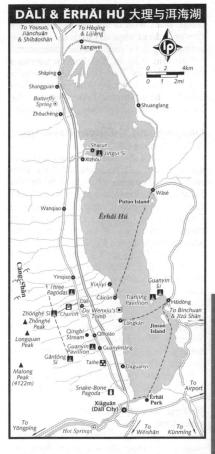

and the island of Jīnsuō Dǎo, so there could be some scope for extended touring. Ferries appear to leave early in the morning (for market) and return around 4pm, though timetables are flexible and departures are somewhat unreliable.

It is possible to do a loop, or partial loop of the lake by mountain bike taking in Xīzhōu, Zhōuchéng, Shāpìng and Wāsè. You could ride around the lake clockwise from Dàlǐ to Hǎidōng and take the ferry back to Lóngkān. A shorter option would be to cycle to Wāsè (57km) and then return to Dàlǐ by ferry.

Lots of local Western-style cafes have connections with boats and horse-cart drivers and can arrange day trips for you. Shop around as prices vary. On the cheaper end, for around Y30 to Y40 per person in a group of around four you can get a round-trip to Ěrhǎi Lake on a horse-cart, then transport to a couple of spots on the lake. Many possible routes exist, so ask around.

Tiānjìng and Guānyīn Pavilions
观音堂 Tiānjìng Gé/Guānyīn Gé

On the eastern shore of Ěrhǎi Lake these two temples couldn't be more different from each other. The somewhat garish white-tiled Tiānjìng Pavilion (also known as the Laotai Temple), wrapped in strings of gargantuan Christmas tree lights, is on a high spot with magnificent views of the lake, especially when the sun shines. Look for the fresco in the ceiling. There's a Y5 admission fee.

On the other side of the bulbous promontory and literally decaying in the weeds amid munching cattle is the better-known Guānyīn Pavilion, also known as the Luoquan Temple. According to legend, this was the place where the clandestine lover of a Nánzhāo princess was turned into a stone donkey by a master when the princess defied her father's arranged marriage.

Private boat owners at Cáicūn offer return trips to Hǎidōng for about Y100 for the boat.

Jīnsuō Island 金梭岛
Jīnsuō Dǎo

Just south of the two temples is tiny Jīnsuō Island, a canoe shaped rock 800m by 2000m. It draws tourists mostly for its **Dragon Jade Palace**, a subterranean network of caves packed with the over-the-top kitsch that is tourist caving in China. Otherwise, just wander around the island through some fairly traditional alleys. After disembarking from your boat, follow the storefronts to the left, and then right on the first alley. You'll come to a small temple and home to a senior citizen centre where old men thwap their plastic checkers around.

The boat fare will cost Y1, admission to the cave is Y12 including the services of a costumed guide.

Zhōnghé Sì 中和寺

Zhōnghé Sì (entry Y2) is a long, steep hike up the mountainside behind Dàlǐ, with fantastic vistas of Dàlǐ and Ěrhǎi Lake. You can cheat and take a new chairlift (Y25 one way, Y35 return). The road leading north to the Three Pagodas crosses the road up to the chairlift - look out for the sign.

Branching out from either side of the temple is a trail that winds along the face of the mountains, taking you in and out of steep lush valleys, past streams and waterfalls. From Zhōnghé Sì it's an amazing 11km up-and-down hike south to Gǎntōng Sì, or alternatively you can take the path to Qīngbì Stream. From both places you can continue to the main road, where you can pick up a Dàlǐ-bound bus.

You could also hike up the hill a sweaty hour. No one path leads directly up; instead, oodles of small tracks wind and switchback through farmland, local cemeteries, and even one off-limits military area (there is a sign in English here!). Walk about 200m north of the chairlift base to the riverbed (often dry). Follow the left bank for about 50m and you'll see lots of ribbony trails leading up. Basically, all roads lead to Rome from here, just keep the chairlift in sight and when in doubt, bear left. You should eventually come upon a well-worn trail and, following that, some steps near the top. You can also take horse trips around here (see Organised Tours & Activities).

One peak south of Zhōnghé Shān is Lóngquán Shān, and halfway up that is Putuo Cliff and Phoenix Cave (Lóngfèngyǎn Dòng), which leads right through the back of the mountain. All in all it's about 9km if you walk from the south-west gate of Dàlǐ to Lóngquán Shān and then up. There are no really good trails, so figure out how to get there before you go.

Guānyīn Temple 观音阁
Guānyīn Táng

The temple is built over a large boulder said to have been placed there by Guānyīn, the Buddhist bodhisattva goddess of mercy, disguised as an old woman, to block an invading enemy's advance. On the 19th of the third, sixth and ninth lunar months, people flock here to worship Guānyīn. It is 5km south of Dàlǐ at the base of Fódǐng Peak.

Gǎntōng Sì 感通寺
This temple is not far south-west of Guānyīntáng Village, which is about 6km from Dàlǐ towards Xiàguān. From Guānyīntáng follow the path uphill for 3km and ask directions. Built during the Tang dynasty, it once had three dozen sub-temples, all of which were destroyed in Qing dynasty uprisings. Supposedly, many poets and government officials retired here as monks and even an emperor of the Ming dynasty considered being a monk there (he wrote a poem about it instead).

Qīngbì Stream 清碧溪
Qīngbì Xī
This scenic picnic spot near the village of Qīlǐqiáo is 3km from Dàlǐ on the way to Xiàguān. Locals say it's the most picturesque of the 20 or so small creeks. After hiking 4km up a path running close to the river, you'll reach three ponds. You could combine a visit to Qīngbì Stream with the hike from Zhōnghé Sì to Gǎntōng Sì.

Xǐzhōu 喜洲
Among the 101 things to do while you're in Dàlǐ, a trip to Xǐzhōu rates fairly highly. It's an old town around 18km north of Dàlǐ, with even better preserved Bai architecture than Dàlǐ. A local bus bound for Ěryuán is the easiest way to get there, but a bicycle trip with an overnight stop in Xǐzhōu is a good idea. The Xǐzhōu Tiánzhuāng Bīnguǎn is an old Bai building with beds for Y30.

Nearby Shācūn village is one of the last places on the lake where you might find cormorant fishing. You could easily combine Xǐzhōu with a bike trip to Zhōuchéng and Shāpíng market

Zhōuchéng 周城
This pretty village is right by the roadside, 7km north of Xǐzhōu and is also worth a visit. The village spreads uphill from a market square, which is dominated by several

ancient trees. About 30m uphill along the main street a side alley leads off to the right. A house at the end of the lane on the left sells indigo cloth that it dyes on the spot.

Butterfly Spring 蝴蝶泉
Húdié Quán
Butterfly Spring is about 30km north of Dàlǐ. The inevitable legend associated with the spring is that two lovers committed suicide here to escape a cruel king. After jumping into the bottomless pond, they turned into two of the butterflies that gather here en masse during May.

If you're energetic you could cycle to the spring but most people find it a bit of a tourist trap. Since it is only 4km from Shāpíng, you could also combine it with a visit to the Shāpíng market.

Shāpíng Market 沙坪赶集
Shāpíng Gǎnjí
Every Monday the town of Shāpíng, about 30km north of Dàlǐ, is host to a colourful Bai market from 10am to around 2.30pm. You can buy everything from tobacco, melon seeds and noodles to meat, pots and wardrobes. In the ethnic clothing line, you can look at shirts, headdresses, embroidered shoes and money belts, as well as local batik. Expect to be quoted ridiculously high prices, get into a bargaining frame of mind and you should have a good time.

Getting to Shāpíng market from Dàlǐ is fairly easy. Some of the hotels and cafes in town run minibuses there on market day for Y15 return. Usually they leave at 9am; ask around and book the day before. Alternatively, you can walk west on Huguo Lu to the main road and catch a local bus bound for Ěryuán. Market day is not the ideal time to test drive a local bus but generally there are enough to cater for the numbers. A ticket to Shāpíng should be around Y6.

Tomb of Generalissimo Du Wenxiu 杜文秀墓
Dùwénxiù Mù
In Xiàduì Village, 4km south-east of Dàlǐ, is the tomb and former residence of Du Wenxiu, a Huí Muslim also known as Sultan

YÚNNÁN

Suleyman who, following the Taiping Rebellion, led a revolt in Dàlǐ. The locals elected him 'generalissimo' and called his office the 'Forbidden City' (now the Dàlǐ Museum). He was later executed by the Qing authorities.

DÀLǏ TO LÌJIĀNG

Most travellers take a direct route between Dàlǐ and Lìjiāng. However, a couple of places may make interesting detours. Transport is a case of pot luck with buses, or hitching.

Shíbǎoshān 石宝山

About 110km north-west of Dàlǐ are the Shíbǎoshān (Stone Treasure Mountain) Grottoes. There are three temple groups: **Stone Bell** (Shízhōng), **Lion Pass** (Shīzi Guān) and **Shadeng village** (Shādēng Cūn). The Stone Bell monastery group includes some of the best Bai stone carvings in southern China and offer insights into life at the Nánzhāo court of the 9th century. One of the best caves features images of Geluofeng, the fourth king of the Nánzhāo kingdom. It also features carvings of female genitalia, which local women visit to boost their fertility. On the way to the complex, 6km from the Stone Bell monastery is the **Bǎoxiāng Temple** at the edge of a huge cliff. At least 1000 steps lead up to the **Golden Summit Temple** (Jīndǐng Sì) on top of the mountain.

To get to Shíbǎoshān, first take a bus to Jiànchuān, 92km north of Dàlǐ on the old Dàlǐ-Lìjiāng road. Get off at the small village of Diànnán, about 8km south of Jiànchuān,

---

The Bai

Of the dozen minority groups represented in the Dàlǐ region, the main inhabitants are the Bai, who comprise 43% – some 430,000 – of Dàlǐ alone. They are the second largest minority nationality in Yúnnán. Related to the Yi of the Tibeto-Burmese group, their language, of the Sino-Tibetan family, has no written form. Their religion is a mix of Buddhism, polytheism and even some Catholicism.

The Bai roots in the Ěrhǎi Lake region, date back some 3000 years. To many observers the Bai have been acculturated to the Han more than most minorities. The Bai definitely have learned how to live with the Han – they are one of only three minority groups whose literacy rates transcend those of the Han and as a result receive zero 'special assistance' in education or university placement by the government. 'Bai' means white in Chinese and that's the predominant colour of Bai traditional dress, which features an embroidered pink apron and pink headdress.

Bai designers and builders are well regarded, having developed the dougong structure where brackets are inserted between the top of a column and a crossbeam. Each bracket is formed of a double bow-shaped 'gong', which supports a black 'dou'. The ingenious interlocking parts were developed to withstand earthquakes. Also of note are the intricate Dàlǐ marble door surrounds and the screen wall that all dwellings have.

The Bai used to shock the Han by preparing and eating pork nearly raw, though the practice isn't as evident today. Mostly Bai meals will include lots of cold, pickled dishes.

Of special interest is the Bai custom of the 'pillow race'. The bride and groom leave the ceremony for the home in which they'll stay. From the threshold they race to the bedchamber, and the one who grabs the pillows first rules the house.

The Bai say the number six augurs good fortune and indicates respect. Gifts must include or show a six somehow, or risk being refused. The practice is thought to reflect that the Bai were one of six 'original' tribes.

where a narrow road branches south-west to the village of Shāxī, 23km away. You'll just have to wait for a bus for this leg. The grottoes are close to Shāxī.

Hèqìng 鹤庆

About 46km south of Lìjiāng, Hèqìng is just off the main Dàlǐ-Lìjiāng highway. In the centre of town is the wooden Yúnhé Pavilion, built during the Míng dynasty. You might be able to catch a glimpse of the pavilion as you speed by on the bus from Lìjiāng to Dàlǐ.

North-West Yúnnán

'Where in all the world is to be found scenery comparable to that which awaits the explorer and photographer in north-western Yúnnán province?'

Joseph Rock, 1928

The region from Lìjiāng to the Tibetan border is one of the most wonderful in China. It boasts Nàxī, Tibetan, Mosu, Lisu and Pumi nationalities, breathtaking scenery, Tibetan monasteries, deep gorges and the backpacker comforts of Lìjiāng's lovely old town.

The region has been declared as one of the world's biodiversity hotspots, thanks to its incredible topography and range of ecosystems. There are proposals to create a 66,000 sq km Great Rivers National Park, 'China's Yellowstone', where the Yangzi, Mekong and Salween all pass within 70km of each other.

Now that all the counties in the region and neighbouring Sìchuān are open to foreigners, there's plenty of scope for exploration. There are countless excursions to be made around Lìjiāng and Zhōngdiàn. Adventurers can explore Wēixī county or routes from Lúgú Lake to the former kingdom of Mùlǐ in Sìchuān, and trek from Bǎoshān to Lúgú Lake or from Tiger Leaping Gorge to Bǐtǎ Hǎi, south-east of Zhōngdiàn.

LÌJIĀNG 丽江
New town ☎ 08891 Old town ☎ 0888
North of Dàlǐ, bordering Tibet, the wonderful old town and surroundings of Lìjiāng is

another great spot to stay a while. It's not until you get into the old town – a delightful maze of cobbled streets, rickety old wooden buildings, gushing canals and the hurly-burly of market life – that you realise Lìjiāng has a lot to offer, including many interesting side trips, most of which can be reached by bicycle, offering a week or more's worth of excursions.

A venerable work on Lìjiāng worth reading if you can find it is *Forgotten Kingdom* (John Murray Co, 1955) by Peter Goullart. A contemporary of sorts of Joseph Rock, Goullart was a White Russian who studied Nàxī culture and lived in Lìjiāng from 1940 to 1949. An excellent epic documentary about Lìjiāng was made a few years ago by Britain's Channel 4 and it's well worth seeking out; see the Film section in the Facts for the Visitor chapter.

In February 1996 an earthquake measuring over seven on the Richter scale rocked the Lìjiāng area, killing more than 300 people – including one foreign tourist – and injuring 16,000. Damage was estimated at over half a billion US dollars. While much of newer Lìjiāng was levelled, the traditional Nàxī architecture held up quite well. The Chinese government took note and sank millions of yuán into rebuilding most of Lìjiāng county with traditional Nàxī architecture, replacing cement with cobblestone and wood. The United Nations was so impressed by the survival of Lìjiāng that it placed all of Lìjiāng county on its World Heritage Site list in 1999.

The town's reconstruction coupled with the unveiling of Lìjiāng's new airport has led to a huge increase in tourists. As one foreign correspondent wise-cracked, 'Forget foreign encroachment, this is civil war!'. The town earned a staggering US$181 million from 2.8 million tourists in 2000. One indirect result has been a cluster of new tourist sights along with fairly high admission fees. More worrying is the influx of Han Chinese entrepreneurs running tourist shops and restaurants for Han tourists, and souvenir sellers pushing out Nàxī stalls. What used to be the preserve of hardy backpackers is now a major tourist destination.

Orientation

Lìjiāng is separated into old and new towns that are as different as day and night. The approximate line of division is Shīzī Shān (Lion Hill), the green hump in the middle of town that's topped by a radio mast and the Wànggǔ Lóu (Looking to the East Pagoda). Everything west of the hill is the new town, and everything east of the hill is the old town.

The easiest way into the old town is from the north, along Dong Dajie. This part of town was largely reconstructed following the 1996 earthquake. From the main bus station head east one block and follow an alley lined with snack bars heading north. The old town is a delightful maze of twists and turns – although it's small, it's easy to get lost in here which, of course, is part of the fun.

Information

Tourist Offices Lìjiāng's cafes and backpacker inns are the best source of information. Most have noticeboards and travellers' books full of useful tips on surrounding sights, especially on the Tiger Leaping Gorge trek.

CITS has a Family & Independent Traveller (FIT) office across the street from the entrance to the Gǔlùwān Bīnguǎn. The staff are helpful, and will give you ideas for local outings and book plane and even train tickets.

Books The Xīnhuá Bookstore on Xin Dajie has postcards, maps of the city and a couple of guidebooks.

Hello Lijiang! by Duan Ping-Hua and Ray Hilsinger is a fairly useful guide to sights around Lìjiāng. It's available for Y30 at the Xīnhuá Bookstore or Lìjiāng Grand Hotel.

PSB The PSB is opposite the Lìjiāng Bīnguǎn and there seems to be no problem getting a first visa extension. Hours are Monday to Friday from 8am to noon, but you can often get in at other times. The office is on the right-hand side of the compound after entering the gate.

Money The Bank of China on Xin Dajie and a branch on Nanguo Zhonglu in the south of town both give cash advances on

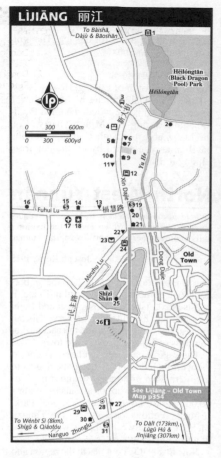

your credit card. There is also a small branch next to the entrance of the Lìjiāng Bīnguǎn. All branches will change travellers cheques.

Post & Communications The China Post and China Telecom office is on Xin Dajie, just south of the turn to the Old Town. It's open 8am to noon and 2pm to 6pm. You should be able to make reverse-charge calls and calling-card calls here. If not, head to the Well Bistro or other local haunts that charge the same (or less) and keep your beer cold as you dial.

LÌJIĀNG

PLACES TO STAY

5 Gǔlùwān
 Bīnguǎn
 古路湾宾馆
9 Red Sun Hotel
 红太阳频
14 Lìjiāng Bīnguǎn
 丽嚣
21 Lìjiāng Dàjiǔdiàn
 丽江人酒店
30 Yúnshān
 Fàndiàn
 云杉饭店

PLACES TO EAT

6 Ali Baba's
 阿里巴巴餐厅
11 Nàxī Restaurant
 纳西风味饭店
13 Love on the
 Bridge Restaurant;
 Gǒubùlǐ Tāngbāo
 桥之情、
 狗不理汤包
22 Belief
 Supermarket
 百信市场
27 Snack Bars
 小吃店

OTHER

1 Museum of Nàxī
 Dōngbā Culture
 东巴博物馆
2 Dōngbā
 Research
 Institute
 东巴研究所
3 Minibuses to
 Bǎoshān
 到宝山的中巴车
4 Cinema
 云岭剧场
7 CITS (FIT);
 Express Bus Station
 中国国际旅行社
8 Mao Square
 毛主席广场
10 Lìjiāng
 International
 Ethnic Cultural
 Exchange Centre
 丽江国际民族文化
 交换中心
12 North Bus
 Station
 北客运站
15 Bank of China
 中国银行

16 CAAC
 民航售票处
17 Hospital
 医院
18 PSB
 公安局
19 Bank of China
 中国银行
20 Xinhua Bookstore
 新华书店
23 China Post;
 China Telecom
 邮电局
24 No 6 Bus to Báishā
 & Jade Dragon
 Mountain
 到白沙和玉龙雪山
 的6路公共车
25 Radio Mast
 狮子山
26 Wànggǔ Lóu
 望古楼
28 Báimǎ Lóngtán Pool
 白马龙潭
29 Long-Distance
 Bus Station
 长途汽车
31 Bank of China
 中国银行

Whatever the disinterested staff tell you, you can mail parcels home from here. If you're not sending parcels home, another post office has opened in the old town north of the Old Market Square on Dong Dajie.

Email & Internet Access Loads of places in the old town offer Internet access for between Y10 and Y12 per hour. Surprisingly, China Telecom is significantly more expensive at Y18 per hour. The cheapest and most convenient places are the Old Town Youth Hostel, the Dōngbā House and the #69 restaurant, though there are plenty of other places.

Dangers & Annoyances In May 1997, two solo Western women were robbed at knifepoint – in separate incidents – atop Elephant Hill in Black Dragon Pool Park. Both attacks occurred in broad daylight in the early afternoon. At least one of the as-

sailants followed his victim for some time before the robbery, so look out for park goers lurking behind you and pair up with at least one other traveller.

Lìjiāng has also had some rather inept pickpockets appear north of old town near the square.

Old Town 老城

Crisscrossed by canals, bridges and a maze of narrow granite streets, the old town is a gem not to be missed. An interesting local historical tidbit has it that the original Nàxī chieftain would not allow the old town to be girdled by a city wall because drawing a box around the Chinese character of his family name would change the character from *mù* (wood) to *kún* (surrounded, or hard pressed).

The old town is dissected by a web of artery-like canals that once brought the city's drinking water from Yuquan Spring, in what is now Black Dragon Pool Park.

The Nàxī

- **population** 286,000
- **locations** Lìjiāng, Wēixī, Zhongdian, Ninglang and Yongsheng.

Lìjiāng has been the base of the Nàxī (also spelt Nakhi and Nahi) minority for about the last 1400 years, though today they only make up about 20% of the prefecture's population. They are descended from Tibetan Qiang tribes of Qinghai and lived until recently in matrilineal families, though since local rulers were always male it couldn't be considered a true matriarchy. Women still seem to do the lion's share of the work.

There are strong matriarchal influences in the Nàxī language. Nouns enlarge their meaning when the word for 'female' is added; the addition of the word for 'male' will decrease the meaning. For example, 'stone' plus 'female' conveys the idea of a boulder; 'stone' plus 'male' a pebble.

Nàxī women wear blue blouses and trousers covered by blue or black aprons. Nàxī women in the Bǎoshān region also wear black turbans. The T-shaped, traditional cape, known as a *yangpi*, not only stops the basket always worn on the back from chafing, but also symbolises the heavens. Day and night are represented by the light and dark halves of the cape; seven embroidered circles symbolise the stars. Two larger circles, one on each shoulder, depict the eyes of a frog, which until the 15th century was an important god to the Nàxī. With the decline of animist beliefs, the frog eyes fell out of fashion, but the Nàxī still call the cape by its original name, 'frog-eye sheepskin'.

The Nàxī created a written language over 1000 years ago using an extraordinary system of over 1300 pictographs – the only hieroglyphic language still in use. You can buy examples of Dōngbā script around town but much is mass produced and the pictographs contain little real meaning. The Dōngbā Research Institute is currently trying to create an extensive Dōngbā dictionary before knowledge of the script dies out. The most famous Nàxī text is the Dōngbā classic, *The Creation*, and ancient copies of it and other texts can still be found in Lijiang, as well as in the archives of some US universities. The Dōngbā (meaning 'wise man') were Nàxī shamans who were caretakers of the written language and mediators between the Nàxī and the spirit world. The Dōngbā religion, itself an offshoot of Tibet's pre-Buddhist Bön religion, eventually absorbed itself into an amalgam of Tibetan Buddhism, Islam and Taoism. The Tibetan origins of the Nàxī are confirmed by references in Nàxī literature to Lake Manasarovar and Mt Kailash, both in Western Tibet.

'Hello' in the Nàxī language is *'nuar lala'*; 'thank you' is *'jiu bai sai'*.

There are several wells and pools still in use around town. Where there are three pools, these were (and still are) designated into pools for drinking, washing clothes and washing vegetables. A famous example of these is the **Báimǎlóng Tán** (White Horse Dragon) pool in the south of the old town. You can see one of the original wells opposite the Well Bistro.

The town once had several water wheels, though the only one now is a reconstructed model at the north edge of the old town. The nearby monument celebrates Lìjiāng's status as a Unesco World Heritage site.

The focus of the old town is the **Market Square** (Sìfāng Jiē). Arrive by mid-morning to see the square full of Nàxī women in traditional dress. You can buy embroidery and lengths of striped cloth in shops around the market. Unfortunately the Nàxī traders are slowly being pushed out by tacky souvenir stalls. To the west of the square is the **Kegong Tower**, which is the scene of celebrations marking the birthday of the local god Sanduo on the eighth day of the second lunar month (March).

Above the old town is a pleasant park, reached by the path leading past the radio antenna. Sit on the slope in the early morning and watch the mist clearing as the old town comes to life. Now acting as a sort of sentinel for the town, is the 33m-high **Wànggǔ Lóu**, a pagoda raised for tourism at a cost of over one million yuán. It's famed for a unique design using dozens of four-storey pillars, but unfortunately these were culled from old-growth forests in northern Yúnnán. Entry is Y15 and isn't really worth it.

Mù Family Mansion 木家大院
Mùshì Shìsìfǔ

This former home of a Nàxī chieftain was heavily renovated (more like built from scratch) after the 1996 earthquake, with funds from the World Bank. The six main halls and courtyards were rebuilt to resemble a mini Forbidden City, some say deliberately, to reinforce historical Chinese ties to Lìjiāng. There's not much to see at the moment, though it's likely that some kind of museum will be installed. The mansion backs onto Shīzī Shān and you should be able to get access from here to the Wànggǔ Lóu.

Tickets are a pricey Y35 and generally considered to be not worth it. Opening hours are 8.30am to 6.30am daily.

Black Dragon Pool Park
黑龙潭公园 Hēilóngtǎn Gōngyuán

This park is on the northern edge of town. Apart from strolling around the pool – its view of **Jade Dragon Snow Mountain** is the most obligatory photo shoot in south-west China – you can visit the **Dōngbā Research Institute** (Dōngbā Wénhuà Yánjiūsuǒ), it is part of a renovated complex on the hillside.

At the far side of the pond are renovated buildings used for an art exhibition, a pavilion with its own five-arch marble bridge across the water and the Ming dynasty **Wǔfèng Lóu** (Five Phoenix Hall), a striking Nàxī 20m-high edifice dating from 1601 but only moved to its current location in 1979. Its three roofs with eight eaves each are supposedly in the shape of phoenixes.

Trails lead straight up **Elephant Hill** to a dilapidated gazebo and then across a spiny ridge past a communications centre and back down the other side. Up and down can take as little as 45 minutes if you push it. Entry to the park costs Y20.

Museum of Nàxī Dōngbā Culture
纳西东巴文化 Nà'ī Dōngbā Wénhuà Bówùguǎn

This new yellow-roofed museum by the north entrance of the park is worth a visit if you have the time. There are displays on Nàxī dress and culture, Dōngbā script, Lìjiāng's old town and the dubious claim that the region is the 'real' Shangri La. The museum is open daily 8.30am to 5.30pm. Entry is Y5.

Xuānkē Museum 宣科住所
Xuānkē Zhùsuǒ

Mr Xuan Ke, a Nàxī scholar, who spent 20 years in labour camps following the suppression of the Hundred Flowers movement, and the leader of the Nàxī Orchestra, has turned his Lìjiāng family home into a small repository for Nàxī and Lìjiāng cultural items. Besides clothing and musical instruments (including an original Persian lute that has been used in Nàxī music for centuries), Mr Xuan Ke's home displays Dr Joseph Rock's large, handmade furniture and has a small library of out-of-print books on Lìjiāng. Joseph Rock was a close family friend.

Xuan Ke speaks English and is always willing to discuss his ideas about world culture. He has taken an active role in preserving traditional Chinese music. His home is in the old town, at No 11 Jishan Alley, just west of the Dōngbā House (see Places to Stay).

Festivals

The 13th day of the third lunar month (late March or early April) is the traditional day to hold a **Fertility Festival**.

July brings the **Torch Festival** (Huǒbǎ Jié), also celebrated by the Bai around Dàlǐ and the Yi around Xīchāng in Sìchuān. The origin of this festival can be traced back to the intrigues of the Nánzhāo kingdom, when the wife of a man burned to death by the king eluded the romantic entreaties of the monarch by leaping into a fire.

Organised Tours

Several agencies offer day trips to Jade Dragon Snow Mountain, Yúnshānpíng, Máoniúpíng, or a combination of these, with Hēishuǐ village often thrown in for good measure. A day trip can cost around Y240, including entry fees. The Máoniúpíng Booking Office in the old town runs good-value tours to Máoniúpíng for Y130, which includes transport, the regional entry fee (Y40) and entry and cable car fees at Máoniúpíng (Y60).

Places to Stay – Budget

Old Town Lìjiāng's old town now has a dozen or so guesthouses with traditional Nàxī architecture. Few of the rooms have much sunlight and so can be cold in winter, but being in the heart of the old town they are close to the majority of restaurants and cafes.

Immediately to the rear of the old Market Square is the *Square Inn* (Sìfāng Kèzhàn; ☎ 512 7487), set on either side of one of the towns canals. Beds in a dark but pleasant triple/quad cost Y20/15. Comfortable doubles cost Y60. The shared bathrooms are clean and there's plenty of hot water in the showers, though the barrierless toilets are a bit disconcerting. There are some nice sitting areas, the staff are very helpful and there's cheap laundry

First Bend Inn (Dìyī Kèzhàn; ☎ 518 1688) is in one of the old city's best-preserved buildings and has one of the prettiest courtyards. Little touches include motion-sensed lights for late-night trips to the facilities. Rooms are comfortable and carpeted and bathrooms are quite clean; showers have reliable hot water in the evenings *and* mornings (8pm to 9am). A bed in a double/ triple/quad is Y40/30/25; all rooms have common bathroom. The staff are attentive and friendly and are full of information on local sights.

A new option nearby is the *Ancient Town Youth Hostel* (Gǔchéng Guójì Qīngnián Lǚguǎn; ☎ 517 5403). The hostel is affiliated with Youth Hostels International (YHI) and card holders get a small discount. There's a range of accommodation. Best value are the bunk-bed dorms at Y15 to Y20 for a bed and locker. Poorer value doubles are Y30 or Y60 per bed with bathroom. Facilities include cheap Internet access, a washing machine available for Y10 per hour and bike hire.

Dōngbā House (☎ 517 5431) is a well-run place which has a great sitting and eating area, though the rooms vary. Bunk-bed

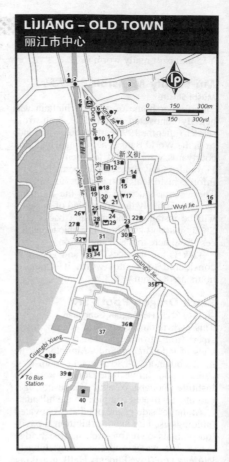

LÌJIĀNG – OLD TOWN
丽江市中心

dorms are Y15; doubles/triples are Y50/90. There's only one bathroom and it isn't up to much. The Tibetan owner also owns the Tibet Café in Zhōngdiàn (and his brother owns the MCA Guesthouse in Dàlǐ) and hopes to establish genuine Tibetan guesthouses from Lìjiāng through Zhōngdiàn to Western Sìchuān and Tibet.

Prague Café (☎ 512 3757) is mostly a cafe but does have rooms round the back for Y10 per bed, or Y25 with a set breakfast. It's not bad if you don't mind the communal atmosphere and close quarters. The *Sakura Café* offers similar rooms for a similar price

LÌJIĀNG – OLD TOWN

PLACES TO STAY
1 Grand Lìjiāng Hotel
  格兰饭店
9 Old Town Inn
  古城客栈
11 Sānhé Nàxī Bīnguǎn
  三河纳西宾馆
13 Dongba House
  东巴豪斯
14 Ancient Town
  Youth Hostel
  古城国际青年旅馆
15 First Bend Inn
  第一湾客栈
16 Yízhōu Kèzhàn
  怡舟客栈
22 Jīnhóng Kèzhàn
  金虹客栈
27 Sakura Cafe Annex
30 Ancient Stone Bridge
  Inn
  古城大石桥客栈
33 Square Inn
  四方客栈
36 Lìjiāng Yuán Kèzhàn
  丽江源客栈
39 Yùlóng Kèzhàn
  玉龙客栈
40 Mùlǎoye Kèzhàn
  木老爷客栈

PLACES TO EAT
5 Nàxī
  Snack Food
  纳西风味小吃
6 Gǔchéng Jiǔlóu
  古城酒楼
8 Snack Bars
  小吃店
17 Well Bistro
  井卓餐馆
20 Prague Cafe
  布拉格咖啡馆
21 #69
24 Ma Ma Fu's
  马马付餐厅
25 Sakura Cafe
26 Delta Cafe
28 Bridge Cafe
32 Old Market Inn
  纳西餐厅

OTHER
2 Yùlóng Bridge
  & Waterwheel
  玉龙桥
3 Fruit
  Market
  水果市场
4 Taxis
  出租汽车

7 Máoniúpíng
  Booking Office
  牦牛坪索道售票处
10 Nàxī Ancient
  Music House
  古乐院
12 Xuānkē
  Museum
  宜科住所
18 Nàxī Music Academy
  纳西音乐
19 Dōngbā Palace
23 Dàshí Bridge
  大石桥
29 China Post
  邮电局
31 Market Square
  四方街
34 CC Bar;
  Camel 3 Bar
35 Gate
  门
37 Mù Family
  Mansion
  木氏土司府
38 Wells
  水井
41 Market
  市场

in a separate building near it's main cafe – reception is in the cafe .

Ancient Stone Bridge Inn *(Gǔchéng Dàshíqiáo Kèzhàn;* ☎ *518 4001)* is a small family run inn with a lovely location. The best thing is the fabulous rooms right on the canal's side for Y60 to Y80 with common bath. Other doubles with bathroom cost Y80 to Y100. There is one good upper-floor double for Y30 per bed. There is only one toilet for everyone.

There are several smaller guesthouses that see fewer foreign tourists but are worth considering.

Jīnhóng Kèzhàn has good-value carpeted rooms for Y20 per bed with clean showers and washing area and a nice courtyard. There's a good Chinese restaurant attached, though there's little English spoken.

Yízhōu Kèzhàn, in a quiet section of the western old town, has the feeling that you are staying in someone's back room. Beds cost Y20 but see a range of rooms as the walls are paper thin and some rooms are claustrophobic.

Yùlóng Kèzhàn is another tiny family run place in the south of the old town with variable rooms for Y20 per bed.

New Town The first place you'll come across when you arrive in town is the ***Yúnshān Fàndiàn*** (☎ *512 1315)*, next to the main southern bus station. The Yúnshān has beds in bright three-bed dorms for Y20, and in two-bed dorms for Y35, though there's little real reason to stay here. Standard doubles with clean bathroom are Y200 but can be discounted as low as Y90.

North of the old town and adjacent to Mao Square, the ***Red Sun Hotel*** *(Hóngtàiyáng Jiǔdiàn;* ☎ *512 1018)* is the next cheapest choice for budget travellers.

YÚNNÁN

The Dǎi

KRAIG LEIB

The Dǎi state is Xīshuāngbǎnnà, annexed by the Mongols and then by the Chinese, and a Chinese governor installed in the regional capital of Jinglan (present-day Jinghong). The Dǎi are Hinayana Buddhists (as opposed to China's majority Mahayana Buddhists) who first appeared 2000 years ago in the Yangzi Valley and who were subsequently driven southwards by the Mongol invasion of the 13th century. Though Xīshuāngbǎnnà was annexed by China, it was done through the Tusi system, which meant that the Chinese were hands-off as long as a consistent supply of gifts was sent northward. Countless Buddhist temples were built in the early days of the Dǎi state and now lie in ruins in the jungles. During the Cultural Revolution Xīshuāngbǎnnà's temples were desecrated and destroyed. Some were saved by being used as granaries, but many are being rebuilt from scratch. Temples are also recovering their role as village schools where young children are accepted for religious training as monks.

In the temple courtyard, look for a cement structure resembling a letterbox; this is an altar to local spirits, a combination of Buddhism and indigenous spirit worship. Spirits exist at every level – home, village, *meung* ('city-state') – of society and humans each have 32 separate spirits that can leave if people become sick or depressed.

To keep themselves off the damp earth, the Dǎi live in spacious wooden houses raised on stilts, with the pigs and chickens below. Buffaloes are widely kept to plough the fields and century-old irrigation methods are still in use. The most common Dǎi foods are sticky rice (*khao nio* in Dǎi) and fish. The common dress for Dǎi women is a straw hat or towel-wrap headdress; a tight, short blouse in a bright colour; and a printed sarong with a belt of silver links. Some Dǎi men tattoo their bodies with animal designs. Betel nut chewing is popular and many Dǎi youngsters get their teeth capped with gold; otherwise they are considered ugly.

Ethnolinguistically, the Dǎi are part of the very large Thai family that includes the Siamese, Lao, Shan, Thai Dam and Ahom peoples found scattered throughout the river valleys of Thailand, Myanmar, Laos, north Vietnam and Assam. The Xīshuāngbǎnnà Dǎi are broken into four subgroups, the Shui (Water) Dǎi, Han (Land) Dǎi, Huayao (Floral Belt) Dǎi and Kemu Dǎi, each distinguished by variations in costume, lifestyle and location. All speak the Dǎi language, which is quite similar to Lao and northern Thai dialects. In fact northern Thai may be somewhat useful once you get off the beaten track a little; those with a firm linguistic background might have fun with a Thai phrasebook, but most newcomers to Thai will be clueless (that is, unless you happen upon one of the many monks who've studied in Thailand). The written language of the Dǎi employs a script that looks like a cross between Lao and Burmese.

Zhang Khap is the name of solo narrative opera, for which the Dǎi have a long tradition. Singers are trained from childhood to perform long songs accompanied by a flute and sometimes a long drum known as the elephant drum. Performances are given at monk initiations, when new houses are built, at weddings and on the birthdays of important people, and often last all night. Westerners generally find it monotonous and even if you understand Dǎi, the lyrics are complex if not fully improvised in a polite language. At the end, the audience shouts, 'Shuay! Shuay!', which is close to 'Hip, hip hooray!'. Even courtship is done via this singing.

From about November to March, the Dǎi celebrate the full moon with raucous music and rocket-launching get-togethers. The first full-moon party, the Tan Ta Festival, is the biggest.

Some Dǎi Phrases

Hello	*dōuzǎo lǐ*
Thank you	*yíndíi*
Goodbye	*gōihán*

Beds in excellent six- to eight-bed dorms cost Y30, with a nice common shower and wash area. There are also doubles with common bathroom for Y100, discounted to Y70. The hotel also has standard rooms for Y200. Some travellers have warned of ear-shattering karaoke.

The old block of the *Gǔlùwān Bīnguǎn*, also known as the No 2 Guesthouse, is pretty charmless but has some of the cheapest dorm beds for Y10 to Y20, with eye-watering common toilets.

Places to Stay – Mid-Range

Old Town Recently a few new places have sprung up catering to Chinese groups, which combine the old town charm with modern rooms and bathrooms.

Sānhé Nàxī Bīnguǎn (☎ 512 0892) on Xinyi Jie has a nicely renovated courtyard and rooms for Y280 to Y320, discounted in winter to Y150 to Y180.

The lovely courtyard is the main draw at the *Old Town Inn* (*Gǔchéng Kèzhàn;* ☎ 518 9000), at the northern end of the old town on Xinyi Jie. Rooms cost Y200 to Y320 (discounts available). There is one double with common bathroom for Y180. The hotel is quite popular with Chinese groups.

In the southern part of the old town, the *Lìjiāng Yuán Kèzhàn* (☎ 512 0181) is a slightly cheaper option, with variable doubles with bathroom for Y200, discounted to Y120 in winter.

Farther south, *Mùlǎoye Kèzhàn* (☎ 512 3877) has nice standard rooms with bathroom for Y138, discounted to excellent value Y100, and there's a sitting area that is pleasant. The new block has less charm but nicer rooms. Doubles/triples without bathroom cost Y82/120.

New Town For more upmarket accommodation, two options are centrally located.

The new block of the Gǔlùwān Bīnguǎn (☎ 512 1446), north of Mao Square on Xin Dajie, has standard doubles for Y200, discounted to Y140. Cheaper single/double/triple rooms are available for Y70/100/120 but these may be booked out by the local workers.

Lìjiāng Dàjiǔdiàn has doubles for Y260 to Y320 with discounts of around 50%. The Mínzúyuàn (Nationality Courtyard) block at the back has a range of single/double rooms around a traditional courtyard for Y60/100 or Y140/180 without/with bathroom. Again discounts of around 40% are available.

Lìjiāng Bīnguǎn (☎ 512 1911), opposite the PSB, has doubles for Y140, Y180 and Y380, and normally offers discounts of 40%.

Grand Lìjiāng Hotel (*Gélán Dàjiǔdiàn;* ☎ 512 8888, fax 512 7878) at the northern edge of the old town is the best luxury option with doubles for around US$55 including tax and breakfast. The hotel is a Sino-Thai joint venture.

Places to Eat

Like Dàlǐ, Lìjiāng has a legion of small, family operated restaurants catering to the culinary fantasies of China backpackers. Kitchens are tiny and waits can be long, but the food is usually interesting.

There are always several 'Nàxī' items on the menu, including the famous 'Nàxī omelette' and 'Nàxī sandwich' (goat's cheese, tomato and fried egg between two pieces of local *baba* flatbread). Try locally produced *yinjiu*, a lychee-based wine with a 500 year history – it tastes like a decent semi-sweet sherry. The Nàxī also have their own variety of Tibetan butter tea, to which they add walnuts, sesame and egg. More exotic are items such as *mabu*, glutinous rice and pig's blood wrapped in intestines. On menus, a Nàxī feast will often be called the 'Eight Bowl' meal because of its requisite number of courses.

Western Food There are some great places to eat in the old part of town. New eateries crop up all the time, so there's never a dearth of choices.

The *Old Market Inn* is oft-mentioned for its atmosphere, though it can be pretty quiet. Seats downstairs look out onto the old Market Square.

Nearby is the easy-to-spend-too-much-time-in *CC Bar*, run by a hip couple. This is the only place you'll hear Louis Armstrong followed by the Beastie Boys, where the owner can expound at length on each.

The **Prague Café** is a bright, modern place run by a Hong Kong couple and their assorted pets. The pizza, milkshakes and deserts are excellent, and there's a computer for Internet access. A major plus in winter is that it catches all the afternoon sun.

Just across the canal is **Ma Ma Fu's**, one of Lìjiāng's long-term stalwarts. There's good food across the board here, and it's the best place to sit outside and sip a cappuccino as the water gurgles by. It's got grand home-baked breads and apple pie (Y7).

Right on Market Square is the **Bridge Café**. It's aimed at Chinese and Japanese visitors (watch out for the expensive teas) but it has cheap Chinese dishes and there's a great sitting area on the 3rd floor that catches the sun and looks over the Market Square.

North of the Market Square, alongside the canal, is the popular and well-run **Sakura Café**, which serves excellent Korean and Japanese food – the outstanding *bimbap* set meal is enough for two. The chocolate cake is well worth the Y7 investment.

Close by is the **Delta Café**, which has good food and better music, heavy on the reggae. In fact, the whole street is now pretty much lined with restaurants.

The **Well Bistro**, around the corner and down from the First Bend Inn, will likely capture your fancy. Everything is made from scratch, including the bread and to-die-for desserts. The pizza is a strong contender for the best in South-West China. Lots of good vegetarian options are available and hip, eclectic music echoes quietly.

Across the alley is **#69**, which serves a good range of vegetarian dishes such as spinach and mushroom pie or baked vegetables in a pot. The food comes without MSG and salt. Set meals from around Y15 are worth the money.

Nàxī & Chinese Food If you get tired of pizza and cappuccino, Lìjiāng also has plenty of good snack bars and local restaurants, often in atmospheric surroundings and catering to Chinese tourists. Look out for places serving *baba*, the Lìjiāng local

speciality – thick flatbreads of wheat, served plain or stuffed with meats, vegetable or sweets. Morning is the best time for the baba selection.

The photogenic **Nàxī Snack Food** (Nàxī Fēngwèi Xiǎochī) on the banks of the main canal serves local Nàxī food and has an English menu of sorts. There's a row of inviting snack bars on Xinyi Jie in the north of the old town. There are also some good snack bars south of the Stone Bridge. Many have anglicised their signs to read 'Old Town Small Eat' and the like, though they haven't actually translated the menu yet.

A bit more upscale is **Gǔchéng Jiǔlóu**. Prices are reasonable at around Y12 for standard dishes. The place is lit up with dozens of lamps at night.

There are several decent places to eat in the new town. For a traveller-free Nàxī meal try the **Nàxī Restaurant** (Nàxī Fēngwèi Fàndiàn) on Xin Dajie near the Red Sun Hotel, where you can get baba bread and yak butter tea. Ask for *nàxī fēngwèi* (Nàxī specialties) as there's not much English spoken.

At the northern edge of Mao Square **Ali Baba's** is a good bet, with good food and friendly people. It's also a good spot to find out about details on Tiger Leaping Gorge and Lúgū Hú. The local bus to Dàjù leaves from near here.

There are a couple of good snack places on Fuhui Lu near the Lìjiāng Bīngǔan. The **Love on the Bridge Restaurant** (Qiáozhiqíng) is a popular place for Across-the-bridge noodles for Y6 to Y45, depending on the ingredients. The nearby **Gǒubùlǐ Tāngbāo** *bāozi* (steamed savoury buns with a meat filling) stand has some of the best bāozi in Yúnnán.

The **Belief Supermarket** (Bǎixìn Shìchǎng) on Minzhu Lu is the place to stock up on food if you are trekking. There's a **fruit market** at the northern end of the old town.

The Grand Lìjiāng Hotel has a good-value dinner buffet of Thai, Chinese and Nàxī dishes for Y40 in its **Jade River Restaurant**. The price includes tax and fruit juice.

Entertainment
One of the few things you can do in the evening in Lìjiāng is attend performances of

the Nàxī Orchestra at the **Nàxī Music Academy** *(Nàxī Gǔyuè Huì)*. These are held nightly in a beautiful old building inside the old town, usually from 8pm to 10pm. All 20 to 24 members are Nàxī, and they play a type of Taoist temple music, known as *dongjing*, that has been lost elsewhere in China. The pieces they perform are renditions of music from the Han, Song and Tang dynasties, played on original instruments. In most of China such instruments didn't survive the Cultural Revolution. Several people in this group hid theirs by burying them. This is a rare chance to hear Chinese music as it must have sounded in classical China. They also play plenty of Han music, so don't be surprised.

The orchestra has been going since 1978 and even toured Europe in 1995. The troupe is getting on in years and loses one or two musicians every year to old age.

Xuan Ke usually speaks for the group at performances, explaining each musical piece and describing the instruments. Usually funny, he's also talkative and always fascinating. Taped recordings, a set of two, cost Y30. Make sure you buy the tape at the show – tapes on sale elsewhere are pirated copies, from which the orchestra receives no revenue.

You should book seats earlier in the day if you want a good seat. Tickets range from Y30 to Y50.

Aware of the popularity of the Nàxī Orchestra, several other troupes have organised 'minority music concerts'. The **Nàxī Ancient Music House** *(Nà'ī Gǔyuèyuàn)*, next to the cinema on Dong Dajie, has a 90-minute

The Conductor

The village schoolmaster was a chivalrous and energetic man with a shock of glinting blue-black hair, who lived with his childlike wife in a wooden house beside the Jade Stream.

A musicologist by training, he had climbed to distant mountain villages to record the folksongs of the Na-Khi tribe. He believed, like Vico, that the world's first languages were in song. Early man, he said, had learnt to speak by imitating the calls of animals and birds, and had lived in a musical harmony with the rest of Creation.

His room was crammed with bric-a-brac salvaged, heaven knows how, from the catastrophes of the Cultural Revolution. Perched on chairs of red lacquer, we nibbled melon seeds while he poured into thimbles of white porcelain a mountain tea known as 'Handful of Snow'.

He played us a tape of Na-Khi chant, sung antiphonally by men and women around the bier of a corpse. *Wooo...Zeee! Wooo...Zeee!* The purpose of the song was to drive away the Eater of the Dead, a fanged and malicious demon thought to feast upon the soul.

He surprised us by his ability to hum his way through the mazurkas of Chopin and an apparently endless repertoire of Beethoven. His father, a merchant in the Lhasa caravan trade, had sent him in the 1940s to study Western music at the Kunming Academy.

On the back wall, above a reproduction of Claude Lorrain's L'Embarquement our Cythère, there were two framed photos of himself: one in white tie and tails behind a concert grand; the other, conducting an orchestra in a street of flag-waving crowds – a dashing and energetic figure, on tiptoe, his arms extended upwards and his baton down.

'In 1949,' he said. 'To welcome the Red Army into Kūnmíng.'

'What were you playing?'

'Schubert's *Marche Militaire*.'

For this – or rather, for his devotion to 'Western culture' – he got twenty-one years in jail.

He held up his hands, gazing at them sadly as though they were long-lost orphans. His fingers were crooked and his wrists were scarred: a reminder of the day when the Guards strung him up to the roof-beams – in the attitude of Christ on the Cross...or a man conducting an orchestra.

Bruce Chatwin, The Songlines, 1987

performance of traditional Nàxī music every night at 8pm. Tickets cost Y35.

The government-run **Dōngbā Palace** on Dong Dajie has a less authentic song and dance show at 8pm (Y35). During the day pop into the hall to look at the black and white photos of old Lìjiāng, mostly taken in the 1930s.

In general, if you see only one concert, you are better off supporting the original Nàxī Orchestra of Xuan Ke.

Getting There & Away

Air Yunnan Airlines can fly you direct from Lìjiāng several times daily to Kūnmíng (Y420) and daily to Jǐnghóng, in Xīshuāngbǎnnà (Y610). You can expect further connections in the coming years, most likely to Guìlín and Guǎngzhōu.

In Lìjiāng, tickets can be booked at the Civil Aviation Administration of China (CAAC) ticket office (☎ 512 0289), and at the Gǔlùwān Bīnguǎn and CITS (both levy a service charge).

Bus Lìjiāng has a northern and larger southern bus station; many, but not all, buses make stops at both. The key is to make sure you know exactly where your bus leaves from. The ticket window for the northern station is just south of the Red Sun Hotel, though most buses depart from the car park of the Gǔlùwān Bīnguǎn across the road. Schedules on the wall are mostly wrong at both.

Minibuses for Xiàguān go via Dàlǐ and leave from both stations every half-hour or so until 5.30pm (Y31.50). Express buses depart from the main southern station at 8.20am, 2.30pm and 6.30pm (Y50). Xiàguān buses will either drop you by the main highway or at the eastern edge of Dàlǐ, from where it's a 20-minute walk or five-minute horse cart ride (Y5) into the centre. Check that your bus will drop you at Dàlǐ (Dàlǐ Gǔchéng) not just Xiàguān.

For Kūnmíng, an express coach leaves the main station at 8.20am (Y154.50, ten hours). Sleeper buses depart from the main bus station between 6pm and 8pm (Y105 to Y115).

If you are headed to Chéngdū you'll need to go to the railhead at Jǐnjiāng. Jǐnjiāng buses leave at 6.30am (Y51.50, ten hours) from the main bus station and 6.45, 7 and 8am from the express bus station. Sleepers leave between 5pm and 6pm from the main and express bus stations (Y65.50). The early bus will allow you to connect with trains to Chéngdū at 6.28pm (No 2152) and 11.05pm (No K114).

Between July and September the Lìjiāng-Jǐnjiāng road can be washed out and Chéngdū-bound travellers then have to book a train ticket from Dàlǐ or Kūnmíng.

It is still impossible for foreigners to book train tickets from Jǐnjiāng in Lìjiāng, though it's easier to get tickets in Jǐnjiāng for same-day travel these days.

Buses to Zhōngdiàn leave from the main bus station every hour or so from 7.30am to 3pm (Y32.50) and pass through Qiáotóu, giving access to Tiger Leaping Gorge.

For buses to Qiáotóu, Dàjù, Shígǔ and Nínglàng (for Lúgū Hú) see those entries later in this chapter.

Getting Around

The modern part of town is a tedious place to walk around. The old town, however, is best seen on foot. Bike hire is available at the Ancient Town Youth Hostel and sometimes from Mao Square and cost around Y15 for the day.

Taxis start at Y6 flag fall but luckily few make it into the old town. Yunnan Airlines has a bus service to the airport 25km away for Y10. A taxi can be bargained down to Y60 if you rise early and prepare for negotiation.

AROUND LÌJIĀNG

Lìjiāng is surrounded by a collection of monasteries that are Tibetan in origin and belong to the Red Hat sect. Most of them were extensively damaged during the Cultural Revolution and there's not much monastic activity but it's worth heading out by bicycle for a look.

Pǔjì Sì 普济寺

Around 5km north-west of town (on a trail that passes the two large ponds to the north

AROUND LÌJIĀNG & ZHŌNGDIÀN 丽江和中甸地区周围

of town) is this monastery whose few monks are usually happy to show a traveller around. Note the copper tiling on the roof interior.

Fùguó Sì 福国寺

Not far from the town of Báishā, this was once the largest of Lìjiāng's monasteries. Much of it was destroyed during the Cultural Revolution and a couple of remaining buildings were moved to Lìjiāng's Black Dragon Pool Park. Look out for the Hufa Hall in the monastery compound; the interior walls have some interesting frescoes. Entry is Y8.

Yùfēng Sì 玉峰寺

This small lamasery, known in English as Jade Peak Temple, is on a hillside at the far south-west foot of the Jade Dragon Snow Mountain, about 5km past the town of Báishā. The last 3km of the track require a steep climb. If you leave your bike at the

foot of the hill, don't leave it too close to the village – local kids might let the air out of the tyres!

The monastery was established in 1756. The monastery's main attraction nowadays is the **Camellia Tree of 10,000 Blossoms** (Wànduǒ Shānchá). Ten thousand might be an exaggeration, but locals claim the tree produces at least 4000 blossoms between February and April. A monk on the grounds risked his life to secretly water the tree during the Cultural Revolution. One camellia in the north-west section is famed as being more than 500 years old.

Not far from Yùfēng is the town of **Yùhú** (Jade Lake), once the home of Joseph Rock (when the town was known as Nguluko). Accommodation is available at the *Nguluko Guesthouse (Xuésōng Kèzhàn)*.

On the way to Yùfēng, about 12km from Lìjiāng is Běiyué Village, the site of another Nàxī temple – devoted to Sanduo a guardian deity – dating from AD 780.

Joseph Rock

Yúnnán was a hunting ground for famous foreign plant-hunters such as Kingdon Ward and Joseph Rock. Rock lived in Lìjiāng between 1922 and 1949, becoming the world's leading expert on Nàxī culture and local botany. At the time of his death in 1963, aged 79, Rock was still working on the definitive Nàxī dictionary. More than his academic pursuits, however, he will be remembered as one of the most enigmatic and eccentric characters to travel in western China.

Rock was born in Austria, the son of a domineering father who insisted he enter the seminary. A withdrawn child, he escaped into imagination and atlases, discovering a passion for China. An astonishing autodidact – he taught himself eight languages, including Sanskrit – he began learning Chinese at 13 years of age. He eventually left Austria, worked his way across Europe and North Africa, and then sailed for the USA. He somehow wound up in Hawaii, and in time became the foremost authority on Hawaiian flora.

Asia always beckoned and he convinced the US Department of Agriculture, and later Harvard University, to sponsor his trips to collect flora for medicinal research. He devoted much of his life to studying Nàxī culture, which he feared was being extinguished by the dominant Han culture. He became *National Geographic* magazine's 'man in China' and it was his exploits in China for the magazine that made him famous.

He sent over 80,000 plant specimens from China – two were named after him – along with 1600 birds and 60 mammals. Amazingly, he was taking and developing the first colour photographic plates in his field in the 1920s! Tragically, container-loads of his collections were lost in 1945 in the Arabian Sea when the boat was torpedoed.

Rock's caravans, which stretched for half a mile, would have rivalled those of the old south-west Silk Road - dozens of servants, including a cook trained in Austrian cuisine (who was fired and re-hired on every trip), trains of pack horses, and hundreds of mercenaries for protection against bandits, not to mention the gold dinner service, a battery-powered gramophone player (with a collection of Caruso recordings) and a collapsible bathtub from Abercrombie & Fitch.

Judged by contemporary standards, Rock comes across as an egomaniac at best, a racist at worst. He certainly alienated other expatriate Westerners, holding a particular disdain for missionaries. (He got along for a spell on one trek with Edgar Snow of *Red Star Over China*-fame, but ultimately dismissed him as naive.) Supporters defend him by pointing out the prevailing attitudes of the day and by arguing that Rock needed to promote himself as a man of great power and importance in the wilds of Yúnnán and Tibet or risk being attacked by warlords and others who held local sway. Many Nàxī remember him fondly as a kind man ferociously devoted to decorum, propriety and honour, who acted as village doctor and risked his life hiding local men from impressment into the Nationalist Army.

Rock lived in Yùhú village (it was called Nguluko when Rock was there) outside Lìjiāng. Many of his possessions are now local family heirlooms. The modest home he shared is now owned and occupied by the grandson of Rock's one-time house mate, his family and a few farm animals. Nearly every day Rock-buffs – sometimes up to six in an afternoon – will come knocking, wishing to look around Rock's old house. The poor – literally – family is left no choice but to spend the day entertaining and serving tea, when they really would rather be working.

The Ancient Nakhi Kingdom of Southwest China (Harvard University Press, 1947) is Joseph Rock's definitive work. Immediately prior to his death, his Nàxī dictionary was also finally prepared for publishing. For a lighter treatment of the man and his work, take a look at *In China's Border Provinces: The Turbulent Career of Joseph Rock, Botanist-Explorer* (Hastings House, 1974) by JB Sutton or the man's many archived articles for *National Geographic*.

Wénbǐ Sì 文笔寺

This monastery, also known as Wenfeng Monastery, involves a fairly steep uphill ride 8km to the south-west of Lìjiāng. The monastery has some distinctive Tibetan features, and dates from 1733. Its two-dozen courtyards once housed 80 lamas. The hill behind the monastery has a sacred cave and spring. In the cave there's a black rock on which a disciple of Sakyamuni is said to have laid a key, so pilgrims headed to Jīzú Shān come to the rock, burn joss, and 'borrow' the key to get to their destination.

Zhǐyún Sì 指云寺

Along the road to Shígǔ, 18km from Lìjiāng by the small Lashi Hai reservoir, is the Zhǐyún Sì (Pointing to the Clouds Monastery) built in 1727. The nearby lake is a wetland reserve popular with birdwatchers and you may get to see black stork and Chinese mergansers. There is an Y10 'entry' fee to the reserve.

Frescoes

Lìjiāng is famed for its temple frescoes. Most were completed during the 15th and 16th centuries by Tibetan, Nàxī, Bai and Han artists. Many were restored during the later Qing dynasty. They depict various Taoist, Chinese and Tibetan Buddhist themes and can be found on the interior walls of temples in the area. Again, the Red Guards came through here slashing and gouging during the Cultural Revolution, but there's still a lot to see.

In Báishā (see section following) ask around for the **Dàbǎojī Palace** (Dàbǎojī Gōng), where the best frescoes are found, and also the **Liúlí Temple** (Liúlí Diàn) or the **Dàdìng Pavilion** (Dàdìng Gé). The Dàbǎojī Palace recently introduced an entry fee. The little shop has reasonably priced Nàxī scrolls and paintings.

In the lovely nearby village of **Lóngquán**, frescoes can also be found on the interior walls of the **Dàjué Temple** (Dàjué Gōng). The village is well worth a visit in its own right.

See the earlier Fùguó Sì section for other frescoes.

Báishā 白沙

Báishā is a small village on the plain north of Lìjiāng near several old temples (see the preceding Frescoes section) and is one of the best day trips out of Lìjiāng, especially if you have a bike. Before Kublai Khan made it part of his Yuan empire (1271 -1368), it was the capital of the Nàxī kingdom. It's hardly changed since then and though it seems like a desultory collection of dirt roads and stone houses, it offers a close-up glimpse of Nàxī culture for those willing to spend some time nosing around.

The star attraction of Báishā will probably hail you in the street. Dr Ho (or He) looks like the stereotypical Taoist physician and has a sign outside his door: 'The Clinic of Chinese Herbs in Jade Dragon Snow Mountain of Lìjiāng'.

The travel writer Bruce Chatwin propelled the good doctor into the limelight when he mythologised Dr Ho as the 'Taoist physician in the Jade-Dragon Mountains of Lìjiāng'. Journalists and photographers turned up from every corner of the world; and Dr Ho, previously an unknown doctor in an unknown town, has achieved worldwide renown. Look out for the John Cleese quote: 'Interesting bloke; crap tea'.

Báishā is an easy bike ride from Lìjiāng. Otherwise take bus No 6 from opposite the post office in Lìjiāng (Y2). The village is about 1km off the main road.

Jade Dragon Snow Mountain
玉龙雪山 Yùlóng Xǔeshān

Around 35km north of Lìjiāng and soaring to 5596m is Mt Satseto, also known as Yùlóng Xǔeshān (Jade Dragon Snow Mountain). The massif is made up of 13 peaks and was climbed for the first time by a research team from Běijīng in 1963.

The mountain is stunning and provincial officials are planning all sorts of awful things: golf courses, resorts and 'parks' that will probably be kitschy minority villages. Plans are underway to make it a year-round ski resort, despite the fact that consultants scream it isn't feasible. All is not lost – one plan introduced by an international consortium would create a 30,000 sq km national

YÚNNÁN

park. Unesco's World Heritage Site status may be the only thing that could save the mountain.

A chairlift has already been built up the mountain. The first section takes you about halfway up, near Love-Suicide Hill, where you can rent horses to ride to a large meadow. The second chairlift, the highest in Asia, takes you to a stunning 4506m, where walkways lead to awesome glacier views. Watch out for the symptoms of altitude sickness here (see the Facts for the Visitor Health section) – Chinese entrepreneurs sell bags of oxygen to chain-smoking Chinese tourists for around Y30.

This outing, aimed mainly at Chinese tourists, is an expensive one. Getting to the mountain requires hitching, hiring your own van for around Y130, or catching a ride on a minibus to Dàjù or Bǎoshān. A bus departs daily at 8.30am from the bus stop across from the post office. Buses take passengers the 4km from the reception centre on the main road to the cable car.

Local tour operators have prohibitively priced tours taking in the mountain and a whole lot else. Once there, the chairlift ride will cost Y110, the optional horse rental another Y20.

Furthermore, there's a Y40 entry fee to the entire area north of Báishā including Jade Dragon Snow Mountain, Yúnshānpíng and Máoniúpíng. If you enter the region from the north (Bǎoshān or Tiger Leaping Gorge) there's no ticket gate. You don't have to pay the fee if you are just travelling by public bus to Bǎoshān or Dàjù.

You can reach the snow line on one of the adjoining peaks if you continue along the base of the hillside near Báishā but ignore the track to Yùfēng Sì. On the other side of the next obvious valley, a well-worn path leads uphill to a lake. Ask locals about conditions in this area before setting out.

Yúnshānpíng 云杉坪

A ski lift has been built at this scenic spot, 36km from Lìjiāng. The lift costs Y42 return and takes you up to a plateau at 3300m, from where there are walking trails. There are plans to make this area a ski resort. To get here take the No 7 bus or any Dàjù- or Bǎoshān-bound bus (Y10.50).

Máoniúpíng 牦牛坪

This scenic area, meaning Yak Meadow, is around 60km from Lìjiāng. Yet another cable car takes tourists up to meadows at 3500m. Xuěhuā Hǎi (Snowflake Lake) is nearby and there are plenty of hiking opportunities. The cable car costs Y60 return and departs from just by the roadside.

As with Yúnshānpíng, take the No 7 bus or any Dàjù- or Bǎoshān-bound bus.

Bǎoshān 保山

Bǎoshān is a fairly interesting Nàxī village about 125km north of Lìjiāng but the main reason to come here is to continue to Shítóuchéng (the Stone City), a lovely walled village of 107 families, perched on a ledge high above the Yangzi River. From the end of the road there's a 20-minute descent to the village. Once inside the walls, the first left and left again will take you up to a viewing platform that is accessed through one family's house. You can make some lovely walks around terraced fields to surrounding villages. The village square at the foot of the entrance gates is the site of occasional Nàxī dances in the evenings. The mountain to the north of the town has connections to Kublai Khan, who is said to have crossed the Yangzi here sometime around 1274.

Many of the eaves of the Nàxī houses have wooden fish decorating the eves; one reason for this is that the Chinese for fish (*yú*) has the same sound as prosperity (*yù*).

Shítóuchéng offers some interesting treks for adventurous travellers. Mu Shangwen, the owner of the Mu Family Guesthouse (see Places to Stay) can act as a guide for three- to seven-day treks to Lúgū Hú for Y60 to Y70 per day (Y50 for solo travellers). You stay in local houses so a sleeping bag is desirable, though you wouldn't need a tent or stove. There are two main routes; north up the Jīnshā Jiāng to Lābó village and then over the mountains to Yǒngníng, or south to Wúmù and east to Cuìyù, from where you can catch a morning bus to the main Nínglàng-Yǒngníng road.

Places to Stay The *Mu Family Guesthouse* in the walled town offers beds for Y15 and excellent food for about the same. The house is the first entrance on the left after entering the old town: look for the white flag and water heaters on the roof.

A second *guesthouse* run by the town's travel company *(Bǎoshān Gǔshíchéng Lüyóu Kāifā Gōngsī Jiēdàichù)* has beds in comfortable doubles for Y30 but doesn't really have the family atmosphere of Mu's (there was a pig carcass in the shower during our visit!). The unsigned guesthouse is outside in the old town, to the right of the main path as you come towards the end of the descent from the road.

Getting There & Away Public buses to Bǎoshān (Y30, 4½ hours) leave Lìjiāng daily between 7am and 7.30am from the road junction in the north of town. From Bǎoshān it's another Y10 and one hour to Shítóuchéng. If you are coming from Dàjù you can catch the bus from the crossroads at around 10am (Y30 to Shítóuchéng).

Buses back to Lìjiāng depart Shítóuchéng sometime between 8am and 9am (give yourself 30 minutes to haul yourself up the hill) but stop for at least an hour in Bǎoshān to pick up passengers and freight, finally leaving around 11am or 11.30am.

An excellent way to leave Shítóuchéng is to hike 3½ to four hours to Bǎoshān. If you leave by 7.30am you should arrive in plenty of time to catch the bus from Bǎoshān. The trail follows the Yangzi River (here known as the Jīnshā Jiāng) past clumps of cacti and after about 1½ hours takes a side valley up to Bǎoshān. After a further 30 minutes the trail crosses a humpbacked bridge to the true right side of the stream. The first half of the trail follows the cliff side and can be dangerous at times so it's a good idea to take a guide; Mu Shangwen can act as a guide for around Y30 or introduce you to someone else.

Tiger Leaping Gorge Viewpoint
If you don't have time to trek the gorge, you can view it from its eastern end near Dàjù. From Dàjù it's a 5km walk to the entry gate

or you can take a taxi for Y10. At the car park there's a Y2 entry fee and a walkway leads down to an observation platform. For more on Dàjù and the gorge see the Tiger Leaping Gorge section later.

Shígǔ 石鼓 & The First Bend of the Yangzi
Shígǔ & Chángjiāng Dìyīwān

The small town of Shígǔ sits on the first bend of China's greatest river. Shígǔ means 'Stone Drum' and refers to a marble plaque shaped like a drum that commemorates a 16th-century Nàxī victory over a Tibetan army. The original stone drum is attributed to Zhuge Liang, the 3rd-century military strategist who crossed the river here during one of his campaigns. The other plaque celebrates the People's Army crossing of the river here in 1936 during the Long March to the north. Kublai Khan is also said to have crossed the river here on inflated sheep skins.

Buses to Shígǔ (Y8, two hours) leave at 10am from Lìjiāng's main bus station. Alternatively, take an 7.30am departure to Wēixī or 8am to Jùdiàn. It's easily visited in a day. First bend fish are reportedly the tastiest in the region.

The Most Important Hill in China

As Simon Winchester notes in his book *The River at the Centre of the World*, China's history hangs in the balance at Cloud Hill, on the first bend of the Yangzi. This pile of rocks in the middle of the oncoming Jīnshā Jiāng funnels China's greatest river north and east into the heartland of China instead of draining south out of China.

Chinese tradition puts the dramatic u-turn down to Yü the Great, China's mythological bureaucrat-deity in charge of water control. Without him, the Yangzi Valley, the cradle of the nation, would never have come into existence and the cultural development of China, and therefore the world, may have been profoundly different.

Límíng 黎明

Halfway to Jùdiàn a road leads to Límíng and then continues to Líguāng, the heart of a 240 sq km scenic area of freak geology, with steep flat-topped hills and crags of every conceivable colour vaulting from the river valley floor. There's plenty of hiking potential here, especially to the **Qiāngui Shān** (1000 Turtle Hill), a weird rock phenomenon that is said to resemble 1000 turtles marching off to the sky.

Occasional buses depart for Límíng at 10.50am from the main bus station. Alternatively take any bus bound for Jùdiàn or Wēixī, get off at the turn-off (near Zhōngxīng Village) and hitch. Accommodation is available at the bus stop in Límíng.

Wēixī County 维西县

Wēixī Lisu Autonomous County lies off the main road to Zhōngdiàn and Déqīn and so gets few visitors but you could visit it as an alternative route to or from Déqīn, or just visit as a return trip from Lìjiāng.

The road to Wēixī passes through Jùdiàn, a transport junction where you may have to change buses. Farther along is Xīnzhŭ village in the Hengduan Shān. These mountains are a treasure trove of botany and have been pegged by Chinese scientists as one of the most diverse in the world. A **botanical garden** showcases the dozens of rare species and several thousand-year-old trees in the region.

Some 40km north of Jùdiàn is Tǎchéng, named for the tower-like mountains rising behind the village. Tǎchéng reportedly has many Neolithic ruins, but most tourists come for the cliffside **Bodhidharma Cave & Temple** (Dámó Zŭshī Dòng or Damo Gompa), often translated as the Damo Founder's Cave, 15km east at the elephant-shaped Dámó Shān. Tibetan pilgrims come to circumambulate the temple complex.

Wēixī is pretty much unexplored. The large county sports **Shuoguo Temple** and the **Pāntiān Gé**, a pavilion 27km north of Wēixī. It also has some lovely Pumi and Lisu villages, including remote **Xiánuò Village**, just over the border in Déqīn county and Tónglè, near Yèzhī town.

Tiger Leaping Gorge 虎跳峡
Hŭtiào Xiá

After making its first turn at Shígŭ the mighty Yangzi River (at this point known as the Jīnshā Jiāng) surges between Hābā and Jade Dragon Snow Mountain, through one of the deepest gorges in the world. The entire gorge measures 16km long, and it's a giddy 3900m from the waters of the Yangzi to the snowcapped mountaintops. The best time is May and the start of June, when the hills are afire with plant and flower life.

Within five years the hike through the gorge has gone from obscure adventure to the can't-miss experience of northern Yúnnán but you'll still probably only encounter several other travellers on the trail. Plan on three or four days away from Lìjiāng. You can do the walk in two days, though some travellers, enchanted with Walnut Grove, have lengthened it to over a week.

First check at cafes in Lìjiāng for the latest gossip on the mini-trek, particularly the weather and its possibly fatal effects on the trail. Most cafes give away hand-drawn maps of the trek. They show paths, walking times and some places to stay but they aren't to scale.

Finishing the walk at Qiáotóu means easier transport links back to Lìjiāng, but finishing at Dàjù gives you the option of continuing north to Báishuĭtái or combining a visit to the gorge with a trip to Băoshān. Waiting a day for a bus to Lìjiāng from Dàjù is not the worst fate. We cover the route in the direction from Qiáotóu to Dàjù.

After three years of Herculean blasting and building, a road now leads right through the gorge from Qiáotóu to Walnut Grove and a dirt track swings north to Báishuĭtái, joining the road to Zhōngdiàn. Tour buses shuttle up and down, kitschy stop-off points are being constructed and a couple of resorts have been started. A ski hill and theme park are just two of the initial proposals; rafting already takes place near Qiáotóu. Buses only reach as far as the upper rapids, halfway through the gorge, but you can expect the fuss to slowly head downstream.

[continued on page 371]

TIGER LEAPING GORGE 虎跳峡
HIGH TRAIL NOTES

JULIET COOMBE

There are two trails – the higher (older route, known as the 24-bend path, though it's more like 30) along an old miners' track, and the lower, along what is now a new road replete with belching tour buses. There's little point hiking along the roadside but it is possible. You could walk both trails, hiking along the high trail and then hitching along the road back to Qiáotóu, stopping at the views of the rapids. As one traveller aptly points out, 'Remember the high road leaves less time for drinking beer in Walnut Grove.'

Via the upper path, from Qiáotóu it's six hours to Bĕndìwán or a strenuous eight hours to Walnut Grove. From Bĕndìwán to Dàjù it's about six hours. Coming in the other direction, from Dàjù it's about four hours to Walnut Grove or six to seven to Bĕndìwán.

There are painted yellow arrows – a godsend – pointing you along the upper path, although some have been obscured and you'll still wander around a bit. To get to the high road from Qiáotóu cross the bridge, turn right and walk toward the gate. After going through the gate, cross a small stream and go 150m. Take a left fork, go through the basketball and football courts of the schoolyard, and join the tractor road. Walk along the tractor road until it ends and then look for the yellow arrow to the right. The path descends to the left and then follows the hillside.

After 1½ hours from Qiáotóu, you cross a stream and see signs for the **Nàxī Family Bed and Breakfast** (Nà'ī Yāgé), a friendly place run by the Li family, which is ideal if you set off late from Qiáotóu or are exhausted from Walnut Grove. Beds cost around Y15 with an extra Y25 for dinner and breakfast and you can hire horses here. The surrounding settlement is the lovely village of Nuòyú.

From here you climb to the ridge, roughly following the telephone poles and then climb the 28 bends, the hardest part of the trek. You reach the top after about 3½ hours from Qiáotóu and get fine views of the gorge and its middle rapids.

Bĕndìwán 本地湾

About six hours from Qiáotóu is the excellent **Halfway Guest House** (Zhōngtú Kèzhàn) at Bĕndìwán Village. Beds cost Y10 or Y15, there are hot showers on request and some of the best food on the trek, listed on a bamboo menu. It's run by the friendly Mr Feng and his family who decided to open a guesthouse at this, the drop-dead point, since so many exhausted and lost travellers came knocking. He gets rave reviews for his treks into the hills for Chinese herb and medicinal plant tours and views of Hābā Peak (5396m). Ask also about the excursion to Guanyin Waterfall. If you are coming from Qiáotóu, this

might be a better option than Walnut Grove, since the Grove is more like three-quarters of the way through and there's no reason to get to Dàjù early the next day anyway because the afternoon bus often doesn't run. Try to get there early to enjoy the views from the balcony of the afternoon sun on the rock wall opposite. It is possible to follow a steep path down to the road from here, thus making a shorter trek.

The next day you cross the pretty Longdong Waterfall after 30 minutes, followed by a short climb and a long descent. After 1½ hours from Běndìwán you descend to the road to *Tina's Guest House* (*Zhōngxiá Lǚdiàn*) (budget more time if you are ascending). Tina's is a friendly place run by relatives of the Halfway Guest House owners and is a convenient place to spend your first night from Dàjù. Beds cost Y10 and many rooms have fine views. A good detour from here leads down 40 minutes to the middle rapids and **Tiger Leaping Stone**, where a tiger is once said to have leapt across the Yangzi, thus giving the gorge its name. The man who restored the path charges Y10 to take people down it (regardless of whether you want him to or not). From Tina's to Walnut Grove it's a 40-minute walk along the road.

A new alternative trail to Walnut Grove keeps high where the path descends to Tina's, crosses a stream and a 'bamboo forest' before descending into Walnut Grove. The guesthouses are scrambling to find ways to avoid the old trails now that busloads of tour groups have taken them over and this is probably just the start.

Walnut Grove 胡桃园

(Hútáoyuán)

There are two hotels nestled among the walnuts. *Sean's Spring Guesthouse* (*Shānquán Kèzhàn; ☎ 0887-880 6300*) is the spot for more lively evenings and socialising. *Chateau de Woody* (*Shānbáiliǎn*), the other option, is considered the quiet alternative. Sean's is probably now the nicer place to stay, since Woody's added a hideously ugly concrete annex full of cramped, charmless rooms. Both places have dorm beds for Y10 or Y15, with a free hot shower (Y5 for a hot bath!). Sean's has electric blankets, mountain bike hire for Y10 per hour (with a Y400 deposit) and can organise camping, horse trips and the hire of horses. There's fine food, cold beer and plenty of local wild herbs. Sean,

Left: Horses tethered to a bridge at Tiger Leaping Gorge. (Photograph by John Borthwick).

Margo and Daisy make very genial hosts. If you are headed to Qiáotóu and want to take the bamboo path (see earlier) ask them to point out the path behind the guesthouse.

The final section of the walk is slightly shorter at around four hours. There are now two ferries and so two route options to get to Dàjù. After 45 minutes you'll see a red marker leading down to the new (winter) ferry *(xīn dùkǒu)*; the descent includes one particularly hairy section over planks with a sheer drop below. The ferry ride across the river costs an extortive Y10 – the boatmen justify it by saying that Y10 is a bargain for a trip from Zhōngdiàn to Lìjiāng (the river divides the

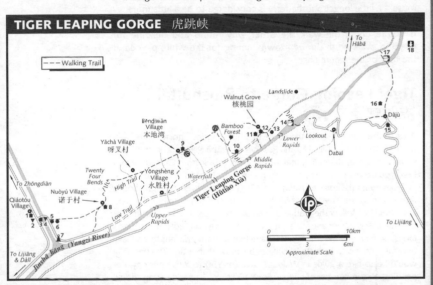

TIGER LEAPING GORGE 虎跳峡

TIGER LEAPING GORGE

PLACES TO STAY
1 Quánxiá Lóu Hotel 泉峡楼
3 Gorge Village Hotel 峡谷村饭店
8 Naxi Family Bed & Breakfast 纳西雅阁
9 Halfway Guest House 中途客栈
10 Tina's Guest House 中峡客栈

11 Sean's Spring Guesthouse 山泉客栈
12 Chateau de Woody 山白脸旅馆
15 Tiger Leaping Gorge Hotel 虎跳峡谷饭店
16 Snowflake Hotel 雪花饭店

PLACES TO EAT
2 Backpacker Cafe
4 Gorged Tiger Cafe 玛佳咖啡馆

OTHER
5 Ticket Office 售票处
6 School 学校
7 Tiger Statue
13 Ticket Office 售票处
14 New (Winter) Ferry
17 Ferry 渡船
18 Pagoda 塔

two counties!). From here it's a hard climb past a look-out point to the car park where you should register with the Lìjiāng PSB. The PSB officer offers a car to take you into Dàjù for Y10, which avoids the fairly dull 1½ hours walk to Dàjù along the road. If you do walk, after 30 minutes look for a red sign pointing to a short cut through a village and down to the road. When you approach Dàjù, follow the short cut straight into town. Basically, all roads lead to Rome from here.

The second, lesser-used option continues along the road from Walnut Grove, past an area prone to landslides, until it reaches the permanent ferry crossing (Y10). From here paths lead to Dàjù. This route is a little longer but the ferry is considered to be a little more reliable and safer in summer, when water levels in the river are higher. If you're doing the walk the other way round and heading for Qiáotóu, walk north through town, aiming for the white pagoda at the foot of the mountains.

Tiger Leaping Gorge to Báishuǐtái
虎跳峡至白水台

An adventurous add-on to the gorge trek is to continue north all the way through the Hābā Shān Nature Reserve to Hābā village and the limestone terraces of Báishuǐtái, making a four-day trek from Qiáotóu. From here you can travel on to Zhōngdiàn. The trek skirts 5396m Hābā Shān.

From Walnut Grove to Hābā, via Jiāngbiān, is seven to eight hours. From here to the Yí village of Sānbā is about the same, following trails. You could just follow the road and hitch on the occasional truck or tractor but this way is longer and less scenic as the trail cuts off most of the road's loops. Some hardy mountain bikers have followed the trail but this is really only fun from north to south, elevations being what they are. The best way would be to hire a guide in Walnut Grove for Y50 to Y100 per day, depending on the number of people. For Y100 to Y120 per day you should be able to get a horse and guide. To hire a car to Sānbā costs around Y300. Eventually buses will make the trip but that is still some time off.

In Hābā most people stay at the *Haba Snow Mountain Inn* (*Hābā Xuěshān Kèzhàn*), which has beds for Y10 and toilets and showers. A second place has no shower. A long day trip from Hābā can take you up to **Hēi Hǎi** (Black Lake), also known as **Qīsè Hǎi** (Seven-Coloured Lake). It's possible to take horses up to the lake. Azaleas bloom spectacularly in the region from June to August.

There are several guesthouses in Sānbā, of which the *Shānzhuāng Lǚguǎn* is probably the most popular. From Sānbā there is an 8am bus to Zhōngdiàn (five hours), or you could get off at the turn-off to Bìtǎ Hǎi and hike to here and Shuòdū Hǎi (see the Around Zhōngdiàn section).

If you decide to take the trek unguided, you'll need specific directions from a local, who are few and far between. Be aware that you'll need your own provisions and equipment for all kinds of weather. Assume the worst and go prepared; you'll have to sleep under the stars if lost.

[continued from page 366]

This currently doesn't affect trekkers as the high path climbs way above the road.

This does mean that you can still see the gorge if you don't want to trek by taking a bus to Qiáotóu and then catching one of the microbuses that shuttle people to the main viewpoint 10km away, just before the road goes through a tunnel (Y10 per person, each way). You could even take a taxi (Y50) the 23km from Qiáotóu to Walnut Grove.

A second road has been built part of the way through the gorge, this time on the south side. It remains to be seen what kind of development occurs here but it might make for quicker access from Lìjiāng.

It is also possible to combine a visit to Jade Dragon Snow Mountain or Bǎoshān with a visit to the eastern look-out point near Dàjù. See the entry earlier in this chapter for details

There is an admission fee to the gorge of Y30. There are check posts about 600m after you cross the bridge at Qiáotóu and at the eastern end of Walnut Grove.

Dangers & Annoyances The gorge trek is not to be taken lightly. Several travellers have died, most because they wandered off the trail, got lost, were unable to return to the trail, or fell. One hiker was buried while trying to scramble over a landslide. Two solo travellers reported being assaulted on the trail, though this couldn't be officially confirmed.

Both roads can be hair-raising during the wet months of July and August – or any time it rains really – when landslides and swollen waterfalls can block the trail.

On a lighter note, several travellers have reported becoming ill after eating in Qiáotóu or from drinking water along the trek.

Speaking of water – one litre of water is definitely *not* enough on this trek. Either take water purification tablets or another bottle to last until the first water in Běndìwān Village.

Be aware that in the high season – particularly late summer – up to 100 people a day can make the trek in each direction, and at those times bed space is short.

Places to Stay & Eat If you have to overnight in Qiáotóu, the best place is the *Gorge Village Hotel*, with clean beds for Y20 in a double or triple with electric blanket, or Y100 for a comfortable double with bathroom and Western toilet. There are hot showers and there's a decent restaurant. This hotel is in front of the bridge leading to the trail.

The *Quánxiá Lóu* across the main road isn't as good but has beds for Y15 and doubles with bathroom for Y50. There are several other hotels.

Directly across from the turn-off to the gorge, on the main highway is the *Backpacker Café*, the nerve-centre of trail information. It has an English menu, staff speak passable English, and there's backpack storage.

A new, perhaps more reliable place to get information on the trail is the *Gorged Tiger Café* run by the same folk who run Sean's Guesthouse. The restaurant is just over the bridge on the right hand side as you walk towards the gorge from Qiáotóu, and is a good place to feed up before or after a trek.

In Dàjù the *Snowflake Hotel (Xuěhuā Fàndiàn)* is the premier vacationer's residence, with beds for Y10 in a lovely courtyard and excellent food. The hotel can arrange the 7.30am bus to Lìjiāng to pick you up at the hotel.

If this is full try the *Tiger Leaping Gorge Hotel (Hǔtiào Xiágǔ Lǚguǎn)* by the central square.

Getting There & Away From Lìjiāng to Qiáotóu, buses run to Zhōngdiàn every hour or so from 7.30am to 3pm from the main bus station and pass through Qiáotóu (Y13).

From Lìjiāng to Dàjù (Y23.50, four to five hours) buses leave from the Gǔlùwān Bīnguǎn at 7.30am and 9am, and 1pm. They can sometimes be persuaded to carry on to the new ferry crossing for an extra Y5 per person.

Returning to Lìjiāng from Qiáotóu, buses start running through from Zhōngdiàn between 8am and 9am; just plop yourself right down on a chair in front of the Backpacker Café and stick your arm out.

The last one rolls through around 7pm, though 5pm is safer (Y10 to Y15). You can also catch a bus north-west to Zhōngdiàn until about 5pm.

Returning to Lìjiāng from Dàjù several buses leave daily at 7.30am. There are sometimes buses at 1.30pm and even rarer buses at 3pm. If you take the early morning bus you'll be able to connect with the bus from Lìjiāng to Bǎoshān.

Eventually the new highway through the gorge will link Qiáotóu, Walnut Grove and the settlement across the river from Dàjù and then bend north to connect Báishuǐtái, allowing travellers to get to Zhōngdiàn from here. Until bus connections start you'll have to hike or hitch.

Lúgū Hú

This remote lake overlaps the Yúnnán-Sìchuān border and is a centre for several Tibetan, Yi and Mosu (a Nàxī subgroup) villages. The lake is fairly high at 2685m and is usually snowbound in winter. The best times to visit are April to May and September to October, when the weather is dry and mild.

Improved roads have resulted in a large rise in numbers of Chinese tourists to the lake. Three- and four-storey hotels have largely replaced the two-storey Mosu cabins in the main tourist town of Luóshuǐ. Roads are planned from Nínglàng to Dàjù and Tiger Leaping Gorge and eventually to south-west Sìchuān. Many people rank the scenery between Lìjiāng and Nínglàng some of their favourite in Yúnnán.

As the road from Nínglàng drops down into the lake basin there is a good lookout point. The lake is dotted with a handful of islets; at the north-west corner is 3756m Gemu Peak, named after a local goddess. Visitors to Lúgū Hú are generally dropped at the lakeside village of Luóshuǐ, which is where most of the accommodation is.

There is now a spurious 'entry' fee of Y30 to the lake that is collected from tourists at a roadside check post. The mini-van drivers usually operate a scam whereby they can get you in for Y20 (a chunk of which goes in their pockets).

The Mosu

The 36,000 Mosu (Mosuo in Chinese) live almost exclusively in the Lúgū region. They are related to their neighbours the Yi, though officially they are considered a sub-group of the Nàxī, a categorisation that many Mosu resent. The Mosu language belongs to the Burmese-Yi group.

The Mosu are most famous for their elements of matriarchal society. They have traditionally maintained flexible arrangements for love affairs. In fact there are no Mosu words for marriage, virginity, husband or wife. The *azhu* (male friend) system allowed a couple to become lovers without setting up joint residence; the boyfriend would spend the nights at his girlfriend's house but return at dawn to live and work at his mother's house. This practise was known as *tisese*, or 'walking back and forth'. Any children born to the couple would grow up in their mother's family and were raised by the mother, grandmother and aunts. It was not uncommon for a child not to know who was its biological mother. The father provided support, but no special effort was made to recognise paternity and family names were passed down from mother to daughter. Women inherited all property, and disputes were adjudicated by female elders. This traditional system was banned during the Cultural Revolution, along with the local form of Tibetan Buddhism.

Elements of this lifestyle still exist but most Mosu are as monogamous as any other ethnic group. Yet the Mosu's reputation for sexual freedom has spread throughout China and Han prostitutes have moved in to service disappointed Chinese visitors.

Things to See & Do In addition to just admiring the gorgeous scenery, you can visit several islands on the lake via large dugout canoes, which the Mosu call 'pig troughs' (*zhūcáo*). The canoes, which are rowed by Mosu who also serve as guides, generally take you out to **Liwubi Island** (Lǐwùbǐ Dǎo), the lake's largest island. From here you can practically wade across to a spit of land in

Sìchuān. It will cost about Y15 per person, Y30 if you want to be rowed around the island as well. The canoes can hold about seven people, but the price should be the same regardless. Canoes leave from near the Mósuōyuàn Hotel and a beach area to the south of the hotel strip.

There are numerous adventurous trips. You can ride a horse or walk around the lake in two days via Lǐgēn, Xiǎo Luòshuǐ and Dàzuǐ. It shouldn't be too difficult to hire a horse and guide. From the other side of the lake you could continue on to Sìchuān (see Getting There & Away).

In the outskirts of nearby Yǒngníng is Zhāměi Sì, a monastery with at least 20 monks in residence. There is also a concrete hot spring (wēnquán), about 10km north of town. A private bus costs Y15 a head for the 30-minute ride and admission is Y1. A bus passes through Luóshuǐ to Yǒngníng for Y5; or you could walk the 19km through pleasant scenery.

Places to Stay & Eat In Luóshuǐ many Mosu homes are guesthouses, where you can stay for Y10 to Y15 per bed. There are no showers but you can wash up from a cistern in the courtyard. There's little to choose between these; pick the one with no tour groups. The three-storey buildings generally have better views of the lake and a balcony is a bonus.

Dinner is normally cooked for you by the Mosu. Little fish, potatoes and barbecued hard-boiled eggs are the order of the day. Prices are Y5 to Y10. Otherwise there are several barbecue places at the north end of town serving up the same dishes.

One Mosu speciality, the 'Boneless Pig' – a gutted, boned, salted and preserved pig carcass (which doubled as a mattress) that was noted by Joseph Rock – has sadly died out. *Ahkejia*, previously known as the Móānyuán (Peace Garden) is good and far away from the clutter. Beds cost Y15.

Of the larger guesthouses, the *Mósuōyuàn* seems to be the centre of action. Occasional Mosu song-and-dance performances are held here and at the *Mósuō Yídiànyuán* at the northern end of the hotel strip.

Husi Teahouse is a backpacker restaurant and guesthouse owned by immigrants from Chóngqìng. There's little Mosu character here but the rooms are glass-fronted and so offer good views of the lake.

The two-star *Mósuō Shānzhuāng*, the lake's only mid-range option, is 3km from Luóshuǐ perched on a bluff above the lake. Rooms cost between Y100 and Y150.

There are less touristed guesthouses in the village by the main road, away from the lakeshore. Some travellers have stayed with families on Ligen Island (*Lǐgēn Dào*) on the north-east side of the lake. To get here take a bus to Yǒngníng and get off where the road branches; from here it's 2km, though it's tough to find at night.

There are also several guesthouses in Yǒngníng, which makes a good base for hiking to the nearby hot spring. The cost of a bed averages Y20.

Getting There & Away From Lìjiāng it's a six-hour bus trip to Nínglàng, the Lúgū county centre, through some fine scenery. Luxury buses leave Lìjiāng's main bus station at 7.50am and 9am (Y54 including a two-hour minibus to Lúgū Hú). Other buses to Nínglàng depart from Lìjiāng's main bus station and express bus station until 11am (Y37). Minibuses meet these buses to take passengers on to the lake but if you get a late bus there's a chance you'll have to overnight in Nínglàng.

Leaving Luóshuǐ, buses leave from the courtyard of the Mósuō Fàndiàn. An 8am minibus to Nínglàng meets the express bus to Lìjiāng (Y57). There is also a 7.30am departure to Jīnjiāng (Y68).

To get to Yǒngníng you'll need to wait at the main road for the bus from Nínglàng.

Some travellers have tried crossing over to Lúgū Zhèn (also known as Zuǒsuǒ), a town on the Sìchuān side, and catching buses on to Yányuán, Mùlǐ or Xīchàng on the Kūnmíng-Chéngdū line (see the Xīchàng section in the Sìchuān chapter for details). You'll need to be very flexible on this route. There's no reason to expect the Tibetan tribespeople you come across to be friendly either. One traveller had a frightening experience with locals while hiking this route, and headed back to Yǒngníng. Most travellers head back to Lìjiāng the same way they came.

For details on trekking here from the east see the Bǎoshān entry in the Around Lìjiāng section.

Nínglàng 宁蒗

For most travellers Nínglàng is just a place to change buses en route to Lúgū Hú but if you break the journey for a couple of hours or overnight, you can see local Yi culture. The town is the centre of the Yi Autonomous County and the streets are often dotted with Yi medicine men, fortune tellers and embroiderers. For more on the Yi see the section in the Sìchuān chapter.

Places to Stay There are several places to stay. The convient *Kèyùnzhàn Zhāodàisuǒ (Bus Station Guesthouse)* near the bus station, has beds for Y15/20 in a triple/double with shared bathroom.

Jiāměi Bīnguǎn, 100m right out of the bus station, has slightly better singles/doubles/triples for Y30/40/50 and a good double with bathroom for Y60.

Diagonally opposite and down a small lane is the *Lúgū Hú Dàjiǔdiàn* (☎ 552 2862), which has rooms with common bathroom for Y30 to Y60 and standard doubles with bathroom for around Y160, discounted to Y100. There are several other hotels in town.

Getting There & Away There are buses to Lìjiāng (Y34) from 7am to noon, though there may be later buses in summer. After this you can still get to Lìjiāng by catching a 2.30pm minibus to Yǒngshèng (Y18) and then catching a passing sleeper from Jīnjiāng onto Lìjiāng.

There are several sleeper buses daily to Kūnmíng (Y115) and an early morning bus to Jīnjiāng (Y45).

ZHŌNGDIÀN 中甸 (GYALTHANG)
☎ 0887

Zhōngdiàn, 198km north-west of Lìjiāng, marks the start of the Tibetan world. At 3200m, the boomtown is a principally Tibetan town, known as Gyeltang or Gyalthang

ZHŌNGDIÀN 中甸

To Nàpà Hǎi (7km) & Déqīn (187km)
To Ganden Sumtseling Gompa (4km)
To Bìtǎ Hǎi (25km), Báishuǐtái (108km) & Lìjiāng (174km)

Huancheng Xīlu
Hongqi Lu
Xiangyang Lu
Jiantang Donglu 建塘东路
To Chörten
To Gyalthang Dzong Hotel
Wenming Jie
Changzheng Lu
Heping Lu
Tuanjie Lu 团结路
Beimen Jie
To Aiport (5km)
To Monastery (1km)
Old Town

in Tibetan, with a heavy Han overlay and a sprinkling of Bai, Huí (Muslim), Yi and Nàxī minorities. A boom in Shangri La driven tourism has fuelled the construction of a bland Han Chinese town but there is still an interesting old town. The main reason to come here is to visit the monastery and to get a taster of Tibet if you can't make it to the real thing.

Zhōngdiàn is also the last stop in Yúnnán for hardy travellers headed on the rough five- or six-day journey to Chéngdū via the Tibetan townships and rugged mountain terrain of western Sìchuān.

ZHŌNGDIÀN

PLACES TO STAY & EAT
6 Tibetan
  Coffee Shop
  金丝咖啡室
8 Jiāotōng Fàndiàn
  交通饭店
11 Díqìng Bīnguǎn
  迪庆宾馆
13 Guānguān
  Jiǔdiàn
  观光酒店
14 Xiāngbālā
  Jiǔdiàn
  香巴拉酒店
15 Lányuègǔ Jiǔdiàn
  蓝月谷酒店
16 Kāngbā Jiǔlóu
  康巴酒楼
17 Tibet Cafe

18 Diànlì Jiǔdiàn
  电力酒店
19 Tibet Hotel
  永生旅馆
20 Tiānchéng Zàngshì
  Jiǔdiàn
  天成藏式酒店

OTHER
1 North Bus Station
  汽车站
2 Market
  市场
3 Bank of China
  中国银行
4 China Post
  邮电局
5 Market
  市场

7 Central
  Bus Station
  汽车总站
9 Market
  市场
10 China
  Telecom
  中国电信
12 Yunnan Airlines/
  CAAC
  云南航空公司、
  中国民航
21 Scripture
  Chamber
  中甸古城藏经堂
22 Guishan Park
  龟山公园
23 CITS
  中国国际旅行社

In the sixth lunar month (mid to late June), Zhōngdiàn plays host to a horse racing festival – three days of dancing, singing, eating and, of course, horse racing in the south-east of town. A new annual minority arts festival, usually in September, features artists from surrounding provinces and Tibet. Accommodation can be a bit tight around these times, so you may want to arrive a day or two early. If you are in Lìjiāng, you can ask CITS about the festival and they might help you book a room.

Information
Tourist offices CITS (☎ 822 2238) in the old town has information on Landcruiser trips to Dàochéng (around US$100 per day for vehicle hire; see the Sìchuān chapter for details) and 12-day overland tours to Tibet (around Y15,000). The staff are happy to show you photos of rarely visited places in the region.

Money The People's Bank of China on Changzheng Lu can change money but can't give cash advances from credit cards.

Email & Internet Access The Internet is available at the China Telecom office on Changzheng Lu for Y8 per hour. The office is open daily from 8.30am to 9pm. Internet access is also available at the Tibet Café (Y12) and at the restaurant of the Tibet Hotel for (Y10).

Dangers & Annoyances Be careful in Zhōngdiàn's bus station, particularly on the early morning Lìjiāng buses and at night, as there's been a spell of push-and-slash bandit bands.

Ganden Sumtseling Gompa
Sōngzànlín Sì
About an hour's walk north of town is this 300-year-old Tibetan monastery complex, home to around 600 monks. The monastery is the most important in South-West China and it is without question worth the trip to Zhōngdiàn.

Construction on the Gelukpa (Yellow Hat) Monastery was initiated in 1679 by the fifth Dalai Lama and was shelled and demolished by the People's Liberation Army (PLA) in 1959. It was reopened in 1981.

There are half a dozen main buildings, including eight colleges, all open to visitors. The monks are generally friendly and the village atmosphere makes it a fine place to while away a few hours. You can walk up into the hills behind the monastery for the views.

YÚNNÁN

There is an admission fee of Y10, of which Y9 goes directly to the monastery. Photography is allowed. By the entrance gates are several shops selling Tibetan accessories.

If you're around during special occasions or festival time, you might see Cham, religious dances in which monks wear masks depicting deities, ghosts, and animals.

To get there, take the No 3 bus from anywhere along Changzheng Lu; it runs past the gate of the Tibet Hotel. The fare is Y1. You could probably walk there in an hour.

Old Town 老城

Exiting the Tibet Hotel to the right, follow side streets south when the road ends and you'll get to **Scripture Chamber** (Gǔchéng Zàngjīngtáng), formerly a memorial hall to the Red Army's Long March. There's only one room to see. Entry costs Y5 and it's open 10am to 5pm.

Across the street **Guishan Park** (Guīshān Gōngyuán) has another temple at the top with commanding views of the area. Entry is Y3.

Farther south, overlooking the old town district, is another **monastery** presided over by two exceedingly friendly monks. Continue south along an alley when Changzheng Lu ends. Bear right, then an immediate left. Paths run up across gardens and along a hill, bypassing a pavilion.

Farther north, atop a hill to the west of Changzheng Lu is a **chörten** (Tibetan stupa) with good views of the town.

Places to Stay

Most travellers head to the **Tibet Hotel** (*Yǒngshèng Fàndiàn; ☎ 822 2488, fax 822 3863*); it's Chinese name means 'Long Life'. It's a clean and friendly spot. A clean dorm bed with electric blanket costs Y20 or Y25, doubles are Y60. Hot showers are available 8pm to midnight in the clean common bathrooms. Comfortable standard doubles go for Y220 but are often discounted to Y150. The hotel also has nice sitting areas, a good restaurant with Internet access, money exchange, a pricey laundry service and an impressively ornate Tibetan-style lobby. Bike rental is relatively steep at Y3

per hour. The hotel can be hard to find so it's worth forking out Y5 on a taxi from the bus station.

The new **Tiānchéng Zàngshì Jiǔdian**, 40m past the Tibet Hotel has clean and comfortable triples for Y30 per bed and standard doubles for Y160, discounted to Y80, though there's no common showers.

The convenient but charmless **Jiāotōng Fàndiàn** next to the bus station has good-value doubles with bathroom for as low as Y60, as well as dorm beds for Y20.

The three-star **Díqìng Bīnguǎn** (*☎ 822 9666*), set back off Changzheng Lu, looks pretty opulent to be offering dorm rooms. Don't get excited, as the rooms are in a dilapidated wing out back. Beds in a quad with common bathroom and showers cost Y20. Standard rooms start at Y280, discounted to Y150.

Along the same lines is the **Xiāngbālā Jiǔdiàn**, which has nice rooms for Y30 to Y40 per bed with common washroom but no shower. Doubles with bathroom run to Y330.

Diànlì Jiǔdiàn, near the Tibet Hotel, is a pretty good mid-range joint that offers rooms with ensuite bathrooms and hot water from Y80 to Y120. Another decent option is the **Lányuègǔ Jiǔdiàn**, which has doubles with ensuite for Y70 to Y100. The **Kāngbā Jiǔlóu** has doubles for Y50 discounted to Y100.

Probably the best mid-range choice is the US joint-venture **Gyalthang Dzong Hotel** (*☎ 822 3646/7583, fax 822 3620, e gylhotel@chengdunet.com, W www.gdh.innerasia.com*). The hotel is built in a Tibetan style in the south of town at the base of the town's two protector hills, near the Longtan Pool. Tibetan rooms are Y300, discounted by 50% between November and March. There's a Tibetan restaurant, crafts centre and herb garden. The hotel runs the region's most professional ecotourism and trekking packages, including botanical tours.

Guānguāng Jiǔdiàn (*☎ 823 0698*) is a three-star monster owned by Yunnan Airlines. Doubles cost Y360 to Y418. Of more relevance to budget travellers are the Western toilets in the marble clad lobby that must be the cleanest in north-west Yúnnán.

It gets cold in Zhōngdiàn, particularly between November and March, so if you're here around this time you may want to ask for extra quilts or an electric blanket. Only the mid-range hotels have any heating (kōngtiáo).

Places to Eat
For all the hoopla of Zhōngdiàn entering the realms of popular tourist destinations, there sure aren't many places to eat.

The main place aimed at foreigners is the **Tibet Café** (☎ 823 0282), run by the owners of the Dōngbā house in Lìjiāng. The cosy place offers decent Western and Chinese food, especially breakfasts (try the 'pancake spank') and is a good place to pick up information on local sights. The maps on the wall and the travellers tips book are especially helpful.

The restaurant at the Tibet Hotel has equally good Western and Chinese food and is another fine place to swap travellers tales.

The **Tibetan Coffee Shop** is a decent place to try a cup of locally grown Golden Ring Tea (Jīnsī Xiāngchá) or even Tibetan yak butter tea. The cafe is the base for the Kawagebo Tibetan Cultural Society, which offers courses in Tibetan and is a good place to meet local English speakers. It is planning to add Tibetan food like thugpa (noodles) to its sparse menu.

There are lots of Sichuanese and Huí Muslim restaurants around town, the latter recognisable by the yak heads and carcasses strewn around the entrance.

The town's main **markets** are generally worth a visit. The one in the northern part of town is a good place to get a snack lunch. Look out for fruit called huangge, which looks like a knobbly tangerine. There are also several decent **supermarkets** along Changzheng Lu.

Shopping
Zhōngdiàn is rife with shops dispensing 'Tibetan' wares. Prices here are decidedly higher than northern Sìchuān, especially for those funky resplendent long yak-fur coats that look like Henry VIII would have worn. Yet competition allows for bargaining.

Regional specialties include bowls crafted from azalea wood, hammered copper kettles, silver ornaments and expensive Tibetan rugs. Zhōngdiàn is a major exporter of exotic mushrooms to Japan – particularly the songrong (matsutake) mushroom, said to be a cancer curative. The region was initially explored by musk merchants, and musk can still be bought in local markets.

Getting There & Away
Air Yunnan Airlines have flights from Zhōngdiàn to Kūnmíng every Tuesday, Thursday, Saturday and Sunday for Y560. China Southwest Airlines has introduced a weekly flight from Chéngdū to Zhōngdiàn via Kūnmíng and on to Lhasa in Tibet. Foreigners face the same restrictions (booking a group tour etc) getting a ticket to Lhasa as they do in Chéngdū and Chóngqìng.

The CAAC office is open daily from 8.30am to noon and 2pm to 5.30pm. The airport is 5km from town and a taxi will cost from Y15 to Y20. The airport opened in 1999 and is sometimes referred to as Shangri La, Díqìng or Deqen – there is currently no airport at Déqīn.

Bus Zhōngdiàn has two bus stations. Most departures are from the central bus station but for destinations north it's worth also checking at the north bus station.

Buses to Lìjiāng (Y29, five hours) depart hourly between 7am and 4pm. Buses pass through Qiáotóu (Y15.50), at the southern-eastern end of the Tiger Leaping Gorge trek.

Sleepers back to Kūnmíng (Y141) and Xiàguān (Y57) leave all day and there are also daytime buses for the latter, including a 9am express coach (Y99).

Buses to Déqīn (Y33, seven hours) depart at 7am, 8am and 9am and take in some stunning scenery on a clear day, stopping for lunch in Bēnzìlán. Minibuses for Bēnzìlán (Y14, three hours) depart at 1pm and 2pm or take the Déqīn bus.

Buses to Sānbā (Y20) depart at 8.30am. There is also an 8am departure from the northern bus station.

Take note that roads out of Zhōngdiàn can be temporarily blocked by snow anytime between November and March. If you are travelling at this time pack lots of warm clothes and a flexible itinerary.

The High Road To Sìchuān The arduous bus-hopping, back-door rollercoaster ride from Zhōngdiàn into western Sìchuān is the next best thing to the road to Tibet. It's a minimum of five to six days' travel at some very high altitudes (4000m-plus passes) past snowy peaks, Tibetan hamlets and isolated monasteries. The road has been off-limits to foreigners for a couple of years but is once again open.

Buses run maybe every three or four days, to Xiāngchéng in Sìchuān (Y50 to Y65). Travellers on a tight timeframe have had to hire a jeep for around Y800. Another option would be to take the 8am bus north to Dōngwàng, get off where it turns off the main road and hitch from here. A third option is to take the daily early morning bus to Déróng (Y37), a town with a decent hotel and a couple of nice monasteries just over the border in Sìchuān, and try to catch onward transport to the main Zhōngdiàn-Lǐtáng road from there.

If you do get through to Xiāngchéng there are several hotels by the bus station and a new monastery in town. Your next destination is Lǐtáng (Y70, 10 hours), though if roads are bad you may be forced to stay overnight in Dáochéng. You may want to detour here anyway as the surrounding scenery is breathtaking. From Lǐtáng it's 12 hours to Kāngdíng and another eight hours on to Chéngdū. (For more details on these towns see the Western Sìchuān & the Road to Tibet section in the Sìchuān chapter.)

Getting Around

Besides the No 3 bus to Sumtseling Gompa, local transport shouldn't be necessary, though there are plenty of taxis that charge Y5 a ride in town, and cheaper autorickshaws.

Bikes can be rented at the Tibet Hotel for Y3 per hour with no ID or deposit.

AROUND ZHŌNGDIÀN

If possible, rustle up other travellers and hire a jeep or minibus for Y250 to Y350 per

day. There are also Chinese day tours of most sights.

Note that many of the roads leading out of Zhōngdiàn, particularly the road to Bìtǎ Hǎi and Báishuǐtái, takes you over 4000m-plus passes. If you fly in direct from Kūnmíng it's important that you give yourself a day or two to acclimatise in Zhōngdiàn.

Nàpà Hǎi 纳帕海

This nearby lake, 7km north-west of Zhōngdiàn, is worth a bike ride in summer, when you might be able to hire horses; the rest of the time it's just a marsh. The best views come from the high ground to the north and you'll get these from the bus to Déqīn or Bēnzilán.

Budding ornithologists will like the place – the 2000 sq metre Nàpà Hǎi Nature Reserve is home to rare bird species, including a winter community of around 200 black-necked cranes. The best time to see bird life is between September and March.

Tiānshēng Bridge & Xiàgěi Hot Spring 天生桥和温泉

Tiānshēng Qiáo & Xiàgěi Wēnquán

This natural limestone bridge over the Suoduogang River is 10km south-east of Zhōngdiàn. A few more kilometres south-east is a subterranean hot spring (Y5). If you can arrange transport to either place, it's worth a stop en route at the Dàbǎo Sì, one of the earliest Buddhist temples in the region.

Bìtǎ Hǎi 碧塔海

Tourists come to this lake, 25km east of Zhōngdiàn, to photograph the island in the middle of the lake that is ablaze with flowers in June and a riot of autumn colours in October. There are also lots of opportunities for hiking and horse riding at the lake. An intriguing sight in summer is the comatose fish that float unconscious for several minutes in the lake after feasting on azalea petals.

There are two entrances to the lake. Nearest to Zhōngdiàn, 4km off the main road is the western entrance, from where it's an additional several kilometres (half-hour by pony) to the lakeshore. Farther along the road to Báishuǐtái is the southern entrance, from where it's a 2km walk to the lake. There is an admission fee of Y30. It's possible to walk or rent boats between the two entrances. You can also hike 10km to Shuòdū Hǎi to the north.

Basic cabins are available at the western end of the lake for between Y15 and Y30.

A daily bus is supposed to depart from Zhōngdiàn at 9am, but don't count on this. You may have to catch the bus to Sānbā, get off at the turn-off and hitch. Getting back you can wait (sometimes forever) for a bus or hike to one of the entrances or main road and look out for taxis – these guys need a fare back to Zhōngdiàn so you might negotiate a good deal. Bìtǎ Hǎi is one of the more ambitious destinations for a bicycle ride.

Báishuǐtái 白水台

At present the most popular option is Báishuǐtái, a limestone deposit plateau 108km south-east of Zhōngdiàn. There's some breathtaking scenery and Tibetan villages en route. The terraces, reminiscent of those found in Pamukkale in Turkey or Huánglóng in Sìchuān, are resplendent in sunlight, but can be tough to get to if rainfall has made trails slick. The terraces are around the small Nàxī village of Baidi. The highlight of the terraces is a 60m-tall cascade and rock cave. Entry to the site is another Y30. There are sometimes horses for hire up to the terraces for around Y25.

The region is also famed as the birthplace and heartland of Nàxī Dōngbā culture (see the aside on the Nàxī for more information).

A couple of *guesthouses* at nearby Baidi have beds for Y10 to Y15. There are also guesthouses at Sānbā, of which the *Shānzhuāng Lǚguǎn* is probably the most popular.

There is a bus to Sānbā (Y20, five hours) leaving Zhōngdiàn daily in summer at 8am and 8.30am. Don't count on this always departing. The starting price to charter a microbus from Zhōngdiàn to Báishuǐtái via Bìtǎ Hǎi is Y400 to Y500.

One adventurous option is to combine a visit to Bìtǎ Hǎi with Báishuǐtái and trek all the way from here to Tiger Leaping Gorge via Sānbā and Hābā villages. You'll need

local expertise to find the paths, though a rough road does lead between the villages. It is probably easier to do this route in reverse, since guesthouses in Walnut Grove along the Tiger Leaping Gorge trek can arrange horses and guides. See the Tiger Leaping Gorge Trail notes for details.

Bǐrǎng Gorge 壁壤峡谷
Bǐrǎng Xiágǔ

This impressive gorge, 100km north of Zhōngdiàn, is worth a visit. It's recently been rechristened Shangri La Gorge (Xiānggélǐlā Xiágǔ) – along, it seems, with half of the sights in north-west Yúnnán. The gorge itself has dramatic 150m high sheer walls but the best part is the trail that leads out from the gorge giving a rare opportunity to do some hiking. Get here quick – shops and restaurants have just been built and the litter is starting to pile up. There is a Y20 admission fee.

Currently you need to stay the night at the gorge or hire your own transport for around Y300. Public buses at 8am to Rongshui (Y21), just north of the gorge, are some of the most hopeless in China, taking up to five hours to cover the 100km and only returning the next morning. You may be able to hitch back in the afternoon in summer.

There is basic accommodation at the *Báimǎ Fàndiàn*, where beds in what is essentially a barn cost Y10. There is also accommodation at the main gate for Y20, which gets you a proper mattress at least. Bring a sleeping bag in winter and be prepared – we were marooned here for several days after heavy snowfalls in November.

Bēnzilán 奔子兰

Approximately halfway to Déqīn is this laidback Tibetan village flanking the Jīnshā Jiāng. The village makes an excellent base from which to explore the Dhondrupling Gompa and surrounding Tibetan villages. Across the water is Sìchuān and a small ferry connects the two provinces. North of town are a temple and chörten; a better temple is on the south side of town. The village is also known for its wooden bowl factory, making use of quality local azalea.

Places to stay include the *Hādá Fàndiàn* (the only place with a shower) and, opposite this, the *Jīnxiágǔ Fàndiàn* and *Tàizi Fànzhuāng* in the centre of town. All offer decent beds for Y20. Uphill and around the bend in the road is the Tibetan-style *Duōwén Lǚguǎn*, which has a prayer wheel by the entrance and pleasant rooms for Y10 to Y20 a bed.

The flashiest place in town is the *Silver Moon Restaurant (Yínyuè Jiǔlóu)*, just renovated. All the hotels have good restaurants as the town is a major truck stop.

Buses to Zhōngdiàn and Déqīn pass through town between 11am and noon. There are local minibuses to Zhōngdiàn (Y15) around 7.30am and an unreliable service to Déqīn around 9am.

Dhondrupling Gompa
Dōngzhúlín Sì
Some 22km north-west of Bēnzǐlán, on the main road, is one of the most important monasteries in the prefecture. The original temple, built in 1667, was up in Báimáng Xuěshān, but after being destroyed by the PLA in the 1950s, it was rebuilt here, in the lee of the mountain. At its peak, more than 700 monks and 10 'living buddhas' resided here; now its main assembly hall and several *kangtsang* (colleges) still house 300 monks and four living buddhas. There is a mask dance festival here in November. There is no entry fee and photos can be taken.

There is lovely scenery in all directions and if you have time it's a great hike to Bēnzǐlán. Monks can show you the short cuts. If you enquire politely it might be possible to spend the night at the monastery.

DÉQĪN 德钦
☎ 0887
If you're in Zhōngdiàn, add a visit to Déqīn, the last town before the Tibetan border. For borderholics, to the east is Sìchuān, to the west is Tibet and Myanmar is to the south-west.

This, Yúnnán's northern-most county, is perched at an average altitude of 3550m and is peppered with views of majestic 'snow mountains' in all directions. One of Yúnnán's – if not China's – most magical mountains, Kawa Karpo (often referred to as Méilǐ Xuěshān) lies to the west of Déqīn. At 6740m, it is Yúnnán's highest peak and straddles the Yúnnán-Tibet border.

During the Tang dynasty, the prefecture was the seat of the Tangbo Tieqiao magistrate, but by the Ming dynasty, Lìjiāng's chieftain held sway. But far-flung Díqìng prefecture was so isolated that it was never really controlled by anyone until the PLA came in force in 1957.

Sparsely populated Déqīn county has only 56,500 people. More than 80% are Tibetan, though a dozen other minorities also live here, including one of the few settlements of non-Huí Muslims in China. A series of recent excavations unearthed stone coffins and tombs with 16 levels dating from the late Han period.

Some travellers are disappointed with the town itself, which is a modern Chinese creation nestling in a side valley of the Mekong River (Láncāng Jiāng) but there's a heavy Tibetan population enlivened by the occasional band of Khampa Tibetans down from the hills on a shopping expedition.

Déqīn is also a jumping-off point for those looking to slip into Tibet by the back door. There are rumours that the Yúnnán route into Tibet will open up in coming years, but at the moment travellers can only go to Déqīn, *not* into Tibet. This route is quite dangerous and the PSB keeps a vigilant eye out for foreigners trying to find their way across. Be warned that even if you find a driver to sneak you into Tibet, more than a few travellers have paid half the fare only to have the driver disappear. Just as importantly, if your driver gets caught smuggling you in he will face a large fine and likely confiscation of his drivers license.

If you are travelling in winter you are crossing some serious ranges here and at any time from mid-October to late spring, heavy snows can close the roads. Pack sensibly and plan for a snow-bound emergency.

Confusingly, Déqīn is the name of the city and county; both are incorporated by the Díqìng Tibetan Autonomous Prefecture.

The county seat (and destination of the bus from Zhōngdiàn) is spelled both ways, but you'll also see other variations.

Thing to See

Along the main road to Tibet, 10km southwest of town is the **Fēilaí Sì**, or Naka Zhashi (or Trashi) Gompa in Tibetan, devoted to the spirit of Kawa Karpo. There's no charge but leave a donation. No photos are allowed inside the tiny hall.

A further 800m along the main road brings you to a row of chörtens and, weather permitting, breathtaking views of the Méilǐ Xuěshān range, including 6740m **Kawa Karpo** (Tàizi Shān in Chinese) to the north. The even more beautiful peak to the south is 6054m **Miacimu** (Shénnǚ in Chinese), whose spirit is the female counterpart of Kawa Karpo. Joseph Rock described Miacimu as 'the most glorious peak my eyes were ever privileged to see...like a castle of a dream, an ice palace of a fairy tale'. A small monument marks the tragic 1991 Sino-Japanese attempt on Kawa Karpo during which 17 people died. Locals come here to burn juniper incense to the wrathful spirit of the mountain. There is a small guesthouse. To get here, go on the road and flag anything that moves.

There's not much to see in town itself. Head to the market at the top end of town and shoot a few games of pool with the local Tibetans.

The Gelukpa (Yellow Hat) sect **Deqin Gompa** is 3km south of Déqīn. The young monks are friendly but there's not a lot to see.

Places to Stay & Eat

Most travellers stay at the **Deqin Tibet Hotel** (*Déxīn Lóu*), a short walk south of the bus station, where dorms cost Y25 and pleasant doubles are Y40, but the walls are paper thin. Bathroom facilities are adequate (ask the owner to turn on the shower heater). There's a nice communal sitting area and an excellent map of the region. The owners can help arrange transport, such as to Fēilaí Sì (Y40 return).

Most other hotels are overpriced. The **Ādūnzi Jiǔdiàn** has rooms for Y228 and very basic dorms for Y20. The deserted three-star monster **Taizi Mount Hotel** (*Tàizifēng Dàjiǔdiàn*) at the southern end of the town has rooms for Y260 (no bathroom) and Y328.

There are several point-and-eat places along the main street. Around the bus station are a couple of shuǐjiǎo and bāozi places. The **Líshí Fàndiàn**, about 100m uphill from the Deqin Tibet Hotel on the left, doesn't look like much but serves consistently good food.

Shuìyuán Cāntīng (*Tax Office Restaurant*) across the road has decent food and an outside eating area; look for the colourful canopy and pool table.

Getting There & Away

Buses depart for Zhōngdiàn at 7.20am, 8am and 8.40am (Y33, seven hours). There is also a 3pm departure to Bēnzǐlán (Y19). There are also buses to Wēixī (Y19) and a 9am departure to Yánjǐng (Salt Well). The latter is just inside the Tibetan Autonomous Region and was once eastern Tibet's major source of salt, an essential commodity in these parts.

AROUND DÉQĪN
Míngyǒng Glacier
Míngyǒng Bīngchuān

Tumbling off the side of Kawa Karpo is the 12km-long Míngyǒng Glacier, the lowest glacier in China. Surrounding villages are known as 'heaven villages' because of the dense fog that hangs about in spring and summer, even permeating into homes. There are plans to create a conservation area around the base of the peak to protect flora that range from subtropical to alpine. The best views of the glacier are from the road to Míngyǒng as it descends from Fēilaí Sì.

For thousands of years the mountain has been a pilgrimage site and you'll still meet a few Tibetan pilgrims, some of whom circumambulate the mountain over seven days in autumn.

Trails up to the glacier lead up from the central square marked by a new chörten. After 45 minutes a path splits off down to the scruffy toe of the glacier. After another 45 minutes you get to the Tàizi Miào, a Tibetan temple currently under renovation. Also here is an orange *guesthouse*, where

YÚNNÁN

clean but basic rooms cost a negotiable Y60 per person, less in winter. Another path leads down from here to the glacier.

If you continue along the main trail for another 30 minutes you come to a second temple known as the **Liánhuā Miào** (Lotus Temple), which offers fantastic views of the glacier framed by prayer flags and chörtens. It's hard to find any trails beyond this point. There is a hefty Y60 entry fee collected at

the start of the trail. Horses can be hired up to the glacier for another Y60.

Places to Stay There are several places to stay in the village. Up some steps from the main square, where the bus drops off, is the **Míngyǒng Shānzhuang**, a government-run place with decent dorm rooms. There's a small restaurant here and a pit toilet a short walk out the back.

Shangri La – Fact and Fiction

At first it seemed like a typically overstated tourist campaign: 'Shangri La Found'. Only they weren't kidding. In November 1997 the *China Daily* reported that the Yúnnán Economy & Technology Research Centre had established with 'certainty' that the fabled 'Shangri La' of James Hilton's 1933 best-seller *Lost Horizon* was, indeed, in Déqīn county.

Hilton's novel (later filmed by Frank Capra and starring Ronald Coleman, Jane Wyatt and John Gielgud) tells the story of four travellers who are hijacked and crash land in a mountain utopia ruled by a 163 year old holy man. This 'Shangri La' is in the Valley of the Blue Moon, a beautiful fertile valley capped by a perfect pyramid peak, Mt Karakul. According to Hilton's book, Shangri La is reached by travelling 'southwest from Peking for many months', and is found 'a few hundred kilometres from a world's end market town...where Chinese coolies from Yúnnán transfer their loads of tea to the Tibetans'.

The Yúnnán Economy & Technology Research Centre based its claim primarily on the fact that Déqīn's Kawa Karpo peak perfectly resembles the 'pyramid-shaped' landmark of Mt Karakul. Also, the county's blood red valleys with three parallel rivers fit a valley from *Lost Horizon*.

One certainly plausible theory is that Hilton, writing the novel in north-west London, based his descriptions of Shangri La on articles by Joseph Rock he had read in *National Geographic* magazine, detailing Rock's expeditions to remote parts of Lìjiāng, Mùlǐ and Déqīn. Others believe that Hilton's 'Shangri La' may just have been a corruption of the word *Shambhala*, a mystical Buddhist paradise.

Tourism authorities wasted little time latching onto the Shangri La phenomenon and today there are Shangri La hotels, travel agencies and a Shangri La airport. Sensing that 'there's money in them there Shangri La hills', rival bids popped up around Yúnnán. Cízhōng in Wéixī county pointed out that its Catholic churches and Tibetan monasteries live side by side in the valley. One local was even told that she was the blood relative of one of the (fictional) characters! Meanwhile, Dàochéng, just over the border in Sìchuān, had a strong bid based around the pyramid peak of its mountain Channa Dorje and the fact that Rock wrote about the region in several articles. Then there's the town of Xionggu, a Nàxī village 40km from near Lìjiāng, which boasts a stone tablet from the Qing dynasty, naming the town 'Xianggeli', from where the name Shangri La is derived.

It's hard for us cynics not to believe that the whole thing has simply been manufactured as a moneymaking exercise. Provincial authorities had long been preparing for an invasion of tourists into the prefecture to provide an alternative income to the recently banned logging trade. Even Xuan Ke, the original proponent of the Shangri La theory, laments that the concept has been hijacked for commercial purposes. No amount of reminding that Shangri La is in a work of fiction will deter local Chinese who are proudly convinced of the authenticity.

And while it may even have been Shangri La to Hilton and millions of readers, Shangri La is at its heart surely a metaphor. As a skinny-dipping Jane Wyatt says in the film version of the book. 'I'm sure there's a wish for Shangri La in everyone's heart...'

Farther towards Déqīn is the **Nuòbù Sāngmù Kèzhàn**, a friendly family run place sadly marred by bathroom tile architecture.

Farther still is the **Biānmǎdìngzhǔ Kèzhàn**. This place definitely has the best location in the lovely original settlement and there's a family feel to the place.

Beds in all guesthouses are around Y20 and toilet facilities are basic. Electricity is iffy so bring a torch or some candles.

Getting There & Away From Déqīn, minibuses to Míngyǒng leave from the bridge, near the market at the top end of town at 4pm (Y13, two hours) and return to Déqīn the next day at 8am. This means that you'll need to spend a minimum of two nights at Míngyǒng or try to hitch back to Déqīn in the afternoon after visiting the glacier.

The road from Déqīn descends into the dramatic Mekong Gorge. Six kilometres before Míngyǒng the road crosses the Mekong River and branches off to Xīdāng. Nearby is the small temple, the **Bǎishūlín Miào**, and a chörten.

Yǔbēng Waterfall
Yǔbēng Shénpù

This could be an adventurous trip. At the bridge over the Mekong River the right hand-fork in the road leads 6km to Xīdāng and another 3km or so to a hot spring. Then it's possible to arrange a pony hire to take you 25km (four to six hours) to Yǔbēng Village, where there is a basic guesthouse. From here it's a half-day return on foot or horseback to the waterfall.

There is a 3pm minibus from Déqīn from Xīdāng that returns the next morning.

Báimáng Xuěshān 白茫雪山

Méilǐ Xuěshān gets all the press, but this mountain nature reserve, part of the Hengduan Shān range, east of Déqīn is impressive. Established in 1985, it's the largest plant and animal reserve in Yúnnán, famous for its dense primeval forests containing many threatened species, including the critically endangered Yúnnán snub-nosed monkey. Botanical gardens and a handful of temples are still on the mountain.

If you are an experienced trekker with a tent, sleeping bag and stove you could get off the Zhōngdiàn-Déqīn bus at the pass and make some fine hikes around the eastern slopes and valleys.

Cizhong Catholic Church
Cízhōng Tiānzhǔjiào Táng

This unexpected church, 80km south of Déqīn in the middle of a quiet village is based on the design of French cathedrals. It was originally built by French missionaries in 1867. It burned down in 1905 but was reconstructed by the local government over a period of 12 years. Wine is still made from vineyards planted by the missionaries. The elderly caretaker still speaks some French. To get here take any bus bound for Wēixī.

The Nùjiāng Valley
怒江峡谷

☎ 0886

This huge river gorge occupies one of the remotest corners of Yúnnán, sandwiched between the Gāolígòng Shān and Myanmar to the west, Tibet to the north and the high Bìluō Shān to the east. Until recently closed to foreigners, the valley is attracting a trickle of hardy travellers.

The main draw is the scenery; waterfalls tumble off high canyon walls into the churning Nù Jiāng (Salween River) – the Chinese name means 'Raging River'. The river is crisscrossed by daredevil suspension and cable bridges and the valley is speckled with traditional villages of thatched houses.

The valley holds an exotic mix of Han, Nu, Lisu, Drung and Tibetan nationalities and even the odd Burmese jade trader. One surprise is the number of Catholic churches, the legacy of hardy French missionaries who arrived here in the 19th century.

The best way to travel is to drop your bags in the capital Liùkù and travel light so that you can jump on and off buses when the scenery looks good. Otherwise you'll have your head craned out of the bus window. The main hassle is that you trundle eight hours up the valley marvelling at the scenery, then head back the way you came but the gorge looks quite different when travelling in the opposite direction.

From maps it looks like you could hike over the mountains into the Mekong Valley, particularly from Gòngshān to Yèzhī or Yànmén in Déqīn prefecture, but once there it's clear that you need a trustworthy guide and camping equipment. Pilgrimage trekking routes lead from the north of the valley into Tibet to join a pilgrimage circuit of Kawa Karpo (see the Around Déqīn section) but again you'd need to arrange this with an expert travel agency.

The Jiaoye Pass in the west side of the valley was a major route marker for the Hump, the air supply route used during WWII. The remoteness of the region is highlighted by the C-53 plane that crashed in the Piànmă region of the valley in 1943 and that remained undiscovered until 1997. Today Piànmă is a border crossing (though not for foreigners) and trading post with Myanmar.

LIÙKÙ 六库

Liùkù is the humdrum capital of the prefecture and an important transport hub, though it's of little intrinsic interest. You will need to get off the bus and register with a police checkpoint about 2km before town.

Information

China Telecom and China Post in the town's north . The Bank of China will change money but you are safest with US dollars. If the bank is closed try the Nùjiāng Bǎiyì Dàjiǔdiàn.

The Xīnhuá Bookstore has a couple of English books and postcards of the valley.

Things to See

About 2km along the road to Bǎoshān is the **golden Buddha** that overlooks the town. You'll have to cross the river and follow trails to the top, from where there are fine views of the valley. **Qingshan Park** at the north end of town might be worth a quick visit.

The **Mabu Hot Springs**, 12km north of town along the road to Fúgòng has an attached hotel complex. A Lisu festival is held here on the 15th of the 1st lunar month (March/April).

Places to Stay & Eat

The *Zhèngfǔ Zhāodàisuǒ (Government Guesthouse)* is probably the best budget

Nationalities of the Nùjiāng Valley

The largest group in the valley are the **Lisu** (587,000 in Yúnnán). The women are recognised by their black pleated skirt, crimson tunic buttoned to one side, hat of plastic shells and beads and ornamental belt. Lisu men sometimes wear black turbans. The Lisu language belongs to the Yi branch of the Sino-Tibetan group. There are over a dozen clans, each with their own totems. A harvest festival is held in the 10th lunar month and a hair-combing festival in the first lunar month. The most spectacular festival is the Kuoshi Festival in the second lunar month, when Lisu braves climb barefoot up 30m-high poles, using sword blades as rungs.

The **Nu** give the valley its name, and number around 26,000. Like the Lisu, the scattered Nu communities grow fields of maize, buckwheat and beans on the hillside and wheat and rice along the valley floors. Also like the Lisu, religion is animist at its heart, with a 19th century overlay of Catholicism.

The 5500 **Drung** are related to the Nu but retain a quite different lifestyle. In remoter areas the extended families live in long houses. Traditional dress consists of a toga of woven cloth wrapped over the shoulder. Facial tattooing is common among older Drung. They trade medicinal herbs and pelts but are fast being integrated into the modern economy.

The Drung have no written language but their spoken tongue is part of the Tibeto-Burman group. Traditionally Drung names consist of the name of the clan, the name of the child's father, a personal name and the infant's position in relation to his siblings. The main spring festival involves the sacrifice of a buffalo.

choice. Clean and pleasant doubles cost Y40 to Y50 while inferior singles cost Y30. The common toilets are clean but have no partitions. There are also triples for Y45 to Y60 and standard doubles for Y80 with bathroom. The dim lighting and luke-warm water are a mild irritation.

Línyè Zhāodàisuǒ (Forestry Guesthouse) has doubles with common bath (in the kitchen!) for Y30. The doubles with bathroom are pretty good value for Y40.

The *Yóudiàn Bīnguǎn (Post Hotel)*, the *Nùjiāng Fàndiàn,* the *Diànxìn Bīnguǎn (Telecom Hotel)* and the *Zhèngfǔ Bīnguǎn (Government Hotel)* all have smoky doubles rooms from Y80 to Y140.

The top-end choice is the *Nùjiāng Bǎiyì Dàjiǔdiàn (☎ 362 7988, 38 Renmin Lu)*, which has doubles for Y180 and Y220, rising to Y420. Buffet breakfasts/lunches cost Y15/30.

Nùjiāng Bīnguǎn, in the north end of town has rooms for Y158 but they aren't worth the price.

There are several decent restaurants around the bus station. The *restaurant* just to the right as you exit the bus station has good bāozi and cheap Chinese dishes.

Getting There & Away

The bus station has luggage storage for Y2 per day, which is useful if you want to travel light up the valley.

There are minibuses every hour or so until 4.30pm to Fúgòng (Y19, five hours). Buses to Gòngshān (Y35, eight hours) depart at 6, 9 and 10am and noon.

Headed out of the valley, there are minibuses to Xiàguān (Y30, 7½ hours) between 6am and noon or you can take the (non-smoking!) express coach at 8am (Y60, six hours) that continues to Kūnmíng (Y126). You can also get sleepers to Kūnmíng at 8pm and 9pm (Y50). Minibuses to Bǎoshān (Y20) depart hourly until 3.30pm.

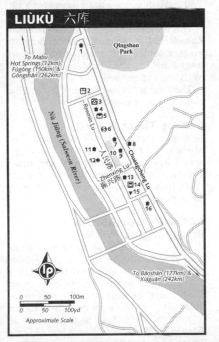

LIÙKÙ 六库

To Mabu
Hot Springs (12km),
Fúgòng (150km) &
Gòngshān (262km)

Nù Jiāng (Salween River)

Qingshan Park

Renmin Lu

Chuangcheng Lu

Zhenxing Lu
振兴桥

To Bǎoshān (177km) &
Xiàguān (242km)

0   50   100m
0   50   100yd
Approximate Scale

LIÙKÙ

1	Nùjiāng Bīnguǎn 怒江宾馆	6	Bank of China 中国银行	12	Xīnhuá Bookstore 新华书店
2	Cinema 电影院	7	Línyè Zhāodàisuǒ 林业招待所	13	Nùjiāng Bǎiyì Dàjiǔdiàn 怒江佰亿大酒店
3	China Telecom 中国电信	8	Nùjiāng Fàndiàn 怒江饭店	14	Bus Station 客运站
4	Diànxìn Bīnguǎn 电信宾馆	9	Yóudiàn Bīnguǎn 邮电宾馆	15	Restaurant 餐厅
5	China Post 中国邮局	10	Market 市场	16	Zhèngfǔ Bīnguǎn 政府宾馆
		11	Zhèngfǔ Zhāodàisuǒ 政府招待所		

YÚNNÁN

FÚGÒNG 福贡
Halfway up the valley, this county capital is a good base. The scenery an hour's ride out of town in either direction is probably the best in the valley. The town itself is a scruffy mix of Lisu, Nu and Han Chinese, which bursts into colour every five days with one of South-West China's best markets.

Places to Stay & Eat
The best place in town is the *Fúgòng Bīnguǎn*, opposite the bus station, where doubles or triples both cost Y120.

Currently the only alternative is the grubby *Zhèngfǔ Zhāodàisuǒ*, 200m away on the main through road, opposite China Telecom. Singles cost Y25 and doubles/triples are Y28/30. The common bathroom will make your eyes water.

The best value is at the *Fúgòng Xiàn Zhèngfǔlì Gōngsī*, but it isn't allowed to take foreigners.

The best restaurants are right by the bus station and the Fúgòng Bīnguǎn. The *Kèyùn Fàndiàn* just east of the bus station is run by a friendly Nàxī woman.

Getting There & Away
Buses to Gòngshān (Y16, four hours) run hourly from 10.30am to 4pm. A private minibus departs from opposite the bus station at 8am. Buses to Liùkù run hourly until 2pm (Y19, five hours).

GÒNGSHĀN 贡山
This friendly one-street town is probably the nicest in the valley and a trading centre for the upper Nùjiāng Valley. There is an interesting Catholic church in the southwest of town. At the northern end of the main street is a square selling Nu, Lisu and Tibetan traditional clothes.

When returning to Fúgòng, watch out for the mountain peak with a huge gape in it in the shape of the moon. The crag is two hours south of Gòngshān, ten minutes north of the village of Lìshādǐ.

Places to Stay
The *Bus Station Hotel (Kèyùn Zhōngxīn Zhāodàisuǒ)* has good singles/doubles for Y60 with squat toilet and shower directly above it. The rooms were recently renovated. Doubles without bathroom cost Y40, plus Y3 for a hot shower. The corner double on the fourth floor has great views over the town.

The *Gòngshān Bīnguǎn* halfway up and set back from the main road has a range of rooms from basic doubles for Y20 per bed to overpriced doubles with bathroom for Y50 and deluxe but smoky rooms for Y120 or Y140.

The only other option is the *Yóudiàn Zhāodàisuǒ* at the north end of the main street. Doubles with a squat bathroom are good value for Y50. Triples without bathroom are Y15 per bed.

There are a few *restaurants* in town but nothing to get excited about.

Getting There & Away
Minibuses leave every hour or so until 2pm to Fúgòng (Y16). To Liùkù (Y35, eight hours) buses depart at 6, 8, 9 and 10am. There are cramped sleeper buses to Xiàguān (Y90, 16 hours) and Kūnmíng (Y150) every day around 10am.

AROUND GÒNGSHĀN
Bǐngzhōngluò 丙中洛
It's worth heading an extra two hours through dramatic scenery to this pleasant village, set in a wide and fertile bowl. There's hikes around the village, either south along the main road for 2km to the impressive 'first bend' of the Salween River or north along a track to the villages of Jiǎshēng (5km) and Qiūnàtǒng (13km). There are impressive gorges north of town along this route.

It's possible to visit Bǐngzhōngluò as a day trip from Gòngshān but if you want to explore the region the *Mínzhèngjú Zhāodàisuǒ* has good value doubles with bathroom for Y40. The *Hóngyuán Jiǔjiā* 30m up the street has cheaper rooms without bathroom.

About two-thirds of the way between Gòngshān and Bǐngzhōngluò, on the east side of the valley is Báihànluò, which has a 125-year-old Catholic church built in Tibetan style. The village is a two-hour hike from the village of Dèmáluò and might be worth a visit if you have the language skills to get directions.

At least three minibuses leave Gòngshān daily for Bǐngzhōngluò, via Wǔqū, all at 9am (Y8, two hours). Private vans loiter at a stand at the north end of town. Buses back to Gòngshān leave at 9am, noon and 2pm and 4pm, so it's easy to take an early one, get off where it looks interesting and walk until the next one comes along.

Drung Valley 独龙峡谷
Dúlóng Jiāng

Separated from the Nùjiāng Valley by the high Gāolígòng Shān range and only reached by road in 1999, this is one of the remotest valleys in China. The valley is home to the Drung ethnic group (see the boxed text 'Minority Nationalities in the Nùjiāng Valley' earlier). The Drung River actually flows out of China into Myanmar, where it eventually joins the Irrawaddy.

At present there are no buses into the valley. You'd have to hire a minivan from Gòngshān for the rough 96km trip to the county capital Dúlóngjiāng. Beyond that, most travel is on foot. There is a *County Guesthouse* (*Xiàn Zhāodàisǔo*) at the county capital Dúlóngjiāng.

Băoshān Region

Travellers often pass through the Băoshān region quickly, staying overnight in Băoshān city on the way to Ruìlì and Wǎndīng. But there are some worthwhile historical sights, the old quarters of Téngchōng and Băoshān make for some good browsing, distinctive minority groups are in abundance, and the Téngchōng area is rich with the signs of past volcanic activity – hot springs and volcanic peaks.

As early as the 4th and 5th centuries BC (two centuries before the northern routes through Central Asia were established), the Băoshān area was an important stage on the southern Silk Road – the Sìchuān-India route. The area did not really come under Chinese control until the time of the Han

dynasty. In 1277 a huge battle waged in the region between the 12,000 troops of Kublai Khan and 60,000 Burmese soldiers and their 2000 elephants. The Mongols won and went on to take Pagan.

BĂOSHĀN 保山
☎ 0875

Băoshān is a small city and easily explored on foot. There are pockets of traditional wooden architecture in the city area and some good walks on the outskirts of town. Marco Polo visited the town in the 13th century when it was known as Yongchang and marvelled at the locals' gold teeth and tattoos. It has innumerable speciality products that range from excellent coffee to leather boots and pepper and silk. Tea connoisseurs might like to try the Reclining Buddha Băoshān Tea, a brand of national repute.

Information

Băoshān is not geared up for foreign visitors, but the Lánhuā Bīnguǎn and the long-distance bus station do sell maps of Băoshan prefecture that show regional sights in Chinese, with some explanations in English.

The Bank of China is next to the Yíndū Dàjiǔdiàn on Baoxiu Donglu, with another branch opposite the Yunnan Airlines office, and the China Post and China Telecom offices are not far away on Xia Gang Jie. You can get slow Internet access at a computer shop on the corner of Shang Gang Jie and Yunwen Lu, for Y3 per hour, or at nearby Kělè Computer Company for Y5 per hour.

Things to See

Băoshān streets are lively and, in many areas, lined with traditional homes, though the city walls have long since gone. The major sight within easy walking distance of the centre of town is **Tàibǎo Shān** and its surrounding park. Just before you head up the steps leading up the hillside you'll see the Ming dynasty **Yùhuáng Pavilion** (Yùhuáng Gé) and the attached **Yùfó Sì** (Jade Buddha Temple) on your right. At the top of the steps is the small park and the **Wǔhòucí Ancestral Temple,** which has a nice garden and teahouse. It's possible to

YÚNNÁN

get here by taxi, following the road that leads around the back of the hill. There's a Y3 admission to the park.

There are paths in the park heading north, west and south. The northern path doubles back to the south and eventually

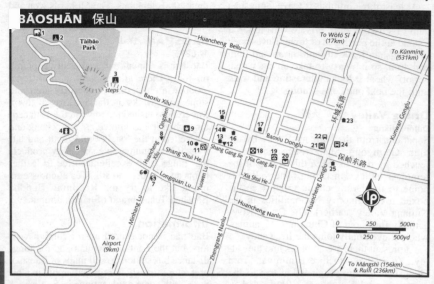

BǍOSHĀN

takes you past a very mediocre zoo (best keep walking).

Continuing to the south you will reach **Yìluó Pond** (Yìluó Chí), also known as the Dragon Spring Pond (Lóngquán Chí) with a view of the 13-tiered pagoda known as the **Wénbǐ Tă**. The pond is a good place to meet English speakers from the nearby Băoshān Teacher's College. You can also walk to the Yìluó Pond from the CAAC office.

Places to Stay

There are plenty of inexpensive places to stay in Băoshān. Along Baoxiu Xilu are a few sprawling Chinese-style hotels. They all take foreigners and most seem fairly friendly.

Huāchéng Bīnguăn (☎ 212 2037), three minutes north of the long-distance bus station on the other side of the road is good value. Doubles/triples cost Y24/30 per bed with common bath. But the best deal may be the doubles with bathroom for Y50 and Y90. Rooms are clean, bright and quiet. The place is popular so you may find it booked out.

At the main roundabout opposite the bus station is the *Shěnyáng Bīnguăn* (☎ 216 0660), a very Chinese-style hotel with spacious double rooms for Y30 to Y40, though the common bathrooms smell. Rooms with bathroom are Y100 to Y120, discounted to Y70 to Y80.

Cheapest in town is the *Yŏngchāng Bīnguăn* (☎ 212 2802), which has beds in the back block from Y10 to Y30 and standard rooms from Y80 to Y360.

Not far up the road is the *Lánhuā Bīnguăn* (☎ 212 2803), with beds in three-bed dorms for Y25. Comfortable doubles/triples with bathroom in the main building are Y150/180 with discounts up to 50%.

Băoshān's premier accommodation is nearby, the *Lándū Bīnguăn* (☎ 212 1888), with fine rooms and slavish service for Y400, though this rapidly crumbles to Y320. Rooms on the fourth floor (without views) cost Y240, discounted to Y200.

Yíndū Dàjiŭdiàn (☎ 212 0948) is set up by the Bank of China. It offers tatty standard doubles for Y80.

The pleasant complex of the *Băoshān Bīnguăn* (☎ 212 2804), a block south, is where the pedicab drivers will probably take you if you stumble off the bus looking confused. Beds in basic doubles with common bathroom are Y60; from there it goes to slightly upmarket but overpriced doubles for Y160 with bathroom.

Places to Eat

Baoxiu Lu, Shang Gang Jie and Xia Gang Jie are good for cheap restaurants. Look for the place selling dumplings and noodles down the road from the Yíndū Dàjiŭdiàn towards the bus station.

Next door to, and part of the Băoshān Bīnguăn, is an *Across-the-Bridge Noodle Restaurant* but it closes quite early. A bowl of noodles costs Y10. The hotel also has a decent restaurant in the main courtyard. Other hotel restaurants seem to be either in mourning or in a drunken karaoke frenzy.

The *Duōwèi Fàndiàn*, just inside the gates of the Yŏngchāng Bīnguăn, serves cheap tasty meals to backpackers. Just point at whatever looks good.

Near the intersection of Baoxiu Xilu and Minhang Lu is Qingzhen Jie (Muslim St), where there are several *Muslim and Burmese restaurants*.

Getting There & Away

Air You can fly daily between Băoshān and Kūnmíng (Y440), though very few Western travellers do. The Yunnan Airlines/CAAC office (☎ 216 1747) is inconveniently located at the intersection of Longquan Lu and Minhang Lu. Look for a large yellow-tiled building. The ticket office is on the 1st floor, facing Longquan Lu and is open daily from 8.30am to 6.30pm. The airport is about 9km south of town.

Bus The Băoshān long-distance bus station is a huge new construction, and buses run from here to a host of destinations around Yúnnán. There are several late afternoon sleeper bus departures between 3pm to 8pm to Kūnmíng (Y70, 18 hours). One express bus leaves for Kūnmíng at 8am (Y116).

Buses for Xiàguān (Dàlǐ) leave every 40 minutes (Y26, five hours). Buses to Téngchōng (Y25, 167km, 4½ hours) also leave every 40 minutes or so. Buses on to Yíngjiāng, past Téngchōng, leave at 9.50am and take forever.

To Ruìlì there are daytime buses at 8.30am and 9am and sleeper buses at 5pm and 7pm (Y36, seven hours). Buses to Ruìlì pass through Mángshì and Wǎndīng. There are also a couple of departures just to Mángshì. For the Nùjiāng Valley there are buses to Liùkù (Y20, four hours) at 6.50, 7.50 and 9am.

There is also a daily sleeper to Jǐnghóng (Y158, 20 hours), though it's a rough ride and most travellers opt to take the direct Dàlǐ-Jǐnghóng bus or return to Kūnmíng. If you want to break the trip to Jǐnghóng there are two morning buses to Líncāng (Y41) where you can overnight and continue on to Mènglián or Jǐnghóng.

Across the street at the city bus station, you can catch a bus to most of the same destinations as from the long-distance station. A sleeper bus to Téngchōng and Yíngjiāng departs at 8.30am. To Ruìlì via Mángshì the first bus departs at 8am. Kūnmíng sleepers depart from 4.30pm. The schedule on the wall is woefully out of date.

Getting Around
Bǎoshān can be comfortably explored on foot. A bicycle would ideal to get to some of the sights around Bǎoshān but there is no evidence of bicycle-hire stands.

Taxis cost Y5 for any ride around the town centre. The three-wheeler motor rickshaws are cheaper but can't travel up the main street Baoxiu Xilu.

AROUND BǍOSHĀN
Just 17km north of town, the **Wòfó Sì** (Reclining Buddha Temple) is one of the most important historical sights near Bǎoshān. The temple dates back to the Tang dynasty, and has a history of 1200 years. The reclining Buddha, in a cave to the rear of the temple area, was severely damaged during the Cultural Revolution and has only recently been restored.

To get to the temple take a microbus from a stand just north of the main bus station to the interesting village of **Běimiào**

and walk or hire a microbus for the rest. A motorcycle with sidecar can take two people there and back from Bǎoshān for Y40. Taxis ask around Y80.

TÉNGCHŌNG 腾冲
☎ 0875
This town on the other side of the Gāolígòng Shān mountain range has about 20 volcanoes in the vicinity and lots of hot springs. It's also prime earthquake territory, having experienced 71 earthquakes measuring over five on the Richter scale since AD 1500.

The town has preserved, on a larger scale, the kind of traditional wooden architecture that has survived only in pockets in Kūnmíng and Bǎoshān. It's not exactly Dàlǐ, but there's a definite charm to the narrow backstreets.

Information
A good English-language map of the town and the surrounding sites is available from the lobby of the Téngchōng Bīnguǎn for Y3.

China Post and China Telecom are together on Fengshan Lu. China Telecom also has an Internet office on Laifeng Dadao, 100m uphill from the main intersection, open 8am to 10pm. Connections are spotty but rates are ridiculously cheap at Y1.8 per hour. The Bank of China towers over the town's main intersection at Fengshan Lu and Yingjian Lu. The bank won't change travellers cheques, so change money before you get to Téngchōng.

Things to See
The best place for a random wander are the backstreets running off Yingjiang Lu. There are a couple of small markets with plenty of colour and activity in the mornings. Walking along Fengshan Lu from Wanshou Lu, the first side street on the left has a small produce market. Farther down on the right is a **Jade market**, where you can see the carving process, though it's a bit tame compared to Ruìlì. A block northwest of the intersection with Guanghua Lu is the town's biggest **produce market**. From here history buffs can head down Huancheng Xilu; about halfway down on

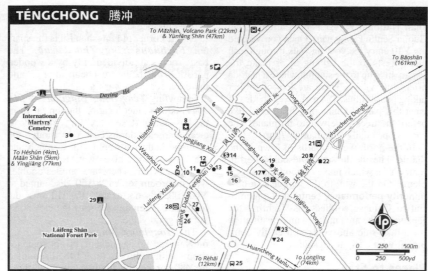

TÉNGCHŌNG 腾冲

TÉNGCHŌNG

PLACES TO STAY
7 Hóngliáng Bīnguǎn
宏粮宾馆
11 Fúzhuāngchǎng
Zhāodàisuǒ
服装厂招待所
15 Téngyún Bīnguǎn;
Myanmar Teahouse
腾云宾馆、
缅甸咖啡厅
20 Gōnglù Zhāodàisuǒ
公路招待所
22 Tōnglìdá Bīnguǎn
通利达宾馆
23 Línyè Dàshà
林业大厦
27 Téngchōng Bīnguǎn;
Five Continent
Travel Service
腾冲宾馆

PLACES TO EAT
17 Yǒuyì Fàndiàn
友谊饭店
24 Ténghé Fàndiàn
腾和饭店

26 Fèngyuán Cāntīng
凤园餐厅

OTHER
1 Xiānlè Sì
仙乐寺
2 Diéshuǐ
Waterfall
叠水瀑布
3 Nationalities
Cultural
Performance
Centre
民族文化表演中心
4 Xīmén Bus Stand
西门车站
5 Former British
Consulate
英国领事馆旧址
(粮食局)
6 Market
市场
8 PSB
公安局
9 Minibuses to Héshùn
到和顺的中巴车

10 Market
市场
12 China Post;
China Telecom
邮电局
13 Jade Market
珠宝玉器交易中心
14 Bank of China
中国银行
16 Market
市场
18 Workers'
Cultural Palace
工人文化宫
19 Bicycle Shop
自行车出租
21 Long-Distance
Bus Station
长途汽车站
25 Minibuses to Rèhǎi
到热海的中巴车
28 China Telecom
(Internet)
网吧
29 Láifēng Sì
米风寺

the north side is the **former British Consulate**, now still a grand old building in the County Grain Department complex. There is another market off Yingjiang Xilu.

On the western edge of town is the **Láifèng Shān National Forest Park** (Láifèng Shān Gúojiā Sēnlín Gōngyuán). Once you've paid the Y10 entry fee you can walk through lush pine forests to the **Láifèng Sì** or make the sweaty hike up to the summit where a pagoda offers fine views. There are lots of further hiking possibilities. The park gives an idea of what this part of China may have been like before the trees gave way to farmland. The park is open daily from 8am to 7pm.

In the north-west suburbs of town is the **Xiānlè Sì** beside the small Diéshuǐ Waterfall (entry Y5), which makes a good place for a picnic. On the way to the temple is a new **minority performance centre** and a memorial to Chinese soldiers lost fighting the Japanese. The area makes a nice destination for a bike ride and you could easily combine it with a trip to Héshùn.

Places to Stay

Téngchōng's accommodation options are fairly spread out and some have no English sign. South-west of the bus station on Huancheng Donglu, the **Gōnglù Zhāodàisuǒ** has beds in a triple for Y10 and other options starting at Y15. It's noisy place but it's close to the bus station – look for the ubiquitous bus steering wheel logo at the top of the entry gate.

Across the street is the better **Tōnglìdá Bīnguǎn** (☎ 518 7787). Beds in spartan but fine double rooms go for Y25 to Y30 per bed; the shared showers and toilets are clean. The rooms on the 4th floor are the best. Fine double rooms with bathroom start at Y70. Hot water is available all day. The only downside is it can be noisy.

Línyè Dàshà (Forestry Building; ☎ 516 4057) is a new hotel that offers bright and clean doubles and triples. A bed in an excellent triple on the 4th floor costs Y40, with a clean common bathroom. Doubles with bathroom cost from Y70 to Y100.

Close to the centre of town, the **Téngyún Bīnguǎn** is dilapidated but has dorm beds for Y10 in pleasant old wooden buildings, and OK singles/doubles in the (somewhat) newer wing for Y40/60, or Y25 for a room with no bathroom. The showers are a bit grim. Look for the little Myanmar Teahouse by the entrance.

On the corner of Fengshan Lu is the spartan **Fúzhuāngchǎng Zhāodàisuǒ**. The basic rooms are divided only by a wooden partition but beds are cheap at Y12 and there's a common wash area.

Sprawling **Téngchōng Bīnguǎn** (☎ 518 1044) is in a quiet location though far from the bus station (take a taxi for Y5). Beds in clean, carpeted dorms cost Y30, though the common bathrooms aren't up to much and the showers are a hike away. Rooms at the back are better. There are singles/doubles with bathroom for Y128/160, discounted to Y60/100. It's not exactly the Hilton – the lights dim when anyone uses the elevator – but it's good value.

The **Hóngliáng Bīnguǎn** (☎ 513 7888) on Nanmen Jie has decent, bright standard rooms with bathroom for Y148, discounted to Y80, or smoky doubles/quads without for Y50/80.

The Fèngyuán Cāntīng has a hotel (zhāodàisuǒ) attached to it. Beds in a double cost Y10, which is probably the best deal in town and rooms with bathroom are Y50. Ask in the restaurant and a waitress will take you to the building around the back.

Places to Eat

There are scores of tiny, inviting eateries in Téngchōng's wooden buildings. Tea aficionados should try the local Qingliang tea.

Look out for the **Yǒuyì Fàndiàn** on Guanghua Lu. It's an open-fronted place and fairly easy to find. The delicious Shandong-style steamed dumplings (zhēngjiǎo) are unlike dumplings anywhere else in China. Also try the spicy pickled vegetables (shuǐyāncài).

Ténghé Fàndiàn on Huancheng Donglu is a friendly family-run place with an English menu of sorts.

For sweet coffee, excellent samosas, Mekong whisky, and a chance to chat with itinerant Burmese jewellery peddlers, stop by the **Myanmar Teahouse** at the entrance to the Téngyún Bīnguǎn. There's usually an English speaker inside.

Farther west on the road to Laifeng Park is the **Fēngyuán Cāntīng**, a nice restaurant set in a traditional Chinese-style courtyard. Dishes are around Y10 each and the atmosphere and service is great.

Getting There & Away

Téngchōng's long-distance bus station must be the only bus station in the whole of the South-West with a board listing information in English. Ignore it – it's completely out of date, though it's a nice thought.

Buses to Băoshān leave every hour or so until around 3.30pm (Y25, five hours). Directly to Xiàguān (Dàlĭ), there is a bus leaving at 7am (Y70, 12 hours) though it would make sense to overnight in Băoshān.

Buses to Ruìlì run via Yíngjiāng and Zhàngfèng twice a day (Y27, 10 hours). Alternatively, take one of the buses that leave every 90 minutes to Yíngjiāng (Y18, four hours), stay overnight there and travel on to Ruìlì by bus the next day (four hours).

There are also buses to Mángshì at 7.30am (Y20, five hours) and at least one sleeper to Kūnmíng in the mid-morning (Y130 to Y140, 24 hours).

Buses to local destinations north such as Măzhàn, Gŭdōng, Ruìdiàn, Diàntān or Zìzhì either leave from, or pass through, Dongximen Jie in the north-east of town.

Getting Around

Téngchōng is small enough to walk around, but a bicycle would be useful for getting to some of the closer sights outside town – the surrounding scenery alone justifies a ride. There is a bicycle shop at 79 Guanghua Lu that rents bikes for Y1 per hour, with a deposit of Y100. The shop is normally open 8am to 10pm.

AROUND TÉNGCHŌNG

There's a lot to see around Téngchōng but getting out to the sights requires a bit of flexibility. You could hire a van, which may be affordable if there are several of you. The Five Continent Travel Service (Wŭzhōu Lǚxíngshè) might be able to help. Alternatively, head down to the minibus stands just off the north end of Dongximen Jie or where minibuses leave for Rèhǎi in the south west of town, where van drivers often wait for business to walk their way.

One of the highlights of the region are the **traditional villages** scattered between Téngchōng and Yùnfēng Shān. The relatively plentiful public transport along this route means that you can jump on and off minibuses as the whim takes you.

Héshùn   和顺乡

If you come to Téngchōng from Ruìlì or Yíngjiāng, 4km before town you come close to the village of Héshùn. It has been set aside as a retirement village but it's more of interest as a quiet, traditional Chinese village with cobbled streets. There are some great old buildings providing lots of photo opportunities. The village also has a **small museum** (àisìqí gǔjū) and a famous **old library** (the largest rural library in China).

To get to Héshùn take a minibus from the corner of Wanshou Lu and Fengshan Lu (Y1.5) or take a No 3 bus that passes nearby. It's an easy bicycle ride out to the village but the ride back is an uphill slog.

Yúnfēng Shān   云蜂山

Yùnfēng (Cloudy Peak) is a Taoist mountain dotted with 17th-century temples and monastic retreats, 47km north of Téngchōng. Most people take the cable car (Y32 one-way, Y54 return), from where it's a 20 minute-walk to the Dà'ióngbǎo Diàn temple at the summit.

Lǚzŭ Diàn, second from the top, serves great vegetarian lunches for Y6. It's a quick walk down but it can be hard on the knees. The mountain has a Y10 entry fee.

To get to the mountain go to the Ximen bus stand and catch a bus to Ruìdiàn or Diàntān and get off at the turnoff to Yúnfēng (Y8), or take a bus to Gŭdōng (Y6) and then a microbus from here to the turnoff (Y2). From the turn-off you'll have to hitch, or it's a lovely walk past the Lisu village of Heping to the pretty villages just before the mountain. The Gāolígòng Reserve fills the skyline to the east. Hiring a vehicle from Téngchōng to take you on a return trip will cost about Y300.

If you want to explore the area in more detail there is accommodation for Y25 at the *Gǔdōng Bīnguǎn* in Gǔdōng.

Volcano Park 火山公园
Huǒshān Gōngyuán

Téngchōng county is renowned for its volcanoes, and although the youngest volcano is 7000 years old there is seismic and geothermal activity in the area. The closest one to town is **Mǎān Shān** (Saddle Mountain), around 5km to the north-west. It's just south of the main road to Yíngjiāng.

Around 22km north of town, near the village of Mǎzhán, is the most accessible cluster of volcanoes. The main central volcano is known as the **Dàkòng Shān**, or Big Empty Hill, which pretty much sums it up. To the left is the black crater of **Hēikòng Shān**. You can haul yourself up the steps for views of the surrounding lava fields (long dormant) but the views of the volcanoes are just as good from the road. A new section featuring volcanic columns is due to open soon.

Minibuses run frequently to Mǎzhàn (Y5) from along Dongximen Jie, or take a Gúdōng-bound minibus. From Mǎzhàn town it's a ten-minute walk or take a motortricycle (Y5) to the volcano area, where there is a Y20 entry fee. Alternatively, hire a van to take you there and back from Téngchōng for around Y150. About 7km north-west from Mǎzhàn is the **Shùnjiāng Volcano Lake** (Shùnjiāng Huǒshān Hú).

Rèhǎi 热海

The 'Sea of Heat', as the Chinese poetically refer to it, is a cluster of hot springs, geysers and streams around 12km south-west of Téngchōng. There's the usual indoor baths, an outdoor hot spring and a warm-water pool just above a river. Admission to the hot springs is Y20, add an extra Y10 for the pool.

The site is a popular local resort and there are a couple of top-end hotels. The three-star **Rehai Grand Hotel** (*Rèhǎi Dàjiǔdiàn;* ☎ 0875-515 0366) has its own swimming pool. Rooms start at Y220 in its main block, though there are cheaper doubles for Y70 inside the springs complex. The *Mínzhū Dàjiǔdiàn* at the other end of the springs is

similarly priced. The *Jiāotōng Bīnguǎn*, outside the main entrance, has decent doubles for Y100; to find it take the path up the hill to the left of the main gate. In summer mosquitoes can wreak havoc – you may opt for just a day's sojourn if it's hot.

Microbuses leave for the hot springs when full from the Huancheng Nanlu turn-off in the south end of town. You can organise a van to the hot springs for around Y5 per person or Y25 for a whole van if you bargain.

Běi Hǎi 北海

Bird spotters might like this small wetland lake, about 10km north-east of Téngchōng. The area is under national level protection. The easiest way to get here is to hire a taxi or minivan, but you can also take a bus to Qùshí and get off en route.

Déhóng Prefecture
德洪地区

Déhóng Lisu and Jingo Autonomous Prefecture, like Xīshuāngbǎnnà, borders Myanmar and is heavily populated by distinctive minority groups, but it hasn't captured travellers' imaginations as 'Bǎnnà has. It's in the far west of Yúnnán and is definitely more off-the-beaten track than Xīshuāngbǎnnà – you're unlikely to bump into more than a couple of other backpackers.

Most Chinese in Déhóng are there for the trade from Myanmar that comes through the towns of Ruìlì and Wǎndīng. Burmese jade is a commodity that many Chinese have grown rich on recently, but countless other items are spirited over the border, some of them illicit. The border with Myanmar is punctuated by many border crossings, some of them almost imperceptible, so be careful if you go wandering close to the border.

The most obvious minority groups in Déhóng are the Burmese, the Dǎi and the Jingpo. The Burmese are normally dressed in their traditional sarong-like *longyi* and the women often wear thanakha paste on their faces as a sun screen. The Jingpo (referred to by Marco Polo as the 'People of the

Golden Teeth') are known today in Myanmar as the Kachin, a minority long-engaged in armed struggle against the Myanmar government. The Jingpo celebrate the large Munao festival on the 15th and 16th of the first lunar month. There are many more smaller groups such as the De'ang and Achang, both found in the Zhāngfēng (Lóngchuān) region. For information on etiquette for visiting temples in the region see the boxed text 'Etiquette in Dǎi Temples' in the Xīshuāngbǎnnà section.

Throughout Déhóng are signs in many languages: Chinese, Burmese, Dǎi and English. This is a border region that is profiting on trade – in the markets you can see old Indian men selling jewellery, tinned fruits from Thailand, Burmese papier-mache furniture; young bloods with huge wads of foreign currency; and Chinese plain-clothes police trying not to look too obvious.

MÁNGSHÌ (LÙXI) 芒市（潞西）
☎ 0692

Mángshì is Déhóng's air link with the outside world. If you fly in from Kūnmíng, there are minibuses running direct from the airport to Ruìlì and most people take this option. But Mángshì has a casual South-East Asian feel to it, and there are a few sights in and around the town that make dallying here worthwhile.

Things to See
There are a couple of markets in Mángshì and a number of temples near the Mángshì Bīnguǎn, where the city gives way to surrounding villages.

If you turn right out of the Mángshì Bīnguǎn you pass the Pútí Sì on the left (Y2 entry), first built in 1674. Continue on to the next road crossing, the more interesting Wǔyún Sì (Five Clouds Temple) is straight ahead down a mud track. Next to the temple is a water tank and a tree wrapped in thread to form a spirit trap. Back at the crossroads a right turn takes you a few hundred metres to the Fóguāng Sì and its cluster of stupas.

Halfway along Youyi Lu, tucked down a side street leading to a primary school is the 200-year-old Shùbāo Tǎ (Embracing Tree Pagoda), so named because over the years it has fused with the surrounding tree. It's only worth a look from a distance, otherwise you'll be hit with an 'admission' ticket (Y2).

The town's most interesting market is in the north-east of town, opposite the Jiànguó Fàndiàn, though there is another market just west of the main square.

Not far from the south bus station is the Nationalities Cultural Palace (Mínzú Wénhuà Gōng), which is more like a large park full of elderly Chinese practising their taijichuan (tai-chi). There's a few small exhibits on nationalities and a couple of reconstructed Dǎi buildings. There's a Y3 admission fee at the main gate.

About 7km south of town are the Fapa Hot Springs (Fǎpà Wēnquán). There are good reports of this site from travellers who have cycled out to them.

If you arrive by plane, en route to town you will pass the attractive Fēngpíng Fótǎ, a pagoda 9km south-west of town.

Places to Stay & Eat
The most popular place to stay is the peaceful, friendly *Mángshì Bīnguǎn*, also signposted as the Déhóng Bīnguǎn. To get there from Tuanjie Dajie, head east down a bizarre-looking block completely redone in Miami Beach Art Deco pastels. Doubles/triples with bathroom, TV and fan are Y45/Y35 per bed, an excellent deal. There is a nice sitting area and surrounding gardens though lower floor rooms are a little damp. Upmarket doubles in the two main blocks range from Y120 to Y180.

On Tuanjie Dajie, *Nánjiāng Fàndiàn* has basic dorm beds from Y20 or less, but you may have to ask to see these. Decent standard doubles/triples go for Y80/90 and up to Y150. The place is nothing to rave about, but it's conveniently situated to catch an early bus or book plane tickets.

Several other small hotels are worth checking out. Just east of the bus station, the *Chángjiāng Bīnguǎn* (☎ 212 3842) has clean pleasant doubles for Y60 to Y70. Nearby, *Mángshì Tángchǎng Dàjiǔjiā* also has good doubles with bathroom for Y50, or Y20 with a clean common bathroom.

YUNNAN

Also try the ***Jīngmào Bīnguǎn,*** which has doubles with bathroom for Y40.

Jiànguó Fàndiàn (☎ 212 5642) has triples with common bathroom for Y60 and

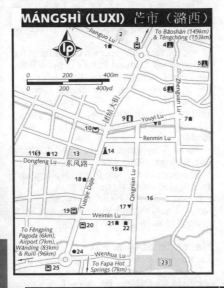

doubles with bathroom for Y80 to Y140, though it's a bit far from anywhere on the north-east edge of town.

Another upper-end place is the ***Tàifēng Bīnguǎn*** (☎ 211 5328) on Dongfeng Lu. Rooms that are listed at Y280 can go for as low as Y100, making this a comfortable mid-range alternative.

Měngzǐ Chuántǒng Guòqiáo Mǐxiàn (*Mengzi Traditional Across-the-Bridge Noodles*) on Youyi Lu is a basic but good place for noodles, costing Y5, Y10, Y15 and Y20. The Y15 option gets you a huge bowl of noodles plus a side dish of herb-infused chicken.

There are several point-and-choose ***restaurants*** along Qingnian Lu, and a ***fruit market***.

Getting There & Away

Air There are daily flights between Mángshì and Kūnmíng for Y530. Buses sometimes leave from Mángshì airport to the town centre 10kms away (Y2) but you might have no choice but to negotiate with the taxi sharks at the airport. The taxi fare into town should cost Y10, though many will try for Y20. A fleet of minibuses to

MÁNGSHÌ (LÙXI)

PLACES TO STAY
1 Jiànguó
  Fàndiàn
  建国饭店
7 Mángshì
  Bīnguǎn
  芒市宾馆
12 Tàifēng
  Bīnguǎn
  泰丰宾馆
15 Jīngmào
  Bīnguǎn
  经贸宾馆
18 Nánjiāng
  Fàndiàn
  南疆饭店
21 Chángjiāng
  Bīnguǎn
  长江宾馆
22 Mángshì
  Tángchǎng
  Dàjiǔjiā
  芒市糖厂大酒家

PLACES TO EAT
8 Měngzǐ Chuántǒng
  Guòqiáo Mǐxiàn
  蒙自传统过桥米线
17 Restaurants
  餐厅

OTHER
2 Market
  市场
3 Long-Distance
  Bus Station
  客运中心
4 Wǔyún Sì
  五云寺
5 Fóguāng Sì
  佛光寺
6 Pútí Sì
  菩提寺
9 Shùbāo Tǎ
  树包塔
10 Post Office
  邮局

11 Bank of China
  中国银行
13 Market
  市场
14 Minorities'
  Monument
16 Fruit market
  水果市场
19 Private
  Bus Station
  私人汽车站
20 Southern
  Bus Station
  客运南站
23 Nationalities
  Cultural Palace
  民族文化宫
24 Yunnan Airlines
  云南航空公司
25 Buses to Wǎndīng
  & Ruìlì
  到畹町和瑞
  丽的汽车

Ruìlì (Y30, two hours) awaits incoming flights.

Buses leave the Mángshì Yunnan Air office for the airport around an hour before flight departures. It is possible to book or reconfirm flights here, or you could wait until you get to Ruìlì. The office is open weekdays 8.30am to 11.30am and 2pm to 5.30pm

Bus Mángshì has several private bus stations. The south bus station is the most useful, though there are also plenty of departures from the long-distance bus station in the north of town. A bus stand a block south-west of the main bus stand has the most frequent departures to Wǎndīng (Y15) and Ruìlì (Y20). Minibuses leave when full so be prepared for a wait.

The long-distance bus station has scheduled departures to Téngchōng (Y22, four hours) at 8am and 1pm and to Bǎoshān (Y25, five hours) at 7am, 8.30am and 9.30am. There are sleeper buses to Xiàguān (Y80, 12 hours) at 8pm and Kunmíng (Y110, 20 hours) at 10.30am and 12.30pm and 6.30pm.

The south bus station and long-distance bus stations offer similar destinations and prices. If you don't find your bus at one, trudge to the other.

WǍNDĪNG   畹町

Many travellers don't make it to Wǎndīng, or do it only as a day trip. It's not as interesting as Ruìlì. The main attraction is that the town is right on the Myanmar border. The Wǎndīng Bīnguǎn and the Yùfēng Dàlóu provide good views of the hills, small township and occasional stupa over on the Myanmar side.

Information

The Bank of China is on the main road that comes in from Ruìlì. The post office, where you will be able to make international phone calls, is next to the Xīnhuá Bookstore on the same road. Staff at the foreign affairs office of the PSB, just across from the Chinese border checkpoint, seem quite easy-going, and although they will not help you sneak into Myanmar, they are otherwise accommodating.

Things to See & Do

The new **Cooperative Border Market** is a vast, multi-storey affair complete with atrium, skylights and hundreds of stalls for would-be border traders. At the time of writing, occupants numbered only several dozen, and the empty, echoing hallways seemed to be waiting for a vast surge of business that was still nowhere in sight. You might want to stop by to see if things have picked up or simply crumbled away.

Two-minutes walk south from the Yùfēng Dàlóu will see you in Myanmar. The only giveaway is the dilapidated customs office. Apparently a Belgian couple did a day trip into Myanmar for US$20 several years ago (the proceeds were shared by those who failed to notice them crossing the bridge), but the guards haven't been interested in allowing a repeat performance.

It's worth climbing up to the north of town to take a look and spend some time at the **Wanding Forest Reserve** (Wǎndīng Sēnlín Gōngyuán). There's a Y2 entry charge and some pleasant walks. Avoid the zoo, home to three psychotic monkeys, a couple of peacocks and an unidentifiable ball of fur that was either fast asleep or dead.

Local places to stay might be able to provide information on river trips that include a barbecue lunch in a minority village. Prices vary depending on the number of participants, but you should be able to do it for around Y50 per person. Alternatively, it is possible to catch a lift on a boat with locals. Take a minibus in the direction of Mángshì and get off at the bridge that connects with the main Ruìlì-Mángshì road. Travellers have caught boats back to the second bridge closer to Ruìlì and then hitched back to Ruìlì or Wǎndīng. Some very strenuous haggling is required for boat trips.

Places to Stay & Eat

The cheapest place to stay is the slightly decayed *Yùfēng Dàlóu*. Dorm beds are Y10 and doubles with bathroom go for Y40.

The better-kept and friendly *Wǎndīng Bīnguǎn* is in a rambling, lonely building up on a hill with good views of Myanmar. Comfortable doubles with bathroom and satellite TV are Y80, or Y60 for single occupancy. Triples are also available for Y90. Look for the alabaster statue of a frolicking maiden holding what looks to be a miniature UFO in her hand, at the front entrance.

Just up the street north of the border, *Zhōngyín Bīnguǎn* is probably the best good choice, with singles/doubles from Y50/60.

The brand new hulking *Jiāotōng Fàndiàn* on the west side of town has smoky and vastly overpriced standard rooms for Y180.

The area around the Yùfēng Dàlóu and opposite the Zhōngyín Bīnguǎn is best for cheap *restaurants*. Most of them are of the pick-and-choose variety, and all are much the same. In the mornings, try the *dumpling stands* opposite the turn-off for the Wǎndīng Bīnguǎn.

Getting There & Away

Minibuses run to Ruìlì for Y10 and to Mángshì for Y15. They leave during the day whenever they are full. You shouldn't have to wait more than 15 minutes for a bus to Ruìlì; buses to Mángshì are less frequent.

RUÌLÌ 瑞丽
☎ 0692

Ruìlì is definately one of the more interesting towns in South-West China. It's just a few kilometres from Myanmar and has a real border-town feel to it. There's a great mix of Han Chinese, Dǎi and Jingpo minorities and Burmese traders hawking jade, and travellers tend to linger longer than they intended, just for the atmosphere. At first it doesn't seem like much (and the place is getting dustier with all the new construction work) but it's worth spending a couple of days here.

Compared with the rest of China, life in Ruìlì seems less restricted, as though people here get away with a lot more. The fact that this atmosphere is generated by proximity to Myanmar and its repressive military

---

The Burma Road

When Japanese troops occupied northern and eastern China in 1937, the Kuomintang government retreated inland to the safety of Chóngqìng. As they looked around for potential supply lines through which to receive Allied reinforcements, they turned back to the ancient overland trade routes with Burma and India, namely the Southwest Silk Road and the old Ambassador's road, once travelled by Marco Polo.

The Kūnmíng-Xiàguān section was built from 1934 to 1935 and in 1937, 200,000 labourers ('coolies' in the parlance of the day) were drafted in to build the section from Xiàguān to Wǎndīng and then on to Mandalay in 1940 via the railhead of Lashio in Burma's Shan state. By February 1939 Allied supplies were being transported by boat to Rangoon, by train to Lashio in northern Burma and then trucked across the jungles and mountain ranges of Burma to Xiàguān and finally Kūnmíng, which rapidly became a major US air base.

In 1942 the Japanese overran Burma and cut the Burma Road and the allies were forced to build another road, from Ledo in north-east India to Bhamo. At one point there were even plans to link Lìjiāng to Assam and US Army engineers went as far as enlisting Joseph Rock's help in mapping the area. The road from Ledo became known as the Stillwell Road, after General Joseph Stillwell, who led the Allied forces in China, Burma and India from his base in Kunming. The road was finally finished in 1944 and disused in 1945.

A short-term stopgap was an air supply line, which ran over the Hump from British India, and over the Himalayan Hump into the airfields of Kūnmíng and Lìjiāng. Over 1000 airmen died crossing the Hump, lost in territory so remote and wild that many bodies have still not been recovered. The US Army is currently investigating two sites in far eastern Tibet as the suspected site of a C-46 plane that crashed in 1946 en route from India.

The importance of the Burma Road diminished after WWII but is enjoying somewhat of a revival, though jade, teak, opium and heroin has replaced the military hardware.

junta makes Ruìlì all the more interesting. There are some minority villages nearby; the stupas are in much better condition than those in Xīshuāngbǎnnà, and it's worth travelling onwards to Wǎndīng and Mángshì, either as day trips or overnight stops.

Hopefully, Myanmar will relax border-crossing restrictions for foreigners in the near future. New highways laid to facilitate border trade should now stretch all the way from Jiěgào, on the border, to Mandalay, making what had been a horrible five-day journey much more sane. Chinese tour groups are already visiting north Myanmar and Ruìlì's travel agencies offer tantalising information on the sights. Soon, foreign travellers may also be able to recreate the 'Southern Silk Route', of which Ruìlì and Mandalay were part.

Information

The shop next to the reception area of the Ruìlì Bīnguǎn has maps and a few brochures on Ruìlì, as does the travel agency next to the Yongchang Dajiudian. The Xīnhuá bookstore sells the useful *Ruili Tour Traffic Map*, published by the Ruìlì Tourism Bureau.

Heading downhill from the Ruìlì Bīnguǎn, at the corner of Minzi Lu and Renmin Lu you'll find China Post and China Telecom, where you can make direct-dial international calls. Just around the corner, you can get Internet access at a China Telecom Business Centre. Access is pricey

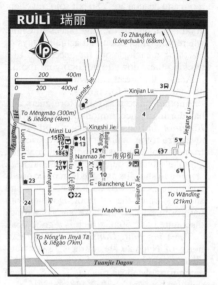

YUNNAN

at Y18 per hour but this rate should fall over time. The office is open weekdays 8am to 6pm.

The speedy and efficient Bank of China is close to the long-distance bus station. In case you're headed to Myanmar, the bank will let you cash travellers cheques for US dollars, which will be likely to come in handy across the border. The 2nd floor of the new ICBC will kindly change cash and travellers cheques but cannot give cash advances on credit cards. Opening hours are 8am to 11.30am and 2.30pm to 5.30pm.

The PSB is just up the road from the Ruìlì Bīnguǎn.

Things to See

There is really nothing specific to see in the town, though it's a great town to wander around, and is small enough to cover in an hour or so. The **market** in the west of town is the most colourful by day, especially in the morning, when the stalls are lined with Burmese smokes, tofu wrapped in banana leaves, snack stalls and charcoal sellers. The centre of the market is arranged around an old tree.

At the other end of town, Ruìlì's **jade market** is worth a visit for its Burmese faces and the fascinating surrounding warren of street stalls.

Nobody really comes to Ruìlì for the *day*life, though. Ruìlì doesn't even open a drowsy eye until 10pm, at which point it transforms itself into an entirely different city. Hundreds of sidewalk restaurants spring open, casinos swing open their doors and tourists get taken everywhere to look at cheap jade while their friends scream into karaoke microphones. The population of Ruìlì seems to triple. The **market** just around the corner from the Ruìlì Bīnguǎn is the liveliest place to hang out. All this fun and madness is lasting till later and later; it isn't quite a city that never sleeps, but it's getting there.

To recover from the night before or escape from the heat, non-guests can currently use the very pleasant pool at the Kaìtōng International Hotel for Y8.

Places to Stay

The most popular place with travellers is currently the well-run *Lìmín Bīnguǎn* on Nanmao Jie. Beds in a clean triple or double cost Y20. The squat common bathrooms are bearable. Tiled standard doubles with bathroom and air-con are Y80 but solo travellers can normally get these for Y50. Staff are good – it's one of the few places in China where your floor attendant actually stays *at the desk*, meaning that, for once, won't be tracking them down to get into your room.

Across the street, the *Míngruì Bīnguǎn* no longer accepts foreigners.

Another place that takes foreigners and has dormitory accommodation is the *Ruìlì Bīnguǎn* on Jianshe Jie. Being a bit farther away from the main strip, it offers refuge from the blaring discos and evil roadside karaoke stands, though the hotel is seriously starting to show its age. Beds in basic quads and doubles are Y20 each. Bathrooms and showers are on the 1st floor. Doubles with bathroom cost Y80; these are sometimes discounted to Y50m, which is a good deal.

The *Yǒngchāng Dàjiǔdiàn* (☎ 414 1808) north of Nanmao Jie, attracts fewer travellers, possibly because of its location, but is a comfortable, clean place to stay. Standard doubles here are Y120, Y148 and Y168.

Back on the main strip, the *Nányáng Bīnguǎn* on Nanmao Jie, has doubles for Y90 and Y120, which rapidly translates into Y50 and Y80. Though this place does not look like much at first, some of the rooms aren't bad, and it has the pluses of 24-hour hot water and a management amenable to price negotiation.

If all of the aforementioned are full (that's not likely), or not to your taste, there are many other hotels, including several down on Biancheng Lu. Standard doubles at these places all share a sense of shabby luxury, and usually cost between Y100 and Y130.

The top hotel in town is currently the three-star *Kaitong International Hotel* (*Kǎitōng Guójì Dàjiǔdiàn;* ☎ 414 9528, fax 414 9526), though top-end resorts are being added all the time for wealthy Chinese holidaymakers. Rooms start at Y360 and facilities include a snooker hall and a nice pool.

Image Problems

You'll hear incessantly of Ruìlì's image problems, for which there is some evidence. The town's pubs, discos and even beauty parlours – lots are simply fronts for an enormous prostitution industry – have always had a rough reputation. And though most of the populace are simple traders, a significant share of the local commerce is of the poppy-derived variety, Ruìlì being an entry point for Burmese opium headed to Hong Kong. This has resulted in a serious intravenous drug use problem in the Déhóng region, along with its pernicious sibling – HIV.

It's claimed that since 1990, virtually all of China's new HIV cases have been reported in Ruìlì and its vicinity, and by 1995, 70% of the nation's cases were in Yúnnán, most in Ruìlì. Déhóng in fact, is home to the China AIDS and IV Drug Centre and the Chinese government is planning to set up AIDS quarantine checkpoints along all its Yúnnán border transit points with Burma and, later, Laos. AIDS is such a serious problem they've earmarked 500 million yuán for the project. The province has also poured over 125 million yuán into anti-drug efforts along the border of Myanmar. In the first three months of 1999 alone 1.8 tonnes of heroin were seized.

Places to Eat

Reports concerning the availability of decent curries in Ruìlì are the result of wishful embellishment, but there is some good food available. Take a stroll up the market street around the corner from the Ruìlì Bīnguǎn in the evening and check out all the snack stands serving everything from hotpot to wontons and seafood.

For good Burmese food, there are several *restaurants* in a small alley off Jiegang Lu. The one at the top of the north-western corner is particularly good, and serves a lot of Burmese patrons. This is also the spot to go for Thai Mekong whisky, served Thai style with soda water and ice. There are also lots of *Chinese restaurants* here.

There are a couple of good *buffet restaurants* south of here on Jiegang Lu, where you choose a selection of pre-cooked food for around Y5.

For good iced coffee and fruit juice drinks, or something stronger, try *Jo Jo's Cold Drinks Shop* (Juéjué Léngyǐndiàn). The shop is on the corner of Nanmao Jie and Baijiang Xigang. Burmese ales costs Y10 but are twice the strength of Chinese beers. You can also get fried noodles and other snacks. A proliferation of other 'beer/coffee/tea/ice-cream/juice' places (many incorporate all those in their names), have cropped up along the main and side drags.

For something different try *Shen Yāzi*, on the corner of Nanmao Jie and Renmin Lu, which specialises in roast duck (kǎoyā). A whole duck costs Y30 (Y15 for a half portion), which comes with hoisin sauce and shallots. There is also a full menu of other cheap dishes. The outdoor seating is very pleasant.

Take the opportunity to try a freshly squeezed lime juice from one of the numerous stands around the town. At Y5 a glass, it's a bit more than your average drink, but the taste is superb.

Entertainment

Ruìlì may be only a small town, but by Chinese standards it packs a lot of punch on the entertainment level. For the Chinese, Ruìlì has a reputation as one of *the* happening places in Yúnnán, and young people with money head down here just for a few nights out. But where discos used to be the venue of choice, now massage parlours have taken over. Prostitution is rampant in Ruìlì, and it's difficult to find a sleaze-free bar or dance hall. This is, of course, still China, and things are much more tame than Bangkok or Manila. Everything closes down around 1am to 2am, and you needn't worry about being flagged down in the street by pimps. Still, be aware if you decide to get adventurous and duck into a dark bar for a drink.

The discos are still in action, though they tend to slow down even earlier, around midnight on a slow night. There is also a *dance hall* opposite the Burmese restaurants on Renmin Jie that has a live band playing most nights. There is usually an admission fee of Y20 or so, depending on where you go, but it's worth it for an insight into China's jiving nightspots.

Getting There & Away
Air Ruìlì has flight connections to Kūnmíng from the town of Mángshì, which is two-hours drive away. See the Mángshì entry for details. Yunnan Airlines (☎ 414 8275) has an office north of the Yǒngchāng Dàjiǔdiàn. Minibuses leave daily for the two-hour trip to the airport; check that day's flight schedule to see what time the buses leave. You can also use the ticket office to book and reconfirm return flights – do so early as this is an increasingly popular flight.

Bus It's still a long, long haul between the Déhóng region and Kūnmíng. You may find that there are customs inspections en route. They're mostly looking for drugs smuggled in from Myanmar, but pornographic magazines and videos are also fair game.

Sleeper buses to Kūnmíng (Y103, 24 hours God willing) leave from the long-distance bus station 11 times daily from 6.20am to 4pm. Sleeper buses to Xiàguān (Dàlǐ) leave at 4, 6 and 7pm (Y80, 10 hours).

Eight buses leave for Bǎoshān between 6.30am and noon (Y40, Y50 for a sleeper, eight hours). Work is progressing on a new highway linking Ruìlì and Bǎoshān.

Buses for Téngchōng leave twice at 6.30am and 7am (Y30, six hours). There are hourly buses for Yíngjiāng via Zhāngfèng (Lóngchuān) between 8am and 2.30pm (Y21, five hours on a good day). A new road is being built. Buses leave for Mángshì frequently between 8am and 3pm from a driveway just east of the long-distance bus station (Y15 to Y20, two hours).

If you're in the mood to rough it, private sleeper buses leave for Jǐnghóng in Xīshuāngbǎnnà at 6.30am, arriving in the afternoon of the third day.

Private entrepreneurs advertise destinations from a few steps west of the bus station's ticket window, so check the signs for more convenient departures or prices.

Minibuses and vans leave for more local destinations from opposite the long-distance bus station. Destinations include Wǎndīng (Y15, one hour), the border checkpoint at Jiěgào (Y4), and the village of Nòngdǎo (Y8). Buses to Zhāngfèng (Y10, one hour) leave from Xinjian Lu.

Getting Around
Ruìlì is easily explored on foot, but all the most interesting day trips require a bicycle. The Lìmín Bīnguǎn rents bikes for Y10, with a Y200 deposit if you aren't staying at the hotel.

A flat rate for a taxi ride inside the city should be Y5, and up for negotiation from there. There are also cheaper motor and cycle rickshaws.

AROUND RUÌLÌ
Most of Ruìlì's sights are outside town, and you'll need a bicycle to visit them. It's worth making frequent detours down the narrow paths leading off the main roads to visit **minority villages**. The people are friendly, and there are lots of photo opportunities. The *Ruili Tour Traffic Map* published by the Ruìlì Tourism Bureau shows the major roads and villages.

The shortest ride is to turn left at the corner north of the post office and continue out of the town proper into the little village of **Měngmǎo**. There are half a dozen Shan temples scattered about; the find is finding them to get a look at the unique interiors.

Nóng'ān Jīnyā Tǎ
A short ride south-west of town, on the main road, the Jīnyā Tǎ, or Golden Duck Pagoda, is an attractive stupa set in a temple courtyard. It was established to mark the arrival of a pair of golden ducks that brought good fortune to what was previously an uninhabited marshy area.

Jiěgào Border Checkpoint
姐告边检点
Straight ahead from the Jīnyā Tǎ, across the Myanmar bridge over the Ruìlì River is

Myanmar Border Crossing

Everyone hoped that with Myanmar's admission to ASEAN in 1997, it would relax its land borders a bit. Not even close. At present absolutely no foreigners get into Myanmar's border town of Muse (Mùjiě in Mandarin). East Asians might be able to sneak across as locals, but definitely not Westerners. The friendly-enough Chinese border guards will wince if you approach – so many foreigners have pleaded for a day pass that the commander and some of his underlings are planning to study English!

The Chinese have actually tried to facilitate border crossings but the Myanmar government doesn't really have control over corruption and lawlessness in the region and claims it doesn't want foreign tourists wandering through that lethal cocktail. Whatever the case, this is a rapidly-developing area and, who knows, things may do an about-face. What will probably happen first is that group tours organised by local agencies will be allowed across in closely supervised day trips.

Jiěgào, a little thumb-shaped piece of land jutting into Myanmar that serves as the main checkpoint for a steady stream of cross-border traffic. See the 'Myanmar Border Crossing' boxed text for more details. You can still marvel at how laid-back everything seems on both sides of the – quite literally – bamboo curtain and indulge the perennial fascination with illicit borders. Wildly popular casinos line the streets of both sides of the border.

Jiěgào is about 7km from Ruìlì. Microbuses shuttle between the border and Ruìlì's long-distance bus station when full for Y4 or you can charter the bus for around Y20. Buses continue until late at night.

Temples

Just past the Jīnyā Tǎ is a crossroad (and a small wooden temple). The road to the right (west) leads to Jiěxiāng and Nòngdǎo, and on the way are a number of small temples, villages and stupas. None are spectacular

but the village life is interesting and there are often small markets near the temples.

The first major Dǎi temple is the **Hánshā Zhuāng Sì**, a fine wooden structure with a few resident monks. It's set a little off the road and a green tourism sign marks the turn-off. The surrounding Dǎi village is interesting.

Ten-minutes cycle past here is the **'One Village, Two Countries'**, so named because the Dǎi village straddles the border.

Another 15 minutes or so down the road, look out for a white stupa on the hillside to the right. This is **Léizhuāngxiāng**, Ruìlì's oldest stupa, which dates back to the middle of the Tang dynasty. There's a nunnery in the grounds of the stupa and fantastic views of the Ruìlì area. Once the stupa comes into view, take the next path to the right that cuts through the fields. There are blue signs in Chinese and Dǎi pointing the way through a couple of Dǎi villages. When you get to market crossroads at the centre of the main village take the right path. You'll need to push your bicycle for the last ascent to the stupa. In all, it takes about 50 minutes to cycle here from the Golden Duck Pagoda.

A few kilometres past the town of Jiěxiāng is the **Děnghánnóng Zhuāng Sì**, a wooden Dǎi temple with pleasant surroundings. Like other temples in the area, the effect is spoiled by the tin roof.

It's possible to cycle all the way to Nòngdǎo, around 29km south-west of Ruìlì. There's a solitary *hotel* in town that has cheap doubles or you can return to Ruìlì on one of the frequent minibuses.

Jiělè Jīn Tǎ 姐勒金塔

A few kilometres to the east of Ruìlì on the road to Wǎndīng is the Jīn Tǎ, or Golden Pagoda, a fine structure that dates back 200 years.

Jiědōng

Another possible cycling route takes you west of Ruìlì, past the old town of Měngmǎo, now a suburb of Ruìlì. After 4km, just past the village of Jiědōng, a turn-off north leads to **Bàngmáhè village**, a Jingpo settlement with a small waterfall nearby.

Xīshuāngbǎnnà
西双版纳

The Xīshuāngbǎnnà Dǎi autonomous prefecture, or usually just 'Bǎnnà, is in the subtropical south of Yúnnán province, bordering Myanmar and Laos. The name Xīshuāngbǎnnà is a Chinese approximation of the original Thai name, Sip Sawng Panna (12 Rice-Growing Districts). The place has a laid-back South-East Asian feel with its small villages, tropical forests and the occasional stupa.

About one-third of the region's population of 800,000 are Dǎi; another third or so are Han Chinese and the rest are minorities including the Hani (20%) Miáo, Yi, Lisu and lesser known hill tribes such as the Aini (a subgroup of the Hani), Jinuo, Bulang, Yao, Lahu and Wa. Many of the women have red-stained teeth and lips from years of chewing betel nut.

Xīshuāngbǎnnà has become China's own mini-Thailand, and Chinese tourists have been heading down in droves for the sunshine, Dǎi minority dancing, water splashing festivals (held daily nowadays) and tour group lures, like the 'Forest of One Tree' and the 'King of Tea Trees' and other trees that suggest something less prosaic than a mere tree. But it is easy to escape the crowds – just jump on a public bus to some small town, and make it your base for exploring the surrounding countryside and villages.

The possibilities for day trips and longer excursions out of Jǐnghóng are endless. First learn the two different characters for 'Měng', since all village names begin with or contain it. Some travellers have hiked and hitched from Měnghǎi to Dàměnglóng, some have cycled up to Měnghǎi and Měngzhē from Jǐnghóng (it's almost impossible on bikes without gears), and one French photographer hitched up with a local medicine man and spent seven days doing house calls in the jungle.

Even with limited time there are interesting possibilities. Probably the best is a stay in Gǎnlǎnbà (also known as Měnghǎn). It's only about 27km from Jǐnghóng, and takes two to three hours, even on a local bike.

Most other destinations in Bǎnnà are only two or three hours away by bus. To get to many villages, you'll often have to bus to a primary village first and overnight, since only one bus a day – if that – travels to the tinier villages.

Markets are another highlight. Most people seem to prefer the Thursday market in Xīdìng, then in Měnghùn, followed by Měnghǎi.

The best advice is to get yourself a good bike or some sturdy hiking boots, pick up a map and get out of town.

Climate

Xīshuāngbǎnnà has wet and dry seasons. The wet season falls between June and August, when it rains almost every day. From September to February there is less rainfall, but thick fog descends in the late evening and doesn't lift until 10am creating 'seas of clouds' that are visible whenever your bus climbs out of the low-lying valleys. Between May and August there are frequent and spectacular thunderstorms. Between November and March temperatures average about 19°C (66°F). The hottest months of the year are from April to September, when you can expect an average of 25°C (77°F).

Flora & Fauna

'Xishuangbanna is known as a beautiful, abundant place; if the forests are destroyed then in the future it will become a desert, we Communists will go down in history as criminals, and later generations will rebuke us.'

Zhou Enlai, 1961, in Jǐnghóng

Like Hǎinán Island, Xīshuāngbǎnnà is home to many unique species of plant and animal life, including over 100 endangered species. Unfortunately, recent scientific studies have demonstrated that the rainforest areas are as acutely endangered as similar areas elsewhere on the planet, even though the Chinese authorities have established 250,000 hectares of protected nature reserve. Studies have indicated that since 1960 Xīshuāngbǎnnà's average temperature

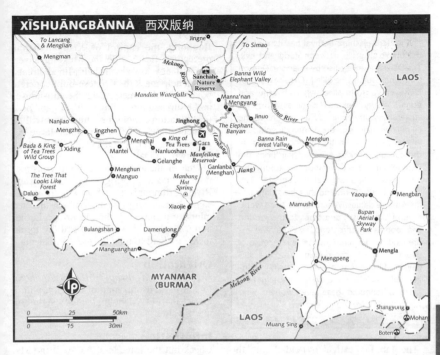

XĪSHUĀNGBǍNNÀ 西双版纳

To Lancang & Menglian

Mengman

Jingne

To Simao

Mekong River

Sanchahe Nature Reserve

Banna Wild Elephant Valley

LAOS

Mandian Waterfalls

Manna'nan Mengyang

Nanjiao

Mengzhe

Jingzhen

Menghai

Jinghong

The Elephant Banyan

Jinuo

Luosuo River

Menglun

Bada & King of Tea Trees Wild Group

Xiding

Mantei

King of Tea Trees

Nanluoshan

Cara

Banna Rain Forest Valley

Menghun

Manguo

Gelanghe

Manfeilong Reservoir

Ganlanba (Menghan)

Jiang

The Tree That Looks Like Forest

Daluo

Manbang Hot Spring

Yaoqu

Mengbán

Xiaojie

Mamushi

Bupan Aerial Skyway Park

Bulangshan

Damenglong

Mengpeng

Mengla

Manguanghan

MYANMAR (BURMA)

Mekong River

Shangyung

Mohan

0   25   50km
0   15   30mi

LAOS

Muang Sing

Boten

has risen 1°C, and rainfall has dropped off 10% to 20%.

Remaining jungle areas still contain dwindling numbers of wild elephants, tigers, leopards and also golden-haired monkeys. The most likely place to see wild elephants is the Banna Wild Elephant Valley in the Sanchahe Nature Reserve north of Jǐnghóng.

It's not all bad news – the elephant population has risen from 195 a decade ago to 250; the government now offers compensation to villagers whose crops are destroyed by elephants, or who assist in wildlife conservation. In 1998 the government banned hunting or processing of animals, though poaching is notoriously difficult to control in these borderlands. In 1999 three Laotians were arrested after killing three wild Asian elephants in Shengyong Reserve.

Festivals

Festivals celebrated by the Dǎi attract hordes of foreigners and Chinese. The **Water-Splashing Festival** held from 13 to 15 April washes away the dirt, sorrow and demons of the old year and brings in the happiness of the new. This is the time when the king of the spirits descends to earth for three days to record man's good and bad deeds. The first day of the festival is devoted to a giant market. The second day features dragon-boat racing (races in Jǐnghóng are held on the Mekong River below the bridge), swimming races and 'gaosheng' rocket launching. The third day features the water-splashing freakout – be prepared to be drenched by the locals all day; the wetter you get, the more luck you will receive. In the evenings there is dancing, launching of hot-air paper balloons and game playing.

During the **Tanpa Festival** in the second lunar month, young boys are sent to the local temple for initiation as novice monks. At about the same time (between February and March), the **Tan Jing Festival** participants honour Buddhist texts housed in local temples.

The Dǎi and the Demon

The Water-Splashing Festival has its roots in the titanic struggle between good and evil. The Dǎi were once ruled by a sadistic Demon king who couldn't be killed. One day one of his seven consorts plied him with wine and good lovin' and extracted the secret of his vulnerability. 'If somebody were to hang me by my own hair,' said the demon, 'I would die immediately'. When the demon fell asleep, the consort plucked a single hair from the Demon king's head, wrapped it around his neck and pulled with all her might. The demon's head fell off and then burst into unquenchable flames. Wherever the head went, it burnt Dǎi houses and crops to the ground and soon flames threatened to engulf the entire land. In desperation, the seven consorts poured water on the burning head for 999 days until the flames were finally extinguished. Since then the Water Splashing Festival has honoured these seven women, who saved the Dǎi from their demons.

The **Tan Ta Festival** is held during the last 10-day period of October or November, with temple ceremonies, rocket launches from special towers and hot-air balloons. The rockets often contain lucky amulets. Those who find the amulets are assured of good luck.

The farming season (from July to October) is the time for the **Closed-Door Festival**, when marriages or festivals are banned. Traditionally, this is also the time that men aged 20 or older ordain as monks. The season ends with the **Open-Door Festival**, when everyone celebrates the harvest.

During festivals, booking same-day airline tickets to Jǐnghóng can be extremely difficult – even with up to 17 flights a day! You can try getting a flight into Sīmáo, 162km to the north, or take the bus. Hotels in Jǐnghóng town are booked solid, but you could stay in a nearby Dǎi village and commute. Festivities take place all over Xīshuāngbǎnnà, so you might be luckier farther away from Jǐnghóng.

JǏNGHÓNG 景洪
☎ 0691

Jǐnghóng, the capital of Xīshuāngbǎnnà prefecture, lies beside the Mekong River. It's a sleepy town with palm-lined streets, which help mask the Chinese-built concrete boxes until they merge with the stilt-houses in the surrounding villages. It's a good base for operations, though eventually it will be as neon-laden as China's other large regional towns. The town's name means 'City of Dawn' in Dǎi.

One of the most eye-catching constructions is the new bridge over the Mekong River. If rumour is true, there was an attempt some years ago by a member of a disaffected minority to blow up the old bridge farther north. Jǐnghóng is such a splendidly torpid town, it's hard to imagine the excitement.

Orientation
Maps The *City Proper Map of Jinghong* (Y2.50) is a useful map of the city, with a tourist map of Xīshuāngbǎnnà's sights on the flip side.

Information
Check out the travellers' books at the Měi Měi, Forest and Mekong cafes for travel tips and some detailed trek notes.

Money The Bank of China is on Jinghong Nanlu, next to the Banna Mansion Hotel. There's another branch on Ganlan Lu. Both are open weekdays 8am to 6pm, minus lunch hours, and less reliably on weekends 8am to 11.30am and 3pm to 6pm.

The China Agricultural Bank, east of the PSB on Jinghong Donglu, takes care of travellers cheques and credit-card advances. Opening hours are weekdays 8am to 8pm and weekends 8am to noon and 3pm to 6pm.

Travel Agencies CITS (☎ 212 4479, 213 0460) has an office across from the entrance to the Xīshuāngbǎnnà Bīnguǎn. The staff are friendly, and can answer questions about sights and accommodation. They also offer several one-day tours (Y50 to Y100 per person) of one or two towns and sights, though they may be able to arrange tours of

Etiquette in Dǎi Temples

Around Dǎi temples the same rules apply as elsewhere: dress appropriately (no tank tops or shorts); take off shoes before entering; don't take monks' photos or interior shots without permission; leave a donation if you do take any shots and consider a token donation even if you don't, since these Buddhists receive no government assistance. Like Thailand, it is polite to *wai* the monks as a greeting and remember to never rub anyone's head, raise yourself higher than a Buddha figure, or point your feet at anyone. This last point applies to secular buildings. If you stay the night in a Dǎi household it is good form to sleep with your feet pointing towards the door.

the Sanchahe Nature Reserve, bamboo rafting, or a visit to a tea of coffee plantation.

The Mengyuan Travel Agency (mobile ☎ 1398 812 27795, ☎ 212 5214, ✉ myluke @bn.yn.cn.info.net) at 3 Jinghong Nanlu, next to the Bank of China, can arrange treks.

The Forest Café and Mekong Café can help with trekking information and can put you in touch with English-speaking guides. It can also help arrange boat trips down the Mekong to Gǎnlǎnbà.

PSB The PSB office on Jinghong Donglu is opposite Peacock Lake Park in the centre of town. It's possible to get visa extensions here, though for a second extension you'll probably have more luck if you have a Lao visa. The office is open weekdays 8.30am to 11.30am and 2.30pm to 5pm.

Post & Communications China Post and China Telecom are in the centre of town at the intersection of Jinghong Xilu and Jinghong Donglu. You can also direct dial from most hotels, but rates are higher. Postal service is available 8am to 8.30pm, with telecommunication services slightly longer.

Email & Internet Access The Internet is available at the Mekong Café and the King

New Network computer shop next to the Měi Měi Café both for Y5 per hour.

China Telecom has slow Internet access at Y3 per hour, with a Y50 refundable deposit. It's open 8am to 11pm.

Laundry The Bǎnnà Jiǔdiàn Service Laundry *(Zhuānyè Xǐyī)* on Manting Lu offers a 24-hour laundry service for Y2 per item.

Dangers & Annoyances There have been reports from travellers regarding drug-and-robbings on the Kūnmíng-Jǐnghóng bus trip. Like other countries in South-East Asia, be careful who your friends are on buses, accept nothing, and leave nothing unattended.

Chunhuan Park 春欢公园
Chūnhuān Gōngyuán

Chunhuan Park, in the south of Jǐnghóng past the Dǎi restaurants, is not really interesting, even if it is the garden of a former Dǎi chieftain. The park contains a couple of replica stupas, Dǎi dancing girls (you'll probably see a Water-Splashing Festival) and a pitiful elephant in chains. All this for just Y12.

The temple in the rear of the park, the *Zǒng Fósì* (or *Wat Bajie* in Dǎi) – is the leading regional temple, described by one anthropologist as the 'Ivy League' of temple schools. The temple was built in 1990 and many of its monks have studied in Thailand and speak Thai.

Just before you get to the park entrance is the **Màntīng Fósí**, a temple claimed to date back 1100 years. Across from the park is the crass 'Peacock Minority Customs Tourist Village'.

Tropical Flower and Plants Garden
Rèdài Huāhuìyuán

A short bicycle ride out of town, and a pleasant walk, the institute is one of Jǐnghóng's better attractions. An entry fee of Y10 gets you into a series of gardens where you can view over 1000 types of plant life. Unless you're a botanist, telling them all apart could be tricky – signs are mainly in Chinese and the rest carry only the botanical names in

YUNNAN

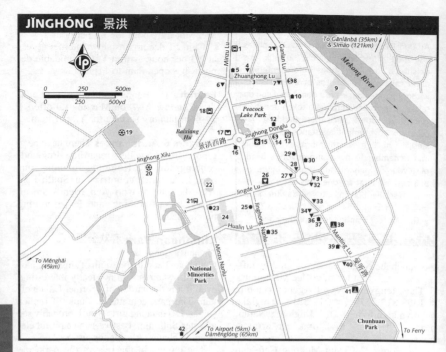

JǏNGHÓNG 景洪

English. Still, it's easy to get a feel for the impressive variety of plants that make up Yúnnán's tropical forests. The admission fee also gets you into the **Zhou Enlai Memorial**, a 2001-like sculpture commemorating a 1961 visit by China's best-loved premier – it sounds better than it is.

A little way back towards town is the **Medicinal Botanical Gardens** (Yàoyòng Zhíwùyuán). Staff at the gate might try to deter you from entering by telling you it's boring. It's not a trick to keep you out... they're telling the truth.

Peacock Lake Park 孔雀湖公园
Kǒngquè Hú Gōngyuán

This artificial lake is in the centre of town and the small park next to it is pleasant. There's a zoo, but it tends to leave you as depressed as the animals seem to be. The English Language Corner takes place here every Sunday evening, this is your chance to practise English with the locals.

National Minorities Park
民族公园 Mínzú Fēngqíng Yuán

This place is firmly aimed at Chinese tourists. Displays on minority customs and houses, a poor zoo and displays (10am and 4pm) of elephant dancing are best avoided. The park closes at 6.30pm (Y20).

Activities

Non-guests can use the swimming pool at the Crown Hotel for Y10. Better yet is the gym (Y15), pool (Y20) and tennis courts (Y40, plus Y20 racket hire) open to the public at the Tai Garden Hotel, south-west of the National Minorities Park.

Jǐnghóng's oft-recommended **Blind Massage School** (Mángrén Ànmó; ☎ 212 5834) offers professional massages between 9am and 1am (Y40 per hour). Massages begin at 9am and continue until 1am and cost Y40 per hour.

There are also freelance masseurs around Peacock Lake Park. For a foot massage try

JǏNGHÓNG

PLACES TO STAY
5   Ruìfēng Bīnguǎn
    瑞丰宾馆
10 Xīshuāngbǎnnà
    Bīnguǎn
    版纳宾馆
12 Jǐngyǒng Fàndiàn
    景咏饭店
16 Banna Mansion
    Hotel;
    Bank of China;
    Mengyuan Travel
    Agency
    版纳大厦、
    中国银行
30 Bǎnnà Jiǔdiàn
    版纳酒店
35 Crown Hotel
    皇冠大酒店
37 Dǎi Building Hotel
    傣家花苑小楼
39 Dǎijiā Zhāodàisuǒ
    傣家招待所
42 Tài Garden
    Hotel
    傣园酒店

PLACES TO EAT
2   Xīngguāng Jiǔjiā
    星光酒家
4   Myanmar
    Mandalay Cafe
    缅甸瓦城风
    味冷饮店
6   Burmese Teahouse
    缅甸茶馆
7   Maung Sein
    Myanmar Muslim
    Restaurant
    缅甸人毛回旅餐部

9   Night Market
    夜市场
27 Měi Měi Cafe;
    King New Network
    (Internet)
    美美咖啡厅、
    劲牛网路
28 Hāěrbīn Shuǐjiǎo
    哈尔滨水饺
31 Lemon Grass Cafe
    香茅草小吃
32 Forest Cafe;
    Xīnjiāng
    Lāmiànguǎn
    森林咖啡厅、
    新疆拉面馆
33 James Cafe
    杰姆斯咖啡馆
34 Wànlǐ Dǎi Guest
    House & Coffee
    Shop; Bǎnnà Jiǔdiàn
    Service Laundry
    婉丽傣味楼、
    专业洗衣
36 Mekong Cafe
    湄公餐馆
40 Barbeque
    Restaurants
    干锅餐厅

OTHER
1   Long-Distance
    Bus Station
    长途汽车站
3   Jade Market
    玉市场
8   Bank of China
    中国银行
11 CITS
    中国国际旅行社

13 Nationality Song &
    Dance Theatre
    歌舞剧院
14 China
    Agricultural Bank
    中国业银行
15 PSB
    公安局
17 China Post;
    China Telecom
    邮电大楼
18 No 2 Bus Station
    第二客运站
19 Tropical Flower &
    Plants Garden
    热带花卉园
20 Medicinal Botanical
    Gardens
    药用植物园
21 Minibuses to
    Airport
    到机场的中巴车
22 Stadium
    体育馆
23 Yunnan
    Airlines/CAAC
    民航售票处
24 Market
    市场
25 Blind Massage
    School
    盲人按摩
26 Hope Club
    好望
29 Honey Shop
    田野蜂园
38 Temple
    曼景兰金狮佛寺
41 Màntīng Fósì
    曼听佛寺

YÚNNÁN

the south-east corner, for back and shoulders try the west side.

A couple of the backpacker cafes can arrange courses such as Chinese language tuition for around Y20 per hour.

Places to Stay

Jǐnghóng definitely does not suffer from a lack of hotel space.

The **Xīshuāngbǎnnà Bīnguǎn** (☎ 212 3679/3559, fax 212 3368, 11 Ganlan Lu), also known as the Bǎnnà Bīnguǎn, in the centre of town, used to be one of those rare Chinese hotels that travellers reminisced about after they had left. It's not quite so idyllic anymore but staff are attentive and friendly. It also has hot water 24-hours a day. Doubles with balcony, bathroom and TV in Building Nos 6 and 7 are not a bad deal at Y80; triples are Y90 and you can pay per bed. Some rooms are less smoky than others.

It's Y150 to Y240 for standard doubles in the Riverview Buildings; look at rooms in a few places, as there's a great deal of difference. If you get a dorm room on the ground floor, leave valuables at the front desk. Reception can help arrange bike hire.

For basic accommodation with a Dǎi flavour, head south on Manting Lu. It's a 25-minutes walk from the bus station. A taxi should cost around Y10.

The **Dǎi Building Hotel** (*Dǎijiā Huāyuán Xiǎolóu*) is a popular backpacker hang-out that you'll either love or hate. All accommodation is in four- or two-bed bamboo bungalows on stilts. Beds with fan cost Y25. The bathrooms are clean and a solar-heated shower has been installed. Downers include a lack of privacy and the occasional rodent visitor.

The cheapest lodging on Manting Lu is the non-Dǎi **Dǎijiā Zhāodàisuǒ** (*☎ 213 9335, 69 Manting Lu*). A hard bed in a spartan triple costs Y15. The toilets are grim and showers mildly warm.

The **Bǎnnà Jiǔdiàn** (*☎ 213 2052*), with a good location at the southern end of Ganlan Lu has less character but better value doubles/triples with bathroom for Y50/70.

The **Ruìfēng Bīnguǎn** (*☎ 213 6449*) is currently an excellent-value modern choice on Minzu Lu. Spotless carpeted rooms with nice bathroom cost Y50.

More centrally located is the **Jǐngyǒng Fàndiàn** (*☎ 212 3430, 12 Jinghong Donglu*). Beds are Y30 in a triple. Clean doubles with fan and bath are Y80. For air-con, you'll pay Y180 for a double.

There are plenty of top-end hotels. In the heart of town, the **Banna Mansion Hotel** (*Bǎnnà Dàshà; ☎ 212 2049*) is Jǐnghóng's luxury option, with air-con doubles for Y238, and triples for Y316.

Probably the top is the **Tài Garden Hotel** (*Tàiyuán Jiǔdiàn; ☎ 212 3888, fax 212 6060, 8 Nonglin Nanlu*) south of town towards the airport. In quiet grounds with its own island, it has singles and doubles for US$70/80 plus 15%. Facilities include a pool, sauna, gym and tennis court.

Places to Eat

Manting Lu is the street to find Dǎi-style food. One drawback (or bonus) is that the majority dish up Dǎi dance performances with their culinary specialities ('singing and dancing hall' are tacked onto restaurant names). Bored-looking Dǎi women thump drums at the entrance and Chinese tourists whoop it up, hollering and generally being festive.

Dǎi dishes include roast fish, eel or beef cooked with lemon grass or served with peanut-and-tomato sauce. Vegetarians can order roast bamboo shoot prepared in the same fashion. Other mouth-watering specialities include fried river moss (excellent with beer) and spicy bamboo shoot soup. And try the glutinous black rice.

The best new place is the **Mekong Café** (*Méigōng Cānguǎn; ☎ 212 8895, 111 Manting Lu*), near the Dǎi Building Guesthouse. Well run and friendly, it has sofas, cold beer and excellent travellers' books. Owners Vicky and Orchid are good sources of travel information. A set Hani vegetarian meal is Y20 and there's Dǎi dishes such as steamed meat in banana leaves and sticky rice in a pineapple and banana flower. There's Western, Japanese and even a few Thai dishes and lots of juices. You can also use the Internet and hire bikes here. The upstairs balcony is a pleasant place to read about the sub-zero temperatures in Běijīng.

For good food, strong coffee, cold beer and all kinds of Western food, stop by the **Měi Měi Café** on the Manting Lu traffic junction, a pleasant little Akha hole-in-the-wall. Azhu, the owner, and her staff are great fun. Měi Měi's just started a laundry service and you can also rent bicycles here.

The **Forest Café**, across the road, is another good spot. It serves a decent hamburger, along with home-baked specialty breads (order ahead), good juices and more books than anywhere else.

There's a good choice of Chinese snack foods nearby. The Muslim **Xīnjiāng Lāmiànguǎn** next to the Forest Café serves excellent Central Asian fried *suoman* noodles for Y6. **Hāěrbīn Shuǐjiǎo** across the road serves great *jiǎozi* (Chinese ravioli), a specialty of north-eastern China.

Nearby, the pleasant **Lemon Grass Café** (*Xiāngyácǎo Xiǎochī*) serves Dǎi barbecue and other Dǎi dishes.

YUNNAN

A place aimed at Western backpackers is *James Café (Jiémǔsī Kāfēi)* on Manting Lu. It's pleasant with balcony tables overlooking Manting Lu.

Farther south down Manting Lu is a collection of grill-it-yourself skillet places, known as *gānguō*.

For Dǎi food in an unpretentious atmosphere, north of the market area on Ganlan Lu is the *Xīnguāng Jiǔjiā*, run by one of Xīshuāngbǎnnà's best-known traditional singers. The place is packed at lunch. No English here, so point and choose.

You can eat really well at the various *street stalls*, which sell kebabs, coconuts, bananas, sugar cane, papayas, pomelos and pineapples served peeled on a stick.

At night there's a huge *food market* by the new bridge over the Mekong. Dozens of stalls serve barbequed everything, from sausages to snails. There are lots of places to get a beer (one brews its own), play pool and stroll along the Mekong. There's also a small fairground.

There are several Burmese teahouses that sell coffee and milk tea (Y3) so sweet that it will peel the enamel from your teeth. The *Myanmar Mandalay Café* on Zhuanghong Lu (the jade sellers' street) has snack food. Look out for *palatar*, a Burmese crepe served hot and doused in sweetened condensed milk. A stall at the east end of Zhuanghong Lu sells it for Y3 and a nearby stall has spicy samosas. The basic *Maung Sein Myanmar Muslim Restaurant* is next door.

The *Burmese Teahouse* at the west end of Zhuanghong Lu also serves palatar along with betel nut and Mekong whisky and it is a good place to meet the local Burmese community.

The Tai Garden Hotel south-west of the National Minorities Park has a breakfast buffet for Y20, with OK coffee and an evening Cantonese buffet for Y30.

Entertainment

If walking around the Manting Lu area listening to minority women bang drums and gongs is not entertainment enough, there are a couple of bars in town. Look for the *Hope Club (Hàowàng)* on Jingde Lu.

The *Nationality Song and Dance Theatre (Mínzú Gēwǔ Jùyuàn)* on Jinghong Xilu has occasional ethnic performances, though it had been taken over by some strippers from Guǎngzhōu.

Shopping

Much of what tourists purchase in Bǎnnà is produced by minorities, usually Dǎi. Popular items include distinctively designed brocade bags, shirts, and wall hangings. Just visit some villages and buy it at the source. You can also get woven bamboo items.

There are plenty of places selling those indigo-and-white tie-dyed T-shirts with elephant patterns. What you think is a steal at one is someone else's starting price.

North of the Xīshuāngbǎnnà Bīnguǎn is Zhuanghong Lu, which is lined with dozens of Burmese jade shops, many of them run by Burmese muslims. It is a fascinating area. You will also find peacock fans, Burmese and Vietnamese dried fruit, Dǎi clothes shops and ridiculously priced carved wooden elephants.

A shop on Ganlan Lu sells locally produced honey.

Getting There & Away

Air More flights and bigger planes (737s) mean that it's usually possible to book the day before. In April (Water-Splashing Festival) you may need to book several days in advance. Be careful if you want to change your flight date on or around a weekend.

There are usually several flights daily to Kūnmíng (Y520) and daily flights to Dàlǐ (Y520), Lìjiāng (Y610) and Bangkok (Y1300). Shanghai Airlines offer a service to Shànghǎi via Kūnmíng (Y1670). Flights can be booked at the Yunnan Airlines booking office (☎ 212 7040) on Jingde Lu, open 8am to noon and 3pm to 6pm.

Bus The Jǐnghóng long-distance bus station has buses to towns around Xīshuāngbǎnnà, but it's mainly useful for more distant destinations. To explore locally go to the No 2 bus station which has frequent buses, minibuses and minivans everywhere from 7am to around 5pm. The ticket office

YÚNNÁN

is efficient but if you have problems walk through the station to the parking lot/departure area, and you'll find vans waiting for passengers. See the around Xīshuāngbǎnnà section for details on these.

There are daily buses between Kūnmíng and Jǐnghóng (see the Kūnmíng Getting There & Away section).

From the long-distance bus station, sleepers leave all day (Y120, 24 hours). There is a luxury express coach (seats not berths) at 4pm (Y146, 15 hours). The price includes bottled water and one meal. The No 2 station has a similar service at 6pm, as well as more sleeper services. Private companies offer more options.

The Jǐnghóng long-distance bus station also has buses to Xiàguān, Bǎoshān and Ruìlì. Seriously consider breaking the trip in Bǎoshān, if for no other reason than to preserve the last traces of pink in your lungs. Trips to Xiàguān, Ruìlì and Bǎoshān should not require an overnight stop if you're on a sleeper, but don't count on it. Non-sleeper buses to Xiàguān may overnight in Zhènyuán; while to Bǎoshān, Líncāng plays midway host to frazzled passengers. Sleepers to both Xiàguān and Bǎoshān (Y150, 28 to 36 hours) leave the long-distance bus station early in the morning and the No 2 bus station at 1.30pm. These routes are served by minibuses at times!

For the marathon trip (about 40 hours) to Ruìlì, seriously consider breaking the trip in Bǎoshān. Roads are quite poor and the buses not much better. If you choose this option, don't do it to save time – many travellers have found their two-day trip stretch to three and even four days as they encounter landslides, floods, roadside inspections, and bus breakdowns.

There is a daily sleeper bus to Gè'jiù (Y123, 24 hours) at 7am from the No 2 bust station. There is also a 7am sleeper to the Vietnamese border at Hékǒu (Y145) via Jiànshuǐ (Y109).

Boat These leave occasionally from the new bridge over the Mekong River for Gǎnlǎnbà and continue to the border with Laos, near Mámùshù. From here it is possible to get a bus to Měnglà. It's hard to find out about departures as people assume you want to charter a whole boat. You could make enquiries at the backpacker cafes.

There are no boats to Laos and Thailand.

Getting Around
Jǐnghóng is small enough to walk to most places, but a bike makes life much easier. The Xīshuāngbǎnnà Bīnguǎn, Mekong Café and Měi Měi Café rent bikes for around Y10 per day, or Y20 for a mountain bike.

Pedicab fares from the Xīshuāngbǎnnà Bīnguǎn to the No 2 bus station should be around Y2 per person.

Taxis are plentiful and cost Y7 for 2km and then Y1.7 per km after that.

To/From the Airport Airport buses meet planes at the airport for the 15 minute, 5km ride (Y2) into town. Buses for the airport leave when full across from the Yunnan Airlines office. A taxi will cost you around Y20.

AROUND JǏNGHÓNG
There are numerous villages near Jǐnghóng that can be reached by bicycle. Most of them are the kinds of places you happen upon by chance.

On the other side of the Mekong, a popular jaunt involves heading south down Manting Lu. If you go far enough you'll hit a ferry crossing point on the Mekong. Pay Y1 and cross, bike and all. After the crossing turn right at the first branch and then right again. There are plenty of lovely villages, temples and pagodas in this area, and many travellers have been invited into Dǎi homes for tea.

Another possible bike ride, for the fit, is from Jǐnghóng to Mandian Waterfall (see following). A much easier bike ride is south along the road to Dàměnglóng; take the left fork near the airport. About 15km from Jǐnghóng is **Manfeilong Reservoir**, a small lake with a tiny resort. Here you can rent jet-skis for Y60 per *minute* – don't worry, they stop timing every time you fall off. Some rooms might be available for about Y60. There's not much else to do on the lake, but it's a nice break if you're continuing south.

Mandian Waterfall 曼典瀑布
Màndiǎn Pùbù

On the road to Měnghǎi, about 6km to 8km outside Jǐnghóng, is a dirt road turn-off to the right near a small market. (If you miss it there should be another fork near Gādōng – take the middle dirt road.) From here it's about 25km to the waterfall that is near some Dǎi villages. Some of the hills can be real bears and during rainy season there's lots of mud. From the end of the bike road, it's about 45 minutes by foot to the falls. It's possible to reach other falls but these are dangerous and require dodgy climbs; take a local guide. The only place to stay here is with Dǎi families. Figure Y30 per person as a top-end price.

Sanchahe Nature Reserve
三岔河自然保护区 Sānchàhé Zìránbǎohùqū

Sānchàhé, 48km north of Jǐnghóng, is one of five enormous forest reserves in southern Yúnnán. This one has an area of nearly 1.5 million hectares.

The part of the park that most tourists visit is the **Banna Wild Elephant Valley** (Bǎnnà Yěxiànggǔ), named after the 40 or so wild elephants who live there. It's aimed squarely at busloads of Chinese tourists.

There are two entrances. The main southern entrance has accommodation, displays on tropical birds and butterflies and peacock shows. The other has 'wild' elephant performances for the shutterbug tourists. A 2km cable car (Y40) leads over the canopy from the main entrance into the heart of the park, or there is a pathway from the other entrance.

Accommodation at the main entrance ranges from Y20 per person in a concrete triple to Y120 for a decent double with views over the lake. There are also rooms for Y180 and Y220 and a couple of restaurants at both entrances. You can stay in a carpeted *canopy treehouse* in the heart of the park for Y220.

It is only possible to get off the main paths with a guide and that will cost Y200 per day. Admission is Y25. Ask about packages that include entry, food and accommodation for Y150.

Just about any bus travelling north from Jǐnghóng to Sīmáo will pass the reserve (Y10, one hour).

En route to the reserve, 8km from Jǐnghóng, you will pass the **Banna Primeval Forest Park** (Bǎnnà Yuánshǐ Sēnlín Gōngyuán), a poor version of the Sanchahe Reserve. Entry is Y25.

Měngyǎng 勐养

Měngyǎng, 34km north-east of Jǐnghóng on the road to Sīmáo, is a centre for the Hani, Lahu and 'Floral-Belt' Dǎi. Chinese tourists stop here to see the 'Banyan Tree Shaped like an Elephant' (Xiàngxíng Róngshù). You could cycle out to the nearby 'Floral Belt' Dǎi village of Manna'nan.

From Měngyǎng, it's 19km to **Jīnuò**, home for the Jinuo minority. Some travellers have reported a cool reception here, so you'll probably have to stay in Měngyǎng. It would help to travel with a local or to have some kind of introduction. Some minorities dislike tourists, and if this is the case with the Jinuo, their views should be respected.

GǍNLǍNBÀ (MĚNGHǍN) 勐罕

Gǎnlǎnbà (Olive Plain), or Měnghǎn as it's sometimes referred to, lies on the Mekong, 27km south-east of Jǐnghóng. The main attraction at Gǎnlǎnbà used to be the boat journey down the Mekong from Jǐnghóng. Passenger boats are now rare, and most tourists can't afford to charter a boat.

Nevertheless, Gǎnlǎnbà remains a wonderful retreat from hectic Jǐnghóng. If you come on a bike (you can hire one in Gǎnlǎnbà) there is plenty of scope to explore the local temples and pagodas.

Information

Check the visitors' book in the Sarlar Restaurant for ideas on bike trips to the surroundings.

Internet access is available for Y5 per hour at the New Century Net Bar, about 200m west of the Gǎnlǎnbà Bīnguǎn.

Things to See & Do

Following Manting Lu to the south-east (past the Gǎnlǎnbà Bīnguǎn) 2km or so brings you to the **Mengbala Banna Xiwang Park** (Měngbàlà Xīwàng Guǒyuánlín), a temple area where there's also tacky minority dancing and water-splashing festivals. The park features the stately **Wat Ban Suan Men** (Chūnmǎn Sì), a gorgeous gold Burmese pagoda, 730 years old. There are a couple of pleasant villages in the park area and a second pagoda, known as the **Màntīng Fósì Dàdú Tǎ**. The park has a pricey admission fee of Y20.

There are numerous temples and villages in the area worth exploring. There's a couple of old decaying temples on the road into town from Jǐnghóng, and nearby is a huge **tourist market** (nóngtè chǎnpǐn gòuwù shìchǎng), where visiting tour groups rush out and try to spend as much money as is humanly possible in six minutes (see the panic in their eyes). You can get all kinds of regional specialities here from mounted butterflies to Dǎi dresses and back scratchers to weird tropical fruit. There are some lovely Dǎi houses nearby decorated with traditional peacock designs. To the south of this, overlooking the Mekong, is a white stupa.

Those who have spent some time here recommend striking off by bike on day trips, heading to the south of town, taking the ferry over the Mekong (Y2 with a bike), and then heading left (east) to Jǐnghā and beyond.

Places to Stay

Currently the most popular backpacker option is the friendly **Sarlar Restaurant** (Shālā Cāntīng), which has a few 'rooms' (a corner of the restaurant partitioned off by a piece of wood) with Dǎi-style mats on the floor for Y10. Check if the sheets are clean and don't expect to get to sleep early – this place isn't for everyone. Still, the bathrooms and shower are clean, the food is good and it's a great place to leaf through the travellers' books. To get here, continue past the Dǎi Bamboo House until just before the road begins to bend to the right. Carved dragons grace the entrance.

The family-run **Dǎi Bamboo House** (Dǎijiā Zhúlóu), on the right-hand side of

Jinlun Donglu, the main road travelling away from Jǐnghóng, has recently gone downhill fast. It still offers a mat on the floor but little else.

More formal lodging is available a block south of the Dǎi Bamboo House on Manting Lu at the **Gǎnlǎnbà Bīnguǎn** (☎ 241 1233). Beds start at Y30 in a quad and passable doubles with bathroom are Y100. There's 24-hour hot water.

Probably the best value is the **Lóngfèng Dàjiǔdiàn**, across the road from the Gǎnlǎnbà Bīnguǎn, where a double with OK bathroom costs Y40.

Places to Eat

If you don't want to eat at either of the Dǎi houses, there's a couple of options. At lunchtime there is a popular buffet-style Dǎi food stall at the main road intersection in the centre of town.

Follow the road south from that intersection to Manting Lu – you'll find several Dǎi restaurants with pleasant wooden balconies.

The **Dǎi Family Restaurant** on the corner has an English menu on the wall but there are no prices so check before you order as food is a little pricey.

Farther along Manting Lu the **Chuānqián Fàndiàn** is a friendly Chinese restaurant that serves good cheap food.

A house on Manting Lu on the left as you cycle to the Mangbala Park sells neat rice wine (chúnmǐjiǔ).

Getting There & Away

Microbuses to Gǎnlǎnbà leave from the Jǐnghóng No 2 bus station every 20 minutes (Y7, 45 minutes). Minibuses depart Gǎnlǎnbà for Jǐnghóng and Měnglún from the main intersection.

It's possible to cycle from Jǐnghóng to Gǎnlǎnbà in a leisurely three hours, and it's a pleasant ride.

Getting Around

The only way to do this is by bicycle or hiking. You can rent a mountain bike at the Sarlar Restaurant or at a private shop a few doors down for Y10 to Y15 per day. If they're all out, walk back towards town to the main intersection where an elderly bicycle repair man rents out Chinese bikes for Y10 per day.

MĚNGLÚN

Often a pit stop for buses to Laos, Měnglún is the next major port of call east of Gǎnlǎnbà, which explains the number of restaurants in town.

Things to See

The major attraction is the **Tropical Botanical Gardens** (Rèdài Zhíwùyuán). The 933 hectares of garden are well laid out, and tour groups give it a festive atmosphere, though the concrete paths and guides toting bullhorns quickly dash any hopes of communing with nature. Over 2000 species of tropical plants have been introduced since 1959 and you'll also find every conceivable species existing in Xīshuāngbǎnnà. Look out for Artiaris Toxicana, which local hunters once used to coat their poisoned arrows. The gardens are over the river, but the entrance is on the northern bank.

To get there, turn left out of the bus station and walk to the first corner. Walk one block and turn left again. You'll come to market hawkers, and a road leading downhill to the right side. Follow this until you reach a footbridge across the Mekong. The ticket booth is just in front of the bridge and the entry fee is Y35, though even the most suspect student card reduces this to Y20.

A ten-minute bus ride west of Měnglún towards Gǎnlǎnbà, at kilometre marker 63, is the **Banna Rain Forest Valley** (Bǎnnà Yǔlíngǔ), a small but fairly pleasant state-level protected area of forest compete with an aerial walkway (though not as good as the walkway at Bupan outside Měnglà – see that section for details). This is primarily a Chinese tourist spot so there's concrete paths and no-smoking signs but if you get there between 4pm and 5pm you should have the place to yourself. Hopping on a bus back to Měnglún is easy. Entry is Y20, or Y16 for students.

There are a couple of lovely Dǎi villages between Měnglún and the valley. If you have time, continue on the Jǐnghóng-Měnglà highway, straight through town for 3km (passing a second entrance to the gardens) to a **forest reserve**. There is no word on whether it's open, but nobody's been kicked out yet so it may be ripe for exploring, following all trail etiquette of course.

Places to Stay & Eat

The best value is the **Bus Station Hotel** with beds in a comfortable quad for Y10, with a bathroom and shower down the hall.

Other options include the **Chūnlín Lǜshè** (☎ 871 7172), 50m in front of the entrance to the gardens, with basic doubles from Y30. Take a look at a number of rooms, as it has many options.

Fēnghuá Jiǔlóu, a block west, has a better range of rooms set around a courtyard from Y20 to Y50. You can get a good room with bathroom for Y30.

There is also accommodation within the gardens. Cross the bridge, follow the main path for about 10 minutes to a group of buildings and a fork in the road, take the left fork and you will find a grungy **zhāodàisuǒ** with dorms beds for Y20, though these can often be booked out by student groups. For a more upmarket stay, take the right fork, go over the hill and to the left of the pond, where there is the damp but clean **Zhíwùyuán Bīnguǎn** *(Botanical Gardens Hotel)*, with doubles/triples with bathroom for Y180/210, the former discounted to Y100.

Otherwise, the top lodgings in town are the **Cùixīnyuán Dàjiǔdiàn** (☎ 871 5711) or the **Grand Sanyang Hotel** *(Sānyáng Dàjiǔdiàn)*, both with rooms for Y80.

Měnglún has loads of restaurants. **The Friendship Restaurant** *(Yǒuyì Cāntīng)* on the main road has lots of dishes made from strange vegetables, ferns and herbs only found locally. The chef is happy for you to go out back and leaf through the options.

Getting There & Away

From Jǐnghóng's No 2 bus station there are buses every 45 minutes until 3pm to Měnglún (Y11 to Y13, two hours). The buses pass through Gǎnlǎnbà. Some travellers have cycled here from Gǎnlǎnbà.

From Měnglún, there are minibuses (Y16, three hours) and faster Iweco buses (Y20, 2½ hours) to Měnglà every 30 minutes or so. Most buses travelling between Jǐnghóng and Měnglà stop here. The last bus back to Jǐnghóng is around 7pm. To get to Jīnuò you'll have to take a Sīmáo-bound bus.

MĚNGLÀ 勐腊

Měnglà sees an increasing number of travellers passing through en route to Laos, via the border crossing at Móhǎn. As the bus journey from Jǐnghóng, or even Měnglún, will take the better part of the day, you will probably overnight here. Don't expect a wild border town; Měnglà is still just a small town trying to find something to do on a Saturday night.

CITS has an office with English-speaking staff at the Měnglà Bīnguǎn, which is about 2km uphill from the northern bus station.

The Bank of China in the southern half of town changes cash and travellers cheques but won't give cash advances for a credit card. To change Renminbi back into US dollars you'll need your original exchange receipts. The bank is open weekdays 8am to 11.30am and 3pm to 6pm.

Things To See

A day trip from Měnglà might include a stop at the **Bupan Aerial Skyway Park** (Wàngtiānshù Zǒuláng), a 45-minute bus ride (Y7) to the north. It has a 500m long rickety walkway 40m above the ground that showcases the rare Chinese parashorea tree (known locally as 'Looking at the Sky Tree' in Chinese because of its height and fast growth). A short trail leads around the forest. Entry is Y20, which includes Y2 life insurance (gulp!); Y17 for students. To get here take an hourly minibus to Měngbàn or Yáoqū. The last bus back is around 5.30pm.

About five minutes out of Měnglá town in the direction of the park is a golden **pagoda** on a distant hillside that makes for a good hike.

There are a couple of basic guesthouses in Měngbàn, which you could use as a base to hike up to surrounding **Yao minority villages**. Don't stray too close to the Lao border.

Places to Stay & Eat

Nánjiāng Bīnguǎn offers pretty good quads with common bathroom for Y15 per bed.

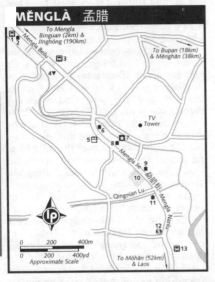

MĚNGLÀ 孟腊

To Mengla Binguan (2km) & Jīnghóng (190km)
To Bupan (18km) & Měnghǎn (38km)
TV Tower
Qingnian Lu
To Móhǎn (52km) & Laos

0   200   400m
0   200   400yd
Approximate Scale

1	Long-Distance Bus Station 长途汽车站	5	Cinema 电影院
2	Jīnqiáo Dàjiǔdiàn 金桥大酒店	6	Nánjiāng Bīnguǎn 南疆宾馆
3	Main Long-Distance Bus Station 汽车总站	7	PSB 公安局
4	Restaurants 饭店	8	Jinxiu Grand Hotel
		9	Suìfēng Bīnguǎn 穗丰宾馆
10	Public Square 广场		
11	Jīnxiàng Bīnguǎn 金象宾馆		
12	Bank of China 中国银行		
13	Southern Bus Station 汽车南站		

YÚNNÁN

A cafe overlooking one of the many flowing canals found in Yúnnán's picturesque Lìjiāng

Walking home after a hard day's work with Guìlín's karst hills as backdrop

A ferryboat ride along the Yangzi River amidst the peaks of Hābā Shān at Tiger Leaping Gorge

JOHN BORTHWICK

Taking a break in Yúnnán's old town Lìjiāng

THOMAS HUHTI

Muslim chef cooking up a storm in Kūnmíng

BILL WASSMAN

The centuries old art of sculpting in Sìchuān

BILL WASSMAN

Bai at the Shāpíng market in Yúnnán

FRANK CARTER

The art of handcrafting wood in Kūnmíng

Tiny singles for Y22 and doubles with bathroom for Y50 are not so good. Standard doubles cost Y80. Look at a few rooms because for one that's passable, another is putrid.

Across from the main square is the chaotic *Suìfēng Bīnguǎn*, which has similar priced rooms that aren't as good.

There are several other places you could try, including the *Jīnqiáo Dàjiǔdiàn* by the northernmost bus station, which has varying rooms from Y30 to Y50 and the new *Jīnxiàng Bīnguǎn*, which has decent doubles with bathroom for Y40.

Měnglà Bīnguǎn, 2km north of town, has dorm beds for around Y20, and doubles with bathroom and TV for Y60. A pedicab should get you there for Y4.

Jīnxiù Grand Hotel in the centre of town is the top-end choice, with an outside pool and rooms for Y148 and Y280.

There are a few basic *restaurants* around town and a couple of buffet style places across from the bus station.

Getting There & Away

There are four or five direct buses a day from Jǐnghóng's No 2 bus station to Měnglà. The long-distance bus station also has departures five times a day between 6.40am and 5.30pm (Y20 to Y25, five to seven hours).

Měnglà has three bus stations. The main long-distance bus station has buses to Kūnmíng at 6.30, 8 and 9.30am (Y138, 24 hours) and many departures to Jǐnghóng via Gǎnlǎnbà (Y26 to Y31). If there's nothing suitable try the other long-distance bus station 200m farther north.

The southern bus station has buses to Móhàn (Y10, 1½ hours) on the border, along with other long-distance buses and a few to Jǐnghóng.

Laos Border Crossing

First off, do *not* expect to turn up at the border and get a visa, tourist or transit, as it's officially impossible. Get one in Kūnmíng before you leave.

This crossing sees a fair amount of traffic. From Měnglà, there are buses to Móhàn from the southern bus station every 30 minutes or so from 8am. Once your passport is

stamped *(double check all stamps!)* you can jump on a tractor *(tuōlājī)* or truck to take you the 3km into Laos for around Y3; drivers will approach you on the Lao side. If you can't find a bus to Móhàn, go to Shàngyǒng and arrange another ride.

Go early. Laos border checkpoints are supposed to be open until 5.30pm on the Lao side (Laos is one hour ahead) but they can occasionally wrap up around noon. If they do remain open, you may have to factor in epic lunch breaks.

On China's side, there's a *guesthouse* opposite the customs office. Look for a sign in English/Lao/Chinese advertising beds from Y15. The showers and bathrooms are out in a compound.

There are reports that the Lao side now has a guesthouse on a dirt road west of the main road with rooms. There's also a National Tourism Authority of Laos office here, but its always closed.

Try to change money in Laos if possible. You can change money in Móhàn at a medical clinic/store underneath the guesthouse but rates are bad. On the Lao side, the duty free shop offers OK rates; otherwise, just change a small amount and wait until you get to Luang Nam Tha.

For more information on crossing from Laos to China see the Land section of the Getting There & Away chapter.

DÀMĚNGLÓNG 大勐龙

Dàměnglóng (written as 'Menglong' on buses) is about 70km south of Jǐnghóng near the Myanmar border. It's another sleepy village that is a good base for hikes around the surrounding hills. The village does rouse itself for the Sunday market, but the surrounding countryside, peppered with decaying stupas and little villages, is more of an attraction.

The town's laid-back feel may change, however. The border crossing point with Myanmar (poetically named 2-4-0) has been designated as the entry point for a planned highway linking Thailand, Myanmar and China. If it opens, life should pick up in Dàměnglóng. This does not mean the Myanmar government will allow border crossings; if they won't allow it at Ruìlì, they probably won't allow it here.

Mànfēilóng Tǎ 曼飞龙塔

This pagoda, built in 1204, is Dàměnglóng's premier attraction. According to legend, the temple was built on the spot of a hallowed footprint left by Sakyamuni, who once visited Xīshuāngbǎnnà. Look for it in a niche below one of the nine stupas. Unfortunately, in recent years a 'beautification' job was done on the temple with a cans of silver paint.

If you're in Xīshuāngbǎnnà in late October or early November, check for the precise dates of the **Tan Ta Festival**. Mànfēilóng Tǎ is host to celebrations that include dancing, rockets, paper balloons and so on.

Mànfēilóng Tǎ is easy to get to: just walk back along the main road towards Jǐnghóng for 2km until you reach a small village with a temple on your left. From here there's a path up the hill; it's about 20-minute walk. There's a Y5 admission fee.

Hēi Tǎ 黑塔

Just above the centre of town is a Dǎi monastery with a steep path beside it that leads up to this pagoda – you will notice it when entering Dàměnglóng. The name means Black Pagoda but it is actually covered in gold paint. Take a stroll up, but the real reason for the climb is the stunning view of Dàměnglóng and the surrounding countryside.

Places to Stay & Eat

To get to the low-key *Dàměnglóng Zhāodàisuǒ*, walk uphill from the traffic circle to the local government building. The hotel is in the grounds to the left, past some ornamental frogs. Basic dorm beds are Y10. Bathrooms are fragrant but passable. Bicycles can be rented for Y3 per hour, or Y15 per day.

Qìchēzhàn Zhāodàisuǒ (Bus Station Guesthouse) still might not take foreigners, but there's another cheap place at the base of the Hēi Tǎ.

Down from the bus station, near the steps leading up to the Hēi Tǎ are a couple of decent *restaurants*. The Chinese signs proclaim

them to be Dǎi restaurants, but it's the old story of going out the back, pointing to your vegetables and getting them five minutes later in a little pool of oil. Dàměnglóng specialises in *shaōkaǒ*, skewers of meat wrapped in banana leaves grilled over wood fires.

Getting There & Away

There are buses to Dàměnglóng (Y13, 2½ hours) every half-hour between 7am and 5pm (occasionally until 7pm) from Jǐnghóng's No 2 bus station. Purchase your tickets on the bus – just walk through the station and across the parking lot to the far left corner. Remember the 'Da' character won't be painted on the bus window. Buses for the return trip run on a similar schedule, though the last bus tends to leave earlier.

AROUND DÀMĚNGLÓNG

The village of **Xiǎojīe**, about 15km northeast of Dàměnglóng, is surrounded by Bulang, Lahu and Hani villages. Lahu women shave their heads; apparently the younger Lahu women aren't happy about this and wear caps. The Bulang may be descended from the Yi of northern Yúnnán. The women wear black turbans with silver decorations; many of the designs are of shells, fish and marine life.

There's plenty of room for exploration, although you're not allowed over the border.

MĚNGHǍI

This uninspiring place serves as a centre for trips into the surrounding area and to visit the markets at Xīdìng and Měnghùn. The Sunday market at Měnghǎi attracts members of the local hill tribes – follow the early morning crowds.

Měnghǎi is famed as the producer of pu'er tea, a noted Xīshuāngbǎnnà speciality hailed by emperors since the Qing dynasty. Wild tea trees, some around 1500 years old, grow everywhere. The Yúnnán Tea Research Institute produces over 30 kinds of tea for sale here including Bincha, a popular iced tea soft drink. The Nestle Company has set up an operational coffee farm. Groups can take tours though it might not be easy for solo travellers.

Trekking in Xīshuāngbǎnnà

Treks around Xīshuāngbǎnnà used to be among the best in China – you'd be invited into a local's home to eat, sleep and drink *báijiǔ*. Increasing numbers of travellers have changed that. But Xīshuāngbǎnnà is a big place, and to quote a long-time walker in the area, 'All you need to do is throw two darts at a map and walk between those two villages along local trails.' Self-directed trekking like this is possible, but, hey, it's a jungle out there, so take a local, go prepared, and make sure somebody knows where you're going and when you should be back.

Travel responsibly; don't expect a welcome mat and free lunch because you are a foreigner, but don't go changing the local economy by throwing money around either. In the rainy season you'll need to be equipped with proper hiking shoes and waterproofs. At any time you'll need water purification, bottled water or a water bottle able to hold boiling water, as well as snacks and sunscreen.

Dàměnglóng-Bùlǎngshān Trek

The most popular walk is this long two-day-or-more, 48km trek through Dǎi, Hani, Bulang and Lahu villages. It can be done in either direction. This is a poor area but the people are still friendly and the jungle pristine. If you do get invited in, try to establish whether payment is expected. If it's not then leave an offering of around Y10 or leave modest gifts such as candles, matches, rice etc, even though the family may insist on nothing. You'll find it easier to arrange accommodation if you arrive in a village before dark.

Start by taking a bus to Dàměnglóng (see Dàměnglóng's Getting There & Away section). From there it's a 10km-or-so walk or hitch on a tractor to the Dǎi village of Manguanghan. One bus should leave Dàměnglóng each day at noon, but this is neither certain nor necessary. Take the path to the right, 200m beyond the end of Manguanghan. It's a steady 12km walk for three-or-so hours to Manpo, a Bulang village. As you cross through Guangmin, an Aini village en route, look out for a temple. After staying overnight in a villager's home in Manpo, the next day is a 24km (5½ to six hours) walk to Weidong via Nuna (Bulang people), Songéer (Lahu people), and Bannankan (Lahu). In Manpo, ask for the right path to Weidong (the path goes down), and there are three or four places where you may lose the trail (particularly just after Songéer) and have to backtrack – but that's part of the fun. Overnight in Weidong and the next day walk another leisurely 10km (three hours) to Bùlǎngshān on a good road. If you just want to spend one night on the trail, a family in Songéer offers accommodation and two meals for Y20 per person. From Manpo to Songéer is three hours walk.

From Bùlǎngshān there are minibuses back to Měnghǎi (via Měnghùn) at 8am and 2.30pm. If you have to spend the night there is a truck stop/karaoke spot in town with dorm beds, but you'll probably be kept awake by drinking truckers offering you smokes. Try to find a local to put you up.

If you're short of time, on the second day you could get to Bùlǎngshān from Manpo without overnighting in Weidong. It's an epic day of trekking but the trail is mostly level, with only a minor uphill grade. Those in shape can probably finish in nine hours.

If you time it right you could stop over in Měnghùn's Sunday market on the way back to Jǐnghóng, or start the trek in Bùlǎngshān and visit the market en route to the town.

Guides

One travel agency catering to these treks is the Mengyuan Travel Service in Jǐnghóng (see the Jǐnghóng Travel Agencies section). For a guide and transport you'll pay a minimum of Y80 to Y100 per person per day. Vicky and Orchid at the Mekong Café and Sarah at the Forest Café, both in Jǐnghòng, can also put you in touch with a guide. One of the main advantages of taking a guide is to communicate with villagers en route; you won't hear much Mandarin Chinese on the trail, let alone any English.

Places to Stay

The flashy *Bus Station Hotel* has comfortable double rooms for Y80 that can be negotiated down to Y60.

The *Liángyuán Bīnguǎn (Grain Hotel)* across the street has beds in triples for Y20 each and doubles/triples for Y60. There are other basic hotels with beds for Y10 to Y15.

A five-minute walk north along the main street is the *Tiānyuánqín Bīnguǎn (Commercial City Hotel)*, which has nice doubles with bathroom for Y168, discounted to Y80.

The top joint in town is the *Jīnfú Jiǔdiàn (☎ 519 0069)* in the south-west end of town, not far from the golden pagoda. Doubles range from Y160 to Y220 and come with hot water and air-conditioning.

Getting There & Away

Buses run from Jínghóng's No 2 bus station to Měnghǎi (Y7, 90 minutes) every half-hour between 7.30am and 5.30pm.

Měnghǎi's flashy new bus station in the south of town has departures throughout the region. Minibuses run to Bùlǎngshān at 9am and 2pm, to Xīdìng (Y10, three hours) at 10.40am and 3.30pm and to Gélǎnghé (Y7.50) at 11am and 4.30pm.

AROUND MĚNGHǍI

On the outskirts of Měnghǎi towards Měnghùn is a **golden pagoda**, a very popular Chinese tourist pit stop.

To the north of Měnghǎi there are pagodas and interesting villages that make for fine exploring on bicycle. Around 5km east of town and then 1km north is another particularly impressive golden pagoda. Farther east, 11km from Měnghǎi (at kilometre marker 3096) is an interesting four-storey **mosque**, replete with minaret.

Měnghùn 勐混

This tiny village is about 26km south-west of Měnghǎi. Some prefer the **Sunday market** here to that of Měnghǎi. It begins buzzing around 7am and lasts until noon. The swirl of hill tribes and women sporting fancy leggings, headdresses, earrings and bracelets alone make the trip worthwhile. The market is a popular day trip from Jínghóng.

Places to Stay & Eat The secluded *White Tower Hotel (Báitǎ Lǚshè)* is a basic place but is quiet and looks out over a lily pond. A hard bed in a basic double costs Y10, and there are squat toilets in the courtyard. To get here from the main intersection, take the road uphill, walk through the archway, bear left across the basketball court then follow a small path; around the corner is the hotel.

In the centre of town where the buses let you off, the *Yúnchuān Lǚshè* also has basic concrete rooms for Y10 to Y20.

Farther down, on the other side of the street, the *Fènghuáng Fàndiàn (Phoenix Hotel)* is cheaper at Y5 a bed, but is noisy.

In between the two is the *Yúnchuān Fàndiàn*, a decent place to get lunch and wait for your bus.

There are several good Dǎi *restaurants* along the main street.

Getting There & Away Buses from Jínghóng to Měnghùn (Y11.50, two hours) leave the Jínghóng No 2 bus station every 20 minutes between 7am and 5.40pm. The earlier you depart the more you'll see of the market.

Going back to Jínghóng you'll just have a short wait on the side of the road until a bus passes by. You could visit Jǐngzhēn on the way back – get off at the main crossroads (where the snack sellers frantically try to sell passengers fish on a stick), catch the first transport headed west and get off about 10km later.

If you are headed to Bùlǎngshān buses pass through Měnghùn at 9.30am and 3pm

Unless you have very good gears, cycling to Měnghùn is not a realistic option. The road up to Měnghǎi is so steep that you'll push the bike most of the way. After Měnghǎi, however, the ride to Měnghùn is good most of the way.

Around Měnghùn

Near Manguo Village, 8km south-east of Měnghùn, is a cluster of **pagodas** atop Guangjingha Hill. Built in 1746, the grouping is one large, 17m-high pagoda ringed by eight more, beneath which lie sacred ashes of Bazaiyapa Pasa. You could hire a tractor

The Hani, Jinuo & Lahu

BRADLEY MAYHEW

The Hani (also known in adjacent countries as the Akha) are of Tibetan origin, but according to folklore they are descended from frogs' eyes. They are closely related to the Yi as a part of the Tibeto-Burman group; the language is Sino-Tibetan but uses Han characters for the written form.

They are famed mostly for their river valley rice terraces, especially in the Red River valley, between the Ailao and Wuliang Shān, where they cultivate rice, corn and the occasional poppy. There is a great variety in dress amongst the Hani, particularly between the Xīshuāngbǎnnà and the Hónghé Hānǐ around Yuányáng. Hani women (especially the Aini, a subgroup of the Hani) wear headdresses of beads, feathers, coins and silver rings, some of which are made with French (Vietnamese), Burmese and Indian coins from the turn of the century.

The Hani have two animated New Year celebrations. The seven-day **Misezha**, New Year festival, takes place in the 10th month of the lunar calendar; this is followed by the **Kuzhazha** god-worshipping celebration in the sixth lunar month, lasting three to six days. As part of festivals, the Hani use an ox hide swing to symbolically ward off bad fortune and augur a favourable year ahead.

The Hani are famed for their hospitality, though whether this endures increasing tourist contact remains to be seen.

The Jinuo, sometimes known as the Youle, were officially 'discovered' as a minority in 1979. The women wear a white cowl, a cotton tunic with bright horizontal stripes and a tubular black skirt. Ear lobe decoration is an elaborate custom – the larger the hole and the more flowers it can contain the better. Their teeth are sometimes painted black with the sap of the lacquer tree, which serves the dual dental purpose of beautifying the mouth and preventing tooth decay and halitosis.

Previously, the Jinuo lived in long houses with as many as 27 families occupying rooms on both sides of the central corridor. Each family had its own hearth, but the oldest man owned the largest hearth, always the closest to the door. Long houses are rarely used now and the Jinuo seem to be quickly losing their distinctive way of life. The **Temaoke Festival** is held in Jinuo villages on the 6th to 8th of the second lunar month.

The Lahu people occupy a narrow belt of land between the Wa and Dǎi people's area, along the Mekong River. Though they've adopted agrarian practices through the Han, the Lahu are still called 'Tiger Hunters' for their one-time prowess at tracking and lack of fear. The Lahu language is of the Sino-Tibetan family; tiger is pronounced as 'la', and 'hu' means 'to roast tiger meat with flavour'. Lahu houses all contain shotguns and crossbows; hunting dogs are still revered, and are even buried by families when they die. Hunters still put tufts of hair or feathers on their weapons for every animal they kill. Not limited to animals, the Lahu in the early 18th century also made their presence known to humans, threatening Luang Prabang, Laos, and border regions of Thailand and Burma. They weren't pacified by China until the end of the 19th century.

The Lahu's distinctive dress is similar to that in certain areas of northern China. The women wear a skirt with a high slit, silver ball buttons and no belt. The men wear a necklace coat buttoned on the right and loose pants. Men and women traditionally shave their heads, leaving a tuft of hair, called their 'soul'. Women usually wrap their heads in a metre of black cloth.

Customarily, a man lives with his wife's family after marriage and there's no preference for sons. But what the Lahu have always been famous for is smoking. If you're a guest, don't offend by neglecting to offer cigarettes to grandma too.

to get to Manguo for about Y15 return, from where you could walk up the hill. Ask in town for more information.

In the village of Manlei, about 7km west of Měnghǎi, are the **twin pagodas**, built in 1746. The taller one is 9m, the shorter one 7m. A temple sits between them.

A few kilometres south-west of Manlei is the **Manduan Wat** in Manduan Village, dating from 1132. Built on 50cm-diameter poles, the heads of each are carved into a lotus or painted like a dragon.

Octagonal Pavilion 八角亭
Bājiǎo Tíng
In the village of Jǐngzhēn, about 14km north-west of Měnghǎi, is this pagoda and temple complex, first built in 1701. The original structure was severely damaged during the Cultural Revolution but renovated in 1978 and the ornate decoration is still impressive. The temple also operates as a monastic school. The paintings on the wall of the temple depict scenes from the Jataka, the life history of Buddha.

Jǐngzhēn is a pleasant rural spot for walks along the river or the fish ponds behind the village. Frequent minibuses from the minibus centre in Měnghǎi go via Jǐngzhēn.

Xīdìng
This village has one of the best markets in the region, every Sunday and Thursday. To get here by public transport you'll probably have to change buses in Měnghǎi (see previous section), from where it's about 1½ hours. If you want to see the market at its most interesting you'll really have to get there the night before. There is a small guesthouse 100m from the bus station.

MÈNGLIÁN 孟连
Although it's technically not in Xīshuāng-bǎnnà, Mènglián is a quick and worthwhile side trip for anyone attempting the epic journey between Jǐnghóng and the Bǎoshān or Déhóng regions. If the Myanmar border regulations are ever relaxed, it would also offer another crossing point.

Mènglián is a big draw for Chinese artists because of its heady dose of minority culture.

Of its 16 minority groups, Dǎi and Lahu are a considerable segment and it's also one of the few places where you experience large numbers of Wa. An old town lined with a few cobblestone walkways rises into the hills.

Information
Internet access is available at the New Tidal Wave Computers (Xīn Lànghú Diànnǎo) for Y9 per hour.

The Mènglián Travel Service (☎ 872 2122), at the entrance to the Kǒngquè Bīnguǎn, can give information on visiting local sights but the staff don't speak much English.

Things to See
Mènglián has an old town up in the hills and a new, soulless part of town built on a grid pattern, where you'll arrive and sleep. In this lower section of town, in the far south-west next to a canal, is the **Jīn Tǎ** (Golden Pagoda). Admission is Y2 and the friendly caretaker might open the temple's cosy interiors to you. You'll find a Buddha statue, other statues, and Dǎi and Burmese script on the walls. If you do get in, leave a donation.

From here, head to the old town and a small **market** where the roadway is lined with Hani, Dǎi and Wa farmers.

Virtually any alley leading up the hill from this point will take you past earthy, traditional mud or wood homes; you can't miss the first alley past the bank.

As you head up through the village you'll see the **Zhōngchéng Fósì**, a Dǎi temple with some pretty gold leaf designs.

MÈNGLIÁN

PLACES TO STAY	OTHER	9	Bank of China
5 Mènglián Bīnguǎn 孟连宾馆	1 Shàngchéng Lóng Miànsì 上城龙缅寺		中国银行
10 Kǒngquè Bīnguǎn 孔雀宾馆	2 Mènglián Dǎi People's House Museum 孟连宣抚司署	11	Mènglián Travel Service 孟连旅行社
16 Kāngfú Bīnguǎn 康福宾馆		12	New Tidal Wave Computers 新浪潮电脑
PLACES TO EAT	3 Zhōngchéng Fósì 中城佛寺	13	Customs House 海关
15 Dǎi Barbeque Vendors 傣味烧烤	4 Bank 银行	14	PSB 公安局
18 Jiāchángwèi Fàndiàn 家常味饭店	6 Local Bus Station 县汽车站	17	Main Bus Station 汽车总站
19 Shùnjūn Fàndiàn 顺君饭店	7 Xīnhuá Bookstore 新华书店	20	Market 集贸市场
21 Dǎijiā Fàndiàn 傣家饭店	8 PSB 公安局	22	Jīn Tǎ 金塔

The real attraction in the old town is the **Mènglián Dǎi People's House Museum** (Mènglián Xuānfǔ Sīshú), the largest and best-preserved of Yúnnán's 18 traditional minority 'clan houses' and used as a residence and meeting hall by the group's elders and high officials. Though Sīmáo now holds sway over the county, Mènglián was once the centre of Dǎi culture, predating Sīmáo and its rulers, which once lavished gifts on the Dǎi leader in Mènglián.

This structure was originally built in 1289 during the Yuan dynasty and held 28 generations of Dǎi rulers. It has now been turned into a museum and the upper floor features historical artefacts ranging from guns to court clothing and Dǎi manuscripts. A side room and shrine was once used as quarters for visiting dignitaries. Admission is Y2 and there are no set hours; generally, there's always somebody about, dawn to dusk.

Farther uphill (take a right just before the museum) is the three-storey **Shàngchéng Lóng Miànsì**, the most active temple in town, with two golden pagodas to the side.

Back in the centre of town the large **central market** is worth a look, especially during the weekly market, held every five days.

Places to Stay

Probably the best bet is the large **Kǒngquè Bīnguǎn** (Peacock Hotel), connected to the Bank of China. There's a range of rooms, with beds for Y10/30 without/with bathroom, and doubles with a spotlessly clean bathroom for Y100, discounted to Y50. Staff are friendly and there's plenty of room for negotiation.

The friendly **Mènglián Bīnguǎn**, at the bridge in the old part of town, has passable rooms with bathroom for Y30, Y50 and Y60 but there's no hot water.

The **Kāngfú Bīnguǎn**, across the street from the bus station has clean smart singles/doubles with squat toilet for Y60/80.

Places to Eat

The friendly **Jiāchángwèi Fàndiàn** next to the bus station serves good food and will try to accommodate you, though there's no English menu.

A block west is the similar **Shùnjūn Fàndiàn**.

Walking towards town from the bus station, turn left at the first intersection and then take the first right to the **Dǎijiā Fàndiàn**, which serves Dǎi specialties.

Mènglián also has some fine street food. Dǎi **barbecue vendors** congregate every afternoon a block west of the bus station but it's all over by around 6.30pm. You'll see local dried sausages all over town, and the odd Burmese vendor selling palatar (see Jinghong Places to Eat for details).

Getting There & Away

If you're headed for Mènglián from Déhóng or Bǎoshān, you're probably looking at an overnight stay in Láncāng to the north-east; buses from Jīnghóng get you there in a morning. Buses from the No 2 bus station in Jīnghóng leave for Mènglián at 8.30am and 11.30am.

The Mènglián bus station has a few buses back up to Láncāng (Y10, 1½ hours), where you may have to go to organise any long-distance transport outside Jīnghóng or Sīmáo. There are buses at 7.30, 8.30, 10 and 11am and 1pm to Jīnghóng (Y39, seven hours). Four buses to Sīmáo leave prior to noon (Y40, seven hours). You may find a sleeper bus to Xiàguān (Y130).

Buses for local destinations, including to Fuai and the border area at Mengma, leave from a second bus station near the Mènglián Bīnguǎn.

AROUND MÈNGLIÁN

About 5km from Mènglián, boats can be rented (around Y10) for riverside tours on the Nanlei River. It's also possible to go swimming and to explore caves nearby. West of Mènglián in the Dǎi village of Mengma there is reportedly another fine pagoda, the **Xiangya Tǎ**, and a waterfall about 10km south of the town.

If nothing else, travellers can hop on a Mengma-bound bus (Y5, one hour) just to sniff around (but not cross!) the markets around the border area.

Minority Villages 民族村

Of the 16 minority groups, you'll mostly encounter Dǎi, Lahu and Wa. Mengma, near the border, has sizeable numbers of Lahu, while Wa are mostly encountered in Fuai to the west or Làlěi to the south. Both Fuai and Làlěi have markets every five days. Buses depart from Mènglián to Fuai (Y7, one hour) at 8am and 11am and 4.30pm. There should be a single afternoon bus to Làlěi at 4pm, which would involve staying the night.

LÁNCĀNG 澜沧

Láncāng is a cheerful if not aesthetically pleasing town, a crossroads between Mènglián, Sīmáo, and Líncāng, leading to Déhóng and Bǎoshān regions. If you plan to head south to Mènglián you'll have to switch buses, if not stay overnight here. Buses from Bǎoshān and Ruìlì often overnight here.

Orientation

Láncāng is dissected into a Y-shape by the highway from Jīnghóng leading to Líncāng, and by the highway south to Myanmar via Mènglián. A large statue sits in the middle of town and is a good place to alight. From the statue, head south-east to the main bus station. South-west is Mènglián. Straight ahead is a long, torturous road to Líncāng.

If you arrive on a Sunday, make sure it's early, as the town market is fairly populated and energetic.

Places to Stay & Eat

Exiting the bus station main entrance head right, turn right at the first intersection and you'll get to the decent *Yínxī Bīnguǎn*. Good-value singles/doubles cost Y20/30 and there are bearable communal squat bathrooms.

Carry on along the street past the post office to the corner you'll find the government-run *Láncāng Xiàn Yíngbīn Jiǔlóu*, which has beds in a decent triple/double for Y10/15 and singles for Y20.

The best place to stay in Láncāng is found to the rear of the departure lot at the main bus station. The new *Commerce Hotel (Shāngyè Bīnguǎn; ☎ 722 7036)* has clean and comfortable rooms with bathroom for Y60 to Y80.

Getting There & Away

To confuse things, Láncāng has three bus stations. From the statue at the crossroads, the main bus station is 100m south-east. Departures to everywhere in all sorts of buses, leave from here. This station should have everything you need, but there's another bus station south-west of the crossroads statue.

To Mènglián there are buses every 40 minutes until 6.30pm (Y10, 1½ hours). To the Wa settlement of Xīméng (Y20, four hours) there are buses three or four times a day from both bus stations.

To Jǐnghóng, buses leave hourly or so until 5.30pm (Y30, five hours). There are hourly buses to Sīmáo (Y29, 3½ hours). A single early morning bus departs for Líncāng (Y45) and there is a sleeper bus to Bǎoshān (Y115, 22 hours) around 6.30pm.

Note that the twisting road from Láncāng to Líncāng, well, basically doesn't exist, especially during the rainy season. To make it worse, hyperactive border agents search buses a lot.

You can also get to Kūnmíng on sleeper buses at 6.50am and 9.30 am.

SĪMÁO 思茅
☎ 0879

Sīmáo, an uninteresting little town, used to be Xīshuāngbǎnnà's air link with the outside world. Nowadays Jǐnghóng has its own airport and only the occasional traveller flies from Kūnmíng to Sīmáo (Y390) and does the final leg to Jǐnghóng by bus if they can't get a flight to Jǐnghóng.

South of Sīmáo is the **Caiyang River Nature Reserve** but apart from that, the scenery between Sīmáo and Jǐnghóng is not exactly a Sumatran jungle, and if you're travelling further afield from Jǐnghóng you'll see plenty of Xīshuāngbǎnnà scenery anyway.

If you do get stuck here, however, east of town is the **Manzhongtian Hot Spring**, set among hundreds of hectares of grassland. Most Chinese tourists come for **Cuìyún Resort** and its oddball karst formations and grottoes, 54km south-west of town.

South-East Yúnnán

This little-visited corner of Yúnnán has its fair share of interesting sights, a good infrastructure and at its outer fringes some of the region's most traditional and off-the-beaten track minority areas. For anyone who wants to avoid the hordes of travellers in Xīshuāngbǎnnà, Dàlǐ and Lìjiāng the region's highlights – the Mongol community near Tōnghǎi, the traditional architecture of Jiànshuǐ and the superb terraces of Yuányáng – may well rank as their low-key favourites.

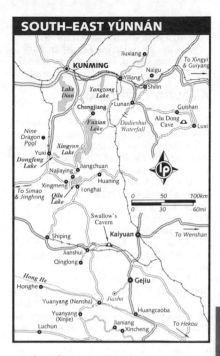

CHÉNGJIĀNG 澄江
☎ 0877

On a highland plateau 65km south-east of Kūnmíng, Chéngjiāng is the seat of the county dubbed the 'Land of Milk and Honey' for its agricultural output. The H-shaped county's population is small – only around 125,000 people – and features sizeable numbers of Huí, Miáo and Yi. The town's picturesque old back alleys make it worth a visit, though it's a bit far from Kūnmíng to do as a day trip. Most Chinese tourists tic in a visit here with Jiāngchuān to the south via Fúxiān and Xingyun lakes, and then perhaps on to Tōnghǎi and Jiànshuǐ.

For details on getting here from Kūnmíng see the Kūnmíng – Getting There & Away secton.

Things to See

On the east side of Chéngjiāng is a massive Ming dynasty **Confucian Temple** (Wénmiào). It takes up 20,000 sq metres and the

Grand Hall of the Honoured Teacher is over 10m high with seven attached rooms.

Also in Chéngjiāng is **Fengshan Park** at the southern base of Feng Shān, built on the site of a long-disappeared Taoist temple.

AROUND CHÉNGJIĀNG
Fúxiān Hú 抚仙湖

The primary point of interest for travellers is this north-south oriented lake separating Chéngjiāng from Jiāngchuān. The north shore lies 5km south of Chéngjiāng. Fúxiān is the deepest lake in Yúnnán (second deepest in China) and though smaller than Lake Dian and Ěrhǎi Lake in Dàlǐ, its volume is 12 times that of Dian, and six times that of Ěrhǎi's. The bluish-green hue comes from phosphorous deposits from surrounding soils.

The northern shore is the most developed. **Bōxī Bay** has a beach of sorts and is a popular resort.

Clockwise, starting from the north-east is **Xiàngbílǐng Shān** and once you see it you'll see why it's English translation is 'Elephant's Trunk Mountain'. The east side has a number of sulphurous **hot springs** – some quite large – and even a warm-water river in Jiǔcūn. As you continue south keep your eyes peeled for the **Serene Lake Bridge** (Hǎiyán Qiáo), 17.5km south of Chéngjiāng near Hǎikǒu, a Qing dynasty stone arch bridge also known as Hǎikǒu Bridge.

Farther south on the western side, a tiny islet called **Solitary Hill** (Gūshān Dǎo) appears. The island was once filled with Ming dynasty temples, a pagoda, pavilions, and nunneries though not much is left (the pagoda was melted down for coins during an uprising). You can normally arrange a boat to take you across to the island.

At the southern tip of the lake, near the village of Hǎimén, a 1km-long river connects Fúxiān Hú to neighbouring Xīngyún Hú. (What's interesting is that fish from both lakes swim to the confluence of the river and Fúxiān Lake, but they are said to never pass the point where a boundary rock overlooks the water.) To the west is **Yùsǔn Shān** (Jade Bamboo Shoots Mountain), known for the platter-shaped rock atop the peak that purportedly is always wet.

JIĀNGCHUĀN 江川
☎ 0877

South-east of Yùxī, 45 minutes by bus, lies Jiāngchuān, the seat of a tiny county of the same name. Occupied since the ancient Dian culture, it wasn't controlled by imperial China until well into the Han dynasty. Villages around Jiāngchuān are filled with Chinese archaeologists, as excavation sites here have unearthed prime sites of Dian, Neolithic and Bronze Age cultures, including 25 tombs of the Warring States Period in Lijiashan near Wengkiaxiang Village.

Located in a small circular basin surrounded by mountains, Yúnnánese say the county's topography resembles the shape of a begonia leaf. The town's major export is water pipes and there are several shops selling every size pipe in the east end of town, plus legions of old men testing them out.

Bronze Age Museum 青铜博物馆
Qīngtóngqì Bówùguǎn

The Bronze Age Museum, west of the bus station, showcases the importance of Jiāngchuān county's archaeological finds, with displays ranging from bronze drums and ritual bells to ornate animal bronzes and ritual weapons.

The Lǐjiāshān excavation site is particularly highlighted, featuring the 25 tombs of the Warring States Period and Western Han dynasty, from which nearly 1000 pristine Bronze Age relics were removed. The local cult of the bull is plain to see. The earliest coins used in Yúnnán were also unearthed at the site. The museum is worth a visit if you are in town but is probably not worth going out of your way for unless you have an interest in early history.

The museum is a five-minute walk along Xingyun Lu west of the bus station. A big bull statue (a replica of one of the bronzes) sits out front. It is open daily 10.30am to 4pm and entry costs Y10.

Places to Stay & Eat

The best option is the *Jiāngchuān Bīnguǎn* (☎ 801 1252) on Ninghai Lu. Beds in a decent double or triple in the side block cost Y20 a bed and the clean shared bathrooms have hot water. The main building has comfortable carpeted singles/doubles with bathroom for Y120, discounted to Y90. From the bus station ticket office turn left, past the market and then right at the major intersection. The hotel is a couple of minutes walk on the right.

Tiānxīng Bīnguǎn has clean doubles with bathroom for Y100 but are reluctant to accept foreign guests.

Jiāngchuān Dàjiǔdiàn, next to the Xīnhuá bookstore, has mid-range doubles for Y120.

For food, good luck. If you turn left out of the bus station ticket office (not the main lot) and walk 200m you'll get to a good *bāozi restaurant*. Otherwise try heading in the direction of the museum; the closer you get, the bigger and better looking the restaurants get. The *market*, one block east of the bus station has a good selection of fruit.

Getting There & Away

The Jiāngchuān bus station is confusing – no schedules and no ticket windows. You'll have to wait for minibuses to regional destinations to fill. There are frequent departures to Yùxī (Y5, one hour) until around 8pm and to Chéngjiāng every hour or so until early afternoon.

Coming from or going to Kūnmíng (Y17), there are a couple of daily services to/from Kūnmíng's east bus station, the last one departing at 3pm; if you go via Yùxī there are plenty of services.

If you don't feel like waiting, head southeast until the first main intersection, Ninghai Lu. Turn right and walk to the highway, from where you could flag down buses. Microvans depart for Tōnghǎi (Y5, one hour) when full throughout the day from here, about 30m outside the Jiāngchuān Bīnguǎn. You could also hook up with the highway by walking west from the Bronze Age Museum.

AROUND JIĀNGCHUĀN
Xīngyún Hú 星云湖

Oval-shaped and somewhat salty, this lake is known locally as the Sea of Broad Waves. The lake has a few hot springs along its shoreline. The lake is also famous for its big-headed fish, supposedly tasty in hot-pot.

Try taking a motor tricycle from the centre of town to the Lakeside Park (Bīnhǎi Gōngyuán), 2km north of town.

TŌNGHǍI 通海
☎ 0877

Tōnghǎi's major attraction is the traditional architecture of its charming avenues and back alleys. To the north 2km or so is icy-looking, windswept Qílù Hú, and a short distance (about 15km) west of town is Yúnnán's only remaining settlement of Mongols. Long famed for their metalworking, dozens of them now sell knives around the bus station.

The town has been occupied since the kingdom of Dian's inception. Its zenith came during the Nánzhāo kingdom, when Tōnghǎi was chosen as the military and economic centre of the kingdom that stretched from Tōnghǎi to Hékǒu. When the later Dàlǐ kingdom was founded after an uprising, the leaders came from Tōnghǎi.

Xiù Shān Park 秀山公园
Xiù Shān Gōngyuán

One of the more pleasant hills to climb in south-east Yúnnán is this green mist-shrouded hump, lush with birds, in the southern section of Tōnghǎi. Original construction of temples began as early as the Tang dynasty and by the Ming dynasty it was revered as one of southern China's most sacred Buddhist sites. Later, the mountain became famous because the section behind the summit supposedly 'predicts' the weather.

It's only about 200m high but it has enough paths to occupy you for hours. Five temples, some Taoist Ming dynasty towers, and over 20 pavilions provide lots of nooks and crannies. Tablets are marked with over 200 couplets left by ancient writers. The first building on the right is the **Sanyuangong Monastery**, which is currently being rebuilt after a tragic fire. The **Puguan Sì** and **Yongjin Sì** higher up, contain a bonsai and camellia garden respectively. From the upper part of the hill a trail leads around the east side of the hill to the **Báilóng Sì** (White Dragon Monastery), a lovely complex whose small hotel that might make a peaceful place to stay a night.

YUNNAN

The views of Qílù Hú and the town are great. Best of all, many of the temples have signs in passable English, giving an insight into the history of the mountain and regional folklore. Admission is Y15.

Xī Shān Park to the west of Tōnghǎi has more trails and a pagoda on its hilltop.

Places to Stay

The new *Jiànhuá Zhāodàisuǒ* (☎ 301 7707) is a clean, good-value option across the roundabout from the bus station. Bright dou-

bles with squat toilet but reliable hot water cost Y50. Singles are smaller but have Western toilet and spotless bathrooms for Y40.

The cheapest place is the small and pretty basic *Gòngxiāoshè Lǚguǎn* at the intersection of Xi Jie and Huancheng Xilu; look for the green and white sign. Dorm beds start at Y5 in no-frills rooms but should be OK; they'll probably try to push you into a Y22 room. Take a look at rooms on different floors, since bathroom hygiene varies. There are no showers.

Close to the town gate at the intersection of Bei, Nan, Dong and Xi Jie, is the glum *Xiùshān Bīnguǎn* (☎ 301 1598), with a glum feel. Dorm beds are available for Y10 to Y20, and rooms cost Y30/40 with common bath or Y40/50 with grim bathroom. Hot water supplies can be dicey.

Lǐyuè Fàndiàn (☎ 301 1651) is a two-star option on Huancheng Xilu that has small standard rooms for Y50/Y100 without/with bathroom. Triples with bathroom cost Y95.

North on Huancheng Beilu the *Xiàn Zhèngfǔ Zhāodàisuǒ* (Government Guesthouse) has spacious rooms in its new wing for Y80 and cell-like single/doubles with a rock-hard bed for Y20/30. Showers are available for an extra Y1.

The top joint in town is the surprisingly glamorous *Tong Print Hotel* (*Tōngyìn Dàjiǔdiàn; ☎ 302 1666, fax 301 6474*). Standard rooms are Y288 always discounted by 50%. Ask for discounts on the Y2880 presidential suite as it is hard to see any

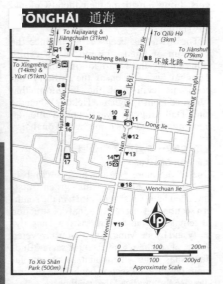

TŌNGHǍI 通海

TŌNGHǍI

1	Microbuses to Jiāngchuān 到江川的小车	7	Xiàn Zhèngfǔ Zhāodàisuǒ 县政府招待所	13	Nánjiē Cāntīng 南街餐厅
2	Restaurants 餐厅	8	Tong Print Hotel 通印大酒店	14	China Post 中国邮局
3	Jiànhuá Zhāodàisuǒ 建华招待所	9	Mosque 清真寺	15	China Telecom 中国电信
4	Buses 公共汽车	10	Xiùshān Bīnguǎn 秀山宾馆	16	Gòngxiāoshè Lǚguǎn 供销社旅馆
5	Bus Station 通海客运总站	11	Town Gate 大门	17	PSB 公安局
6	Lǐyuè Fàndiàn 礼乐饭店	12	Xueshan Cold Drinks Shop 雪山冷饮部	18	Xīnhuá Bookstore 新华书店
				19	Snack Bars 小吃店

presidents ever making it to Tōnghǎi. Facilities include a 16th-floor sightseeing bar, a bowling alley, tennis court, sauna and pool in summer. Bizarrely, the reception won't let you see a room until you've already paid.

Places to Eat

There are plenty of good *restaurants* across from the bus station. Most offer a buffet of pre-cooked food but you are better off ordering something fresh. Itinerant musicians sometimes sing here.

Down a side street by the Jiànhuá Zhaodàisuǒ is a good *night food market* with all kinds of barbecued critters and snacks (though there's not much for vegetarians). All around the central part of town are a number of grilled *tofu snack bars*.

South of the town gate is the *Xueshan Cold Drinks Shop* (*Xuěshān Bīngyǐnbù*). Nearby is a *fast food place*.

Tōnghǎi's best-known eatery is the *Nánjiē Cāntīng*, south of the cold drink shop on Nan Jie. You pay a couple of yuán for a bowl of noodles served quickly at the back of the restaurant. Or, pick and point and they'll whip it up pronto. It's an excellent meal.

Across town look out for hot and peppery stews cooked in Tōnghǎi-made copper pots. There are several *Muslim restaurants* around town serving this and other dishes, especially around the main mosque.

Getting There & Away

Tōnghǎi's bus station is just south of the Huancheng Beilu and Huangcheng Xilu intersection. But most regional buses leave from a stop west around the corner along Huancheng Beilu at the Hubin Lu intersection. Buses to Jiànshuǐ (Y10, two hours), Gèjiù and Yùxī leave every half-hour or so when full. There are minibuses to Kūnmíng (Y20) every hour until 6.30pm. Cramped microbuses leave for Jiāngchuān from across the road when full (Y5, one hour).

AROUND TŌNGHǍI
Qílù Hú 杞麓湖

This Indigo-blue lake, 1km north of town, was famed from Tang dynasty times as one of the emperor's eight favourite south-east

Yúnnán getaways. The lake once rose much higher along the cliffs of the eastern shoreline and legends tell of how an ancient monk poked a hole in the ground to drain the water for farmers; his story is told at a temple in Xiù Shān Park, Tōnghǎi. The easiest option is to travel north of Tōnghǎi to a lakeside park around 3km north of town. You could walk, or a motorcycle taxi would cost around Y5.

Xīngmēng

At the base of Feng Shān, in a compact village 14km west of Tōnghǎi just off the main highway, some 4000 **Mongolian** descendants of members of Kublai Khan's expeditionary force still reside. Over the last 700 years, most have switched from the nomadic rough-riding lifestyle to fishing on Qílù Hú, but dwindling water levels over the past three decades have forced most onto the land as farmers or builders. The traditional stone and sun-dried brick village is still a nice place to wander.

The Mongolian faces and language have become diluted over the years but the dress is still distinct and most people wear green or blue tunics with brightly embroidered sleeves. An annual early-winter festival called **Nadaam** is held here every three years (the next one is scheduled for 2002), just as it is during summer on the grasslands several thousand kilometres north.

Najiaying Mosque 纳家营清真寺

A half-hour by bus up the western shoreline of the lake is the village of Najiaying, home to one of the oldest mosques in Yúnnán, predating the Ming dynasty. The mosque's three sections include a gate, a courtyard, hall and two flanking rooms that total over 5000 sq metres. The mosque is most impressive if viewed from the heights descending along the road from Jiāngchuān. Any bus to Jiāngchuān from Tōnghǎi will pass through Najiaying.

JIÀNSHUǏ 建水
☎ 0873

Probably the most traditional town remaining in south-east Yúnnán, Jiànshuǐ expects

YÚNNÁN

to start pulling in lots more tourists with its old-style architecture, friendly folk, and a quotient of tourist sights second to none in the region. Jiànshuǐ's even got one of the cooler little markets left too, abuzz on Sundays. The town is also famous for its traditional purple pottery.

Known in ancient times as Butou or Badian, Jiànshuǐ's history dates back to the Western Jin period, when it was under the auspices of the Ningzhou kingdom. It was handed around to other authorities until its most important days as part of the Tōnghǎi Military Command of the Nánzhāo kingdom. The Yuan dynasty established what would eventually become the contemporary town.

Jiànshuǐ figured prominently in the 1911 Revolution. On 1 November a group within the army staged a rebellion here inside the Tianjun Temple and established the military government of the Southern Garrison Army. Later, Marshal Zhu De would station his troops here.

Yúnnán & Kublai Khan

Travellers to Tōnghǎi are surprised to discover distinct Mongolian dress and non-Han features throughout the town and region. (Not to mention the ornate knives and scabbards sold on every street corner.) In fact there are around 13,000 ethnic Mongolians in Yúnnán; all descended from the great Khan, Kublai.

Genghis (Chingiz) Khan died in 1227 and was succeeded as Great Khan by his third son Ögedei, under whose rule the Mongol empire expanded. One of his major accomplishments was the final vanquishment of the Chin empire in northern China. Ögedei died in 1241, and for the first time since Genghis Khan, a power struggle erupted in the Mongol realm, eventually won by Möngke, from a rival familial branch. He dispatched his brothers to all parts of the Mongol empire; Kublai was given the task of subjugating the nemesis of the Mongols – southern China.

As part of his campaign in southern China, Kublai and his armies had to enter what today is Yúnnán, one of China's most isolated and long-unconquered regions. In fact, the Mongols thought it a separate country – their name Qandahar for the region is from an Indian language meaning 'great country'; it was also called Nan-chao or 'southern kingdom' in Chinese (Polo knew it as Caragan). Yúnnán was to provide material and provisions for a struggling army as it swept through in 1256 in a sustained effort to outflank the Song armies and smash their economic links with India and Burma. Completely unprepared for the enormity of the land and population opposing them, the Mongol horsemen were also baffled by the strange, river valley topography. Yet Kublai's two armies managed to cross western China mountain by mountain, river by river, opposed by ethnic minority groups at every step. They converged on Dàlǐ and somehow nearly took it without shedding blood.

In the interim Möngke died and a four-year civil war ensued, in which Kublai was victorious in 1264. He could now focus his full attention on defeating southern China.

Khan's armies would not subdue the Song and southern China until 1279, some 70 years after they had made initial advances. In the process they brought Yúnnán into the great Chinese fold. Indeed the inclusion of Yúnnán into the country is considered one of Kublai Khan's greatest achievements as he established the Yuan (Mongol) dynasty. North and south China had been forced to find each other.

Kublai Khan's period was an intriguing one for Chinese culture and society. Kublai was much more open-minded than his Mongol counterparts. He realised Chinese culture had much to offer, and even moved his capital to Běijīng. He would never have been victorious if he hadn't persuaded entire divisions of the Song land and naval forces to switch allegiances; once in control in Yúnnán he also left a number of Dǎi princes in autonomous control. The Chinese were prohibited from most high positions, those being reserved for Mongols. But as a hands-off emperor, Kublai also allowed many aspects of Chinese high culture to flower, the educated elite of Chinese society quietly 'retiring' and concentrating on artistic endeavours.

Orientation

You can easily cover all the city sights in a day. The eastern perimeter of the city consists of a curved line connecting the bus station, Chaoyang Gate, and the train station along Chaoyang Nanlu and Chaoyang Beilu. The main road downtown is Jianzhong Lu, leading west from Chaoyang Gate. To the north, Chaoyang Beilu curves away from Chaoyang Gate and reaches a traffic roundabout, where you'll find the Lìnán Jiǔdiàn. Qīngyuan Lu is as far west as you'll need to go.

Maps The most reliable place to get a map is the Jiànshuǐ Travel Agency (see following). The only map available is in Chinese.

Information

The Jiànshuǐ Travel Agency (☎ 765 2241) can help with information on the surrounding sights but there's little English spoken. Contact them either at the main office next to the Lìnán Jiǔdiàn or at a branch office next to the Zhū Family Gardens.

The Jiāhuá Diànnǎo Kèjì computer shop on Beizheng Jie offers fast Internet access for Y4 per hour. There's a laundry close to the Zhéngfǔ Zhāodàisuǒ.

Confucian Temple 文庙
Wénmiào

Jiànshuǐ's tourism linchpin is this famous temple west of the town centre. Modelled after the temple in Confucius' hometown of Qufu (Shandong province) and finished in 1285, it covers 7.5 hectares and is the third largest Confucian temple in China.

The place is so large that you first walk through a gate on Jianzong Lu and all the way around Xue Lake (the Chinese word is actually 'sea') just to get to another gate, then up a walkway before the main structures loom magnificently before you. The structure includes a main hall, two side rooms, two central halls, two pavilions and eight glazed-tile archways. **Dacheng Hall**, the epicentre, is supported by 22 5m pillars, two engraved with two dragons rising through the mist.

Remarkably, the temple has operated as a school for nearly 750 years and was so successful that over half of all Yúnnán's *juren*

(successful candidates in imperial examinations) came from Jiànshuǐ. Many of the names of buildings in Jiànshuǐ use the ideogram *(wén)*, or 'literacy'. A couple of entrance fees are levied, totalling Y3, though you can expect this to rise after renovation work is completed. The complex is open daily 7am to 6pm.

Zhū Family Garden 朱家花园
Zhūjiā Huāyuán

A 10-minute walk east from the Confucian Temple and then left down an alley, is an outstanding example of a Qing dynasty traditional ancestral home. The spacious 20,000 sq metre complex comprises ancestral buildings, family homes, ponds and lovely gardens and took 30 years to build. Some of the courtyards have recently been converted into a hotel.

Travellers will like the small museum in the rear, with dozens of photographs of local architecture, with a heavy focus on bridges. There is also an exhibit on the history of the Zhū family. The Zhū family made its name through its mill and tavern and dabbled in everything from tin in Gèjiù to opium in Hong Kong, eventually falling victim to the political chaos following the 1911 revolution.

Admission is Y11 and the gardens are open daily 7.30am to 10pm.

Zhǐlín Sì 指林寺

One of the few remaining examples of intricate woodworking on a large scale, and the largest preserved wooden structure in Yúnnán, this monastery is tucked away in a tiny alley south-west of the Confucian Temple.

Built during the latter stages of the Yuan dynasty, the monastery's distinctive design feature is the brackets between columns and crossbeams. A set of 600-year-old frescoes were recently discovered here, though they have since been moved to local museums.

Chaoyang Gate 朝阳门
Cháoyáng Lóu

Guarding the centre of town is this imposing Ming dynasty edifice, modelled on the Huanghe Tower in Wǔhàn and Yueyang Tower in Hunan and bearing more than a

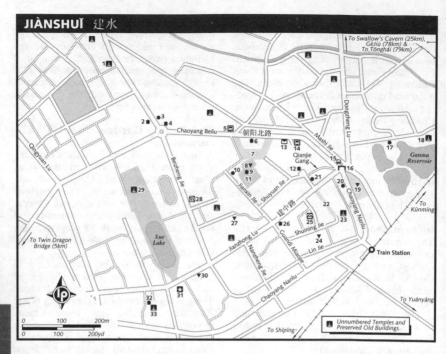

JIÀNSHUǏ 建水

To Swallow's Cavern (25km),
Gèjiù (78km) &
To Tōnghǎi (79km)

Chaoyang Beilu 朝阳北路

Qingyuan Lu

Beizheng Jie

Dongzheng Lu

Mashi Jie

Ganma
Reservoir

Qianjie
Gang

Jianxin Jie

Shuyuan Jie

建中路

Chaoyang Nanlu

To Künming

Xue
Lake

Jianzhong Lu

Nanzheng Jie

Guandi Miaojie

Shuining Jie

Lin Jie

Train Station

To Twin Dragon
Bridge (5km)

To Yuányáng

Chaoyang Nanlu

To Shípíng

Unnumbered Temples and
Preserved Old Buildings

0   100   200m
0   100   200yd

passing resemblance to Tian'anmen Gate in
Běijīng. Recent renovations have resulted
in a nice sitting area where you can grab a
tea or beer, a pricier interior teahouse and
an upper-floor exhibit of local history (Y2).
There's no charge to walk up into the gate
and admire the building and views close up.

Traditional Architecture Tour
Classic architecture is everywhere in Jiànshuǐ, and not just in the old-style back alleys
either. Virtually every main street has a historically significant traditional structure.
The architecture is especially intriguing because of the obvious mixture of central
plains and local styles. Many old buildings,
despite official decrees positing them as
state treasures, have been coopted for other
purposes and the trick – and truthfully the
great fun – is trying to find them.

A good place to start your explorations is
Chaoyang Gate. Head south and then right
up a short hill. After 200m on the right is the

Grain Bureau (Liángshi Jú). Walk confi-
dently inside, past two old storehouses to the
Chóngwén Tǎ, an elegant 14-storey pagoda.
From here continue round Guilin Jie and
you'll come across the four **wells** and shrine.

Back at Chaoyang Gate, head north and
then east to the Workers Club (Gōngrén
Jùlèbù). Around the back are several interlocking **lakes**, banked by a throng of elderly
card players. A little farther east is the former **Fúdōng Sì**, a temple which houses the
town's Education Department.

Places to Stay – Budget
*Zhèngfǔ Zhāodàisuǒ (Government Guest-
house)*, close to Chaoyang Gate on Jianzong Lu, is popular so try to get a room
early. Fair doubles with common bathroom
cost Y30. Singles/doubles with bathroom in
the front building are Y45/60; pricier rooms
for Y60/70 are almost identical. There's a
nice restaurant in a traditional style building, though it seems to hardly ever open.

YÚNNÁN

JIÀNSHUǏ

PLACES TO STAY
2 Hóngyùn Jiǔdiàn;
  Bus Station Hotel
  红运酒店
4 Lín'ān Jiǔdiàn
  临安酒店
6 Shānluóluo Dàjiǔdiàn
  山倮罗大酒店
9 Zhūjiā Huāyuán
  Kèzhàn
  朱家花园客栈
12 Zhèngfǔ Zhāodàisuǒ
  政府招待所
26 Garden Hotel
  花园招待所
32 Dǎngxiào Zhāodàisuǒ
  党校招待所

PLACES TO EAT
8 Garden Hotel
  Restaurant
  花园饭店
19 Jiànshuǐ Fēngwèi
  Guòqiáo Chéng
  建水风味过桥城
22 Roast Tofu
  Vendors

24 Míngchéng Yúlè
  Zhongxīn
  名城娱乐中心
27 Restaurant's
  餐厅
30 Zìxīng Kǎoyādiàn
  自兴烤鸭店

OTHER
1 Lǜwǎ Sì
  绿瓦寺
3 Jiànshuǐ Travel
  Agency
  建水旅行社
5 Bus Station
  汽车站
7 Market
  市场
10 Jiànshuǐ Travel
  Agency
  建水旅行社
11 Zhū Family Gardens
  朱家花园
13 China Post
  邮电局
14 Main Bus Station
  汽车站

15 Microbuses to
  Qīnglóng
  到青龙的小车
16 Cháoyáng Gate
  朝阳楼
17 Workers Club
  工人俱乐部
18 Fúdōng Sì
  福东寺
20 Xīnhuá
  Bookstore
  新华书店
21 Laundry
  洗衣店
23 Chóngwén Tǎ
  崇文塔
25 China Telecom
  中国电信
28 Jiāhuá Diànnǎo Kējì
  (Internet)
  嘉华电脑科技
29 Confucian Temple
  文庙
31 PSB
  公安局
33 Zhǐlín Sì
  指林寺

Farther down Jianzhong Lu is the *Garden Hotel (Huāyuán Bīnguǎn)* with a range of rooms around a flowery courtyard. Good value doubles cost Y20 with a common bathroom and hot shower. The mid-priced rooms aren't really worth it for Y40 to Y50 but the Y80 rooms, discounted to Y60, come with a hot shower and Western toilet. Triples are Y25 and Y90. The restaurant is classic Chinese – huge and a bit grungy but with good food.

One rarely used option is the *Dǎngxiào Zhāodàisuǒ*; rooms with bathroom surround the beautiful Zhǐlín Sì for Y50, and Y80, the latter with reliable hot water.

Bus Station Hotel, attached to the Hóngyùn Jiǔdiàn has very basic doubles with bathroom for Y20 a bed.

Places to Stay – Mid-Range

There are several good mid-range options that offer some character as well as comfort. A 10-minute walk west of the bus station along Chaoyang Beilu brings you to the *Lín'ān Jiǔdiàn* (☎ 765 1888, fax 765 4888), set off the street and in pleasant gardens. Comfortable and clean Y170 doubles will come with air-con and heater. Cheaper doubles are dark and poorer value at Y130.

Across the road is *Hóngyùn Jiǔdiàn* (☎ 765 8648), where clean and fresh doubles cost Y80 or Y60.

The *Shānluóluo Dàjiǔdiàn* on the 6th floor of a deserted shopping hall currently offers huge discounts bringing its Y180 rooms down to Y88.

The classiest place in town is the *Zhūjiā Huāyuán Kèzhàn* (☎ 766 7988) in the Zhu Family Gardens. Four of the courtyards have been converted into rooms for Y220 and Y280, which although they are dark, have lovely furniture and traditional old style beds. It's worth splashing out on the Y280 rooms, as the Y220 are really small and pokey.

TUNNAN

Places to Eat

Try a dish making use of the local specialty – grass sprout (*cǎoyā*), also known as elephant's tooth grass root. It tastes like bamboo. Only found in Jiànshuǐ county, it's often used in broth or fried with liver or pork. Non-meat eaters might find a place that will substitute tofu. Another local specialty is tonic soup made from bird nests from Swallow's Cavern – don't gulp at the price.

Like Gèjiù, you'll find lots of cubbyhole restaurants full of braziers roasting tofu and perhaps goat cheese. In the evenings Jianzhong Lu becomes a pedestrian area with vendors offering sugar cane, skinned pineapples and kebabs.

The alley east of Chaoyang Gate is lined with restaurants and tofu grills. The *Jiànshuǐ Fēngwèi Guòqiáo Chéng* here is rumoured to be the source of Yúnnán's Across-the-bridge noodles, which it serves for Y50 or Y10.

A couple of places sell Běijīng duck, including the takeaway stall called the *Zìxīng Kǎoyādiàn*, near the Zhǐlín Sì. *Míngchéng Yúlè Zhōngxīn* also serves duck and other local dishes in the shadow of a 1950s Communist building.

There are *restaurants* down the winding alley that leads off Jianxin Jie. Finally, dozens of stalls set up every evening in the courtyard of the Hóngyùn Jiǔdiàn in the north of town.

The *juice bar* on Jianzhong Lu offers everything from coconut juice to banana milkshakes and coffee. It also serves *tāngyuán*, sweet balls of gum that the Chinese go loopy over. Try the excellent mango juice (*mángguǒ zhī*) for Y1.50.

There's a formal *restaurant* attached to the Garden Hotel on the 2nd floor with an English menu (copied from the back of this book!) and cheap prices. This is one place to try *cǎoyā*.

A branch is at the back of the Zhu Family Gardens. In the heat of summer you can dine on a raised platform overlooking the garden. Prices are very reasonable at around Y10 per dish. If you book in advance you don't have to pay the Y11 gardens entry fee.

Getting There & Away

Bus Jiànshuǐ has several bus stations. The main one is on the south side of Chaoyang Beilu. If there's nothing there, try the second small bus station a couple of minutes walk west. The third and least useful is on the main roundabout at the north of town and has mostly local departures.

There are buses continually leaving for Gèjiù (Y10), Yuányáng (Y13) and Tōnghǎi (Y10), as well as Měngzì, Shípíng and Kāiyuán.

Farther afield, Kūnmíng is served 8am to noon by frequent buses (Y30) and 6.30pm to 11.30pm by sleepers (Y35, six hours). Hékǒu-bound travellers have three morning buses (Y33). The masochistic can take the sleeper to Jǐnghóng (Y110, 24 hours), scheduled for 7.50am and 4pm.

Train Jiànshuǐ is on the narrow-gauge train line from between Shípíng and Kūnmíng but trains are slow and most people take the bus. Trains to Kūnmíng leave at around 5pm (Y65, 14 hours). For Hékǒu change at Kāiyuán and wait a couple of hours for the midnight train to the Vietnamese border.

AROUND JIÀNSHUǏ
Swallow's Cavern 燕子洞
Yúnzǐ Dòng

This freak of nature and ornithology is halfway between Jiànshuǐ and Gèjiù. The karst formations (the largest in Asia) are a lure, but what you'll want to see are the hundreds of thousands of swallows flying around in spring and summer. The cave is split into two, high and dry and low and wet. The higher one is so large that a three-storey pavilion and a tree fit inside. Plank walkways link up with other pavilions outside on the rock formations. Look out for the inscribed plaques hanging from the roof at the entrance to the cave. The Lu River runs through the lower cave for about 8km and you can tour the caverns in 'dragon-boats'. The cacophony of river and bird is insane.

Getting to the cave is easy. Just take any bus bound for Měngzì, Kāiyuán or Gèjiù (there may be others). Forty-five minutes to an hour later and five to 10 minutes after you pass through Miàndiàn village, at the entrance to another tiny village, you should see signs saying 'Welcome to Swallow's Cave', among other things, all in English. The fare is Y4. Entry to the caves is a steep Y35.

Twin Dragon Bridge 双龙桥
Shuānglóng Qiáo
Traditionally styled bridges abound – check out the photos at the Zhu Family Garden – but you must see this bridge across the confluence of the Lu and Tachong rivers, 5km from the west edge of town. The bridge features 17 arches, so many that it took two periods of the Qing dynasty to complete the project. A three-storey pavilion sits in the middle, with two smaller ones at either end. In the right light at the right times, it's a great photo opportunity.

To get there take minibus No 4 from in front of the bus station (Y1, five minutes). The No 4 bus continues to **Huánglóng Sì**, a small temple. Some 13km beyond here is the **Zhang Family Gardens** (Zhangjiā Huāyuán) in Tuánshān Village, a similar but smaller complex to the gardens in Jiànshuǐ.

Wénbǐ Tà 文笔塔
South-west of town, a few kilometres on the road to Qīnglóng, this Ming-dynasty pagoda is certainly distinctive, shaped like a calligraphy brush. The perimeter of the base matches the height, exactly 31.4m. To get here take a Qīnglóng-bound minibus (Y2) from the north-west side of Chaoyang Gate or a taxi for Y10. It's a pleasant ride on a bicycle.

YUÁNYÁNG 元阳
The southern part of the Hónghé Hani and Yi Autonomous Prefecture is largely made up of Yi, Dǎi and mostly Hani settlements. The region is dominated by the Hóng Hé (also known as the Red River and also the Yuán Jiāng), which rises near Dàlǐ and flows into Vietnam at Hékǒu.

On the south side of the Hóng Hé rises a wall of fog-shrouded mountains, the Ailao Shan, which hide some of the most stupendous rice terraces in the world, carved out over generations by Hani farmers. The ter-

races are particularly resplendent at sunrise and sunset and from November to April when they are full of water. They take in Yuányáng and Lüchūn counties and the Jīnpíng Miáo, Yao and Yi Autonomous county, but they are most accessible outside Yuányáng.

There are two towns called Yuányáng. The new town of Yuányáng lies on the banks of the Hóng Hé and is also known as Nánshā. This town has a couple of restaurants and hotels but is of little interest. You want the old town of Yuányáng, also known as Xīnjiē. If the weather is cloudy, the terraces will be invisible.

Xīnjiē is populated largely by traditionally dressed Hani, who wear embroidered trousers, tunics and embroidered squares of cloth wrapped around their back. Many people still use hemp back covers when carrying goods. The market stretches down hill from the Zhéngfǔ Zhāodàisuǒ.

Places to Stay
Zhéngfǔ Zhāodàisuǒ (Government Guesthouse), across the road from the bus station, has good rooms with beds from Y10 to Y20. The common toilets are clean and there's hot water in the evenings. Standard doubles with bathroom and Western toilet are Y80. Solo travellers can often stay in them for Y40.

Backpacker Rendezvous is a private guesthouse run by a guy from Hong Kong that many travellers have recommended. Dorm beds and hot showers cost Y30.

Getting There & Away
Coming from Jiànshuǐ or Gèjiù, don't get off at new Yuányáng (Nánshā). If you stop here you'll have to catch a microbus for the 40-minute (Y5) ride up into the hills to old Yuányáng (Xīnjiē). Sleeper buses leave Kūnmíng at around 6.30pm (Y64, 12 hours).

There's minibuses every 30 minutes or so until 5pm for Jiànshuǐ (Y13, 3½ hours). Minibuses to Gèjiù (Y22, six hours) run until 2pm. The tortuous route follows the Hóng Hé before climbing up into the hills at Huángcǎobà.

To get to the terraces for sunrise catch the 7am minibus to Jiáníáng and get off where it looks good (there are fine terraces 15km from Yuányáng). There are later buses at noon, and 1.30pm and 2.30pm, as well as a 1.40pm bus to Xīnchéng, which will take you past some fine terraces.

GÈJIÙ 个旧
☎ 0873

Virtually everyone going to Hékǒu on the Vietnam border whizzes through this city. Too bad, they don't know what they missed. It's like an alpine town against a backdrop of craggy cliffs, and the views over the steely blue lake approach picture-postcard realms. It's got a European feel, which is ironic as the tropic of Cancer passes through its northern end of town.

This counteracts the grim nickname 'Tin City' because of its local industry. Extraction of tin dates from the Han dynasty, though the first commercial enterprise wasn't until 1883, during the Qing dynasty. Tin extraction and smelting, still accounts for 95% of Gèjiù's economic base.

Gèjiù isn't a must-see for most travellers but it's a pleasant place for a visit, after you've been to Jiànshuǐ or Yuányáng. The lake is circled by a lovely promenade, there's lots of greenery, boating, and a teahouse or two perched above the water. A park in the south-eastern section houses one of the most significant temples in south-east Yúnnán. You can even take a chairlift up to the summit of the mountains ringing the town.

Orientation

Gèjiù is built on a north-south axis, divided by a lake, Jīn Hú. The bus station is nearly 1.5km from the city centre. The main artery, Jinhu Xilu, branches along the west side of the lake; it becomes Renmin Lu at its first major intersection south of the lake. Jinhu Nanlu leads east from here, along the south shore, 300m to the base of the hills. South of this is the real Gèjiù – half modern and half a warren of old-world architecture. The southern part of the city is buttressed by Bǎohuá Park, the site of Bàohuá Sì.

Maps Hawkers outside the main bus station sell good detailed maps of Gèjiù (Y3.50), but they're all in Chinese.

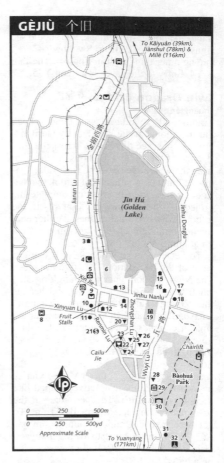

Information

The Hónghégǔ Travel Agency, next to China Post on Renmin Lu, has some tourist pamphlets covering local sights, though not much English is spoken.

The China Telecom Business Centre on Xin Jie offers slow Internet access for Y9 per hour.

Jīn Hú

Otherwise known as Golden Lake, Jīn Hú was created in 1954 when torrential rains created a sinkhole into a limestone cavern, swallowing half of the downtown. It's a

GÈJIÙ

PLACES TO STAY
3 Golden Lake Hotel
   金湖宾馆
12 Grand Hotel Honghe
   红河大酒店
13 Shìgōngānjú
   Zhùsùlóu
   市公安局住宿楼
14 Liángyǒu Jiǔdiàn
   良友酒店
15 Dìshíhàolóu
   第十号楼
16 Gèjiù Bīnguǎn
   个旧宾馆

PLACES TO EAT
17 Buffet Restaurant
   餐厅
20 Buffet Restaurant
   餐厅
23 Restaurant of
   Tin Metropolis
   锡都饭店
24 Běijīng Fàndiàn
   北京饭店

25 Pújīng Ice Cream
   Store
   葡京冰淇淋
26 Blue Baron
   蓝爵士
27 Chōuchōu
   Pósūbāo
   丑丑破酥包
28 Yìxīng Jiǔlóu
   义兴酒楼

OTHER
1 Bus Station
   汽车站
2 Post Office
   邮局
4 Mosque
   清真寺
5 China Telecom
   中国电信
6 Railway Market
   火车市场
7 China Telecom
   Business Centre
   电信新业务演示厅

8 South Bus Station
   南城客运站
9 China Post
   中国邮局
10 Hónghégú Travel
   Agency
   红河谷旅行社
11 Xīnhuá Bookstore
   新华书店
18 Xīnhuá Bookstore
   新华书店
19 Workers Cultural
   Palace
   工人文化宫
21 Bank of China
   中国银行
22 House Disco
29 Gèjiù Museum
   个旧博物馆
30 Bǎohuá Gate
   宝华门
31 Monastery
   寺庙
32 Bǎohuá Sì
   宝华寺

pleasant stroll around the wide promenade. You might be able to hire boats for a spin.

Bǎohuá Park 宝华公园
Bǎohuá Gōngyuán
A largish park on the south-eastern outskirts of downtown Gèjiù, Bǎohuá Park is built around **Bǎohuá Sì**.

The monastery was constructed from 1670 to 1675 during the Qing dynasty by a Taoist monk. Later expansions took place in the 20th century. Many of the pavilions and temples have faded but the Lingguan Pavilion, Liang Hall, and Baiyuan Tower have all been preserved.

Footpaths wind through the park, taking in some gardens and memorials. The lowlight is another zoo full of mopey camels, agitated bears and psychotic monkeys.

A chairlift up Qiling Shān departs from near the northern entrance to the park. A one-way trip is Y15; Y20 for a return. At the top is a restaurant. You could do some good ridge walks around here and walk back to town. The top of the hill is lit by incredible coloured floodlights. The chairlift operates from 10am to 11pm. Admission to the park is Y2.

Other Sights
If you are headed to Bàohuá Park, the old town offers interesting backstreets en route to Wuxi Lu. As you head up Wuxi Lu, stop off at the **Yìxīng Jiǔlóu**, a restaurant converted from the courtyard of the former Yunmiao Temple.

Nearby, the **Gèjiù Museum** has some dull exhibits on local 2000-year-old Eastern Han dynasty excavations. The attached Caishendian Sí has some fine statues.

Just up the road, by the entrance to the Bǎohuá Park is the **Bǎohuá Gate**, also known as the **Línyún Gé**, built in 1921 by the Republican government.

Places to Stay
Budget accommodation is a problem in Gèjiù. *Shìgōngānjú Zhùsùlóu (PSB Guesthouse)*, along Jinhu Nanlu, just east of the Jinhu Xilu intersection has beds in clean singles/doubles with decent common bath

for Y30/40. Rooms with bathroom cost Y60/80. The hotel is reluctant to take foreigners and so is often 'full' but you should get in with some friendly persuasion.

Probably the best budget option is the **Grand Hotel Honghe** (Hónghé Dàjiǔdiàn; ☎ 215 5598). While the main building has doubles/quads for Y120/200, the No 2 Building has doubles with bathroom for Y80 and Y50. A bed in a triple/quad is Y20/15. Shared bathrooms are clean and there are hot showers on the 2nd floor in the evening.

South of here around the corner on Jinhu Nanlu is the **Gèjiù Bīnguǎn**. A bed in a knackered triple with shared bathroom is Y20. This is one of the few places to mix Chinese and foreigners in the same room. Otherwise doubles start at Y140, triples at Y160.

Liángyǒu Jiǔdiàn (Good Friend Hotel; ☎ 214 2168) has excellent doubles for Y148, discounted to Y100, and triples or quads for Y140. Karaoke blasts until midnight.

Tops in Gèjiù are rooms at the **Golden Lake Hotel** (Jīnhú Bīnguǎn; ☎ 212 3348) on the south-west corner of the lake along Jinhu Xilu. This gleaming new complex provides panoramic views. Doubles cost Y180, discounted to Y160, including breakfast, and triples cost Y220, discounted to Y180. Try to get a lake view. The old block has doubles with bathroom for Y100, as well as doubles/triples with common bathroom for Y80/90.

Dìshíhàolóu (No 10 Guest Hotel; ☎ 212 2514, fax 212 2830, 124 Jinhu Donglu), along the far south-east shore of the lake, is being renovated to make it a three-star hotel.

Places to Eat

Lunch is easy. There are plenty of **buffet-style restaurants** where you pick out three or so dishes and rice for around Y3. The stalls set up around 11.30am and it's all over by 1.30pm. There are places by the Gèjiù Hotel, outside the Liángyǒu Jiǔdiàn and in the southern part of town.

For some of Yunnan's best bāozi and dòujiāng (soy bean milk) try **Chǒuchǒu Pòsūbāo** on Zhongshan Lu.

Across the road is the **Pújīng Ice Cream Store**, and nearby is the **Blue Baron** (Lán-juéshì), a pseudo-Western cafe for beer, coffee and Western food.

Roast tofu and goat cheese can be found all over. Head to the **railway market** between the south shore of the lake and Jinhu Nanlu, the inside of which is lined with stalls offering braziers to roast your own tofu, goat cheese, potatoes and even little sausages. Many of these are Muslim.

There are vendors selling yoghurt on most street corners. There's a **fruit market** in the alley between Jinhu Nanlu and Xinyuan Lu.

One of the nicest restaurants is the **Yìxīng Jiǔlóu** (☎ 212 4288), housed in the former Yunmiao temple. Prices are higher but veggie dishes are around Y6. The surroundings are fantastic, with seats in the side rooms of the former temple or by the pool.

Other choices include the **Restaurant of the Tin Metropolis** (Xīdū Fàndiàn) on Cailu Jie (for a real treat, be here on a Saturday when the wedding crowds invade).

Only moderately less **rènào** ('hot and noisy') is the **Běijīng Fàndiàn**, south of here on Renmin Lu.

Entertainment

At the intersection of Cailu Jie and Renmin Lu, is an entrance to an underground **House Disco**. It's worth checking out if you are curious about provincial Chinese nightlife.

The **Workers Cultural Palace** has a fine bowling alley.

Getting There & Away

Bus Gèjiù's new bus station has lots of private bus companies. Buses to Kāiyuán (Y5, one hour) depart constantly. There are buses every ten minutes to Jiànshuǐ (Y10), Měngzǐ and Kāiyuán. To Jiāngchuān, buses leave at 6.20am and 9am (Y20, 5½ hours).

Going to Shílín, take any Kūnmíng-bound bus and get off at Lùnán (Y30, three hours). One bus leaves at 9.40am for Yùxī though it would make sense to stop off somewhere in between. Buses to Tōnghǎi (Y16, five hours) leave at 6.20, 9.20 and 9.40am. To Qiūběi there is one bus at 8.20am (Y25). To Lúxī there are hourly buses between 8am and 3pm (Y26).

To Hékǒu, buses depart hourly between 7am and 10am (Y22, seven hours). There are also twice daily buses at 9.40am and 2pm straight to the Vietnamese border (Y38). A sleeper bus departs 2pm for Jǐnghóng in Xīshuāngbǎnnà (Y120 for a sleeper, 20 hours).

Buses going to Kūnmíng leave frequently from 6.20am to 10pm on a range of buses (Y30/Y40 regular/sleeper; Y48/Y60 Iweco/luxury coach, five hours).

Another regional bus station is downtown on the south-west end of Xinyuan Lu. You should find a bus here to Jiāshā (Y7, 2½ hours) for the hot springs, but otherwise the buses are all to nearby destinations.

Getting Around

The No 3 bus runs from in front of Bàohuá Park's south entrance all the way along Wuxi Lu to the main bus station north of Jīn Hú. The No 1 bus runs north from downtown to the bus station.

AROUND GÈJIÙ
Jiāshā Hot Spring

About 60km south-west of Gèjiù and on the banks of the Longcha River is this small but pleasant hot spring that maintains a temperature of 70°C.

Transport is a bit tricky. To start, roads to Jiāshā are in pretty sad shape. Gèjiù's local bus station – not the main bus station – on Xinyuan Lu has buses to Jiāshā, leaving when they are full. Departures vary seasonally. From Jiāshā it's another 10km to 15km to the spring.

Měngzì 蒙自

Měngzì, due to bad roads, is a 1½-hour ride away. It might be worth a day trip for the 200-year-old architecture. This town also claims – along with Jiànshuǐ – to being the source of Yúnnán's Across-the-bridge noodles.

Mílè 弥勒

If you're heading north for Lúxī or Qūjìng, maybe hop off for a look at Mílè. A few temples dot the town, but it's famous for its Red River cigarette brand, produced from

field-to-carton here. The Báilóng Dòng (White Dragon Cave) is the highlight.

LÚXĪ 泸西
☎ 0873

The capital of a county of 298,000 people, Lúxī county produces a wealth of coal and dried red peppers, which it exports throughout China. You'll probably see dozens and dozens of market hawkers, blankets everywhere, drying peppers in the sun.

Things to See

In the north-east section of town stands **Xiushan Hill**, a park known for its forests and scenery. A 25m-high Ming-dynasty hexagonal pavilion sits atop. Behind the park is the impressive **Confucius Temple** (Wénmiào), which is open weekdays.

The big feature in Lúxī is the **Alu Caves** (Ālù Gǔdòng), 3km north of town. This set of caves lies ensconced within a large karst formation and takes its name from a resident tribe that inhabited the area during the Song dynasty. The main cavern stretches 3000m and is broken into three caves and the crystal clear Yusun subterranean stream coursing some 800m, 15m underground (look out for transparent fish). This is overall one of the more pleasant experiences in Yúnnán. The last cave looks like a million melted candles.

Entry to the three caves, a short boat ride and a short cable car to the third cave costs Y35, or Y25 with student card. The caves are open 8am to 4.30pm. To get to the caves take minibus No 1 from the main Jiuhua Lu; it picks up at the exit of the last cave. Ticket sellers will want you to take a guide who will turn on the cave lights but if you take a torch and lose your group it's great fun exploring by torchlight.

Places To Stay & Eat

One long block from the bus station is the *Zhōngxiù Bīnguǎn*, which has doubles with bathroom for Y206, discounted to Y100. The side building is better value with triples with squat toilet for Y40 per bed. Best are the Y15 beds in a quad in the No 7 Building just outside the main gate. Foreigners almost always get the rooms to themselves. The No 7 Building is officially known as the *Xiàn Zhèngfŭ Zhāodăisŭo Qīhàolóu*. There are a couple of other hotels in town.

Ālù Dàjiŭdiàn at the entrance to the caves has doubles with bathroom for Y150 and doubles/quads with common bathroom for Y55/75.

Yíngxiāng Fàndiàn, opposite the entrance to Building No 7 has good food. There is a group of *barbecue places* in the market north of the intersection leading to the Zhōngxiù Bīnguăn.

Getting There & Away

From Lúxī there are lots of buses to Kūnmíng (Y26, 3½ hours) via Lùnán, as well as to other local destinations such as Gèjiù and Qiūběi. Coming from Kūnmíng you can explore the Stone Forest, and then either hop on a Lúxī-bound bus, or head into Lùnán, from where buses depart for Lúxī.

Sìchuān 四川

Sìchuān at a Glance

Northern Sìchuān p514

Jiŭzhàigōu p522
Sōngpān p520
Around Dégé p508 Mǎěrkāng p518
Qīngchéng Shān p462 Dūjiāngyàn p463
Chéngdū p446
Lǐtáng p510 Éméi Shān p469
Kāngdìng p495 Lèshān p470
Around Zìgòng p476
Kāngdìng p498 Yíbīn p480
Xīchāng p488 Bamboo Sea p483
Around Yíbīn p482

Area: 488,000 sq km

Population: 86 million

Capital: Chéngdū

Highlights

- Chéngdū, with fantastic backstreets, great teahouses, Sìchuān Opera and giant pandas

- Jiŭzhàigōu, a national park set in pristine alpine scenery with brightly coloured lakes

- Western Sìchuān, with soaring snow-capped peaks, grasslands, glaciers and a heavy Tibetan influence

- Dà Fó, the world's largest Buddha statue, which sits in splendour across from the city of Lèshān

- Éméi Shān, one of China's four Buddhist sacred mountains, great for hiking and monastery-hopping

The Chinese often refer to Sìchuān as Tiānfǔ Zhīguó (Heavenly Kingdom), a reference to the province's abundance of natural resources and cultural heritage. Its name means 'four rivers', referring to four of the more than 80 mighty rivers spilling across the province, weaving their way down through the soaring mountains of the north-west and across the Chūanxī plain in the east.

As the largest province, Sìchuān's population abounds with as much diversity as its landscape. While the east supports one of the densest rural populations in the world, the west rises in giant steps to the Tibetan plateau, where green tea turns to butter tea and Confucianism yields to Buddhism. These windswept grasslands and deep forests are home to the Qiang and Tibetans. Farther south, tobacco smoke curls from long pipes and vibrant embroidery brightens the mountain villages of the Yi people. The province forms the spicy heartland of South-West China.

Sìchuān's wild, mountainous terrain and fast rivers have kept it relatively isolated. Its inaccessibility has given Sìchuān its own food, dialect and character and made it the site of various breakaway kingdoms throughout Chinese history. It was here that the Kingdom of Shu ruled as an independent state during the Three Kingdoms Period (AD 220–280) and the beleaguered Kuomintang Party spent its last days before being vanquished and fleeing to Taiwan. The latest breakaway region is Chóngqìng, which split from Sìchuān in March 1997. With the split, Sìchuān lost almost 30 million people out of a total of 110 million and a quarter of its arable land – a clear sign from Běijīng that the province had become too powerful for its own good.

Sìchuān became famous during the Warring States Period (453–221 BC), when a famed engineer, Li Bing, managed to harness the Dū Hé on the Chūanxī plain with his weir system, allowing Sìchuān some 2200 continuous years of irrigation and prosperity.

Today the province continues to get rich, having played an active role in China's economic reforms over the past two decades. Zhao Ziyang, who soared from the post of First Party Secretary of Sìchuān

SÌCHUĀN 四川

HÚBĚI

Shiyan

To Xiangfan

Ankang

SHAANXI

Hanzhong

To Xi'an

Wuxi

Wushan (Yangzi)

Jiang

Wanxian

Daxian

HÚNÁN

Qianjiang

Jiang

Wu

Fengdu Fuling

CHONGQING

Youtingpu

GUIZHŌU

GUIYANG

To Luzhou

Zunyi

Anshun

GĀNSÙ

Guangyuan

Zhaohua

Bazhong

Sìchuān Basin

Nanchong

Dazu

Luzhou

Chishui

To Xingyi

Bijie

To Luzhou

Jiangyou

Mianyang

Suining

Chengdu Expressway

Neijiang

Yibin

Bamboo Sea

Bo Hanging Coffins

Luzhou

Nanping

Pingwu

Huanglong

Maowen

Xuebao Shan (5588m)

Wenchuan

CHENGDU

Dujiangyan

Meishan

Leshan

Zigong

Jiuzhaigou

Songpan

Qionglai Shan Range

Qingcheng Shan

Xinjin

Ya'an

Emei Shan (3099m)

Emei

Ebin

Wushe

Langmusi

Zöigê

Aba

Siguniang Shan (6250m)

Wolong Nature Reserve

Wolong

Danba

Tagong Grasslands

Kangding

Moxi

Hanyuan

Shimian

Meigu

Zhaojue

Butuo

Puge

GĀNSÙ

Sertar

Maerkang

Luhuo

Daofu

Yajiang

Hailuogou Glacier

Gongga Shan (7556m)

Ludig

Tuowu

Xichang

Luoji Shan (4358m)

Panzhihua (Jinjiang)

QĪNGHǍI

Sêrxü

Dzogchen

Manigango

Rongpatsa

Gānzī

Daxue Shan Range

Tro La

Tro La (Chola) Shan (6168m)

Horpo

Baiyu

Xinlong

Sìchuān-Tibet Hwy

Litang

Batang

Sìchuān-Tibet Hwy

Genyen Feng Shan (6204m)

Yalong Jiang

Daocheng

Xiangcheng

Riwa

Yading Nature Reserve

Lugu Hai

Muli

Yanyuan

Ninglang

Lijiang

To Kunming

To Lanzhou

To Yushu (Jyekundo)

Dêgê

Mesho

Peipung

Tro La Pass

To Chamdo & Lhasa

TIBET

Zhongdian

YÚNNÁN

MYANMAR (BURMA)

150km

90mi

75

45

0

0

Suggested Itineraries

The following are only a few of the countless options in this vastly varied province. Western Sìchuān, in particular, is fantastic to explore, although not a good place to be on a tight schedule.

Kūnmíng to Chéngdū

Most travellers see Sìchuān's main sites en route from Kūnmíng (or Lìjiāng) to Chéngdū. An overnight train from Kūnmíng or Jīnjiāng (the railhead for Lìjiāng) brings you to the popular Buddhist mountain of Éméi Shān, where you can follow pilgrim trails up the mountain for a couple of days, staying in monasteries en route. From here you could take a short bus ride to Lèshān, site of the biggest Buddha in the world.

From Lèshān, express buses run the four-hour trip to **Chéngdū**, where you can get some great food, take in some Sìchuān opera and check out the **Panda Research Base**. All this can be done in a week.

Northern Sìchuān

From Chéngdū take one week or a 10-day round trip to **Sōngpān** to horse trek, and wander around the gorgeous lakes and Tibetan settlements of **Jiǔzhàigōu National Park**.

You can tack on another seven to 10 days by continuing north-west from Sōngpān to the peaceful Tibetan village of **Lángmùsì**, with its many monasteries set amidst mountains and grasslands. From there, either head north into Gānsù province or return to Chéngdū via **Ābà** and **Mǎěrkāng**.

Western Sìchuān

For remote mountain travel, head south-east from Chéngdū to **Kāngdìng**, from where you can spend about 10 days following the northern route of the **Sìchuān-Tibetan Hwy** through the **Tǎgōng Grasslands** as far as **Dégé**, with its fascinating **Tibetan Printing Monastery**. Alternatively, follow the southern route of the highway to **Lǐtáng** and then continue south through the backdoor of Yúnnán, taking about a week.

If you want a taste of Sìchuān's wild Tibetan west, visit Tǎgōng village from Kāngdìng, making it there and back from Chéngdū in four days.

South-East Sìchuān

In a seven-day trip south of Chéngdū, you can take in **Zìgòng** and its fantastic **dinosaur museum** and then continue south to the **Bamboo Sea** and the **Bo Hanging Coffins**, then east to Chóngqìng or south to Guìzhōu.

---

to General Secretary of the Communist Party before falling from grace in the wake of the Tiānānmén massacre, made his reputation by instituting pioneering agricultural reforms. Under the so-called 'responsibility system', plots of land were let to farmers on the condition that a portion of the crops be sold back to the government. By 1984 the reforms had spread throughout China and were later applied to the industrial sector.

While the fruits of these economic reforms are evident in Chéngdū, one of the most prosperous, liberal and fashionable cities in the region, a less fortunate result has been soaring unemployment. With downsized bureaucracies, Sìchuān has the lion's share of China's 130 million-strong 'surplus labour force', and the first rumblings of labour unrest.

Meanwhile, worlds away from urban renewal and economic reform, the remote mountains of Sìchuān, bordering Gānsù and Qīnghǎi provinces, are the natural habitat of the giant panda. This shy animal is the one that Westerners are quickest to associate with China, landing it a new job as 'little ambassador' for the government.

SÌCHUĀN

CHÉNGDŪ 成都
☎ 028 • pop 11.3 million • elevation 500m

Chéngdū is Sìchuān's capital and its administrative, educational and cultural centre, as well as a major industrial base. It is unquestionably the economic, political and military linchpin of the South-West.

At first glance it may seem easy to write off Chéngdū as just another massive urban construction site, however with a bit of exploring you may be pleasantly surprised. With a friendly, easy-going population and some worthwhile sights, Chéngdū is a great place to spend a few days.

Comparisons between Chéngdū and Běijīng are tempting but Chéngdū has an altogether different character, with more greenery, overhanging wooden housing in the older parts of town and a very different kind of energy. You'll quickly encounter its artisans: basket-weavers, cobblers, itinerant dentists, tailors, houseware merchants and snack hawkers who swarm the streets and contribute to the city's atmosphere.

Chéngdū also abounds with new-found affluence and is bent on modernising. Many of the city's older wooden buildings have been pushed aside and replaced with trendy, opulent department stores and high-rise commercial and residential blocks. This may well be a positive change for residents who associate the older buildings with the poverty of generations past. Despite the transformation, the city has managed to retain much of its charm.

The majority of Chéngdū's streets provide an interesting wander and there are many miles of side streets to explore. Free markets, flea markets, black markets, pedlar markets, commercial districts, underground shopping malls – you'll stumble over them as you explore. Add to this the indoor food markets, the countless tiny restaurants specialising in Sìchuānese snacks, the old men walking their song birds or huddled over a game of Chinese chess, and you're looking at one of the more intriguing cities.

History
Built in 316 BC during the late Warring States Period, when the Dūjiāngyàn dam and irrigation system was put into place, Chéngdū boasts a 2300-year history, which is linked closely with the arts and crafts trades.

Running through Chéngdū is the Jǐn Jiāng, or Brocade River, carrying with its name a reminder of the city's silk brocade industry, which thrived during the Eastern Han dynasty (AD 25–220). The city's name eventually shifted from Jǐnchéng (Brocade City) to 'Lotus City', still used today by locals.

Festivals in Sìchuān

festival	location	lunar calendar	2002	2003	2004
Zìgòng Lantern Festival	Zìgòng	1st lunar month	12 Feb–13 Mar	1 Feb–2 Mar	22 Jan–19 Feb
Chéngdū Flower Fair	Qīngyáng Sì	15th of 2nd	28 Mar	17 Mar	5 Mar
Walking Around the Mountain Festival	Kāngdìng	8th of 4th	19 May	8 May	26 May
Dragon Boat Festival	Lèshān	5th of 5th	15 Jun	4 Jun	22 Jun
Huánglóng Festival	Huánglóng	10–16th of 6th	19–25 Jul	9–15 Jul	26 Jul–1 Aug
Lǐtáng Festival	Lǐtáng	13th of 6th	22 Jul	12 Jul	29 Jul
Yi Torch Festival	Puge, Butuo (Daliangshan)	24–26th of 6th	2–4 Aug	23–25 Jul	9–11 Aug
Horse Racing Festival	Tǎgòng	1st of 8th	7 Sep	28 Aug	14 Sep

NB *Dates are approximate and subject to change. Check with local authorities before setting off.*

The name Chéngdū means 'Perfect Metropolis', and by the Tang dynasty (AD 618–907) Chéngdū had become a cornerstone of Chinese society. Three hundred years later, during the Song dynasty, the city began to issue the world's first paper money.

Like other major Chinese cities, it has had its share of turmoil. First, it was devastated by the Mongols in retaliation to the fierce resistance put up by the Sìchuānese. From 1644–1647 it was presided over by the rebel Zhang Xiangzhong, who set up an independent state in Sìchuān, ruling by terror and mass executions. Three centuries later the city became one of the last strongholds of the Kuomintang.

The original city was walled and surrounded by a moat. Gates were built at the four compass points with the Viceroy's Palace (14th century) at the city's heart. The remains of the city walls were demolished in the early 1960s, and the Viceroy's Palace was blown up at the height of the Cultural Revolution. In its place was erected the Russian-style Exhibition Centre with a massive Mao statue outside, waving merrily down Renmin Lu. The Great Helmsman's gaze used to take in enormous portraits of Marx, Engels, Lenin and Stalin, but the forefathers of communism have been removed in favour of advertisements for cognac and imported watches – more in keeping with China's modern aspirations.

Orientation

Chéngdū has echoes of boulevard-sweeping Běijīng, except that here flowering shrubs and foliage line many of the expanses. As in Běijīng, there are ring roads right around the outer city (Yīhuán Lu and Èrhuán Lu), which are divided into numbered segments (duàn). The main boulevard through the centre is Renmin Lu, with its northern (běi), central (zhōng) and southern (nán) manifestations.

At the nucleus of the city is a square that interrupts the progress of Renmin Lu with administrative buildings, the Sìchuān Exhibition Centre, a sports stadium and, at its southern extent, the colossal Mao presiding over the city

Streetwise

Chéngdū is a true Asian city in its nonchalant disregard of systematic street numbering and naming. It's not unusual, when following street numbers in one direction, to meet another set coming the other way, often leaving the poor family in the middle with five sets of numbers over their doorway. Street names also seem to change every 100m or so, with very little apparent logic. When you're looking for somewhere in particular, rely more on nearby landmarks and relative locations on maps than on street numbers and names.

The area where Renmin Nanlu crosses the Jǐn Jiāng, between the Jǐnjiāng and Traffic hotels, has become the city's backpackers' ghetto. This is where you'll find many of the Western-style restaurants and coffee shops and, just south of here down Renmin Nanlu, a multiplying number of bars.

Maps The most useful map for foreigners is the English-language *Chéngdū – the Latest Tourist Map*, published by China National Import and Export Corporation and available from the Foreign Languages Bookstore.

City maps in Chinese can be found at train and bus stations, the Traffic Hotel and Foreign Languages Bookstore, and can be useful for tracing bus routes even if you can't read Chinese. Chinese maps also provide excellent detail of Sìchuān and Chéngdū's surrounding areas, though not even the best ones can hope to fully capture the insanity that is Chéngdū's street naming (see the boxed text).

Information

Tourist Offices Unless you're interested in group tours, there's no point in bothering with China International Travel Service. The main office is on Renmin Nanlu, opposite the Jǐnjiāng Bīnguǎn (☎ 665 8731, ✉ citsfit@sc .homeway.com.cn). Staff here are friendly but they can't book train tickets and don't have much information on other tours. The office is open 8.30am to 5pm daily.

SICHUAN

CHÉNGDŪ 城都

To Giant Panda Breeding
Research Base (6km), Xīndū (18km)
& Guānghàn (40km)

1
2

0   0.5   1km
0   0.25   0.5mi

3

4 ← Bei Erhuan Lu－北二路

5

To Dūjiāngyàn (60km)
& Wòlóng (140km)

6
Xīnhua Xīlu

Bei Yihuan Lu

北 一 环 路

7

Renmin Beilu

Jiefang Lu－华粹路

Sha Hé

Fu Hé

8

12

10

Renmin Zhonglu

11

Caoshi Jie

13

14

Xinhua Donglu

Xi Yulong Jie

15

红星路

Shier Qiao Lu

9

To Dù Fǔ's
Cottage (400m)

Xī'an Lu

Shahtongren Lu

Xiatongren Lu

Dongchengnen Jie

16

Xishuncheng Jie

Taisheng Nanlu

Shuwa Beijie

17   18
19

Huanxingzheng Jie

Hongxing Lu

Qinghua Jie

41

Wenhua
Park
40

Baihuatan
Park

Nan Hé

Jin He Lu

Renmin
Park
39

Renmin Donglu

35
37   36   34
33   32
46   48   30
47
38
45

Shannxi Jie

31 29
28
27   26
20 21
25
23 24

Dongfeng Lu

Chunxi Lu

22

Wuhou Renmin Lu

44

50

Shandong Dajie

Xinkai Lu

Xiadong Dajie

Nanjiao
Park

42

43

Nan Dajie

Wenmiaohou Jie

(Jin Jiang)

51
52
54   53 58
55   57
56

59

Dong Yihuan Lu

To Airport (18km),
Éméi Shān (130km) &
Lèshān (140km)

Xinnan Qiao Jie

Jiangxi Jie

62   61 60

63

Renmin Nanlu

Nan Yihuan Lu

南 一 环 路

64

Xinnan Lu

Kehua Lu

67

Wangjiang Lu

Park

68

69
70

To South Train
Station (1.5km)

Renmin Nanlu

人 民 南 路

71

Nanerhuan Lu

南 二 环 路

Fu Hé

SICHUAN

CHÉNGDŪ

PLACES TO STAY
5 Chéngdū Dàjiǔdiàn
成都大酒店
9 Chéngdū
Bǎoyuántáng Jiǔlóu;
Chengdu College of
Traditional Medicine
Guesthouse
成都保元堂酒楼
成都中医药大学招
待所
14 Jīndì Fàndiàn
金地饭店
15 Sheraton Chengdu
Lido Hotel
天府丽都喜
来登饭店
28 Holiday Inn
Crowne Plaza;
Sichuan Bīnguǎn
总府皇冠假日酒店
33 Yínhé Dynasty Hotel
银河王朝大酒店
38 Sam's Guesthouse;
Róngchéng Fàndiàn
蓉城饭店
55 Jǐnjiāng Bīnguǎn
锦江宾馆
57 Mínshān Fàndiàn
岷山饭店
61 Traffic Hotel
交通饭店

PLACES TO EAT
13 Chén Mápó Dòufu
Restaurant
陈麻婆豆腐
20 Shìměixuān Cāntīng
市美轩餐厅
23 Lóngchāoshǒu
Cāntīng
龙抄手餐厅
25 Shì Qiǎoshǒumiàn
市巧手面
30 Chéngdū Cāntīng
成都餐厅
41 Chén Mápó Dòufu
Restaurant
陈麻婆豆腐
51 Hotpot Restaurants
火锅

59 Paul's Oasis
62 Carol's by the River
卡罗西餐
63 Highfly Cafe
高飞咖啡
65 Red Brick Cafe Pub
& Pizzeria
红砖西餐厅
66 Grandma's Kitchen
祖母的厨房
70 Bāguó Bùyī
Fēngwèijiǔbù;
Grandma
Sunflower Cafe
巴国布衣风味酒部

OTHER
1 Chéngdū Zoo
成都动物园
2 Zhàojué Sì
照觉寺
3 North Train Station
火车北站
4 North Bus Station
城北汽车客运中心
6 General Post
Office/EMS
市邮电局
7 Xīmén Bus Station
西门汽车站
8 Tomb of Wáng Jiàn
王建墓
10 No 3 Hospital
三医院
11 PSB
公安局
12 Wénshū Temple
文殊院
16 Municipal Sports
Stadium
市体育场
17 Cultural Palace
文化宫
18 Main Post Office
市电信局
19 Jǐnjiāng Jùchǎng
锦江剧场
21 Sichuan Foreign
Language Bookstore
省外文书店
22 Dàcí Sì
大慈寺

24 Lido Plaza
利都广场
26 Chūnxī Commercial
District
春熙路商业区
27 Tàipíngyáng
Department Store
太平洋百货
29 Bank of China
中国银行大厦
31 Cinema
32 China Life
Insurance
Company
中国人民保险公司
34 China Telecom
电话电报大楼
35 Sìchuān Exhibition
Centre
省展览馆
36 Mao Statue
毛主席像
37 Sìchuān Fine Arts
Exhibition Hall
四川美术展览馆
39 China Post
邮电局
40 Qīngyáng Temple
青羊宫
42 Wǔhóu Temple;
Nánjiāo Park
武侯祠南郊公园
43 Tibetan Shops
西藏专卖店
44 PSB (Foreign
Affairs Section)
省公安局外事科
45 Internet Cafe
网吧
46 Chéngdū
Department Store
成都百货大楼
47 People's Market
人民商场
48 Advance Rail
Booking Office
火车站售票处
49 Yánshìkǒu Plaza
盐市口广场
50 South-West
Book Centre
西南书城

continued over

SÌCHUĀN

CHÉNGDŪ

52	Sìchuān Airlines 四川航空公司	58	Qīngshíqiáo Sìcháng 青石桥市场	68	River Viewing Pavilion Park 望江楼公园
53	China Southwest Airlines 中国西南航空公司	60	Xīnnánmén Bus Station 新南门汽车站	69	Wild Goose Cafe; Seventh Sensation; Twelve Oaks
54	Bank of China 中国银行	64	Sìchuān Provincial Museum 省博物馆	71	US Consulate 美国领事馆
56	CITS 中国国际旅行社、 中国民航	67	Sìchuān University Museum 四大博物馆		

More useful are the travel agencies in and around the Traffic Hotel (see Travel Agencies later in this section). Sam of Sam's Guesthouse is also a great source of information.

Consulates The US consulate (☎ 558 3992, fax 558 3520) is in a small fortress at 4 Lingshiguan Lu, just off Renmin Nanlu between the first and second ring roads.

Public Security Bureau The main PSB office (Zhōu Gōngānjú) is about 1.5km north of the centre on Wenwu Lu, east of the intersection with Renmin Zhonglu. However, whether you're seeking visa extensions or even reporting a theft, you'll probably be better off at the Foreign Affairs section (☎ 630 1454). It's a single-storey building at 40 Wenmiaohou Jie, off Nan Dajie to the west of the Jīnjiāng Bīnguǎn. Some staff members speak excellent English. This office is open 8am to 11am and 2.30pm to 5pm Monday to Friday, and 8.30am to 11am Sunday. Saturday hours are hit and miss.

Money Many hotels, including the Traffic and Jinjiang, have foreign-exchange counters, although they may offer poor rates. There are two useful branches of the Bank of China: one next to the Jīnjiāng Bīnguǎn, on Renmin Nanlu, and the other at the eastern end of Renmin Donglu. Both change money painlessly, have ATMs and offer cash advances on credit cards. Banking hours are 8.30am to 11.30am and 2.30pm to 5pm Monday to Friday.

Post & Communications China Post's main office is housed in a converted church on the corner of Huaxingzheng Jie and Shuwa Beijie, close to the Cultural Palace in the centre of town. It's open 8.30am to 6pm daily.

Numerous other little post offices are scattered throughout the city centre. For poste restante you will need to go to the general post office (the EMS building) on Shawan Lu, near the intersection of Bei Erhuan Lu. To get there, take bus No 48 from Xishuncheng Jie, east of Mao's statue, to the second-to-last stop, just past the large overpass. Walk east along the second ring road until you see a statue, and turn right. It'll be ahead on the left.

More convenient might be the poste restante service at the Traffic Hotel, which holds letters and parcels for 15 days at the luggage storage counter. Items should be mailed care of the Traffic Hotel, 77 Linjiang Rd, Xīnnánmén, Chéngdū 610041.

The best place in town for making reverse-charge (collect) calls is China Telecom (Diànxìn Shāngchéng), east of the Sìchuān Exhibition Centre. You can also make direct-dial overseas calls and faxes from here. Card phones for home-country direct calls are along a wall to the left after entering. The telecommunications service is supposed to be open 24 hours but don't count on it.

Email & Internet Access There's no problem getting online in Chéngdū. You'll find countless Internet cafes offering access for Y3 per hour. There are three offices across from Sam's Guesthouse and more

Carrying a heavy load of water home along a winding country road in Xīshuāngbǎnnà, Yúnnán

JOHN BORTHWICK

Window cleaners scaling a Kūnmíng building

BILL WASSMAN

The city lights of Chéngdū

MARTIN MOOS

Guìzhōu's magical Huángguǒshù Falls plunging down into Rhinoceros Pool at night

around Bean Café and Paul's Oasis. A number of restaurants (such as Grandma's Kitchen) also offer access, although at slightly higher rates.

Travel Agencies There are several travel agencies and private entrepreneurs in the vicinity of the Traffic Hotel offering useful services. There are at least five different agencies in the hotel itself.

Common tour destinations aimed at backpackers are Hǎiluógōu Glacier Park, Wòlóng, Jiǔzhàigōu, Éméi Shān and Sōngpān. There are also daytrips to the Giant Panda Breeding Research Centre, local operas and the Traditional Chinese Medicine Centre. Prices vary but are generally good value. Agencies can often arrange Yangzi River cruise tickets, train and flight tickets and permits to Lhasa.

You may also encounter Mr Lee (☎ 139-0803 5353, @ lee_tray@hotmail.com) who frequents the Renmin Park teahouses. He'll provide free information and can arrange tours of everything from artists' quarters to silk factories to kindergartens. For a tour of a local Sìchuān opera including a backstage tour contact Mike (☎ 626 6510) after 8.30pm (see the Entertainment section later).

Bookshops The Sìchuān Foreign Languages Bookstore has good maps and tourist literature, English-teaching materials, novels such as *Jane Eyre*, short story collections and Grimm's fairy tales. The front of the shop is devoted to VCDs, music and electronic goods. To find the books, head to the back left corner of the shop. There is also a selection of postcards here. The bookshop is just off the intersection of Dongfeng Lu and Hongxing Lu.

South of here, on the corner of Shangdong Dajie and Zouma Jie, is the new, colossal South-West Book Centre, with more English-teaching materials as well as Chinese art books.

A number of guesthouses and cafes, including Paul's Oasis, Sam's Guesthouse and Bean Cafe, have book exchanges. This is likely your best bet for picking up some new reading material.

Medical Services The Global Doctor (☎/fax 678 6746, @ chengdu@eglobal doctor.com, W www.eglobaldoctor.com) at room 402 of the Holiday Inn Crowne Plaza is an Australian clinic that offers English-speaking doctors.

Dangers & Annoyances There have been several reports of foreigners becoming targets for rip-offs and theft. As always ask the price in taxis and pedicabs, and in restaurants, at the start of proceedings. You can also check notice boards and notebooks in cafes and guesthouses for tourist agencies to avoid.

Pickpockets are common around bus and train stations and post offices. Watch out for gangs who use razors to slit your bags on buses. In trains, make a note of your ticket numbers. Then if the tickets are stolen you'll be given replacements.

While Chéngdū feels like a safe city, there have been a couple of incidents on the riverside path between the Jǐnjiāng and Traffic Hotels. (One foreigner was stabbed.) Take care late at night – it's best not to walk alone. Should things get out of hand, ring the Foreign Affairs section of the PSB. English is spoken and the staff do their best to assist.

Wenshu (God of Wisdom) Temple 文殊院
Wénshū Yuàn

This Tang dynasty temple, a monastery located in the north of town, is Chéngdū's largest and best-preserved Buddhist place of worship. It was originally known as Xinxiang Temple, but was renamed after a Buddhist monk who lived there in the late 17th century. It is believed that his presence literally illuminated the monastery.

A bustling crowd of worshippers flock to the place. Together with the exquisite relief carvings that decorate many of the buildings in the complex, they render the temple well worth a visit.

In the monastery grounds, check out the teahouse, one of the largest in Chéngdū, with what seems like acres of tables. If you want to join in, sit on the west side of the path, closest to the main temple, where tea costs Y1. The tea must be greener on the other side of the path where it costs Y10. The vegetarian restaurant next door has great food at good prices. Buy food tickets in a booth outside the restaurant and exchange them at the kitchen window for overflowing dishes.

The alley off Renmin Zhonglu, on which the monastery is located, is a curiosity in itself, with joss-stick vendors, foot-callus removers, beggars, blind fortune-tellers with bamboo spills, and flower and fireworks sellers.

The monastery is open 6am to 8.30pm daily, and there's an entry charge of Y1. Some travellers have reported not being able to enter until 8am.

Tomb of Wáng Jiàn 王建墓
Wángjiàn Mù

In the north-west of town, the Tomb of Wáng Jiàn was, until 1942, thought to be Zhuge Liang's music pavilion (see Wǔhóu Temple later in this section). Wang Jian (AD 847–918) was a Tang general who established the Former Shu kingdom in the aftermath of the collapse of the Tang in 907.

The tomb in the central building is surrounded by statues of 24 musicians all playing different instruments, and is considered to be the best surviving record of a Tang dynasty musical troupe.

Also featured are relics taken from the tomb itself, including a jade belt, mourning books and imperial seals. The tomb is open 8.30am to 6pm daily. Entry costs Y3.

Qīngyáng Temple 青羊宫
Qīngyáng Gōng

West of Mao, on the western section of the circular road, is Wénhuà Gōngyuán. This park is home to Qīngyáng (Green Ram) Temple, the oldest and most extensive Taoist temple in the area.

The story goes that Laotzu, the shadowy originator of Taoism and reputed author of the *Daodejing (The Way and Its Power)*, asked a friend to meet him there. When the friend arrived he saw only a boy leading two goats on a leash and, in a fabulous leap of lateral thinking, realised the boy was Laotzu.

The goats are represented in bronze in the rear building. If the one with only one horn looks slightly ungoat-like, it is because it combines features of all the Chinese zodiac animals: a mouse's ears, a cow's nose, a horse's mouth, the back of a rabbit, a snake's tail, the neck of a monkey and a pig's bum. The solitary horn was borrowed from a dragon. For its goatish qualities, take a look at the beard. The other goat can vanquish life's troubles and pains if you stroke its flank.

In the centre of the temple grounds is an eight-sided pagoda that is an architectural embodiment of Taoist philosophy. There are no bolts or pegs holding the building together. Instead each piece fits into the next and the building balances as a whole.

The park is open 6am to 8pm and costs Y1.50 to enter. The temple is open 8am to 5pm; entry costs Y1. While here check out **Qintai Lu**, just east of Wenhua Park, whose old-world charm has been tarted up for tourists and is now home to a number of plush teahouses and restaurants. At the southern end of the road is the pleasant **Baihuatan Park**.

Dù Fǔ's Cottage 杜甫草堂
Dùfǔ Cǎotáng

Qīngyáng Temple can be combined with a visit to Dù Fǔ's Cottage, former home of the celebrated Tang dynasty poet. Dù Fǔ (AD 712–770) was born in Hénán but left his home province at the tender age of 20 to see China. He was an official in Chang'an (the ancient capital on the site of modern-day Xī'ān) for 10 years, was later captured by rebels after an uprising and fled to Chéngdū, where he stayed for four years. He built himself a humble cottage and penned over 200 poems on simple themes around the lives of the people who lived and worked nearby.

The present grounds – 20 hectares of leafy bamboo and luxuriant vegetation – are a much-enlarged version of Dù Fǔ's original poetic retreat. This is also the centre of the Chéngdū Dù Fǔ Study Society, and several display halls house examples of the poet's work.

From the time of his death in exile (in Húnán), Dù Fǔ acquired cult status, and his poems have been a major source of inspiration. His statue is accompanied by statues of two lesser poets: Li You and Huang Tingjian.

Dù Fǔ's Cottage is open 7am to 11pm. Fee is Y5 to the grounds, Y15 to the cottage.

Wǔhóu Temple 武侯祠
Wǔhóu Cí

To the west of the Jǐnjiāng Bīnguǎn and next to Nánjiāo Park is Wǔhóu Temple. Wuhou might be translated as 'Minister of War', the title given to Zhuge Liang, a famous military strategist of the Three Kingdoms Period (AD 220–280) immortalised in one of the classics of Chinese literature, *The Tale of the Three Kingdoms*.

For the Chinese, Zhuge Liang is not the main attraction of the temple. The front shrine is dedicated to Liu Bei, Zhuge Liang's emperor. Liu's temple, the Hanzhaolie Temple, was moved here and rebuilt during the Ming dynasty, but the Wǔhóu Temple name stuck.

Liu is a common Chinese surname, and many make a point of visiting the temple while they are in Chéngdū on the glorious off chance that the emperor is a distant ancestor. The park and temple each cost Y2 to enter. The park opens at 6am and the temple at 6.30am; both close at 10pm.

Renmin Park 人民公园
Rénmín Gōngyuán

To the south-west of the city centre, Renmin (People's) Park is well worth visiting. The teahouse here is excellent (see the Entertainment section later) and a perfect perch for people-watching.

The park also holds a bonsai rockery, a children's playground, a few swimming pools, and the Monument to the Martyrs of the Railway-Protecting Movement (1911). This obelisk, decorated with shunting manoeuvres and railway tracks, marks an uprising of the people against officers who pocketed cash raised for the construction of the Chéngdū to Chóngqìng line. Since the park was also at the time a private officers'

garden, it was a fitting place to erect the structure.

Across the lake from the teahouse is the entry to an underground museum/funhouse that is one of Chéngdū's weirder experiences. An entry fee of Y10 buys you a tour through a converted air-raid shelter where, after a maze of cafeterias and arcades, you can hop on a shuttle-train and travel through aging scenes from the wild west, space, the dinosaur age and straight into the mouth of a shark. There's also endless display cases of beautiful shells from the world's seas.

Renmin Park opens at 6.30am and stays open until 2am to allow free access to patrons of a disco dance hall located on the park grounds. Admission is Y2.

Sìchuān Provincial Museum
四川省博物馆 Sìchuān Shěng Bówùguǎn

This is the largest provincial museum in the South-West, with more than 150,000 items on display. The displays of tiled murals and frescoes taken from nearby tombs offer a wide-ranging depiction of ancient daily activities, from agriculture to dance.

The museum is open 9am to 4pm weekdays and 10am to 4pm weekends. Admission is Y10. The museum is down Renmin Nanlu in the direction of the south train station and within cycling distance of the city centre.

Sìchuān University Museum
四川大学博物馆 Sìchuān Dàxué

Founded in 1914 by US scholar DS Dye, this museum reopened under its current name in 1984. The four exhibition rooms display over 40,000 items. The collection is particularly strong in the fields of ethnology, folklore and traditional arts.

The ethnology room exhibits artefacts from the Yi, Qiang, Miáo, Jingpo, Nàxī and Tibetan cultures. The Chinese painting and calligraphy room displays works from the Tang, Song, Yuan, Ming and Qing dynasties. Some labels are in English.

The museum is open 8.30am to 11.30am and 2.40pm to 5.30pm Monday to Friday. Entry costs Y10. The museum is in the south-east of the city; from the university's main entrance off Wangjiang Lu, go straight until the road ends at a T-junction. The museum is the first building on the right.

Dàcí Sì 大慈寺

East on Dongfeng Lu is Dàcí Sì (Temple of Mercy). A few small buildings display calligraphy and paintings, but the grounds are filled with small bamboo tables overflowing with teacups, mahjong pieces and sunflower seeds, and Chéngdū's older folks. Admission to this spectacle costs Y1.

River Viewing Pavilion
Wàngjiāng Lóu

Near Sìchuān University is a four-storey wooden pavilion overlooking the Jǐn Jiāng. The Qing dynasty pavilion was built to the memory of Xue Tao, a female Tang dynasty poet with a great love for bamboo. Nearby is a well, where she drew water to dye her writing paper.

The surrounding park is famous for its lush bamboo forests and boasts over 150 types of bamboo from China, Japan and South-East Asia. The varieties of bamboo range from bonsai-sized potted plants to towering giants, creating a shady retreat in the heat of summer.

The park is open 9am to 6pm and the entry fee is Y2.

Chéngdū Zoo 动物园
Chéngdū Dòngwùyuán

Chinese zoos are always slightly depressing, and although now upstaged by the nearby Giant Panda Breeding Research Base, this zoo still has a respectable collection of around six pandas.

The zoo is about 6km north-east of the city centre and is open 7.30am to 8pm daily. Admission is Y3. There are minibuses running direct to the zoo from the north train station. Cycling isn't advisable unless you don't mind riding along clogged motorways.

Zhàojué Sì 照觉寺

Next door to the zoo, this temple is a Tang dynasty building dating from the 7th century. During the early Qing dynasty it underwent extensive reconstruction under the supervision of Po Shan, a famous Buddhist monk who established waterways and groves of trees around the temple. The temple has since served as a model for many Japanese and South-East Asian Buddhist temples.

Unsurprisingly, it went through hard times during the Cultural Revolution but has been restored and is worth combining with a trip to the zoo. There's a vegetarian restaurant on the grounds that serves lunch from 11am to 2pm, as well as an adjacent teahouse. The temple is open from 7am to 7pm and admission is Y1.

Giant Panda Breeding Research Base 大熊猫繁殖研究中心
Dà'ióngmaō Fánzhí Yánjiū Zhōngxīn

About 6km north of the zoo, this research station and breeding ground for giant and lesser pandas has been in operation since 1990 and was first opened to the public in 1995.

Some 10 to 12 giant pandas currently reside at the base, in quarters somewhat more humane than those at the zoo, although still fairly small. There is also a breeding area that has been partially opened and where some of China's animal ambassadors are allowed to 'freely roam'. The result has been a number of baby pandas and if you're lucky, in autumn you may get to see tiny newborns in the 'nursery'.

Just past the entrance gate, the base museum has detailed exhibits on panda evolution, habits (including rather graphic displays on the, um, more private physiology and reproductive aspects of the bears), habitats and conservation efforts, all with English captions.

Once the breeding area is completed the base will cover over 230 hectares. This is just the beginning though, as there are long-term plans to build a US$70 million theme park around the site. The base is open 8am to 6pm daily, but the best time to visit is between 8.30am and 10am: feeding time is around 9.30am and soon thereafter the pandas return to their other predominant pastime, sleeping.

The entry fee of Y30 is a bit steep, but at least some of the money goes to a good cause and you are guaranteed a look at these elusive animals.

The Elusive Panda

Distributed almost entirely in the north and north-west of Sìchuān are the world's surviving thousand or so giant pandas. Living at high altitudes in mountainous regions, this endangered mammal is shrouded as much by mystery as by perpetual mist and cloud. Sightings are rare and our knowledge remains patchy.

Some sources claim that the giant panda has existed for around 600,000 years while others date earliest remains of the panda as far back as the Ice Age, between one and three million years ago. Scientists have spent over a century debating whether pandas belong to the bear family, the raccoon family, or are a separate family of their own.

As good climbers and solitary animals, pandas are adept at evading observation. But if you manage to spot one in the wild you'd quickly recognise it, with its black-and-white face having been popularised as the emblem of the World Wide Fund for Nature and as the logo on Chinese cigarettes. Chinese literature has references to pandas (xióngmāo or 'bear cats' in Chinese) going back over 3,000 years; however, it wasn't until 1869 that the West found out about the panda, when a French missionary brought a pelt back with him to Paris. Now, in the 21st century, this stout, pigeon-toed animal is facing extinction.

An obvious factor in the depletion of the giant panda population is the encroachment of humans as China's land and resources attempt to meet the needs of its massive population. To counter this, the Government has set up 11 panda reserves and attempted to diminish the threat of panda hunting by imposing life sentences and public executions on convicted poachers.

Pandas are also threatened by their exclusive eating habits. They consume enormous amounts of food – up to 20kg a day – with bamboo accounting for around 95% of their diet. They spend 10 to 16 hours a day munching on it, but will only eat around 20 of China's 300 species of bamboo. In the mid-1970s more than 130 pandas starved to death when one of these favoured species flowered and withered in the Mín Shān Range of Sìchuān.

Perhaps the greatest difficulty faced by conservationists is the panda's slow reproductive rate. Pandas remain solitary throughout the year, except during their three-month mating season each spring. Then pandas not only have a tricky time finding one another, they're also rather particular about who they'll mate with, especially in captivity.

Females generally birth only one cub. When two cubs are born the mother, unable to care for both, tends to leave one behind or crush it in its sleep. An amazing 60% of panda cubs die shortly after being born. For the first month after birth, the mother carries the cub in one of her paws at all times, even as she sleeps and eats. Good news came in 1998 as zoologists discovered a cure for panda gastro-enteritis, the biggest killer of panda cubs.

Conservationists have had low success rates with breeding pandas in captivity. Artificial insemination has been attempted at Běijīng Zoo and even Viagra has been introduced to spice up the panda's sex life. Cloning remains a further option. Six cubs were born in one week alone in Wòlóng in August 2000 (45 cubs have been born here since 1963) and the first panda triplets were born in 1999.

With world attention on the survival of the panda, Chinese laws now strictly forbid locals to hunt, fell trees or make charcoal in the panda habitats. Farmers in these areas are offered rewards equivalent to up to five times their annual salary if they save a starving panda, which is exactly what happened when an emaciated panda stumbled into a farmer's backyard in Shenxi village near Dūjiāngyàn in 1999. And despite a constant battle with budget deficits, China's central government maintains its funding to the Breeding and Research Base in Chéngdū which continues in its struggle to find solutions to preserve pandas and their habitats.

SICHUAN

Getting to the base is a bit tricky. Cycling is not recommended as you'll mainly be travelling along congested motorways. The base is not served by any bus routes, so your other options are to take a taxi or a tour. The Traffic Hotel and Sam's Guesthouse offer tours for Y50 per person, including the admission fee. This is definitely the best deal.

Places to Stay – Budget

Chéngdū has some excellent foreigner-friendly budget accommodation.

Once upon a time, Sam's Guesthouse was located west of downtown on the grounds of the Chéngdū College of Traditional Medicine, and many travellers continue to head there in search of a budget bed. There are two guesthouses on the campus; neither is particularly quiet, and you'll likely need to bargain for a decent price.

As you enter the grounds off Shi'er Qiao Lu, and walk straight up the drive, the first guesthouse you'll come to on your left is the *Chéngdū Bǎoyuán Tāngjiúlōu* (☎ 777 0511) with dorm beds for Y40 and doubles with bath for Y150. If you take a left just before this guesthouse and then a right, you'll find the *Chéngdū College Of Traditional Medicine Guesthouse* (*Chéngdū Dūzhōngyīyào Dà'ué Zhāodāisuǒ;* ☎ 775 3909), with similar rooms. Doubles are Y160 and dorms (if you can get them) range from Y20 to Y50.

Sam has moved to the Róngchéng Fàndiàn, where he leases a wing for *Sam's Guesthouse* (☎ 609 9022, ℮ Samtour@ yahoo.com), now only a few steps away from the heart of downtown. Enter through the gate on the hotel's left, head into the building straight ahead and you'll find Sam's reception down the first hall on the left. Clean and surprisingly quiet rooms overlook a garden, with dorm beds going for Y20 and doubles with bath and hot water for Y80 to Y120. You'll also find VCD rental, left luggage, cafe, email, travel service, laundry, bike rental, book exchange and an information/notice board.

Across the river and conveniently located next to the Xīnnánmén Bus Station is the ever-popular *Traffic Hotel* (*Jiāotōng Fàndian;* ☎ 545 1017, fax 558 2777). Although a little less cosy than Sam's, this place has similar services including a large array of tours. A bed in a triple with satellite TV and air-con (a lifesaver in summer) is Y40, with showers and toilet down the hall. Doubles/ triples with satellite TV and bathroom cost Y200/300. All prices include a decidedly uninspiring breakfast. To get here from the north train station, take bus No 16 and get off past the bridge just south of the Jǐnjiāng Bīnguǎn; from there it's a 10-minute walk east along the south bank of the river.

Places to Stay – Mid-Range

Chéngdū hasn't much in the way of mid-range options. North-west of downtown is the *Jǐndì Fàndiàn* (☎ 691 5339 ext 281), a two-star hotel with bright, clean singles/ doubles with bath, air con and a private safe for Y160/230.

Chéngdū Dàjiǔdiàn (☎ 317 3888 ext 3105) is feeling the competition of the army of new top-end hotels appearing all over town and, with clean, comfortable rooms conveniently located for early morning trains, it's well worth seeing if they're offering a deal. Large, heated doubles with bath and minibar are posted at Y300 to Y400 but go for Y120 to Y240.

Róngchéng Fàndiàn (☎ 611 2933), west off Renmin Nanlu, used to be dirt-cheap but has endured an overhaul and now has somewhat overpriced doubles starting at Y240. The hotel is conveniently located but the rooms are mediocre and a few travellers have reported nocturnal visitations by Mr Rat.

Places to Stay – Top End

If you're looking for plush accommodation, Chéngdū has a sea of top-end hotels to choose from. With continuously growing competition, huge discounts (up to 40%) are often available during the low season so it's worth shopping around. The prices listed below are the posted rates that you can expect to pay during high season.

Mínshān Fàndiàn (☎ 558 3333, ℮ m hotel@swww.com.cn), near the river on Renmin Lu, has bright, four-star rooms starting at Y800. The hotel has a couple of bars, a coffee shop and five restaurants, and is a popular option for tour groups.

Across the street, *Jīnjiāng Bīnguǎn* (☎ 558 2222, fax 558 23448, [e] *ajjhsw@shell .scsti.ac.cn*) is a five-star giant with pricey standards starting from Y1180 in the new wing and singles/doubles in the older building for Y788/960. Rooms aren't half as nice as those across the road, but they do have the option of non-smoking rooms. There are good views to be had from the rooftop Chinese restaurant here, but at a high price: beer and soft drinks are around Y30 each.

Downtown you'll find the *Holiday Inn Crowne Plaza* (*Zǒngfǔ Huángguàn Rì Jiǔdiàn;* ☎ 678 6666, fax 678 6599, *31 Zongfu Jie*), the *Yínhé Dynasty Hotel* (*Yínhé Wǎngsháo Dàfàndiàn;* ☎ 661 8888, [e] *dynasty@mail.sc.cninfo.net, 99 Xiaxishuncheng Jie*) and the brand-new *Sheraton Chéngdū Lido Hotel* (*Tiānhū Lìdō Dūxǐláidēng Fàndiàn;* ☎ 676 8999, *15 Section 1, Renminzhong Lu*). All three offer five-star services and plush international restaurants and shops. Standard doubles start from around US$140.

Attached to the Holiday Inn, the *Sìchuan Bīnguǎn* (☎ 675 9147, *31 Zongfu Lu*) offers similar rooms for slightly cheaper, with singles/doubles from Y580/800.

Places to Eat
Chinese Restaurants For an excellent bowl of noodles, try the *Shì Qiǎoshǒumiàn*, just south of Dongfeng Lu on Hongxin Lu. You can watch noodles being made fresh on the premises and the friendly staff are happy to cater to vegetarians. A huge, filling bowl of noodles costs Y2. Also try the spicy radish pickles.

In the north of the city, on Jiefang Lu, *Chén Mápó Dòufu (Pockmarked Grandma Chen's Bean Curd)* serves *mapo doufu* with a vengeance. Soft, fresh bean curd is served up with a fiery meat sauce of garlic, minced beef, salted soybean, chilli oil and nasty little peppercorns for Y3 a bowl. Beer is served to cool the fires. Also served are spicy chicken and duck and plates of tripe. As the story goes, the woman with the

pockmarked face set up shop here a century ago, providing food and lodging for itinerant peddlers.

Be sure to sit downstairs, as the 2nd floor has been redone to look like a typical Chinese banquet hall and carries a Y5 'seating charge'. Don't worry about the grotty decor – those spices should kill any lurking bugs. This place appears to have franchised, with a second, more pleasant version across from Wénhuà Park.

Chéngdū Cāntīng (134 Shangdong Dajie) is one of Chéngdū's most famous and authentic restaurants. It has a good atmosphere, decent food and reasonable prices; downstairs serves set courses of appetisers, while full meals can be had upstairs. Try to assemble a group before venturing forth as you get to sample more. Arrive early: the place starts shutting down around 8.30pm.

For *guoba roupian*, you can't beat the *Shìměixuān Cāntīng* opposite the Jinjiang Theatre on Huaxingzheng Jie. A large plate of crispy rice in pork and lychee sauce costs around Y10, plenty for two. The proprietors don't seem to mind if you walk through the kitchen and point out what you want. Large, clean dining rooms with wooden tables and ceiling fans make eating here even more enjoyable.

Bāguó Bùyī Fēngwèijiǔbù, south along Renmin Nanlu, is named after the traditional cotton clothing worn by peasants in an ancient state of eastern Sìchuān. Best described as down-home country Sìchuān, you wander and point. Be careful – it isn't cheap.

Vegetarian A special treat for vegetarians is to head out to the Wénshū Temple, where there is an excellent *vegetarian restaurant* with an English menu.

Zhàojué Sì also serves up vegetarian dishes for lunch. If you're really keen, you might ride out to the Monastery of Divine Light in Xīndū in time for lunch (11am to noon). For details of the bus service, see Around Chéngdū later in this chapter.

Snacks Many of Chéngdū's specialities originated as *xiǎo chī* (little eats). The snack bars are great fun and will cost you next to nothing. In fact, the offerings here can be outdone in no other.

Still going strong is **Lóngchāoshǒu Cāntīng**. It has sampler courses that allow you to experience the whole gamut of Chéngdū snacks. The Y5 course gives you a range of sweet and savoury items, while the Y10 and Y15 courses are basically the same deal on a grander and more filling scale. Apparently they haven't much to offer vegetarians. The restaurant is on the corner of Chunxi Lu and Dong Dajie.

You'll see lots of sidewalk hotpot operations in the older section of town near the Chunxi Lu market. Skewers of veggies or meat are around two máo to five máo each.

Unlike hotpots, shākǎo is a popular lunchtime snack as well. You'll find roadside stalls all over the city as well as portable grills on bikes.

Gastronomic Delights

With influences from most areas of China, the 4,000 Sìchuānese speciality dishes are a delight of taste and variety. It is, however, undoubtedly China's hottest and spiciest cuisine – often made with *huājiāo* (flower pepper), a crunchy devil that leaves an unusual aftertaste and numbs your mouth. When restaurant proprietors see your face begin to turn purple and steam shooting out your ears, they'll quickly serve you some peanut milk, reportedly the best thing for cooling the fires.

Sìchuān chefs have a catch-cry that draws attention to the diversity of Sìchuānese cooking styles: '*bǎicài, bǎiwèi*', literally, 'a hundred dishes, a hundred flavours'. It's true that there's a bewildering profusion of sauces and culinary preparation techniques; so many that you could spend a couple of months eating out in Chéngdū and still only scratch the surface.

Some of the better-known varieties include *yúxiāng wèi*, a tasty fish-flavoured sauce that draws heavily on vinegar, soy sauce and mashed garlic and ginger; *málà wèi*, a numbingly spicy sauce that is often prepared with bean curd; *yānxūn wèi*, a 'smoked flavour' sauce, mostly used with smoked duck; and, perhaps most famous of all, the hot and sour sauce *suānlà wèi*. The hot and sour soup, *suānlà tāng*, is popular throughout China and is great on a cold day – provided you've got some peanut milk handy.

Sìchuān's most popular dishes include *gōngbǎo jīdīng* (spicy chicken fried with peanuts) and *mápó dòufu* (bean curd, pork and chopped spring onions prepared in a chilli sauce). Also try *kǒudài dòufu* ('pocket bean curd', which are cubes of stuffed bean curd), *guàiwèi jīsī* ('strange taste chicken'; diced chicken prepared with a sweet yet spicy sauce) and *zhāngchá yāzi* (smoked-tea duck). *Dāndān miàn* are oily noodles whose name translates as 'carrying pole noodles'. The best-named snack must be *mǎyǐ shàngshù*, or 'ants climbing the tree' – thin noodles tossed with bits of spicy meat.

A favourite with travellers and worth trying simply for the novelty value is *guōbā ròupiàn*. Guoba refers to the crispy bits of rice, uncannily similar to Rice Krispies, that get stuck to the bottom of the rice pot – they are served on a plate, and pork and gravy are added at your table.

Two favourites throughout Sìchuān are *huǒguō*, or hotpot, and *shāokǎo*, Sìchuānese barbecue. Hotpot originated in Chóngqìng and involves dipping skewers of meat and veggies into a wok of hot, spiced oil, fondue style. Barbecue is generally found at street stalls and is similar to hotpot except that the skewered food is brushed with oil and chilli and grilled while you wait. With both, you pay by the skewer and it's best to ask the price first. During the winter months the skewered items on offer tend to be meat or vegetables like potatoes. In the summer months lighter, mostly vegetarian fare is the norm.

Both hotpot and barbecue can be ferociously hot – even some Sìchuānese can't take it. If you want it a little tame, ask for *báiwèi*, the hotpot for wimps, or *bùlà*, the barbecue equivalent. Some will turn their noses up at this, claiming that it's not the real thing – toast them with your peanut milk and dig in, knowing your tastebuds will live to taste another dish.

Western Food For amazing North American cuisine head to *Grandma's Kitchen* (*Zǔmǔ Dēchúfang; 75 Kehau Beilu,* ☎ 524 2835). Here you can fill up on baked macaroni and cheese, steak, pizza, salads, soup, fluffy pancakes and excellent desserts. Grandma is also stocked with a huge variety of beer. At *Grandma's Sunflower Café* on Renmin Lu you can choose from a more limited version of the same menu in front of a roaring log fire.

Next door to Grandma's Kitchen is the *Red Brick Café Pub and Pizzeria* (*Hóng Zhuānxī Cāntīng*). Specialising in pizza and pasta, they also offer moderately priced appetisers, chicken dishes and even some pan-Asian and African dishes.

Backpacker-friendly Western-style cafes have exploded all over Chéngdū. One of the most popular is *Paul's Oasis* (☎ 672 3074), where you can get fries, pizza and cheap ice-cold beer. The place often sees patrons moving furniture outside and dancing into the morning. Across the river, *Carol's by the River* (*Kǎluó Xīcàn*) serves up good food with south-western US and Mexican overtones. South-west of here is the *Highfly Café* (*Gāofēi Kāfēi*), one of Chéngdū's longest-running cafes and famous for its brownies. Finally, Sam's Guesthouse has a small cafe with oatmeal, pancakes and excellent vegetarian pizza.

Entertainment

Finding entertainment can be fruitful hunting in Chéngdū, but you will have to hunt. If you don't speak Chinese, ask around among the English-speaking staff at the Traffic Hotel or the travel outfits nearby.

If something strikes your fancy, get it written down in Chinese, and get a good map location – these places are often hard to find, especially at night. If you have more time, try and get advance tickets. Among other things there's teahouse entertainment, acrobatics, cinema, Sìchuān opera, Běijīng opera, drama, art exhibits, traditional music, storytelling and shadow plays.

Opera Sìchuān opera has a 200-year tradition and features slapstick, men dressed as women, eyeglass shattering songs and gymnastics. Several opera houses are scattered throughout the older sections of town. As attendances fall, however, most cut back performances to only once or twice per week.

If you are interested in seeing a local Sìchuān opera, contact Mike (☎ 626 6510) after 8.30pm. He'll take you to a small, local opera house hidden in the depths of a market. While the cast, costume and make-up is all very professional, the audience use the theatre as a meeting place and chat and slurp tea throughout the performance. Mike is a friendly, English-speaking local who will give you a running translation of the opera. You'll also get a backstage tour, tea and a taxi to and from the opera for Y60 per person. It is an entertaining and worthwhile experience. Try to go on the weekend when the performance is a combination of the highlights from a number of operas.

Local English-speaking tour guides around the Traffic Hotel and Sam's Guesthouse also organise backstage tours for around Y40 to Y50 per person, with tours leaving around 2pm.

If you'd rather go on your own, one of the easier Sìchuān opera venues to find is the Jinjiang Theatre on Huaxingzheng Jie, which is a combination teahouse, opera theatre and cinema. High standard Sìchuān opera performances are given here every Sunday afternoon.

Teahouses There are a number of excellent teahouses. The *Rénmín Cháguǎn* in Renmin Park is a leisurely tangle of bamboo armchairs, sooty kettles and ceramics, with a great outdoor location by a lake. It's a family-type teahouse, crowded on weekends. In the late afternoon, workers roll up to soothe factory shattered nerves and some doze off in their armchairs. Tourists are welcome to do the same after a hard day's sightseeing. A most pleasant afternoon can be spent here over a bottomless cup of stone-flower tea.

Another charming indoor family-type teahouse is in Wénshū Temple, with an amazingly crowded and steamy ambience. This is in addition to the huge tea garden

SÌCHUĀN

outside (see Wénshū Temple earlier in this section). As well, try the Dàcí Sì.

Pubs & Bars New bars are appearing like bamboo shoots after the spring rains and some of those mentioned may have been superseded or relocated by the time you arrive.

South of the river on Renmin Lu is a strip of Western-style bars including the *Wild Goose Cafe*, *Seventh Sensation* and the *Twelve Oaks*, which regularly has live music. Most of these bars have similar prices with cocktails for Y25 to Y30 and beer for about Y15. You may also be served plates of fruit and seeds.

If you're looking for somewhere to go dancing, it's probably best to ask at Paul's Oasis for the current clubbing hotspot.

Shopping

Downtown shopping extends from the eastern end of Renmin Lu south to Shangdong Dajie, and has taken on the look of most modern cities with trendy clothing shops and department stores. If you delve into the narrow alleys between the main streets you'll find arcades of smaller shops and stalls selling similar items at cheaper prices.

On Chunxi Lu, halfway between Dongfeng Lu and Shangdong Dajie, is the Arts & Crafts Service Department Store (Chéngdū Měishùpǐn Fúwùbù), which deals in such specialities as lacquerware, silverwork and bamboo. Also check out the Derentang Chemist, the oldest and largest of all Chéngdū's Chinese pharmacies, on the left at the southern end of the street.

One of the most interesting and busiest places to wander is the Qīngshíqiáo Shìcháng, a large market north-east of the Mínshān Fàndiàn. Shops and stalls sell brightly coloured seafood, flowers, cacti, birds, pets and a thousand dried foods. To get there, turn right just north of the Mínshān Fàndiàn and then take the second road to the left.

Directly behind the Mínshān Fàndiàn are antique stores, and in the evening dozens of stalls appear and turn the street into an antique market. Across from the Mínshān Fàndiàn, Renmin Lu turns into an evening

art gallery as street hawkers sell paintings, calendars and intricate paper cut-outs.

South of the river, on a small street across from the entrance of the Wǔhóu Temple, is a small Tibetan neighbourhood. There are prayer papers, colourful scarves, beads and brass goods for sale. You won't find the variety of things (nor the bargains) that you'll find in the north-west of Sìchuān, but it still makes for an interesting wander and you can sit and sip yak butter tea and eat bowls of spicy, fried potatoes with the sheepskin robed Tibetans.

Getting There & Away

Air Shangliu airport is 18km west of the city and services many destinations.

Major internal destinations include Běijīng (Y1150, daily), Shànghǎi (Y1290, daily), Kūnmíng (Y560, daily), Guǎngzhōu (Y1040, daily), Xī'ān (Y500, four days per week) and Chóngqìng (Y190, three days per week). You can purchase tickets from the CAAC office (☎ 664 7163) opposite the Jǐnjiāng Bīnguǎn. The office is open 8am to 7.30pm weekdays and 8.30am to 7.30pm on Saturday and Sunday.

China Southwest (☎ 666 5911) has flights to Hong Kong (Y2550, daily), Bangkok (Y2480, four days per week), Singapore (Y3300, two days per week), Seoul (Y3480, two days per week) and Lhasa (Y1200, daily). Their office is a few doors south of the CAAC office on Renmin Lu. Dragon Air (☎ 675 5555 ext 6105) has an office in the Sìchuān Bīnguǎn.

Tibet The most frequently asked question in Chéngdū must be 'Can I fly to Lhasa?'. If you're on your own, China Southwest's official answer is 'No'. To get around this, travel agents in the Traffic Hotel, Sam's Guesthouse and elsewhere can sign you onto a 'tour', which usually includes a one-way ticket to Lhasa, the transfer to Chéngdū airport and a Tibet Tourism Bureau permit that you will probably never see. At the height of summer, you may have to book the two-hour transfer from Gonggar airport to Lhasa and three nights' dormitory accommodation and tour in Lhasa. The fact that members of the tour group have never seen each other prior to the flight and split up immediately after is overlooked by the authorities.

At the time of research these packages were priced at about Y2000 to Y2700 (the ticket alone costs Y1270) and were the most cost-effective way of getting into Tibet (though the regulations could change tomorrow). CITS runs its own four-day tours for around Y3500, or will get you a one-way ticket and permit for Y2600.

Rumour is that the whole permit system may be dismantled in the next year or two.

Sìchuān's land borders into Tibet are still closed to foreigners. Some travellers attempt to sneak across but the majority are turned away.

Bus Transport connections in Chéngdū are more comprehensive than in other parts of the South-West. High-speed expressways from Chéngdū to both Chóngqìng and Lèshān have cut down travel time to a mere two hours.

The main bus station is Xīnnánmén, next to the Traffic Hotel; it sells tickets to most destinations around Sìchuān. For northern destinations you will need to trek over to the Xīmén bus station in the north-west of the city and for eastern destinations such as Chóngqìng, your best bet is to try the northern bus station, near the north train station.

Xīnnánmén Bus Station From Xīnnánmén bus station, regular buses head for Lèshān and Éméi from 7am. For Éméi you can get a seat for Y20 if you're willing to spend four or five hours on it, or you can opt for the Y31 tickets and be there in two hours. Likewise, Lèshān has slow buses for Y26 or an express bus for Y46.

Between 7am and 10am there are about four departures to Dūjiāngyàn (Y18.50).

Early morning buses for Lúdìng and Kāngdìng (Y98, seven hours) leave daily and travel through the 4km-long Erlangshan Pass. There is a sleeper departing at 4pm but it will dump you off at Kāngdìng around midnight. You won't be able to buy a Kāngdìng ticket without proof of insurance.

Xīmén Bus Station This station is for travellers heading up to Jiǔzhàigōu or taking the overland route to Xiàhé in Gānsù province by way of northern Sìchuān.

There is a daily departure from here to Sōngpān at 7am (Y46) and a sleeper leaving for Jiǔzhàigōu at 7.20am (Y86.5, 12 hours). Daily buses also run to Xiaojin at 6.30am (Y43) and Hóngyuán 10.30am (Y67.50).

There are a number of departures each day to Dūjiāngyàn from 9.50am (Y11) from where you can change for Qīngchéng Shān or Wòlóng. There is a direct bus to Wòlóng at 11.40am (Y20). One departure leaves daily for Lèshān at 3.30pm (Y35), although you'd be better off trying Xīnnánmén Station.

North Bus Station Chéngdū's north bus station has seemingly constant minibuses to Chóngqìng between 6.30am and 9.30pm (Y112). There are also morning departures to Dàzú. Buses depart every 15 minutes for Dūjiāngyàn between 7am and 6pm (Y7.5), every half-hour to Bàogúo Sì between 7.30am to 3pm (Y25) and regularly to Lèshān from 6.30am to 6pm (Y25).

Train In recent years the advance-booking offices around town have become more user-friendly. While it's possible to reserve tickets, you won't be able to make same-day reservations for hard-sleeper tickets to popular destinations such as Kūnmíng or Xī'ān.

Alternatively, you can spend an extra Y30 or so and get Sam's Guesthouse or the Traffic Hotel to arrange the tickets for you. You'll usually need to organise this a day and a half in advance. Don't even bother with CITS.

Trains to Kūnmíng take either 19 hours (express) or 21½ hours, and cost Y222/338 for a hard/soft sleeper. An afternoon train departs at 1.57pm and arrives in Kūnmíng at 9.05am the following morning and an evening train departs at 9.15pm, arriving at 5.48pm the next evening.

For Lìjiāng or Dàlǐ, take the train to Pānzhīhūa (Jìnjiāng) on the Chéngdū-Kūnmíng route, from where you can catch a bus or minibus to either destination. Trains depart at 6.12, 7.03 and 8.27pm and arrive in Pānzhīhūa about 12 hours later.

Hard/soft sleepers for the 6.12pm departure cost Y112/182 or Y166/248 for the two later departures.

All trains headed for Kūnmíng or Pānzhǐhūa stop in Éméi. Express trains take two hours, while fast trains take three hours (both are Y9).

There are daily trains to Chóngqìng and Yóutíng (for Dàzú) however they do take much longer than the buses that continuously plough down the new expressway

(12 hours to Chóngqìng). The same is true for trains to Yíbīn and Zígòng, cities now linked by expressways to Lèshān.

Other daily departures include Běijīng (Y241 to Y418 hard sleeper, 28 to 34 hours), Shànghǎi (Y269 to Y499 hard sleeper, 36 to 40 hours), Xī'ān (Y122, 16 hours) Guǎngzhōu, Guìyáng, Lánzhōu and Ürümqi. Xī'ān is the most popular destination besides Kūnmíng and you'll most likely need to hang out in Chéngdū for at least a day and a half waiting for a ticket.

Getting Around
To/From the Airport Shuāngliu airport is 18km west of the city. CAAC runs a bus every half-hour between the ticket office on Renmin Nanlu and Shuangliu airport (Y8). Taxi drivers will take you for Y10 per person (minimum two people) from outside the office. A taxi to the airport costs around Y60.

Bus The most useful bus is No 16, which runs from Chéngdū's north train station to the south train station along Renmin Nanlu. Regular buses cost Y1, while the double-deckers cost Y2. Bus No 81 runs from the Mao Statue to Qīngyáng Temple and Bus No 12 circles the city along Yihuan Lu, starting and ending at the north train station.

Taxi There is a flag fall of Y5 (Y6 at night), plus Y1.40 per kilometre. From the Traffic Hotel to the Xīmén bus station, the direct route should cost around Y15.

Bicycle Both Sam's Guesthouse and the Traffic Hotel rent bikes for about Y10 per day, plus around Y200 deposit. The bikes are in fairly good condition but the usual rules apply – check your bike before you cycle off and make an effort to park it in a designated parking area. Bicycle theft is a problem here as in most cities.

AROUND CHÉNGDŪ
Monastery of Divine Light 宝光寺
Bǎoguāng Sì
In the north of Xīndū county, this monastery is an active Buddhist temple,

with five halls and 16 courtyards sur-rounded by bamboo groves. It's popular with pilgrims, monks and tourists and at-tracts a fine line-up of hawkers.

Founded in the 9th century, the monastery was subsequently destroyed and recon-structed in the 17th century. Among the treasures here are a white jade Buddha from Myanmar (Burma), Ming and Qing paint-ings and calligraphy, a stone tablet engraved with 1000 Buddhist figures (AD 540) and ceremonial musical instruments. Unfortu-nately, most of the more valuable items are locked away and require special permission to be viewed – you may be able to get this if you can find whoever's in charge.

The Arhat Hall, built in the 19th century, contains 500 two-metre-high clay figurines representing Buddhist saints. Well, not all of them: among this spaced-out lot are two earthlings – emperors Kangxi and Qianlong. They're distinguishable by their royal cos-tumes, beards, boots and capes. One of the impostors, Kangxi, is shown with a pock-marked face, perhaps a whim of the sculptor.

About 1km from the monastery is **Os-manthus Lake** with its bamboo groves and osmanthus trees. If you visit in the early au-tumn, you will also see lotuses in bloom. In the middle of the lake is a small **memorial hall** for the Ming scholar Yang Shengan.

The monastery has an excellent vegetar-ian *restaurant* where a huge array of dishes is prepared by monastic chefs. It's open 10am to 3pm, though it is best to be here around lunchtime, when there are more dishes available. The monastery itself is open 8am to 5.30pm daily.

Getting There & Away Xīndū is 18km north of Chéngdū. Buses leave from in front of Chéngdū's north train station and from the north bus station from around 6am to 6pm. The trip takes just under an hour.

On bicycle, the round trip would be 40km, or at least four hours.

Sanxingdui Museum 三星堆博物馆
Sānxīngduī Bówùguǎn

This fairly new museum, situated 40km north-east of Chéngdū, was opened in late 1997 to preserve the remains of what the Chinese authorities have called 'one of the most important archaeological discoveries of the century'.

The Sanxingdui site, discovered in 1985, was once an important commercial centre of the Shu kingdom, which ruled present-day Sìchuān from the 16th to the 3rd century BC. Remains include city walls, two large sacrificial pits and several bronze masks.

To get to the museum take a bus to the town of Guanghan, on the road to Deyang, and then take a taxi or motor-tricycle for the remaining few kilometres out of town.

Qīngchéng Shān 青城山

A holy Taoist mountain 65km west of Chéngdū, with a summit of only 1600m, Qīngchéng Shān is an excellent day trip into the subtropics. While not a rigorous work-out, Qīngchéng Shān offers beautiful trails lined with ginko, plum and palm trees, pic-turesque vistas and plenty of atmospheric sights along its rather short four-hour return route. In nasty weather, it's a good alterna-tive to Éméi Shān as its somewhat sturdier steps are stone rather than slate (and there-fore less slippery) and the views here are less likely to be obscured by mist and cloud. Qīngchéng Shān is a popular destination year-round and there is a small army of sou-venir hawkers permanently stationed here.

Situated outside the **Qīngchéng Shān Gate, Jianfu Temple** (Jiànfú Gōng) is the best-preserved of the mountain's temples. Of the 500 or so Taoist monks resident here prior to liberation, there are still about 100 living here.

Further up the hill, both **Cháoyáng Dòng** and **Tiānshī Dòng** are temples built into hal-lows in the side of the mountain (*dòng* means cave). In the courtyard of Tiānshī Dòng (Taoist Master Cave) are ancient twin ginkos planted during the Han dynasty and aged over 1000 years. Only 500m from the mountain's summit is **Shàngqīng Temple** (Shàngqīng Gōng), established in the Jin dynasty.

The most popular way of ascending Qīngchéng Shān is by gliding across **Yuèchéng Hú** on a small ferry (Y6) and then riding the chairlift up (Y25 one way, Y40

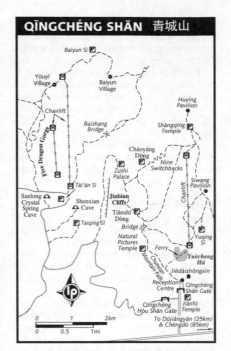

QĪNGCHÉNG SHĀN 青城山

Map labels:
Baiyun Sì
Yòuyí Village
Baiyun Village
Chairlift
Huying Pavilion
Baizhang Bridge
Shàngqīng Temple
Five Dragon Gorge
Cháoyáng Dòng
Nine Switchbacks
Zushi Palace
Sìwang Pavilion
Tài'ān Sì
Sanlong Crystal Spring Cave
Shenxian Cave
Jinbian Cliffs
Chairlift
Tiānshī Dòng
Taiqing Sì
Bridge
Natural Pictures Temple
Yuging Sì
Ferry
Yuècheng Hú
Chunxian Mountain Path
Jiēdàizhōngxīn
Reception Centre
Qīngchéng Shān Gate
Jiānfú Temple
Qīngchéng Hòu Shān Gate
To Dūjiāngyàn (25km) & Chéngdū (85km)

0   1   2km
0   0.5   1mi

return) to within a 20-minute walk of Shàngqīng Temple. This removes most of the hard work and makes it very easy to fit Qīngchéng Shān into a day trip. If you do walk only one way, the western trail past Cháoyáng Dòng and Tiānshī Dòng offers the most sites and views. At the southern end of this route is the lush **Chunxian Mountain Path** created early in the 19th century by headmaster Chunxian Peng who had each visitor to the mountain plant a tree along the path.

Entry to the mountain costs Y40 plus Y1 insurance.

Places to Stay Accommodation is available at three spots on the mountain. *Shàngqīng Temple* and *Tiānshī Dòng* both have clean, basic doubles starting at Y50 with common balconies that look out over the surrounding forests. While staying at Shàngqīng Gōng gives you an easier walk to the summit for sunrise, Tiānshī Dòng has

loads of atmosphere, is likely to be quieter and also has slightly fancier doubles with bath available for Y80.

At the bottom of the hill the *Jiēdà izhōngxìn* has damp and somewhat dingy triples for Y120. While they will bargain all the way down to Y40, you're better off heading back into Dūjiāngyàn or Chéngdū.

On the road to Qīngchéng Shān are a growing number of resort-style hotels.

Places to Eat You will likely be met at the base of the mountain by women keen to drag you away for a meal. The restaurants they'll herd you to are generally a short way up the mountain and quite good.

There are a number of *restaurants* along Qīngchéng Shān's trails, as well as *snack stands* at the top of the chairlift and noodles available inside Tiānshī Dòng. You are also likely to find fruit and boiled eggs for sale along the way.

Getting There & Away To reach Qīngchéng Shān from Chéngdū, catch a bus from Xīmén station to Dūjiāngyàn (Y12, one hour). These run 7am to 7pm. From Dūjiāngyàn, it's a minibus ride (Y4, 20 minutes) to the foot of the mountain. The last minibus returns from the mountain to Dūjiāngyàn at 6pm. During the high season there are likely to be buses running directly between Chéngdū's Xīmén station and Qīngchéng Shān.

Qīngchéng Hòu Shān 青城后山

In a bid to bolster tourism, the local authorities have opened up Qīngchéng Hòu Shān to trekkers. Its base lies about 15km north-west of the base of Qīngchéng Shān proper. With 20km of hiking trails, this mountain offers a more natural environment than the temple-strewn slopes of Qīngchéng Shān, with **Five Dragon Gorge** (Wǔlóng Gōu) offering dramatic vistas. There is a cable car to help with part of the route, but climbing the mountain will still require an overnight stay, either at the mountain itself or in nearby Dūjiāngyàn: doing it as a day trip from Chéngdū isn't really practical.

SICHUĀN

There's accommodation in the ***Tài'ān Sì***, a temple at the mountain's base, or at Yòuyī village, about halfway up. Dorm beds at both are around Y15.

Getting There & Away One of the easiest ways to reach Qīngchéng Hòu Shān is via Dūjiāngyàn, from where buses run to the base of both Qīngchéng Shān and Qīngchéng Hòu Shān from early morning until 6pm. During the high season you should also be able to catch direct buses from Chéngdū's Xīmén station to the foot of the mountain (see Getting There & Away in the previous section).

Dūjiāngyàn 都江堰

The Dūjiāngyàn irrigation project, some 60km north-west of Chéngdū, was undertaken in the 3rd century BC by famed prefect and engineer Li Bing to divert the fast-flowing Mín Hé into irrigation canals. The Mín was subject to flooding at this point, yet when it subsided, droughts could ensue. A weir system was built to split the force of the river and a trunk canal was cut through a mountain to irrigate the Chéngdū plain.

Li Bing's brilliant idea was to devise an annual maintenance plan to remove silt build-up. Thus the mighty Mín was tamed, with a temple, **Fúlóng Guàn**, erected in AD 168 to commemorate the occasion. This temple can still be seen in the pleasant **Líduī Park**. The temple contains a gallery of proud propaganda photographs showing, among many others, former US president Jimmy Carter visiting the site. China has applied to Unesco to award the site World Heritage status. Admission to the park and temple is Y4.

The project is ongoing – while it originally irrigated over a million hectares of land, this has expanded to three million hectares. Most of the present dams, reservoirs, pumping stations, hydroelectric works, bridgework and features are modern. A good overall view of the outlay can be gained from **Èrwáng Miào** (Two Kings Temple), which dates from AD 494 and commemorates Li Bing and his son, Er Lang. Inside the temple is a statue of Li Bing, shockingly lifelike; in the rear hall is a standing figure of his son holding a dam tool. There's also a Qing dynasty project map.

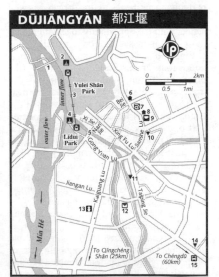

DŪJIĀNGYÀN

1	Anlán Cable Bridge 安澜索桥
2	Èrwáng Temple 二王庙
3	Chairlift 索道
4	Fúlóng Temple 伏龙观
5	South Bridge 南桥
6	China Travel Service Hotel 中旅饭店
7	Internet Cafe
8	Jīnqiú Bīnguǎn 金球宾馆
9	Coffee House
10	Barbecue Stalls
11	Barbecue Stalls
12	China Post 邮电大楼
13	Kuíguāng Pagoda 奎光塔
14	Restaurants
15	Bus Station; Shìkèyùn Zhōngxīn Zhāodàisuǒ 市客运中心招待所

SÌCHUĀN

A chairlift runs from Lídūi Park to Èrwáng Miào and on to Yulei Hill Park and costs Y16 to Y25 per segment.

While the idea of visiting a massive irrigation project may not sound thrilling, Dūjiāngyàn is a friendly enough place to stay overnight and a visit to the teahouses lining the river around the funky south bridge is a pleasant way to while away the afternoon. You could also get lost for weeks in **Yulei Shān Park** (open 8am to 6pm).

Places to Stay and Eat Should you decide to stay overnight in Dūjiāngyàn, perhaps to tackle Qīngchéng Shān the next day or en route to Wòlóng, the cheapest beds you're likely to find are at the *Shìkèyùn Zhōngxīn Zhāodàisuǒ* (☎ 720 2300), attached to the bus station. Beds in very basic, damp and rather drab doubles are Y20. There are also doubles with bath at Y60 per bed. The staff, however, is keen to bargain. While the hotel is conveniently located for catching an early morning bus, it's rather far from the town centre.

A better option is the *Jīnqiú Bīnguǎn* (☎ 711 5616), which has clean, comfortable doubles with bath for Y100 to Y150. For the most upmarket option in town, head a few blocks north to the new *China Travel Service Hotel* (*Zhōnglǚ Fàndiàn*; ☎ 713 1188), which has plush singles/doubles for Y280/298.

There isn't much food to recommend in Dūjiāngyàn. You'll find the usual *barbecue stalls* along the streets in the evening, particularly on the western half of Jianshe Lu and along Taiping Jie. There are a few *restaurants* across from the bus station and, if you're looking for a pricey cup of coffee in comfortable surroundings, try the *coffee house* next door to Jīnqiǔ Bīnguǎn.

Getting There & Away The bus station is inconveniently located south of town. To find downtown from here, turn left out of the station (towards the giant statue), and bear right onto what is eventually called Taiping Jie. Follow this north into town.

Buses run regularly between Chéngdū and Dūjiāngyàn from 7am to 7pm (Y12, one

hour). Buses to and from Qīngchéng Shān also run frequently until 6pm. One bus leaves daily for Wòlóng at 8am (Y13, 2½ hours).

ÉMÉI SHĀN 峨眉山
☎ 0842 • elevation 3099m

Éméi Shān, locked in a medieval time warp, receives a steady stream of happy pilgrims with their straw hats, makeshift baggage, walking canes and fans, as well as those visiting from the city in their business suits and dress shoes, ready for a day's climb. The monasteries, with their cheerful Buddhist monks, clouds of incense and firewood and coal lumped in the courtyards for the winter months, echo with the tinkle of bells.

The mountain climb is filled with what seems like hundreds of views of luxuriant scenery and millions of stairs. Particularly admirable are the hardened affiliates of Grannies' Alpine Club, who slog it out with the best of them, walking sticks at the ready for the marauding monkeys. They come every year, and burn paper money as a Buddhist offering for longevity. And the climb, filled with fresh alpine air, may well add to your longevity too. For the traveller itching to do something, the Éméi climb is a good opportunity to air the respiratory organs, as well as to observe post-1976 religious freedoms in action, with the opportunity to stay in the atmospheric monasteries along the trail.

Éméi Shān is one of the Middle Kingdom's four famous Buddhist mountains (the others are Pǔtuó, Wǔtái and Jiǔhuá). The original temple structures dated from as long ago as the advent of Buddhism itself in China; by the 14th century, the estimated 100 or so holy structures housed several thousand monks. Unfortunately, Éméi Shān has little of its original temple-work. The glittering Jīndǐng Sì, with its brass tiling engraved with Tibetan script, was completely gutted by fire. A similar fate befell numerous other temples and monasteries. War with the Japanese and Red Guard looting haven't helped either.

After a Cultural Revolution hiatus, around 20 temples are now active, regaining traces of their original splendour. Since 1976 the remnants have been renovated, access to the

ÉMÉI SHĀN 峨眉山

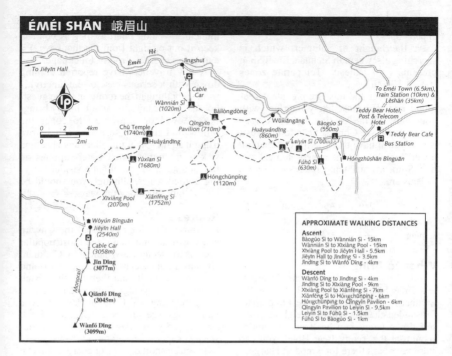

APPROXIMATE WALKING DISTANCES

Ascent
Bàogúo Sì to Wànnián Sì - 15km
Wànnián Sì to Xīxiàng Pool - 15km
Xīxiàng Pool to Jiēyǐn Hall - 5.5km
Jiēyǐn Hall to Jīndǐng Sì - 3.5km
Jīndǐng Sì to Wànfó Dǐng - 4km

Descent
Wànfó Dǐng to Jīndǐng Sì - 4km
Jīndǐng Sì to Xīxiàng Pool - 9km
Xīxiàng Pool to Xiānfēng Sì - 7km
Xiānfēng Sì to Hóngchūnpíng - 6km
Hóngchūnpíng to Qīngyīn Pavilion - 6km
Qīngyīn Pavilion to Leiyīn Sì - 9.5km
Leiyīn Sì to Fúhǔ Sì - 1.5km
Fúhǔ Sì to Bàogúo Sì - 1km

mountain has been improved, hiking paths widened, lodgings added, and tourists permitted to climb to the sacred summit.

The pilgrims, tourists and hawkers who line the path during the high season may remove the chance of finding solitude on the mountain; however, it does add to the atmosphere. The crowds hover largely around the monasteries; once away from them, the path is lined with fir, pine and cedar trees that clothe the slopes. Lofty crags, cloud-kissing precipices, butterflies and azaleas form a nature reserve of sorts. The mountain was added to Unesco's list of World Heritage sites in 1996, joining Lèshān and Jiǔzhàigōu.

The major scenic goal of Chinese hikers is to witness a sunrise or sunset over the sea of clouds at the summit. On the rare afternoon there is also a phenomenon known as 'Buddha's Aureole' where rainbow rings, produced by refraction of water particles, attach themselves to a person's shadow in a cloud bank below the summit. Devout

Buddhists, thinking this was a call from yonder, used to jump off the Cliff of Self-Sacrifice in ecstasy, leading officials of the Ming and Qing dynasties to set up iron poles and chain railings to prevent suicides.

Tickets

Entrance to Éméi Shān is Y60. The ticket is dated and so theoretically you can re-enter the grounds at different points throughout the day. You also get your mugshot scanned onto the ticket and can even have it laminated for Y1 – not a bad idea if it's raining. Entry to Bàogúan Sì and Fúhǔ Sì at the foot of the mountain do not require this ticket; they have tickets of their own.

Climate

The best time to visit is from May to October. Visiting in winter is not impossible, but will present some trekking problems – iron soles with spikes can be hired to deal with encrusted ice and snow on the trails. Snowfall generally starts around November on the upper slopes.

At the height of summer, which is scorching elsewhere in Sìchuān, Éméi Shān presents cool majesty. Temperate zones start at 1000m.

Cloud cover and mist are prevalent year round and will most likely interfere with your view of the sunrise. If you're *very* lucky, you'll see Gòngga Shān to the west; if not, you'll have to settle for the telecom tower 'temple' and the meteorological station. Some average temperatures in degrees Celsius are:

	Jan	Apr	Jul	Oct
Éméi Town	7°	21°	26°	17°
Summit	-6°	3°	12°	-1°

What to Bring

Definitely not your entire pack. Nevertheless, Éméi Shān is a tall one at 3099m, so the weather is uncertain and it's best to prepare for sudden changes without weighing yourself down (steps can be steep). If you're staying at the Teddy Bear Hotel, you can store your bags there for a modest charge.

There is no heating or insulation in the monasteries, but blankets – albeit damp ones – are provided. A couple of places now even have electric blankets and you can also hire overcoats at the top. Heavy rain can be a problem, as even a light mist can make the slate steps slippery and extremely treacherous. A good pair of rough-soled shoes or boots is a must. When it does rain, big, flimsy, plastic bags with hoods are sold by enterprising vendors on the slopes. They appear to do the trick, at least for a little while.

A fixed-length umbrella would be most useful – for the rain, as a walking stick and for scaring the hell out of those monkeys by pressing auto-release! You should be able to find one in Éméi town for Y30 to Y45. If you want to look even more authentic, you can buy yourself a handcrafted walking stick (very cheap) for sale along the way. A torch (flashlight) is important if you're spending the night or planning to hike at dawn. Food supplies are not necessary with food stalls along the way, nevertheless, a pocket of munchies wouldn't hurt as long as you can keep it out of sight from the monkeys. Finally, don't forget a roll of toilet paper.

A few travellers have reported coming down with a serious case of conjunctivitis from something in the rooms in some guesthouses. You can try to avoid this by bringing a towel or pillowcase to cover the pillow and then be sure to wash before using it again. Other travellers have become sick from contaminated water supplies on the mountain, so you might consider carrying bottled water, although you should be able to buy this along the way.

Routes

For those planning to hike all the way up and down the mountain, the most popular route is to ascend via Wànnián Sì, Chūdián, Xǐxiàng Pool (Elephant Bathing Pool) and on to the summit, and then to climb back down via Xǐxiàng Chí, Xiānfēng Sì, Hóngchūnpíng and Qīngyīn Pavilion. The paths converge just below Xǐxiàng Pool. The majority of hikers agree that the descent is superior in sights and views.

If you're short on time or energy, you can be carried up on the sturdy back of a porter. If this doesn't sound like your cup of tea, there is now a bus that runs up the mountain from the bus station in Bàoguó, next door to the Teddy Bear Cafe. You can either take a bus up to Wǔxiǎngǎng and begin your hike there or continue on the bus up to the village of Jìngshuǐ where a cable car (Y30/Y20/Y45 up/down/return, open 6am to 6pm) awaits you for a lift up to Wànnián Sì. From the top of the cable car, you can pick up the route to the summit. Buses also run as far up the mountain as Jiēyǐn Hall (two hours) from where it's a two-hour hike or five-minute cable car ride to the top. This cable car ride costs Y40 to ascend and Y30 to descend.

Bus routes and prices are posted at the Bàoguó bus station as well as at the stops en route. A ride to the top costs Y30, to Wǔxiǎngǎng costs Y15 and a return trip with a number of stops en route is Y60. Buses run from approximately 6am to 6pm but you don't want to cut it too close on the way down – if you miss the last bus, it's a 15km walk down from Wànnián Sì.

If for some reason you wish to do the whole mountain in one day, most hotels can book you on a bus leaving at 3.30am(!). This is supposed to get you to the summit in time to see the sunrise, and is a popular option. Unfortunately, so many buses make this early-morning run now that there's usually an immense traffic jam at the entrance gate – up to a 45-minute wait – and then the clog of tourists up the mountainside slows to a snail's crawl, with the result that very, very few people make it to Jīndǐng Sì for sunrise. There's also only one good photo-opportunity vantage point, half an hour below the summit, and it's generally crowded with other shutterbugs.

The buses head down from Jiēyǐn Hall around mid-morning, stopping at various temples along the way and finally bringing you back to Bàoguó at around 5pm. The round trip costs about Y40 and will probably leave your head spinning. It's best to do it in segments – buy your ticket (Y15) at the Teddy Bear Café the day before, so once you're there you can decide if, when and how you return.

Duration

It's difficult to estimate how long you will need to make it up and back down Éméi Shān by foot. While you don't require any particular hiking skills, it is nonetheless a tough climb. You will be quoted wildly differing times by locals and other hikers. Many say that two days is enough time to make it to the summit from Wànnián Sì and back down to Bàoguó Sì; however, this is only possible if you're able and willing to spend at least 10 hours hiking each day and are fortunate enough to have optimum conditions. Crowds and weather (heavy rainfall in particular) can dampen these plans. The altitude may also play havoc with your breathing, and ascending too quickly will only increase this. Finally, you may want to explore the many temples and monasteries en route and to enjoy the vistas. It's wise to leave yourself three days for the trek.

To get an idea of how long it's going to take you (remember you are climbing a steep staircase), time yourself on the first kilometre or two and then average out your own probable climbing duration using the trail distance chart found with the Éméi Shān map.

Things to See

Éméi Shān is dotted with monasteries and temples, many of which have their histories posted for visitors in both English and in Chinese. If not, you are likely to encounter a friendly monk or caretaker to answer your questions.

Bàoguó Sì The 'Protecting the State' Monastery was constructed in the 16th century, enlarged in the 17th century by Emperor Kangxi and recently renovated. Its 3.5m porcelain Buddha, made in 1415, is housed near the Sutra Library. To the left of the gate is a rockery for potted miniature trees and rare plants. There's a good vegetarian *restaurant* and a *teahouse* here. Admission to the temple is Y8.

A museum is diagonally across the road from the monastery, around the side of the knoll. Admission is Y4.

Fúhǔ Sì The renovated 'Crouching Tiger' Monastery is deep within the forest. Inside is a 7m-high copper pagoda inscribed with Buddhist images and texts. Admission is Y6.

Qīngyīn Pavilion Named 'Pure Sound' Pavilion because of the sound effects produced by rapid waters coursing around rock formations in the area, the temple is built on an outcrop in the middle of a fast-flowing stream.

There are several small pavilions from which to observe the waterworks and appreciate the natural music. It's possible to swim here, although the water is only likely to be warm enough during the summer months.

Wànnián Sì The 'Long Life' Monastery is the oldest surviving Éméi temple (reconstructed in the 9th century). It's dedicated to the man on the white elephant, the

Bodhisattva Puxian (Samantabhadra in Sanskritt), who was one of Sakyamuni Buddha's two main disciples and the protector of the mountain. This 8.5m-high statue dates from AD 980, is cast in copper and bronze and weighs an estimated 62,000kg. If you can manage to rub the elephant's back, good luck will come to you.

The statue is housed in Brick Hall, a domed building with small stupas on it. When the temple was damaged by fire in 1945, Brick Hall was the only building left unharmed. There is also a **graveyard** to the rear of the temple.

Xiāngfēng Sì Somewhat off the beaten track, the 'Magic Peak' Monastery backs onto rugged cliffs, surrounded by fantastic scenery and oozing with character. The nearby **Jiulao Cave** is inhabited by big bats.

Xīxiàng Pool According to legend, the Elephant Bathing Pool (Xīxiàng Chí) is the spot where Puxian flew his elephant in for a big scrub, but today there's not much of a pool to speak of. Being almost at the crossroads of the major trails, the temple here is something of a hang-out and often crowded with pilgrims.

Jīndǐng Sì At 3077m, the magnificent 'Golden Summit' Temple is as far as most hikers get. It has been rebuilt since being gutted by a fire several years ago. Covered with glazed tiles and surrounded by white marble balustrades, the temple now occupies 1695 sq metres.

The original temple had a bronze-coated roof, which is how it got the name Jīndǐng (which can also mean 'Gold Top'). However, it's constantly overrun with tourists, pilgrims and monks, and you'll be continuously bumped and jostled. The sun rarely forces its way through the mists up here and the result is that it is usually impossible to see very far past your own nose.

From Jīndǐng it was once possible to hike to Wànfó Dǐng (Ten Thousand Buddhas Summit) but pilgrims now take a monorail – a one-hour return ticket costs Y50.

Places to Stay and Eat

On the Mountain The old monasteries offer food, shelter and sights all rolled into one. While some travellers complain about the spartan and somewhat damp conditions, others find what may be as many as a thousand years of character a delightful change from the regular tourist hotels.

There are a number of monastery guesthouses: at Bàoguó Monastery, Qīngyīn Pavilion, Wànnián Sì, Xīxiàng Pool, Xiānfēng Sì, Hóngchūnpíng, Fúhǔ Sì, Leiyin Sì and Jīndǐng Sì. There's also a host of smaller lodgings at Chu Sì, Jiēyīn Hall, Yúxiān Sì, Báilòngdòng, and Huayanding, among others. The smaller places will accept you if the main monasteries are full. Failing those, if night is falling, you can kip virtually anywhere – a teahouse, a restaurant.

During the high season, be prepared to backtrack or advance under cover of darkness, as key points are often full of pilgrims – old women two to a bed, filling the

---

Monkey Etiquette

The monkeys have got it all figured out – Xīxiàng Pool is the place to be. If you come across a monkey 'tollgate', the standard procedure is to thrust open palms towards the outlaw to show you have no food. The Chinese find the monkeys an integral part of the Éméi trip, and many like to tease them.

Monkeys form an important part of Chinese mythology. There is a saying in Chinese, 'With one monkey in the way, not even 10,000 men can pass' – which may be truer than you think!

Some of these chimps are buggers, and staying cool when they look like they might make a leap at you is easier said than done. There is debate as to whether it's better to give them something to eat or to fight them off.

One thing is certain, if you do throw them something, don't apply too much moderation. They get annoyed very quickly if they think they are being undersold.

corridors, or camping out in the hallowed temple itself, on the floor.

You won't often find a reception desk at the monasteries. Instead, find a monk or caretaker and ask to be pointed in the right direction. A few of the monasteries at key junctions have posted prices but at others you may well have to bargain with the monks. You can expect to pay between Y15 and Y40 for a bed in a dorm room, with plumbing and electricity provided in those at the higher end of the scale. The following should give you an idea as to where to head for the cheapest beds:

Bàoguó Sì Y20	Fúhǔ Sì Y30
Wànnián Sì Y10–40	Xīxiàng Pool Y30–40
Jīndǐng Sì Y15–40	
Qīngyīn Gé dorms Y15–20, doubles Y150	

There are a growing number of *guesthouses* cropping up on Éméi Shān. Many of the cheaper ones do not accept foreigners. Others are closed during the off season. On average you can expect to pay between Y100 and Y250 for a room, depending on the availability of hot water and whether you opt for a private bath. The majority of these guesthouses are clumped behind Jīndǐng Sì, to the west of the temple.

Wòyún Bīnguǎn, located just under the cable car station, is the only hotel on the summit that can boast round-the-clock hot water and heating. Standard doubles range from Y280 to Y480.

Vegetarian meals are included with the price of a bed at many of the monasteries. There is also often a small *food stall* or *shop* near the monastery grounds selling biscuits, instant noodles, peanuts and drinks – not to mention a wide variety of fungus.

You will also come across a large number of *food stalls* and *restaurants* along the route. Food becomes more expensive and less varied the higher you climb, due to cartage surcharges and difficulties. Be wary of teahouses or restaurants serving *shénshuǐ* (divine water), or any type of tea or food said to possess mystical healing qualities. Miracles are not guaranteed, but the price of at least Y10 for the cup of water or tea is.

Around the Base The stretch of road leading up to Bàoguó Sì witnesses the rise and fall of many hotels. Most are nondescript and overpriced but will accept foreigners if you catch them in the right mood. It's best to have a wander and check out a few options.

The *Teddy Bear Hotel* is run from a wing of the Post and Telecommunications Hotel, directly across from the Teddy Bear Café. At Y30 a bed (either in a dorm or a double), this is the best and most popular deal in town. Standards in the *Post and Telecommunications Hotel* (☎ 559 3367) itself are much pricier at Y238.

If the Teddy Bear Hotel is full and you don't feel you're getting value for money anywhere else, you might want to try the *Hóngzhūshān Bīnguǎn* (☎ 652 3666 ext 3010). Doubles in building No 7 go for Y280 and, while they may not appear particularly special, the tranquil setting of lush forests and the view easily make it feel like money well spent.

The *Teddy Bear Café* has friendly staff who serve up Chinese and a few Western dishes, which you can order off an English menu. They can also help with information on transport up the hill as well as with buses and trains farther afield.

The street leading up to Bàoguó Sì is lined with *restaurants* including *huǒguō* (hotpot) and *shāokǎo* (barbecue) *stalls*, which begin to appear as the evening approaches. There are also a large number of *shops* along here that stock food supplies for your trek up the mountain.

Getting There & Away

The hubs of the transport links to Éméi Shān are Bàoguó village and Éméi town. Éméi town itself is best skipped although it does have markets, some cheap hotels, restaurants and a long-distance bus station and train station.

Bus Éméi town lies 6.5km from Bàoguó village and the base of Éméi Shān. To Bàoguó from Éméi town, frequent microbuses (Y2) depart from the first intersection exiting the bus station to the left. You can also try to negotiate a taxi for Y20.

Minibuses and taxis run back from Bàogúo to Éméi town for the same prices. You'll find them lurking around the bus station, next to the Teddy Bear Café.

Buses from Éméi town to Chéngdū run frequently from the main bus terminal throughout the day (Y30, two hours). Buses departing from Chéngdū to Bàogúo leave from both the north and Xīmén bus stations in the mornings. While all of Chéngdū's bus stations have departures throughout the day for Éméi town, the Xīnnánmén station offers the most choice in times and prices.

Buses run between Lèshān and Éméi town every half-hour (Y6, one hour) from 7am to 6.30pm. Buses to Yǎ'ān depart at 7.40am, 8.40am, 12.10pm, and 2.10pm and return between 7am and 4pm. This is the route you want for Móxī and Kāngdìng.

From the bus station at Bàogúo, hourly buses head to Chéngdū (Y35, two hours) from 6.30am to 6pm. You can also catch buses from here to Chóngqìng (Y95) at 7.30am and 4.30pm.

Train Éméi train station is on the Chéngdū-Kūnmíng line and lies 3.5km from the centre of Éméi town. Bus No 4 (Y0.50) runs between the train station and the long-distance bus station.

Morning trains bound for Chéngdū depart Éméi town at 7.40am and 11.18am and an evening train passes through at 7.40pm (Y9, three hours). To Kūnmíng, trains leave at 12.50pm, 6.40pm and 7.30pm. To Wūshīhè (another route to Móxī and Kāngdìng) trains go at 11.14am and 9pm.

LÈSHĀN 乐山
☎ 0833 • pop 3.5 million

Once a sleepy counterpart to Éméi Shān and now a Unesco World Heritage site, Lèshān has taken off as a popular tourist destination thanks to its main attraction – the towering Grand Buddha (Dà Fó). Prospering from increasing droves of tourists, Lèshān has revamped many of its old quarters, levelling old residential districts to make way for new apartment towers and department stores. Nevertheless, Lèshān has managed to retain a friendly, relaxed atmosphere and a wander

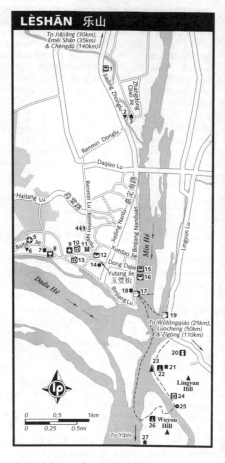

through its markets and side streets will unearth some of its unique character, along with some excellent food. All in all, it's a good place to either rest those Éméi-weary legs or to give them a test-run on the Dà Fó grounds.

Information
PSB The PSB is at 29 Shanxi Jie, not far from the Jiāzhōu Bīnguǎn, and is claimed by many to be one of the best places in China to try for a visa extension.

Money The efficient main branch of the Bank of China is on Renmin Nanlu, just

SICHUAN

LÈSHĀN

PLACES TO STAY
3　Lèshān Jiàoyù
　Bīnguǎn
　乐山教育宾馆
7　Jiāzhōu Bīnguǎn
　嘉州宾馆
18　Táoyuán
　Bīnguǎn
　桃源宾馆
21　Nánlóu
　Bīnguǎn
　南楼宾馆
27　Xiāndǎo
　Bīnguǎn
　仙岛宾馆

PLACES TO EAT
2　Hotpot Restaurant
　火锅饭店
6　The Yangs'
　Restaurant
　杨家餐厅

OTHER
1　Long-Distance
　Bus Station
　长途汽车站
4　Bank of China
　中国银行
5　Hospital
　医院
8　Newcastle Arms Pub
9　PSB
　公安局
10　Internet Cafe
11　Workers' Cultural
　Palace
　劳动人民文化宫
12　China Post
　邮电局
13　Internet Cafe
14　Xinhua Bookstore
　新华书店
15　Central Bus Station
　省汽车客运中心站

16　Small Tour Boats &
　Ticket Office
　小旅游船及售票处
17　Ferry Ticket Office;
　Ferry Dock
　渡轮售票处、
　渡轮码头
19　Ferry Dock
20　Língbǎo Pagoda
　灵宝塔
22　Dàfó Sì
　大佛寺
23　Grand Buddha
　人佛
24　Máhào Tombs
　Museum
　麻浩崖博物馆
25　Oriental Buddha
　Park
　东方佛都公园
26　Wǔyōu Sì
　乌尤寺

past Yueertang Jie. There is also an ATM here that accepts Plus and Cirrus cards as well as major credit cards.

Post China Post's main office is on the corner of Yutang Jie and Fu Jie.

Email and Internet Access China Telecom runs an Internet service from the third floor of the main post office. Access costs Y3 per hour. There is also a cafe.

Private Internet cafes are sprouting up throughout the city. The one on Baita Jie, just east of the PSB, offers access for Y2 per hour and is open until 11pm. There's another one on Binjiang Lu with similar rates.

Travel Agencies For a long time, Mr. Yang of The Yangs' Restaurant (☎ 211 2046, 49 Baita Jie) has been the guru of travel information in Lèshān. While he can organise almost anything – a visit to a local doctor, a local family, a silk or tea factory, nearby villages – he has recently been getting mixed reviews from travellers who feel he has doled out dubious information in order to encourage them to patronise his services. While he's a great source of information and fantastic at

arranging boat tickets along the Yangzi River (he can often get you tickets for one class higher than you pay), you may want to double check some of his information.

Things to See
The Grand Buddha & Around Carved into a cliff face overlooking the confluence of the Dàdù Hé and Mín Hé, the **Grand Buddha** (Dà Fó) measures an overwhelming 71m high. Qualifying as the largest Buddha in the world (the nearest contender, the Buddhas of Bamiyan in Afghanistan, were recently destroyed by the Taliban), his ears are 7m long, his insteps 8.5m broad, and you could picnic on the nail of his big toe – the toe itself is 8.5m long.

This mammoth project was begun in AD 713, engineered by a Buddhist monk called Haitong who organised fundraising and hired workers; it was completed 90 years later. Below the Buddha (actually Maitreya, or the Future Buddha) was a hollow where boatmen used to vanish – Haitong hoped that the Buddha's presence would subdue the swift currents and protect the boatmen. And the Grand Buddha did do a lot of good, as the surplus rocks from the sculpting filled the river hollow. Haitong gouged out his own eyes in an effort to protect funding from disappearing into the hands of officers, but he died before the completion of his life's work.

Inside the body, hidden from view, is a water-drainage system to prevent weathering, although the stone statue has had its fair share of it. A building once sheltered the giant statue, but it was destroyed during a Ming dynasty war. Today, the Grand Buddha is so old that foliage is trying to reclaim him – flowers grow on the giant hands, his chest is bushy, there are ferns in his topknot, and weeds wind out of his ears.

Officials are worried about the possibility of collapse due to soil erosion; one suggestion that has not met with an enthusiastic response is to cover the Buddha with a huge transparent shell.

It's worth looking at the Grand Buddha from several angles. While the easiest way to see him is to walk along the riverfront on Binjiang Lu (an especially attractive spectacle in the evening when the site is lit), you need to get closer to him to really appreciate his magnitude. You can go to the top, opposite the head, and then descend a stairway to the feet for a Lilliputian perspective. Tour boats pass by for a frontal view, revealing two guardians in the cliffside not visible from land.

Locals also point out that from a certain angle the hills surrounding the Grand Buddha resemble another Buddha lying in the water, with Wūyóu Shān as his head and Língyún Shān as his shoulders. If you can't quite make it out yourself, artistic liberty taken on posters around town will attempt to convince you.

To make a round tour that encompasses the many views of the Grand Buddha, take a boat from the dockside along Binjiangnan Lu. You currently have a choice of three types of boat. Best value is the ferry which charges the bargain fare of Y1 (plus an extra Y1 to sit on the top deck) and goes from just south of the Táoyuán Bīnguǎn to Wūyóu, continues on to the Lèshān paper mill and its opposite bank and then returns by the same route. The only snag with this is that you don't get much time in front of the Grand Buddha – one shot with the camera and you've passed it. It helps to sit on

the upper deck facing the dock, since the boat turns around when leaving.

The two other options are on a large tour boat (Y30) or a smaller speedboat for the same price. You won't see anything different on these boats but you will have more time to enjoy it, as the boats will hover for five to 10 minutes in front of the Buddha. Boats leave from north of the ferry dock approximately every 30 minutes from 7am to 5pm.

All the boats pass close by the Grand Buddha and then stop at the **Wūyōu Sì**. Like the Buddha, this monastery dates from the Tang dynasty with Ming and Qing renovations. It commands panoramic views and is a museum piece containing calligraphy, painting and artefacts, many with English captions.

Wūyōu Sì also has a hall of 1000 terracotta arhat monks displaying an incredible variety of postures and facial expressions – no two are alike. The arhats are housed in the **Luohan Hall,** which dates back to 1909. Inside is also a fantastic statue of Avalokiteshvara, the Bodhisattva of Mercy.

The temple's vegetarian restaurant is famed for its imitation meat dishes: spare ribs and beef strips that look like the real thing. The taste, however, is another matter, and you'll probably be better off with straight vegetables.

If you get off the boat at Wūyóu Sì, a visit through the temple will take you across Wūyóu Shān and down to a small bridge that crosses over to Língyún Shān (Towering Cloud Hill). Here you can visit **Oriental Buddha Park** (Dōngfāng Fódū Gōngyuán), a newly assembled collection of 3000 Buddha statutes and figurines.

The centrepiece is a 170m-long reclining Buddha, said to be the world's longest. Though touted by local tourist authorities as a major attraction, the park seems more about cashing in on Buddha-mania. Still, it's an interesting walk, albeit a pricey one at Y25.

Next door is the **Máhàoya Tombs Museum** (Máhàoyámù Bówùguǎn), which has a modest collection of tombs and burial artefacts dating from the Eastern Han dynasty (AD 25–220). Entry costs Y2.

Continuing past the Buddha Park and up Língyún Shān brings you to the entrance gate to **Dàfó Sì** (Y40). This temple gives views over the Grand Buddha's head and from here you are at the correct angle to have a picture taken of you sticking your finger in his ear – surely what you've always wanted. You can also follow a narrow staircase down to reach his feet before hauling yourself back up to the top again. Nearby is the **Língbǎo Pagoda**.

To return to Lèshān, there are local ferries (Y1) departing from the first dock north of the main exit. The service is sporadic and the last runs are awfully early – around mid-afternoon sometimes. Buses also run from the exit back to town.

This whole exercise can be done in less than 1½ hours from the Lèshān dock; however, it's worth making a day of it.

During winter you can get another angle on Dà Fó from the island in the middle of the two rivers' confluence. Boatmen ferry passengers onto the island, from where you can walk along the spit. In summer you should be careful of how far you wander, as river levels are generally higher. Get local advice before attempting this.

Thousand Buddhas Cliffs About 30km north of Lèshān, 2.5km west of the train station at Jiājiāng, are the Thousand-Buddha Cliffs (Jiājiāng Qiānfóyán). For once, the name is not an exaggeration: over 2400 Buddhas dot the cliffs, dating from as early as the Eastern Han dynasty. The statues show a few signs of wear and tear but, considering their age, are in fairly good condition.

Set in a rather pretty location along a riverbank and on the edge of the countryside, this site takes something of an effort to reach. Catch one of the many buses from Lèshān's main bus station down the bumpy road to Jiājiāng (Y5, one hour). From Jiājiāng bus station, take a pedicab (Y10) or taxi (Y15) to the site. The last bus returning to Lèshān leaves Jiājiāng at 6pm.

The site is open 8am to 4.45pm. Tickets cost Y30.

Other Things to See & Do There are some pleasant walks in Lèshān itself. The area around the ferry docks and the old town buzzes with market activity and, in season,

the markets yield a surprising array of fresh fruit and vegetables. The newly constructed walkway along Binjiang Lu follows the river's edge from the confluence of the Min Hé and Dadu Hé, up past the Jiāzhōu Bīnguǎn. Popular strolling grounds in the evenings, if you follow it as far as the Jiāzhōu Bīnguǎn, you'll see fan dancers practicing in a square near the intersection of Binjiang Lu and Baita Jie. You can also take bus No 6 out to the big new **Town Square** where a 27m high fountain attracts crowds in the evenings.

Recommended day trips to villages outside Lèshān, include **Lúochéng**, 50km south-east, famed for its old 'boathouse' architecture, and **Wǔtōngqiáo**, 25km south. Check with The Yangs' Restaurant.

Places to Stay Located down by Lèshān's pier, the *Táoyuán Bīnguǎn* (☎ 212 7784, fax 212 9904) has been receiving mixed reviews. This is likely because the hotel is housed in two separate buildings, practically next door to one another, with separate receptions and very different conditions. The building to the south offers doubles without bath for as low as Y50; but the rooms are somewhat grotty, with reports of cockroaches living it up at night. Three doors north, the second building advertises standards with bath for Y160 to Y260, but may well offer these comfortable, clean rooms for Y50.

Near the long-distance bus station, the *Lèshān Jiàoyù Bīnguǎn* (☎ 213 4257, 156 Liren Jie) was once a favourite, but the hike in prices seems to have been matched with a plunge in quality. Damp and dingy doubles go for Y100 to Y180 and triples start at Y180. Business is slow these days and they may be willing to slash prices in half.

Over on the Grand Buddha's side of the river, in the backyard of Dàfó Sì, is the *Nánlóu Bīnguǎn*. Perhaps due to the Buddha's drainage system, the cliff around here is wet and the dampness can extend to the rooms. Doubles/suites are Y120/180, all with bathrooms, air-con and hot water. The greatest bonus is that in the morning you can beat the rush to the Grand Buddha. To find the hotel simply walk through the temple to the last courtyard where you'll find reception.

South-east of Wǔyóu Sì is the *Xiāndǎo Bīnguǎn* (☎ 230 1988). Near the temple, rooms are clean but somewhat pricey with standards from Y168.

Top-of-the-line is the three-star *Jiāzhōu Bīnguǎn* (☎ 213 9888, fax 213 3233, 19 Baita Lu). Doubles/triples start at Y360 and suites at Y600, both with breakfast. The hotel is in a pleasant area; to get there from the long-distance bus station take the No 1 bus to the end of the line.

Places to Eat
Restaurants abound in Lèshān, with the best food served at the dozens of small cubby-hole *restaurants* and *street stalls*. Try Xuedao Jie, north of the pier, but be sure to check prices before ordering. Also try the fantastically popular *hotpot restaurant* just north of the intersection of Jiading Zhonglu and Renmin Lu.

For a home-style meal and good conversation, wander into *The Yangs' Restaurant* (49 Baita Jie), a wooden hole-in-the-wall with an English menu and Chinese prices.

There are also dozens of *restaurants* overlooking the river at the bottom end of Binjiangnan Duan. If you're craving a more relaxed atmosphere or a pint of beer with your meal, try the *Newcastle Arms Pub* next door to the Jiāzhōu Bīnguǎn.

Getting There & Away
Transportation links in Lèshān are both expanding and improving. The expressway from Chéngdū has reached Lèshān, cutting travel time down to a mere two hours. An expressway from Lèshān to Chóngqìng is also near completion, resulting in a triangular transportation conduit. Plans are also being finalised for an enormous new airport 20km outside Lèshān.

Bus There are two bus stations in Lèshān. The long-distance bus station is somewhat inconveniently located in the northern reaches of the city. The central bus station is closer to the centre of town, next to the Mín Hé.

From the long-distance station, buses to Chéngdū leave every 10 to 20 minutes from 6.30am to 7pm (Y37, two hours).

Watch out for the buses' Chéngdū destination. While most go to Xīnnánmén bus station next to the Traffic Hotel, several go to the north bus station or train station, which are inconveniently located for Chéngdū's budget accommodation.

Buses leave for Éméi town from both bus stations at least once every half-hour between 6.30am and 6pm (Y5.50, one hour). Those running from the central bus station seem to stop far more frequently than those departing from the long-distance bus station.

From the long-distance bus station, buses to Chóngqìng (Y84) depart hourly from 7.10am until 2.10pm and then at 3.30pm and 5pm. Buses for Yǎ'ān (for connections to Lúdìng and Kāngdìng) depart hourly from 7.10am to 10.10am and at 11.50am and 9pm (Y21, three hours). Note that connecting buses to Lúdìng leave Yǎ'ān every other day.

Early-morning buses also go south from the long-distance bus station to Mabian, Meigu and Zhāojué in the Liángshān Yi Autonomous Prefecture (see the Around Xīchàng section for information on this area).

Train It doesn't matter what anyone says, there simply is no train service to Lèshān. Ticket sellers in other cities will swear blind they can sell you a ticket to Lèshān but in reality they will only sell you a ticket to Éméi Shān, or more likely Jiājiāng, both about 40 minutes away by bus.

Boat At one time there was a regular boat service between Lèshān and Yíbīn, with further services to Chóngqìng. River fluctuations and bad management means there are currently no services. The new expressways have made bus travel faster, safer and understandably more popular, and the resulting lack of customers for boat travel has left it in the lurch. If you're lucky, you may find private high-speed boats to Yíbīn (Y80, 2½ hours) running from June to August.

Getting Around
Bus Nos 1 and 8 run the length of Jiading Lu and connect the pier area with the long-distance bus station. Buses run 6am to 6pm at roughly 20-minute intervals.

On foot, it's an hour's walk from one end of town to the other. A pedicab from the main long-distance bus station to the Táoyuán Bīnguǎn should cost about Y5 and from the pier to Jiāzhōu Bīnguǎn about Y2. Pedicab operators in Lèshān all split up the fares, so don't be paranoid when one of them stops halfway and tells you to get on his buddy's pedicab. Just pay him half and pay the remainder when you arrive. Taxis in Lèshān start at a flat rate of Y3 for the first 3km.

Unfortunately, there doesn't seem to be any bicycle hire in Lèshān.

MÉISHĀN 眉山

Méishān, 90km south-west of Chéngdū by road or rail (it's on the Kūnmíng-Chéngdū railway line), is largely of interest to those with a knowledge of Chinese language, literature and calligraphy.

The town is famed as the former residence of Su Xun and his two sons, Su Shi and Su Zhe, the three noted literati of the Northern Song dynasty (960–1126). Their home was converted into a temple in the early Ming dynasty, with renovations under the Qing emperor Hongwu (1875–1909).

The mansion and pavilions now operate as a museum for the study of the writings of the Northern Song period. Historical documents, relics of the Su family, writings, calligraphy – some 4500 items all told – are on display at the Sansu (Three Sus) shrine.

Southern Sìchuān

Few Westerners head south of Lèshān unless they're catching a train to Kūnmíng or branching off west to Lìjiāng. There are, however, a few overlooked and offbeat sites in the south and the region is quite popular with local Chinese tourists. You could easily spend a few days wandering the back-streets of Zígòng and Yíbīn or exploring the Bamboo Forest and Hanging Coffins of the ancient Bo. If you're looking for an offbeat route on to Guìzhōu or Chóngqìng, then the region has some interesting sites to detain you. Be forewarned that travel isn't as smooth in these areas as in the more popu-

lar destinations and hotels may be nervous of foreigners.

ZÌGÒNG 自贡
☎ 0813

Roughly halfway between Chéngdū and Chóngqìng, Zìgòng sees very few visitors and is one of the best-kept secrets of the South-West. It has narrow backstreets overflowing with colourful market stalls, some of the most atmospheric teahouses in the region and a collection of extinct dinosaurs rivalled only by the amazing set of *Jurassic Park*.

The town has been important for centuries because of its huge underground salt wells. Salt has been refined here for more than 2000 years. As early as the 10th century, boreholes were being drilled thousands of feet into the ground. The salt-laden brine was then brought to the surface, boiled, and dried by burning the natural gas that accompanied it.

Salt was a valuable commodity so far from the sea and an important way to both pay and raise taxes. Merchants grew wealthy and decorated the town with halls and temples to protect the source of their wealth.

Today, Zìgòng remains an important centre of salt production and the natural gas is used to power local buses in Zìgòng and Yíbīn. You'll see it carried on the bus roof in huge floppy bags.

Information
The main Bank of China is next door to the Shāwān Fàndiàn and changes money and travellers cheques fairly easily. There is also an ATM here that accepts most major credit and bank cards. A second ATM can be found at the smaller Bank of China on Ziyou Lu.

China Post and Telecom is in the centre of town on Jiefang Lu. Internet access is available for Y3 per hour in two Internet cafes side by side, just north of the Támúlín Bīnguǎn.

Walking Tour
Zìgòng is a nice place to explore on foot. Start from the **Wángyé Sì**, on the river near the Shāwān Fàndiàn. The temple is now an excellent teahouse with a view across the river to **Fǎzàng Sì**. Both temples were built to protect the salt trade and ensure a safe

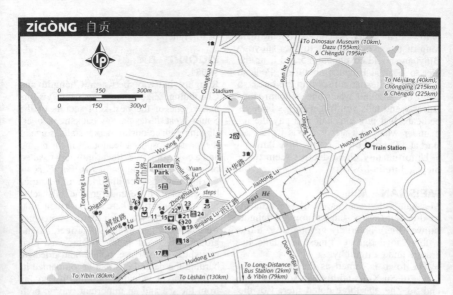

ZÌGÒNG

PLACES TO STAY
1 Xīnxīng Fàndiàn
新星饭店
3 Tánmùlín
Bīnguǎn
檀木林宾馆
13 Huáhuá Lǚguǎn
华华旅馆
19 Shāwān Fàndiàn
沙湾饭店
21 Zhōngxìn Dà
Fàndiàn
中信大饭店
25 Tiānxiáng Dà
Jiǔdiàn
天祥大酒店

PLACES TO EAT
6 Hotpot Stalls
11 Night Market
夜市场

22 Restaurants
饭馆
23 Huáběi Shítáng
华北食堂

OTHER
2 Internet Cafes
网吧
4 Market
市场
5 Colourful
Lantern
Museum
彩灯博物馆
7 Bank of China
中国银行
8 Annie Teahouse;
Cinema
阿细餐饮
9 Xiǎoqiáo Wěll
小桥井

10 Market
市场
12 China Post & Telecom
邮电局
14 Teahouse
茶馆
15 Camel Bar
16 Bus No 3 to
Dinosaur Museum
到恐龙博物馆
的公共汽车
17 Fǎzàng Sì
法藏寺
18 Wángyé Sì;
Disco
王爷茶馆
20 Bank of China
24 Shaanxi Guild Hall; Salt
Industry History
Museum
西秦会馆

journey for the cargo boats transporting salt downstream.

From here, walk north on Binjiang Lu, past the Shāwan Fàndiàn. Take the first right and then right again onto Jiefang Lu. A little farther on you'll find the **Shaanxi**

Guild Hall (Xīqín Huìguǎn), home to the **Salt Industry History Museum**. This beautifully ornate building was built by salt merchants from Shaanxi in 1736 and later renovated in 1872. The exuberantly up-turned eaves cleverly screen the 2nd floor from the outside and the 4th floor from the inside. The inside is decorated with clay statues and paintings depicting scenes from local opera.

The salt museum has a few interesting pictures of derricks and 19th-century salt workers but few English captions. Entry to the Guild Hall is Y10 and opening hours are 8.30am to 5pm.

From here, continue east and take the staircase on the left leading up to Xinmin Jie. There are several interesting back streets in this area, filled with markets. **Xinmin Jie** itself is crammed with older people playing mahjong under huge lines of laundry or whiling away the hours sipping tea.

If you continue north along this narrow alley, you'll reach Yuan Lu. Turn left and then take the first right onto an alley filled with stalls selling plants and brightly coloured birds. At the end of the alley, you'll find the entrance to **Lantern Park** (Dēnglóng Gōngyán), a popular family meeting place. It may be lacking somewhat in greenery but it's still a pleasant place to wander around or to sip a cup of tea at the bamboo teahouse built over the park's lake. There are also small boats, ponies and mechanical elephants for hire. Entry is Y1.

On the western side of the park is the looming **Colourful Lantern Museum** (Cǎidēng Bówūguǎn). Here you can see some of the huge floats that are paraded in Zìgòng's Lantern Festival, held in the park for 40 days during the first and second lunar months (normally February). The floats are spectacular when lit; however, the museum doesn't appear to see many visitors and seems to be saving its yuán by keeping the electricity switched off. Admission is Y4.

From Lantern Park, walk back down to Zhonghua Lu and head west. Here you'll find Zìgòng's most incredible **teahouse** on the right. From the outside, it looks like it may have been Dracula's Chinese holiday home – there are even a few bats circling it in the evening. Inside is a large courtyard brimming with plants, bamboo tables and chairs and red lanterns. You can sip a bottomless cup here for Y2.

Continuing west on Jiefang Lu takes you through a commercial shopping street, also the site of the night market. Crossing Ziyou Lu, the road narrows and you enter yet another busy market, this one selling everything from slippers to sausages. If you follow the bend in the river at the end of Jiefang Lu, you will come to **Xiǎoqiáo Well**, one of Zìgòng's ancient salt wells (*jǐng*). The well itself is filled in, but you can still see the wooden poles and pulleys used to haul the brine up to the surface.

Zigong Dinosaur Museum

自贡恐龙博物馆 Zìgòng Kǒnglóng Bówùguǎn
In 1972, at the end of the Cultural Revolution, dinosaurs were discovered in the Dashanpu suburbs of Zìgòng, 10km northeast of the town centre. After the cultural chaos subsided, excavations started in earnest and since then over 100 dinosaurs ('terrible dragons' in Chinese) have been found.

Initially, scientists were puzzled as to why so many fossils were concentrated at one site, but it is now believed that the already-dead animals were washed here from the surrounding areas during a massive flood. This created a huge jam of dinosaur carcasses, which were then covered by silt and compressed over the millennia.

The museum is made up of three main halls. To the left of the entrance is the Hall of Specimens, which includes a historical exhibit (mainly in Chinese) and houses the astounding reconstructed dinosaurs.

It's hard to miss the star attractions of the hall, two huge *Omeisaurus*, over 20m long and once weighing in at 40 tonnes. Their immense weight and huge necks suggest that they spent most of their time in marshy bogs or lakes with just their heads poking above the surface. There are also a number of huge, ancient dino bones that are out for visitors to touch.

A typical plant of the Jurassic period, and thus prime dinosaur food, is the *Spinulosa* tree fern, which still grows to this day near Chìshuǐ in northern Guìzhōu (see the Around Chìshuǐ section in the Guìzhōu chapter).

In the middle of the hall and in the large room next door are the main excavations

SÌCHUĀN

where work is still being carried out. Watch out for the little lights on the display above the main excavations, which help identify the mish-mash of bones. Tracing the various spines, legs and flippers of the 170-million-year-old animals is fascinating.

Upstairs is a collection of the rarest bones and fossils and a photographic history of the excavation and museum itself. Across the grounds, to the right of the entrance, are some creaky animatronic dinos. Photography throughout the museum is prohibited.

The museum is open 8.30am until 5pm daily and tickets are Y30. To get here from town catch bus No 3 (25 minutes) heading east on Binjiang Lu and ask to be let off at the museum. The bus will drop you a further 10-minute walk south of the museum.

Places to Stay

The best budget rooms can be found at the **Huáhuá Lǚguǎn**, where you can get clean, spacious double rooms with bath for Y30 a bed. The traffic outside is a bit noisy but the staff are friendly and it's the best value you'll find in town. Reception is in an office downstairs but if nobody is around, head up a set of stairs on the right side of the building where the rooms are.

The **Shāwān Fàndiàn** (☎ 220 8888; fax 220 1168, e swfd@zg-public.sc.cninfo.nt, 3 Binjiang Lu) is a flashy three-star, marble-clad monster. Rooms in the main hotel range from Y280 to Y380; but don't panic, what you're here for (after pretending to consider the top-end suites) is the old block of cheapo rooms around the side. Here Y60 will get you a threadbare, dark double and 24-hour hot water. More expensive doubles at Y120 or Y190 in the same building aren't nearly as good value. The floor attendants can arrange pricey laundry, and the hotel's travel agency in front of the hotel can arrange train and plane tickets.

A mid-range option is the **Tánmùlín Bīnguǎn**, set in its own spacious grounds up the hill past Zhongua Lu. Doubles are posted at Y280 but may be offered for Y140, which is still more than they seem worth. Beds in a triple are Y100 apiece. It looks as if a new building may be going up soon.

In the centre of town, the **Zhōngxìn Dà Fàndiàn** (☎ 230 1888) and the **Tiānxiáng Dà Jiǔdiàn** (☎ 220 9868) both have average doubles with hot water and bath starting at Y138.

A definite last option is the unpleasant-smelling **Xīnxīng Fàndiàn**, way to the north of town on Guanghua Lu. The staff are likely to warn you flat out that the place is **bùhǎo** (no good); however, the rooms are much cleaner than the rest of the building suggests and a bed in a triple with bath goes for Y30.

Places to Eat

The **night market** on Jiefang Lu is a good place to fill up on snacks and shop for shoes at the same time. You'll find **shāokǎo stalls** with oodles of barbecued goodies to choose from, as well as bowls of fresh noodles. If you're looking for **huǒguō** (hotpot), head up Ziyou Lu where you'll find excellent stalls with covered seating in the evening.

Halfway between Shawan Fàndiàn and the Shaanxi Guild Hall is the excellent canteen-style **Huáběi Shítáng**. The speciality is excellent **shuǐjiǎo** (dumplings; seven for Y1). There are also several family-run **restaurants** up the side alley beside the Húaběi.

Entertainment

Besides the buzzing night market, Zìgòng has a couple of evening hotspots. **Wángyé Sì** – teahouse by day – turns into a disco at night where you can groove to Chinese dance music in one of the most atmospheric clubs imaginable. Get there early though, as it shuts down at 11.20pm.

If this sounds like a bit too much, the **Camel Bar** is a cosy, relaxing French place that serves cocktails and has live jazz(ish) music. **Annie's Teahouse** (Āxìchānyǐn) is also open until the wee hours and has loads of tea to choose from in posh, warm surroundings.

Getting There & Away

Bus Zígòng's long-distance bus station is south of the town centre and connected by a fume-filled tunnel that is regularly clogged with traffic. A taxi from downtown to the bus station will cost about Y7.

Express buses to Chéngdū (Y51 to Y61, four hours) run between 6.30am and 6.30pm. At 9.40am there is a slower bus (Y41) and even slower ones between 11am and noon (Y35). Sleepers run at 7.30am and 10.30am (Y51) daily.

To Chóngqìng, express buses (Y49.50, four hours) run from 6.15am to 6.20pm with four slower (and cheaper) buses going between 11.25am and 2.30pm. Sleepers (Y46) depart at 9.40pm and 10.30pm. Buses to Dàzú leave daily (Y40) at 8.30am, 11.30am and 3.30pm. Buses to Néijiāng run down the expressway from 7.20am until 7pm (Y13).

Comfortable minibuses zip to Yíbīn from early morning until late at night along a new expressway (Y26). The trip takes under an hour. Slower buses take the long route (Y14, three hours) from 6.10am to 5pm.

If you're headed west, buses to Lèshān (Y23) run from 6.30am to 6.30pm with express versions running from 8am to 5pm in half the time for twice the price. Buses also run directly to Éméi town from 6.10am to 5.30pm (Y27).

Finally, heading south, one bus runs daily to Chángníng at 1.10pm (Y33). You're better off catching the express bus to Yíbīn and then one of the regular buses south from the Niumachang bus station.

Train With those great bus connections, Zìgòng's train station is fairly quiet. Trains to Yíbīn depart at 3pm (Y9), 4pm (Y4.5) and 5pm (Y4). To Chéngdū there is a morning train at 10.46am (Y35). A night train bound for Chéngdū passes through at 11.46pm, but you can't reserve sleepers in Zìgòng. To Chóngqìng, the train pulls out at 11am (Y25).

Getting Around
A taxi between the town centre and train station will cost around Y7. Bus No 3 goes out to the dinosaur museum, No 9 to the train station and No 11 to Xīnxīng Fàndiàn.

YÍBĪN 宜宾
☎ 0831
Yíbīn, 79km south of Zìgòng, gained fame in China as the first port on the Yangzi River. East of town, the Yangzi is known as the Cháng Jiāng, or Long River; west of town it is called the Jīnshā, or Golden Sands. Yíbīn itself spreads over a spit of land where the Jīnshā joins the Mín Hé. For many years the Mín was considered to be the source of the Cháng Jiāng, but the Jīnshā is by far the longer tributary – by the time it gets to Yíbīn it has already covered over 2200km.

Improved surface travel throughout the area has brought passenger boats along the river to a grinding halt; today only cargo ships visit Yíbīn's port. Nevertheless, this doesn't seem to have slowed Yíbīn down as it rapidly transforms itself into a modern city. With a cheerful population, some interesting backstreets, nice teahouses and street stalls galore, Yíbīn is a pleasant enough place to visit en route to intriguing sights further south.

Unfortunately, the accommodation scene is not so good in Yíbīn. At least you can drown your worries about the hotel bill in the strong brews of the city's famous liquor distilleries. Try Wuliangye (Five Grain Liquor) or Yishouye. There's even a joint venture distillery outside of town that blends Scotch whisky with local firewater to produce Chinese whisky for the really brave.

Information
The Bank of China is on Qingnian Gai, an alley off Nan Jie. Despite its inauspicious appearance, it is the main branch and you can change money or travellers cheques here or make a cash advance on your credit card.

China Post's main office is also on Nan Jie, a block or so north of the bank. Further south, where Nan Jie becomes Wainan Jie, China Telecom is on the brink of opening a huge office that will offer Internet access.

Things to See & Do
The geographical centre of town is the **Grand Viewing Pavilion** (Dàguan Lóu), the heart of a traditional town layout that has roads leading off to city gates at the four cardinal points. The ground floor of the pavilion is now a shop selling books, stationery and an odd assortment of plastic goods. The 1st floor houses a pricey teahouse and the 2nd floor is a library.

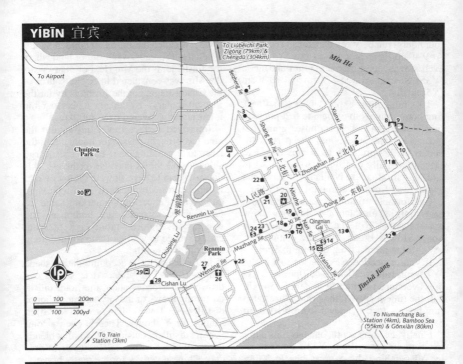

YÍBĪN 宜宾

YÍBĪN

PLACES TO STAY

7 Jiŭdū Fàndiàn
酒都饭店

11 Xīyuàn Bīnguǎn
西苑宾馆

22 Xùfǔ Bīnguǎn
叙府宾馆

23 Yíbīn
Grand Hotel
宜宾大酒店

28 Jīnyuàn
Bīnguǎn
金苑宾馆

PLACES TO EAT

5 Dàkuàilè Western
Food Restaurant
大快乐中西
快餐咖啡店

25 Street Stalls

27 Yùlǎoxiāng
Miànguǎn
玉老乡面馆

OTHER

1 Teahouses
茶馆

2 Market
市场

3 CAAC
中国民航售票处

4 Beimen
Bus Station
北门汽车站

6 Clock Tower
钟鼓楼

8 East Gate
东门

9 Ferry Boat
(Across Min River)
渡轮

10 Teahouses

12 Teahouse

13 Kuíxīng Pavilion
魁星阁

14 Bank of China
中国银行

15 China Telecom

16 China Post &
Telecom
邮电局

17 United Industrial &
Commercial
Teahouse
工商联茶厅

18 Grand Viewing
Pavilion
大观楼

19 Xinhua Bookstore
新华书店

20 PSB
公安局

21 Train Ticket Office
火车售票处

24 ATM

26 Catholic Church
天主堂

29 Nánmén Bus Station
南门汽车站

30 Dàojiào Sì

For a cup of tea head south for 100m to a wonderful but dilapidated old building that has been converted into the proletarian **United Industrial and Commercial Teahouse** (Gōngshānglián Chátíng). Here you can get a cup of tea for six máo.

There are still a number of areas around the edges of Yíbīn that have managed to retain some of their traditional wooden buildings, narrow streets and the flavour of the old port. The streets surrounding the site of the North Gate, itself long since disappeared, are worth a wander. At the northern end of Beizheng Jie there are a number of small traditional teahouses. The street itself is a meat market that isn't likely to fire up the appetites of even the most devoted carnivores. Looking for a haircut or a shave? Heading north on Beizheng Jie, take the last left and follow it under the bridge where you'll find a number of busy, outdoor barber stalls.

The area around the **East Gate**, along the Mín Hé, is also worth exploring. This gate is the last remaining example of the four city gates and has been smartened up into a teahouse/restaurant overlooking the harbour. A new pathway has been built along the edge of the rivers, which you can wander along from the East Gate around to an outdoor teahouse beside the Jīnshā Jiāng.

Also in this area, a block or so inland from the East Gate, are a number of small teahouses filled with Yíbīn's older folk playing mahjong. It is questionable as to how long these wooden buildings will survive as, at the time of writing, those just inland from the confluence of the two rivers were being bulldozed.

Yíbīn has two main parks. **Liúbēichí Park** to the north of town is not up to much. A better option is to climb up to the top of **Chuípíng Park**, where a less-than-beautiful concrete pagoda gives good views of the city below. Look out for the White Pagoda on a hilltop east of town and its counterpart, the Black Pagoda, high on the ridge to the south.

In the south of Chuípíng Park is a Taoist temple, **Dàojiào Sì**. The temple was rebuilt in the early 90s by a Taiwanese religious leader. After awaking from a dream in which Laotzu (Lǎozǐ) had appeared to him

and told him of the decrepit state of the temple of his birth, the Taiwanese leader scoured China in search of this temple, determined to salvage it. Although Laotzu was supposedly born in Húnán, the leader found the likeness of his dream, both in the temple and its surroundings, here in Yíbīn. He urged Taiwanese Taoist followers to donate money for the temple's reconstruction and for a few years this drew a great number of tourists from Taiwan, strengthening the tourist infrastructure in and around Yíbīn.

Other places of interest are the **traditional pharmacies** along Wenxing Jie, near the People's Park, and the dilapidated **Kuíxīng Pavilion** in the south-east of town.

Places to Stay
The best place to stay if visiting Yíbīn is in Zìgòng, one hour away by bus. All of Yíbīn's budget options have been closed to foreigners, leaving a few mid-range to top-end hotels that don't offer very good value for money.

The cheapest beds are at *Jīnyuàn Bīnguǎn* (☎ 822 5634) across from the Nánmén bus station. Newly refurbished it now offers clean, heated doubles with bath and hot water for Y120. For Y10 more you can get a slightly plusher but older room in the towering *Xùfǔ Bīnguǎn* (☎ 822 1883). Newer rooms begin at Y280.

In the east of the city, the *Xīyuàn Bīnguǎn* (☎ 822 7884, 13 Fuxin Jie) has doubles from Y180 to Y230.

The *Jiǔdū Fàndiàn* (☎ 822-3399, fax 822 3961, 5 Kaoshu Jie) has drab doubles starting at Y200; however, the early stages of refurbishment were underway so perhaps it will soon be worth a second look.

The nicest hotel in town is the new *Yíbīn Grand Hotel* (Yíbīn Dà Fàndiàn) on Mazhong Jie with comfortable rooms and real showers for Y280 to Y380.

Places to Eat
The streets of Yíbīn are lined with countless *stalls* dishing up a fantastic array of food. Every corner off the main streets will present you with barbecues, fresh noodles, pancakes, sweets, and yam chips. The small road crossing Mazhang Jie, alongside

Renmin Park, is particularly good, as is the small road north of the Xùfǔ Bīnguǎn.

On Wenxing Jie, *Yùlǎoxiāng Miànguǎn* is a noodle bar that serves 10 kinds of noodles for a tasty snack. For the price (Y3 a bowl) you could try them all. The *ránmiàn* (literally, 'burning noodles') are recommended if you like spicy food. The noodles are fried and then served with onions, chillies, peanuts, chives and a side serving of sauce.

If you fancy something a bit more sophisticated, head for the *Jìngshèng Cháfǎng* in the north of town. Although fairly new, the decor is very traditional and the place oozes 19th-century atmosphere. Tea is a bit pricey by local standards (eg, Y10 for a pot) but the food isn't bad value at around Y20 a dish.

Go down to the riverfront, where a number of the boats that once cruised between here and Chóngqìng have been converted into terrace-style *restaurants* with great views.

The *Dàkuàilè Western Food Restaurant* (*Dàkuàilè Hōngxīkuàicāi Kāfēidiàn*) is a Western restaurant with salads, pizza, steaks, pasta, burgers, cocktails and milkshakes.

Getting There & Away

Air Yíbīn airport, 7km north-east of town, has flights to Kūnmíng (Y470, daily except Tuesday), Běijīng (Y1400, Monday, Thursday and Saturday), Guǎngzhōu (Y1040, daily except Tuesday and Friday) and Shànghǎi (Y1350, Wednesday and Sunday). Flights to Chéngdū, Guìyáng and Chóngqìng have been discontinued.

Bus Yíbīn has the usual confusing array of bus stations. The Nánmén (South Gate) station has buses to Chéngdū (Y90) more than hourly between 6am and 11.40am and then at 3pm and 5.30pm. To Chóngqìng (Y50) there are morning services at 6.40am, 9am and 11am and then hourly 1.30pm to 5.30pm.

From the Beimen (North Gate) station, minibuses depart for Zìgòng (Y26) every half-hour from 7.20am to 6.50pm. The new expressway has cut the journey down to less than an hour. You can also get buses hourly to Chéngdū (Y80) from 7am to noon and to Lèshān (Y50) at 8am. There is one sleeper service daily to Xīchàng (Y108, 17 hours).

For destinations south, you'll have to trek out to the Niumachang station, about 4km south-east of Yíbīn. Regular buses to Gǒngxiàn (Y8.50) and Xīngwén (Y12.50) run between 6am and 6.30pm. Buses to Chángníng (Y7.50, two hours) run from 6am to 7.30pm. To reach Niumachang station, you can catch a super-slow city bus from the south-east side of Daguan Pavilion for eight máo. A taxi from town will cost about Y8.

Train Yíbīn's train station is 3km south of the town centre but there's a ticket office on Renmin Lu where you can get train information and hard-seat tickets. The office is open 8am to noon and 1pm to 6pm

There is an early morning train to Chóngqìng (Y34, nine hours) departing at 6am as well as an overnight sleeper at 9.22pm (Y74). To Chéngdū there is a slow train leaving at 9.08am (Y28) or a faster one at 10pm (Y47). Two departures a day stop

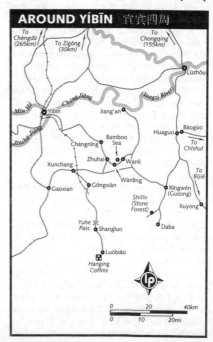

AROUND YÍBĪN 宜宾四周

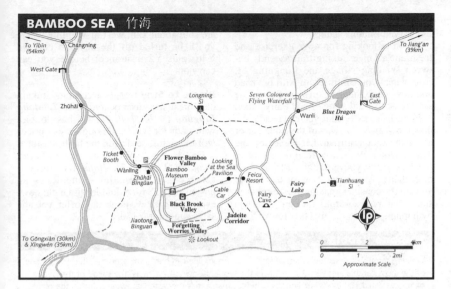

BAMBOO SEA 竹海

at Zigòng, the faster one at 9.08am (Y12); however, it's much faster to take a minibus.

AROUND YÍBĪN 宜宾四周
Bamboo Sea 竹海
Zhúhǎi

Some 61km south-east of Yíbīn lies one of South-West China's largest stretches of bamboo forest. About 12,000 acres of saturated green, waterfalls and inky black pools spread over crumpled valleys and mountains. There are some 30 types of bamboo in the park, including Nan, Mao, Golden, Fishpole, Turtleback and Flower Bamboo, all of which have been used to produce almost everything the local people have ever needed over the centuries. Today it is sold commercially, and the forest is dotted with processing factories and roads and trails established to transport felled bamboo.

Although strong tourist infrastructure has developed in the forest, business has slowed down; the low season is silent and you're only likely to see tour groups here in the summer. Nevertheless, if you arrive to find crowds and are looking for some peace and quiet, the best thing to do is to head out along one of the many narrow trails leading off the roads. It's probably not wise to stray too far off the trails, however, as one bamboo tree quickly begins to look like the next and it would be extremely easy to get lost.

Things to See The main park starts at the eastern edge of Wànlǐng town. Buses go to the car park, from where one road heads south across a bridge and up towards the Bamboo Sea Hotel while a second heads south-east towards the **Bamboo Museum**.

From the museum you can either continue south to the waterfalls of **Forgetting Worries Valley** (Wàngyōu Gǒu) or turn left for the inky pools of **Black Brook Valley** (Heixī) and the cable car which gives you a worthwhile bird's-eye view of the forest, its pools and waterfalls (Y30/40 one way/return).

At the top of the cable car is **Looking at the Sea Pavilion** (Guānhǎi Lóu), which gives a view down onto the billowing canopy of wispy bamboo heads that give the Bamboo Sea its name. A short walk away is **Jadeite Corridor** (Fěicùi Chángláng), a red-dirt road cutting through towering 20m-high bamboo – a scene captured on everything from bus station walls to baseball caps. You can also head north-east from here to **Fairy**

Lake (Xiānnǔ Hú), to see its less-than-life-like carved Buddha statues.

If you're looking for some exercise and fresh air, a longer hiking trail ascends between Wànlǐng village and Longning Sì, from where you can meet up with the road and carry on to Jadeite Corridor or continue south-east to **Tianhuang Sì** and Fairy Lake.

From Jadeite Corridor you can head back down to Wànlǐng by way of the cable car or along the southern road that passes by the Traffic Hotel. While this road does offer a few nice views, you aren't going to see a lot more than pavement and bamboo trunks and you might consider making this 8km trek somewhat more exciting (and much faster) by hopping on a motorbike taxi for Y15.

Entry Fees Tickets to the Bamboo Forest are sold about 1km west of Wànlǐng where you'll be turfed off the bus and charged Y40 (plus Y2 insurance) before you can carry on.

Places to Stay Budget accommodation in the forest has disappeared. The *Jiāotōng Bīnguǎn* (☎ 0831-498 0919) has doubles with bath for Y150, although these prices will likely inflate during the high season.

Overlooking Wànlǐng, the *Zhǔhǎi Bīnguǎn (Bamboo Sea Hotel)* has comfortable rooms in a beautiful setting. Rates are posted at Y228 for a double with bath; however, if it's slow, they may offer you the same room for Y180.

Bamboo Babble

Walking through a graceful thicket of sinewy bamboo, one can hardly imagine that this grass is one of the most durable and versatile plants in the world. Known in China as 'the friend of the people', bamboo existed 100 to 200 million years before man and is the fastest growing plant on the planet, recorded at growing over 47 inches in a 24-hour period.

Proving its durability, bamboo was the closest living thing to ground zero during the attack on Hiroshima, one small thicket suffering only a singed side. It's not surprising, then, that bamboo is also bullet proof, thus providing shelter to Japanese soldiers during WWII. In the event of an earthquake or typhoon, a bamboo thicket is the most stable environment in which to seek shelter. Bamboo is so resilient it can tolerate drought or exist in 250 inches of annual rainfall.

Nearly 200 different species of bamboo provide over 1000 different uses, making it one of the most versatile resources in the world. While bamboo is used for the obvious baskets, mats and chopsticks, it was also used for the first phonograph needles and for the filaments in Thomas Edison's lightbulbs. Bamboo leaves are used for medicine, bamboo pulp is formed into paper and sauteed bamboo shoots make a satisfying snack. From the vain nail cases worn at night by the China's imperial elite to protect finely sharpened fingernails, to the aesthetic sounds of the Chinese *sheng* (mouth organ) or Miáo *lusheng*, to the fundamental structure of modern villages, the function of bamboo seems as limitless as the imagination.

The myriad other uses of bamboo include: acupuncture needles, airplane wings, alcohol, aphrodisiacs, ashtrays, blowguns, bracelets, bridges, buttons, caulking, colanders, crutches, cultures (for bacteria in lab tests), curtains, deodorisers, fertiliser, fireworks, furniture, gutters, hairpins, helmets, humidors, kites, lamps, looms, medicines, sewing needles, opium pipes, poison, polo mallets, puppets, ropes, rulers, sake, ski poles, splints, textiles, tongue depressors, toothpicks, wicks, writing brushes, xylophones and zithers.

In addition, bamboo is pivotal in the prevention of deforestation in China because its sturdy anchor prevents landslides and washouts and because the thick canopy conserves moisture as well as providing shade to suppress shrubs, thereby providing area for timber growth. Although bamboo is often cut back in the hope of growing more timber and despite the over 100 anti-bamboo bugs in China, the plant continues to thrive.

Kelli Hahn

There are also a couple of hotels on the road heading to the museum; at the time of writing they were all closed and in the process of being rebuilt.

Your other option is to stay in Chángníng where the **Shǔnán Zhúhǎi Jiāotōng Bīnguǎn** has clean if somewhat drab doubles with hot water for Y150. To find the hotel head south down the road out of Chángníng's bus station, take the first left over the river and then the first right. The hotel is ahead of you at the end of the road.

Also in Chángníng is the **Gentleman's Hotel** (*Jūnzǐ Bīnguǎn;* ☎ 0831-462 2027), which has transformed itself into a top-end hotel with doubles for Y228. With a little luck you might be able to get a dorm bed for Y120. To find it, follow directions to the Shǔnán Zhúhǎi Jiāotōng Bīnguǎn, go left, and the hotel is on the left side of the road. If you go on to the T-junction, you'll find lots of small restaurants and street stalls.

Places to Eat There are a number of *restaurants* around the car park at Wànlǐng as well as across from the Zhǔhǎi Bīnguǎn and near Looking at the Sea Pavilion. Check prices first or you may automatically be served special 'bamboo rice' in a bamboo container for Y8.

Getting There & Away From Yíbīn's Niumachang bus station, take a bus to Chángníng (Y7.50, two hours); they run regularly between 6am and 7.30pm. From Chángníng get on a bus to Wànlǐng (Y4.50). A bus also runs from Zìgòng to Chángníng at 1.10pm (Y33). Going the other way, the last bus departs Chángníng for Yíbīn at 6pm.

To head south-west from Wànlǐng, it's easiest to return to Chángníng and pick up a bus to Gǒngxiàn which heads out at 10.35am (Y7.50, two hours).

Bo Hanging Coffins 悬棺
Xuánguān

Some 106km south of Yíbīn, perched precariously up on the cliffs of the Deying Valley, are dozens of wooden coffins erected by the ancient Bo people. Nobody knows why they are there, how they got there or

who put them there, but the mystery just adds to the enigma of the place. There's not much else to see once you've gawked at the coffins, but the surrounding valley is pleasant and you could do some nice walks.

Admission to the area is Y10. While you can see a few of the coffins on a cliff before the entrance gate (ie, without buying a ticket), once inside there are a greater number of coffins and stairs that allow a closer look. Despite what the back of the ticket implies, there are only one or two coffin-hung cliffs within easy walking distance.

To get to the coffins first take a bus to Gǒngxiàn. Buses run there from Yíbīn (Y8.50) from 6.10am to 6.30pm and from Chángníng at 10.35am (Y7.50, two hours). From Gǒngxiàn take another bus south over the Yuhe Pass to Luòbiǎo (Y8.50, 2½ hours). The coffins are a further 3km walk south of Luòbiǎo, just past the village of Matangba. The bus will drop you at a fork in the road; head down the road on the right.

Buses return hourly to Gǒngxiàn between 6am and 5pm. To reach Xīngwén (also known as Gǔsòng; Y8, two hours), you'll have to take a short bus ride from Gǒngxiàn to Xucheng (Y3) and then pick up a through bus heading east to Xīngwén. These run until 5pm or 6pm.

The coffins are not easily visited as a day trip. If you decide to stay in Luòbiǎo, the unnamed *hotel* where the bus drops you has very basic but clean rooms for Y10 per bed. This hotel is on the east side, before the fork in the road. A few doors down (also on the east side but just past the fork) is a *guesthouse* that has similar rooms for Y30 a bed.

Locals may show you *Luòbiǎofánxiāng Bīnguǎn*, a prison-like maze with basic, nondescript rooms with beds at Y30.

There are a number of *restaurants* and a few shops where the bus drops you. Take the left at the fork in the road and then the first right to find more of both plus a *bakery* and some *fruit stalls*.

Stone Forest
Shíhǎi Dòngxiāng

Xīngwén Stone Forest is a beautiful hilly area of bizarre, fractured limestone rocks

The Bo

The only remaining legacy of the mysterious Bo people are the collections of 400-year-old wooden coffins, dangling off the sides of high cliff faces. There are 23 sites in southern Sìchuān where you can see these hanging coffins, the most popular of which is just over 100km from Yíbīn.

The Bo were only briefly recorded in ancient Chinese chronicles as the *Yaze* (Sons of the Cliffs) or *Tutian* (Subjugators of the Sky). Marco Polo was as mystified as everyone else by their bizarre habits. In the heat of the summer sun, the Bo wore heavy leather coats and warmed themselves round fires; in winter they wore a single layer and carried huge fans around with them. In a final act of defiance, the leader of the Bo declared himself emperor during a local rebellion and the entire group was beaten and driven off by the Imperial Army, vanishing during the 16th century. Some anthropologists suggest that the modern-day Tujia or north-eastern Guìzhōu and Hunan are distant relatives of the Bo.

What little else we know of the Bo has been garnered from the coffins themselves, ten of which were examined by archaeologists in 1974. Implements dating back to the 12th century indicate that the Bo were good horsemen, with a sharp social divide. One wealthy man was discovered wearing 29 shirts and 13 pairs of hemp or silk trousers, hinting that the Bo were preparing their deceased for a spiritual journey of some sort. Some see the hanging coffins as an attempt by the Bo to aid the spirits in their journey up to the heavens.

Another intriguing fact is that all the adult skeletons had had their side teeth removed well before death, suggesting that the Bo deliberately knocked out their own teeth for religious or decorative purposes. Murals also depict a hairstyle similar to that of the modern-day Yi of the Liángshān region, with a horn of hair protruding to one side.

As you look up at the 250kg coffins, you'll likely wonder how the Bo managed to get them up there. The niches in the cliff face suggest scaffolding. Don't look too closely though – the coffins continue to decay and have been known occasionally to plummet to the ground.

that form pinnacles and splintered, craggy outcrops. There is a primeval feel about this place – you almost expect to see a dinosaur come wandering around the bend. Also, one of the largest caves in China is here, an enormous funnel that is definitely worth a look.

Despite the occasional tour group that might have a wander through the cave in the summer, you are almost guaranteed to be the only foreign tourist around, making this an excellent place for a quiet walk. The main trail begins in Shílín village. To find it, cross the road from the Shílín Bīnguǎn and take the stairs up on the left. You'll pass a number of small cottages and villagers farming. While there isn't a lot of soil here, it is fertile, and lush crops and gardens grow anywhere that's flat.

If you follow the main stone path in a general north-westerly direction, you'll reach a dirt road after about 45 minutes. Here you can either head down the Confusing Path of Stones to the **Peak of Seven Ladies** or head

north down the dirt road towards the **Heavenly Basin**, a giant depression. Also in this direction is the **Big Funnel Cave**. En route to the cave, it's worth taking a two-minute detour off to see **Couple Peak**, where a large rock is balanced between two huge towers of limestone. The way is signposted.

The cave itself is magnificent – running water, natural skylights, more pinnacles of limestone and a brilliant echo. The admission fee is a hefty Y31 and they may try to stick you with a Y50 guide but this doesn't appear to be obligatory. While there are some lights in the cave, it's a good idea to bring a flashlight. The opposite end of the cave opens onto the road from Xīngwén. This is where tour buses hover in the summer and there are a few restaurants and souvenir shops. A bus to Xīngwén passes here every hour or so. To head back to the village, turn right.

Places to Stay & Eat While you can easily follow the trail from the village through the stone forest and out through the cave in a couple of hours, if you'd like to take in some of the smaller paths, it's worth spending a night in the village and making a day of it. *Shílín Bīnguǎn* has beds in clean, basic rooms for Y25. Rooms on the 2nd floor are the same but twice the price. A few doors down on the same side of the road, *Xiandongxiang Bīnguǎn* has beds for Y20.

There are a couple of *restaurants* in Shilin, including one at Xiandongxiang Bīnguǎn. The *very* friendly proprietor will likely find you before you find him. There are also a couple of shops in the village where you can buy water, however, if you want any snacks for the trail, you'd be better off bringing them with you.

Accommodation in Xīngwén itself is not so good, especially for budget travellers. The *Xīngwén Bīnguǎn* (☎ 882 2289) has singles/doubles starting at Y100/160.

Getting There & Away Shílín village and the Stone Forest can be reached via Xīngwén. To reach Xīngwén (also known as Gǔsòng), take a bus from Yíbīn (Y12.50, four hours) from between 6am and 6.30pm. You can also reach Xīngwén from Xunchang (Y8, two hours) or Lúzhōu (Y15, seven hours).

From Xīngwén, buses run hourly from the west bus station to Shílín village (Y5, one hour), 21km away. Be sure to ask for the village itself or you'll be dropped at the entrance to the cave. From Shílín village, buses run hourly(ish) back to Xīngwén. Catch them at the crossroads leading into the village.

Xīngwén has two bus stations, a few kilometres from each other. A motorcab between the two costs Y2. From the west station there are regular buses to Yíbīn and Xunchang until about 5.30pm. From the north station, sleepers head to Chóngqìng and Chéngdū at 4.30pm. A number of buses also head to Lúzhōu (Y15) with the last departing at 2pm.

The road heading north from Xīngwén up to the Chéngdū-Chóngqìng expressway is under construction and in abominable shape. Until it's finished, you might consider breaking your journey in Lúzhōu, a friendly, busy town on the Yangtze River. The *Lúzhōu Bīnguǎn* (☎ 229 3888) has

clean doubles with bath and hot water for Y60. You can catch regular onward superspeedy Iweco minivans on to Chóngqìng or Chéngdū from Lúzhōu.

If you are heading from Xīngwén on to Chìshuǐ in northern Guìzhōu, you will have to take a morning bus to Lúzhōu (Y15, four hours), get off at the road junction at Huaguo and wait there for a through bus to Chìshuǐ, some 2½ hours east. Next to Huaguo is the village of Bàogúo (Defend the Country), which has a great market every third day.

Another route into Guìzhōu takes you south via Xuyong, from where you can catch a bus to Bìjié in northern Guìzhōu and then continue on to Guìyáng, Ānshùn or Wēiníng.

XĪCHĀNG 西昌
☎ 0834

About halfway between Chéngdū and Kūnmíng, Xīchāng is a friendly mix of Han, Yi and Huí Muslims. On arrival, it may appear like just another Chinese town hellbent on modernisation, but with a little delving a more traditional side reveals itself.

Xīchāng's main draw is as a base from which to visit surrounding Yi villages. As the capital of the Liángshān (Cool Mountains) Yi Autonomous Prefecture, Xīchāng itself is a major centre for local Yi. In the centre of town is a statue depicting the brotherhood of the Han and Yi peoples, with the Red Army commander Liu Bocheng downing a toast of blood and wine with a local Yi chieftain after securing a safe passage for the Long Marchers in 1935.

Xīchāng has also been known for centuries as the 'City of the Moon' and so it's apt that China's major satellite launching operation should take place nearby. You will see a statue or two in recognition of this as well as some 'unique' satellite souvenirs for sale.

On the edge of town is the large Qiónghǎi Hú where you can watch the fishermen. There is also a big torch festival here in July.

Information
Tourist Office Xīchāng International Travel Service (XITS; ☎/fax 323 2161, ⓔ xits@moon.ls.scsti.ac.cn), just around the corner from the main bus station, is a

SÌCHUĀN

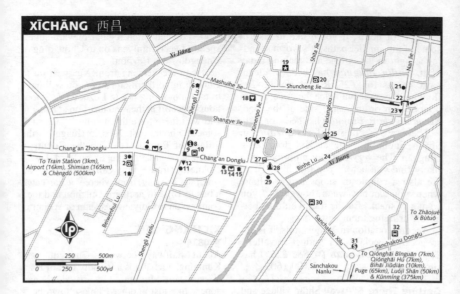

XĪCHĀNG 西昌

friendly source of information. For a Y30 commission, the staff can book onward train sleepers. They can also arrange tours of the Satellite Launching Centre.

Xīnlǒng Bīnguǎn (☎ 366 9760, e xin long@xc-public.sc.cningo.net) has a travel service and can help with local information.

PSB At the time of writing, permits were no longer necessary to visit any of the nearby villages; however, foreigners still require a special permit to cross into Yúnnán via Lúgū Hú. Staff here can get you this permit and can extend your visa.

Money The huge, new, main Bank of China is on Sanchakou Lu and changes travellers cheques and cash.

Post & Communications The China Post and Telecom Office is on Chang'an Donglu and is open until 9pm.

Email & Internet Access Small Internet cafes with access for Y3 per hour have appeared in Xīchāng. One is on Beiwenhui Lu, just south of the train ticket office. Another three are on Shita Jie, in the north of town.

Things to See

The most interesting part of town is the **old quarter** in the north-east, centred around the south gate of the old walled city. Here you'll see Yi traders selling vegetables and medicines by the riverside market and gossiping in wooden teahouses. There is also a large **market** through the centre of town on the pedestrianised Shangye Jie, where you can buy everything from shoes to noodles.

Seven kilometres south-east of town is the large **Qiónghǎi Hú**, often dotted with small fishing boats. You can visit the lakeside at Qiónghǎi Park (Y5) where, in the summer, you can rent windsurfing equipment and small boats. To reach the park take bus No 22, which will drop you off at the entrance.

The Buddhist and Taoist complex of **Lu Shān** rises from the western shore of the lake. The majority of the eight temples were razed during the Cultural Revolution; however, a walk up the hill takes you past 2000-year-old cypress trees that date from the Han dynasty and offers excellent views of the lake and surrounding mountains.

About 15 minutes' walk up Lu Shān lies the **Liángshān Yi Minority Slave Museum**. All of the captions are in Chinese only;

SICHUAN

XĪCHĀNG

PLACES TO STAY

1 Rénhé Bīnguǎn
  人和宾馆
6 Golden Bridge Hotel
  金桥宾馆
7 Liángshān Bīnguǎn
  凉山宾馆
9 Jiāotōng Gōngyù
  交通公寓
15 Wùmào Bīnguǎn
  物贸宾馆

PLACES TO EAT

12 Restaurants
  饭馆
16 Night Market
  夜市
23 Teahouses;
  Restaurants
  茶馆

OTHER

2 Internet Cafe
3 Bǐhǎiyuàn Teahouse
  壁海苑

4 Train Ticket Office
  火车售票处
5 Post Office
  邮电局
8 XITS
  西昌旅行社
10 Main Bus Station
  汽车站
11 CAAC
  中国民航售票处
13 Xīnlóng Bīnguǎn
  鑫龙
14 China Post &
  Telecom
  中国电信
17 Xinhua Bookstore
  新华书店
18 Báiyè Pub
  白液酒吧
19 PSB
  公安局
20 Internet Cafes
  网吧
21 Teahouses
  茶馆

22 South Gate
  南门
24 Market
  市场
25 Fountain
  喷泉
26 Market
  市场
27 No 6 Buses
  to Train Station
  汽车到火车站
28 Statue
  塑像
29 Minority
  Products Store
  少数民族用品商店
30 Nánqiáo
  Bus Station
  南桥汽车站
31 Bank of
  China
  中国银行
32 South-East
  Bus Station
  西昌车站

however, there is a collection of black-and-white photos as well as detailed local maps. The museum is open from 8.30am to 4pm, and closed Monday and Tuesday. Admission is Y3.

To reach Lu Shān and the museum, take bus No 22 to the Qiónghǎi Bīnguǎn, continue walking south-east and take the second small road uphill on the right. This will take you to the bottom of the stairs leading up the hill. You'll find the museum on your right; look for a large stone fence and a small white-tiled ticket office.

Places to Stay – Budget

The *Wùmào Bīnguǎn* (☎ 322 3374), a five-minute walk east of the main bus station, is the best budget choice. Beds in a clean triple with common bath cost Y15. Clean doubles with bath cost Y60 to Y80. Hot water comes on at 8pm.

The only other budget option open to foreigners is the *Jiāotōng Gōngyù*, above the main bus station, which has a range of cheap beds starting at Y12. It may be con-

venient for early morning travel, but it's also maddeningly noisy and often full.

Places to Stay – Mid-Range to Top-End

Xīchāng has a number of mid-range hotels. The *Liángshān Bīnguǎn* (☎ 322 3007) is a little run down but has nice triples for Y160 with heat, hardwood floors and a quiet garden out back. There is even a bowling alley where you can get a game for Y20 in the evening or Y10 at lunchtime. Posted rates begin at Y269.

Up the road, *Golden Bridge Hotel* (*Jīnqiáo Bīnguǎn;* ☎ 322 0088) is a shiny two-star hotel with nicer standard rooms for Y188 and suites for Y288. Prices include breakfast.

South of Cháng'ān Dōnglù, *Rénhé Bīnguǎn* (☎ 323 3234) is the best mid-range hotel in town with comfortable, good-as-new doubles for Y188.

On the banks of the lake, 7km south of town, is the *Qiónghǎi Bīnguǎn* (☎ 395 2096). Doubles with a balcony overlooking the lake start at Y268, with the possibility

SÌCHUĀN

of a discount during low season. The hotel also has a peaceful garden and tennis courts.

Further down the road is the unique *Bìhǎi Jiǔdiàn* (☎/fax 395 2888). Shaped like a cruise liner, the hotel has gorgeous, peaceful doubles with large windows overlooking the lake for Y268 to Y388. There is also a fancy glassed-in teahouse in the lounge.

Places to Eat & Drink

A local speciality is *qìguō*, an earthenware pot has it's soupy contents heated up by steam through a hole in the middle. *Restaurants* all over town serve qìguō; try the northern end of Shengli Nanlu. Unfortunately, it's hard to get a veggie version. Another local treat is steamed oat bread made by Yi people and sold on the roadside in the mornings.

If you're looking for a snack, check out the street vendors in the *market* along Shangye Jie, where you can find yam pancakes, fries and corn on the cob. In the evening, Ximenpo Jie, between Shangye Jie and Changan Donglu, turns into a large *night market*. Hundreds of little plastic chairs and tables are set up along the pavement and cooks whip up noodles, veggies and the like. You'll also find *barbecue stalls* at night, especially across from the Nánqiáo bus station. Many serve small fish caught in the nearby lake.

In addition to the small teahouses in the north-east of town, fancier versions are cropping up in Xīchāng where you get a small aperitif and little bowls of peanuts and seeds along with your tea or coffee. The *Bǐhǎiyuàn* serves coffee for Y30 to Y40 a cup, or the *Xīlǒng Bīnguǎn* has a more affordable version with tea/coffee for Y18/20.

If you're looking for a pint, the *Báiyè Pub* (*Báiyè Jiǔbā*) is a comfy bar.

Shopping

A few shops in town sell Yi wares – red, yellow and black lacquered bowls and dishes, long pipes and embroidered clothing. Some of these shops are found along Shangye Jie. You might also see leather belts for sale with a secret zipped pocket on the inside for stashing money. Finally, a number of shops sell scale models of the 'Long March' rocket and 'The East is Red' satellite.

Getting There & Away

Xīchāng is a bit of a black hole. Buy your onward ticket as soon as possible.

Air China Southwest Airlines flies three times a week to Chéngdū (Y450). Flights leave at 10.10am on Tuesday, Friday and Sunday. The once-weekly flight to Kūnmíng has been cancelled.

The CAAC ticket office (☎ 322 3194) is on Shengli Nanlu and is open 8am to 11.30am and 2.30pm to 5.30pm.

The airport is 16km north of town. An airport bus departs from the CAAC office at 8.30am (Y5) on the mornings of scheduled flights.

Bus There are three bus stations in town. Xīchāng's main bus station is on Chang'an Donglu and has departures to Chéngdū (Y86) at 2pm and, when there are enough passengers, at 3.30pm and 5pm as well, arriving in Chéngdū the following afternoon. To Kāngdìng there is an early morning bus at 6.30am (Y58) and sometimes a second bus at 7.30am. There are also buses to Shímǐ (Y29) at 5.30am, 6.30am, 9.30am and 11.30am. From Shímǐ you can change for Lúdìng and then Kāngdìng.

Heading west, a number of buses depart for Mùlǐ (Y49) between 6.30am and 8.30am.

For Yúnnán, an afternoon bus heads south to Kūnmíng each afternoon and buses to Pānzhīhūa (Y35 to Y46) depart at 7.30am and 11.30am. From here you can change for a bus to Lìjiāng.

Xīchāng's Nánqiáo bus station, over the bridge on Sanchakou Xilu, has three buses to Zhāojué (Y18) between 6.20am and 7am. There is also a bus to Bùtuō (Y21) at 6.30am and almost hourly buses to Pǔgé (Y14) between 7.10am and 3.40pm.

Further south, the south-east bus station also has buses to Zhāojué (Y18). These run every 20 minutes between 6am and 9am. Buses to Bùtuō (Y21) depart every half-hour between 6am and 3.30pm. To Leibo (Y50), there are five departures between 6.20am and 7.40am with a sixth at noon.

Attempting to head east to Yíbīn can be rather frustrating. A sleeper bus originating in Pānzhīhūa pulls into the south-east bus station between 8pm and 9pm and heads off for Yíbīn along an extremely rough, slide-prone and often snowy road (17 hours).

Train Xīchāng's train station is a few kilometres west of town but there's a useful ticket office on Chang'an Zhonglu. It's open 9.40am to noon and 1pm to 3pm. Bus No 6 runs from the town centre to the train station along Chang'an Donglu. There is also a ticket window on the main intersection near the bus station but it's less user-friendly and will usually only sell hard-seat tickets.

Trains to Jiājiāng (for Lèshān; eight hours) and Chéngdū (Y73, 11 hours) leave at 8.57pm and 11.21pm. Originating in Xīchāng, the earlier train is easier to get tickets on. There is one train that continues north all the way to Xī'ān, departing daily at noon. A train to Kūnmíng passes through town at 11pm (Y71) and is notoriously crowded.

If you haven't bought your ticket well in advance, your only option may be to buy a Y1 platform ticket from the information desk at the station and attempt to hunt down a bunk on the train once it pulls in.

AROUND XĪCHĀNG
Satellite Launching Centre
Wēixīng Fāshè Zhōngxīn

Hidden in the Shaba Valley 65km north of Xīchāng is China's major satellite rocket launching centre. In the true spirit of Dengism, the centre now acts as a commercial venture and has launched several countries' satellites on the back of its Long March rockets. As they say with a grin at the launch centre, business is really taking off.

China's own satellites are the wonderfully named 'The East is Red' satellite system. China launched its first satellites during the Cultural Revolution and the first thing it did was to broadcast the speeches of Chairman Mao around the world.

Unfortunately, the rockets have had a nasty habit of plummeting back down to earth onto unsuspecting villages. It is believed that there have been several major accidents in the area with considerable (four-figure) loss of life.

Remarkably enough, Chinese tour groups still regularly visit the launch centre, though foreigners require a special permit to join them. Tourists can visit the control centre and launch pads and then grab a bite to eat in the space canteen. In Xīchāng, both XITS (☎/fax 0834-323 2161, e xits@moon.ls.scsti.ac.cn) and the Xīlǒng International Travel Service (☎ 366 7760) can arrange tours for you for between Y120 and Y150. This usually includes a quick detour to Luójì Shān as well.

XITS can also assist you in applying for your permit, done through the local military rather than the PSB; unfortunately, this can take up to 15 days. You can attempt to speed up the process by emailing or telephoning ahead and faxing a copy of your passport to them. Whether you actually get the permit seems a bit hit and miss, but it's certainly worth a try. You definitely *won't* get one if there are any launches imminent or if there have been any recent catastrophes.

Liángshān Yi Autonomous Region
凉山彝族自治州 Liángshān Yìzú Zìzhìzhōu

If you're interested in exploring Yi territory beyond the metropolis of Xīchāng, head out to one of the smaller towns or villages in the area that make up the Liángshān Yi Autonomous Region.

About 2½ hours south-east of Xīchāng lies **Pǔgé**. It's a busy market town populated almost entirely by traditionally dressed Yi. The bus journey to Pǔgé passes through some beautiful scenery and tiny Yi villages where you can hop off for an hour or two until the next bus from Xīchāng passes by.

Pǔgé can easily be visited as a day trip. If you do decide to stay (perhaps to scale the nearby Luójì Shān the next day), the next-to-new *Liángmào Bīnguǎn* (☎ 0834 447 5649) has spacious, comfortable doubles with bath and hot water for a steal at Y50 per bed.

Buses for Pǔgé (Y14) depart almost hourly from Xīchāng's Nánqiáo bus station from 7.10am to 3.40pm, with the last bus returning from Pǔgé at 4pm.

Other Yi towns in the region include **Bùtuō**, famous for having perhaps the largest torch festival, and **Zhāojué**, which has the highest percentage of Yi in its population.

The Yi

- **population** 6.57 million in China, 4.2 million in Yúnnán
- **location** Daliangshan mountains of southern Sìchuān; western and north-western Guìzhōu (Wēiníng); Chǔxióng and Honghe in Yúnnán.

The Yi are the second-largest minority group in the South-West after the Zhuang, and the fourth-largest in China. In Sìchuān, by far the largest single community of Yi (two million) live in the Dàliáng Shān, or 'Great Cool Mountains' in the south of the province. There are also around four million Yi scattered through north-central and eastern Yúnnán, with Yi-related ethnic groups in neighbouring Vietnam and Laos. There are many different sub-groups, each with very different traditional dress, from the reds and yellows of Pǔgé to the green and pinks of Dàlǐ. Their common language belongs to the Tibeto-Burmese family.

It's difficult to trace the Yi's history due to the number of subgroups which have historically gone by different names. The use of the character 'yi' has only recently been adopted as an ethnic name, with rumours that Mao Zedong started it by substituting it to a homophonous character meaning 'barbarian'. Worse than this is the derogatory term Luoluo (or Lolo) that the Han Chinese traditionally used to refer to the Yi. The Yi prefer to call themselves Nuosu (the Black People).

The Yi originally migrated to the South-West from areas around Qīnghǎi and Gānsù. A thousand years ago they lived around Lake Dian and, with the Bai of Dàlǐ, formed part of the Nanzhao kingdom in the 8th and 9th centuries. The Yi fiercely resisted assimilation with the Han, assisted by the inhospitable terrain of their mountain homeland. Eventually, they gained fame in communist history by entering into an alliance with the Red Army when the Long March passed through their territory.

The Yi society is based on clans and even today the clan remains the dominant social institution, with clan elders in charge of social order. Each clan belongs to a caste and, up until the 1950's, these were the basis of a slave society.

The Black Yi, the aristocrats and landowners of this society, made up 7% of the population and owned 80% of the land. The White Yi made up around 50% of the population and had no freedom of movement. A Black Yi who had committed murder could offer a White Yi as compensation to the family of the deceased. The White Yi also had to offer a fixed amount of time each year working in the Black Yi's fields. The lowest two classes, the Aija (33%) and Xiaxi (10%), were freely bought and sold as slaves and had no rights.

You can reach both towns by bus down the rather rough road east of Xīchāng (see Getting There & Away in the previous section).

If you are headed up to Kāngdìng or Lúdìng you will also see many remote Yi villages around Tuowu. It's possible for die-hard explorers to visit more remote Yi towns by heading overland to Lèshān and stopping in Zhāojué, Meigu and Ebian; or by going to Yíbīn via Zhāojué, Meigu, Leibo and Mabian. **Mahu Hú**, 56km east of Meigu, has the ruined Hailong Sì set on an island in the middle of the lake. It's a good idea to check with the PSB in Xīchāng as to whether or not you require a permit to do this. The route sees very few (if any) foreign visitors.

Luójǐ Shān 螺山

Also in this region is **Luójǐ Shān**, a 4358m mountain named for its resemblance to a spiral snail shell. With hot springs, waterfalls and glacial lakes, Luójǐ Shān has become a popular spot for local tourism.

The climb to the top, however, is not as popular, although the steep ascent to the billowing summit is estimated to take only three or four hours. The forested range in which Luójǐ Shān is situated offers further opportunities for exploration. Places to head for are **Five Colour Lake** (Wǔsè Hú) and **Big Lake** (Dà Hǎizi). April and May are usually the best times for hiking. You need to bring your own camping equipment, all

The Yi

The Yi were famous for their slave-raiding trips into Han territory. Han traders only dared enter the Liàng Shān under the protection of a local chief. During the Nationalist era, several powerful Sìchuānese warlords were of Yi descent. Slave society existed in the Liàng Shān region until 1959, when the Communists forced the tricky transition to socialist society. Reports state that some 700,000 slaves were freed during Liberation. One famous story, later made into a Chinese film, tells of a US airforce pilot who was captured by the Yi during WWII and kept as a slave for 12 years.

The Yi are fairly tall, with aquiline features and an air of nobility, despite living in the third-poorest of China's 30 autonomous prefectures. They are often seen smoking a long pipe held in the ball of the hand. Most men wear a black turban and a black woollen felt or sheepskin cloak with tassels, or *charwa*, which doubles as both a coat and blanket. Yi noblemen traditionally shaved their heads except for a topknot, which was pulled forward and tied into a horn-shaped bulge.

Women wear beautiful red, black and yellow embroidered waistcoats and headscarves and are famed for their intricate embroidery – they may work on one jacket for two to three months. Some women wear big square hats like university mortarboards. Married women often pile layers of cloth on top of their hats and tie it in place with a braid to act as a sunshade. Big earrings and pompoms finish the grand effect. Oats are a common staple in the Yi diet and were grown in their original hill settlements. The oats are ground into a flour to produce steamed buns that you'll find for sale in the markets. A favourite meat is 'twice-cooked piglet', often slaughtered in honour of a guest. Food is served in the famous Yi yellow, black and red lacquerware.

Shamans are still popular in Yi culture for divining the future, as they are among the few who can decipher the Yi's religious, medical and historical texts, written in the Yi's own remarkable 13th-century script. You may see shamans squatting by the side of the road, reading palms and offering advice on market days. The traditional Yi calender is divided into five seasons, each of two 36-day months.

The **Torch Festival**, on the 24th of the sixth lunar month, is the Yi's biggest festival. It commemorates the time when local settlements lit reeds to disperse locusts sent by a local god after people refused to pay an unfair grain tax. Activities include a torch parade, horse racing, bullfighting, wrestling, singing and dancing. Women carry yellow umbrellas, traditionally made of oilskin, and torches are planted everywhere. Important guests are served maize wine out of a horn or through straws out of a communal jar. Bùtuō is said to be the best place to see this, though the festival is celebrated in all Yi areas.

food supplies and a good map of the area. For more information see XITS in Xīchāng.

From Pǔgé, buses head north-east for 20 minutes to the trailhead. Tour buses also cover the 50km to the mountain from countless hotels and agencies in Xīchāng.

Mùlǐ 木里

Mùlǐ is a remote Tibetan autonomous prefecture set deep in the 4500m Taiyang Shān Range, or Mountains of the Sun, 245km west of Xīchāng. The region has several Tibetan monasteries and backs onto the Konkaling, the three holy peaks of the **Yàdīng Nature Reserve** (see the boxed text 'Trekking to Paradise' in the Dégé section later).

At the time of writing, foreigners did not require a special permit to visit Mùlǐ, however it's best to check at XITS in Xīchāng on these ever-fluctuating regulations.

Several buses depart Xīchāng's main bus station between 6.30am and 8.30am for Mùlǐ (Y49). You could combine a visit to Mùlǐ with a trip to Lúgū Hú and then continue on to Lìjiāng, however you do require a permit to cross the Yúnnán border.

Lúgù Hú 泸沽湖

About 280km south-west from Xīchāng is the pretty Lúgū Hú, inhabited by the Mosu people, a minority group closely related to the Nàxī.

SÌCHUĀN

Buses to the lake go via Yányuán where there are a couple of hotels. From Yányuán you will have to find transport to Lúgū Zhèn (also known as Zuǒsuǒ), on the northeast side of the lake, where there is basic accommodation. Roads skirt the lake, but they are often impassable in summer due to slides and in winter because of heavy snowfall. As an alternative, you can take a boat across the lake to Luòshuǐ village on the south-western shore where there is plenty of accommodation. From here there are buses to Nínglàng and Lìjiāng.

For more information on the southern side of the lake see the Lúgū Hú section of the Yúnnán chapter.

Western Sìchuān & the Road to Tibet

The Sìchuān mountains to the north and west of Chéngdū rise above 5000m with deep valleys, vast grasslands and rapid rivers. To Tibetans, this area is part of the 'province' of Kham that covers the eastern third of the Tibetan plateau, taking in the eastern Tibetan Autonomous Region (TAR) and western Sìchuān. To most Chinese, it is a backward borderland. For travellers, it is an opportunity to visit 'Tibet' without the permit hassles involved in crossing the border.

Tibetans and Tibetan-related peoples (Qiang) live here by herding yaks, sheep and goats on the high-altitude Kangba Plateau grasslands. The further out you go from Kāngdìng, the more readily evident the Tibetan customs and clothing.

Towns in these areas experience cold temperatures, with up to 200 freezing days per year; summers are blistering by day and the high altitude invites particularly bad sunburn. Lightning storms are frequent from May to October when cloud cover can shroud the scenic peaks. On a more pleasant note, there appear to be sufficient hot springs in these areas to have a solid bath along the route.

The Sìchuān-Tibet Hwy, begun in 1950 and finished in 1954, is one of the world's highest, roughest, most dangerous and most beautiful roads. It has been split into northern and southern routes, forking 70km west of Kāngdìng.

Much of this area was only opened to foreigners in 1999 and, as yet, does not have a lot of tourist facilities. Levels of noise and staring are higher than elsewhere in Sìchuān and hotel and bus standards are lower. Be forewarned: it is not possible to change money or travellers cheques or to get advances on credit cards in Sìchuān's north-west. Bring your Rénmínbì with you.

For more information on off-the-beaten-track travel in western Sìchuān check out the Web site at Ⓦ www.khamaid.org.

KĀNGDÌNG   康定
(DARDO OR DARTSEDO)
☎ 0836 • elevation 2560m
Kāngdìng is a large town nestled in a steep river valley at the confluence of the Zheduo and Yala rivers, known as the Dar and Tse in Tibetan (the 'do' of the town's name means 'river confluence'). Swift currents from the rapids of the Zheduo River provide Kāngdìng with hydroelectric power, the source of heating and electricity for the town. If you're en route to western Sìchuān it's worth staying for a day to take in the surrounding sights and scenery that inspired a popular Chinese love song.

Arriving in Kāngdìng, there is a tangible sense that you've reached the end of the Chinese world and the beginning of the Tibetan. The town has been a trade centre between the two cultures for centuries with the exchange of yak hides, wool, Tibetan herbs and, especially, bricks of tea from Yǎ'ān wrapped in yak hide. It also served as an important staging post on the road to Lhasa, as indeed it does today. Kāngdìng was historically the capital of the local Tibetan kingdom of Chakla (or Chala) and later, from 1939 to 1951, the capital of the short-lived province of Xikang, when it was controlled by the opium-dealing warlord Liu Wenhui.

Today Kāngdìng is largely a Chinese town, though you'll still see plenty of Khambas down from the hills shopping or selling huge blocks of yak butter in the local market. You'll also spot monks wandering around town in crimson robes.

Information

The PSB (☎ 281 1415 ext 6035) is on the 4th floor of a building five minutes' walk south-

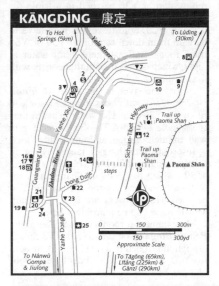

east of the Black Tent Hotel. They process visa extensions here quickly and painlessly.

China Post and Telecom is next to the river on Yanhe Xilu. The Bank of China is next door but does not change money.

Several places around town offer Internet access for around Y3 per hour, especially around the Pǎomǎ Bīnguǎn.

Travel Agencies The Kāngdìng Tour Service (Kāngdìng Lǚyǒu Fúwùahōngxīn; ☎ 283 4000, fax 283 1946, @ js@ganzi.scst .ac.cn) offers information and tours of nearby sites such as treks, horse tours and buses to Gōnggà (Konka) Gompa and Minya Konka (Gōnggà Shān). The staff speak English and seem happy to tailor tours and to give advice.

Things to See & Do

There are several monasteries in and around Kāngdìng. Just behind the Black Tent Hotel, the **Ngachu Gompa** (Ānjué Sì in Chinese) is a fairly quiet temple built in 1654, home to around 20 monks and a few old prayer wheels. A new Maitreya Chapel has been added to the side of the main prayer hall.

The **Nánwù Gompa** is the most active monastery in the area with around 80 lamas in residence. Set in the western part of town

KĀNGDÌNG

PLACES TO STAY

9   Tàiníng Jiǔdiàn
    泰宁酒店
16 Pàomǎ Bīnguǎn
    跑马宾馆
19 Kāngdìng Bīnguǎn
    康定宾馆
21 Black Tent Hotel;
    Teahouse
    贡嘎山旅社
22 Jīnlù Bīnguǎn
    金路宾馆

PLACES TO EAT

3   Bakery
7   Barbecue Stalls
    小吃店
17 Pǎomǎshān
    Cāntīng
    跑马山餐厅

23 Jíxiáng Fàndiàn
    吉祥饭店
24 Restaurant
    饭馆

OTHER

1   Kāngdìng Tour
    Service; Teahouse;
    Tibetan Restaurant
    康巴旅游服务中心
    西藏餐馆
2   Bank of China
    中国银行
4   China Telecom
    (Internet Service)
5   China Post
    邮电局
6   Market
    市场
8   Bus Station
    汽车站

10 Taxis to Lúding
    & Tǎgōng
    出租汽车站
11 Entrance to
    Pǎomǎ Shān
    跑马山公园门口
12 Gompa
13 Entrance to
    Pǎomǎ Shān
    跑马山公园门口
14 Mosque
    清真寺
15 Catholic Church
    天主教堂
18 Internet Cafes
    网吧
20 Ngachu
    Gompa
    安觉寺
25 PSB
    公安局

SICHUAN

on the northern bank of the river, it affords good views of Kāngdìng and the valley. Walk south along the main road and follow its bend to the left for 2km, cross the bridge at the southern end of town and go another 300m. Next to a walled Han Chinese cemetery you will find a dirt path leading uphill alongside a stream that leads right to the monastery. Next door is Dorje Drak Gompa (Jīn'gāng Sì), which is also worth a visit

In town, the **market** on Dong Dajie is worth a look. You can also head up Pǎomǎ Shān for excellent views of Kāngdìng, the surrounding mountains and valleys and – if you're lucky – Minya Konka. The ascent takes you past oodles of prayer flags, several Buddhist temples and up to a white *chörten* (stupa). Take particular care when wandering around Pǎomǎ Shān and try to avoid hiking around on your own. A British tourist was murdered here in the spring of 2000.

To reach the hill, bear left at the fork in the road just south of the bus station and walk for 10 minutes until you reach a temple on the left; a stairway leads up the hill from here. A second, more direct route, heads up the hill further south, beginning above the staircase on Dong Dajie.

About 5km north of Kāngdìng are the **Erdao Bridge Hot Springs** (Èrdàoqiáo Wēnquán). Private half-hour baths in slightly eggy-smelling, warm, sulphur water cost Y10. Go in on your own or get a larger bath for a group soak. Take your own towel. You can reach the springs by taxi for about Y8.

The **Walking around the Mountain Festival** (Zhuànshānjie) takes place on Pǎomǎ Shān on the eighth day of the fourth lunar month to commemorate the birthday of the historical Buddha, Sakyamuni. White and blue Tibetan tents cover the hillside and there's plenty of wrestling, horse racing and visitors from all over western Sìchuān.

Places to Stay

Next to Ngachu Gompa, **Black Tent Hotel** (*Hei Zhanpeng Zhuse*) has beds in triples for Y17 to Y27 and double for Y42. Quiet, clean and with electric blankets and a teahouse on the ground floor, this is the place to come to if you want to relax or meet other travellers. The toilets are relatively good for this part of the world and washing facilities consist of the usual basin and heated water.

Immediately behind this is the chaotic *Kāngdìng Bīnguǎn* (☎ 282 3153), once the best in town but no longer. Weary-looking rooms start at Y36 per bed in a triple for foreigners; with a student card of any type it's only Y20. Solo travellers may have to bargain them down to around Y50 or Y60 for a room. At least there's hot water at night, which comes on simultaneously with the rousing karaoke sessions.

Across the river is the *Jīnlù Bīnguǎn* (☎ 283 3216), with beds in spacious, clean rooms for Y30 each. Hot water in bathrooms is available 24 hours. To find the reception, walk through the gate and turn right.

Just south of the long-distance bus station is the friendly *Tàiníng Jiǔdiàn* (☎ 282 4530), which has beds in clean triples for Y30 each and one six-room dorm for Y20 per bed. Hot showers are down the hall. Traffic noise can be a problem here.

More upmarket rooms are on offer at the *Pǎomǎ Bīnguǎn* (☎ 283 3110). The cheapest option is a bed in a quad with bathroom for Y70, or Y35 with a student card. Doubles are Y240.

Places to Eat

For a rousing cup of yak butter tea, try the *teahouse* adjacent to the Black Tent Hotel. They also carry a wide selection of other types of teas from these parts but it's best to ask the price first. For inexpensive meals, the Black Tent Hotel will likely recommend the *restaurant* across the road.

Across the river from the Black Tent Hotel is the *Jíxiáng Fàndiàn*. The friendly owners have an English menu and serve fantastic local cuisine at good prices. Try the potato pancake (Y5) or the black bean fish (Y18).

At the Kāngdìng Tour Service you'll also find a *teahouse* and *Tibetan restaurant* offering such delicacies as Tibetan butter dumplings and *tsampa* (roasted barley flour).

For a huge hotpot extravaganza, the *Pǎomǎsān Cāngtíng* serves exotic looking veggies, fish, meat, prawns, squid and – of course – chicken feet. You can stuff your-

The Tibetans

- **population** 4.6 million in China, one million in the South-West
- **location** Western Sìchuān (Gānzı and Ābà autonomous prefectures and Mùlĭ autonomous county); north-western Sìchuān (Zhōngdiàn and Déqīn counties); north-west Yúnnán (Déqīn prefecture).

Western Sìchuān and the extreme north-west of Yúnnán were once part of the Tibetan province of Kham and remain distinctly Tibetan to this day, despite large-scale Han Chinese immigration. Almost the entire region is comprised of Tibetan autonomous prefectures, the largest of which are centred upon the Ābà, Gānzī, Déqīn and Mùlĭ regions. The grasslands of the extreme north-west of Sìchuān once formed part of the Tibetan region of Amdo, (in)famous for its bandits and caravan-raiders.

Khamba men can be seen swaggering along the streets of most settlements west of Kāngdìng. Most wear a *chuba* (Tibetan cloak), normally lined with sheepskin and properly worn hanging off the right shoulder. Many wear broad-rimmed cowboy hats (fur-lined hats in winter) and big boots, sporting at least one gold tooth, an amulet around their neck and a knife by their side. Women traditionally wear elaborate coral and amber jewellery and arrange their hair into 108 braids.

Khambas are known as the most religious and warlike of all Tibetans and were depicted by most early travellers as either saints or murderers. In 1959 the region around Lĭtáng saw the fiercest guerilla resistance to the encroaching Chinese troops and many rebels fled to India and Nepal to organise armed resistance from Mustang (with CIA assistance).

Almost all Tibetans are Buddhists, though north-western Sìchuān is also a strong centre of Bön, the indigenous pre-Buddhist faith of Tibet. Bön blends the shamanistic spirit worship of rivers, mountains and trees with a veneer of Tibetan Buddhism (which itself has been influenced by the Bön pantheon of gods). Followers of Bön are most easily recognised by the fact that they circumambulate *koras* (pilgrim circuits) and rotate prayer wheels anticlockwise, as opposed to Buddhists who do this clockwise.

The most famous Tibetan Buddhist monastery in the region is the printing college of Dégé. Many others were destroyed in the 1959 rebellion or during the Cultural Revolution. As you travel through Tibetan territory, you'll see plenty of chörtens and prayer flags adorning the countryside.

Tibetan food you might taste in the region includes *tsampa* (roast barley), *momos* (dumplings) and *thugpa* noodles. Drinks include yak butter tea and *chang*, Tibetan barley beer.

Basic Tibetan Phrases

Hello	*tashi delek*	Where is...?	*...kaba du?*
Thanks	*tujay chay*	straight ahead	*shar gya*
Goodbye	*kaliy shu*	right	*yay chola*
(if you are leaving)		left	*yon chola*
Goodbye	*kaliy pay*	far	*tha ringpo*
(if someone is leaving)		monastery	*gompa*
What is your name?	*kayrang gi mingla karay ray?*	shrine	*lhakhang*
My name is...	*ngay mingla...ray*	beautiful	*nying-jepo*
I am from (America)	*nga (Amerika) nay yin*	good	*yakpo*
...Australia	*...ositaliya*	boiled water	*chu khoma*
...England	*...injiy lungpa*	I don't understand	*ha ko masong*

For a comprehensive guide to the Tibetan language see Lonely Planet's *Tibetan phrasebook*.

self for Y38 a person. The *Tàiníng Jiŭdiàn* also has a good restaurant with reasonable prices (Y8 to Y20 per dish), considering its fancy decor.

There are also numerous point-and-choose *restaurants* near the bus station and a couple of noodle and baozi places in the market. In the evening, numerous covered

Chinese *barbecue stalls* set up camp at the northern end of town with arguably the widest selection of skewered meat, veggies and fish in Sìchuān. There is also a late night *bakery* on the road behind the post office.

Getting There & Away

The completion of the Èrláng Shān tunnel has cut the ride down to eight short hours.

Buses leave hourly for Chéngdū from 8am to 4pm (Y98, eight hours). If you are headed to the Traffic Hotel make sure your bus is bound for the Xīnnánmén station.

To Lúdìng (for Móxī and Hǎiluógōu Glacier), taxis and minivans depart a stand south of the bus station. Drivers will bargain high but you can get a seat for around Y15.

Going west from Kāngdìng, a bus departs daily to Lǐtáng (Y78, seven hours) at 6.50am. There is a 6.40am bus for Gānzī (Y103, 12 hours) and a 7.50am bus for Bātáng (Y134, 11 hours). For Dégé there is a departure daily at 7am (Y162, two days). Local minibuses run to Yǎjiāng, Dáofú and Luohu.

There are also departures for Xiāngchéng (Y130) and Dàochéng (Y121) that depart at 7am every other day (or so) and overnight in Lǐtáng.

AROUND KĀNGDÌNG 康定四周
Mùgécuò Lake

There are several mountain lakes and hot springs in the vicinity of Kāngdìng. Lying 21km to the north of town up the Yala Valley, Mùgécuò Hú is one of the highest lakes in north-western Sìchuān at 3700m. Locals also boast that it's one of the most beautiful.

Mùgécuò Hú is part of a series of lakes. Trails around it lead to other smaller lakes such as **Hóng Hǎi** (Red Sea). Also worth checking out is **Qīsè Hǎi** (Seven Colour Lake), which lies a few kilometres before Mùgécuò. The area of 'Wild Men's Lake,' as Mùgécuò means in Tibetan, is home to wolves and other wild beasts.

There are occasional early morning minibuses to Mùgécuò from in front of the bus station, dependent on the number of passages. Idle taxi drivers will be more than pleased to shuttle you there and back for Y150 to Y200 (1½ hours). You can also talk to the Kāngdìng Tour Service to see if they have any tours going there.

Mùgécuò Hú can easily be done as a day trip from Kāngdìng but if you choose to stay out there, both the *Qīsèhai Bīnguǎn* and *Mùgécuò Bīnguǎn* have beds you may get for as low as Y30.

Gònggā Gompa 贡嘎寺

Gònggā (Konka or Kongkar) Gompa is situated at the western foot of Gòngga Shān. The monastery was ravaged during the Cultural Revolution but is currently enjoying something of a revival. It is of the Kagyu sect of Tibetan Buddhism and forms part of a pilgrimage route around the holy Minya Konka, the local Tibetan name for Gònggà Shān. The monastery is very remote and can only be reached on foot or with a 4WD.

This trip is difficult but not impossible to do on your own. You first need to get yourself to the trailhead at Liùbā. There is no bus service to Liùbā but you may be able to get

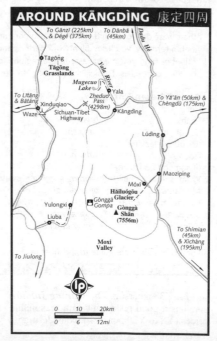

AROUND KĀNGDÌNG 康定四周

To Gānzī (225km) & Dégé (375km)
To Dānbā (45km)
Dadu Hé
Tǎgōng
Tǎgōng Grasslands
Yala River
Mugecuo Lake
Yala
To Lǐtáng & Bātáng
Xinduqiao
Zheduo Pass (4298m)
Kāngdìng
To Yǎ'ān (50km) & Chéngdū (175km)
Waze
Sichuan-Tibet Highway
Lúdìng
Maoziping
Móxī
Hǎiluógōu Glacier
Yulongxi
Gònggà Gompa
Gònggà Shān (7556m)
Liuba
To Shímian (45km) & Xīchāng (195km)
Moxi Valley
To Jiulong

0   10   20km
0   6   12mi

one heading for Jiǔlóng, which leaves Kāngdìng at 7.10am.. This will take you to the crossroads leading to Liùbā from where you'll have to walk or hitch the remaining 10km. From Liùbā you can hitch or trek the 25 or so kilometres to Yulongxi, where you may be able to arrange accommodation. From here you will have to trek over into the Móxī Valley, where the monastery is situated. Another option is to start from Laoyulin, just south of Kāngdìng, where it's possible to hire pack animals. For details on the trek see Gary McCue's *Trekking in Tibet*.

You may be able to stay in the monastery, from where you could do any number of day hikes up and down the Móxī Valley, before retracing your steps back to Kāngdìng. A more difficult option involves following the Móxī Valley downstream (eastwards) for around 60km until you reach the main Lúdìng-Shími road, where you can flag down a bus.

This is a wild, difficult and untouristed route. Only experienced hikers should attempt it with sufficient food, a tent and warm clothes. If you aren't self-sufficient, Kāngdìng Tour Service arranges two- to four-day tours to Gònggā Gompa, some of which include horseback riding. These tours start at around Y400 per person (minimum three people). They can also provide up-to-date details of conditions on the trek if you are planning to venture out on your own.

LÚDÌNG 泸定

Lúdìng is a small, bustling town about halfway between Kāngdìng and Móxī. As a major connection point for buses between western Sìchuān and Chéngdū, Lèshān and Móxī, you are likely to find yourself here. For those with a keen interest in China's communist history, it may be worth a brief stop.

Lúdìng is famous throughout China as the site of what is often regarded as the most glorious moment of the Long March. The key element in this story is the **Luding Bridge** (Lúdìng Qiáo), a 100m-long chain suspension bridge over the Dadu Hé.

On 29 May 1935, the communist troops approached the Lúdìng Bridge, only to discover that Kuomintang troops had beaten

---

Minya Konka

Towering above Kāngdìng is the mighty peak of Gònggà Shān (7556m); Minya Konka (or Minyak Gangkar) in Tibetan. To behold it is worth 10 years of meditation, says an inscription in the ruined monastery by the base. Unfortunately the mountain is often covered with cloud so some patience is required for the beholding. The best places to view it are from the upper sections of Hǎiluógōu Park or from the top of Pǎomǎ Shān. When Joseph Rock saw the mountain for the first time he was convinced he had discovered the highest in the world.

Minya Konka is on the open list for foreign mountaineers and in 1981 it buried eight Japanese climbers in an avalanche. This awesome 'goddess' has been conquered, however. Two Americans in 1939, six Chinese in 1957, and more recently, a group of students from the UK in 2000 have all made successful conquests.

---

them to it. The Kuomintang had removed the planks from the bridge, set the bridge-head alight and had it covered with fire-power. In response, 22 communist troops armed with grenades inched their way precariously along the 13 chains, dodging enemy fire as they went, and then proceeded to overcome the Kuomintang troops on the other side. Only three out of the 22 soldiers were lost. This heroic action allowed the Long March to continue before the main body of the Kuomintang forces could catch up with them.

The Lúdìng Bridge is five minutes' walk south along the river from the northern bus station and has an admission fee of Y5. The original bridge was first constructed in 1705 and was an important link in the Sìchuān-Tibet road. On the main street in town you might also want to check out the **Lúdìng Bridge Revolutionary Artefacts Museum** (Lúdìng Qiáo Gémìng Wénwù Chénlièguǎn), which houses a collection of some 150 items left behind by members of the Long March.

SÌCHUĀN

You can also get a gander at some of Mao's calligraphy on a shelter near the Buddhist Temple on the hillside above town.

Places to Stay & Eat

The hotel situation in Lúdìng is not great. As they gear up in anticipation for the tourist boom headed for Móxī, hotel proprietors have inflated their prices but left concern for the quality of rooms behind.

Chēzhàn Lüǎn, across the street from the southern bus station, has beds in triples for Y30. They're fairly drab and some are kind of stinky, but this is the best value you'll find.

Turning right out of the south bus station and walking back to where the town's main street meets the through highway, you'll find the *Yagudu Bīnguǎn*. Look for 'Yagudu Restaurant' stencilled on the window. Here, shabby doubles with bath go for Y70. Hot water kicks in after 9pm.

Between the Lúdìng Bridge and the north bus station is the county government's *Xiàn Zhāodàisuǒ*. Rooms here are cleaner and perhaps a bit brighter than elsewhere in town, but they're still overpriced at Y120 for a double with bath or Y100 without bath. On the upside, there is 24-hour hot water.

Clustered around the southern bus station are a number of nondescript *restaurants* as well as a *teahouse* where you can while away your time until the next bus pulls into town.

Getting There & Away

For some unknown reason, Lúdìng has two bus stations. Getting information on buses out of staff at either station is excruciating. They'll claim there is only one bus each morning for every destination, despite buses pulling in and out all day. If you don't want to wait around, you can get shared taxis to Móxī and Kāngdìng for practically the same price as the bus or you can try flagging down through buses as they pass by town.

The town itself is built up along two roads – the through highway to Kāngdìng, which runs along the river, and the more bustling main street, which arcs in a half-moon shape, meeting the highway at each end.

On the highway, where it bends to cross the river, you'll find the north bus station.

Here you can get the 8am bus to Móxī (Y15, two hours) or bargain a shared taxi down to Y20 per person (minimum four passengers; one hour). The bus to Chéngdū (Y90) leaves at 7am every other day, or you can try to flag down buses for Chéngdū as they pass by from Kāngdìng.

A bus for Kāngdìng (Y40) leaves Lúdìng's north bus station at 7am. Again, you can attempt to flag down buses on route from Yǎ'ān and Chéngdū. You can also bargain a taxi down to Y20 to Y30 for the trip to Kāngdìng (one hour).

At the other end of town, on the main street, is the southern bus station. It looks more like a parking lot than a bus station; you'll find the ticket office (which doubles as the reception for the Chēzhàn Lüǎn) across the street. One bus a day departs from here to Shími (Y15) at 6am. The bus for Yǎ'ān (Y55) leaves at 7am.

Lúdìng – Yǎ'ān – Lèshān

If you're travelling east from Kāngdìng or Móxī to Éméi Shān or Lèshān, you may decide (or be forced) to break the journey in Yǎ'ān. Buses from Lèshān leave for Yǎ'ān (four hours) more or less hourly from 7.10am until 9pm. From Éméi Shān, buses leave at 8.40am, 12.10pm, and 2.10pm.

Buses between Yǎ'ān and Lúdìng (where you can change for Móxī or carry on to Kāngdìng) are somewhat trickier. The Erlang Shan Pass, renowned for its steep climb, blind corners and landslides, is being conquered by a new 4km-long tunnel cutting through the mountainside. This and other road works have made the already narrow road even narrower. The result: bus service runs in each direction only every other day – one day west from Yǎ'ān, the next day east from Lúdìng. Traffic must also wait on either side of the tunnel for designated times to pass through it, meaning that it's best to head out of Yǎ'ān no earlier than 9.30am or risk facing a four- or five-hour wait. The trip to Lúdìng is supposed to take four hours, but due to queues it may well take closer to eight. Once road works are completed, it is likely that travel will resume daily from both directions.

Nevertheless, you may still want to overnight in Yǎ'ān.

A friendly town during the day, Yǎ'ān really comes to life at nightfall with **Music Square**. Visit the square during the day and find it desolate. Return in the evening and find the entire town out, gathered around a huge, lit fountain and moving to the beat of Chinese and Euro house music. Tiny children bop up and down; kids and teenagers practice dance routines; groups of middle-aged women practice fan-dance routines (minus the fans) at high speed to Aqua. This is definitely worth a visit.

Be warned, however – as a foreigner, you may well become the object of interest to what can quickly become a frenzied mob of 12-year-olds, screaming for your signature on scraps of paper, their arms and T-shirts. To find Music Square, turn right out of the bus station and cross the bridge.

If you're spending the night in Yǎ'ān, there are a few hotels near the bus station. As you exit the station, along the road directly ahead of you is the *Xīka Fàndiàn* (☎ 0835-262 3583). Clean doubles range from Y40 to Y80 per bed. Check out a couple of rooms as size and quality vary. The staff is friendly and will fill you in with information on bus schedules. To get into town, turn right out of the bus station and cross the bridge. Here you'll find oodles of *restaurants*, *street hawkers* and *stalls*.

A second route between Éméi Shān and Lúdìng, without doubling back to Chéngdū, is south via Wūsīhé. There is usually one bus at 6am from Lúdìng to Wūsīhé (Y15) but if it doesn't appear, jump on a bus to Shímǐ, from where there is frequent onward transport. Once you reach Wūsīhé you'll need to hop on a train to Éméi town. The train departs Wūsīhé in the afternoon, so you shouldn't have to overnight here. Should you need to, there are several cheap hotels around the train station. Coming from Éméi town, the train to Wūsīhé leaves at 11.14am or 9pm (Y10, 3½ hours). If you're headed south to Pānzhīhūa or Hunming, note that you can only buy hard-seat tickets in Wūsīhé and very few onward trains stop here.

MÓXĪ 磨西
☎ 0836

Nestled in the mountains around 50km south-west of Lúdìng, this peaceful one-street village is the gateway to the Hǎiluógōu Glacier Park (see the following section).

With lots of character, Móxī itself is worth a visit. The older, traditional wooden buildings are at the bottom of the village. Also at this end is a somewhat out-of-place, multi-coloured **Catholic Church**. Boarded up and sprouting grass on its steeple, the Church's principal claim to fame these days is that Mao camped out in it during the Long March.

From here, the village climbs its way up a hill. If you follow the dirt up, about 200m past the main crossroad on the right is **Guānyīnggǔ Gompa**, a 400-year-old Bön temple. Across the road from the temple is a small pagoda from where you can get a view of some of the surrounding scenery.

Places to Stay

Next to the Catholic Church is *Lǚyóu Fàndiàn*. Quiet, all-wood rooms are in a building at the back of the courtyard. The rooms are simple and clean and a good deal at Y15 per bed. The owner and his family are friendly and can help with bus and transport information.

Up the hill about 300m from here is the *Hǎiluógōu Bīnguǎn*, which is currently being rebuilt but promises to offer upmarket rooms and facilities.

Continuing uphill, you'll arrive at the *Aurum Conch Guesthouse*. Dorm beds go for Y30, doubles with bath for Y120. Better value is the *Hó Fàndiàn* (☎ 326 6296), directly next door. Extremely clean and comfortable doubles are Y60, with hot showers down the hall. There is also a rooftop terrace that offers views of the glacier.

At the top of the hill, over the crossroad, is a second *Hǎiluógōu Bīnguǎn*. This is where buses and taxi drivers generally drop their passengers and then try their mightiest to convince them to stay. Doubles are Y80 and dorm beds go for Y30. The staff seems willing to bargain.

If you continue further uphill, the *Shāhǎigoujīnxué* is 175m on the right.

SÌCHUĀN

Brand-new doubles with hot water are Y120/60 with/without bath.

Places to Eat

The Lǚyóu Fàndiàn will bring on a feast for you at very good prices. You'll also find a fair number of *restaurants* along the main road as well as *barbecue stalls*. Móxī's shops and fruit stands are well stocked if you need to buy some supplies for a trip to Hǎiluógōu.

Getting There & Away

If you're arriving from the south via Shími, you can either carry on to Lúdìng and backtrack or get off at Maoziping and flag down a minicab to Móxī from there. To reach Móxī from Lúdìng, you can try to catch the 7am bus (Y15) or hunt down a minibus for the same price. You can also bargain a taxi down to about Y20 per person.

From Móxī there is a 7am bus to Lúdìng (Y15, two hours) which can be flagged down outside the Lǚyóu Fàndiàn. Change at Lúdìng for Chéngdū, Yǎ'ān and Kāngdìng. If you're headed to Shími, get off the bus at Maoziping, on the other side of the bright orange Rainbow Bridge. From here you can flag down a southbound bus.

The main draw to Móxī is, of course, Hǎiluuógōu Glacier Park. The entrance to the park is within easy walking distance from Móxī. Turn left at Móxī's main crossroads at the top of the hill; the ticket office is about 400m up the road.

HǍILUÓGŌU GLACIER PARK

海螺沟冰川公园

Magnificent Hǎiluógōu Glacier (Hǎiluógōu Bīngchuān) tumbles off the eastern slopes of Gòngga Shān to form the lowest glacier in Asia. The main glacier (No 1) is 14km long and covers an area of 16 sq km. It's relatively young as glaciers go: around 1600 years.

The top of Hǎiluógōu offers incredible vistas of Gòngga Shān and surrounding peaks, above 6000m, but how much you can see is entirely up to Mother Nature. Always framed with a backdrop of snowy peaks, the surrounding tropical forests are very beautiful.

The rainy season for this area is July and August, although the locals say they get 200 days of rain a year. The best time to visit is between late September and November, when skies are generally clear. Autumn colours are particularly beautiful at this time, though it can be cold up at Camp No 3.

By Foot Once a popular foot or pony trek, the park has fallen under the watchful eye of the government's tourism board. Today there is not a bray to be heard for miles, the path is neglected and overgrown and a cable car should be up and running by the time you read this. Trekking to the top is still possible; however, many trekkers have complained of finding the path difficult to follow as both use and maintenance fall away. Other parts of the route are now paved road used by the minibuses. You are also likely to be discouraged from walking (if not told flat out that you can't) by workers at the park entrance. While you can attempt to avoid them by taking a shortcut west of Móxī and around the gate, you may well find you're not allowed onto the glacier once you reach it, as you've arrived without an 'official' guide. The atmosphere of Hǎiluógōu Glacier Park is quickly changing and will continue to do so, with increased tour buses racing up and down the mountain and tourists hanging out of the cable cars above the glacier.

If you do plan to trek, come prepared with warm clothes and sunglasses. You'll also need to bring food and water, as you might not find much to buy en route until you reach Camp No 3 and its pricey restaurants. Maps of the park are available from the entrance gate; however, marked trails may be less than accurate and some may have disappeared. For information on specific camps en route, see the following section.

By Bus If your main interest is seeing and even walking across a glacier, then the park is still worth a visit. The most popular way to ascend the mountain is now by minibus (Y50 return, 30 minutes one way), departing from the park entrance at 7.30am.

The Y60 admission fee to the park includes a guide, compulsory for all tourists going out on the glacier and handy for keeping you away from deep crevices and melting points, as well as for pointing out wind tunnels and naming mountain peaks. Guides will not depart for the glacier from Camp No 3 after 2pm.

From Camp No 3, you have a 3km walk to the top of the road. From there you will eventually be able to take a cable car over the glacier, or it's about an hour's walk up to the glacier's base. Although this walk is short, it affords some beautiful mountain views and takes you through lovely forest. During the summer, it is possible to hire horses to take you from Camp No 3 up to the base from a stand just up the road from the hotels. During the low season you may be able to arrange this through the Gold Mountain Hotel.

En route to the base is the **Glacier Waterfall Viewing Platform** (Bīngchua Guānjīngtái) at 3000m. From here you view the main glacier tongue, plus glacier No 2 and Golden Peak (6368m). From its base, you can walk up onto the glacier, although how far depends on the conditions of the ice.

If you want to head back down the mountain the same day, your guide and driver will agree a return time with you and the bus will wait for you at Camp No 3. If you spend the night, your return bus ticket remains valid until you use it.

Places to Stay & Eat
Cheap accommodation in the park is quickly becoming a thing of the past. *Camp No 1* (*Yīhào Yíngdì*), at 1940m, still offers budget dorm beds but conditions are damp and dirty. *Camp No 2* (*Èrhào Yíngdì*) sits at 2620m and has beds for Y150, although this does include a dip into the hot springs. *Camp No 3* is the highest camp, at 2940m, and is taking on resort proportions. The *Golden Mountain Hotel* (☎ 0836-326 6433) has doubles from Y400 to Y500 and a second, even plusher, hotel is about to open with doubles from Y350 to Y400.

The park authorities frown upon camping and there isn't a great deal in the way of flat ground on the way up in any case.

The camps sell some food and drinks, but in the low season you can only count on this at Camp No 3. Mineral water, soft drinks,

beer and instant noodles are usually available. The food isn't bad, though prices are naturally higher than in Móxī and rise with the altitude.

Getting There & Away
Hǎiluógōu is accessible via the town of Móxī, which in turn can be reached by bus from Lúdìng (see Lúdìng and Móxī Getting There & Away sections earlier). A bus up the mountains departs from the park entrance gate at 7.30am, and more are likely to race up the mountain during the high season season.

SÌCHUĀN-TIBET HWY – NORTHERN ROUTE
Of the two routes to Tibet, this is the less heavily travelled. This may be because, at 2412km, it is 300km longer than the southern route; however, it likely has more to do with the fact that it crosses the Chola (or Trola) Shān Range, over one of the most notorious passes this side of Lhasa. The highway also crosses through the Tǎgōng Grasslands, with its blue-green rivers and velvety hills, studded with Tibetan prayer flags and watched over by gracefully soaring eagles.

For travellers, this highway leads to the town of Dégé, with its internationally revered Printing Monastery. It also takes you to the north where it is possible to work your way up to Qīnghǎi via Sêrxu (*Shíqú* in Chinese) and the Tibetan town of Yùshù (Jyekundo).

If you do come this way, be sure to bring some warm clothing; this area reaches high, frozen altitudes. Remember that bus services can be erratic – this is no place to be if you're in a hurry. It's also not possible to change money or travellers cheques up here so come prepared.

Tǎgōng 塔贡草原
North-west of Kāngdìng lie the Tǎgōng Grasslands (Tǎgōng Cǎoyuán), a vast expanse of green meadow surrounded by snow-capped peaks and dotted with Tibetan herdsmen and tents. In the midst of this lies Tǎgōng village, a vibrant Tibetan community.

Tǎgōng's active Buddhist community is evident in the prayer wheels in constant motion, the monks chanting in the corners of the temples and the old women circumambulating the monastery walls. At the northern end of the village stands **Tǎgōng Gompa**, a monastery that blends Han Chinese and Tibetan styles and dates back to the Qing dynasty. The large collection of chörtens (*tǎ* in Chinese), gives the monastery its Chinese name.

Tǎgōng's monastery appears to have survived the ravages of time amazingly well, though two of the three main halls have been rebuilt recently. The holiest statue in the far right building is a replica of Lhasa's Jowo Sakyamuni Buddha, said to have been carved in situs when the original passed through en route to Lhasa in the seventh century. Note also the beautiful thousand-armed Chenresig or Avalokiteshvara (Qiānshǒu Guānyīn), the Bodhisattva of Mercy, in the building to the left. Be sure to visit the stunning collection of over 100 chörtens behind the monastery and finish off a visit with a clockwise kora (*circuit*) of the site. Admission is Y10.

The velvety hills around Tǎgōng, topped with prayer flags and chörtens, offer a great opportunity to wander in the fresh air while getting views of the rolling grasslands, the new gold-roofed college and the stunning 5820m pyramid peak of Hǎizi Shān (*Zhare Lhatse* in Tibetan). Walk up to the hill above town, which is topped by a chörten surrounded by votive rags, amulets and beads left by pilgrims. The grasslands are also the stage for an annual **Horse Racing Festival** (Sàimǎhuì), held at the beginning of the eighth lunar month (mid-July to August) and attended by thousands of local Tibetan herdsmen. You might get to see Tibetan opera here at this time. A 20-minute walk west of town, over the river, leads to shedra, or Buddhist college, which has a large collection of Buddhist rock carvings in the plain below.

Tǎgōng remains a great stopover en route north from Kāngdìng and a perfect place to get the flavour of Sìchuān's wild west.

Places to Stay & Eat The *Tǎgōng Hotel* (*Tǎgōng Luèshè*) has beds in bearable doubles and triples for Y10. To find the hotel,

head 50m south down the main street away from the monastery, and it's on your right in a government compound.

A better option is the two-storey building diagonally opposite the monastery entrance – look for the English sign that says 'Tibetan Food and Butter Tea'. A karaoke pitstop for Chinese tourists during the day, the ornately decorated Tibetan-style room moonlights as a guesthouse in the evenings, with Tibetan-style beds for Y20. Privacy and traffic noise can be a problem during the day but things quieten down at night.

If all else fails, wander down the main street and you will likely receive offers from locals for beds in private homes.

Along the main street you will also find a number of *restaurants* and *noodle shops*. If you're staying in a private home, the family may offer you meals for a small charge.

Getting There & Away Buses to Tǎgōng village run every day from Kāngdìng (Y27, three hours) at 7.20am and drop you outside the monastery.

If you're headed on to Gānzī, you can pick up the same bus the next day at about 10am as it passes through town. A bus heading north to Lúhùo also passes through Tǎgōng around 9.30am or 10am (Y40, 5½ hours). From Lúhùo you can catch the Kāngdìng-Gānzī bus (Y20, three hours), with a better chance of getting a seat than in Tǎgōng.

Afternoon buses returning to Kāngdìng can be flagged down in Tǎgōng. You can also catch a minibus or shared taxi (Y20) on the main street, which will take you to the Xīndūqiáo crossroads from where there are buses to Chéngdū or Lǐtáng.

Tǎgōng to Gānzī

While most travellers whiz along the main road to Gānzī on the bus, several bustling towns en route offer impressive monasteries and at least basic accommodation.

Bāměi (Garthar) is a lunch stop about 20km north of Tǎgōng which has a pretty series of chörtens in the south of town. Eight kilometres north-east of town along the road to Dānbā is the Garthar Chörten Gompa (Hǎiyuán Sí in Chinese), built by the seventh Dalai Lama. Bāměi is famous as the birthplace of the 11th Dalai Lama.

A further 75km is **Dáofú**, with a huge chörten dedicated to the Panchen Lama and a hillside monastery. **Lúhuó** (Drango) is a newly rebuilt town a further 70km away and has the Drango Gompa.

About 20km before Gānzī the road passes the lake and monastery of Kasuo Hu, from where the road rises to a high pass before dropping down into Gānzī.

Gānzī 甘孜 (Kandze or Garzê)

The noisy market town of Gānzī sits in a valley at 3400m, surrounded by the sleeping giants of the **Chola Shān Range**. Now open to tourism, a growing number of foreigners have sojourned here as an intermediate stop between Sêrxu and Kāngdìng or on their way west to Dégé. The gorgeous surrounding countryside is peppered with Tibetan villages and resurgent monasteries.

Over 540 years old, **Garzê Gompa** is just north of the town's Tibetan quarter and is the region's largest monastery with over 500 monks. Encased in the walls of the main prayer hall are hundreds of small golden Sakyamunis. In a smaller hall just west of the main hall is an impressive statue of Jampa (Maitreya or Future Buddha), dressed in silk.

To find the monastery, take a left out of the bus station and head north for about 10 minutes until you reach the Tibetan neighbourhood. You'll see the monastery long before you reach it. A kora pilgrim path winds around and above the monastery. To follow it take one of the roads to the left when you reach the Tibetan quarter and look for a huge chörten and then a hall of prayer wheels from where the path winds uphill.

Den Gompa in the southern part of town is smaller but older and more atmospheric. The inner chapel is surrounded by three pilgrimage paths and houses fierce statues of the protector god Mahakala. Upstairs are several Mao slogans from the Cultural Revolution and a small printing press.

Gānzī has the region's best antique shops and many general stores that sell Tibetan goods like clothes and jewellery.

Places to Stay The easiest option is the *Hóngyuèliàng* (☎ 752 2676), which is the former Post Office Hotel. To find it, turn left out of the bus station, cross the main intersection, and continue on for about a block. It's on the left. There is no English sign outside but look for the hotel's telephone number on the lit up blue, yellow and red sign. Decent doubles and triples cost Y20. Unfortunately the toilets are a bit grim and the karaoke kicks in nightly. There's a public hot shower (Y3) in a nearby building.

The government-run *Kāngbā Bīnguǎn* (☎ 752 3214) in the east end of town is a quieter option with rooms for Y25 per bed and suites with bathroom for Y120.

The *Jīnmáoniú Jiǔdián* above the bus station has decent doubles with attached hot water bathroom for Y50 per person.

Places to Eat A number of small restaurants are located around the main intersection, just north of the bus station. A row of *Muslim restaurants* just east of here double as video bars and offer good noodles if you can stand the ear-shattering sounds of kung fu.

The best restaurant in town is the *Gānzī Sí Xīnfú Fàndiàn*, a block east of the intersection and recognisable by its purple sign. The sweet red pepper and pork *(tiánqíng chǎoróu)* is sublime.

Getting There & Away Buses to Gānzī (Y104, 12 hours) leave Kāngdìng daily at 6.50am and 7.30am. From Gānzī, a bus leaves each morning at 6.30am for Kāngdìng. A rather decrepit bus leaves at 8.30am for Dégé (Y60, 10 hours) and often continues to Báiyù (Pelyul).

You can head north from Gānzī to Yùshù (Jyekundo) in Qīnghǎi via Sêrxu. Buses to Sêrxu originate in Kāngdìng every day or two, overnight in Dàofú and stop in Gānzī around 10am before resuming their drive.

Around Gānzī

For a nice half-day walk head south from the bus station over the Yǎlóng Jiāng. The right path leads through barley fields for 20 minutes to **Dongtong (or Dontok) Gompa** and the new but impressive **Dingkhor chörten**.

The left path leads to Pongo Gompa after about an hour or so.

About 7km along the road to Kāngdìng, sheltered in the lee of a hill is the **Burana Ani Gompa**, a large nunnery by the roadside that might be worth checking out.

Headed 15km west on the road to Dégé, on the north side of the river, is the Gelukpa sect **Beri Gompa**. There are several other monasteries in the pretty village.

Another 15km or so, near the village of **Rongbatsa**, are the circular walls of **Dargye Gompa** (Dàjīn Sí). Set against white-capped mountains, the monastery is a relaxing place to rest for a day or two. A local lama named Gyalten Rinpoche is said to operate an excellent *guesthouse* nearby (Y35 to Y100 per person) or try the monastery itself. The nearby hot springs, although more lukewarm than hot, may be the only bath you get for some time. From here it's a two-hour walk north along the Yălóng Jiāng to **Hadhi Nunnery**, home to around 60 nuns who operate a basic shop and are happy to receive short-term guests.

To reach Beri Gompa and Dargye Gompa, catch the morning bus to Dégé or one of the sporadic local buses heading west.

Manigango

You'll have to change transport at this crossroads village if headed for Dzogchen Gompa (see later). The *Manigango Guesthouse* by the river has decent rooms for Y15 per bed and the restaurant here is where the buses stop for lunch. There are several Muslim noodle restaurants and shops at the crossroads.

Thirteen kilometres south-west of Manigango is **Yilhun Lhatso** (Xīnlù Hǎi) a stunning holy alpine lake bordered by chörtens and dozens of rock carvings. The lake is backed by the huge glaciers of 6018m Trola Peak (Què'ér Shān) and it's possible to walk an hour or two up the left (east) side of the lakeshore for glacier views. The lake has great places to camp but you'll need to guard against mosquitos. To get here you'll have to hitch on Dégé-bound traffic to the turn-off where there's a bridge and trail 1km to the lake. The entry fee is Y20 to the lake.

Dzogchen Gompa (Zhùqíg Sí)

This important Nyingmapa monastery, 50km north of Manigango, has a stunning location at the foot of a glacial valley that could have been lifted straight from the Canadian Rockies (think Lake Louise). The monastery is the home of the Dzogchen school, the most popular form of Tibetan Buddhism in the West. Several important high Nyingmapa lamas, now exiled abroad, originate from nearby valleys.

The site consists of the small town, 1.5km off the road, which has a few shops, chörtens and a chapel with huge prayer wheels. Up the small gorge is the main monastery and a further 1km is the college, or **shedra**. The monastery was destroyed in the Cultural Revolution and reconstruction is continuing.

The college offers beds for Y15 per bed though you need a sleeping bag and your own food. There are a couple of well-stocked shops in the village below.

Buses to Yùshù and Sêrxu run every other day past Dzogchen but in practice it's easier to hitch.

Hikes Around Dzogchen Gompa There are several excellent day hikes around Dzogchen. First head straight up the main valley (south) to the reconstructed Pemathong chapel and then head up the left (true right) side of the river past prayer flags to a small hermitage not far from a waterfall. From here a hard to find path heads steeply through rhododendrons to a couple of ridges and then an alpine meadow (2½ hours from the monastery) with awesome views of the glacier.

A second day hike takes you west behind the college up to the ridge, then left along the ridge following a small stream (at first hidden) for 1½ hours to a stunning turquoise lake (cross to the right side of the stream early on). From here it's another 30 minutes uphill to a second lake at the foot of an immense rock wall. A hard to find trail leads from here to a third lake. On the descent there are fine views of Dzogchen monastery.

A long day's walk from Dzogchen is **Shechen Gompa**, which could make for a fine overnight trip. Follow the main road north 10km and then follow a side road north-east up the Sānchà Hé valley for 8km or so. It should be possible to stay at the monastery. There are hot springs nearby.

Dégé 德格 (Dêgê)
☎ 0836 • elevation 4000m

Resting in a valley with Chola Shān Range to the east and the Tibetan border to the west, Dégé is steeped in living tradition and sees little of the distant, outside world, other than the truckers and few travellers who pass through. While the Chinese influence is evident in some of the newer, tiled buildings, the village is mainly Tibetan and the military presence that you might expect so near to the Tibetan border is not prevalent in the town itself.

Getting to Dégé is a long haul. En route you'll see the towering snowy peaks of the Chola Shān Range stretching up 6000m. Chola Shān was first scaled in 1988 and you might begin to wonder if your bus driver is attempting the same as the bus inches its way uphill to the top of the peaks. At the 4916m **Tro La Pass** (La means pass in Tibetan) Tibetans on board will throw coloured prayer papers out the window and chant something that you can only hope will carry your bus down to safety through deep gorges and more spectacular scenery.

Bakong Scripture Printing Lamasery

At the heart of Dégé is the Bakong Scripture Printing Lamasery. While the present structure dates from 1744, the printing house has existed on this site for over 270 years with printing blocks dating from early in the 18th century. The lamasery currently houses over 217,000 engraved blocks of Tibetan scriptures from the five Tibetan Buddhist sects, including Bön. Texts include ancient works on astronomy, geography, music, medicine and Buddhist classics, including two of the most important Tibetan sutras. A history of Indian Buddhism, comprising 555 woodblock plates, is the only surviving copy in the world (written in Hindi, Sanskrit and Tibetan).

Within the lamasery, dozens of workers hand-produce over 2,500 prints each day. A visit will give you the opportunity to witness this rare sight as ink, paper and brushes fly through the workers' hands at lightening speed. Upstairs is an older crowd of printers who produce larger prints of Tibetan gods on paper or coloured cloth that later find their way to hills and temples as prayer flags. If you catch them with a free moment, they'll print one of your choice for Y10.

You can also examine storage chambers, paper cutting and binding rooms and the main hall of the lamasery itself. Protecting the monastery from fire and earthquake is a guardian goddess, a green Tara (*Drölma* in Tibetan). There are some nice murals in the two ground floor chapels so bring a torch. You can get a close up look at the workers who carve the printing blocks in the administrative building across from the monastery.

Admission to the lamasery is Y35 and includes an English-language brochure and obligatory guide. Photography is not allowed.

To reach the printing house, turn left out of the bus station and right over the bridge. Continue up this road to the south-east of town and it will bring you to the monastery's front door. The monastery is closed noon to 2pm.

Other things to See & Do Just uphill behind the printing house, **Gonchen Gompa** is a large Sakyapa sect monastery that is well worth a look. Restored during the 1980s, the three inner sanctums are dedicated to the Indian sage Guru Rinpoche, Buddha Sakayamuni and Jampa (the Future Buddha).

Also worth seeking out is the **Tangtong Gyelpo chapel** (Tangyel Lhakhang) – as you head uphill to the printing press look out for the small alley leading to the right. Gyelpo was an 18th century bridge builder, medic and inventor of Tibetan opera – a kind of Tibetan Leonardo Da Vinci. He is depicted with characteristic long white hair and beard.

Places to Stay and Eat The only place in town that is open to foreigners is the *Dégé Bīnguǎn* (☎ 836-822 2167). Clean but damp doubles/triples go for Y35/Y30 per bed.

There are a number of point and choose restaurants around town.

SICHUAN

Getting There & Away Buses to Gānzī (Y61) and Kāngdìng (Y163, two days) leave at 7am and there may also be seats on the bus from Báiyù to Gānzī that passes through about lunchtime. The ticket office sells tickets for next day buses between 3.30pm and 5pm. The occasional sleeper bus trundles through to and from Chamdo in Tibet but rarely has berths. You may find transport in Jomda over the Tibet border but you are likely to be stopped at the bridge over the Jīnshā Jiāng (Yangzi), which forms the Tibetan border.

Around Dégé

South of Dégé, draining into the Jīnshā Jiāng is a series of forested side valleys that hide some of Kham's largest and most important monasteries. Visiting them is hard work: food is limited mainly to instant noodles, transport is almost non-existent and accommodation is basic at best (most of the monastery guesthouses are infested with rats). The only public transport is the daily Báiyù-Dégé bus. Beyond this it's down to hiring a vehicle, trekking (see the boxed text 'Trekking Around Dégé') or hitching.

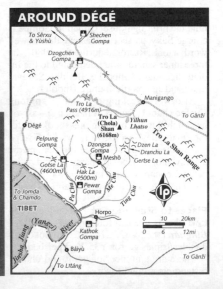

AROUND DÉGÉ

Pelpung Gompa This monastery, known as Bābāng Sí in Chinese, is 30km up the beautiful Pa Chu valley. Three hours walk up the valley from the Dégé-Báiyù road brings you to Pewar Gompa (Báiyā Sí) set at the foot of a ruined dzong *(fort)* and home to a set of 270 year-old murals which fuse Nepalese, Chinese and Tibetan styles. The unfriendly monks charge an outrageous Y50 entry fee, that is ironic as the murals were restored with foreign aid. It's possible to stay in the monastery for Y20.

A further four-hour hike gets you to Pelpung, set high (20- to 30-minutes hike) above the auspicious confluence of five rivers. It's possible to look around the huge main building and there are lots of potential day hikes, for example south-west to Dordra Gompa, north-east to Trandra Gompa and up to the hillside to the famed footprint of the Karmarpa. The monastery can provide guides, though the site is almost deserted of monks from May to November.

Accommodation at the monastery costs around Y25 and there's a small monastery shop. Trucks head up the valley to Pelpung every day or two so you might get a lift out. It's possible to hire horses in the village or through the monastery for about Y70 per day.

Dzongsar Gompa About 40km up the Me Chu valley this large Sakyapa monastery towers above the fertile Meshö valley. A pilgrim path leads steeply up to the monastery and around the chörtens at the rear. The main hall has many hanging thangkas and murals of Jamyang Khentse Wangdrup, a prominent lama. The monastery's current *rinpoche* (reincarnate lama) made a rare visit to the monastery from exile in India in 2001.

It's possible to hire horses and a horseman at the monastery for about Y65 per day. One excellent overnight trek or horse trip takes you north and then east up to the dramatic rock spires of the Dophu Valley. Another fantastic trip is to take horses and a Tibetan guide for the two-day trek to Manigango.

Accommodation is available at the monastery or there's a well-run guesthouse in the village (Y20 per person). There are

Trekking Around Dégé

There are great opportunities for trekking between the monasteries south of Dégé. You can even do one or two of the walks without a tent or stove, staying at monasteries en route. It's possible to hire horses to carry your gear for around Y65 to Y80 per day. Maps to the area are sketchy so it's a good idea to hire a guide to show you the paths, though these are generally quite clear. For security always trek with a partner. For more on treks in the region see Gary MacCue's *Trekking in Tibet*.

Dégé to Pelpung over the Gotse La (4600m) – two days

Firstly, hitch or take a bus south from Dégé and get off at the prominent white chörten, from where it's 5km south-east to a village where you might be able to arrange accommodation. From here it's a hard six- to seven-hour climb to the double pass of Gotse La. Take plenty of water on this trek.

An easier alternative is to take the Dégé-Báiyú bus and get off at the turn-off to Pelpung. From here it's an easy seven-hour walk up the valley along the road to Pelpung via Pewar Gompa.

Pelpung-Dzongsar over the Hak La (4500m) – one day

This eight-hour trek is pretty easy follow the telephone poles from Pelpung village cross the main river and follow the side valley east. There's plenty of water on this trek. After the pass (four hours from Pelpung) the trail descends for two hours and then swings north reaching Handa village in another 1½ hours or so. You can hire a horse in Pelpung to take your gear to the top of Hak La for around Y70.

Dzongsar to Manigango over the Gertse La, Dranchu La and Dzen La – two days

For this two-day trek you'll need a tent, sleeping bag, food and a way to purify water. A guide is strongly recommended. Horses make for a lovely trip and can be hired for Y65 per day with a horseman in Pelpung – you'll have to pay for his return trip. Even if you ride he will probably walk.

The trail leads east of Meshō village along the road for an hour and then swings north up the Ngandra Chu, past the side valley of the Karmo Chu and then above a small lake created by a landslide in 1989 (1½ hours from the road). The road ascends above the river and then descends through forest before revealing stunning views of the south side of Trola Peak (known locally as Ngandra) after two hours. The trail then takes a side valley east and climbs for 1½ hours through rhododendrons to the high Gertse La. From here the trail descends a little but keeps high and swings north for an hour over boulders to the Dranchu La pass. The trail then descends past a glacial lake to join the main Ting Chu valley, which makes for good camping (nine hours from Dzongsar).

The second day head north up the wide Ting Chu valley for an hour past nomad camps before the trail starts to climb and swing east up a side valley, eventually reaching the Dzen La 2½ hours from the camp. From here there are amazing views of Trola Peak on one side and a huge glacier on the other. The trail descends northwards and follows the valley downstream. Two hours from the pass you'll reach a beautiful lake and from here on the valley is populated by nomadic herders. About 2½ hours from the lake you'll join the main road from Dégé from where it's a two-hour walk northeast to Manigango (nine hours total from the camp). Alternatively it is possible to head south-west and spend that night at Yilhun Lhatso before heading back to Manigango.

---

several shops in the village but no restaurant so bring some of your own food.

Kathok Gompa This large 12th century Nyingmapa monastery is a punishing five-

hour climb uphill from the village of Horpo (Hépō), itself 7km east off the main Dégé-Báiyù road. The main buildings include the large prayer hall surrounded by a circuit of prayer wheels, an unusual multi-storey chörten overlooking the main courtyard and a new college, all set in a stunning location. The monastery has a dramatic **cham festival** on the tenth day of the sixth Tibetan month (July) on the birthday of Guru Rinpoche.

It's normally possible to stay at the monastery. Otherwise Horpo has a *government hotel* and a better private *guesthouse* (Y25 per bed) and *restaurant* by the only road intersection.

Báiyù The pleasant tree-lined town of Báiyù (*Pelyul* in Tibetan) is the only one in the region with reliable transport links, a hotel and several restaurants. The brooding monastery above town is well worth a visit.

The friendly *Báiyù Sí Jiēdàisuǒ* has doubles for Y20 or triples with rock hard beds for Y10. The plusher *Báiyù Bīnguǎn* over the bridge was undergoing renovations during our visit.

A daily bus leaves at 7am for Gānzī. It currently goes north via Dégé (Y40, four hours) but may switch to the more direct eastern route via Barong if the road improves. The roads south to Bātáng and east to Gānzī are not well travelled and locals still warn of bandits. The paranoid PSB have forbidden foreigners from using the Internet in Báiyù.

SÌCHUĀN-TIBET HWY – SOUTHERN ROUTE

A journey along this 2140km route takes you through vast, open landscapes with horizons of majestic peaks. Tibetan homes dot the landscape like small stone castles. Huge vultures soar overhead while roaming yaks munch on frosty grass. Solitary Tibetans watch your bus pass from a distance and you may be miles down the road before you spot the black tents of these nomadic herdsmen.

With roads and transport improving and restrictions for foreign visitors lifted, it is no wonder that the southern route of the Sìchuān-Tibet Highway is seeing a considerable rise in the number of foreign tourists. In particular, the Kāngdìng-Lǐtáng-Xiāngchéng-Zhōngdiàn route has become a popular backdoor route into Yúnnán.

As with the rest of north-west Sìchuān, warm clothing is a must. Some travellers experience difficulties with the high altitudes here; be on the look-out for side effects and if you're feeling unwell, head to somewhere lower. There are no money-changing facilities here.

Lǐtáng 理塘

Surrounded by snow-capped peaks and resting on open grassland at an altitude of 4680m, Lǐtáng will leave you breathless in more ways than one. This is Sìchuān's wild west, where tall fur hats and silver embossed knives are the on-going fashion rage and where neighbouring herdsmen can be seen kicking up a trail of dust at dawn. Tibetan culture abounds here. Markets are filled with yak-skin coats, wooden and silver teacups and brightly coloured woven cloth. 'Tashi Delek', the Tibetan greeting, is more commonly used than 'Nǐ Hǎo', and traditional stone and dirt homes fill the northern half of town. A horse racing festival in late July/early August sees the town swell with Tibetan visitors. In recent years dates have been fixed to August 1-7, with the first four days seeing the most action.

Lǐtáng has an amazingly relaxed and friendly atmosphere. While there may not be much in the way of sights, this is an excellent small town to spend a few days hanging out with the local people under a blazing sun, in the blustering winds and under the starry night skies.

There are also some spectacular walks into the surrounding hills. Advice on where

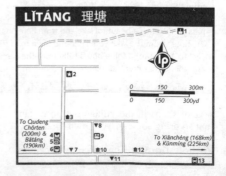

LǏTÁNG 理塘

to go should be sought from locals. Be sure to allow yourself to acclimatise to the altitude before you set out.

If you do find yourself suffering from altitude sickness and can't get out of town, there is a local remedy consisting of medicated pills and rehydration drinks. The woman running Xiānhè Bīnguǎn may be able to help you out.

Information None of Lǐtáng's streets appear to be named, but the town is small enough that you can find your way around regardless. China Post is on the main north-south street. Next door is China Telecom which has an Internet service for Y5 per hour, open until midnight.

Things to See At the northern end of town is the **Lǐtáng Chöede Gompa**, a Tibetan monastery, built for the Third Dalai Lama. Inside is a statue of Sakyamuni, which is said to have been carried from Lhasa by foot. Tibetan homes lead up to the monastery and you are likely to encounter friendly monks en route who may offer to give you a tour.

On the eastern edge of Lǐtáng is **Qūdēnggābù**, a newly erected chörten that active worshippers seem to be perpetually circling, reciting mantras and spinning prayer wheels. Dozens of smaller chörtens fill the courtyard which itself is edged with a corridor of prayer wheels.

Places to Stay Take a left out of the bus station and head about 350m east into town to the *Xiānhè Bīnguǎn*. The hotel is not easily spotted; it's on the right side of the

road and the Chinese-only sign over the entrance has a painting of a bird (something like a heron). The two women running the hotel are cheerful and the rooms are impeccably clean with fresh sheets and electric blankets – a great deal at Y25 a bed. Toilets are across the courtyard and washing facilities consist of basins and all the boiling water you can stand.

Lǐtáng Zhāodàisuǒ (☎ 0836-532 3089) is on the same side of the road, further east. Beds in slightly grotty dorm rooms cost Y25. Toilets and washing facilities are the same as above.

North of here, the *High City Hotel* (*Gāochéng Bīnguǎn*) has beds for only Y10. They seem to have an abundance of rooms but the conditions are something of a mystery as the staff was unable to unlock any of the doors when we last visited.

Places to Eat Lǐtáng has countless hole-in-the-wall *restaurants*, the majority of which are on the south side of the main road running east-west or over the road from the High City Hotel. Serving plates of extremely tasty veggies and meat and huge, steaming bowls of noodles is the *Lǎoqī Xiǎochī*, near the Lǐtáng Zhāodàisuǒ.

There is also a *bakery* and a *market* in town where you can stock up for long bus journeys, and lots of *barbecue stalls* grilling spicy potatoes, tofu and meat.

Getting There and Away Lǐtáng's bus schedule is in something of a muddle. Tickets are sold for buses that don't exist and oversold for those that do. When you

LÍTÁNG

1	Chöde Gompa 相切寺	6	Minibuses and Taxis 面包车和出租车	10 Lǐtáng Zhāodàisuǒ 理塘招待所
2	PSB 公安局	7	Market 市场	11 Lǎoqī Xiǎochī 老七小吃
3	High City Hotel 高城宾馆	8	Bakery 饼店	12 Xiānhè Bīnguǎn 仙鹤宾馆
4	China Post 中国电信	9	VCD Theatres 播映厅	13 Long-Distance Bus Station 长途汽车站
5	Internet Cafe 网吧			

attempt to buy a ticket in advance, you'll likely be told to go away and come back in the morning but don't give up, especially if you plan to travel on the weekend or a holiday when buying tickets for same-day travel is next to impossible.

Double-check the following times before you make your travel plans. All but the road to Bātáng have been vastly improved in this area, reducing travel times immensely.

From Kāngdìng there is a daily departure for Lǐtáng at 6.20am and for Xiāngchéng (passing through Lǐtáng) at 7am.

There are buses leaving Lǐtáng for Kāngdìng daily at 8.30am as well as a Kāngdìng-bound bus or two passing through from Bātáng and Xiāngchéng.

Buses for Bātáng (Y60, 5½ hours) depart Lǐtáng daily at 7am and 7.30am and for Xiāngchéng (Y60, five hours) at 7am. If the bus to Xiāngchéng is full (or oversold), you may be able to hire a minivan to take you and a group of buddies there for about Y600.

Bātáng   八塘

Lying 32km from the Tibetan border and 5½ bumpy hours down a dirt track from Lǐtáng, Bātáng's strict security and remote location has kept it off the tourist route. The town is now open to foreigners, but there's little to see or do here other than to contemplate the surrounding mountains from one of the many sidewalk teahouses. There is a strong Han Chinese presence in Bātáng and your attempts at Tibetan phrases may not always be well received.

Across the river from the town proper lies farmland, beautiful Tibetan homes and a chörten; it is a pleasant place to stroll. The suspension bridge across the river is at the eastern end of town and is a little hairy; it's missing more than a few planks.

Many travellers trying to sneak into Tibet by land have made their attempts from Bātáng. Unsurprisingly, the local PSB is suspicious of foreigners and may pay you a visit to suss you out. It might help to buy your return ticket upon arrival as proof that you don't intend to sneak across the border. It's also a good idea to double-check with the PSB in Chéngdū that Bātáng is still

open to tourists, as penalties for crossing into ever-changing restricted zones can be high – up to Y400.

Places to Stay The *Kèyùn Fàndiàn* has rooms with lumpy beds for Y10 to Y15 each, with grotty common toilets down the hall. Late-night karaoke is on the ground floor should you get bored. Take a left out of the bus station and the hotel is in the first courtyard on the left.

If you continue into town and take the first right after the huge, hard-to-miss golden bird, you'll find the comfortable *Jīnhùi Bīnguǎn* (☎ 0836-562 2700), about a block down on the left. Clean doubles with/without bath go for Y70/50 and dorm beds range from Y10 to Y20.

Getting There & Away One bus heads east from Bātáng daily at 6.30am. It stops in Lǐtáng (Y60, 5½ hours) and Kāngdìng (Y140, 13 hours) en route to Chéngdū. Before reaching Kāngdìng, this bus overnights in Yǎjiāng, where there is a *hotel* in town charging Y50 for doubles. To find the hotel, turn right out of the station, take the stairs on the left until you reach a main road and stay to the right when the road forks. The hotel is on the left.

From Kāngdìng, a bus leaves for Bātáng (Y110) each morning at 7am, overnighting in Lǐtáng. Buses from Lǐtáng to Bātáng leave daily at 7am and 7.30am. While you're attempting to ignore the plunging cliffs that the bus careens ever so close to between Lǐtáng and Bātáng, you can take in some stunning scenery.

Lǐtáng to Zhōngdiàn – The Back Door To Yúnnán

As an alternative route to Yúnnán that takes you through 400km of spectacular scenery and Tibetan territory, the route from Lǐtáng to Zhōngdiàn has once again been opened up to foreigners.

Buses from Kāngdìng and Lǐtáng head for Xiāngchéng in Sìchuān (see the Getting There & Away sections of Kāngdìng and Lǐtáng), from where you can catch an onward bus to Zhōngdiàn in Yúnnán the next morning between 7am and 8am. Going the other way, buses from Xiāngchéng head back to Lǐtáng at around the same time. Try to buy your onward ticket on arrival in Xiāngchéng as the ticket seller may not show up in the morning before your bus departs.

Xiāngchéng is a small bordertown that is quickly expanding. Nevertheless, a hike up to the **Tibetan Gompa** offers views over the valley and what's left of the town's traditional square stone houses. The monastery itself is being rebuilt by hand and is worth a visit to watch carvers and painters at work.

The gompa is at the opposite end of town from the bus station. To find it, follow the dirt track up on the left as you reach the edge of town.

Bámùshān Bīnguǎn is the only hotel in town with a permit to accept foreigners. Don't let its fancy exterior scare you – while doubles start at Y240, beds in clean dorm rooms are available from Y25. The hotel is the huge building on the right as you exit the bus station.

Dàochéng
☎ 0836

The county town of Dàochéng (Dabpa in Tibetan) is really just a staging post for travellers en route to Yàdīng (see later in this section), though if you have time you could visit the **Xiongdeng Gompa** in town. After a trek in Yàdīng, soak your weary limbs in the Rubu Chaka Hot Springs, 4km out of town. North of town is the Hǎizi Shān nature reserve, with its estimated 1000 or so lakes.

The main hotel in town is the *Blue Moon Valley Hotel* (*Lányuègōu Bīnguǎn;* ☎ 572 8752), with rooms for Y80 to Y100. Here is the Yàdīng Travel Agency (☎ 572 8262). There are a couple of other hotels in town, including the *Diànlì Bīnguǎn*.

Buses run to Dàochéng from Kāngdìng (Y121, two days), overnighting in Lǐtáng en route. There are reports that an airport is being built at Dàochéng, which will eventually have direct flights to Chéngdū.

The turn-off to Dàochéng is at Sāngduī, from where it's 28km to Dàochéng.

Sāngduī has the *Happy Times Guesthouse* with beds for Y10. North of Sāngduī is the recently rebuilt Bangpu Gompa.

Yàdīng Nature Reserve

Six hours drive south from Dàochéng is this stunning reserve, the real reason to come all the way out to this remote area. There's no public transport to the reserve so you'll have to hire a jeep in Dàochéng or try your luck hitching. Some intrepid travellers have reached the reserve on horseback from Zhōngdiàn in two to three days.

The reserve is based around the three holy peaks of **Jampelyang** (Yāngmàiyǒng Shénshān 5958m) to the south, **Chana Dorje** (Xiárì Duōjí Shénshān 5958m) and **Chenresig** (Xiānnàirí Shénshān 6032m). The mountains are named after the Tibetan Buddhist trinity of Bodhisattvas known as the Rigsum Gonpo. None have ever been climbed. The reserve is a strong contender for the title 'Shangri La' (see the boxed text 'Shangri La – Fact and Fiction' in the Zhōngdiàn section).

The region was once part of the old kingdom of Mùlǐ and was visited by the fifth Dalai Lama in the 17th century. Joseph Rock, who counted the corpulent King of Mùlǐ as a close personal friend, visited in the 1930s and first described the famed 'Bandit Monastery', whose 400 monks would regularly head out on plundering expeditions before returning to prayer and contemplation. En route to the reserve, before Rìwǎ, 60km from Dàochéng, is the **Konkaling Gompa** (Gònglíng Sì).

At the reserve entrance there is a hefty Y180 entry fee and you can hire horses (with an obligatory guide) for around Y80 per day. There are several tent hotels here though it's only a 45-minute walk to **Tsongu Gompa** (Chōnggǔ Sì), where there is a *tent hotel* (Y20 to Y40 per bed) and *restaurant*. It is also possible to camp near the monastery (paid to the monastery), though some campers have complained that they've been pressured into staying at the tent hotels.

Three-hours walk south-east of the monastery is **Luorong Pasture** (Luóróg

SÌCHUĀN

Mùhǎg) where there is another *tent hotel* and *restaurant*. Three hours past here is a trail to Niúnǎi Hǎi (Milk Lake) at 4720m.

From this point most Chinese tourists return the way they came but it is possible to do a kora (circuit) of the mountain if you have camping equipment for one night. From Niúnǎi Hǎi the kora continues for one hour to a 4400m pass, and then branches right to some meadows, a popular place to camp. The next day, two hours hiking north-east gets you to another higher pass, from where it's a four hour descent beneath the north face of Chenresig Peak. The trail then passes Tara Lake (Drölma Tso) en route back to Tsongu Gompa.

Northern Sìchuān

With dense alpine forests and wide grasslands, northern Sìchuān is a great place to commune with nature. Pony treks around

Sōngpān and hiking in the stunning nature preserve of Jiǔzhàigōu have made this area increasingly popular with travellers. Also in this area is Wòlóng, one of China's most famous nature reserves.

Northern Sìchuān is home to the Ābà Tibetan and Qiang Autonomous Prefecture. In the extreme north-west, the region around Ābà and Lángmùsì is the territory of the Goloks, nomads who speak their own dialect of Tibetan, distinct from the local Amdo dialect. The meadows are speckled with their black and white tents, yaks and livestock. While these Tibetan destinations are less visited, you can incorporate them as an alternative route into Gānsù or into a scenic loop taking in Mǎěkāng, Ābà, Lángmùsì, Jiǔzhàigōu, Sōngpān and Chéngdū. You'll need at least two weeks for this last route.

Most of northern Sìchuān is between 2000m and 4000m in altitude, so make sure you take warm clothing. The grassland plateau in the north-west averages more than 4000m and even in summer temperatures can dip to 15°C at night. The rainy season lasts from June to August.

Beyond the Sōngpān-Jiǔzhaōu route, roads in the region aren't always in the best condition; many of the buses are in worse condition. Roads are particularly hazardous in summer when heavy rains prompt frequent landslides, and you might want to think about planning this trip for the spring or autumn, when the weather is better.

As in the rest of Sìchuān, travellers are required to purchase Chinese insurance. The difference in this area is that you may actually need it. If you're coming from Chéngdū, the insurance will be included in the cost of the ticket. However, once you're in northern Sìchuān without insurance, you'll either be charged a huge surcharge or may not be allowed onto the onward or returning bus. You won't have an easy time purchasing insurance once you're up here either. This is the one area where we felt that buying insurance in Chéngdū had paid off (see the boxed text 'Warning' in the Chéngdū Getting There & Away section.)

While you're getting prepared, bear in mind that there is virtually nowhere to

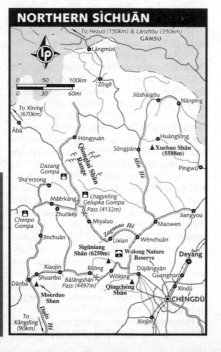

NORTHERN SÌCHUĀN

change money in this region, so bring sufficient cash Rénmínbì.

WOLONG NATURE RESERVE
卧龙自然保护区 Wòlóng Zìrán Bǎohùqū

Wòlóng Nature Reserve lies 140km northwest of Chéngdū, about four hours by bus (via Dūjiāngyàn). It was set up in the late 1970s and is the largest of the 16 reserves set aside by the government for panda conservation. (Of these 16 reserves, 11 are in Sìchuān.)

The reserve is estimated to have some 3000 kinds of plants and covers an area of 200,000 hectares. To the north-west rises Sìgūniang Shān (6250m); to the east the reserve drops as low as 155m. Pandas like to dine on fang cane and fountain bamboo in the zone from 2300m to 3600m, ranging lower in winter. Other animals protected here are the golden monkey, golden langur, musk deer and snow leopard.

Before setting out for Wòlóng be forewarned: there is little chance of seeing a panda in the wild. Dr George Schaller, invited by China to help with panda research and conservation efforts, spent two months trekking in the mountains before he saw one. The pandas have a hard enough time finding each other; in spring, the park is closed so that trekkers don't disturb the pandas' hunt for each other during their mating season.

The **China Research and Conservation Center for the Giant Panda**, on the edge of the reserve, has about 30 pandas cooped up in small cages that you can visit for Y18. However, to see a live panda in something resembling its natural habitat, you'd be

better off visiting the Giant Panda Breeding Research Base in Chéngdū.

If you're just out to commune with nature, Wòlóng is nice, but your time may be better spent making the trip to Sōngpān and Jiǔzhàigōu. The rainy season is a bad time to be in Wòlóng as the leeches take over the park. Summer is the most popular time to visit, especially for Japanese tourists who are looking for the two rare types of azalea that bloom here.

Trekking here is fairly tough and the trails are faint. The Park Administration Office in Shawan village, at the centre of the reserve, can give information on hiking trails and researchers at the Conservation Centre (some of whom speak English) are good sources of info on conditions. Trails along **Silver Mine Valley** (Yínchǎng) and **Hero Valley** (Yingxióng Gǔ) cross fields covered in wildflowers and grazing yaks and give you views of Balong Shān. At **Wuyue Valley** there are observation decks and accommodation, but you'll need to check at the administration office as to whether or not it's open. Admission to the park is Y20. Be sure to bring your own supplies, including warm clothing.

At the Conservation Centre, 6km from Shawan, the ***Panda Inn*** has clean, comfortable doubles with hot showers and heaters for Y200. There is also a ***restaurant*** here and ***barbecue stalls*** across the road.

Getting There & Away
The opening of the research base in Chéngdū and improved access to northern Sìchuān has dampened demand for tours of the Wòlóng reserve. Though most travel outfits at the Traffic Hotel in Chéngdū have dropped this tour, one or two still offer packages that include transport, entry to the reserve and one night's accommodation in Wòlóng town. Sam's Guesthouse in Chéngdū will organise a tour here for you.

There is theoretically at least one bus a day from Chèngdū's Xīmén Bus Station to Wòlóng at 11.40am (Y20). The village (also called Shawan) is at the centre of the reserve and is where you'll find onward transport. There are also a number of daily departures from Chéngdū to Dūjiāngyàn (Y12) – if you

Yaks can be found all over South-West China

SÌCHUĀN

catch the first one at 7am you might just make it for the 8am bus from Dūjiāngyàn to Wòlóng (Y13.50, 2½ hours). If you want to get dropped at the Conservation Centre, rather than Wòlóng Village, watch for it on the left and ask the bus driver for the Xióngmāo Yuán (Panda Garden).

Buses continue irregularly over the 4497m Bālǎngshān Pass to Rìlóng (see the next entry) and Xiaojin, from where you can catch buses to Dānbā, Kāngdìng and Mǎěrkāng.

SÌGŪNIANG SHĀN 四姑娘山

The western borders of the Wòlóng Nature Reserve are defined by the 6250m Sìgūniang Shān or 'Four Girl Mountain'. The mountain is actually a cluster of four peaks, of which the highest is Yaomei Feng, named after the youngest of the 'four girls'. The name stems from a Tibetan legend about four girls who lost their lives protecting a panda from a ferocious snow leopard. The mountain is the highest peak in the Qionglai Range and marks a steep jump in the transition zone between the Tibetan plateau and the Sìchuān basin.

From the town of Rìlóng, 25km west of Wòlóng, you could hike or arrange a horse ride 20km up the Changping Valley, and use this as a base for trekking up side valleys like Haizigou or Shuangqiaogou. The region has great trekking potential but you'll need to be well equipped, totally self-sufficient and know exactly what you're doing, as it's extremely remote territory. Travel agencies in Chéngdū and Kāngdìng can help with logistics.

WÉNCHUĀN 汶川
☎ 0837

Wénchuān is halfway between Chéngdū and Sōngpān, strategically placed at a river confluence and the turn-off to Mǎěrkāng and Ābà. A rather dull Chinese town, Wénchuān hasn't much to offer tourists. Its main attraction is the scenery of the nearby Zagunao Valley and the surrounding villages of Qiang people.

If you've got time to kill in Wénchuān, you can cross the footbridge 100m north of the northern bus station and climb up the hill

to get a good view of the town. From here you can see the old defensive **city walls** to the east and several Qiang stone **watchtowers** up on the ridge behind you. If you continue over the second bridge you'll reach a **Monument to the Revolutionary Masses**.

Places to Stay & Eat

Wénchuān is seriously lacking in budget accommodation. The PSB appears to have placed the majority of hotels out of reach of foreigners. Next to the Monument to the Revolutionary Masses, the somewhat run down **Sāngpíng Bīnguǎn** is Wénchuān's cheapest option, with clean doubles from around Y60.

Ābà Zhōuyín Bīnguǎn (☎ 622 2360), about 300m north of the northern bus station, has new, comfortable doubles with bath and hot water starting at Y150.

Two doors down from the southern bus station is **Jiǎhuán Bīnguǎn** (☎ 622 5242), with run down doubles for Y80. The rooms are clean enough but the bathrooms are grim. Turn right out of the station to find the hotel.

As a last resort, halfway between the north and south bus stations is the new **Telecom Hotel** with doubles from Y600.

Wénchuān has no shortage of restaurants, many of which line the main street. Heading south out of the north bus station to where the road forks left, are a large number of hotpot restaurants. The **Cāngyué Fándiàn** is the first one on the right and offers unlimited grazing for Y30 per person. If you carry on up the road you'll find less fancy versions where you pay by the skewer. There are also lots of **barbecue stalls** and **fruit stands** along this street.

Getting There & Away

There are two bus stations in Wénchuān. While you may get dropped off at the southern station, buses from here only head to Chéngdū, with departures every hour or so from 4.25am to 4.30pm.

From the northern station, there are departures at 7am for Mǎěrkāng (Y44.50), 9am for Ābà (Y56) and 10am for Hóngyuán. There are also regular buses for Maoxian (Y17) from 7.40am to 5.50pm. A bus heads north to Sōngpān (Y37) at 9am; however, it

The Qiang

The Qiang are a small ethnic group centred around the upper Min Valley in Wénchuān. They derive their name from an ancient kingdom that settled in the region 2000 years ago and which is mentioned still earlier in ancient oracle bone transcriptions. This ancient tribe is said to be the progenitor of both the Qiang and Tibetan peoples. There are still many ethnological and linguistic links between the Qiang and Tibetans and the two live in close proximity in the valleys of north-western Sichuán.

Qiang women wear dresses slit down the sides over blue trousers. Over the top of this are work aprons and black waistcoats. Most women wear black or white turbans and as much silver and amber jewellery as they can afford.

The villages have their own character and you may spot many from the bus on the way to Sōngpān and Mǎěrkāng. The Qiang are famed as stonemasons and many villages are guarded by tall stone watchtowers (gŭdiāo). Fires lit on these rooftops would have warned surrounding villages of impending attack.

Most Qiang houses are three-storey constructions. The bottom floor is for livestock, the middle floor for living quarters and the top floor is for storing grain and drying crops. The sharp corners of these fortress-like houses are lined with whitewash and the window frames are painted in bright colours. The sombre stone walls are often lined with bright yellow maize, red chillies and green lucerne drying over the upper balconies.

You'll also see many cable and pulley bridges in Qiang areas and locals hauling themselves nonchalantly over raging rivers as they make their precarious way home.

originates in Chéngdū and you'll have to cross your fingers for a seat.

AROUND WÉNCHUĀN

A pleasant day excursion takes you up the beautiful **Zagunao Valley** towards Lixian, 46km east of Wénchuān. The 90-minute trip shows you Qiang watchtowers and beautiful hamlets of stone houses and apple orchards. If you have time, it's worth continuing on to **Miyaluo village** (three hours by bus from Wénchuān) where there are a couple of basic *guesthouses*. The villages around here are very picturesque and the scenery is particularly beautiful in late autumn.

Local buses run frequently from Wénchuān to Lixian. For Miyaluo (Y20) you can pick up the bus originating in Mǎěrkāng, which passes through Wénchuān at 11.30am. You'll have to spend the night in Miyaluo as there isn't a bus returning until the following morning.

MǍĚRKĀNG 马尔康 (BARKAM)

Resting in a deep gorge, Mǎěrkāng is the capital of the Ābà Autonomous Prefecture and largest town in the region. While the Chinese influence here is predominant, Mǎěrkāng continues to carry some Tibetan flavour. The main draw of the town is its scenic neighbouring valleys. You might consider spending a day or two busing up and down the main roads, stopping where you like to explore some of the surrounding villages.

In town, a path leads north up the hill to the restored **Gelugpa Gompa**. This small Tibetan monastery has a friendly caretaker and affords good views of the valley. To get there, take the alley to the right of the post office and then follow the steps up by the Tibetan Cultural Translation Bureau for about half an hour.

There's not much else to do in town except sip tea in the sun at the numerous friendly teahouses or browse the Tibetan handicraft shops.

Information

The China Post and Telecom office is at the opposite end of the road from the bus station. China Telecom should be opening its own Internet office soon but, in the meantime, snail-paced access is available for Y5 per hour in an office on the eastern side of town.

There is also a PICC office in town where you can attempt to buy Chinese insurance for onward journeys (see the boxed text 'Warning' in the Chéngdū Getting There & Away section). This rather time-consuming process takes numerous faxes to Chéngdū and just as many cups of tea, but the staff is friendly and helpful.

Places to Stay

The *Mǎěrkāng Fàndiàn*, on the corner of Tuanjie Lu and 100m from the bus station, isn't the quietest or cleanest place you could wish for, and its inconsistent pricing means you aren't likely to get much of a deal. Beds range anywhere from Y20 to Y60 with doubles with bath starting at around Y120.

A better option is a few doors down at the *Mǎěrkāng Bīnguǎn*, where you can get a bed in a clean triple for Y30 with spotless toilets and a hot shower down the hall. Doubles start at Y120 and go up to Y180 for rooms with bath and electric blankets.

Places to Eat

East of the hotels is the *Nóngmù Fàndiàn*, which serves Chinese dishes at reasonable prices. Watch for the gold writing on blue windows.

If you're hungry for a steak, the *Yīsīlán Cāntīng* is around the corner and specialises in beef dishes. Half a block further south is the busy *Huímín Fàndiàn (Huí Nationality Restaurant)*, which has excellent food and seems happy to cater to vegetarians.

Just up from the bus station is *Jolly Good*, a fast food burger joint where you can get your fix of ice cream and French fries. West of the hotels are a number of *bakeries* and *barbecue snack bars*. In the *market*, vendors sell corn bread and lots of fruit.

Getting There & Away

Early morning buses leave for Chéngdū (Y72) at 5.30am and 6.40am and for Dānbā (Y26) at 7am. A bus departs at 6am, for Hóngyuán (Y52.5) at 7am and for Zöigê (Y134) at 6am. If you're planning to travel on a weekend, buy your tickets as soon as possible – they disappear quickly.

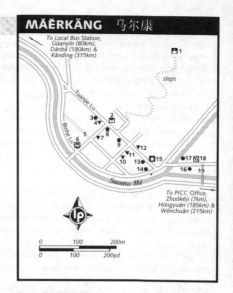

Local buses head west to Sha'erzong and Guanyin from the local bus station on the western edge of town.

AROUND MǍĚRKĀNG

The forested valley around Mǎěrkāng is speckled with Tibetan stone villages and it's worth spending a day exploring. Farther away are remote monasteries. Hitching is generally no problem here, though most of the bus drivers will try to overcharge you for short trips.

About 7km east of Mǎěrkāng, at the turn-off south to Xiaojin, is the compact Tibetan village of **Zhuōkéji** (*Choktse* in Tibetan). The village consists of beautiful layered stone houses with open roofs lined with drying corn cobs and strings of red chillies. Just above the town is a derelict watchtower/fortress that once belonged to a local chieftain and in which Mao Zedong is said to have slept when the Long March passed by.

Continuing east past Zhuōkéji and then north along the same road, 10km past the turn-off to Wénchuān, is the **Lhagyeling Gelupka Gompa** (Shuājīng Sì), 65km from Mǎěrkāng. Any bus to Ābà, Hóngyuán or Zöigê can drop you off here.

MĂĚRKĀNG

PLACES TO STAY
8 Măěrkāng Fàndiàn
马尔康饭店
9 Măěrkāng Bīnguăn
马尔康宾馆

PLACES TO EAT
4 Snack Bars
& Bakeries
5 Market
市场
7 Jolly Good
10 Huímín Fàndiàn
回民饭店

11 Yīsīlán Cāntīng
伊斯兰餐厅
12 Nóngmù Fàndiàn
农牧饭店

OTHER
1 Gelugpa Gompa
喇嘛庙
2 China Post & Telecom
3 Tibetan Shop
藏族用品商店
6 Long-Distance
Bus Station
汽车站

13 Tibetan Shop
藏族用品商店
14 Teahouses
茶馆
15 PSB
公安局
16 Teahouse
茶馆
17 Teahouses
茶馆
18 Internet Access
网吧
19 Footbridge
步行桥

A more challenging trip can be taken to **Dazang Gompa**, around 50km north of Măěrkāng, up the Jiaomuzu and then Qingping valleys. To get there you'll have to take a bus to Sha'erzong (Sher Dzong) and then hitch or hike the remaining 10km or so. It would be wise to take a sleeping bag and food in case you have to spend the night there.

Further exploration could take you to **Chenpo Gompa** (Guānyīn Sì), a monastery 80km west of Măěrkāng. Buses run in the morning to Guanyin town, from where it's about an hour's walk up to the small monastery. Ask locals for directions.

Măěrkāng – Dānbā – Kāngdìng

If you haven't yet had your fill of long bus rides, it is possible to travel between Măěrkāng and Kāngdìng without backtracking through Chéngdu. This route follows a deep gorge through stunning scenery, especially true on either side of **Jīnchuān**, a friendly town that is home to a small Huí population. Sunbathing cows loll on sandy riverbanks that are often edged with orchards and cornfields. There are also a number of Qiang stone watchtowers, and Tibetan homes climb the barren mountains bedecked in prayer flags.

This journey is broken mid-way in Dānbā where beds in the surprisingly clean and comfortable **Kèyù Fàndiàn** go for Y15 and doubles for Y36.

While there isn't much to do in Dānbā itself, 5km south-east of town is **Mòěrduō Shān**, revered by Tibetans. At the base of the mountain is **Dāsíbāo Gompa** and behind this monastery is the start of the pilgrim route to the mountain's summit. You'll need two days to reach the top and climb back down again. Accommodation is available at a second monastery halfway up the mountain. To reach Mòěrduō Shān, take a local bus or taxi to the village of Yazha.

About 4km north-east of Dānbā is **Shuānbō**, a village where you can visit a number of Qiang watch towers (*gŭdiāo*).

Buses to Dānbā leave Kāngdìng at 7.30am (Y34, six hours) and Măěrkāng at 7am (Y24). Buses to Kāngdìng and Măěrkāng leave Dānbā very early in the morning.

The southern half of this journey, between Dānbā and Kāngdìng, is particularly rough with only a narrow, uneven dirt and gravel path.

SŌNGPĀN 松潘
☎ 0837

Although largely viewed as a stopover point on the road to Jiǔzhàigōu or as a base for horse treks, it's worth having a wander around Sōngpān. While the downtown area is filled with modern tourist shops selling Tibetan wares (yak-skin coats are said to be cheaper here than elsewhere), old wooden buildings still line many of the side streets and residential areas. The ancient gates from Sōngpān's days as a walled city are also still intact and a couple of old wooden bridges cross over the Mín Hé. On the far, eastern side of the river is **Guānyīn Gé**, a small Chinese temple. Walking up to it will take you through a village-like setting and offer views over Sōngpān.

Be sure to bring a flashlight with you to Sōngpān, which is often plagued with faulty electricity.

Horse Treks

Several kilometres outside of Sōngpān lies idyllic mountain forest and emerald-green lakes. One of the most popular ways to experience this is to join a horse trek from Sōngpān. Guides can take you out from one to seven days through pristine, peaceful valleys and forests, aboard a very tame horse.

There are two prominent horse trekking operators in Sōngpān. Don't worry about finding them – they'll find you. Those who go out on treks with either company return with rave reviews.

Shùnjiāng Horse Treks (Shùnjiāng Lüóu Mǎdù) was the first trekking operation in Sōngpān catering to backpackers. Happy Trails, next door, is run by ex-guides of the former and has bikes for rent, laundry and a book exchange. Employees of both are friendly and helpful.

The companies' tours appear to be virtually identical. It's probably best to visit both offices and see which one takes your fancy or has room on a tour already organised. The basic three-day trip takes you to a series of mountain lakes and a hot spring at **Erdao Hai**, and then on to the **Zhaga Waterfall**. They're amenable to suggestions, and will tailor a trip to suit you. For Y60 per day, you get a horse, three meals a day, tents, bedding, warm jackets and raincoats. The guides take care of everything: you won't touch a tent pole or a cooking pot unless you want to.

The only additional charge is entrance to the different sites (around Y30 each), but the tour companies will warn you of these before you set out. As food consists mainly of green veggies, potatoes and bread, you may want to take along some extra snacks for variety.

Places to Stay

With Sōngpān's faulty electricity also comes a shortage of hot water (apparently

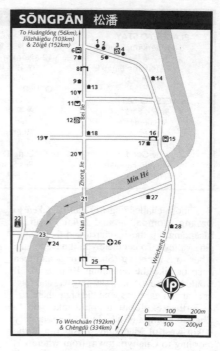

SŌNGPĀN 松潘

the water pumps halt), something you might want to consider before splashing out on an expensive room with en suite. If you're coming in from a horse trek, be prepared to remain grimy. There are two public bathhouses in town where you can take a steaming shower if the hot water is flowing.

There are two budget options in town: *Līnyè Bīnguǎn* and *Sōngzhōu Bīnguǎn*. Both offer comparable basic rooms for Y15 per bed. While the Sōngzhōu is cheerier, the Līnyè is quieter. Washing facilities in both are a bowl and thermos of hot water, and both have shared toilets.

Once a popular budget choice, the *Jīnyuán Bīnguǎn (Songpan County Government Guesthouse)* appears to have been recently refurbished; its cheapest rooms are now doubles with bath for Y100. Down the road, the run down *Huánglóng Bīnguǎn* has beds for Y30 with rank toilets outside.

Gǔchéng Bīnguǎn (☎ 723 2575), next to the East Gate, has comfortable, clean rooms

SŌNGPĀN

PLACES TO STAY
7 Tàiyáng Dàjiǔdiàn
   太阳大酒店
9 Sōngzhōu
   Bīnguǎn
   松州宾馆
13 Jìnyuán Bīnguǎn
   县政府招待所
14 Línyè Bīnguǎn
   林业宾馆
17 Gǔchéng
   Bīnguǎn
   古城宾馆
18 Huánglóng
   Bīnguǎn
   黄龙宾馆
27 Dájí Bīnguǎn
   达吉宾馆
28 Sōngpān Bīnguǎn
   松潘宾馆

PLACES TO EAT
10 Yùlán Fànguǎn
   玉兰饭馆
19 Hotpot Restaurant
20 Muslim Restaurant
   穆斯林餐厅
24 Teahouse
   茶馆

OTHER
1 Happy Trails
   快乐的小路
   骑马旅游
2 Shùnjiāng Horse
   Treks
   顺江旅游马
3 Internet Cafe
   网吧
4 Public Showers
5 Public Showers

6 North Bus Station
   汽车北站
8 North Gate
   北门
11 China Post
   邮局
12 Internet Cafe
15 East Bus Station
   汽车站
16 East Gate; Teahouse
   东门、茶馆
21 Covered Bridge
   古松桥
22 Guānyīn Gé
   观音阁
23 Covered Bridge
25 South Gate
   南门
26 Hospital
   医院

for Y50 per person. Unfortunately, at the time of writing the plumbing wasn't working and toilets were a bucket in each room. At the southern end of town, the friendly **Dájí Bīnguǎn** (☎ 723 2080) has sparkling new rooms with bath for Y100 per person.

Tàiyáng Dàjiǔdiàn is one of the most upmarket hotels. Almost next door to the north bus station, it has doubles for Y280. At the other end of town, the **Sōngpān Bīnguǎn** (closed in the off season) has doubles/triples for Y260/360.

Places to Eat & Drink

Sōngpān has an excellent assortment of breads for sale, made and sold fresh all day at small **stalls** along Zhong Jie – big crusty loaves, dumplings, Tibetan flatbread and sweet breads.

There are also a huge number of restaurants along Zhong Jie including **hotpot** and **noodle shops**. Many have English signs and menus. There are numerous hole-in-the-wall **restaurants** on the eastern side of town, between the Linye Bīnguǎn and the East Gate. They aren't likely to have a menu, much less an English one, but you can point out what you want. You'll find a large **hotpot restaurant** in what was the town's cinema. Head west from the Huánglóng Bīnguǎn.

A favourite hangout for foreign travellers is the friendly **Yùlán Fànguǎn**, where you can get pancakes, hot chocolate and tasty Chinese dishes. Their English menu includes phrases such as 'I'm a vegetarian' and 'Not too spicy'. This is probably not the place to be if you're attempting to steer clear of the horse-trekking operators.

South of the intersection on Zhong Jie, the **Muslim Restaurant** is clean and has great food. Prices are a bit higher, especially for chicken and fish, and there's no English menu, but you can easily pick out what you want in the kitchen. The yúxiāng qiézi (fish-flavoured eggplant) is particularly good.

Along the Mín Hé, on the western edge of town, is a fantastic outdoor **teahouse** where you can enjoy views of the covered wooden bridge, Guānyīn Sì and wooden houses. There is another **teahouse** atop the eastern gate that is also a good place to relax.

Getting There & Away

Sōngpān has two bus stations. You'll need to buy your ticket at the station from which your bus originates. This is the north station for all destinations except Píngwǔ.

A bus to Chéngdū departs every morning at 6am (Y41.50, 10 hours). A Chéngdū-bound sleeper bus from Nánpíng also passes through town at around 9.30am; however, you can't be guaranteed a bunk. From Chéngdū, a bus departs the Xīmén bus station at 7am (Y46, 10 hours).

Heading north to Jiǔzhàigōu, a bus leaves Sōngpān's north station at 7am (Y26, four hours) and continues on to Nánpíng. For Zöigê, a daily bus departs at 6am (Y31).

From the south bus station, a bus leaves each morning for Píngwǔ. This takes you within hiking distance of Huánglóng (Y40).

HUÁNGLÓNG 黄龙

Named Yellow Dragon, this valley is studded with waterfalls and terraced, coloured limestone ponds of blue, yellow, white and green. The most spectacular terraced ponds are behind the **Huánglóng Sì**, located 7.5km and about a four-hour round trip from the road, returning through dense (and dark) forest. The valley, temple and surrounding area were designated a national park in 1983. While some people rave about the valley's beauty and love the peace and quiet here, others find it disappointing and prefer an extra day at Jiǔzhàigōu.

A great time to visit is during the annual **Miáo Hui** (Temple Fair). Held here around the middle of the sixth lunar month (usually July), it attracts large numbers of traders from the Qiang minority.

Admission is Y75, Y50 for students. There are no vendors, so bring some water and supplies.

In the national park there are several small *guesthouses* with cheap beds – no frills, just hard beds and maybe a coal burner in the winter. The *Huánglóng Zhāodàisuǒ* is slightly more upmarket, with dorm beds in triples and standard doubles.

Around 56km from Sōngpān, Huánglóng is almost always included on the itinerary of the seven-day Jiǔzhàigōu tours run out of Chéngdū as well as on the horse trekking tours out of Sōngpān. Unfortunately, unless you've signed up on a tour, the valley can be difficult to reach. Buses from Sōngpān to Píngwǔ pass within hiking distance of the entrance but you may then be stuck for transport back. You might be able to jump on a tour bus setting out from either

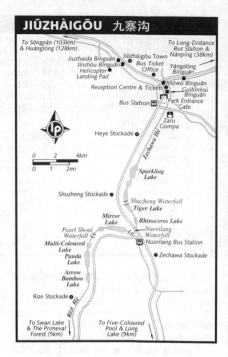

JIǓZHÀIGŌU 九寨沟

To Sōngpān (103km) & Huánglóng (128km)
To Long-Distance Bus Station & Nánpíng (38km)
Jiuzhaida Binguan
Jinshòu Binguan
Helicopter Landing Pad
Jiǔzhàigōu Town
Bus Ticket Office
Yángdòng Binguan
Reception Centre & Tickets
Mùwū Binguan
Guibīnlóu Binguan
Bus Station
Park Entrance Gate
Zaru Gompa
Heye Stockade
Zechawa Hé
0 2 4km
0 1 2mi
Sparkling Lake
Shuzheng Stockade
Shuzheng Waterfall
Tiger Lake
Mirror Lake
Rhinoceros Lake
Pearl Shoal Waterfall
Nuorilang Waterfall
Multi-Coloured Lake
Nuorilang Bus Station
Panda Lake
Zechawa Stockade
Arrow Bamboo Lake
Rize Stockade
Rize Hé
To Swan Lake & The Primeval Forest (5km)
To Five-Coloured Pool & Long Lake (9km)

Sōngpān or Jiǔzhàigōu early in the morning, but drivers are often reluctant to take foreigners, citing the risk of insurance liability.

JIǓZHÀIGŌU 九寨沟

Just inside Sìchuān's northern border lies Jiǔzhàigōu, a gorgeous alpine valley studded with dazzling lakes as clear and bright as gemstones. Heavily forested and surrounded by snowy peaks, Jiǔzhàigōu is a national nature reserve and home to the protected takins, golden monkeys and pandas. There are also a number of Tibetan villages here and the valley is lightly sprinkled with Bön prayer flags, chörtens and prayer wheels that spin anti-clockwise, powered by the current of the rivers. As a reflection of the number of lakes that are said to be within the park, the local Tibetan women wear 108 braids in their hair during festivals.

The park is in pristine condition; however, it has also been groomed for the rapidly increasing influx of tourists.

Jiǔzhàigōu was first pinpointed for tourism in the 1970s. Judging by the number of new resort-style hotels being built along the highway leading to the park entrance, the number of visitors is only expected to grow. Don't let this put you off, as most tourists only visit Jiǔzhàigōu for the day, hopping on and off the tourist bus and not venturing far from the roadside sights.

The scenery here is spectacular and unique and you can easily spend three or four days hiking between the sites and beyond the tourist route. While autumn can plunge the park into icy temperatures, it's also quieter, with beautiful snowy scenes and colourful trees.

The Park
Buses from Chéngdū and Sōngpān will drop you outside the park reception centre and ticket office, just north of the park entrance. Admission is Y153, or Y113 if you can produce something resembling a student card. The price includes entrance to all areas of the park and a bus service within the park for as long as you're there (see Getting Around later in this section).

The first official site inside the park is the Tibetan monastery, **Zaru Gompa**. It's a short walk down the first fork off the main road.

If you continue on the main road, you'll follow the Zechawa Hé as it runs past Heye village to **Sparkling Lake**, the first in a series of lakes filled by the Shuzheng Waterfall. Keep your eyes open for trees growing unexpectedly out of the middle of the river, lakes and waterfalls. This is caused by fertile pockets of calcium in the waterways that create impromptu flowerpots.

A walking trail begins north of Sparkling Lake and runs along the eastern edge of the river as far as Shuzheng Stockage. Here it crosses back over, leading you to a number of water-powered prayer wheels. The trail then continues up to the Shuzheng Waterfall.

South from here, just past Nuorilang Waterfall, the road branches in two, with the eastern road leading to Long Lake and Five-Coloured Pool and the western road to Swan Lake. If you're looking to stretch your legs and clear your lungs, you'd be better off

heading along the western route where there are a number of scattered sites and a forest trail leading from Mirror Lake to Panda Lake. Views from this trail are particularly good, especially of Pearl Shoal Waterfall.

The eastern route is almost better done by bus, as the narrow road sees a great deal of traffic. Nevertheless, the two lakes at the far end are both well worth a visit.

You can either base yourself at one village and bus to different areas for walks each day, or walk from one settlement to the next – an ambitious itinerary. From the park entrance to Nuorilang Waterfall is about 14km. It's a further 17.5km along the western road to the primary forest and 18km down the eastern road to Long Lake.

Organised Tours
During summer, various companies in Chéngdū operate tours to Jiǔzhàigōu and the surrounding area. Most trips are advertised for a certain day, but the bus will only go if it's full. If you are unlucky you may have to spend days waiting so it's best to try to register first and then pay before departure.

A standard tour includes Huánglóng and Jiǔzhàigōu, lasts seven days and costs a minimum of Y250 to Y300 per person. Hotels, food and entry fees are not included in the price. There are longer tours that include visits to the Tibetan grassland areas of Mǎěrkāng and Zöigê. Prices vary.

Chéngdū travel agencies in the Traffic Hotel, Sam's Guesthouse, the Xīmén bus station, the Jǐnjiāng Bīnguǎn and CITS all offer tours. The last two are the most expensive. Check around and compare prices.

A word of warning: several tour operators in Chéngdū have been blacklisted by travellers for lousy service, rip-offs and rudeness. Ask around among travellers to pinpoint a reliable agency and look in the travellers' notebooks in cafes such as Sam's Guesthouse or Paul's Oasis.

Places to Stay
Unless you're catching an early bus the next day, it's worth staying in the park amidst the scenery. Lodging is found in three places: Heye village, Shuzheng Stockade

SÌCHUĀN

and Zechawa Stockade. During the high season your options will increase considerably with a choice between concrete block 'guesthouses' or basic, wooden Tibetan-style rooms with the lingering scent of pine. The latter rooms are usually family-run and you may be invited in to warm your hands around the kitchen fire and sip an endless cup of yak butter tea.

At all three villages you are meant to report to the 'central desk' – often located somewhere in the middle of the village. Here you'll be asked to choose a hotel from a number of outdated photographs. If you're not interested in the pricey rooms, the folks at the office are unlikely to be interested in you. It seems easiest to have a look around yourself, and to deal directly with the guesthouse proprietors. You can find beds in the villages for Y15 to Y20.

Heye village is the place where most travellers don't stay, since it's the furthest from the local sights (but closest to the park entrance). More popular is **Shuzheng village** where many of the rooms have beautiful views of turquoise pools. For cheap, comfortable rooms, check out the Tibetan *guesthouses* at the back of the village, up the hill.

On the northern edge of **Zechewa village** is a *guesthouse* offering doubles with bath for Y50, as well as Y15 beds in wooden rooms. Located in the middle of the park near the main junction, this is a great location for those planning to set out on long walks. The hotel is on the road to Long Lake, a five-minute walk south of Nuorilang. Look for the wooden building peeking out from behind a yellow-tiled building.

If you're wanting to stay outside the park, the cheapest option is the *Jīnshòu Bīnguǎn* (☎ 773 4129), a 15-minute walk west of the park entrance. Beds in doubles with bath and heated blankets go for Y30.

Head east from the park entrance to find the *Yángdóng Bīnguǎn* (☎ 773 9770) where comfortable, clean doubles with bath are Y50 per bed.

If you're looking for something more up-market, options are plentiful. The *Mùwū Bīnguǎn*, next to the park reception centre on the main road, has wooden chalet-style doubles with showers and a heater for Y258. On the other side of the reception centre, the *Guìbīnlóu Bīnguǎn* has plush doubles for Y668.

Places to Eat

While there are a number of small *restaurants* in the village west of the park reception centre, inside the park options are more limited, especially if you visit during the off season. You can also expect to pay slightly more for food inside the park.

On the northern edge of the main parking lot at Shuzheng village is a *restaurant* that serves up greasy Chinese dishes at lunch and dinner. At the other end of the parking lot is a tiny *shop* that will make you a cheap bowl of noodles at almost any time of day.

Further up the road at Nuorilang is another *restaurant* that opens for an early lunch. A set price of Y30 gives you a number of dishes, rice and tea.

Getting Around

Included in your admission fee is a bus service within the park on minibuses that zip between the sites. Unfortunately, these buses are often commandeered by tour groups who hop off at each site, take their obligatory photos and hop back on 15 minutes later to race to the next site. This can become rather tedious if you're just trying to get from A to B.

Buses run from about 7am until the sun begins to sink behind the mountains. They often don't go beyond Panda Lake. If you're wandering around in the afternoon, it's best to make sure you're within easy walking distance of your base, as buses seem to travel more by the whim of their tour group than by any sort of schedule or route.

Getting There & Away

While local authorities are planning to build an airport, the local bus remains the best means of transport. It can be taken in one dose or as part of a bus/train combination.

Between October and April snow often cuts off access to Jiǔzhàigōu for weeks on end. Even at the best of times, transport is not plentiful. Hitching to Jiǔzhàigōu on tour buses has supposedly happened, but it's a rare occurrence indeed.

Take the Nánpíng sleeper bus (Y86.50) at 7.20am from Chéngdū's Xīmén station. If you're coming from Gānsù via Zöigê, you'll have to go through Sōngpān. From Sōngpān to Jiŭzhàigōu (Y26, four hours), the road goes up and over some gorgeous scenery. Buses drop you outside the entrance to the park.

Bus/train combinations are more troublesome but can be done. The most popular option has been to travel north on the Chéngdū-Baoji train line as far as Zhāohuā, where you will have to stay overnight. From there you need to catch a bus heading back to Chéngdū that travels via Nánpíng and Jiŭzhàigōu (check to be certain). Buses from Nánpíng to Zhāohua have been discontinued. Whether or not you'll find one heading the other way is a risk. If you do, you may well have to overnight in Nánpíng as well. Added to this, the road between Zhāohuā and Nánpíng is notoriously dangerous.

A second train/bus option is to take a train to Miányáng, north of Chéngdū. You should be able to get a Nánpíng bus from Miányáng on Jiŭzhàigōu. This road is reportedly much better. You could also get a train to Jiāngyóu from where you can catch a bus to Píngwŭ. From there you can get a Sōngpān-bound bus and stop at Huánglóng, and then continue on to Sōngpān and Jiŭzhàigōu.

Returning from Jiŭzhàigōu to Sōngpān or Chéngdū, you are more likely to get a seat by heading north to Nánpíng and purchasing your ticket there. As buses leave Nánpíng at the break of day, you will have to overnight there (see the Nánpíng Getting There & Away section later). Minicabs run back and forth between Jiŭzhàigōu and Nánpíng (Y10 to Y15, one hour).

If you do want to chance buying a ticket in Jiŭzhàigōu, you'll find the bus station a few kilometres east of the park, on the road to Nánpíng. In the high season, a bus ticket office is also open on the main road, across from the entrance to Jiŭzhàigōu, and you can attempt to purchase your onward tickets from there. Theoretically, this office has six berths reserved daily on the Nánpíng-

Chéngdū sleeper. Even so, it's best to book your tickets in advance.

NÁNPÍNG 南坪
☎ 0837

East of Jiŭzhàigōu, Nánpíng doesn't see many foreign visitors except for those searching for a seat on a Chéngdū- or Sōngpān-bound bus. If you do find yourself overnighting here, there isn't much to see or do, but the town is friendly and pleasant to wander through.

Places to Stay & Eat
Minibuses and taxis from Jiŭzhàigōu will drop you outside the *Jiŭzhài Bīnguǎn* (☎ 773 0686), across from the river at the northern edge of town. Comfortable rooms with bathroom and hot water are posted at Y150 but may be offered for Y120.

For a cheaper version of the same, continue up the street, bearing to the right, to the *Jìnsuí Bīnguǎn* (☎ 773 3168). Doubles here go for Y80.

For something to eat, take the first right after the Jiŭzhài Bīnguǎn into the centre of town where there are numerous *hotpot restaurants* and *barbecue stalls*. You'll also find well-stocked *fruit stalls* and *bakeries*. Across from the Jìnsuí Bīnguǎn is a small shop selling tasty, fresh flatbread.

Getting There & Away
Minibuses from Jiŭzhàigōu will drop you outside the Jiŭzhài Bīnguǎn, attached to which is a small bus ticket office. Unfortunately, it won't likely sell tickets to foreigners and, if it does, a nasty insurance charge will be added. Instead, you'll need to haul yourself uphill to the other side of town where the long-distance bus station is hidden.

To find the long-distance bus station, turn left out of the Jiŭzhài Bīnguǎn, walk about 25m and take a left into a narrow pedestrian market street. Follow this all the way to the top of the hill, about 15 minutes' walk. At the top is the bus station. There is a second station a few doors west of here; however, it's far easier to purchase tickets from this first station, where the buses originate and

SICHUAN

where you are unlikely to be questioned about insurance.

A sleeper bus to Chéngdū leaves at an ungodly 5.30am (Y45, 12 hours). In the high season you may also find a night bus on this route. There are two buses daily to Sōngpān at 7am and noon (Y25, four hours) and departures to Miányáng at 5.30, 7.50 and 9.10am (Y50). Buses to Zhouhua have been discontinued; however, if you want to head down this road, it's worth asking to see if they've been reinstated.

THE NORTH-WEST ROUTE TO GĀNSÙ

This journey through the extreme north-west of Sìchuān has emerged as a popular backdoor route into Gānsù province. Even if you're not headed north beyond the Sìchuān border, this area offers an opportunity to explore remote Tibetan towns and villages in what was once known as the Tibetan province of Amdo. At an average altitude of 3500m to 4000m, travel through this grassland bog is not recommended for those in a hurry – bus transport is slow and sporadic. If you plan to explore any of the towns or Tibetan monasteries on the way, you'll need a minimum of five days, more if you make a side trip to Jiǔzhàigōu.

In winter months, roads often become impassable and temperatures plummet way past the tolerance levels of most mere mortals. Early autumn, however, sees clear and

Sky Burial

The white cloth is removed from the body while those in attendance are bathed in the incense of the juniper fire. The *Tomden* sharpens his large knife on a nearby stone, circles around a small Buddhist monument while reciting mantras, and slices into the body lying before him on the stone slab. The flesh is cut into large chunks while the bones and brain are smashed and mixed with barley flour.

By this time, the smell of the flesh and the incense have drawn a large number of vultures who circle high above. The Tomden steps away and the huge birds descend into a feeding frenzy, devouring every bit of the body and carrying it up to the heavens, witnessed by the family of the deceased from a nearby hilltop.

This is sky burial, an ancient Tibetan burial tradition. While it may at first seem a gruesome af-front to Western sensibilities, in this corner of the world it makes sense both spiritually and practically. According to Buddhist beliefs, the body is merely a vehicle to carry you through this life; once a body dies, the spirit leaves it and the body is no longer of use. Giving one's body as food for the vultures is a final act of generosity to the living world and provides a link in the cycle of life. Vultures themselves are revered and believed to be a manifestation of the flesh-eating god *Dakinis*.

On a more practical note, sky burial provides an ecologically sound way to dispose of bodies in a terrain where wood is scarce and the ground is often too hard to dig. Traditionally, only people of high stature were cremated while those with smallpox or other infectious ailments were chopped up and disposed of as fish food through water burial, perhaps accounting for the unpopularity of fish in the Tibetan diet.

The Chinese banned sky burials in the 1960s and '70s and it wasn't until the '80s, as Tibetans regained limited religious rights, that the practice was once again legalised. Chinese officials continue to regard sky burial as a primitive practice. The fact that one Buddhist sect has been known to keep the tops of the skulls from the deceased and use them as enlarged sacred teacups has often been touted as proof of Tibetan savagery.

In Lhasa, tourists require official permission to attend a sky burial; however, in the more remote areas of Sìchuān, you may well be told where and when the burials are to take place. Nevertheless, local Tibetans have been Unsurprisingly offended by travellers who have turned these funerals into a 'tourist outing'. Common decency applies – if you aren't invited, don't go and whatever you do, don't attempt to make it a Kodak moment.

sunny skies, although you'll still need to dress warmly. If you are travelling in the autumn or winter, it's best to buy your onward tickets as soon as possible as, during these colder months, the nomadic Goloks stay closer to main roads and towns and do much of their travel by bus.

There are a number of places where you can pick up this route. The most obvious way is to begin in Chéngdū and travel to Sōngpān (see the Sōngpān Getting There & Away section earlier). Most travellers take a side trip from Sōngpān to Jiǔzhàigōu at this point. From Sōngpān you can travel 168km northwest to your next overnight stop in Zöigê, a dusty little town surrounded by sweeping grasslands. From here it's worth heading to Lángmùsì, just inside the Sìchuān border, for a day or two before crossing into Gānsù.

Another option is to head west from Sōngpān via Hóngyuán to the grassland settlement of Ābà, where you can cross into Qīnghǎi province or continue on to Zöigê and Gānsù. Ābà can also be reached from Wénchuān via Mǎěrkāng.

You can also pick up this route from Kāngdìng by heading north to Mǎěrkāng via Dānbā.

Ābà 阿坝

Ābà (*Ngawa* in Tibetan) is a rough-edged Tibetan town on the border of Qīnghǎi. If you find yourself here on a stopover en route to Xīníng in Qīnghǎi, it's worth spending a day exploring a couple of the 30 monasteries in the vicinity.

To the north of town, set at the top of a pretty valley, is the **Nazhi Gompa**, a Bön monastery that is home to around 1100 monks. Also resident in this peaceful place is the monastery's 17-year-old 39th Lama.

The main hall of the temple reveals subtle differences between Bön monasteries and those of Tibetan Buddhism. Look, for instance, at the features of the 1139 small gold Buddhas. If you tour the elaborate interior, be sure to circle it anticlockwise, as is customary with Bönpo pilgrims.

To reach Nazhi Gompa, head east out of town. Just before you reach the Tibetan Middle School (with its English sign) on

your right, you'll find a path leading off to the left between a concrete and a mud wall. This path will take you out into the valley and to the monastery, an enjoyable 3km or 4km walk. You can also take a taxi from town that will cost you an exorbitant Y30 for the 6km drive.

At the western edge of town is the Kirti Gompa, a large Tibetan monastery with over 2,000 monks in residence, many of whom are under the age of ten. The huge, brightly painted **chörten** here is worth a visit.

Places to Stay Down the first road on the left as you enter town is the *Xiànwei Zhāodàisŭo*. Dorm beds cost Y10 to Y15; however, staff will push you towards the new building where doubles without bath are overpriced at Y80. Washing facilities are the usual bowl and hot water and, while the women's toilets are down the hall, men have to trudge out into the cold to dirty facilities.

Next to the western bus ticket window is the *Kèyùn Fàndiàn*, where a very friendly family charges Y10 for a bed in the usual bus station hotel conditions.

At the far east end of town, behind an elaborately painted gate, is the *Jíxiǎngxīnjū Bīnguǎn*. Conditions here are a little better with beds for Y20, but it's a bit of a trudge to catch your early-morning bus.

Getting There & Away Ābà has two bus ticket windows at the eastern end of town, about half a block from each other on opposite sides of the road. Both sell tickets for the same buses; however, the office farther west, on the left side of the road as you enter town, is less likely to charge you a foreign surcharge and more likely to recognise PICC insurance if you have it. Buses depart from in front of the ticket windows.

Buses leave Ābà early – between 5.30am and 6am. Destinations include Zöigê (Y30), Mǎěrkāng, Hóngyuán (Y17) and Wénchuān (Y47). You can also get an early bus to Xīníng in Qīnghǎi.

About 100km south-east of Ābà, you'll pass through **Hóngyuán** (Red Plain) en route to Zöigê. The town derives its name from its associations with the Long March,

SICHUAN

when the Red Army slogged its way through the bogs during August 1935, trying to avoid the roaming packs of Golok nomads. Many marchers remember this section as the worst of the entire march. The town itself isn't much of a destination, though you'll probably have to overnight here if you're headed east from Ābà to Sōngpān. You'll find accommodation at the *Xiànwei Zāodàisǔo*.

Zöigê 若尔盖

Other than as a resting point en route to Lángmùsì and north to Gānsù, Zöigê does not have much pull for travellers. It is easy to spend a day here sipping tea in the sun, and at the western edge of town is a **gompa** with pleasant, peaceful grounds. While the town's Chinese name is Ruòěrgài, it is most commonly referred to by its Tibetan name, Zöigê.

The Foreigner's Registration Office in town once charged travellers for a permit, but thankfully no longer seems to be in business as Zöigê is officially open to foreigners.

Behind Zöigê's closed-down cinema, a trail leads up a hill to a few rather dilapidated **pagodas**. From here you can get views of the town and surrounding grasslands. To find the cinema, take a right out of the west bus station, the first left onto the main road and then left again.

China Post and China Telecom are one block west of the Liángjú Bīnguǎn, on the same side of the road.

Places to Stay & Eat Conveniently located across the road from the western bus station is *Liyuán Bīnguǎn (☎ 0837-299 1885)*. Rooms are clean but rather bleak, with toilets outside and central heating that isn't likely to be working. As the hotel serves as a guesthouse for truckers, it can be noisy through to the wee hours as these big rigs pull into town. Beds are Y15 each.

The *Pānchuán Bīnguǎn* is not much better, but the staff seems friendly and toilets and showers are indoors. Beds are also Y15 here. Take a right out of the western bus station and the hotel is up the road on the right, just before the crossroads.

Probably the best option in town is *Liángjú Bīnguǎn (☎ 229 8360)*. Beds are a bit more expensive at Y25 each, but it's quieter, cleaner and more cheerful. And the central heating works! Head right out of the western bus station, take the first left onto the main street and walk for about 15 minutes. The white and yellow hotel will be on your left. The small sign is in Chinese only, but you can watch for the telephone number.

Between the Liángjú Bīnguǎn and the western end of the main street are a number of small restaurants including *hotpot* and *noodle shops*. Across from the ever-popular pool tables is the *Gābāfǎngjiǎo Cāguǎn*, a teahouse where you can sit outside on the balcony, eat fresh bread and sip delicious eight-treasure tea.

There are also small *restaurants* next to the western bus station, which sell fresh bread and dumplings in the mornings.

Getting There & Away Zöigê has two bus stations, one at the western edge of town and the other, on the same road, at the south-eastern edge of town. The more conveniently located western bus station has services to all destinations while the south-eastern only has buses to Sōngpāng. If you're heading to Sōngpān and can't get a ticket at the western station, it's worth trying at the south-eastern one.

Arriving in Zöigê, you are likely to end up at the south-eastern station if you arrive from Sōngpān.

The bus to Hóngyuán and on to Mǎěrkāng leaves at 6.20am daily (nine hours). To Sōngpān there is a departure at 6.30am (Y62), and to Ābà a bus leaves at 7am (Y62, nine hours).

Buses to Lángmùsì leave every other day at 6.30 (Y28, four hours). This bus carries on to Hezuo in Gānsù, which is only a few hours from Xiàhé. From Xiàhé you have the option of travelling on to Lánzhōu or taking the more unusual option of heading to Xīníng in Qīnghǎi, via Tongren.

Lángmùsì 朗木寺

Lǎngmùsì (Namu) is an unexpected oasis on Sìchuān's northern border. This small, remote village is nestled between alpine scenery to the west and grasslands to the east. It is home to a friendly population of Tibetans, Huí Muslims and Han Chinese. Surrounded by countless gompas and temples with numerous possibilities for hikes and horse treks, it is easy to spend a few relaxing days here. The hills surrounding this area are also traditional sites for sky burials.

The village is built around one main dirt road that runs east to west along the river. Crossing the first bridge north over the river will take you up a hill scattered with chörtens and gompas. The largest **gompa** on this side of the river is 900 years old. Hidden from view as you start up the hill, you'll eventually see it to your east. Its entrance is carved with scenes from ancient Tibetan Buddhist scriptures.

If you follow the small road beyond here, you will eventually come to a trail that leads to the top of the hill from where you can enjoy fantastic views of the village and surrounding mountains and grasslands.

Continuing west along the village's main road leads to the **Dacheng Lamo Kerti Gompa**. Built in 1413, this monastery is home to around 700 monks who study medicine, astrology and the sutras and tantrics. Admission is Y10.

Also on the eastern side of the village is a **Huí mosque**. You'll spot its slightly decrepit minaret that you can climb at your own risk.

If you follow the river beyond the western edge of the village, you will eventually come to a number of small caves, grottoes and Tibetan mantras carved into the foot of the hills. The largest **cave** occurs just before the river disappears underground, at the point where the aqueduct begins. The cave is marked with prayer flags, and is the source of the village's water. The entrance to the cave is very low but it opens up inside. You may see monks in here hanging prayer flags or washing their faces in the river's underground flow.

In addition to hiking out on your own, the Lǎngmùsì Bīnguǎn offers two-day horse treks with an English-speaking Tibetan guide to nearby rivers, hot springs or simply out across the grasslands.

Places to Stay & Eat There are a number of hotels offering similar facilities and beds for Y15. The *Hóngyuán Lǚguǎn* is on the right as you enter town, above China Post. Rooms are clean and simple with your own coal stove lit at 7pm.

A block up on the left hand corner is *Lǎngmùsì Lǚguǎn*. Next door to this is the *Lǎngmùsì Bīnguǎn*, with central heating and steaming hot common showers.

For its size, there is a large number of restaurants in Lǎngmùsì, many of which boast English signs and menus. The restaurant downstairs from the Lǎngmùsì Bīnguǎn serves good pancakes and sandwiches as well as local dishes like fish and yak. *Lesha's Coffee Shop* is just past the hotels on the main road. Inside this tiny place, Lesha whips up amazing fare including fresh apple pie, coffee (the real thing!), yak burgers and chips. Be warned – the servings are huge!

Getting There & Away Buses to Hezuo leave Lǎngmùsì around 11am. Buses to Zöigê pass by the Lǎngmùsì junction northeast of town every other day between noon and 1pm. To reach the junction, hop on the back of a blue taxi-truck (Y5, 15 minutes). If you're coming from Zöigê, Buses leave the western station at 6:30am every other morning and drop you at the Lǎngmùsì junction. Here, blue taxi-trucks will be waiting to give you a lift into the village.

Chóngqìng 重庆

Chóngqìng at a Glance

Chóngqìng p531

Chóngqìng to Yíchāng p547

Chóngqìng p532

Area: 82,400 sq km

Population: 30.4 million

Highlights

- Dàzú, the site of some of China's most celebrated Buddhist cave sculptures and grotto art

- Yangzi River Cruises – sail down the Cháng Jiāng for a look at the famous Three Gorges before they are submerged

CHÓNGQÌNG CITY

☎ 0236 • pop 5.8 million • elevation 261m

Perched on steep hills overlooking the confluence of the Yangzi River (Cháng Jiāng) and its longest tributary, the Jiālíng Jiāng, Chóngqìng is one of China's more unusual cities. Dusty grey tenements and shining office towers cling to the precipitous hillsides that make up much of the city centre.

Chóngqìng is quite pleasant to stroll around, and even if it's not exactly brimming with 'sights' there's nevertheless a certain picturesque quality to this grey city. For Chinese tourists the 'sights' are usually connected with the Communist Revolution, most being linked to the city's role as the wartime capital of the Kuomintang from 1938 to 1945.

Something immediately noticeable in Chóngqìng is the absence of bicycles. There's barely a cyclist to be found, as the hill climbs make it coronary country for any would-be rider. As a replacement, Chóngqìng is the largest producer of motorbikes in China. Despite this dependence on motor transport, you may also notice a certain silence on the city streets. In 1997 the city banned outright the use of car horns to reduce noise pollution on the congested peninsula.

Chóngqìng is a city with big plans, most of them connected with the hype surrounding the Three Gorges Dam. It already rates as the chief industrial city of south-western China, with its production equal to a quarter of the industrial output of neighbouring Sìchuān. Cheap electricity from the dam and faster communications with Wǔhàn and Shànghǎi are set to boost the city's industries further and kick-start economic growth throughout the South-West. Either that or it will place the city right at the end of the largest toilet in China (see the boxed text 'The Damned Yangzi' later in this chapter).

With all this, the city long lobbied for a special status akin to that of Shànghǎi. In 1997 what it got was not quite provincial status, but the 30-odd million residents of the three-county area separated from Sìchuān and became a 'special' municipality directly under central government control. On many measures, Chóngqìng is now the largest city in China.

Within China, Chóngqìng is famous for its searing summers, when temperatures can exceed 40°C. This lovely climate has earned the city a place among the country's 'three furnaces', the other two being Wǔhàn and Nánjīng. Outside of summer, the city is regularly shrouded in fog.

History

Chóngqìng (known in pre-Pinyin China as 'Chungking') was opened as a treaty port in

CHÓNGQÌNG MUNICIPALITY 重庆市

1890, but not many foreigners made it up the river to this isolated outpost, and those who did had little impact.

A program of industrialisation got under way in 1928, but it was in the wake of the Japanese invasion that Chóngqìng really took off as a major centre, after the Kuomintang retreated to set up its wartime capital here. Refugees from all over China flooded in, swelling the population to over two million.

The irony of this overpopulated, overstrained city with its bomb-shattered houses is that its name means something like 'double jubilation' or 'repeated good luck'. Originally named Gongzhou, Emperor Zhao Dun of the Song dynasty renamed it in 1190 when he succeeded the throne. As he had previously been made the prince of the city, he called it Chóngqìng in celebration of these two happy events.

Living in the shadow of Kuomintang military leaders, representatives of the CCP (including Zhou Enlai) acted as 'liaisons' between Chóngqìng and the Communists' headquarters at Yán'ān, in Shaanxi province. Repeated efforts to bring the two sides together in a unified front against the Japanese

CHÓNGQÌNG CITY 重庆

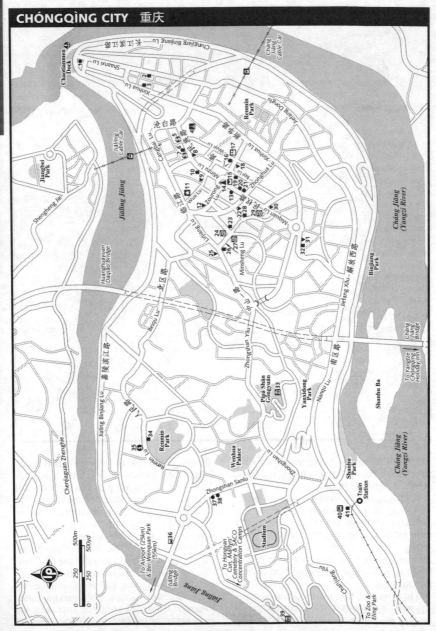

CHÓNGQÌNG

PLACES TO STAY

2 Chóngqìng Shípǐn
Dàshà
重庆食品大厦

3 Chung King Hotel
重庆饭店

6 Peace Hotel
和平饭店

10 Huìxiānlóu Bīnguǎn
会仙楼宾馆

16 Harbour Plaza
重庆海逸酒店

19 Yúdū Bīnguǎn
渝都宾馆

23 Milky Way Hotel
银河大宾馆

26 Chóngqìng
Guesthouse
重庆宾馆

28 Marriott Hotel
重庆万豪酒店

32 Mosque
(Qīngzhēnsì)
清真寺

34 Rénmín Bīnguǎn
人民宾馆

41 Fùyuàn Bínguǎn
富苑宾馆

PLACES TO EAT

8 Yángròu Guǎn
羊肉馆

9 California Beef
Noodles
加州牛肉面

12 Yízhìshí Cāntīng
颐之时大酒店

18 Whale World
蓝鲸湾

22 Noah's Ark
诺亚方舟

25 Sophie's Coffee
House
苏菲亚

30 Ziyi Coffee House;
Old Tree Café
子怡西餐厅;
老树咖啡

31 Lǎojiēshè Bātīlóu
老街十八梯楼

OTHER

1 Chaotianmen
Booking Hall
朝天门码头
(售票处)

4 Luóhàn Sì
罗汉寺

5 Bank of China
中国银行

7 ATM
自动柜员机

11 PSB
公安局外事科

13 Xinhua
Bookstore
新华书店

14 Liberation
Monument
解放碑

15 China Post
邮电局

17 Cinema
电影院

20 Foreign Languages
Bookstore
外文书店

21 Qinyuan Bakery
沁园饼屋

24 Intel Internet Café
英特花园

27 Xinhua Bookstore
& Internet Café
新华书店与网吧

29 Internet Café
网吧

33 Chóngqìng
Museum
重庆博物馆

35 CITS
中国国际旅行社

36 Buses to SACO
Prisons
至中美合作
所汽车站

37 China Southwest
Airlines
中国西南航空公司

38 CAAC
中国民航

39 Stillwell Museum
史迪威将军旧居

40 Long-Distance
Bus Station
长途汽车站

failed, largely due to mutual distrust and Chiang Kaishek's obsession with wiping out the Communists, even at the cost of yielding Chinese territory to an invading army.

The wartime offices and living quarters of the Communist officials form the bulk of Chóngqìng's tourist attractions, along with museums depicting atrocities committed by the Kuomintang and its US backers.

Orientation

The heart of Chóngqìng spreads across a hilly peninsula of land wedged between the Jiālíng Jiāng to the north and the Cháng Jiāng to the south. The rivers meet at the tip of the peninsula at the eastern end of the city.

For most visitors the central focus of this congested peninsula of winding streets is the now neon-shrouded Liberation Monument (Jiěfàng Bēi), which is within walking distance from most of Chóngqìng's accommodation. Originally a wooden structure built to commemorate Sun Yat Sun's death, the monument was rebuilt in 1945 to celebrate the end of China's war with Japan.

Chóngqìng is a good city to explore on foot. The distances are manageable, and there's always an interesting alley to duck into. Between the Liberation Monument and Chaotianmen Dock are a number of steep, laddered alleyways, usually lined with little shops. Also within walking distance of the

Liberation Monument are the two cable cars over the Jiālíng and Cháng rivers.

Maps Good maps in Chinese and less detailed ones in English are available from street vendors around the Liberation Monument, as well as at the train and bus stations.

Information

Public Security Bureau The office (☎ 383 1830) is officially on Linjiang Lu, however the entrance is off Wusi Lu. You can apply for visa extensions here but if you're after anything less than usual, it is best to wait until you get to Chéngdū.

Money The main Chóngqìng branch of the Bank of China is on Minzu Lu, just up the road from the Huíxiānlóu Bīnguǎn. Inside is an ATM. A few doors east is another ATM at the Huaxia Bank and a couple of doors west is a 24-hour ATM centre for Visa and Plus card holders. Many of the larger hotels have exchange desks.

Post & Communications There is a China Post on Minzu Lu, within walking distance of the Chung King and Huìxiānlóu hotels. It claims to have 24-hour service but we're sceptical. Most of the top-end hotels offer limited postal services.

Email & Internet Access A huge Xīnhuá Bookstore has opened on Minsheng Lu. There are close to 100 computers on the 3rd floor, where you can surf the net and drink coffee, 24-hours a day. Access is Y3 an hour. Across the street, Intel offers the same services on the 3rd floor of a shopping mall, past the glitzy shops and ping-pong tables.

Down an alley behind the Marriot Hotel is yet another Internet cafe, this one with beer and slightly cheaper rates (Y2 per hour).

Luóhàn Sì 罗汉寺

Built around 1000 years ago, Luóhàn Sì has since been sandwiched between the skyscrapers and apartments of the city. At its peak, this temple was home to 70 monks; there are only around 18 in residence these days. Nonetheless, the temple is still popular with local worshippers, who burn tonnes of fragrant incense, and it's worth a brief visit.

Luóhàn is the Chinese rendering of the Sanskrit *arhat*, which is a Buddhist term referring to people who have released themselves from the psychological bondage of greed, hate and delusion. There are 500 life-like terracotta arhat sculptures inside the temple. You'll also find a large golden Buddha figure, behind which is an Indian-style *jataka* mural depicting Prince Siddhartha (the Buddha) in the process of cutting his hair to renounce the world.

The temple's most remarkable feature is its long entrance flanked by rock carvings, many of which have survived the onslaught of time, the Cultural Revolution and the city's pollution.

The vegetarian restaurant here has been spiffed up for tour groups. Some of its dishes are good, others (like the fake turkey carcass) are just interesting; all are pricey.

The temple is open 8am to 5pm and admission is Y2.

Hóngyán Village 红岩村
Hóngyán Cūn

During the Kuomintang-Communist alliance against the Japanese during WWII, Hóngyán (Red Cliff) village outside Chóngqìng was used as the offices and living quarters of the Communist representatives to the Kuomintang.

Among others, Ye Jianying, Zhou Enlai and Zhou's wife Deng Yingchao lived here. After the Japanese surrender in 1945, Mao Zedong also arrived in Chóngqìng – at the instigation of US ambassador Patrick Hurley – to join in the peace negotiations with the Kuomintang. The talks lasted 42 days and resulted in a formal agreement that Mao described as 'words on paper'.

One of China's better revolutionary history museums now stands at the site and has a large collection of photos, although all of the captions are in Chinese only.

A short walk from the museum stands the old headquarters of the South Bureau of the Communist Party's Central Committee and the office of the representatives of the Eighth Route Army. There are only

Deng Xiaoping (1904–1997)

Deng Xixian was born on 22 August 1904 in Paifen (or Baifang) village in Xiexing township, Guang'an county, 100km north of Chóngqìng. He later changed his name to Deng Bin, before finally taking the name Xiaoping, or Little Peace. The words *xiao ping* sound just like 'little bottle' in Chinese and this was to become Deng's political symbol over the years.

No stranger to violence, Deng suffered a turbulent family history. His father, a prosperous landlord, was beheaded by bandits in 1938. His brother committed suicide in 1967 at the height of the Cultural Revolution. Roughly the same time, Deng's eldest son, Deng Pufang, fell (or was pushed) out of a 4th floor window after being hounded by radicals at Běijīng University, fracturing his spine and leaving him a paraplegic.

Deng married his first wife, Zhang Xiyuan, in 1928, but she died two years later during a miscarriage. His second wife, Jin Weiying, divorced him during his first political purge and went to live with his political persecutor. He married his third wife, Zhuo Lin, in 1939 and together they had three daughters and two sons.

Deng's political career began in Guǎngxī during the 1920s, where he established one of the original Red Armies. He took part in the Long March under Lin Biao and worked with Liu Bocheng in Jiāngxī during the civil war. He was appointed the leading party cadre in the South-West in 1949, during which time it is said he sanctioned, or at least knew of, the execution of thousands of local landlords.

Known as a political pragmatist, Deng's most famous quote, 'It doesn't matter if a cat is black or white as long as it catches mice' was first uttered in the early 1960s in reaction to the Great Leap Forward. He was purged from office in 1933, 1966 and 1976 and each time rehabilitated. During the Cultural Revolution he was accused of being the 'No 2 Capitalist Roader' in China, responsible for the 'Right Deviationist Wind' and was sent down to the countryside to work in a tractor repair factory. His 1977 rehabilitation led him to the post of vice premier and he became a popular figure to redress the wrongs of the Cultural Revolution, especially as he himself had suffered as much as anyone.

Deng's cosmopolitan persona gave rise to his popularity in the West and stands in sharp contrast to Mao. Deng was educated in Chóngqìng before moving to Paris in 1920, where he developed a lifelong love of croissants and communism. In the early 1980s the diminutive Deng (he was 148cm tall) became the world's favourite communist when he donned a ten-gallon hat at a Texas rodeo. He listened to John Denver and watched the Harlem Globetrotters; back home he chain-smoked Panda cigarettes and spat profusely. In 1985 Deng Xiaoping was even voted *Time Magazine*'s Man of the Year.

Deng's achievements are manifold. It was he who reversed much of the madness of the Mao years and brought China into the world community. He also led the negotiations over the return of Hong Kong, though he never lived to see the final handover.

The Tiananmen Square massacre turned everyone's favourite uncle into the 'Butcher of Běijīng'. It emphasised that, although Deng was a firm believer in economic development, he never once doubted the one-party system. He was adamant that the fifth modernisation – democracy – had no role to play in Communist China. As Mao sardonically noted, Deng was indeed a 'needle wrapped in cotton'.

Throughout his life Deng retained many connections to the South-West. Colleagues complained that his thick Sichuānese accent was almost incomprehensible. It was no coincidence that the first experiments in economic reform took place in Sichuān during the late 1970s.

In the three years before his death Deng made no public appearances, fuelling rumours that he had actually died months, if not years before. Even in death he was a pragmatic moderniser, donating his corneas and body to medical research – a spit in the eye of Confucian tradition. Unlike Mao, Deng did not want a mausoleum or open casket, requesting instead that his ashes be cast into the sea.

Bradley Mayhew

CHONGQING

Red Star Over Chóngqìng

In 1939, Edgar Snow arrived in Chóngqìng to find a city living in fear of Japanese raids. It was, he said:

...a place of moist heat, dirt and wide confusion, into which, between air raids, the imported central government...made an effort to introduce some technique of order and construction. Acres of buildings had been destroyed in the barbaric raids of May and June.

The Japanese preferred moonlit nights for their calls, when from their base in Hankow they could follow the silver banner of the Yangzi up to its confluence with the Jiālíng, which identified the capital in a way no blackout could obscure.

The city had no defending air force and only a few anti-aircraft guns... Spacious public shelters were being dug, but it was estimated that a third of the population still had no protection. Government officials, given advance warning, sped outside the city in their motor cars – cabinet ministers first, then vice-ministers, then minor bureaucrats.

The populace soon caught on; when they saw a string of official cars racing to the west, they dropped everything and ran. A mad scramble of rickshaws, carts, animals and humanity blew up the main streets like a great wind, carrying all before it.

a few sparse furnishings and photographs to see.

To get to Hóngyán village, take bus No 104 from its terminal on Beiqu Lu, just north of the Liberation Monument. The site is open daily 8am to 5.30pm and admission is Y6.

US–Chiang Kaishek Criminal Acts Exhibition Hall & SACO Prisons
Zhōngměi Hézuòsuǒ Jízhōngyíng Jiùzhǐ

In 1943, the USA and Chiang Kaishek signed a secret agreement setting up the Sino-American Cooperation Organisation (SACO) under which the USA helped to train and dispatch secret agents for the Kuomintang. As an extension of SACO, a number of prison camps were also built here. The chief of SACO was Tai Li, the notorious head of the Kuomintang military

secret service; the deputy chief was a US Navy officer, Commodore ME Miles.

The Kuomintang never recognised the Communist Party as a legal political entity, although in theory it recognised its army as allies in the struggle against the Japanese invaders. Civilian Communists remained subject to repressive laws and hundreds of Communists were kept captive as political prisoners by the Kuomintang in these prisons and others. According to the Communists, many were also executed.

Unfortunately, the site has Chinese captions only, making it fairly uninteresting for Western visitors. The exhibition hall has lots of photos on display; there are manacles and chains but nothing too ghoulish. The hall opens 8am to 7pm and admission is Y2.

To get there take bus No 215 or 217 just south of Zhongshan Sanlu, not far from Jiālíng Bridge. It's about a 45-minute ride. Make sure that the driver knows where you want to get off, as the place is not obvious. The SACO prisons are an hour's walk from the hall.

Alternatively, if you are keen to see these sights, there are tour buses leaving from the Chaotianmen Dock and train station areas. For a pricey Y60, the four-hour tour takes in both the hall and the prisons and throws in some other revolutionary sights as well.

Stillwell Museum
Located in the west of the city, this museum is rather unique in China as it focuses on the involvement of the US in WWII without putting it under a negative spotlight. The museum is housed in the former VIP guesthouse of the Kuomintang and residence of General Stillwell, who was commander of China-Burma-Indian theatre and chief of staff to Chiang Kaishek in 1942. On display are mostly USA-supplied photos, documents, articles and videos that may be of interest to American history buffs.

The museum is open 9am to 6pm (closed January and February). Entry costs Y5.

Parks
Chóngqìng's two temple parks are neglected by many visitors, but they are pleasant places

to while away an afternoon. At 345m, **Pípá Shān Park** (Pípá Shān Gōngyuán) marks the highest point on the Chóngqìng peninsula. The hill is supposedly shaped like the classical Chinese instrument, giving the park its name. Can't see it? Don't worry, others can't either and claim that the park was in fact named after the loquats that once covered the hill. (The Chinese word for loquat is a homonym of pípá.) The Hongxing Pavilion at the top of the park provides good views of Chóngqìng. The park is open 6am to 10pm. Admission is Y5, plus Y3 for the temple.

Élíng Park (Élíng Gōngyuán), at the neck of the peninsula, is more of a hike and not really worth a special trip. You can find the Liangjiang Pavilion here.

Along the Cháng Jiāng, just east of the bus station, is **Coral Park** (Shānhú Gōngyuán), opened in 1997. Designed as a theme park, inside are paths, palms and gardens. While it's not somewhere you can really commune with nature, it's a pleasant place to wander or wait for your bus. In summer, musical performances are hosted here. Admission to the park is a steep Y10.

Bridges
As you tour around Chóngqìng, it's hard to miss the enormous Jiālíng and Cháng bridges. The **Jiālíng Bridge**, which crosses the river north of central Chóngqìng, was built between 1963 and 1966. It is 150m long and 60m high and for 15 years was one of the few means of access to the rest of China. The **Cháng Bridge** was finished in 1981 and, in 1989, the **Shímén Bridge** over the Cháng Jiāng was completed.

Cable Car Trips
There are cable cars spanning the Jiālíng and Cháng rivers that carry you over precipitously stacked housing and polluting industrial estates for a bird's-eye view of the murky waters. The cost is Y1 each way and both cable cars run 6.30am to 9.30pm.

Chóngqìng Museum 博物馆
Chóngqìng Bówùguǎn
The dinosaur skeletons on display at this museum were unearthed between 1974 and 1977 at Zígòng, Yangchuan and elsewhere in Sìchuān province. The museum is at the foot of Pípá Shān Park. It's open 9am to 5pm and entry is Y10, plus an extra Y10 for the dinosaur exhibits.

Northern Hot Springs 北温泉公园
Běi Wēnquán Gōngyuán
Fifty-five kilometres north-east of the city, at the foot of Jinyun Shān and overlooking the Jiālíng Jiāng, the Northern Hot Springs are in a large park that is also the site of a 5th-century Buddhist temple.

The springs have an Olympic-size swimming pool where you can bathe to an audience. There are also private rooms with hot baths – big tubs where the water comes up to your neck if you sit and up to your waist if you stand. Water temperature averages around 32°C. There are also gardens and a water-slide that should be open by the time you read this. Swimsuits can be hired here – they're coloured red, symbolising happiness.

To get to the springs take bus No 306 from the Liberation Monument.

There's another group of springs 20km south of Chóngqìng, with hotter waters, that may be quieter than the northern springs.

Places to Stay – Budget
If you're thinking of splurging, Chóngqìng is the place to do it as there is next to nothing in the way of budget accommodation here.

You will undoubtedly be met by touts at the bus/train station. They will certainly insist that foreign friends can stay at their cheap hotel (figure Y40 for the cheapest), but remember that these folks only get paid to bring you there and are often clueless about the rules. The hotel may well turn you away anyway but you might not mind as many are grotty and unsafe.

The only dorms in the central part of the city are the seven-bed rooms at the *Huìxiānlóu Bīnguǎn* (☎ 384 5101) close to the Liberation Monument, where a bed will set you back Y50. This place is well located and the remodelled, air-conditioned dorms are quite good. From the train station, walk up to Zhongshan Lu and take bus No 405 to the Liberation Monument.

A more pleasant option is *Chóngqìng Shípǐn Dàshà* (☎ 384 7300, 72 Shaanxi Lu) near the Chaotianmen Dock. This place has pleasant, clean doubles with bathroom and air-con for Y150 and triples for Y180. There are also 'deluxe' doubles for Y200. You can book boat and train tickets here.

Places to Stay – Mid-Range

In the centre of town is the *Peace Hotel* (Hèpíng Bīnguǎn; ☎ 384 7800), with singles/doubles in refurbished, comfortable rooms for Y158/210.

A remodelled *mosque* (☎ 374 0018) at the southern edge of town has views of the river below. While the rooms are large they are somewhat musty and frayed. Doubles start at Y190.

Next to the bus station is the *Fùyuàn Bīnguǎn* (☎ 389 3994, 38 Caiyuan Ba), which has standard twins/triples for Y160/180. These are inevitably full and you'll be shown deluxe twins for Y220 instead. While this place is quite a haul out of town, it's convenient for early morning buses and trains.

On the edge of Rénmín Park, *Rénmín Bīnguǎn* (☎ 385 1421, fax 385 2076) appears from the outside to be a palace, with a design that seems inspired by the Temple of Heaven and the Forbidden City in Běijīng. Constructed in 1953, the hotel comprises three wings (north, south and east) that are separated by an enormous 65m-high circular concert hall that seats 4000 people. Unfortunately this grandeur doesn't extend to the rooms inside, considering the price of a standard room (Y600 to Y1700). Nevertheless, competition is steep in the big city and you may land a good mid-range deal here, with a double for around Y200. From the train station, the best way to get to the hotel is to head up to Zhongshan Lu and catch bus No 401 or 405 to the traffic circle and walk east down Renmin Lu.

Places to Stay – Top End

There is definitely no shortage of top-end hotels in Chóngqìng. During the off-season it's worth shopping around as you can find some excellent deals.

The *Chung King Hotel* (Chóngqìng Fàndiàn; ☎ 384 9301, fax 384 3085) is a three-star joint-venture operation on Xinhua Lu near the Chaotianmen Dock area. Singles/doubles cost Y198/268 and facilities include a small gift shop (with a few English titles), foreign exchange, post and telecommunications, taxi and clinic. The hotel has its own shuttle bus to and from the train station and the airport.

The *Milky Way Hotel* (Yínhéda Bīnguǎn; ☎ 380 8585, 49 Datong Lu) has comfortable, like-new doubles for Y298. Down the street the *Chóngqìng Guesthouse* (Chóngqìng Bīnguǎn; ☎ 384 5888), on Minsheng Lu, has transformed itself into a four-star luxury hotel. Comfortable singles/doubles in the old wing are Y228/260, while rooms in the new VIP wing start at Y435, breakfast included. Check here for bargains. The hotel has all amenities including a pool.

Next to the Liberation Monument, the *Yúdū Jiǔdiàn* boasts a good location, with rooms from Y280.

Across the street, the brand-new *Harbour Plaza* (Chǒngxìhǎiyì Jiǔdiàn; ☎ 370 0888, W www.harbour-plaza.com/hpcq) has five-star facilities. Rooms are posted at Y1330, however, if you're lucky you may get these for as little as Y465. Not far away, the flashy *Marriott Hotel* (Wànháo Jiǔdiàn; ☎ 388 8888) has similar service, rates and deals.

Places to Eat

The central business district, in the eastern section of the city near the docks, abounds with small restaurants and street vendors. For tasty noodles and *baozi*, check out Xinhua Lu and Shaanxi Lu towards Chaotianmen Dock. There are some good *night markets* behind the Huìxiānlóu Bīnguǎn, in the vicinity of Luóhàn Sì and near the Yúdū Bīnguǎn.

Chóngqìng's number-one speciality is *huǒguō*, or hotpot. While it's usually cheap, it's a good idea to check prices as you go along. Although hotpot can be found wherever there are street vendors or small restaurants, *Wuyi Lu* has the greatest variety and is locally known as *huǒguō jiē*, or 'hotpot street'. Wuyi Lu runs off Minzu Lu, parallel to Xinhua Lu, a couple of blocks away from the Huìxiānlóu and Chung King hotels. Bayi Lu is also a great street for snack hunting.

Zourong Lu is a good street for larger, sit-down restaurants when you've got a group and feel like feasting on Sìchuānese main courses. Among them is the well-known *Yízhīshí Cāntīng*, which serves Sìchuān-style pastries in the morning and local specialities like tea-smoked duck and dry-stewed fish at lunch and dinner. The 2nd floor has full-course meals; go up to the 3rd floor and Y25 will buy you a sampler course of famous Chóngqìng snacks. Draught beer and special 'eight-treasure tea' *(bābǎochá)* do a fine job of washing it all down.

The area around Huìxiānlóu Bīnguǎn is teeming with restaurants. Try the *Yángròu Guǎn (Lamb Restaurant)* up the road from the hotel. The dishes here are spicy, but the kebabs aren't too punishing on the tongue.

On Wusi Lu is *California Beef Noodles*, one of seemingly dozens of Chinese restaurants employing the name 'Califor-nia' for no apparent reason. It's pretty good, but the small, hole-in-the-wall restaurants along this street serve up more interesting noodles in clay pots.

At the southern end of Miquan Lu, *Ziyi Coffee House (Zīyìxī Cāntīng)* has excellent pizzas, soups and pasta at reasonable prices. Just down the street, the mosque runs a fairly busy *Muslim restaurant*.

Across from the Harbour Plaza, *Whale World (Lánjīngwān)* has a pan-Asian menu and a relaxed atmosphere; it's open 9am until 1am. The Harbour Plaza itself has a number of *restaurants* with a Western buffet breakfast/dinner for Y60/128.

Entertainment
Coffee & Tea Houses The *Old Tree Café (Lǎosu Kāfēi)* has a long menu of freshly ground coffee.

Down the street is the beautiful *Lǎojiēshí Bātīlǒu*, with wooden and bamboo decor and old teapots, cups and photos on display. There's lots of tea here although it's fairly pricey – around Y25 for a bottomless cup.

Noah's Ark (Nuòyáfāngzhōu), with its four cosy floors, has coffee, tea, popcorn, ice-cream and an international collection of beer.

Across from the Chongqing Guesthouse, the keen staff at *Sophie's Coffee House (Sūfēiyà)* serve coffees, teas and snacks.

Finally, the Harbour Plaza has a *coffee-house/bar* on its ground floor with live Singaporean music in the evenings.

Bars Bars come and go with great frequency in Chóngqìng. At the time of writing, the *Cool Bar* served inexpensive beer near the Monument in something akin to a Western bar. Your best bet is to ask around.

Getting There & Away
Air Chóngqìng's new Jiangbei airport is 25km north of the city. You can buy airline tickets at the Civil Aviation Administration of China (CAAC) office (☎ 360 3144) on Zhongshan Sanlu, in the west of the city. China Southwest Airlines (☎ 785 3191) has an office a couple of doors down and Drag-onair (☎ 6280 3380) has an office at the Yangzi Chóngqìng Holiday Inn, in the south of the city. You can also book flights at the Chung King Hotel and in numerous ticket offices around the Liberation Monument.

Connections within the South-West include Chéngdū (Y220, daily), Guìlín (Y670, daily), Guìyáng (Y420, Monday, Wednesday, Saturday), Kūnmíng (Y660, daily) and Nánníng (Y700, daily). Flights to other major cities include Běijīng (Y1400, daily), Guǎngzhōu (Y1080, daily), Lhasa (Y1300, Sunday), Shànghǎi (Y1340, daily), Ürümqi (Y1610, Wednesday and Saturday), Wǔhàn (Y720, daily) and Xī'ān (Y530, daily).

China Southwest and Dragonair also have flights to Hong Kong (Y2320, daily except Wednesday), Bangkok (Y2860, Friday) and Nagoya in Japan (Y3600, Tuesday and Friday).

Bus Transport between Chóngqìng, Chéngdū and Lèshān is much faster with the completion of the new expressways.

Buses from Chóngqìng depart from the two-storey long-distance bus terminal next to the train station. With two ticket halls, two waiting halls and dozens of gates, the station can process 800 to 1000 buses daily.

To Chéngdū, there are buses running from 6.30am to 9.30pm (Y112, four hours). For Dàzú, most buses are of the micro variety, departing from 6am to 6pm (Y80, three hours). To Lèshān buses depart from 6.15am to 6pm (Y80) and to Zìgòng from 6.15am to 7.30pm (Y54).

You can also catch buses to Chéngdū (the speedy, plush air-con type) in the mornings from in front of Chaotianmen Dock.

Train While you're much better off taking the bus to Chéngdū than the morning train (Y64 hard seat, 6.37am), which takes 11 hours, it might be worth taking the overnight train at 11.17pm (Y83 hard sleeper) to save a night's pricey accommodation in Chóngqìng.

There are a couple of trains a day that stop at Dàzú, however the station is 30km from Dàzú town. The train is far more inconvenient and time-consuming than the buses that speed down the expressway.

Trains to Shànghǎi also take in Guìyáng, before making a long haul through the sticks to Hángzhōu and on to the final destination. A daily train departs Chóngqìng at 6.12pm (Y475 hard sleeper, 43 hours). There is another train to Guìyáng at 8.34pm (Y103 hard sleeper, 10 hours).

There are daily trains to Kūnmíng at 9.19am and 2.39pm (Y200 hard sleeper, 23 hours). These trains pass through Chéngdū and Pānzhīhūa (for Lìjiāng or Dàlǐ).

There are three trains daily to Guǎngzhōu (40 hours) and two trains each day to Běijīng (30 hours). Daily trains also depart for Xī'ān (28 hours) and Zhèngzhōu (25 hours).

Boat It certainly seems that zillions of boats make the run from Chóngqìng down the Cháng Jiāng to Wǔhàn. The ride is a popular tourist trip, a good way of getting away from the trains and an excellent way to get to Wǔhàn. Consider doing it before the Chinese government finishes its massive dam project and floods the Three Gorges (see 'The Dammed Yangzi' boxed text later in this chapter. For details, see the following section 'Down the Cháng Jiāng (Yangzi River): Chóngqìng to Wǔhàn' later in this chapter.

Travelling upriver by boat has not been a viable option since the government put all of its money behind the expressway and pulled it out of the ferry business. You may find private boats selling tickets for Yíbīn or Lèshān in the summer, however it's considered by locals to be a risky ride.

Getting Around

To/From the Airport CAAC runs shuttle buses between the airport and the ticket office, timed to coincide with flights. Buses to the airport leave 2½ hours before scheduled flight times (Y15).

Bus Buses in Chóngqìng can be tediously slow, and since there are no bicycles they're even more crowded than in other Chinese cities. Useful routes include: No 401, which runs between the Chaotianmen Dock and the intersection of Renmin Lu and Zhongshan Lu, near the CAAC office; No 405, running up Zhongshan Lu up to the Liberation Monument; and No 102, which connects the train station and Chaotianmen Dock.

There are also minibuses running between the dock and the train station for Y1.

Taxi Nowadays, as in most other Chinese cities, flagging down a taxi is no problem. Flag fall is Y6, although can be slightly higher depending on the size of the car. Expect to pay Y10 to Y15 from the city centre to the bus station.

DÀZÚ 大足县

The grotto art of Dàzú county, 160km north-west of Chóngqìng, is rated alongside China's other great Buddhist cave sculptures at Dūnhuáng, Luòyáng and Dàtóng.

Historical records for Dàzú are sketchy. The cliff carvings and statues (with Buddhist, Taoist and Confucian influences) amount to thousands of pieces, large and small, scattered over the county in some 40-odd places. The main groupings are at Běi Shān (North Hill) and the more interesting Bǎodǐng. They date from the Tang dynasty (9th century) to the Song (13th century).

The town of Dàzú is small and relatively unhurried. Despite the tour buses that visit the grottoes in the summer, the town itself sees few tourists, especially of the foreign type.

Běi Shān 北山

According to inscriptions, the Běi Shān site was originally a military camp, with the earliest carvings commissioned by a general. The dark niches hold small statues, many in poor condition; only one or two really stand out.

Niche No 136 depicts Puxian, the patron saint (male) of Éméi Shān, riding a white elephant. The same niche has the androgynous Sun and Moon Guanyin. Niche 155 has the Peacock King.

Běi Shān is about a 30-minute hike from Dàzú town – aim straight for the pagoda visible from the bus station. From the top of the hill there are good overall views. There's a Y5 entry fee for the park and a further Y40 entry fee for the sculptures. The park is open 8am to 5pm.

Bǎodǐng Shān 宝顶山

Fifteen kilometres north-east of Dàzú town, the Bǎodǐng sculptures are definitely more interesting than those at Běi Shān. It is believed the sculptures were completed over 70 years, between AD 1179 and 1249. It's easy to spend a few hours wandering around this area.

The founding work is attributed to Zhao Zhifeng, a monk from an obscure Yoga sect of Tantric Buddhism. A monastery with nice woodwork and throngs of pilgrims sits atop a hill; on the lower section of the hill is a 125m horseshoe-shaped cliff sculptured with coloured figures, some of them up to 8m high.

The centrepiece is a 31m-long, 5m-high reclining Buddha, depicted in the state of entering nirvana, the torso sunk into the cliff face. Next to the Buddha there is a mesmerising, gold Avalokitesvara (Goddess of Mercy) with 1007 arms, each with an eye, the symbol of wisdom.

Statues surrounding the rest of the horseshoe vary considerably: Buddhist preachers and sages, historical figures, realistic scenes (on the rear of a postcard one is described as 'Pastureland – Cowboy at Rest') and

delicate sculptures a few centimetres high. Some of them have been eroded by wind and rain, some have lost layers of paint, but overall there is a remarkable survival rate. Fanatical Red Guards did descend on the Dàzú area, bent on defacing the sculptures, but were stopped – so the story goes – by an urgent order from Zhou Enlai.

Bǎodǐng differs from other grottoes in that it was based on a preconceived plan that incorporated some of the area's natural features – a sculpture next to the reclining Buddha, for example, makes use of an underground spring.

Admission into Bǎodǐng is Y50 or Y80 for a combined ticket to Bǎodǐng and Běi Shān. The sites are open 8am to 5pm.

Minibuses to Bǎodǐng leave the Dàzú bus station every 30 minutes or so (or as soon as they fill up) throughout the day, though they start to thin out by about 4pm, with the last one at 6pm. The fare is Y2, however if you look foreign you'll be charged Y5. To avoid paying this surcharge (which really *isn't* a requirement, no matter what the ticket seller tells you), have the correct change ready and hand it over before they have time to tell you the price. The trip takes anywhere from 30 to 45 minutes. For a much quicker ride, hop on the back of a motorcycle taxi, which you can bargain down to Y15.

As you pass by in the bus, keep an eye on the cliff faces for solo sculptures.

Places to Stay & Eat

The local Public Security Bureau (PSB) has done a good job of swaying most hotels into refusing foreigners, leaving you with only two options in Dàzú, neither of which are particularly cheap.

The *Běishān Bīnguǎn*, near the base of Běi Shān, is musty, unkempt and horrendously overpriced at Y180 for a room. The only real reason to come here is to make the Dàzú Bīnguǎn seem like that much more of a deal

The *Dàzú Bīnguǎn* has doubles for Y180 that are clean and comfortable with good service and a Chinese breakfast included. The hotel also has new, fancier doubles with all amenities from Y489. To find the hotel, turn left out of the bus station, cross over the bridge and take the road branching to the right. This will bring you to one of the hotel's two main gates. This one may be locked, but don't panic; walk around the left side to the back entrance.

Finding a bite to eat in Dàzú is no problem. Shizi Jie (the first right up from the roundabout) comes alive at night with dozens of *street stalls* serving noodles, dumplings, hotpot and wok-fried dishes. If you head straight up the main road from the roundabout, you'll come to a number of *restaurants* serving fresh noodles for Y2 a bowl.

Getting There & Away

Bus There are four departures for Chéngdū from Dàzú between 6.30am and 9.30am (Y51, four hours). There are also frequent departures to Chóngqìng between 6.30am and 5.30pm (Y29).

From Chóngqìng, buses leave the main bus terminal for Dàzú between 7am and 7pm. Regular morning buses leave Chéngdū's north bus station for Dàzú.

Train Travelling to Dàzú by train is impractical and time-consuming. You're better off taking a bus down the new expressways.

To get to Dàzú by train, you need to get off the Chéngdū-Chóngqìng railway line at Yóutíngpù (five hours from Chóngqìng, seven hours from Chéngdū), which is the nearest stop to Dàzú. Despite the fact that the town is around 30km from Dàzú, train timetables refer to it as Dàzú station. There are frequent minibuses running from the train station to Dàzú.

Down the Yangzi River: Chóngqìng to Wǔhàn

The dramatic scenery and rushing waters of China's greatest river, called Cháng Jiāng by the Chinese, has been inspirational to many of China's painters and poets. This is little consolation for those negotiating its twists and turns. Since early navigation of the Cháng Jiāng, a journey along this dangerous stretch of water has been sheer hard work. A large boat pushing upstream often needed hundreds of coolies (trackers), who lined the riverbanks and hauled the boat with long ropes against the surging waters. Even today smaller boats are pulled up the river by their crews. For more on the Cháng Jiāng see the boxed text 'The Long River' in the Facts about South-West China chapter.

Between the towns of Fèngjié in Sìchuān and Yíchāng in Húběi lie three great gorges (*sānxiá*), regarded as one of the great scenic attractions of China. At least for now. When the Three Gorges Dam is completed in 2009, the famous Three Gorges will be completely submerged and over 1.5 million people will be displaced. (See boxed text 'The Damned Yangzi' later in this chapter.) If anything, this has made the sight even more popular and boats run continuously, filled with tourists wanting to see it while they still can.

Unfortunately, many people who do take the steamer ride from Chóngqìng to Wǔhàn find the trip a bit dull, perhaps due to high expectations. The scenery is pleasant but don't expect to be dwarfed by mile-high cliffs.

The ride downriver from Chóngqìng to Wǔhàn takes two nights and the better part of three days (upriver the ride takes five days). One possibility is to take the boat as far as Yíchāng, which will let you see the Three Gorges and the huge Gězhōu Dam, the most scenic parts.

You may also be able to shave one day off the trip by taking a hydrofoil from Chóngqìng to Wànxiàn, where you can usually hook up with another ferry for the Three Gorges section. How much time you save depends on what boats are in Wànxiàn when you arrive, when they're leaving and whether there are any empty berths.

From Yíchāng you can take direct trains to Běijīng, Wǔhàn and Xī'ān. Trains also run south to Huáihuà, where you can connect with trains to Chángshā, Guǎngzhōu, Guìlín or Liǔzhōu. If you continue the boat ride you can get off at Yuèyáng and take the train to Guǎngzhōu, or you can carry on to Wǔhàn.

There are also a few boats that go beyond Wǔhàn. If you change at Wǔhàn, you can connect with a boat travelling all the way to Shànghǎi, which is 2400km downriver – a week's journey.

Tickets

You can buy tickets for the boats from China International Travel Service (CITS) in Chóngqìng, from the booking office at the Chaotianmen Dock terminal building or from private operators who hover around the terminal. While it's good to book two or three days ahead of your intended departure, increases in the number of Cháng Jiāng cruise operators means that tickets for same- or next-day travel, especially outside of the autumn tourist season, are readily available.

CITS adds a service charge of Y15 to the price of the tickets. If you do book tickets with CITS, make sure you're not being put on one of the luxury liners reserved solely for foreigners: the price could inflict mortal damage on your cash reserves.

The main booking office at Chaotianmen Dock is open daily 6am to 11pm. Outside this main hall are lots of small agencies that also sell boat tickets – often marked-up. It's worth trying them if the main office doesn't have tickets for the day you want. Tickets for foreigners used to carry a 50% surcharge. This is no longer the case.

Once you've bought your ticket and boarded, a steward will exchange your ticket for a numbered, colour-coded tag that denotes your bed assignment. Hang onto the tag, since it must be exchanged for your ticket at the end of the voyage – without it they may not let you off the boat.

Classes

In a sign of the changing times in what was once egalitarian China, some boats now boast 1st-class cabins. These come with two beds, bathrooms, television and air-con.

Second-class cabins have two to four berths, with soft beds, a small desk and chair and a washbasin. Showers and toilets are private cubicles shared by the passengers. Third class usually has from six to 12 beds.

Fourth class has eight to 12, but older vessels can have more than 20 beds. Fifth class can be anything from 15 beds to deck-space. Toilets and showers are communal, though you should be able to use the toilets and showers in 2nd class. If they don't let you into the 2nd-class area then have a look around the boat; some boats have toilet cubicles with doors and partitions on the lower deck.

Lounges with soft seating and karaoke can normally be found adjacent to the 2nd-class cabins or on the top deck.

Some boats also have a couple of large cabins the entire width of the boat that accommodate about 40 people on triple-tiered bunks. Foreigners are not often given tickets for this class. If you get one, remember that this part of China is very cold in winter and very hot in summer. Petty thieves have also been reported in the dorms, so keep valuable items safe – particularly at night.

In addition to the Chinese tour boats described here, there are several 'foreigner only' vessels plying the waters of the Cháng Jiāng. These are mostly reserved for large tour groups that can afford the hundreds of US dollars that these trips cost. CITS and some of the independent booking agents around the Chaotianmen Dock area can arrange tickets for these luxury liners.

destination	2nd class (Y)	3rd class (Y)	4th class (Y)
Yíchāng	464	218	155
Wǔhàn (Hankou)	684	320	229
Nánjīng	920	429	305
Shànghǎi	1031	480	339

Fares It's advisable that you shop around. Prices will be higher if you book through CITS or one of the independent operators around the dock area, though it's possible to bargain with the private touts if there are several of you.

Note that there are also 1st and 5th classes; the former most travellers won't go for (with 100% price mark-up over 2nd class) and the latter is dirt-cheap but not always easy to get.

The Damned Yangzi

The Three Gorges Dam is China's biggest engineering project since the construction of the Great Wall. When completed in 2009, it will back the Cháng Jiāng up for 550km, flood an area the size of Singapore and wash away the homes of up to two million people. It will rank as the world's largest dam – an epic show of Communist might, definitive proof of man's dominance of capricious nature and the 21st-century symbol of a new superpower.

A cherished vision since the early years of Republican China, the dam proposal was finally given government go-ahead in April 1992, despite having been originally proposed by Sun Yatsen in 1919. It has enjoyed the staunch support over the years of other political heavyweights such as Mao Zedong and, most recently, Premier Li Peng, himself a Moscow-trained engineer.

The colossal project involves the construction of a 2km-wide, 185m-high dam wall across the Cháng Jiāng at Sandouping, 38km upstream from the existing Gezhou Dam. The Cháng Jiāng has already been blocked and its water diverted; images of the final few boulders filling in the plug were broadcast simultaneously on all of China's TV channels in November 1997. Now that the riverbed is dry, 60,000 workers work around the clock on pouring the concrete for the main dam, construction of which will continue until 2003 when water levels are expected to rise significantly. River traffic currently travels along a diversion canal through a temporary lock.

The Three Gorges Dam is a cornerstone of government efforts to channel economic growth from the dynamic coastal provinces into the more backward western regions, somehow transforming hinterland into heartland. The Cháng Jiāng is likened by enthusiastic officials to a dragon with its head in Shanghai and its tail in Chóngqìng, or to a crossbow shooting Shanghai's economic energy up into Chóngqìng and beyond. In between the two will be the 220-million-people-strong Yangzi Economic Region, stretched over nine provinces. The dam's hydroelectric production – the equivalent of 18 nuclear power plants and reckoned to equal almost one-fifth of China's current generating capacity – is intended to power this continuing industrialisation and relieve the region's environmentally damaging dependency on coal and other fossil fuels.

The dam will also improve navigation on the Cháng Jiāng, which already transports 70% of the entire country's shipping. Although passing the dam itself will be an inconvenience (the dam will have five locks, raising boats over 100m) the navigability of the upper Cháng Jiāng will be drastically improved by the widening of shipping lanes and the creation of a constant water level within the new lake.

At least as important will be the dam's role in flood control. The Cháng Jiāng is prone to repeated flooding (the most recent in 1998), often causing great loss of life. Catastrophic floods have been recorded for the past millennium and in the past 100 years alone, more than one million lives have been claimed by them.

However, the massive scale of the Three Gorges Dam project has caused disquiet among environmentalists and economists, arousing some of the most outspoken criticism of government policy in China since 1989. The official debate by the National Congress recorded the largest number of negative votes ever recorded against government policy. Free discussion has hardly been encouraged: Dai Qing's outspoken book *Yangzi! Yangzi!* earned her a 10-month spell in prison.

Construction of the dam is expensive, and the initial estimates of US$20 to US$30 billion have now risen to as high as US$70 billion. The dam is a magnet for graft: In 2000 a local government official in Chóngqìng was executed for taking over US$1 million in bribes relating to the dam and

Prices for upper and lower desks can also differ: quoted earlier are upper-deck prices but you may find cheaper beds on the lower deck.

Food

You'll usually be able to find a couple of restaurants on the boat. Those on the lower decks cater for the masses and can be terrible.

The Damned Yangzi

another 96 officials were arrested. Economists both in China and abroad have warned that it may be imprudent for the government to concentrate so much investment into one single project and that epic dam constructions are simply an anachronism. The World Bank has refused to back the project. The US government has advised American companies not to get involved. Nevertheless, given the political and economic investment to date, work is most likely too far along to be halted.

The social implications of the dam are profound indeed. An estimated 1.5 million people living in inundated areas will need to be relocated and, more importantly, given a new livelihood. Compensation packages range from US$2000 to US$4000 and Chóngqìng municipality alone has to resettle over one million people, the price it must pay for economic clout. That is, if the money is still there: Government auditors estimate that US$52 million of resettlement funds is now unaccounted for, with other sources quoting figures as high as US$600 million.

Perhaps the greatest fears relate to the dam's environmental impact. Friends of the Earth has described the dam as 'the most socially and environmentally destructive dam in history'. It is thought that as the river slows so will its ability to oxygenate. The untreated waste that pours into the river from over 40 towns and 400 factories, as well as the toxic materials and pollutants from the inundated industrial sites, could well create another world record for the dam: a 480km-long septic tank – the largest toilet in the world. The slowing of the river will also lead to more silt deposits, which in turn could block the turbines of the dam or silt up Chóngqìng's port. The dam will also disrupt the environments of such endangered species as the Yangzi River dolphin, Chinese sturgeon and Siberian crane. Some say that the massive waters could even induce a localised earthquake. The same experts suggest that a series of smaller dams further downstream would provide a far more effective and less damaging system of flood control.

The rising waters will cover countless cultural artefacts at over 8000 important archaeological sites in the Cháng Jiāng basin, many of which offer clues to China's early political development that have not yet been properly studied. Despite an ambitious plan of relocation and preservation, time is running out and archaeologists are racing smugglers to collect as much of the region's cultural heritage as time allows.

Some destruction of the natural and scenic splendour of the Three Gorges is certain, though how the dam will affect Cháng Jiāng tourism is uncertain. Boat trips of the Three Gorges are running overtime as local and foreign tourists rush to see one of China's most famous sights before the concrete slabs begin to spell the demise of a great river.

Fears about the project were heightened when information was released about two dams that collapsed in Hénán province in 1975. After 20 years as a state secret, it is now apparent that as many as 230,000 people died in the catastrophe. If a similar accident was to happen on the Cháng Jiāng, the population of nearby Yíchāng would be dead within an hour.

Planners insist that the Three Gorges Dam will be constructed according to safety regulations that make such disasters impossible. Still, the collapse of the walls holding back the world's largest storage reservoir, in one of the world's most densely populated pieces of real estate, is a thought that must keep even the most gung-ho supporters of the project awake at night.

Check Ⓦ www.coxnews.com/washington/GORGES.HTM for more information on the progress of the dam.

Bradley Mayhew

If there's a restaurant on the upper deck, chances are it's a bit better. Prices seem to vary from boat to boat. It's a good idea to bring some of your own food with you.

When the boat stops at a town for any length of time, passengers may disembark and eat at one of the little restaurants near the pier.

The Route

Boats stop frequently during the cruise to visit cities, towns and a slew of tourist sights. What you will see during daylight hours depends on what time your boat sets sail from Chóngqìng. Departure times can change from season to season, depending on the river level, so check on the signboards at the main ticket hall to be sure. Note that on the signboard, Wǔhàn is listed as Hankou, since this is the district of Wǔhàn where the boat docks.

The afternoon and evening boats are more popular and plentiful, as they stop at more sights, spending the first night docked at Fēngdū, then continuing on to tie up for the second night in Fèngjiē. The following morning they enter the Three Gorges, and then proceed to Yíchāng and Wǔhàn.

If you do get a morning departure your trip will be shorter and you may be able to sleep on the boat the night before for a nominal charge (Y25 to Y35). Morning boats usually end their first day at Wànxiàn, leave before dawn the following day and pass through the Three Gorges around midday or later, before heading to Yíchāng and Wǔhàn.

Almost all boats stop between the first and second gorge for six hours for tours of the 'Little Three Gorges' (see later Wànxiàn to Yíchāng). For travellers who want to avoid this, there are some boats that pass directly through, but you'll have to ask around for these.

Chóngqìng to Wànxiàn

For the first few hours the river is lined with factories. This eventually gives way to some pretty, green, terraced countryside with the occasional small town.

One of the first stops is usually the town of Fúlíng. The town overlooks the mouth of the Wū Hé, which flows from Guìzhōu in the south and controls the river traffic between Guìzhōu and eastern Sìchuān.

Near Fúlíng, in the middle of the Cháng Jiāng, is a huge rock called Baihe Ridge. On one side of the rock are three carvings known as 'stone fish' that date back to ancient times and are thought to have served as watermarks – the rock can be seen only

when the river is at its very lowest. In addition to the carvings, there are many inscriptions describing the culture, art and technology of these ancient times.

The next major settlement is Fēngdū. Nearby Pingdu Shān is said to be the abode of devils. The story goes that during the Han dynasty two men, Yin Changsheng and Wang Fangping, lived on the mountain, and when their family names were joined together they were taken to be that of Yinwang, the king of hell.

Numerous temples containing sculptures of demons and devils have been built on the mountain since the Tang dynasty, with heartening names like 'Between the Living and the Dead', 'Bridge of Helplessness' and 'Palace of the King of Hell'. You'll also see the huge 'Ghost King', some 138m high and 217m wide. While many people find it all a bit too much – especially the Y55 admission fee – it's hard not to be impressed as you walk up the King's 81m-long tongue. All of this is due to be submerged; watch for the white cliffside markers that show how high the water is expected to rise.

The boat then passes through Zhōngxiàn county. North-east of the county seat of Zhōngzhōu is the Qian Jinggou site, where primitive stone artefacts, including axes, hoes and stone weights (for fishing nets), were unearthed.

Soon after comes the Shíbǎozhai (Stone Treasure Stronghold) on the northern bank of the river. Shíbǎozhai is a 30m-high rock that is supposed to look something like a stone seal. During the early years of Emperor Qianlong's reign (1736–97), an impressive red wooden temple, the Lanruodian, shaped like a pagoda and 11 storeys high, was built on the rock. It houses a statue of Buddha and inscriptions that commemorate its construction.

Next is the large town of Wànxiàn, where most morning boats tie up for the night. Wànxiàn is the transport and communications hub along the river between eastern Sìchuān and western Húběi and has traditionally been known as the gateway to Sìchuān. It was opened to foreign trade in 1917. Today it's a neat, hilly town and a

CHÓNGQÌNG TO YÍCHĀNG 重庆至宜昌

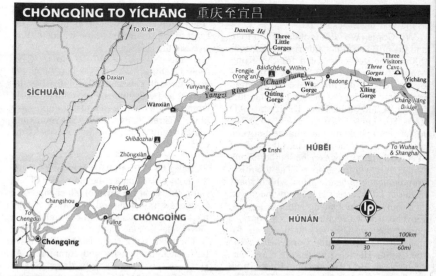

great place to wander around for a few hours while the boat is in port. There's a pleasant park around the tower in the centre of town. A long flight of steps leads from the pier up the riverbank to a bustling night market where you can get something to eat or buy very cheap wickerwork baskets, chairs and stools.

Wànxiàn to Yíchāng Boats overnighting at Wànxiàn generally depart before dawn. Before entering the gorges, they pass by (and may stop at) the town of **Fèngjiē** (Yong'an). This ancient town was the capital of the state of Kui during the Spring, Autumn and Warring States Periods from 722 to 221 BC.

The town overlooks the Qútáng Gorge, the first of the three Cháng Jiāng gorges. Just east of Fèngjiē, outside **Báidìchéng**, is the remains of stone piles that can be seen when the water is low. These piles were erected during the Stone and Bronze ages, possibly for commemorative and sacrificial purposes.

At the entrance to the Qútáng Gorge, Báidìchéng, or White King Town, is on the river's northern bank. The story goes that an official proclaimed himself king during the Western Han dynasty, and moved his capi-

tal to this town. A well was discovered that emitted a fragrant white vapour; this struck him as such an auspicious omen that he renamed himself the White King and his capital 'White King Town'.

The spectacular **Three Gorges** (Qútáng, Wū and Xīlíng) start just after Fèngjiē and end near Yíchāng, a stretch of about 200km. The gorges vary in size from 300m at their widest to less than 100m at their narrowest. The seasonal difference in water level can be as much as 50m.

Qútáng Gorge (Qūtáng Xiá) is the smallest and shortest gorge (only 8km long), though the water flows most rapidly here. The Song-dynasty poet Su Dongpo described it as 'one thousand seas poured into one cup'. High on the north bank, at a place called Feng Xiá (Bellows Gorge), are a series of crevices. There is said to have been an ancient tribe in this area whose custom was to place the coffins of their dead in high mountain caves, like the Bo people in southern Sìchuān (see the boxed text in the Around Yíbīn section of the Sìchuān chapter). Nine coffins were discovered in these crevices, some containing bronze swords, armour and other artefacts, but they are believed to date back only as far as the Warring States Period.

Wū Gorge (Wū Xiá) is about 40km long and the cliffs on either side rise to just over 900m. The gorge is noted for the Kong Ming tablet, a large slab of rock at the foot of the Peak of the Immortals. Kong Ming was prime minister of the state of Shu during the period of the Three Kingdoms (AD 220–280). On the tablet is a description of his stance upholding the alliance between the states of Shu and Wu against the state of Wei. **Badong** is a town on the southern bank of the river within the gorge. The town is a communications centre from which roads span out into western Húběi province.

In between the Qútáng and Wū gorges, most boats will stop for five to six hours so passengers can shift to smaller boats for tours of the **Little Three Gorges**. Flanking the Daning Hé, these gorges are much narrower than their larger counterparts and, some travellers say, more dramatic. The tour usually costs about Y60 – a foreigner's surcharge may still exist. Though some travellers have complained of the cost, many enjoy the chance to get out and view the rock formations up close.

On the way to the Little Three Gorges the boats usually stop at several gratuitous tourist traps, most of which are not worth the entry fee. For example, one stop promises views of a mysterious mountain cave coffin, which turns out to mean a brief look through a pair of binoculars.

Xīlíng Gorge (Xīlíng Xiá) is the longest of the Three Gorges at 80km. At the end of the gorge everyone crowds out onto the deck to watch the boat pass through the locks of the huge Gězhōu Dam.

The next stop is the industrial town of **Yíchāng**. From here you can take a train to Xiāngfán and points north, east and west, or to Huáihuà, where you can catch trains to southern destinations. Yíchāng is regarded as the gateway to the upper Cháng Jiāng. Once a walled city, it dates back at least as far as the Sui dynasty. The town was opened to foreign trade in 1877 by a treaty

between Britain and China, and a foreign concession area was set up along the riverfront to the south-east of the walled city.

Near the Yíchāng train station you can take bus No 10 to **White Horse Cave** (Báimǎ Dòng), where you can boat and walk through caverns with impressive stalactites and stalagmites. Five minutes' walk from the other end is an equally impressive place – **Three Visitors Cave** (Sānyǒu Dòng) – along with a cliff trail that overlooks the Cháng Jiāng.

Yíchāng to Wǔhàn After leaving Yíchāng, the boat passes under the immense **Cháng Jiāng Bridge** at the town of Zhichéng. The bridge is 1700m long and supports a double-track train with roads for trucks and cars on either side. It came into operation in 1971.

The next major town is **Shāshì**, a town built on light-industry and commerce. As early as the Tang dynasty dates, Shāshì was a trading centre of some importance, enjoying great prosperity during the Taiping Rebellion when trade lower down the Cháng Jiāng was largely at a standstill. The town was opened up to foreign trade in 1896 by the Treaty of Shimonoseki signed between China and Japan. Though an area outside the town was assigned as a Japanese concession, it was never developed. About 7.5km from Shāshì is the ancient town of **Jīngzhōu**, to which you can catch a bus.

After Shāshì there's not much to look at: you're out on the flat plains of central China. The river widens immensely and you can see little of the shore. The boat continues down the river to pass by (and possibly stop at) the town of **Chénglíngjī**, which lies at the confluence of Dòngtíng Hé and the Cháng Jiāng.

East of Dòngtíng Hé is the town of **Yuèyáng**, from where you can catch trains heading either towards Chángshā, Guìlín and Guǎngzhōu, or towards Wǔhàn and points north. Another nine hours will bring you to Wǔhàn, at which point most travellers are quite ready to part ways with their boat.

Language

The official language of the PRC is the dialect spoken in Beijing. It is usually referred to in the west as 'Mandarin', but the Chinese call it *Putonghua* (common speech). While Putonghua is referred to as the 'Han language' *(hànyǔ)*, most of the minorities of the South-West speak their own language and understand Chinese only as a second or even third language.

Discounting ethnic minority languages, China has eight principal dialect groups. The major one in the South-West is Sichuanese, though this is as much accent as dialect. Deng Xiaoping gave most of his speeches in a thick Sichuanese accent. Changes are slight but enough to throw you off course; *hùzhào* (passport) is pronounced 'fuzhao', *méi yǒu* (no; don't have) becomes 'mo de'. Most overseas Chinese and people from Hong Kong speak Cantonese, a southern dialect that originated in Guangdong Province. It differs from Mandarin as much as French does from Spanish, and although speakers of both dialects can read Chinese characters, many words are pronounced differently. Cantonese also has a more complex tone system than Mandarin, with at least seven tones compared to Mandarin's four.

Grammar

Chinese grammar is much simpler than that of European languages. There are no articles such as 'a' and 'the', no tenses and no plurals. There isn't even a simple word for 'yes' or 'no'. The basic point to bear in mind is that, like English, Chinese word order is subject-verb-object. In other words, a basic English sentence like 'I (subject) love (verb) you (object)' is constructed in exactly the same way in Chinese. The hard part with Chinese is mastering the tones.

Writing System

Chinese is often referred to as a language of pictographs. Many of the basic Chinese characters are in fact highly stylised pictures of what they represent, but most Chinese characters (around 90%) are compounds of a 'meaning' element and a 'sound' element.

Characters are made up of 'radicals' which add to the sound or meaning of the word. Many characters which express feeling have a heart radical. The word for 'good' is a woman and a child radical together, 'home' is a roof over a pig, a 'forest' consists of three tree radicals together.

Just how many Chinese characters are there? It's possible to verify the existence of some 56,000 characters but the vast majority of these are archaic. The general consensus is that a well-educated, contemporary Chinese might know and use between 6000 and 8000 characters. To read a Chinese newspaper you'll need to know 2000 to 3000 but 1200 to 1500 would be enough to get the gist.

Each Chinese character represents a spoken syllable, leading many people to declare that Chinese is a 'monosyllabic language.' Actually, while the building block of the Chinese language is indeed the mono-syllabic Chinese character, Chinese words are usually a combination of two or more characters. Chinese has used this system of compound words to create new words to express modern concepts. Thus a computer is an 'electric brain' in Chinese, a film is an 'electric shadow' and rugby is the 'olive ball game'.

Theoretically, all Chinese dialects share the same written system so a Mandarin and Cantonese speaker can at the very least communicate by writing. This is why some Chinese will draw a character (often in the air or in the dust) if you don't understand their meaning.

Traditional texts are read from the back page to the front, right to left and top to bottom, though most newspapers follow western layout.

Simplification It's estimated that that it takes a Chinese child on average two years longer to read and write compared to his or her alphabet-using counterpart. Therefore, in the interests of promoting universal literacy, the Committee for Reforming the

Chinese Sayings and Expressions

Chinese is an extremely rich idiomatic language. Many sayings are four-character phrases that combine a great balance of rhythm and tone with a clever play on the multiple meanings of similar-sounding characters. Perhaps most interesting is how many phrases have direct English equivalents.

缘木求鱼 *(yuánmù qiúyú)*
Like climbing a tree to catch fish (a waste of time)

问道于盲 *(wèndào yú máng)*
Like asking a blind man for directions (another waste of time)

同床异梦 *(tóngchuáng yìmèng)*
To sleep in the same bed but have different dreams

坐井观天 *(zuòjǐng guāntiān)*
Like looking at the sky from the bottom of a well (not seeing the whole picture)

水落石出 *(shuǐluò shíchū)*
When the tide goes out the rocks are revealed (the truth will out)

守株待兔 *(shǒuzhū dàitù)*
Like a hunter waiting for a rabbit to kill itself by running into a tree (trusting to dumb luck)

殊途同归 *(shūtú tóngguī)*
Different roads all reach the same end

临阵磨枪 *(línjūn móqiāng)*
To not sharpen your weapons until the battle is upon you (to do things at the last minute)

热锅上的蚂蚁 *(règuōshàng demǎyǐ)*
Like ants on top of a hot stove (full of worries)

新瓶装旧酒 *(xīnpíng zhuāng jiùjiǔ)*
A new bottle filled with old wine (a superficial change)

削足适履 *(xiāozú shìlǚ)*
Like trimming the foot to fit the shoe

种瓜得瓜 *(zhòngguā déguā)*
If a man plants melons, so will he reap melons

酒肉朋友 *(jiǔròu péngyou)*
An eating and drinking friend (fair-weather friend)

晴天霹雳 *(qíngtiān pīlì)*
Like thunder from a blue sky (a bolt from the blue)

沐猴而冠 *(mù hóu ér guàn)*
A monkey dressed in a tall hat (a petty official)

燃眉之急 *(ránméi zhījí)*
A fire that is burning one's eyebrows (extremely urgent)

Chinese Language was set up by the Beijing government in 1954. Around 2200 Chinese characters were simplified. Taiwan, Hong Kong and overseas Chinese communities, however, continue to use traditional full-form (complex) characters.

In the last few years there has been a return to the full-form characters to China, probably as a result of tourism and large-scale investment by Overseas Chinese. They're seen mainly on restaurant, hotel and shop signs, and in advertising (where the traditional characters are considered more attractive). While the government is adamant that the simplified characters are the only officially-recognised system, there are indications that the two systems are coming into competition in China.

Romanisation

In 1958 the Chinese officially adopted a system known as *pinyin* (literally, 'same sound') as a method of rendering Mandarin into the Roman alphabet. The original idea was to do away with characters altogether at some stage and use only pinyin with accent marks showing tones. Most people resisted this and the plan was eventually abandoned.

Pinyin is often used on shop fronts, street signs and advertising billboards in China, but don't expect most people to be able to use it, as it never really took off as the main form of written Chinese.

In the countryside and the smaller towns you may not see any signs in pinyin at all, so unless you speak Chinese you'll need a phrasebook with Chinese characters.

Pronunciation

The following is a rough description of the sounds you'll hear in spoken Mandarin Chinese. In pinyin, apostrophes are occasionally used to separate syllables. So, you can write *ping'an* to prevent the word being pronounced as *pingan*.

Vowels
Most pinyin vowels and consonants are pronounced as they would be in English, but a few may cause difficulty.

a	as in 'father'
ai	as the 'i' in 'high'
ao	as the 'ow' in 'cow'
e	as the 'u' in 'fur'
ei	as in 'weigh'
i	as the 'ee' in 'meet' or as the 'oo' in 'book' after **c, ch, r, s, sh, z** or **zh**
ian	as the word 'yen'
ie	as the word 'yeah'
o	like 'or' but with no 'r' sound
ou	as the 'oa' in 'boat'
u	as in 'flute'
ui	as the word 'way'
uo	as 'w' followed by the 'o' in 'or'
yu	as the German 'ü'; purse your lips and say 'ee'
ü	as the German 'ü'

Consonants
The English 'v' sound doesn't occur in Chinese. For beginners, the trickiest consonants are **c, q** and **x** because their pronunciation isn't remotely similar to English. Other than **n, ng** and **r**, consonants never occur at the end of a syllable.

c	as the 'ts' in 'bits'
ch	as in 'chicken', but with the tongue curled back
h	articulated from the throat as in the 'ch' of Scottish *loch*
q	as the 'ch' in 'chicken'
r	a difficult letter; pronounced roughly as the 's' in 'pleasure'
sh	as in 'ship', but with the tongue curled back
x	as the 'sh' in 'ship'
z	as the 'ds' in 'suds'
zh	as the 'j' in 'judge' but with the tongue curled back

Gestures
Hand signs are frequently used in China. The 'thumbs-up' sign has a long tradition as an indication of excellence. Another way to indicate excellence is to gently pull your earlobe between thumb and index finger.

Finger counting is widely used in China but usually as a confirmation of a spoken number. One of the disadvantages of finger counting is that there are regional differences. The sign for 10, for instance, can also be made with a single fist or by crossing the fore and index finger of the same hand.

Tones
Four basic tones are used in Mandarin, which makes the language easier to learn than Cantonese. As in Cantonese, changing the tone changes the meaning. For example, in Mandarin the word *ma* can have quite different meanings, depending on which tone is used:

high tone	*mā* (mother)
rising tone	*má* (hemp, numb)
falling-rising tone	*mǎ* (horse)
falling tone	*mà* (scold, swear)

Getting Started
The following list of phrases will help get you started. If you want something more in-depth, arm yourself with a copy of Lonely Planet's *Mandarin phrasebook*.

Pronouns
I
wǒ	我

you
nǐ	你

he, she, it
tā	他/她/它

we, us
wǒmen	我们

you (plural)
nǐmen	你们

they, them
tāmen	他们

Greetings & Civilities
Hello.
nǐ hǎo	你好

Goodbye.
zàijiàn	再见

Thank you.
xièxie	谢谢

You're welcome.
búkèqi	不客气

I'm sorry.
duìbùqǐ	对不起

Small Talk

May I ask your name?
  nín guìxìng? 您贵姓？
My (sur)name is ...
  wǒ xìng ... 我姓 ...
Where are you from?
  nǐ shì cōng 你是从 ...
  nǎr láide? 哪儿来的？
I'm from ...
  wǒ shì cōng ... láide 我是从 ... 来的
No. (don't have)
  méi yǒu 没有
No. (not so)
  búshì 不是
I'm a foreign student.
  wǒ shì liúxuéshēng 我是留学生
What's to be done now?
  zěnme bàn? 怎么办？
It doesn't matter.
  méishì 没事
I want ...
  wǒ yào ... 我要 ...
No, I don't want it.
  búyào 不要

Language Difficulties

I understand.
  wǒ tīngdedǒng 我听得懂
I don't understand.
  wǒ tīngbudǒng 我听不懂
Do you understand?
  dǒng ma? 懂吗？
Could you speak
more slowly please?
  qīng nǐ shuō màn 请你说慢
  yīdiǎn, hǎo ma? 一点，好吗？

Toilets

Men/Women (signs) 男/女
toilet (restroom)
  cèsuǒ 厕所
toilet paper
  wèishēng zhǐ 卫生纸
bathroom (washroom)
  xǐshǒu jiān 洗手间

Money

How much is it?
  duōshǎo qián? 多少钱？
Is there anything
cheaper?
  yǒu piányi yìdiǎn 有便宜一点
  de ma? 的吗？

Emergencies

I'm sick.
  wǒ shēng bìng 我生病
I'm injured.
  wǒ shòushāng 我受伤
Fire!
  huǒ zāi! 火灾
Help!
  jiùmìng a! 救命啊
Thief!
  xiǎo tōu! 小偷
emergency
  jǐnjí qíngkuàng 紧急情况
police
  jǐngchá 警察
foreign affairs police
  wàishì jǐngchá 外事警察
pickpocket
  páshǒu 扒手
rapist
  qiángjiānzhě 强奸者

That's too expensive.
  tài guìle 太贵了
Bank of China
  zhōngguó yínháng 中国银行
change money
  huàn qián 换钱

Accommodation

Is there a room vacant?
  yǒu méiyǒu kōng fángjiān?
  有没有空房间？
Yes, there is/No, there isn't.
  yǒu/méiyǒu
  有/没有
Can I see the room?
  wǒ néng kànkan fángjiān ma?
  我能看看房间吗？
I don't like this room.
  wǒ bù xǐhuan zhèijiān fángjiān
  我不喜欢这间房
Are there any messages for me?
  yǒu méiyǒu liú huà?
  有没有留话？
May I have a hotel namecard?
  yǒu méiyǒu lǚguǎn de míngpiàn?
  有没有旅馆的名片？
Could I have these clothes washed, please?
  qǐng bǎ zhè xiē yīfu xǐ gānjìng, hǎo ma?
  请把这些衣服洗干净，好吗？

hotel
   lǚguǎn   旅馆
tourist hotel
   bīnguǎn/fàndiàn/   宾馆/饭店/
   jiǔdiàn   酒店
reception desk
   zǒng fúwù tái   总服务台
dormitory
   duōrénfáng   多人房
single room
   dānrénfáng   单人房
twin room
   shuāngrénfáng   双人房
bed
   chuángwèi   床位
economy room (no bath)
   pǔtōngfáng   普通房
standard room
   biāozhǔn fángjiān   标准房
deluxe suite
   háohuá tàofáng   豪华套房

Post

post office
   yúojú   邮局
letter
   xìn   信
envelope
   xìnfēng   信封
package
   bāoguǒ   包裹
air mail
   hángkōng xìn   航空信
surface mail
   píngyóu   平邮
stamps
   yóupiào   邮票
postcard
   míngxìnpiàn   明信片
aerogramme
   hángkōng xìnjiàn   航空邮件
poste restante
   cúnjú hòulǐnglán   存局候领栏
express mail (EMS)
   yóuzhèng tèkuài
   zhuāndì   邮政特快专递
registered mail
   guà hào   挂号

Telecommunications

telephone
   diànhuà   电话

telephone office
   diànxùn dàlóu   电讯大楼
telephone card
   diànhuà kǎ   电话卡
international call
   guójì diànhuà   国际电话
collect call
   duìfāng fùqián
   diànhuà   对方付费电话
direct-dial call
   zhíbō diànhuà   直拨电话
fax
   chuánzhēn   传真

Directions

Where is the ...?
   ... zài nǎlǐ?   ... 在哪里?
I'm lost.
   wǒ mílùle   我迷路了
Turn right.
   yòu zhuǎn   右转
Turn left.
   zuǒ zhuǎn   左转
Go straight ahead.
   yìzhí zǒu   一直走
Turn around.
   wàng huí zǒu   往回走

alley
   nòng   弄
boulevard
   dàdào   大道
lane
   xiàng, hútóng   巷\胡同
map
   dìtú   地图
road
   lù   路
section
   duàn   段
street
   jiē, dàjiē   街，大街
No 21
   21 hào   21号

Time

What's the time?
   jǐ diǎn?   几点?
... hour ... minute
   ... diǎn ... fēn   ... 点 ... 分
3.05
   sān diǎn wǔ fēn   3点5分

now
 xiànzài 现在

today
 jīntiān 今天

tomorrow
 míngtiān 明天

day after tomorrow
 hòutiān 后天

yesterday
 zuótiān 昨天

Wait a moment.
 děng yī xià 等一下

Transport

I want to go to ...
 wǒ yào qù ... 我要去 ...

I want to get off.
 wǒ yào xiàchē 我要下车

What time does it
depart/arrive?
 jǐdiǎn kāi/dào? 几点开/到?

How long does the
trip take?
 zhècì lǚxíng yào huā 这次旅行要花
 duōcháng shíjiān? 多长时间?

Please use the meter.
 dǎ biǎo 打表

luggage
 xíngli 行李

left-luggage room
 jìcún chù 寄存处

one ticket
 yìzhāng piào 一张票

two tickets
 liǎngzhāng piào 两张票

buy a ticket
 mǎi piào 买票

refund a ticket
 tuì piào 退票

taxi
 chūzū chē 出租车

microbus taxi
 miànbāo chē, miǎndī 面包车、面的

Air

airport
 fēijīchǎng 飞机场

charter flight
 bāojī 包机

one way ticket
 dānchéng piào 单程票

return ticket
 láihuí piào 来回票

boarding pass
 dēngjì kǎ 登记卡

reconfirm
 quèrèn 确认

cancel
 qǔxiāo 取消

bonded baggage
 cúnzhàn xínglǐ 存栈行李

CAAC ticket office
 zhōngguó mínháng 中国民航
 shòupiào chù 售票处

Bus

When is the first bus?
 tóubān qìchē jǐdiǎn kāi?
 头班汽车几点开?

When is the last bus?
 mòbān qìchē jǐdiǎn kāi?
 末班汽车几点开?

When is the next bus?
 xià yìbān qìchē jǐdiǎn kāi?
 下一班汽车几点开?

bus
 gōnggòng qìchē 公共汽车

minibus
 xiǎo gōnggòng qìchē 小公共汽车

long-distance bus
station
 chángtú qìchē zhàn 长途汽车站

Train

train
 huǒchē 火车

ticket office
 shòupiào chù 售票处

railway station
 huǒchē zhàn 火车站

hard-seat
 yìngxí, yìngzuò 硬席、硬座

soft-seat
 ruǎnxí, ruǎnzuò 软席、软座

hard-sleeper
 yìngwò 硬卧

soft-sleeper
 ruǎnwò 软卧

platform ticket
 zhàntái piào 站台票

Which platform?
 dìjǐhào zhàntái? 第几号站台?

upgrade ticket (after
boarding)
  bǔpiào   补票
subway (underground)
  dìxiàtiě   地下铁
subway station
  dìtiě zhàn   地铁站

Bicycle
bicycle
  zìxíngchē
  自行车
I want to hire a bicycle.
  wǒ yào zū yíliàng zìxíngchē
  我要租一辆自行车
How much is it per day?
  yìtiān duōshǎo qián?
  一天多少钱?
How much is it per hour?
  yíge xiǎo shí duōshǎo qián?
  一个小时多少钱?
How much is the deposit?
  yājīn duōshǎo qián?
  押金多少钱?

Health
hospital
  yīyuàn   医院
laxative
  xièyào   泻药
anti-diarrhoea
medicine
  zhǐxièyào   止泻药
rehydration salts
  shūwéizhí dīnà   舒维质低钠
  fā pàodìng   发泡锭
aspirin
  āsīpīlín   阿斯匹林
antibiotics
  kàngjūnsù   抗菌素
condom
  bìyùn tào   避孕套
tampon
  wèishēng mián tiáo   卫生棉条
sanitary napkin (Kotex)
  wèishēng mián   卫生棉
sunscreen (UV) lotion
  fáng shài yóu   防晒油
mosquito coils
  wénxiāng   蚊香
mosquito coils (electric)
  diàn wénxiāng   电蚊香

Numbers

0	*líng*	零
1	*yī, yāo!*	一、幺
2	*èr, liǎng*	二、两
3	*sān*	三
4	*sì*	四
5	*wǔ*	五
6	*liù*	六
7	*qī*	七
8	*bā*	八
9	*jiǔ*	九
10	*shí*	十
11	*shíyī*	十一
12	*shí'èr*	十二
20	*èrshí*	二十
21	*èrshíyī*	二十一
100	*yìbǎi*	一百
200	*liǎngbǎi*	两百
1000	*yìqiān*	一千
2000	*liǎngqiān*	两千
10,000	*yíwàn*	一万
20,000	*liǎngwàn*	两万
100,000	*shíwàn*	十万
200,000	*èrshíwàn*	二十万

FOOD
For more information about Chinese food,
see the Food section in Facts for the Visitor.

At the Restaurant   在餐馆
I don't eat dog.
  wó bú chī góuròu   我不吃狗肉
I don't want MSG.
  wó bú yào wèijīng   我不要味精
I'm vegetarian.
  wǒ chī sù   我吃素
not too spicy.
  bú yào tài là   不要太辣
restaurant
  cāntīng   餐厅
menu
  cài dān   菜单
bill (cheque)
  mǎi dān/jiézhàng   买单(结帐)
set meal (no menu)
  tàocān   套餐
to eat/let's eat
  chī fàn   吃饭
chopsticks
  kuàizi   筷子

Rice 饭

steamed white rice
mǐfàn 米饭
fried rice with beef
niúròusī chǎofàn 牛肉丝炒饭
fried rice with pork
ròusī chǎofàn 肉丝炒饭
fried rice with vegetables
shūcài chǎofàn 蔬菜炒饭
fried rice with egg
jīdàn chǎofàn 鸡蛋炒饭

Popular Dishes 二十大常见菜肴

spicy chicken with peanuts
gōngbào jīdīng 宫爆鸡丁
shredded pork and green beans
biǎndòu ròusī 扁豆肉丝
pork and sizzling rice crust
guōbā ròupiàn 锅巴肉片
double cooked fatty pork
huíguō ròu 回锅肉
sweet and sour pork fillets
tángcù lǐjǐ/ 糖醋里脊/
gǔlǎo ròu 古老肉
'wooden ear' mushrooms and pork
mùěr ròu 木耳肉
pork and green peppers
qīngjiāo ròupiàn 青椒肉片
'strange tasting' pork
guàiwèi ròusī 怪味肉丝
dry cooked beef
gānbiǎn niúròusī 干煸牛肉丝
beef and tomato
fānqié niúròupiàn 番茄牛肉片
sizzling beef on a platter
tiěbǎn niúròu 铁板牛肉
egg and tomato
fānqié chǎodàn 番茄炒蛋
red cooked aubergine
hóngshāo qiézi 红烧茄子
'fish-resembling' aubergine
yúxiāng qiézi 鱼香茄子
garlic beans
sùchǎo biǎndòu 素炒扁豆
spicy tofu
málà dòufu 麻辣豆腐
'homestyle' tofu
jiācháng dòufu 家常豆腐
fried vegetables
sùchǎo sùcài 素炒素菜

Sauces & Styles 调味汁与烹调法

'fish-resembling'
yúxiāng 鱼香
fried
chǎo 炒
oyster sauce
háoyóu 蚝油
red cooked
hóngshāo 红烧
sweet & sour
tángcù 糖醋
yellow bean
huángdòu 黄豆

Vegetables 素菜

bean curd casserole
shāguō dòufǔ 沙锅豆腐
fried beansprouts
sùchǎo dòuyá 素炒豆芽
bok choy and mushrooms
xiānggū báicài 香菇白菜
fried tomato and cauliflower
chǎo fānqié càihuā 炒番茄菜花
mushroom and tomato
mógu chǎo fànqiè 蘑菇炒番茄
aubergine
qiézi 茄子
beans
hélándòu 荷兰豆
bok choy
báicài 白菜
broccoli
gānlán 甘蓝
cauliflower
càihuā 菜花
four season beans
sìjìdòu 四季豆
French beans
biǎndòu 扁豆
mushroom
mógu 蘑菇
potato
tǔdòu 土豆
pumpkin
nánguā 南瓜
spinach
bōcài 菠菜
sweet potato
yùtou 芋头
tofu
dòufu 豆腐
wooden ear mushroom
mùěr 木耳

Other Dishes 其它菜肴

pocket bean curd (stuffed with meat)
  kǒudài dòufǔ 口袋豆腐
beef with green peppers
  qīngjiāo niúròu piàn 青椒牛肉片
beef and potato
  tǔdòu shāoniúròu 土豆烧牛肉
beef with oyster sauce
  háoyóu niúròu 蚝油牛肉
pork and fried onions
  yángcōng chǎo ròupiàn 洋葱炒肉片
pork, eggs and black fungus
  mùxū ròu 木须肉
pork with oyster sauce
  háoyóu ròus 蚝油肉丝
spicy pork cubelets
  làzi roudīng 辣子肉丁
shredded pork fillet
  chǎo lǐjǐ sī 炒里脊丝
fried pork slices
  liūròupiàn 熘肉片
ribs
  páigǔ 排骨
crispy chicken
  xiāngsū jī 香酥鸡
chicken & cashew nuts
  yāoguǒ jīdīng 腰果鸡丁
chicken braised in soy sauce
  hóngshāo jīkuài 红烧鸡块
lemon chicken
  níngméng jī 柠檬鸡
steampot chicken
  qìguōjī 汽锅鸡
tangerine chicken
  júzi jī 桔子鸡
Beijing duck
  běijīng kǎoyā 北京烤鸭

Seafood Dishes 海鲜

diced shrimp with peanuts
  gōngbào xiārén 宫爆虾仁
fish braised in soy sauce
  hóngshāo yú 红烧鱼
sour soup fish
  suāntāng yú 酸汤鱼

Miscellanea 其它

dogmeat
  gǒu ròu 狗肉
goat's cheese
  rǔbìng 乳饼

goat, mutton
  yáng ròu 羊肉
ratmeat
  lǎoshǔ ròu 老鼠肉
snake
  shé ròu· 蛇肉

Condiments 佐料

black pepper
  hújiāo 胡椒
garlic
  dàsuàn 大蒜
ginger
  jiāng 姜
hot sauce
  làjiāo jiàng 辣椒酱
honey
  fēngmì 蜂蜜
jam
  guǒ jiàng 果酱
ketchup
  fānqié jiàng 蕃茄酱
salt
  yán 盐
soy sauce
  jiàng yóu 酱油
sugar
  táng 糖

Soup 汤

bean curd and vegetable soup
  dòufǔ cài tāng 豆腐菜汤
egg drop soup
  jīdàn tāng 鸡蛋汤
hot and sour soup
  suānlà tāng 酸辣汤
mushroom and egg soup
  mógu dànhuā tāng 蘑菇蛋花汤
vegetable soup
  shūcài tāng 蔬菜汤
wanton soup
  húndùn tāng 馄饨汤

Desserts 甜点

caramelised banana
  básī xiāngjiāo 拔丝香蕉
eight treasure rice
  bābǎofàn 八宝饭
sweet glutinous ball
  tāngyuán 汤圆

Fruit 水果

apple
  píngguǒ 苹果

banana
   xiāngjiāo   香蕉
longan
   lóngyǎn   龙眼
loquat
   pípa   枇杷
lychees
   lìzhī   荔枝
mandarins
   gānzi   柑子
mango
   mángguǒ   芒果
pear
   lízi   梨子
persimmon
   shìzi   柿子
pineapple
   bōluó   菠萝
pomelo
   yòuzi   柚子
rambutan
   hóngmáodān   红毛丹

Snacks   小吃

across the bridge noodles
   guòqiáo mǐxiàn   过桥米线
ants climbing tree (noodles & mince-meat)
   mǎyǐ shàngshū   蚂蚁上树
beef noodles in a soup
   niúròu miàn   牛肉面
chinese ravioli
   shuǐjiǎo   水饺
dough stick
   yóutiáo   油条
dry 'burning' noodles
   rán miàn   燃面
egg and flour omelette
   jiān bǐng   煎饼
fried noodles ('chaomein')
   chǎomiàn   炒面
fried noodles with beef
   niúròu chǎomiàn   牛肉炒面
hotpot
   huǒguō   火锅
noodles and egg
   jīdàn miàn   鸡蛋面
soupy casserole
   qìguō   汽锅
steamed bun
   mántou   馒头
steamed dumpling
   bāozi   包子

steamed shuijiao
   zhēngjiǎo   蒸饺

DRINKS
For more information, see Drinks in Facts for the Visitor.

beer
   píjiǔ   啤酒
Coca-Cola
   kěkǒu kělè   可口可乐
tea
   chá   茶
coffee
   kāfēi   咖啡
boiling water
   kāi shuǐ   开水
mineral water
   kuàng quán shu   矿泉水
red grape wine
   hóng pútáo jiǔ   红葡萄酒
white grape wine
   bái pútáo jiǔ   白葡萄酒
whisky
   wēishìjì jiǔ   威士忌酒
vodka
   fútèjiā jiǔ   伏特加酒
rice wine
   mǐ jiǔ   米酒
Chinese spirits
   báijiǔ   白酒
milk
   niúnǎi   牛奶
soybean milk
   dòujiāng   豆浆
yogurt
   suānnǎi   酸奶
fruit juice
   guǒzhī   果汁
orange juice
   liǔchéng zhī   柳橙汁
coconut juice
   yézi zhī   椰子汁
pineapple juice
   bōluó zhī   菠萝汁
mango juice
   mángguǒ zhī   芒果汁
hot
   rède   热的
ice cold
   bīngde   冰的
ice cube
   bīng kuài   冰块

Glossary

antiphonal – a form of singing involving echoing refrains, duets and choruses
apsaras – Buddhist celestial beings, similar to angels
arhat – Buddhist, especially a monk who achieves enlightenment and passes to nirvana at death

baba – thick flatbreads of wheat
bābǎo chá – eight treasure tea
báijiǔ – literally 'white alcohol', a type of face numbing rice wine served at banquets and get-togethers
bāozi – steamed buns with meat inside
běi – north
bīnguǎn – guesthouse
Bodhisattva – one worthy of nirvana but who remains on earth to help others attain enlightenment
Bön – the pre-Buddhist indigenous faith of Tibet, pockets of which survive in western Sìchuān

cadre – Chinese government bureaucrat
cāntīng – restaurant
cǎoyā – grass sprouts
chang – a Tibetan brew made from fermented barley
chop – see *name chop*
chörten – Tibetan *stupa*
chuba – cloak (Tibetan)
chúnmǐjiǔ – rice wine
cūn – village

dàjiǔdiàn – hotel
dāndān miàn – oily noodles
dānwèi – work unit, the cornerstone of China's social control
dǎo – island
dàpùbù – large waterfall
dōng – east
dòng – cave
dzong – Tibetan fort

fàndiàn – a hotel or restaurant
fànguǎn – restaurant
feng – peak

fēngshuǐ – geomancy, literally 'wind and water', the art of using ancient principles to maximise the flow of 'qì', or universal energy

gompa – Tibetan Buddhist monastery
gōngbǎo jīdīng – spicy chicken fried with peanuts
gōngyuán – park
guānxì – advantageous social or business connections
guiding – regulations

hǎi – lake (literally 'sea')
hé – river
hú – lake
huājiāo – flower pepper
Huí – ethnic Chinese Muslims
huǒguō – hotpot

jiāng – river
jiaozi – Chinese-style ravioli
jīdòu liángfěn – cold chickpea jelly
jiē – street
jié – festival
jīnsī xiāngchá – golden ring tea
jun – prefecture
jùyuàn – theatre

kǎoyā – roast duck
karst – denotes the characteristically eroded landscape of limestone regions, eg, the whimsical scenery of Guìlín and Yángshuò
Kham – traditional name for eastern Tibet, encompassing western Sichuan
Khamba – person from Kham
kǒndài dòufu – pocket bean curd
kōngtiáo – heating
kora – the walking circuit of a Tibetan holy site
kuài – colloquial term for the yuán

lama – a Buddhist priest of the Tantric or Lamaist school
lǎoshǔ ròu – rat meat
lù – road
luohan – see *Arhat*

lúshēng – a reed pipe that features in many festivals in Guìzhōu

máo – colloquial term for the jiǎo (currency), 10 of which equal one kuài
mǎyǐ shàngshù – thin noodles tossed with bits of spicy meat
meiyou – 'No.' 'There isn't any.' 'We don't have.' Possibly the first word you'll hear in China
Miào – Chinese ethnic group
miào – monastery
momos – Tibetan dumplings
motor-tricycle – an enclosed three-wheeled vehicle with a driver at the front, a small motorbike engine below and seats for two passengers in the back

name chop – a carved name seal that acts as a signature
nán – south

palatar – Burmese crepe
Pangolin – a scaly anteater which is a protected species that nonetheless crops up on restaurant menus
pedicab – pedal-powered tricycle with a seat to carry passengers
Pīnyīn – the official system to transliterate Chinese script into roman characters
prefecture – political subdivision, between a province and a county in size
pùbù – waterfall

qì – vital energy (life force) or cosmic currents manipulated in acupuncture and massage
qìgōng – form of exercise which channels one's qì

ránmiàn – 'burning noodles' served with onions, chillies, peanuts, chives and a side serving of sauce
rènào – a Chinese saying that translates into 'hot and noisy'
Rénmínbì – literally 'peoples money', the formal name for the currency of China

rimpoche – abbot of a gompa

sāndàochá – three course tea
shāguō fěn – a noodle and seafood, meat or vegetable combination put in a casserole pot and fired over a flame of rocket-launch proportion.
shān – mountain
shāokǎo – skewers of meat wrapped in banana leaves and grilled over wood fires
shìchǎng – market
shuijiao – a form of steamed *jiaozi*
sì – monastery
special municipality – the name given to centrally-administered regions such as Běijīng, Chóngqìng and Shànghǎi
stupa – hemispherical Buddhist religious structure; always walk around stupas clockwise
suānlà – hot and sour

tàijíquán – taichi, the graceful, flowing exercise that has its roots in China's martial arts
tán – pool
tāng – soup
tāngyuán – sweet balls of gum
thugpa – noodles (Tibetan)
tiánqíng chǎorón – sweet red pepper and pork
tsampa – roasted barley flour (Tibetan)
tuōlājī – tractor

wèi – sauce

xi – west

yinyin – lychee-based wine
yuán – the Chinese unit of currency; also referred to as RMB
yúxiāng wèi – fish-flavoured sauce

zhāngchá yāzi – smoked-tea duck
zhāodàisuǒ – basic hotel or guesthouse
zhēngjiǎo – Shāndōng-style dumplings, steamed
zhōng – middle

LONELY PLANET

You already know that Lonely Planet produces more than this one guidebook, but you might not be aware of the other products we have on this region. Here is a selection of titles that you may want to check out as well:

Beijing
ISBN 1 86450 144 8

China
ISBN 0 86442 755 7

Healthy Travel Asia & India
ISBN 1 86450 051 4

Laos
ISBN 1 86450 373 4

Vietnam
ISBN 1 86450 189 8

Cantonese phrasebook
ISBN 0 86442 645 3

Hong Kong Condensed
ISBN 1 86450 253 3

Shanghai
ISBN 0 86442 507 4

Mandarin phrasebook
ISBN 0 86442 652 6

Beijing City Map
ISBN 1 86450 255 X

Read This First: Asia & India
ISBN 1 86450 049 2

World Food Hong Kong
ISBN 1 86450 288 6

Hong Kong City Map
ISBN 1 86450 007 7

Hong Kong & Macau
ISBN 1 86450 230 4

Karakoram Highway
ISBN 0 86442 531 7

Myanmar
ISBN 0 86442 703 4

Available wherever books are sold

LONELY PLANET

ON THE ROAD

Travel Guides explore cities, regions and countries, and supply information on transport, restaurants and accommodation, covering all budgets. They come with reliable, easy-to-use maps, practical advice, cultural and historical facts and a rundown on attractions both on and off the beaten track. There are over 200 titles in this classic series, covering nearly every country in the world.

 Lonely Planet Upgrades extend the shelf life of existing travel guides by detailing any changes that may affect travel in a region since a book has been published. Upgrades can be downloaded for free from **www.lonelyplanet.com/upgrades**

For travellers with more time than money, **Shoestring** guides offer dependable, first-hand information with hundreds of detailed maps, plus insider tips for stretching money as far as possible. Covering entire continents in most cases, the six-volume shoestring guides are known around the world as 'backpackers bibles'.

For the discerning short-term visitor, **Condensed** guides highlight the best a destination has to offer in a full-colour, pocket-sized format designed for quick access. They include everything from top sights and walking tours to opinionated reviews of where to eat, stay, shop and have fun.

CitySync lets travellers use their Palm™ or Visor™ hand-held computers to guide them through a city with handy tips on transport, history, cultural life, major sights, and shopping and entertainment options. It can also quickly search and sort hundreds of reviews of hotels, restaurants and attractions, and pinpoint their location on scrollable street maps. CitySync can be downloaded from **www.citysync.com**

MAPS & ATLASES

Lonely Planet's **City Maps** feature downtown and metropolitan maps, as well as transit routes and walking tours. The maps come complete with an index of streets, a listing of sights and a plastic coat for extra durability.

Road Atlases are an essential navigation tool for serious travellers. Cross-referenced with the guidebooks, they also feature distance and climate charts and a complete site index.

LONELY PLANET

ESSENTIALS

Read This First books help new travellers to hit the road with confidence. These invaluable predeparture guides give step-by-step advice on preparing for a trip, budgeting, arranging a visa, planning an itinerary and staying safe while still getting off the beaten track.

Healthy Travel pocket guides offer a regional rundown on disease hot spots and practical advice on predeparture health measures, staying well on the road and what to do in emergencies. The guides come with a user-friendly design and helpful diagrams and tables.

Lonely Planet's **Phrasebooks** cover the essential words and phrases travellers need when they're strangers in a strange land. They come in a pocket-sized format with colour tabs for quick reference, extensive vocabulary lists, easy-to-follow pronunciation keys and two-way dictionaries.

Miffed by blurry photos of the Taj Mahal? Tired of the classic 'top of the head cut off' shot? **Travel Photography: A Guide to Taking Better Pictures** will help you turn ordinary holiday snaps into striking images and give you the know-how to capture every scene, from frenetic festivals to peaceful beach sunrises.

Lonely Planet's **Travel Journal** is a lightweight but sturdy travel diary for jotting down all those on-the-road observations and significant travel moments. It comes with a handy time-zone wheel, a world map and useful travel information.

Lonely Planet's eKno is an all-in-one communication service developed especially for travellers. It offers low-cost international calls and free email and voicemail so that you can keep in touch while on the road. Check it out on **www.ekno.lonelyplanet.com**

FOOD & RESTAURANT GUIDES

Lonely Planet's **Out to Eat** guides recommend the brightest and best places to eat and drink in top international cities. These gourmet companions are arranged by neighbourhood, packed with dependable maps, garnished with scene-setting photos and served with quirky features.

For people who live to eat, drink and travel, **World Food** guides explore the culinary culture of each country. Entertaining and adventurous, each guide is packed with detail on staples and specialities, regional cuisine and local markets, as well as sumptuous recipes, comprehensive culinary dictionaries and lavish photos good enough to eat.

Lonely Planet Guides by Region

Lonely Planet is known worldwide for publishing practical, reliable and no-nonsense travel information in our guides and on our Web site. The Lonely Planet list covers just about every accessible part of the world. Currently there are 16 series: Travel guides, Shoestring guides, Condensed guides, Phrasebooks, Read This First, Healthy Travel, Walking guides, Cycling guides, Watching Wildlife guides, Pisces Diving & Snorkeling guides, City Maps, Road Atlases, Out to Eat, World Food, Journeys travel literature and Pictorials.

AFRICA Africa on a shoestring • Botswana • Cairo • Cairo City Map • Cape Town • Cape Town City Map • East Africa • Egypt • Egyptian Arabic phrasebook • Ethiopia, Eritrea & Djibouti • Ethiopian Amharic phrasebook • The Gambia & Senegal • Healthy Travel Africa • Kenya • Malawi • Morocco • Moroccan Arabic phrasebook • Mozambique • Namibia • Read This First: Africa • South Africa, Lesotho & Swaziland • Southern Africa • Southern Africa Road Atlas • Swahili phrasebook • Tanzania, Zanzibar & Pemba • Trekking in East Africa • Tunisia • Watching Wildlife East Africa • Watching Wildlife Southern Africa • West Africa • World Food Morocco • Zambia • Zimbabwe, Botswana & Namibia
Travel Literature: Mali Blues: Traveling to an African Beat • The Rainbird: A Central African Journey • Songs to an African Sunset: A Zimbabwean Story

AUSTRALIA & THE PACIFIC Aboriginal Australia & the Torres Strait Islands •Auckland • Australia • Australian phrasebook • Australia Road Atlas • Cycling Australia • Cycling New Zealand • Fiji • Fijian phrasebook • Healthy Travel Australia, NZ & the Pacific • Islands of Australia's Great Barrier Reef • Melbourne • Melbourne City Map • Micronesia • New Caledonia • New South Wales • New Zealand • Northern Territory • Outback Australia • Out to Eat – Melbourne • Out to Eat – Sydney • Papua New Guinea • Pidgin phrasebook • Queensland • Rarotonga & the Cook Islands • Samoa • Solomon Islands • South Australia • South Pacific • South Pacific phrasebook • Sydney • Sydney City Map • Sydney Condensed • Tahiti & French Polynesia • Tasmania • Tonga • Tramping in New Zealand • Vanuatu • Victoria • Walking in Australia • Watching Wildlife Australia • Western Australia
Travel Literature: Islands in the Clouds: Travels in the Highlands of New Guinea • Kiwi Tracks: A New Zealand Journey • Sean & David's Long Drive

CENTRAL AMERICA & THE CARIBBEAN Bahamas, Turks & Caicos • Baja California • Belize, Guatemala & Yucatán • Bermuda • Central America on a shoestring • Costa Rica • Costa Rica Spanish phrasebook • Cuba • Cycling Cuba • Dominican Republic & Haiti • Eastern Caribbean • Guatemala • Havana • Healthy Travel Central & South America • Jamaica • Mexico • Mexico City • Panama • Puerto Rico • Read This First: Central & South America • Virgin Islands • World Food Caribbean • World Food Mexico • Yucatán
Travel Literature: Green Dreams: Travels in Central America

EUROPE Amsterdam • Amsterdam City Map • Amsterdam Condensed • Andalucía • Athens • Austria • Baltic States phrasebook • Barcelona • Barcelona City Map • Belgium & Luxembourg • Berlin • Berlin City Map • Britain • British phrasebook • Brussels, Bruges & Antwerp • Brussels City Map • Budapest • Budapest City Map • Canary Islands • Catalunya & the Costa Brava • Central Europe • Central Europe phrasebook • Copenhagen • Corfu & the Ionians • Corsica • Crete • Crete Condensed • Croatia • Cycling Britain • Cycling France • Cyprus • Czech & Slovak Republics • Czech phrasebook • Denmark • Dublin • Dublin City Map • Dublin Condensed • Eastern Europe • Eastern Europe phrasebook • Edinburgh • Edinburgh City Map • England • Estonia, Latvia & Lithuania • Europe on a shoestring • Europe phrasebook • Finland • Florence • Florence City Map • France • Frankfurt City Map • Frankfurt Condensed • French phrasebook • Georgia, Armenia & Azerbaijan • Germany • German phrasebook • Greece • Greek Islands • Greek phrasebook • Hungary • Iceland, Greenland & the Faroe Islands • Ireland • Italian phrasebook • Italy • Kraków • Lisbon • The Loire • London • London City Map • London Condensed • Madrid • Madrid City Map • Malta • Mediterranean Europe • Milan, Turin & Genoa • Moscow • Munich • Netherlands • Normandy • Norway • Out to Eat – London • Out to Eat – Paris • Paris • Paris City Map • Paris Condensed • Poland • Polish phrasebook • Portugal • Portuguese phrasebook • Prague • Prague City Map • Provence & the Côte d'Azur • Read This First: Europe • Rhodes & the Dodecanese • Romania & Moldova • Rome • Rome City Map • Rome Condensed • Russia, Ukraine & Belarus • Russian phrasebook • Scandinavian & Baltic Europe • Scandinavian phrasebook • Scotland • Sicily • Slovenia • South-West France • Spain • Spanish phrasebook • Stockholm • St Petersburg • St Petersburg City Map • Sweden • Switzerland • Tuscany • Ukrainian phrasebook • Venice • Vienna • Wales • Walking in Britain • Walking in France • Walking in Ireland • Walking in Italy • Walking in Scotland • Walking in Spain • Walking in Switzerland • Western Europe • World Food France • World Food Greece • World Food Ireland • World Food Italy • World Food Spain **Travel Literature:** After Yugoslavia • Love and War in the Apennines • The Olive Grove: Travels in Greece • On the Shores of the Mediterranean • Round Ireland in Low Gear • A Small Place in Italy

Lonely Planet Mail Order

onely Planet products are distributed worldwide. They are also available by mail order from Lonely Planet, so if you have difficulty finding a title please write to us. North and South American residents should write to 150 Linden St, Oakland, CA 94607, USA; European and African residents should write to 10a Spring Place, London NW5 3BH, UK; and residents of other countries to Locked Bag 1, Footscray, Victoria 3011, Australia.

INDIAN SUBCONTINENT & THE INDIAN OCEAN Bangladesh • Bengali phrasebook • Bhutan • Delhi • Goa • Healthy Travel Asia & India • Hindi & Urdu phrasebook • India • India & Bangladesh City Map • Indian Himalaya • Karakoram Highway • Kathmandu City Map • Kerala • Madagascar • Maldives • Mauritius, Réunion & Seychelles • Mumbai (Bombay) • Nepal • Nepali phrasebook • North India • Pakistan • Rajasthan • Read This First: Asia & India • South India • Sri Lanka • Sri Lanka phrasebook • Tibet • Tibetan phrasebook • Trekking in the Indian Himalaya • Trekking in the Karakoram & Hindukush • Trekking in the Nepal Himalaya • World Food India **Travel Literature:** The Age of Kali: Indian Travels and Encounters • Hello Goodnight: A Life of Goa • In Rajasthan • Maverick in Madagascar • A Season in Heaven: True Tales from the Road to Kathmandu • Shopping for Buddhas • A Short Walk in the Hindu Kush • Slowly Down the Ganges

MIDDLE EAST & CENTRAL ASIA Bahrain, Kuwait & Qatar • Central Asia • Central Asia phrasebook • Dubai • Farsi (Persian) phrasebook • Hebrew phrasebook • Iran • Israel & the Palestinian Territories • Istanbul • Istanbul City Map • Istanbul to Cairo • Istanbul to Kathmandu • Jerusalem • Jerusalem City Map • Jordan • Lebanon • Middle East • Oman & the United Arab Emirates • Syria • Turkey • Turkish phrasebook • World Food Turkey • Yemen **Travel Literature:** Black on Black: Iran Revisited • Breaking Ranks: Turbulent Travels in the Promised Land • The Gates of Damascus • Kingdom of the Film Stars: Journey into Jordan

NORTH AMERICA Alaska • Boston • Boston City Map • Boston Condensed • British Columbia • California & Nevada • California Condensed • Canada • Chicago • Chicago City Map • Chicago Condensed • Florida • Georgia & the Carolinas • Great Lakes • Hawaii • Hiking in Alaska • Hiking in the USA • Honolulu & Oahu City Map • Las Vegas • Los Angeles • Los Angeles City Map • Louisiana & the Deep South • Miami • Miami City Map • Montreal • New England • New Orleans • New Orleans City Map • New York City • New York City City Map • New York City Condensed • New York, New Jersey & Pennsylvania • Oahu • Out to Eat – San Francisco • Pacific Northwest • Rocky Mountains • San Diego & Tijuana • San Francisco • San Francisco City Map • Seattle • Seattle City Map • Southwest • Texas • Toronto • USA • USA phrasebook • Vancouver • Vancouver City Map • Virginia & the Capital Region • Washington, DC • Washington, DC City Map • World Food New Orleans **Travel Literature:** Caught Inside: A Surfer's Year on the California Coast • Drive Thru America

NORTH-EAST ASIA Beijing • Beijing City Map • Cantonese phrasebook • China • Hiking in Japan • Hong Kong & Macau • Hong Kong City Map • Hong Kong Condensed • Japan • Japanese phrasebook • Korea • Korean phrasebook • Kyoto • Mandarin phrasebook • Mongolia • Mongolian phrasebook • Seoul • Shanghai • South-West China • Taiwan • Tokyo • Tokyo Condensed • World Food Hong Kong • World Food Japan **Travel Literature:** In Xanadu: A Quest • Lost Japan

SOUTH AMERICA Argentina, Uruguay & Paraguay • Bolivia • Brazil • Brazilian phrasebook • Buenos Aires • Buenos Aires City Map • Chile & Easter Island • Colombia • Ecuador & the Galapagos Islands • Healthy Travel Central & South America • Latin American Spanish phrasebook • Peru • Quechua phrasebook • Read This First: Central & South America • Rio de Janeiro • Rio de Janeiro City Map • Santiago de Chile • South America on a shoestring • Trekking in the Patagonian Andes • Venezuela **Travel Literature:** Full Circle: A South American Journey

SOUTH-EAST ASIA Bali & Lombok • Bangkok • Bangkok City Map • Burmese phrasebook • Cambodia • Cycling Vietnam, Laos & Cambodia • East Timor phrasebook • Hanoi • Healthy Travel Asia & India • Hill Tribes phrasebook • Ho Chi Minh City (Saigon) • Indonesia • Indonesian phrasebook • Indonesia's Eastern Islands • Java • Lao phrasebook • Laos • Malay phrasebook • Malaysia, Singapore & Brunei • Myanmar (Burma) • Philippines • Pilipino (Tagalog) phrasebook • Read This First: Asia & India • Singapore • Singapore City Map • South-East Asia on a shoestring • South-East Asia phrasebook • Thailand • Thailand's Islands & Beaches • Thailand, Vietnam, Laos & Cambodia Road Atlas • Thai phrasebook • Vietnam • Vietnamese phrasebook • World Food Indonesia • World Food Thailand • World Food Vietnam

ALSO AVAILABLE: Antarctica • The Arctic • The Blue Man: Tales of Travel, Love and Coffee • Brief Encounters: Stories of Love, Sex & Travel • Buddhist Stupas in Asia: The Shape of Perfection • Chasing Rickshaws • The Last Grain Race • Lonely Planet ... On the Edge: Adventurous Escapades from Around the World • Lonely Planet Unpacked • Lonely Planet Unpacked Again • Not the Only Planet: Science Fiction Travel Stories • Ports of Call: A Journey by Sea • Sacred India • Travel Photography: A Guide to Taking Better Pictures • Travel with Children • Tuvalu: Portrait of an Island Nation

Index

Abbreviations

Text

Bold indicates maps.

Bold indicates maps.

Boxed Text

Bold indicates maps.

MAP LEGEND

CITY ROUTES

Highway .... Primary Road
Road .... Secondary Road
Street .... Street
)= = = ... Tunnel
.... Footbridge
Lane .... Lane

REGIONAL ROUTES

.... Tollway, Freeway
.... Primary Road
.... Secondary Road

BOUNDARIES

.... International
.... Province
.... Fortified Wall

HYDROGRAPHY

.... River, Creek
.... Canal
.... Lake
.... Dry Lake; Salt Lake
.... Spring; Rapids
.... Waterfalls

TRANSPORT ROUTES & STATIONS

.... Train
.... Metro
.... Cable Car, Chairlift
.... Ferry
.... Walking Trail
.... Aerial Cable

AREA FEATURES

.... Building
.... Park, Gardens
.... Market
.... Sports Ground
.... Beach
.... Cemetery
.... Campus
.... Forest

POPULATION SYMBOLS

CAPITAL .... National Capital
CAPITAL .... Provincial Capital
CITY .... City
Town .... Town
Village .... Village
.... Urban Area

MAP SYMBOLS

.... Place to Stay
.... Place to Eat
.... Point of Interest

.... Airport, Airfield
.... Bank
.... Battle Site
.... Bus Terminal, Stop
.... Buddhist Temple
.... Café
.... Camping Ground
.... Castle
.... Cave
.... Church

.... Cinema
.... Confucian Temple
.... Embassy
.... Gate
.... Golf Course
.... Gompa
.... Hospital
.... Internet
.... Lookout
.... Mine

.... Monument
.... Mountain
.... Museum
.... National Park
.... Pagoda
.... Parking, Toilet
.... Pass
.... Pavillion, Shelter
.... Police Station
.... Post Office

.... Pub or Bar
.... Shopping Centre
.... Swimming Pool
.... Stately Home
.... Taoist Temple
.... Telephone
.... Theatre
.... Tomb
.... Tourist Information
.... Zoo

Note: not all symbols displayed above appear in this book

LONELY PLANET OFFICES

Australia
Locked Bag 1, Footscray, Victoria 3011
☎ 03 8379 8000 fax 03 8379 8111
email: talk2us@lonelyplanet.com.au

USA
150 Linden St, Oakland, CA 94607
☎ 510 893 8555 TOLL FREE: 800 275 8555
fax 510 893 8572
email: info@lonelyplanet.com

UK
10a Spring Place, London NW5 3BH
☎ 020 7428 4800 fax 020 7428 4828
email: go@lonelyplanet.co.uk

France
1 rue du Dahomey, 75011 Paris
☎ 01 55 25 33 00 fax 01 55 25 33 01
email: bip@lonelyplanet.fr
www.lonelyplanet.fr

World Wide Web: www.lonelyplanet.com or AOL keyword: lp
Lonely Planet Images: lpi@lonelyplanet.com.au